PHILOSOPHY

PHILOSOPHY
An Introduction Through Literature

Lowell Kleiman & Stephen Lewis

PARAGON HOUSE
St. Paul, Minnesota

First paperback edition, 1992

Published in the United States by
Paragon House
2700 University Avenue West
St. Paul, MN 55114-1016

Copyright © 1990 by Paragon House

10 9 8 7 6 5

Library of Congress Cataloging-in-Publication Data

Kleiman, Lowell, 1942–
    Philosophy : an introduction through literature / by Lowell
Kleiman and Stephen Lewis. — 1st ed.
      p.   cm.
   ISBN 1-55778-539-2
    1. Philosophy—Introductions.   2. Philosophy in literature.
I. Lewis, Stephen, 1942–   II. Title.
BD21.K27   1989
100—dc20   89-37253
                                         CIP

Manufactured in the United States of America

To Larry Lewis
A very special father,
and
To the memory of
Joe, Rose, and Manny

Contents

PART
——5——
JUSTICE

PART
——6——
RELIGIOUS BELIEF

PART
___7___
FREEDOM, FATALISM, AND DETERMINISM

Preface

We have attempted in this book to offer beginning students the best of philosophy through the medium of literature. The two disciplines are natural allies—philosophy supplying perennial themes raised anew from one generation to the next, literature providing vivid illustrations of the meaning and poignancy of abstract thought.

Other books, including some introductory philosophy texts, have attempted to bring together philosophical writings and literary works. Our approach, however, is unique in several respects. First, we introduce each part with one or two literary selections that raise the philosophical issue. Second, in order to make the alliance work, we have been careful to pick the right combination of literary piece and philosophical issue. Our criterion throughout was that the story or play lend itself to philosophical scrutiny. The issue should emerge from the plot or character development without force.

Third, we have attempted to include not just selections but complete literary pieces. Fully realized literary works match the complexity of the issues themselves. Too often, especially in introductory philosophy classes, subtlety or insight is lost for want of a rich example. By primarily using short stories, we have avoided this problem.

Fourth, we have included some of the best philosophical writings available, and chosen them from both classical and contemporary sources. In each chapter, we have attempted to include the clearest presentation of a particular point of view, which sometimes meant going back to an earlier article not generally found in other current texts. On the whole, we have sought balance, drawing not only on what is called the "analytic" tradition, but on hermeneutics and feminist philosophy as well.

Fifth, rather than simply classifying interesting philosophical and literary pieces under some common heading and leaving to the instructor or the more ambitious student the task of finding a unifying thread, we have attempted to introduce each piece and to integrate the philosophy with the literature through extensive discussion. We hope in this way to show clearly how useful the approach of combining philosophy and literature can be—how much fun there can be in thinking about a well-written story philosophically—how illuminating to think philosophically with a good example in mind.

In our efforts, we have been helped by many people, to some of whom we would like to give special thanks: to David Seiple (Columbia University), Harry James Cargas

(Webster University), and Malcolm Reid (Gorden College) for their critical and constructive evaluation of the manuscript; to Eddy Zemach (Hebrew University) and Ed Erwin (University of Miami, Coral Gables) for their stimulating and challenging conversations over the years that have helped shape the character of this book; to our editor, Don Fehr, and assistant editor, Jo Glorie, for their insightful suggestions and support; and to our wives, Sheila and Carolyn, for their patience, good humor, and especially their wisdom and guidance throughout.

PART
1
Knowledge

Literary Introduction:
What Do We Know?

During the special Senate Committee Watergate hearings, then Senator Howard Baker from Tennessee phrased the central question of the investigation in a way that captured the concerns of the American public. Over and over again, to a variety of witnesses, Baker asked, "What did the President know, and when did he know it?" The issue involved not only President Nixon's awareness of the illegal break-in into the Democratic Party Headquarters in the Watergate Hotel complex, but equally important, the extent of his awareness, and its moral and legal implications.

The question of what constitutes knowledge is both perplexing and compelling. Not only do we hold other people accountable, as in the Watergate affair, on the basis of their knowledge, but we are driven in our own everyday lives by a thirst to know. We read newspapers, or listen to the news on the radio, or watch it on television, all to find out what is happening in the world. Science provides knowledge of the laws that seem to govern the physical world. Technology, as an extension of science, provides practical uses for scientific knowledge. Our lives and well-being depend on our knowledge of other people, of politics, and of international relations. Clearly, the idea of knowledge, in all of its manifestations, is of central importance.

The question of what knowledge is can take a variety of forms, but perhaps underlying all of them is the following question: "Can we be certain we know what we think we know?"

It is often difficult to be sure what other people know. Examinations, for example, are designed to test students. But such measures are not always fair. In some cases the students might be tired, distracted, or nervous when they take the examinations.

If certainty about what other people know is difficult to establish, the problem does not become easier when we evaluate self-knowledge. There are many times in our lives when we are uncertain of what we ourselves know. We frequently hear the advice that it is a good thing to think before we act. One interpretation of that common wisdom is that we ought to assess the certitude of our beliefs about a situation, especially before we do something we might regret.

But the evidence for belief might be confusing. In a famous passage from Melville's *Moby Dick*, this problem is presented in metaphorical form. Ishmael, the narrator of the novel, ponders the physical fact of the size of a whale's head and the placement of the animal's eyes on either side of its body:

> A curious and most puzzling question might be started concerning this visual matter as touching the Leviathan. But I must be content with a hint. So long as a man's eyes are open in the light, the act of seeing is involuntary; that is, he cannot then help mechanically seeing whatever objects are before him. Nevertheless, any one's experience will teach him, that though he can take in an undiscriminating sweep of things at one glance, it is quite impossible for him, attentively, and completely, to examine any two things—however large or however small—at one and the same instant of time; never mind if they lie side by side and touch each other. But if you now come to separate these two objects, and surround each by a circle of profound darkness; then, in order to see one of them, in such a manner as to bring your mind to bear on it, the other will be utterly excluded from your contemporary consciousness. How is it, then, with the whale? True, both his eyes, in themselves, must simultaneously act; but is his brain so much more comprehensive, combining, and subtle than man's, that he can at the same moment of time attentively examine two distinct prospects, one on one side of him, and the other in an exactly opposite direction? If he can, then is it as marvellous a thing in him, as if a man were able simultaneously to go through the demonstrations of two distinct problems in Euclid. Nor, strictly investigated, is there any incongruity in this comparison.
>
> It may be but an idle whim, but it has always seemed to me, that the extraordinary vacillations of movement displayed by some whales when beset by three or four boats; the timidity and liability to queer frights, so common to such whales; I think that all this indirectly proceeds from the helpless perplexity of volition, in which their divided and diametrically opposite powers of vision must involve them.

Ishmael finds the fact that a whale cannot focus both eyes on the same object puzzling. If we assume that one source of human knowledge is perception of the physical world through our senses (our eyes, let us say), and if we further understand that human eyes work in conjunction with each other to bring a coherent visual stimulus to the brain which then processes the image, what, Ishmael wonders, do we make of the whale? For the leviathan's eyes must work independently of each other: it is impossible for both eyes to focus on the same object. Therefore, the whale's brain must simultaneously receive two disparate visual stimuli, perhaps of very different objects. Sensory knowledge for a whale, according to this reasoning, must inevitably present the animal with an irresolvable dichotomy. Therefore, Ishmael concludes, the whale's behavior when it is surrounded by several boats exhibits terror bred from confusion. Simply put, the whale in that circumstance does not *know* what is happening because his visual senses provide him with conflicting evidence.

The extension of this line of thought to human terms moves beyond purely physical sources of knowledge. We can conjecture, along with Ishmael, that whenever a person is confronted by two or more pieces of evidence, especially if they seem in conflict, the individual may become confused, and may be incapable of a rational decision. Like the whale, he or she may thrash around, making meaningless circles in the waters of his or her life.

Knowledge as a basis for action is at the heart of James Joyce's "Araby." The story takes place in Dublin in the early years of this century, and it is told through the eyes of a young boy, just moving into adolescence, who becomes obsessed with his friend's somewhat older sister. Because he is experiencing feelings of sexuality for the first time, he does not understand what to make of them. He only knows that she has become the center of his life, that her image "accompanied . . . [him] . . . even in places the most hostile to romance." In trying to deal with the feelings produced by his imagined romance, he translates them into the language of the medieval romances he has read. He declares, "I imagined that I bore my chalice safely through a throng of foes," as though he were a knight on a quest for the Holy Grail, and that in bringing it safely back he will win the affection of his ladylove.

The narrator of "Araby" finds himself as confused as Ishmael's whale. Whereas the whale encounters separate visual images, the boy in the story experiences a conflict between the actual facts of his situation and his imagined sense of those facts. His mind's eye proves far more persuasive than his actual experience with the woman. In his mind, he is involved in a romantic adventure to win the love of Mangan's sister. In actuality, he barely exists in the world of this young woman: he is only her kid brother's friend. So strong, however, is the power of his imagination that be becomes blind to his place in the young woman's life.

The young narrator of the story seems not to know what he thinks he knows. He thinks his friend's sister shares his feelings for him. More specifically, he believes that, instead of recapturing the Holy Grail, she wants him to bring back a gift from the bazaar—from Araby. He has no direct evidence for this belief, yet he clearly believes that he knows it to be the case. Consequently, he devotes all his energy to fulfilling his commitment to bring back a present for her from Araby.

The conclusion to the story involves a reconciliation between the boy's fantasy and a revelation that he acquires in the very act of attempting to buy the present. The boy declares that he has been a fool, "a creature driven and derided by vanity." The reader understands that his "vanity" was his belief that Mangan's sister could be seriously interested in him. He thought he knew this to be the case, but as he came to realize, he did not.

JAMES JOYCE
Araby

North Richmond Street, being blind, was a quiet street except at the hour when the Christian Brothers' School set the boys free. An uninhabited house of two storeys stood at the blind end, detached from its neighbours in a square ground. The other houses of the street, conscious of decent lives within them, gazed at one another with brown imperturbable faces.

The former tenant of our house, a priest, had died in the back drawing-room. Air, musty from having been long enclosed, hung in all the rooms, and the waste room behind the kitchen was littered with old useless papers. Among these I found a few papercovered books, the pages of which were curled and damp: *The Abbot*, by Walter Scott, *The Devout Communicant* and *The Memoirs of Vidocq*. I liked the last best because its leaves were yellow. The wild garden behind the house contained a central apple-tree and a few straggling bushes under one of which I found the late tenant's rusty bicycle-pump. He had been a very charitable priest; in his will he had left all his money to institutions and the furniture of his house to his sister.

When the short days of winter came dusk fell before we had well eaten our dinners. When we met in the street the houses had grown sombre. The space of sky above us was the colour of everchanging violet and towards it the lamps of the street lifted their feeble lanterns. The cold air stung us and we played till our bodies glowed. Our shouts echoed in the silent street. The career of our play brought us through the dark muddy lanes behind the houses where we ran the gantlet of the rough tribes from the cottages, to the back doors of the dark dripping gardens where odours arose from the ashpits, to the dark odorous stables where a coachman smoothed and combed the horse or shook music from the buckled harness. When we returned to the street light from the kitchen windows had filled the areas. If my uncle was seen turning the corner we hid in the shadow until we had seen him safely housed. Or if Mangan's sister came out on the doorstep to call her brother in to his tea we watched her from our shadow peer up and down the street. We waited to see whether she would remain or go in and, if she remained, we left our shadow and walked up to Mangan's steps resignedly. She was waiting for us, her figure defined by the light from the half-opened door. Her brother always teased her before he obeyed and I stood by the railings looking at her. Her dress swung as she moved her body and the soft rope of her hair tossed from side to side.

Every morning I lay on the floor in the front parlour watching her door. The blind was pulled down to within an inch of the sash so that I could not be seen. When she came out on the doorstep my heart leaped. I ran to the hall, seized my books and followed her. I kept her brown figure always in my eye and, when we came near the point at which our ways diverged, I quickened my pace and passed her. This happened morning after morning. I had never spoken to her, except for a few casual words, and yet her name was like a summons to all my foolish blood.

Her image accompanied me even in places the most hostile to romance. On Saturday evenings when my aunt went marketing I had to go to carry some of the parcels. We walked through the flaring streets, jostled by drunken men and bargaining women, amid the curses of labourers, the shrill litanies of shop-boys who stood on guard by the barrels of pigs' cheeks, the nasal chanting of street-singers, who sang a *come-all-you* about O'Donovan Rossa, or a ballad about the troubles in our native land. These noises converged in a single sensation of life for me: I imagined that I bore my chalice safely through a throng of foes. Her name sprang to my lips at moments in strange prayers and praises which I myself did not understand. My eyes were often full of tears (I could not tell why) and at times a flood from my heart seemed to pour itself out into my bosom. I thought little of the future. I did not know whether I would ever speak to her or not or, if I spoke to her, how I could tell her of my confused adoration. But my body was like a harp and her words and gestures were like fingers running upon the wires.

One evening I went into the back drawing-room in which the priest had died. It was a dark rainy evening and there was no sound in the house. Through one of the broken panes I heard the rain impinge upon the earth, the fine incessant needles of water playing in the sodden beds. Some distant lamp or lighted window gleamed below me. I was thankful that I could see so little. All my senses seemed to desire to veil themselves and, feeling that I was about to slip from them, I pressed the palms of my hands together until they trembled, murmuring: *O love! O love!* many times.

At last she spoke to me. When she addressed the first words to me I was so confused that I did not know what to answer. She asked me was I going to Araby. I forget whether I answered yes or no. It would be a splendid bazaar, she said; she would love to go.

—And why can't you? I asked.

While she spoke she turned a silver bracelet round and round her wrist. She could not go, she said, because there would be a retreat that week in her convent. Her brother and two other boys were fighting for their caps and I was alone at the railings. She held one of the spikes, bowing her head towards me. The light from the lamp opposite our door caught the white curve of her neck, lit up her hair that rested there and, falling, lit up the hand upon the railing. It fell over one side of her dress and caught the white border of a petticoat, just visible as she stood at ease.

—It's well for you, she said.

—If I go, I said, I will bring you something.

What innumerable follies laid waste my waking and sleeping thoughts after that evening! I wished to annihilate the tedious intervening days. I chafed against the work of school. At night in my bedroom and by day in the classroom her image came between me and the page I strove to read. The syllables of the word *Araby* were called to me through the silence in which my soul luxuriated and cast an Eastern enchantment over me. I asked for leave to go to the bazaar on Saturday night. My aunt was surprised and hoped it was not some Freemason affair. I answered few questions in class, I watched my master's face pass from amiability to sternness; he hoped I was not beginning to idle. I could not call my wandering thoughts together. I had hardly any patience with the serious work of life which, now that it stood between me and my desire, seemed to me child's play, ugly monotonous child's play.

On Saturday morning I reminded my uncle that I wished to go to the bazaar in the evening. He was fussing at the hallstand, looking for the hat-brush, and answered me curtly:

—Yes, boy, I know.

As he was in the hall I could not go into the front parlour and lie at the window. I left the

house in bad humour and walked slowly towards the school. The air was pitilessly raw and
already my heart misgave me.

When I came home to dinner my uncle had
not yet been home. Still it was early. I sat staring at the clock for some time and, when its
ticking began to irritate me, I left the room. I
mounted the staircase and gained the upper part
of the house. The high cold empty gloomy
rooms liberated me and I went from room to
room singing. From the front window I saw my
companions playing below in the street. Their
cries reached me weakened and indistinct and,
leaning my forehead against the cool glass, I
looked over at the dark house where she lived. I
may have stood there for an hour, seeing nothing but the brown-clad figure cast by my imagination, touched discreetly by the lamplight at
the curved neck, at the hand upon the railings
and at the border below the dress.

When I came downstairs again I found Mrs.
Mercer sitting at the fire. She was an old gar-
rulous woman, a pawnbroker's widow, who collected used stamps for some pious purpose. I had
to endure the gossip of the tea-table. The meal
was prolonged beyond an hour and still my uncle did not come. Mrs. Mercer stood up to go:
she was sorry she couldn't wait any longer, but it
was after eight o'clock and she did not like to be
out late, as the night air was bad for her. When
she had gone I began to walk up and down the
room, clenching my fists. My aunt said:

—I'm afraid you may put off your bazaar
for this night of Our Lord.

At nine o'clock I heard my uncle's latchkey
in the halldoor. I heard him talking to himself
and heard the hallstand rocking when it had received the weight of his overcoat. I could interpret these signs. When he was midway through
his dinner I asked him to give me the money to
go to the bazaar. He had forgotten.

—The people are in bed and after their first
sleep now, he said.

I did not smile. My aunt said to him energetically:

—Can't you give him the money and let
him go? You've kept him late enough as it is.

My uncle said he was very sorry he had for-

gotten. He said he believed in the old saying:
All work and no play makes Jack a dull boy. He
asked me where I was going and, when I had
told him a second time he asked me did I know
The Arab's Farewell to his Steed. When I left
the kitchen he was about to recite the opening
lines of the piece to my aunt.

I held a florin tightly in my hand as I strode
down Buckingham Street towards the station.
The sight of the streets thronged with buyers
and glaring with gas recalled to me the purpose
of my journey. I took my seat in a third-class
carriage of a deserted train. After an intolerable
delay the train moved out of the station slowly.
It crept onward among ruinous houses and over
the twinkling river. At Westland Row Station a
crowd of people pressed to the carriage doors;
but the porters moved them back, saying that
it was a special train for the bazaar. I remained
alone in the bare carriage. In a few minutes the
train drew up beside an improvised wooden
platform. I passed out on to the road and saw
by the lighted dial of a clock that it was ten
minutes to ten. In front of me was a large building which displayed the magical name.

I could not find any sixpenny entrance and,
fearing that the bazaar would be closed, I
passed in quickly through a turnstile, handing a
shilling to a weary-looking man. I found myself
in a big hall girdled at half its height by a gallery. Nearly all the stalls were closed and the
greater part of the hall was in darkness. I recognised a silence like that which pervades a
church after a service. I walked into the centre
of the bazaar timidly. A few people were gathered about the stalls which were still open. Before a curtain, over which the words *Café
Chantant* were written in coloured lamps, two
men were counting money on a salver. I listened
to the fall of the coins.

Remembering with difficulty why I had
come I went over to one of the stalls and examined porcelain vases and flowered teasets. At
the door of the stall a young lady was talking
and laughing with two young gentlemen. I remarked their English accents and listened
vaguely to their conversation.

—O, I never said such a thing!

—O, but you did!

—O, but I didn't!

—Didn't she say that?

—Yes! I heard her.

—O, there's a . . . fib!

Observing me the young lady came over and asked me did I wish to buy anything. The tone of her voice was not encouraging; she seemed to have spoken to me out of a sense of duty. I looked humbly at the great jars that stood like eastern guards at either side of the dark entrance to the stall and murmured:

—No, thank you.

The young lady changed the position of one of the vases and went back to the two young men. They began to talk of the same subject. Once or twice the young lady glared at me over her shoulder.

I lingered before her stall, though I knew my stay was useless, to make my interest in her wares seem the more real. Then I turned away slowly and walked down the middle of the bazaar. I allowed the two pennies to fall against the sixpence in my pocket. I heard a voice call from one end of the gallery that the light was out. The upper part of the hall was now completely dark.

Gazing up into darkness I saw myself as a creature driven and derided by vanity; and my eyes burned with anguish and anger.

QUESTIONS ABOUT "ARABY"

1. What *objective* evidence is there in the story concerning Mangan's sister's attitude toward the narrator?
2. Review their conversation about Araby. Did she ask him to bring her back a present?
3. Read the descriptions of the young woman. What about her seems to capture the boy's imagination?
4. Most of the action of the story occurs in the boy's mind. What kind of mental reality does he create for himself and Mangan's sister?
5. Joyce uses language to suggest the boy's mental processes. Look for particular words that offer either a romantic or a religious connotation. For example, the narrator talks about his feelings of "adoration" for the young woman. What does this word choice tell us about how the boy views her? What other examples of suggestive word choice can you find?
6. On the night the boy intends to go to Araby, his uncle arrives home late and drunk. Do you see any significance in this scene in terms of the tension between the boy's fantasy and the real world?
7. Review the last scene. Why does the boy fail to buy a present? What does he realize? What does he see in the behavior of the shop girl that opens his eyes to his situation?
8. The story begins and ends with references to blindness and darkness. How do these images pull the story together?

Philosophical Discussion:
What Is Knowledge?

The young hero of James Joyce's short story, "Araby," suffers from a youthful malady—infatuation. He thinks that he is in love with his friend Mangan's sister, a girl he knows only from a distance. Yet he is convinced, after she speaks to him briefly of Araby, a certain bazaar, that he must go there (at considerable inconvenience and some expense) to bring his "true love" a gift. So all-encompassing is his fantasy that the "serious work of life" becomes "ugly monotonous child's play." Does she care for him? Does she even notice him? She pays him little heed aside from when she speaks those few words. Our hero is unconcerned. What counts is Araby, the very sound of which "cast an Eastern enchantment" over him.

We can sympathize with Joyce's hero. Perhaps we can recall our own Araby, our own follies, when we, too, were deluded, beguiled, misled, duped, gulled, or deceived. Yet, we often see through the error of our ways as Joyce's hero does at the end of the story. "Gazing into the darkness I saw myself as a creature driven and derided by vanity. . . ." Araby, after all, is just a market. And Mangan's sister? Well, perhaps she is just Mangan's sister.

Human beings are prone to error. Thinking or believing that something is the case, even when we do so with all our heart and soul, does not make it so. The study of knowledge, or "epistemology" as philosophers call this field, is the problem of distinguishing between thinking that we know something and actually knowing it. Without this distinction, for all we know we might just be living in a fantasy, like the hero of "Araby."

Joyce's story is about the awakening of a boy, but the problem of knowledge runs much deeper. Our western tradition has apparently undergone similar awakenings, not the least of which was the revolution in scientific thinking led by Copernicus, Galileo and others in the sixteenth and early seventeenth centuries. Although these thinkers were not infatuated with romantic illusions, they, not unlike the hero of Joyce's story, experienced a kind of revelation.

Until the sixteenth century, most scholars believed, with Aristotle, that the earth was the center of the universe and that all celestial objects, including the sun, revolved about us. The Church, too, following the teachings of St. Thomas Aquinas, accepted the Aristotelian view, especially as it coincided with Judeo-Christian theology. If

God created Man in His image, then certainly the Creator would place His creation at the center of His universe. Moreover, the Aristotelian view was commonsensical. Everyone could plainly see that the sun rose in the east and set in the west, and that the earth was stationary.

Nevertheless, despite apparent widespread agreement among scientists, theists and laymen, the Aristotelian system was mistaken. The earth is not the center of the universe, nor does everything revolve about us.

It seems that the people of the ancient and medieval worlds were systematically beguiled. Like Joyce's protagonist, they too were living in a kind of dream. Worse. Unlike Joyce's hero, who apparently suffered his foolish beliefs for only a few days, the Aristotelian tradition was alive for 2,000 years. "Araby," by itself, presents no great epistemological crisis. A young man gets caught up in a romantic fantasy. This is not earthshaking. But when, for generations, a whole civilization appears to be taken in by a set of beliefs that turn out to have no more foundation than a boy's daydream, something more profound is at stake. If so many people can be so wrong, how can anybody ever be sure of anything? Can our present beliefs in astronomy, physics, biology, politics, and morality turn out to be no more well-founded than those of our intellectual predecessors—than those, for example, of a child dreaming of Araby?

In order to answer these and other related questions, let us consider what we mean when we speak of knowledge or, more commonly, of knowing. As we shall see, the terms "knowing" and "knowledge" are not always used in the same sense and it may prove useful to see how they differ. To begin, we speak of knowing in at least two different, though related contexts.

Human beings know how to do things, for example, to play the piano, drive a car, build a birdhouse. Philosophers call this *knowing how*. Animals, too, know how to do things. A dog, for example, can be trained to fetch a stick, a laboratory rat to run a maze. Following the lead of Ivan Pavlov, J. B. Watson, and B. F. Skinner, behavioral psychologists claim that *knowing how* is the result of either classical or instrumental conditioning, methods designed to reinforce desired behaviors and extinguish others.

Behaviorists have suggested that, except for certain reflexes, human conduct can be explained entirely as the result of conditioning. This is controversial, however, especially in light of those situations in which we speak of, and in which human actions seem partly determined by, *knowing that* something is the case. We may be conditioned in the army, for example, to salute a superior officer. But as soon as we know that we are officially discharged from the service, we no longer behave in this way. Of course, we may continue to salute as the result of habit. But we need no special training to behave in a more civilian manner. We need only know that saluting is no longer called for—and perhaps bear this in mind as we pass individuals who are still in uniform.

Knowing that is typically human. A supermarket scanner that correctly identifies a container of milk does not know that it *is* a container of milk; a rat that knows how to run a maze does not know that it *is* a maze, or that it is running through one. A person, unlike a supermarket scanner or a laboratory rat, cannot only recognize things, and know how to do things, but can also know that something is the case. A person can have knowledge.

Because we can have knowledge, the need arises for distinguishing between knowing something and thinking that we do, since we can think we know that something is so, when we do not. For example, a checkout clerk who mistakenly gives a customer a ten-dollar bill, thinks that it is a one. By contrast, a computer that misidentifies a ten-dollar item as a one-dollar item is malfunctioning. Similarly, a rat that takes an incorrect turn does not think that it is taking a correct turn. Rather, it just does not know how to negotiate the maze.

Knowledge involves thinking and other higher-order cognitive powers, such as reasoning, inferring, deducing, deliberating, speculating, pondering, meditating, ruminating, and musing. To help illuminate the concept of knowledge, let us turn to a traditional analysis of knowledge inspired by Plato. According to the Platonic tradition, a person (call the individual ''S'') knows that something is the case (let's call what S knows ''p''—for example, that *the earth revolves about the sun,* or that *water freezes at 32° farenheit*) when, and only when, three conditions are satisfied:

(a) S believes that p;
(b) S's belief that p is justified;
(c) It is true that p.

In brief, according to this approach, knowledge is *true justified belief.* Let us consider why philosophers have regarded each of these conditions as necessary. According to the first condition, without beliefs there can be no knowledge. For example, inanimate objects or plants do not know anything. A geranium, for example, faces the sun not because it believes that that's where the sunlight comes from, but because of photosynthesis, a chemical-mechanical process that automatically adjusts the position of the plant's leaves for maximum exposure. Some people, nevertheless, think that geraniums have beliefs. They talk to their plants in hopes of keeping them in good spirits so that they will blossom. But plants, like stones, do not have the central nervous system necessary for awareness. Without awareness, an individual cannot have hopes, fears, wants, desires, or beliefs.

Let us now consider the third condition, that ''it is true that p.'' According to this Platonistic suggestion, one of the main differences between knowledge and belief is that a person can believe what is false, but cannot know what is false. If a person knows something, then what the individual knows must be the case. For example, Aristotelians thought they knew that the earth was motionless. They certainly believed that this was so. But since the earth revolves about the sun, they did not know what they thought they knew. Otherwise, medieval scholars knew that the earth is stationary when, in fact, the earth is moving—which seems contradictory.

It may be suggested, in deference to Aristotle, that he did have knowledge. Thinkers from the fourth century B.C. until the time of Galileo, knew that the earth was stable and central in the universe. This is what was taught. This is what students of astronomy studied. This is what the accepted texts proclaimed to be the case. To insist that truth be a condition of knowing seems to be an ideal that we need not attain in the actual practice of human speculation and scholarship. History suggests a standard other than Plato's for whether a person knows or does not know.

But what other standard is there? If truth is not a condition of knowledge, then what exactly is the difference between knowing that something is so, and merely imagining that it is? Without truth, fantasizing that Mangan's sister is one's true love would be no different from knowing that she is. This means that dreaming that something is so would make it so, which, unfortunately for both Joyce's hero and Aristotelian scholars, seems not to be the case. (For more on Truth, see Part II.)

Is true belief enough to have knowledge? The Platonic tradition says no, and for good reason. Consider the following scenario. Watching the 1988 presidential election returns on television, Jack dozes off and dreams. In his dream he is watching the same election returns on a similar TV set and hears that George Bush is pronounced the winner. Jack wakes up, not realizing he has dozed off, believing that George Bush is indeed the winner. Moreover, while Jack was asleep, George Bush actually won the election. Jack now has a true belief. But does he have knowledge? It seems not. Otherwise, a person could learn not only about an election, but any other event, simply by dreaming about it—which seems unrealistic.

Something more is needed, but what? In the "Theaetetus," Plato suggests that in addition to having true beliefs about a thing, we must be able to give "an account" of it. However, in the dialogue, this suggestion proves inadequate. Others, agreeing with Plato that true belief is not enough, have suggested that a justification is needed. Edmund Gettier points this out in his article, "Is Justified True Belief Knowledge?" According to this approach, a person who dreams that something is the case is not justified in believing that it is and thus lacks knowledge. But what counts as justification? Dreaming is not a reliable method of finding something out. Does this mean that our source of information must be reliable? Do we know that George Bush won the election if we read the results in the *New York Times* or the *Christian Science Monitor*? Perhaps, just as we can find out who won the election of 1888 by looking it up in an encyclopedia or reading about it in some history textbook. Newspapers, encyclopedias, and textbooks are common sources of information which provide us, it seems, with a wealth of knowledge.

But is this so? Consider a scenario similar to the one described above, with one apparently minor modification. As before, Jack wakes up believing truly that George Bush has won the election. This time, however, he tells Jill. Jill believes Jack—Jack is a reliable source of information, at least as trustworthy as the *New York Times,* a textbook, or an encyclopedia. Jill now has a true belief. Moreover, if justification consists in acquiring a belief from a reliable source, then Jill's belief is justified. But does Jill know who won the election? Here we face a puzzle. If Jill knows, why doesn't Jack? Aside from the fact that Jill acquires her belief from Jack, there does not seem to be any other significant epistemological difference between them. For example, Jack has as much (or as little) evidence for the belief as Jill. But if Jack knows, then justification does not seem necessary, since Jack is not justified. Jack falsely believes that he acquired the information about the election from a reliable source, a TV broadcast, while he really got it from his own dream. Under the supposition that Jill has knowledge, knowledge is nothing more than true belief, which we have already rejected.

Let us suppose that Jill does not know. If this is so, then having a justified true belief would seem to be insufficient for knowledge, since Jill has a justified true belief. Gettier makes a similar point. Under this supposition, something more seems needed, but what can that be?

The general response is that a certain kind of justification is needed. For example, religious believers have generally appealed to *authority,* either to some leader such as the Pope, or a sacred text, like the Bible, or to God Himself. And they are right that most people initially acquire their beliefs, both religious and otherwise, from some authority or other. The problem is that there is not just one recognized leader nor just one holy book. Moreover, the leaders and the books do not all agree. To be sure, the Judaic, Christian, and Moslem traditions teach that there is one deity. About this there is agreement. Nevertheless, since God is thought of as revealing His intentions through each of these different traditions, it is not clear how this apparent agreement helps.

Some individuals claim to converse directly with God. Tradition is less important than accepting God into one's heart or reading holy writ literally. But since not all who claim direct contact with the Almighty agree about His message, we seem to have the same difficulty all over again.

The problem goes deeper. When a person thinks that he or she hears the voice of God, how does that person know that it is God's voice and not, for example, that of some evil genius? René Descartes raises this question in "Meditation I." How would we know, if we thought we heard the voice of God, that it was God's voice? This question brings us back to the basic problem of knowledge: how do we distinguish between knowing and only thinking that we know? The authoritarian approach does not seem to solve the problem.

Proponents of science have generally taken a different approach: that people must ultimately justify their beliefs by appeal to experience. This approach is termed *empiricism*. (A selection of David Hume, the eighteenth-century empiricist, is included in Part VI, Religious Belief.) Indeed, established scientific beliefs are supported by empirical observation, often obtained through some experiment. But is there one common set of experiences that all people share, to which an appeal can be made, especially when people disagree in their beliefs? Empiricists since David Hume have attempted to define some such set, but with limited success. Earlier in this century, theorists attempted to define a basic kind of data obtained through the senses, called *sense data*, that any adequate experiment must be designed to yield (for example, a needle deflection on an ammeter, or a red color in a spectroscope). The idea was to describe the data in a way that stood neutrally between competing theories so that any observer, regardless of theoretical orientation, could test his or her beliefs accordingly. But, as critics of the sense-datum approach have argued, the distinction between what one observes and what one believes, especially when the beliefs are of the theoretical kind found in science, is not clear. For example, two different physicians may hear the same "hiss" when listening through a stethoscope to a person's chest. One of them hears the sound as a mitral valve heart murmur, the other as endocarditis. However the correct diagnosis is to be determined, it seems that getting more auditory sense data will not suffice. Somehow the data, to be of any use, must be interpreted. But interpretation seems to require other beliefs. The idea that there are certain bits of independent data seems as much a myth for science as for the young boy in "Araby." Experience alone, even when defined as "sense data," seems inadequate to explain how we know what we think we know.

The hero of "Araby" sees what he wants to see. Is this true of us all? There is, after all, a difference between an adolescent male just coming of age and those of us who are more mature, not just in age, but in judgment. It may appear to be almost a mathematical certainty that if you add one boy and one girl of post-pubescent age, the result is romantic illusion—and it stands to reason that the judgment of people under an illusion is impaired. But how certain can we be of mathematical or quasi-mathematical equations? Some philosophers following Descartes' rationalistic approach (consider, for example, Descartes' "Meditation V") have argued that if we know anything, we know the basic truths of arithmetic and geometry. Beyond a certain age, (say six), we need no special training or even experience to appreciate the obvious truth that in all cases $1 + 1 = 2$. If someone denies this, we automatically question his or her judgment rather than the mathematics, just as we would question the judgment of an adolescent who feels that his love is confirmed after only a few brief words with a mere acquaintance.

The rationalist solution to the problem of knowledge is that we know that which is self-evident or that which is logically derived from the self-evident. For example, we can know that our checkbook balances, not because the balance itself is self-evident, but because we can analyze and reduce our accounts to a series of relatively simple arithmetical equations, each one of which is clear and distinct, as Descartes would suggest. Putting them all together, our result is no less certain than any of the parts.

What advice would the rationalist give to Joyce's hero? Be a little more analytic, a little more critical. Before rushing off to Araby on what might turn out to be a wild goose chase, try to decide whether your own experience is most revealing or whether the experiences of other, cooler, heads can be more trustworthy. Sounds like good advice.

However, certain mathematical assumptions, long held to be self-evident, have themselves been called into question. For example, in the nineteenth century Nicholas Lobachevesky and other mathematicians showed how a consistent geometry need not assume Euclid's axiom that parallel lines can never meet. The subsequent development of non-Euclidean geometries and their application to physical space, as in Einsteinian relativity, is regarded as a dislocation in our thinking at least as profound as the Copernican revolution in the seventeenth century. These developments alone should not make us skeptical of mathematics. It is as certain now as in the past that in a non-curved Euclidean space, parallel lines never meet. The problem is this: since there are several incompatible yet self-consistent geometries, we cannot rely on mathematics alone to decide the shape of real space. The problem can be generalized. In any field of enquiry we may expect to find self-consistent and apparently incompatible principles, each of which seems self-evident when expressed in the abstract. For example, Thomas Jefferson, Alexander Hamilton, and other founders of American democracy, influenced by seventeenth-century rationalism, held certain principles of equality and human rights to be self-evident. But as we see more clearly today, the attempt to bring about a more egalitarian society, through such programs as progressive taxation and social-welfare legislation, seems to conflict with the apparent rights of individuals to keep what they earn and spend their resources as they will. (For a more extensive discussion of this issue, see Part V, Justice.) How we know that a certain social policy is right, no less than how a physicist knows that the real world conforms to a certain geometry, seems not to be explained on the rationalist model. The rationalist's advice to the hero of "Araby" would thus appear to be just as abstract—and, by itself, just as empty.

Where does this leave us? Neither the authoritarian, empiricist nor rationalist seems to answer our question about justification. Each offers a necessary part of the answer, but not one, not even all together, provides a sufficient solution. In the absence of a clear account of the distinction between knowing and thinking that we know, should we be skeptical that there is a distinction? What would this mean?

Those who favor *skepticism* as an approach seem to think that there is no more foundation for believing in subatomic particles than there is for believing in earth, air, fire, and water (the four elements of ancient physics) as the basis of matter, or no more reason for believing in equality and human rights than for believing in slavery or apartheid. According to the skeptic, our beliefs are as much the product of cultural upbringing as they are of science and philosophy, which is to say that much of what we take for granted derives from historical accident. Had we been raised among the Kali cultists of Northern India we too would believe in ritual human sacrifice, just as European and American physicians until the twentieth century believed in bloodletting. And although our current beliefs appear to be particularly successful—as the technological advancement in the last seventy-five years would indicate, from horse-and-buggy to space rocketry—in its day bloodletting, too, seemed to work. Of course, there were dramatic failures. George Washington died as the result of his physician applying too many leeches. But our technology has had its failures as well—the tragic loss of the U.S. space shuttle, *Challenger,* for example. If pre-twentieth-century technology worked, the skeptic would argue, it was largely a matter of good luck. The skeptic would say the same about twentieth-century technology.

Before we embrace the skeptical attitude, however, let us examine this philosophy more clearly, especially since there are at least two forms of skepticism, an ordinary and an extreme view. We should be clear which one we are adopting.

Ordinary skepticism is the view that
> (O) Some beliefs are unjustified.

Extreme skepticism holds that
> (E) No belief is justified.

Notice that neither skeptic, as we are using the term "skeptic," doubts that people have beliefs, nor that some beliefs are true. On the contrary, the skeptic, whether ordinary or extreme, believes to be true almost everything that we do—that the earth revolves about the sun, for example, or that water freezes at 32° farenheit, or perhaps that apartheid ought to be abandoned. The issue is not whether some beliefs are true but whether we know which ones they are.

The two varieties of skepticism are closely related. But the difference is important. Ordinary skepticism is a common attitude that most people attempt to cultivate and for good reason. One alternative to thinking that some beliefs are unjustified is the view that all beliefs are justified. But this is naive. Only a very young child, for example, thinks that he or she can believe everything. Some skepticism is certainly healthy.

But how skeptical should we be? Our discussion thus far seems to indicate that the main attempts to explain knowledge have been unsuccessful. Should we allow the skeptic to win the debate by default? We think not. On the contrary, a healthy skeptical attitude suggests that we be at least as skeptical of skepticism, especially the extreme variety, as of any of the other views.

Extreme skepticism seems self-defeating. Anyone who expresses doubts about everything, who thinks that deep down nothing can be proven, that there is no sufficient evidence for believing anything, that no belief is justified, must apply this same attitude to his or own beliefs, including (E), the principle that no belief is justified. Otherwise, such an individual is an ordinary, not an extreme, skeptic. But if extreme skepticism implies that (E) is unjustified, then there can be no reason for extreme skepticism. Otherwise, no belief is justified and, at least one belief is justified, which is a contradiction. By its own lights, (E) is unjustifiable, and hence, extreme skepticism is an unacceptable view.

Are there extreme skeptics? David Hume, the eighteenth-century empiricist, expressed an extremely skeptical attitude toward religious, ethical, mathematical, and eventually even empirical belief. He is regarded as the ultimate skeptic. Recently, Peter Unger defended a new form of skepticism which he suggests avoids the paradox described above. (We leave it to the reader to decide whether Unger is successful.) Richard Rorty has suggested that epistemology, rather than providing basic guidance in all forms of life, is just one among many intellectual pastimes. He expressed his skepticism of the whole enterprise in his recent book, *Philosophy and the Mirror of Nature.*

In the selection that follows he recommends hermeneutics, the study of textual interpretation, as a substitute.

Most people, except perhaps for adolescents who feel the stirrings of young love, are skeptics. This is the way things ought to be, provided we do not fall into an extreme and untenable version of this philosophy. If our review of epistemology teaches anything, it suggests that at present there are no easy formulas for distinguishing between knowing and thinking that we know. It also suggests that there is no reason for rejecting the distinction altogether. The lesson seems to be that there is more philosophical work to be done.

PLATO
Knowledge as Justified True Belief

SOCRATES: . . . what is one to say that knowledge is? For surely we are not going to give up yet.

THEAETETUS: Not unless you do so.

SOCRATES: Then tell me, what definition can we give with the least risk of contradicting ourselves?

THEAETETUS: The one we tried before, Socrates. I have nothing else to suggest.

SOCRATES: What was that?

THEAETETUS: That true belief is knowledge. Surely there can at least be no mistake in believing what is true and the consequences are always satisfactory.

SOCRATES: Try, and you will see, Theaetetus, as the man said when he was asked if the river was too deep to ford. So here, if we go forward on our search, we may stumble upon something that will reveal the thing we are looking for. We shall make nothing out, if we stay where we are.

THEAETETUS: True. Let us go forward and see.

SOCRATES: Well, we need not go far to see this much. You will find a whole profession to prove that true belief is not knowledge.

THEAETETUS: How so? What profession?

SOCRATES: The profession of those paragons of intellect known as orators and lawyers. There you have men who use their skill to produce conviction, not by instruction, but by making people believe whatever they want them to believe. You can hardly imagine teachers so clever as to be able, in the short time allowed by the clock, to instruct their hearers thoroughly in the true facts of a case of robbery or other violence which those hearers had not witnessed.

THEAETETUS: No, I cannot imagine that, but they can convince them.

SOCRATES: And by convincing you mean making them believe something.

THEAETETUS: Of course.

SOCRATES: And when a jury is rightly convinced of facts which can be known only by an eyewitness, then, judging by hearsay and accepting a true belief, they are judging

Reprinted from *The Collected Dialogues of Plato* (1961) pgs. 907–917, edited by Edith Hamilton and Huntington Cairns by permission of Routledge and Methuen Publishers. **Plato** (ca. 428 to 348 B.C.), one of the giants of Western philosophy, is best known for his classical theory of ideal forms. He was a student of Socrates and the teacher of Aristotle.

without knowledge, although, if they find the right verdict, their conviction is correct?

THEAETETUS: Certainly.

SOCRATES: But if true belief and knowledge were the same thing, the best of jurymen could never have a correct belief without knowledge. It now appears that they must be different things.

THEAETETUS: Yes, Socrates, I have heard someone make the distinction. I had forgotten, but now it comes back to me. He said that true belief with the addition of an account (λόγος) was knowledge, while belief without an account was outside its range. Where no account could be given of a thing, it was not 'knowable'—that was the word he used—where it could, it was knowable.

SOCRATES: A good suggestion. But tell me how he distinguished these knowable things from the unknowable. It may turn out that what you were told tallies with something I have heard said.

THEAETETUS: I am not sure if I can recall that, but I think I should recognize it if I heard it stated.

SOCRATES: If you have had a dream, let me tell you mine in return. I seem to have heard some people say that what might be called the first elements of which we and all other things consist are such that no account can be given of them. Each of them just by itself can only be named; we cannot attribute to it anything further or say that it exists or does not exist, for we should at once be attaching to it existence or nonexistence, whereas we ought to add nothing if we are to express just it alone. We ought not even to add 'just' or 'it' or 'each' or 'alone' or 'this', or any other of a host of such terms. These terms, running loose about the place, are attached to everything, and they are distinct from the things to which they are applied. If it were possible for an element to be expressed in any formula exclusively belonging to it, no other terms ought to enter into that expression. But in fact there is no formula in which any element can be expressed; it can only be named, for a name is all there is that belongs to it. But when we come to

things composed of these elements, then, just as these things are complex, so the names are combined to make a description (λόγος), a description being precisely a combination of names. Accordingly, elements are inexplicable and unknowable, but they can be perceived, while complexes ('syllables') are knowable and explicable, and you can have a true notion of them. So when a man gets hold of the true notion of something without an account, his mind does think truly of it, but he does not know it, for if one cannot give and receive an account of a thing, one has no knowledge of that thing. But when he has also got hold of an account, all this becomes possible to him and he is fully equipped with knowledge.

Does that version represent the dream as you heard it, or not?

THEAETETUS: Perfectly.

SOCRATES: So this dream finds favor and you hold that a true notion with the addition of an account is knowledge?

THEAETETUS: Precisely.

SOCRATES: Can it be, Theaetetus, that, all in a moment, we have found out today what so many wise men have grown old in seeking and have not found?

THEAETETUS: I, at any rate, am satisfied with our present statement, Socrates.

SOCRATES: Yes, the statement just in itself may well be satisfactory, for how can there ever be knowledge without an account and right belief? But there is one point in the theory as stated that does not find favor with me.

THEAETETUS: What is that?

SOCRATES: What might be considered its most ingenious feature. It says that the elements are unknowable, but whatever is complex ('syllables') can be known.

THEAETETUS: Is not that right?

SOCRATES: We must find out. We hold as a sort of hostage for the theory the illustration in terms of which it was stated.

THEAETETUS: Namely?

SOCRATES: Letters—the elements of writing—and syllables. That and nothing else was the prototype the author of this theory had in mind, don't you think?

THEAETETUS: Yes, it was.

SOCRATES: Let us take up that illustration, then, and put it to the question, or rather put the question to ourselves. Did we learn our letters on that principle or not? To begin with, is it true that an account can be given of syllables, but not of letters?

THEAETETUS: It may be so

SOCRATES: I agree, decidedly. Suppose you are asked about the first syllable of 'Socrates.' Explain, Theaetetus, what is SO? How will you answer?

THEAETETUS: S and O.

SOCRATES: And you have there an account of the syllable?

THEAETETUS: Yes.

SOCRATES: Go on, then, give me a similar account of S.

THEAETETUS: But how can one state the elements of an element? The fact is, of course, Socrates, that S is one of the consonants, nothing but a noise, like a hissing of the tongue, while B not only has no articulate sound but is not even a noise, and the same is true of most of the letters. So they may well be said to be inexplicable, when the clearest of them, the seven vowels themselves, have only a sound, and no sort of account can be given of them.

SOCRATES: So far, then, we have reached a right conclusion about knowledge.

THEAETETUS: Apparently.

SOCRATES: But now, have we been right in declaring that the letter cannot be known, though the syllable can?

THEAETETUS: That seems all right.

SOCRATES: Take the syllable then. Do we mean by that both the two letters or, if there are more than two, all the letters? Or do we mean a single entity that comes into existence from the moment when they are put together?

THEAETETUS: I should say we mean all the letters.

SOCRATES: Then take the case of the two letters S and O. The two together are the first syllable of my name. Anyone who knows that syllable knows both the letters, doesn't he?

THEAETETUS: Naturally,

SOCRATES: So he knows the S and the O.

THEAETETUS: Yes.

SOCRATES: But has he, then, no knowledge of *each* letter, so that he knows both without knowing either?

THEAETETUS: That is a monstrous absurdity, Socrates.

SOCRATES: And yet, if it is necessary to know each of two things before one can know both, he simply must know the letters first, if he is ever to know the syllable, and so our fine theory will vanish and leave us in the lurch.

THEAETETUS: With a startling suddenness.

SOCRATES: Yes, because we are not keeping a good watch upon it. Perhaps we ought to have assumed that the syllable was not the letters but a single entity that arises out of them with a unitary character of its own and different from the letters.

THEAETETUS: By all means. Indeed, it may well be so rather than the other way.

SOCRATES: Let us consider that. We ought not to abandon an imposing theory in this poor-spirited manner.

THEAETETUS: Certainly not.

SOCRATES: Suppose, then, it is as we say now. The syllable arises as a single entity from any set of letters which can be combined, and that holds of every complex, not only in the case of letters.

THEAETETUS: By all means.

SOCRATES: In that case, it must have no parts.

THEAETETUS: Why?

SOCRATES: Because, if a thing has parts, the whole thing must be the same as all the parts. Or do you say that a whole likewise is a single entity that arises out of the parts and is different from the aggregate of the parts?

THEAETETUS: Yes, I do.

SOCRATES: Then do you regard the sum (τò zso παν) as the same thing as the whole, or are they different?

THEAETETUS: I am not at all clear, but you tell me to answer boldly, so I will take the risk of saying they are different.

SOCRATES: Your boldness, Theaetetus, is right; whether your answer is so, we shall have to consider.

THEAETETUS: Yes, certainly.

SOCRATES: Well, then, the whole will be different from the sum, according to our present view.

THEAETETUS: Yes.

SOCRATES: Well but now, is there any difference between the sum and all the things it includes? For instance, when we say, 'one, two, three, four, five, six,' or 'twice three' or 'three times two' or 'four and two' or 'three and two and one,' are we in all these cases expressing the same thing or different things?

THEAETETUS: The same.

SOCRATES: Just six, and nothing else?

THEAETETUS: Yes.

SOCRATES: In fact, in each form of expression we have expressed all the six.

THEAETETUS: Yes.

SOCRATES: But when we express them all, is there no sum that we express?

THEAETETUS: There must be.

SOCRATES: And is that sum anything else than 'six'?

THEAETETUS: No.

SOCRATES: Then, at any rate in the case of things that consist of a number, the words 'sum' and 'all the things' denote the same thing.

THEAETETUS: So it seems.

SOCRATES: Let us put our argument, then, in this way. The number of [square feet in] an acre, and the acre are the same thing, aren't they?

THEAETETUS: Yes.

SOCRATES: And so too with the number of [feet in] a mile?

THEAETETUS: Yes.

SOCRATES: And again with the number of [soldiers in] an army and the army, and so on, in all cases. The total number is the same as the total thing in each case.

THEAETETUS: Yes.

SOCRATES: But the number of [units in] any collection of things cannot be anything but *parts* of that collection?

THEAETETUS: No.

SOCRATES: Now, anything that has parts consists of parts.

THEAETETUS: Evidently.

SOCRATES: But all the parts, we have agreed, are the same as the sum, if the total number is to be the same as the total thing.

THEAETETUS: Yes.

SOCRATES: The whole, then, does not consist of parts, for if it were all the parts it would be a sum.

THEAETETUS: Apparently not.

SOCRATES: But can a part be a part of anything but its whole?

THEAETETUS: Yes, of the sum.

SOCRATES: You make a gallant fight of it, Theaetetus. But does not 'the sum' mean precisely something from which nothing is missing?

THEAETETUS: Necessarily.

SOCRATES: And is not a whole exactly the same thing—that from which nothing whatever is missing? Whereas, when something is removed, the thing becomes neither a whole nor a sum; it changes at the same moment from being both to being neither.

THEAETETUS: I think now that there is no difference between a sum and a whole.

SOCRATES: Well, we were saying, were we not, that when a thing has parts, the whole or sum will be the same thing as all the parts?

THEAETETUS: Certainly.

SOCRATES: To go back, then, to the point I was trying to make just now, if the syllable is not the same thing as the letters, does it not follow that it cannot have the letters as parts of itself; otherwise, being the same thing as the letters, it would be neither more nor less knowable than they are?

THEAETETUS: Yes.

SOCRATES: And it was to avoid that consequence that we supposed the syllable to be different from the letters.

THEAETETUS: Yes.

SOCRATES: Well, if the letters are not parts of the syllable, can you name any things, other than its letters, that are parts of a syllable?

THEAETETUS: Certainly not, Socrates. If I admitted that it had any parts, it would surely be absurd to set aside the letters and look for parts of any other kind.

SOCRATES: Then, on the present showing, a syllable will be a thing that is absolutely one and cannot be divided into parts of any sort?

THEAETETUS: Apparently.

SOCRATES: Do you remember then, my dear Theaetetus, our accepting a short while ago a statement that we thought satisfactory—that no account could be given of the primary things of which other things are composed, because each of them, taken just by itself, was incomposite, and that it was not correct to attribute even 'existence' to it, or to call it 'this,' on the ground that these words expressed different things that were extraneous to it, and this was the ground for making the primary thing inexplicable and unknowable?

THEAETETUS: I remember.

SOCRATES: Then is not exactly this, and nothing else, the ground of its being simple in nature and indivisible into parts? I can see no other.

THEAETETUS: Evidently there is no other.

SOCRATES: Then has not the syllable now turned out to be a thing of the same sort, if it has not parts and is a unitary thing?

THEAETETUS: Certainly.

SOCRATES: To conclude, then, if, on the one hand, the syllable is the same thing as a number of letters and is a whole with the letters as its parts, then the letters must be neither more nor less knowable and explicable than syllables, since we made out that all the parts are the same thing as the whole.

THEAETETUS: True.

SOCRATES: But if, on the other hand, the syllable is a unity without parts, syllable and letter likewise are equally incapable of explanation and unknowable. The same reason will make them so.

THEAETETUS: I see no way out of that.

SOCRATES: If so, we must not accept this statement—that the syllable can be known and explained, the letter cannot.

THEAETETUS: No, not if we hold by our argument.

SOCRATES: And again, would not your own experience in learning your letters rather incline you to accept the opposite view?

THEAETETUS: What view do you mean?

SOCRATES: This—that all the time you were learning you were doing nothing else but trying to distinguish by sight or hearing each letter by itself, so as not to be confused by any arrangement of them in spoken or written words.

THEAETETUS: That is quite true.

SOCRATES: And in the music school the height of accomplishment lay precisely in being able to follow each several note and tell which string it belonged to, and notes, as everyone would agree, are the elements of music.

THEAETETUS: Precisely.

SOCRATES: Then, if we are to argue from our own experience of elements and complexes to other cases, we shall conclude that elements in general yield knowledge that is much clearer than knowledge of the complex and more effective for a complete grasp of anything we seek to know. If anyone tells us that the complex is by its nature knowable, while the element is unknowable, we shall suppose that, whether he intends it or not, he is playing with us.

THEAETETUS: Certainly.

SOCRATES: Indeed we might, I think, find other arguments to prove that point. But we must not allow them to distract our attention from the question before us, namely, what can really be meant by saying that an account added to true belief yields knowledge in its most perfect form.

THEAETETUS: Yes, we must see what that means.

SOCRATES: Well then, what is this term 'account' intended to convey to us? I think it must mean one of three things.

THEAETETUS: What are they?

SOCRATES: The first will be giving overt expression to one's thought by means of vocal sound with names and verbs, casting an image of one's notion on the stream that flows through the lips, like a reflection in a mirror or in water. Do you agree that expression of that sort is an 'account'?

THEAETETUS: I do. We certainly call that expressing ourselves in speech (λέγειν).

SOCRATES: On the other hand, that is a thing that anyone can do more or less readily. If a man is not born deaf or dumb, he can signify what he thinks on any subject. So in this sense anyone whatever who has a correct notion evidently will have it 'with an account,' and there will be no place left anywhere for a correct notion apart from knowledge.

THEAETETUS: True.

SOCRATES: Then we must not be too ready to charge the author of the definition of knowledge now before us with talking nonsense. Perhaps that is not what he meant. He may have meant being able to reply to the question, what any given thing is, by enumerating its elements.

THEAETETUS: For example, Socrates?

SOCRATES: For example, Hesiod says about a wagon, 'In a wagon are a hundred pieces of wood.' I could not name them all; no more, I imagine, could you. If we were asked what a wagon is, we should be content if we could mention wheels, axle, body, rails, yoke.

THEAETETUS: Certainly.

SOCRATES: But I dare say he would think us just as ridiculous as if we replied to the question about your own name by telling the syllables. We might think and express ourselves correctly, but we should be absurd if we fancied ourselves to be grammarians and able to give such an account of the name Theaetetus as a grammarian would offer. He would say it is impossible to give a scientific account of anything, short of adding to your true notion a complete catalogue of the elements, as, I think, was said earlier.

THEAETETUS: Yes, it was.

SOCRATES: In the same way, he would say, we may have a correct notion of the wagon, but the man who can give a complete statement of its nature by going through those hundred parts has thereby added an account to his correct notion and, in place of mere belief,

has arrived at a technical knowledge of the wagon's nature, by going through all the elements in the whole.

THEAETETUS: Don't you approve, Socrates?

SOCRATES: Tell me if you approve, my friend, and whether you accept the view that the complete enumeration of elements is an account of any given thing, whereas description in terms of syllables or of any larger unit still leaves it unaccounted for. Then we can look into the matter further.

THEAETETUS: Well, I do accept that.

SOCRATES: Do you think, then, that anyone has knowledge of whatever it may be, when he thinks that one and the same thing is a part sometimes of one thing, sometimes of a different thing, or again when he believes now one and now another thing to be part of one and the same thing?

THEAETETUS: Certainly not.

SOCRATES: Have you forgotten, then, that when you first began learning to read and write, that was what you and your school-fellows did?

THEAETETUS: Do you mean, when we thought that now one letter and now another was part of the same syllable, and when we put the same letter sometimes into the proper syllable, sometimes into another?

SOCRATES: That is what I mean.

THEAETETUS: Then I have certainly not forgotten, and I do not think that one has reached knowledge so long as one is in that condition.

SOCRATES: Well, then, if at that stage you are writing 'Theaetetus' and you think you ought to write T and H and E and do so, and again when you are trying to write 'Theodorus,' you think you ought to write T and E and do so, can we say that you know the first syllable of your two names?

THEAETETUS: No, we have just agreed that one has not knowledge so long as one is in that condition.

SOCRATES: And there is no reason why a person should not be in the same condition with respect to the second, third, and fourth syllables as well?

THEAETETUS: None whatever.

SOCRATES: Can we, then, say that whenever in writing 'Theaetetus' he puts down all the letters in order, then he is in possession of the complete catalogue of elements together with correct belief?

THEAETETUS: Obviously.

SOCRATES: Being still, as we agree, without knowledge, though his beliefs are correct?

THEAETETUS: Yes.

SOCRATES: Although he possesses the 'account' in addition to right belief. For when he wrote he was in possession of the catalogue of the elements, which we agreed was the 'account.'

THEAETETUS: True.

SOCRATES: So, my friend, there is such a thing as right belief together with an account, which is not yet entitled to be called knowledge.

THEAETETUS: I am afraid so.

SOCRATES: Then, apparently, our idea that we had found the perfectly true definition of knowledge was no better than a golden dream. Or shall we not condemn the theory yet? Perhaps the meaning to be given to 'account' is not this, but the remaining one of the three, one of which we said must be intended by anyone who defines knowledge as correct belief together with an account.

THEAETETUS: A good reminder. There is still one meaning left. The first was what might be called the image of thought in spoken sound, and the one we have just discussed was going all through the elements to arrive at the whole. What is the third?

SOCRATES: The meaning most people would give—being able to name some mark by which the thing one is asked about differs from everything else.

THEAETETUS: Could you give me an example of such an account of a thing?

SOCRATES: Take the sun as an example. I dare say you will be satisfied with the account of it as the brightest of the heavenly bodies that go round the earth.

THEAETETUS: Certainly.

SOCRATES: Let me explain the point of this example. It is to illustrate what we were just saying—that if you get hold of the difference distinguishing any given thing from all others, then, so some people say, you will have an 'account' of it, whereas, so long as you fix upon something common to other things, your account will embrace all the things that share it.

THEAETETUS: I understand. I agree that what you describe may fairly be called an 'account.'

SOCRATES: And if, besides a right notion about a thing, whatever it may be, you also grasp its difference from all other things, you will have arrived at knowledge of what, till then, you had only a notion of.

THEAETETUS: We do say that, certainly.

SOCRATES: Really, Theaetetus, now I come to look at this statement at close quarters, it is like a scene painting. I cannot make it out at all, though, so long as I kept at a distance, there seemed to be some sense in it.

THEAETETUS: What do you mean? Why so?

SOCRATES: I will explain, if I can. Suppose I have a correct notion about you; if I add to that the account of you, then, we are to understand, I know you. Otherwise I have only a notion.

THEAETETUS: Yes.

SOCRATES: And 'account' means putting your differentness into words.

THEAETETUS: Yes.

SOCRATES: So, at the time when I had only a notion, my mind did not grasp any of the points in which you differ from others?

THEAETETUS: Apparently not.

SOCRATES: Then I must have had before my mind one of those common things which belong to another person as much as to you.

THEAETETUS: That follows.

SOCRATES: But look here! If that was so, how could I possibly be having a notion of you rather than of anyone else? Suppose I was thinking, Theaetetus is one who is a man and has a nose and eyes and a mouth and so forth, enumerating every part of the body. Will thinking in that way result in my thinking of Theaetetus rather than of Theodorus or, as they say, of the man in the street?

THEAETETUS: How should it?

SOCRATES: Well, now suppose I think not merely of a man with a nose and eyes, but of one with a snub nose and prominent eyes. Once more shall I be having a notion of you any more than of myself or anyone else of that description?

THEAETETUS: No.

SOCRATES: In fact, there will be no notion of Theaetetus in my mind, I suppose, until this particular snubness has stamped and registered within me a record distinct from all the other cases of snubness that I have seen, and so with every other part of you. Then, if I meet you tomorrow, that trait will revive my memory and give me a correct notion about you.

THEAETETUS: Quite true.

SOCRATES: If that is so, the correct notion of anything must itself include the differentness of that thing.

THEAETETUS: Evidently.

SOCRATES: Then what meaning is left for getting hold of an 'account' in addition to the correct notion? If, on the one hand, it means adding the notion of how a thing differs from other things, such an injunction is simply absurd.

THEAETETUS: How so?

SOCRATES: When we have a correct notion of the way in which certain things differ from other things, it tells us to add a correct notion of the way in which they differ from other things. On this showing, the most vicious of circles would be nothing to this injunction. It might better deserve to be called the sort of direction a blind man might give. To tell us to get hold of something we already have, in order to get to know something we are already thinking of, suggests a state of the most absolute darkness.

THEAETETUS: Whereas, if . . . ? The supposition you made just now implied that you would state some alternative. What was it?

SOCRATES: If the direction to add an 'account' means that we are to get to *know* the differentness, as opposed to merely having a notion of it, this most admirable of all definitions of knowledge will be a pretty business, because 'getting to know' means acquiring knowledge, doesn't it?

THEAETETUS: Yes.

SOCRATES: So, apparently, to the question, 'What is knowledge?' our definition will reply, 'Correct belief together with knowledge of a differentness,' for, according to it, 'adding an account' will come to that.

THEAETETUS: So it seems.

SOCRATES: Yes, and when we are inquiring after the nature of knowledge, nothing could be sillier than to say that it is correct belief together with a *knowledge* of differentness or of anything whatever.

So, Theaetetus, neither perception, nor true belief, nor the addition of an 'account' to true belief can be knowledge.

THEAETETUS: Apparently not.

SOCRATES: Are we in labor, then, with any further child, my friend, or have we brought to birth all we have to say about knowledge?

THEAETETUS: Indeed we have, and for my part I have already, thanks to you, given utterance to more than I had in me.

SOCRATES: All of which our midwife's skill pronounces to be mere wind eggs and not worth the rearing?

THEAETETUS: Undoubtedly.

SOCRATES: Then supposing you should ever henceforth try to conceive afresh, Theaetetus, if you succeed, your embryo thoughts will be the better as a consequence of today's scrutiny, and if you remain barren, you will be gentler and more agreeable to your companions, having the good sense not to fancy you know what you do not know. For that, and no more, is all that my art can effect; nor have I any of that knowledge possessed by all the great and admirable men of our own day or of the past. But this midwife's art is a gift from heaven; my mother had it for women, and I for young men of a generous spirit and for all in whom beauty dwells.

Now I must go to the portico of the King-Archon to meet the indictment which Meletus has drawn up against me. But tomorrow morning, Theodorus, let us meet here again.

EDMUND L. GETTIER
Is Justified True Belief Knowledge?

Various attempts have been made in recent years to state necessary and sufficient conditions for someone's knowing a given proposition. The attempts have often been such that they can be stated in a form similar to the following:[1]

(a) S knows that P	*IFF*	(i) P is true,
		(ii) S believes that P, and
		(iii) S is justified in believing that P.

For example, Roderick Chisholm has held that the following gives the necessary and sufficient conditions for knowledge:[2]

(b) S knows that P	*IFF*	(i) S accepts P,
		(ii) S has adequate evidence for P, and
		(iii) P is true.

A. J. Ayer has stated the necessary and sufficient conditions for knowledge as follows:[3]

(c) S knows that P	*IFF*	(i) P is true,
		(ii) S is sure that P is true, and
		(iii) S has the right to be sure that P is true.

I shall argue that (a) is false in that the conditions stated therein do not constitute a *sufficient* condition for the truth of the proposition that S knows that P. The same argument will show that (b) and (c) fail if 'has adequate evidence for' or 'has the right to be sure that' is substituted for 'is justified in believing that' throughout.

I shall begin by noting two points. First, in that sense of 'justified' in which S's being justified in believing P is a necessary condition of S's knowing that P, it is possible for a person to be justified in believing a proposition that is in fact false. Secondly, for any proposition P, if S is justified in believing P, and P entails Q, and S

"Is True Justified Belief Knowledge?" is reprinted from *Analysis,* 23 (1963) by permission of the author.
Edmund L. Gettier is a contemporary American philosopher affiliated with the University of Massachusetts. Ever since this article first appeared over twenty-five years ago, Gettier's argument has been the center of an ongoing controversy concerning the classical definition of knowledge.

deduces Q from P and accepts Q as a result of this deduction, then S is justified in believing Q. Keeping these two points in mind, I shall now present two cases in which the conditions stated in (a) are true for some proposition, though it is at the same time false that the person in question knows that proposition.

CASE I

Suppose that Smith and Jones have applied for a certain job. And suppose that Smith has strong evidence for the following conjunctive proposition:

>   (d) Jones is the man who will get the job, and Jones has ten coins in his pocket.

Smith's evidence for (d) might be that the president of the company assured him that Jones would in the end be selected, and that he, Smith, had counted the coins in Jones's pocket ten minutes ago. Proposition (d) entails:

>   (e) The man who will get the job has ten coins in his pocket.

Let us suppose that Smith sees the entailment from (d) to (e), and accepts (e) on the grounds of (d), for which he has strong evidence. In this case, Smith is clearly justified in believing that (e) is true.

But imagine, further, that unknown to Smith, he himself, not Jones, will get the job. And, also, unknown to Smith, he himself has ten coins in his pocket. Proposition (e) is then true, though proposition (d), from which Smith inferred (e), is false. In our example, then, all of the following are true: (*i*) (e) is true, (*ii*) Smith believes that (e) is true, and (*iii*) Smith is justified in believing that (e) is true. But it is equally clear that Smith does not *know* that (e) is true; for (e) is true in virtue of the number of coins in Smith's pocket, while Smith does not know how many coins are in Smith's pocket, and bases his belief in (e) on a count of the coins in Jones's pocket, whom he falsely believes to be the man who will get the job.

CASE II

Let us suppose that Smith has strong evidence for the following proposition:

>   (f) Jones owns a Ford.

Smith's evidence might be that Jones has at all times in the past within Smith's memory owned a car, and always a Ford, and that Jones has just offered Smith a ride while driving a Ford. Let us imagine, now, that Smith has another friend, Brown, of whose whereabouts he is totally ignorant. Smith selects three place names quite at random and constructs the following three propositions:

>   (g) Either Jones owns a Ford, or Brown is in Boston.
>   (h) Either Jones owns a Ford, or Brown is in Barcelona.
>   (i) Either Jones owns a Ford, or Brown is in Brest-Litovsk.

Each of these propositions is entailed by (f). Imagine that Smith realizes the entailment of each of these propositions he has constructed by (f), and proceeds to accept (g), (h), and (i) on the basis of (f). Smith has correctly inferred (g), (h), and (i) from a proposition for which he has strong evidence. Smith is therefore completely justified in believing each of these three propositions. Smith, of course, has no idea where Brown is.

But imagine now that two further conditions hold. First, Jones does *not* own a Ford, but is at present driving a rented car. And secondly, by the sheerest coincidence, and entirely unknown to Smith, the place mentioned in proposition (h) happens really to be the place where Brown is. If these two conditions hold, then Smith does *not* know that (h) is true, even though (*i*) (h) *is* true, (*ii*) Smith does believe that (h) is true, and (*iii*) Smith is justified in believing that (h) is true.

These two examples show that definition (a) does not state a *sufficient* condition for someone's knowing a given proposition. The same cases, with appropriate changes, will suffice to show that neither definition (b) nor definition (c) do so either.

NOTES

1. Plato seems to be considering some such definition at *Theaetetus* 201, and perhaps accepting one at *Meno* 98.

2. Roderick M. Chisholm, *Perceiving: a Philosophical Study,* Cornell University Press (Ithaca, New York, 1957), p. 16.

3. A. J. Ayer, *The Problem of Knowledge,* Macmillan (London, 1956), p. 34.

RENÉ DESCARTES
Meditations on First Philosophy

SYNOPSIS OF THE SIX FOLLOWING MEDITATIONS

In the first Meditation I set forth the reasons for which we may, generally speaking, doubt about all things and especially about material things, at least so long as we have no other foundations for the sciences than those which we have hitherto possessed. But although the utility of a Doubt which is so general does not at first appear, it is at the same time very great, inasmuch as it delivers us from every kind of prejudice, and sets out for us a very simple way by which the mind may detach itself from the senses; and finally it makes it impossible for us ever to doubt those things which we have once discovered to be true.

In the second Meditation, mind, which making use of the liberty which pertains to it,

Reprinted from *The Philosophical Works of Descartes* VOL. I "Meditations on First Philosophy," (1931) pgs. 131–199, translated by Elizabeth S. Haldane and G. R. T. Ross, by permission of Cambridge University Press. **René Descartes** (1596–1650) was the first modern philosopher to recognize clearly the profound significance of the skeptical problem. His rationalistic solution influenced much subsequent thinking throughout the seventeenth century.

takes for granted that all those things of whose existence it has the least doubt, are non-existent, recognises that it is however absolutely impossible that it does not itself exist. This point is likewise of the greatest moment, inasmuch as by this means a distinction is easily drawn between the things which pertain to mind—that is to say to the intellectual nature—and those which pertain to body.

But because it may be that some expect from me in this place a statement of the reasons establishing the immortality of the soul, I feel that I should here make known to them that having aimed at writing nothing in all this Treatise of which I do not possess very exact demonstrations, I am obliged to follow a similar order to that made use of by the geometers, which is to begin by putting forward as premises all those things upon which the proposition that we seek depends, before coming to any conclusion regarding it. Now the first and principal matter which is requisite for thoroughly understanding the immortality of the soul is to form the clearest possible conception of it, and one which will be entirely distinct from all the conceptions which we may have of body; and in this Meditation this has been done. In addition to this it is requisite that we may be assured that all the things which we conceive clearly and distinctly are true in the very way in which we think them; and this could not be proved previously to the Fourth Meditation. Further we must have a distinct conception of corporeal nature, which is given partly in this Second, and partly in the Fifth and Sixth Meditations. And finally we should conclude from all this, that those things which we conceive clearly and distinctly as being diverse substances, as we regard mind and body to be, are really substances essentially distinct one from the other; and this is the conclusion of the Sixth Meditation. This is further confirmed in this same Meditation by the fact that we cannot conceive of body excepting in so far as it is divisible, while the mind cannot be conceived of excepting as indivisible. For we are not able to conceive of the half of a mind as we can do of the smallest of all bodies; so that we see that not only are their natures

different but even in some respects contrary to one another. I have not however dealt further with this matter in this Treatise, both because what I have said is sufficient to show clearly enough that the extinction of the mind does not follow from the corruption of the body, and also to give men the hope of another life after death, as also because the premises from which the immortality of the soul may be deduced depend on an elucidation of a complete system of Physics. This would mean to establish in the first place that all substances generally—that is to say all things which cannot exist without being created by God—are in their nature incorruptible, and that they can never cease to exist unless God, in denying to them his concurrence, reduce them to nought; and secondly that body, regarded generally, is a substance, which is the reason why it also cannot perish, but that the human body, inasmuch as it differs from other bodies, is composed only of a certain configuration of members and of other similar accidents, while the human mind is not similarly composed of any accidents, but is a pure substance. For although all the accidents of mind be changed, although, for instance, it think certain things, will others, perceive others, etc., despite all this it does not emerge from these changes another mind: the human body on the other hand becomes a different thing from the sole fact that the figure or form of any of its portions is found to be changed. From this it follows that the human body may indeed easily enough perish, but the mind [or soul of man (I make no distinction between them)] is owing to its nature immortal.

In the Third Meditation it seems to me that I have explained at sufficient length the principal argument of which I make use in order to prove the existence of God. But none the less, because I did not wish in that place to make use of any comparisons derived from corporeal things, so as to withdraw as much as I could the minds of readers from the senses, there may perhaps have remained many obscurities which, however, will, I hope, be entirely removed by the Replies which I have made to the Objections which have been set before me. Amongst others there is, for example, this one, 'How the idea in us of a being supremely perfect possesses so much objective reality (that is to say participates by representation in so many degrees of being and perfection) that it necessarily proceeds from a cause which is absolutely perfect.' This is illustrated in these Replies by the comparison of a very perfect machine, the idea of which is found in the mind of some workman. For as the objective contrivance of this idea must have some cause, i.e. either the science of the workman or that of some other from whom he has received the idea, it is similarly impossible that the idea of God which is in us should not have God himself as its cause.

In the Fourth Meditation it is shown that all these things which we very clearly and distinctly perceive are true, and at the same time it is explained in what the nature of error or falsity consists. This must of necessity be known both for the confirmation of the preceding truths and for the better comprehension of those that follow. (But it must meanwhile be remarked that I do not in any way there treat of sin—that is to say of the error which is committed in the pursuit of good and evil, but only of that which arises in the deciding between the true and the false. And I do not intend to speak of matters pertaining to the Faith or the conduct of life, but only of those which concern speculative truths, and which may be known by the sole aid of the light of nature.)

In the Fifth Meditation corporeal nature generally is explained, and in addition to this the existence of God is demonstrated by a new proof in which there may possibly be certain difficulties also, but the solution of these will be seen in the Replies to the Objections. And further I show in what sense it is true to say that the certainty of geometrical demonstrations is itself dependent on the knowledge of God.

Finally in the Sixth I distinguish the action of the understanding [*intellectio*] from that of the imagination [*imaginatio*]; the marks by which this distinction is made are described. I here show that the mind of man is really distinct from the body, and at the same time that the two are so closely joined together that they form, so to speak, a single thing. All the errors which proceed from the senses are then surveyed, while the means of avoiding them are demonstrated, and finally all the reasons from which we may deduce the existence of material things are set forth. Not that I judge them to be very useful in establishing that which they prove, to wit, that there is in truth a world, that men possess bodies, and other such things which never have been doubted by anyone of sense; but because in considering these closely we come to see that they are neither so strong nor so evident as those arguments which lead us to the knowledge of our mind and of God; so that these last must be the most certain and most evident facts which can fall within the cognizance of the human mind. And this is the whole matter that I have tried to prove in these Meditations, for which reason I here omit to speak of many other questions with which I dealt incidentally in this discussion.

MEDITATION I
Of the things which may be brought within the sphere of the doubtful.

It is now some years since I detected how many were the false beliefs that I had from my earliest youth admitted as true, and how doubtful was everything I had since constructed on this basis; and from that time I was convinced that I must once for all seriously undertake to rid myself of all the opinions which I had formerly accepted, and commence to build anew from the foundation, if I wanted to establish any firm and permanent structure in the sciences. But as this enterprise appeared to be a very great one, I waited until I had attained an age so mature that I could not hope that at any later date I should be better fitted to execute my design. This reason caused me to delay so long that I should feel that I was doing wrong were I to occupy in deliberation the time that yet remains to me for action. To-day, then, since very opportunely for the plan I have in view I have delivered my mind from every care [and am happily agitated by no passions] and since I have procured for myself an assured leisure in a peaceable retirement, I shall at last seriously and freely address myself to the general upheaval of all my former opinions.

Now for this object it is not necessary that I should show that all of these are false—I shall perhaps never arrive at this end. But inasmuch as reason already persuades me that I ought no less carefully to withhold my assent from matters which are not entirely certain and indubitable than from those which appear to me manifestly to be false, if I am able to find in each one some reason to doubt, this will suffice to justify my rejecting the whole. And for that end it will not be requisite that I should examine each in particular, which would be an endless undertaking; for owing to the fact that the destruction of the foundations of necessity brings with it the downfall of the rest of the edifice. I shall only in the first place attack those principles upon which all my former opinions rested.

All that up to the present time I have accepted as most true and certain I have learned either from the senses or through the senses; but it is sometimes proved to me that these senses are deceptive, and it is wiser not to trust entirely to any thing by which we have once been deceived.

But it may be that although the senses sometimes deceive us concerning things which are hardly perceptible, or very far away, there are yet many others to be met with as to which we cannot reasonably have any doubt, although we recognize them by their means. For example, there is the fact that I am here, seated by the fire, attired in a dressing gown, having this paper in my hands and other similar matters. And how could I deny that these hands and this body are mine, were it not perhaps that I compare myself to certain persons, devoid of sense, whose cerebella are so troubled and clouded by the violent vapours of black bile,

that they constantly assure us that they think they are kings when they are really quite poor, or that they are clothed in purple when they are really without covering, or who imagine that they have an earthenware head or are nothing but pumpkins or are made of glass. But they are mad, and I should not be any the less insane were I to follow examples so extravagant.

At the same time I must remember that I am a man, and that consequently I am in the habit of sleeping, and in my dreams representing to myself the same things or sometimes even less probable things, than do those who are insane in their waking moments. How often has it happened to me that in the night I dreamt that I found myself in this particular place, that I was dressed and seated near the fire, whilst in reality I was lying undressed in bed! At this moment it does indeed seem to me that it is with eyes awake that I am looking at this paper; that this head which I move is not asleep, that it is deliberately and of set purpose that I extend my hand and perceive it; what happens in sleep does not appear so clear nor so distinct as does all this. But in thinking over this I remind myself that on many occasions I have in sleep been deceived by similar illusions, and in dwelling carefully on this reflection I see so manifestly that there are no certain indications by which we may clearly distinguish wakefulness from sleep that I am lost in astonishment. And my astonishment is such that it is almost capable of persuading me that I now dream.

Now let us assume that we are asleep and that all these particulars, e.g. that we open our eyes, shake our head, extend our hands, and so on, are but false delusions; and let us reflect that possibly neither our hands nor our whole body are such as they appear to us to be. At the same time we must at least confess that the things which are represented to us in sleep are like painted representations which can only have been formed as the counterparts of something real and true, and that in this way those general things at least, i.e. eyes, a head, hands, and a whole body, are not imaginary things, but things really existent. For, as a matter of fact, painters, even when they study with the greatest skill to represent sirens and satyrs by forms the most strange and extraordinary, cannot give them natures which are entirely new, but merely make a certain medley of the members of different animals; or if their imagination is extravagant enough to invent something so novel that nothing similar has ever before been seen, and that then their work represents a thing purely fictitious and absolutely false, it is certain all the same that the colours of which this is composed are necessarily real. And for the same reason, although these general things, to wit, [a body], eyes, a head, hands, and such like, may be imaginary, we are bound at the same time to confess that there are at least some other objects yet more simple and more universal, which are real and true; and of these just in the same way as with certain real colours, all these images of things which dwell in our thoughts, whether true and real or false and fantastic, are formed.

To such a class of things pertains corporeal nature in general, and its extension, the figure of extended things, their quantity or magnitude and number, as also the place in which they are, the time which measures their duration, and so on.

That is possibly why reasoning is not unjust when we conclude from this that Physics, Astronomy, Medicine and all other sciences which have as their end the consideration of composite things, are very dubious and uncertain; but that Arithmetic, Geometry and other sciences of that kind which only treat of things that are very simple and very general, without taking great trouble to ascertain whether they are actually existent or not, contain some measure of certainty and an element of the indubitable. For whether I am awake or asleep, two and three together always form five, and the square can never have more than four sides, and it does not seem possible that truths so clear and apparent can be suspected of any falsity [or uncertainty].

Nevertheless I have long had fixed in my mind the belief that an all-powerful God existed by whom I have been created such as I am. But how do I know that He has not brought it to pass that there is no earth, no heaven, no extended body, no magnitude, no place, and that

nevertheless [I possess the perceptions of all these things and that] they seem to me to exist just exactly as I now see them? And, besides, as I sometimes imagine that others deceive themselves in the things which they think they know best, how do I know that I am not deceived every time that I add two and three, or count the sides of a square, or judge of things yet simpler, if anything simpler can be imagined? But possibly God has not desired that I should be thus deceived, for He is said to be supremely good. If, however, it is contrary to His goodness to have made me such that I constantly deceive myself, it would also appear to be contrary to His goodness to permit me to be sometimes deceived, and nevertheless I cannot doubt that He does permit this.

There may indeed be those who would prefer to deny the existence of a God so powerful, rather than believe that all other things are uncertain. But let us not oppose them for the present, and grant that all that is here said of a God is a fable; nevertheless in whatever way they suppose that I have arrived at the state of being that I have reached—whether they attribute it to fate or to accident, or make out that it is by a continual succession of antecedents, or by some other method—since to err and deceive oneself is a defect, it is clear that the greater will be the probability of my being so imperfect as to deceive myself ever, as is the Author to whom they assign my origin the less powerful. To these reasons I have certainly nothing to reply, but at the end I feel constrained to confess that there is nothing in all that I formerly believed to be true, of which I cannot in some measure doubt, and that not merely through want of thought or through levity, but for reasons which are very powerful and maturely considered; so that henceforth I ought not the less carefully refrain from giving credence to these opinions than to that which is manifestly false, if I desire to arrive at any certainty [in the sciences].

But it is not sufficient to have made these remarks, we must also be careful to keep them in mind. For these ancient and commonly held opinions still revert frequently to my mind, long and familiar custom having given them the right to occupy my mind against my inclination and rendered them almost masters of my belief; nor will I ever lose the habit of deferring to them or of placing my confidence in them, so long as I consider them as they really are, i.e. opinions in some measure, doubtful, as I have just shown, and at the same time highly probable, so that there is much more reason to believe in than to deny them. That is why I consider that I shall not be acting amiss, if, taking of set purpose a contrary belief, I allow myself to be deceived, and for a certain time pretend that all these opinions are entirely false and imaginary, until at last, having thus balanced my former prejudices with my latter [so that they cannot divert my opinions more to one side than to the other], my judgment will no longer be dominated by bad usage or turned away from the right knowledge of the truth. For I am assured that there can be neither peril nor error in this course, and that I cannot at present yield too much to distrust, since I am not considering the question of action, but only of knowledge.

I shall then suppose, not that God who is supremely good and the fountain of truth, but some evil genius not less powerful than deceitful, has employed his whole energies in deceiving me; I shall consider that the heavens, the earth, colours, figures, sound, and all other external things are nought but the illusions and dreams of which this genius has availed himself in order to lay traps for my credulity; I shall consider myself as having no hands, no eyes, no flesh, no blood, nor any senses, yet falsely believing myself to possess all these things; I shall remain obstinately attached to this idea, and if by this means it is not in my power to arrive at the knowledge of any truth, I may at least do what is in my power [i.e. suspend my judgment], and with firm purpose avoid giving credence to any false thing, or being imposed upon by this arch deceiver, however powerful and deceptive he may be. But this task is a laborious one, and insensibly a certain lassitude leads me into the course of my ordinary life. And just as a captive who in sleep enjoys an imaginary liberty, when he begins to suspect that his liberty is but a dream, fears to awaken, and conspires with these agreeable illusions that the deception may be prolonged, so insensibly of my own accord I fall back into my former opinions, and I dread awakening from this slumber, lest the laborious wakefulness which would follow the tranquility of this repose should have to be spent not in daylight, but in the excessive darkness of the difficulties which have just been discussed.

MEDITATION II

Of the Nature of the Human Mind; and that it is more easily known than the Body.

The Meditation of yesterday filled my mind with so many doubts that it is no longer in my power to forget them. And yet I do not see in what manner I can resolve them; and, just as if I had all of a sudden fallen into very deep water, I am so disconcerted that I can neither make certain of setting my feet on the bottom, nor can I swim and so support myself on the surface. I shall nevertheless make an effort and follow anew the same path as that on which I yesterday entered, i.e. I shall proceed by setting aside all that in which the least doubt could be supposed to exist, just as if I had discovered that it was absolutely false; and I shall ever follow in this road until I have met with something which is certain, or at least, if I can do nothing else, until I have learned for certain that there is nothing in the world that is certain. Archimedes, in order that he might draw the terrestrial globe out of its place, and transport it elsewhere, demanded only that one point should be fixed and immovable; in the same way I shall have the right to conceive high hopes if I am happy enough to discover one thing only which is certain and indubitable.

I suppose, then, that all the things that I see are false; I persuade myself that nothing has ever existed of all that my fallacious memory represents to me. I consider that I possess no senses; I imagine that body, figure, extension, movement and place are but the fictions of my mind. What, then, can be esteemed as true? Perhaps nothing at all, unless that there is nothing in the world that is certain.

But how can I know there is not something different from those things that I have just considered, of which one cannot have the slightest doubt? Is there not some God, or some other being by whatever name we call it, who puts these reflections into my mind? That is not necessary, for is it not possible that I am capable of producing them myself? I myself, am I not at least something? But I have already denied that I had senses and body. Yet I hesitate, for what follows from that? Am I so dependent on body and senses that I cannot exist without these? But I was persuaded that there was nothing in all the world, that there was no heaven, no earth, that there were no minds, nor any bodies: was I not then likewise persuaded that I did not exist? Not at all; of a surety I myself did exist since I persuaded myself of something [or merely because I thought of something]. But there is some deceiver or other, very powerful and very cunning, who ever employs his ingenuity in deceiving me. Then without doubt I exist also if he deceives me, and let him deceive me as much as he will, he can never cause me to be nothing so long as I think that I am something. So that after having reflected well and carefully examined all things, we must come to the definite conclusion that this proposition: I am, I exist, is necessarily true each time that I pronounce it, or that I mentally conceive it.

But I do not yet know clearly enough what I am, I who am certain that I am; and hence I must be careful to see that I do not imprudently take some other object in place of myself, and thus that I do not go astray in respect of this knowledge that I hold to be the most certain and most evident of all that I have formerly learned. That is why I shall now consider anew what I believed myself to be before I embarked upon these last reflections; and of my former opinions I shall withdraw all that might even in a small degree be invalidated by the reasons which I have just brought forward, in order that there may be nothing at all left beyond what is absolutely certain and indubitable.

What then did I formerly believe myself to be? Undoubtedly I believed myself to be a man. But what is a man? Shall I say a reasonable animal? Certainly not; for then I should have to inquire what an animal is, and what is reasonable; and thus from a single question I should insensibly fall into an infinitude of others more difficult; and I should not wish to waste the little time and leisure remaining to me in trying to unravel subtleties like these. But I shall rather stop here to consider the thoughts which of themselves spring up in my mind, and which were not inspired by anything beyond my own nature alone when I applied myself to the consideration of my being. In the first place, then, I considered myself as having a face, hands, arms, and all that system of members composed of bones and flesh as seen in a corpse which I designated by the name of body. In addition to this I considered that I was nourished, that I walked, that I felt, and that I thought, and I referred all these actions to the soul: but I did not stop to consider what the soul was, or if I did stop, I imagined that it was something extremely rare and subtle like a wind, a flame, or an ether, which was spread throughout my grosser parts. As to body I had no manner of doubt about its nature, but thought I had a very clear knowledge of it; and if I had desired to explain it according to the notions that I had then formed of it, I should have described it thus: By the body I understand all that which can be defined by a certain figure: something which can be confined in a certain place, and which can fill a given space in such a way that every other body will be excluded from it; which can be perceived either by touch, or by sight, or by hearing, or by taste, or by smell: which can be moved in many ways not, in truth, by itself, but by something which is foreign to it, by which it is touched [and from which it receives impressions]: for to have the power of self-movement, as also of feeling or of thinking, I did not consider to appertain to the nature of body: on the contrary, I was rather astonished to find that faculties similar to them existed in some bodies.

But what am I, now that I suppose that there is a certain genius which is extremely powerful, and, if I may say so, malicious, who employs all his powers in deceiving me? Can I affirm that I possess the least of all those things which I have just said pertain to the nature of body? I pause to consider, I revolve all these things in my mind, and I find none of which I can say that it pertains to me. It would be tedious to stop to enumerate them. Let us pass to the attributes of soul and see if there is any one which is in me? What of nutrition or walking [the first mentioned]? But if it is so that I have no body it is also true that I can neither walk nor take nourishment. Another attribute is sensation. But one cannot feel without body, and besides I have thought I perceived many things during sleep that I recognised in my waking moments as not having been experienced at all. What of thinking? I find here that thought is an attribute that belongs to me; it alone cannot be separated from me. I am, I exist, that is certain. But how often? Just when I think; for it might possibly be the case if I ceased entirely to think, that I should likewise cease altogether to exist. I do not now admit anything which is not necessarily true: to speak accurately I am not more than a thing which thinks, that is to say a mind or a soul, or an understanding, or a reason, which are terms whose significance was formerly unknown to me. I am, however, a real thing and really exist; but what thing? I have answered: a thing which thinks.

And what more? I shall exercise my imagination [in order to see if I am not something more]. I am not a collection of members which we call the human body: I am not a subtle air distributed through these members, I am not a wind, a fire, a vapour, a breath, or anything at all which I can imagine or conceive; because I have assumed that all these were nothing. Without changing that supposition I find that I only leave myself certain of the fact that I am somewhat. But perhaps it is true that these same things which I supposed were non-existent because they are unknown to me, are really not

different from the self which I know. I am not sure about this, I shall not dispute about it now; I can only give judgment on things that are known to me. I know that I exist, and I inquire what I am, I whom I know to exist. But it is very certain that the knowledge of my existence taken in its precise significance does not depend on things whose existence is not yet known to me; consequently it does not depend on those which I can feign in imagination. And indeed the very term *feign* in imagination proves to me my error, for I really do this if I image myself a something, since to imagine is nothing else than to contemplate the figure or image of a corporeal thing. But I already know for certain that I am, and that it may be that all these images, and, speaking generally, all things that relate to the nature of body are nothing but dreams [and chimeras]. For this reason I see clearly that I have as little reason to say, 'I shall stimulate my imagination in order to know more distinctly what I am,' than if I were to say, 'I am now awake, and I perceive somewhat that is real and true: but because I do not yet perceive it distinctly enough, I shall go to sleep of express purpose, so that my dreams may represent the perception with greatest truth and evidence.' And, thus, I know for certain that nothing of all that I can understand by means of my imagination belongs to this knowledge which I have of myself, and that it is necessary to recall the mind from this mode of thought with the utmost diligence in order that it may be able to know its own nature with perfect distinctness.

But what then am I? A thing which thinks. What is a thing which thinks? It is a thing which doubts, understands, [conceives], affirms, denies, wills, refuses, which also imagines and feels.

Certainly it is no small matter if all these things pertain to my nature. But why should they not so pertain? Am I not that being who now doubts nearly everything, who nevertheless understands certain things, who affirms that one only is true, who denies all the others, who desires to know more, is averse from being deceived, who imagines many things, sometimes indeed despite his will, and who perceives many likewise, as by the intervention of the bodily organs? Is there nothing in all this which is as true as it is certain that I exist, even though I should always sleep and though he who has given me being employed all his ingenuity in deceiving me? Is there likewise any one of these attributes which can be distinguished from my thought, or which might be said to be separated from myself? For it is so evident of itself that it is I who doubt, who understand, and who desire, that there is no reason here to add anything to explain it. And I have certainly the power of imagining likewise; for although it may happen (as I formerly supposed) that none of the things which I imagine are true, nevertheless this power of imagining does not cease to be really in use, and it forms part of my thought. Finally, I am the same who feels, that is to say, who perceives certain things, as by the organs of sense, since in truth I see light, I hear noise, I feel heat. But it will be said that these phenomena are false and that I am dreaming. Let it be so; still it is at least quite certain that it seems to me that I see light, that I hear noise and that I feel heat. That cannot be false; properly speaking it is what is in me called feeling; and used in this precise sense that is no other thing than thinking.

From this time I begin to know what I am with a little more clearness and distinction than before; but nevertheless it still seems to me, and I cannot prevent myself from thinking, that corporeal things, whose images are framed by thought, which are tested by the senses, are much more distinctly known than that obscure part of me which does not come under the imagination. Although really it is very strange to say that I know and understand more distinctly these things whose existence seems to me dubious, which are unknown to me, and which do not belong to me, than others of the truth of which I am convinced, which are known to me and which pertain to my real nature, in a word, than myself. But I see clearly how the case stands: my mind loves to wander, and cannot yet suffer itself to be retained within the just limits of truth. Very good, let us once more give it the freest rein, so that, when afterwards we seize

the proper occasion for pulling up, it may the more easily be regulated and controlled.

Let us begin by considering the commonest matters, those which we believe to be the most distinctly comprehended, to wit, the bodies which we touch and see; not indeed bodies in general, for these general ideas are usually a little more confused, but let us consider one body in particular. Let us take, for example, this piece of wax: it has been taken quite freshly from the hive, and it has not yet lost the sweetness of the honey which it contains; it still retains somewhat of the odour of the flowers from which it has been culled; its colour, its figure, its size are apparent; it is hard, cold, easily handled, and if you strike it with the finger, it will emit a sound. Finally all the things which are requisite to cause us distinctly to recognise a body, are met with in it. But notice that while I speak and approach the fire what remained of the taste is exhaled, the smell evaporates, the colour alters, the figure is destroyed, the size increases, it becomes liquid, it heats, scarcely can one handle it, and when one strikes it, no sound is emitted. Does the same wax remain after this change? We must confess that it remains; none would judge otherwise. What then did I know so distinctly in this piece of wax? It could certainly be nothing of all that the senses brought to my notice, since all these things which fall under taste, smell, sight, touch, and hearing, are found to be changed, and yet the same wax remains.

Perhaps it was what I now think, viz, that this wax was not that sweetness of honey, nor that agreeable scent of flowers, nor that particular whiteness, nor that figure, nor that sound, but simply a body which a little while before appeared to me as perceptible under these forms, and which is now perceptible under others. But what, precisely, is it that I imagine when I form such conceptions? Let us attentively consider this, and, abstracting from all that does not belong to the wax, let us see what remains. Certainly nothing remains excepting a certain extended thing which is flexible and movable. But what is the meaning of flexible and moveable? Is it not that I imagine that this piece of wax being round is capable of becoming square and of passing from a square to a triangular figure? No, certainly it is not that, since I imagine it admits of an infinitude of similar changes, and I nevertheless do not know how to compass the infinitude by my imagination, and consequently this conception which I have of the wax is not brought about by the faculty of imagination. What now is this extension? Is it not also unknown? For it becomes greater when the wax is melted, greater when it is boiled, and greater still when the heat increases; and I should not conceive [clearly] according to truth what wax is, if I did not think that even this piece that we are considering is capable of receiving more variations in extension than I have ever imagined. We must then grant that I could not even understand through the imagination what this piece of wax is, and that it is my mind alone which perceives it. I say this piece of wax in particular, for as to wax in general it is yet clearer. But what is this piece of wax which cannot be understood excepting by the [understanding or] mind? It is certainly the same that I see, touch, imagine, and finally it is the same which I have always believed it to be from the beginning. But what must particularly be observed is that its perception is neither an act of vision, nor of touch, nor of imagination, and has never been such although it may have appeared formerly to be so, but only an intuition of the mind, which may be imperfect and confused as it was formerly, or clear and distinct as it is at present, according as my attention is more or less directed to the elements which are found in it, and of which it is composed.

Yet in the meantime I am greatly astonished when I consider [the great feebleness of mind] and its proneness to fall [insensibly] into error; for although without giving expression to my thoughts I consider all this in my own mind, words often impede me and I am almost deceived by the terms of ordinary language. For we say that we see the same wax, if it is present, and not that we simply judge that it is the same from its having the same colour and figure. From this I should conclude that I knew the wax by means of vision and not simply by the intuition of the mind; unless by chance I remember that, when looking from a window and saying I see men who pass in the street, I really do not see them, but infer that what I see is men, just as I say that I see wax. And yet what do I see from the window but hats and coats which may cover automatic machines? Yet I judge these to be men. And similarly solely by the faculty of judgment which rests in my mind, I comprehend that which I believed I saw with my eyes.

A man who makes it his aim to raise his knowledge above the common should be ashamed to derive the occasion for doubting from the forms of speech invented by the vulgar; I prefer to pass on and consider whether I had a more evident and perfect conception of what the wax was when I first perceived it, and when I believed I knew it by means of the external senses or at least by the common sense as it is called, that is to say by the imaginative faculty, or whether my present conception is clearer now that I have most carefully examined what it is, and in what way it can be known. It would certainly be absurd to doubt as to this. For what was there in this first perception which was distinct? What was there which might not as well have been perceived by any of the animals? But when I distinguish the wax from its external forms, and when, just as if I had taken from it its vestments, I consider it quite naked, it is certain that although some error may still be found in my judgment, I can nevertheless not perceive it thus without a human mind.

But finally what shall I say of this mind, that is, of myself, for up to this point I do not admit in myself anything but mind? What then, I who seem to perceive this piece of wax so distinctly, do I not know myself, not only with much more truth and certainty, but also with much more distinctness and clearness? For if I judge that the wax is or exists from the fact that I see it, it certainly follows much more clearly that I am or that I exist myself from the fact that I see it. For it may be that what I see is not really wax, it may also be that I do not possess eyes with which to see anything; but it cannot be that when I see, or (for I no longer take account of the distinction) when I think I see, that I myself who think am nought. So if I judge that the wax exists from the fact that I touch it, the same thing will follow, to wit, that I am; and if I judge that my imagination, or some other cause, whatever it is, persuades me that wax exists, I shall still conclude the same. And what I have here remarked of wax may be applied to all other things which are external to me [and which are met with outside of me]. And further, if the [notion or] perception of wax has seemed to me clearer and more distinct, not only after the sight or the touch, but also after many other causes have rendered it quite manifest to me, with how much more [evidence] and distinctness must it be said that I now know myself, since all the reasons which contribute to the knowledge of wax, or any other body whatever, are yet better proofs of the nature of my mind! And there are so many other things in the mind itself which may contribute to the elucidation of its nature, that those which depend on body such as these just mentioned, hardly merit being taken into account.

But finally here I am, having insensibly reverted to the point I desired, for, since it is now manifest to me that even bodies are not properly speaking known by the senses or by the faculty of imagination, but by the understanding only, and since they are not known from the fact that they are seen or touched, but only because they are understood, I see clearly that there is nothing which is easier for me to know than my mind. But because it is difficult to rid oneself so promptly of an opinion to which one was accustomed for so long, it will be well that I should halt a little at this point, so that by the length of my meditation I may more deeply imprint on my memory this new knowledge.

MEDITATION III
Of God: That He exists.

I shall now close my eyes, I shall stop my ears, I shall call away all my senses, I shall efface even from my thoughts all the images of corporeal things, or at least (for that is hardly possible) I shall esteem them as vain and false; and thus holding converse only with myself and considering my own nature, I shall try little by little to reach a better knowledge of and a more familiar acquaintanceship with myself. I am a thing that thinks, that is to say, that doubts, affirms, denies, that knows a few things, that is ignorant of many [that loves, that hates], that wills, that desires, that also imagines and perceives; for as I remarked before, although the things which I perceive and imagine are perhaps nothing at all apart from me and in themselves, I am nevertheless assured that these modes of thought that I call perceptions and imaginations, inasmuch only as they are modes of thought, certainly reside [and are met with] in me.

And in the little that I have just said, I think I have summed up all that I really know, or at least all that hitherto I was aware that I knew.

In order to try to extend my knowledge further, I shall now look around more carefully and see whether I cannot still discover in myself some other things which I have not hitherto perceived. I am certain that I am a thing which thinks; but do I not then likewise know what is requisite to render me certain of a truth? Certainly in this first knowledge there is nothing that assures me of its truth, excepting the clear and distinct perception of that which I state, which would not indeed suffice to assure me that what I say is true, if it could ever happen that a thing which I conceived so clearly and distinctly could be false; and accordingly it seems to me that already I can establish as a general rule that all things which I perceive very clearly and very distinctly are true.

At the same time I have before received and admitted many things to be very certain and manifest, which yet I afterwards recognised as being dubious. What then were these things? They were the earth, sky, stars and all other objects which I apprehended by means of the senses. But what did I clearly [and distinctly] perceive in them? Nothing more than that the ideas or thoughts of these things were presented to my mind. And not even now do I deny that these ideas are met with in me. But there was yet another thing which I affirmed, and which, owing to the habit which I had formed of believing it, I thought I perceived very clearly, although in truth I did not perceive it at all, to wit, that there were objects outside of me from which these ideas proceeded, and to which they were entirely similar. And it was in this that I erred, or, if perchance my judgment was correct, this was not due to any knowledge arising from my perception.

But when I took anything very simple and easy in the sphere of arithmetic or geometry into consideration, e.g. that two and three together made five, and other things of the sort, were not these present to my mind so clearly as to enable me to affirm that they were true? Certainly if I judged that since such matters could be doubted, this would not have been so for any other reason than that it came into my mind that perhaps a God might have endowed me with such a nature that I may have been deceived even concerning things which seemed to me most manifest. But every time that this preconceived opinion of the sovereign power of a God presents itself to my thought, I am constrained to confess that it is easy to Him, if He wishes it, to cause me to err, even in matters in which I believe myself to have the best evidence. And, on the other hand, always when I direct my attention to things which I believe myself to perceive very clearly, I am so persuaded of their truth that I let myself break out into words such as these: Let who will deceive me, He can never cause me to be nothing while I think that I am, or some day cause it to be true to say that I have never been, it being true now to say that I am, or that two and three make more or less than five, or any such thing in which I see a manifest contradiction. And, certainly, since I have no reason to believe that there is a God who is a deceiver, and as I have not yet satisfied myself that there is a God at all, the reason for doubt which depends on this opinion alone

is very slight, and so to speak metaphysical. But in order to be able altogether to remove it, I must inquire whether there is a God as soon as the occasion presents itself; and if I find that there is a God, I must also inquire whether He may be a deceiver; for without a knowledge of these two truths I do not see that I can ever be certain of anything.

And in order that I may have an opportunity of inquiring into this in an orderly way [without interrupting the order of meditation which I have proposed to myself, and which is little by little to pass from the notions which I find first of all in my mind to those which I shall later on discover in it] it is requisite that I should here divide my thoughts into certain kinds, and that I should consider in which of these kinds there is, properly speaking, truth or error to be found. Of my thoughts some are, so to speak, images of the things, and to these alone is the title 'idea' properly applied; examples are my thought of a man or of a chimera, of heaven, of an angel, or [even] of God. But other thoughts possess other forms as well. For example in willing, fearing, approving, denying, though I always perceive something as the subject of the action of my mind; yet by this action I always add something else to the idea which I have of that thing; and of the thoughts of this kind some are called volitions or affections, and others judgments.

Now as to what concerns ideas, if we consider them only in themselves and do not relate them to anything else beyond themselves, they cannot properly speaking be false; for whether I imagine a goat or a chimera, it is not less true that I imagine the one than the other. We must not fear likewise that falsity can enter into will and into affections, for although I may desire evil things, or even things that never existed, it is not the less true that I desire them. Thus there remains no more than the judgments which we make, in which I must take the greatest care not to deceive myself. But the principal error and the commonest which we may meet with in them, consists in my judging that the ideas which are in me are similar or conformable to the things which are outside me; for without doubt if I considered the ideas only as certain modes of my thoughts, without trying to relate them to anything beyond, they could scarcely give me material for error.

But among these ideas, some appear to me to be innate, some adventitious, and others to be formed [or invented] by myself; for, as I have the power of understanding what is called a thing, or a truth, or a thought, it appears to me that I hold this power from no other source than my own nature. But if now I hear some sound, if I see the sun, or feel heat, I have hitherto judged that these sensations proceeded from certain things that exist outside of me; and finally it appears to me that sirens, hippogryphs, and the like, are formed out of my own mind. But again I may possibly persuade myself that all these ideas are of the nature of those which I term adventitious, or else that they are all innate, or all fictitious: for I have not yet clearly discovered their true origin.

And my principal task in this place is to consider, in respect to those ideas which appear to me to proceed from certain objects that are outside me, what are the reasons which cause me to think them similar to these objects. It seems indeed in the first place that I am taught this lesson by nature; and, secondly, I experience in myself that these ideas do not depend on my will nor therefore on myself—for they often present themselves to my mind in spite of my will. Just now, for instance, whether I will or whether I do not will, I feel heat, and thus I persuade myself that this feeling, or at least this idea of heat, is produced in me by something which is different from me, i.e. by the heat of the fire near which I sit. And nothing seems to me more obvious than to judge that this object imprints its likeness rather than anything else upon me.

Now I must discover whether these proofs are sufficiently strong and convincing. When I say that I am so instructed by nature, I merely mean a certain spontaneous inclination which impels me to believe in this connection, and not a natural light which makes me recognise that it is true. But these two things are very different; for I cannot doubt that which the natural light causes me to believe to be true, as, for exam-

ple, it has shown me that I am from the fact that I doubt, or other facts of the same kind. And I possess no other faculty whereby to distinguish truth from falsehood, which can teach me that what this light shows me to be true is not really true, and no other faculty that is equally truthworthy. But as far as [apparently] natural impulses are concerned, I have frequently remarked, when I had to make active choice between virtue and vice, that they often enough led me to the part that was worse; and this is why I do not see any reason for following them in what regards truth and error.

And as to the other reason, which is that these ideas must proceed from objects outside me, since they do not depend on my will, I do not find it any the more convincing. For just as these impulses of which I have spoken are found in me, notwithstanding that they do not always concur with my will, so perhaps there is in me some faculty fitted to produce these ideas without the assistance of any external things, even though it is not yet known by me; just as, apparently, they have hitherto always been found in me during sleep without the aid of any external objects.

And finally, though they did proceed from objects different from myself, it is not a necessary consequence that they should resemble these. On the contrary, I have noticed that in many cases there was a difference between the object and its idea. I find, for example, two completely diverse ideas of the sun in my mind; the one derives its origin from the senses, and should be placed in the category of adventitious ideas; according to this idea the sun seems to be extremely small; but the other is derived from astronomical reasonings, i.e. is elicited from certain notions that are innate in me, or else it is formed by me in some other manner; in accordance with it the sun appears to be several times greater than the earth. These two ideas cannot, indeed, both resemble the same sun, and reason makes me believe that the one which seems to have originated directly from the sun itself, is the one which is most dissimilar to it.

All this causes me to believe that until the present time it has not been by a judgment that was certain [or premeditated], but only by a sort of blind impulse that I believed that things existed outside of, and different from me, which, by the organs of my senses, or by some other method whatever it might be, conveyed these ideas or images to me [and imprinted on me their similitudes].

But there is yet another method of inquiring whether any of the objects of which I have ideas within me exist outside of me. If ideas are only taken as certain modes of thought, I recognise amongst them no difference or inequality, and all appear to proceed from me in the same manner; but when we consider them as images, one representing one thing and the other another, it is clear that they are very different one from the other. There is no doubt that those which represent to me substances are something more, and contain so to speak more objective reality within them [that is to say, by representation participate in a higher degree of being or perfection] than those that simply represent modes or accidents; and that idea again by which I understand a supreme God, eternal, infinite, [immutable], omniscient, omnipotent, and Creator of all things which are outside of Himself, has certainly more objective reality in itself than those ideas by which finite substances are represented.

Now it is manifest by the natural light that there must at least be as much reality in the efficient and total cause as in its effect. For, pray, whence can the effect derive its reality, if not from its cause? And in what way can this cause communicate this reality to it, unless it possessed it in itself? And from this it follows, not only that something cannot proceed from nothing, but likewise that what is more perfect—that is to say, which has more reality within itself—cannot proceed from the less perfect. And this is not only evidently true of those effects which possess actual or formal reality, but also of the ideas in which we consider merely what is termed objective reality. To take an example, the stone which has not yet existed not only cannot now commence to be unless it has been produced by something which possesses within itself, either formally or eminently, all that enters into the composition of the stone [i.e. it must possess the same things or other more excellent things than those which exist in the stone] and heat can only be produced in a subject in which it did not previously exist by a cause that is of an order [degree or kind] at least as perfect as heat, and so in all other cases. But further, the idea of heat, or of a stone, cannot exist in me unless it has been placed within me by some cause which possesses within it at least as much reality as that which I conceive to exist in the heat or the stone. For although this cause does not transmit anything of its actual or formal reality to my idea, we must not for that reason imagine that it is necessarily a less real cause; we must remember that [since every idea is a work of the mind] its nature is such that it demands of itself no other formal reality than that which it borrows from my thought, of which it is only a mode [i.e. a manner or way of thinking]. But in order that an idea should contain some one certain objective reality rather than another, it must without doubt derive it from some cause in which there is at least as much formal reality as this idea contains of objective reality. For if we imagine that something is found in an idea which is not found in the cause, it must then have been derived from nought; but however imperfect may be this mode of being by which a thing is objectively [or by representation] in the understanding by its idea, we cannot certainly say that this mode of being is nothing, nor, consequently, that the idea derives its origin from nothing.

Nor must I imagine that, since the reality that I consider in these ideas is only objective, it is not essential that this reality should be formally in the causes of my ideas, but that it is sufficient that it should be found objectively. For just as this mode of objective existence pertains to ideas by their proper nature, so does the mode of formal existence pertain to the causes of those ideas (this is at least true of the first and principal) by the nature peculiar to them. And although it may be the case that one idea gives birth to another idea, that cannot continue to be so indefinitely; for in the end we must reach an idea whose cause shall be so to speak an archetype, in which the whole reality [or perfection] which is so to speak objectively [or by representation] in these ideas is contained formally [and really]. Thus the light of nature causes me to know clearly that the ideas in me are like [pictures or] images which can, in truth, easily fall short of the perfection of the objects from which they have been derived, but which can never contain anything greater or more perfect.

And the longer and the more carefully that I investigate these matters, the more clearly and distinctly do I recognise their truth. But what am I to conclude from it all in the end? It is this, that if the objective reality of any one of my ideas is of such a nature as clearly to make me recognise that it is not in me either formally or eminently, and that consequently I cannot myself be the cause of it, it follows of necessity that I am not alone in the world, but that there is another being which exists, or which is the cause of this idea. On the other hand, had not such an idea existed in me, I should have had no sufficient argument to convince me of the existence of any being beyond myself; for I have made very careful investigation everywhere and up to the present time have been able to find no other ground.

But of my ideas, beyond that which represents me to myself, as to which there can here be no difficulty, there is another which represents a God, and there are others representing corporeal and inanimate things, others angels, others animals, and others again which represent to me men similar to myself.

As regards the ideas which represent to me other men or animals, or angels, I can however easily conceive that they might be formed by an admixture of the other ideas which I have of myself, of corporeal things, and of God, even although there were apart from me neither men nor animals, nor angels, in all the world.

And in regard to the ideas of corporeal objects, I do not recognise in them anything so great or so excellent that they might not have possibly proceeded from myself; for if I consider them more closely, and examine them individually, as I yesterday examined the idea of wax, I find that there is very little in them which I perceive clearly and distinctly. Magnitude or extension in length, breadth, or depth, I do so perceive; also figure which results from a termination of this extension, the situation which bodies of different figure preserve in relation to one another, and movement or change of situation; to which we may also add substance, duration and number. As to other things such as light, colours, sounds, scents, tastes, heat, cold and the other tactile qualities, they are thought by me with so much obscurity and confusion that I do not even know if they are true or false, i.e. whether the ideas which I form of these qualities are actually the ideas of real objects or not [or whether they only represent chimeras which cannot exist in fact]. For although I have before remarked that it is only in judgments that falsity, properly speaking, or formal falsity, can be met with, a certain material falsity may nevertheless be found in ideas, i.e. when these ideas represent what is nothing as though it were something. For example, the ideas which I have of cold and heat are so far from clear and distinct that by their means I cannot tell whether cold is merely a privation of heat, or heat a privation of cold, or whether both are real qualities, or are not such. And inasmuch as [since ideas resemble images] there cannot be any ideas which do not appear to represent some things, if it is correct to say that cold is merely a privation of heat, the idea which represents it to me as something real and positive will not be improperly termed false, and the same holds good of other similar ideas.

To these it is certainly not necessary that I should attribute any author other than myself. For if they are false, i.e. if they represent things which do not exist, the light of nature shows me that they issue from nought, that is to say, that they are only in me in so far as something is lacking to the perfection of my nature. But if they are true, nevertheless because they exhibit so little reality to me that I cannot even clearly distinguish the thing represented from nonbeing, I do not see any reason why they should not be produced by myself.

As to the clear and distinct idea which I have of corporeal things, some of them seem as though I might have derived them from the idea which I possess of myself, as those which I have of substance, duration, number, and such like. For [even] when I think that a stone is a substance, or at least a thing capable of existing of itself, and that I am a substance also, although I conceive that I am a thing that thinks and not one that is extended, and that the stone on the other hand is an extended thing which does not think, and that thus there is a notable difference between the two conceptions—they seem, nevertheless, to agree in this, that both represent substances. In the same way, when I perceive that I now exist and further recollect that I have in former times existed, and when I remember that I have various thoughts of which I can recognise the number, I acquire ideas of duration and number which I can afterwards transfer to any object that I please. But as to all the other qualities of which the ideas of corporeal things are composed, to wit, extension, figure, situation and motion, it is true that they are not formally in me, since I am only a thing that thinks; but because they are merely certain modes of substance [and so to speak the vestments under which corporeal substance appears to us] and because I myself am also a substance, it would seem that they might be constrained in me eminently.

Hence there remains only the idea of God, concerning which we must consider whether it is something which cannot have proceeded from me myself. By the name God I understand a substance that is infinite [eternal, immutable], independent, all-knowing, all-powerful, and by which I myself and everything else, if anything else does exist, have been created. Now all these characteristics are such that the more diligently I attend to them, the less do they appear capable of proceeding from me alone; hence, from what has been already said, we must conclude that God necessarily exists.

For although the idea of substance is within me owing to the fact that I am substance, nevertheless I should not have the idea of an infinite substance—since I am finite—if it had not proceeded from some substance which was veritably infinite.

Nor should I imagine that I do not perceive the infinite by a true idea, but only by the negation of the finite, just as I perceive repose and darkness by the negation of movement and of light; for, on the contrary, I see that there is manifestly more reality in infinite substance than in finite, and therefore that in some way I have in me the notion of the infinite earlier than the finite—to wit, the notion of God before that of myself. For how would it be possible that I should know that I doubt and desire, that is to say, that something is lacking to me, and that I am not quite perfect, unless I had within me some idea of a Being more perfect than myself, in comparison with which I should recognise the deficiencies of my nature?

And we cannot say that this idea of God is perhaps materially false and that consequently I can derive it from nought [i.e. that possibly it exists in me because I am imperfect], as I have just said is the case with ideas of heat, cold and other such things; for, on the contrary, as this idea is very clear and distinct and contains within it more objective reality than any other, there can be none which is of itself more true, nor any in which there can be less suspicion of falsehood. The idea, I say, of this Being who is absolutely perfect and infinite, is entirely true; for although, perhaps, we can imagine that such a Being does not exist, we cannot nevertheless imagine that His idea represents nothing real to me, as I have said of the idea of cold. This idea is also very clear and distinct; since all that I conceive clearly and distinctly of the real and the true, and of what conveys some perfection, is in its entirety contained in this idea. And this does not cease to be true although I do not comprehend the infinite, or though in God there is an infinitude of things which I cannot comprehend, nor possibly even reach in any way by thought; for it is of the nature of the infinite that my nature, which is finite and limited, should not comprehend it; and it is sufficient that I should understand this, and that I should judge that all things which I clearly perceive and in which I know that there is some perfection, and possibly likewise an infinitude of properties of which I am ignorant, are in God formally or eminently, so that the idea which I have of Him may become the most true, most clear, and most distinct of all the ideas that are in my mind.

But possibly I am something more than I suppose myself to be, and perhaps all those perfections which I attribute to God are in some way potentially in me, although they do not yet disclose themselves, or issue in action. As a matter of fact I am already sensible that my knowledge increases [and perfects itself] little by little, and I see nothing which can prevent it from increasing more and more into infinitude; nor do I see, after it has thus been increased [or perfected], anything to prevent my being able to acquire by its means all the other perfections of the Divine nature; nor finally why the power I have of acquiring these perfections, if it really exist in me, shall not suffice to produce the ideas of them.

At the same time I recognise that this cannot be. For, in the first place, although it were true that every day my knowledge acquired new degrees of perfection, and that there were in my nature many things potentially which are not yet there actually, nevertheless these excellences do not pertain to [or make the smallest approach to] the idea which I have of God in whom there is nothing merely potential [but in whom all is present really and actually]; for it is an infallible token of imperfection in my knowledge that it increases little by little. And further, although my knowledge grows more and more, nevertheless I do not for that reason believe that it can ever be actually infinite, since it can never reach a point so high that it will be unable to attain to any greater increase. But I understand God to be actually infinite, so that He can add nothing to His supreme perfection. And finally I perceive that the objective being of an idea cannot be produced by a being that exists potentially only, which properly speaking is nothing, but only a being which is formal or actual.

To speak the truth, I see nothing in all that I have just said which by the light of nature is not manifest to anyone who desires to think atten-

tively on the subject; but when I slightly relax my attention, my mind, finding its vision somewhat obscured and so to speak blinded by the images of sensible objects, I do not easily recollect the reason why the idea that I possess of a being more perfect than I, must necessarily have been placed in me by a being which is really more perfect; and this is why I wish here to go on to inquire whether I, who have this idea, can exist if no such being exists.

And I ask, from whom do I then derive my existence? Perhaps from myself or from my parents, or from some other source less perfect than God; for we can imagine nothing more perfect than God, or even as perfect as He is.

But [were I independent of every other and] were I myself the author of my being, I should doubt nothing and I should desire nothing, and finally no perfection would be lacking to me; for I should have bestowed on myself every perfection of which I possessed any idea and should thus be God. And it must not be imagined that those things that are lacking to me are perhaps more difficult of attainment than those which I already possess; for, on the contrary, it is quite evident that it was a matter of much greater difficulty to bring to pass that I, that is to say, a thing or substance that thinks, should emerge out of nothing, than it would be to attain to the knowledge of many things of which I am ignorant, and which are only the accidents of this thinking substance. But it is clear that if I had of myself possessed this greater perfection of which I have just spoken [that is to say, if I had been the author of my own existence], I should not at least have denied myself the things which are the more easy to acquire [to wit, many branches of knowledge of which my nature is destitute]; nor should I have deprived myself of any of the things contained in the idea which I form of God, because there are none of them which seem to me specially difficult to acquire; and if there were any that were more difficult to acquire, they would certainly appear to me to be such (supposing I myself were the origin of the other things which I possess) since I should discover in them that my powers were limited.

But though I assumed that perhaps I have always existed just as I am at present, neither can I escape the force of this reasoning, and imagine that the conclusion to be drawn from this is, that I need not seek for any author of my existence. For all the course of my life may be divided into an infinite number of parts, none of which is in any way dependent on the other; and thus from the fact that I was in existence a short time ago it does not follow that I must be in existence now, unless some cause at this instant, so to speak, produces me anew, that is to say, conserves me. It is as a matter of fact perfectly clear and evident to all those who consider with attention the nature of time, that, in order to be conserved in each moment in which it endures, a substance has need of the same power and action as would be necessary to produce and create it anew, supposing it did not yet exist, so that the light of nature shows us clearly that the distinction between creation and conservation is solely a distinction of the reason.

All that I thus require here is that I should interrogate myself, if I wish to know whether I possess a power which is capable of bringing it to pass that I who now am shall still be in the future; for since I am nothing but a thinking thing, or at least since thus far it is only this portion of myself which is precisely in question at present, if such a power did reside in me, I should certainly be conscious of it. But I am conscious of nothing of the kind, and by this I know clearly that I depend on some being different from myself.

Possibly, however, this being on which I depend is not that which I call God, and I am created either by my parents or by some other cause less perfect than God. This cannot be, because, as I have just said, it is perfectly evident that there must be at least as much reality in the cause as in the effect; and thus since I am a thinking thing, and possess an idea of God within me, whatever in the end be the cause assigned to my existence, it must be allowed that it is likewise a thinking thing and that it possesses in itself the idea of all the perfections which I attribute to God. We may again inquire whether this cause derives its origin from itself or from some other thing. For if from itself, it follows by the reasons before brought forward, that this cause must itself be God; for since it possesses the virtue of self-existence, it must also without doubt have the power of actually possessing all the perfections of which it has the idea, that is, all those which I conceive as existing in God. But if it derives its existence from some other cause than itself, we shall again ask, for the same reason, whether this second cause exists by itself or through another, until from one step to another, we finally arrive at an ultimate cause, which will be God.

And it is perfectly manifest that in this there can be no regression into infinity, since what is in question is not so much the cause which formerly created me, as that which conserves me at the present time.

Nor can we suppose that several causes may have concurred in my production, and that from one I have received the idea of one of the perfections which I attribute to God, and from another the idea of some other, so that all these perfections indeed exist somewhere in the universe, but not as complete in one unity which is God. On the contrary, the unity, the simplicity or the inseparability of all things which are in God is one of the principal perfections which I conceive to be in Him. And certainly the idea of this unity of all Divine perfections cannot have been placed in me by any cause from which I have not likewise received the ideas of all the other perfections; for this cause could not make me able to comprehend them as joined together in an inseparable unity without having at the same time caused me in some measure to know what they are [and in some way to recognise each one of them].

Finally, so far as my parents [from whom it appears I have sprung] are concerned, although all that I have ever been able to believe of them were true, that does not make it follow that it is they who conserve me, nor are they even the authors of my being in any sense, in so far as I am a thinking being; since what they did was merely to implant certain dispositions in that matter in which the self—i.e. the mind, which alone I at present identify with myself—is by me deemed to exist. And thus there can be no difficulty in their regard, but we must of necessity conclude from the fact alone that I exist, or that the idea of a Being supremely perfect—that is of God—is in me, that the proof of God's existence is grounded on the highest evidence.

It only remains to me to examine into the manner in which I have acquired this idea from God; for I have not received it through the senses, and it is never presented to me unexpectedly, as is usual with the ideas of sensible things when these things present themselves, or seem to present themselves, to the external organs of my senses; nor is it likewise a fiction of my mind, for it is not in my power to take from or to add anything to it; and consequently the only alternative is that it is innate in me, just as the idea of myself is innate in me.

And one certainly ought not to find it strange that God, in creating me, placed this idea within me to be like the mark of the workman imprinted on his work; and it is likewise not essential that the mark shall be something different from the work itself. For from the sole fact that God created me it is most probable that in some way he has placed his image and similitude upon me, and that I perceive this similitude (in which the idea of God is contained) by means of the same faculty by which I perceive myself—that is to say, when I reflect on myself I not only know that I am something [imperfect], incomplete and dependent on another, which incessantly aspires after something which is better and greater than myself, but I also know that He on whom I depend possesses in Himself all the great things towards which I aspire [and the ideas of which I find within myself], and that not indefinitely or potentially alone, but really, actually and infinitely; and that thus He is God. And the whole strength of the argument which I have here made use of to prove the existence of God consists in this, that I recognise that it is not possible that my nature should be what it is, and indeed that I should have in myself the idea of a God, if God did not veritably exist—a God, I say, whose idea is in me, i.e. who possesses all those supreme perfections of which our mind may indeed have some idea but without understanding them all, who is liable to no errors or defect [and who has none of all those marks which denote imperfection]. From this it is manifest that He cannot be a deceiver, since the light of nature teaches us that fraud and deception necessarily proceed from some defect.

But before I examine this matter with more care, and pass on to the consideration of other truths which may be derived from it, it seems to me right to pause for a while in order to contemplate God Himself, to ponder at leisure His marvellous attributes, to consider, and admire, and adore, the beauty of this light so resplendent, at least as far as the strength of my mind, which is in some measure dazzled by the sight, will allow me to do so. For just as faith teaches us that the supreme felicity of the other life consists only in this contemplation of the Divine Majesty, so we continue to learn by experience that a similar meditation, though incomparably less perfect, causes us to enjoy the greatest satisfaction of which we are capable in this life.

MEDITATION IV
Of the True and the False.

I have been well accustomed these past days to detach my mind from my senses, and I have accurately observed that there are very few things that one knows with certainty respecting corporeal objects, that there are many more which are known to us respecting the human mind, and yet more still regarding God Himself; so that I shall now without any difficulty abstract my thoughts from the consideration of [sensible or] imaginable objects, and carry them to those which, being withdrawn from all contact with matter, are purely intelligible. And certainly the idea which I possess of the human mind inasmuch as it is a thinking thing, and not extended in length, width and depth, nor participating in anything pertaining to body, is incomparably more distinct than is the idea of any corporeal thing. And when I consider that I doubt, that is to say, that I am an incomplete and dependent being, the idea of a being that is complete and independent, that is of God, presents itself to my mind with so much distinctness and clearness—and from the fact alone that this idea is found in me, or that I who possess this idea exist, I conclude so certainly that God exists, and that my existence depends entirely on Him in every moment of my life—that I do not think that the human mind is capable of knowing anything with more evidence and certitude. And it seems to me that I now have before me a road which will lead us from the contemplation of the true God (in whom all the treasures of science and wisdom are contained) to the knowledge of the other objects of the universe.

For, first of all, I recognise it to be impossible that He should ever deceive me; for in all fraud and deception some imperfection is to be found, and although it may appear that the power of deception is a mark of subtilty or power, yet the desire to deceive without doubt testifies to malice or feebleness, and accordingly cannot be found in God.

In the next place I experienced in myself a certain capacity for judging which I have doubtless received from God, like all the other things that I possess; and as He could not desire to deceive me, it is clear that He has not given me a faculty that will lead me to err if I use it aright.

And no doubt respecting this matter could remain, if it were not that the consequence would seem to follow that I can thus never be deceived; for if I hold all that I possess from God, and if He has not placed me in the capacity for error, it seems as though I could never fall into error. And it is true that when I think only of God [and direct my mind wholly to Him], I discover [in myself] no cause of error, or falsity; yet directly afterwards, when recurring to myself, experience shows me that I am nevertheless subject to an infinitude of errors, as to which, when we come to investigate them more closely, I notice that not only is there a real and positive idea of God or of a Being of supreme perfection present to my mind, but also, so to speak, a certain negative idea of nothing, that is, of that which is infinitely removed from any kind of perfection; and that I am in a sense something intermediate between God and nought, i.e. placed in such a manner between the supreme Being and non-being, that there is in truth nothing in me that can lead to error in so far as a sovereign Being has formed me; but that, as I in some degree participate likewise in nought or in non-being, i.e. in so far as I am not myself the supreme Being, and as I find myself subject to an infinitude of imperfections, I ought not to be astonished if I should fall into error. Thus do I recognise that error, in so far as it is such, is not a real thing depending on God, but simply a defect; and therefore, in order to fall into it, that I have no need to possess a special faculty given me by God for this very purpose, but that I fall into error from the fact that the power given me by God for the purpose of distinguishing truth from error is not infinite.

Nevertheless this does not quite satisfy me; for error is not a pure negation [i.e. is not the simple defect or want of some perfection which ought not to be mine], but it is a lack of some knowledge which it seems that I ought to possess. And on considering the nature of God it does not appear to me possible that He should have given me a faculty which is not perfect of its kind, that is, which is wanting in some perfection due to it. For if it is true that the more skillful the artisan, the more perfect is the work of his hands, what can have been produced by this supreme Creator of all things that is not in all its parts perfect? And certainly there is no doubt that God could have created me so that I could never have been subject to error; it is also certain that He ever wills what is best; is it then better that I should be subject to err than that I should not?

In considering this more attentively, it occurs to me in the first place that I should not be astonished if my intelligence is not capable of comprehending why God acts as He does; and that there is thus no reason to doubt of His existence from the fact that I may perhaps find many other things besides this as to which I am able to understand neither for what reason nor how God has produced them. For, in the first place, knowing that my nature is extremely feeble and limited, and that the nature of God is on the contrary immense, incomprehensible, and infinite, I have no further difficulty in recognising that there is an infinitude of matters in His power, the causes of which transcend my knowledge; and this reason suffices to convince me that the species of cause termed final, finds no useful employment in physical [or natural] things; for it does not appear to me that I can without temerity seek to investigate the [inscrutable] ends of God.

It further occurs to me that we should not consider one single creature separately, when we inquire as to whether the works of God are perfect, but should regard all his creations together. For the same thing which might possibly seem very imperfect with some semblance of reason if regarded by itself, is found to be very perfect if regarded as part of the whole universe; and although, since I resolved to doubt all things, I as yet have only known certainly my own existence and that of God, nevertheless since I have recognised the infinite power of God, I cannot deny that He may have produced many other things, or at least that He has the power of producing them, so that I may obtain a place as a part of a great universe.

Whereupon, regarding myself more closely, and considering what are my errors (for they alone testify to there being any imperfection in me), I answer that they depend on a combination of two causes, to wit, on the faculty of knowledge that rests in me, and on the power of choice or of free will—that is to say, of the understanding at the same time of the will. For by the understanding alone I [neither assert nor deny anything, but] apprehend the ideas of things as to which I can form a judgment. But no error is properly speaking found in it, provided the word error is taken in its proper signification; and though there is possibly an infinitude of things in the world of which I have no idea in my understanding, we cannot for all that say that it is deprived of these ideas [as we might say of something which is required by its nature], but simply it does not possess these; because in truth there is no reason to prove that God should have given me a greater faculty of knowledge than He has given me; and however skillful a workman I represent Him to be, I should not for all that consider that He was bound to have placed in each of His works all the perfections which He may have been able to place in some. I likewise cannot complain that God has not given me a free choice or a will which is sufficient, ample and perfect, since as a matter of fact I am conscious of a will so extended as to be subject to no limits. And what seems to me very remarkable in this regard is that of all the qualities which I possess there is no one so perfect and so comprehensive that I do not very clearly recognise that it might be yet greater and more perfect. For, to take an example, if I consider the faculty of comprehension which I possess, I find that it is of very small extent and extremely limited, and at the same time I find the idea of another faculty much more ample and even infinite, and seeing that I can form the idea of it, recognise from this very fact that it pertains to the nature of God. If in the same way I examine the memory, the imagination, or some other faculty, I do not find any which is not small and circumscribed, while in God it is immense [or infinite]. It is free will alone or liberty of choice which I find to be so great in me that I can conceive no other idea to be more great; it is indeed the case that it is for the most part this will that causes me to know that in some manner I bear the image and similitude of God. For although the power of will is incomparably greater in God than in me, both by reason of the knowledge and the power which, conjoined with it, render it stronger and more efficacious, and by reason of its object, inasmuch as in God it extends to a great many things; it nevertheless does not seem to me greater if I consider it formally and precisely in itself: for the faculty of will consists alone in our having the power of choosing to do a thing or choosing not to do it (that is, to affirm or deny, to pursue or to shun it), or rather it consists alone in the fact that in order to affirm or deny, pursue or shun those things placed before us by the understanding, we act so that we are unconscious that any outside force constrains us in doing so. For in order that I should be free it is not necessary that I should be indifferent as to the choice of one or the other of two contraries; but contrariwise the more I lean to the one—whether I recognise clearly that the reasons of the good and true are to be found in it, or whether God so disposes my inward thought—the more freely do I choose and embrace it. And undoubtedly both divine grace and natural knowledge, far from diminishing my liberty, rather increase it and strengthen it. Hence this indifference which I feel, when I am not swayed to one side rather than to the other by lack of reason, is the lowest grade of liberty, and rather evinces a lack or negation in knowledge than a perfection of will: for if I always recognised clearly what was true and good, I should never have trouble in deliberating as to what judgment or choice I should make, and then I should be entirely free without ever being indifferent.

From all this I recognise that the power of will which I have received from God is not of itself the source of my errors—for it is very ample and very perfect of its kind—any more than is the power of understanding; for since I understand nothing but by the power which God has given me for understanding, there is no doubt that all that I understand, I understand as I ought, and it is not possible that I err in this. Whence then come my errors? They come from the sole fact that since the will is much wider in its range and compass than the understanding, I do not restrain it within the same bounds, but extend it also to things which I do not understand: and as the will is of itself indifferent to these, it easily falls into error and sin, and chooses the evil for the good, or the false for the true.

For example, when I lately examined whether anything existed in the world, and found that from the very fact that I considered this question it followed very clearly that I myself existed, I could not prevent myself from believing that a thing I so clearly conceived was true: not that I found myself compelled to do so by some external cause, but simply because from great clearness in my mind there followed a great inclination of my will; and I believed this with so much the greater freedom or spontaneity as I possessed the less indifference towards it. Now, on the contrary, I not only know that I exist, inasmuch as I am a thinking thing, but a certain representation of corporeal nature is also presented to my mind; and it comes to pass that I doubt whether this thinking nature which is in me, or rather by which I am what I am, differs from this corporeal nature, or whether both are not simply the same thing; and I here suppose that I do not yet know any reason to persuade me to adopt the one belief rather than the other. From this it follows that I am entirely indifferent as to which of the two I affirm or deny, or even whether I abstain from forming any judgment in the matter.

And this indifference does not only extend to matters as to which the understanding has no knowledge, but also in general to all those which are not apprehended with perfect clearness at the moment when the will is deliberating upon them: for, however probable are the conjectures which render me disposed to form a judgment respecting anything, the simple knowledge that I have that those are conjectures alone and not certain and indubitable reasons, suffices to occasion me to judge the contrary. Of this I have had great experience of late when I set aside as false all that I had formerly held to be absolutely true, for the sole reason that I remarked that it might in some measure be doubted.

But if I abstain from giving my judgment on any thing when I do not perceive it with sufficient clearness and distinctness, it is plain that I act rightly and am not deceived. But if I determine to deny or affirm, I no longer make use as I should of my free will, and if I affirm what is not true, it is evident that I deceive myself;

even though I judge according to truth, this comes about only by chance, and I do not escape the blame of misusing my freedom; for the light of nature teaches us that the knowledge of the understanding should always precede the determination of the will. And it is in the misuse of the free will that the privation which constitutes the characteristic nature of error is met with. Privation, I say, is found in the act, in so far as it proceeds from me, but it is not found in the faculty which I have received from God, nor even in the act in so far as it depends on Him.

For I have certainly no cause to complain that God has not given me an intelligence which is more powerful, or a natural light which is stronger than that which I have received from Him, since it is proper to the finite understanding not to comprehend a multitude of things, and it is proper to a created understanding to be finite; on the contrary, I have every reason to render thanks to God who owes me nothing and who has given me all the perfections I possess, and I should be far from charging Him with injustice, and with having deprived me of, or wrongfully withheld from me, these perfections which He has not bestowed upon me.

I have further no reason to complain that He has given me a will more ample than my understanding, for since the will consists only of one single element, and is so to speak indivisible, it appears that its nature is such that nothing can be abstracted from it [without destroying it]; and certainly the more comprehensive it is found to be, the more reason I have to render gratitude to the giver.

And, finally, I must also not complain that God concurs with me in forming the acts of the will, that is, the judgment in which I go astray, because these acts are entirely true and good, inasmuch as they depend on God; and in a certain sense more perfection accrues to my nature from the fact that I can form them, than if I could not do so. As to the privation in which alone the formal reason of error or sin consists, it has no need of any concurrence from God, since it is not a thing [or an existence], and since it is not related to God as to a cause, but

should be termed merely a negation [according to the significance given to these words in the Schools]. For in fact it is not an imperfection in God that He has given me the liberty to give or withhold my assent from certain things as to which He has not placed a clear and distinct knowledge in my understanding; but it is without doubt an imperfection in me not to make a good use of my freedom, and to give my judgment readily on matters which I only understand obscurely. I nevertheless perceive that God could easily have created me so that I never should err, although I still remained free, and endowed with a limited knowledge, viz, by giving to my understanding a clear and distinct intelligence of all things as to which I should ever have to deliberate; or simply by His engraving deeply in my memory the resolution never to form a judgment on anything without having a clear and distinct understanding of it, so that I could never forget it. And it is easy for me to understand that, in so far as I consider myself alone, and as if there were only myself in the world, I should have been much more perfect than I am, if God had created me so that I could never err. Nevertheless I cannot deny that in some sense it is a greater perfection in the whole universe that certain parts should not be exempt from error as others are than that all parts should be exactly similar. And I have no right to complain if God, having placed me in the world, has not called upon me to play a part that excels all others in distinction and perfection.

And further I have reason to be glad on the ground that if He has not given me the power of never going astray by the first means pointed out above, which depends on a clear and evident knowledge of all the things regarding which I can deliberate, He has at least left within my power the other means, which is firmly to adhere to the resolution never to give judgment on matters whose truth is not clearly known to me; for although I notice a certain weakness in my nature in that I cannot continually concentrate my mind on one single thought, I can yet, by attentive and frequently repeated meditation, impress it so forcibly on my memory that I shall never fail to recollect it whenever I have need of it, and thus acquire the habit of never going astray.

And inasmuch as it is in this that the greatest and principal perfection of man consists, it seems to me that I have not gained little by this day's Meditation, since I have discovered the source of falsity and error. And certainly there can be no other source than that which I have explained; for as often as I so restrain my will within the limits of my knowledge that it forms no judgment except on matters which are clearly and distinctly represented to it by the understanding, I can never be deceived; for every clear and distinct conception is without

doubt something, and hence cannot derive its origin from what is nought, but must of necessity have God as its author—God, I say, who being supremely perfect, cannot be the cause of any error; and consequently we must conclude that such a conception [or such a judgment] is true. Nor have I only learned to-day what I should avoid in order that I may not err, but also how I should act in order to arrive at a knowledge of the truth; for without doubt I shall arrive at this end if I devote my attention sufficiently to those things which I perfectly understand; and if I separate from these that which I only understand confusedly and with obscurity. To these I shall henceforth diligently give heed.

MEDITATION V
Of the essence of material things, and, again, of God that he exists.

Many other matters respecting the attributes of God and my own nature or mind remain for consideration; but I shall possibly on another occasion resume the investigation of these. Now (after first noting what must be done or avoided, in order to arrive at a knowledge of the truth) my principal task is to endeavour to emerge from the state of doubt into which I have these last days fallen, and to see whether nothing certain can be known regarding material things.

But before examining whether any such objects as I conceive exist outside of me, I must consider the ideas of them in so far as they are in my thought, and see which of them are distinct and which confused.

In the first place, I am able distinctly to imagine that quantity which philosophers commonly call continuous, or the extension in length, breadth, or depth, that is in this quantity, or rather in the object to which it is attributed. Further, I can number in it many different parts, and attribute to each of its parts many sorts of size, figure, situation and local movements, and, finally, I can assign to each of these movements all degrees of duration.

And not only do I know these things with distinctness when I consider them in general,

but, likewise [however little I apply my attention to the matter], I discover an infinitude of particulars respecting numbers, figures, movements, and other such things, whose truth is so manifest, and so well accords with my nature, that when I begin to discover them, it seems to me that I learn nothing new, or recollect what I formerly knew—that is to say, that I for the first time perceive things which were already present to my mind, although I had not as yet applied my mind to them.

And what I here find to be most important is that I discover in myself an infinitude of ideas of certain things which cannot be esteemed as pure negations, although they may possibly have no existence outside of my thought, and which are not framed by me, although it is within my power either to think or not to think them, but which possess natures which are true and immutable. For example, when I imagine a triangle, although there may nowhere in the world be such a figure outside my thought, or ever have been, there is nevertheless in this figure a certain determinate nature, form, or essence, which is immutable and eternal, which I have not invented, and which in no wise depends on my mind, as appears from the fact that diverse properties of that triangle can be demonstrated, viz, that its three angles are equal to two right angles, that the greatest side is subtended by the greatest angle, and the like, which now, whether I wish it or do not wish it, I recognise very clearly as pertaining to it, although I never thought of the matter at all when I imagined a triangle for the first time, and which therefore cannot be said to have been invented by me.

Nor does the objection hold good that possibly this idea of a triangle has reached my mind through the medium of my senses, since I have sometimes seen bodies triangular in shape; because I can form in my mind an infinitude of other figures regarding which we cannot have the least conception of their ever having been objects of sense, and I can nevertheless demonstrate various properties pertaining to their nature as well as to that of the triangle, and these must certainly all be true since I conceive them clearly. Hence they are something, and not pure negation; for it is perfectly clear that all that is true is something, and I have already fully demonstrated that all that I know clearly is true. And even although I had not demonstrated this, the nature of my mind is such that I could not prevent myself from holding them to be true so long as I conceive them clearly; and I recollect that even when I was still strongly attached to the objects of sense, I counted as the most certain those truths which I conceived clearly as regards figures, numbers, and the other matters which pertain to arithmetic and geometry, and, in general, to pure and abstract mathematics.

But now, if just because I can draw the idea of something from my thought, it follows that all which I know clearly and distinctly as pertaining to this object does really belong to it, may I not derive from this an argument demonstrating the existence of God? It is certain that I no less find the idea of God, that is to say, the idea of a supremely perfect Being, in me, than that of any figure or number whatever it is; and I do not know any less clearly and distinctly that an [actual and] eternal existence pertains to this nature than I know that all that which I am able to demonstrate of some figure or number truly pertains to the nature of this figure or

number, and therefore, although all that I concluded in the preceding Meditations were found to be false, the existence of God would pass with me as at least as certain as I have ever held the truths of mathematics (which concern only numbers and figures) to be.

This indeed is not at first manifest, since it would seem to present some appearance of being a sophism. For being accustomed in all other things to make a distinction between existence and essence, I easily persuade myself that the existence can be separated from the essence of God, and that we can thus conceive God as not actually existing. But, nevertheless, when I think of it with more attention, I clearly see that existence can no more be separated from the essence of God than can its having its three angles equal to two right angles be separated from the essence of a [rectilinear] triangle, or the idea of a mountain from the idea of a valley; and so there is not any less repugnance to our conceiving a God (that is, a Being supremely perfect) to whom existence is lacking (that is to say, to whom a certain perfection is lacking), than to conceive of a mountain which has no valley.

But although I cannot really conceive of a God without existence any more than a mountain without a valley, still from the fact that I conceive of a mountain with a valley, it does not follow that there is such a mountain in the world; similarly although I conceive of God as possessing existence, it would seem that it does not follow that there is a God which exists; for my thought does not impose any necessity upon things, and just as I may imagine a winged horse, although no horse with wings exists, so I could perhaps attribute existence to God, although no God existed.

But a sophism is concealed in this objection; for from the fact that I cannot conceive a mountain without a valley, it does not follow that there is any mountain or any valley in existence, but only that the mountain and the valley, whether they exist or do not exist, cannot in any way be separated one from the other. While from the fact that I cannot conceive God without existence, it follows that existence is inseparable from Him, and hence that He really exists; not that my thought can bring this to pass, or impose any necessity on things, but, on the contrary, because the necessity which lies in the thing itself, i.e. the necessity of the existence of God determines me to think in this way. For it is not within my power to think of God without existence (that is of a supremely perfect Being devoid of a supreme perfection) though it is in my power to imagine a horse either with wings or without wings.

And we must not here object that it is in truth necessary for me to assert that God exists after having presupposed that He possesses every sort of perfection, since existence is one of these, but that as a matter of fact my original supposition was not necessary, just as it is not necessary to consider that all quadrilateral figures can be inscribed in the circle; for supposing I thought this, I should be constrained to admit that the rhombus might be inscribed in the circle since it is a quadrilateral figure, which, however, is manifestly false. [We must not, I say, make any such allegations because] although it is not necessary that I should at any time entertain the notion of God, nevertheless whenever it happens that I think of a first and a sovereign Being, and, so to speak, derive the idea of Him from the storehouse of my mind, it is necessary that I should attribute to Him every sort of perfection, although I do not get so far as to enumerate them all, or to apply my mind to each one in particular. And this necessity suffices to make me conclude (after having recognised that existence is a perfection) that this first and sovereign Being really exists; just as though it is not necessary for me ever to imagine any triangle, yet, whenever I wish to consider a rectilinear figure composed only of three angles, it is absolutely essential that I should attribute to it all those properties which serve to bring about the conclusion that its three angles are not greater than two right angles, even though I may not then be considering this point in particular. But when I consider which figures are capable of being inscribed in the circle, it is in no wise necessary that I should think that all quadrilateral figures are of this number; on the

contrary, I cannot even pretend that this is the case, so long as I do not desire to accept anything which I cannot conceive clearly and distinctly. And in consequence there is a great difference between the false suppositions such as this, and the true ideas born within me, the first and principal of which is that of God. For really I discern in many ways that this idea is not something factitious, and depending solely on my thought, but that it is the image of a true and immutable nature; first of all, because I cannot conceive anything but God himself to whose essence existence [necessarily] pertains; in the second place because it is not possible for me to conceive two or more Gods in this same position; and, granted that there is one such God who now exists, I see clearly that it is necessary that He should have existed from all eternity, and that He must exist eternally; and finally, because I know an infinitude of other properties in God, none of which I can either diminish or change.

For the rest, whatever proof or argument I avail myself of, we must always return to the point that it is only those things which we conceive clearly and distinctly that have the power of persuading me entirely. And although amongst the matters which I conceive of in this way, some indeed are manifestly obvious to all, while others only manifest themselves to those who consider them closely and examine them attentively; still, after they have once been discovered, the latter are not esteemed as any less certain than the former. For example, in the case of every right-angled triangle, although it does not so manifestly appear that the square of the base is equal to the squares of the two other sides as that this base is opposite to the greatest angle; still, when this has once been apprehended, we are just as certain of its truth as of the truth of the other. And as regards God, if my mind were not pre-occupied with prejudices, and if my thought did not find itself on all hands diverted by the continual pressure of sensible things, there would be nothing which I could know more immediately and more easily than Him. For is there anything more manifest than that there is a God, that is to say, a Supreme Being, to whose essence alone existence pertains?

And although for a firm grasp of this truth I have need of a strenuous application of mind, at present I not only feel myself to be as assured of it as of all that I hold as most certain, but I also remark that the certainty of all other things depends on it so absolutely, that without this knowledge it is impossible ever to know anything perfectly.

For although I am of such a nature that as long as I understand anything very clearly and distinctly, I am naturally impelled to believe it to be true, yet because I am also of such a nature that I cannot have my mind constantly fixed on the same object in order to perceive it clearly, and as I often recollect having formed a past judgment without at the same time properly recollecting the reasons that led me to make it, it may happen meanwhile that other reasons present themselves to me, which would easily cause me to change my opinion, if I were ignorant of the facts of the existence of God, and thus I should have no true and certain knowledge, but only vague and vacillating opinions. Thus, for example, when I consider the nature of a [rectilinear] triangle, I who have some little knowledge of the principles of geometry recognise quite clearly that the three angles are equal to two right angles, and it is not possible for me not to believe this so long as I apply my mind to its demonstration; but so soon as I abstain from attending to the proof, although I still recollect having clearly comprehended it, it may easily occur that I come to doubt its truth, if I am ignorant of there being a God. For I can persuade myself of having been so constituted by nature that I can easily deceive myself even in those matters which I believe myself to apprehend with the greatest evidence and certainty, especially when I recollect that I have frequently judged matters to be true and certain which other reasons have afterwards impelled me to judge to be altogether false.

But after I have recognised that there is a God—because at the same time I have also rec-ognised that all things depend upon Him, and that He is not a deceiver, and from that have inferred that what I perceive clearly and distinctly cannot fail to be true—although I no longer pay attention to the reasons for which I have judged this to be true, provided that I recollect having clearly and distinctly perceived it, no contrary reason can be brought forward which could ever cause me to doubt of its truth; and thus I have a true and certain knowledge of it. And this same knowledge extends likewise to all other things which I recollect having formerly demonstrated, such as the truths of geometry and the like; for what can be alleged against them to cause me to place them in doubt? Will it be said that my nature is such as to cause me to be frequently deceived? But I already know that I cannot be deceived in the judgment whose grounds I know clearly. Will it be said that I formerly held many things to be true and certain which I have afterwards recognised to be false? But I had not had any clear and distinct knowledge of these things, and not as yet knowing the rule whereby I assure myself of the truth, I had been impelled to give my assent from reasons which I have since recognised to be less strong than I had at the time imagined them to be. What further objection can then be raised? That possibly I am dreaming (an objection I myself made a little while ago), or that all the thoughts which I now have are no more true than the phantasies of my dreams? But even though I slept the case would be the same, for all that is clearly present to my mind is absolutely true.

And so I very clearly recognise that the certainty and truth of all knowledge depends alone on the knowledge of the true God, in so much that, before I knew Him, I could not have a perfect knowledge of any other thing. And now that I know Him I have the means of acquiring a perfect knowledge of an infinitude of things, not only of those which relate to God Himself and other intellectual matters, but also of those which pertain to corporeal nature in so far as it is the object of pure mathematics [which have no concern with whether it exists or not].

MEDITATION VI

Of the Existence of Material Things, and of the real distinction between the Soul and Body of Man.

Nothing further now remains but to inquire whether material things exist. And certainly I at least know that these may exist in so far as they are considered as the objects of pure mathematics, since in this aspect I perceive them clearly and distinctly. For there is no doubt that God possesses the power to produce everything that I am capable of perceiving with distinctness, and I have never deemed that anything was impossible for Him, unless I found a contradiction in attempting to conceive it clearly. Further, the faculty of imagination which I possess, and of which, experience tells me, I make use when I apply myself to the consideration of material things, is capable of persuading me of their existence; for when I attentively consider what imagination is, I find that it is nothing but a certain application of the faculty of knowledge to the body which is immediately present to it, and which therefore exists.

And to render this quite clear, I remark in the first place the difference that exists between the imagination and pure intellection [or conception]. For example, when I imagine a triangle, I do not conceive it only as a figure comprehended by three lines, but I also apprehend these three lines as present by the power and inward vision of my mind, and this is what I call imagining. But if I desire to think of a chiliagon, I certainly conceive truly that it is a figure composed of a thousand sides, just as easily as I conceive of a triangle that it is a figure of three sides; but I cannot in any way imagine the thousand sides of a chiliagon [as I do the three sides of a triangle], nor do I, so to speak, regard them as present [with the eyes of my mind]. And although in accordance with the habit I have formed of always employing the aid of my imagination when I think of corporeal things, it may happen that in imagining a chiliagon I confusedly represent to myself some figure, yet it is very evident that this figure is not a chiliagon, since it in no way differs from that which I represent to myself when I think of a myriagon or any other many-sided figure; nor does it serve my purpose in discovering the properties which go to form the distinction between a chiliagon and other polygons. But if the question turns upon a pentagon, it is quite true that I can conceive its figure as well as that of a chiliagon without the help of my imagination; but I can also imagine it by applying the attention of my mind to each of its five sides, and at the same time to the space which they enclose. And thus I clearly recognise that I have need of a particular effort of mind in order to effect the act of imagination, such as I do not require in order to understand, and this particular effort of mind clearly manifests the difference which exists between imagination and pure intellection.

I remark besides that this power of imagination which is in one, inasmuch as it differs from the power of understanding, is in no wise a necessary element in my nature, or in [my essence, that is to say, in] the essence of my mind; for although I did not possess it I should doubtless ever remain the same as I now am, from which it appears that we might conclude that it depends on something which differs from me. And I easily conceive that if some body exists with which my mind is conjoined and united in such a way that it can apply itself to consider it when it pleases, it may be that by this means it can imagine corporeal objects; so that this mode of thinking differs from pure intellection only inasmuch as mind in its intellectual activity in some manner turns on itself, and considers some of the ideas which it possesses in itself; while in imagining it turns towards the body, and there beholds in it something conformable to the idea which it has either conceived of itself or perceived by the senses. I easily understand, I say, that the imagination could be thus constituted if it is true that body exists; and because I can discover no other convenient mode of explaining it, I conjecture with probability that body does exist; but this is only with probability, and although I examine all things with care, I nevertheless do not find that from this distinct idea of corporeal nature, which I have in my imagination, I can derive any argument from which there will necessarily be deduced the existence of body.

But I am in the habit of imagining many other things besides this corporeal nature which is the object of pure mathematics, to wit, the colours, sounds, scents, pain, and other such things, although less distinctly. And inasmuch as I perceive these things much better through the senses, by the medium of which, and by the memory, they seem to have reached my imagination, I believe that, in order to examine them more conveniently, it is right that I should at the same time investigate the nature of sense perception, and that I should see if from the ideas which I apprehend by this mode of thought, which I call feeling, I cannot derive some certain proof of the existence of corporeal objects.

And first of all I shall recall to my memory those matters which I hitherto held to be true, as having perceived them through the senses, and the foundations on which my belief has rested; in the next place I shall examine the reasons which have since obliged me to place them in doubt; in the last place I shall consider which of them I must now believe.

First of all, then, I perceived that I had a head, hands, feet, and all other members of which this body—which I considered as a part, or possibly even as the whole, of myself—is composed. Further I was sensible that this body was placed amidst many others, from which it was capable of being affected in many different ways, beneficial and hurtful, and I remarked that a certain feeling of pleasure accompanied those that were beneficial, and pain those which were harmful. And in addition to this pleasure and pain, I also experienced hunger, thirst, and other similar appetites, as also certain corporeal inclinations towards joy, sadness, anger, and other similar passions. And outside myself, in addition to extension, figure, and motions of bodies, I remarked in them hardness, heat, and

all other tactile qualities, and, further, light and colour, and scents and sounds, the variety of which gave me the means of distinguishing the sky, the earth, the sea, and generally all the other bodies, one from the other. And certainly, considering the ideas of all these qualities which presented themselves to my mind, and which alone I perceived properly or immediately, it was not without reason that I believe myself to perceive objects quite different from my thought, to wit, bodies from which those ideas proceeded; for I found by experience that these ideas presented themselves to me without my consent being requisite, so that I could not perceive any object, however desirous I might be, unless it were present to the organs of sense; and it was not in my power not to perceive it, when it was present. And because the ideas which I receive through the senses were much more lively, more clear, and even, in their own way, more distinct than any of those which I could of myself frame in meditation, or than those I found impressed on my memory, it appeared as though they could not have proceeded from my mind, so that they must necessarily have been produced in me by some other things. And having no knowledge of those objects excepting the knowledge which the ideas themselves gave me, nothing was more likely to occur to my mind than that the objects were similar to the ideas which were caused. And because I likewise remembered that I had formerly made use of my senses rather than my reason, and recognised that the ideas which I formed of myself were not so distinct as those which I perceived through the senses, and that they were most frequently even composed of portions of these last, I persuaded myself easily that I had no idea in my mind which had not formerly come to me through the senses. Nor was it without some reason that I believed that this body (which by a certain special right I call my own) belonged to me more properly and more strictly than any other; for in fact I could never be separated from it as from other bodies; I experienced in it and on account of it all my appetites and affections, and finally I was touched by the feeling of pain and titillation of pleasure in its parts, and not in the parts of other bodies which were separated from it. But when I inquired, why, from some, I know not what, painful sensation, there follows sadness of mind, and from the pleasurable sensation there arises joy, or why this mysterious pinching of the stomach which I call hunger causes me to desire to eat, and dryness of throat causes a desire to drink, and so on, I could give no reason excepting that nature taught me so; for there is certainly no affinity (that I at least can understand) between the craving of the stomach and the desire to eat, any more than between the perception of whatever causes pain and the thought of sadness which arises from this perception. And in the same way it appeared to me that I had learned from nature all the other judgments which I formed regarding the objects of my senses, since I remarked that these judgments were found in me before I had the leisure to weigh and consider any reasons which might oblige me to make them.

But afterwards many experiences little by little destroyed all the faith which I had rested in my senses; for I from time to time observed that those towers which from afar appeared to me to be round, more closely observed seemed square, and that colossal statues raised on the summit of these towers, appeared as quite tiny statues when viewed from the bottom; and so in an infinitude of other cases I found error in judgments founded on the external senses. And not only in those founded on the external senses, but even in those founded on the internal as well; for is there anything more intimate or more internal than pain? And yet I have learned from some persons whose arms or legs have been cut off, that they sometimes seemed to feel pain in the part which had been amputated, which made me think that I could not be quite certain that it was a certain member which pained me, even though I felt pain in it. And to those grounds of doubt I have lately added two others, which are very general; the first is that I never have believed myself to feel anything in waking moments which I cannot also sometime believe myself to feel when I sleep, and as I do not think that these things

which I seem to feel in sleep, proceed from objects outside of me, I do not see any reason why I should have this belief regarding objects which I seem to perceive while awake. The other was that being still ignorant, or rather supposing my self to be ignorant, of the author of my being, I saw nothing to prevent me from having been so constituted by nature that I might be deceived even in matters which seemed to me to be most certain. And as to the grounds on which I was formerly persuaded of the truth of sensible objects, I had not much trouble in replying to them. For since nature seemed to cause me to lean towards many things from which reason repelled me, I did not believe that I should trust much to the teachings of nature. And although the ideas which I receive by the senses do not depend on my will, I did not think that one should for that reason conclude that they proceeded from things different from myself, since possibly some faculty might be discovered in me—though hitherto unknown to me—which produced them.

But now that I begin to know myself better, and to discover more clearly the author of my being, I do not in truth think that I should rashly admit all the matters which the senses seem to teach us, but, on the other hand, I do not think that I should doubt them all universally.

And first of all, because I know that all things which I apprehend clearly and distinctly can be created by God as I apprehend them, it suffices that I am able to apprehend one thing apart from another clearly and distinctly in order to be certain that the one is different from the other, since they may be made to exist in separation at least by the omnipotence of God; and it does not signify by what power this separation is made in order to compel me to judge them to be different: and, therefore, just because I know certainly that I exist, and that meanwhile I do not remark that any other thing necessarily pertains to my nature or essence, excepting that I am a thinking thing, I rightly conclude that my essence consists solely in the fact that I am a thinking thing [or a substance whose whole essence or nature is to think]. And although possibly (or rather certainly, as I shall say in a moment) I possess a body with which I am very intimately conjoined, yet because, on the one side, I have a clear and distinct idea of myself inasmuch as I am only a thinking and extended thing, and as, on the other, I possess a distinct idea of body, inasmuch as it is only an extended and unthinking thing, it is certain that this I [that is to say, my soul by which I am what I am], is entirely and absolutely distinct from my body, and can exist without it.

I further find in myself faculties employing modes of thinking peculiar to themselves, to wit, the faculties of imagination and feeling, without which I can easily conceive myself clearly and distinctly as a complete being; while, on the other hand, they cannot be so conceived apart from me, that is, without an intelligent substance in which they reside, for [in the notion we have of these faculties, or, to use the language of the Schools] in their formal concept, some kind of intellection is comprised, from which I infer that they are distinct from me as its modes are from a thing. I observe also in me some other faculties such as that of change of position, the assumption of different figures and such like, which cannot be conceived, any more than can the preceding, apart from some substance to which they are attached, and consequently cannot exist without it; but it is very clear that these faculties, if it be true that they exist, must be attached to some corporeal or extended and not to an intelligent substance, since in the clear and distinct conception of these there is some sort of extension found to be present, but no intellection at all. There is certainly further in me a certain passive faculty of perception, that is, of receiving and recognising the ideas of sensible things, but this would be useless to me [and I could in no way avail myself of it], if there were not either in me or in some other thing another active faculty capable of forming and producing these ideas. But this active faculty cannot exist in me [inasmuch as I am a thing that thinks] seeing that it does not presuppose thought, and also that those ideas are often produced in me without my contributing in any way to the same, and often even against my will; it is thus neces-

sarily the case that the faculty resides in some substance different from me in which all the reality which is objectively in the ideas that are produced by this faculty is formally or eminently contained, as I remarked before. And this substance is either a body, that is, a corporeal nature in which there is contained formally [and really] all that which is objectively [and by representation] in those ideas, or it is God Himself, or some other creature more noble than body in which that same is contained eminently. But since God is no deceiver, it is very manifest that He does not communicate to me these ideas immediately and by Himself, nor yet by the intervention of some creature in which their reality is not formally, but only eminently, contained. For since He has given me no faculty to recognise that this is the case, but, on the other hand, a very great inclination to believe [that they are sent to me or] that they are conveyed to me by corporeal objects, I do not see how He could be defended from the accusation of deceit if these ideas were produced by causes other than corporeal objects. Hence we must allow that corporeal things exist. However, they are perhaps not exactly what we perceive by the senses, since this comprehension by the senses is in many instances very obscure and confused; but we must at least admit that all things which I conceive in them clearly and distinctly, that is to say, all things which, speaking generally, are comprehended in the object of pure mathematics, are truly to be recognised as external objects.

As to other things, however, which are either particular only, as, for example, that the sun is of such and such a figure, etc., or which are less clearly and distinctly conceived, such as light, sound, pain and the like, it is certain that although they are very dubious and uncertain, yet on the sole ground that God is not a deceiver, and that consequently He has not permitted any falsity to exist in my opinion which He has not likewise given me the faculty of correcting, I may assuredly hope to conclude that I have within me the means of arriving at the truth even here. And first of all there is no doubt that in all things which nature teaches me there is some truth contained; for by nature, considered in general, I now understand no other thing than either God Himself or else the order and disposition which God has established in created things; and by my nature in particular I understand no other thing than the complexus of all the things which God has given me.

But there is nothing which this nature teaches me more expressly [nor more sensibly] than that I have a body which is adversely affected when I feel pain, which has need of food or drink when I experience the feelings of hunger and thirst, and so on; nor can I doubt there being some truth in all this.

Nature also teaches me by the sensations of pain, hunger, thirst, etc., that I am not only lodged in my body as a pilot in a vessel, but that I am very closely united to it, and so to speak so intermingled with it that I seem to compose with it one whole. For if that were not the case, when my body is hurt, I, who am merely a thinking thing, should not feel pain, for I should perceive this wound by the understanding only, just as the sailor perceives by sight when something is damaged in his vessel; and when my body has need of drink or food, I should clearly understand the fact without being warned of it by confused feelings of hunger and thirst. For all these sensations of hunger, thirst, pain, etc. are in truth none other than certain confused modes of thought which are produced by the union and apparent intermingling of mind and body.

Moreover, nature teaches me that many other bodies exist around mine, of which some are to be avoided, and others sought after. And certainly from the fact that I am sensible of different sorts of colours, sounds, scents, tastes, heat, hardness, etc., I very easily conclude that there are in the bodies from which all these diverse sense-perceptions proceed certain variations which answer to them, although possibly these are not really at all similar to them. And also from the fact that amongst these different sense-perceptions some are very agreeable to me and others disagreeable, it is quite certain that my body (or rather myself in my entirely, inasmuch as I am formed of body and soul)

may receive different impressions agreeable and disagreeable from the other bodies which surround it.

But there are many other things which nature seems to have taught me, but which at the same time I have never really received from her, but which have been brought about in my mind by a certain habit which I have of forming inconsiderate judgments on things; and thus it may easily happen that these judgments contain some error. Take, for example, the opinion which I hold that all space in which there is nothing that affects [or makes an impression on] my senses is void; that in a body which is warm there is something entirely similar to the idea of heat which is in me; that in a white or green body there is the same whiteness or greenness that I perceive; that in a bitter or sweet body there is the same taste, and so on in other instances; that the stars, the towers, and all other distant bodies are of the same figure and size as they appear from far off to our eyes, etc. But in order that in this there should be nothing which I do not conceive distinctly, I should define exactly what I really understand when I say that I am taught somewhat by nature. For here I take nature in a more limited signification than when I term it the sum of all the things given me by God, since in this sum many things are comprehended which only pertain to mind (and to these I do not refer in speaking of nature) such as the notion which I have of the fact that what has once been done cannot ever be undone and an infinitude of such things which I know by the light of nature [without the help of the body]; and seeing that it comprehends many other matters besides which only pertain to body, and are no longer here contained under the name of nature, such as the quality of weight which it possesses and the like, with which I also do not deal; for in talking of nature I only treat of those things given by God to me as a being composed of mind and body. But the nature here described truly teaches me to flee from things which cause the sensation of pain, and seek after the things which communicate to me the sentiment of pleasure and so forth; but I do not see that beyond this it teaches me that from those diverse sense-perceptions we should ever form any conclusion regarding things outside of us, without having [carefully and maturely] mentally examined them beforehand. For it seems to me that it is mind alone, and not mind and body in conjunction, that is requisite to a knowledge of the truth in regard to such things. Thus, although a star makes no larger an impression on my eye than the flame of a little candle there is yet in me no real or positive propensity impelling me to believe that it is not greater than that flame; but I have judged it to be so from my earliest years, without any rational foundation. And although in approaching fire I feel heat, and in approaching it a little too near I even feel pain, there is at the same time no reason in this which could persuade me that there is in the fire something resembling this heat any more than there is in it something resembling the pain; all that I have any reason to believe from this is, that there is something in it, whatever it may be, which excites in me these sensations of heat or of pain. So also, although there are spaces in which I find nothing which excites my senses, I must not from that conclude that these spaces contain no body; for I see in this, as in other similar things, that I have been in the habit of perverting the order of nature, because these perceptions of sense having been placed within me by nature merely for the purpose of signifying to my mind what things are beneficial or hurtful to the composite whole of which it forms a part, and being up to that point sufficiently clear and distinct, I yet avail myself of them as though they were absolute rules by which I immediately determine the essence of the bodies which are outside me, as to which, in fact, they can teach me nothing but what is most obscure and confused.

But I have already sufficiently considered how, notwithstanding the supreme goodness of God, falsity enters into the judgments I make. Only here a new difficulty is presented—one respecting those things the pursuit or avoidance of which is taught me by nature, and also respecting the internal sensations which I possess, and in which I seem to have sometimes detected error [and thus to be directly deceived by my own nature]. To take an example, the agreeable taste of some food in which poison has been intermingled may induce me to partake of the poison, and thus deceive me. It is true, at the same time, that in this case nature may be excused, for it only induces me to desire food in which I find a pleasant taste, and not to desire poison which is unknown to it; and thus I can infer nothing from this fact, except that my nature is not omniscient, at which there is certainly no reason to be astonished, since man, being finite in nature, can only have knowledge the perfectness of which is limited.

But we not unfrequently deceive ourselves even in those things to which we are directly impelled by nature, as happens with those who when they are sick desire to drink or eat things hurtful to them. It will perhaps be said here that the cause of their deceptiveness is that their nature is corrupt, but that does not remove the difficulty, because a sick man is none the less truly God's creature than he who is in health; and it is therefore as repugnant to God's goodness for the one to have a deceitful nature as it is for the other. And as a clock composed of wheels and counterweights no less exactly observes the laws of nature when it is badly made, and does not show the time properly, than when it entirely satisfies the wishes of its maker, and as, if I consider the body of a man as being a sort of machine so built up and composed of nerves, muscles, veins, blood and skin, that though there were no mind in it at all, it would not cease to have the same motions as at present, exception being made of those movements which are due to the direction of the will, and in consequence depend upon the mind [as opposed to those which operate by the disposition of its organs], I easily recognise that it would be as natural to this body, supposing it to be, for example, dropsical, to suffer the parchedness of the throat which usually signifies to the mind the feeling of thirst, and to be disposed by this parched feeling to move the nerves and other parts in the way requisite for drinking, and thus to augment its malady and do harm to itself, as it is natural to it, when it has no indisposition, to be impelled to drink for its good by a similar cause. And although, considering the use to which the clock has been destined by its maker, I may say that it deflects from the order of its nature when it does not indicate the hours correctly; and as, in the same way, considering the machine of the human body as having been formed by God in order to have in itself all the movements usually manifested there, I have reason for thinking that it does not follow the order of nature when, if the throat is dry, drinking does harm to the conservation of health, nevertheless I recognise at the same time that this last mode of explaining nature is very different from the other. For this is but a purely verbal characterisation depending entirely on my thought, which compares a sick man and a badly constructed clock with the idea which I have of a healthy man and a well made clock, and it is hence extrinsic to the things to which it is applied; but according to the other interpretation of the term nature I understand something which is truly found in things and which is therefore not without some truth.

But certainly although in regard to the dropsical body it is only so to speak to apply an extrinsic term when we say that its nature is corrupted, inasmuch as apart from the need to drink, the throat is parched; yet in regard to the composite whole, that is to say, to the mind or soul united to this body, it is not a purely verbal predicate, but a real error of nature, for it to have thirst when drinking would be hurtful to it. And thus it still remains to inquire how the goodness of God does not prevent the nature of man so regarded from being fallacious.

In order to begin this examination, then, I here say, in the first place, that there is a great difference between mind and body, inasmuch as body is by nature always divisible, and the mind is entirely indivisible. For, as a matter of fact, when I consider the mind, that is to say, myself inasmuch as I am only a thinking thing, I cannot distinguish in myself any parts, but apprehend myself to be clearly one and entire; and although the whole mind seems to be united to the whole body, yet if a foot, or an arm, or some other part, is separated from my body, I am aware that nothing has been taken away

from my mind. And the faculties of willing, feeling, conceiving, etc. cannot be properly speaking said to be its parts, for it is one and the same mind which employs itself in willing and in feeling and understanding. But it is quite otherwise with corporeal or extended objects, for there is not one of these imaginable by me which my mind cannot easily divide into parts, and which consequently I do not recognise as being divisible; this would be sufficient to teach me that the mind or soul of man is entirely different from the body, if I had not already learned it from other sources.

I further notice that the mind does not receive the impressions from all parts of the body immediately, but only from the brain, or perhaps even from one of its smallest parts, to wit, from that in which the common sense is said to reside, which, whenever it is disposed in the same particular way, conveys the same thing to the mind, although meanwhile the other portions of the body may be differently disposed, as is testified by innumerable experiments which it is unnecessary here to recount.

I notice, also, that the nature of body is such that none of its parts can be moved by another part a little way off which cannot also be moved in the same way by each one of the parts which are between the two, although this more remote part does not act at all. As, for example, in the cord ABCD [which is in tension] if we pull the last part D, the first part A will not be moved in any way differently from what would be the case if one of the intervening parts B or C were pulled, and the last part D were to remain unmoved. And in the same way, when I feel pain in my foot, my knowledge of physics teaches me that this sensation is communicated by means of nerves dispersed through the foot, which, being extended like cords from there to the brain, when they are contracted in the foot, at the same time contract the inmost portions of the brain which is their extremity and place of origin, and then excite a certain movement which nature has established in order to cause the mind to be affected by a sensation of pain represented as existing in the foot. But because these nerves must pass through the tibia, the thigh, the loins, the back and the neck, in order to reach from the leg to the brain, it may happen that although their extremities which are in the foot are not affected, but only certain ones of their intervening parts [which pass by the loins or the neck], this action will excite the same movement in the brain that might have been excited there by a hurt received in the foot, in consequence of which the mind will necessarily feel in the foot the same pain as if it had received a hurt. And the same holds good of all the other perceptions of our senses.

I notice finally that since each of the movements which are in the portion of the brain by which the mind is immediately affected brings about one particular sensation only, we cannot under the circumstances imagine anything more likely than that this movement, amongst all the sensations which it is capable of impressing on it, causes mind to be affected by that one which is best fitted and most generally useful for the conservation of the human body when it is in health. But experience makes us aware that all the feelings with which nature inspires us are such as I have just spoken of; and there is therefore nothing in them which does not give testimony to the power and goodness of the God [who has produced them]. Thus, for example, when the nerves which are in the feet are violently or more than usually moved, their movement, passing through the medulla of the spine to the inmost parts of the brain, gives a sign to the mind which makes it feel somewhat, to wit, pain, as though in the foot, by which the mind is excited to do its utmost to remove the cause of the evil as dangerous and hurtful to the foot. It is true that God could have constituted the nature of man in such a way that this same movement in the brain would have conveyed something quite different to the mind; for example, it might have produced consciousness of itself either in so far as it is in the brain, or as it is in the foot, or as it is in some other place between the foot and the brain, or it might finally have produced consciousness of anything else whatsoever; but none of all this would have contributed so well to the conservation of the body. Similarly, when we desire to drink, a cer-

tain dryness of the throat is produced which moves its nerves, and by their means the internal portions of the brain; and this movement causes in the mind the sensation of thirst, because in this case there is nothing more useful to us than to become aware that we have need to drink for the conservation of our health; and the same holds good in other instances.

From this it is quite clear that, notwithstanding the supreme goodness of God, the nature of man, inasmuch as it is composed of mind and body, cannot be otherwise than sometimes a source of deception. For if there is any cause which excites, not in the foot but in some part of the nerves which are extended between the foot and the brain, or even in the brain itself, the same movement which usually is produced when the foot is detrimentally affected, pain will be experienced as though it were in the foot, and the sense will thus naturally be deceived; for since the same movement in the brain is capable of causing but one sensation in the mind, and this sensation is much more frequently excited by a cause which hurts the foot than by another existing in some other quarter, it is reasonable that it should convey to the mind pain in the foot rather than in any other part of the body. And although the parchedness of the throat does not always proceed, as it usually does, from the fact that drinking is necessary for the health of the body, but sometimes comes from quite a different cause, as is the case with dropsical patients, it is yet much better that it should mislead on this occasion than if, on the other hand, it were always to deceive us when the body is in good health; and so on in similar cases.

And certainly this consideration is of great service to me, not only in enabling me to recognise all the errors to which my nature is subject, but also in enabling me to avoid them or to correct them more easily. For knowing that all my senses more frequently indicate to me truth than falsehood respecting the things which concern that which is beneficial to the body, and being able almost always to avail myself of many of them in order to examine one particular thing, and, besides that, being able to make use of my memory in order to connect the present with the past, and of my understanding which already has discovered all the causes of my errors, I ought no longer to fear that falsity may be found in matters every day presented to me by my senses. And I ought to set aside all the doubts of these past days as hyperbolical and ridiculous, particularly that very common uncertainty respecting sleep, which I could not distinguish from the waking state; for at present I find a very notable difference between the two, inasmuch as our memory can never connect our dreams one with the other, or with the whole course of our lives, as it unites events which happen to us while we are awake. And, as a matter of fact, if someone, while I was awake, quite suddenly appeared to me and disappeared as fast as do the images which I see in sleep, so that I could not know from whence the form came nor whither it went, it would not be without reason that I should deem it a spectre or a phantom formed by my brain [and similar to those which I form in sleep], rather than a real man. But when I perceive things as to which I know distinctly both the place from which they proceed, and that in which they are, and the time at which they appeared to me; and when, without any interruption, I can connect the perceptions which I have of them with the whole course of my life, I am perfectly assured that these perceptions occur while I am waking and not during sleep. And I ought in no wise to doubt the truth of such matters, if, after having called up all my senses, my memory, and my understanding, to examine them, nothing is brought to evidence by any one of them which is repugnant to what is set forth by the others. For because God is in no wise a deceiver, it follows that I am not deceived in this. But because the exigencies of action often oblige us to make up our minds before having leisure to examine matters carefully, we must confess that the life of man is very frequently subject to error in respect to individual objects, and we must in the end acknowledge the infirmity of our nature.

PETER UNGER
A Defense of Skepticism

The skepticism that I will defend is a negative thesis concerning what we know. I happily accept the fact that there is much that many of us correctly and reasonably believe, but much more than that is needed for us to know even a fair amount. Here I will not argue that nobody knows anything about anything, though that would be quite consistent with the skeptical thesis for which I will argue. The somewhat less radical thesis which I will defend is this one: every human being knows, at best, hardly anything to be so. More specifically, I will argue that hardly anyone knows that 45 and 56 are equal to 101, if anyone at all. On this skeptical thesis, no one will know the thesis to be true. But this is all right. For I only want to argue

"A Defense of Skepticism" is reprinted from *Philosophical Review*, Vol. LXXX No. 2 (April 1971), by permission of the *Philosophical Review*. **Peter Unger,** a contemporary American philosopher affiliated with New York University, has stirred many heated debates in his various papers and presentations defending skepticism.

that it may be reasonable for us to suppose the thesis to be true, not that we should ever know it to be true.

Few philosophers now take skepticism seriously. With philosophers, even the most powerful of traditional skeptical argument has little force to tempt them nowadays. Indeed, nowadays, philosophers tend to think skepticism interesting only as a formal challenge to which positive accounts of our common-sense knowledge are the gratifying responses. Consequently, I find it at least somewhat natural to offer a defense of skepticism.[1]

My defense of skepticism will be quite unlike traditional arguments for this thesis. This is largely because I write at a time when there is a common faith that, so far as expressing truths is concerned, all is well with the language that we speak. Against this common, optimistic assumption, I shall illustrate how our language habits might serve us well in practical ways, even while they involve us in saying what is false rather than true. And this often does occur, I will maintain, when our positive assertions contain terms with special features of a certain kind, which I call *absolute* terms. Among these terms, ''flat'' and ''certain'' are *basic* ones. Due to these terms' characteristic features, and because the world is not so simple as it might be, we do not speak truly, at least as a rule, when we say of a real object, ''That has a top which is flat'' or when we say of a real person, ''He is certain that it is raining.'' And just as basic absolute terms generally fail to apply to the world, so other absolute terms, which are at least partially defined by the basic ones, will fail to apply as well. Thus, we also speak falsely when we say of a real object or person, ''That is a cube'' or ''He knows that it is raining.'' For an object is a cube only if it has surfaces which are flat, and, as I shall argue, a person knows something to be so only if he is certain of it.

I. SOPHISTICATED WORRIES ABOUT WHAT SKEPTICISM REQUIRES

The reason contemporary sophisticated philosophers do not take skepticism seriously can be stated broadly and simply. They think that skepticism implies certain things which are, upon a bit of reflection, quite impossible to accept. These unacceptable implications concern the functioning of our language.

Concerning our language and how it functions, the most obvious requirement of skepticism is that some common terms of our language will involve us in error systematically. These will be such terms as ''know'' and ''knowledge,'' which may be called the ''terms of knowledge.'' If skepticism is right, then while we go around saying ''I know,'' ''He knows,'' and so on, and while we believe what we say to be true, all the while what we say and believe will actually be false. If our beliefs to the effect that we know something or other are so consistently false, then the terms of knowledge lead us into error systematically. But if these beliefs really are false, should we not have experiences which force the realization of their falsity upon us, and indeed abandon these beliefs? Consequently, shouldn't our experiences get us to stop thinking in these terms which thus systematically involve us in error? So, as we continue to think in the terms of knowledge and to believe ourselves to know all sorts of things, this would seem to show that the beliefs are not false ones and the terms are responsible for no error. Isn't it only reasonable, then, to reject a view which requires that such helpful common terms as ''knows'' and ''knowledge'' lead us into error systematically?

So go some worrisome thoughts which might lead us to dismiss skepticism out of hand. But it seems to me that there is no real need for our false beliefs to clash with our experiences in any easily noticeable way. Suppose, for instance, that you falsely believe that a certain region of space is a vacuum. Suppose that, contrary to your belief, the region does contain some gaseous stuff, though only the slightest trace. Now, for practical purposes, we may suppose that, so far as gaseous contents go, it is not important whether that region really is a vacuum or whether it contains whatever gaseous stuff it does contain. Once this is supposed, then it is reasonable to suppose as well that, for practical purposes, it makes no important difference whether you falsely believe that the region is a vacuum or truly believe this last thing—namely, that, for practical purposes, it is not important whether the region is a vacuum or whether it contains that much gaseous stuff.

We may notice that this supposed truth is entailed by what you believe but does not entail it. In other words, a region's being a vacuum entails that, for practical purposes, there is no important difference between whether the region is a vacuum or whether it contains whatever gaseous stuff it does contain. For, if the region is a vacuum, whatever gas it contains is nil, and so there is no difference at all, for any sort of purpose, between the region's being a vacuum and its having that much gaseous stuff. But the entailment does not go the other way, and this is where we may take a special interest. For while a region may not be a vacuum, it may contain so little gaseous stuff that, so far as gaseous contents go, for practical purposes there is no important difference between the region's being a vacuum and its containing whatever gaseous stuff it does contain. So if this entailed truth lies behind the believed falsehood, your false belief, though false, may not be harmful. Indeed, generally, it may even be helpful for you to have this false belief rather than having none and rather than having almost any other belief about the matter that you might have. On this pattern, we may have many false beliefs about regions being vacuums even while these beliefs will suffer no important clash with the experiences of life.

More to our central topic, suppose that, as skepticism might have it, you falsely believe that you *know* that there are elephants. As before, there is a true thing which is entailed by what you falsely believe and which we should notice. The thing here, which presumably you do not actually believe, is this: that, with respect to the matter of whether there are elephants, for practical purposes there is no important difference between whether you know that there are elephants or whether you are in that position with respect to the matter that you actually are in. This latter, true thing is entailed by the false thing you believe—namely, that you know that there are elephants. For if you do know, then, with respect to the matter of the elephants, there is no difference at all, for any purpose of any sort, between your knowing and your being in the position you actually are in. On the other hand, the entailment does not go the other way and, again, this is where our pattern allows a false belief to be helpful. For even if you do not really know, still, it may be that for practical purposes you are in a position with respect to the matter (of the elephants) which is not importantly different from knowing. If this is so, then it may be better, practically speaking, for you to believe falsely that you know than to have no belief at all here. Thus, not only with beliefs to the effect that specified regions are vacuums, but also with beliefs to the effect that we know certain things, it may be that there are very many of them which, though false, it is helpful for us to have. In both cases, the beliefs will not noticeably clash with the experiences of life. Without some further reason for doing so, then, noting the smooth functioning of our "terms of knowledge" give us no powerful reason for dismissing the thesis of skepticism.

There is, however, a second worry which will tend to keep sophisticates far from embracing skepticism, and this worry is, I think, rather more profound than the first. Consequently, I shall devote most of the remainder to treating this second worry. The worry to which I shall be so devoted is this: that, if skepticism is right, then the terms of knowledge, unlike other terms of our language, will never or hardly ever be used to make simple, positive assertions that are true. In other words, skepticism will require the terms of knowledge to be isolated freaks of our language. But even with familiar, persuasive arguments for skepticism, it is implausible to think that our language is plagued by an isolated little group of troublesome freaks. So, by being so hard on knowledge alone, skepticism seems implausible once one reflects on the exclusiveness of its persecution.

II. ABSOLUTE TERMS AND RELATIVE TERMS

Against the worry that skepticism will require the terms of knowledge to be isolated freaks, I shall argue that, on the contrary, a variety of other terms is similarly troublesome. As skepticism becomes more plausible with an examination of the terms of knowledge, so other originally surprising theses become more plausible once their key terms are critically examined. When all of the key terms are understood to have essential features in common, the truth of any of these theses need not be felt as such a surprise.

The terms of knowledge, along with many other troublesome terms, belong to a class of terms that is quite pervasive in our language. I call these terms *absolute terms.* The term "flat," in its central, literal meaning, is an absolute term. (With other meanings, as in "His voice is flat" and "The beer is flat," I have no direct interest.) To say that something is flat is no different from saying that it is absolutely, or perfectly, flat. To say that a surface is flat is to say that some things or properties *which are matters of degree* are *not* instanced in the surface *to any degree at all.* Thus, something which is flat is not at all bumpy, and not at all curved. Bumpiness and curvature are matters of degree. When we say of a surface that it is bumpy, or that it is curved, we use the *relative terms* "bumpy" and "curved" to talk about the surface. Thus, absolute terms and relative terms go together, in at least one important way, while other terms, like "unmarried," have only the most distant connections with terms of either of these two sorts.

There seems to be a syntactic feature which is common to relative terms and to certain absolute terms, while it is found with no other terms. This feature is that each of these terms may be modified by a variety of terms that serve to indicate (matters of) degree. Thus, we find "The table is *very* bumpy" and "The table is *very* flat" but not "The lawyer is *very* unmarried." Among those absolute terms which admit such qualification are all those absolute terms which are *basic* ones. A basic absolute term is an absolute term which is not (naturally) defined in terms of some other absolute term, not even partially so. I suspect that "straight" is such a term, and perhaps "flat" is as well. But in its central (geometrical) meaning, "cube" quite clearly is not a basic absolute term even though it is an absolute term. For "cube" means, among other things, "having edges that are *straight* and surfaces which are *flat*": and "straight" and "flat" are absolute terms. While "cube" does not admit of qualification of degree, "flat" and "straight" do admit of such qualification. Thus, all relative terms and all basic absolute terms admit of constructions of degree. While this is another way in which these two sorts of terms go together, we must now ask: how may we distinguish terms of the one sort from those of the other?

But is there now anything to distinguish here? For if absolute terms admit of degree construction, why think that any of these terms is not a relative term, why think that they do not purport to predicate things or properties which are, as they now look to be, matters of degree? If we may say that a table is very flat, then why not think flatness a matter of degree? Isn't this essentially the same as our saying of a table that it is very bumpy, with bumpiness being a matter of degree? So perhaps "flat," like "bumpy" and like all terms that take degree constructions, is, fittingly, a relative term. But basic absolute terms may be distinguished from relatives even where degree constructions conspire to make things look otherwise.

To advance the wanted distinction, we may look to a procedure for paraphrase. Now, we have granted that it is common for us to say of a surface that it is pretty, or very, or extremely, flat. And it is also common for us to say that, in saying such things of surfaces, we are saying *how* flat the surfaces are. What we say here seems of a piece with our saying of a surface that it is pretty, or very, or extremely, bumpy, and our then saying that, in doing this, we may notice a difference here. For only with our talk about "flat," we have the idea that these locutions are only convenient means for saying how closely a surface approximates, or *how close it comes to being,* a surface which is (absolutely) flat. Thus, it is intuitively plausible, and far from being a nonsensical interpretation, to paraphrase things so our result with our "flat" locutions is this: what we have said of a surface is that it is pretty *nearly* flat, or very *nearly* flat, or extremely *close to being* flat and, in doing that, we have said, not simply how flat the surface is, but rather *how close* the surface is *to being* flat. This form of paraphrase gives a plausible interpretation of our talk of flatness while allowing the term "flat" to lose its appearance of being a relative term. How will this form of paraphrase work with "bumpy," where, presumably, a genuine relative term occurs in our locutions?

What do we say when we say of a surface that it is pretty bumpy, or very bumpy, or extremely so? Of course, it at least appears that we say *how* bumpy the surface is. The paraphrase has it that what we are saying is that the surface is pretty *nearly* bumpy, or very *nearly* bumpy, or extremely *close to being* bumpy. In other words, according to the paraphrase, we are saying *how close* the surface is *to being* bumpy. But anything of this sort is, quite obviously, a terribly poor interpretation of what we are saying about the surface. Unfortunately for the paraphrase, if we say that a surface is very bumpy it is entailed by what we say that the surface is bumpy, while if we say that the surface is very close to being bumpy it is entailed that the surface is *not* bumpy. Thus, unlike the case with "flat," our paraphrase cannot apply with "bumpy." Consequently, by means of our paraphrase we may distinguish between absolute terms and relative ones.

Another way of noticing how our paraphrase lends support to the distinction between absolute and relative terms is this: the initial data are that such terms as "very," which standardly serve to indicate that there is a great deal of something, serve with opposite effect when they modify terms like "flat"—terms which I have called basic absolute terms. That is, when we say, for example, that something is (really) very flat, then, so far as flatness is concerned, we seem to say less of the thing than when we say, simply, that it is (really) flat. The augmenting function of "very" is turned on its head so that the term serves to diminish. What can resolve this conflict? It seems that our paraphase can. For on the paraphrase, what are we saying of the thing is that it is very *nearly* flat, and so, by implication, that it is *not* flat (but only very nearly so). Once the paraphrase is exploited, the term "very" may be understood to have its standard augmenting function. At the same time, "very" functions without conflict with "bumpy." Happily, the term "very" is far from being unique here; we get the same results with other augmenting modifiers: "extremely," "especially," and so on.

For our paraphrastic procedure to be comprehensive, it must work with contexts containing explicitly comparative locutions. Indeed, with these contexts, we have a common form of talk where the appearances of relativeness is most striking of all. What shall we think of our saying, for example, that one surface is not as flat as another, where things strikingly look to be a matter of degree? It seems that we must allow that in such a suggested comparison, the surface which is said to be the *flatter* of the two may be, so far as logic goes, (absolutely) flat. Thus, we should *not* paraphrase this comparative context as "the one surface is not as *nearly* flat as the other." For this form of paraphrase would imply that the second surface is not flat, and so it gives us a poor interpretation of the original, which has no such implication. But then, a paraphrase with no bad implications is not far removed. Instead of simply inserting our "nearly" or our "close to being," we may allow for the possibility of (absolute) flatness by putting things in a way which is only somewhat more complex. For we may paraphrase our original by saying: the first surface is *either not flat though the second is, or else it is* not as *nearly* flat as the second. Similarly, where we say that one surface is flatter than another, we may paraphrase things like this: the first surface is *either flat though the second is not or else it is closer to being flat* than the second. But in contrast to all this, with comparisons of bumpiness, no paraphrase is available. To say that one surface is not as bumpy as another is not to say either that the first surface is not bumpy though the second is, or else that it is not as nearly bumpy as the second one.

Our noting the availability of degree constructions allows us to class together relative terms and basic absolute terms, as against any other terms. And our noting that only with the absolute terms do our constructions admit of our paraphrase allows us to distinguish between the relative terms and the basic absolute terms. Now that these terms may be quite clearly distinguished, we may restate without pain of vacuity those ideas on which we relied to introduce our terminology. Thus, to draw the *connection* between terms of the two sorts we may now say this: every basic absolute term, and so every absolute term whatever, may be defined, at least partially, by means of certain relative terms. The defining conditions presented by means of the relative terms are negative ones; they say that what the relative term purports to denote is *not* present *at all,* or *in the least,* where the absolute term correctly applies. Thus, these negative conditions are logically necessary ones for basic absolute terms, and so for absolute terms which are defined by means of the basic ones. Thus, something is flat, in the central, literal sense of "flat," only if it is not at all, or not in the least, curved or bumpy. And similarly, something is a cube, in the central, literal sense of "cube," only if it has surfaces which are not at all, or not in the least, bumpy or curved. In noting these demanding *negative relative requirements,* we may begin to appreciate, I think, that a variety of absolute terms, if not all of them, might well be quite troublesome to apply, perhaps even failing consistently in application to real things.

In a final general remark about these terms, I should like to motivate my choice of terminology for them. A reason I call terms of the one sort "absolute" is that, at least in the case of the basic ones, the term may always be modified, grammatically, with the term "absolutely." And indeed, this modification fits so well that it is, I think, always redundant. Thus, something is flat if and only if it is absolutely flat. In contrast, the term "absolutely" never gives a standard, grammatical modification for any of our relative terms: nothing which is bumpy is absolutely bumpy. On the other hand, each of the relative terms takes "relatively" quite smoothly as a grammatical modifier. (And, though it is far from being clear, it is at least arguable, I think, that this modifier is redundant for these terms. Thus, it is at least arguable that something is bumpy if and only if it is relatively bumpy.) In any event, with absolute terms, while "relatively" is grammatically quite all right as a modifier, the construction thus obtained must be understood in terms of our paraphrase. Thus, as before, something is relatively flat if and only if it is relatively close to being (absolutely) flat, and so only if it is not flat.

In this terminology, and in line with our linguistic tests, I think that the first term of each of the following pairs is a relative term while the second is an absolute one: "wet" and "dry," "crooked" and "straight," "important" and "crucial," "incomplete" and "complete," "useful" and "useless," and so on. I think that both "empty" and "full" are absolute terms, while "good" and "bad," "rich" and "poor," and "happy" and "unhappy" are all relative terms. Finally, I think that, in the sense defined by our tests, each of the following is neither an absolute term nor a relative one: "married" and "unmarried," "true" and "false," and "right" and "wrong." In other plausible senses, though, some or all of this last group might be called "absolute."

III. ON CERTAINTY AND CERTAIN RELATED THINGS

Certain terms of our language are standardly followed by propositional clauses, and, indeed, it is plausible to think that wherever they occur they *must* be followed by such clauses on pain of otherwise occurring in a sentence which is elliptical or incomplete. We may call terms which take these clauses *propositional terms* and we may then ask: are some propositional terms absolute ones, while others are relative terms? By means of our tests, I will argue that "certain" is an absolute term, while "confident," "doubtful," and "uncertain" are all relative terms.

With regard to being certain, there are two ideas which are important: first, the idea of something's being certain, where that which is certain is *not* certain *of* anything, and, second, the idea of a being's being certain, where that which is certain *is* certain *of* something. A paradigm context for the first idea is the context "It is certain that it is raining" where the term "it" has no apparent reference. I will call such contexts *impersonal* contexts, and the idea of certainty which they serve to express, thus, the impersonal idea of certainty. In contrast, a paradigm context for the second idea is this one: "He is certain that it is raining"—where, of course, the term "he" purports to refer as clearly as one might like. In the latter context, which we may call the *personal* context, we express the personal idea of certainty. This last may be allowed, I think, even though in ordinary conversations we may speak of dogs as being certain; presumably, we treat dogs there the way we typically treat persons.

Though there are these two important sorts of context, I think that "certain" must mean the same in both. In both cases, we must be struck by the thought that the presence of certainty amounts to the complete absence of doubt, or doubtfulness. This thought leads me to say that "It is certain that *p*" means, within the bounds of nuance, "It is not at all doubtful that *p*." The idea of personal certainty may then be defined accordingly; we relate what is said in the impersonal form to the mind of the

person, or subject, who is said to be certain of something. Thus, "He is certain that *p*" means, within the bounds of nuance, *"In his mind*, it is not at all doubtful that *p*."* Where a man is certain of something, then, concerning that thing, all doubt is absent in that man's mind. With these definitions available, we may now say this: connected negative definitions of certainty suggest that, in its central, literal meaning, "certain" is an absolute term.

But we should like firmer evidence for thinking that "certain" is an absolute term. To be consistent, we turn to our procedure for paraphrase. I will exhibit the evidence for personal contexts and then say a word about impersonal ones. In any event, we want contrasting results for "certain" as against some related relative terms. One term which now suggests itself for contrast is, of course, "doubtful." Another is, of course, "uncertain." And we will get the desired results with these terms. But it is, I think, more interesting to consider the term "confident."

In quick discussions of these matters, one might speak indifferently of a man's being confident of something and of his being certain of it. But on reflection there is a difference between confidence and certainty. Indeed, when I say that I am certain of something, I tell you that I am not confident of it but that I am *more than* that. And if I say that I am confident that so-and-so, I tell you that I am *not so much as* certain of the thing. Thus, there is an important difference between the two. At least part of this difference is, I suggest, reflected by our procedure for paraphrase.

We may begin to apply our procedure by resolving the problem of augmenting modifiers. Paradoxically, when I say that I am (really) very certain of something, I say *less* of myself, so far as a certainty is concerned, than I do when I say, simply, that I am (really) certain of the thing. How may we resolve this paradox? Our paraphrase explains things as before. In the first case, what I am really saying is that I am very *nearly* certain, and so, in effect, that I am not really certain. But in the second case, I say that I really am. Further, we many notice that, in contrast, in the case of "confident" and "uncertain," and "doubtful" as well, no problem with augmenting arises in the first place. For when I say that I am very confident of something, I say more of myself, so far as confidence is concerned, than I do when I simply say that I am confident of the thing. And again our paraphrastic procedure yields us the lack of any problems here. For the augmented statement cannot be sensibly interpreted as saying that I am very nearly confident of the thing. Indeed, with any modifier weaker than "absolutely," our paraphrase works well with "certain" but produces only a nonsensical interpretation with "confident" and other contrasting terms. For example, what might it mean to say of someone that he was rather confident of something? Would this be to say that he was rather close to being confident of the thing? Surely not.

Turning to comparative constructions, our paraphrase separates things just as we should expect. For example, from "He is more certain that *p* than he is that *q*" we get "He is either certain that *p* while not certain that *q,* or else he is more nearly certain that *p* than he is that *q*." But from "He is more confident that *p* than he is that *q*" we do *not* get "He is either confident that *p* while not confident that *q,* or else he is more nearly confident that *p* than he is that *q*." For he may well already be confident of both things. Further comparative constructions are similarly distinguished when subjected to our paraphrase. And no matter what locutions we try, the separation is as convincing with impersonal contexts as it is with personal ones, so long as there are contexts which are comparable. Of course, "confident" has no impersonal contexts; we cannot say "It is confident that *p,*" where the "it" has no purported reference. But where comparable contexts do exist, as with "doubtful" and "uncertain," further evidence is available. Thus, we may reasonably assert that "certain" is an absolute term while "confident," "doubtful," and "uncertain" are relative terms.

IV. THE DOUBTFUL APPLICABILITY OF SOME ABSOLUTE TERMS

If my account of absolute terms is essentially correct, then, at least in the case of some of these terms, fairly reasonable suppositions about the world make it somewhat doubtful that the terms properly apply. (In certain contexts, generally where what we are talking about divides into discrete units, the presence of an absolute term need cause no doubts. Thus, considering the absolute term "complete," the truth of "His set of steins is now complete" may be allowed without hesitation, but the truth of "His explanation is now complete" may well be doubted. It is with the latter, more interesting contexts, I think, that we shall be concerned in what follows.) For example, while we say of many surfaces of physical things that they are flat, a rather reasonable interpretation of what we do observe makes it at least somewhat doubtful that these surfaces actually *are* flat. When we look at a rather smooth block of stone through a powerful microscope, the observed surface appears to us to be rife with irregularities. And this irregular appearance seems best explained, not by being taken as an illusory optical phenomenon, but by taking it to be a finer, more revealing look of a surface which is, in fact, rife with smallish bumps and crevices. Further, we account for bumps and crevices by supposing that the stone is composed of much smaller things, molecules and so on, which are in such a combination that, while a large and sturdy stone is the upshot, no stone with a flat surface is found to obtain.

Indeed, what follows from my account of "flat" is this: that, as a matter of logical necessity, if a surface is flat, then there never is any surface which is flatter than it is. For on our paraphrase, if the second surface is flatter than the first, then either the second surface is flat while the first is not, or else the second is more nearly flat than the first, neither surface being flat. So if there is such a second, flatter surface, then the first surface is not flat after all, contrary to our supposition. Thus there cannot be any second, flatter surface. Or in other words,· if it is logically possible that there be a surface which is flatter than a given one, then that given surface is not really a flat one. Now, in the case of the observed surface of the stone, owing to the stone's irregular composition, the surface is *not* one such that it is logically impossible that there be a flatter one. (For example, we might veridically observe a surface through a microscope of the same power which did not appear to have any bumps or crevices.) Thus it is only reasonable to suppose that the surface of this stone is not really flat.

Our understanding of the stone's composition, that it is composed of molecules and so on, makes it reasonable for us to suppose as well that any similarly sized or larger surfaces will fail to be flat just as the observed surface fails to be flat. At the same time, it would be perhaps a bit rash to suppose that much smaller surfaces would fail to be flat as well. Beneath the level of our observation perhaps there are small areas of the stone's surface which are flat. If so, then perhaps there are small objects that have surfaces which are flat, like this area of the stone's surface: for instance, chipping off a small part of the stone might yield such a small object. So perhaps there are physical objects with surfaces which are flat, and perhaps it is not now reasonable for us to assume that there are no such objects. But even if this strong assumption is not now reasonable, one thing which does seem quite reasonable for us now to assume is this: we should at least suspend judgment on the matter of whether there are any physical objects with flat surfaces. That there are such objects is something it is not now reasonable for us to believe.

It is at least somewhat doubtful, then, that "flat" ever applies to actual physical objects or to their surfaces. And the thought must strike us that if "flat" has no such application, this must be due in part to the fact that "flat" is an ab-

solute term. We may then do well to be a bit doubtful about the applicability of any other given absolute term and, in particular, about the applicability of the term "certain." As in the case of "flat," our paraphrase highlights the absolute character of "certain." As a matter of logical necessity, if someone is certain of something, then there never is anything of which he is more certain. For on our paraphrase, if the person is more certain of any other thing, then either he is certain of the other thing while not being certain of the first, or else he is more nearly certain of the other thing than he is of the first; that is, he is certain of neither. Thus, if it is logically possible that there be something of which a person might be more certain than he now is of a given thing, then he is not really certain of that given thing.

Thus it is reasonable to suppose, I think, that hardly anyone, if anyone at all, is certain that 45 and 56 are 101. For it is reasonable to suppose that hardly anyone, if anyone at all, is so certain of that particular calculation that it is impossible for there to be anything of which he might be yet more certain. But this is not surprising; for hardly anyone *feels* certain that those two numbers have that sum. What, then, about something of which people commonly do feel absolutely certain—say, of the existence of automobiles?

Is it reasonable for us now actually to believe that many people are certain that there are automobiles? If it is, then it is reasonable for us to believe as well that for each of them it is not possible for there to be anything of which he might be more certain than he now is of there being automobiles. In particular, we must then believe of these people that it is impossible for any of them ever to be more certain of his own existence than all of them now are of the existence of automobiles. While these people *might* all actually be as certain of the automobiles as this, just as each of them *feels* himself to be, I think it somewhat rash for us actually to believe that they *are* all so certain. Certainty being an absolute and our understanding of people being rather rudimentary and incomplete, I think it more reasonable for us now to suspend judgment on the matter. And, since there is nothing importantly peculiar about the matter of the automobiles, the same cautious position recommends itself quite generally; so far as actual human beings go, the most reasonable course for us now is to suspend judgment as to whether any of them is certain of more than hardly anything, if anything at all.[2]

V. DOES KNOWING REQUIRE BEING CERTAIN

One tradition in philosophy holds that knowing requires being certain. As a matter of logical necessity, a man knows something only if he is certain of the thing. In this tradition, certainty is not taken lightly; rather, it is equated with absolute certainty. Even that most famous contemporary defender of common sense, G. E. Moore, is willing to equate knowing something with knowing the thing with absolute certainty.[3] I am rather inclined to hold with this traditional view, and it is now my purpose to argue that this view is at least a fairly reasonable one.

To a philosopher like Moore, I would have nothing left to say in my defense of skepticism. But recently some philosophers have contended that not certainty, but only belief, is required for knowing.[4] According to these thinkers, if a man's belief meets certain conditions not connected with his being certain, that mere belief may properly be counted as an instance or a bit of knowledge. And even more recently some philosophers have held that not even so much as belief is required for a man to know that something is so.[5] Thus, I must argue for the traditional view of knowing. But then what has led philosophers to move further and further away from the traditional strong assertion that knowing something requires being certain of the thing?

My diagnosis of the situation is this. In everyday affairs we often speak loosely, charitably, and casually; we tend to let what we say pass as being true. I want to suggest that it is by being wrongly serious about this casual talk that philosophers (myself included) have come to think it rather easy to know things to be so. In particular, they have come to think that certainty is not needed. Thus typical in the contemporary literature is this sort of exchange. An examiner asks a student when a certain battle was fought. The student fumbles about and, eventually, unconfidently says what is true: "The Battle of Hastings was fought in 1066." It is supposed, quite properly, that this correct answer is a result of the student's reading. The examiner, being an ordinary mortal, allows that the student knows the answer; he judges that the student knows that the Battle of Hastings was fought in 1066. Surely, it is suggested, the examiner is correct in his judgment even though this student clearly is not certain of the thing; therefore, knowing does not require being certain. But is the examiner really correct in asserting that the student knows the date of this battle? That is, do such exchanges give us good reason to think that knowing does not require certainty?

My recommendation is this. Let us try focusing on just those words most directly employed in expressing the concept whose conditions are our object of inquiry. This principle is quite generally applicable and, I think, quite easily applied. We may apply it by suitably juxtaposing certain terms, like "really" and "actually," with the terms most in question (here, the term "knows"). More strikingly, we may *emphasize* the terms in question. Thus, instead of looking at something as innocent as "He knows that they are alive," let us consider the more relevant "He (really) *knows* that they are alive."

Let us build some confidence that this principle is quite generally applicable, and that it will give us trustworthy results. Toward this end, we may focus on some thoughts about definite descriptions—that is, about expressions of the form "the so-and-so." About these expressions, it is a tradition to hold that they require uniqueness, or unique satisfaction, for their proper application. Thus, just as it is traditional to hold that a man knows something only if he is certain of it, so it is also traditional to hold that there is something which is the chair with seventeen legs only if there is exactly one chair with just that many legs. But, again, by being wrongly serious about our casual everyday talk, philosophers may come to deny the traditional view. They may do this by being wrongly serious, I think, about the following sort of ordinary exchange. Suppose an examiner asks a student, "Who is the father of Nelson Rockefeller, the present Governor of New York State?" The student replies, "Nelson Rockefeller is the son of John D. Rockefeller, Jr." No doubt, the examiner will allow that, by implication, the student got the right answer; he will judge that what the student said is true even though the examiner is correctly confident that the elder Rockefeller sired other sons. Just so, one might well argue that definite descriptions, like "the son of X," do not require uniqueness. But against this argument from the everyday flow of talk, let us insist that we focus on the relevant conception by employing our standard means for emphasizing the most directly relevant term. Thus, while we might feel nothing contradictory at first in saying "Nelson Rockefeller is the son of John D. Rockefeller, Jr., and so is Winthrop Rockefeller," we must confess that even initially we would have quite different feelings about our saying "Nelson Rockefeller is actually *the* son of John D. Rockefeller, Jr., and so is Winthrop Rockefeller." With the latter, where emphasis is brought to bear, we cannot help but feel that what is asserted is inconsistent. And, with this, we feel differently about the original remark, feeling it to be essentially the same assertion and so inconsistent as well. Thus, it seems that when we focus on things properly, we may assume that definite descriptions do require uniqueness.

Let us now apply our principle to the question of knowing. Here, while we might feel nothing contradictory at first in saying "He

knows that it is raining, but he isn't certain of it," we would feel differently about our saying "He really *knows* that it is raining, but he isn't certain of it." And, if anything, this feeling of contradiction is only enhanced when we further emphasize, "He really *knows* that it is raining, but he isn't actually *certain* of it." Thus it is plausible to suppose that what we said at first is actually inconsistent, and so that knowing does require being certain.

For my defense of skepticism, it now remains only to combine the result we have just reached with that at which we arrived in the previous section. Now, I have argued that each of two propositions deserves, if not our acceptance, at least the suspension of our judgment:

> That, in the case of every human being, there is hardly anything, if anything at all, of which he is certain.
> That (as a matter of necessity), in the case of every human being, the person knows something to be so only if he is certain of it.

But I think I have done more than just that. For the strength of the arguments given for this position on each of these two propositions is, I think, sufficient for warranting a similar position on propositions which are quite obvious consequences of the two of them together. One such consequential proposition is this:

> That, in the case of every human being, there is hardly anything, if anything at all, which the person knows to be so.

And so this third proposition, which is just the thesis of skepticism, also deserves, if not our acceptance, at least the suspension of our judgment. If this thesis is not reasonable to accept, then neither is its negation, the thesis of "common sense."

VI. A PROSPECTUS AND A RETROSPECTIVE

I have argued that we know hardly anything, if anything, because we are certain of hardly anything, if anything. My offering this argument

will strike many philosophers as peculiar, even many who have some sympathy with skepticism. For it is natural to think that, except for the requirement of the truth of what is known, the requirement of "attitude," in this case of personal certainty, is the *least* problematic requirement of knowing. Much more difficult to fulfill, one would think, would be requirements about one's justification, about one's grounds, and so on. And, quite candidly, I am inclined to agree with these thoughts. Why, then, have I chosen to defend skepticism by picking on what is just about the easiest requirement of knowledge? My thinking has been this: the requirement of being certain will, most likely, not be independent of more difficult requirements; indeed, any more difficult requirement will entail this simpler one. Thus one more difficult requirement might be that the knower be completely *justified* in being certain, which entails the requirement that the man be certain. And, in any case, for purposes of establishing some clarity, I wanted this defense to avoid the more difficult requirements because they rely on normative terms—for example, the term "justified." The application of normative terms presents problems which, while worked over by many philosophers, are still too difficult to handle at all adequately. By staying away from more difficult requirements, and so from normative terms, I hoped to raise doubts in a simpler, clearer context. When the time comes for a more powerful defense of skepticism, the more difficult requirements will be pressed. Then normative conditions will be examined and, for this examination, declared inapplicable. But these normative conditions will, most likely, concern one's being certain; no justification of mere belief or confidence will be the issue in the more powerful defenses. By offering my defense, I hoped to lay part of the groundwork for more powerful defenses of skepticism.

I would end with this explanation but for the fact that my present views contradict claims I made previously, and others have discussed critically these earlier claims about knowledge.[6] Before, I strove to show that knowledge was rather easy to come by, that the conditions of knowledge could be met rather easily. To connect my arguments, I offered a unified analysis:

> For any sentential value of *p*, (at a time *t*) a man know that *p* if and only if (at *t*) it is not at all accidental that the man is right about its being the case that *p*.

And, in arguing for the analysis, I tried to understand its defining condition just so liberally that it would allow men to know things rather easily. Because I did this, I used the analysis to argue against skepticism—that is, against the thesis which I have just defended.

Given my present views, while I must find the criticisms of my earlier claims more interesting than convincing, I must find my analysis to be more accurate than I was in my too liberal application of it. For, however bad the analysis might be in various respects, it does assert that knowledge is an absolute. In terms of my currently favored distinctions, "accidental" is quite clearly a relative term, as are other terms which I might have selected in its stead: "coincidental," "matter of luck," "lucky," and so on. Operating on these terms with expressions such as "not at all" and "not in the least degree" will yield us absolute expressions, the equivalent of absolute terms. Thus, the condition that I offered is not at all likely to be one that is easily met. My main error, then, was not that of giving too vague or liberal a defining condition, but rather that of too liberally interpreting a condition which is in fact strict.

But I am quite uncertain that my analysis is correct in any case, and even that one can analyze knowledge. Still, so far as analyzing knowledge goes, the main plea of this paper must be this: whatever analysis of knowledge is adequate, if any such there be, it must allow that the thesis of skepticism be at least fairly plausible. For this plea only follows from my broader one: that philosophers take skepticism seriously and not casually suppose, as I have often done, that this unpopular thesis simply must be false.[7]

NOTES

1. Among G. E. Moore's most influential papers against skepticism are "A Defense of Common Sense," "Four Forms of Scepticism," and "Certainty." These papers are now available in Moore's *Philosophical Papers* (New York, 1962). More recent representatives of the same anti-skeptical persuasion include A. J. Ayer's *The Problem of Knowledge* (Baltimore, 1956) and two books by Roderick M. Chisholm: *Perceiving* (Ithaca, 1957) and *Theory of Knowledge* (Englewood Cliffs, N.J., 1966). Among the many recent journal articles against skepticism are three papers of my own: "Experience and Factual Knowledge," *Journal of Philosophy*, vol. 64, no. 5 (1967), "An Analysis of Factual Knowledge," *Journal of Philosophy*, vol. 65, no. 6 (1968), and "Our Knowledge of the Material World," *Studies in the Theory of Knowledge American Philosophical Quarterly Monograph* No. 4 (1970). At the same time, a survey of the recent journal literature reveals very few papers where skepticism is defended or favored. With recent papers which do favor skepticism, however, I can mention at least two. A fledgling skepticism is persuasively advanced by Brian Skyrms in his "The Explication of 'X Knows that *p*,' " *Journal of Philosophy*, vol 64, no. 12 (1967). And in William W. Rozeboom's "Why I Know So Much More Than You Do," *American Philosophical Quarterly*, vol. 4, no. 4 (1967), we have a refreshingly strong statement of skepticism in the context of recent discussion.

2. For an interesting discussion of impersonal certainty, which in some ways is rather in line with my own discussion while in other ways against it, one might see Michael Anthony Slote's "Empirical Certainty and the Theory of Important Criteria," *Inquiry*, vol. 10 (1967). Also, Slote makes helpful references to other writers in the philosophy of certainty.

3. See Moore's cited papers, especially "Certainty," p. 232.

4. An influential statement of this view is Roderick M. Chisholm's, to be found in the first chapter of each of his cited books. In "Experience and Factual Knowledge," I suggest a very similar view.

5. This view is advanced influentially by Colin Radford in "Knowledge by Examples," *Analysis*, 27 (October, 1966). In "An Analysis of Factual Knowledge," and especially in "Our Knowledge of The Material World," I suggest this view.

6 See my cited papers and these interesting discussions of them: Gilbert H. Harman, "Unger on Knowledge," *Journal of Philosophy*, 64 (1967), 353–359; Ruth Anna Putnam, "On Empirical Knowledge," *Boston Studies in the Philosophy of Science*, IV, 392–410; Arthur C. Danto, *Analytical Philosophy of Knowledge* (Cambridge, 1968), pp. 130 ff. and 144 ff.; Keith Lehrer and Thomas Paxson, Jr., "Knowledge: Undefeated Justified True Belief," *Journal of Philosophy*, 66 (1969), 225–237; J. L. Mackie, "The Possibility of Innate Knowledge," *Proceedings of the Aristotelian Society* (1970), pp. 245–257.

7. Ancestors of the present paper were discussed in philosophy colloquia at the following schools: Brooklyn College of The City University of New York, The University of California at Berkeley, Columbia University, The University of Illinois at Chicago Circle, The Rockefeller University, Stanford University, and The University of Wisconsin at Madison. I am thankful to those who participated in the discussion. I would also like to thank each of these many people for help in getting to the present defense: Peter M. Brown, Richard Cartwright, Fred I. Dretske, Hartry Field, Bruce Freed, H. P. Grice, Robert Hambourger, Saul A. Kripke, Stephen Schiffer, Michael A. Slote, Sydney S. Shoemaker, Dennis W. Stampe, Julius Weinberg, and Margaret Wilson, *all* of whom remain at least somewhat skeptical. Finally, I would like to thank the Graduate School of The University of Wisconsin at Madison for financial assistance during the preparation of this defense.

RICHARD RORTY
Philosophy Without Mirrors

HERMENEUTICS AND EDIFICATION

Our present notions of what it is to be a philosopher are so tied up with the Kantian attempt to render all knowledge-claims commensurable that it is difficult to imagine what philosophy without epistemology could be. More generally, it is difficult to imagine that any activity would be entitled to bear the name "philosophy" if it had nothing to do with knowledge—if it were not in some sense a theory of knowledge, or a method for getting knowledge, or at least a hint as to where some supremely important kind of knowledge might be found. The difficulty stems from a notion shared by Platonists, Kantians, and positivists: that man has an essence—namely, to discover essences. The notion that our chief task is to mirror accurately, in our own Glassy Essence, the universe around us is the complement of the notion, common to Democritus and Descartes, that the universe is made up of very simple, clearly and distinctly knowable things, knowledge of whose essences provides the master-vocabulary which permits commensuration of all discourses.

This classic picture of human beings must be set aside before epistemologically centered philosophy can be set aside. "Hermeneutics," as a polemical term in contemporary philosophy, is a name for the attempt to do so. The use

of the term for this purpose is largely due to one book—Gadamer's *Truth and Method*. Gadamer there makes clear that hermeneutics is not a "method for attaining truth" which fits into the classic picture of man: "The hermeneutic phenomenon is basically not a problem of method at all."[1] Rather, Gadamer is asking, roughly, what conclusions might be drawn from the fact that we have to practice hermeneutics—from the "hermeneutic phenomenon" as a fact about people which the epistemological tradition has tried to shunt aside. "The hermeneutics developed here," he says, "is not . . . a methodology of the human sciences, but an attempt to understand what the human sciences truly are, beyond their methodological self-consciousness, and what connects them with the totality of our experience of the world."[2] His book is a redescription of man which tries to place the classic picture within a larger one, and thus to "distance" the standard philosophical problematic rather than offer a set of solutions to it.

For my present purposes, the importance of Gadamer's book is that he manages to separate off one of the three strands—the romantic notion of man as self-creative—in the philosophical notion of "spirit" from the other two

strands with which it became entangled. Gadamer (like Heidegger, to whom some of his work
is indebted) makes no concessions either to Cartesian dualism or to the notion of "transcendental constitution" (in any sense which could be
given an idealistic interpretation).[3] He thus
helps reconcile the "naturalistic" point I tried
to make in the previous chapter—that the "ir-
reducibility of the *Geisteswissenschaften*" is not
a matter of a metaphysical dualism—with our
"existentialist" intuition that redescribing ourselves is the most important thing we can do.
He does this by substituting the notion of *Bildung* (education, self-formation) for that of
"knowledge" as the goal of thinking. To say
that we become different people, that we "re-
make" ourselves as we read more, talk more,
and write more, is simply a dramatic way of
saying that the sentences which become true of
us by virtue of such activities are often more
important to us than the sentences which become true of us when we drink more, earn
more, and so on. The events which make us able
to say new and interesting things about ourselves are, in this nonmetaphysical sense, more
"essential" to us (at least to us relatively lei-
sured intellectuals, inhabiting a stable and prosperous part of the world) than the events which
change our shapes or our standards of living
("remaking" us in less "spiritual" ways). Gadamer develops his notion of *wirkungsgeschichtliches Bewusstsein* (the sort of consciousness of
the past which changes us) to characterize an
attitude interested not so much in what is out
there in the world, or in what happened in history, as in what we can get out of nature and
history for our own uses. In this attitude, getting the facts right (about atoms and the void,
or about the history of Europe) is merely propaedeutic to finding a new and more interesting
way of expressing ourselves, and thus of coping
with the world. From the educational, as opposed to the epistemological or the technological, point of view, the way things are said is
more important than the possession of truths.[4]

Since "education" sounds a bit too flat,
and *Bildung* a bit too foreign, I shall use "edification" to stand for this project of finding
new, better, more interesting, more fruitful

ways of speaking. The attempt to edify (ourselves or others) may consist in the hermeneutic
activity of making connections between our
own culture and some exotic culture or historical period, or between our own discipline and
another discipline which seems to pursue incommensurable aims in an incommensurable
vocabulary. But it may instead consist in the
"poetic" activity of thinking up such new
aims, new words, or new disciplines, followed
by, so to speak, the inverse of hermeneutics: the
attempt to reinterpret our familiar surroundings
in the unfamiliar terms of our new inventions.
In either case, the activity is (despite the etymological relation between the two words) edifying
without being constructive—at least if "constructive" means the sort of cooperation in the
accomplishment of research programs which
takes place in normal discourse. For edifying
discourse is *supposed* to be abnormal, to take us
out of our old selves by the power of strange-
ness, to aid us in becoming new beings.

The contrast between the desire for edification and the desire for truth is, for Gadamer, not
an expression of a tension which needs to be
resolved or compromised. If there is a conflict,
it is between the Platonic-Aristotelian view that
the *only* way to be edified is to know what is
out there (to reflect the facts accurately—to realize our essence by knowing essences) and the
view that the quest for truth is just one among
many ways in which we might be edified. Gadamer rightly gives Heidegger the credit for
working out a way of seeing the search for
objective knowledge (first developed by the
Greeks, using mathematics as a model) as one
human project among others.[5] The point is,
however, more vivid in Sartre, who sees the
attempt to gain an objective knowledge of the
world, and thus of oneself, as an attempt to
avoid the responsibility for choosing one's
project.[6] For Sartre, to say this is not to say that
the desire for objective knowledge of nature,
history, or anything else is bound to be unsuccessful, or even bound to be self-deceptive. It is
merely to say that it presents a temptation to
self-deception insofar as we think that, by
knowing which descriptions within a given set of
normal discourses apply to us, we thereby know

ourselves. For Heidegger, Sartre, and Gadamer, objective inquiry is perfectly possible and frequently actual—the only thing to be said against it is that it provides only some, among many, ways of describing ourselves, and that some of these can hinder the process of edification.

To sum up this "existentialist" view of objectivity, then: objectivity should be seen as conformity to the norms of justification (for assertions and for actions) we find about us. Such conformity becomes dubious and self-deceptive only when seen as something more than this—namely, as a way of obtaining access to something which "grounds" current practices of justification in something else. Such a "ground" is thought to need no justification, because it has become so clearly and distinctly perceived as to count as a "philosophical foundation." This is self-deceptive not simply because of the general absurdity of ultimate justification's reposing upon the unjustifiable, but because of the more concrete absurdity of thinking that the vocabulary used by present science, morality, or whatever has some privileged attachment to reality which makes it *more* than just a further set of descriptions. Agreeing with the naturalists that redescription is not "change of essence" needs to be followed up by abandoning the notion of "essence" altogether.[7] But the standard philosophical strategy of most naturalisms is to find some way of showing that our own culture has indeed got hold of the essence of man—thus making all new and incommensurable vocabularies merely "noncognitive" ornamentation.[8] The utility of the "existentialist" view is that, by proclaiming that we have no essence, it permits us to see the descriptions of ourselves we find in one of (or in the unity of) the *Naturwissenschaften* as on a par with the various alternative descriptions offered by poets, novelists, depth psychologists, sculptors, anthropologists, and mystics. The former are not privileged representations in virtue of the fact that (at the moment) there is more consensus in the sciences than in the arts. They are simply among the repertoire of self-descriptions at our disposal.

This point can also be put as an extrapolation from the commonplace that one cannot be counted as educated—*gebildet*—if one knows *only* the results of the normal *Naturwissenschaften* of the day. Gadamer begins *Truth and Method* with a discussion of the role of the humanist tradition in giving sense to the notion of *Bildung* as something having "no goals outside itself."[9] To give sense to such a notion we need a sense of the relativity of descriptive vocabularies to periods, traditions, and historical accidents. This is what the humanist tradition in education does, and what training in the results of the natural sciences cannot do. Given that sense of relativity, we cannot take the notion of "essence" seriously, nor the notion of man's task as the accurate representation of essences. The natural sciences, by themselves, leave us convinced that we know both what we are and what we can be—not just how to predict and control our behavior, but the limits of that behavior (and, in particular, the limits of our significant speech). Gadamer's attempt to fend off the demand (common to Mill and Carnap) for "objectivity" in the *Geisteswissenschaften* is the attempt to prevent education from being reduced to instruction in the results of normal inquiry. More broadly, it is the attempt to prevent abnormal inquiry from being viewed as suspicious solely because of its abnormality.

This "existentialist" attempt to place objectivity, rationality, and normal inquiry within the larger picture of our need to be educated and edified is often countered by the "positivist" attempt to distinguish learning facts from acquiring values. From the positivist point of view, Gadamer's exposition of *wirkungsgeschichtliche Bewusstsein* may seem little more than reiteration of the commonplace that even when we know all the objectively true descriptions of ourselves, we still may not know what to do with ourselves. From this point of view, *Truth and Method* (and chapters six and seven above) are just overblown dramatizations of the fact that entire compliance with all the demands for justification offered by normal inquiry would still leave us free to draw our own morals from the assertions so justified. But from the viewpoints of Gadamer, Heidegger, and Sartre, the trouble with the fact-value distinction is that it is contrived precisely to blur the fact that alternative descriptions are possible in addition to those offered by the results of normal inquiries.[10] It suggests that once "all the facts are in" nothing remains except "noncognitive" adoption of an attitude—a choice which is not rationally discussable. It disguises the fact that to use one set of true sentences to describe ourselves is already to choose an attitude toward ourselves, whereas to use another set of true sentences is to adopt a contrary attitude. Only if we assume that there is a value-free vocabulary which renders these sets of "factual" statements commensurable can the positivist distinction between facts and values, beliefs and attitudes, look plausible. But the philosophical fiction that such a vocabulary is on the tips of our tongues is, from an educational point of view, disastrous. It forces us to pretend that we can split ourselves up into knowers of true sentences on the one hand and choosers of lives or actions or works of art on the other. These artificial diremptions make it impossible to get the notion of edification into focus. Or, more exactly, they tempt us to think of edification as having nothing to do with the rational faculties which are employed in normal discourse.

So Gadamer's effort to get rid of the classic picture of man-as-essentially-knower-of-essences is, among other things, an effort to get rid of the distinction between fact and value, and thus to let us think of "discovering the facts" as one project of edification among others. This is why Gadamer devotes so much time to breaking down the distinctions which Kant made among cognition, morality, and aesthetic judgment.[11] There is no way, as far as I can see, in which to *argue* the issue of whether to keep the Kantian "grid" in place or set it aside. There is no "normal" philosophical discourse which provides common commensurating ground for those who see science and edification as, respectively, "rational" and "irrational," and those who see the quest for objectivity as one possibility among others to be taken account of in *wirkungsgeschichtliche Bewusstsein*. If there is no such common ground, all we can do is to show how the other side looks from our point of view. That is, all we can do is be hermeneutic about the opposition—trying to show how the odd or paradoxical or offensive things they say hang together with the rest of what they want to say, and how what they say looks when put in our own alternative idiom. This sort of hermeneutics with polemical intent is common to Heidegger's and Derrida's attempts to deconstruct the tradition.

NOTES

1. Hans-Georg Gadamer, *Truth and Method* (New York, 1975), p. xi. Indeed, it would be reasonable to call Gadamer's book a tract against the very idea of method, where this is conceived of as an attempt at commensuration. It is instructive to note the parallels between this book and Paul Feyerabend's *Against Method*. My treatment of Gadamer is indebted to Alasdair MacIntyre; see his "Contexts of Interpretation," *Boston University Journal* 24 (1976), 41–46.

2. Gadamer, *Truth and Method*, p. xiii.

3. Cf. ibid., p. 15. "But we may recognize that *Bildung* is an element of spirit without being tied to Hegel's philosophy of absolute spirit, just as the insight into the historicity of consciousness is not tied to his philosophy of world history."

4. The contrast here is the same as that involved in the traditional quarrel between "classical" education and "scientific" education, mentioned by Gadamer in his opening section on "The Significance of the Humanist Tradition." More generally, it can be seen as an aspect of the quarrel between poetry (which cannot be omitted from the former sort of education) and philosophy (which, when conceiving of itself as super-science, would like to become foundational to the latter sort of education). Yeats asked the spirits (whom, he believed, were dictating *A Vision* to him through his wife's mediumship) why they had come. The spirits replied, "To bring you metaphors for poetry." A philosopher might have expected some hard facts about what it was like on the other side, but Yeats was not disappointed.

5. See the section called "The Overcoming of the Epistemological Problem . . ." in *Truth and Method*, pp. 214ff., and compare Martin Heidegger, *Being and Time*, trans. John Macquarrie and Edward Robinson (New York, 1962), sec. 32.

6. See Jean-Paul Sartre, *Being and Nothingness*, trans. Hazel Barnes (New York, 1956), pt. two, chap. 3, sec. 5, and the "Conclusion" of the book.

7. It would have been fortunate if Sartre had followed up his remark that man is the being whose essence is to have no essence by saying that this went for all other beings also. Unless this addition is made, Sartre will appear to be insisting on the good old metaphysical distinction between spirit and nature in other terms, rather

than simply making the point that man is always free to choose new descriptions (for, among other things, himself).

8. Dewey, it seems to me, is the one author usually classified as a "naturalist" who did not have this reductive attitude, despite his incessant talk about "scientific method." Dewey's peculiar achievement was to have remained sufficiently Hegelian not to think of natural science as having an inside track on the essences of things, while becoming sufficiently naturalistic to think of human beings in Darwinian terms.

9. Gadamer, *Truth and Method*, p. 12.
10. See Heidegger's discussion of "values" in *Being and Time*, p. 133, and Sartre's in *Being and Nothingness*, pt. two, chap. 1, sec. 4. Compare Gadamer's remarks on Weber (*Truth and Method*, pp. 461ff.).
11. See Gadamer's polemic against "the subjectivization of the aesthetic" in Kant's Third Critique (*Truth and Method*, p. 87) and compare Heidegger's remarks in "Letter on Humanism" on Aristotle's distinctions among physics, logic, and ethics (Heidegger, *Basic Writings*, ed. Krell [New York, 1976], p. 232).

QUESTIONS ABOUT KNOWLEDGE

1. What is the problem of knowledge? Can you offer some original illustrations?
2. Explain the proposed difference between *knowing that and knowing how*.
3. It has been suggested that *knowing that* is the basic form of knowing, since a person cannot know how to do something unless the individual knows that something is the case. How do you respond?
4. Plato's proposal in the "Theaetetus" is that, in order to have knowledge, a person must not only have true belief, but must also be able to give an account of what he or she believes. What does this mean and how does it differ from the standard approach of knowledge as true justified belief?
5. Most people rely on authority for their beliefs. Is this an error according to the previous discussion?
6. Think about your study of science, in high school or college. Is it fair to say that science, as currently taught, does not rely on authority?
7. Seeing is believing, some people say, but is experience enough for knowing? What is Descartes's argument against experience as the foundation of knowledge? Would the appeal to *sense data* satisfy Descartes's doubts?
8. Does the rationalist think that experience is irrelevant for knowledge? Can we find out about the world without making any observations or performing any experiments? If not, exactly how does rationalism differ from empiricism?
9. Peter Unger argues that knowledge implies certainty and since we cannot be as certain as we might think we are, we do not know what we think we know. Why can't we be as certain as we might think we are? What is Unger's argument?
10. Why does the extreme skeptic think, as most of us do, that water freezes at 32° farenheit? Shouldn't the skeptic think that water does not freeze at this temperature? Otherwise, why is the skeptic a skeptic?

Knowledge:
Suggestions for Further Study

The problem of knowledge has long been discussed in an extensive and continually growing literature. The modern treatment of the issue is generally traced to René Descartes, whose *Meditations* we have reproduced in its entirety to illustrate both the beginnings of modern skepticism and a certain rationalistic attempt to answer the skeptic.

For the empiricist response to seventeenth-century rationalism, see John Locke's *Essay Concerning Human Understanding,* and George Berkeley's *Treatise Concerning the Principles of Human Knowledge.* More recent discussion of the basic issues can be found in Bertrand Russell's *Human Knowledge, Its Scope and Limits* (New York: Simon & Schuster, 1948) and A. J. Ayer's *The Problem of Knowledge* (London: Penguin, 1956), which treats the problem as an ongoing attempt to answer the skeptic. In his earlier writings, Ayer, along with many other epistemologists, favored the sense-data approach, until the publication of J. L. Austin's *Sense and Sensibilia* (New York: Oxford University Press, 1962) which effectively challenged the sense-data theorist's basic assumptions. Ayer responded in "Has Austin Refuted the Sense-Datum Theory?" in *Metaphysics and Common Sense* (London: Macmillan, 1969).

In recent years, theorists have turned to the history of science for insight into the problem of knowledge. See, for example, Thomas Kuhn's *Structure of Scientific Revolutions* (Chicago: University of Chicago Press, 1973). Others, in response to Edmund L. Gettier's challenge to the analysis of knowledge as true justified belief, have developed what is called a *causal approach* to knowledge. See, for example, Alvin I. Goldman's "A Causal Theory of Knowledge" (*Journal of Philosophy,* 64, 1967).

David Hume is regarded as the great skeptic of modern philosophy, based on his two main works, *The Treatise on Human Nature* and *An Enquiry Concerning Human Understanding.* In recent literature, Peter Unger defends skepticism in *Ignorance* (New York: Oxford University Press, 1975). Benson Mates also defends the skeptical attitude in "Our Knowledge of the External World," in *Skeptical Essays* (Chicago: University of Chicago Press, 1981). Peter D. Klein has attempted to answer recent skeptical arguments in *Certainty: A Refutation of Scepticism* (Minneapolis: University of Minnesota Press, 1981).

PART

2

Truth

Literary Introduction:
What Is the Truth?

Beauty is truth, truth beauty,—that is all
Ye know on earth, and all ye need to know.

These, the concluding lines to Keats' "Ode on a Grecian Urn," have puzzled readers since they first appeared in 1820. Was Keats declaring that only beautiful things are true? Where would that explanation leave the admittedly ugly things? Do we have to see an automobile junkyard as either "beautiful" or "untrue"? That interpretation seems to deny common sense. We know junkyards exist, and we know that they are not beautiful.

It seems that we should search for another reading of these lines. The rest of the poem describes how the figures painted on the urn, two youthful lovers about to kiss, will never touch. Keats suggests that the young man should accentuate the positive in this situation because "For ever wilt thou love, and she be fair!" We, however, can reasonably wonder what the advantage is to a love that can never be consummated.

Keats's answer would be that such a question misses the point. To demand a physical realization of love is to misread the surface for the reality, and the surface is always flawed. The poem expresses the romantic notion, derived from Plato, that the idea of love is necessary in order for the physical manifestation to have meaning. The idea of love is beautiful precisely because it exists beyond the senses. It is an ideal to which the physical must correspond to be true.

Truth as correspondence to an ideal has influenced both creative artists and philosophers alike. Writers, for example, create a representation of reality as they imagine it to be. A poet such as Keats depends on symbolic language to convey a sense of truth. Others use narrative. Earnest Hemingway, for example, attempted to write objectively. His contemporary William Faulkner, by contrast, emphasized the individual's feelings and perception. In a Hemingway novel, the reader finds a clear and unobstructed view of the world, but has to uncover the less obvious subtleties of emotion and motivation. A Faulkner novel provides a rich matrix of psychological insight which obscures, however, the readers view of what actually takes place.

Which representation is best? Can the truth emerge at the point where both approaches converge? This section begins with a short story that defines the problem but does not offer a solution.

Written by the twentieth-century Japanese author Ryunosuke Akutagawa, ''In a Grove'' concisely and brilliantly confronts the question of truth. Akutagawa sets his narrative in the Japanese feudal period and peoples it with three main characters: a husband, his wife, and a bandit. The action occurs in a wooded area, and at the end of the story we know that the husband is dead, that the woman has found sanctuary in a temple, and that the bandit is in police custody.

However, we do not know precisely what happened in the grove. By telling the story through a series of first-person accounts, and by refusing to impose a narrative voice to color the reader's perception of these accounts, Akutagawa leaves the question open. This technique is a blend of Hemingway's and Faulkner's approaches. We do see the surface clearly, as in a Hemingway novel, but several times and from different subjective points of view, as in a Faulkner narrative. The combination is strikingly effective in raising the issue of truth.

RYUNOSUKE AKUTAGAWA
In a Grove

THE TESTIMONY OF A WOODCUTTER QUESTIONED BY A HIGH POLICE COMMISSIONER

Yes, sir. Certainly, it was I who found the body. This morning, as usual, I went to cut my daily quota of cedars, when I found the body in a grove in a hollow in the mountains. The exact location? About 150 meters off the Yamashina stage road. It's an out-of-the-way grove of bamboo and cedars.

The body was lying flat on its back dressed in a bluish silk kimono and a wrinkled head-dress of the Kyoto style. A single sword-stroke had pierced the breast. The fallen bamboo-blades around it were stained with bloody blossoms. No, the blood was no longer running. The wound had dried up, I believe. And also, a gad-fly was stuck fast there, hardly noticing my footsteps.

You ask me if I saw a sword or any such thing?

No, nothing, sir. I found only a rope at the root of a cedar near by. And . . . well, in addition to a rope, I found a comb. That was all. Apparently he must have made a battle of it before he was murdered, because the grass and fallen bamboo-blades had been trampled down all around.

"A horse was near by?"

No, sir. It's hard enough for a man to enter, let alone a horse.

THE TESTIMONY OF A TRAVELING BUDDHIST PRIEST QUESTIONED BY A HIGH POLICE COMMISSIONER

The time? Certainly, it was about noon yesterday, sir. The unfortunate man was on the road from Sekiyama to Yamashina. He was walking toward Sekiyama with a woman accompanying him on horseback, who I have since learned was his wife. A scarf hanging from her head

"In a Grove" is reprinted from *Rashomon and Other Stories* by Ryunosuke Akutagawa, translated by Takashi Kojima, with the permission of Liveright Publishing Corporation. Copyright © 1952, 1970 by Liveright Publishing Corporation. **Ryunosuke Akutagawa** (1892–1927) based much of his work on traditional Japanese tales, and set them in earlier historical periods while writing from a very modern perspective.

hid her face from view. All I saw was the color of her clothes, a lilac-colored suit. Her horse was a sorrel with a fine mane. The lady's height? Oh, about four feet five inches. Since I am a Buddhist priest, I took little notice about her details. Well, the man was armed with a sword as well as a bow and arrows. And I re-member that he carried some twenty odd ar-rows in his quiver.

Little did I expect that he would meet such a fate. Truly human life is as evanescent as the morning dew or a flash of lightning. My words are inadequate to express my sympathy for him.

THE TESTIMONY OF A POLICEMAN QUESTIONED BY A HIGH POLICE COMMISSIONER

The man that I arrested? He is a notorious brig-and called Tajomaru. When I arrested him, he had fallen off his horse. He was groaning on the bridge at Awataguchi. The time? It was in the early hours of last night. For the record, I might say that the other day I tried to arrest him, but unfortunately he escaped. He was wearing a dark blue silk kimono and a large plain sword. And, as you see, he got a bow and arrows somewhere. You say that this bow and these ar-rows look like the ones owned by the dead man? Then Tajomaru must be the murderer. The bow wound with leather strips, the black lac-quered quiver, the seventeen arrows with hawk feathers—these were all in his possession I be-lieve. Yes, sir, the horse is, as you say, a sorrel with a fine mane. A little beyond the stone bridge I found the horse grazing by the road-side, with his long rein dangling. Surely there is some providence in his having been thrown by the horse.

Of all the robbers prowling around Kyoto, this Tajomaru has given the most grief to the women in town. Last autumn a wife who came to the mountain back of the Pindora of the Tor-ibe Temple, presumably to pay a visit, was murdered, along with a girl. It has been sus-pected that it was his doing. If this criminal murdered the man, you cannot tell what he may have done with the man's wife. May it please your honor to look into this problem as well.

THE TESTIMONY OF AN OLD WOMAN QUESTIONED BY A HIGH POLICE COMMISSIONER

Yes, sir, that corpse is the man who married my daughter. He does not come from Kyoto. He was a samurai in the town of Kokufu in the province of Wakasa. His name was Kanazawa no Takehiko, and his age was twenty-six. He was of a gentle disposition, so I am sure he did nothing to provoke the anger of others.

My daughter? Her name is Masago, and her age is nineteen. She is a spirited, fun-loving girl, but I am sure she has never known any man except Takehiko. She has a small, oval, dark-complected face with a mole at the corner of her left eye.

Yesterday Takehiko left for Wakasa with my daughter. What bad luck it is that things should have come to such a sad end! What has become of my daughter? I am resigned to giving up my son-in-law as lost, but the fate of my daughter worries me sick. For heaven's sake leave no stone unturned to find her. I hate that robber Tajomaru, or whatever his name is. Not only my son-in-law, but my daughter . . . (Her later words were drowned in tears.)

TAJOMARU'S CONFESSION

I killed him, but not her. Where's she gone? I can't tell you. Oh, wait a minute. No torture can make me confess what I don't know. Now things have come to such a head, I won't keep anything from you.

Yesterday a little past noon I met that couple. Just then a puff of wind blew, and raised her hanging scarf, so that I caught a glimpse of her face. Instantly it was again covered from my view. That may have been one reason; she looked like a Bodhisattva. At that moment I made up my mind to capture her even if I had to kill her man.

Why? To me killing isn't a matter of such great consequence as you might think. When a woman is captured, her man has to be killed anyway. In killing, I use the sword I wear at my side. Am I the only one who kills people? You, you don't use your swords. You kill people with your power, with your money. Sometimes you kill them on the pretext of working for their good. It's true they don't bleed. They are in the best of health, but all the same you've killed them. It's hard to say who is a greater sinner, you or me. (An ironical smile.)

But it would be good if I could capture a woman without killing her man. So, I made up my mind to capture her, and do my best not to kill him. But it's out of the question on the Yamashina stage road. So I managed to lure the couple into the mountains.

It was quite easy. I became their traveling companion, and I told them there was an old mound in the mountain over there, and that I had dug it open and found many mirrors and swords. I went on to tell them I'd buried the things in a grove behind the mountain, and that I'd like to sell them at a low price to anyone who would care to have them. Then . . . you see, isn't greed terrible? He was beginning to be moved by my talk before he knew it. In less than half an hour they were driving their horse toward the mountain with me.

When he came in front of the grove, I told them that the treasures were buried in it, and I asked them to come and see. The man had no objection—he was blinded by greed. The woman said she would wait on horseback. It was natural for her to say so, at the sight of a thick grove. To tell you the truth, my plan worked just as I wished, so I went into the grove with him, leaving her behind alone.

The grove is only bamboo for some distance. About fifty yards ahead there's a rather open clump of cedars. It was a convenient spot for my purpose. Pushing my way through the grove, I told him a plausible lie that the treasures were buried under the cedars. When I told him this, he pushed his laborious way toward the slender cedar visible through the grove. After a while the bamboo thinned out, and we came to where a number of cedars grew in a row. As soon as we got there, I seized him from behind. Because he was a trained, sword-bearing warrior, he was quite strong, but he was taken by surprise, so there was no help for him. I soon tied him up to the root of a cedar. Where did I get the rope? Thank heaven, being a robber, I had a rope with me, since I might have to scale a wall at any moment. Of course it was easy to stop him from calling out by gagging his mouth with fallen bamboo leaves.

When I disposed of him, I went to his woman and asked her to come and see him, because he seemed to have been suddenly taken sick. It's needless to say that this plan also worked well. The woman, her sedge hat off, came into the depths of the grove, where I led her by the hand. The instant she caught sight of her husband, she drew a small sword. I've never seen a woman of such violent temper. If I'd been off guard, I'd have got a thrust in my side. I dodged, but she kept on slashing at me. She might have wounded me deeply or killed me. But I'm Tajomaru. I managed to strike down her small sword without drawing my own. The most spirited woman is defenseless without a weapon. At last I could satisfy my desire for her without taking her husband's life.

Yes . . . without taking his life. I had no wish to kill him. I was about to run away from the grove, leaving the woman behind in tears, when she frantically clung to my arm. In broken fragments of words, she asked that either her husband or I die. She said it was more trying than death to have her shame known to two men. She gasped out that she wanted to be the wife of whichever survived. Then a furious desire to kill him seized me. (Gloomy excitement.)

Telling you in this way, no doubt I seem a crueler man than you. But that's because you didn't see her face. Especially her burning eyes at that moment. As I saw her eye to eye, I wanted to make her my wife even if I were to be struck by lightning. I wanted to make her my wife . . . this single desire filled my mind. This was not only lust, as you might think. At that time if I'd had no other desire than lust, I'd surely not have minded knocking her down and running away. Then I wouldn't have stained my sword with his blood. But the moment I gazed at her face in the dark grove, I decided not to leave there without killing him.

But I didn't like to resort to unfair means to kill him. I untied him and told him to cross swords with me. (The rope that was found at the root of the cedar is the rope I dropped at the time.) Furious with anger, he drew his thick sword. And quick as thought, he sprang at me ferociously, without speaking a word. I needn't tell you how our fight turned out. The twenty-third stroke . . . please remember this. I'm impressed with this fact still. Nobody under the sun has ever clashed swords with me twenty strokes. (A cheerful smile.)

When he fell, I turned toward her, lowering my blood-stained sword. But to my great astonishment she was gone. I wondered to where she had run away. I looked for her in the clump of cedars. I listened, but heard only a groaning sound from the throat of the dying man.

As soon as we started to cross swords, she may have run away through the grove to call for help. When I thought of that, I decided it was a matter of life and death to me. So, robbing him of his sword, and bow and arrows, I ran out to the mountain road. There I found her horse still grazing quietly. It would be a mere waste of words to tell you the later details, but before I entered town I had already parted with the sword. That's all my confession. I know that my head will be hung in chains anyway, so put me down for the maximum penalty. (A defiant attitude.)

THE CONFESSION OF A WOMAN WHO HAS COME TO THE SHIMIZU TEMPLE

That man in the blue silk kimono, after forcing me to yield to him, laughed mockingly as he looked at my bound husband. How horrified my husband must have been! But no matter how hard he struggled in agony, the rope cut into him all the more tightly. In spite of myself I ran stumblingly toward his side. Or rather I tried to run toward him, but the man instantly knocked me down. Just at that moment I saw an indescribable light in my husband's eyes. Something beyond expression . . . his eyes make me shudder even now. That instantaneous look of my husband, who couldn't speak a word, told me all his heart. The flash in his eyes was neither anger nor sorrow . . . only a cold light, a look of loathing. More struck by the look in his eyes than by the blow of the thief, I called out in spite of myself and fell unconscious.

In the course of time I came to, and found that the man in blue silk was gone. I saw only my husband still bound to the root of the cedar. I raised myself from the bamboo-blades with difficulty, and looked into his face; but the expression in his eyes was just the same as before.

Beneath the cold contempt in his eyes, there was hatred. Shame, grief, and anger . . . I don't know how to express my heart at that time. Reeling to my feet, I went to my husband.

"Takejiro," I said to him, "since things have come to this pass, I cannot live with you. I'm determined to die . . . but you must die, too. You saw my shame, I can't leave you alive as you are."

This was all I could say. Still he went on gazing at me with loathing and contempt. My heart breaking, I looked for his sword. It must have been taken by the robber. Neither his sword nor his bow and arrows were to be seen in the grove. But fortunately my small sword was lying at my feet. Raising it over head, once more I said, "Now give me your life. I'll follow you right away."

When he heard these words, he moved his lips with difficulty. Since his mouth was stuffed with leaves, of course his voice could not be heard at all. But at a glance I understood his words. Despising me, his look said only, "Kill me." Neither conscious nor unconscious, I stabbed the small sword through the lilac-colored kimono into his breast.

Again at this time I must have fainted. By the time I managed to look up, he had already breathed his last—still in bonds. A streak of sinking sunlight streamed through the clump of cedars and bamboos, and shone on his pale face. Gulping down my sobs, I untied the rope from his dead body. And . . . and what has become of me since I have no more strength to tell you. Anyway I hadn't the strength to die. I stabbed my own throat with the small sword, I threw myself into a pond at the foot of the mountain, and I tried to kill myself in many ways. Unable to end my life, I am still living in dishonor. (A lonely smile.) Worthless as I am, I must have been forsaken even by the most merciful Kwannon. I killed my own husband. I was violated by the robber. Whatever can I do? Whatever can I . . . I . . . (Gradually, violent sobbing.)

THE STORY OF THE MURDERED MAN, AS TOLD THROUGH A MEDIUM

After violating my wife, the robber, sitting there, began to speak comforting words to her. Of course I couldn't speak. My whole body was tied fast to the root of a cedar. But meanwhile I winked at her many times, as much as to say "Don't believe the robber". I wanted to convey some such meaning to her. But my wife, sitting dejectedly on the bamboo leaves, was looking hard at her lap. To all appearances, she was listening to his words. I was agonized by jealousy. In the meantime the robber went on with his clever talk, from one subject to another. The robber finally made his bold, brazen proposal. "Once your virtue is stained, you won't get along well with your husband, so won't you be my wife instead? It's my love for you that made me be violent toward you."

While the criminal talked, my wife raised her face as if in a trance. She had never looked so beautiful as at that moment. What did my beautiful wife say in answer to him while I was sitting bound there? I am lost in space, but I have never thought of her answer without burning with anger and jealousy. Truly she said . . . "Then take me away with you wherever you go."

This is not the whole of her sin. If that were all, I would not be tormented so much in the dark. When she was going out of the grove as if in a dream, her hand in the robber's, she suddenly turned pale, and pointed at me tied to the root of the cedar, and said, "Kill him! I cannot marry you as long as he lives." "Kill him!" she cried many times, as if she had gone crazy. Even now these words threaten to blow me headlong into the bottomless abyss of darkness. Has such a hateful thing come out of a human mouth ever before? Have such cursed words ever struck a human ear, even once? Even once such a . . . (A sudden cry of scorn.) At these words the robber himself turned pale. "Kill him," she cried, clinging to his arms. Looking hard at her, he answered neither yes nor no . . . but hardly had I thought about his answer before she had been knocked down into the bamboo leaves. (Again a cry of scorn.) Quietly folding his arms, he looked at me and said, "What will you do with her? Kill her or save her? You have only to nod. Kill her?" For these words alone I would like to pardon his crime.

While I hesitated, she shrieked and ran into the depths of the grove. The robber instantly snatched at her, but he failed even to grasp her sleeve.

After she ran away, he took up my sword, and my bow and arrows. With a single stroke he cut one of my bonds. I remember his mumbling, "My fate is next." Then he disappeared from the grove. All was silent after that. No, I heard someone crying. Untying the rest of my bonds, I listened carefully, and I noticed that it was my own crying. (Long silence.)

I raised my exhausted body from the root of the cedar. In front of me there was shining the small sword which my wife had dropped. I took it up and stabbed it into my breast. A bloody lump rose to my mouth, but I didn't feel any pain. When my breast grew cold, everything was silent as the dead in their graves. What profound silence! Not a single bird-note was heard in the sky over this grave in the hollow of the mountains. Only a lonely light lingered on the cedars and mountains. By and by the light gradually grew fainter, till the cedars and bamboo were lost to view. Lying there, I was enveloped in deep silence.

Then someone crept up to me. I tried to see who it was. But darkness had already been gathering round me. Someone . . . that someone drew the small sword softly out of my breast in its invisible hand. At the same time once more blood flowed into my mouth. And once and for all I sank down into the darkness of space.

QUESTIONS ABOUT "IN A GROVE"

1. Make a list of those details about which all the characters in the story agree. Do these details provide a basis to decide what actually happened?
2. Make a similar list of those details about which the characters *do not* agree. Do these differences make one version of the incident more credible than the others?
3. Consider the personalities of the main characters: the husband, the wife, and the bandit. Does Akutagawa give the reader enough evidence about them to test their stories? Think about the pride of the men, and about the wife's concern for her reputation.
4. Do you think we should attach any special significance to the manner in which we receive the husband's testimony?
5. Given the conflicting evidence in the story, do you think Akutagawa wants us to conclude that knowledge of the truth is beyond our capabilities?
6. Do you feel that a writer should be clearer about *the truth* of his or her work? If you do, what assumptions about the relationship between art and truth would support your feeling?

Philosophical Discussion:
What Is Truth?

A body is found. A crime has been committed. Three people confess. Who did it? Tajomaru, the notorious brigand, Masago, the wife of the victim, or Takejiro, the dead man himself?

Ryunosuke Akutagawa's "In a Grove" is a mystery, a kind of "whodunit." But unlike the stories of Agatha Christie or Sir Arthur Conan Doyle, the truth, at the end, is not revealed. Is this a flaw? Part of the fun of the murder mystery is finding out who the real murderer is. Speculation, guesswork, hypothesis, deduction have their place. But come the end, we want to know. We don't just want the pieces to fit, a là Sherlock Holmes, or the different alternative theories neatly laid out, in the style of Hercule Poirot. We want the truth. And we want it unvarnished, untainted, unadorned, pure and simple.

Readers of murder mysteries are not alone. In real life, too, the truth is important to us. Though much of contemporary courtroom drama is played out behind the scenes in plea bargaining and out-of-court settlements, the British-American adversarial system is designed not just to produce winners and losers, but to allow the truth to emerge. Otherwise, guilty and innocent alike are punished, and the court system is unnecessary.

In finance, business, medicine, advertising, science, even politics, we expect the truth. And even if we cannot always get the whole truth, we do expect something that at least comes close. Otherwise, the resources we expend on research, the money and energies we invest in planning, the decisions we make that will affect our futures, all would seem pointless. If there is no truth, we might just as well turn to soothsaying as to science, meditation as to medicine.

What is the truth? Philosophers have debated the question for generations. Three main answers have emerged: the correspondence, coherence, and pragmatic theories of truth. Each makes an important contribution to our understanding of this fundamental concept. Yet, like almost every significant theory, each leaves something to be desired. Before considering these theories, however, let us first ask what exactly we are looking for.

What should a theory of truth do for us? There are many apparently true things— "2+2=4," "The earth is a planet," "Water boils at 212° Farenheit," "A crime was committed in a grove,'' etc. The philosopher's task, as commonly understood, is not to add to this corpus nor to duplicate the work of the mathematician, astronomer, or magistrate. Rather, the philosopher's job is to find out what all of these things have in common. We might say that a theory of truth should answer the question, *What do all true things have in common?*

Why should this be of interest? Unless there is something that all these things have in common, it is doubtful that there is any such thing as truth. In the previous chapter we considered the skeptical claim that there is no ultimate justification of belief. This does not mean that the skeptic disbelieves that $2+2=4$, or any other apparent truth. On the contrary, the skeptic believes almost everything that we believe. However, the skeptical idea is that calling something true is like calling someone a witch. Just as those who were accused of witchcraft in seventeenth-century Salem, Massachusetts, had little in common other than that they were so accused, so those things we say are true have nothing more in common either. And just as there were no witches in Salem, so there is no truth. If there is some such thing as truth, then a philosophical theory is needed to answer the question, *What do all true things have in common other than that we call them true?*

The skeptic's assumption is that just as we can call almost anyone a witch, so too, we can call almost anything true. But is this so? Just as there are certain minimal conditions for someone to be called a witch, for example, that the person be female (males with alleged special powers of sorcery are called warlocks), so there appear to be certain minimal conditions for something to be called true, namely that it be (1) independent of belief; (2) immutable; and (3) public. Let us consider each separately.

First, why should we think of truth as something that is independent of belief? To think otherwise is to commit what may be called the *"wishful thinking fallacy,"* the mistake, often made by children, of thinking that something is so because we want it to be so. Growing up, in part, consists in realizing that things are not always as we want them to be. Nevertheless, even the best of thinkers is subject to this error. Einstein, for example, admitted that one of his greatest blunders was to try to avoid the apparent implication of his theory of general relativity that the universe is expanding. Despite his apparent wish for a static universe, the truth seems to be otherwise, as the observational astronomer Edwin Hubble later confirmed.

Second, it has long been felt that if there is some such thing as truth, it is immutable. For example, that $2+2=4$ would seem to be as true today as ever. But are all apparent truths like those of mathematics? Consider, for example, ''The airplane is an available means of transportation.'' A hundred years ago people traveled by horse-and-buggy. Does this mean that what is true today was not true then, that truth changes? Obviously many things have changed over the past hundred years. But has the truth changed along with them? To say that the truth has changed seems to suggest that although it was once true that a hundred years ago the airplane was not available, it is now true that a hundred years ago it was. But this cannot be. It cannot be the case that the airplane was and was not available. One way to avoid the apparent contradiction is to speak of the statement a person makes on a particular occasion as either true or false. The truth (or falsity) of a statement need not change, since, on a different occasion, a different statement is made. For example, this particular instance of the statement, ''People travel by automobile,'' is as true today as it ever was and ever will be.

Third, in what way is truth public? The idea is that truth, whatever else it is, is the same for all, that what is true for me, so to speak, is true for everybody, and *vice versa*. Or more simply, what is true is true, and there is no need to add "for me," "for you," or "for anybody." But how can this be since, for the ancients, including Aristotle, it was true that the earth was the immovable center of the universe but not true for us today. To say, for example, that it was true for Aristotle that the sun revolves about the earth, while it is true for us that the earth revolves about the sun suggests misleadingly that our planetary solar system has undergone a cataclysmic reversal since the time of Aristotle, that somehow between the fourth century B.C. and the present day, the earth jumped out of its stationary and central position and was replaced by the sun. But this is not so. To avoid false impressions, let us say that the ancients *believed* that the earth was stationary. If the earth rotates and revolves as we believe, then it was as mobile then as it is today.

One other consideration. We've seen in the previous section that truth is a necessary condition of knowledge. Hence, a desirable feature of a theory of truth is that it illuminate, in some way, this relationship. Otherwise, if there is no apparent relationship between knowledge and truth, why should we think that truth is necessary at all? If a theory of truth cannot help us decide, for example, who killed the man in the grove, of what practical use can it be?

Let us begin by considering a view that Aristotle adopted in opposition to certain pre-Socratic philosophers. According to Aristotle,

To say of what is, that it is not, or of what is not, that it is, is false, while to say of what is that it is, or of what is not that it is not, is true. . . .

The view seems little more than a truism and has come to be known as *the correspondence theory of truth*, which can be defined as follows:

Something is true if and only if it corresponds to the facts.

According to this approach, there are certain facts, and in order for something to be true it must correspond to them, or be false otherwise. For example, if the facts are as Masago, the wife in Akutagawa's story, says, then what she says is true; otherwise not. Facts seem to be independent of belief. Takejiro may have killed himself, even though not everyone believes this. Moreover, if it is a fact that Tajomaru is the murderer, then it will always be a fact. And the facts, whatever they are, are the same for all. The correspondence theory can account for all three minimal conditions.

According to the correspondence theorist, we need only ascertain the facts and the truth will be revealed. But what are facts? Sometimes the facts are apparent. I attend a loud rock concert at the end of which I have a splitting headache. Whatever the ultimate cause may be—the music itself, the loudness of the music, the constriction of certain blood vessels in the brain—the fact is that I have a headache. But in what exactly does this fact consist? Is it identical with the headache? Apparently not. The headache seems to be going on in my head. The fact that I have a headache does not seem to be going on at all, let alone in my head. Is the fact something other than the headache, an object, an event? But where exactly is this object and when does this event take place?

Questions such as these have led philosophers to doubt that there really are facts, suggesting that what we mean by *fact* is nothing more than *true statement*. After all, whenever the facts are discussed, true statements are asserted. If this is so, then the correspondence theory would collapse into the triviality that a statement is true if and only if it corresponds to a true statement.

Perhaps this is desirable. To identify a fact with a true statement would avoid populating the world with negative facts, general facts, and whatever other kind of fact would seem to be needed to correspond to the variety of statements there are. But the identification of fact with true statement cannot be correct. Although there cannot be a true statement unless there is a corresponding fact, it seems that there can be a fact without a corresponding true statement. Not every fact is stated. Otherwise, every true thing that can be said has been said, which is absurd.

What then is a fact? Perhaps we are not absolutely clear about this. But the notion of a fact is not new or technical. We commonly speak of, infer on the basis of, disagree about, seek out, guess, meditate upon, and discover some such things. A theory of fact would be interesting. But the correspondence theory is a theory of truth. It *uses* the notion of fact; it does not try to explain it. Every theory must use some notion that it leaves unexplained. Otherwise, no theory could explain anything.

The question is, is the notion of fact helpful? It is, at least in that it can account for the minimal conditions of truth. But is that enough? Earlier it was suggested that an acceptable theory should also illuminate the relationship between truth and knowledge. Except for situations where the facts are apparent, it is not always clear how the facts are to be ascertained. In the story, "In A Grove," for example, how is the magistrate supposed to get at the facts? He might decide to visit the scene of the crime. But the crime took place in the past, and no one can travel back in time. The magistrate does what most people do when the facts are not immediately accessible: he tries to piece together, from conflicting reports, a single coherent story. Any account that contains conflicting statements or outright contradictions cannot correspond to the facts. But if coherence can provide a test for ascertaining the facts, what need is there to speak of facts at all? Let us consider coherence as a theory of truth.

The coherence theory of truth can be defined as follows:

Something is true if and only if it is coherent.

The idea is that truth is not to be found in the abstract, but always within a context of other accepted beliefs. For example, the magistrate, or we as readers, might decide to reject the dead man's testimony on the grounds that, given other assumptions we make about life and death, dead men cannot give testimony. If this is so, then truth is not completely independent of belief. Otherwise, we can believe that a dead man cannot testify and accept the testimony of a dead man, which seems incoherent.

Does this mean that the coherence theorist commits the wishful thinking fallacy? That truth is not completely independent of belief does not mean that we can believe what we will. What we accept as true must be coherent. Wanting or wishing a belief or a system of beliefs to be coherent does not make it so.

How do we decide between conflicting reports? For example, both the bandit's and the wife's stories seem independently coherent, yet they appear to conflict with each other. If the bandit's testimony is correct, he was enticed into killing the husband. If the wife's testimony is accepted, Tajomaru left the grove while the husband was still alive. What is true for one does not seem to be true for the other, so to speak. But the truth must be the same for all. How can this be, since there is no coherent story that is the same for all?

Coherence seems to provide a necessary test of truth. But can this approach suffice as a full theory? In his discussion, Brand Blanshard, a coherence theorist, addresses the problem. We will leave it to the reader to decide whether he succeeds. David Ingram addresses a similar problem from the point of view of hermeneutics, the study of textual interpretation. Again, we will let the reader decide whether the hermeneuticist provides an acceptable alternative to the correspondence theory.

Other philosophers, recognizing this difficulty and not willing to return to a correspondence approach, have proposed a practical solution: if faced with choosing between two coherent stories, theories, or sets of beliefs, pick the one which is most predictive, less *ad hoc,* simpler, or more explanatory. The American philosopher, Charles Sanders Peirce, pioneered this approach, which he called pragmaticism, but which has come to be called *pragmatism. The pragmatic theory of truth* may be defined as follows:

Something is true if and only if it is part of an "inference to the best explanation."

The expression "inference to the best explanation" was introduced into recent philosophical discussion by Gilbert Harman, not as a way of attempting to explain truth, but as a way of designating a certain form of reasoning. Nevertheless, Harman's suggestion is useful in understanding the pragmatic approach. Given that a certain hypothesis would explain the evidence, we can infer that the hypothesis is true. For example, if the hypothesis that Tajomaru killed the husband would explain, among other things, why a dead man's body was in a grove, then we can infer that the bandit is the murderer. But first we must discount all competing hypotheses. To do this we may consider *more* than what we are explicitly told. For example, according to Tajomaru, the dead man was killed with a sword, but according to the wife's story, he was killed with a smaller weapon. We are not told what sort of wounds were found on the body. Perhaps we are not given enough information to make a practical choice. But the evidence is available. One need not travel back in time to inspect the body more carefully. Modern investigators would perform an autopsy. If the wounds were inflicted by a warrior's weapon, then Tajomaru's explanation would seem best. But what if the wounds were the result of a small sword? Both the wife's and husband's account seem to agree on this. According to the pragmatist, considerations other than direct empirical evidence may be relevant. For example, did the wife have any motive to lie? Was the husband trying to save face? Without more information, from a practical point of view, it does seem that the husband had reason to commit suicide. He was a warrior. He allowed himself to be tricked by a brigand and failed to protect his wife from rape. On the other hand, the wife claims that she "stabbed the small sword into his breast," but admits that she was neither conscious nor unconscious. How much credence can we give her testimony? Tajomaru is too much of a braggart and too willing to take the blame. "I know that my head will be hung in chains anyway, so put me down for the maximum penalty," he says defiantly. But if he is truly guilty, why is he defiant? Can he be challenging the authorities to find him truly innocent even though he knows that they are prejudiced against him?

Did the dead man kill himself? Pragmatic considerations would make this hypothesis plausible. But is it true? If we say that it is, we should be prepared to allow that additional evidence may yet be uncovered to support some other theory. But then it appears that the truth can change, and the pragmatic approach has failed to account for the condition of immutability. Some theorists consider this a benefit, suggesting that science, for example, is always somewhat tentative in its judgments, and never dogmatic. But a magistrate, unlike a scientist, must make decisions about life and death and cannot always afford the luxury of suspending final judgment.

Peirce suggested that the truth will be revealed in whatever explanation stands at the end of enquiry. The idea is that our beliefs may appear to differ, but with open enquiry, they will evolve and eventually converge. Recent work by Thomas Kuhn and others in the philosophy and history of science, however, suggest a different picture, that competing theories in science are incommensurable and incompatible. The history of science is the history of scientific revolution, not evolution. If Kuhn is correct, then there is no ultimate convergence.

Where does this leave us? The coherence theory fails to account for truth as the same for all. The pragmatic approach leaves out immutability. Only the correspondence theory seems to account for all minimum conditions. Is truth correspondence to the facts? If so, how can this help us?

Akutagawa's "In A Grove" brilliantly raises a deep skeptical problem. If the same event can appear so differently to different people, in what sense is there a "same event"? This question, in one form or another, has been raised throughout Western philosophy and in other traditions as well. Akutagawa is not alone. The correspondence theory answers that, despite appearances, there is something that is independent of belief, immutable, and public. By itself this does not tell us who the murderer is. The coherence and pragmatic approaches may also be needed, not as competing theories of truth, but as methods for discovering what it is. Without correspondence, however, it seems that there is nothing to discover.

ARISTOTLE
from *Metaphysics*

BOOK FOUR
Chapter Five

From the same opinion proceeds the doctrine of Protagoras, and both doctrines must be alike true or alike untrue. For on the one hand, if all opinions and appearances are true, all statements must be at the same time true and false. For many men hold beliefs in which they conflict with one another, and think those mistaken who have not the same opinions as themselves; so that the same thing must both be and not be. And on the other hand, if this is so, all opinions must be true; for those who are mistaken and those who are right are opposed to one another in their opinions; if, then, reality is such as the view in question supposes, all will be right in their beliefs.

Evidently, then, both doctrines proceed from the same way of thinking. But the same method of discussion must not be used with all opponents; for some need persuasion, and others compulsion. Those who have been driven to this position by difficulties in their thinking can easily be cured of their ignorance; for it is not their expressed argument but their thought that one has to meet. But those who argue for the sake of argument can be cured only by refuting the argument as expressed in speech and in words.

Those who really feel the difficulties have been led to this opinion by observation of the sensible world. (I) They think that contradictories or contraries are true at the same time, because they see contraries coming into existence out of the same thing. If, then, that which is not cannot come to be, the thing must have existed before as both contraries alike, as Anaxagoras says all is mixed in all, and Democritus too; for *he* says the void and the full exist alike in every part, and yet one of these is being, and the other non-being. To those, then, whose belief rests on these grounds, we shall say that in a sense they speak rightly and in a sense they err. For 'that which is' has two meanings, so that in some sense a thing can come to be out of that which is not, while in some sense it cannot, and the same thing can at the same time be in being and not in being—but not in the same respect. For the same thing can be potentially at the same time two contraries, but it cannot actually. And again we shall ask them to believe that among existing things there is also another kind

Reprinted from Aristotle's "Metaphysics," translated by W. D. Ross from *The Oxford Translation of Aristotle*, edited by W. D. Ross, Vol. 9 (1928) by permission of Oxford University Press. **Aristotle** (384–322 B.C.), a student of Plato, and the teacher of Alexander the Great, is universally respected. Writing in almost every major branch of philosophy, his careful attention to detail is still a model of philosophical analysis.

of substance to which neither movement nor destruction nor generation at all belongs.

And (2) similarly some have inferred from observation of the sensible world the truth of appearances. For they think that the truth should not be determined by the large or small number of those who hold a belief, and that the same thing is thought sweet by some when they taste it, and bitter by others, so that if all were ill or all were mad, and only two or three were well or sane, these would be thought ill and mad, and not the others.

And again, they say that many of the other animals receive impressions contrary to ours; and that even to the senses of each individual, things do not always seem the same. Which, then, of these impressions are true and which are false is not obvious; for the one set is no more true than the other, but both are alike. And this is why Democritus, at any rate, says that either there is no truth or to us at least it is not evident.

And in general it is because these thinkers suppose knowledge to be sensation, and this to be a physical alteration, that they say that what appears to our senses must be true; for it is for these reasons that both Empedocles and Democritus and, one may almost say, all the others have fallen victims to opinions of this sort. For Empedocles says that when men change their condition they change their knowledge,

For wisdom increases in men according
to what is before them.

And elsewhere he says that

So far as their nature changed, so far to
them always
Came changed thoughts into mind.

And Parmenides also expresses himself in the same way:

For as at each time the much-bent limbs
are composed,
So is the mind of men; for in each and all
men

'Tis one thing thinks—the substance of
their limbs:
For that of which there is more is
thought.

A saying of Anaxagoras to some of his friends is also related—that things would be for them such as they supposed them to be. And they say that Homer also evidently had this opinion, because he made Hector, when he was unconscious from the blow, lie 'thinking other thoughts'—which implies that even those who are bereft of thought have thoughts, though not the same thoughts. Evidently, then, if both are forms of knowledge, the real things also are at the same time 'both so and not so'. And it is in this direction that the consequences are most difficult. For if those who have seen most of such truth as is possible for us (and these are those who seek and love it most)—if these have such opinions and express these views about the truth, is it not natural that beginners in philosophy should lose heart? For to seek the truth would be to follow flying game.

But the reason why these thinkers held this opinion is that while they were inquiring into the truth of that which is, they thought 'that which is' was identical with the sensible world; in this, however, there is largely present the nature of the indeterminate—of that which exists in the peculiar sense which we have explained; and therefore, while they speak plausibly, they do not say what is true (for it is fitting to put the matter so rather than as Epicharmus put it against Xenophanes). And again, because they saw that all this world of nature is in movement, and that about that which changes no true statement can be made, they said that of course, regarding that which everywhere in every respect is changing, nothing could truly be affirmed. It was this belief that blossomed into the most extreme of the views above mentioned, that of the professed Heracliteans, such as was held by Cratylus, who finally did not think it right to say anything but only moved his finger, and criticized Heraclitus for saying that it is impossible to step twice into the same river; for *he* thought one could not do it even once.

But we shall say in answer to this argument also, that while there is some justification for their thinking that the changing, when it is changing, does not exist, yet it is after all disputable; for that which is losing a quality has something of that which is being lost, and of that which is coming to be, something must already be. And in general if a thing is perishing, there will be present something that exists; and if a thing is coming to be, there must be something from which it comes to be and something by which it is generated, and this process cannot go on *ad infinitum.*—But, leaving these arguments, let us insist on this, that it is not the same thing to change in quantity and in quality. Grant that in quantity a thing is not constant; still it is in respect of its form that we know each thing.—And again, it would be fair to criticize those who hold this view for asserting about the whole material universe what they saw only in a minority even of sensible things. For only that region of the sensible world which immediately surrounds us is always in process of destruction and generation; but this is—so to speak—not even a fraction of the whole, so that it would have been juster to acquit this part of the world because of the other part, than to condemn the other because of this.—And again, obviously we shall make them also the same reply that we made long ago; we must show them and persuade them that there is something whose nature is changeless. Indeed, those who say that things at the same time are and are not, should in consequence say that all things are at rest rather than that they are in movement; for there is nothing into which they can change, since all attributes belong already to all subjects.

Regarding the nature of truth, we must maintain that not everything which appears is true; firstly, because even if sensation—at least of the object peculiar to the sense in question—is not false, still appearance is not the same as sensation.—Again, it is fair to express surprise at our opponents' raising the question whether magnitudes are as great, and colours are of such a nature, as they appear to people at a distance, or as they appear to those close at hand, and whether they are such as they appear to the healthy or to the sick, and whether those things

are heavy which appear so to the weak or those which appear so to the strong, and those things true which appear to the sleeping or to the waking. For obviously they do not think these to be open questions; no one, at least, if when he is in Libya he has fancied one night that he is in Athens, starts for the concert hall.—And again with regard to the future, as Plato says, surely the opinion of the physician and that of the ignorant man are not equally weighty, for instance, on the question whether a man will get well or not.—And again, among sensations themselves the sensation of a foreign object and that of the appropriate object, or that of a kindred object and that of the object of the sense in question, are not equally authoritative, but in the case of colour sight, not taste, has the authority, and in the case of flavour taste, not sight; each of which senses never says at the same time of the same object that it simultaneously is 'so and not so'.—But not even at different times does one sense disagree about the quality, but only about that to which the quality belongs. I mean, for instance, that the same wine might seem, if either it or one's body changed, at one time sweet and at another time not sweet; but at least the sweet, such as it is when it exists, has never yet changed, but one is always right about it, and that which is to be sweet is of necessity of such and such a nature. Yet all these views destroy this necessity, leaving nothing to be of necessity, as they leave no essence of anything; for the necessary cannot be in this way and also in that, so that if anything is of necessity, it will not be 'both so and not so.'

And, in general, if only the sensible exists, there would be nothing if animate things were not; for there would be no faculty of sense. Now the view that neither the sensible qualities nor the sensations would exist is doubtless true (for they are affections of the perceiver), but that the substrata which cause the sensation should not exist even apart from sensation is impossible. For sensation is surely not the sensation of itself, but there is something beyond the sensation, which must be prior to the sensation; for that which moves is prior in nature to that which is moved, and if they are correlative terms, this is no less the case.

BOOK FOUR
Chapter Six

There are, both among those who have these convictions and among those who merely profess these views, some who raise a difficulty by asking, who is to be the judge of the healthy man, and in general who is likely to judge rightly on each class of questions. But such inquiries are like puzzling over the question whether we are now asleep or awake. And all such questions have the same meaning. These people demand that a reason shall be given for everything; for they seek a starting-point, and they seek to get this by demonstration, while it is obvious from their actions that they have no conviction. But their mistake is what we have stated it to be; they seek a reason for things for which no reason can be given for the starting-point of demonstration is not demonstration.

These, then, might be easily persuaded of this truth, for it is not difficult to grasp; but those who seek merely compulsion in argument seek what is impossible; for they demand to be allowed to contradict themselves—a claim which contradicts itself from the very first. But if not all things are relative, but some are self-existent, not everything that appears will be true; for that which appears is apparent to someone, so that he who says all things that appear are true, makes all things relative. And, therefore, those who ask for an irresistible argument, and at the same time demand to be called to account for their views, must guard themselves by saying that the truth is not that what appears exists, but that what appears exists *for him to whom* it appears, and *when*, and *to the sense to which*, and *under the conditions under which* it appears. And if they give an account of their view, but do not give it in this way, they will soon find themselves contradicting themselves. For it is possible that the same thing may appear to be honey to the sight, but not to the taste, and that, since we have two eyes, things may not appear the same to each, if their sight is unlike. For to those who for the reasons named some time ago say that what appears is true, and therefore that all things are alike

false and true, for things do not appear either the same to all men or always the same to the same man, but often have contrary appearances at the same time (for touch says there are two objects when we cross our fingers, while sight says there is one),—to these we shall say 'yes, but not to the same sense and in the same part of it and under the same conditions and at the same time', so that what appears will be with these qualifications true. But perhaps for this reason those who argue thus not because they feel a difficulty but for the sake of argument, should say that this is not true, but true for this man. And as has been said before, they must make everything relative—relative to opinion and perception, so that nothing either has come to be or will be without some one's first thinking so. But if things *have* come to be or will be, evidently not all things will be relative to opinion.—Again, if a thing is one, it is in relation to one thing or to a definite number of things; and if the same thing is both half and equal, it is not to the double that the equal is correlative. If, then, in relation to that which thinks, man and that which is thought are the same, man will not be that which thinks, but only that which is thought. And if each thing is to be relative to that which thinks, that which thinks will be relative to an infinity of specifically different things.

Let this, then suffice to show (1) that the most indisputable of all beliefs is that contradictory statements are not at the same time true, and (2) what consequences follow from the assertion that they are, and (3) why people do assert this. Now since it is impossible that contradictories should be at the same time true of the same thing, obviously contraries also cannot belong at the same time to the same thing. For of contraries, one is a privation no less than it is a contrary—and a privation of the essential nature; and privation is the denial of a predicate to a determinate genus. If, then, it is impossible to affirm and deny truly at the same time, it is also impossible that contraries should belong to a subject at the same time, unless both belong to it in particular relations, or one in a particular relation and one without qualification.

BOOK FOUR
Chapter Seven

But on the other hand there cannot be an intermediate between contradictories, but of one subject we must either affirm or deny any one predicate. This is clear, in the first place, if we define what the true and the false are. To say of what is that it is not, or of what is not that it is, is false, while to say of what is that it is, and of what is not that it is not, is true; so that he who says of anything that it is, or that it is not, will say either what is true or what is false; but neither what is nor what is not is said to be or not to be.—Again, the intermediate between the contradictories will be so either in the way in which grey is between black and white, or as that which is neither man nor horse is between man and horse. *(a)* If it were of the latter kind, it could not change into the extremes (for change is from not-good to good, or from good to not-good), but as a matter of fact when there is an intermediate it is always observed to change into the extremes. For there is no change except to opposites and to their intermediates. *(b)* But if it is really intermediate, in this way too there would have to be a change to white, which was not from not-white; but as it is, this is never seen.—Again, every object of understanding or reason the understanding either affirms or denies—this is obvious from the definition—whenever it says what is true or false. When it connects in one way by assertion or negation, it says what is true, and when it does so in another way, what is false.—Again, there must be an intermediate between *all* contradictories, if one is not arguing merely for the sake of argument; so that it will be possible for a man to say what is neither true nor untrue, and there will be a middle between that which is and that which is not, so that there will also

be a kind of change intermediate between generation and destruction.—Again, in all classes in which the negation of an attribute involves the assertion of its contrary, even in these there will be an intermediate; for instance, in the sphere of numbers there will be number which is neither odd nor not-odd. But this is impossible, as is obvious from the definition.—Again, the process will go on *ad infinitum,* and the number of realities will be not only half as great again, but even greater. For again it will be possible to deny this intermediate with reference both to its assertion and to its negation, and this new term will be some definite thing; for its essence is something different.—Again, when a man, on being asked whether a thing is white, says 'no', he has denied nothing except that it is; and its not being is a negation.

Some people have acquired this opinion as other paradoxical opinions have been acquired; when men cannot refute eristical arguments, they give in to the argument and agree that the conclusion is true. This, then, is why some express this view; others do so because they demand a reason for everything. And the starting-point in dealing with all such people is definition. Now the definition rests on the necessity of their meaning something; for the form of words of which the word is a sign will be its definition.—While the doctrine of Heraclitus, that all things are and are not, seems to make everything true, that of Anaxagoras, that there is an intermediate between the terms of a contradiction, seems to make everything false; for when things are mixed, the mixture is neither good nor not-good, so that one cannot say anything that is true.

J. L. AUSTIN
Truth

1. 'What is truth?' said jesting Pilate, and would not stay for an answer. Pilate was in advance of his time. For 'truth' itself is an abstract noun, a camel, that is, of a logical construction, which cannot get past the eye even of a grammarian. We approach it cap and categories in hand: we ask ourselves whether Truth is a substance (the Truth, the Body of Knowledge), or a quality (something like the colour red, inhering in truths), or a relation ('correspondence').[1] But philosophers should take something more nearly their own size to strain at. What needs discussing rather is the use, or certain uses, of the word 'true'. *In vino,* possibly, *'veritas',* but in a sober symposium *'verum'*.

2. What is that we say is true or is false? Or, how does the phrase 'is true' occur in English sentences? The answers appear at first multifarious. We say (or are said to say) that beliefs are true, that descriptions or accounts are true, that propositions or assertions or statements are true, and that words or sentences are true: and this is to mention only a selection of the more obvious candidates. Again, we say (or are said to say) 'It is true that the cat is on the mat', or 'It is true to say that the cat is on the mat', or ' "The cat is on the mat" ' is true'. We also remark on occasion, when someone else has said

something, 'Very true' or 'That's true' or 'True enough'.

Most (though not all) of these expressions, and others besides, certainly do occur naturally enough. But it seems reasonable to ask whether there is not some use of 'is true' that is primary, or some generic name for that which at bottom we are always saying 'is true'. Which, if any, of these expressions is to be taken *au pied de la lettre?* To answer this will not take us long, nor, perhaps, far: but in philosophy the foot of the letter is the foot of the ladder.

I suggest that the following are the primary forms of expression:

> It is true (to say) that the cat is on the mat.
> That statement (of his, &c.) is true.
> The statement that the cat is on the mat is true.

But first for the rival candidates.

(a) Some say that 'truth is primarily a property of beliefs. But it may be doubted whether the expression 'a true belief' is at all common outside philosophy and theology: and it seems clear that a man is said to hold a true belief when and in the sense that he believes (in)

"Truth" is reprinted from J. L. Austin's *Philosophical Papers*, edited by J. O. Urmson and G. J. Warnock (3rd ed., 1979) by permission of Oxford University Press. **John Langshaw Austin** (1911–1960) spearheaded a movement called *ordinary language philosophy* in post-World War II Britain which professed no special philosophical theory other than the general suspicion of philosophical doctrines expressed in what would appear to be unnecessary technical jargon.

something which is true, or believes that *something which* is true is true. Moreover if, as some also say, a belief is 'of the nature of a picture', then it is of the nature of what cannot be true, though it may be, for example, faithful.[2]

(b) True descriptions and true accounts are simply varieties of true statements or of collections of true statements, as are true answers and the like. The same applies to propositions too, in so far as they are genuinely said to be true (and not, as more commonly, sound, tenable and so on).[3] A proposition in law or in geometry is something portentous, usually a generalization, that we are invited to accept and that has to be recommended by argument: it cannot be a direct report on current observation—if you look and inform me that the cat is on the mat, that is not a proposition though it is a statement. In philosophy, indeed 'proposition' is sometimes used in a special way for 'the meaning or sense of a sentence or family of sentences': but whether we think a lot or little of this usage, a proposition in this sense cannot, at any rate, be what we say is true or false. For we never say 'The meaning (or sense) of this sentence (or of these words) is true'; what we do say is what the judge or jury says, namely that *The words* taken in this sense, or if we assign to them such and such a meaning, or so interpreted or understood, *are true*'.

(c) Words and sentences are indeed said to be true, the former often, the latter rarely. But only in certain senses. Words as discussed by philologists, or by lexicographers, grammarians, linguists, phoneticians, printers, critics (stylistic or textual) and so on, are not true or false: they are wrongly formed, or ambiguous or defective or untranslatable or unpronounceable or mis-spelled or archaistic or corrupt or what not.[4] Sentences in similar contexts are elliptic or involved or alliterative or ungrammatical. We may, however, genuinely say 'His closing words were very true' or 'The third sentence on page 5 of his speech is quite false': but here 'words' and 'sentence' refer, as is shown by the demonstratives (possessive pronouns, temporal verbs, definite descriptions, &c.), which in this usage consistently accompany them, to the words or sentence *as used by a certain person on a certain occasion*. That is, they refer (as does 'Many a true word spoken in jest') to *statements*.

A statement is made and its making is an historic event, the utterance by a certain speaker or writer of certain words (a sentence) to an audience with reference to an historic situation, event or what not.[5]

A sentence is made *up of* words, a statement is made *in* words. A sentence is not English or not good English, a statement is not in English or not in good English. Statements are made, words or sentences are used. We talk of *my* statement, but of *the English* sentence (if a sentence is mine, I coined it, but I do not coin statements). The *same* sentence is used in making *different* statements (I say 'It is mine', you say 'It is mine'): it may also be used on two occasions or by two persons in making the *same* statement, but for this the utterance must be made with reference to the same situation or event.[6] We speak of 'the statement that S,' but of 'the sentence "S" ', not of 'the sentence that S'.[7]

When I say that a statement is what is true, I have no wish to become wedded to one word. 'Assertion', for example, will in most contexts do just as well, though perhaps it is slightly wider. Both words share the weakness of being rather solemn (much more so than the more general 'what you said' or 'your words')—though perhaps we are generally being a little solemn when we discuss the truth of anything. Both have the merit of clearly referring to this historic use of a sentence by an utterer, and of being therefore precisely not equivalent to 'sentence'. For it is a fashionable mistake to take as primary '(The sentence) "S" is true (in the English language)'. Here the addition of the words 'in the English language' serves to emphasize that 'sentence' is not being used as equivalent to 'statement', so that it precisely is not what can be true or false (and moreover, 'true in the English language' is a solecism . . . mismodelled presumably, and with deplorable effect, on expressions like 'true in geometry').

3. When is a statement true? The temptation is to answer (at least if we confine ourselves to 'straightforward' statements): 'When it corresponds to the facts'. And as a piece of standard English this can hardly be wrong. Indeed, I must confess I do not really think it is wrong at all: the theory of truth is a series of truisms. Still, it can at least be misleading.

If there is to be communication of the sort that we achieve by language at all, there must be a stock of symbols of some kind which a communicator ('the speaker') can produce 'at will' and which a communicatee ('the audience') can observe: these may be called the 'words', though, of course, they need not be anything very like what we should normally call words—they might be signal flags, &c. There must also be something other than the words, which the words are to be used to communicate about: this may be called the 'world'. There is no reason why the world should not include the words, in every sense except the sense of the actual statement itself which on any particular occasion is being made about the world. Further, the world must exhibit (we must observe) similarities and dissimilarities (there could not be the one without the other): if everything were either absolutely indistinguishable from anything else or completely unlike anything else, there would be nothing to say. And finally (for present purposes—of course there are other conditions to be satisfied too) there must be two sets of conventions:

Descriptive conventions correlating the words (= sentences) with the *types* of situation, thing, event &c., to be found in the world.

Demonstrative conventions correlating the words (=statements) with the *historic* situations, &c., to be found in the world.[8]

A statement is said to be true when the historic state of affairs to which it is correlated by the demonstrative conventions (the one to which it refers) is of a type[9] with which the sentence used in making it is correlated by the descriptive conventions.[10]

3a. Troubles arise from the use of the word 'facts' for the historic situations, events, &c., and in general, for the world. For 'fact' is regularly used in conjunction with 'that' in the sentences 'The fact is that S' or 'It is a fact that S' and in the expression 'the fact that S', all of which imply that it would be true to say that S.[11]

This may lead us to suppose that
(i) 'fact' is only an alternative expression for 'true statement'. We note that when a detective says 'Let's look at the facts' he does not crawl round the carpet, but proceeds to utter a string of statements: we even talk of 'stating the facts';
(ii) for every true statement there exists 'one' and its own precisely corresponding fact—for every cap the head it fits.

It is (i) which leads to some of the mistakes in 'coherence' or formalist theories; (ii) to some of those in 'correspondence' theories. Either we suppose that there is nothing there but the true statement itself, nothing to which it corresponds, or else we populate the world with linguistic *Doppelgänger* (and grossly overpopulate it—every nugget of 'positive' fact overlaid by a massive concentration of 'negative' facts, every tiny detailed fact larded with generous general facts, and so on).

When a statement is true, there is, *of course*, a state of affairs which makes it true and which is *toto mundo* distinct from the true statement about it; but equally of course, we can only *describe* that state of affairs *in words* (either the same or, with luck, others). I can only describe the situation in which it is true to say that I am feeling sick by saying that it is one in which I am feeling sick (or experiencing sensations of nausea):[12] yet between stating, however truly, that I am feeling sick and feeling sick there is a great gulf fixed.[13]

'Fact that' is a phrase designed for use in situations where the distinction between a true statement and the state of affairs about which it is a truth is neglected; as it often is with advantage in ordinary life, though seldom in philosophy—above all in discussing truth, where it is precisely our business to prise the words off the world and keep them off it. To ask 'Is the fact that S the true statement that S or that which it is true of?' may beget absurd answers. To take an analogy: although we may sensibly ask 'Do we *ride* the word "elephant" or the animal?' and equally sensibly 'Do we *write* the word or word and animal (do we focus the image or the battleship?); and so speaking about 'the fact that' is a compendious way of speaking about a situation involving both words and world.[14]

3*b*. 'Corresponds' also gives trouble, because it is commonly given too restricted or too colourful a meaning, or one which in this context it cannot bear. The only essential point is this: that the correlation between the words (= sentences) and the type of situation, event, &c., which is to be such that when a statement in those words is made with reference to an historic situation of that type the statement is then true, is *absolutely and purely* conventional. We are absolutely free to appoint *any* symbol to describe *any* type of situation, so far as merely being true goes. In a small one-spade language tst nuts might be true in exactly the same circumstances as the statement in English that the National Liberals are the people's choice.[15] There is no need whatsoever for the words used in making a true statement to 'mirror' in any way, however indirect, any feature whatsoever of the situation or event; a statement no more needs, in order to be true, to reproduce the 'multiplicity,' say, or the 'structure' or 'form' of the reality, than a word needs to be echoic or writing pictographic. To suppose that it does, is to fall once again into the error of reading back into the world the features of language.

The more rudimentary a language, the more, very often, it will tend to have a 'single' word for a highly 'complex' type of situation: this has such disadvantages as that the language becomes elaborate to learn and is incapable of dealing with situations which are non-standard, unforeseen, for which there may just be no word. When we go abroad equipped only with a phrase-book, we may spend long hours learning by heart—

A¹moest-fa¹nd-ᵉtschâʳwoumᵉn,
Ma¹hwîl-iz-wauʳpt (bènt),

and so on and so on, yet faced with the situation where we have the pen of our aunt, find ourselves quite unable to say so. The characteristics of a more developed language (articulation, morphology, syntax, abstractions, &c.), do not make statements in it any more capable of being true or capable of being any more true, they make it more adaptable, more learnable, more comprehensive, more precise, and so on; and *these* aims may no doubt be furthered by making the language (allowance made for the nature of the medium) 'mirror' in conventional ways features described in the world.

Yet even when a language does 'mirror' such features very closely (and does it ever?) the truth of statements remains still a matter, as it was with the most rudimentary languages, of the words used being the ones *conventionally appointed* for situations of the type to which that referred to belongs. A picture, a copy, a replica, a photograph—these are *never* true in so far as they are reproductions, produced by natural or mechanical means; a reproduction can be accurate or lifelike (true *to* the original), as a gramophone recording or a transcription may be, but not true (*of*) as a record of proceedings can be. In the same way a (natural) sign *of* something can be infallible or unreliable but only an (artificial) sign *for* something can be right or wrong.[16]

There are many intermediate cases between a true account and a faithful picture, as here somewhat forcibly contrasted, and it is from the study of these (a lengthy matter) that we can get the clearest insight into the contrast. For example, maps: these may be called pictures, yet they are highly conventionalized pictures. If a map can be clear or accurate or misleading, like a statement, why can it not be true or exaggerated? How do the 'symbols' used in map-making differ from those used in statement-making? On the other hand, if an air-mosaic is not a map, why is it not? And when does a map become a diagram? These are the really illuminating questions.

4. Some have said that—

To say that an assertion is true is not to make any further assertion at all.

In all sentences of the form '*p* is true' the phrase 'is true' is logically superfluous.

To say that a proposition is true is just to assert it, and to say that it is false is just to assert its contradictory.

But wrongly. TstS (except in paradoxical cases of forced and dubious manufacture) refers to the world or any part of it exclusive of tstS, i.e. of itself.[17] TstST refers to the world or any part of it *inclusive* of tstS, though once again exclusive of itself, i.e. of tstST. That is, tstST refers to something to which tstS cannot refer. TstST does not, certainly, include any statement referring to the world exclusive of tstS which is not included already in tstS—more, it seems doubtful whether it does include that statement about the world exclusive of tstS which is made when we state that S. (If I state that tstS is true, should we really agree that I have stated that S? Only 'by implication'.)[18] But all this does not go any way to show that tstST is not a statement different from tstS. If Mr. Q writes on a notice-board 'Mr. W. is a burglar', then a trial is held to decide whether Mr. Q's published statement that Mr. W. is a burglar is a libel: finding 'Mr. Q's statement was true (in substance and in fact)'. Thereupon a second trial is held, to decide whether Mr. W is a burglar, in which Mr. Q's statement is no longer under consideration; verdict 'Mr. W is a burglar'. It is an arduous business to hold a second trial: why is it done if the verdict is the same as the previous finding?[19]

What is felt is that the evidence considered in arriving at the one verdict is the same as that considered in arriving at the other. This is not strictly correct. It is more nearly correct that whenever tstS is true then tstST is also true and conversely, and that whenever tstS is false tstST is also false and conversely.[20] And it is argued that the words 'is true' are logically superfluous because it is believed that generally if any two statements are always true together and always false together then they must mean the same. Now whether this is in general a sound view may be doubted: but even if it is, why should it not break down in the case of so obviously 'peculiar' a phrase as 'is true'? Mistakes in philosophy notoriously arise through thinking that what holds of 'ordinary' words like 'red' or 'growls' must also hold of extraordinary words like 'real' or 'exists'. But that 'true' is just such another extraordinary word is obvious.[21]

There is something peculiar about the 'fact' which is described by tstST, something which may make us hesitate to call it a 'fact' at all; namely, that the relation between tstS and the world which tstST asserts to obtain is a *purely conventional* relation (one which thinking makes so). For we are aware that this relation is one which we could alter at will, whereas we like to restrict the word 'fact' to *hard* facts, facts which are natural and unalterable, or anyhow not alterable at will. Thus, to take an analogous case, we may not like calling it a fact that the word elephant means what it does, though we can be induced to call it a (soft) fact—and though, of course, we have no hesitation in calling it a fact that contemporary English speakers use the word as they do.

An important point about this view is that it confuses falsity with negation: for according to it, it is the same thing to say 'He is not at home' as to say 'It is false that he is at home'. (But what if no one has said that he *is* at home? What if he is lying upstairs dead?) Too many philosophers maintain, when anxious to explain away negation, that a negation is just a second order affirmation (to the effect that a certain first order affirmation is false), yet, when anxious to explain away falsity, maintain that to assert that a statement is false is just to assert its negation (contradictory). It is impossible to deal with so fundamental a matter here.[22] Let me assert the following merely. Affirmation and negation are exactly on a level, in this sense, that no language can exist which does not contain conventions for both and that both refer to the world equally directly, not to statements about the world: whereas a language can quite well exist without any device to do the work of 'true' and 'false'. Any satisfactory theory of truth must be able to cope equally with falsity:[23] but 'is false' can only be maintained to be logically superfluous by making this fundamental confusion.

5. There is another way of coming to see that the phrase 'is true' is not logically superfluous, and to appreciate what sort of a state-

ment it is to say that a certain statement is true. There are numerous other adjectives which are in the same class as 'true' and 'false', which are concerned, that is, with the relations between the words (as uttered with reference to an historic situation) and the world, and which nevertheless no one would dismiss as logically superfluous. We say, for example, that a certain statement is exaggerated or vague or bald, a description somewhat rough or misleading or not very good, an account rather general or too concise. In cases like these it is pointless to insist on deciding in simple terms whether the statement is 'true or false'. Is it true or false that Belfast is north of London? That the galaxy is the shape of a fried egg? That Beethoven was a drunkard? That Wellington won the battle of Waterloo? There are various *degrees and dimensions* of success in making statements: the statements fit the facts always more or less loosely, in different ways on different occasions for different intents and purposes. What may score full marks in a general knowledge test may in other circumstances get a gamma. And even the most adroit of languages may fail to 'work' in an abnormal situation or to cope, or cope reasonably simply, with novel discoveries: is it true or false that the dog goes round the cow?[24] What, moreover, of the large class of cases where a statement is not so much false (or true) as out of place, *inept* ('All the signs of bread' said when the bread is before us)?

We become obsessed with 'truth' when discussing statements, just as we become obsessed with 'freedom' when discussing conduct. So long as we think that what has always and alone to be decided is whether a certain action was done freely or was not, we get nowhere: but so soon as we turn instead to the numerous other adverbs used in the same connexion ('accidentally', 'unwillingly', 'inadvertently', &c.), things become easier, and we come to see that no concluding inference of the form 'Ergo, it was done freely (or not freely)' is required. Like freedom, truth is a bare minimum or an illusory ideal (the truth, the whole truth and nothing but the truth about, say, the battle of Waterloo or the *Primavera).*

6. Not merely is it jejune to suppose that all a statement aims to be is 'true', but it may further be questioned whether every 'statement' does aim to be true at all. The principle of Logic, that 'Every proposition must be true or false', has too long operated as the simplest, most persuasive and most pervasive form of the descriptive fallacy. Philosophers under its influence have forcibly interpreted all 'propositions' on the model of the statement that a certain thing is red, as made when the thing concerned is currently under observation.

Recently, it has come to be realized that many utterances which have been taken to be statements (merely because they are not, on grounds of grammatical form, to be classed as commands, questions, &c.) are not in fact descriptive, nor susceptible of being true or false. When is a statement not a statement? When it is a formula in a calculus: when it is a performatory utterance: when it is a value-judgment: when it is a definition: when it is part of a work of fiction—there are many such suggested answers. It is simply not the business of such utterances to 'correspond to the facts' (and even genuine statements have other businesses besides that of so corresponding).

It is a matter for decision how far we should continue to call such masqueraders 'statements' at all, and how widely we should be prepared to extend the uses of 'true' and 'false' in 'different senses'. My own feeling is that it is better, when once a masquerader has been unmasked, *not* to call it a statement and *not* to say it is true or false. In ordinary life we should not call most of them statements at all, though philosophers and grammarians may have come to do so (or rather, have lumped them all together under the term of art 'proposition'). We make a difference between 'You said you promised' and 'You stated that you promised': the former can mean that you said 'I promise', whereas the latter must mean that you said 'I promised': the latter, which we say you 'stated', is something which is true or false, whereas for the former, which is not true or false, we use the wider verb to 'say'. Similarly, there is a difference between 'You say this is (call this) a good picture' and

'You state that this is a good picture'. More-over, it was only so long as the real nature of arithmetical formulae, say, or of geometrical axioms remained unrecognized, and they were thought to record information about the world, that it was reasonable to call them 'true' (and perhaps even 'statements'—though were they ever so called?): but, once their nature has been recognized, we no longer feel tempted to call them 'true' or to dispute about their truth or falsity.

In the cases so far considered the model 'This is red' breaks down because the 'state-ments' assimilated to it are not of a nature to correspond to facts at all—the words are not descriptive words, and so on. But there is also another type of case where the words *are* de-scriptive words and the 'proposition' does in a way have to correspond to facts, but precisely not in the way that 'This is red' and similar statements setting up to be true have to do.

In the human predicament, for use in which our language is designed, we may wish to speak about states of affairs which have not been ob-served or are not currently under observation (the future, for example). And although we *can* state anything 'as a fact' (which statement will then be true or false[25]) we need not do so: we need only say 'The cat *may be* on the mat'. This utterance is quite different from tstS—it is not a statement at all (it is not true or false; it is compatible with 'The cat may *not* be on the mat'). In the same way, the situation in which we discuss whether and state that tstS is *true* is different from the situation in which we discuss whether it is *probable* that S. Tst it is probable that S is out of place, inept, in the situation where we can make tstST, and, I think, con-versely. It is not our business here to discuss probability: but is worth observing that the phrases 'It is true that' and 'It is probable that' are in the same line of business,[26] and in so far incompatibles.

7. In a recent article in *Analysis* Mr. Straw-son has propounded a view of truth which it will be clear I do not accept. He rejects the 'se-mantic' account of truth on the perfectly correct ground that the phrase 'is true' is not used in talking about *sentences,* supporting this with an ingenious hypothesis as to how meaning may have come to be confused with truth: but this will not suffice to show what he wants—that 'is true' is not used in talking about (or that 'truth is not a property of') *anything.* For it *is* used in talking about *statements* (which in his article he does not distinguish clearly from sentences). Further, he supports the 'logical superfluity' view to this extent, that he agrees that to say that ST is not to make any further assertion at all, beyond the assertion that S: but he dis-agrees with it in so far as he thinks that to say that ST *is* to *do* something more than just to assert that S—it is namely to *confirm* or to *grant* (or something of that kind) the assertion, made or taken as made already, that S. It will be clear that and why I do not accept the first part of this: but what of the second part? I agree that to say that ST 'is' very often, and according to the all-important linguistic occa-sion, to confirm tstS or to grant it or what not; but this cannot show that to say that ST is not also and at the same time to make an assertion about tstS. To say that I believe you 'is' on oc-casion to accept your statement; but it is also to make an assertion, which is not made by the strictly performatory utterance 'I accept your statement'. It is common for quite ordinary statements to have a performatory 'aspect': to say that you are a cuckold may be to insult you, but it is also and at the same time to make a statement which is true or false. Mr. Strawson, moreover, seems to confine himself to the case where I *say* 'Your statement is true' or some-thing similar—but what of the case where you state that S and I *say* nothing but '*look and see*' that your statement is true? I do not see how this critical case, to which nothing analogous occurs with strictly performatory utterances, could be made to respond to Mr. Strawson's treatment.

One final point: if it is admitted (*if*) that the rather boring yet satisfactory relation between words and world which has here been discussed does genuinely occur, why should the phrase 'is true' not be our way of describing it? And if it is not, what else is?

NOTES

1. It is sufficiently obvious that 'truth' is substantive, 'true' an adjective and 'of' in 'true of' a preposition.
2. A likeness is true *to* life, but not true *of* it. A *word* picture can be true, just because it is *not* a picture.
3. Predicates applicable also to 'arguments', which we likewise do not say are true, but, for example, valid.
4. Peirce made a beginning by pointing out that there are two (or three) different senses of the word 'word', and adumbrated a technique ('counting' words) for deciding what is a 'different sense'. But his two senses are not well defined, and there are many more—the 'vocable' sense, the philologist's sense in which 'grammar' is the same word as 'glamour', the textual critic's sense in which the 'the' in 1.254 has been written twice, and so on. With all his 66 division of signs, Peirce does not, I believe, distinguish between a sentence and a statement.
5. 'Historic' does not, of course, mean that we cannot speak of future or possible statements. A 'certain' speaker need not be any definite speaker. 'Utterance' need not be public utterance—the audience may be the speaker himself.
6. 'The same' does not always mean the same. In fact it has no meaning in the way that an 'ordinary' word like 'red' or 'horse' has a meaning: it is a (the typical) device for establishing and distinguishing the meanings of ordinary words. Like 'real', it is part of our apparatus *in* words for fixing and adjusting the semantics *of* words.
7. Inverted commas show that the words, though uttered (in writing), are not to be taken as a statement by the utterer. This covers two possible cases, (i) where what is to be discussed is the sentence, (ii) where what is to be discussed is a statement made elsewhere in the words 'quoted'. Only in case (i) is it correct to say simply that the token is doing duty for the type (and even here it is quite incorrect to say that 'The cat is on the mat' is the *name* of an English sentence—though possibly *The Cat is on the Mat* might be the title of a novel, or a bull might be known as *Catta est in matta*). Only in case (ii) is there something true or false, *viz.* (not the quotation but) the statement made in the words quoted.
8. Both sets of conventions may be included together under 'semantics'. But they differ greatly.
9. 'Is of a type with which' means 'is sufficiently like those standard states of affairs with which'. Thus, for a statement to be true one state of affairs must be *like* certain others, which is a natural relation, but also *sufficiently* like to merit the same 'description', which is no longer a purely natural relation. To say 'This is red' is not the same as to say 'This is like those', nor even as to say 'This is like those which were called red'. That things are *similar,* or even 'exactly' similar, I may literally see but that they are the *same* I cannot literally see—in calling them the same colour a convention is involved additional to the conventional choice of the name to be given to the colour which they are said to be.
10. The trouble is that sentences contain words or verbal devices to serve both descriptive and demonstrative purposes (not to mention other purposes), often both at once. In philosophy we mistake the descriptive for the demonstrative (theory of universals) or the demonstrative for the descriptive (theory of monads). A sentence as normally distinguished from a mere word or phrase is characterized by its containing a minimum of verbal demonstrative devices (Aristotle's 'reference to time'); but many demonstrative conventions are non-verbal (pointing, &c.), and using these we can make a statement in a single word which is not a 'sentence'. Thus, 'languages' like that of (traffic, &c.) *signs* use quite distinct media for their descriptive and demonstrative elements (the sign on the post, the site of the post). And however many verbal demonstrative devices we use as auxiliaries, there must *always* be a non-verbal *origin* for these co-ordinates, which is the point of utterance of the statement.
11. I use the following *abbreviations:*

    S for the cat is on the mat.
    ST for it is true that the cat is on the mat.
    tst for the statement that.

    I take tstS as my example throughout and not, say, tst Julius Casear was bald or tst all mules are sterile, because these latter are apt in their different ways to make us overlook the distinction between sentence and statement: we have, apparently, in the one case a sentence capable of being used to refer to only one historic situation, in the other a statement without reference to at least (or to any particular) one).

    If space permitted other types of statement (existential, general, hypothetical, &c.) should be dealt with: these raise problems rather of meaning than of truth, though I feel uneasiness about hypotheticals.
12. If this is what was meant by '"It is raining" is true if and only if it is raining', so far so good.
13. It takes two to make a truth. Hence (obviously) there can be no criterion of truth in the sense of some feature detectable in the statement itself which will reveal whether it is true or false. Hence, too, a statement cannot without absurdity refer to itself.
14. 'It is true that S' and 'It is a fact that S' are applicable in the same circumstances; the cap fits when there is a head it fits. Other words can fill the same role as 'fact': we say, e.g. 'The situation is that S'.
15. We could use 'nuts' even now as a code-word: but a code, as a transformation of a language, is distinguished from a language, and a code-word dispatched is not (called) 'true'.
16. Berkeley confuses these two. There will not be books in the running brooks until the dawn of hydro-semantics.
17. A statement may refer to 'itself' in the sense, for example, of the sentence used or the utterance uttered in making it ('statement' is not exempt from all ambiguity). But paradox does result if a statement purports to refer to itself in a more full-blooded sense, purports, that is, to state that it itself is true, or to state what it itself refers to ('This statement is about Cato').
18. And 'by implication' tstST asserts something about the making of a statement which tstS certainly does not assert.
19. This is not quite fair: there are many legal and personal reasons for holding two trials—which, however, do not

affect the point that the issue being tried is not the same.

20. Not *quite* correct, because tstST is only in place at all when tstS is envisaged as made and has been verified.

21. *Unum, verum, bonum*—the old favourites deserve their celebrity. There *is* something odd about each of them. Theoretical theology is a form of onomatolatry.

22. The following sets of logical axioms are, as Aristotle (though not his successors) makes them, quite distinct:

   (a) No statement can be both true and false.
      No statement can be neither true nor false.
   (b) Of two contradictory statements—
      Both cannot be true.
      Both cannot be false.

The second set demands a definition of contradictories, and is usually joined with unconscious postulate that for every statement there is one and only one other statement such that the pair are contradictories. It is doubtful how far any language does or must contain contradictories, however defined, such as to satisfy both this postulate and the set of axioms *(b)*.

Those of the so-called 'logical paradoxes' (hardly a genuine class) which concern 'true' and 'false' are *not* to be reduced to cases of self-contradiction, any more than 'S but I do not believe it' is. A statement to the effect that it is itself true is every bit as absurd as one to the effect that it is itself false. There are *other* types of sentence which offend against the fundamental conditions of all communication in ways *distinct from* the way in which 'This is red and is not red' offends—e.g.

'This does (I do) not exist', or equally absurd 'This exists (I exist)'. There are more deadly sins than one; nor does the way to salvation lie through any hierarchy.

23. To be false is (not, of course, to correspond to a non-fact, but) to mis-correspond with a fact. Some have not seen how, then, since the statement which is false does not describe the fact with which it mis-corresponds (but mis-describes it), we know which fact to compare it with: this was because they thought of all linguistic conventions as descriptive—but it is the demonstrative conventions which fix which situation it is to which the statement refers. No statement can state what it itself refers to.

24. Here there is much sense in 'coherence' (and pragmatist) theories of truth, despite their failure to appreciate the trite but central point that truth is a matter of the relation between words and world, and despite their wrong-headed *Gleichschaltung* of all varieties of statemental failure under the lone head of 'partly true' (thereafter wrongly equated with 'part of the truth'). 'Correspondence' theorists too often talk as one would who held that every map is either accurate or inaccurate; that accuracy is a single and the sole virtue of a map; that every country can have but one accurate map; that a map on a larger scale or showing different features must be a map of a different country; and so on.

25. Though it is not yet in place to call it either. For the same reason, one cannot lie or tell the truth about the future.

26. Compare the odd behaviours of 'was' and 'will be' when attached to 'true' and to 'probable'.

Brand Blanshard
The Nature of Truth

1. It has been contended in the last chapter that coherence is in the end our sole criterion of truth. We have now to face the question whether it also gives us the nature of truth. We should be clear at the beginning that these are different questions, and that one may reject coherence as the definition of truth while accepting it as the test. It is conceivable that one thing should be an accurate index of another and still be extremely different from it. There have been philosophers who held that pleasure was an accurate gauge of the amount of good in experience, but that to confuse good with pleasure was a gross blunder. There have been a great

''The Nature of Truth'' is reprinted from Brand Blanshard's *The Nature of Thought* (1939), pgs. 253–261, by permission of Unwin Hyman Limited. Throughout his writings, **Brand Blanshard** (b. 1892) maintains a rationalistic line of reasoning inspired by the idealist tradition of the late-nineteenth and early-twentieth centuries.

many philosophers who held that for every change in consciousness there was a change in the nervous system and that the two corresponded so closely that if we knew the laws connecting them we could infallibly predict one from the other; yet it takes all the hardihood of a behaviourist to say that the two are the same. Similarly it has been held that though coherence supplies an infallible measure of truth, it would be a very grave mistake to identify it with truth.

2. The view that truth *is* coherence rests on a theory of the relation of thought to reality, and since this is the central problem of the theory of knowledge, to begin one's discussion by assuming the answer to it or by trying to make one out of whole cloth would be somewhat ridiculous. But as this was our main problem in the long discussions of Book II, we may be pardoned here for brevity. First we shall state in *résumé* the relation of thought to reality that we were there driven to accept, and sketch the theory of truth implicit in it. We shall then take up one by one the objections to this theory and ask if they can pass muster.

To think is to seek understanding. And to seek understanding is an activity of mind that is marked off from all other activities by a highly distinctive aim. This aim, as we saw in our chapter on the general nature of understanding, is to achieve systematic vision, so to apprehend what is now unknown to us as to relate it, and relate it necessarily, to what we know already. We think to solve problems; and our method of solving problems is to build a bridge of intelligible relation from the continent of our knowledge to the island we wish to include in it. Sometimes this bridge is causal, as when we try to explain a disease; sometimes teleological, as when we try to fathom the move of an opponent over the chess board; sometimes geometrical, as in Euclid. But it is always systematic; thought in its very nature is the attempt to bring something unknown or imperfectly known into a subsystem of knowledge, and thus also into that larger system that forms the world of accepted beliefs. That is what explanation is. *Why* is it that thought desires this ordered vision? Why

should such a vision give satisfaction when it comes: To these questions there is no answer, and if there were, it would be an answer only because it had succeeded in supplying the characteristic satisfaction to this unique desire.

But may it not be that what satisfies thought fails to conform to the real world? Where is the guarantee that when I have brought my ideas into the form my ideal requires, they should be *true?* Here we come round again to the tortured problem of Book II. In our long struggle with the relation of thought to reality we saw that if thought and things are conceived as related only externally, then knowledge is luck; there is no necessity whatever that what satisfies intelligence should coincide with what really is. It may do so, or it may not; on the principle that there are many misses to one bull's-eye, it more probably does not. But if we get rid of the misleading analogies through which this relation has been conceived, of copy and original, stimulus and organism, lantern and screen, and go to thought itself with the question what reference to an object means, we get a different and more hopeful answer. To think of a thing is to get that thing itself in some degree within the mind. To think of a color or an emotion is to have that within us which if it *were developed and completed,* would identify itself with the object. In short, if we accept its own report, thought is related to reality as the partial to the perfect fulfillment of a purpose. The more adequate its grasp the more nearly does it approximate, the more fully does it realize in itself, the nature and relations of its objects.

3. Thought thus appears to have two ends, one immanent, one transcendent. On the one hand it seeks fulfillment in a special kind of satisfaction, the satisfaction of systematic vision. On the other hand it seeks fulfillment in its object. Now it was the chief contention of our second book that these ends are one. Indeed unless they are accepted as one, we could see no alternative to scepticism. If the pursuit of thought's own ideal were merely an elaborate self-indulgence that brought us no nearer to reality, or if the apprehension of reality did not lie in the line of thought's interest, or still more if

both of these held at once, the hope of knowledge would be vain. Of course it may really be vain. If anyone cares to doubt whether the framework of human logic has any bearing on the nature of things, he may be silenced perhaps, but he cannot be conclusively answered. One may point out to him that the doubt itself is framed in accordance with that logic, but he can reply that thus we are taking advantage of his logico-centric predicament; further, that any argument we can offer accords equally well with his hypothesis and with ours, with the view that we are merely flies caught in a logical net and the view that knowledge reveals reality. And what accords equally well with both hypotheses does not support either to the exclusion of the other. But while such doubt is beyond reach by argument, neither is there anything in its favor. It is a mere suspicion which is, and by its nature must remain, without any positive ground; and as such it can hardly be discussed. Such suspicions aside, we can throw into the scale for our theory the impressive fact of the advance of knowledge. It has been the steadfast assumption of science whenever it came to an unsolved problem that there was a key to it to be found, that if things happened thus rather than otherwise they did so for a cause or reason, and that if this were not forthcoming it was never because it was lacking, but always because of a passing blindness in ourselves. Reflection has assumed that pursuit of its own immanent end is not only satisfying but revealing, that so far as the immanent end is achieved we are making progress toward the transcendent end as well. Indeed, that these ends coincide is the assumption of every act of thinking whatever. To think is to raise a question; to raise a question is to seek an explanation; to seek an explanation is to assume that one may be had; so to assume is to take for granted that nature in that region is intelligible. Certainly the story of advancing knowledge unwinds as if self-realization in thought meant also a coming nearer to reality.

4. That these processes are really one is the metaphysical base on which our belief in coherence is founded. If one admits that the pursuit of a coherent system has actually carried us to what everyone would agree to call knowledge, why not take this ideal as a guide that will conduct us farther? What better key can one ask to the structure of the real? Our own conviction is that we should take this immanent end of thought in all seriousness as the clue to the nature of things. We admit that it may prove deceptive, that somewhere thought may end its pilgrimage in frustration and futility before some blank wall of the unintelligible. There are even those who evince their superior insight by taking this as a foregone conclusion and regarding the faith that the real is rational as the wishful thinking of the "tender-minded." Their attitude appears to us a compound made up of one part timidity, in the form of a refusal to hope lest they be disillusioned; one part muddled persuasion that to be sceptical is to be sophisticated; one part honest dullness in failing to estimate rightly the weight of the combined postulate and success of knowledge; one part genuine insight into the possibility of surds in nature. But whatever its motives, it is a view that goes less well with the evidence than the opposite and brighter view. That view is that reality is a system, completely ordered and fully intelligible, with which thought in its advance is more and more identifying itself. We may look at the growth of knowledge, individual or social, either as an attempt by our own minds to return to union with things as they are in their ordered wholeness, or the affirmation through our minds of the ordered whole itself. And if we take this view, our notion of truth is marked out for us. Truth is the approximation of thought to reality. It is thought on its way home. Its measure is the distance thought has travelled, under guidance of its inner compass, toward that intelligible system which unites its ultimate object with its ultimate end. Hence at any given time the degree of truth in our experience as a whole is the degree of system it has achieved. The degree of truth of a particular proposition is to be judged in the first instance by its coherence with experience as a whole, ultimately by its coherence with that further whole, all-comprehensive and fully articulated, in which thought can come to rest.

5. But it is time we defined more explicitly what coherence means. To be sure, no fully satisfactory definition can be given; and as Dr. Ewing says, "it is wrong to tie down the advocates of the coherence theory to a precise definition. What they are doing is to describe an ideal that has never yet been completely clarified but is none the less immanent in all our thinking."[1] Certainly this ideal goes far beyond mere consistency. Fully coherent knowledge would be knowledge in which every judgment entailed, and was entailed by, the rest of the system. Probably we never find in fact a system where there is so much of interdependence. What it means may be clearer if we take a number of familiar systems and arrange them in a series tending to such coherence as a limit. At the bottom would be a junk-heap, where we could know every item but one and still be without any clue as to what that remaining item was. Above this would come a stone-pile, for here you could at least infer that what you would find next would be a stone. A machine would be higher again, since from the remaining parts one could deduce not only the general character of a missing part, but also its special form and function. This is a high degree of coherence, but it is very far short of the highest. You could remove the engine from a motorcar while leaving the other parts intact, and replace it with any one of thousands of other engines, but the thought of such an interchange among human heads or hearts shows at once that the interdependence in a machine is far below that of the body. Do we find then in organic bodies the highest conceivable coherence? Clearly not. Though a human hand, as Aristotle said, would hardly be a hand when detached from the body, still it would be something definite enough; and we can conceive systems, in which even this something would be gone. Abstract a number from the number series, and it would be a mere unrecognizable *x;* similarly, the very thought of a straight line involves the thought of the Euclidean space in which it falls. It is perhaps in such systems as Euclidean geometry that we get the most perfect examples of coherence that have been constructed. If any proposition were

lacking, it could be supplied from the rest; if any were altered, the repercussions would be felt through the length and breadth of the system. Yet even such a system as this falls short of an ideal system. Its postulates are unproved; they are independent of each other, in the sense that none of them could be derived from any other or even from all the others together; its clear necessity is bought by an abstractness so extreme as to have left out nearly everything that belongs to the character of actual things. A completely satisfactory system would have none of these defects. No proposition would be arbitrary, every proposition would be entailed by the others jointly and even singly,[2] no proposition would stand outside the system. The integration would be so complete that no part could be seen for what it was without seeing its relation to the whole, and the whole itself could be understood only through the contribution of every part.

6. It may be granted at once that in common life we are satisfied with far less than this. We accept the demonstrations of the geometer as complete, and do not think of reproaching him because he begins with postulates and leaves us at the end with a system that is a skeleton at the best. In physics, in biology, above all in the social sciences, we are satisfied with less still. We test judgments by the amount of coherence which in that particular subject-matter it seems reasonable to expect. We apply, perhaps unconsciously, the advice of Aristotle, and refrain from asking demonstration in the physical sciences, while in mathematics we refuse to accept less. And such facts may be thought to show that we make no actual use of the ideal standard just described. But however much this standard may be relaxed within the limits of a particular science, its influence is evident in the grading of the sciences generally. It is precisely in those sciences that approach most nearly to system as here defined that we achieve the greatest certainty, and precisely in those that are most remote from such system that our doubt is greatest whether we have achieved scientific truth at all. Our immediate exactions shift with the subject-matter; our ultimate standard is unvarying.

7. Now if we accept coherence as the test of truth, does that commit us to any conclusions about the *nature* of truth or reality? I think it does, though more clearly about reality than about truth. It is past belief that the fidelity of our thought to reality should be rightly measured by coherence if reality itself were not coherent. To say that the nature of things may be *in*coherent, but we shall approach the truth about it precisely so far as our thoughts become coherent, sounds very much like nonsense. And providing we retained coherence as the test, it would still be nonsense even if truth were conceived as correspondence. On this supposition we should have truth when, our thought having achieved coherence, the correspondence was complete between that thought and its object. But complete correspondence between a coherent thought and an incoherent object seems meaningless. It is hard to see, then, how anyone could consistently take coherence as the test of truth unless he took it also as a character of reality.

8. Does acceptance of coherence as a test commit us not only to a view about the structure of reality but also to a view about the nature of truth? This is a more difficult question. As we saw at the beginning of the chapter, there have been some highly reputable philosophers who have held that the answer to "What is the test of truth?" is "Coherence," while the answer to "What is the nature or meaning of truth?" is "Correspondence." These questions are plainly distinct. Nor does there seem to be any direct path from the acceptance of coherence as the test of truth to its acceptance as the nature of truth. Nevertheless there is an indirect path. If we accept coherence as our test, we must use it everywhere. We must therefore use it to test the suggestion that truth *is* other than coherence. But if we do, we shall find that we must reject the suggestion as leading to *in*coherence. Coherence is a pertinacious concept and, like the well-known camel, if one lets it get its nose under the edge of the tent, it will shortly walk off with the whole.

Suppose that, accepting coherence as the test, one rejects it as the nature of truth in favour of some alternative; and let us assume, for example, that this alternative is correspondence. This, we have said, is incoherent; why? Because if one holds that truth is correspondence, one cannot intelligibly hold either that it is tested by coherence or that there is any dependable test at all. Consider the first point. Suppose that we construe experience into the most coherent picture possible, remembering that among the elements included will be such secondary qualities as colors, odors, and sounds. Would the mere fact that such elements as these are coherently arranged prove that anything precisely corresponding to them exists "out there"? I cannot see that it would, even if we knew that the two arrangements had closely corresponding patterns. If on one side you have a series of elements a,b,c, . . . , and on the other a series of elements α, β, γ . . . , arranged in patterns that correspond, you have no proof as yet that the *natures* of these elements correspond. It is therefore impossible to argue from a high degree of coherence within experience to its correspondence in the same degree with anything outside. And this difficulty is typical. If you place the nature of truth in one sort of character and its test in something quite different, you are pretty certain, sooner or later, to find the two falling apart. In the end, the only test of truth that is not misleading is the special nature or character that is itself constitutive of truth.

Feeling that this is so, the adherents of correspondence sometimes insist that correspondence shall be its own test. But then the second difficulty arises. If truth does consist in correspondence, no test can be sufficient. For in order to know that the experience corresponds to fact, we must be able to get at that fact, unadulterated with idea, and compare the two sides with each other. And we have seen in the last chapter that such fact is not accessible. When we try to lay hold of it, what we find in our hands is a judgment which is obviously not itself the indubitable fact we are seeking, and which must be checked by some fact beyond it. To this process there is no end. And even if we did get at the fact directly, rather than through the veil of our ideas, that would be no less fatal to correspondence. This direct seizure of fact presumably gives us truth, but since that truth no longer consists in correspondence of idea with fact, the main theory has been abandoned. In short, if we can know fact only through the medium of our own ideas, the original forever eludes us; if we can get at the facts directly, we have knowledge whose truth is not correspondence. The theory is forced to choose between scepticism and self-contradiction.

Thus the attempt to combine coherence as the test of truth with correspondence as the nature of truth will not pass muster by its own test. The result is *in*coherence. We believe than an application of the test to other theories of truth would lead to a like result. The argument is: assume coherence as the test, and you will be driven by the incoherence of your alternatives to the conclusion that it is also the nature of truth. . . .

NOTES

1. *Idealism*, p. 231.
2. Coherence can be defined without this point, which, as Dr. Ewing remarks (*Idealism*, 231), makes the case harder to establish. In no mathematical system, for example, would anyone dream of trying to deduce all the other propositions from any proposition taken singly. But when we are describing an ideal, such a fact is not decisive, and I follow Joachim in holding that in a perfectly coherent system every proposition would entail all others, if only for the reason that its meaning could never be fully understood without apprehension of the system in its entirety.

CHARLES SANDERS PEIRCE
Truth

I. TRUTH AS CORRESPONDENCE

A *state of things* is an abstract constituent part of reality, of such a nature that a proposition is needed to represent it. There is but one *individual*, or completely determinate, state of things, namely, the all of reality. A *fact* is so highly a prescisively abstract state of things, that it can be wholly represented in a simple proposition, and the term, "simple," here, has no absolute meaning, but is merely a comparative expression.

A *mathematical form* of a state of things is such a representation of that state of things as represents only the samenesses and diversities involved in that state of things, without definitely qualifying the subjects of the samenesses and diversities. It represents not necessarily all of these; but if it does represent all, it is the *complete* mathematical form. Every mathematical form of a state of things is the complete mathematical form of *some* state of things. The complete mathematical form of any state of things, real or fictitious, represents every ingredient of that state of things except the qualities of feeling connected with it. It represents whatever importance or significance those qualities may have; but the qualities themselves it does not represent.

Before any conclusion shall be made to rest upon this almost self-evident proposition, a way of setting it quite beyond doubt shall be explained. As at present enunciated, it is merely put forward as a private opinion of the writer's which will serve to explain the great interest he attaches to the emphatic dualism of the three normative sciences, which may be regarded as being the sciences of the conditions of truth and falsity, of wise and foolish conduct, of attractive and repulsive ideas. Should the reader become convinced that the importance of everything resides entirely in its mathematical form, he, too, will come to regard this dualism as worthy of close attention. Meantime that it exists, and is more marked in these sciences than in any others, is an indisputable fact. To what is this circumstance to be attributed? Skipping the easy reasoning by which it can be shown that this dualism cannot be due to any peculiar quality of feeling that may be connected with these sciences, nor to any intellectual peculiarity of them, which negative propositions will become obtrusively plain at a later stage of our reasoning, we may turn at once to the affirmative reason for attributing the dualism to the reference of the normative sciences to action. It is curious how this reason seems to seek to escape detection, by putting forward an apparent indication that it is not there. For it is evident that it is in esthetics that we ought to seek for the deepest characteristics of normative science, since esthetics, in dealing with the very ideal itself whose mere materialization engrosses the attention of practics and of logic, must contain the heart, soul, and spirit of normative science. But the dualism which is so much marked in the True and False, logic's object of study, and in the Useful and Pernicious of the confessional of Practics, is softened almost to obliteration in esthetics. Nevertheless, it would be the height of stupidity to say that esthetics knows no good and bad. It must never be forgotten that evil of any kind is none the less bad though *the occurrence of it* be a good. Because in every case the ultimate in some measure abrogates, and ought

to abrogate, the penultimate, it does not follow that the penultimate ought not to have abrogated the antepenultimate in due measure. On the contrary, just the opposite follows.

Esthetic good and evil are closely akin to pleasure and pain. They are what would be pleasure or pain to the fully developed superman. What, then, are pleasure and pain? The question has been sufficiently discussed, and the answer ought by this time to be ready. They are secondary feelings or generalizations of such feelings; that is, of feelings attaching themselves to, and excited by, other feelings. A toothache is painful. It is not pain, but pain *accompanies* it; and if you choose to say that pain is an ingredient of it, that is not far wrong. However, the quality of the feeling of toothache is a simple, positive feeling, distinct from pain; though pain accompanies it. To use the old consecrated terms, pleasure is the feeling that a feeling is "sympathetical," pain that it is "antipathetical." The feeling of pain is a symptom of a feeling which repels us; the feeling of pleasure is the symptom of an attractive feeling. Attraction and repulsion are kinds of action. Feelings are pleasurable or painful according to the kind of action which they stimulate. In general, the good is the attractive—not to everybody, but to the sufficiently matured agent; and the evil is the repulsive to the same. Mr. Ferdinand C. S. Schiller[1] informs us that he and James have made up their minds that the true is simply the satisfactory. No doubt; but to say "satisfactory" is not to complete any predicate whatever. Satisfactory to what end?

That truth is the correspondence of a representation with its object is, as Kant[2] says, merely the nominal definition of it. Truth belongs exclusively to propositions. A proposition has a subject (or set of subjects) and a predicate. The subject is a sign; the predicate is a sign; and the proposition is a sign that the predicate is a sign of that of which the subject is a sign. If it be so, it is true. But what does this correspondence or reference of the sign, to its object, consist in? The pragmaticist answers this question as follows. Suppose, he says, that the angel Gabriel were to descend and communicate to me the answer to this riddle from the breast of omniscience. Is this supposable; or does it involve an essential absurdity to suppose the answer to be brought to human intelligence? In the latter case, "truth," in this sense, is a useless word, which never can express a human thought. It is real, if you will; it belongs to that universe entirely disconnected from human intelligence which we know as the world of utter nonsense. Having no use for this meaning of the word "truth," we had better use the word in another sense presently to be described. But if, on the other hand, it be conceivable that the secret should be disclosed to human intelligence, it will be something that thought can compass. Now thought is of the nature of a sign. In that case, then, if we can find out the right method of thinking and can follow it out—the right method of transforming signs—then truth can be nothing more nor less than the last result to which the following out of this method would ultimately carry us. In that case, that to which the representation should conform, is itself something in the nature of a representation, or sign—something noumenal, intelligible, conceivable, and utterly unlike a thing-in-itself.

Truth is the conformity of a representamen to its object, *its* object, ITS object, mind you. The International Dictionary at the writer's elbow, the Century Dictionary which he daily studies, the Standard which he would be glad sometimes to consult, all contain the word *yes;* but that word is not true simply because he is going to ask on this eighth of January 1906, in Pike County, Pennsylvania, whether it is snowing. There must be an action of the object upon the sign to render the latter true. Without that, the object is not the representamen's object. If a colonel hands a paper to an orderly and says, "You will go immediately and deliver this to Captain Hanno," and if the orderly does so, we do not say the colonel told the truth; we say the orderly was obedient, since it was not the orderly's conduct which determined the colonel to say what he did, but the colonel's speech which determined the orderly's action. Here is a view of the writer's house: what makes that house to be the object of the view? Surely not the similarity of appearance. There are ten thousand others in the country just like it. No, but the photographer set up the film in such a way that according to the laws of optics, the film was forced to receive an image of this house. What the sign virtually has to do in order to indicate its object—and make it its—all it has to do is just to seize its interpreter's eyes and forcibly turn them upon the object meant: it is what a knock at the door does, or an alarm or other bell, or a whistle, a cannonshot, etc. It is pure physiological compulsion; nothing else.

So, then, a sign, in order to fulfill its office, to actualize its potency, must be compelled by its object. This is evidently the reason of the dichotomy of the true and the false. For it takes two to make a quarrel, and a compulsion involves as large a dose of quarrel as is requisite to make it quite impossible that there should be compulsion without resistance.

II. TRUTH AND SATISFACTION

It appears that there are certain mummified pedants who have never waked to the truth that the act of knowing a real object alters it. They are curious specimens of humanity, and as I am one of them, it may be amusing to see how I think. It seems that our oblivion to this truth is due to our not having made the acquaintance of a new analysis that the True is simply that in cognition which is Satisfactory. As to this doctrine, if it is meant that True and Satisfactory are synonyms, it strikes me that it is not so much a doctrine of philosophy as it is a new contribution to English lexicography.

But it seems plain that the formula does express a doctrine of philosophy, although quite vaguely; so that the assertion does not concern two words of our language but, attaching some other *meaning* to the True, makes it to be *coextensive with* the Satisfactory in cognition.

In that case, it is indispensable to say what is meant by the True: until this is done the statement has no meaning. I suppose that by the

True is meant that at which inquiry aims.

It is equally indispensable to ascertain what is meant by Satisfactory; but this is by no means so easy. Whatever be meant, however, if the doctrine is true at all, it must be necessarily true. For it is the very object, conceived in entertaining the purpose of the inquiry, that is asserted to have the character of satisfactoriness.

Is the Satisfactory meant to be whatever excites a certain peculiar feeling of satisfaction? In that case, the doctrine is simply hedonism in so far as it affects the field of cognition. For when hedonists talk of ''pleasure,'' they do not mean what is so-called in ordinary speech, but what excites a feeling of satisfaction.

But to say that an action or the result of an action is Satisfactory is simply to say that it is congruous to the aim of that action. Consequently, the aim must be determined before it can be determined, either in thought or in fact, to be satisfactory. An action that had no other aim than to be congruous to its aim would have no aim at all, and would not be a deliberate action.

The hedonists do not offer their doctrine as an induction from experience but insist that, *in the nature of things,* that is, from the very essence of the conceptions, an action can have no other aim than ''pleasure.'' Now it is *conceivable* that an action should be disconnected from every other in its aim. Such an action, then, according to hedonistic doctrine, can have no other aim than that of satisfying its own aim, which is absurd.

But if the hedonist replies that his position does not relate to satisfaction, but to a feeling that only arises upon satisfaction, the rejoinder will be that feeling is incomprehensible; so that no necessary truth can be discovered about it. But as a matter of observation we do, now and then, meet with persons who very largely behave with a view of experiencing this or that feeling. These people, however, are exceptional, and are wretched beings sharply marked off from the mass of busy and happy mankind.

It is, however, no doubt true that men act, especially in the action of inquiry, *as if* their sole purpose were to produce a certain state of feeling, in the sense that when that state of feeling is attained, there is no further effort. It was upon that proposition that I originally based pragmaticism, laying it down in the article that in November 1877 prepared the ground for my argument for the pragmaticistic doctrine (*Pop. Sci. Monthly* for January, 1878). In the case of inquiry, I called that state of feeling ''firm belief,'' and said, ''As soon as a firm belief is reached we are entirely satisfied, whether the belief be true or false,'' and went on to show how the action of experience consequently was to create the conception of real truth. Early in 1880, in the opening paragraphs of my memoir in Vol. III of the *American Journal of Mathematics,* I referred the matter to the fundamental properties of protoplasm, showing that purposive action must be action *virtually* directed toward the removal of stimulation.

My paper of November 1877, setting out from the proposition that the agitation of a question ceases when satisfaction is attained with the settlement of belief, and then only, goes on to consider how the conception of truth gradually develops from that principle under the action of experience; beginning with willful belief, or self-mendacity, the most degraded of all intellectual conditions; thence rising to the imposition of beliefs by the authority of organized society; then to the idea of a settlement of opinion as the result of a fermentation of ideas; and finally reaching the idea of truth as overwhelmingly forced upon the mind in experience as the effect of an independent reality.

III DEFINITIONS OF TRUTH

Logical. (1) Truth is a character which attaches to an abstract proposition, such as a person might utter. It essentially depends upon that proposition's not professing to be exactly true. But we hope that in the progress of science its error will indefinitely diminish, just as the error of 3.14159, the value given for π, will indefinitely diminish as the calculation is carried to more and more places of decimals. What we call π is an ideal limit to which no numerical expression can be perfectly true. If our hope is vain; if in respect to some question—say that of the freedom of the will—no matter how long the discussion goes on, no matter how scientific our methods may become, there never will be a time when we can fully satisfy ourselves either that the question has no meaning, or that one answer or the other explains the facts, then in regard to that question there certainly is no *truth*. But whether or not there would be perhaps any *reality* is a question for the metaphysician, not the logician. Even if the metaphysician decides that where there is no truth there is no reality, still the distinction between the character of truth and the character of reality is plain and definable. Truth is that concordance of an abstract statement with the ideal limit towards which endless investigation would tend to bring scientific belief, which concordance the abstract statement may possess by virtue of the confession of its inaccuracy and one-sidedness, and this confession is an essential ingredient of truth. A further explanation of what this concordance consists in will be given below. Reality is that mode of being by virtue of which the real thing is as it is, irrespectively of what any mind or any definite collection of minds may represent it to be. The truth of the proposition that Caesar crossed the Rubicon consists in the fact that the further we push our archaeological and other studies, the more strongly will that conclusion force itself on our minds forever—or would do so, if study were to go on forever. An idealist metaphysician may hold that therein also lies the whole *reality* behind the proposition; for though men may for a time persuade themselves that Caesar did *not* cross the Rubicon, and may contrive to render this belief universal for any number of generations, yet ultimately research—if it be persisted in—must bring back the contrary belief. But in holding that doctrine, the idealist necessarily draws the distinction between truth and reality.

In the above we have considered positive scientific truth. But the same definitions equally hold in the normative sciences. If a moralist describes an ideal as the *summum bonum*, in the first place, the perfect truth of his statement requires that it should involve the confession that the perfect doctrine can neither be stated nor conceived. If, with that allowance, the future development of man's moral nature will only lead to a firmer satisfaction with the described ideal, the doctrine is true. A metaphysician may hold that the fact that the ideal thus forces itself upon the mind, so that minds in their development cannot fail to come to accept it, argues that the ideal is *real;* he may even hold that that fact (if it be one) constitutes a *reality*. But the two ideas, *truth* and *reality,* are distinguished here by the same characters given in the above definitions.

These characters equally apply to pure mathematics. Projective geometry is not pure mathematics, unless it be recognized that whatever is said of rays holds good of every family of curves of which there is one and one only through any two points, and any two of which have a point in common. But even then it is not pure mathematics until for points we put any complete determinations of any two-dimensional continuum. Nor will that be enough. A proposition is not a statement of perfectly pure mathematics until it is devoid of all definite meaning, and comes to this—that a property of a certain icon is pointed out and is declared to belong to anything like it, of which instances are given. The perfect truth cannot be stated, except in the sense that it confesses its imperfection. The pure mathematician deals exclusively with hypotheses. Whether or not there is any corresponding real thing, he does not care. His hypotheses are creatures of his own imagination; but he discovers in them relations which surprise him sometimes. A metaphysician may hold that this very forcing upon the mathematician's acceptance of propositions for which he was not prepared, proves, or even constitutes, a mode of being independent of the mathematician's thought, and so a *reality*. But whether there is any reality or not, the truth of the pure mathematical proposition is constituted by the impossibility of ever finding a case in which it fails. This, however, is only possible if we confess the impossibility of precisely defining it.

The same definitions hold for the propositions of practical life. A man buys a bay horse, under a warranty that he is sound and free from vice. He brings him home and finds he is dyed, his real colour being undesirable. He complains of false representations; but the seller replies, "I never pretended to state every fact about the horse; what I said was true, so far as it professed to be true." In ordinary life all our statements, it is well understood, are, in the main, rough approximations to what we mean to convey. A tone or gesture is often the most definite part of what is said. Even with regard to perceptual facts, or the immediate judgments we make concerning our single percepts, the same distinction is plain. The percept is the reality. It is not in propositional form. But the most immediate judgment concerning it is abstract. It is therefore essentially unlike the reality, although it must be accepted as true to that reality. Its truth consists in the fact that it is impossible to correct it, and in the fact that it only professes to consider one aspect of the percept.

But even if it were impossible to distinguish between truth and reality, that would not in the least prevent our defining what it is that truth consists in. Truth and falsity are characters confined to propositions. A proposition is a sign which separately indicates its object. Thus, a portrait with the name of the original below it is a proposition. It asserts that if anybody looks at it, he can form a reasonably correct idea of how the original looked. A sign is only a sign *in actu* by virtue of its receiving an interpretation, that is, by virtue of its determining another sign of the same object. This is as true of mental judgments as it is of external signs. To say that a proposition is true is to say that every interpretation of it is true. Two propositions are equivalent when either might have been an interpretant of the other. This equivalence, like others, is by an act of abstraction (in the sense in which forming an abstract noun is abstraction) conceived as identity. And we speak of

believing in a proposition, having in mind an entire collection of equivalent propositions with their partial interpretants. Thus, two persons are said to have the same proposition in mind. The interpretant of a proposition is itself a proposition. Any necessary inference from a proposition is an interpretant of it. When we speak of truth and falsity, we refer to the possibility of the proposition being refuted; and this refutation (roughly speaking) takes place in but one way. Namely, an interpretant of the proposition would, if believed, produce the expectation of a certain description of percept on a certain occasion. The occasion arrives: the percept forced upon us is different. This constitutes the falsity of every proposition of which the disappointing prediction was the interpretant.

Thus, a false proposition is a proposition of which some interpretant represents that, on an occasion which it indicates, a percept will have a certain character, while the immediate perceptual judgment on that occasion is that the percept has not that character. A true proposition is a proposition belief in which would never lead to such disappointment so long as the proposition is not understood otherwise than it was intended.

All the above relates to *complex truth,* or the truth of propositions. This is divided into many varieties, among which may be mentioned *ethical truth,* or the conformity of an assertion to the speaker's or writer's belief, otherwise called *veracity,* and *logical truth,* that is, the concordance of a proposition with reality, in such way as is above defined.

(2) The word *truth* has also had great importance in philosophy in widely different senses, in which it is distinguished as *simple truth,* which is that truth which inheres in other subjects than propositions.

Plato in the *Cratylus* (385B) maintains that words have truth; and some of the scholastics admitted that an incomplex sign, such as a picture, may have truth.

But *truth* is also used in senses in which it is not an affection of a sign, but of things as things. Such truth is called *transcendental truth.*

The scholastic maxim was Ens est unum, verum, bonum. Among the senses in which transcendental truth was spoken of was that in which it was said that all science has for its object the investigation of *truth,* that is to say, of the real characters of things. It was, in other senses, regarded as a subject of metaphysics exclusively. It is sometimes defined so as to be indistinguishable from reality, or real existence. Another common definition is that truth is the conformity, or conformability, of things to reason. Another definition is that truth is the conformity of things to their essential principles.

(3) *Truth* is also used in logic in a sense in which it inheres only in subjects more complex than propositions. Such is *formal truth,* which belongs to an argumentation which conforms to logical laws.

NOTES

1. Cf. *Studies in Humanism,* p. 83.

2. *Kritik der Reinen Vernunft,* A58, B82.

GILBERT HARMAN
Inference to the Best Explanation[1]

I wish to argue that enumerative induction should not be considered a warranted form of nondeductive inference in its own right.[2] I claim that, in cases where it appears that a warranted inference is an instance of enumerative induction, the inference should be described as a special case of another sort of inference, which I shall call "the inference to the best explanation."

The form of my argument in the first part of this paper is as follows: I argue that even if one accepts enumerative induction as one form of nondeductive inference, one will have to allow for the existence of "the inference to the best explanation." Then I argue that all warranted inferences which may be described as instances of enumerative induction must also be described as instances of the inference to the best explanation.

So, on my view, either (a) enumerative induction is not always warranted or (b) enumerative induction is always warranted but is an uninteresting special case of the more general inference to the best explanation. Whether my view should be expressed as (a) or (b) will depend upon a particular interpretation of "enumerative induction."

In the second part of this paper, I attempt to show how taking the inference to the best explanation (rather than enumerative induction) to be the basic form of nondeductive inference enables one to account for an interesting feature of our use of the word "know." This provides an additional reason for describing our inferences as instances of the inference to the best explanation rather than as instances of enumerative induction.

"Inference To The Best Explanation" is reprinted from the *Philosophical Review,* Vol. LXXIV (1965), by permission of *Philosophical Review* and **Gilbert Harman,** a contemporary American philosopher affiliated with Princeton University, has contributed greatly to the philosophy of language, the theory of reasoning, and epistemology.

I

"The inference to the best explanation" corresponds approximately to what others have called "abduction," "the method of hypothesis," "hypothetic inference," "the method of elimination," "eliminative induction," and "theoretical inference." I prefer my own terminology because I believe that it avoids most of the misleading suggestions of the alternative terminologies.

In making this inference one infers, from the fact that a certain hypothesis would explain the evidence, to the truth of that hypothesis. In general, there will be several hypotheses which might explain the evidence, so one must be able to reject all such alternative hypotheses before one is warranted in making the inference. Thus one infers, from the premise that a given hypothesis would provide a "better" explanation for the evidence than would any other hypothesis, to the conclusion that the given hypothesis is true.

There is, of course, a problem about how one is to judge that one hypothesis is sufficiently better than another hypothesis. Presumably such a judgment will be based on considerations such as which hypothesis is simpler, which is more plausible, which explains more, which is less *ad hoc,* and so forth. I do not wish to deny that there is a problem about explaining the exact nature of these considerations; I will not, however, say anything more about this problem.

Uses of the inference to the best explanation are manifold. When a detective puts the evidence together and decides that it *must* have been the butler, he is reasoning that no other explanation which accounts for all the facts is plausible enough or simple enough to be accepted. When a scientist infers the existence of atoms and subatomic particles, he is inferring the truth of an explanation for various data which he wishes to account for. These seem the obvious cases; but there are many others. When we infer that a witness is telling the truth, our inference goes as follows: (i) we infer that he says what he does because he believes it; (ii) we infer that he believes what he does because he

actually did witness the situation which he describes. That is, our confidence in his testimony is based on our conclusion about the most plausible explanation for that testimony. Our confidence fails if we come to think there is some other possible explanation for his testimony (if, for example, he stands to gain a great deal from our believing him). Or, to take a different sort of example, when we infer from a person's behavior to some fact about his mental experience, we are inferring that the latter fact explains better than some other explanation what he does.

It seems to me that these examples of inference (and, of course, many other similar examples) are easily described as instances of the inference to the best explanation. I do not see, however, how such examples may be described as instances of enumerative induction. It may seem plausible (at least prima facie) that the inference from scattered evidence to the proposition that the butler did it may be described as a complicated use of enumerative induction; but it is difficult to see just how one would go about filling in the details of such an inference. Similar remarks hold for the inference from testimony to the truth of that testimony. But whatever one thinks about these two cases, the inference from experimental data to the theory of subatomic particles certainly does not seem to be describable as an instance of enumerative induction. The same seems to be true for most inferences about other people's mental experiences.

I do not pretend to have a conclusive proof that such inferences cannot be made out to be complicated uses of enumerative induction. But I do think that the burden of proof here shifts to the shoulders of those who would defend induction in this matter, and I am confident that any attempt to account for these inferences as inductions will fail. Therefore, I assert that even if one permits himself the use of enumerative induction, he will still need to avail himself of at least one other form of nondeductive inference.

As I shall now try to show, however, the opposite does not hold. If one permits himself the use of the inference to the best explanation, one will not still need to use enumerative induction (as a separate form of inference). Enumerative induction, as a separate form of nondeductive inference, is superfluous. All cases in which one appears to be using it may also be seen as cases in which one is making an inference to the best explanation.

Enumerative induction is supposed to be a kind of inference that exemplifies the following form. From the fact that all observed A's are B's we may infer that all A's are B's (or we may infer that at least the next A will probably be a B). Now, in practice we always know more about a situation than that all observed A's are B's, and before we make the inference, it is good inductive practice for us to consider the total evidence. Sometimes, in the light of the total evidence, we are warranted in making our induction, at other times not. So we must ask ourselves the following question: under what conditions is one permitted to make an inductive inference?

I think it is fair to say that, if we turn to inductive logic and its logicians for an answer to this question, we shall be disappointed. If, however, we think of the inference as an inference to the best explanation, we can explain when a person is and when he is not warranted in making the inference from "All observed A's are B's" to "All A's are B's." The answer is that one is warranted in making this inference whenever the hypothesis that all A's are B's is

(in the light of all the evidence) a better, simpler, more plausible (and so forth) hypothesis than is the hypothesis, say, that someone is biasing the observed sample in order to make us think that all A's are B's. On the other hand, as soon as the total evidence makes some other, competing hypothesis plausible, one may not infer from the past correlation in the observed sample to a complete correlation in the total population.

The inference from "All observed A's are B's" to "The next observed A will be B" may be handled in the same way. Here, one must compare the hypothesis that the next A will be different from the preceding A's with the hypothesis that the next A will be similar to preceding A's. As long as the hypothesis that the next A will be similar is a better hypothesis in the light of all the evidence, the supposed induction is warranted. But if there is no reason to rule out a change, then the induction is unwarranted.

I conclude that inferences which appear to be applications of enumerative induction are better described as instances of the inference to the best explanation. My argument has been (1) that there are many inferences which cannot be made out to be applications of enumerative induction but (2) that we can account for when it is proper to make inferences which appear to be applications of enumerative induction, if we describe these inferences as instances of the inference to the best explanation.

II

I now wish to give a further reason for describing our inferences as instances of the inference to the best explanation rather than enumerative induction.[3] Describing our inference as enumerative induction disguises the fact that our inference makes use of certain lemmas, whereas, as I show below, describing the inference as one to the best explanation exposes these lemmas. These intermediate lemmas play a part in the analysis of knowledge based on inference. Therefore, if we are to understand such knowledge, we must describe our inference as infer-

ence to the best explanation.

Let me begin by mentioning a fact about the analysis of "know" which is often overlooked.[4] It is now generally acknowledged by epistemologists that, if a person is to know, his belief must be both true and warranted. We shall assume that we are now speaking of a belief which is based on a (warranted) inference.[5] In this case, it is not sufficient for knowledge that the person's final belief be true. If these intermediate propositions are warranted but false, then the person cannot be correctly described as *knowing* the conclusion. I will refer to this necessary condition of knowledge as "the condition that the lemmas be true."

To illustrate this condition, suppose I read on the philosophy department bulletin board that Stuart Hampshire is to read a paper at Princeton tonight. Suppose further that this warrants my believing that Hampshire will read a paper at Princeton tonight. From this belief, we may suppose I infer that Hampshire will read a paper (somewhere) tonight. This belief is also warranted. Now suppose that, unknown to me, tonight's meeting was called off several weeks ago, although no one has thought to remove the announcement from the bulletin board. My belief that Hampshire will read a paper at Princeton tonight is false. It follows that I do not know whether or not Hampshire will read a paper (somewhere) tonight, even if I am right in believing that he will. Even if I am accidentally right (because Hampshire has accepted an invitation to read a paper at N.Y.U.), I do not know that Hampshire will read a paper tonight. The condition that the lemmas be true has not been met in this case.

I will now make use of the condition that the lemmas be true in order to give a new reason for describing the inferences on which belief is based as instances of the inference to the best explanation rather than of enumerative induction. I will take two different sorts of knowledge (knowledge from authority and knowledge of mental experiences of other people) and show how our ordinary judgment of when there is and when there is not knowledge is to be accounted for in terms of our belief that the inference involved must make use of certain lemmas. Then I will argue that the use of these lemmas can be understood only if the inference is in each case described as the inference to the best explanation.

First, consider what lemmas are used in obtaining knowledge from an authority. Let us imagine that the authority in question either is a person who is an expert in his field or is an authoritative reference book. It is obvious that much of our knowledge is based on authority in this sense. When an expert tells us something about a certain subject, or when we read about

the subject, we are often warranted in believing that what we are told or what we read is correct. Now one condition that must be satisfied if our belief is to count as knowledge is that our belief must be true. A second condition is this: what we are told or what we read cannot be there by mistake. That is, the speaker must not have made a slip of the tongue which affects the sense. Our belief must not be based on reading a misprint. Even if the slip of the tongue or the misprint has changed a falsehood into truth, by accident, we still cannot get knowledge from it. This indicates that the inference which we make from testimony to truth must contain as a lemma the proposition that the utterance is there because it is believed and not because of a slip of the tongue or typewriter. Thus our account of this inference must show the role played by such a lemma.

My other example involves knowledge of mental experience gained from observing behavior. Suppose we come to know that another person's hand hurts by seeing how he jerks it away from a hot stove which he has accidentally touched. It is easy to see that our inference here (from behavior to pain) involves as lemma the proposition that the pain is responsible for the sudden withdrawal of the hand. (We do not know the hand hurts, even if we are right about the pain being there, if in fact there is some alternative explanation for the withdrawal.) Therefore, in accounting for the inference here, we will want to explain the role of this lemma in the inference.

My claim is this: if we describe the inferences in the examples as instances of the inference to the best explanation, then we easily see how lemmas such as those described above are an essential part of the inference. On the other hand, if we describe the inferences as instances of enumerative induction,[6] then we obscure the role of such lemmas. When the inferences are described as basically inductive, we are led to think that the lemmas are, in principle, eliminable. They are not so eliminable. If we are to account properly for our use of the word "know," we must remember that these inferences are instances of the inference to the best explanation.

In both examples, the role of the lemmas in our inference is explained only if we remember that we must infer an explanation of the data. In the first example we infer that the best explanation for our reading or hearing what we do is given by the hypothesis that the testimony is the result of expert belief expressed without slip of tongue or typewriter. From this intermediate lemma we infer the truth of the testimony. Again, in making the inference from behavior to pain, we infer the intermediate lemma that the best explanation for the observed behavior is given by the hypothesis that this behavior results from the agent's suddenly being in pain.

If in the first example we think of ourselves as using enumerative induction, then it seems in principle possible to state all the relevant evidence in statements about the correlation between (on the one hand) testimony of a certain type of person about a certain subject matter, where this testimony is given in a certain manner, and (on the other hand) the truth of that testimony. Our inference appears to be completely described by saying that we infer from the correlation between testimony and truth in the past to the correlation in the present case. But, as we have seen, this is not a satisfactory account of the inference which actually does back up our knowledge, since this account cannot explain the essential relevance of whether or not there is a slip of the tongue or a misprint. Similarly, if the inference used in going from behavior to pain is thought of as enumerative induction, it would again seem that getting evidence is in principle just a matter of finding correlations between behavior and pain. But this description leaves out the essential part played by the lemma whereby the inferred mental experience must figure in the explanation for the observed behavior.

If we think of the inferences which back up our knowledge as inferences to the best explanation, then we shall easily understand the role of lemmas in these inferences. If we think of our knowledge as based on enumerative induction (and we forget that induction is a special case of the inference to the best explanation), then we will think that inference is solely a matter of finding correlations which we may project into the future, and we will be at a loss to explain the relevance of the intermediate lemmas. If we are adequately to describe the inferences on which our knowledge rests, we must think of them as instances of the inference to the best explanation.

I have argued that enumerative induction should not be considered a warranted form of inference in its own right. I have used two arguments: (a) we can best account for when it is proper to make inferences which appear to be applications of enumerative induction by describing these inferences as instances of the inference to the best explanation; and (b) we can best account for certain necessary conditions of one's having knowledge (for example, which is knowledge from authority or which is knowledge of another's mental experience gained through observing his behavior) if we explain these conditions in terms of the condition that the lemmas be true and if we think of the inference on which knowledge is based as the inference to the best explanation rather than as enumerative induction.

NOTES

1. This paper is based on one read at the December 1963 meetings in Washington of the Eastern Division of the American Philosophical Association. I wish to thank J. J. Katz, R. P. Wolff, and a reader for the *Philosophical Review* for their helpful comments.

2. Enumerative induction infers from observed regularity to universal regularity or at least to regularity in the next instance.

3. In what follows, when I speak of "describing an inference as an instance of enumerative induction," I understand this phrase to rule out thought of the inference as an instance of the inference to the best explanation. I have no objection to talking of enumerative induction where one recognizes the inference as a special case of the inference to the best explanation.

4. But see Edmund L. Gettier, "Is Justified True Belief Knowledge?" *Analysis*, 23 (1963), 121–123 and Clark, "Knowledge and Grounds: A Comment on Mr. Gettier's Paper," *Analysis*, 24 (1963), 46–48.

5. Cf. "How Belief Is Based on Inference," *The Journal of Philosophy*, LXI (1964), 353–360.

6. See note 3.

DAVID INGRAM
Hermeneutics and Truth

Recently, some philosophers in the Anglo-American and Continental traditions, having rid themselves of the antiquated presuppositions and taxonomies of classical epistemology and metaphysics, have turned their attention toward various holistic doctrines to account for the nature of truth and being. Classical epistemology held that truth was a property which denoted the adequation, or correspondence, of knowledge and reality, conceived as absolutely self-subsisting, univocal being. Attempts to explain this correspondence invariably invoked such metaphors as mirroring, picturing, reflecting, etc.[1]

The major difficulties with the correspondence theory of truth became perspicuous, the holists maintain, with the advent of post-Cartesian philosophy. It is Descartes to whom we owe the idea that the *cogito* and the peculiar conviction which accompanies it are to be regarded as the *sine qua non* of knowledge as such. The path leading from immediate subjectivity to external reality is now to be guaranteed by way of indubitable evidence. Henceforth, epistemology becomes the chief concern of philosophy, which is delegated the task of showing how our knowledge claims (or mental representations) can be justified as objectively valid.

According to the holists, neither transcendental nor empirical epistemologies have satisfactorily carried out this task. As Quine and others pointed out, the 'theory-ladenness' of observation statements—the fact that meaning and reference are a function, not of atomic acts of ostensive definition, but of syncategorematic inclusion within a specific semantic totality—necessarily frustrates any attempt to define the meaning of so-called referring expressions in terms of a neutral operationalist description of expected sensory presentations.[2]

To be sure, the transcendental approach to the problem inaugurated by Kant was intended to obviate the aforementioned difficulties encountered by empiricism through the postulation and deduction of *a priori* categories. Hegel notwithstanding, however, the assumption that all particular conceptual worldviews are commensurable and converge upon an absolute set of Archimedian points has been dealt a serious blow by philosophers of science such as Kuhn and Feyerabend.

This takes us to the topic of my paper. The significance of hermeneutics for the problem of truth, I shall argue, is two-fold. On the one hand, contemporary philosophical hermeneutics is the pre-eminent defender of epistemological holism. The major proponents of this posture argue that truth-claims which purport to say something about reality are relative to irreducible interpretative schemas. The lack of a uni-

"Hermeneutics and Truth" is reprinted from the *Journal of the British Society for Phenomenology*, Vol. 15, No. 1 (January 1984), by permission of Haigh and Hochland Ltd. **David Ingram,** a contemporary philosopher, brings to the discussion of truth a style generally associated with continental philosophers, but gaining in popularity both in the United States and Great Britain.

versal language in terms of which every epistemic frame of reference might be univocally translated in turn seems to entail relativism—an implication which Rorty and Derrida wholeheartedly embrace and defend. On the other hand, the philosophical hermeneutics developed by Gadamer is introduced as an alternative to the holistic relativism advanced by Rorty (though Rorty conveniently elides this fact in his commentary of the former's work). Gadamer, I contend, not only seeks to refute the classical theory of truth and its correlative methodological presuppositions but he also undertakes the justification of a different concept of truth which still retains a link to the idea of universal agreement.

The question addressed by this essay is whether Gadamer's concept of truth fully succeeds in overcoming holistic relativism. My investigation of this problem will proceed as follows. In section one I will examine Heidegger's defense of hermeneutic holism and his theory of historicity with the aim of demonstrating its implications for a theory of truth. Section two will join the issue of truth as it is taken up by Gadamer in *Wahrheit und Methode*. I shall endeavor to show that Gadamer elaborates a dialogical model of hermeneutic experience which draws its basic impetus from Heidegger's theory of historicity and Hegel's concept of experience. Finally, section three will conclude with a critical examination of the problem deriving normative conditions from hermeneutic experience.

I

In *Sein und Zeit* Heidegger addresses the separate issues of truth and being as aspects of the same problem. By improperly formulating the question of being as one of substance ontology replete with its taxonomic division of beings into hierarchies of genera and species, Western metaphysics, Heidegger observes, concealed from itself the primary question of being as the *ground* and *possibility* of beings.[3] The classical notion of being conceived as an independently subsisting substratum of intrinsically determinate properties—what Aristotle called *hypokeimenon*—abstracts from the contextual background against which discrete 'things' appear as possible beings. Hence, the difficulty arises concerning the relation of correspondence which obtains between two separate existents, *res* and *intellectus*.[4]

According to Heidegger, beings are not originally encountered as isolable objects with substantive properties such as color, weight, extension, etc., but are rather disclosed as implements of use, what he calls *ready-to-hands (Zuhanden)*. The disclosure of pragmata, which includes such items as tools, equipment, construction materials, etc., is essentially teleo-logical and practical, viz., their *meaning* and *identity* are defined with reference to a *totality* of assignments and functions, all or which are referred back to the intentional vector of our aims.[5]

Heidegger elaborates the holistic nature of experience by designating *understanding (Verstehen)* as the primary structure of our insertion in the world. Understanding so conceived is neither a subjective faculty of sympathetic concern nor a specific epistemic method for deciphering symbolic objectifications, but rather denotes the way in which human beings inhabit a world. For Heidegger, understanding is assigned the status of an ontological 'clearing' whereby a world-horizon, or contextual background, is originally projected. The anticipatory, protensive orientation of projection (*Entwerfen*) is analogous to that foresight which guides our reading of a text. In the case of textual comprehension, the meaning of each sentence is syncategorematically determined by situating it within a not-yet-completed sequence of interrelated actions and events which are tied together in a coherent totality by way of an anticipatory completion of the narrative. Similarly, from an ontological perspective, specific involvements with persons and entities are thrown into relief against the anticipatory projection of a world-horizon. In both instances there exists a semantic interdependence of part and whole.[6]

The significance of Heidegger's hermeneutic holism for the problem of truth can be grasped once we understand the derivative nature of the proposition as that which refers to an object. In the pre-propositional circumspective concern (*Umsicht*) which typifies our 'sighting' of tools, there is no contemplative detachment separating 'subject' from 'object'; the implement is inconspicuous and merges with the manipulator. Though it is impossible to piece together the tool from an isolated subject and object, one can trace the emergence of the 'thing', or *present-at-hand*, in breakdowns and disruptions within the equipmental network. Once the tool loses its functionality, the unity of the referential *Gestalt* dissolves and we are left with a lifeless 'object' which manifests itself as a potential subject of predicates.

The origin of the thing, then, roughly coincides with the possibility of the proposition as that which explicitly predicates properties of an object.[7] Once the proposition is further removed from immediately indicating something within our experimental horizon and is reified into a piece of information for purposes of transmission, it becomes possible to view it as a thing to be compared with an objective state-of-affairs. Hence, just as 'thinghood' is revealed as a limited manner of projecting a scientific, theoretical world which is parasitic on an *a priori* matrix of practical involvements, so too, Heidegger argues that the correspondence theory of truth is likewise possible only against the background of a more universal experience of truth conceived as 'disclosedness' (*aletheia*).[8] Heidegger's analysis of truth as disclosedness is essentially congruent with our commonsensical understanding of the notion. Heidegger asserts that the truth of a proposition manifests itself when it is demonstrated to be true. Such demonstration has nothing to do with comparing proposition with object, but involves providing evidence in support of the proposition, e.g., by pointing something out or by proffering reasoned justification. The fact that the truth of a proposition is a function of its being *warranted* rather than of its being related in some mysterious way to brute sense-data shows that a prior *context of discourse* determining the semantic domain of reference is already presupposed. The presentation of evidence in support of a proposition, for example, merely singles out those salient aspects of the data that have already been previously located by an agreed upon set of conventional signifiers. In other words, ostensive reference presupposes that the referent already be semantically highlighted, named, and thereby ontologically determined *vis-à-vis* the entire linguistic totality of which the atomic signifiers are but a part.[9]

Now it is Heidegger's contention that understanding is itself ontologically embedded in a prior, culturally determined matrix of presuppositions which delimit the range of possible meaningfulness. This dimension of Heidegger's theory of understanding, which will occupy the remainder of our treatment of his hermeneutic theory, leads directly to a confrontation with the issue of relativism.

According to Heidegger, presuppositions operate below the threshold of conscious intent as a *vis a tergo* which comprises the familiar referential background guiding our search for possible meaning. This dependence upon a pre-reflective sedimentation of orientations, what Heidegger calls the *facticity* of human existence, signifies the state of being delivered over to a situation, a mood, a cultural identity, etc.[10] Now Heidegger believes that this dependency has ontological import for the way in which human being and world are codeterminative. Projected possibilities which do not facilitate understanding, or in some other way fail to mesh with the horizon of expectations, exert a counter-thrust that alters this horizon, and therewith, our self-identity.[11] The reciprocal reinterpretation of world and self (*Auslegung*), which transpires as a result of this critical interplay is further elaborated by Heidegger in his discussion of historicity (*Geschichtlichkeit*).

The linguistic forms and traditions that are inculcated in us map out a sort of destiny (*Geschick*) or pre-determined manner of viewing reality in terms of which we understand ourselves and our world. Not only is the being of individuals and their world relative to tradition, but this ontological circle is itself modulated through cultural transmission. A cultural heritage is not a static accumulation of anachronisms, but is a dynamic process whereby what is handed down and preserved is necessarily reinterpreted in light of the interests and concerns of the present.[12]

We can summarize the preceding discussion by saying that Heidegger's holistic account of truth conceived as a contextual clearing for possible denotation is essentially tied to the way in which historical languages and traditions open-up horizons of meaning. From a synchronic perspective, particular entities appear in a determinate light only insofar as they are hermeneutically located within a referential *Gestalt* that ultimately refers back to our purposes and aims. Seen diachronically, however, these referential totalities are themselves determined by historical possibilities that have been handed down.

The aforementioned account of truth clearly has relativistic implications. If disclosure is structurally defined by an ontological circle in which every interpretation continually discloses new possibilities and thereby transcends itself, then understanding and truth will necessarily be *partial* and *incomplete*. There can in principle be no final, absolute interpretation of reality which escapes revision in view of the open horizon of future projects. Indeed, because world-horizons are projections of sedimented presuppositions, they essentially remain relative to concrete historical circumstances.

II

Heidegger's hermeneutic holism undermines the foundations of classical epistemology in both its empirical and transcendental forms. The semantic interdependence which obtains between isolated propositions and the linguistic totality entails that objective reference and correlatively, ontological commitment, can hardly be conceived as a function of ostensive grounding in reality any more than can verification be regarded as a function of adducing interpretation-free sense-data statements in support of objective facts.[13]

The correspondence criterion of truth is operational only as long as the categories determining ontological commitments are shared alike by one and all. For this reason, Rorty correctly observes that traditional epistemology is possible only within the parameters of a shared discourse.[14] As the framework progressively succeeds in expanding its explanatory purview to include ever new horizons of discourse, it can be said to approach asymptotically an ideal of universal agreement. Charles Peirce, for one, believed that the hypothetico-deductive methodology of the natural sciences established the possibility for achieving such an ideal consensus, though as Kuhn and Feyerabend have pointed out, there is no rational consensus regarding the acceptance of this paradigm.[15] Nevertheless, there is no gainsaying the fact that hermeneutic holism condones coherence, or consensus, as a criterion of truth. The progressive translation of alien discourses into the unitary idiom of a given paradigm in a manner which enhances the overall explanatory power and consistency of the system also facilitates pragmatic utility.[16]

Transcendental idealism, however, rests its case on the existence of a *consensus gentium* concerning such pragmatic values. Recently, Jürgen Habermas and K. O. Apel have attempted to revive the transcendentalist program by grounding the methodologies of the natural sciences, the humanities, and the social sciences in distinct *a priori* cognitive interests (*kenntnisleitende Interesse*).[17] Though such interests straddle the line separating biological instincts and cultural dispositions, these philosophers concede that their precise meaning and value is contingent upon historically variable interpretations. Assuming that Heidegger is correct, the historicity of human understanding would indeed preclude the possibility of attaining a complete consensus uniting all historical interpretations. Because living languages undergo constant mutation in the open horizon of possible interpretation, the Hegelian project of sublating all historical worldviews to a unified system appears to be a fantastic chimera.

The incompleteness and relativity of cultural horizons brings into question the very possibility of discovering a viable model of truth. Nietzsche, we know, took the perspectivalism of our condition as proof of the infeasibility of such a notion. "Truth is the kind of error without which a certain species of living being could not live."[18] Derrida, following Nietzsche, has drawn the most radical conclusions from the hermeneutic interdependence which subsists between the signifier and the signified. According to Derrida, every signifier is a metaphor for the signified. Referent, symbol, and concept (meaning) are co-determinative and the total signifier only acquires a meaning metonymically by way of further reference to the entire system of signs.

> There is thus no phenomenality reducing the sign or the representer so that the thing signified may be allowed to glow finally in the luminosity of its presence. The so-called "thing itself" is always already a *representamen* shielded from the simplicity of intuitive evidence. The *representamen* functions only by giving rise to an *interpretant* that itself becomes a sign and so on to infinity.[19]

In opposition to structuralism, Derrida maintains that the system of signs—the field of possible reference—is indefinite and infinite. The semiological enterprise of connecting *nominatum* and sense as dual functions of the sign must give way to a grammatological study of the geneology of infinitely extending sign chains which never refer beyond themselves to a pristine signified. For Derrida, the primacy of spoken communication (conceived as immediate comprehension of a plenitude of meaning complete in itself) over writing must be reversed. Language is essentially haunted by the "trace" of "arche-writing" (*archiécriture*), namely, a fundamental alterity (*differance*) or spacing which designates both the inclusion of every sign within the semantic horizon of every other sign and the internal dialectical structure of the sign itself.[20] As a unity of difference and identity, the sign opens-up an exteriority (the world of extant signifieds) which in its very "otherness" and opacity reflects the alterity within the semantic interiority of the sign. Is this radical alterity which resides at the heart of the sign not already present in Heidegger's notion of historicity?

If human understanding, as an event of linguistic disclosure, is a continually self-transcending movement which loses itself in the indefinite horizon of possible interpretation, then the hermetic relativity of self-enclosed sign structures is indeed shattered, but only at the expense of dissolving into a play of de-centered acts of signification. Lacking a transcendental referent, it appears that no possible notion of truth can be salvaged out of this arbitrary play of signifiers.

There remains, however, an alternative to this radical relativism. Gadamer observes that the process of interpretation "which we are" is itself teleologically oriented toward a state of openness (*Offenheit*) and mutual recognition. Even Rorty, who bases his understanding of hermeneutics principally on Gadamer's work, acknowledges that hermeneutic holism entails a commitment of sorts to refrain from epistemological reductionism.

> . . . hermeneutics is an expression of hope that the cultural space left by the demise of epistemology will not be filled—that our culture should become one in which the demand for constraint and confrontation is no longer felt. The notion that there is a permanent neutral framework whose "structure" philosophy can

display is the notion that the objects to be confronted by the mind, or the rules which constrain inquiry, are common to all discourse, or at least to every discourse on a given topic. Thus epistemology proceeds on the assumption that all contributions to a given discourse are commensurable. Hermeneutics is largely a struggle against this assumption.[21]

Despite this admission, Rorty denies that hermeneutics is in the business of showing that discourse and interpretation in general presuppose a consensus regarding the very rules of hermeneutic interplay. Hermeneutics, he informs us, has relinquished the search for absolutes and is content to "settle back into the 'relativism' which assumes that our only useful notions of 'true' and 'real' and 'good' are extrapolations . . . from practices and beliefs."[22]

No doubt, if truth is conceived as correspondence to an *antecedently* existing ground of agreement, one which is itself removed from the historical process of interpretation, then Rorty and Gadamer would concur that the search for such a truth must be in vain. Nevertheless, though there may not be any discourse which is capable of uniting speakers standing in incommensurable world-horizons, there still remains the *meta-hermeneutical* pre-condition which binds them together in a common effort to achieve agreement, namely, mutual recognition and openness. This pre-condition, Gadamer argues, is not adventitiously related to the process of generating consensus, notwithstanding the fact that it has only become a conscious demand since the "practices and beliefs" of the Enlightenment. That Gadamer himself espouses a faith in reason reminiscent of his predecessors in the German Idealist tradition is certainly ignored by most of his commentators, who prefer to concentrate their attention upon his more notable objection to the Enlightenment's "prejudice against prejudices"—a fact which may explain why they have strangely ignored the teleological dimension of his hermeneutics. Consequently, a propaedeutic examination of his hermeneutic

theory must begin with a discussion of this objection in order to place it in proper perspective.

Romantic hermeneutics, Gadamer maintains, succumbs to historicism precisely because it never entirely succeeded in extricating itself from the enlightenment credo of scientific objectivity. The hermeneutic tradition extending from Schleiermacher to Dilthey viewed cultural artifacts as spiritual objectivities whose very being was alien to the interpreter in much the same way that extended substance was regarded as alien to the subjectivity of the scientist by post-Cartesian empiricism.[23] Dilthey, whose *Lebensphilosophie* laid the epistemological foundations of the tradition, uncritically appropriated the classical idea of truth in his transcendental deduction of the *Geisteswissenschaften,* insisting that the proper aim of textual interpretation be methodologically secured by way of an empathetic re-living (*Nacherleben*) of the original *Weltanschauungen* of alien spiritualities.[24] Buttressing this methodology was the assumption that human understanding is capable of transcending its own horizon of cultural prejudices, a presupposition which stands discredited from the standpoint articulated in *Sein und Zeit.*[25] Retrieving the Kerygmatic orientation of biblical hermeneutics, Gadamer argues that human understanding is not to be conceived as an act of psychological transposition, but is rather like a conversation in which a shared understanding (agreement) is reached that resists reduction to either of the interlocutors' privileged intentions.[26]

It will be recalled that Heidegger's analysis of historicity overcomes the hermetic relativism of historicism by showing that the semantic elisions separating the past from the present, the interpreter from tradition, subject and object, etc., are at least partially bridged in a continuous movement of reinterpretation. Nevertheless, the lack of closure endemic to our ever changing protensive reflection upon our past introduces a new element of relativity. Gadamer's *Wahrheit und Methode,* I believe, can be seen as an attempt to justify a theory of truth which takes into consideration this new relativity with

out, however, abandoning the idea of a teleological advance.

For Gadamer, true understanding is dialectical rather than reductive, viz., it is neither a
blind repetition of an alien spirituality—a self-
defeating act which, if possible, would only
succeed in retaining meaningless anachronisms—nor an uncritical assimilation to the parochial present, which would equally obscure
the novel meaning of the past. True understanding occupies a middle ground which preserves
tradition as of vital consequence for the present
only by critically excising both parochial prejudices and anachronisms.

Gadamer observes that the temporal distance separating the interpreter from tradition
establishes the setting for hermeneutical reflection in two senses. First, the opacity of something which is partially anachronistic and resists
immediate assimilation to one's familiar horizon of discourse challenges one's prejudices and
stimulates critical reflection. Second, whatever
universal value the text may have beyond what
was understood by its original audience only
emerges *ex post facto*, from the vantage point of
a retrospective comprehension of the totality of
past interpretations.[27] Finally, the true meaning
of the text, Gadamer reminds us, is not identifiable with any one canonical interpretation, but
is essentially relative to a changing horizon of
discourse.

> . . . the discovery of the true meaning of
> (tradition) is never finished; it is, in fact,
> an infinite process. Not only are fresh
> sources of error constantly excluded, so
> that the true meaning has filtered out all
> kinds of things that obscure it but there
> emerge continually new sources of under-
> standing which reveal unsuspected ele-
> ments of meaning . . . the filtering
> process is not a closed dimension, but is
> itself undergoing constant movement and
> extension.[28]

The continuity which ties together diverse
historical interpretations in the unitary phenomenon of a cultural truth may be illustrated in a
number of ways, so long as the eternal 'contem-
poraneity' of the phenomenon is not construed
as an immutable Platonic essence.[29]

Gadamer's wedding of temporality and truth
strikes one *prima facie* as nothing more than a
re-affirmation of relativism. However, what
Rorty and others lose sight of is that Gadamer
also conceives the temporal dimension as teleological in nature.

In *Sein und Zeit* Heidegger already realized
that the possibility of true (or authentic) understanding presupposed making "a reciprocative
rejoinder to the possibility of that existence
which has already been there".[30] Gadamer further adumbrates the contours of such a hermeneutic reciprocity in terms of the concept of
Bildung, which informs Hegel's treatment of
experience in the *Phenomenology of Spirit*.[31]

Bildung denotes a process of cultivation, or
education whereby egoistic individuality is elevated to the moral plane of free, universal self-
consciousness. Hegel observes that civic
acculturation is a necessary condition for individual freedom because the private moral conscience which follows its own dictates must
inevitably encounter the resistance of other such
agents. This objective resistance is only overcome at the level of political life where individuals conduct themselves in accordance with
legally promulgated norms and customary
codes which they collectively acknowledge as
representing their mutual interest.[32] If one continues one's *Bildung* further by familiarizing
oneself with the languages, customs, and literary accomplishments of other historical peoples, one may even achieve a modicum of
freedom from the narrow outlook of one's own
cultural horizon and, by so doing, gradually
learn to open oneself up to ever broader horizons of fresh experience. Contrary to Dilthey,
freedom from parochial prejudices is not
achieved by methodologically eclipsing one's
entire cultural background and restoring it to
the state of a *tabula rasa*. Rather, growth into
cultural horizons and the freedom which is
thereby acquired is possible only by translating
the unfamiliar into the familiar. Stated differently, freedom is not an event which transpires

sub specie aeternitatis but is only actuated in the play of historical possibilities.[33]

Gadamer elucidates the structure of *Bildung* with respect to two concepts which recall Hegel's concept of experience: synthesis (*Aufhebung*) and dialogue. Gadamer compares *Bildung* to a progressive *fusion of horizons* in which interpreter and tradition are elevated to participation in a higher universality. This fusion is at once the cancellation of both the parochial prejudices of the interpreter which impede access to the unique message of the tradition and the dead anachronisms implicit in the latter as well as the *preservation* and *extension* of what is common to both of them.[34] The moment of cancellation results in a dual negation whereby both the being of the interpreter and the being of the tradition are altered.[35] However, in contradistinction to Hegel's dialectic of experience, hermeneutic experience does not culminate in a complete identity of subject and object (absolute knowledge) but only issues in progressively higher states of reflexive openness, what Gadamer calls *effective-historical consciousness* (*Wirkungsgeschichtliches Bewusstsein*).[36]

The reflexivity of hermeneutic experience has the structure of a dialogue. Figuratively speaking, the interpreter and the text can be regarded as advancing potentially conflicting truth claims. The ebb and flow of questions and answers which arises from this encounter is like a game (*Spiel*) in which the play, more than the conscious intentions of the players, determines what happens. As in any conversation, what is said is "put at risk"; one's answer may not elicit the expected response from the other, but the dialogical process continues with the aim of achieving as much agreement as possible.[37]

Significantly, Gadamer argues that openness and mutual recognition are necessary conditions of true dialogue and he underscores the importance of this concept for hermeneutic theory by defining it in the normative phraseology of political rights.

> The experience of the 'thou' throws light on the idea of effective historical experience. The experience of the 'thou' also manifests the paradoxical element that something standing over against me asserts its own rights and requires absolute recognition and in that very process is understood . . . It is the same with tradition.[38]

Again, hermeneutic reciprocity enjoins against any reductionistic attempt on the part of the interpreter to assimilate the meaning of the other by 'prejudging' it in advance.

> In human relations the important thing is . . . to experience the 'thou' as 'thou', i.e., not overlook his claim and listen to what he has to say to us. To this end openness is necessary. Without this kind of openness to one another there is no human relationship.[39]

III

In retrospect, Gadamer's theory of truth reaffirms relativism, albeit, not without qualification. To be sure, the "hermetic" relativism typical of historicist doctrines of truth loses much of its appeal once the historicity of cultural transmission is acknowledged. Nevertheless, the relativity of truth-claims with respect to culture-bound discourses which cannot in principle command universal assent is not thereby discounted. Even if there were to exist a clear etymological descent linking historically disparate traditions so that a "shared meaning" were to emerge, it is apparent that each concrete interpretation of this meaning would yield an irreducibly unique and, therefore, different content. The meaning which is preserved and extended in cultural transmission is not an immutable essence, but undergoes cultural alteration in application to new historical circumstances. The higher universality of meaning which arises from the concourse of traditions is no more reducible to its constitutive cultural "moments" than is a vital organism reducible to its molecular, inorganic components. Gadamer cites Aristotle's example of natural law to illustrate the relativity of universal truth-claims, which are neither entirely conventional in the way that traffic regulations are nor absolutely unchangeable and independent of human convention in the way that physical laws are.[40] Moreover the achievement of a universal consensus uniting all present discourses would hardly mitigate the problem of relativism, for such a consensus would itself require reinterpretation in light of future events. Subsequently, it cannot be denied that Gadamer's theory of truth is inimical to traditional epistemic absolutism.

Despite the above conclusion, Gadamer's elucidation of the *process* of human understanding does contain something of a qualification of relativism. To recapitulate, according to Gadamer every successful clarification of the "thou" which truly captures its provocative meaning without distortion or diminution involves hermeneutical reflection. The latter, in turn, contributes to a process of *Bildung* whereby our parochial horizons are liberated from restrictive prejudices and broadened. The maturation of free, self-conscious, universal spirituality is itself impelled by a dialogical interplay of prejudices which progressively evolves higher levels of openness and reciprocity. Thus, the very *modus operandi* of human understanding is teleologically oriented toward a recognition of the "thou" as one whose individuality merits an equal right to be respected and understood. Though such an attitude no doubt informs any search for new meaning, it is especially definitive of communicative understanding. Indeed, Gadamer regards reciprocity as in some sense a transcendental condition for the very possibility of human communication as such.

Might not Gadamer's analysis of reciprocity procure for humanity a *normative* direction which is not subject to the relativistic vicissitudes of time and place? Unfortunately, Gadamer does not give us an unequivocal response to this question. On the one hand, he endorses the view that dialogical reciprocity is a necessary and universal condition founding all possible communication. One the other hand, he just as emphatically repudiates the possibility of any transcendentally justified ethic.[41] Wherein, then, does the normative status of reciprocity reside?

In his social and political writings, Gadamer occasionally likens the fundamental consensus which unites and harmonizes the different social strata of a community (*Gemeinschaft*) to the equilibrium (*Gleichgewicht*) of forces which secures the well-being of a biological organism.[42] Language is here regarded as the ultimate medium of consensual solidarity and organic metaphors are introduced to underscore the egalitarian interaction which constitutes its syncretic unity. Language is a "game of interpretation" in which "everyone is at the center".[43] The egalitarianism of this dialogue is primarily a reflection of the primacy of social process over individual and corporate will. Inasmuch as social life consists of a vast web of intersecting contracts, norms and other forms of mutual agreement linking a plurality of autonomous wills, it essentially extends beyond the unitary control of particular agencies. Even totalitarian governments, it would seem, must respect established customs and practices which foster harmonious interaction if their authority is to be freely recognized as legitimate. The tendency of this line of thought is to treat relations of authority and inequality, to the extent that they typify stable communities, as epiphenomenal manifestations of a prior consent freely given by those occupying subordinate positions in the social hierarchy. Consequently, we find Gadamer arguing, for example, that the rhetorical hegemony which corporate powers apparently exercise with respect to formation of public opinion is illusory because it is dialogically checked and countered by individual consumers whose scales of preference function as the decisive factor regulating production in the free market.

On the above reading, the normative scope of dialogical reciprocity is universal and necessary for all "true" (i.e., harmonious) communities, regardless of the specific forms of institutionalized authority and inequality they possess. Because the meaning of reciprocity has now been extended to cover a seemingly *indefi-*

nite range of social arrangements, it is doubtful whether any *concrete, prescriptive* content can be generated from it. Gadamer reminds us that this is in perfect keeping with the general tenor of his philosophical hermeneutics, which extrudes methodological and prescriptive considerations in favor of *ontological description*.[44] Habermas here correctly observes that Gadamer's ontological hermeneutics harbours a neo-Kantian prejudice which perpetuates a suspect dichotomy separating facts and values.[45] The corollary to such a view is a relativism which condones all *de facto* social consensus, no matter how *ideologically* constrained it might be due to covert disparities in economic and political power, as dialogically well-founded so long as it is sustained by tacit consent.[46]

Notwithstanding this rather negative assessment of Gadamer's theory of truth, it is perfectly obvious that Gadamer does attach some prescriptive import to dialogical reciprocity. This is particularly evident in his debate with Habermas, where he argues that there is an *a priori* limit to social engineering, including the kind of psycho-therapeutic sociology advocated by Habermas, which ostensibly authorizes the "critic of ideology" to question others as pathologically affected, as lacking the qualifications for rational accountability, and, therefore, as unreliable in matters of speech. Apropos of the above remark, Gadamer has pointed out that Habermas's critical sociology has the paradoxical consequence of subverting the very fabric of societal reciprocity which it seeks to restore under the aegis of therapy.[47] Yet, one can detect in his more recent pronouncements concerning the deleterious impact of mass-media manipulation something of a rapprochement with the "critical" position espoused by his opponent.[48] Gadamer now submits that even in modern Western democracies which formally institutionalize procedural rules guaranteeing freedom of speech and association, the balance of dialogical give and take is so tilted in favor of corporate powers that the *lingua franca* by means of which society as a whole reaches consensus is inevitably distorted. This is a surprising admission, for Gadamer here seems to be saying that true dialogical reciprocity is *not* compatible

with a state of affairs in which socio-economic disparities and political privileges constrain the "natural equilibrium" of dialogical checks and balances—*be they acknowledged legitimate or otherwise.*

> The real political activity of the citizen has become . . . restricted to the participation in elections . . . In the old days it was the personal participation of the citizens in the administrative work which controlled and neutralized the impact of special interest groups . . . on the common welfare. Today it is much more difficult to control and neutralize the organization of powerful economic interests. Even the opinions which form the patterns of social life and constitute the conditions for solidarity are today dominated to a great extent by the technical and economic organizations within our civilization.[49]

Eschewing a social psycho-therapeutic solution to the problem of post-modern dystopia, Gadamer prefers to advocate mutual restraint on the part of would-be social engineers and media technocrats. Rhetorical manipulation, Gadamer concludes, though indispensable as a means of generating societal consensus, needs to be counterbalanced by greater dialogical self-determination.

> Both rhetoric and the transmission of scientific knowledge are monological in form; both need the counterbalance of hemeneutical appropriation, which works in the form of dialogue. And precisely and especially practical and political reason can only be realized and transmitted dialogically. I think, then, that the chief task of philosophy is to justify this way of reason and to defend practical and political reason against the domination of technology based upon science . . . it vindicates again the noblest task of the citizen . . . decision-making according to one's own responsibility . . .[50]

Is the above citation not a moral *recommendation* to promote the cause of a more democratic society? If so, how can it be squared with Gadamer's earlier contention that philosophical hermeneutics essentially prescinds from value commitments?

There are two possible ways to interpret Gadamer on this score which will render his hermeneutics consistent. On the one hand, it is possible to construe his recommendation as a particular, culture-bound interpretation of an *a priori* pre-condition which lends it vital, imperative significance for the historical present. However, the peculiar egalitarian and libertarian contours of this interpretation could not on this view of the matter be themselves transcendentally justified. Whatever authority these values command for the present age must be seen as accruing to them in virtue of their historical relation to past tradition, especially the secular rationalism of our Enlightenment heritage. This is just to say that an ideal of uncoercive dialogue would be legitimated to the degree that this legacy is accepted as a convincing source of value which has "proven" its worth for contemporary society.

The above interpretation of Gadamer's position is unsatisfactory chiefly because it would have him defend a *philosophically sanctioned* ethics on the basis of a particular historical tradition whose "worth" is clearly questionable to him and whose acknowledged authority is limited to a rather small segment of humanity. The other alternative is to interpret Gadamer's ontological hermeneutics as axiological in the strong sense of the word, i.e., as implying a *definite* normative commitment. This is the option pursued by Habermas, who takes as his point of departure Heidegger's analysis of the "fore-completion" of interpretative understanding. In his review of *Wahrheit und Methode*, Habermas insisted that the protensive orientation of understanding necessarily ties every historical and sociological interpretation of human action to the anticipated future. The historian is not a mere chronicler of events, but ties them together into a coherent narrative. Some intimation about the significance of entire cultures,

their relation to one another in the broader expanse of human history *as a whole,* and what the latter, *qua* process striving for completion, means to the individual historian given his own practical situation (e.g., the arena in which human emancipation is achieved, the setting for the eschatological redemption of the world, etc.) implicitly if not explicitly informs the narrative colligation of data into a meaningful whole. Thus, historical narrative, like literary criticism, involves evaluation as well as description. Inasmuch as philosophical hermeneutics too seeks to understand the meaning of human being it cannot renounce the projection of a universal history from a practical standpoint. For Habermas, the practical standpoint which imposes itself on us with compelling force is none other than a visionary interest in an emancipated speech community in which dialogical reciprocity is substantively guaranteed.[51]

In his rejoinder to Habermas, Gadamer did not contest the view that "the goal, the end-thought of freedom" possesses a "compelling evidentness" which "one can as little get beyond" as "one can get beyond consciousness itself".[52] In a more recent reply he agrees that the "living idea of reason" cannot renounce the ideal of a general agreement grounded in "a shared life under conditions of uncoercive communication".[53] However, he qualifies these remarks by denying that a *fixed* end-point of the historical process can be determined once and for all. The projection of a universal history is always provisional, for it is subject to revision in light of new circumstances. Despite this important qualification, there is no getting around the fact that Gadamer does subscribe to a teleology which specifies, if not the *terminus ad quem,* at least the *terminus a quo,* i.e., the ideal presupposition and direction, of all human understanding. Surely, this is tantamount to a transcendental justification of a norm having considerable prescriptive, critical impact.[54]

In effect, the aforementioned reconciliation of ontology and axiology which one increasingly detects in Gadamer's recent philosophy provides something of an "absolute" reference point for human practice, albeit, one which cannot entirely escape the historical relativity of finite understanding. Every general ethical principle, regardless of its status, must be reinterpreted to accommodate the unique circumstances of our historical condition. The parameters of ethical conduct, however, are nonetheless definite, even if they do permit an indeterminate number of possible responses. Indeed, it is only in and through the living application of tradition that continuity and value are preserved. But following Hegel, is this not to concede that history is at once the realization and the Golgotha of the absolute, that the advent of truth is only played out in the eternal recurrence of concrete interpretation? If I am not mistaken, our reflection on hermeneutics inexorably leads to this conclusion. Consequently, it is appropriate to end this essay by recalling the dialectic of truth which resonates in the denouement of *Wahrheit und Methode:*

In understanding we are drawn into an event of truth and arrive, as it were, too late if we want to know what we ought to believe.[55]

NOTES

1. Cf. Augustine, *Confessions*, I. 8. and L. Wittgenstein, *Tractatus Logico-Philosophicus*, London, Kegan Paul, 1922.
2. Quine argues that the analytic/synthetic distinction and the verificationist theory of truth are untenable because they presuppose a bogus distinction between semantics, language, and logic on the one hand, and practice, experience, and psychology on the other. (W. V. -O. Quine, "The Two Dogmas of Empiricism" in *From a Logical Point of View*, New York, 1953.) In connection with this critique of epistemological atomism also see Wittgenstein's refutation of the ostensive theory of meaning. (L. Wittgenstein, *Philosophical Investigations*, New York, Macmillan, 1953.)
3. M. Heidegger, *Being and Time*, trans. by E. Robinson, and J. Macquarrie, New York, 1962, pp. 21–4, 30 2.
4. Ibid., p. 258.
5. Ibid., pp. 96–102.
6. Ibid., pp. 182–88.
7. Ibid., pp. 102–7, 189–203. Clearly, everyday practical understanding and "know-how" does not get articulated in the mind in the form of explicit propositions—a point which Gilbert Ryle eloquently makes in *The Concept of Mind* (New York, 1949, pp. 25–61).
8. Ibid., pp. 114–124, 262–93. There has been much controversy generated by Heidegger's etymological derivation of *aletheia* understood as disclosedness. Cf. "Friedländer vs. Heidegger: *Aletheia* controversy," by C. S. Nwodo in the *Journal of the British Society for Phenomenology*, 2, 1979.
9. Ibid., pp. 261, 269–73. Cf. G. Schufrieder, "Art and the Problem of Truth" in *Man and World*, 13, 1980, for a discussion of the different levels of truth in the Heideggerian corpus.
10. *BT*, pp. 174, 435–6.
11. Ibid., p. 192.
12. Ibid., pp. 434–6.
13. Cf. J. Fell, *Heidegger and Sartre: An Essay on Being and Place*, New York, 1979, pp. 395–8.
14. R. Rorty, *Philosophy and the Mirror of Nature*, Princeton, 1970, p. 317.
15. For Peirce, the superiority of the scientific method of investigation resides in its capacity to generate an uncompelled and permanent consensus about reality. (C. Peirce, "The Logic of 1873", VII, p. 319 in *Collected Papers*, Cambridge, 1931–35.) Kuhn and Feyerabend, however, deny that the methods, values, and standards which inform modern scientific research have any privileged claim over other methods of discovering the truth in this respect. Cf. T. Kuhn, *The Structure of Scientific Revolutions*, Chicago, 1961, pp. 108–9, and Feyerabend "Against Method, Outline of an Anarchistic Theory of Knowledge" in *Minnesota Studies in the Philosophy of Science*, IV, 1970.
16. Cf. L. Versenyi, *Heidegger, Being, and Truth*, New Haven, 1965, pp. 49–51.
17. J. Habermas, *Knowledge and Human Interests*, trans. by J. Shapiro, Boston, 1971, p. 196. K.-O. Apel, "The A Priori of Communication and the Foundations of the Humanities" in *Man and World*, 1975, 3.
18. F. Nietzsche, *Will to Power*, trans. by W. Kaufmann, Vintage Books, 1968, p. 272.
19. J. Derrida, *Of Grammatology*, trans. by G. Chakravorty Spivak, Johns Hopkins, 1976, p. 49.
20. Ibid., p. 70.
21. Rorty, loc. cit., pp. 315–6.
22. Ibid., p. 377.
23. H.-G. Gadamer, *Truth and Method (TM)*, trans. by G. Garret and J. Cumming, Seabury, 1975, p. 210.
24. W. Dilthey, *Pattern and Meaning in History*, ed. and trans. by H. P. Rickman, New York, 1962, pp. 72–4.
25. Ibid., pp. 167–8. Also see *TM*, p. 200.
26. *TM*, p. 158–9.
27. Ibid., p. 365. Though Gadamer states that true understanding is possible only when *all* relations to the past have faded away, this would, as he notes elsewhere, render understanding impossible. For the importance of sharing a common tradition and the possibility of cross-cultural understanding, see *TM*, p. 425.
28. Ibid., p. 265–6.
29. Claus von Bormann notes that there remains a residual element of Platonism in *TM*. ("Die Zweideutigkeit der hermeneutischen Erfahrung" in *Hermeneutik und Ideologiekritik* (HI), Frankfurt, 1971, pp. 93–4).
30. *BT*, p. 438.
31. *TM*, pp. 306–8. (*TM*, p. 15.)

32. Cf. *Vernunft im Zeitalter der Wissensschaft*, Frankfurt, 1976, p. 64.
33. *TM*, p. 273. (*TM*, p. 272.)
34. *TM*, p. 318. (*TM*, p. 319.)
35. *TM*, p. 320.
36. Ibid., p. 245.
37. Ibid., pp. 259, 320.
38. Ibid., p. 324.
39. Ibid., pp. 233–4.
40. *TM*, p. 285.
41. Cf. H.-G. Gadamer, "Über die Möglichkeit einer philosophischen Ethik" in *Kleine Schriften* I. (Tübingen, 1967), p. 184–8.
42. H.-G. Gadamer, "Über die Planung der Zunkunft", in *Kleine Schriften*, Vol. I, Tübingen, 1967, pp. 172–4.
43. H.-G Gadamer, "On the Scope and Function of Hermeneutical Reflection," in *Philosophical Hermeneutics*, ed., D. Linge, (Berkeley, 1976), p. 32.
44. *TM*, p. xvi.
45. Cf. J. Habermas, *Zur Logik der Sozialwissenschaften*, Frankfurt, 1967, p. 291. It was the unresolved tension between axiology and ontology in Hegel's own philosophy that led to the controversy among his followers posing "conservative" right Hegelians against "critical" left Hegelians—a controversey which bears striking resemblance to the Gadamer/Habermas debate. Echoing the conservatives, Gadamer asserts that philosophical hermeneutics retraces the path marked out by Hegel's *Phenomenology of Spirit*, which describes the *substance* of social life from the vantage point of a retrospective synopsis (*TM*, p. 269). The problem for historical practice arises because understanding can only grasp the true meaning of history in its dead past, not in its living present or future. According to Habermas (and Marx), the contemplative objectivity of philosophy is contested by the fact that it, too, is an activity situated in practical life and therefore, anticipates the ideal fulfillment of that life. Hence, in contrast to the conservative's emphasis upon the justification of the present in terms of the past the radical is inclined to criticize the present in terms of its unfulfilled promises. Rudiger Bubner ("Theory and Practice in Light of the Hermeneutic-Criticist Controversy" in *Cultural Herme-*

neutics, 2, 1975, pp. 240–2) and Paul Ricoeur (*The Conflict of Interpretations*, Evanston, 1974, pp. 13–14 and "Ethics and Culture" in *Philosophy Today* 17, 1973, pp. 153–75) attempts to bridge the hiatus separating the conservative and critical aspects of hermeneutical reflection.
46. *TM*, p. 289.
47. H.-G Gadamer, "On the Scope and Function of Hermeneutical Reflection" in *Philosophical Hermeneutics*, trans. by D. Linge, Berkeley, 1976, pp. 40–1.
48. The major shortcomings of Gadamer's ontological conception of dialogue, Habermas avers, is that it ignores the socio-economic constraints which covertly impinge upon the equilibrium of democratic checks and balances from outside the context of dialogue (*KHI*, pp. 314–5). Habermas's more recent attempts to combine philosophical hermeneutics and the speech act theories of Austin and Searle have led him to develop a consensus theory of truth which shows how our interest in an emancipated speech community constitutes an essential condition of human knowledge. The *Ideal speech situation* articulates the pragmatic conditions of rational discourse, which specify a symmetrical distribution of chances to select and employ speech acts without hindrance from external coercion (e.g., threats of violence, economic and political pressure, etc.) and internal ideological constraint. (J. Habermas, "Wahrheitstheorien", in *Wirklichkeit und Reflexion: Festschrift für Walter Schutz*. Pfülligen, 1973, pp. 245–58.)
49. H.-G Gadamer, *Vernunft im Zeitalter der Wissenschaft*, Frankfurt, 1976, p. 64.
50. H.-G Gadamer, "Hermeneutics and Social Science" in *Cultural Hermeneutics*, 2, 1975, p. 314.
51. *Knowledge and Human Interests*, p. 284. (Cf. ft. 50). Also see Arthur Danto, *Analytical Philosophy of History*, Cambridge, 1965, p. 115.
52. H.-G. Gadamer, "On the Scope and Function of Hermeneutical Reflection" in *Philosophical Hermeneutics*, trans. by D. Linge, Berkeley, 1976, p. 37.
53. H.-G. Gadamer, "Replik" in *HI*, p. 316.
54. See my dissertation, "Truth, Method, and Understanding in the Human Sciences: The Gadamer/Habermas Controversy," University of California, 1980.
55. *TM*, p. 446.

QUESTIONS ABOUT TRUTH

1. Why is a theory of truth needed?
2. If the philosopher does not add to the corpus of truths, then the philosopher has no significant task to perform. How do you respond?
3. Explain why the *correspondence theory* is truistic but not trivial.
4. Coherence may be a useful test of truth even though it may not serve as a full-fledged theory. What exactly is the difference?
5. The pragmatist considers more than direct evidence. What is the rationale?

6. Aristotle seems to attribute to Protagoras (and other pre-Socratic philosophers) a kind of "appearance" theory of truth. What do you suppose this is and what is Aristotle's criticism?

7. How does J. L. Austin avoid "negative" facts? What would he say about "general" facts?

8. What exactly is Brand Blanshard's argument for coherence as "the nature of truth"?

9. Pick out Charles Sanders Peirce's clearest statement of his notion of truth and explain your choice.

10. Compare Peirce's statement (as picked out in question 9) with Harman's "inference to the best explanation." Does Harman's expression help to illuminate Peirce's view?

Truth:
Suggestions for Further Study

Ludwig Wittgenstein developed, in his *Tractatus Logico-Philosophicus* (London: Rout-ledge & Kegan Paul, 1961), an influential and widely discussed theory of truth as *picturing,* a variation of the correspondence approach. There is an extensive literature on Wittgenstein. G. E. M. Anscombe provides a helpful guide in *An Introduction to Wittgenstein's Tractatus* (New York: Harper & Row, 1959).

Brand Blanshard, in his defense of the coherence theory, represents a philosophical school called *idealism,* popular in the late-nineteenth and early-twentieth centuries. Other well-known idealists were F. H. Bradley and Bernard Bosanquet. See, for example, Bradley's *Appearance and Reality* (New York: Macmillan & Co., 1893) and Bernard Bosanquet's *Implication and Linear Inference* (London: Macmillan & Co., 1920). A more recent treatment of the coherence approach may be found in Nicholas Rescher's *The Coherence Theory of Truth* (Oxford: Clarendon Press, 1973.)

All of Peirce's papers, both published and previously unpublished, can be found in his *Collected Papers,* edited by Charles Hartshorne and Paul Weiss (Cambridge: Harvard University Press, 1965). Another famous pragmatist was William James; see, for example, his essays on truth in *Pragmatism* (New York: World, 1967). Equally famous was the pragmatist John Dewey; see, for example, his *Reconstruction in Philosophy* (Boston: Beacon Press, 1963).

PART
3

*Personal
Identity*

Literary Introduction:
Is This The Same Individual?

In Shakespeare's *Romeo and Juliet*, (II, ii, 38–49), Juliet declares to her lover:

> 'Tis but thy name that is my enemy;
> Thou art thyself, though not a Montague.
> What's Montague? It is nor hand nor foot,
> Nor arm nor face, {nor any other part}
> Belonging to man. O, be some other name!
> What's in a name? That which we call a rose
> By any other word would smell as sweet;
> So Romeo would, were he not Romeo call'd,
> Retain that dear perfection which he owes
> Without that title. Romeo, doff thy name,
> And for thy name, which is no part of thee,
> Take all myself.

Though it may be true, as Juliet asserts, "a rose/By any other word would smell as sweet," and though names are not the things themselves, it is also true, as the lovers in the play discover, that names can be insuperable barriers to happiness.

Moreover, perhaps Juliet misses an even more important point. She believes that Romeo would be Romeo, even if his name were Herman, and that she would love him. Perhaps so. But the question is, *whom* would she love? *Who*, in fact, is Romeo? If Juliet does not love the name Romeo, what exactly does she love?

Were we able to question Juliet, she would no doubt respond that she loves this certain young man. Pressed further, she might declare that she loves his physical attractiveness and his charming personality. If we were to push the question one step more, we could ask Juliet if she would love Romeo when he was old, wrinkled, and complaining constantly about his gout or his bad teeth. Our imagined interview would probably end on that question, with Juliet expressing her contempt for our unromantic inquiry. If she responded at all, she might say that of course her love for Romeo would endure, no matter how much he might change.

That answer serves well enough in the interests of romance, but it begs the question: namely, would the stooped, potbellied, short-tempered old man, that Romeo might become, be the same person Juliet so passionately loves? The quick answer is that, naturally, all people change over time, and their family and mates adapt to the changes. While this observation might seem true, it contains the kernel of the riddle of personal identity.

To say that a person changes over time assumes that part of the person does not change. If the person somehow were to change completely, in every possible way, then we would be forced to admit that we were dealing with at least two people. Since we cannot easily accept that proposition, we must find a way to understand the unchanging part, however we want to define it, that is the person.

In our example, it is the *essential* Romeo to whom Juliet vows her undying love. There is always an essential somebody that we understand to be a particular person. Recently, for example, a woman was arrested for allegedly participating in a hijacking of a commercial flight nineteen years ago. The woman who was arrested was living under a different name. She was married and seemed much more the suburban housewife than the radical political activist who committed the crime a generation ago. In fact, the hijacking involved the kidnapping of a young child on board the flight who was returned safely to his parents. When the woman was arrested, he could not be reached for comment because, now a young man, he was traveling abroad.

The jury hearing the evidence in the case will try to determine whether this woman is guilty of the offense with which she is charged. Put simply, if the FBI has done its job accurately, it has found the same women it has been looking for for nineteen years. And the jurors will assume that the woman before them is indeed the same person who has for so long occupied a position on the FBI's wanted list. A jury's job is to decide if this particular person is guilty of the crime: the identity of the defendant cannot, however, be open to question. If it were, we would have to ask exactly who is on trial.

Many areas of our lives demand an assured sense of personal identity. When we vote for a candidate, we reasonably assume we know who the person is. In business, we contract with a certain person, acting either for himself or herself, or on behalf of a company. In our personal relationships and especially in our romantic relationships, we believe we are involved with a particular individual. Only when reading fiction about the world of super espionage, of double and triple agents, are we sometimes unsure of who is who. But even in that case, we believe that there is a single person behind all the deceitful masks of the spy business. There simply has to be someone who is, in fact, disguising his or her identity.

What, then, constitutes this identity? No simple answer seems to work. Our physical bodies change dramatically from birth through maturity to old age. Fingerprints can be changed and faces rebuilt. And even if a reliable physical criterion for identity could be found, we would still not be comfortable in thinking that this physical criterion is the person. If dental records, for example, were infallible physical markers, would we be content to say we are our teeth?

We seem to hunger for something more, something that eludes definition, the something that Juliet loves in Romeo. Perhaps the idea of the mind, or more vaguely, the personality of a person answers this need. But minds change, as in the case of amnesia that can rob a person of memory, or in the case of emotional trauma that can alter an individual's personality. When we say a person has "lost" his or her mind, do we also mean that the person is gone?

It seems that neither physical characteristics nor mental qualities adequately identifies personhood. In "The Metamorphosis," Franz Kafka addresses this question of personal identity in a bizarre yet strikingly direct way. Kafka's fiction often presents the unthinkable in such believable terms that we are invited to contemplate an issue in a new and startling way. His fiction seems surrealistic, that is, it seems to involve people in circumstances that have more in common with dreams or nightmares than with what we generally understand to be the "real" world. Yet these surrealistic stories are told in a narrative voice that is as objective and natural as that which we find in our daily newspapers. Such a story is "The Metamorphosis," in which we are asked to accept, as simple fact, the transformation of Gregor Samsa, one morning, into a giant insect.

If we can believe that Gregor has literally turned into a dung beetle, (a cockroach in some translations), then we read the story as science fiction in which such events can occur without disturbing our sense of ordinary reality. Yet nothing else in the story seems to fit this kind of reading. All the other details are absolutely mundane: the sister wants to go to a music conservatory, the father has lost money in business, the family has taken in boarders to supplement its income, and so on. Even Gregor's boss appears to be a typically rigid bureaucrat of the early twentieth century, the time frame of the story. Therefore, the story does not fit the usual science fiction category.

We could read the story as the rendering of a nightmare and assume that Gregor has dreamed the metamorphosis. However, the story does not work this way either. For one thing, everybody else in the story goes about his or her usual business, stepping around, as it were, the presence of the insect Gregor. It is possible that the other characters might behave in that fashion in a dream. But more tellingly, Gregor dies; he is disposed of by the charwoman. The family moves on to a happier life after he is gone. If the dreamer dies, how do we have access to the dream? And from a more technical perspective, the narrative point of view (the angle of vision through which a story is told) changes from Gregor's while he is alive to an objective narrator describing the family after he is dead. All of this argues against seeing the story as a nightmare.

We are left, fittingly, to take the story as Kafka gives it to us, to accept its reality on its own terms. If we don't want to see it as science fiction, or as nightmare, we can approach it as a unique combination of these two genres. Perhaps the key to this approach is to see the story as an externalization of the main character's personality, or more precisely, of his perception of himself.

When we look at the story this way, it begins to yield a coherent message. Gregor Samsa has always thought of himself as a victim—of his father's disabling trauma, of his boss's unreasonable demands upon him, of the economic pressure that has made him the mainstay of the family at the expense of his youth. But it seems that this unhappy lot is one he feels he deserves. Even when he discovers, in his insect state, that his father has squirreled some money away after the collapse of his business, money that could have relieved some of the financial burden on Gregor, Gregor does not get angry. Rather, he congratulates his father for his foresight. He thinks of himself as of no worth in comparison to the other members of his family, and probably in comparison to the world at large. He sees himself as an insect, perhaps a drone working to keep the family hive together, but also a being that arouses disgust in others and that should be exterminated when it serves no useful purpose. That, of course, is precisely what happens at the end of the story, once the family members realize they can no longer depend on Gregor and start taking care of business for themselves.

The story demands attention on many levels, and predictably has drawn a variety of interpretations from literary critics. Some have seen Gregor's self-loathing as the consequence of an unresolved Oedipal complex wherein he has reluctantly usurped his father's role as breadwinner. Others have suggested that the father represents a distant, godlike figure, one whom Gregor can never hope to please. These interpretations explain the story, which is all we can ask of any interpretation, and they are not really inconsistent with each other. Both, and others like them, begin with the recognition of Gregor's lack of respect for himself.

However we read the story, it raises the question of personal identity in a unique way. Gregor wakes up as a giant insect. He thinks, however, like his old human self, even to the point of trying to dress and rush off to catch his train. The other members of his family believe he is still Gregor, perhaps even blaming him for his transformation. His sister tries to take care of him for a while. She obviously considers the insect that squeezes itself beneath the couch her brother, as do his mother, and more negatively, his father. And, of course, Gregor still thinks he is Gregor.

But *is* he? If he is, then physical appearance would seem irrelevant to the question of personal identity. Toward the end of the story, Gregor's mind becomes more insect-like. He refuses to eat anything but rotted food, for example, so that we can say that his mind, as well as his body, has undergone a significant change. What right, then, do we have to continue to see him as Gregor?

Perhaps an answer to the riddle can be found in the general approach to the story outlined above. If the story is an externalization of Gregor's sense of himself, then it is this perception of him, now a reality shared by the other characters, that defines the "true" Gregor.

The point, it seems, is that each of us has an "invisible" or "unknowable" identity that cannot be pinned down either by ourselves or by others. Unless, that is, one morning we awake and find ourselves turned into the physical manifestation of this identity. "The Metamorphosis" asks us to consider what we might see in the mirror on a morning when our "real" identity stares back at us.

Would we shrink back in horror or smile in delight? In a sense, that unknown is what Kafka asks us to ponder.

FRANZ KAFKA
The Metamorphosis

I

As Gregor Samsa awoke one morning from uneasy dreams he found himself transformed in his bed into a gigantic insect. He was lying on his hard, as it were armor-plated, back and when he lifted his head a little he could see his dome-like brown belly divided into stiff arched segments on top of which the bed quilt could hardly keep in position and was about to slide off completely. His numerous legs, which were pitifully thin compared to the rest of his bulk, waved helplessly before his eyes.

What has happened to me? he thought. It was no dream. His room, a regular human bedroom, only rather too small, lay quiet between the four familiar walls. Above the table on which a collection of cloth samples was unpacked and spread out—Samsa was a commercial traveler—hung the picture which he had recently cut out of an illustrated magazine and put into a pretty gilt frame. It showed a lady, with a fur cap on and a fur stole, sitting upright and holding out to the spectator a huge fur muff into which the whole of her forearm had vanished!

Gregor's eyes turned next to the window, and the overcast sky—one could hear rain drops beating on the window gutter—made him quite melancholy. What about sleeping a little longer and forgetting all this nonsense, he thought, but it could not be done, for he was accustomed to sleep on his right side and in his present condition he could not turn himself over. However violently he forced himself towards his right side he always rolled on to his back again. He tried it at least a hundred times, shutting his eyes to keep from seeing his struggling legs, and only desisted when he began to feel in his side a faint dull ache he had never experienced before.

Oh God, he thought, what an exhausting job I've picked on! Traveling about day in, day out. It's much more irritating work than doing the actual business in the office, and on top of that there's the trouble of constant traveling, of worrying about train connections, the bed and irregular meals, casual acquaintances that are always new and never become intimate friends. The devil take it all! He felt a slight itching up on his belly; slowly pushed himself on his back nearer to the top of the bed so that he could lift his head more easily; identified the itching place which was surrounded by many small white spots the nature of which he could not understand and made to touch it with a leg, but drew the leg back immediately, for the contact made a cold shiver run through him.

He slid down again into his former position. This getting up early, he thought, makes one quite stupid. A man needs his sleep. Other commercials live like harem women. For instance, when I come back to the hotel of a morning to write up the orders I've got, these others are only sitting down to breakfast. Let me just try that with my chief; I'd be sacked on the spot. Anyhow, that might be quite a good thing for me, who can tell? If I didn't have to hold my hand because of my parents I'd have given notice long ago. I'd have gone to the chief and told him exactly what I think of him. That would knock him endways from his desk! It's a queer way of doing, too, this sitting on high at a desk and talking down to employees, especially when they have to come quite near because the chief is hard of hearing. Well, there's still hope; once I've saved enough money to pay back my parents' debts to him— that should take another five or six years—I'll do it without fail. I'll cut myself completely loose then. For the moment, though, I'd better get up, since my train goes at five.

He looked at the alarm clock ticking on the chest. Heavenly Father! he thought. It was half-past six o'clock and the hands were quietly moving on, it was even past the half-hour, it was getting on toward a quarter to seven. Had the alarm clock not gone off? From the bed one could see that it had been properly set for four o'clock; of course it must have gone off. Yes, but was it possible to sleep quietly through that ear-splitting noise? Well, he had not slept quietly, yet apparently all the more soundly for that. But what was he to do now? The next train went at seven o'clock; to catch that he would need to hurry like mad and his samples weren't even packed up, and he himself wasn't feeling particularly fresh and active. And even if he did catch the train he wouldn't avoid a row with the chief, since the firm's porter would have been waiting for the five o'clock train and would have long since reported his failure to turn up. The porter was a creature of the chief's, spineless and stupid. Well, supposing he were to say

he was sick? But that would be most unpleasant and would look suspicious, since during his five years' employment he had not been ill once. The chief himself would be sure to come with the sick-insurance doctor, would reproach his parents with their son's laziness and would cut all excuses short by referring to the insurance doctor, who of course regarded all mankind as perfectly healthy malingerers. And would he be so far wrong on this occasion? Gregor really felt quite well, apart from a drowsiness that was utterly superfluous after such a long sleep, and he was even unusually hungry.

As all this was running through his mind at top speed without his being able to decide to leave his bed—the alarm clock had just struck a quarter to seven—there came a cautious tap at the door behind the head of his bed. "Gregor," said a voice—it was his mother's—"it's a quarter to seven. Hadn't you a train to catch?" That gentle voice! Gregor had a shock as he heard his own voice answering hers, unmistakably his own voice, it was true, but with a persistent horrible twittering squeak behind it like an undertone, that left the words in their clear shape only for the first moment and then rose up reverberating round them to destroy their sense, so that one could not be sure one had heard them rightly. Gregor wanted to answer at length and explain everything, but in the circumstances he confined himself to saying: "Yes, yes, thank you, Mother, I'm getting up now." The wooden door between them must have kept the change in his voice from being noticeable outside, for his mother contented herself with this statement and shuffled away. Yet this brief exchange of words had made the other members of the family aware that Gregor was still in the house, as they had not expected, and at one of the side doors his father was already knocking, gently, yet with his fist. "Gregor, Gregor," he called, "what's the matter with you?" And after a little while he called again in a deeper voice: "Gregor! Gregor!" At the other side door his sister was saying in a low, plaintive tone: "Gregor? Aren't you well? Are you needing anything?" He answered them both at once: "I'm just ready," and did his best to make his voice sound as normal as possible by enunciating the words very clearly and leaving long pauses between them. So his father went back to his breakfast, but his sister whispered: "Gregor, open the door, do." However, he was not thinking of opening the door, and felt thankful for the prudent habit he had acquired in traveling of locking all doors during the night, even at home.

His immediate intention was to get up quietly without being disturbed, to put on his clothes and above all eat his breakfast, and only then to consider what else was to be done, since in bed, he was well aware, his meditations would come to no sensible conclusion. He remembered that often enough in bed he had felt small aches and pains, probably caused by awkward postures, which had proved purely imaginary once he got up, and he looked forward eagerly to seeing this morning's delusions gradually fall away. That the change in his voice was nothing but the precursor of a severe chill, a standing ailment of commercial travelers, he had not the least possible doubt.

To get rid of the quilt was quite easy; he had only to inflate himself a little and it fell off by itself. But the next move was difficult, especially because he was so uncommonly broad. He would have needed arms and hands to hoist himself up; instead he had only the numerous little legs which never stopped waving in all directions and which he could not control in the least. When he tried to bend one of them it was the first to stretch itself straight; and did he succeed at last in making it do what he wanted, all the other legs meanwhile waved the more wildly in a high degree of unpleasant agitation. "But what's the use of lying idle in bed," said Gregor to himself.

He thought that he might get out of bed with the lower part of his body first, but this lower part, which he had not yet seen and of which he could form no clear conception, proved too difficult to move; it shifted so slowly; and when finally, almost wild with annoyance, he gathered his forces together and thrust out recklessly, he had miscalculated the direction and bumped heavily against the lower end of the bed, and the stinging pain he felt informed him that precisely this lower part of his body was at the moment probably the most sensitive.

So he tried to get the top part of himself out first, and cautiously moved his head towards the edge of the bed. That proved easy enough, and despite its breadth and mass the bulk of his body at last slowly followed the movement of his head. Still, when he finally got his head free over the edge of the bed he felt too scared to go on advancing, for after all if he let himself fall in this way it would take a miracle to keep his head from being injured. And at all costs he must not lose consciousness now, precisely now; he would rather stay in bed.

But when after a repetition of the same efforts he lay in his former position again, sighing, and watched his little legs struggling against each other more wildly than ever, if that were possible, and saw no way of bringing any order into this arbitrary confusion, he told himself again that it was impossible to stay in bed and that the most sensible course was to risk everything for the smallest hope of getting away from it. At the same time he did not forget meanwhile to remind himself that cool reflection, the coolest possible, was much better than desperate resolves. In such moments he focused his eyes as sharply as possible on the window, but, unfortunately, the prospect of the morning fog, which muffled even the other side of the narrow street, brought him little encouragement and comfort. "Seven o'clock already," he said to himself when the alarm clock chimed again, "seven o'clock already and still such a thick fog." And for a little while he lay quiet, breathing lightly, as if perhaps expecting such complete repose to restore all things to their real and normal condition.

But then he said to himself: "Before it strikes a quarter past seven I must be quite out of this bed, without fail. Anyhow, by that time someone will have come from the office to ask for me, since it opens before seven." And he set himself to rocking his whole body at once in a regular rhythm, with the idea of swinging it out of the bed. If he tipped himself out in that way he could keep his head from injury by lifting it at an acute angle when he fell. His back seemed to be hard and was not likely to suffer from a fall on the carpet. His biggest worry was the loud crash he would not be able to help making, which would probably cause anxiety, if not terror, behind all the doors. Still he must take the risk.

When he was already half out of bed—the new method was more a game than an effort, for he needed only to hitch himself across by rocking to and fro—it struck him how simple it would be if he could get help. Two strong people—he thought of his father and the servant girl—would be amply sufficient; they would only have to thrust their arms under his convex back, lever him out of bed, bend down with their burden and then be patient enough to let him turn himself right over on to the floor, where it was to be hoped his legs would then find their proper function. Well, ignoring the fact that the doors were all locked, ought he really to call for help? In spite of his misery he could not suppress a smile at the very idea of it.

He had got so far that he could barely keep his equilibrium when he rocked himself strongly, and he would have to nerve himself very soon for the final decision since in five minutes' time it would be a quarter past seven—when the front doorbell rang. "That's someone from the office," he said to himself, and grew almost rigid, while his little legs only jigged about all the faster. For a moment everything stayed quiet. "They're not going to open the door," said Gregor to himself, catching at some kind of irrational hope. But then of course the servant girl went as usual to the door with her heavy tread and opened it. Gregor needed only to hear the first good morning of the visitor to know immediately who it was—the chief clerk himself. What a fate, to be condemned to work for a firm where the smallest omission at once gave rise to the gravest suspicion! Were all employees in a body nothing but scoundrels, was there not among them one single loyal devoted man who, had he wasted only an hour or so of the firm's time in a morning, was so tormented by conscience as to be driven out of his

mind and actually incapable of leaving his bed? Wouldn't it really have been sufficient to send an apprentice to inquire—if any inquiry were necessary at all—did the chief clerk himself have to come and thus indicate to the entire family, an innocent family, that this suspicious circumstance could be investigated by no one less versed in affairs than himself? And more through the agitation caused by these reflections than through any act of will Gregor swung himself out of bed with all his strength. There was a loud thump, but it was not really a crash. His fall was broken to some extent by the carpet, his back, too, was less stiff than he thought, and so there was merely a dull thud, not so very startling. Only he had not lifted his head carefully enough and had hit it; he turned it and rubbed it on the carpet in pain and irritation.

"That was something falling down in there," said the chief clerk in the next room to the left. Gregor tried to suppose to himself that something like what had happened to him today might some day happen to the chief clerk; one really could not deny that it was possible. But as if in brusque reply to this supposition the chief clerk took a couple of firm steps in the next-door room and his patent leather boots creaked. From the right-hand room his sister was whispering to inform him of the situation: "Gregor, the chief clerk's here." "I know," muttered Gregor to himself; but he didn't dare to make his voice loud enough for his sister to hear it.

"Gregor," said his father now from the left-hand room, "the chief clerk has come and wants to know why you didn't catch the early train. We don't know what to say to him. Besides, he wants to talk to you in person. So open the door, please. He will be good enough to excuse the untidiness of your room." "Good morning, Mr. Samsa," the chief clerk was calling amiably meanwhile. "He's not well," said his mother to the visitor, while his father was still speaking through the door, "he's not well, sir, believe me. What else would make him miss a train! The boy thinks about nothing but his work. It makes me almost cross the way he never goes out in the evenings; he's been here the last eight days and has stayed at home every single evening. He just sits there quietly at the table reading a newspaper or looking through railway timetables. The only amusement he gets is doing fretwork. For instance, he spent two or three evenings cutting out a little picture frame; you would be surprised to see how pretty it is; it's hanging in his room; you'll see it in a minute when Gregor opens the door. I must say I'm glad you've come, sir; we should never have got him to unlock the door by ourselves; he's so obstinate; and I'm sure he's unwell, though he wouldn't have it to be so this morning.'' "I'm just coming," said Gregor slowly and carefully, not moving an inch for fear of losing one word of the conversation. "I can't think of any other explanation, madam,'' said the chief clerk, "I hope it's nothing serious. Although on the other hand I must say that we men of business—fortunately or unfortunately—very often simply have to ignore any slight indisposition, since business must be attended to.'' "Well, can the chief clerk come in now?" asked Gregor's father impatiently, again knocking on the door. "No," said Gregor. In the left-hand room a painful silence followed this refusal, in the right-hand room his sister began to sob.

Why didn't his sister join the others? She was probably newly out of bed and hadn't even begun to put on her clothes yet. Well, why was she crying? Because he wouldn't get up and let the chief clerk in, because he was in danger of losing his job, and because the chief would begin dunning his parents again for the old debts? Surely these were things one didn't need to worry about for the present. Gregor was still at home and not in the least thinking of deserting the family. At the moment, true, he was lying on the carpet and no one who knew the condition he was in could seriously expect him to admit the chief clerk. But for such a small discourtesy, which could plausibly be explained away somehow later on, Gregor could hardly be dismissed on the spot. And it seemed to Gregor that it would be much more sensible to leave him in peace for the present than to trouble him

with tears and entreaties. Still, of course, their uncertainty bewildered them all and excused their behavior.

"Mr. Samsa," the chief clerk called now in a louder voice, "what's the matter with you? Here you are, barricading yourself in your room, giving only 'yes' and 'no' for answers, causing your parents a lot of unnecessary trouble and neglecting—I mention this only in passing—neglecting your business duties in an incredible fashion. I am speaking here in the name of your parents and of your chief, and I beg you quite seriously to give me an immediate and precise explanation. You amaze me, you amaze me. I thought you were a quiet, dependable person, and now all at once you seem bent on making a disgraceful exhibition of yourself. The chief did hint to me early this morning a possible explanation for your disappearance—with reference to the cash payments that were entrusted to you recently—but I almost pledged my solemn word of honor that this could not be so. But now that I see how incredibly obstinate you are, I no longer have the slightest desire to take your part at all. And your position in the firm is not so unassailable. I came with the intention of telling you all this in private, but since you are wasting my time so needlessly I don't see why your parents shouldn't hear it too. For some time past your work has been most unsatisfactory; this is not the season of the year for a business boom, of course, we admit that, but a season of the year for doing no business at all, that does not exist, Mr. Samsa, must not exist.''

"But, sir," cried Gregor, beside himself and in his agitation forgetting everything else, "I'm just going to open the door this very minute. A slight illness, an attack of giddiness, has kept me from getting up. I'm still lying in bed. But I feel all right again. I'm getting out of bed now. Just give me a moment or two longer! I'm not quite so well as I thought. But I'm all right, really. How a thing like that can suddenly strike one down! Only last night I was quite well, my parents can tell you, or rather I did have a slight presentiment. I must have showed some sign of it. Why didn't I report it at the office! But one always thinks that an indisposition can be got over without staying in the house. Oh sir, do spare my parents! All that you're reproaching me with now has no foundation; no one has ever said a word to me about it. Perhaps you haven't looked at the last orders I sent in. Anyhow, I can still catch the eight o'clock train, I'm much the better for my few hours' rest. Don't let me detain you here, sir; I'll be attending to business very soon, and do be good enough to tell the chief so and to make my excuses to him!''

And while all this was tumbling out pell-mell and Gregor hardly knew what he was saying, he had reached the chest quite easily, perhaps because of the practice he had had in bed, and was now trying to lever himself upright by means of it. He meant actually to open the door, actually to show himself and speak to the chief clerk; he was eager to find out what the others, after all their insistence, would say at the sight of him. If they were horrified then the responsibility was no longer his and he could stay quiet. But if they took it calmly, then he had no reason either to be upset, and could really get to the station for the eight o'clock train if he hurried. At first he slipped down a few times from the polished surface of the chest, but at length with a last heave he stood upright; he paid no more attention to the pains in the lower part of his body, however they smarted. Then he let himself fall against the back of a nearby chair, and clung with his little legs to the edges of it. That brought him into control of himself again and he stopped speaking, for now he could listen to what the chief clerk was saying.

"Did you understand a word of it?'' the chief clerk was asking; "surely he can't be trying to make fools of us?'' "Oh dear,'' cried his mother, in tears, "perhaps he's terribly ill and we're tormenting him. Grete! Grete!'' she called out then. "Yes Mother?'' called his sister from the other side. They were calling to each other across Gregor's room. "You must go this minute for the doctor. Gregor is ill. Go for the doctor, quick. Did you hear how he was speaking?'' "That was no human voice,'' said the chief clerk in a voice noticeably low beside the shrillness of the mother's. "Anna! Anna!'' his father was calling through the hall to the kitchen, clapping his hands, "get a locksmith at once!'' And the two girls were already running through the hall with a swish of skirts—how could his sister have got dressed so quickly?—and were tearing the front door open. There was no sound of its closing again; they had evidently left it open as one does in houses where some great misfortune has happened.

But Gregor was now much calmer. The words he uttered were no longer understandable, apparently, although they seemed clear enough to him, even clearer than before, perhaps because his ear had grown accustomed to the sound of them. Yet at any rate people now believed that something was wrong with him, and were ready to help him. The positive certainty with which these first measures had been taken comforted him. He felt himself drawn once more into the human circle and hoped for great and remarkable results from both the doctor and the locksmith, without really distinguishing precisely between them. To make his voice as clear as possible for the decisive conversation that was now imminent he coughed a little, as quietly as he could, of course, since this noise too might not sound like a human cough for all he was able to judge. In the next room meanwhile there was complete silence. Perhaps his parents were sitting at the table with the chief clerk, whispering, perhaps they were all leaning against the door and listening.

Slowly Gregor pushed the chair towards the door, then let go of it, caught hold of the door for support—the soles at the end of his little legs were somewhat sticky—and rested against it for a moment after his efforts. Then he set himself to turning the key in the lock with his mouth. It seemed, unhappily, that he hadn't really any teeth—what could he grip the key with?—but on the other hand his jaws were certainly very strong; with their help he did manage to set the key in motion, heedless of the fact that he was undoubtedly damaging them somewhere, since a brown fluid issued from his mouth, flowed over the key and dripped on the floor. "Just listen to that,'' said the chief clerk next door; "he's turning the key.'' That was a great encouragement to Gregor; but they should all have shouted encouragement to him, his father and mother too: "Go on, Gregor," they should have called out, "keep going, hold on to that key!" And in the belief that they were all following his efforts intently, he clenched his jaws recklessly on the key with all the force at his command. As the turning of the key progressed he circled round the lock, holding on now only with his mouth, pushing on the key, as required, or pulling it down again with all the weight of his body. The louder click of the finally yielding lock literally quickened Gregor. With a deep breath of relief he said to himself, "So I didn't need the locksmith," and laid his head on the handle to open the door wide.

Since he had to pull the door towards him, he was still invisible when it was really wide open. He had to edge himself very slowly round the near half of the double door, and to do it very carefully if he was not to fall plump upon his back just on the threshold. He was still carrying out this difficult manoeuvre, with no time to observe anything else, when he heard the chief clerk utter a loud "Oh!"—it sounded like a gust of wind—and now he could see the man, standing as he was nearest to the door, clapping one hand before his open mouth and slowly backing away as if driven by some invisible steady pressure. His mother—in spite of the chief clerk's being there her hair was still undone and sticking up in all directions—first clasped her hands and looked at his father, then took two steps towards Gregor and fell on the floor among her outspread skirts, her face quite hidden on her breast. His father knotted his fist with a fierce expression on his face as if he meant to knock Gregor back into his room, then looked uncertainly round the living room, covered his eyes with his hands and wept till his great chest heaved.

Gregor did not go now into the living room, but leaned against the inside of the firmly shut wing of the door, so that only half his body was visible and his head above it bending sideways to look at the others. The light had meanwhile strengthened; on the other side of the street one could see clearly a section of the endlessly long, dark gray building opposite—it was a hospital—abruptly punctuated by its row of regular windows; the rain was still falling, but only in large singly discernible and literally singly splashing drops. The breakfast dishes were set out on the table lavishly, for breakfast was the most important meal of the day to Gregor's father, who lingered it out for hours over various newspapers. Right opposite Gregor on the wall hung a photograph of himself on military service, as a lieutenant, hand on sword, a carefree smile on his face, inviting one to respect his uniform and military bearing. The door leading to the hall was open, and one could see that the front door stood open too, showing the landing beyond and the beginning of the stairs going down.

"Well," said Gregor, knowing perfectly that he was the only one who had retained any composure, "I'll put my clothes on at once, pack up my samples and start off. Will you only let me go? You see, sir, I'm not obstinate, and I'm willing to work; traveling is a hard life, but I couldn't live without it. Where are you going, sir? To the office? Yes? Will you give a true account of all this? One can be temporarily incapacitated, but that's just the moment for remembering former services and bearing in mind that later on, when the incapacity has been got over, one will certainly work with all the more industry and concentration. I'm loyally bound to serve the chief, you know that very well. Besides, I have to provide for my parents and my sister. I'm in great difficulties, but I'll get out of them again. Don't make things any worse for me than they are. Stand up for me in the firm. Travelers are not popular there, I know. People think they earn sacks of money and just have a good time. A prejudice there's no particular reason for revising. But you, sir, have a more comprehensive view of affairs than the rest of the staff, yes, let me tell you in confidence, a more comprehensive view than the chief himself, who, being the owner, lets his judgment easily be swayed against one of his employees. And you know very well that the traveler, who is never seen in the office almost the whole year round, can so easily fall a victim to gossip and ill luck and unfounded complaints, which he mostly knows nothing about, except when he comes back exhausted from his rounds, and only then suffers in person from their evil consequences, which he can no longer trace back to the original causes. Sir, sir, don't go away without a word to me to show that you think me in the right at least to some extent!''

But at Gregor's very first words the chief clerk had already backed away and only stared at him with parted lips over one twitching shoulder. And while Gregor was speaking he did not stand still one moment but stole away towards the door, without taking his eyes off Gregor, yet only an inch at a time, as if obeying some secret injunction to leave the room. He was already at the hall, and the suddenness with which he took his last step out of the living room would have made one believe he had burned the sole of his foot. Once in the hall he stretched his right arm before him towards the staircase, as if some supernatural power were waiting there to deliver him.

Gregor perceived that the chief clerk must on no account be allowed to go away in this frame of mind if his position in the firm were not to be endangered to the utmost. His parents did not understand this so well; they had convinced themselves in the course of years that Gregor was settled for life in this firm, and besides they were so occupied with their immediate troubles that all foresight had forsaken them. Yet Gregor had this foresight. The chief clerk must be detained, soothed, persuaded and finally won over; the whole future of Gregor and his family depended on it! If only his sister had been there! She was intelligent; she had begun to cry while Gregor was still lying quietly on his back. And no doubt the chief clerk, so partial to ladies, would have been guided by her; she would have shut the door of the flat and in the hall talked him out of his horror. But she was not there, and Gregor would have to handle the situation himself. And without remembering that he was still unaware what powers of movement he possessed, without even remembering that his words in all possibility, indeed in all likelihood, would again be unintelligible, he let go the wing of the door, pushed himself through the opening, started to walk to-

wards the chief clerk, who was already ridiculously clinging with both hands to the railing on the landing; but immediately, as he was feeling for a support, he fell down with a little cry upon all his numerous legs. Hardly was he down when he experienced for the first time this morning a sense of physical comfort; his legs had firm ground under them; they were completely obedient, as he noted with joy; they even strove to carry him forward in whatever direction he chose; and he was inclined to believe that a final relief from all his sufferings was at hand. But in the same moment as he found himself on the floor, rocking with suppressed eagerness to move, not far from his mother, indeed just in front of her, she, who had seemed so completely crushed, sprang all at once to her feet, her arms and fingers outspread, cried: ''Help, for God's sake, help!'' bent her head down as if to see Gregor better, yet on the contrary kept backing senselessly away; had quite forgotten that the laden table stood behind her; sat upon it hastily, as if in absence of mind, when she bumped into it; and seemed altogether unaware that the big coffee pot beside her was upset and pouring coffee in a flood over the carpet.

''Mother, Mother,'' said Gregor in a low voice, and looked up at her. The chief clerk, for the moment, had quite slipped from his mind; instead he could not resist snapping his jaws together at the sight of the streaming coffee. That made his mother scream again, she fled from the table and fell into the arms of his father, who hastened to catch her. But Gregor had now no time to spare for his parents; the chief clerk was already on the stairs; with his chin on the banisters he was taking one last backward look. Gregor made a spring, to be as sure as possible of overtaking him; the chief clerk must have divined his intention, for he leaped down several steps and vanished; he was still yelling ''Ugh!'' and it echoed through the whole staircase.

Unfortunately, the flight of the chief clerk seemed completely to upset Gregor's father, who had remained relatively calm until now, for instead of running after the man himself, or at least not hindering Gregor in his pursuit, he seized in his right hand the walking stick which the chief clerk had left behind on a chair, together with a hat and greatcoat, snatched in his left hand a large newspaper from the table and began stamping his feet and flourishing the stick and the newspaper to drive Gregor back into his room. No entreaty of Gregor's availed, indeed no entreaty was even understood; however humbly he bent his head his father only stamped on the floor the more loudly. Behind his father his mother had torn open a window, despite the cold weather, and was leaning far out of it with her face in her hands. A strong draught set in from the street to the staircase, the window curtain blew in, the newspapers on the table fluttered, stray pages whisked over the floor. Pitilessly Gregor's father drove him back, hissing and crying "Shoo!" like a savage. But Gregor was quite unpracticed in walking backwards, it really was a slow business. If he only had a chance to turn round he could get back to his room at once, but he was afraid of exasperating his father by the slowness of such a rotation and at any moment the stick in his father's hand might hit him a fatal blow on the back or on the head. In the end, however, nothing else was left for him to do since to his horror he observed that in moving backwards he could not even control the direction he took; and so, keeping an anxious eye on his father all the time over his shoulder, he began to turn round as quickly as he could, which was in reality very slowly. Perhaps his father noted his good intentions, for he did not interfere except every now and then to help him in the manoeuvre

from a distance with the point of the stick. If only he would have stopped making that unbearable hissing noise! It made Gregor quite lose his head. He had turned almost completely round when the hissing noise so distracted him that he even turned a little the wrong way again. But when at last his head was fortunately right in front of the doorway, it appeared that his body was too broad simply to get through the opening. His father, of course, in his present mood was far from thinking of such a thing as opening the other half of the door, to let Gregor have enough space. He had merely the fixed idea of driving Gregor back into his room as quickly as possible. He would have never suffered Gregor to make the circumstantial preparations for standing up on end and perhaps slipping his way through the door. Maybe he was now making more noise than ever to urge Gregor forward, as if no obstacle impeded him; to Gregor, anyhow, the noise in his rear sounded no longer like the voice of one single father; this was really no joke, and Gregor thrust himself—come what might—into the doorway. One side of his body rose up, he was tiled at an angle in the doorway, his flank was quite bruised, horrid blotches stained the white door, soon he was stuck fast and, left to himself, could not have moved at all, his legs on one side fluttered trembling in the air, those on the other were crushed painfully to the floor—when from behind his father gave him a strong push which was literally a deliverance and he flew far into the room, bleeding freely. The door was slammed behind him with the stick, and then at last there was silence.

II

Not until it was twilight did Gregor awake out of a deep sleep, more like a swoon than a sleep. He would certainly have waked up of his own accord not much later, for he felt himself sufficiently rested and well-slept, but it seemed to him as if a fleeting step and a cautious shutting of the door leading into the hall had aroused him. The electric lights in the street cast a pale

sheen here and there on the ceiling and the upper surfaces of the furniture, but down below, where he lay, it was dark. Slowly, awkwardly trying out his feelers, which he now first learned to appreciate, he pushed his way to the door to see what had been happening there. His left side felt like one single long, unpleasantly tense scar, and he had actually to limp on his two rows of legs. One little leg, moreover, had been severely damaged in the course of that morning's events—it was almost a miracle that only one had been damaged—and trailed uselessly behind him.

He had reached the door before he discovered what had really drawn him to it: the smell of food. For there stood a basin filled with fresh milk in which floated little sops of white bread. He could almost have laughed with joy, since he was now still hungrier than in the morning, and dipped his head almost over the eyes straight into the milk. But soon in disappointment he withdrew it again; not only did he find it difficult to feed because of his tender left side—and he could only feed with the palpitating collaboration of his whole body—he did not like the milk either, although milk had been his favorite drink and that was certainly why his sister had set it there for him, indeed it was almost with repulsion that he turned away from the basin and crawled back to the middle of the room.

He could see through the crack of the door that the gas was turned on in the living room, but while usually at this time his father made a habit of reading the afternoon newspaper in a loud voice to his mother and occasionally to his sister as well, not a sound was now to be heard. Well, perhaps his father had recently given up this habit of reading aloud, which his sister had mentioned so often in conversation and in her letters. But there was the same silence all around, although the flat was certainly not empty of occupants. "What a quiet life our family has been leading," said Gregor to himself, and as he sat there motionless staring into the darkness he felt great pride in the fact that he had been able to provide such a life for his parents and sister in such a fine flat. But what if all the quiet, the comfort, the contentment were now to end in horror? To keep himself from being lost in such thoughts Gregor took refuge in movement and crawled up and down the room.

Once during the long evening one of the side doors was opened a little and quickly shut again, later the other side door too; someone had apparently wanted to come in and then thought better of it. Gregor now stationed himself immediately before the living room door, determined to persuade any hesitating visitor to come in or at least to discover who it might be; but the door was not opened again and he waited in vain. In the early morning, when the doors were locked, they had all wanted to come in, now that he had opened one door and the other had apparently been opened during the day, no one came in and even the keys were on the other side of the doors.

It was late at night before the gas went out in the living room, and Gregor could easily tell that his parents and his sister had all stayed awake until then, for he could clearly hear the three of them stealing away on tiptoe. No one was likely to visit him, not until the morning, that was certain; so he had plenty of time to meditate at his leisure on how he was to arrange his life afresh. But the lofty, empty room in which he had to lie flat on the floor filled him with an apprehension he could not account for, since it had been his very own room for the past five years—and with a half-unconscious action, not without a slight feeling of shame, he scuttled under the sofa, where he felt comfortable at once, although his back was a little cramped and he could not lift his head up, and his only regret was that his body was too broad to get the whole of it under the sofa.

He stayed there all night, spending the time partly in a light slumber, from which his hunger kept waking him up with a start, and partly in worrying and sketching vague hopes, which all led to the same conclusion, that he must lie low for the present and, by exercising patience and the utmost consideration, help the family to bear the inconvenience he was bound to cause them in his present condition.

Very early in the morning, it was still almost night, Gregor had the chance to test the strength of his new resolutions, for his sister, nearly fully dressed, opened the door from the hall and peered in. She did not see him at once, yet when she caught sight of him under the sofa—well, he had to be somewhere, he couldn't have flown away, could he?—she was so startled that without being able to help it she slammed the door shut again. But as if regretting her behavior she opened the door again immediately and came in on tiptoe, as if she were visiting an invalid or even a stranger. Gregor had pushed his head forward to the very edge of the sofa and watched her. Would she notice that he had left the milk standing, and not for lack of hunger, and would she bring in some other kind of food more to his taste? If she did not do it of her own accord, he would rather starve than draw her attention to the fact, although he felt a wild impulse to dart out from under the sofa, throw himself at her feet and beg her for something to eat. But his sister at once noticed, with surprise, that the basin was still full, except for a little milk that had been spilt all around it, she lifted it immediately, not with her bare hands, true, but with a cloth and carried it away. Gregor was wildly curious to know what she would bring instead, and made various speculations about it. Yet what she actually did next, in the goodness of her heart, he could never have guessed at. To find out what he liked she brought him a whole selection of food, all set out on an old newspaper. There were old, half-decayed vegetables, bones from last night's supper covered with a white sauce that had thickened; some raisins and almonds; a piece of cheese that Gregor would have called uneatable two days ago; a dry roll of bread, a buttered roll, and a roll both buttered and salted. Besides all that, she set down again the same basin, into which she had poured some water, and which was apparently to be reserved for his exclusive use. And with fine tact, knowing that Gregor would not eat in her presence, she withdrew quickly and even turned the key, to let him understand that he could take his ease as much as he liked. Gregor's legs all whizzed towards the food. His wounds must have healed completely, moreover, for he felt no disability, which amazed him and made him reflect how more than a month ago he had cut one finger a little with a knife and had still suffered pain from the wound only the day before yesterday. Am I less sensitive now? he thought, and sucked greedily at the cheese, which above all the other edibles attracted him at once and strongly. One after

another and with tears of satisfaction in his eyes he quickly devoured the cheese, the vegetables and the sauce; the fresh food, on the other hand, had no charms for him, he could not even stand the smell of it and actually dragged away to some little distance the things he could eat. He had long finished his meal and was only lying lazily on the same spot when his sister turned the key slowly as a sign for him to retreat. That roused him at once, although he was nearly asleep, and he hurried under the sofa again. But it took considerable self-control for him to stay under the sofa, even for the short time his sister was in the room, since the large meal had swollen his body somewhat and he was so cramped he could hardly breathe. Slight attacks of breathlessness afflicted him and his eyes were starting a little out of his head as he watched his unsuspecting sister sweeping together with a broom not only the remains of what he had eaten but even the things he had not touched, as if these were now of no use to anyone, and hastily shoveling it all into a bucket, which she covered with a wooden lid and carried away. Hardly had she turned her back when Gregor came from under the sofa and stretched and puffed himself out.

In this manner Gregor was fed, once in the early morning while his parents and the servant girl were still asleep, and a second time after they had all had their midday dinner, for then his parents took a short nap and the servant girl could be sent out on some errand or other by his sister. Not that they would have wanted him to starve, of course, but perhaps they could not have borne to know more about his feeding than from hearsay, perhaps too his sister wanted to spare them such little anxieties wherever possible, since they had quite enough to bear as it was.

Under what pretext the doctor and the locksmith had been got rid of on that first morning Gregor could not discover, for since what he said was not understood by the others it never struck any of them, not even his sister, that he could understand what they said, and so whenever his sister came into his room he had to content himself with hearing her utter only a sigh now and then and an occasional appeal to the saints. Later on, when she had got a little used to the situation—of course she could never get completely used to it—she sometimes threw out a remark which was kindly meant or could be so interpreted. "Well, he liked his dinner today," she would say when Gregor had made a good clearance of his food; and when he had not eaten, which gradually happened more and more often, she would say almost sadly: "Everything's been left standing again."

But although Gregor could get no news directly, he overheard a lot from the neighboring rooms, and as soon as voices were audible, he would run to the door of the room concerned and press his whole body against it. In the first few days especially there was no conversation that did not refer to him somehow, even if only indirectly. For two whole days there were family consultations at every mealtime about what should be done; but also between meals the same subject was discussed, for there were always at least two members of the family at home, since no one wanted to be alone in the flat and to leave it quite empty was unthinkable. And on the very first of these days the household cook—it was not quite clear what and how much she knew of the situation—went down on her knees to his mother and begged leave to go, and when she departed, a quarter of an hour later, gave thanks for her dismissal with tears in her eyes as if for the greatest benefit that could have been conferred on her, and without any prompting swore a solemn oath that she would never say a single word to anyone about what had happened.

Now Gregor's sister had to cook too, helping her mother; true, the cooking did not amount to much, for they ate scarcely anything. Gregor was always hearing one of the family vainly urging another to eat and getting no answer but: "Thanks, I've had all I want," or something similar. Perhaps they drank nothing either. Time and again his sister kept asking his father if he wouldn't like some beer and offered kindly to go and fetch it herself, and when he made no answer suggested that she could ask the concierge to fetch it, so that he need feel no

sense of obligation, but then a round "No" came from his father and no more was said about it.

In the course of that very first day Gregor's father explained the family's financial position and prospects to both his mother and his sister. Now and then he rose from the table to get some voucher or memorandum out of the small safe he had rescued from the collapse of his business five years earlier. One could hear him opening the complicated lock and rustling papers out and shutting it again. This statement made by his father was the first cheerful information Gregor had heard since his imprisonment. He had been of the opinion that nothing at all was left over from his father's business, at least his father had never said anything to the contrary, and of course he had not asked him directly. At that time Gregor's sole desire was to do his utmost to help the family to forget as soon as possible the catastrophe which had overwhelmed the business and thrown them all into a state of complete despair. And so he had set to work with unusual ardor and almost overnight had become a commercial traveler instead of a little clerk, with of course much greater chances of earning money, and his success was immediately translated into good round coin which he could lay on the table for his amazed and happy family. These had been fine times, and they had never recurred, at least not with the same sense of glory, although later on Gregor had earned so much money that he was able to meet the expenses of the whole household and did so. They had simply got used to it, both the family and Gregor; the money was gratefully accepted and gladly given, but there was no special uprush of warm feeling. With his sister alone had he remained intimate, and it was a secret plan of his that she, who loved music, unlike himself, and could play movingly on the violin, should be sent next year to study at the Conservatorium, despite the great expense that would entail, which must be made up in some other way. During his brief visits home the Conservatorium was often mentioned in the talks he had with his sister, but always merely as a beautiful dream which could never come true, and his parents discouraged even these innocent references to it; yet Gregor had made up his mind firmly about it and meant to announce the fact with due solemnity on Christmas Day.

Such were the thoughts, completely futile in his present condition, that went through his head as he stood clinging upright to the door and listening. Sometimes out of sheer weariness he had to give up listening and let his head fall negligently against the door, but he always had to pull himself together again at once, for even the slight sound his head made was audible next door and brought all conversation to a stop. "What can he be doing now?" his father would say after a while, obviously turning towards the door, and only then would the interrupted conversation gradually be set going again.

Gregor was not informed as amply as he could wish—for his father tended to repeat himself in his explanations, partly because it was a long time since he had handled such matters and partly because his mother could not always grasp things at once—that a certain amount of investments, a very small amount it was true, had survived the wreck of their fortunes and had even increased a little because the dividends had not been touched meanwhile. And besides that, the money Gregor brought home every month—he had kept only a few dollars for himself—had never been quite used up and now amounted to a small capital sum. Behind the door Gregor nodded his head eagerly, rejoiced at this evidence of unexpected thrift and foresight. True, he could really have paid off some more of his father's debts to the chief with this extra money, and so brought much nearer the day on which he could quit his job, but doubtless it was better the way his father had arranged it.

Yet this capital was by no means sufficient to let the family live on the interest of it; for one year, perhaps, or at the most two, they could live on the principal, that was all. It was simply a sum that ought not to be touched and should be kept for a rainy day; money for living expenses would have to be earned. Now his father was still hale enough for an old man, and he had done no work for the past five years and

could not be expected to do much; during these five years, the first years of leisure in his laborious though unsuccessful life, he had grown rather fat and become sluggish. And Gregor's old mother, how was she to earn a living with her asthma, which troubled her even when she walked through the flat and kept her lying on a sofa every other day panting for breath beside an open window? And was his sister to earn her bread, she who was still a child of seventeen and whose life hitherto had been so pleasant, consisting as it did in dressing herself nicely, sleeping long, helping in the housekeeping, going out to a few modest entertainments and above all playing the violin? At first whenever the need for earning money was mentioned Gregor let go his hold on the door and threw himself down on the cool leather sofa beside it, he felt so hot with shame and grief.

Often he just lay there the long nights through without sleeping at all, scrabbling for hours on the leather. Or he nerved himself to the great effort of pushing an armchair to the window, then crawled up over the window sill and, braced against the chair, leaned against the window panes, obviously in some recollection of the sense of freedom that looking out of a window always used to give him. For in reality day by day things that were even a little way off were growing dimmer to his sight; the hospital across the street, which he used to execrate for being all too often before his eyes, was not quite beyond his range of vision, and if he had not known that he lived in Charlotte Street, a quiet street but still a city street, he might have believed that his window gave on a desert waste where gray sky and gray land blended indistinguishably into each other. His quick-witted sister only needed to observe twice that the armchair stood by the window; after that whenever she had tidied the room she always pushed the chair back to the same place at the window and even left the inner casements open.

If he could have spoken to her and thanked her for all she had to do for him, he could have borne her ministrations better; as it was, they oppressed him. She certainly tried to make as light as possible of whatever was disagreeable in her task, and as time went on she succeeded, of course, more and more, but time brought more enlightenment to Gregor too. The very way she came in distressed him. Hardly was she in the room when she rushed to the window, without even taking time to shut the door, careful as she was usually to shield the sight of Gregor's room from the others, and as if she were almost suffocating tore the casements open with hasty fingers, standing then in the open draught for a while even in the bitterest cold and drawing deep breaths. This noisy scurry of hers upset Gregor twice a day; he would crouch trembling under the sofa all the time, knowing quite well that she would certainly have spared him such a disturbance had she found it at all possible to stay in his presence without opening the window.

On one occasion, about a month after Gregor's metamorphosis, when there was surely no reason for her to be still startled at his appearance, she came a little earlier than usual and found him gazing out of the window, quite motionless, and thus well placed to look like a bogey. Gregor would not have been surprised had she not come in at all, for she could not immediately open the window while he was there, but not only did she retreat, she jumped back as if in alarm and banged the door shut; a stranger might well have thought that he had been lying in wait for her there meaning to bite her. Of course he hid himself under the sofa at once, but he had to wait until midday before she came again, and she seemed more ill at ease than usual. This made him realize how repulsive the sight of him still was to her, and that it was bound to go on being repulsive, and what an effort it must cost her not to run away even from the sight of the small portion of his body that stuck out from under the sofa. In order to spare her that, therefore, one day he carried a sheet on his back to the sofa—it cost him four hours' labor—and arranged it there in such a way as to hide him completely, so that even if she were to bend down she could not see him. Had she considered the sheet unnecessary, she would certainly have stripped it off the sofa again, for it was clear enough that this curtaining and confining of himself was not likely to

conduce Gregor's comfort, but she left it where it was, and Gregor even fancied that he caught a thankful glance from her eye when he lifted the sheet carefully a very little with his head to see how she was taking the new arrangement.

For the first fortnight his parents could not bring themselves to the point of entering his room, and he often heard them expressing their appreciation of his sister's activities, whereas formerly they had frequently scolded her for being as they thought a somewhat useless daughter. But now, both of them often waited outside the door, his father and his mother, while his sister tidied his room, and as soon as she came out she had to tell them exactly how things were in the room, what Gregor had eaten, how he had conducted himself this time and whether there was not perhaps some slight improvement in his condition. His mother, moreover, began relatively soon to want to visit him, but his father and sister dissuaded her at first with arguments which Gregor listened to very attentively and altogether approved. Later, however, she had to be held back by main force, and when she cried out: "Do let me in to Gregor, he is my unfortunate son! Can't you understand that I must go to him?" Gregor thought that it might be well to have her come in, not every day, of course, but perhaps once a week; she understood things, after all, much better than his sister, who was only a child despite the efforts she was making and had perhaps taken on so difficult a task merely out of childish thoughtlessness.

Gregor's desire to see his mother was soon fulfilled. During the daytime he did not want to show himself at the window, out of consideration for his parents, but he could not crawl very far around the few square yards of floor space he had, nor could he bear lying quietly at rest all during the night, while he was fast losing any interest he had ever taken in food, so that for mere recreation he had formed the habit of crawling crisscross over the walls and ceiling. He especially enjoyed hanging suspended from the ceiling; it was much better than lying on the floor. One could breathe more freely; one's body swung and rocked lightly; and in the almost blissful absorption induced by this suspension it could happen to his own surprise that he let go and fell plump on the floor. Yet he now had his body much better under control than formerly, and even such a big fall did him no harm. His sister at once remarked the new distraction Gregor had found for himself—he left traces behind him of the sticky stuff on his soles wherever he crawled—and she got the idea in her head of giving him as wide a field as possible to crawl in and of removing the pieces of furniture that hindered him, above all the chest of drawers and the writing desk. But that was more than she could manage all by herself, she did not dare ask her father to help her; and as for the servant girl, a young creature of sixteen who had had the courage to stay on after the cook's departure, she could not be asked to help, for she had begged as an especial favor that she might keep the kitchen door locked and open it only on a definite summons; so there was nothing left but to apply to her mother at an hour when her father was out. And the old lady did come, with exclamations of joyful eagerness, which, however, died away at the door of Gregor's room. Gregor's sister, of course, went in first, to see that everything was in order before letting his mother enter. In great haste Gregor pulled the sheet lower and tucked it more in folds so that it really looked as if it had been thrown accidentally over the sofa. And this time he did not peer out from under it; he renounced the pleasure of seeing his mother on this occasion and was only glad that she had come at all. "Come in, he's out of sight," said his sister, obviously leading her mother by the hand. Gregor could now hear the two women struggling to shift the heavy old chest from its place, and his sister claiming the greater part of the labor for herself, without listening to the admonitions of her mother who feared she might overstrain herself. It took a long time. After at least a quarter of an hour's tugging his mother objected that the chest had better be left where it was, for in the first place it was too heavy and could never be got out before his father came home, and standing in the middle of the room like that it would only hamper Gregor's movements, while in the second place it was not at all certain that removing the furniture would be doing a service to Gregor. She was inclined to think to the contrary; the sight of the naked walls made her own heart heavy, and why shouldn't Gregor have the same feeling, considering that he had been used to his furniture for so long and might feel forlorn without it. "And doesn't it look," she concluded in a low voice—in fact she had been almost whispering all the time as if to avoid letting Gregor, whose exact whereabouts she did not know, hear even the tones of her voice, for she was convinced that he could not understand her words—"doesn't it look as if we were showing him, by taking away his furniture, that we have given up hope of his ever getting better and are just leaving him coldly to himself? I think it would be best to keep his room exactly as it has always been, so that when he comes back to us he will find everything unchanged and be able all the more easily to forget what has happened in between."

On hearing these words from his mother Gregor realized that the lack of all direct human speech for the past two months together with the monotony of family life must have confused his mind, otherwise he could not account for the fact that he had quite earnestly looked forward to having his room emptied of furnishing. Did he really want his warm room, so comfortably fitted with old family furniture, to be turned into a naked den in which he would certainly be able to crawl unhampered in all directions but at the price of shedding simultaneously all recollection of his human background? He had indeed been so near the brink of forgetfulness that only the voice of his mother, which he had not heard for so long, had drawn him back from it. Nothing should be taken out of his room; everything must stay as it was; he could not dispense with the good influence of the furniture on his state of mind; and even if the furniture did hamper him in his senseless crawling round and round, that was no drawback but a great advantage.

Unfortunately his sister was of the contrary opinion; she had grown accustomed, and not without reason, to consider herself an expert in Gregor's affairs as against her parents, and so her mother's advice was now enough to make her determined on the removal not only of the chest and the writing desk, which had been her first intention, but of all the furniture except the indispensable sofa. This determination was not, of course, merely the outcome of childish recalcitrance and of the self-confidence she had recently developed so unexpectedly and at such cost; she had in fact perceived that Gregor needed a lot of space to crawl about in, while on the other hand he never used the furniture at all, so far as could be seen. Another factor might have been also the enthusiastic temperament of an adolescent girl, which seeks to indulge itself on every opportunity and which now tempted Grete to exaggerate the horror of her brother's circumstances in order that she might do all the more for him. In a room where Gregor lorded it all alone over empty walls no one save herself was likely ever to set foot.

And so she was not to be moved from her resolve by her mother who seemed moreover to be ill at ease in Gregor's room and therefore unsure of herself, was soon reduced to silence and helped her daughter as best she could to push the chest outside. Now, Gregor could do without the chest, if need be, but the writing desk he must retain. As soon as the two women had got the chest out of his room, groaning as they pushed it, Gregor stuck his head out from under the sofa to see how he might intervene as kindly and cautiously as possible. But as bad luck would have it, his mother was the first to return, leaving Grete clasping the chest in the room next door where she was trying to shift it all by herself, without of course moving it from the spot. His mother however was not accustomed to the sight of him, it might sicken her and so in alarm Gregor backed quickly to the other end of the sofa, yet could not prevent the sheet from swaying a little in front. That was enough to put her on the alert. She paused, stood still for a moment and then went back to Grete.

Although Gregor kept reassuring himself that nothing out of the way was happening, but only a few bits of furniture were being changed round, he soon had to admit that all this trotting to and fro of the two women, their little ejaculations and the scraping of furniture along the floor affected him like a vast disturbance coming from all sides at once, and however much he tucked in his head and legs and cowered to the very floor he was bound to confess that he would not be able to stand it for long. They were clearing his room out; taking away everything he loved; the chest in which he kept his fret saw and other tools was already dragged off, they were now loosening the writing desk which had almost sunk into the floor, the desk at which he had done all his homework when he was at the commercial academy, at the grammar school before that, and, yes, even at the primary school—he had no more time to waste in weighing the good intentions of the two women, whose existence he had by now almost forgotten, for they were so exhausted that they were laboring in silence and nothing could be heard but the heavy scuffling of their feet.

And so he rushed out—the women were just leaning against the writing desk in the next room to give themselves a breather—and four times changed his direction, since he really did not know what to rescue first, then on the wall opposite, which was already otherwise cleared, he was struck by the picture of the lady muffled in so much fur and quickly crawled up to it and pressed himself to the glass, which was a good surface to hold on to and comforted his hot belly. This picture at least, which was entirely hidden beneath him, was going to be removed by nobody. He turned his head towards the door of the living room so as to observe the women when they came back.

They had not allowed themselves much of a rest and were already coming; Grete had twined her arm round her mother and was almost supporting her. "Well, what shall we take now?" said Grete, looking round. Her eyes met Gregor's from the wall. She kept her composure, presumably because of her mother, bent her head down to her mother, to keep her from looking up, and said, although in a fluttering unpremeditated voice: "Come, hadn't we better go back to the living room for a moment?" Her intentions were clear enough to Gregor, she wanted to bestow her mother in safety and then chase him down from the wall. Well, just let her try it! He clung to his picture and would not give it up. He would rather fly in Grete's face.

But Grete's words had succeeded in disquieting her mother, who took a step to one side, caught sight of the huge brown mass on the flowered wallpaper, and before she was really conscious that what she saw was Gregor screamed in a loud, hoarse voice: "Oh God, oh God! fell with outspread arms over the sofa as if giving up and did not move. "Gregor!" cried his sister, shaking her fist and glaring at him. This was the first time she had directly addressed him since his metamorphosis. She ran into the next room for some aromatic essence with which to rouse her mother from her fainting fit. Gregor wanted to help too—there was still time to rescue the picture—but he was stuck fast to the glass and had to tear himself loose; he then ran after his sister into the next room as if he could advise her, as he used to do; but then had to stand helplessly behind her; she meanwhile searched among various small bottles and when she turned round started in alarm at the sight of him; one bottle fell on the floor and broke; a splinter of glass cut Gregor's face and some kind of corrosive medicine splashed him; without pausing a moment longer Grete gathered up all the bottles she could carry and ran to her mother with them; she banged the door shut with her foot. Gregor was now cut off from his mother, who was perhaps nearly dying because of him; he dared not open the door for fear of frightening away his sister, who had to stay with her mother; there was nothing he could no but wait; and harassed by self-reproach and worry he began now to crawl to and fro, over everything, walls, furniture and ceiling, and finally in his despair, when the whole room seemed to be reeling round him, fell down on to the middle of the big table.

A little while elapsed, Gregor was still lying there feebly and all around was quiet, perhaps that was a good omen. Then the doorbell rang. The servant girl was of course locked in her kitchen, and Grete would have to open the door. It was his father. "What's been happening?" were his first words; Grete's face must have told him everything. Grete answered in a muffled voice, apparently hiding her head on his breast: "Mother has been fainting, but she's better now.

Gregor's broken loose." "Just what I expected," said his father, "just what I've been telling you, but you women would never listen." It was clear to Gregor that his father had taken the worst interpretation of Grete's all too brief statement and was assuming that Gregor had been guilty of some violent act. Therefore Gregor must now try to propitiate his father, since he had neither time nor means for an explanation. And so he fled to the door of his own room and crouched against it, to let his father see as soon as he came in from the hall that his son had the good intention of getting back into his room immediately and that it was not necessary to drive him there, but that if only the door were opened he would disappear at once.

Yet his father was not in the mood to perceive such fine distinctions. "Ah!" he cried as soon as he appeared, in a tone which sounded at once angry and exultant. Gregor drew his head back from the door and lifted it to look at his father. Truly, this was not the father he had imagined to himself, admittedly he had been too absorbed of late in his new recreation of crawling over the ceiling to take the same interest as before in what was happening elsewhere in the flat, and he ought really to be prepared for some changes. And yet, and yet, could that be his father? The man who used to lie wearily sunk in bed whenever Gregor set out on a business journey; who welcomed him back of an evening lying in a long chair in a dressing gown; who could not really rise to his feet but only lifted his arms in greeting, and on the rare occasions when he did go out with his family, on one or two Sundays a year and on high holidays, walked between Gregor and his mother, who were slow walkers anyhow, even more slowly than they did, muffled in his old greatcoat, shuffling laboriously forward with the help of his crook-handled stick which he set down most cautiously at every step and, whenever he wanted to say anything, nearly always came to a full stop and gathered his escort around him? Now he was standing there in fine shape; dressed in a smart blue uniform with gold buttons, such as bank messengers wear; his strong double chin bulged over the stiff high collar of his jacket; from under his bushy eye-brows his black eyes darted fresh and penetrat-ing glances; his one-time tangled white hair had been combed flat on either side of a shining and carefully exact parting. He pitched his cap, which bore a gold monogram, probably the badge of some bank, in a wide sweep across the whole room on to a sofa and with the tail-ends of his jacket thrown back, his hands in his trou-ser pockets, advanced with a grim visage to-wards Gregor. Likely enough he did not himself know what he meant to do; at any rate he lifted his feet uncommonly high, and Gregor was dumbfounded at the enormous size of his shoe soles. But Gregor could not risk standing up to him, aware as he had been from the very first day of his new life that his father believed only the severest measures suitable for dealing with him. And so he ran before his father, stopping when he stopped and scuttling forward again when his father made any kind of move. In this way they circled the room several times without anything decisive happening, indeed the whole operation did not even look like a pursuit be-cause it was carried out so slowly. And so Gre-gor did not leave the floor, for he feared that his father might take as a piece of peculiar wicked-ness any excursion of his over the walls or the ceiling. All the same, he could not stay this course much longer, for while his father took one step he had to carry out a whole series of movements. He was already beginning to feel breathless, just as in his former life his lungs had not been very dependable. As he was stagger-ing along, trying to concentrate his energy on running, hardly keeping his eyes open; in his dazed state never even thinking of any other es-

cape than simply going forward; and having al-most forgotten that the walls were free to him, which in this room were well provided with finely carved pieces of furniture full of knobs and crevices—suddenly something lightly flung landed close behind him and rolled before him. It was an apple; a second apple followed imme-diately; Gregor came to a stop in alarm; there was no point in running on, for his father was determined to bombard him. He had filled his pockets with fruit from the dish on the side-board and was now shying apple after apple, without taking particularly good aim for the moment. The small red apples rolled about the floor as if magnetized and cannoned into each other. An apple thrown without much force grazed Gregor's back and glanced off harm-lessly. But another following immediately landed right on his back and sank in; Gregor wanted to drag himself forward, as if this star-tling, incredible pain could be left behind him; but he felt as if nailed to the spot and flattened himself out in a complete derangement of all his senses. With his last conscious look he saw the door of his room being torn open and his mother rushing out ahead of his screaming sis-ter, in her underbodice, for her daughter had loosened her clothing to let her breathe more freely and recover from her swoon, he saw his mother rushing towards his father, leaving one after another behind her on the floor her loos-ened petticoats, stumbling over her petticoats straight to his father and embracing him, in complete union with him—but here Gregor's sight began to fail—with her hand clasped round his father's neck as she begged for her son's life.

III

The serious injury done to Gregor, which dis-abled him for more than a month—the apple went on sticking in his body as a visible re-minder, since no one ventured to remove it—seemed to have made even his father recollect that Gregor was a member of the family, de-spite his present unfortunate and repulsive

shape, and ought not to be treated as an enemy, that, on the contrary, family duty required the suppression of disgust and the exercise of pa-tience, nothing but patience.

And although his injury had impaired, prob-ably for ever, his power of movement, and for the time being it took him long, long minutes to creep across his room like an old invalid—there was no question now of crawling up the wall—yet in his own opinion he was sufficiently compensated for this worsening of his condition by the fact that towards evening the living-room door, which he used to watch intently for an hour or two beforehand, was always thrown open, so that lying in the darkness of his room, invisible to the family, he could see them all at the lamplit table and listen to their talk, by general consent as it were, very different from his earlier eavesdropping.

True, their intercourse lacked the lively character of former times, when he had always called to mind with a certain wistfulness in the small hotel bedrooms where he had been wont to throw himself down, tired out, on damp bedding. They were now mostly very silent. Soon after supper his father would fall asleep in his armchair; his mother and sister would admonish each other to be silent; his mother, bending low over the lamp, stitched at fine sewing for an underwear firm; his sister, who had taken a job as a salesgirl, was learning shorthand and French in the evenings on the chance of bettering herself. Sometimes his father woke up, and as if quite unaware that he had been sleeping said to his mother: "What a lot of sewing you're doing today!" and at once fell asleep again, while the two women exchanged a tired smile.

With a kind of mulishness his father persisted in keeping his uniform on even in the house; his dressing gown hung uselessly on its peg and he slept fully dressed where he sat, as if he were ready for service at any moment and even here only at the beck and call of his superior. As a result, his uniform, which was not brand-new to start with, began to look dirty, despite all the loving care of the mother and sister to keep it clean, and Gregor often spent whole evenings gazing at the many greasy spots on the garment, gleaming with gold buttons always in a high state of polish, in which the old man sat sleeping in extreme discomfort and yet quite peacefully.

As soon as the clock struck ten his mother tried to rouse his father with gentle words and to persuade him after that to get into bed, for sitting there he could not have a proper sleep and that was what he needed most, since he had to go to duty at six. But with the mulishness that had obsessed him since he became a bank messenger he always insisted on staying longer at the table, although he regularly fell asleep again and in the end only with the greatest trouble could be got out of his armchair and into his bed. However insistently Gregor's mother and sister kept urging him with gentle reminders, he would go on slowly shaking his head for a quarter of an hour, keeping his eyes shut, and refuse to get to his feet. The mother plucked at his sleeve, whispering endearments in his ear, the sister left her lessons to come to her mother's help, but Gregor's father was not to be caught. He would only sink down deeper in his chair. Not until the two women hoisted him up by the armpits did he open his eyes and look at them both, one after the other, usually with the remark: "This is a life. This is the peace and quiet of my old age." And leaning on the two of them he would heave himself up, with difficulty, as if he were a great burden to himself, suffer them to lead him as far as the door and then wave them off and go on alone, while the mother abandoned her needlework and the sister her pen in order to run after him and help him farther.

Who could find time, in this overworked and tired-out family, to bother about Gregor more than was absolutely needful? The household was reduced more and more; the servant girl was turned off; a gigantic bony charwoman with white hair flying round her head came in morning and evening to do the rough work; everything else was done by Gregor's mother, as well as great piles of sewing. Even various family ornaments, which his mother and sister used to wear with pride at parties and celebrations, had to be sold, as Gregor discovered of an evening from hearing them all discuss the prices obtained. But what they lamented most was the fact that they could not leave the flat which was much too big for their present circumstances, because they could not think of any way to shift Gregor. Yet Gregor saw well enough that consideration for him was not the main difficulty preventing the removal, for they could have easily shifted him in some suitable box with a few air holes in it; what really kept them from moving into another flat was rather their own complete hopelessness and the belief that they had been singled out for a misfortune such as had never happened to any of their relations or acquaintances. They fulfilled to the uttermost all that the world demands of poor people, the father fetched breakfast for the small clerks in the bank, the mother devoted her energy to making underwear for strangers, the sister trotted to and fro behind the counter at the behest of customers, but more than this they had not the strength to do. And the wound in Gregor's back began to nag at him afresh when his mother and sister, after getting his father into bed, came back again, left their work lying, drew close to each other and sat cheek by cheek; when his mother, pointing towards his room, said: "Shut that door now, Grete," and he was left again in darkness, while next door the women mingled their tears or perhaps sat dry-eyed staring at the table.

Gregor hardly slept at all by night or by day. He was often haunted by the idea that next time the door opened he would take the family's affairs in hand again just as he used to do; once more, after this long interval, there appeared in his thoughts the figures of the chief and the chief clerk, the commercial travelers and the apprentices, the porter who was so dull-witted, two or three friends in other firms, a chambermaid in one of the rural hotels, a sweet and fleeting memory, a cashier in a milliner's shop, whom he had wooed earnestly but too slowly—they all appeared, together with strangers or people he had quite forgotten, but instead of helping him and his family they were one and all unapproachable and he was glad when they vanished. At other times he would not be in the mood to bother about his family, he was only filled with rage at the way they were neglecting him, and although he had no clear idea of what he might care to eat he would make plans for getting into the larder to take the food that was after all his due, even if he were not hungry. His sister no longer took thought to bring him

what might especially please him, but in the morning and at noon before she went to business hurriedly pushed into his room with her foot any food that was available, and in the evening cleared it out again with one sweep of the broom, heedless of whether it had been merely tasted, or—as most frequently happened—left untouched. The cleaning of his room, which she now did always in the evenings, could not have been more hastily done. Streaks of dirt stretched along the walls, here and there lay balls of dust and filth. At first Gregor used to station himself in some particularly filthy corner when his sister arrived, in order to reproach her with it, so to speak. But he could have sat there for weeks without getting her to make any improvements; she could see the dirt as well as he did, but she had simply made up her mind to leave it alone. And yet, with a touchiness that was new to her, which seemed anyhow to have infected the whole family, she jealously guarded her claim to be the sole caretaker of Gregor's room. His mother once subjected his room to a thorough cleaning, which was achieved only by means of several buckets of water—all this dampness of course upset Gregor too and he lay widespread, sulky and motionless on the sofa—but she was well punished for it. Hardly had his sister noticed the changed aspect of his room that evening than she rushed in high dudgeon into the living room and, despite the imploringly raised hands of her mother, burst into a storm of weeping, while her parents—her father had of course been startled out of his chair—looked on at first in helpless amazement; then they too began to go into action; the father reproached the mother on his right for not having left the cleaning of Gregor's room to his sister; shrieked at the sister on his left that never again was she to be allowed to clean Gregor's room; while the mother tried to pull the father into his bedroom, since he was beyond himself with agitation; the sister, shaken with sobs, then beat upon the table with her small fists; and Gregor hissed loudly with rage because not one of them thought of shutting the door to spare him such a spectacle and so much noise.

Still, even if the sister, exhausted by her daily work, had grown tired of looking after Gregor as she did formerly, there was no need for his mother's intervention or for Gregor's being neglected at all. The charwoman was there. This old widow, whose strong bony frame had enabled her to survive the worst a long life could offer, by no means recoiled from Gregor. Without being in the least curious she had once by chance opened the door of his room and at the sight of Gregor, who, taken by surprise, began to rush to and fro although no one was chasing him, merely stood there with her arms folded. From that time she never failed to open his door a little for a moment, morning and evening, to have a look at him. At first she even used to call him to her, with words which apparently she took to be friendly; such as: "Come along, then, you old dung beetle!" or "Look at the old dung beetle, then!" To such allocutions Gregor made no answer, but stayed motionless where he was, as if the door had never been opened. Instead of being allowed to disturb him so senselessly whenever the whim took her, she should rather have been ordered to clean out his room daily, that charwoman! Once, early in the morning—heavy rain was lashing on the windowpanes, perhaps a sign that spring was on the way—Gregor was so exasperated when she began addressing him again that he ran for her, as if to attack her, although slowly and feebly enough. But the charwoman instead of showing fright merely lifted high a chair that happened to be beside the door, and as she stood there with her mouth wide open it was clear that she meant to shut it only when she brought the chair down on Gregor's back. "So you're not coming any nearer?" she asked, as Gregor turned away again, and quietly put the chair back into the corner.

Gregor was now eating hardly anything. Only when he happened to pass the food laid out for him did he take a bit of something in his mouth as a pastime, kept it there for an hour at a time and usually spat it out again. At first he thought it was chagrin over the state of his room that prevented him from eating, yet he soon got used to the various changes in his room. It had become a habit in the family to push into his room things there was no room for elsewhere, and there were plenty of these now, since one of the rooms had been let to three lodgers. These serious gentlemen—all three of them with full beards, as Gregor once observed through a crack in the door—had a passion for order, not only in their own room but, since they were now members of the household, in all its arrangements, especially in the kitchen. Superfluous, not to say dirty, objects they could not bear. Besides, they had brought with them most of the furnishings they needed. For this reason many things could be dispensed with that it was no use trying to sell but that should not be thrown away either. All of them found their way into Gregor's room. The ash can likewise and the kitchen garbage can. Anything that was not needed for the moment was simply flung into Gregor's room by the charwoman, who did everything in a hurry; fortunately Gregor usually saw only the object, whatever it was, and the hand that held it. Perhaps she intended to take the things away again as time and opportunity offered, or to collect them until she could throw them all out in a heap, but in fact they just lay wherever she happened to throw them, except when Gregor pushed his way through the junk heap and shifted it somewhat, at first out of necessity, because he had not room enough to crawl, but later with increasing enjoyment, although after such excursions, being sad and weary to death, he would lie motionless for hours. And since the lodgers often ate their supper at home in the common living room, the living-room door stayed shut many an evening, yet Gregor reconciled himself quite easily to the shutting of the door, for often enough on evenings when it was opened he had disregarded it entirely and lain in the darkest corner of his room, quite unnoticed by the family. But on one occasion the charwoman left the door open a little and it stayed ajar even when the lodgers came in for supper and the lamp was lit. They set themselves at the top end of the table where formerly Gregor and his father and mother had eaten their meals, unfolded their napkins and took knife and fork in hand.

At once his mother appeared in the doorway with a dish of meat and close behind her his sister with a dish of potatoes piled high. The food steamed with a thick vapor. The lodgers bent over the food set before them as if to scrutinize it before eating, in fact the man in the middle, who seemed to pass for an authority with the other two, cut a piece of meat as it lay on the dish, obviously to discover if it were tender or should be sent back to the kitchen. He showed satisfaction, and Gregor's mother and sister, who had been watching anxiously, breathed freely and began to smile.

The family itself took its meals in the kitchen. None the less, Gregor's father came into the living room before going into the kitchen and with one prolonged bow, cap in hand, made a round of the table. The lodgers all stood up and murmured something in their beards. When they were alone again they ate their food in almost complete silence. It seemed remarkable to Gregor that among the various noises coming from the table he could always distinguish the sound of their masticating teeth, as if this were a sign to Gregor that one needed teeth in order to eat, and that with toothless jaws even of the finest make one could do nothing. "I'm hungry enough," said Gregor sadly to himself, "but not for that kind of food. How these lodgers are stuffing themselves, and here am I dying of starvation!"

On that very evening—during the whole of his time there Gregor could not remember ever having heard the violin—the sound of violin-playing came from the kitchen. The lodgers had already finished their supper, the one in the middle had brought out a newspaper and given the other two a page apiece, and now they were leaning back at ease reading and smoking. When the violin began to play they pricked up their ears, got to their feet, and went on tiptoe to the hall door where they stood huddled together. Their movements must have been heard in the kitchen, for Gregor's father called out: "Is the violin-playing disturbing you gentlemen? It can be stopped at once." "On the contrary," said the middle lodger, "could not Fräulein Samsa come and play in this room, be-

side us, where it is much more convenient and comfortable?" "Oh certainly," cried Gregor's father, as if he were the violin player. The lodgers came back into the living room and waited. Presently Gregor's father arrived with the music stand, his mother carrying the music and his sister with the violin. His sister quietly made everything ready to start playing; his parents who had never let rooms before and so had an exaggerated idea of the courtesy due to lodgers, did not venture to sit down on their own chairs; his father leaned against the door, the right hand thrust between two buttons of his livery coat, which was formally buttoned up; but his mother was offered a chair by one of the lodgers and, since she left the chair just where he had happened to put it, sat down in a corner to one side.

Gregor's sister began to play; the father and mother, from either side, intently watched the movements of her hands. Gregor, attracted by the playing, ventured to move forward a little until his head was actually inside the living room. He felt hardly any surprise at his growing lack of consideration for the others; there had been a time when he prided himself on being considerate. And yet just on this occasion he had more reason that ever to hide himself, since owing to the amount of dust which lay thick in his room and rose into the air at the slightest movement, he too was covered with dust; fluff and hair and remnants of food trailed with him, caught on his back and along his sides; his indifference to everything was much too great for him to turn on his back and scrape himself clean on the carpet, as once he had done several times a day. And in spite of his condition, no shame deterred him from advancing a little over the spotless floor of the living room.

To be sure, no one was aware of him. The family was entirely absorbed in the violin-playing; the lodgers, however, who first of all had stationed themselves, hands in pickets, much too close behind the music stand so that they could all have read the music, which must have bothered his sister, had soon retreated to the window, half-whispering with downbent heads, and stayed there while his father turned an anxious eye on them. Indeed, they were making it more than obvious that they had been disappointed in their expectation of hearing good or enjoyable violin-playing, that they had had more than enough of the performance and only out of courtesy suffered a continued disturbance of their peace. From the way they all kept blowing the smoke of their cigars high in the air through nose and mouth one could divine their irritation. And yet Gregor's sister was playing so beautifully. Her face leaned sideways, intently and sadly her eyes followed the notes of music. Gregor crawled a little farther forward and lowered his head to the ground so that it might be possible for his eyes to meet hers. Was he an animal, that music had such an effect upon him? He felt as if the way were opening before him to the unknown nourishment he craved. He was determined to push forward till he reached his sister, to pull at her skirt and so let her know that she was to come into his room with her violin, for no one here appreciated her playing as he would appreciate it. He would never let her out of his room, at least, not so long as he lived; his frightful appearance would become, for the first time, useful to him; he would watch all the doors of his room at once and spit at intruders; but his sister should need no constraint, she should stay with him of her own free will; she should sit beside him on the sofa, bend down her ear to him and hear him confide that he had had the firm intention of sending her to the Conservatorium, and that, but for his mishap, last Christmas—surely Christmas was long past?—he would have announced it to everybody without allowing a single objection. After this confession his sister would be so touched that she would burst into tears, and Gregor would then raise himself to her shoulder and kiss her on the neck, which, now that she went to business, she kept free of any ribbon or collar.

"Mr. Samsa!" cried the middle lodger, to Gregor's father, and pointed, without wasting any more words, at Gregor, now working himself slowly forwards. The violin fell silent, the middle lodger first smiled to his friends with a shake of the head and then looked at Gregor again. Instead of driving Gregor out, his father seemed to think it more needful to begin by soothing down the lodgers, although they were not at all agitated and apparently found Gregor more entertaining than the violin-playing. He hurried towards them and, spreading out his arms, tried to urge them back into their own room and at the same time to block their view of Gregor. They now began to be really a little angry, one could not tell whether because of the old man's behavior or because it just dawned on them that all unwittingly they had such a neighbor as Gregor next door. They demanded explanations of his father, they waved their arms like him, tugged uneasily at their beards, and only with reluctance backed towards their room. Meanwhile Gregor's sister, who stood there as if lost when her playing was so abruptly broken off, came to life again, pulled herself together all at once after standing for a while holding violin and bow in nervelessly hanging hands and staring at her music, pushed her violin into the lap of her mother, who was still sitting in her chair fighting asthmatically for breath, and ran into the lodgers' room to which they were now being shepherded by her father rather more quickly than before. One could see the pillows and blankets on the beds flying under her accustomed fingers and being laid in order. Before the lodgers had actually reached their room she had finished making the beds and slipped out.

The old man seemed once more to be so possessed by his mulish self-assertiveness that he was forgetting all the respect he should show to his lodgers. He kept driving them on and driving them on until in the very door of the bedroom the middle lodger stamped his foot loudly on the floor and so brought him to a halt. "I beg to announce," said the lodger, lifting one hand and looking also at Gregor's mother and sister, "that because of the disgusting conditions prevailing in his household and family"—here he spat on the floor with emphatic brevity—"I give you notice on the spot. Naturally I won't pay you a penny for the days I have lived here, on the contrary I shall consider bringing an action for damages against you, based on claims—believe me—that will be easily susceptible of proof.'' He ceased and stared straight in front of him, as if he expected something. In fact his two friends at once rushed into the breach with these words: ''And we too give notice on the spot.'' On that he seized the door-handle and shut the door with a slam.

Gregor's father, groping with his hands, staggered forward and fell into his chair; it looked as if he were stretching himself there for his ordinary evening nap, but the marked jerkings of his head, which was as if uncontrollable, showed that he was far from asleep. Gregor had simply stayed quietly all the time on the spot where the lodgers had espied him. Disappointment at the failure of his plan, perhaps also the weakness arising from extreme hunger, made it impossible for him to move. He feared, with a fair degree of certainty, that at any moment the general tension would discharge itself in a combined attack upon him, and he lay waiting. He did not react even to the noise made by the violin as it fell off his mother's lap from under her trembling fingers and gave out a resonant note.

''My dear parents,'' said his sister, slapping her hand on the table by way of introduction, ''things can't go on like this. Perhaps you don't realize that, but I do. I won't utter my brother's name in the presence of this creature, and so all I say is: we must try to get rid of it. We've tried to look after it and to put up with it as far as is humanly possible, and I don't think anyone could reproach us in the slightest.''

''She is more than right,'' said Gregor's father to himself. His mother, who was still choking for lack of breath, began to cough hollowly into her hand with a wild look in her eyes.

His sister rushed over to her and held her forehead. His father's thoughts seemed to have lost their vagueness at Grete's words, he sat more upright, fingering his service cap that lay among the plates still lying on the table from the lodgers' supper, and from time to time looked at the still form of Gregor.

''We must try to get rid of it,'' his sister now said explicitly to her father, since her mother was coughing too much to hear a word, ''it will be the death of both of you, I can see that coming. When one has to work as hard as

we do, all of us, one can't stand this continual torment at home on top of it. At least I can't stand it any longer.'' And she burst into such a passion of sobbing that her tears dropped on her mother's face, where she wiped them off mechanically.

''My dear,'' said the old man sympathetically, and with evident understanding, ''but what can we do?''

Gregor's sister merely shrugged her shoulders to indicate the feeling of helplessness that had now overmastered her during her weeping fit, in contrast to her former confidence.

''If he could understand us,'' said her father, half questioningly; Grete, still sobbing, vehemently waved a hand to show how unthinkable that was.

''If he could understand us,'' repeated the old man, shutting his eyes to consider his daughter's conviction that understanding was impossible, ''then perhaps we might come to some agreements with him. But as it is—''

''He must go,'' cried Gregor's sister, ''that's the only solution, Father. You must just try to get rid of the idea that this is Gregor. The fact that we've believed it for so long is the root of all our trouble. But how can it be Gregor? If this were Gregor, he would have realized long ago that human beings can't live with such a creature, and he'd have gone away on his own accord. Then we wouldn't have any brother, but we'd be able to go on living and keep his memory in honor. As it is, this creature persecutes us, drives away our lodgers, obviously wants the whole apartment to himself and would have us all sleep in the gutter. Just look, Father,'' she shrieked all at once, ''he's at it again!'' And in an access of panic that was quite incomprehensible to Gregor she even quitted her mother, literally thrusting the chair from her as if she would rather sacrifice her mother than stay so near to Gregor, and rushed behind her father, who also rose up, being simply upset by her agitation, and half-spread his arms out as if to protect her.

Yet Gregor had not the slightest intention of frightening anyone, far less his sister. He had only begun to turn round in order to crawl back to his room, but it was certainly a startling operation to watch, since because of his disabled condition he could not execute the difficult turning movements except by lifting his head and then bracing it against the floor over and over again. He paused and looked round. His good intentions seemed to have been recognized; the alarm had only been momentary. Now they were all watching him in melancholy silence. His mother lay in her chair, her legs stiffly outstretched and pressed together, her eyes almost closing for sheer weariness; his father and his sister were sitting beside each other, his sister's arm around the old man's neck.

Perhaps I can go on turning round now, thought Gregor, and began his labors again. He could not stop himself from panting with the effort, and had to pause now and then to take breath. Nor did anyone harass him, he was left entirely to himself. When he had completed the turn-round he began at once to crawl straight back. He was amazed at the distance separating him from his room and could not understand how in his weak state he had managed to accomplish the same journey so recently, almost without remarking it. Intent on crawling as fast as possible, he barely noticed that not a single word, not an ejaculation from his family, interfered with his progress. Only when he was already in the doorway did he turn his head round, not completely, for his neck muscles were getting stiff, but enough to see that nothing had changed behind him except that his sister had risen to her feet. His last glance fell on his mother, who was not quite overcome by sleep.

Hardly was he well inside his room when the door was hastily pushed shut, bolted and locked. The sudden noise in his rear startled him so much that his little legs gave beneath him. It was his sister who had shown such haste. She had been standing ready waiting and had made a light spring forward. Gregor had not even heard her coming, and she cried, "At last!" to her parents as she turned the key in the lock.

"And what now?" said Gregor to himself, looking round in the darkness. Soon he made the discovery that he was now unable to stir a limb. This did not surprise him, rather it seemed unnatural that he should ever actually have been able to move on these feeble little legs. Otherwise he felt relatively comfortable. True, his whole body was aching, but it seemed that the pain was gradually growing less and would finally pass away. The rotting apple in his back and the inflamed area around it, all covered with soft dust, already hardly troubled him. He thought of his family with tenderness and love. The decision that he must disappear was one that he held to even more strongly than his sister, if that were possible. In this state of vacant and peaceful meditation he remained until the tower clock struck three in the morning. The first broadening of light in the world outside the window entered his consciousness once more. Then his head sank to the floor of its own accord and from his nostrils came the last faint flicker of his breath.

When the charwoman arrived early in the morning—what between her strength and her impatience she slammed all the doors so loudly, never mind how often she had been begged not to do so, that no one in the whole apartment could enjoy any quiet sleep after her arrival—she noticed nothing unusual as she took her customary peep into Gregor's room. She thought he was lying motionless on purpose, pretending to be in the sulks; she credited him with every kind of intelligence. Since she happened to have the longhandled broom in her hand she tried to tickle him up with it from the doorway. When that too produced no reaction she felt provoked and poked him a little harder, and only when she had pushed him along the floor without meeting any resistance was her attention aroused. It did not take her long to establish the truth of the matter, and her eyes widened, she let out a whistle, yet did not waste much time over it but tore open the door of the Samsas' bedroom and yelled into the darkness at the top of her voice: "Just look at this, it's dead; it's lying here dead and done for!"

Mr. and Mrs. Samsa started up in their double bed and before they realized the nature of the charwoman's announcement had some difficulty in overcoming the shock of it. But then they got out of bed quickly, one on either side, Mr. Samsa throwing a blanket over his shoulders, Mrs. Samsa in nothing but her night-gown; in this array they entered Gregor's room. Meanwhile the door of the living room opened, too, where Grete had been sleeping since the advent of the lodgers; she was completely dressed as if she had not been to bed, which seemed to be confirmed also by the paleness of her face. "Dead?" said Mrs. Samsa, looking questioningly at the charwoman, although she could have investigated for herself, and the fact was obvious enough without investigation. "I should say so," said the charwoman, proving her words by pushing Gregor's corpse a long way to one side with her broomstick. Mrs. Samsa made a movement as if to stop her, but checked it. "Well," said Mr. Samsa, "now thanks be to God." He crossed himself, and the three women followed his example. Grete, whose eyes never left the corpse, said: "Just see how thin he was. It's such a long time since he's eaten anything. The food came out again just as it went in." Indeed Gregor's body was completely flat and dry, as could only now be seen when it was no longer supported by the legs and nothing prevented one from looking closely at it.

"Come in beside us, Grete, for a little while," said Mrs. Samsa with a tremulous smile, and Grete, not without looking back at the corpse, followed her parents into their bed-room. The charwoman shut the door and opened the window wide. Although it was so early in the morning a certain softness was perceptible in the fresh air. After all, it was already the end of March.

The three lodgers emerged from their room and were surprised to see no breakfast; they had been forgotten. "Where's our breakfast?" said the middle lodger peevishly to the charwoman. But she put her finger to her lips and hastily, without a word, indicated by gestures that they should go into Gregor's room. They did so and stood, their hands in the pockets of their some-what shabby coats, around Gregor's corpse in the room where it was now fully light.

At that the door of the Samsas' bedroom opened and Mr. Samsa appeared in his uniform, his wife on one arm, his daughter on the other.

They all looked a little as if they had been crying; from time to time Grete hid her face on her father's arm.

"Leave my house at once!" said Mr. Samsa, and pointed to the door without disengaging himself from the women. "What do you mean by that?" said the middle lodger, taken somewhat aback, with a feeble smile. The two others put their hands behind them and kept rubbing them together, as if in gleeful expectation of a fine set-to in which they were bound to come off the winners. "I mean just what I say," answered Mr. Samsa, and advanced in a straight line with his two companions towards the lodger. He stood his ground at first quietly, looking at the floor as if his thoughts were taking a new pattern in his head. "Then let us go, by all means." he said and looked up at Mr. Samsa as if in a sudden access of humility he were expecting some renewed sanction for this decision. Mr. Samsa merely nodded briefly once or twice with meaning eyes. Upon that the lodger really did go with long strides into the hall, his two friends had been listening and had quite stopped rubbing their hands for some moments and now went scuttling after him as if afraid that Mr. Samsa might get into the hall before them and cut them off from their leader. In the hall they all three took their hats from the rack, their sticks from the umbrella stand, bowed in silence and quitted the apartment. With a suspiciousness which proved quite unfounded Mr. Samsa and the two women followed them out to the landing; leaning over the banister they watched the three figures slowly but surely going down the long stairs, vanishing from sight at a certain turn of the staircase on every floor and coming into view again after a moment or so; the more they dwindled, the more the Samsa family's interest in them dwindled, and when a butcher's boy met them and passed them on the stairs coming up proudly with a tray on his head, Mr. Samsa and the two women soon left the landing and as if a burden had been lifted from them went back into their apartment.

They decided to spend this day in resting and going for a stroll; they had not only deserved such a respite from work, but absolutely needed it. And so they sat down at the table and wrote three notes of excuse, Mr. Samsa to his board of management, Mrs. Samsa to her employer and Grete to the head of her firm. While they were writing, the charwoman came in to say that she was going now, since her morning's work was finished. At first they only nodded without looking up, but as she kept hovering there they eyed her irritably. "Well?" said Mr. Samsa. The charwoman stood grinning in the doorway as if she had good news to impart to the family but meant not to say a word unless properly questioned. The small ostrich feather standing upright on her hat, which had annoyed Mr. Samsa ever since she was engaged, was waving gaily in all directions. "Well, what is it then?" asked Mrs. Samsa, who obtained more respect from the charwoman than the others. "Oh," said the charwoman, giggling so amiably that she could not at once continue, "just this, you don't need to bother about how to get rid of the thing next door. It's been seen to already." Mrs. Samsa and Grete bent over their letters again, as if preoccupied; Mrs. Samsa, who perceived that she was eager to begin describing it all in detail, stopped her with a decisive hand. But since she was not allowed to tell her story, she remembered the great hurry she was in, being obviously deeply huffed: "Bye, everybody," she said, whirling off violently, and departed with a frightful slamming of doors.

"She'll be given notice tonight," said Mr. Samsa, but neither from his wife nor his daughter did he get any answer, for the charwoman seemed to have shattered again the composure they had barely achieved. They rose, went to the window and stayed there, clasping each other tight. Mr. Samsa turned in his chair to look at them and quietly observed them for a little. Then he called out: "Come along, now, do. Let bygones be bygones. And you might have some consideration for me." The two of them complied at once, hastened to him, caressed him and quickly finished their letters.

Then they all three left the apartment together, which was more than they had done for months, and went by tram into the open country outside the town. The tram, in which they were the only passengers, was filled with warm sunshine. Leaning comfortably back in their seats they canvassed their prospects for the future, and it appeared on closer inspection that these were not at all bad, for the jobs they had got, which so far they had never really discussed with each other, were all three admirable and likely to lead to better things later on. The greatest immediate improvement in their condition would of course arise from moving to another house; they wanted to take a smaller and cheaper but also better situated and more easily run apartment than the one they had, which Gregor had selected. While they were thus conversing, it struck both Mr. and Mrs. Samsa, almost at the same moment, as they became aware of their daughter's increasing vivacity, that in spite of all the sorrow of recent times, which had made her cheeks pale, she had bloomed into a pretty girl with a good figure. They grew quieter and half unconsciously exchanged glances of complete agreement, having come to the conclusion that it would soon be time to find a good husband for her. And it was like a confirmation of their new dreams and excellent intentions that at the end of their journey their daughter sprang to her feet first and stretched her young body.

QUESTIONS ABOUT "THE METAMORPHOSIS"

1. What evidence do we have at the beginning of the story that Gregor thinks of himself as human?
2. Kafka's prose style is understated, reading almost like a newspaper story. How does this style influence the reader's acceptance of the metamorphosis?

3. At what point, if any, does Gregor cease believing he is human? Is there a point at which the reader, too, begins to view him as an insect?

4. How does Gregor perceive authority figures such as his employer and his father? Do these perceptions support his sense of unworthiness?

5. From a psychological point of view, Gregor seems to be terribly guilty about usurping his father's breadwinning function as well as seeming to come between his father and his mother. Find evidence for this line of interpretation.

6. Gregor's self-esteem is obviously minimal. How does he, in fact, think of himself? Does he ever put himself first? What details can you find to characterize Gregor's self-image?

7. The charwoman seems to be clearest about Gregor: to her, he is an insect and she disposes of him accordingly. How does her presence in the story influence our reading of it?

8. After Gregor's death, the narrative point of view, which had been limited to Gregor's sensibility, shifts to an observer's perspective in detailing the family's activities. How does this shift affect our sense of Gregor? Do we think that Gregor has died, or the insect he became? or somehow both?

Philosophical Discussion:
What Is a Person?

Gregor Samsa is facing an identity crisis. Is he a human being or an insect, a person or a giant beetle? Happily, none of us will ever have to face Gregor's problem. However, we might appreciate what it's like to feel as he does. For five years, Gregor has been a commercial traveler—a traveling salesman—trying to make train connections, eating irregularly, never developing any intimate friendships. And for what? Not only to pay off his parents, debts, but to support them, his sister and several household servants in the comfortable style to which they have all become accustomed. Without Gregor how would his father spend his long leisurely breakfasts reading various newspapers? How would his mother malinger in the apartment for days on end? How would his sister continue to sleep late, dress well, and go out for her entertainments?

That the family has money is not to the point. Even Gregor could see the wisdom in not using up the savings on his account. The important thing is to send his sister to study music at the conservatorium. His own interests are secondary, his life subservient, his personal wants, desires, and hopes are of little or no consequence, like that of some loathsome lower creature, a cockroach or spider. No wonder Gregor Samsa feels like a "dung beetle."

But Kafka tells us that the creature that wakes up in Gregor Samsa's bed actually is Gregor Samsa. How can that be? Samsa is a human being. This creature is not. It does not look like Samsa. It does not sound like Samsa. On the contrary, it looks and sounds like a bug. What reason, if any, is there to identify this thing as Kafka suggests? Even Gregor's trusting sister, Grete, finally announces in desperation,

> You must try to get rid of the idea that this is Gregor. The fact that we've believed it for so long is the root of all our trouble. But how can it be Gregor? If this were Gregor, he would have realized long ago that human beings can't live with such a creature, and he'd have gone away on his own accord.

Get rid of the idea that this is Gregor. But how can we do this? Grete seems to be missing something. The creature seems to have Gregor's feelings. It even thinks like Gregor. Though it wakes up in the grotesque form of a beetle, its main concern is making the five o'clock train.

Gregor Samsa's problem is extreme, but not unique. We all undergo a metamorphosis in life, though not usually as sudden and dramatic as Gregor's. We are born into infancy, physically helpless and as yet undeveloped emotionally and intellectually, and then we gradually grow, through childhood, adolescence, and adulthood to old age. Weighing no more than six or seven pounds at birth and measuring perhaps twenty inches in length, the average male attains the weight of between 150 and 200 pounds at maturity and approaches six feet in height. Hair, bone, muscle, skin, and overall configuration undergo equally significant alterations. The very cells of our bodies, physiologists tell us, are also eventually replaced.

Our thoughts and beliefs change as well. We give up believing in Santa Claus and the tooth fairy, and, usually at puberty, start thinking more seriously about school, sports, friends, career, sex, marriage, children, and, a bit further down the line, social security.

Since the changes are gradual, at any one moment or period in our lives they are virtually imperceptible, or sufficiently insignificant so as not to affect our self-image, let alone our identity. By middle age we may have changed quite dramatically. Elvis Presley, for example, was eighty pounds heavier in his later years than when he first became a star. Nevertheless, despite his excessive weight, Elvis Presley was the same performer in 1976 who had recorded "Heartbreak Hotel" in 1956. However little he resembled his former self when he died in 1977, the man who is now buried in Graceland was the very same person who was hailed thirty years ago as the "King of Rock and Roll."

How can a person, any person—Elvis Presley, Gregor Samsa—be the same individual? The philosophical problem of personal identity is to explain how an individual can be the same person through time and change, especially the kind of extreme change a person undergoes in the course of a lifetime. This problem is not only of interest to metaphysical philosophers concerned with the ultimate mysteries of the universe, it is also of profound importance to thinkers in the fields of law, politics, and science; for without an understanding of personal identity, it would be difficult to make sense of the idea of personal responsibility. If we cannot be sure what makes an individual the same person, how can we, in clear conscience, punish old men—ex-Nazis now in their late seventies and eighties—for crimes committed over forty years ago by much younger men? What sense is there in electing a politician to public office if the person elected is not the same person as the one who eventually takes the post? How can medical investigators study the long-term effects of breathing asbestos dust if the individuals studied are not the *same* individuals throughout the study?

In an attempt to solve the problem of personal identity, theorists have proposed two main approaches, what we will call *the soul theory*, and *the biological theory*. But before we examine each one separately, let us first briefly consider what exactly we are looking for.

First, any acceptable theory should tell us not only what distinguishes each of us from everyone else but also what we have in common with ourselves, aside from the obvious fact that, along with an appropriate possessive pronoun, we call ourselves *selves*. This may seem obvious, but we should bear in mind that unless there is something more than just a linguistic appellation, we would not be speaking of anything special when we apparently speak of ourselves. (David Hume argues that there is no self as such, although he does propose a so-called "bundle" theory of personal identity—that a person is essentially a collection of experiences.)

Second, a theory of personal identity should illuminate, to some extent, how we actually identify people. This may also seem obvious, even trivially true, but identifying a person is one thing; what makes a person the same individual over time is something else. For example, Albert Einstein can be identified in photographs by a great shock of unruly hair. No other well-known contemporary person resembles him in this way. Yet he would still be Einstein even if his hair were neatly combed. His hair is an identifying characteristic; but it does not make Einstein *Einstein*.

Third, a theory of personal identity should help to explain the sense of intimate knowledge we have of ourselves, especially in identifying ourselves. While we tend to identify others perceptually, by their looks, their walk, their mannerisms, their voice, we need not peek at ourselves in the mirror or hear ourselves speak to know who we are. We can identify ourselves straight out. For example, Phil and Steve Mahre, the famous Olympic skiers who are also twins, are often misidentified by others. But Phil never mistakes himself for Steve, nor does Steve ever mistake himself for Phil. They know who they are even when others confuse them. No matter what other people say or think, we know who we are.

We begin by considering a very old view traceable to Plato: *the soul theory*. In this view, a person not only *has* a soul, as Christian theists tend to say, but *is* a soul. The difference is significant. In the Christian sense, having a soul suggests moral worth. A person can lose his soul, for example, to temptation or to the devil, and thus forfeit any hope of salvation. But he does not thus give up his identity (for all it may be worth). The Platonic sense is more metaphysical and more interesting as a theory of personal identity. As a soul, a human being is an embodied spirit, a simple, unchanging substance that can be freed, upon the death of the body, to exist eternally in a realm of nonphysical and incorruptible ideal forms.

But what exactly is it? The Platonic tradition is not clear about this. If the soul were truly metaphysical, then it would seem to be beyond all appearance, and remain an ultimate mystery. Could such a mysterious entity help to answer any of the questions raised above? Apparently so. If a person is a simple, unchanging substance, then all *apparent* changes in the life of an individual are not real changes at all. The person is the same despite the appearance of change. Gregor Samsa, for example, can be the same person despite the physical alteration that he endures. The first consideration above appears to be satisfactorily dealt with by this theory.

With respect to items two and three, however, the view is problematic. The Platonic version of the soul theory does not tell us clearly, or illuminate in any way, how we actually identify either ourselves or others. Since, strictly speaking, a person viewed from this perspective has no appearance, we have no explanation of why we can identify Einstein in a photograph by his hair, or Elvis by his sideburns. For all we know, no matter what physical description or telltale sign (tattoo, birthmark, scar, fingerprint, or DNA coding) we use to identify an individual, we might be wrong. And not just in some highly improbable way, but also in the way we might be wrong if we picked someone out of a crowd blindfolded. Our closest friend or loved one may not be the same person today as yesterday, since that special something may have transmigrated to some other realm or some other body. In this view, despite years of intimate contact with people we think we know—wives, husbands, parents, children—they may all be total strangers. Worse. Since we are in no better position to identify our own soul than anyone else's, we, too, may not be who we think we are. We may be strangers to ourselves.

There are, of course, some people who would applaud this situation. Such people believe that the human condition, especially in the modern, postindustrial world, is essentially one of alienation. According to this view, we are profoundly alienated, not just from society in general but from the people around us, and even from ourselves. This may be so. But if this *is* so, it is because people do know, full well, who they are. Otherwise, they wouldn't know that they are alienated. Clearly, the soul theory, in its Platonic form, is inadequate.

Despite these drawbacks, however, theorists have been drawn to the soul theory as holding out the best hope of solving the original problem. Largely for this reason, philosophers have attempted to demystify it by making it more empirical in what may be termed *the Cartesian approach.*

René Descartes suggested that the essence of a person is the mind, a nonphysical substance that thinks, as well as doubts, imagines, believes, and has all the other higher-order functions we associate with cognition. (Descartes's discussion of this issue can be found in his "Meditation II," reproduced in Part I of this volume.) Since we know our own mind, perhaps better than we know anything else, according to Descartes, we can know who we are with absolute certainty. This is not only reassuring: it helps to explain item three listed above. We can identify ourselves without any special physical cues because we are aware of ourselves as such. No mirrors, special surveys, or investigations are needed. If we are fully conscious, then we know who we are. Gregor Samsa, on this view, can have no doubts about who he is.

Of course, others may still have their doubts. Gregor's sister Grete, for example, does not know his thoughts. She does not know what is running through his mind, or even if the thing in Gregor's room has a mind. For all she knows it is just a large bug. It seems, however, that if this creature really is Samsa, some way should be available for getting the information across. People do manage to communicate their thoughts even if they are no longer easily recognizable by others, or are no longer in complete control of their bodies. A gesture, a movement, a blink of the eye, under the right circumstances, can convey much information. This may be why the Samsa family accepts this strange animal. There is something about its behavior that is reminiscent of their son and brother.

But the Cartesian approach does not explain clearly what this something is. What connection, if any, is there between a person's thoughts and the expression of those thoughts? On the Cartesian view, it is as if a person is a diaphanous ghost inside a robot. Exactly how the mechanism gets manipulated, however, is not made plain. (Gilbert Ryle eloquently expresses the difficulty of what he calls "the ghost in the machine.") The problem of the relationship of mind and body has proven to be one of the most vexing issues in Cartesian philosophy, warranting the name, *the mind-body problem.*

It seems that unless the mind-body problem is solved, the Cartesian approach does not adequately explain how we identify others, especially on the basis of their thoughts. But a person's thinking seems crucial. Someone you do not immediately recognize at a party claims to be Harry, a long-forgotten childhood friend. You are skeptical until the fellow recalls the time you and he broke the window in your father's Chevy. It must be Harry. He was the only one, other than yourself, who knew about it.

In what may be termed *the memory theory,* memory plays a critical role as a criterion for identifying a person. But does it make us who we are? John Locke thought so. His proposal was that a person is the sum total of his or her memories. But unlike

Descartes, Locke did not suggest that a person is a nonphysical substance. On the contrary, a person is not a substance at all, but a quasi-legal or moral entity which, at different times, may be composed of different substances. For example, the same Arnold Shwartzenegger that at one time had the immature body of a young boy now has the developed physique of a professional body builder. What makes him the same person is not the body, since he seems to have been composed of at least two different bodies, but that he can remember being a certain ninety-pound weakling. Because the same consciousness extends back through the changes, we credit Arnold with the development. He, not his body, wins the Mr. Olympia award, although without the body he would not win anything. As Anthony Quinton suggests, a person must have some body or other, but not necessarily the same body. On the Lockean-Quinton view, so long as the memories (Quinton also includes character) of the beetle are those of the human being, then the same person, Gregor Samsa, who went to bed with the body of one, woke up with the body of the other.

There are, however, at least two difficulties with this view. People not only forget (we leave the reader to decide whether Locke deals with this problem adequately); they also seem to misremember. Suppose the creature who wakes up in Samsa's bed really isn't Gregor, but only thinks it is. Somehow the beetle has taken on the memories of a human being in the same way that we ourselves sometimes *seem* to remember an event that a parent or guardian attributes to us—falling out of a crib, for example—that actually happened to a close sibling. We, like the bug, would be misremembering. And just as we would not be our sibling, so the bug would not be Gregor Samsa.

It seems that the memory theory is adequate only if the alleged memories are genuine. But what makes memories genuine? It might be suggested that if we could determine that we were there, having the experience of falling out of the crib, we could be assured that the memories are truly ours. But this suggests that there is something other than memory that determines who we are. If that were the case, the basic Lockean approach would seem to be unnecessary. (Quinton attempts to address this issue.)

Let us now consider the main alternative approach, what we are calling *the biological theory,* the view that we are essentially members of the species homo sapien. Although the human body has been both exalted and deprecated throughout the history of Western civilization, the modern idea that our identity is intimately related to our body is traceable to the publication in 1871 of Charles Darwins's *Descent of Man.* Darwin himself did not argue that people are essentially animals. The theory of evolution, the idea that one living species can arise from another, seems to undermine the idea that species have essences. The homo sapien, for example, was a simian in years past, according to the evolutionist. But as Saul Kripke and others have argued in recent literature, individuals have essences. With this, the biological theory may take on new impetus in the sense that although persons could have arisen (and may actually exist on some presently unknown planet) in a form other than the biological, people that are in fact human beings, namely us, could not have arisen in any other form. The upshot— not so farfetched when you think about it—is that we, persons that we are, are necessarily human beings.

But how can we be our bodies? Our bodies undergo radical change throughout the average life span. Is there something about our physical makeup that makes us who we are? Hair and eye color clearly won't do. We can dye our hair and with contact lenses even change the color of our eyes. A birthmark, scar, tattoo? They can be altered or removed by cosmetic surgery without changing who we are. Fingerprints? Important though they are, especially in law enforcement, a person who loses a limb, and thus loses his fingerprints, has not thus lost his identity. What about genetics, the particular set of genes that ultimately determine all our basic physical characteristics? This suggestion, too, seems inadequate. Identical twins have the same genetic structure but are not the same person.

Kripke's point, however, would seem to avoid these difficulties. A person, or his parts, could change. But an individual could not have been different originally—or, at least, could not have had a different origin. A particular lecturn that was originally milled from certain wood, may, over time, become petrified and turn to stone. But that same lecturn could not have been made from stone originally. Otherwise, it would not be *that* lecturn. On this view, while Gregor Samsa may become a dung beetle, he, homo sapien that he was originally, could not have been a cockroach from the beginning.

Could the same object have had a different origin? Perhaps not. But it seems that different individuals could have had the same origin. For example, when the W-particle, a high-energy bit of physical material, disintegrates, according to physicists, it gives birth, so to speak, to a neutrino and electron, two different particles— different particles that have the same origin. Different human beings, too, seem to have the same origin—identical twins, for example, evolve from the same sperm and ovum. (To be sure, human babies are rarely, if ever, born at exactly the same time or precisely the same place to the same mother, but this seems to be more a matter of female physiology rather than metaphysical necessity. The birth of subatomic particles does not seem to be attendant with the same difficulties.)

Unless the concept of origin is more clearly defined, the biological theorist does not tell us who we are nor whether the creature in the next room is brother Gregor. For example, knowing that the beetle ultimately has the same origin as the human being would not be enough to determine that each is a different stage in the life of Gregor Samsa. Something more seems needed. What can that be?

Kafka proposes the idea of metamorphosis, the dramatic and radical transformation of the same individual from one physical form to another. But what exactly is metamorphosis? Just as a caterpillar can apparently become something other than a caterpillar, or a tadpole can become something other than a tadpole, so, Kafka suggests, a human being can become something other than a human being. And just as we need not speak of the soul or body of a caterpillar so it seems, we need not speak of Gregor Samsa's soul or body either. But what else is there?

In contrast to the dominant schools of philosophic thought, which hold that a particular individual such as Gregor Samsa, is either a soul, a set of memories, or a certain body, Kafka seems to suggest that Gregor Samsa is not essentially any of these things. (Eddy Zemach defends an anti-essentialist approach in "Looking Out For Number One.") We, like Gregor Samsa, are many things—child, sibling, wage earner, traveler, what have you. Just as we can lose our youth, family, and livelihood, so, in the absence of some special theory to the contrary, it seems that we can even lose our humanity. With respect to his identity, Gregor Samsa is not essentially different from an insect. Moreover, if Kafka is right, neither are we.

PLATO
from *Phaedo*

"Then," said he, "when does the soul get hold of the truth? For whenever the soul tries to examine anything in company with the body, it is plain that it is deceived by it."

"Quite true."

"Then it is not clear that in reasoning, if anywhere, something of the realities becomes visible to it?"

"Yes."

"And I suppose it reasons best when none of these senses disturbs it, hearing or sight, or pain, or pleasure indeed, but when it is completely by itself and says good-bye to the body, and so far as possible has no dealings with it, when it reaches out and grasps that which really is."

"That is true."

"And is it not then that the philosopher's soul chiefly holds the body cheap and escapes from it, while it seeks to be by itself?"

"So it seems."

"Let us pass on, Simmias. Do we say there is such a thing as justice by itself, or not?"

"We do say so, certainly!"

"Such a thing as the good and beautiful?"

"Of course!"

"And did you ever see one of them with your eyes?"

"Never," said he.

"By any other sense of those the body has did you ever grasp them? I mean all such things, greatness, health, strength, in short everything that really is the nature of things whatever they are: Is it through the body that the real truth is perceived? Or is this better—whoever of us prepares himself most completely and most exactly to comprehend each thing which he examines would come nearest to knowing each one?"

"Certainly."

"And would he do that most purely who should approach each with his intelligence alone, not adding sight to intelligence, or dragging in any other sense along with reasoning, but using the intelligence uncontaminated alone by itself, while he tries to hunt out each essence uncontaminated, keeping clear of eyes and ears and, one might say, of the whole body, because he thinks the body disturbs him and hinders the soul from getting possession of truth and wisdom when body and soul are companions—is not this the man, Simmias, if anyone, who will hit reality?"

"Nothing could be more true, Socrates," said Simmias.

"Then from all this," said Socrates, "genuine philosophers must come to some such opinion as follows, so as to make to one an-

Reprinted from *Great Dialogues of Plato*, translated by W. H. D. Rouse, edited by Eric H. Warmington and Philip G. Rouse (1957). Copyright © 1984 by John Clive Graves Rouse, reprinted by agreement of New American Library, a Division of Penguin Books USA Inc. **Plato** (ca. 428–348 B.C.), one of the great philosophers in the Western tradition, envisioned a realm of abstract thought which is still at the heart of much philosophical controversy.

other statements such as these: 'A sort of direct path, so to speak, seems to take us to the conclusion that so long as we have the body with us in our enquiry, and our soul is mixed up with so great an evil, we shall never attain sufficiently what we desire, and that, we say, is the truth. For the body provides thousands of busy distractions because of its necessary food; besides, if diseases fall upon us, they hinder us from the pursuit of the real. With loves and desires and fears and all kinds of fancies and much rubbish, it infects us, and really and truly makes us, as they say, unable to think one little bit about anything at any time. Indeed, wars and factions and battles all come from the body and its desires, and from nothing else. For the desire of getting wealth causes all wars, and we are compelled to desire wealth by the body, being slaves to its culture; therefore we have no leisure for philosophy, from all these reasons. Chief of all is that if we do have some leisure, and turn away from the body to speculate on something, in our searches it is everywhere interfering, it causes confusion and disturbance, and dazzles us so that it will not let us see the truth; so in fact we see that if we are ever to know anything purely we must get rid of it, and examine the real things by the soul alone; and then, it seems, after we are dead, as the reasoning shows, not while we live, we shall possess that which we desire, lovers of which we say we are, namely wisdom. For if it is impossible in company with the body to know anything purely, one thing of two follows: either knowledge is possible nowhere, or only after death; for then alone the soul will be quite by itself apart from the body, but not before. And while we are alive, we shall be nearest to knowing, as it seems, if as far as possible we have no commerce of communion with the body which is not absolutely necessary, and if we are not infected with its nature, but keep ourselves pure from it, until God himself shall set us free. And so, pure and rid of the body's foolishness, we shall probably be in the company of those like ourselves, and shall know through our own selves complete incontamination, and that is perhaps the truth. But for the impure to grasp the pure is not, it seems, allowed.' So we must think, Simmias, and so we must say to one another, all who are rightly lovers of learning; don't you agree?''

''Assuredly, Socrates.''

''Then,'' said Socrates, ''if this is true, my comrade, there is great hope that when I arrive where I am travelling, there if anywhere I shall sufficiently possess that for which all our study has been pursued in this past life. So the journey which has been commanded for me is made with good hope, and the same for any other man who believes he has got his mind purified, as I may call it.''

''Certainly,'' replied Simmias.

''And is not purification really that which has been mentioned so often in our discussion, to separate as far as possible the soul from the body, and to accustom it to collect itself together out of the body in every part, and to dwell alone by itself as far as it can, both at this present and in the future, being freed from the body as if from a prison?''

''By all means,'' said he.

''Then is not this called death—a freeing and separation of soul from body?''

''Not a doubt of that,'' said he.

''But to set it free, as we say, is the chief endeavour of those who rightly love wisdom, nay of those alone, and the very care and practice of the philosophers is nothing but the freeing and separation of soul from body, don't you think so?''

''It appears to be so.''

''Then, as I said at first, it would be absurd for a man preparing himself in his life to be as near as possible to death, so to live, and then when death came, to object?''

''Of course.''

''Then in fact, Simmias,'' he said, ''those who rightly love wisdom are practicing dying, and death to them is the least terrible thing in the world. Look at it in this way: If they are everywhere at enmity with the body, and desire the soul to be alone by itself, and if, when this very thing happens, they shall fear and object—would not that be wholly unreasonable? Should they not willingly go to a place where there is good hope of finding what they were in love with all through life (and they loved wisdom), and of ridding themselves of the companion which they hated? When human favourites and wives and sons have died, many have been willing to go down to the grave, drawn by the hope of seeing there those they used to desire, and of being with them; but one who is really in love with wisdom and holds firm to this same hope, that he will find it in the grave, and nowhere else worth speaking of—will he then fret at dying and not go thither rejoicing? We must surely think, my comrade, that he will go rejoicing, if he is really a philosopher; he will surely believe that he will find wisdom in its purity there and there alone. If this is true, would it not be most unreasonable, as I said just now, if such a one feared death?''

"Unreasonable, I do declare,'' said he.

"Then this is proof enough,'' he said, "that if you see a man fretting because he is to die, he was not really a philosopher, but a philosōma—not a wisdom-lover but a body-lover. And no doubt the same man is money-lover and honours-lover, one or both. . . .''

"Since the soul is clearly immortal, this or something like this at any rate is what happens in regard to our souls and their habitations—that this is so seems to me proper and worthy of the risk of believing; for the risk is noble. Such things he must sing like a healing charm to himself, and that is why I have lingered so long over the story. But these are the reasons for a man to be confident about his own soul, when in his life he has bidden farewell to all other pleasures, the pleasures and adornments of the body, thinking them alien and such as do more harm than good, and has been earnest only for the pleasure of learning; and having adorned the soul with no alien ornaments, but with her own—with temperance and justice and courage and freedom and truth, thus he awaits the journey to the house of Hades, ready to travel when the doom ordained shall call. You indeed,'' he said, "Simmias and Cebes and all, hereafter at some certain time shall each travel on that journey: but me—'Fate calls me now,' as a man might say in a tragedy, and it is almost time for

me to travel towards the bath; for I am sure you think it better to have a bath before drinking the potion, and to save the women the trouble of washing a corpse.''

When he had spoken, Criton said, "Ah well, Socrates, what injunctions have you for these friends or for me, about your children or anything else? What could we do for you to gratify you most?''

"What I always say, Criton,'' he said, "nothing very new: Take good care of yourselves, and you will gratify me and mine and yourselves whatever you do, even if you promise nothing now. But if you neglect yourselves, and won't take care to live your lives following the footsteps, so to speak, of both this last conversation and those we have had in former times, you will do no good even if you promise ever so much at present and ever so faithfully.''

"Then we will do our best about that,'' he said; "but how are we to bury you?''

"How you like,'' said he, "if you catch me and I don't escape you.'' At the same time, laughing gently and looking towards us, he said, "Criton doesn't believe me, my friends, that this is I, Socrates now talking with you and laying down each of my injunctions, but he thinks me to be what he will see shortly, a corpse, and asks, if you please, how to bury me! I have been saying all this long time, that when I have drunk the potion, I shall not be here then with you; I shall have gone clear away to some bliss of the blest, as they call it. But he thinks I am talking nonsense, just to console myself, yes and you too. Then go bail for me to Criton,'' he said, "the opposite of the bail he gave to those judges. He gave bail that I would remain; you please, give bail that I will not remain after I die, but I shall get off clear and clean, that Criton may take it more easily, and may not be vexed by seeing my body either being burnt or buried; don't let him worry for me and think I'm in a dreadful state, or say at the funeral that he is laying out or carrying or digging in Socrates. Be sure, Criton, best of friends,'' he said, "to use ugly words not only is out of tune with the event, but it even infects the soul with something evil. Now, be confident and say you are burying my body, and then bury it as you please and as you think would be most according to custom.''

With these words, he got up and retired into another room for the bath, and Criton went after him, telling us to wait. So we waited discussing and talking together about what had been said, or sometimes speaking of the great misfortune which had befallen us, for we felt really as if we had lost a father and had to spend the rest of our lives as orphans. When he had bathed, and his children had been brought to see him—for he had two little sons, and one big—and when the women of his family had come, he talked to them before Criton and gave what instructions he wished. Then he asked the women and children to go, and came back to us. It was now near sunset, for he had spent a long time within. He came and sat down after his bath, and he had not talked long after this when the servant of the Eleven came in, and standing by him said, ''O Socrates! I have not to complain of you as I do of others, that they are angry with me, and curse me, because I bring them word to drink their potion, which my officers make me do! But I have always found you in this time most generous and gentle, and the best man who ever came here. And now too, I know well you are not angry with me, for you know who are responsible, and you keep it for them. Now you know what I came to tell you, so farewell, and try to bear as well as you can what can't be helped.''

Then he turned and was going out, with tears running down his cheeks. And Socrates looked up at him and said, ''Farewell to you also, I will do so.'' Then, at the same time turning to us, ''What a nice fellow!'' he said. ''All the time he has been coming and talking to me, a real good sort, and now how generously he sheds tears for me! Come along, Criton, let's obey him. Someone bring the potion, if the stuff has been ground; if not, let the fellow grind it.''

Then Criton said, ''But, Socrates, I think the sun is still over the hills, it has not set yet. Yes, and I know of others who, having been told to drink the poison, have done it very late;

they had dinner first and a good one, and some enjoyed the company of any they wanted. Please don't be in a hurry, there is time to spare.''

But Socrates said, ''Those you speak of have very good reason for doing that, for they think they will gain by doing it; and I have good reasons why I won't do it. For I think I shall gain nothing by drinking a little later, only that I shall think myself a fool for clinging to life and sparing when the cask's empty. Come along,'' he said, ''do what I tell you, if you please.''

And Criton, hearing this, nodded to the boy who stood near. The boy went out, and after spending a long time, came in with the man who was to give the poison carrying it ground ready in a cup. Socrates caught sight of the man and said, ''Here, my good man, you know about these things; what must I do?''

''Just drink it,'' he said, ''and walk about till your legs get heavy, then lie down. In that way the drug will act of itself.''

At the same time, he held out the cup to Socrates, and he took it quite cheerfully, Echecrates, not a tremble, not a change in colour or looks; but looking full at the man under his brows, as he used to do, he asked him. ''What do you say about this drink? What of a libation to someone? Is that allowed, or not?''

He said, ''We only grind so much as we think enough for a moderate potion.''

''I understand,'' he said, ''but at least, I suppose, it is allowed to offer a prayer to the gods and that must be done, for good luck in the migration from here to there. Then that is my prayer, and so may it be!''

With these words he put the cup to his lips and, quite easy and contented, drank it up. So far most of us had been able to hold back our tears pretty well; but when we saw him begin drinking and end drinking, we could no longer. I burst into a flood of tears for all I could do, so I wrapped up my face and cried myself out; not for him indeed, but for my own misfortune in losing such a man and such a comrade. Criton had got up and gone out even before I did, for he could not hold the tears in. Apollodoros had never ceased weeping all this time, and now he burst out into loud sobs, and by his weeping and lamentations completely broke down every man there except Socrates himself. He only said, "What a scene! You amaze me. That's just why I sent the women away, to keep them from making a scene like this. I've heard that one ought to make an end in decent silence. Quiet yourselves and endure."

When we heard him we felt ashamed and restrained our tears. He walked about, and when he said that his legs were feeling heavy, he lay down on his back, as the man told him to do; at the same time the one who gave him the potion felt him, and after a while examined his feet and legs; then pinching a foot hard, he asked if he felt anything; he said no. After this, again, he pressed the shins; and, moving up like this, he showed us that he was growing cold and

stiff. Again he felt him, and told us that when it came to his heart, he would be gone. Already the cold had come nearly as far as the abdomen, when Socrates threw off the covering from his face—for he had covered it over—and said, the last words he uttered, "Criton," he said, "we owe a cock to Asclepios; pay it without fail."

"That indeed shall be done," said Criton. "Have you anything more to say?"

When Criton had asked this, Socrates gave no further answer, but after a little time, he stirred, and the man uncovered him, and his eyes were still. Criton, seeing this, closed the mouth and eyelids.

This was the end of our comrade, Echecrates, a man, as we would say, of all then living we had ever met, the noblest and the wisest and most just.

GILBERT RYLE
Descartes' Myth

I The Official Doctrine

There is a doctrine about the nature and place of minds which is so prevalent among theorists and even among laymen that it deserves to be described as the official theory. Most philosophers, psychologists and religious teachers subscribe, with minor reservations, to its main articles and, although they admit certain theoretical difficulties in it, they tend to assume that these can be overcome without serious modifications being made to the architecture of the theory. It will be argued here that the central

principles of the doctrine are unsound and conflict with the whole body of what we know about minds when we are not speculating about them.

The official doctrine, which hails chiefly from Descartes, is something like this. With the doubtful exceptions of idiots and infants in arms every human being has both a body and a mind. Some would prefer to say that every human being is both a body and a mind. His body and his mind are ordinarily harnessed together, but after

Reprinted from *The Concept of Mind*, chapter I, by permission of Hertford College, Oxford. **Gilbert Ryle** (1900–1976), a leading proponent, along with J. L. Austin (1911–1960), of a largely British movement called *ordinary language philosophy*, inspired the current debate within the philosophy of mind.

the death of the body his mind may continue to exist and function.

Human bodies are in space and are subject to the mechanical laws which govern all other bodies in space. Bodily processes and states can be inspected by external observers. So a man's bodily life is as much a public affair as are the lives of animals and reptiles and even as the careers of trees, crystals and planets.

But minds are not in space, nor are their operations subject to mechanical laws. The workings of one mind are not witnessable by other observers; its career is private. Only I can take direct cognisance of the states and processes of my own mind. A person therefore lives through two collateral histories, one consisting of what happens in and to his body, the other consisting of what happens in and to his mind. The first is public, the second private. The events in the first history are events in the physical world, those in the second are events in the mental world.

It has been disputed whether a person does or can directly monitor all or only some of the episodes of his own private history; but, according to the official doctrine, of at least some of these episodes he has direct and unchallengeable cognisance. In consciousness, self-consciousness and introspection he is directly and authentically apprised of the present states and operations of his mind. He may have great or small uncertainties about concurrent and adjacent episodes in the physical world, but he can have none about at least part of what is momentarily occupying his mind.

It is customary to express this bifurcation of his two lives and of his two worlds by saying that the things and events which belong to the physical world, including his own body, are external, while the workings of his own mind are internal. This antithesis of outer and inner is of course meant to be construed as a metaphor, since minds, not being in space, could not be described as being spatially inside anything else, or as having things going on spatially inside themselves. But relapses from this good intention are common and theorists are found speculating how stimuli, the physical sources of which are yards or miles outside a person's skin, can generate mental responses inside his skull,

or how decisions framed inside his cranium can set going movements of his extremities.

Even when 'inner' and 'outer' are construed as metaphors, the problem how a person's mind and body influence one another is notoriously charged with theoretical difficulties. What the mind wills, the legs, arms and the tongue execute; what affects the ear and the eye has something to do with what the mind perceives; grimaces and smiles betray the mind's moods and bodily castigations lead, it is hoped, to moral improvement. But the actual transactions between the episodes of the private history and those of the public history remain mysterious, since by definition they can belong to neither series. They could not be reported among the happenings described in a person's autobiography of his inner life, but nor could they be reported among those described in some one else's biography of that person's overt career. They can be inspected neither by introspection nor by laboratory experiment. They are theoretical shuttlecocks which are forever being bandied from the physiologist back to the psychologist and from the psychologist back to the physiologist.

Underlying this partly metaphorical representation of the bifurcation of a person's two lives there is a seemingly more profound and philosophical assumption. It is assumed that there are two different kinds of existence or status. What exists or happens may have the status of physical existence, or it may have the status of mental existence. Somewhat as the faces of coins are either heads or tails, or somewhat as living creatures are either male or female, so, it is supposed, some existing is physical existing, other existing is mental existing. It is a necessary feature of what has physical existence that it is in space and time, it is a necessary feature of what has mental existence that it is in time but not in space. What has physical existence is composed of matter, or else is a function of matter; what has mental existence consists of consciousness, or else is a function of consciousness.

There is thus a polar opposition between mind and matter, an opposition which is often brought out as follows. Material objects are situated in a common field, known as 'space', and what happens to one body in one part of space is mechanically connected with what happens to other bodies in other parts of space. But mental happenings occur in insulated fields, known as 'minds', and there is, apart maybe from telepathy, no direct causal connection between what happens in one mind and what happens in another. Only through the medium of the public physical world can the mind of one person make a difference to the mind of another. The mind is its own place and in his inner life each of us lives the life of a ghostly Robinson Crusoe. People can see, hear and jolt one another's bodies, but they are irremediably blind and deaf to the workings of one another's minds and inoperative upon them.

What sort of knowledge can be secured of the workings of a mind? On the one side, according to the official theory, a person has direct knowledge of the best imaginable kind of the workings of his own mind. Mental states and processes are (or are normally) conscious states and processes, and the consciousness which irradiates them can engender no illusions and leaves the door open for no doubts. A person's present thinkings, feelings and willings, his perceivings, rememberings and imaginings are intrinsically 'phosphorescent'; their existence and their nature are inevitably betrayed to their owner. The inner life is a stream of consciousness of such a sort that it would be absurd to suggest that the mind whose life is that stream might be unaware of what is passing down it.

True, the evidence adduced recently by Freud seems to show that there exist channels tributary to this stream, which run hidden from their owner. People are actuated by impulses the existence of which they vigorously disavow; some of their thoughts differ from the thoughts which they acknowledge; and some of the actions which they think they will perform they do not really will. They are thoroughly gulled by some of their own hypocrisies and they successfully ignore facts about their mental lives which on the official theory ought to be patent to them. Holders of the official theory tend, however, to maintain that anyhow in normal cir-

cumstances a person must be directly and authentically seized of the present state and workings of his own mind.

Besides being currently supplied with these alleged immediate data of consciousness, a person is also generally supposed to be able to exercise from time to time a special kind of perception, namely inner perception, or introspection. He can take a (non-optical) 'look' at what is passing in his mind. Not only can he view and scrutinize a flower through his sense of sight and listen to and discriminate the notes of a bell through his sense of hearing; he can also reflectively or introspectively watch, without any bodily organ of sense, the current episodes of his inner life. This self-observation is also commonly supposed to be immune from illusion, confusion or doubt. A mind's reports of its own affairs have a certainty superior to the best that is possessed by its reports of matters in the physical world. Sense-perceptions can, but consciousness and introspection cannot, be mistaken or confused.

On the other side, one person has no direct access of any sort to the events of the inner life of another. He cannot do better than make problematic inferences from the observed behaviour of the other person's body to the states of mind which, by analogy from his own conduct, he supposes to be signalised by that behaviour. Direct access to the workings of a mind is the privilege of that mind itself; in default of such privileged access, the workings of one mind are inevitably occult to everyone else. For the supposed arguments from bodily movements similar to their own to mental workings similar to their own would lack any possibility of observational corroboration. Not unnaturally, therefore, an adherent of the official theory finds it difficult to resist this consequence of his premises, that he has no good reason to believe that there do exist minds other than his own. Even if he prefers to believe that to other human bodies there are harnessed minds not unlike his own, he cannot claim to be able to discover their individual characteristics, or the particular things that they undergo and do. Absolute solitude is on this showing the ineluctable destiny of the soul. Only our bodies can meet.

As a necessary corollary of this general scheme there is implicitly prescribed a special way of construing our ordinary concepts of mental powers and operations. The verbs, nouns and adjectives, with which in ordinary life we describe the wits, characters and higher-grade performances of the people with whom we have do, are required to be construed as signifying special episodes in their secret histories, or else as signifying tendencies for such episodes to occur. When someone is described as knowing, believing or guessing something, as hoping, dreading, intending or shirking something, as designing this or being amused at that, these verbs are supposed to denote the occurrence of specific modifications in his (to us) occult stream of consciousness. Only his own privileged access to this stream in direct awareness and introspection could provide authentic testimony that these mental-conduct verbs were correctly or incorrectly applied. The onlooker, be he teacher, critic, biographer or friend, can never assure himself that his comments have any vestige of truth. Yet it was just because we do in fact all know how to make such comments, make them with general correctness and correct them when they turn out to be confused or mistaken, that philosophers found it necessary to construct their theories of the nature and place of minds. Finding mental-conduct concepts being regularly and effectively used, they properly sought to fix their logical geography. But the logical geography officially recommended would entail that there could be no regular or effective use of these mental-conduct concepts in our descriptions of, and prescriptions for, other people's minds.

II. The Absurdity of the Official Doctrine

Such in outline is the official theory. I shall often speak of it, with deliberate abusiveness, as 'the dogma of the Ghost in the Machine'. I hope to prove that it is entirely false, and false not in detail but in principle. It is not merely an assemblage of particular mistakes. It is one big mistake and a mistake of a special kind. It is, namely, a category mistake. It represents the facts of mental life as if they belonged to one logical type or category (or range of types or categories), when they actually belong to another. The dogma is therefore a philosopher's myth. In attempting to explode the myth I shall probably be taken to be denying well-known facts about the mental life of human beings, and my plea that I aim at doing nothing more than rectify the logic of mental-conduct concepts will probably be disallowed as mere subterfuge.

I must first indicate what is meant by the phrase, 'Category-mistake'. This I do in a series of illustrations.

A foreigner visiting Oxford or Cambridge for the first time is shown a number of colleges, libraries, playing fields, museums, scientific departments and administrative offices. He then asks 'But where is the University? I have seen where the members of the Colleges live, where the Registrar works, where the scientists experiment and the rest. But I have not yet seen the University in which reside and work the members of your University.' It has then to be explained to him that the University is not another collateral institution, some ulterior counterpart to the colleges, laboratories and offices which he has seen. The University is just the way in which all that he has already seen is organized. When they are seen and when their co-ordination is understood, the University has been seen. His mistake lay in his innocent assumption that it was correct to speak of Christ Church, the Bodleian Library, the Ashmolean Museum *and* the University, to speak, that is, as if 'the University' stood for an extra member of the class of which these other units are members. He was mistakenly allocating the University to the same category as that to which the other institutions belong.

The same mistake would be made by a child witnessing the march-past of a division, who, having had pointed out to him such and such battalions, batteries, squadrons, etc., asked when the division was going to appear. He would be supposing that a division was a counterpart to the units already seen, partly similar to them and partly unlike them. He would be shown his mistake by being told that in watching the battalions, batteries and squadrons marching past he had been watching the division marching past. The march-past was not a parade of battalions, batteries, squadrons *and* a division; it was a parade of the battalions, batteries and squadrons *of* a division.

One more illustration. A foreigner watching his first game of cricket learns what are the functions of the bowlers, the batsmen, the fielders, the umpires and the scorers. He then says 'But there is no one left on the field to contribute the famous element of team-spirit. I see who does the bowling, the batting and the wicket-keeping; but I do not see whose role it is to exercise *esprit de corps.*' Once more, it would have to be explained that he was looking for the wrong type of thing. Team-spirit is not another cricketing-operation supplementary to all of the other special tasks. It is, roughly, the keenness with which each of the special tasks is performed, and performing a task keenly is not performing two tasks. Certainly exhibiting team-spirit is not the same thing as bowling or catching, but nor is it a third thing such that we can say that the bowler first bowls *and* then exhibits team-spirit or that a fielder is at a given moment *either* catching *or* displaying *esprit de corps.*

These illustrations of category-mistakes have a common feature which must be noticed. The mistakes were made by people who did not know how to wield the concepts *University, division* and *team-spirit.* Their puzzles arose from inability to use certain items in the English vocabulary.

The theoretically interesting category-mistakes are those made by people who are perfectly competent to apply concepts, at least in the situations with which they are familiar, but are still liable in their abstract thinking to allocate those concepts to logical types to which they do not belong. An instance of a mistake of this sort would be the following story. A student of politics has learned the main difference between the British, the French and the American Constitutions, and has learned also the differences and connections between the Cabinet, Parliament, the various Ministries, the Judicature and the Church of England. But he still becomes embarrassed when asked questions about the connections between the Church of England, the Home Office and the British Constitution. For while the Church and the Home Office are institutions, the British Constitution is not another institution in the same sense of that noun. So inter-institutional relations which can be asserted or denied to hold between the Church and the Home Office cannot be asserted or denied to hold between either of them and the British Constitution. 'The British Constitution' is not a term of the same logical type as 'the Home Office' and 'the Church of England'. In a partially similar way, John Doe may be a relative, a friend, an enemy or a stranger to Richard Roe; but he cannot be any of these things to the Average Taxpayer. He knows how to talk sense in certain sorts of discussions about the Average Taxpayer, but he is baffled to say why he could not come across him in the street as he can come across Richard Roe.

It is pertinent to our main subject to notice that, so long as the student of politics continues to think of the British Constitution as a counterpart to the other institutions, he will tend to describe it as a mysteriously occult institution; and so long as John Doe continues to think of the Average Taxpayer as a fellow-citizen, he will tend to think of him as an elusive insubstantial man, a ghost who is everywhere yet nowhere.

My destructive purpose is to show that a family of radical category-mistakes is the source of the double-life theory. The representation of a person as a ghost mysteriously ensconced in a machine derives from this argument. Because, as is true, a person's thinking, feeling and purposive doing cannot be described solely in the idioms of physics, chemistry and physiology, therefore they must be described in counterpart idioms. As the human body is a complex organised unit, so the human mind must be another complex organised unit, though one made of a different sort of stuff and with a different sort of structure. Or, again, as the human body, like any other parcel of matter, is a field of causes and effects, so the mind must be another field of causes and effects, though not (Heaven be praised) mechanical causes and effects.

III. The Origin of the Category-mistake

One of the chief intellectual origins of what I have yet to prove to be the Cartesian category-mistake seems to be this. When Galileo showed that his methods of scientific discovery were competent to provide a mechanical theory which should cover every occupant of space, Descartes found in himself two conflicting motives. As a man of scientific genius he could not but endorse the claims of mechanics, yet as a religious and moral man he could not accept, as Hobbes accepted, the discouraging rider to those claims, namely that human nature differs only in degree of complexity from clockwork. The mental could not be just a variety of the mechanical.

He and subsequent philosophers naturally but erroneously availed themselves of the following escape-route. Since mental-conduct words are not to be construed as signifying the occurrence of mechanical processes, they must be construed as signifying the occurrence of non-mechanical processes; since mechanical laws explain movements in space as the effects of other movements in space, other laws must explain some of the non-spatial workings of minds as the effects of other non-spatial workings of minds. The difference between the human behaviours which we describe as intelligent and those which we describe as unintelligent must be a difference in their causation; so, while some movements of human tongues and limbs are the effects of mechanical causes, others must be the effects of non-mechanical causes, i.e. some issue from movements of particles of matter, others from workings of the mind.

The differences between the physical and the mental were thus represented as differences inside the common framework of the categories of 'thing', 'stuff', 'attribute', 'state', 'process', 'change', 'cause' and 'effect'. Minds are things, but different sorts of things from bodies; mental processes are causes and effects, but different sorts of causes and effects from bodily movements. And so on. Somewhat as the foreigner expected the University to be an extra edifice, rather like a college but also considerably different, so the repudiators of mechanism represented minds as extra centres of causal processes, rather like machines but also considerably different from them. Their theory was a para-mechanical hypothesis.

That this assumption was at the heart of the doctrine is shown by the fact that there was from the beginning felt to be a major theoretical difficulty in explaining how minds can influence and be influenced by bodies. How can a mental process, such as willing, cause spatial movements like the movements of the tongue? How can a physical change in the optic nerve have among its effects a mind's perception of a flash of light? This notorious crux by itself shows the logical mould into which Descartes pressed his theory of the mind. It was the self-same mould into which he and Galileo set their mechanisms. Still unwittingly adhering to the grammar of mechanics, he tried to avert disaster by describing minds in what was merely an obverse vocabulary. The workings of minds had to be described by the mere negatives of the specific descriptions given to bodies; they are not in space, they are not motions, they are not modifications of matter, they are not accessible to public observation. Minds are not bits of clockwork, they are just bits of not-clockwork.

As thus represented, minds are not merely ghosts harnessed to machines, they are themselves just spectral machines. Though the human body is an engine, it is not quite an ordinary engine, since some of its workings are governed by another engine inside it—this interior governor-engine being one of a very special sort. It is invisible, inaudible and it has no size or weight. It cannot be taken to bits and the laws it obeys are not those known to ordinary engineers. Nothing is known of how it governs the bodily engine.

A second major crux points the same moral. Since, according to the doctrine, minds belong to the same category as bodies and since bodies are rigidly governed by mechanical laws, it seemed to many theorists to follow that minds must be similarly governed by rigid non-mechanical laws. The physical world is a deterministic system, so the mental world must be a deterministic system. Bodies cannot help the modifications that they undergo, so minds cannot help pursuing the careers fixed for them. *Responsibility, choice, merit* and *demerit* are therefore inapplicable concepts—unless the compromise solution is adopted of saying that the laws governing mental processes, unlike those governing physical processes, have the congenial attribute of being only rather rigid. The problem of the Freedom of the Will was the problem how to reconcile the hypothesis that minds are to be described in terms drawn from the categories of mechanics with the knowledge that higher-grade human conduct is not a piece with the behaviour of machines.

It is an historical curiosity that it was not noticed that the entire argument was broken-backed. Theorists correctly assumed that any sane man could already recognise the differences between, say, rational and non-rational utterances or between purposive and automatic behaviour. Else there would have been nothing requiring to be salved from mechanism. Yet the explanation given presupposed that one person could in principle never recognise the difference between the rational and the irrational utterances issuing from other human bodies, since he could never get access to the postulated immaterial causes of some of their utterances. Save for the doubtful exception of himself, he could never tell the difference between a man

and a Robot. It would have to be conceded, for example, that, for all that we can tell, the inner lives of persons who are classed as idiots or lunatics are as rational as those of anyone else. Perhaps only their overt behaviour is disappointing; that is to say, perhaps 'idiots' are not really idiotic, or 'lunatics' lunatic. Perhaps, too, some of those who are classed as sane are really idiots. According to the theory, external observers could never know how the overt behaviour of others is correlated with their mental powers and processes and so they could never know or even plausibly conjecture whether their applications of mental-conduct concepts to these other people were correct or incorrect. It would then be hazardous or impossible for a man to claim sanity or logical consistency even for himself, since he would be debarred from comparing his own performances with those of others. In short, our characterisations of persons and their performances as intelligent, prudent and virtuous or as stupid, hypocritical and cowardly could never have been made, so the problem of providing a special causal hypothesis to serve as the basis of such diagnoses would never have arisen. The question, 'How do persons differ from machines?' arose just because everyone already knew how to apply mental-conduct concepts before the new causal hypothesis was introduced. This causal hypothesis could not therefore be the source of the criteria used in those applications. Nor, of course, has the causal hypothesis in any degree improved our handling of those criteria. We still distinguish good from bad arithmetic, politic from impolitic conduct and fertile from infertile imaginations in the ways in which Descartes himself distinguished them before and after he speculated how the applicability of these criteria was compatible with the principle of mechanical causation.

He had mistaken the logic of his problem. Instead of asking by what criteria intelligent behaviour is actually distinguished from non-intelligent behaviour, he asked 'Given that the principle of mechanical causation does not tell us the difference, what other causal principle will tell it us?' He realised that the problem was not one of mechanics and assumed that it must therefore be one of some counterpart to mechanics. Not unnaturally psychology is often cast for just this role.

When two terms belong to the same category, it is proper to construct conjunctive propositions embodying them. Thus a purchaser may say that he bought a left-hand glove and a right-hand glove, but not that he bought a left-hand glove, a right-hand glove and a pair of gloves. 'She came home in a flood of tears and a sedan-chair' is a well-known joke based on the absurdity of conjoining terms of different types. It would have been equally ridiculous to construct the disjunction 'She came home either in a flood of tears or else in a sedan-chair'. Now the dogma of the Ghost in the Machine does just this. It maintains that there exist both bodies and minds; that there occur physical processes and mental processes; that there are mechanical causes of corporeal movements and mental causes of corporeal movements. I shall argue that these and other analogous conjunctions are absurd; but, it must be noticed, the argument will now show that either of the illegitimately conjoined propositions is absurd in itself. I am not, for example, denying that there occur mental processes. Doing long division is a mental process and so is making a joke. But I am saying that the phrase 'there occur mental processes' does not mean the same sort of thing as 'there occur physical processes', and, therefore, that it makes no sense to conjoin or disjoin the two.

If my argument is successful, there will follow some interesting consequences. First, the hallowed contrast between Mind and Matter will be dissipated, but dissipated not by either of the equally hallowed absorptions of Mind by Matter or of Matter by Mind, but in quite a different way. For the seeming contrast of the two

will be shown to be as illegitimate as would be the contrast of 'she came home in a flood of tears' and 'she came home in a sedan-chair'. The belief that there is a polar opposition between Mind and Matter is the belief that they are terms of the same logical type.

It will also follow that both Idealism and Materialism are answers to an improper question. The 'reduction' of the material world to mental states and processes, as well as the 'reduction' of mental states and processes to physical states and processes, presuppose the legitimacy of the disjunction 'Either there exist minds or there exist bodies (but not both)'. It would be like saying, 'Either she bought a left-hand and a right-hand glove or she bought a pair of gloves (but not both)'.

It is perfectly proper to say, in one logical tone of voice, that there exist minds and to say, in another logical tone of voice, that there exist bodies. But these expressions do not indicate two different species of existence, for 'existence' is not a generic word like 'coloured' or 'sexed'. They indicate two different senses of 'exist', somewhat as 'rising' has different senses in 'the tide is rising', 'hopes are rising', and 'the average age of death is rising'. A man would be thought to be making a poor joke who said that three things are now rising, namely the tide, hopes and the average age of death. It would be just as good or bad a joke to say that there exist prime numbers and Wednesdays and public opinions and navies; or that there exist both minds and bodies. In the succeeding chapters I try to prove that the official theory does rest on a batch of category-mistakes by showing that logically absurd corollaries follow from it. The exhibition of these absurdities will have the constructive effect of bringing out part of the correct logic of mental-conduct concepts.

IV. HISTORICAL NOTE

It would not be true to say that the official theory derives solely from Descartes' theories, or even from a more widespread anxiety about the

implications of seventeenth century mechanics. Scholastic and Reformation theology had schooled the intellects of the scientists as well as of the laymen, philosophers and clerics of that age. Stoic-Augustinian theories of the will were embedded in the Calvinist doctrines of sin and grace; Platonic and Aristotelian theories of the intellect shaped the orthodox doctrines of the immortality of the soul. Descartes was reformulating already prevalent theological doctrines of the soul in the new syntax of Galileo. The theologian's privacy of conscience became the philosopher's privacy of consciousness, and what had been the bogy of Predestination reappeared as the bogy of Determinism.

It would also not be true to say that the two-worlds myth did no theoretical good. Myths often do a lot of theoretical good, while they are still new. One benefit bestowed by the para-mechanical myth was that it partly superannuated the then prevalent para-political myth. Minds and their Faculties had previously been described by analogies with political superiors and political subordinates. The idioms used were those of ruling, obeying, collaborating and rebelling. They survived and still survive in many ethical and some epistemological discussions. As, in physics, the new myth of occult Forces was a scientific improvement on the old myth of Final Causes, so, in anthropological and psychological theory, the new myth of hidden operations, impulses and agencies was an improvement on the old myth of dictations, deferences and disobediences.

JOHN LOCKE
The Prince and the Cobbler

. . . If the identity of *soul alone* makes the same *man*, and there be nothing in the nature of matter why the same individual spirit may not be united to different bodies, it will be possible that those men, living in distant ages, and of different tempers, may have been the same man: which way of speaking must be from a very strange use of the word man, applied to an idea out of which body and shape are excluded. . . .

An animal is a living organized body; and consequently the same animal, as we have observed, is the same continued *life* communicated to different particles of matter, as they happen successively to be united to that organized living body. And whatever is talked of other definitions, ingenious observation puts it past doubt, that the idea in our minds, of which the sound "man" in out mouths is the sign, is nothing else but of an animal of such a certain form. . . .

I presume it is not the idea of a thinking or rational being alone that makes the *idea of a man* in most people's sense: but of a body, so and so shaped, joined to it; and if that be the idea of a man, the same successive body not shifted all at once, must, as well as the same immaterial spirit, go to the making of the same man.

This being premised, to find wherein personal identity consists, we must consider what *person* stands for;—which, I think, is a thinking intelligent being, that has reason and reflection,

Reprinted from John Locke's "Of Ideas of Identity and Diversity" in *An Essay Concerning Human Understanding,* Book II, Chap. 27 (First published in 1690). **John Locke** (1632–1704) is considered the first British empiricist, although empiricism as a movement did not take hold until the eighteenth century.

and can consider itself as itself, the same thinking thing, in different times and places; which it does only by that consciousness which is inseparable from thinking, and, as it seems to me, essential to it: it being impossible for any one to perceive without *perceiving* that he does perceive. When we see, hear, smell, taste, feel, meditate, or will anything, we know that we do so. Thus it is always as to our present sensations and perceptions: and by this every one is to himself that which he calls self:—it not being considered, in this case, whether the same self be continued in the same or divers substances. For, since consciousness always accompanies thinking, and it is that which makes every one to be what he calls self, and thereby distinguishes himself from all other thinking things, in this alone consists personal identity, i.e. the sameness of a rational being: and as far as this consciousness can be extended backwards to any past action or thought, so far reaches the identity of that person; it is the same self now it was then; and it is by the same self with this present one that now reflects on it, that that action was done.

But it is further inquired, whether it be the same identical substance. This few would think they had reason to doubt of, if these perceptions, with their consciousness, always remained present in the mind, whereby the same thinking thing would be always consciously present, and, as would be thought, evidently the same to itself. But that which seems to make the difficulty is this, that this consciousness being interrupted always by forgetfulness, there being no moment of our lives wherein we have the whole train of all our past actions before our eyes in one view, but even the best memories losing the sight of one part whilst they are viewing another; and we sometimes, and that the greatest part of our lives, not reflecting on our past selves, being intent on our present thoughts, and in sound sleep having no thoughts at all, or at least none with that consciousness which remarks our waking thoughts,—I say, in all these cases, our consciousness being interrupted, and we losing the sight of our past selves, doubts are raised whether we are the same thinking thing, i.e. the same *substance* or no. Which, however, reasonable or unreasonable, concerns not *personal* identity at all. The question being what makes the same person; and not whether it be the same identical substance, which always thinks in the same person, which, in this case, matters not at all: different substances, by the same consciousness (where they do partake in it) being united into one person, as well as different bodies by the same life are united into one animal, whose identity is preserved in that change of substances by the unity of one continued life. For it being the same consciousness that makes a man be himself to himself, personal identity depends on that only, whether it be annexed solely to one individual substance, or can be continued in a succession of several substances. For as far as any intelligent being can repeat the idea of any past action with the same consciousness it had of it at first, and with the same consciousness it has of any present action; so far it is the same personal self. For it is by the consciousness it has of its present thoughts and actions, that it is *self to itself* now, and so will be the same self, as far as the same consciousness can extend to actions past or to come; and would be by distance of time, or change of substance, no more two persons, than a man be two men by wearing other clothes today than he did yesterday, with a long or a short sleep between: the same consciousness uniting those distant actions in the same person, whatever substances contributed to their production.

That this is so, we have some kind of evidence in our very bodies, all whose particles, whilst vitally united to this same thinking conscious self, so that *we feel* when they are touched, and are affected by, and conscious of good or harm that happens to them, are a part of ourselves; i.e. of our thinking conscious self. Thus, the limbs of his body are to every one a part of himself; he sympathizes and is concerned for them. Cut off a hand, and thereby separate it from that consciousness he had of its heat, cold, and other affections, and it is then no longer a part of that which is himself, any more than the remotest part of matter. Thus, we see the *substance* whereof personal self consisted at one time may be varied at another, without the change of personal identity; there being no question about the same person, though the limbs which but now were a part of it, be cut off. . . .

And thus may we be able, without any difficulty, to conceive the same person at the resurrection, though in a body not exactly in make or parts the same which he had here—the same consciousness going along with the soul that inhabits it. But yet the soul alone, in the change of bodies, would scarce to any one but to him that makes the soul the man, be enough to make the same man. For should the soul of a prince, carrying with it the consciousness of the prince's past life, enter and inform the body of a cobbler, as soon as deserted by his own soul, every one sees he would be the same *person* with the prince, accountable only for the prince's actions: but who would say it was the same *man*? The body too goes to the making the man, and would, I guess, to everybody determine the man in this case, wherein the soul, with all its princely thoughts about it, would not make another man, but he would be the same cobbler to every one besides himself. I know that, in the ordinary way of speaking, the same person, and the same man, stand for one and the same thing. And indeed every one will always have a liberty to speak as he pleases, and to apply what articulate sounds to what ideas he thinks fit, and change them as often as he pleases. But yet, when we will inquire what makes the same *spirit, man,* or *person,* we must fix the ideas of spirit, man, or person in our minds; and having resolved with ourselves what we mean by them, it will not be hard to determine in either of them, or the like, when it is the same, and when not.

But though the immaterial substance or soul does not alone, wherever it be, and in whatsoever state, make the same *man;* yet it is plain, consciousness, as far as ever it can be extended—should it be to ages past—unites existences and actions very remote in time into the same *person,* as well as it does the existences

and actions of the immediately preceding moment: so that whatever has the consciousness of present and past actions, is the same person to whom they both belong. Had I the same consciousness that I saw the ark and Noah's flood, as that I saw an overflowing of the Thames last winter, or as that I write now, I could no more doubt that I who write this now, that saw the Thames overflowed last winter, and that viewed the flood at the general deluge, was the same *self*—place that self in what *substance* you please—than that I who write this am the same *myself* now whilst I write (whether I consist of all the same substance, material or immaterial, or no) that I was yesterday. For as to this point of being the same self, it matters not whether this present self be made up of the same or other substances—I being as much concerned, and as justly accountable for any action that was done a thousand years since, appropriated to me now by this self-consciousness, as I am for what I did the last moment. . . .

But yet possibly it will still be objected—Suppose I wholly lose the memory of some parts of my life, beyond a possibility of retrieving them, so that perhaps I shall never be conscious of them again; yet am I not the same person that did those actions, had those thoughts that I once was conscious of, though I have now forgot them? To which I answer, that we must here take notice what the word *I* is applied to; which, in this case, is the *man* only. And the same man being presumed to be the same person, I is easily here supposed to stand also for the same person. But it is possible for the same man to have distinct incommunicable consciousness at different times, it is past doubt the same man would at different times make different persons; which, we see, is the sense of mankind in the solemnest declaration of their opinions, human laws not punishing the mad man for the sober man's actions, nor the sober man for what the mad man did—thereby making them two persons: which is somewhat explained by our way of speaking in English when we say such as one is "not himself," or is "beside himself"; in which phrases it is insinuated, as if those who now, or at least first used them, thought that self was changed; the selfsame person was no longer in that man.

But yet it is hard to conceive that Socrates, the same individual man, should be two persons. To help us a little in this, we must consider what is meant by Socrates, or the same individual *man*.

First, it must be either the same individual, immaterial, thinking substance; in short, the same numerical soul, and nothing else.

Secondly, or the same animal, without any regard to an immaterial soul.

Thirdly, or the same immaterial spirit united to the same animal.

Now, take which of these suppositions you please, it is impossible to make personal identity to consist in anything but consciousness; or reach any further than that does.

DAVID HUME
Of Personal Identity

There are some philosophers who imagine we are every moment intimately conscious of what we call our *self;* that we feel its existence and its continuance in existence; and are certain, beyond the evidence of a demonstration, both of its perfect identity and simplicity. The strongest sensation, the most violent passion, say they, instead of distracting us from this view, only fix it the more intensely, and make us consider their influence on *self* either by their pain or pleasure. To attempt a further proof of this were to weaken its evidence; since no proof can be derived from any fact of which we are so intimately conscious; nor is there anything of which we can be certain if we doubt of this.

Unluckily all these positive assertions are contrary to that very experience which is pleaded for them; nor have we any idea of *self,* after the manner it is here explained. For, from what impression could this idea be derived?

This question it is impossible to answer without a manifest contradiction and absurdity; and yet it is a question which must necessarily be answered, if we would have the idea of self pass for clear and intelligible. It must be some one impression that gives rise to every real idea. But self or person is not any one impression, but that to which our several impressions and ideas are supposed to have a reference. If any impression gives rise to the idea of self, that impression must continue invariably the same, through the whole course of our lives; since self is supposed to exist after that manner. But there is no impression constant and invariable. Pain and pleasure, grief and joy, passions and sensations succeed each other, and never all exist at the same time. It cannot therefore be from any of these impressions, or from any other, that the idea of self is derived; and consequently there is no such idea.

Reprinted from David Hume's "Of Personal Identity" in *A Treatise of Human Nature*, Part IV (1961), by permission of Doubleday, a Division of Bantam, Doubleday, Dell Publishing Group, Inc. **David Hume** (1711–1776), one of the leading proponents of eighteenth-century British empiricism, is universally recognized as one of the great skeptics of all time.

But further, what must become of all our particular perceptions upon this hypothesis? All these are different, and distinguishable, and separable from each other, and may be separately considered, and may exist separately, and have no need of anything to support their existence. After what manner therefore do they belong to self, and how are they connected with it? For my part, when I enter most intimately into what I call *myself,* I always stumble on some particular perception or other, of heat or cold, light or shade, love or hatred, pain or pleasure. I never can catch *myself* at any time without a perception, and never can observe anything but the perception. When my perceptions are removed for any time, as by sound sleep, so long am I insensible of *myself,* and may truly be said not to exist. And were all my perceptions removed by death, and could I neither think, nor feel, nor see, nor love, nor hate, after the dissolution of my body, I should be entirely annihilated, nor do I conceive what is further requisite to make me a perfect nonentity. If any one, upon serious and unprejudiced reflection, thinks he has a different notion of *himself,* I must confess I can reason no longer with him. All I can allow him is, that he may be in the right as well as I, and that we are essentially different in this particular. He may, perhaps, perceive something simple and continued, which he calls *himself;* though I am certain there is no such principle in me.

But setting aside some metaphysicians of this kind, I may venture to affirm of the rest of mankind, that they are nothing but a bundle or collection of different perceptions, which succeed each other with an inconceivable rapidity, and are in a perpetual flux and movement. Our eyes cannot turn in their sockets without varying our perceptions. Our thought is still more variable than our sight; and all our other senses and faculties contribute to this change; nor is there any single power of the soul, which remains unalterably the same, perhaps for one moment. The mind is a kind of theatre, where several perceptions successively make their appearance; pass, repass, glide away, and mingle in an infinite variety of postures and situations.

There is properly no *simplicity* in it at one time, nor *identity* in different, whatever natural propension we may have to imagine that simplicity and identity. The comparison of the theatre must not mislead us. They are the successive perceptions only, that constitute the mind; nor have we the most distant notion of the place where these scenes are represented, or of the materials of which it is composed.

What then gives us so great a propension to ascribe an identity to these successive perceptions, and to suppose ourselves possessed of an invariable and uninterrupted existence through the whole course of our lives? In order to answer this question we must distinguish betwixt personal identity, as it regards our thought or imagination, and as it regards our passions or the concern we take in ourselves. The first is our present subject; and to explain it perfectly we must take the matter pretty deep, and account for that identity, which we attribute to plants and animals; there being a great analogy betwixt it and the identity of a self or person.

We have a distinct idea of an object that remains invariable and uninterrupted through a supposed variation of time; and this idea we call that of *identity* or *sameness.* We have also a distinct idea of several different objects existing in succession, and connected together by a close relation; and this to an accurate view affords as perfect a notion of *diversity* as if there was no manner of relation among the objects. But though these two ideas of identity, and a succession of related objects, be in themselves perfectly distinct, and even contrary, yet it is certain that, in our common way of thinking, they are generally confounded with each other. That action of the imagination, by which we consider the uninterrupted and invariable object, and that by which we reflect on the succession of related objects, are almost the same to the feeling; nor is there much more effort of thought required in the latter case than in the former. The relation facilitates the transition of the mind from one object to another, and renders its passage as smooth as if it contemplated one continued object. This resemblance is the cause of the confusion and mistake, and makes

us substitute the notion of identity, instead of
that of related objects. However at one instant
we may consider the related succession as variable or interrupted, we are sure the next to ascribe to it a perfect identity, and regard it as
invariable and uninterrupted. Our propensity to
this mistake is so great from the resemblance
above mentioned, that we fall into it before we
are aware; and though we incessantly correct
ourselves by reflection, and return to a more accurate method of thinking, yet we cannot long
sustain our philosophy, or take off this bias
from the imagination. Our last resource is to
yield to it, and boldly assert that these different
related objects are in effect the same, however
interrupted and variable. In order to justify to
ourselves this absurdity, we often feign some
new and unintelligible principle, that connects
the objects together, and prevents their interruption or variation. Thus we feign the continued
existence of the perceptions of our senses, to remove the interruption; and run into the notion
of a *soul*, and *self*, and *substance*, to disguise
the variation. But, we may further observe, that
where we do not give rise to such a fiction, our
propension to confound identity with relation is
so great, that we are apt to imagine something
unknown and mysterious, connecting the parts,
beside their relation; and this I take to be the
case with regard to the identity we ascribe to
plants and vegetables. And even when this does
not take place, we still feel a propensity to confound these ideas, though we are not able fully
to satisfy ourselves in that particular, nor find
anything invariable and uninterrupted to justify
our notion of identity.

Thus the controversy concerning identity is
not merely a dispute of words. For when we attribute identity, in an improper sense, to variable or interrupted objects, our mistake is not
confined to the expression, but is commonly attended with a fiction, either of something invariable and uninterrupted, or of something
mysterious and inexplicable, or at least with a
propensity to such fictions. What will suffice to
prove this hypothesis to the satisfaction of every
fair inquirer, is to show, from daily experience
and observation, that the objects which are
variable or interrupted, and yet are supposed to

continue the same are such only as consist of a
succession of parts connected together by resemblance, contiguity, or causation. For as such
a succession answers evidently to our notion of
diversity, it can only be by mistake we ascribe
to it an identity; and as the relation of parts,
which leads us into this mistake, is really nothing but a quality, which produces an association
of ideas, and an easy transition of the imagination from one to another, it can only be from
the resemblance, which this act of the mind
bears to that by which we contemplate one continued object, that the error arises. Our chief
business, then, must be to prove, that all objects, to which we ascribe identity, without
observing their invariableness and uninterrupt-
edness, are such as consist of a succession of
related objects.

In order to this, suppose any mass of matter,
of which the parts are contiguous and connected, to be placed before us; it is plain we
must attribute a perfect identity to this mass,
provided all the parts continue uninterruptedly
and invariably the same, whatever motion or
change of place we may observe either in the
whole or in any of the parts. But supposing
some very *small* or *inconsiderable* part to be
added to the mass, or subtracted from it; though
this absolutely destroys the identity of the
whole, strictly speaking, yet as we seldom think
so accurately, we scruple not to pronounce a
mass of matter the same, where we find so trivial an alteration. The passage of the thought
from the object before the change to the object
after it, is so smooth and easy, that we scarce
perceive the transition, and are apt to imagine,
that it is nothing but a continued survey of the
same object.

There is a very remarkable circumstance
that attends this experiment; which is, that
though the change of any considerable part in a
mass of matter destroys the identity of the
whole, yet we must measure the greatness of
the part, not absolutely, but by its *proportion* to
the whole. The addition or diminution of a
mountain would not be sufficient to produce a
diversity in a planet; thought the change of a
very few inches would be able to destroy the
identity of some bodies. It will be impossible to

account for this, but by reflecting that objects operate upon the mind, and break or interrupt the continuity of its actions, not according to their real greatness, but according to their proportion to each other; and therefore, since this interruption makes an object cease to appear the same, it must be the uninterrupted progress of the thought which constitutes the imperfect identity.

This may be confirmed by another phenomenon. A change in any considerable part of a body destroys its identity; but it is remarkable, that where the change is produced *gradually* and *insensibly,* we are less apt to ascribe to it the same effect. The reason can plainly be no other, than that the mind, in following the successive changes of the body, feels an easy passage from the surveying its condition in one moment, to the viewing of it in another, and in no particular time perceives any interruption in its actions. From which continued perception, it ascribes a continued existence and identity to the object.

But whatever precaution we may use in introducing the changes gradually, and making them proportionable to the whole, it is certain, that where the changes are at last observed to become considerable, we make a scruple of ascribing identity to such different objects. There is, however, another artifice, by which we may induce the imagination to advance a step further; and that is, by producing a reference of the parts to each other, and a combination to some *common end* or purpose. A ship, of which a considerable part has been changed by frequent reparations, is still considered as the same; nor does the difference of the materials hinder us from ascribing an identity to it. The common end, in which the parts conspire, is the same under all their variations, and affords an easy transition of the imagination from one situation of the body to another.

But this is still more remarkable, when we add a *sympathy* of parts to their *common end,* and suppose that they bear to each other the reciprocal relation of cause and effect in all their actions and operations. This is the case with all animals and vegetables; where not only the several parts have a reference to some general pur-

pose, but also a mutual dependence on, and connection with, each other. The effect of so strong a relation is, that though every one must allow, that in a very few years both vegetables and animals endure a *total* change, yet we still attribute identity to them, while their form, size, and substance, are entirely altered. An oak that grows from a small plant to a large tree is still the same oak, though there be not one particle of matter or figure of its parts the same. An infant becomes a man, and is sometimes fat, sometimes lean, without any change in his identity.

We may also consider the two following phenomena, which are remarkable in their kind. The first is, that though we commonly be able to distinguish pretty exactly betwixt numerical and specific identity, yet it sometimes happens that we confound them, and in our thinking and reasoning employ the one for the other. Thus, a man who hears a noise that is frequently interrupted and renewed, says it is still the same noise, though it is evident the sounds have only a specific identity or resemblance, and there is nothing numerically the same but the cause which produced them. In like manner it may be said, without breach of the propriety of language, that such a church, which was formerly of brick, fell to ruin, and that the parish rebuilt the same church of freestone, and according to modern architecture. Here neither the form nor materials are the same, nor is there anything common to the two objects but their relation to the inhabitants of the parish; and yet this alone is sufficient to make us denominate them the same. But we must observe, that in these cases the first object is in a manner annihilated before the second comes into existence; by which means, we are never presented, in any one point of time, with the idea of difference and multiplicity; and for that reason are less scrupulous in calling them the same.

Secondly, we may remark, that though, in a succession of related objects, it be in a manner requisite that the change of parts be not sudden nor entire, in order to preserve the identity, yet where the objects are in their nature changeable and inconstant, we admit of a more sudden transition than would otherwise be consistent with that relation. Thus, as the nature of a river consists in the motion and change of parts, though in less than four-and-twenty hours these be totally altered, this hinders not the river from continuing the same during several ages. What is natural and essential to anything is, in a manner, expected; and what is expected makes less impression, and appears of less moment than what is unusual and extraordinary. A considerable change of the former kind seems really less to the imagination than the most trivial alteration of the latter; and by breaking less the continuity of the thought, has less influence in destroying the identity.

We now proceed to explain the nature of *personal identity,* which has become so great a question in philosophy, especially of late years, in England, where all the abstruser sciences are studied with a peculiar ardour and application. And here it is evident the same method of reasoning must be continued which has so successfully explained the identity of plants, and animals, and ships, and houses, and of all compounded and changeable productions either of art or nature. The identity which we ascribe to the mind of man is only a fictitious one, and of a like kind with that which we ascribe to vegetable and animal bodies. It cannot therefore have a different origin, but must proceed from a like operation of the imagination upon like objects.

But lest this argument should not convince the reader, though in my opinion perfectly decisive, let him weigh the following reasoning, which is still closer and more immediate. It is evident that the identity which we attribute to the human mind, however perfect we may imagine it to be, is not able to run the several different perceptions into one, and make them lose their characters of distinction and difference, which are essential to them. It is still true that every distinct perception which enters into the composition of the mind, is a distinct existence, and is different, and distinguishable, and separable from every other perception, either contemporary or successive. But as, notwithstanding this distinction and separability, we suppose the whole train of perceptions to be united by identity, a question naturally arises concerning this relation of identity, whether it

be something that really binds our several perceptions together, or only associates their ideas in the imagination; that is, in other words, whether, in pronouncing concerning the identity of a person, we observe some real bond among his perceptions, or only feel one among the ideas we form of them. This question we might easily decide, if we would recollect what has been already proved at large, that the understanding never observes any real connection among objects, and that even the union of cause and effect, when strictly examined, resolves itself into a customary association of ideas. For from thence it evidently follows, that identity is nothing really belonging to these different perceptions, and uniting them together, but is merely a quality which we attribute to them, because of the union of their ideas in the imagination when we reflect upon them. Now, the only qualities which can give ideas a union in the imagination, are these three relations above mentioned. These are the uniting principles in the ideal world, and without them every distinct object is separable by the mind, and may be separately considered, and appears not to have any more connection with any other object than if disjoined by the greatest difference and remoteness. It is therefore on some of these three relations of resemblance, contiguity, and causation, that identity depends; and as the very essence of these relations consists in their producing an easy transition of ideas, it follows that our notions of personal identity proceed entirely from the smooth and uninterrupted progress of the thought along a train of connected ideas, according to the principles above explained.

The only question, therefore, which remains is, by what relations this uninterrupted progress of our thought is produced, when we consider the successive existence of a mind or thinking person. And here it is evident we must confine ourselves to resemblance and causation, and must drop contiguity, which has little or no influence in the present case.

To begin with *resemblance;* suppose we could see clearly into the breast of another, and observe that succession of perceptions which constitutes his mind or thinking principle, and suppose that he always preserves the memory of a considerable part of past perceptions, it is evident that nothing could more contribute to the bestowing a relation on this succession amidst all its variations. For what is the memory but a faculty, by which we raise up the images of past perceptions? And as an image necessarily resembles its object, must not the frequent placing of these resembling perceptions in the chain of thought, convey the imagination more easily from one link to another, and make the whole seem like the continuation of one object? In this particular, then, the memory not only discovers the identity, but also contributes to its production, by producing the relation of resemblance among the perceptions. The case is the same, whether we consider ourselves or others.

As to *causation*, we may observe that the true idea of the human mind, is to consider it as a system of different perceptions or different existences, which are linked together by the relation of cause and effect, and mutually produce, destroy, influence, and modify each other. Our impressions give rise to their correspondent ideas; and these ideas, in their turn, produce other impressions. One thought chases another, and draws after it a third, by which it is expelled in its turn. In this respect, I cannot compare the soul more properly to anything than to a republic or commonwealth, in which the several members are united by the reciprocal ties of government and subordination, and give rise to other persons who propagate the same republic in the incessant changes of its parts. And as the same individual republic may not only change its members, but also its laws and constitutions; in like manner the same person may vary his character and disposition, as well as his impressions and ideas, without losing his identity. Whatever changes he endures, his several parts are still connected by the relation of causation. And in this view our identity with regard to the passions serves to corroborate that with regard to the imagination, by the making our distant perceptions influence each other, and by giving us a present concern for our past or future pains or pleasures.

As memory alone acquaints us with the continuance and extent of this succession of perceptions, it is to be considered, upon that account chiefly, as the source of personal identity. Had we no memory, we never should have any notion of causation, nor consequently of that chain of causes and effects, which constitute our self or person. But having once acquired this notion of causation from the memory, we can extend the same chain of causes, and consequently the identity of our persons beyond our memory, and can comprehend times, and circumstances, and actions, which we have entirely forgot, but suppose in general to have existed. For how few of our past actions are there, of which we have any memory? Who can tell me, for instance, what were his thoughts and actions on the first of January 1715, the eleventh of March 1719, and the third of August 1733? Or will he affirm, because he has entirely forgot the incidents of these days, that the present self is not the same person with the self of that time; and by that means overturn all the most established notions of personal identity? In this view, therefore, memory does not so much *produce* as *discover* personal identity, by showing us the relation of cause and effect among our different perceptions. It will be incumbent on those who affirm that memory produces entirely our personal identity, to give a reason why we can thus extend our identity beyond our memory.

The whole of this doctrine leads us to a conclusion, which is of great importance in the present affair, viz. that all the nice and subtile questions concerning personal identity can never possibly be decided, and are to be regarded rather as grammatical than as philosophical difficulties. Identity depends on the relations of ideas; and these relations produce identity, by means of that easy transition they occasion. But as the relations, and the easiness of the transition may diminish by insensible degrees, we have no just standard by which we can decide any dispute concerning the time when they acquire or lose a title to the name of identity. All the disputes concerning the identity of connected objects are merely verbal, except so far as the relation of parts gives rise to some fiction or imaginary principle of union, as we have already observed.

What I have said concerning the first origin and uncertainty of our notion of identity, as applied to the human mind, may be extended with little or not variation to that of *simplicity*. An object, whose different coexistent parts are bound together by a close relation, operates upon the imagination after much the same manner as one perfectly simple and indivisible, and requires not a much greater stretch of thought in order to its conception. From this similarity of operation we attribute a simplicity to it, and feign a principle of union as the support of this simplicity, and the centre of all the different parts and qualities of the object.

Thus we have finished our examination of the several systems of philosophy, both of the intellectual and moral world; and, in our miscellaneous way of reasoning, have been led into several topics, which will either illustrate and confirm some preceding part of this discourse, or prepare the way for our following opinions. It is now time to return to a more close examination of our subject, and to proceed in the accurate anatomy of human nature, having fully explained the nature of our judgment and understanding.

ANTHONY QUINTON
The Soul

I. THE SOUL AND SPIRITUAL SUBSTANCE

Philosophers in recent times have had very little to say about the soul. The word, perhaps, has uncomfortably ecclesiastical associations, and the idea seems to be bound up with a number of discredited or at any rate generally disregarded theories. In the history of philosophy the soul has been used for two distinct purposes: first, as an explanation of the vitality that distinguishes human beings, and also animals and plants, from the broad mass of material objects, and, secondly, as the seat of consciousness. The first of these, which sees the soul as an ethereal but nonetheless physical entity, a volatile collection of fire-atoms or a stream of animal spirits, on some views dissipated with the dissolution of the body, on others absorbed at death into the cosmic soul, and on others again as capable of independent existence, need not detain us. The second, however, the soul of Plato and Descartes, deserves a closer examination than it now usually receives. For it tends to be identified with the view that in each person there is to be found a spiritual substance which is the subject of his mental states and the bearer of his personal identity. But on its widest interpretation, as the nonphysical aspect of a person, its acceptance need not involve either the existence of a spiritual substance over and above the mental states that make up a person's inner, conscious life or the proposition that this spiritual substance is what ultimately determines a person's identity through time. When philosophers

"The Soul" is reprinted from *The Journal of Philosophy*, LIX, 15 (July 19, 1962) by permission of *The Journal of Philosophy* and Anthony Quinton. **Anthony Quinton,** a contemporary British philosopher affiliated with Oxford University, has made major contributions in many areas of philosophy.

dismiss the soul it is usually because they reject one or both of these supposed consequences of belief in it.

It is worth insisting, furthermore, that the existence of a spiritual substance is logically distinct from its being the criterion of personal identity. So the strong, and indeed fatal, arguments against the substance theory of personal identity do not at the same time refute the proposition, self-evident to Berkeley and many others, that there can be no conscious state that is not the state of some subject.

As a criterion of identity spiritual substance has three main weaknesses. First, it is regressive in just the same way as is an account of the identity of a material object through time in terms of its physical components. No general account of the identity of a kind of individual thing can be given which finds that identity in the presence of another individual thing within it. For the question immediately arises, how is the identity through time of the supposed identifier to be established? It, like the thing it is supposed to identify, can present itself at any one time only as it is at that time. However alike its temporally separate phases may be, they still require to be identified as parts of the same, continuing thing. In practice we do identify some wholes through their parts, normally where the parts are more stable and persistent unities than the wholes they compose and where, in consequence, the parts are more readily identifiable, as, for example, when we pick out one person's bundle of laundry from the bundles of others after the labels have been lost. But this can be only a practical expedient, not a theoretical solution.

A second difficulty is to find any observable mental entity that can effectively serve as a criterion in this case. The only plausible candidate is that dim, inchoate background, largely composed of organic sensations, which envelops the mental states occupying the focus of attention. This organic background is a relatively unchanging environment for the more dramatic episodes of conscious life to stand out against. But both the fixity and the peripheral status of this background are only relative. It does

change, and it, or its parts, can come or be brought into the focus of attention. Even if its comparatively undisturbed persistence of character suggests it as a criterion, its vagueness makes it even less accessible to public application than the general run of mental criteria and leaves it with little power to distinguish between one person and another. The organic background is, of course, as regressive a criterion as any other part of a person's mental life. Its only virtues are that it is observable and that it does seem to be a universal constituent of the momentary cross sections of a person's experience. In this last respect it is preferable to most distinguishable features of a person's mental life. For, generally speaking, the parts of a complex and enduring thing are not necessary to the identity of that thing. Just as a cathedral is still the same cathedral if a piece has been knocked off it, whatever the piece may be, so a person is the same person if he ceases to have a particular belief or emotion, whatever that belief or emotion may be.

Finally, if it is held that the spiritual substance is nevertheless a permanent and unaltering constituent of a person's conscious life, it follows that it must be unobservable and so useless for purposes of identification. Suppose that from its very first stirrings my consciousness has contained a continuous whistling sound of wholly unvarying character. I should clearly never notice it, for I can only notice what varies independently of my consciousness—the whistles that start and stop at times other than those at which I wake up and fall asleep. It is this fact that ensured from the outset that Hume's search for a self over and above his particular perceptions was bound to fail. The unobservability of spiritual substance, and its consequent inapplicability as a criterion, can also be held to follow directly from taking its status as substance seriously, as an uncharacterized substratum for qualities and relations to inhere in with no recognizable features of its own.

But to admit that spiritual substance cannot possibly be the criterion of a person's identity and that it cannot be identified with any straightforwardly observable part of a person's mental life does not mean that it does not exist. It has seemed self-evident to many philosophers that every mental state must have an owner. To believe this is not to commit oneself to the existence of something utterly unobservable. If it is true, although both subjects and mental states are unobservable in isolation, each can be observed in conjunction with the other. There is a comparison here with the relations and observability of the positions and qualities of material things. One cannot be aware of a color except as present at some place and at some time or of a position except as the place and time where some discernible characteristics are manifested. So it might be argued that one can be aware of a conscious subject only as in some mental state or other and of a mental state only as belonging to some subject or other. Critics of the Berkeleyan principle sometimes suggest that it is no more than a faulty inference from the subject-object structure of the sentences in which mental facts are reported. It would certainly be a mistake to infer that a conscious subject is something entirely distinct from all its states from the linguistic fact that we commonly assign mental states to owners. We say of a chair that it has a back, a seat, arms, and legs, but this should not and does not lead us to conclude that the chair is something over and above the parts that it has, appropriately arranged. A more usual argument for the principle starts from the premise that mental states are acts that cannot be conceived without an agent in the same way as there cannot be a blow without a striker or a journey without a traveler. The premise of this argument has been much criticized by recent philosophers. A feeling of depression or a belief in the trustworthiness of a friend is not a precisely datable occurrence but a more or less persisting dispositional state. Nor is it an instance of agency in the sense of being the intentional execution of a decision. But these mistaken implications do not affect the validity of the argument under consideration. A disposition requires a possessor as much as an act requires an agent, and the blow I get from a swinging door still presupposes the existence of the door even though it did not mean to hit me.

The strength of the argument lies in the fact that we can assert the existence of some mental state, a feeling of anger let us say, only when we are in a position to assert either that we ourselves are angry or that somebody else is. We have given no sense to the words "discovering the existence of a mental state that is not my own or anyone else's." The nearest we come to speaking in this way is when we say, for example, "there is a sadness about the place," when walking about some ruins in a contemplative frame of mind. What we mean in this case is that the place inclines us to feel sad and might well give rise to the same inclination in others. And this capacity for producing sad feelings in myself and others, as a disposition, has its own substance, so to speak: the broken columns and collapsed walls with which it is bound up.

The subject in this rather thin and formal sense is not borne down in the ruin of that concept of spiritual substance in which it is proposed as the determinant of personal identity. It could be argued that it is a loose way of referring to the related series of other mental states or to the body or both with which any given mental state is universally associated by our manner of reporting such states. If it is something distinct from both of these, as it has traditionally been believed to be, it is not properly to be called the soul. It could not exist without any states at all, and even if it could it would be an emotionally useless form of survival of bodily death. Its existence, in fact, is irrelevant to the problem of the soul, which is that of whether a person is essentially mental in character and so distinct from his body, a connected sequence of mental states and not a physical object. It is irrelevant whether the sequence of mental states composing a person on this theory presupposes a distinguishable subject or not.

Spiritual substance cannot be the criterion of personal identity, and it may or may not be presupposed by the existence of conscious mental states. Whether as part or presupposition of our mental life, it should not be identified with the soul when this is conceived as the non-bodily aspect of a person. The well-founded conviction that there is no spiritual substance in the first sense and widespread doubts as to its existence in the second should not be allowed to obscure the issue of whether there is a unitary nonbodily aspect to a person and, if there is, whether it is the fundamental and more important aspect. Locke saw that spiritual substance could not account for personal identity and, although he believed in its existence, speculated whether it might not have been possible for God to endow a material substance with the power

of thinking. Yet he clearly believed in the soul as the connected sequence of a person's conscious states, regarded this sequence as what a person essentially was, and held it to be capable of existing independently of the body. I want to consider whether an empirical concept of the soul, which, like Locke's, interprets it as a sequence of mental states logically distinct from the body and is neutral with regard to the problem of the subject, can be constructed.

II. THE EMPIRICAL CONCEPT OF THE SOUL

It will be admitted that among all the facts that involve a person there is a class that can be described as mental in some sense or other. Is it enough to define the soul as the temporally extended totality of mental states and events that belong to a person? It will not be enough to provide a concept of the soul as something logically distinct from the body if the idea of the series of a person's mental states involves some reference to the particular human body that he possesses. In the first place, therefore, a nonbodily criterion of personal identity must be produced. For if the soul were the series of mental states associated with a given body, in the sense of being publicly reported by it and being manifested by its behavior, two temporally separate mental states could belong to the history of the same soul only if they were in fact associated with one and the same human body. This notion of the soul could have no application to mental states that were not associated with bodies. The soul must, then, be a series of mental states that is identified through time in virtue of the properties and relations of these mental states themselves. Both the elements of the complex and the relations that make an identifiable persisting thing out of them must be mental. To establish the possibility of such a mental criterion of identity will be the hardest part of the undertaking.

Locke's criterion of memory has been much criticized, and it is certainly untenable in some of the interpretations it has been given. It will not do to say that two mental states belong to

the same soul if and only if whoever has the later one can recollect the earlier one if the possibility of recollection involved is factual and not formal. For people forget things, and the paradox of the gallant officer is generated in which he is revealed as identical with both his childish and his senile selves while these are not identical with each other. However, a more plausible criterion can be offered in terms of continuity of character and memory. Two soul-phases belong to the same soul, on this view, if they are connected by a continuous character and memory path. A soul-phase is a set of contemporaneous mental states belonging to the same momentary consciousness. Two soul-phases are directly continuous if they are temporally juxtaposed, if the character revealed by the constituents of each is closely similar, and if the later contains recollections of some elements of the earlier. Two soul-phases are indirectly continuous and connected by a continuous character and memory path if there is a series of soul-phases all of whose members are directly continuous with their immediate predecessors and successors in the series and if the original soul-phases are the two end points of the series. There is a clear analogy between this criterion and the one by means of which material objects, including human bodies, are identified. Two object-phases belong to the same object if they are connected by a continuous quality and position path. Direct continuity in this case obtains between two temporally juxtaposed object-phases which are closely similar in qualities and are in the same position or in closely neighboring positions. Indirect continuity is once again the ancestral of direct continuity. There is no limit to the amount of difference in position allowed by the criterion to two indirectly continuous object-phases, but in normal discourse a limit is set to the amount of qualitative difference allowed by the requirement that the two phases be of objects of the same kind. Character in the mental case corresponds to quality in the physical and memory to spatial position. The soul, then, can be defined empirically as a series of mental states connected by continuity of character and memory.

Now there is an objection to the idea that memory can be any sort of fundamental criterion of identity which rests on the view that a memory criterion presupposes a bodily criterion. I shall defer the consideration of this issue, however, until two less serious difficulties have been met. These are that the construction suggested requires an exploded Cartesian dualism about the nature of mental states and, arising out of this, that a person's character is not clearly distinguishable from his body. The former, Rylean, objection can be met without difficulty. Even if the most extreme and reductive version of logical behaviorism were correct, even if a person's mental states were simply and solely behavioral dispositions, actual or potential, his character a complex property of these dispositions, and his memory a particular disposition to make first-person statements in the past tense without inference or reliance on testimony, the empirical concept of the soul would still apply to something distinct from any particular human body, though some body or other, not necessarily human perhaps, would be required to manifest the appropriate dispositions in its behavior and speech. In other words, an extreme, reductive, logical behaviorism is perfectly compatible with reincarnation, with the manifestation by one body of the character and memories that were previously manifested by another body that no longer exists. The second objection is that the soul as here defined and the body cannot be clearly distinguished, since the possession of some sorts of character trait requires the possession of an appropriate sort of body. I do not see that there is much empirical foundation for this to start with. It would be odd for a six-year-old girl to display the character of Winston Churchill, odd indeed to the point of outrageousness, but it is not utterly inconceivable. At first, no doubt, the girl's display of dogged endurance, a world-historical comprehensiveness of outlook, and so forth, would strike one as distasteful and pretentious in so young a child. But if she kept it up the impression would wear off. We do not, after all, find the story of Christ disputing with the doctors in the temple literally unintelligible. And a very large number of character traits seem to presume nothing about the age, sex, build, and general physical condition of their host. However, even if this were an empirically well-founded point, it would not be a relevant one. It would merely show that the possession of a given trait of character required the possession of an appropriate *kind* of body, a large one or a male one or an old one, and not the possession of a *particular* body. As things are, characters can survive large and even emotionally disastrous alterations to the physical type of a person's body, and these changes may have the effect of making it hard to others to recognize the continuity of character that there is. But courage, for example, can perfectly well persist even though the bodily conditions for its more obvious manifestations do not.

III. MENTAL AND BODILY CRITERIA OF IDENTITY

In recent philosophy there have been two apparently independent aspects to the view that the mind is logically dependent on the body. On the one hand, there are the doctrines that hold mental states either to be or necessarily to involve bodily states, whether bodily movement and dispositions thereto or neural events and configurations. With these doctrines, I have argued, the empirical concept of the soul can be reconciled. On the other hand, many philosophers have insisted that the basic and indispensable criterion of personal identity is bodily. Even mind-body dualists like A. J. Ayer, who have accepted the existence of a categorically clear-cut class of mental events, have sometimes taken this position. In his first treatment of the problem he appears at first to give a mental account of the concept of a person as being a series of experiences. But the relation that connects them in his theory involves an indispensable reference to a particular persisting human body. A person is made up of those total mental states which contain organic sensations belonging to one particular human body, presumably to be identified itself in terms of continuity of qualities and spatial position. Ayer draws the conclusion that properly follows from this and from any other account of personal identity that involves reference to a particular human body, namely that the notion of a person's disembodied existence is a self-contradictory one and, further, that even the association of a personality with different bodies at different times is inconceivable. These conclusions may well seem to constitute a reductio ad absurdum of the bodily criterion of personal identity rather than a disproof of the possibility of a person's survival of death. To explore them a little further will help to present the claims of mental as against bodily criteria in a clearer light.

At the outset it must be admitted that the theory of a bodily criterion has a number of virtues. It has, first, the theoretical attraction of simplicity, in that it requires only one mode of treatment for the identification through time of all enduring things, treating human beings as just one variety of concrete objects. Second, it has a practical appeal, in that its application yields uncontentiously correct answers in the very great majority of the actual cases of personal identification with which we are called upon to deal. Finally, it has the merit of realism, for it is, in fact, the procedure of identification that we do most commonly apply. Even where, for lack of relevant evidence, it is inap-

plicable, as in the case of the Tichborne claimant, it would not be supposed that the result of applying other criteria such as memory would conflict with what the bodily evidence would have shown if it had been forthcoming. Is there anything better to set against these powerful recommendations in favor of a bodily criterion than that it entails that things many people have wanted very deeply to say about the survival of death are inconsistent? A supporter of the bodily criterion might argue that it was so much the worse for them, that their inconsistent assertions arose from attempting to assert and deny at the same time that the person no longer existed.

It does seem strange, all the same, to say that all statements about disembodied or reincarnated persons are self-contradictory. Is it really at all plausible to say this about such familiar things as the simpler type of classical ghost story? It may be argued that there are plenty of stories which are really self-contradictory and yet which can be, in a way, understood and enjoyed, stories about time machines, for example. To try to settle the case we had better consider some concrete instances. Suppose I am walking on the beach with my friend A. He walks off a fair distance, treads on a large mine that someone has forgotten to remove, and is physically demolished in front of my eyes. Others, attracted by the noise, draw near and help to collect the scattered remains of A for burial. That night, alone in my room, I hear A's voice and see a luminous but intangible object, of very much the shape and size of A, standing in the corner. The remarks that come from it are in A's characteristic style and refer to matters that only A could have known about. Suspecting a hallucination, I photograph it and call in witnesses who hear and see what I do. The apparition returns afterwards and tells of where it has been and what it has seen. It would be very peculiar to insist, in these circumstances, that A no longer existed, even though his body no longer exists except as stains on the rocks and in a small box in the mortuary. It is not essential for the argument that the luminous object look like A or that it speak in A's voice.

If it were a featureless cylinder and spoke like a talking weighing machine we should simply take longer becoming convinced that it really was *A*. But if continuity of character and memory were manifested with normal amplitude, we surely should be convinced.

Consider a slightly different case. I know two men *B* and *C*. *B* is a dark, tall, thin, puritanical Scotsman of sardonic temperament with whom I have gone on bird-watching expeditions. *C* is a fair, short, plump, apolaustic Pole of indestructible enterprise and optimism with whom I have made a number of more urban outings. One day I come into a room where both appear to be, and the dark, tall, thin man suggests that he and I pursue tonight some acquaintances I made with *C*, though he says it was with him, a couple of nights ago. The short, fair, plump, cheerful-looking man reminds me in a strong Polish accent of a promise I had made to *B*, though he says it was to him, and which I had forgotten about, to go in search of owls on this very night. At first I suspect a conspiracy, but the thing continues far beyond any sort of joke, for good perhaps, and is accompanied by suitable amazement on their part at each other's appearance, their own reflections in the mirror, and so forth.

Now what would it be reasonable to say in these circumstances: that *B* and *C* have changed bodies (the consequence of a mental criterion), that they have switched character and memories (the consequences of a bodily criterion), or neither? It seems to me quite clear that we should not say that *B* and *C* had switched characters and memories. And if this is correct, it follows that bodily identity is not a logically complete criterion of personal identity; at best it could be a necessary condition of personal identity. Of the other alternatives, that of refusing to identify either of the psychophysical hybrids before us with *B* or *C* may seem the most scrupulous and proper. But the refusal might take a number of different forms. It might be a categorical denial that either of the hybrids is *B* or *C*. It might, more sophisticatedly, be an assertion that the concept of personal identity had broken down and that there was no correct answer, affirmative or negative, to the question: which of these two is *B* and which *C*? It might, uninterestingly, be a state of amazed and inarticulate confusion.

What support is there for the conclusion required by the empirical concept of the soul, that *B* and *C* have substituted bodies? First of all, the rather weak evidence of imaginative literature. In F. Anstey's story *Vice Versa* the corpulent and repressive Mr. Bultitude and his athletic and impulsive schoolboy son are the victims of a similar rearrangement. The author shows not the smallest trace of hesitation in calling the thing with the father's character and memories the father and the thing with the father's body the son. (Cf. also Conan Doyle's *Keinplatz Experiment*.) A solider support is to be found by reflecting on the probable attitude after the switch of those who are most concerned with our original pair, *B* and *C*, as persons, those who have the greatest interest in answering the question of their personal identity: their parents, their wives, their children, their closest friends. Would they say that *B* and *C* had ceased to exist, that they had exchanged characters and memories or that they had exchanged bodies? It is surely plain that if the character and memories of *B* and *C* really survived intact in their new bodily surroundings those closely concerned with them would say that the two had exchanged bodies, that the original persons were where the characters and memories were. For why, after all, do we bother to identify people so carefully? What is unique about individual people that is important enough for us to call them by individual proper names? In our general relations with other human beings their bodies are for the most part intrinsically unimportant. We use them as convenient recognition devices enabling us to locate without difficulty the persisting character and memory complexes in which we are interested, which we love or like. It would be upsetting if a complex with which we were emotionally involved came to have a monstrous or repulsive physical appearance, it would be socially embarrassing if it kept shifting from body to body while most such complexes stayed put, and it would be confusing and tiresome if such shifting around were generally widespread, for it would be a laborious business finding out where one's friends and family were. But that our concern and affection would follow the character and memory complex and not its original bodily associate is surely clear. In the case of general shifting about we should be in the position of people trying to find their intimates in the dark. If the shifts were both frequent and spatially radical we should no doubt give up the attempt to identify individual people, the whole character of relations between people would change, and human life would be like an unending sequence of shortish ocean trips. But, as long as the transfers did not involve large movements in space, the character and memory complexes we are concerned with could be kept track of through their audible identification of themselves. And there is no reason to doubt that the victim of such a bodily transfer would regard himself as the person whom he seems to remember himself as being. I conclude, then, that although, as things stand, our concept of a person is not called upon to withstand these strains and, therefore, that in the face of a psychophysical transfer we might at first not know what to say, we should not identify the people in question as those who now have the bodies they used to have and that it would be the natural thing to extend our concept of a person, given the purposes for which it has been constructed, so as to identify anyone present to us now with whoever it was who used to have the same character and memories as he has. In other words the soul, defined as a series of mental states connected by continuity of character and memory, is the essential constituent of personality. The soul, therefore, is not only logically distinct from any particular human body with which it is associated; it is also what a person fundamentally is.

It may be objected to the extension of the concept of personal identity that I have argued for that it rests on an incorrect and even sentimental view of the nature of personal relations. There are, it may be said, personal relationships which are of an exclusively bodily character and which would not survive a change of body but which would perfectly well survive a change of soul. Relations of a rather unmitigatedly sexual type might be instanced and also those where the first party to the relationship has violent racial feelings. It can easily be shown that these objections are without substance. In the first place, even the most tired of entrepreneurs is going to take some note of the character and memories of the companion of his later nights at work. He will want her to be docile and quiet, perhaps, and to remember that he takes two parts of water to one of scotch, and no ice. If she ceases to be plump and red-headed and vigorous he may lose interest in and abandon her, but he would have done so anyway in response to the analogous effects of the aging process. If he has any idea of her as a person at all, it will be as a unique cluster of character traits and recollections. As a body, she is simply an instrument of a particular type, no more and no less interesting to him than a physically identical twin. In the case of a purely sexual relationship no particular human body is required, only one of a more or less precisely demarcated kind. Where concern with the soul is wholly absent there is no interest in individual identity at all, only in identity of type. It may be said that this argument cuts both ways: that parents and children are concerned only that they should have round them children and parents with the same sort of character and memories as the children and parents they were with yesterday. But this is doubly incorrect. First, the memories of individual persons cannot be exactly similar, since even the closest of identical twins must see things from slightly different angles; they cannot be in the same place at the same time. More seriously, if more contingently, individual memories, even of identical twins, are seldom, if ever, closely similar. To put the point crudely, the people I want to be with are the people who remember me and the experiences we have shared, not those who remember someone more or less like me with whom they have shared more or less similar experiences. The relevant complexity of the memories of an individual person is of an altogether different order of magnitude from that of the bodily properties of an entrepreneur's lady-friend. The lady friend's bodily type is simply enough defined for it to have a large number of instances. It is barely conceivable that two individual memories should be similar enough to be emotionally adequate substitutes for each other. There is the case of the absolutely identical twins who go everywhere together, side by side, and always have done so. Our tendency here would be to treat the pair as a physically dual single person. There would be no point in distinguishing one from the other. As soon as their ways parted sufficiently for the question of which was which to arise, the condition of different memories required for individuation would be satisfied.

It may be felt that the absolutely identical twins present a certain difficulty for the empirical concept of the soul. For suppose their characters and memories to be totally indistinguishable and their thoughts and feelings to have been precisely the same since the first dawning of consciousness in them. Won't the later phases of one of the twins be as continuous in respect of character and memory with the earlier phases of the other as they are with his own earlier phases? Should we even say that there are two persons there at all? The positional difference of the two bodies provides an answer to the second question. Although they are always excited and gloomy together, the thrills and pangs are manifested in distinct bodies and are conceivable as existing separately. We might ignore the duality of their mental states, but we should be able in principle to assert it. As to the matter of continuity, the environment of the two will be inevitably asymmetrical, each will at various times be nearer something than the other, each will block some things from the other's field of vision or touch; so there will always be some, perhaps trivial, difference in the memories of the two. But even if trivial, the difference will be enough to allow the application in this special case of a criterion that normally relies on radical and serious differences. However alike the character and memories of twin no. 1 on Tuesday and twin no. 2 on Wednesday, they will inevitably be less continuous than those of twin no. 2 on the two days.

IV. MEMORY AND BODILY IDENTITY

I must now return to the serious objection to the use of memory as a criterion of personal identity whose consideration was postponed earlier. This has been advanced in an original and interesting article on personal identity recently published by Sydney S. Shoemaker in this *Journal*.* He argues that memory could not be the sole or fundamental criterion for the identity of other people, because in order to establish what the memories of other people are I have to be able to identify them in a bodily way. I cannot accept sentences offered by other people beginning with the words "I remember" quite uncritically. I must be assured, first, that these utterances really are memory claims, that the speaker understands the meaning of the sentences he is using, and, secondly, that his memory claims are reliable. Mr. Shoemaker contends that it is essential, if either of these requirements is to be satisfied, for me to be able to identify the maker of the apparent memory claims in an independent, bodily way. In order to be sure that his remarks really are intended as memory claims, I have to see that he generally uses the form of words in question in connection with antecedent states of affairs of which he has been a witness. And to do this I must be assured that he is at one time uttering a memory sentence and at another, earlier, time is a witness of the event he purports to describe; in other words I must be able to identify him at different times without taking his apparent memories into account. The point is enforced by the second requirement about the conditions under which I can take his memory claims as trustworthy. To do this I must be able to establish at least that he was physically present at and, thus, in a position to observe the state of affairs he now claims to recollect.

There is a good deal of force in these arguments, but I do not think they are sufficient to prove that the soul is not logically distinct from the particular body with which it happens to be associated at any given time. In the first place, the doubt about the significance of someone's current memory claims is not one that I must positively have laid to rest before taking these claims as evidence of his identity. The doubt could seriously arise only in very special and singular circumstances. If someone now says to me, "I remember the battle of Hastings," I will presume him to be slightly misusing the words, since I have good reasons for thinking that no one now alive was present at that remote event. I shall probably take him to be saying that he remembers that there was such a thing as the battle of Hastings, having learnt of it at school, or that it took place in 1066, that Harold was killed at it, that it was the crucial military factor in the Norman conquest, and so forth. But if, on being questioned, he says that these reinterpretations distort the meaning he intended, that he remembers the battle of Hastings in the same way as he remembers having breakfast this morning, if perhaps a little more dimly, then I cannot reasonably suppose that he doesn't understand the meaning of his remark though I may well think that it is false, whether deliberately or not. Mr. Shoemaker admits that in a case of apparent bodily transfer the significance of a person's memory claims could be established by considering the way in which he used memory sentences after the transfer had taken place. So at best this part of his argument could prove that in order to identify people we need to be able to make at least local applications of the criterion of bodily identity. They must be continuous in a bodily way for a period of time sufficient to enable us to establish that they are using memory sentences correctly. But in view of the somewhat strained and artificial character of the doubt in question, I am inclined to reject even this modest conclusion. At best it is a practical requirement: people must be suffi-

ciently stable in a bodily way for me to be able to accumulate a large enough mass of apparent memory claims that are prima facie there to infer from the coherence of these apparent claims that they really are memory claims and not senseless noises.

The reliability of the memory claims of others is a more substantial issue. For, unlike significance, it is a feature of apparent memory claims that we commonly do have serious reason to doubt. It must be admitted, further, that if I have independent reasons for believing that Jones's body was physically present at an event that Jones now claims to remember, I have a piece of strong evidence in support of the correctness of his claim. It is not, of course, conclusive. Even if he were looking in the direction at the time, he might have been in a condition of day-dreaming inattentiveness. The question is, however: is it in any sense a necessary condition for the correctness of my acceptance of a man's present memory claim that I should be able, in principle, to discover that the very same body from which the claim under examination now emerges was actually present at the event now purportedly remembered? I cannot see that it is. To revert to the example of a radical psychological exchange between *B* and *C*. Suppose that from *B*'s body memory claims emerge about a lot of what I have hitherto confidently taken to be *C*'s experiences. I may have good reason to believe that *C*'s body was present at the events apparently recalled. If the claims are very numerous and detailed, if they involve the recollection of things I didn't know *B* had seen although I can now establish that they were really present for *C* to observe, and if the emission of apparent *C* memories from *B*'s body and vice versa keeps up for a fair period, it would be unreasonable not to conclude that the memory claims emerging from *B*'s body were in fact correct, that they were the memory claims of *C* not of *B*, and that therefore the person with *B*'s body was in fact not now *B* but *C*. Here again a measure of local bodily continuity seems required. I shall not say that *C* inhabits *B*'s body at all unless he seems to do so in a fairly substantial way and over a fair period of time. But as long as the possibility of psycho-physical exchange is established by some salient cases in which the requirement of local bodily continuity is satisfied I can reasonably conjecture that such exchange has taken place in other cases where the translocation of memory claims is pretty short-lived. At any rate it is only the necessity of local bodily continuity that is established, not the necessary association of a person with one particular body for the whole duration of either. Bodily continuity with a witness is a test of the reliability of someone's memory claims, and it is an important one, but it is not a logically indispensable one.

V. THE PROBLEM OF DISEMBODIMENT

Nothing that I have said so far has any direct bearing on the question whether the soul can exist in an entirely disembodied state. All I have tried to show is that there is no necessary connection between the soul as a series of mental states linked by character and memory and any particular continuing human body. The question now arises: must the soul be associated with some human body? The apparent intelligibility of my crude ghost story might seem to suggest that not even a body is required, let alone a human one. And the same point appears to be made by the intelligibility of stories in which trees, toadstools, pieces of furniture, and so on are endowed with personal characteristics. But a good deal of caution is needed here. In the first place, even where these personal characteristics are not associated with any sort of body in the physiological sense, they are associated with a body in the epistemological sense; in other words, it is an essential part of the story that the soul in question have physical manifestations. Only in our own case does it seem that strictly disembodied existence is conceivable, in the sense that we can conceive circumstances in which there would be some good reason to claim that a soul existed in a disembodied state. Now how tenuous and nonhuman could these physical manifestations be? To take a fairly mild example, discussed by Professor Norman Malcolm, could we regard a tree as another person? He maintains with great firmness that we could not, on the rather flimsy ground that trees haven't got mouths and, therefore, could not be said to speak or communicate with us or make memory claims. But if a knothole in a tree trunk physically emitted sounds in the form of speech, why should we not call it a mouth? We may presume that ventriloquism, hidden record-players and microphones, dwarfs concealed in the foliage, and so forth have all been ruled out. If the remarks of the tree were coherent and appropriate to its situation and exhibited the type of continuity that the remarks of persons normally do exhibit, why shouldn't we regard the tree as a person? The point is that we might, by a serious conceptual effort, allow this in the case of one tree or even several trees or even a great many nonhuman physical things. But the sense of our attribution of personality to them would be logically parasitic on our attributions of personality to ordinary human bodies. It is from their utterances and behavior that we derive our concept of personality, and this concept would be applicable to nonhuman things only by more or less far-fetched analogy. That trees should be personal presupposes, then, the personality of human beings. The same considerations hold in the extreme case of absolutely minimal embodiment, as when a recurrent and localized voice of a recognizable tone is heard to make publicly audible remarks. The voice might give evidence of qualitative and positional continuity sufficient to treat it as an identifiable body, even if of an excessively diaphanous kind. The possibility of this procedure, however, is contingent on there being persons in the standard, humanly embodied sense to provide a clear basis for the acquisition of the concept that is being more or less speculatively applied to the voice.

Whatever the logic of the matter, it might be argued, the causal facts of the situation make the whole inquiry into the possibility of a soul's humanly or totally disembodied existence an entirely fantastic one. That people have the memories and characters that they do, that they have memories and characters at all, has as its causally necessary condition the relatively undisturbed persistence of a particular bit of physiological apparatus. One can admit this without concluding that the inquiry is altogether without practical point. For the bit of physiological apparatus in question is not the human body as a whole, but the brain. Certainly lavish changes in the noncerebral parts of the human body often affect the character and perhaps even to some extent the memories of the person whose body it is. But there is no strict relationship here. Now it is sometimes said that the last bit of the body to wear out is the brain, that the brain takes the first and lion's share of the body's nourishment, and that the brains of people who have starved to death are often found in perfectly good structural order. It is already possible to graft bits of one human body on to another, corneas, fingers, and, even, I believe, legs. Might it not be possible to remove the brain from an otherwise worn-out human body and replace it either in a manufactured human body or in a cerebrally untenanted one? In this case we should have a causally conceivable analogue of reincarnation. If this were to become possible and if the resultant creatures appeared in a coherent way to exhibit the character and memories previously associated with the brain that had been fitted into them, we could say that the original person was still in existence even though only a relatively minute part of its original mass and volume was present in the new physical whole. Yet if strict bodily identity is a necessary condition of personal identity, such a description of the outcome would be ruled out as self-contradictory. I conclude, therefore, not only that a logically adequate concept of the soul is constructible but that the construction has some possible utility even in the light of our knowledge of the causal conditions of human life.

NOTE

*"Personal Identity and Memory." *The Journal of Philosophy*, 56, 22 (Oct. 22, 1959): 868.

E. VICTORIA SPELMAN
Woman as Body

and what
pure happiness to know
all our high-toned questions
breed in a lively animal.

    Adrienne Rich, from "Two Songs"

What philosophers have had to say about women typically has been nasty, brutish, and short. A page or two of quotations from those considered among the great philosophers (Aristotle, Hume, and Nietzsche, for example) con-

"Woman As Body" is reprinted from *Twenty Questions: An Introduction to Philosophy* (1988) edited by G. Lee Bowie, Meredith W. Michaels and Robert C. Solomon, copyright © 1988 by Harcourt Brace Jovanovich, Inc., by permission of the publisher. **E. Victoria Spelman,** affiliated with Smith College, brings to the debate on personal identity a new feminist perspective.

stitutes a veritable litany of contempt. Because philosophers have not said much about women, and, when they have, it has usually been in short essays or chatty addenda which have not been considered to be part of the central body of their work, it is tempting to regard their expressed views about women as asystemic: their remarks on women are unofficial asides which are unrelated to the heart of their philosophical doctrines. After all, it might be thought, how could one's views about something as unimportant as women have anything to do with one's views about something as important as the nature of knowledge, truth, reality, freedom? Moreover—and this is the philosopher's move par excellence—wouldn't it be charitable to consider those opinions about women as coming merely from the *heart*, which all too easily responds to the tenor of the times, while philosophy "proper" comes from the *mind*, which resonates not with the times but with the truth?

Part of the intellectual legacy from philosophy "proper," that is, the issues that philosophers have addressed which are thought to be the serious province of philosophy, is the soul/body or mind/body distinction (differences among the various formulations are not crucial to this essay). However, this part of philosophy might have not merely accidental connections to attitudes about women. For when one recalls that the Western philosophical tradition has not been noted for its celebration of the body, and that women's nature and women's lives have long been associated with the body and bodily functions, then a question is suggested. What connection might there be between attitudes toward the body and attitudes toward women?

PLATO'S LESSONS ABOUT THE SOUL AND THE BODY

Plato's dialogues are filled with lessons about knowledge, reality, and goodness, and most of the lessons carry with them strong praise for the soul and strong indictments against the body. According to Plato, the body, with its deceptive senses, keeps us from real knowledge; it rivets us in a world of material things which is far removed from the world of reality; and it tempts us away from the virtuous life. It is in and through the soul, if at all, that we shall have knowledge, be in touch with reality, and lead a life of virtue. Only the soul can truly know, for only the soul can ascend to the real world, the world of the Forms or Ideas. That world is the perfect model to which imperfect, particular things we find in matter merely approximate. It is a world which, like the soul, is invisible, unchanging, not subject to decay, eternal. To be good, one's soul must know the Good, that is, the Form of Goodness, and this is impossible when one is dragged down by the demands and temptations of bodily life. Hence, bodily death is nothing to be feared: immortality of the soul not only is possible, but greatly to be desired, because when one is released from the body one finally can get down to the real business of life, for this real business of life is the business of the soul. Indeed, Socrates describes his own commitment, while still on earth, to encouraging his fellow Athenians to pay attention to the real business of life.

> [I have spent] all my time going about trying to persuade you, young and old, to make your first and chief concern not for your bodies nor for your possessions, but for the highest welfare of your souls.

Plato also tells us about the nature of beauty. Beauty has nothing essentially to do with the body or with the world of material things. *Real* beauty cannot "take the form of a face, or of hands, or of anything that is of the flesh." Yes, there are beautiful things, but they only are entitled to be described that way because they "partake in" the form of Beauty, which itself is not found in the material world. Real beauty has characteristics which merely beautiful *things* cannot have; real beauty is an everlasting loveliness which neither comes nor goes, which neither flowers nor fades, for such beauty is the same on every hand, the same then as now, here as there, this way as that way, the same to every worshipper as it is to every other.

Because it is only the soul that can know the Forms, those eternal and unchanging denizens of Reality, only the soul can know real Beauty; our changing, decaying bodies only can put us in touch with changing, decaying pieces of the material world.

Plato also examines love. His famous discussion of love in the *Symposium* ends up being a celebration of the soul over the body. Attraction to and appreciation for the beauty of another's body is but a vulgar fixation unless one can use such appreciation as a stepping stone to understanding Beauty itself. One can begin to learn about Beauty, while one is still embodied, when one notices that this body is beautiful, that that body is beautiful, and so on, and then one begins to realize that Beauty itself is something beyond any particular beautiful body or thing. The kind of love between people that is to be valued is not the attraction of one body for another, but the attraction of one soul for another. There is procreation of the spirit as well as of the flesh. All that bodies in unison can create are more bodies—the children women bear—which are mortal, subject to change and decay. But souls in unison can create "something lovelier and less mortal than human seed," for spiritual lovers "conceive and bear the things of the spirit," that is, "wisdom and all her sister virtues." Hence, spiritual love between men is preferable to physical love between men and women. At the same time, physical love between men is ruled out, on the grounds that "enjoyment of flesh by flesh" is "wanton shame," while desire of soul for soul is at the heart of a relationship that "reverences, aye and worships, chastity and manhood, greatness and wisdom." The potential for harm in sexual relations is very great—harm not so much to one's body or physique, but to one's soul. Young men especially shouldn't get

caught up with older men in affairs that threaten their "spiritual development," for such development is "assuredly and ever will be of supreme value in the sight of gods and men alike."

So, then, one has no hope of understanding the nature of knowledge, reality, goodness, love, or beauty unless one recognizes the distinction between soul and body; and one has no hope of attaining any of these unless one works hard on freeing the soul from the lazy, vulgar, beguiling body. A philosopher is someone who is committed to doing just that, and that is why philosophers go willingly unto death; it is, after all, only the death of their bodies, and finally, once their souls are released from their bodies, these philosophical desiderata are within reach. . . .

The division among parts of the soul is intimately tied to one other central and famous aspect of Plato's philosophy that hasn't been mentioned so far: Plato's political views. His discussion of the parts of the soul and their proper relation to one another is integral to his view about the best way to set up a state. The rational part of the soul ought to rule the soul and ought to be attended by the spirited part in keeping watch over the unruly appetitive part; just so, there ought to be rulers of the state (the small minority in whom reason is dominant), who, with the aid of high-spirited guardians of order, watch over the multitudes (whose appetites need to be kept under control).

What we learn from Plato, then, about knowledge, reality, goodness, beauty, love, and statehood, is phrased in terms of a distinction between soul and body, or alternatively and roughly equivalent, in terms of a distinction between the rational and irrational. And the body, or the irrational part of the soul, is seen as an enormous and annoying obstacle to the possession of these desiderata. If the body gets the upper hand over the soul, or if the irrational part of the soul overpowers the rational part, one can't have knowledge, one can't see beauty, one will be far from the highest form of love, and the state will be in utter chaos. So the soul/body distinction, or the distinction between the rational and irrational parts of the soul, is a highly charged distinction. An inquiry into the distinction is no mild metaphysical musing. It is quite clear that the distinction is heavily value-laden. Even if Plato hadn't told us outright that the soul is more valuable than the body, and the rational part of the soul is more important than the irrational part, that message rings out in page after page of his dialogues. The soul/body distinction, then, is integral to the rest of Plato's views, and the higher worth of the soul is integral to that distinction.

PLATO'S VIEW OF THE SOUL AND BODY, AND HIS ATTITUDE TOWARD WOMEN

Plato, and anyone else who conceives of the soul as something unobservable, cannot of course speak as if we could point to the soul, or hold it up for direct observation. At one point, Plato says no mere mortal can really understand the nature of the soul, but one perhaps could tell what it resembles. So it is not surprising to find Plato using many metaphors and analogies to describe what the soul is *like,* in order to describe relations between the soul and the body or relations between parts of the soul. For example, thinking, a function of the soul, is described by analogy to talking. The parts of the soul are likened to a team of harnessed, winged horses and their charioteer. The body's relation to the soul is such that we are to think of the body vis-à-vis the soul as a tomb, a grave or prison, or as barnacles or rocks holding down the soul. Plato compares the lowest or bodylike part of the soul to a brood of beasts.

But Plato's task is not only to tell us what the soul is like, not only to provide us with ways of getting a fix on the differences between souls and bodies, or differences between parts of the soul. As we've seen, he also wants to convince us that the soul is much more important than the body, and that it is to our peril that we let ourselves be beckoned by the rumblings of the body at the expense of harkening to the call of the soul. And he means to convince us of this by holding up for our inspection the silly and sordid lives of those who pay too much attention to their bodies and do not care enough for their souls; he wants to remind us of how unruly, how without direction, are the lives of those in whom the lower part of the soul holds sway over the higher part. Because he can't

point to an adulterated soul, he points instead to those embodied beings whose lives are in such bad shape that we can be sure that their souls are adulterated. And whose lives exemplify the proper soul/body relationship gone haywire? The lives of women (or sometimes the lives of children, slaves, and brutes).

For example, how are we to know when the body has the upper hand over the soul, or when the lower part of the soul has managed to smother the higher part? We presumably can't see such conflict, so what do such conflicts translate into, in terms of actual human lives? Well, says Plato, look at the lives of women. It is women who get hysterical at the thought of death; obviously, their emotions have overpowered their reason, and they can't control themselves. The worst possible model for young men could be "a woman, young or old or wrangling with her husband, defying heaven, loudly boasting, fortunate in her own conceit, or involved in misfortune or possessed by grief and lamentation—still less a woman that is sick, in love, or in labor". . . .

Moreover, Plato on many occasions points to women to illustrate the improper way to pursue the things for which philosophers are constantly to be searching. For example, Plato wants to explain how important and also how difficult the attainment of real knowledge is. He wants us to realize that not just anyone can have knowledge, there is a vital distinction between those who really have knowledge and those who merely think they do. Think, for example, about the question of health. If we don't make a distinction between those who know what health is, and those who merely have unfounded and confused opinions about what health is, then "in the matter of good or bad health . . . any woman or child—or animal, for that matter—knows what is wholesome for it and is capable of curing itself." The implication is clear: if any old opinion were to count as real knowledge, then we'd have to say that women, children, and maybe even animals have knowledge. But surely *they* don't have knowledge! And why not? For one thing, because they don't recognize the difference between the material, changing world of appearance, and the invisible, eternal world of Reality. In matters of beauty, for example, they are so taken by the physical aspects of things that they assume that they can see and touch what is beautiful; they don't realize that what one knows when one has knowledge of real Beauty cannot be something that is seen or touched. Plato offers us, then, as an example of the failure to distinguish between Beauty itself, on the one hand, and beautiful things, on the other, "boys and women when they see bright-colored things." They don't realize that it is not through one's senses that one knows about beauty or anything else, for real beauty is eternal and invisible and unchangeable and can only be known through the soul.

So the message is that in matters of knowledge, reality, and beauty, don't follow the example of women. They are mistaken about those things. In matters of love, women's lives serve as negative examples also. Those men who are drawn by "vulgar" love, that is, love of body for body, "turn to women as the object of their love, and raise a family"; those men drawn by a more "heavenly" kind of love, that is, love of soul for soul, turn to other men. But there are strong sanctions against physical love between men: such physical unions, especially between older and younger men, are "unmanly." The older man isn't strong enough to resist his lust (as in woman, the irrational part of the soul has overtaken the rational part), and the younger man, "the impersonator of the female," is reproached for this "likeness to the model." The problem with physical love between men, then, is that men are acting like women.

To summarize the arguments so far: the soul/body distinction is integral to the rest of Plato's views; integral to the soul/body distinction is the higher worth and importance of the soul in comparison to the body; finally, Plato tries to persuade his readers that it is to one's peril that one does not pay proper attention to one's soul—for if one doesn't, one will end up acting and living as if one were a woman. We know, Plato says, about lives dictated by the demands and needs and inducements of the body instead of the soul. Such lives surely are not good models for those who want to understand and undertake a life devoted to the nurturance of the best parts of us: our souls.

To anyone at all familiar with Plato's official and oft-reported views about women, the above recitation of misogynistic remarks may be quite surprising. Accounts of Plato's views about women usually are based on what he says in book 5 of the *Republic*. In that dialogue, Plato startled his contemporaries, when as part of his proposal for the constitution of an ideal state, he suggested that

there is no pursuit of the administrators of a state that belongs to woman because she is a woman or to a man because he is a man. But the natural capacities are distributed alike among both creatures, and women naturally share in all pursuits and men in all. . . .

Well now, what are we to make of this apparent double message in Plato about women? What are we to do with the fact that on the one hand, when Plato explicitly confronts the question of women's nature, in the *Republic,* he seems to affirm the equality of men and women; while on the other hand, the dialogues are riddled with misogynistic remarks? . . .

So the contradictory sides of Plato's views about women are tied to the distinction he makes between soul and body and the lessons he hopes to teach his readers about their relative values. When preaching about the overwhelming importance of the soul, he can't but regard the kind of body one has as of no final significance, so there is no way for him to assess differentially the lives of women and men; but when making gloomy pronouncements about the worth of the body, he points an accusing finger at a class of people with a certain kind of body—women—because he regards them, as a class, as embodying the very traits he wishes no one to have. In this way, women constitute a deviant class in Plato's philosophy, in the sense that he points to their lives as the kinds of lives that are not acceptable philosophically: they are just the kind of lives no one, especially philosophers, ought to live. . . .

In summary, Plato does not merely embrace a distinction between soul and body; for all the good and hopeful and desirable possibilities for human life (now and in an afterlife) are aligned with the soul, while the rather seedy and undesirable liabilities of human life are aligned with the body (alternatively, the alignment is with the higher or lower parts of the soul). There is a highly polished moral gloss to the soul/body distinction in Plato. One of his favorite devices for bringing this moral gloss to a high luster is holding up, for our contempt and ridicule, the lives of women. This is one of the ways he tries to make clear that it makes no small difference whether you lead a soul-directed or a bodily-directed life.

FEMINISM AND "SOMATOPHOBIA"

There are a number of reasons why feminists should be aware of the legacy of the soul/body distinction. It is not just that the distinction has been bound up with the depreciation and degradation of women, although, as has just been shown, examining a philosopher's view of the distinction may give us a direct route to his views about women.

First of all, as the soul or mind or reason is extolled, and the body or passion is denounced by comparison, it is not just women who are both relegated to the bodily or passionate sphere of existence and then chastised for belonging to that sphere. Slaves, free laborers, children, and animals are put in "their place" on almost the same grounds as women are. The images of women, slaves, laborers, children, and animals are almost interchangeable. For example, we find Plato holding that the best born and best educated should have control over "children, women and slaves . . . and the base rabble of those who are free in name," because it is in these groups that we find "the mob of motley appetites and pleasures and pains." As we saw above, Plato lumps together women, children, and animals as ignoramuses. (For Aristotle, there is little difference between a slave and an animal, because both "with their bodies attend to the needs of life.") A common way of denigrating a member of any one of these groups is to compare that member to a member of one of the other groups—women are thought to have slavish or childish appetites, slaves are said to be brutish. Recall too, that Plato's way of ridiculing male homosexuals was to say that they imitated women. It is no wonder that the images and insults are almost interchangeable, for there is a central descriptive thread holding together the images of all these groups. The members of these groups lack, for all intents and purposes, mind or the power of reason; even the humans among them are not considered fully human.

It is important for feminists to see to what extent the images and arguments used to denigrate women are similar to those used to denigrate one group of men vis-à-vis another, children vis-à-vis adults, animals vis-à-vis humans, and even—though I have not discussed it here—the natural world vis-à-vis man's will (yes, man's will). For to see this is part of understanding how the oppression of women occurs in the context of, and is related to, other forms of oppression or exploitation.

There is a second reason why feminists should be aware of the legacy of the soul/body distinction. Some feminists have quite happily adopted both the soul/body distinction and relative value attached to soul and to body. But in doing so, they may be adopting a position inimical to what on a more conscious level they are arguing for.

For all her magisterial insight into the way in which the image of woman as body has been foisted upon and used against us, Simone de Beauvoir can't resist the temptation to say that woman's emancipation will come when woman, like man, is freed from this association with—according to the male wisdom of the centuries—the less important aspect of human existence. According to *The Second Sex*, women's demand is "not that they be exalted in their femininity; they wish that in themselves, as in humanity in general, transcendence may prevail over immanence." But in de Beauvoir's own terms, for "transcendence" to prevail over "immanence" is for spirit or mind to prevail over matter or body, for reason to prevail over passion and desire. This means not only that the old images of women as mired in the world of "immanence"—the world of nature and physical existence—will go away. It will also happen that women won't lead lives given over mainly to their "natural" functions: "the pain of childbirth is on the way out"; "artificial insemination is on the way in." Although de Beauvoir doesn't explicitly say it, her directions for women are to find means of leaving the world of immanence and joining the men in the realm of transcendence. Men have said, de Beauvoir reminds us, that to be human is to have mind prevail over body; and no matter what disagreements she has elsewhere with men's perceptions and priorities, de Beauvoir here seems to agree with them.

. . . can we as a species sustain negative attitudes and negative ideologies about the bodily aspects of our existence and yet keep those attitudes and ideologies from working in behalf of one group of people as it attempts to oppress other groups?

. . . in *The Feminist Mystique*, [Betty] Friedan remarks on the absence, in women's lives, of "the world of thought and ideas, the life of the mind and spirit." She wants women to be "culturally" as well as "biologically" creative—she wants us to think about spending

our lives "mastering the secrets of the atoms, or the stars, composing symphonies, pioneering a new concept in government or society." And she associates "mental activity" with the "professions of highest value to society." Friedan thus seems to believe that men have done the more important things, the mental things; women have been relegated in the past to the less important human tasks involving bodily functions, and their liberation will come when they are allowed and encouraged to do the more important things in life.

Friedan's analysis relies on our old friend, the mind/body distinction, and Friedan, no less than Plato or de Beauvior, quite happily assumes that mental activities are more valuable than bodily ones. Her solution to what she refferred to as the "problem that has no name" is for women to leave (though not entirely) women's sphere and "ascend" into man's. Certainly there is much pleasure and value in the "mental activities" she extolls. But we can see the residue of her own negative attitude about tasks associated with the body: the bodily aspects of our existence must be attended to, but the "liberated" woman, who is on the ascendant, can't be bothered with them. There is yet another group of people to whom these tasks will devolve: servants. Women's liberation—and of course it is no secret that by "woman," Friedan could only have meant middle-class white women—seems to require woman's dissociation and separation from those who will perform the bodily tasks which the liberated woman has left behind in pursuit of "higher,"mental activity. So we find Friedan quoting, without comment, Elizabeth Cady Stanton:

> I now understand the practical difficulties most women had to contend with in the isolated household and the impossibility of women's best development if in contact the chief part of her life with servants and children. . .

Friedan at times seems to chide those women who could afford to have servants but don't: the women pretend there's a "servant problem" when there isn't, or insist on doing their own menial work. The implication is that women could find servants to do the "menial work," if they wanted to, and that it would be desirable for them to do so. But what difference is there between the place assigned to women by men and the place assigned to some women (or men) by Friedan herself? . . .

What I have tried to do here is bring attention to the fact that various versions of women's liberation may themselves rest on the very same assumptions that have informed the depreciation and degradation of women, and other groups which, of course, include women. Those assumptions are that we must distinguish between soul and body, and that the physical part of our existence is to be devalued in comparison to the mental. Of course, these two assumptions alone don't mean that women or other groups have to be degraded; it's these two assumptions, along with the further assumption that woman is body, or is bound to her body, or is meant to take care of the bodily aspects of life, that have so deeply contributed to the degradation and oppression of women. And so perhaps feminists would like to keep the first two assumptions (about the difference between mind and body, and the relative worth of each of them) and somehow or other get rid of the last—in fact, that is what most of the feminists previously discussed have tried to do. Nothing that has been said so far has amounted to an argument against those first two assumptions: it hasn't been shown that there is no foundation for the assumptions that the mind and body are distinct and that the body is to be valued less than the mind.

There is a feminist thinker, however, who has taken it upon herself to chip away directly at the second assumption and to a certain extent at the first. Both in her poetry, and explicitly in her recent book, *Of Woman Born,* Adrienne Rich has begun to show us why use of the mind/body distinction does not give us appropriate descriptions of human experience; and she has begun to remind us of the distance we keep from ourselves when we try to keep a distance from our bodies. She does this in the process of trying to redefine the dimensions of the experience of childbirth, as she tries to show us why

childbirth and motherhood need not mean what they have meant under patriarchy.

We are reminded by Rich that it is possible to be alienated from our bodies not only by pretending or wishing they weren't there, but also by being "incarcerated" in them. The institution of motherhood has done the latter in its insistence on seeing woman only or mainly as a reproductive machine. Defined as flesh by flesh-loathers, woman enters the most "fleshly" of her experiences with that same attitude of flesh-loathing—surely "physical self-hatred and suspicion of one's own body is scarcely a favorable emotion with which to enter an intense physical experience."

But Rich insists that we don't have to experience childbirth in that way—we don't have to experience it as a "torture rack"; but neither do we have to mystify it as a "peak experience." The experience of childbirth can be viewed as a way of recognizing the integrity of our experience, because pain itself is not usefully catalogued as something just our minds or just our bodies experience. . . . The point of "natural childbirth" should be thought of not as enduring pain, but as having an active physical experience—a distinction we recognize as crucial for understanding, for example, the pleasure of athletics.

Rich recognizes that feminists have not wanted to accept patriarchal versions of female biology, of what having a female body means. It has seemed to feminists, she implies, that we must either accept that view of being female, which is, essentially, to be a body, or deny that view and insist that we are "disembodied spirits." It perhaps is natural to see our alternatives in that way:

> We have been perceived for too many centuries as pure Nature, exploited and raped like the earth and the solar system; small wonder if we not try to become Culture: pure spirit, mind.

But we don't *have* to do that, Rich reminds us; we can appeal to the physical without denying what is called "mind." We can come to regard our physicality as "resource, rather than a destiny":

> In order to live a fully human life we require not only *control* of our bodies (though control is a prerequisite); we must touch the unity and resonance of our physicality, our bond with the natural order, the corporeal ground of our intelligence.

Rich doesn't deny that we will have to start thinking about our lives in new ways; she even implies that we'll have to start thinking about thinking in new ways. Maybe it will give such a project a small boost to point out that philosophers for their part still squabble about mind/body dualism; the legacy of dualism is strong, but not unchallenged by any means. And in any event . . . one can hardly put the blame for sexism (or any other form of oppression) on dualism itself. Indeed, the mind/body distinction can be put to progressive political ends, for example, to assert equality between human beings in the face of physical differences between them. There is nothing intrinsically sexist or otherwise oppressive about dualism, that is, about the belief that there are minds and there are bodies and that they are distinct kinds of things. But historically, the story dualists tell often ends up being a highly politicized one: although the story may be different at different historical moments, often it is said not only that there are minds (or souls) and bodies, but also that one is meant to rule and control the other. And the stage is thereby set for the soul/body distinction, now highly politicized and hierarchically ordered, to be used in a variety of ways in connection with repressive theories of the self, as well as oppressive theories of social and political relations. Among the tasks facing feminists is to think about the criteria for an adequate theory of self. Part of the value of Rich's work is that it points to the necessity of such an undertaking, and it is no criticism of her to say that she does no more than remind us of some of the questions that need to be raised.

A FINAL NOTE ABOUT THE SIGNIFICANCE OF SOMATOPHOBIA IN FEMINIST THEORY

In the history of political philosophy, the grounds given for the inferiority of women to men often are quite similar to those given for the inferiority of slaves to masters, children to fathers, animals to humans. In Plato, for example, all such subordinate groups are guilty by association with one another and each group is guilty by association with the bodily. In their eagerness to end the stereotypical association of women and body, feminists such as de Beauvior, Friedan, Firestone, and Daly have overlooked the significance of the connections—in theory and in practice—between the derogation and oppression of women on the basis of our sexual identity and the derogation and oppression of other groups on the basis of, for example, skin color and class membership. It is as if in their eagerness to assign women a new place in the scheme of things, these feminist theorists have by implication wanted to dissociate women from other subordinate groups. One problem with this, of course, is that those other subordinate groups include women.

What is especially significant about Rich's recent work is that in contrast to these other theorists she both challenges the received tradition about the insignificance and indignity of bodily life and bodily tasks and explicitly focuses on racism as well as sexism as essential factors in women's oppression. I believe that it is not merely a coincidence that someone who attends to the first also attends to the second. Rich pauses not just to recognize the significance attached to the female body, but also to reevaluate that significance. "Flesh-loathing" is loathing of flesh by some particular group under some particular circumstances—the loathing of women's flesh by men, but also the loathing of black flesh by whites. (Here I begin to extrapolate from Rich, but I believe with some warrant.) After all, bodies are always particular bodies—they are male or female bodies (our deep confusion when we can't categorize a body in either way supports and does not belie the general point); but they are black or brown or biscuit or yellow or red bodies as well. We cannot seriously attend to the social significance attached to embodiment without recognizing this. I believe that it is Rich's recognition of this that distinguishes her work in crucial ways from that of most other white feminists. Although the topic of feminism, sexism, and rac-

ism deserves a much fuller treatment, it is important to point out in the context of the present paper that not only does Rich challenge an assumption about the nature of the bodily that has been used to oppress women, but unlike other feminists who do not challenge this assumption, she takes on the question of the ways in which sexism and racism interlock. Somatophobia historically has been symptomatic not only of sexism, but also of racism, so it is perhaps not surprising that someone who has examined that connection between flesh-loathing and sexism would undertake an examination of racism.

SAUL KRIPKE
from *Naming and Necessity*

Let's try and refine the question a little bit. The question really should be, let's say, could the Queen—could this woman herself—have been born of different parents from the parents from whom she actually came? Could she, let's say, have been the daughter instead of Mr. and Mrs. Truman? There would be no contradiction, of course, in an announcement that (I hope the ages do not make this impossible), fantastic as it may sound, she was indeed the daughter of Mr. and Mrs. Truman. I suppose there might even be no contradiction in the discovery that— it seems very suspicious anyway that on either hypothesis she has a sister called Margaret— that these two Margarets were one and the same person flying back and forth in a clever way. At

any rate we can imagine discovering all of these things.

But let us suppose that such a discovery is not in fact the case. Let's suppose that the Queen really did come from these parents. Not to go into too many complications here about what a parent is, let's suppose that the parents are the people whose body tissues are sources of the biological sperm and egg. So you get rid of such recherché possibilities as transplants of the sperm from the father, or the egg from the mother, into other bodies, so that in one sense other people might have been her parents. If that happened, in another sense her parents were still the original king and queen. But other than that, can we imagine a situation in which it

Reprinted from "Naming and Necessity" by Saul Kripke, in *Semantics of Natural Language*, edited by Donald Davidson and Gilbert Harman, D. Reidel Publishing, 1972. Copyright © 1972 D. Reidel Publishing Co. Reproduced by permission of Kluwer Academic Publishers, Dordrecht, Holland. **Saul Kripke,** affiliated with Princeton University, is credited with fundamental breakthroughs in modal logic and the renewal of Aristotelian essentialism.

would have happened that this very woman came out of Mr. and Mrs. Truman? They might have had a child resembling her in many properties. Perhaps in some possible world Mr. and Mrs. Truman even had a child who actually became the Queen of England and was even passed off as the child of other parents. This still would not be a situation in which *this very woman* whom we call Elizabeth the Second was the child of Mr. and Mrs. Truman, or so it seems to me. It would be a situation in which there was some other woman who had many of the properties that are in fact true of Elizabeth. Now, one question is, in this world, was Elizabeth herself ever born? Let's suppose she wasn't ever born. It would then be a situation in which, though Truman and his wife have a child with many of the properties of Elizabeth, Elizabeth herself didn't exist at all. One can only become convinced of this by reflection on how you would describe this situation. (That, I suppose, means in some cases that you won't become convinced of this, at least not at the moment. But it is something of which I personally have been convinced.)

What right would you have to call this baby from completely different parents—in what sense would she be—*this very woman?* One can imagine, *given* the woman, that various things in her life could have changed: that she should have become a pauper; that her royal blood should have been unknown, and so on. One is given, let's say, a previous history of the world up to a certain time, and from that time it diverges considerably from the actual course. This seems to be possible. And so it's possible that even though she were born of these parents she never became queen. Even though she were born of these parents, like Mark Twain's character she was switched off with another girl. But what is harder to imagine is her being born of different parents. It seems to me that anything coming from a different origin would not be this object.

In the case of this table, we may not know what block of wood the table came from. Now could *this table* have been made from a completely *different* block of wood, or even of water cleverly hardened into ice—water taken from the Thames River? We could conceivably discover that, contrary to what we now think, this table is indeed made of ice from the river. But let us suppose that it is not. Then, though we can imagine making a table out of another block of wood or even from ice, identical in appearance with this one, and though we could have put it in this very position in the room, it seems to me that this is *not* to imagine *this* table as made of wood or ice, but rather it is to imagine another table, *resembling* this one in all external details, made of another block of wood, or even of ice.

EDDY M. ZEMACH
Looking Out for Number One

I. THE RATIONAL EGOIST

More often than not, people try to achieve a state which they believe will be good for them. Our society is based on the belief that prudential, or egoistic, action is rational and almost self-justifying; an action should benefit its agent. For this belief to be justified, there must be a clear distinction between what is, and what is not, that very same agent. In a number of articles published over the last twenty years[1] I have argued, however, that no such distinction exists. The very conceptual framework necessary for formulating such claims is flawed— what survives is (by the egoist's lights) valueless, and what is valuable cannot possibly survive. In the present article I recast some of those arguments in a new, uniform way, avoiding what I take to be Parfit's failure to distinguish between (1) a genuine (e.g., Schlick-like) no-ownership model of mental life, where there is no substance which is oneself; and (2) a framework which has an enduring subject of ex-

periences, oneself, albeit to a higher or lower degree. It is one thing to reject the concept of self-regarding interest altogether, and quite another to say that it is open-textured, because in some far-out and recherché cases the identity conditions of persons are not clearly defined.[2] Arguing that only the first of these positions is viable I also suggest what can replace self-interest as a motive for action. (Parfit's "moderate" solution is, I think, a clear case of confusing the two frameworks.)

Let us start by assuming that prudential behavior is rational, and try to identify the putative beneficiary of such action by looking at what rational people cherish, care for, and value, using the following rule as a criterion: If some x has no value at all for me, as a rational self-seeker, I can conclude that I am not x. Since I am the intended beneficiary of my prudential behavior we shall also see, in this way, whether prudential action can ever be successful.

II. I AM NOT MY BODY

At first blush it seems that my body passes the test with flying colors. Do I not take great care

of this body, clothe it, wash it, feed it, heal it when it is damaged, shelter it and defend it as

"Looking Out for Number One" is reprinted from *Philosophy and Phenomenological Research* 48 (December 1987), by permission of *Philosophy and Phenomenological Research*. **Eddy Zemach**, a contemporary Israeli philosopher affiliated with Hebrew University, specializes in aesthetics and the philosophy of mind. He has also made contributions to the philosophy of language, the theory of knowledge, and to Wittgensteinian scholarship.

best I can? Yet it is clear, I think, that in fact I do not care about this body in the least.

When I cut my nails or my hair, parts of this body are thrown away and dumped as garbage. If the welfare of this body is dear to me, why do I let these parts of it rot away? Why do I not rush to their rescue? Suppose that I have lost a limb or two in an accident; say, ten percent of this body. If this body is really I, should I not earmark ten percent of my property to provide future maintenance for the unfortunate dismembered limbs? But I, and other people who are not usually considered terribly irrational or self-destructive, do not behave in this way.

An obvious answer would be that a severed part of a body is a *former* part, and not a part, of a body; hence, the above argument is irrelevant. Let us call this view of the body the Winner Takes All Principle. At the barber shop, or as a result of the accident, this body was indeed divided, but, using the above principle, we let that part of it which has the most claim to be the continuer of the body that was, take all. We consider it the sole heir of the body as it was before the split. All the other parts are not this body at all; hence my complete lack of interest in their fate.

Let us consider, then, only unsevered parts of this body. Do I care about them, in any degree? The answer is that I do not. Suppose that through a simple, painless and safe operation I can replace these two hands by a pair of visually indistinguishable bionic hands which are far stronger and better. Using them, I play the piano like Rubinstein, have the punch of Muhammad Ali, and open locks like Houdini. Of course I shall not hesitate to get rid of my old, worn out hands (or heart, or lungs, or liver, or legs, or what have you) to get the better, sturdier, and more efficient replacement! In doing so I never show any regard to those actual parts of my body which, as a result of that operation, will be thrown out and crushed into pulp. Yet these condemned parts are organic, undetached parts of this body. Thus, this body fails the test.

I see no reason why I would not be just as eager to replace defective, worn out, or ineffi-

cient parts of my brain, as I am eager to replace such parts elsewhere in my body. Suppose that I can avail myself of synthetic parts which are exact (only more durable) replicas of my existing brain cells, containing every bit of information contained in the present ones and functioning in exactly the same way; surely, I would be willing to discard the fast-deteriorating original carbon-based cells and replace them with the new ones. But if I am willing to do that, I do not place any value in this brain itself. I regard it, too, as a tool, replaceable when worn out, just like any other tool, without any compunction or sense of self-sacrifice. On the other hand, *I* am not such a tool: I would most strenuously object if one were to inform me that since I am old and do not function as well as I used to, I shall be treated as refuse and totally annihilated, so that I could be replaced by some other person, more efficient and durable than I am. But if it is my wish that this brain, or parts thereof, be eliminated and replaced, and it is not my wish that I be eliminated and replaced, then I am not identical with this brain.

Some philosophers may consider this argument faulty since it substitutes terms in an opaque context. It is often said that one may desire *a* but not *b* although *a* = *b*, because one may not realize that *a* = *b*. In such cases, however, the subject's attitude would change as soon as he or she is appraised of the facts of the matter. That is, if *p* and *q* are the same state of affairs, a rational person would express a desire that *p* be the case and indifference toward *q* only if that person is unaware of their identity. But this is not the case in our thought experiment. There is no fact which I must assume I am ignorant of when I desire to have the decaying parts of my brain replaced by new ones. It will not do, of course, to say that the fact of which I am ignorant is that I am my brain, since the identity of *a* and *b* is defined as *a* and *b* sharing all their other properties (Leibniz's Law). But in this case I know all the facts about my psychological makeup (which I know would not be affected by the operation) and my physiology (which I know would). When all relevant facts are known to the subject, contexts governed by propositional attitude operators are not opaque, and substitution of coreferentials is perfectly in order.

I think that Parfit is right in arguing that the difference between a gradual replacement of all my brain cells and replacing them all at once is trivial, and cannot assume the momentous significance we attribute to the difference between life and death.[3] A rational person who is willing to undergo a whole series of operations for replacement of brain cells would gladly have one operation instead, if the end result is the same. Now a rational person would be willing to undergo the series of replacement operations, since he is risking nothing: those cells are replaced anyway, in the natural course of events. If one's identity is not jeopardized by the natural process, it cannot be ruined by accelerating it. (Note: I am not claiming that one can survive a brain-change; what I say is that the concept of one's own survival, which I want to discard, does not preclude it.)

Moreover, as far as we know, it is possible that the whole brain is replaced at one time in the natural course of events. Suppose that elementary particles always pulsate in and out of existence (this assumption is closer to science fact than to science fiction). Let us say that an elementary particle "flashes" in and out of existence, on the average, a million times a second. Given the number of elementary particles in the brain we can calculate how often all its particles go out of existence simultaneously. Suppose that this happens once a year. I therefore get a wholly new brain every year. Since I have a new brain, do I lose all my possessions, my rights and my duties every year, having violated the brain-identity criterion? To avoid this preposterous conclusion, an advocate of the I Am My Brain theory may claim that the criteria for brain identity are molar and are not affected by the identity (or lack of it) of its constituents at any time. In that case, the concept of brain identity becomes trivial: there is no reason why we cannot say that the same brain has survived the simultaneous replacement of all its cells, using molar criteria such as sameness of function

and location. The criteria of brain identity are thus tailored to fit our intuitions about personal survival, and the I Am My Brain thesis becomes trivially true, i.e., true by definition. The suggestion that I am my brain is therefore either false (because it violates our intuitions about one's own survival) or (if it is forced to adhere to those intuitions) empty.

Another argument is this: I care about my body only because changes in it can occasion pleasant or unpleasant experiences in me; otherwise I would not have been interested in it at all. Suppose, e.g., that a massive damage is caused to your body, but you are assured that this damage cannot result in your having any untoward experience, nor can it deprive you of any experience which you would otherwise have had. Surely you would not care one bit? Similarly, I am not overly concerned with the deterioration of my body after I die, if I do not expect to rise one day from the dead and need it for having sensations, emotions, intentions and thoughts.

The sophisticated materialist may protest at this point that my argument presupposes a dualistic position. Indeed, he would say, I am (as a rational egoist) exclusively interested in having pleasant experiences; yet that does not show that I have no inherent interest in the states of this body. On the contrary, my experiences, the materialist claims, are themselves physical processes taking place in that (my) body. Thus even if it is true that physical processes in my body matter to me only to the extent that they bring about the presence or absence of certain mental processes, this fact only proves that not all physical processes in me, i.e., in this body, are equally valuable to me. Some of them, i.e., those brain processes which are my experiences, are all that I value and identify with, while other processes have value only insofar as they make the above brain processes possible.

Let us assume, for the argument's sake, that the materialist is right. Let us say that pleasant experiences are identical with certain processes in my brain, e.g., the production of certain currents or particles which we may refer to, from now on, as *hedons*. Now, if I value my pleasures, those hedons must be extremely valuable for me, and their existence in my brain should be what I cherish above all else. Yet a rational hedonist would not place such a high value on the hedons in his brain; he would not value them at all. What I want is pleasure, and if this means having hedons in the brain, I want hedons in the brain. But I do not care about *these* particular hedons: I am perfectly content to have all of them destroyed if they are to be generously replaced by others, qualitatively identical, or better and more numerous, hedons. I do

not mind in the least if the pleasure I have is the set of hedons *a* (which are actually in my brain) or another set of hedons *b*. On the other hand, the existence or nonexistence of myself seems to be of great value to me, and I would not be willing to have myself destroyed and replaced by someone who is much happier than I am. Therefore, whether my pleasures are physical entities or not, I know that I am not any physical entity; I am not my hands or my heart or my brain or my hedons. I am not a body at all.

III. I AM NOT A SET OF MENTAL CONTENTS

If I am not a body, perhaps I am a set of mental contents: a set of experiences, including sensations, feelings, emotions, memories, thoughts, beliefs, intentions, desires, etc., as well as dispositions for certain mental states, all tied together by similarity, temporal contiguity, and causality. Those mental states are causally connected in a twofold way: first, they causally influence each other, such that the occurrence of later experiences is partially explained by reference to earlier mental contents in the series; second, the occurrence of all items in this series is partially explained by reference to the same body. Let us call the said relation, 'P'. The present suggestion, then, is that persons are sets of P-connected mental contents. What I am is *this* set of mental contents which stand to each other in the P relation.

This view can be subscribed to by materialists who take mental contents to be syntactically identified and semantically interpreted brain states. They, too, deny that the criteria determining the identity of persons can be stated in terms descriptive of the body (i.e., the hardware); a certain kind of software, which they identify with a P-ly related set of mental contents, is what makes people what they are; it is what really counts. This view of a person as a set of mental contents (originally suggested by John Locke) is widely accepted.

I shall not challenge Lockeans to give a precise formulation of the relation P which will be

neither too wide, nor too narrow, but exactly fit our intuitions about personal identity; such an account has never been given. Nor shall I expect the Lockean to spell out what is the exact nature of P's causal ingredient, although here, too, no hint was ever given on what this unique (this "right causal connection") has to be. But let this pass, too (relegate it to the general story of woes which is Modern Functionalism). Let us give the Lockeans the best starting position they can hope for, and merely ask: can this view pass the test I have suggested at the beginning of this article? I do not think so.

If I were this set of P-ly connected experiences, I would have regarded it as a most valuable thing, resisting any attempt to compromise its existence. Do I, in fact, behave in this way? Of course not. I often regret having, having had, or having to have, a certain experience, desire, or thought. There is no reason why a rational self-seeker cannot wish his past, present or future experiences to be more pleasant than they were, or are, or will be. Have I not often regretted having done *a*, wishing I would have done *b* instead? But if I *am* the set A (which includes the experience of having done *a* and subsequent memories and regrets) and I wish that I were the set B (which, I say, includes the quite different experience of having done *b*, etc.) then I must be either quite mad or hopelessly suicidal. If I know that I = A and that A ≠ B, and I have learned some set theory, I know that it is quite impossible, logically impossible, that $I = B$. If the egoist wishes for something which he knows to be logically impossible, he must be mad: how can anyone not completely innocent of logic wish for one set (A, i.e., I) to be identical with another set (B) which he knows to have a different membership? Alternatively, the said wish may be interpreted as a death wish: not that $A = B$, which is logically inconceivable, but that instead of A existing, B would exist. But if I am A, and know that, to wish for A's nonexistence is to wish for my own nonexistence, and the existence of someone else (that one who is B) in my stead. In this case I am a self-hater, and not an egoist at all. Therefore, no rational self-seeker who accepts this version of Locke's view should ever regret anything or wish for any experience of his not to have occurred (or, occur). Since this is a bit too much to ask, Locke's model of the self cannot be used for any prudential (egoistic) centered theory of rational action.

There is a way around this objection: a Lockean may try to define the set of experiences that I am in a different way. One may choose some privileged experience, e.g., my present experience at the present moment, e, and say that whatever stands in the relation P to that experience, e, is a segment of me, a stage in my career. Thus, the wish that a certain experience of mine would not have existed amounts to a wish for a change *in* me, e.g., that some part of my career does not exist, and this does not amount to a desire that I do not exist. Rather, it is a wish that instead of the experience d bearing P to the present experience e, c would stand in that relation to e. This solution, however, makes it impossible to wish that one's present experience would not have occurred. But what if e is an experience of dire pain? The problem cannot be solved by taking some other experience, d, instead of e as the privileged one since, first, what makes d my (rather than someone else's) experience? And, second, I can wish that it, too, would have never occurred. Another way for the Lockean is to say that I am a certain (say, weighted) majority of that set of mental contents. But this too runs against our

basic intuitions. Propositions such as, "Had I married Jane rather than Sue, my entire life would have been different"; "Had my parents not immigrated to this country when I was a baby, I would have perished in the holocaust" do not seem self-contradictory, but, if I *am* the majority of my actual experiences, they must be considered logically false.

Here, then, are some of the reasons why Parfit's position is a nonstarter. According to Parfit, what really matters to me is not survival, but the existence of a P-ly related (Parfit uses the letter 'R') set of experiences. (Even this is not quite clear, because Parfit often talks as if the existence of a P-ly related set of experiences is his *explicandum* for the vulgar 'survival'). But the existence of *which* of the many P-ly related sets of mental contents is valuable to me? Or (on the other reading of Parfit) which one of them I partially am? Parfit does not raise this question. Let us, however, supplement his account by saying that what matters to me is that this very experience be P-ly connected to others. We must remember, however, that Parfit waives the special-causal-connection condition which other Lockeans require in their explications of personal identity; in Parfit's view, "The right kind of cause could be any cause."[4] The result is quite catastrophic: let us suppose that one of my experiences, e, fits very neatly (it is both continuous with and closely connected to) the mental life of someone else. Suppose, e.g., that my experience e is a total absorption in Fermat's last theorem, which also happens to occupy Dr. Cube, who continues to work on it for the next thirty years, while I tire after five minutes and go to watch a ball game. The set of Dr. Cube's experiences is continuous with and connected to e more than mine; hence, on Parfit's view, my life is really continued by Dr. Cube; or (according to the other reading of Parfit) what I should now value above all are Cube's experiences. Most of one's normal experience fits a huge number of psychologically connected sets, carefully collated from various people. Parfit needs a much richer psychological basis, including mental states which are manifested only over a long period of time and dispositions, as the core I, to which further experiences may be P-ly connected. Such a rich basis is not available if one starts from *e;* who is to say *which* long-term dispositions, skills, attitudes, etc., are continuous with, and connected to, *e?* On the other hand if one takes the mental life of a *person* over a long period of time, one is using some other criterion (e.g., a certain dependence on a given brain) and not the mere connectedness-cum-continuity criterion. Parfit's requirement of *some* causal connection is trivial, since it is satisfied by any event whatsoever in *e*'s light cone, an astronomical number indeed. If after a discussion with my twin brother I find myself accepting his views and coming closer to the way he was before our discussion than to what I was then, do I become a "branch" of my brother, and not a continuation of who I think I was?

Conceptual analysis of an existing framework and (to use Strawson's expression) revisionary metaphysics do not mix; this Parfit fails to see. Why is the existence of experiences P-ly connected to *e* so important to me? Is it because *e* itself is so inherently valuable that it would be a great loss to the world if it is not continued? Of course not; *e* is important to me because it is what I am now, I *live* it, and I want to survive. But if I cannot survive then it is a sort of fetishism to hold that the mere occurrence of *e*-like experiences is a source of consolation for me. Closing his eyes to this obvious truism, Parfit is forced to say, e.g., that if he were to die tomorrow he would find great consolation in the fact that someone who is very much like him will come from Mars to take possession of his house, sleep with his wife, finish and publish the book he (Parfit) has been working on, and get the total love and devotion of his (Parfit's) children! If all this is candid (which I doubt) Parfit must be very different from most of us, less saintly, people. Where Parfit errs is in thinking that if P-connectedness is the only item in the new metaphysical framework which roughly corresponds to personal self-sameness in the old metaphysical framework, then it takes on (albeit in an attenuated form) the function of the old concept in the old framework. This is a methodological mistake and psychologically absurd. It does not please me in the least to know that you are actually doing all the things I always wanted to do; it makes me mad. If, however, Parfit believes that survival as conceived of in the old framework is impossible but we *ought* to cherish P-connectedness *instead,* he is wrong again, for now it all depends on the nature of the experiences which are to be continued. If *e* is morally valueless, there is no reason why it should be perpetuated.

The self-justificatory status of egoistic statements does not rub off on their Lockean counterparts. If a set of items which I took to be holy relics are in fact all produced by Dr. Crook, I won't take the property of being produced by Dr. Crook as the closest I can get to the property of being holy. The *sense* of 'my own' is not closer to P-relatedness than it is to any other kind of relation. If, on the other hand, 'P-ly related to *e*' is taken as an *analysis* of 'my own experience,' then it is impossible to explain the special significance to me of experiences P-ly related to *e* by saying that they are my own experiences. It reduces to the following tautology: what is P-ly related to *e* is significant because it is P-ly related to *e*. The plausible-sounding egoistic credo degenerates into the following idiotic statement: "Only happy experiences shall be P-ly related to my present experience, because they are P-ly related to it." This justification is no more cogent than the following silly piece of reasoning: "I shall devote all my efforts to have all experiences Q-ly related to this one happy, because they are Q-ly related to it," for any Q whatsoever. He who endorses such a maxim is certainly not a rational self-seeker; he is, rather, crazy.

What reasons can I have for valuing states P-ly related to *e?* One may cite the similarity of proximate experiences in such a set; but this is hardly a reason for an egoist. Why should an egoist cherish, rather than hate, those who share her every wish and goal and would compete with her for everything, having every advantage she has? To devote all your efforts to benefit those who are similar to you is not to be an egoist: think of a state which allows only one of two identical clones to stay alive, and imagine yourself fighting your identical clone with (mutual) ferocity and hate, in order to survive.

Another answer to our question ("Why on earth should I regard those items which are P-ly, rather than Q-ly, related to my present experience, as constituting parts of the person that I am?") is that this is the way the term 'I' is used in my society. That is, in order to master the use of 'I' in my language I have to apply it to items P-ly related to my present experience, and to no other items. This is doubtlessly true, but irrelevant, since I can imagine other societies where 'I' is used with the same meaning we use it (i.e., 'the utterer of this very token') which chart the boundaries of that utterer somewhat wider, or narrower, than we do (e.g., including what we call "one's children," or not including what we call, "one's childhood," in it). Prudential action is possible only if certain future experiences are part of the life of its agent. But if the question of whether those experiences and the said action do or do not belong to the career of the same person is a mere matter of linguistic convention, of conveniently classifying P-ly connected experiences as constituting a single life, when other classifications are possible, exclusive devotion to those items which by one of those filing systems belong together with my present experience seems utterly silly. Suppose that in another society it is items Q-ly related to *e* which are considered as belonging to the same life with *e*. Which items should I cherish more? If everything (except my present experi-ence, *e*) can be deemed either mine or not mine, according to the kind of relation (P, Q, R, . . .) we use for classifying, an egoist cannot do anything at all, since the beneficiary is never that which is truly himself.

The traditional model of the self as a simple, indivisible (and hence immaterial) object, a substance distinct from, and independent of, anything else, i.e., a soul, came to answer this need. The only way to maintain egoistic justifications for action is by accepting a model of the self where the beneficiary of an action can literally be the same substance as the agent, not something which may, if we so wish, be classified as a part of a complex whole which includes the agent and the beneficiary as its temporal parts. That model of the self is impossible for the egoist, because distinct parts which may be classified as belonging to the same whole can also be classified, with little or no trouble, as belonging to distinct wholes. If I am not an indivisible monad, even if there are only two components in me, x and y, one need not consider x and y as parts of the same object. If my action occurs at t and the result enjoyed at $t + n$, I can distinguish the agent from the beneficiary, as two temporal parts of the same person. But then they can also be classified as belonging to different, say, schmersons; who, then, is the beneficiary—myself (the same person) or someone else (another schmerson)? Thus, the egoist must believe that he is a soul, a simple, seamless substance, which has no temporal, or any other, parts.

IV. I AM NOT A SOUL

The main argument for the existence of the soul is that it is needed to hold together a multitude of experiences, e.g., the parts of a thought, various aspects in a perception, etc. It is what impressions are present *to*. Otherwise, how could you think, e.g., that the house is on fire if by the time you think about the fire the thought of the house is already gone? If thinking takes time, and experiences are momentary, we need a trans-temporal unity in which the entire thought is held. This basically Kantian argument has often been, and still is, used (e.g., by Chisholm[5] and Madell[6]) in a way explicitly rejected by Kant, i.e., to prove the existence of the soul as a simple substance, to which all my representations are present.

In either form, this argument is invalid. If my soul does exist in time, it must represent different contents at different times. E.g., I may be in pain at t_1, but not at t_2. My soul's career must, therefore, have at least these two stages, $s1$, at which it represents pain, and $s2$, at which it does not. Thus the same question returns: since thoughts are extended in time, consequent soul-parts which exist at t_1 . . . t_2 respectively represent each a part of the thought. Who, then, thinks the thought itself? The introduction of a temporally extended observer adds nothing to the account given in terms of sets of experiences. The soul must therefore represent thoughts outside time. But then I cannot be that soul, because I, for sure, take time to think. Perhaps it only *appears* to me as if I need time to think, while in fact this is only how the thought is represented to me, and not how it really is (this is Sellars' position[7]). But in this case the whole problem disappears, and I can say that the fact that the content of what I think of is temporal does not imply the temporality of the experiences of thinking that content. The soul is therefore not needed in either explanation.

I am sure, however, that a simpler answer is available. A Humean model of mental activity includes ideas of reflexion, i.e., experiences of other experiences, perhaps summarizing a great many of them in an instant. Mental processes need be neither egalitarian or pointillistic; that is, experiences may be accumulative, with later stages richer in content than earlier ones, including summaries and overviews of larger sections of past experience. Moreover, we need not suppose that, if a thought is extended in time, then infinitesimal parts of this time would each contain an infinitesimal part of the thought. Consider, e.g., a semi-Leibnizian model (which is useful provided that it is not taken too literally) where one's mental life is like a line, some points on which are holographic representations of the immediate vicinity, on both the mental and the (perpendicular) physical dimension. The radius of the represented area need not be identical for all points. Another model may describe experiences as stretching to cover the entire span of one's specious present, containing not only information about the content of earlier bits of awareness, but that content itself, which is thus integrated with the new content. At any rate, a fixed transendent scanner is redundant; that model has all the drawbacks of the Humean picture and none of its advantages.

But let us indulge the egoist once more. Let us assume that the soul does exist, exactly as he conceives it to be. It is a simple, indivisible substance, one for each person; it is the organ of feeling, thinking, willing, etc. Let us, now, apply our test. Suppose, for the argument's sake, that with the demise of the body the soul, too, ceases to exist, but an illustrious thaumaturgist, a soul scientist of absolute integrity, finds a (very costly) way of keeping the soul from disintegration after the body's destruction. What is preserved is the soul itself, and not its past states. This scientist now offers you immortality, a perpetual existence. Indeed, your present mental contents will be lost, but the organ of thought, the substance which is the soul, shall stay intact. He will lodge it in a container filled with ambrosia, which will protect it forever against mortality. No feelings, thoughts or desires will ever mar its crystalline purity; it shall have no experiences, but live for all eternity. If you, yourself, are this soul, you will have achieved everlasting life. Immortality, however, does not come cheap: the price tag is one million dollars.

Is there any rational person who is ready to pay a million dollars, or any amount of money, for that matter, for such a treatment? I doubt it. What you will say to the soul-scientist is probably this: "What makes you think that you will have *me* in that container of ambrosia? I am not identical with my thinking-organ any more than I am identical with any other organ of mine. In fact, I do not care which organ it is whose states are my thoughts, just as it is immaterial to me which pump is used to circulate blood in my body. A preserved soul is therefore no more valuable to me than a preserved heart, or left ear, after I die: I am none of these organs, material or otherwise. Moreover," you shall continue, "that soul will be blank and featureless, having no mental life. It will be indistinguishable from any of the other souls you keep in your ambrosia jars. How can it be I, myself, if it is quite indistinguishable from any other soul?

Just because I have used it for thinking? But then I have also used my ears for hearing. Would I pay the pathologist a million dollars so that he will keep my dismembered ears in perpetuity?'' I think this argument is right: a thinking organ, that which produces thoughts, is nothing but a spiritual engine. As such, it has no desires, no feelings and no thoughts; in short, it is very much unlike what I am; if it has no feelings, it has a history of production, but not life. If it is feelings, it is a Humean evanescent succession, and not an enduring, simple, indivisible soul. If it has feelings, it makes it possible for me to exist, but it is certainly not identical with me, because I do not care how those feelings come to be.

One may think that this argument is unfair, since I chose to describe the soul as preserved without experiences, a mere capacity to think without actually thinking or feeling. Such a soul (one may argue) is not better than a dead soul, and hence is indeed not worth a dime for me. But what if the thaumaturgist can keep my soul not only in working condition, but actually working, producing a succession of mental states? Will it be me?

Suppose, then, that my soul goes on performing, implanted into a newborn baby. Say, it is a girl, growing up in Soviet Uzbekistan. There is absolutely no difference between the experiences that girl is having now (using a secondhand soul, the one which was mine) and what she would have experienced were she to be equipped with a brand new soul, directly from the Creator's workshop. The only difference is that now those states are produced by that soul which once produced my experiences. Thus, my soul continues to function. I can have that immortality for the same price: a million dollars (or some other huge sum which I can raise only by selling all that I have and going deeply into debt). There is hardly anything people want more than immortality, and hence there is no doubt that ordinary people would be willing to pay a huge amount for eternal life. But is there anyone who is ready to pay that amount of money for such a ridiculous deal?

Would you be willing to sell your house and your car, and, for the rest of your natural life, live in abject poverty so that some Uzbek girl (and, after her, some other person) will use your soul? This deal is not different, in principle, from that one: you pay me a million dollars and, in return, I shall transplant your heart, after your death, into another person. Will you pay a huge sum of money for that? Certainly not.

Thus, even if people have souls, we have shown that they *are* not souls. Acting so as to preserve my soul and provide for it is not to act so as to preserve my own existence and provide for myself. But let us, once more, grant the egoist what he needs and assume that I am my soul, and hence I should provide for it as best I can. Still, I can do nothing, for I have no idea which soul is mine. Is the soul with which I went to sleep last night the same one which animates me today? Perhaps that soul, whose yesterday thoughts and actions I remember, is now quickening Mr. Gorbachev, while his yesterday soul is now besouling humble me, erroneously believing that it has worked on this article on the previous day. Suppose that, while I am about to make a bank deposit, I am informed that the said exchange will take place. Is it clear that it is in my best interest to deposit the money in Mr. Gorbachev's account? I doubt it. In whose account should I, then, deposit the money? This is the point which Parfit misses: our intuitions are silent, dumbfounded. Within the Aristotelian-Egoistic framework there *is* no answer.

One may think that such exchanges are unlikely to occur. But how do we know that? We have no evidence that the same soul always animates the same body. Perhaps souls switch memories and control over bodies every hour. Thus, if I am a soul, I know not what to do: perhaps my rival will host my soul tomorrow; should I play to win or to lose? All attitudes, personal relations, and legal systems become absurd, because we do not know who is who. Under such conditions, no prudential action is conceivable.

V. I AM NOT ANY COMBINATION OF THE ABOVE

The reader may complain that all I have shown so far is that I (that which I care about) am neither my body, nor my mental contents, nor my soul, *exclusively*. Whenever I considered one of those candidates, showing our indifference to it, I have tacitly kept the other two intact. Thus, perhaps the only conclusion is that I am a complex thing; perhaps I am a combination of a soul, a body, and mental contents.

Let us suppose, then, that I am third soul, third body, and third mental contents, all put together. In that case, any harm done, e.g., to my body, is harming me, damaging something that I am. But we saw that this is not so at all. What happens to this body, in and of itself, is no concern of mine, and I am willing to see it utterly destroyed. Hence, it is not a part of me, because I am valuable to me, and so my parts have, also, some inherent value for me; but this body has none. The same argument, as we saw earlier, works for my soul and my mental contents: none of those is, therefore, any part of me, if I am that which I cherish for its own sake.

Moreover, as I have argued in section III, on the egoistic-based view of the ego I cannot have any parts at all. Since this point is crucial, let me use an example. Call the present temporal stage of my house 'a'. Now, I can gradually replace all the bricks in the house, so that the form and location of the house are preserved, but its matter is not. Call the resulting house-stage 'b'. Or I can do the opposite: retain all the original bricks, but use them in a different way, so that by the end of the period I have a house of a completely different form, built of the same matter, on the same location. Call the resulting house-stage, 'c'. Or else I may retain the same bricks and keep the same form, but have the house reassembled in a different location. Call the result this time, 'd'. There are, of course, infinitely many other permutations, which leave open the question whether the resulting house-stage is, or is not, a stage of the house I have started with. This question, however, seems merely linguistic (i.e., "how shall we *call* the resulting stage?") since all the facts are known. Like all empirical concepts, the concept *house* is open-textured and hence does not determine, for all possible house-stages i and j, whether i and j are or are not stages of the same house. When such problem cases become pressing, we can make the old concept more determinate by stipulation, or leave it intact and coin two new subconcepts. Thus, if H is the concept which leaves open the question whether i and j are stages of the same H or not, we coin two new concepts, F and G, and say that i and j are the same F but not the same G. In our example, we simply coin three new concepts (subconcepts of the concept, *house*); call these new concepts, 'haus' (stressing identity of matter), 'aous' (stressing identity of form) and 'hows' (stressing identity of location). Thus, a and b are stages of different hauses, but they are stages of the same aous and of the same hows; a and c are different aouses but they are the same haus and the same hows; finally a and d are different howses, but they are the same aous and also the same haus.

Similar cases can be described for any kind of thing whatsoever; the kinds we discern in nature are not disjoint: in the great majority of cases they widely overlap. Hence to ask whether two spatiotemporally-defined items, i and j, are stages of the same object or else are stages of two distinct objects is strictly senseless. It all depends on what sortal concept we have in mind. In our example, a, b, c, and d are, all of them, houses, hauses, aouses, and howses; yet we saw that they are the same thing with respect to some of those sortals and different things with respect to other sortals. In general, therefore, we can put it like that: for *any* two not completely overlapping items i and j there are two sortal concepts F and G, and hence two kinds of objects, Fs and Gs, such that for some F, i and j are stages in its career, i.e., they are phases of the same F; and for some G, i and j are stages in the careers of two numerically distinct Gs.

The only way to avoid this conclusion is to adopt Aristotelian Essentialism, holding that each item we *can* individuate ("genuine thing") falls under one sortal only. If *a* is a stage of a haus, it cannot be also a stage of a hows, etc. But such an injunction against overlapping classification is arbitrary, and blatantly anti-scientific. There is no justification for such high-handed metaphysical tyranny, decreeing that there can be only one way to individuate and classify, one taxonomy for all things and all purposes. The pious belief in natural kinds which neatly divide the world and allow no cross-filing (denying, e.g., that several kinds of classification may be equally important) is nothing but a superstition. On the contrary, we can see that any item we single out may be said to fall under several distinct sortals, and it therefore has different identity conditions as a specimen of (i.e., relative to) each of those sortals.

As long as egoistic considerations are not involved, cross-classification gives us no trouble; therefore, when it does clash with our ideas concerning the justification of action, it is probably our ideas about rational action which are at fault, and not the ubiquitously useful principle of cross-classification. Suppose, for example, that my house (call it 'Charlie') is a live and conscious being. When Charlie is at stage *a* I tell it what I intend to do; say, I intend to make it into *c*, that is, retain all the bricks but redesign the shape of the house. Charlie listens with growing apprehension and then asks: "all this is well and good, sir; I understand exactly what you intend to do; but you have not told me the most important thing yet—will *c* be me, myself, so that I shall survive the change and will only have a different form when I become *c*, or is *c* another house, not I, to whom you intend to give the bricks which constituted me before my demise? In other words, is the transition from *a* to *c* a change in the *same* substance or the annihilation of one substance and the creation of another?" How can I answer this question? Of course, I cannot. The best I can do is try to explain that the very Aristotelian framework within which this question is formulated is inadequate and should be rejected. I can say to Charlie that *a* and *c* are, e.g., the same

haus, and therefore, as a haus, he will survive, but that *a* and *c* are different aouses, and therefore, as an aous, he will not survive. But suppose that Charlie was brought up (as we are) to think and reason in the Aristotelian framework. In that case, it shall find my answer extremely paradoxical: "How can I," Charlie will say, "perish as one thing and survive as another? This makes no sense; I either exist or else I do not exist. Thus if you say that I shall survive as a haus but not as an aous, what I need to know is what I really and truly, i.e., essentially, am. If I am essentially a haus, I can rejoice and look forward to this adventure; but if I am in my true nature an aous, I shall mourn my untimely destruction." What can one say now? Only that this talk of essences and true natures is nonsense, that Charlie is a haus just as much as it is a hows and an aous. I can say that the distinction between perishing and merely changing is strictly language dependent and has no application except relative to some understood sortal. I cannot, however, answer the question "shall I survive, or not?" It does make perfectly good sense within the Aristotelian framework, but none outside it. But if, as I have been arguing, the Aristotelian framework is at fault and ought to be discarded, the said question must go with it. For *any* complex thing it makes no sense at all.

Thus, when Parfit says that the question "shall I survive" has no definite, yes-or-no, answer, he is absolutely right; but he is entirely wrong about the reasons for this situation. The explanation for this situation is the general rule of cross-classification, and the sortal-dependent nature of the question of survival. Things have no essences, and any of their properties can be elevated to that status in the appropriate classification and relative to the appropriate sortal. You have no essence; you can be classified under a huge number or sortals. With respect to some of them, what shall there be is the same thing as you, and hence, you shall survive. With respect to others, you shall not. The answer to the question "who am I" is, "it depends." "Whom am I, then?" says Alice, "Tell me that, and then, if I like being that person, I'll come up; if not, I'll stay down here till I'm somebody else."[8]

VI. INDEXICALS

The illusion which the egoist belabors under is hiding under the cloak of a linguistic error. The term 'I' is an indexical term, denoting that entity whose life history overlaps the event of uttering the given token of 'I'. But 'I' is not a sortal, and it does not delimit the boundaries of that entity. Since there are infinitely many entities whose boundaries may be so drawn that they include the event of uttering the said token of 'I', 'I' itself does not denote any entity in particular. The meaning of 'I' entirely parallels that of 'here' (i.e., the place which overlaps the location in which this token of 'here' was uttered), 'now' (i.e., the time which overlaps the moment at which this token of 'now' was uttered), etc. Can one imagine a more fantastically absurd position than that of a here-chauvinist, who intends to do all he can in order to preserve, maintain and defend the area *here?* If no boundaries are arbitrarily, or conventionally demarcated which decree how far it is still *here,* and where does not-here begin, the said chauvinist can do nothing at all, because there is nothing which does not (initially) qualify as here. The egoist's intention is (initially) equally void of any significance: which one of all those infinitely many entities is you?

The non-vacuity of the egoist's policy derives from his arbitrary choice of one of those entities as the intended reference of his term 'I'. The entity in question is, of course, the *person* whose life-history includes the event of uttering the said token of 'I'. This is the sleight of hand which gives egoism its air of reasonability, of almost tautological validity: If we retain the strict meaning of 'I,' the egoistic principle is indeed logically sound, but it is absolutely empty. If we supplement that meaning by some sortal, then it does mandate a course of action—without any justification. Egoists ignore this crucial linguistic fact. Instead of regarding the *person* who uttered 'I' as the referent of that token of 'I' we could have chosen some other sortal, say, *schmerson,* and say that the said token of 'I' refers to the schmerson who uttered it. If that schmerson includes the entire people of Uzbekistan, should I, as an egoist, strive from now on to benefit the Uzbeks?

"This" I hear the reader protesting, "is preposterous. Of course you can put the said utterance-event (call it '*e*') in the same basket with any collection of items, including, if you want, the Uzbek nation. But this collection is artificial, nothing unites those items except your whim. If you look for real wholes, that is, you look for those items to which the utterance event *e* is closely related—by causal connections, by similarity, by spatiotemporal proximity—you shall find that the most significant whole which includes the said event is a person." I think the weakness of this answer is evident. First of all, it is far from clear that if we look for the most "significant" whole which includes the said event we shall come up with one candidate only. Indeed, there are strong causal connections between the said event, *e,* and some of my brain cells, my childhood experiences, and the events of my birth. But there are also quite strong and "significant" causal connections between *e,* the event of my father proposing to my mother, your ear (which I turn to when I say 'I'), and your experience of hearing my sentence. If anyone protests again, that the latter events, although closely related, are not related in *the right way,* i.e., are not P-ly related, let me ask (assuming that there is a workable definition of that way, which to put it mildly, I strongly doubt), why is this way (the P-like connection) the right one? What makes this connection "more right" than other causal and explanatory connections? Its rightness amounts to its being chosen, by our society, as the one to use in drawing up the boundaries between individuals. Indeed, it is very important for us to have such a standard way of carving separate subjects, or else it would be impossible for us to assign responsibilities and rights, rewards and punishments. My point is only that the current division, useful as it is, is conventional: there is no one thing which 'I' denotes (although there is one thing which 'the *person* which overlaps *e*' denotes); hence, in a very serious sense, I do not exist.

The egoist is not doing philosophy of science, and Parfitian arguments like "it will make a rather smooth and elegant division of nature if we classify *e* together with such and such items as belonging together in one whole," or like "the laws of psychology can be more succinctly phrased in terms of persons than in terms of schmersons" cut no ice with him. He is not in the business of helping those who make nice wholes when put together with the event *e;* he is in the business of helping himself. If any of his actions is to make sense he must assume that prudence is smart rather than pretty, and that the life he fashions is his own: no artist, or Good Samaritan, he! Yet the identity conditions of the entity referred to by 'I' are given not by that indexical, but by the sortal term which we have chosen to use in such cases (e.g., 'person,' a P-ly connected set of items), and sortals are chosen precisely because they make nice wholes, and for no other reason. Many other sortals may be used instead; we can imagine a society of people who consider themselves to be consummate rationalists and exclusive egoists, yet in our eyes their behavior is (because their notion of the self is much wider than ours) altruistic, to the point of self-abnegation, or (because their notion of the self is much narrower than ours) irrational and short-sighted, lacking all prudence and consideration for one's own overall utility. We have, then, three radically different kinds of behavior: which one is the truly egoistic? No answer to this pseudo-question can possibly be given. The very notion that some of the things I do are beneficial to me (i.e., to the one entity which I really am) and others are harmful to me, although they are beneficial to others (i.e., to entities entirely distinct from the entity which I am) is confused, an utter chimera. Our practical philosophy, which distinguishes between prudential or egoistic motivation on the one hand, and altruistic or moral motivation on the other hand, is rooted in error: Our individualistic culture is built on sand. We use, for the most important decisions we can make, an utterly inadequate conceptual framework.

VII. WHAT SHOULD I DO?

Obviously, you should do your duty. Thus Parfit has the right idea when he suggests that, "since we must reject the Classical Self-Interest Theory, we should expand the area covered by morality."[9] But the only suggestion he gives on how to do this is the maxim that "we ought not to do to our future selves what it would be wrong to do to other people."[10] This suggestion is, perhaps, sufficient to prevent "great imprudence"; it does not give one a reason to pursue one's career and do anything at all. If self-interest reasons are invalid, why should I bother? The reason can only be moral duty, and it has to be spelled out, not in a Kantian language, but in a utilitarian one.

It is the duty of the agent to bring about the existence of the best of all possible worlds. This task is, of course, very hard for a limited and weak being, who acts in a given situation which she can only marginally influence. Therefore, it is the duty of the (limited) agent to bring, through her action, as much good as can be achieved in the given situation. That means that it is one's duty to be efficient, not to waste one's action, but, appraising oneself of one's abilities and limitations under the existing circumstances, act so as to produce an optimal amount of good. Now, given the biological reality in which I find myself as an agent, it should be quite clear where and to whom I can be of most use. It would be a very wasteful world in which you would dress me, wash me, feed me and read for me when I can do all these things for myself in a fraction of the time it will take you, and do those things in a manner which will please me much more, knowing which food I prefer, which clothes I like, and where exactly is the pebble in my shoe. All these things are better done by me than by you, and therefore in the great majority of cases the most good I can generate by my action is by an action labelled by Aristotelians 'self-seeking' or 'prudential'. The label would, in this case, be wrong, since the motive behind those actions is the duty to do maximum good, in an impartial way (which is the only way one can act if survival is impossible). Self-seekers are therefore doing, most of the time, the right thing out of a wrong motive, and through a mistaken interpretation of the existing conditions (believing in the existence of a substantial, enduring self). In this case two wrongs do make one good. Moral considerations, which are the *only* motives for a rational agent, tell us to carry on pretty much as before.

An agent who can bring about the situation *p,* or else the situation *q,* ought to bring about the existence of the better of these situations. The value of a situation, I maintain, is an objective property of that situation; it is determined and verified by empirical observation. That the situation of my finger being in fire is *bad* is a fact that I clearly observe; to attribute badness to that situation is no more and no less justified than to attribute motion or color to the flame. In either case, the ensuing theory cannot be used to predict the existence of the observations in question (neither experiences of motion nor experiences of badness can be predicted by physical theory *only*), but, assuming that the observer is a standard and attentive one, we can attribute his experiencing the badness of the situation (or the motion of the flame) to his being a reliable observer of such properties under the given conditions.

Relativists and other opponents of the view that moral value is an objective feature of states of affairs claim that, unlike motion, value is relative to the particular observer and his desires: given a desire *d,* state *p* may be said to be good for *p,* but not good *tout court*. This, however, is again a feature of all observations; they are all relative to the measuring device (e.g., the human perceptual system) used. We take some observations to be veridical not because they are revelatory of reality in an unmediated fashion, "in the buff," so to speak, but because they

can be systematically expanded into a coherent explanatory system. Harman and other relativists to the contrary, there is no reason to think that ethics cannot pass *that* test.

To take an ethical observation as veridical is to say that not only is *p* bad relative to a given desire *d,* but that the situation as such is bad. For example, the situation in which a flame impacts on my finger is bad, *tout court*. The older ethical relativists, as well as the emotivists, did not see that 'good' as a two-place predicate (i.e., *p* is good relative to *d*) is worthless for ethics; in no case can it be used to enjoin an action, since desires are no more ineluctibly given than the situations that satisfy or frustrate them. We spend more on manipulation of desires (e.g., by education, advertisement, propaganda, by chemical and surgical means, and soon by genetic programming) than on their satisfaction. With technological advance, we become responsible for the desires we have, since desires may be reinforced or extinguished. Since *any* situation would satisfy *some* desire, ethical relativism is pointless; it is no help at all to know that action A will satisfy the desire *d* that *s* happens to have, since we do not know whether *d* should or should not be maintained.

To avoid such pitfalls, contemporary relativists (Harman, Rorty, Davidson, etc.) refuse to say that 'good' is relative to a conceptual framework or value system. Instead, they take the meaning of 'good' to be determined by the way *we* use it, given our present desires and beliefs. This parochialism (the term is Quine's), however, also ignores the above noted fact, i.e., that we can and do change our desires. No agent is tied to his current system of preferences and is not bound to do the bidding of his desires, because one *can* envisage another desire-system, and, sometimes, bring it about that one adopts it. Knowing the contingent circumstances in which the desires that I now happen to have were inculcated into me, or into my forefathers, I need neither value having them nor identify with them; I may replace them rather than do what they bid. It therefore seems, in conclusion, that personalistic ethics, grounding morality on there being rigidly distinct agents having rigid desires (an assumption necessary for all conventional, contractual, and emotivistic ethical systems) is not only metaphysically bankrupt, as I have tried to argue in previous sections, but also irrelevant, being unable to constrain action.

Personalistic systems of ethics not only fail to direct action; they cannot uphold the elementary intuitions that they were supposed to ground. Take, e.g., the case of murder. If my obligation to satisfy s's craving for p is derived, not from the absolute goodness of situations of satisfied desire (thus placing me under a *prima facie* obligation to realize p) but rather from the existence of s's desire d for p, why am I not allowed to discharge my duty by swiftly and painlessly killing s, thus eliminating d and the need to bring about p? Personalist philosophers claim that by killing s I have frustrated s's past desire to continue living, to enjoy life, to carry out certain plans, etc., and hence killing s infringes upon s's right to pursue his desires (this is, e.g., the answer given by Tom Nagel). I cannot see, however, that this answer has any force at all. Surely, I am under an obligation not to interfere with your pursuit of your desire for p, and assist you in securing p, only as long as you desire p. If you cease to desire p then it is *not* incumbent upon me to bring about the existence of p or not to bring about not-p. Now, as long as you existed, and desired to exist, you did exist. Having instantaneously killed you, you no longer desire to exist. But if there is no time at which you desire to exist and do not exist, how can I be accused of having frustrated your desire? It is only your *past* desire that I thwart; but the fact that *once* you wanted p to be the case (you do not want it any more) does not put me under any, even *prima facie*, obligation to secure p for you. Killing would be entirely unobjectionable. But, while person-based ethics cannot find anything wrong with murder, value-based ethics can. If p is not only good for d, but also the situation of d being satisfied by p is good *simpliciter*, then we can justify our moral objection to murder and to similar atrocities which eliminate the desire for the states

denied (e.g., by frontal lobotomy) by reference to their negative moral value.

Let me try to respond to three objections to value-based ethics; the first two very briefly, the third in some detail. The first objection is Parfit's argument[11] (also discussed by others, e.g., T. Narveson[12] and B. Anglin[13]) that value-based ethics is committed to the "Repugnant Conclusion," i.e., that as long as life is even minimally worth living, we ought to further populate the world by procreating billions upon billions of new people. This conclusion, however, can be avoided by placing a relatively high value on the quality of life, on the importance of beauty and knowledge. A world of billions with no art or science is worse, not better, than a world of millions that supports Bachs, Einsteins, and Shakespeares. The rejoinder to that answer, i.e., that such valuation would sanction killing the less fortunate among us to increase overall value, can be easily dismissed on the usual rule-utilitarian grounds. The second strongly counter intuitive alleged result of value-based ethics was actually adopted by Moore, i.e., that an uninhabited garden world is morally better than an uninhabited junk world. But I deny the validity of this reasoning: a garden world is beautiful given the reference-scheme of humans (creatures of certain size, sensitive to certain colors, etc.). For intelligent rats, a different order would be manifest in these worlds. In general, for every situation p one can find some perceptual framework m such that, given m, p is beautiful. Thus, unless the existence of humans is tacitly assumed, Moore cannot even say that the garden world is more beautiful than the dump. To put it otherwise, a painful experience is self-sentient, and hence bad in and of itself, while an ugly object is indeed ugly, and therefore bad, only relative to a given mode of sentience.

Thirdly, it is alleged that, like Kant, value based ethics cannot allow a special duty to those closest to one, e.g., one's family, or nation. But love and affection are values which ought to be preserved, and they cannot exist unless a special duty to those one loves is rightly recognized. Such love can encompass one's special relation to what the Aristotelian would call, one's own person, i.e., the so-called "self love." Even if one does not feel such love, however, being better placed than others to preserve and pursue some values places one under an obligation to do so. Thus, one may, first of all, *adopt* some people or values or ties to love and cherish, and the freedom to do so is an important part of one's humanity, which ought to be recognized and respected by those who are not so chosen. Secondly, the very fact that with respect to some (e.g., personal, cultural and national) values and ties one *happens* to be in a position effectively to safeguard and maintain them makes one a custodian of those values, and places one under a special responsibility for them. Metaphorically speaking, even though one did not elect to be in charge of the family jewels, falling heir to them makes one responsible for them, due to the objective value of the jewels, and to one's being, *de facto*, in the best position to keep them. Thus, although one does not choose one's family or culture or nation, it is treason for one to forsake them. This is because nations, cultures, families and persons are items of great value, and

one's duty to maximize value is especially relevant to those values that one can actually realize. Some duties (e.g., to one's parents) do not therefore entirely depend on one's feelings or contractual obligations (Jane English[14] to the contrary, that duty cannot be uniquely based on friendship, which may or may not exist in the family). It may, however, be derived from the principle that mandates, and therefore sanctions, prudential behavior. That duty, like all other duties, is only *prima facie* duty that may be overridden by other duties, but it is a moral duty nonetheless.

One's obligation to maximize value can therefore often be fulfilled most successfully by providing for those one loves, or by devoting oneself to *proximal* causes and values. In both cases, this would tend to benefit the *person* that Aristotelians mistakenly identify with the agent, the family of that person, his ethnic group, nation, culture, and species. Thus, even though it is wrong to *identify* the agent with any particular chunk of reality, there are particular chunks of reality that, although not more meritorious than others, it is the agent's special duty to benefit, and that by providing for which one would be doing the right thing.

VIII. THE MYTH OF PASSAGE

The best vindication of a theory is its ability to shed light on an area other than the one for the explanation of which it was originally designed. I would like, therefore, to conclude this essay by a few remarks on a completely different problem which, if I am right, the theory here offered can satisfactorily solve.

There is no way in which the Russell-Reichenbach-Smart, etc., theory of time can be challenged: Time does not pass. It cannot pass. The very idea of time's flowing is nonsensical and self-contradictory. There is no dimension with respect to which time itself could change its "location," at a certain "velocity." For some object x to move is for it to have parts located at adjacent spatiotemporal points: hence

Time itself cannot move. Each spatiotemporal event is where it is in spacetime, and events have certain spatiotemporal distances between them. With respect to a given frame of reference we can say which events are (tenselessly) before other events, but it is meaningless to say that some events are past and some are future (using those predicates monadically; in the dyadic sense, *any* event defines its past, its future, and its elsewhere). To speak about what has been as ontologically different from what is going to be requires a "successive" becoming of time itself, but there are no "metatemporal" dates such that time $t1$ comes into being at "metatemporal date" $m1$ and time $t2$ comes into being at a "later metatemporal date" $m2$.

It makes no sense to speak of time's passing in a Newtonian world, and it is even more absurd to speak of it in an Einsteinian universe. (I am not arguing for this thesis: I cannot do so in this paper. I am merely stating what I take to be the consensus among the vast majority of philosophers of science in the last sixty years.)

Yet it is an undeniable fact, a scandal which we cannot quite explain, that precisely those modes of speech, these categories of viewing the world as having temporal passage, and absolute past and future, are fundamental to our common sense. We do think that World War II, for example, is absolutely (for every real observer) past, not only that it (tenselessly) occurs before the event of uttering this sentence. We all instinctively believe that events come to be and cease to be, and that time passes, while we watch, and notice, how it moves, becoming later and later all the time!

If all this is nonsense, an illusion which cannot possibly be true, why are we so addicted to it? How did we, all of us, fall victim to this logically ludicrous world picture? I think I have an answer. The culprit is, as you expected, the fictitious substance I, which is so dear to us that we wish to retain it at all costs. In a block universe, filled with spatiotemporally related events, *nothing* endures. To endure, in four-space, *is* for there to be a certain similarity between adjacent spatiotemporal points. ("The book stayed in this place between $t1$ and $t2$" becomes, "the events $t1p1 \ldots t2p1$ are bookish.") All you have is events, some of which are more or less like others, and you can group them together as you well please. Now suppose that you postulate the existence of the simple

(partless) substance *self*. To endure, it must *(per impossibile)* travel in four-space. If I am strictly the very same thing at various times, then I must *travel in time*. I existed on Sunday, and I exist on Monday. If this is *not* to be understood as, "I am a four-dimensionally extended thing with one part in Sunday and another part in Monday," i.e., if it is strictly *the very same thing* present at both temporal points, then the only way for me to achieve that remarkable fiat is by travelling uptime, from my temporal location at Sunday to my present location, at Monday. In this way I portray myself as able to be present, *all of me,* at one time (Sunday), and "then" be, again, *all of me,* at another time (Monday). This picture of the self as a point moving from one temporal location to another can also be represented in a different way: the self stays stationary while the river of time flows downstream, in front of one. Thus, while staying stationary and unmoved, I first see one time (Sunday) flowing by, and "then," "after a while," another time (Monday) comes along; "pretty soon" a third time (Tuesday), which is still upstream now, will make its way and arrive to the "metatemporal place" where I stand.

These two absurd pictures, that of the simple, yet enduring, self, and that of the flowing and passing time, are the two sides of the same worthless coin. It is a world picture which, against all odds, against reason, against science and against logic, we insist on clinging to. We are simply afraid, dead afraid, to lose our selves. If the argument of this paper is cogent, however, we have no reason to be so frightened. A world where morality takes the place of self-interest cannot be all that bad.

NOTES

1. "Sensations, Raw Feels, and Other Minds," *Review of Metaphysics* 20 (1966): 317–40; "Personal Identity Without Criteria," *Australasian Journal of Philosophy* 47 (1969): 344–53; "The Unity and Indivisibility of the Self," *International Philosophical Quarterly* 10 (1970): 542–55; "Pains and Pain Feelings," *Ratio* 13 (1971): 150–57; "The Reference of 'I'," *Philosophical Studies* 23 (1972): 65–75; "Strawson's Transcendental Deduction," *Philosophical Quarterly* 25 (1975): 114–25; "Egoism and Altruism," *Midwest Studies in Philosophy* 3 (1978): 148–58; "Time and Self," *Analysis* 39 (1979): 143–47; "De Se and Descartes," *Nous* 19 (1985): 181–204.

2. Derek Parfit, *Reasons and Persons* (Oxford: Clarendon Press, 1984), pp. 199–320.

3. Ibid., pp. 276, 474–75.

4. Ibid., p. 262.

5. R. Chisholm, *The First Person* (Minneapolis: University of Minnesota Press, 1981), pp. 75–91.

6. G. Madell, *The Identity of the Self* (Edinburgh: Edinburgh University Press, 1981).

7. W. Sellars, "Naturalism and Process," *The Monist* 64 (1981): 37–65.

8. Lewis Carrol, *Alice in Wonderland*, Chapter II.

9. Parfit, op. cit., p. 319.
10. Ibid., p. 320.
11. Parfit, op. cit., pp. 425–41.
12. J. Narveson, "Moral Problems of Population," *The Monist* 57 (1973): 62–86; "Further People and Us," in P. I. Sikora and B. Barry, eds., *Obligations to Future Generations* (Philadelphia: Temple, 1978) pp. 38–60.

13. B. Anglin, "The Repugnant Conclusion," *Canadian Journal of Philosophy* 7 (1977): 745–54; also G. S. Kavka, "The Paradox of Future Individuals," *Philosophy and Public Affairs* 11 (1982): 93–112.
14. J. English, "What Do Grown Children Owe Their Parents?" in C. H. Sommers, ed., *Vice and Virtue in Everyday Life* (Harcourt, Brace, 1985) pp. 460–67.

QUESTIONS ABOUT PERSONAL IDENTITY

1. What exactly is the problem of personal identity?
2. What is the difference between a person's identity and a person's identification, as philosophers use these terms? Can the same person be identified differently? Can the same person have a different identity?
3. Why does Socrates seem to ridicule the question, "How are we to bury you?" What assumptions does he make about his own identity that seem to warrant his apparently favorable attitude toward death?
4. Descartes identifies himself as a "thing which thinks." (See his Meditation II, in Part 1 if this volume.) Is this enough to establish his identity as René Descartes?
5. What exactly is the *mind-body problem?* How does Descartes's reasoning seem to lead to this difficulty?
6. Gilbert Ryle ridicules Descartes's philosophy as the myth of "the ghost in the machine." What basis, if any, does Ryle have for his criticism?
7. How does John Locke answer the criticism that people forget? What do you make of his distinction between the same person and the same man? Is the distinction useful?
8. How does Anthony Quinton respond to the objection that a memory criterion presupposes a bodily criterion? Do you think Quinton's response is successful?
9. Does the problem of personal identity, and its proposed solutions, have social and political implications? What exactly is E. Victoria Spelman's point about the soul, "somatophobia," sexism, and racism?
10. Eddy Zemach suggests that the problem of personal identity, especially in puzzling cases such as that of Gregor Samsa, is "merely linguistic." What does he mean by this, and do you agree?

Personal Identity:
Suggestions for Further Study

The problem of personal identity is at the center of a host of diverse but closely related psychological, religious, and metaphysical issues concerning human nature. Though the groundwork for much of the current discussion was laid by Plato and Aristotle—Plato favoring an otherworldly approach; Aristotle, especially in his *De Anima*, proposing something more biological—the modern treatment is traceable to René Descartes's seventeenth century *Meditations*. Descartes was a dualist, believing that a person is composed of both a physical and a mental substance. However, as early critics recognized, the relationship between the two substances is not clear. Descartes seemed to suggest that an interaction between mind and body takes place in the pineal gland. But exactly how something that is physical can affect, and be affected by, something that is not, whether in the pineal gland or anywhere else, was not made plain. The trend in contemporary philosophy has been against Cartesian dualism, though the view has not been completely abandoned. C. J. Ducasse, for example, following a Cartesian approach, has argued in a number of articles in favor of life after death. See his "A Critical Examination of the Belief in a Life After Death" (Springfield, Ill.: Charles C. Thomas, 1961).

Perhaps more than any other contemporary philosopher, Gilbert Ryle has influenced current thinking about mind and body—ironically enough, not so much for his success as for his apparent failure. In the *Concept of Mind*, Ryle attempted to analyze, in terms of either overt behavior or certain dispositions to behave, what we mean when we speak of a person's mind. But basic sensations, such as itches, tingles, and pains, seemed to resist his analysis. Others, such as U. T. Place, in "Is Consciousness a Brain Process?" (*British Journal of Psychology* XLVII, 1956, 44–50) and J. J. C. Smart in "Sensations and Brain Processes" (*Philosophical Review* LXVIII, 1959, 141–56) helped pioneer what has come to be called *the identity theory*—the idea that sensations are nothing more than brain processes. The identity theory, at least in some of its versions, has proven resilient in withstanding very sharp criticism, including the powerful objections raised by Saul Kripke in "Identity and Necessity" in *Naming, Necessity, and Natural Kinds* (Ithaca, New York: Cornell University Press, 1977, 66–101).

The main alternative to the identity approach has been *functionalism,* the view that mind is not identical with, but rather a function of, the brain. Human beings need not be the only intelligent creatures; machines too, as well as noncarbon-based aliens from outer space (if they exist), can be intelligent, according to Hilary Putnam and other proponents of this approach, including D. C. Dennett in *Content and Consciousness* (London: Routledge & Kegan Paul, 1969), and Jerry Fodor in *Psychological Explanations* (New York: Random House, 1982).

The debate over personal identity has been waged within the framework of the broader mind-body issue. On the one side are those favoring a memory, or quasi-memory, approach, such as John Locke, Anthony Quinton, and H. P. Grice in his "Personal Identity" (*Mind* 50, October 1941). Another who favors this approach is John Perry; see his "Personal Identity, Memory and the Problem of Circularity" in *Personal Identity*, edited by John Perry (Berkeley: University of California Press, 1975). On the other side of the debate are those exploring a bodily alternative. Among them are David Wiggins in *Identity and Spatio-Temporal Continuity* (Oxford: Oxford University Press, 1967) and Bernard Williams in "On Transfer of Bodies" in *Problems of the Self* (Cambridge: Cambridge University Press, 1973). Finally, following the lead of P. F. Strawson in *Individuals* (Garden City, New York: Doubleday, 1963), Derek Parfit has attempted to show that the concept of personhood is more basic than, and not reducible to, either the concept of mind or of body; see his "Personal Identity" (*Philosophical Review*, 80, 1971).

PART

4

Ethics

Literary Introduction:
What To Do?

Raskolnikov, the tormented hero of Dostoyevsky's *Crime and Punishment*, proposes that some individuals can transgress the law:

> The first category, [of ordinary people], generally speaking are men conservative in temperament and law-abiding; they live under control and love to be controlled. To my thinking it is their duty to be controlled, because that's their vocation, and there is nothing humiliating in it for them. The second category all transgress the law; they are destroyers or disposed to destruction according to their capacities. The crimes of these men are of course relative and varied; for the most part they seek in very varied ways the destruction of the present for the sake of the better. But if such a one is forced for the sake of his idea to step over a corpse or wade through blood, he can, I maintain, find within himself, in his conscience, a sanction for wading through blood—that depends on the idea and its dimensions. . . .

Raskolnikov's notion challenges traditional morality. Moral guidelines, whether they are drawn from religious teachings, the law, or simply community standards, constitute the moral precepts we learn as we grow up. For example, stealing violates Biblical teaching, secular law, and communal demands to respect the property of our neighbors.

Raskolnikov suggests that moral precepts apply only to "ordinary" people. For those whose talents provide them the opportunity to build a "better future" by destroying the present, the traditional guidelines do not apply. Though it is clear that Raskolnikov is a deeply troubled young man, one who acts out his theory in the senseless murder of a money lender and who later repents of his action, we should not dismiss his ideas out of hand. For example, Henry David Thoreau "marched to his own drummer" in protesting the American government's expansionist war against Mexico and its tacit support of the institution of slavery in the middle of the nineteenth century. Thoreau deliberately broke the law by refusing to pay his taxes to the State of Massachusetts. The state did not share his moral vision and imprisoned him briefly, but later generations would confirm the rightness of his views. His seminal essay describing his protest—"Civil Disobedience"— is a document that is credited with influencing other great social activists such as Ghandi and Martin Luther King, Jr.

If we concede that these extraordinary individuals, possessed of a special moral vision, should violate the usual guidelines in the interest of a higher calling, what can we say about the distinctly ordinary person who has no claim to a unique moral perception? Most of us do not undertake the task of correcting society's ills, but rather try to lead decent, law-abiding, and honest lives, and for us the precepts we learn as we grow up are adequate for the kinds of everyday decisions we must make.

We know that we should not call in sick when we are not, especially if this ruse would burden others with our responsibilities, nor should we steal a pair of Reeboks, no matter how much we might want stylish footwear. The moral choices in these cases present no special problem other than the obvious one of resisting temptation.

But sometimes people find themselves in extraordinary situations that offer no acceptable choices. Frank O'Connor's "Guests of the Nation" presents such a situation.

The story is set in Ireland during a rebellion of the Irish against English rule, a struggle that eventually produced the compromise of a free, predominantly Catholic, Irish state in the south of the country, and a largely Protestant protectorate of the English government in the north. (For another story set in this time frame, see James Joyce's "Araby" in Part I, Knowledge.) That this "solution" to the conflict has not worked is evident in the recurrent stories in our newspapers, well over fifty years after the time of "Guests of the Nation," of acts of violent terrorism and retribution by both sides in the continuing struggle. This conflict is centuries old and seems to defy satisfactory resolution, perhaps because the emotions of patriotism, heavily leavened with religious passion, are simply too strong and too deep, so that generations have grown up nurtured on a blind antagonism toward the "enemy."

"Guests of the Nation" directly confronts the consequences of these feelings, and in so doing, challenges us to reflect upon the clear basis for right behavior. The story raises our awareness of how difficult making an ethical decision can be.

We can see that Bonaparte (probably a code name taken on when he joined the obviously illegal Irish Republican Army), the narrator of the story, is a rather young man of limited experience. We can assume that he joined the IRA in response to the pull of the patriotic urge to free his country from the English. Ironically, he finds himself, along with his companion, Noble, as "host" to two of these soldiers, the "guests" of the title. He and Noble have been put in charge of guarding Belcher and Hawkins, but it becomes very clear that the latter have no interest in escaping and are, in fact, perfectly happy as prisoners of war. Consequently, a friendship develops between the young Irish partisans and their captives. The first part of the story shows us an interaction among the four as individuals, rather than as guards and prisoners. Then, at the pivotal point of the story, the war intrudes its ugly presence and demands an action that is an utter and contemptuous rejection of the bonds of friendship that have evolved among the four characters.

This action is nothing less than a political murder. Hawkins and Belcher must be executed as retribution for the killing of Irish prisoners by the British—to even the score, as it were. Bonaparte is devastated, as well he should be. How can he reconcile holding a revolver to the back of the head of a man with whom he had been playing cards and living with congenially for so long? How can he see such a man as the "enemy" to whom a message must be sent?

O'Connor underscores the poignancy of his theme by insisting on the individual characteristics of the two English soldiers: physically, Hawkins is short and Belcher tall; in terms of personality, Hawkins is argumentative and volatile while his companion is mellow and laconic; at the moment of the execution, Belcher accepts his fate while Hawkins tries to make a deal for his life. Because they are so different, it is that much more difficult for Bonaparte, and the reader, to think of them simply as "the enemy."

Faced with the fact of his prisoners' differences, and in view of the friendship that he feels for them as individuals, Bonaparte is shattered when he learns that they are to be shot. When Donovan informs him that the two English soldiers must pay with their lives for the execution of "some of our lads," Bonaparte complains that it was very "unforeseen" of Donovan not to have made it clear from the beginning that Belcher and Hawkins were hostage to the fate of the Irish prisoners held by the English army. Perhaps, had he known, he would have kept a more professional distance between himself and the two English soldiers.

But even if that were the case, the conflict would have been profound. Bonaparte would still have experienced the conflict between loyalty to his own cause and the recognition that these two soldiers, Hawkins and Belcher, did not deserve to die. They are the victims of a struggle they do not seem to care very much about; they have committed no crime that justifies capital punishment; in fact, their only "crime" was being captured. Bonaparte could not have failed to see all this, even had he not developed a friendship with his prisoners, and therefore, he would still have had to deal with the apparent injustice of killing.

Bonaparte's ethical conflict seems to deny a proper solution. He has dedicated himself to a worthy cause—ridding his homeland of a foreign and repressive force—and it appears right that he should enthusiastically serve that cause. But he also recognizes the claims of friendship, and the trust that binds him to Hawkins and Belcher. If he responds to the orders of his army, he must execute his friends; if he spares his friends, he will be disloyal to his cause.

Further, the story raises perhaps a deeper question: even if Bonaparte has persuaded himself that it is morally correct for Hawkins and Belcher to die, why should *he* pull the trigger? We can believe that Bonaparte did not envision this kind of duty when he joined the IRA. Even though we can argue that he must follow orders, particularly in an army where his superiors would deal harshly with any sign of disloyalty, why must he undertake this brutally harsh assignment? He says at the end of the story, that after the execution, "anything that happened to me afterwards, I never felt the same about again," and that he "felt very small and very lost and lonely like a child astray in the snow."

O'Connor asks us to share his young narrator's agony, and to understand that whatever the authority for moral decisions, it appears that such conflicts cannot be avoided, and that when they occur they make us question our most basic assumptions about right and wrong.

FRANK O'CONNOR
Guests of the Nation

I

At dusk the big Englishman, Belcher, would shift his long legs out of the ashes and say "Well, chums, what about it?" and Noble or me would say "All right, chum" (for we had picked up some of their curious expressions), and the little Englishman, Hawkins, would light the lamp and bring out the cards. Sometimes Jeremiah Donovan would come up and supervise the game and get excited over Hawkins's cards, which he always played badly, and shout at him as if he was one of our own "Ah, you divil, you, why didn't you play the tray?"

But ordinarily Jeremiah was a sober and contented poor devil like the big Englishman, Belcher, and was looked up to only because he was a fair hand at documents, though he was slow enough even with them. He wore a small cloth hat and big gaiters over his long pants, and you seldom saw him with his hands out of his pockets. He reddened when you talked to him, tilting from toe to heel and back, and looking down all the time at his big farmer's feet. Noble and me used to make fun of his broad accent, because we were from the town.

I couldn't at the time see the point of me and Noble guarding Belcher and Hawkins at all, for it was my belief that you could have planted that pair down anywhere from this to Claregalway and they'd have taken root there like a native weed. I never in my short experience seen two men to take to the country as they did.

They were handed on to us by the Second Battalion when the search for them became too hot, and Noble and myself, being young, took over with a natural feeling of responsibility, but Hawkins made us look like fools when he showed that he knew the country better than we did.

"You're the bloke they calls Bonaparte," he says to me. "Mary Brigid O'Connell told me to ask you what you done with the pair of her brother's socks you borrowed."

For it seemed, as they explained it, that the Second used to have little evenings, and some of the girls of the neighborhood turned in, and, seeing they were such decent chaps, our fellows couldn't leave the two Englishmen out of them. Hawkins learned to dance "The Walls of Limerick," "The Siege of Ennis," and "The Waves of Tory" as well as any of them, though, naturally, we couldn't return the compliment, because our lads at that time did not dance foreign dances on principle.

So whatever privileges Belcher and Hawkins had with the Second they just naturally took with us, and after the first day or two we gave up all pretense of keeping a close eye on them. Not that they could have got far, for they had accents you could cut with a knife and wore khaki tunics and overcoats with civilian pants and boots. But it's my belief that they never had any idea of escaping and were quite content to be where they were.

It was a treat to see how Belcher got off with the old woman of the house where we were staying. She was a great warrant to scold, and cranky even with us, but before ever she had a chance of giving our guests, as I may call them, a lick of her tongue, Belcher had made her his friend for life. She was breaking sticks, and Belcher, who hadn't been more than ten minutes in the house, jumped up from his seat and went over to her.

"Allow me, madam," he says, smiling his queer little smile, "please allow me"; and he takes the bloody hatchet. She was struck too paralytic to speak, and after that, Belcher would be at her heels, carrying a bucket, a basket, or a load of turf, as the case might be. As Noble said, he got into looking before she leapt, and hot water, or any little thing she wanted, Belcher would have it ready for her. For such a huge man (and though I am five foot ten myself I had to look up at him) he had an uncommon shortness—or should I say lack?—of speech. It took us some time to get used to him, walking in and out, like a ghost, without a word. Especially because Hawkins talked enough for a platoon, it was strange to hear big Belcher with his toes in the ashes come out with a solitary "Excuse me, chum," or "That's right, chum." His one and only passion was cards, and I will say for him that he was a good cardplayer. He could have fleeced myself and Noble, but whatever we lost to him Hawkins lost to us, and Hawkins played with the money Belcher gave him.

Hawkins lost to us because he had too much old gab, and we probably lost to Belcher for the same reason. Hawkins and Noble would spit at one another about religion into the early hours of the morning, and Hawkins worried the soul out of Noble, whose brother was a priest, with a string of questions that would puzzle a cardinal. To make it worse, even in treating of holy subjects, Hawkins had a deplorable tongue. I never in all my career met a man who could mix such a variety of cursing and bad language into an argument. He was a terrible man, and a fright to argue. He never did a stroke of work, and when he had no one else to talk to, he got stuck in the old woman.

He met his match in her, for one day when he tried to get her to complain profanely of the drought, she gave him a great come-down by blaming it entirely on Jupiter Pluvius (a deity neither Hawkins nor I had ever heard of, though Noble said that among the pagans it was believed that he had something to do with the rain). Another day he was swearing at the capitalists for starting the German war when the old lady laid down her iron, puckered up her little crab's mouth, and said: "Mr. Hawkins, you can say what you like about the war, and think you'll deceive me because I'm only a simple poor country-woman, but I know what started the war. It was the Italian Count that stole the heathen divinity out of the temple in Japan. Believe me, Mr. Hawkins, nothing but sorrow and want can follow the people that disturb the hidden powers."

A queer old girl, all right.

II

We had our tea one evening, and Hawkins lit the lamp and we all sat into cards. Jeremiah Donovan came in too, and sat down and watched us for a while, and it suddenly struck me that he had no great love for the two Englishmen. It came as a great surprise to me, because I hadn't noticed anything about him before.

Late in the evening a really terrible argument blew up between Hawkins and Noble, about capitalists and priests and love of your country.

"The capitalists," says Hawkins with an angry gulp, "pays the priests to tell you about the next world so as you won't notice what the bastards are up to in this."

"Nonsense, man!" says Noble, losing his temper. "Before ever a capitalist was thought of, people believed in the next world."

Hawkins stood up as though he was preaching a sermon.

"Oh, they did, did they?" he says with a sneer. "They believed all the things you believe, isn't that what you mean? And you believe that God created Adam, and Adam created Shem, and Shem created Jehoshaphat. You believe all that silly old fairytale about Eve and Eden and the apple. Well, listen to me, chum. If you're entitled to hold a silly belief like that, I'm entitled to hold my silly belief—which is that the first thing your God created was a bleeding capitalist, with morality and Rolls-Royce complete. Am I right, chum?" he says to Belcher.

"You're right, chum," says Belcher with his amused smile, and got up from the table to stretch his long legs into the fire and stroke his moustache. So, seeing that Jeremiah Donovan was going, and that there was no knowing when the argument about religion would be over, I went out with him. We strolled down to the village together, and then he stopped and started blushing and mumbling and saying I ought to be behind, keeping guard on the prisoners. I didn't like the tone he took with me, and anyway I was bored with life in the cottage, so I replied by asking him what the hell we wanted guarding them at all for. I told him I'd talked it over with Noble, and that we'd both rather be out with a fighting column.

"What use are those fellows to us?" says I.

He looked at me in surprise and said: "I thought you knew we were keeping them as hostages."

"Hostages?" I said.

"The enemy have prisoners belonging to us," he says, "and now they're talking of shooting them. If they shoot our prisoners, we'll shoot theirs."

"Shoot them?" I said.

"What else did you think we were keeping them for?" he says.

"Wasn't it very unforeseen of you not to warn Noble and myself of that in the beginning?" I said.

"How was it?" says he. "You might have known it."

"We couldn't know it, Jeremiah Donovan," says I. "How could we when they were on our hands so long?"

"The enemy have our prisoners as long and longer," says he.

"That's not the same thing at all," says I.

"What difference is there?" says he.

I couldn't tell him, because I knew he wouldn't understand. If it was only an old dog that was going to the vet's, you'd try and not get too fond of him, but Jeremiah Donovan wasn't a man that would ever be in danger of that.

"And when is this thing going to be decided?" says I.

"We might hear tonight," he says. "Or tomorrow or the next day at latest. So if it's only hanging round here that's a trouble to you, you'll be free soon enough."

It wasn't the hanging round that was a trouble to me at all by this time. I had worse things to worry about. When I got back to the cottage the argument was still on. Hawkins was holding forth in his best style, maintaining that there was no next world, and Noble was maintaining that there was; but I could see that Hawkins had had the best of it.

"Do you know what, chum?" he was saying with a saucy smile. "I think you're just as big a bleeding unbeliever as I am. You say you believe in the next world, and you know just as much about the next world as I do, which is sweet damn-all. What's heaven? You don't know. Where's heaven? You don't know. You know sweet damn-all! I ask you again, do they wear wings?"

"Very well, then," says Noble, "they do. Is that enough for you? They do wear wings."

"Where do they get them, then? Who makes them? Have they a factory for wings?

Have they a sort of store where you hands in your chit and takes your bleeding wings?''

"You're an impossible man to argue with," says Noble. "Now, listen to me—" And they were off again.

It was long after midnight when we locked up and went to bed. As I blew out the candle I told Noble what Jeremiah Donovan was after telling me. Noble took it very quietly. When we'd been in bed about an hour he asked me did I think we ought to tell the Englishmen. I didn't think we should, because it was more than likely that the English wouldn't shoot our men, and even if they did, the brigade officers, who were always up and down with the Second Battalion and knew the Englishmen well, wouldn't be likely to want them plugged. "I think so too," says Noble. "It would be great cruelty to put the wind up them now."

"It was very unforeseen of Jeremiah Donovan anyhow," says I.

It was next morning that we found it so hard to face Belcher and Hawkins. We went about the house all day scarcely saying a word. Belcher didn't seem to notice; he was stretched into the ashes as usual, with his usual look of waiting in quietness for something unforeseen to happen, but Hawkins noticed and put it down to Noble's being beaten in the argument of the night before.

"Why can't you take a discussion in the proper spirit?" he says severely. "You and your Adam and Eve! I'm a Communist, that's what I am. Communist or anarchist, it all comes to much the same thing." And for hours he went round the house, muttering when the fit took him. "Adam and Eve! Adam and Eve! Nothing better to do with their time than picking bleeding apples!"

III

I don't know how we got through that day, but I was very glad when it was over, the tea things were cleared away, and Belcher said in his peaceable way: "Well, chums, what about it?" We sat round the table and Hawkins took out the cards, and just then I heard Jeremiah Donovan's footstep on the path and a dark presentiment crossed my mind. I rose from the table and caught him before he reached the door.

"What do you want?" I asked.

"I want those two soldier friends of yours," he says, getting red.

"Is that the way, Jeremiah Donovan?" I asked.

"That's the way. There were four of our lads shot this morning, one of them a boy of sixteen."

"That's bad," I said.

At that moment Noble followed me out, and the three of us walked down the path together, talking in whispers. Feeney, the local intelligence officer, was standing by the gate.

"What are you going to do about it?" I asked Jeremiah Donovan.

"I want you and Noble to get them out; tell them they're being shifted again; that'll be the quietest way."

"Leave me out of that," says Noble under his breath.

Jeremiah Donovan looks at him hard.

"All right," he says. "You and Feeney get a few tools from the shed and dig a hole by the far end of the bog. Bonaparte and myself will be after you. Don't let anyone see you with the tools. I wouldn't like it to go beyond ourselves."

We saw Feeney and Noble go round to the shed and went in ourselves. I left Jeremiah Donovan to do the explanations. He told them that he had orders to send them back to the Second Battalion. Hawkins let out a mouthful of curses, and you could see that though Belcher didn't say anything, he was a bit upset too. The old woman was for having them stay in spite of us, and she didn't stop advising them until Jeremiah Donovan lost his temper and turned on her. He had a nasty temper, I noticed. It was pitch-dark in the cottage by this time, but no one thought of lighting the lamp, and in the darkness the two Englishmen fetched their top-coats and said good-bye to the old woman.

"Just as a man makes a home of a bleeding place, some bastard at headquarters thinks you're too cushy and shunts you off," says Hawkins, shaking her hand.

"A thousand thanks, madam," says Belcher. "A thousand thanks for everything"—as though he'd made it up.

We went round to the back of the house and down towards the bog. It was only then that Jeremiah Donovan told them. He was shaking with excitement.

"There were four of our fellows shot in Cork this morning and now you're to be shot as a reprisal."

"What are you talking about?" snaps Hawkins. "It's bad enough being mucked about as we are without having to put up with your funny jokes."

"It isn't a joke," says Donovan. "I'm sorry, Hawkins, but it's true," and begins on the usual rigmarole about duty and how unpleasant it is.

I never noticed that people who talk a lot about duty find it much of a trouble to them.

"Oh, cut it out!" says Hawkins.

"Ask Bonaparte," says Donovan, seeing that Hawkins isn't taking him seriously. "Isn't it true, Bonaparte?"

"It is," I say, and Hawkins stops.

"Ah, for Christ's sake, chum."

"I mean it, chum," I say.

"You don't sound as if you meant it."

"If he doesn't mean it, I do," says Donovan, working himself up.

"What have you against me, Jeremiah Donovan?"

"I never said I had anything against you. But why did your people take out four of our prisoners and shoot them in cold blood?"

He took Hawkins by the arm and dragged him on, but it was impossible to make him understand that we were in earnest. I had the Smith and Wesson in my pocket and I kept fingering it and wondering what I'd do if they put up a fight for it or ran, and wishing to God they'd do one or the other. I knew if they did run for it, that I'd never fire on them. Hawkins wanted to know was Noble in it, and when we said yes, he asked us why Noble wanted to plug him. Why did any of us want to plug him? What had he done to us? Weren't we all chums? Didn't we understand him and didn't he understand us? Did we imagine for an instant that he'd shoot us for all the so-and-so officers in the so-and-so British Army?

By this time we'd reached the bog, and I was so sick I couldn't even answer him. We walked along the edge of it in the darkness, and every now and then Hawkins would call a halt and begin all over again, as if he was wound up, about our being chums, and I knew that nothing but the sight of the grave would convince him that we had to do it. And all the time I was hoping that something would happen; that they'd run for it or that Noble would take over the responsibility from me. I had the feeling that it was worse on Noble than on me.

IV

At last we saw the lantern in the distance and made towards it. Noble was carrying it, and Feeney was standing somewhere in the darkness behind him, and the picture of them so still and silent in the bogland brought it home to me that we were in earnest, and banished the last bit of hope I had.

Belcher, on recognizing Noble, said: "Hallo, chum," in his quiet way, but Hawkins

flew at him at once, and the argument began all over again, only this time Noble had nothing to say for himself and stood with his head down, holding the lantern between his legs.

It was Jeremiah Donovan who did the answering. For the twentieth time, as though it was haunting his mind, Hawkins asked if anybody thought he'd shoot Noble.

"Yes, you would," says Jeremiah Donovan.

"No, I wouldn't, damn you!"

"You would, because you'd know you'd be shot for not doing it."

"I wouldn't, not if I was to be shot twenty times over. I wouldn't shoot a pal. And Belcher wouldn't—isn't that right, Belcher?"

"That's right, chum," Belcher said, but more by way of answering the question than of joining in the argument. Belcher sounded as though whatever unforeseen thing he'd always been waiting for had come at last.

"Anyway, who says Noble would be shot if I wasn't? What do you think I'd do if I was in his place, out in the middle of a blasted bog?"

"What would you do?" asks Donovan.

"I'd go with him wherever he was going, of course. Share my last bob with him and stick by him through thick and thin. No one can ever say of me that I let down a pal."

"We had enough of this," says Jeremiah Donovan, cocking his revolver. "Is there any message you want to send?"

"No, there isn't."

"Do you want to say your prayers?"

Hawkins came out with a cold-blooded remark that even shocked me and turned on Noble again.

"Listen to me, Noble," he says. "You and me are chums. You can't come over to my side, so I'll come over to your side. That show you I mean what I say? Give me a rifle and I'll go along with you and the other lads."

Nobody answered him. We knew that was no way out.

"Hear what I'm saying?" he says. "I'm through with it. I'm a deserter or anything else you like. I don't believe in your stuff, but it's no worse then mine. That satisfy you?"

Noble raised his head, but Donovan began to speak and he lowered it again without replying.

"For the last time, have you any messages to send?" says Donovan in a cold, excited sort of voice.

"Shut up, Donovan! You don't understand me, but these lads do. They're not the sort to make a pal and kill a pal. They're not the tools of any capitalist."

I alone of the crowd saw Donovan raise his Webley to the back of Hawkins's neck, and as he did so I shut my eyes and tried to pray. Hawkins had begun to say something else when Donovan fired, and as I opened my eyes at the bang, I saw Hawkins stagger at the knees and lie out flat at Noble's feet, slowly and as quiet as a kid falling asleep, with the lantern-light on his lean legs and bright farmer's boots. We all stood very still, watching him settle out in the last agony.

Then Belcher took out a handkerchief and began to tie it about his own eyes (in our excitement we'd forgotten to do the same for Hawkins), and, seeing it wasn't big enough, turned and asked for the loan of mine. I gave it to him and he knotted the two together and pointed with his foot at Hawkins.

"He's not quite dead," he says. "Better give him another."

Sure enough, Hawkins's left knee is beginning to rise. I bend down and put my gun to his head; then, recollecting myself, I get up again. Belcher understands what's in my mind.

"Give him his first," he says. "I don't mind. Poor bastard, we don't know what's happening to him now."

I knelt and fired. By this time I didn't seem to know what I was doing. Belcher, who was fumbling a bit awkwardly with the handkerchiefs, came out with a laugh as he heard the shot. It was the first time I heard him laugh and it sent a shudder down my back; it sounded so unnatural.

"Poor bugger!" he said quietly. "And last night he was so curious about it all. It's very queer, chums, I always think. Now he knows as much about it as they'll ever let him know, and last night he was all in the dark."

Donovan helped him to tie the handkerchiefs about his eyes. "Thanks chum," he said. Donovan asked if there were any messages he wanted sent.

"No, chum," he says. "Not for me. If any of you would like to write to Hawkins's mother, you'll find a letter from her in his pocket. He and his mother were great chums. But my missus left me eight years ago. Went away with another fellow and took the kid with her. I like the feeling of a home, as you may have noticed, but I couldn't start again after that.''

It was an extraordinary thing, but in those few minutes Belcher said more than in all the weeks before. It was just as if the sound of the shot had started a flood of talk in him and he could go on the whole night like that, quite happily, talking about himself. We stood round like fools now that he couldn't see us any longer. Donovan looked at Noble, and Noble shook his head. Then Donovan raised his Webley, and at that moment Belcher gives his queer laugh again. He may have thought we were talking about him, or perhaps he noticed the same thing I'd noticed and couldn't understand it.

"Excuse me, chums," he says. "I feel I'm talking the hell of a lot, and so silly, about my being so handy about a house and things like that. But this thing came on me suddenly. You'll forgive me, I'm sure.''

"You don't want to say a prayer?" asked Donovan.

"No, chum," he says. "I don't think it would help. I'm ready, and you boys want to get it over.''

"You understand that we're only doing our duty?'' says Donovan.

Belcher's head was raised like a blind man's, so that you could only see his chin and the tip of his nose in the lantern-light.

"I never could make out what duty was myself," he said. "I think you're all good lads, if that's what you mean. I'm not complaining.''

Noble, just as if he couldn't bear any more of it, raised his fist at Donovan, and in a flash Donovan raised his gun and fired. The big man went over like a sack of meal, and this time there was no need of a second shot.

I don't remember much about the burying, but that it was worse than all the rest because we had to carry them to the grave. It was all mad lonely with nothing but a patch of lantern-light between ourselves and the dark, and birds hooting and screeching all round, disturbed by

the guns. Noble went through Hawkins's belongings to find the letter from his mother, and then joined his hands together. He did the same with Belcher. Then, when we'd filled in the grave, we separated from Jeremiah Donovan and Feeney and took our tools back to the shed. All the way we didn't speak a word. The kitchen was dark and cold as we'd left it, and the old woman was sitting over the hearth, saying her beads. We walked past her into the room, and Noble struck a match to light the lamp. She rose quietly and came to the doorway with all her cantankerousness gone.

"What did ye do with them?" she asked in a whisper, and Noble started so that the match went out in his hand.

"What's that?" he asked without turning round.

"I heard ye," she said.

"What did you hear?" asked Noble.

"I heard ye. Do ye think I didn't hear ye, putting the spade back in the houseen?''

Noble struck another match and this time the lamp lit for him.

"Was that what ye did to them?" she asked.

Then, by God, in the very doorway, she fell on her knees and began praying, and after looking at her for a minute or two Noble did the same by the fireplace. I pushed my way out past her and left them at it. I stood at the door, watching the stars and listening to the shrieking of the birds dying out over the bogs. It is so strange what you feel at times like that you can't describe it. Noble says he saw everything ten times the size, as though there were nothing in the whole world but that little patch of bog with the two Englishmen stiffening into it, but with me it was as if the patch of bog where the Englishmen were was a million miles away, and even Noble and the old woman, mumbling behind me, and the birds and the bloody stars were all far away, and I was somehow very small and very lost and lonely like a child astray in the snow. And anything that happened to me afterwards, I never felt the same about again.

QUESTIONS ABOUT "GUESTS OF THE NATION"

1. Exposition in fiction is background information that helps the reader understand the circumstances of the story. What crucial piece of exposition do we not know until Jeremiah Donovan speaks with Bonaparte?
2. We do not know this detail because Bonaparte, who is our narrator, does not. How else does out understanding depend on Bonaparte's perception of the action?
3. How do we see Jeremiah Donovan? How does his attitude contrast with that of Bonaparte?
4. What details make us see Hawkins and Belcher as very different human beings?
5. How do the differences between Belcher and Hawkins underscore Bonaparte's problem in carrying out their execution?
6. What evidence do we have that the English soldiers are not very concerned about the outcome of the war?
7. Why does Bonaparte hope the prisoners will try to escape? Would such an attempt solve his moral problem?
8. How do you suppose Bonaparte will view his service in the IRA?
9. What does Bonaparte learn about life as the result of this experience?

Philosophical Discussion:
What is the Difference Between Right and Wrong?

Noble and Bonaparte are not killers. They have no intention of taking the lives of Belcher and Hawkins, their British prisoners. Noble just wants to win an argument about religion; Bonaparte just wants to win a few rounds of cards. They have come to know their British captives almost as well as they know each other. They're all practically chums.

Yet, here Noble and Bonaparte stand, weapons drawn, graves dug, waiting to put a bullet into each of these two British heads. How can this be? Noble and Bonaparte seem to be basically moral individuals. How can they kill two other human beings? What authority, what deity has proclaimed that two Irish patriots must snuff out the lives of two British nationals? What rational basis, if any, can there be for Noble and Bonaparte to carry out this deed?

Do they have a moral duty to obey the orders of Jeremiah Donovan? He is, admittedly, their superior officer. But Donovan is just another human being. What right does he have to issue such orders? What right does anybody have to order, or to personally carry out, the execution of another individual?

Noble and Bonaparte are soldiers in the Irish Republican Army, fighting the British. For all the appearance of camaraderie, they are mortal enemies of Belcher and Hawkins. In war, a soldier's first obligation is to destroy the enemy. Morality, itself, seems to demand this. Yet if morality can demand that we kill each other, why should anyone be moral? (Plato raised a similar question about justice in the story of Gyges's ring. See the selection from *The Republic*, in Part V, Justice.)

The basic problem for philosophers of morality is to explain how, under certain circumstances, we must do things that we would not otherwise want to do—even if this means taking the life of another human being. Noble and Bonaparte's dilemma is extreme, but not unique. We all face conflicts between what we are supposed to do and what we would prefer to do, between watching a ball game and mowing the lawn, eating a second helping of chocolate cake and sticking to a diet, spending a week's salary on a night out and saving the money for next semester's tuition payment.

Of course, not every conflict poses a *moral* dilemma. There is nothing apparently immoral about watching a ball game, eating chocolate cake or spending some money on entertainment. Still, if we've promised to mow the lawn, or resolved to resist rich foods, or could only obtain the needed fee by borrowing it from someone else, then moral questions are involved.

We've all learned that we ought to keep our promises, resist temptation, and not harm others. Traditional morality, when we start to think about it, seems little more than a set of relatively simple rules that we must bear in mind as we go about our lives. But we cannot always satisfy these injunctions. Bonaparte, for example, is morally bound to the Irish cause. Yet he is tempted to allow the British soldiers to escape. Would he be wrong to do so? Would he be a better person, more noble, to shoot them instead? And how in good conscience could he carry out his obligation if, as we have all learned, killing is wrong? When facing a moral conflict what exactly is a person to do?

Doing nothing, of course, is no solution. Refraining from acting, when action is called for, can be as morally damaging as doing the wrong thing. For example, if Hawkins were truly a maniacal murderer, allowing him to escape would be a mistake.

Is there a right thing to do? The traditional moralist's appeal to the familiar rules of conduct seems inadequate, especially when we face moral conflict. What more is needed? Ethicists, or moral philosophers, have tended to emphasize either an *authoritarian*, a *teleological*, or a *deontological* approach. Religious moralists, for example, have emphasized the need for moral authority. Most religious institutions, such as the Catholic Church, subscribe to an authoritarian system which holds that an act is right only if it is properly sanctioned. (Consider, for example, Bishop Robert C. Mortimer's discussion of moral authority in the selection that follows this introduction.)

Nowadays there is a tendency, especially among those of us who have been nurtured on the ideals of democracy, freedom of choice, and individual conscience, to deride the appeal to *authority*. Nevertheless, we should not overlook the significant role authority actually plays. Most of our beliefs, in one way or another, are sanctioned by authority. Life is too short to investigate personally everything we tend to take for granted, whether it be the acceptability of the water we drink, the quality of the food we eat, or the safety of the cars we drive. Even those of us who drink only bottled water, eat only health food, or carefully study the various consumer magazines before purchasing a new car, are relying on authority, be it only the authority of the magazines or books we choose to read. The appeal to authority does seem necessary, in most practical circumstances, in order to know what to believe. But, in conjunction with the basic rules of morality, is it enough?

Not all groups share the same authority. For the Catholic Church, ultimately, authority derives from the Pope, inspired by an all-knowing, all-good Supreme being. Jews ultimately appeal to the Torah, a work that is equally inspired. The Moslem appeals to the Koran, and so it goes. The problem is that, except for moral platitudes, recognized moral authorities do not always agree. For example, many Jews and Protestants are not, in principle, opposed to abortion, while the Catholic Church has taken a strong stand against the practice. The point is not that all moral authority is suspect. On the contrary, if one group says that abortion is right and another says it is wrong, it is difficult to see how they can both be mistaken. Rather, the problem is this: Just as moral rules seem to conflict, so do moral authorities. If appealing to the rules is inadequate to resolve a moral dilemma, it seems that the additional appeal to moral authority would not, by itself, resolve the difficulty either.

Again we must ask whether there is some independent appeal that might work. There is a so-called *teleological alternative* to the religious tradition which may be traced back to Aristotle in ancient times. The teleologist is an empiricist (see the discussion of empiricism in Part I, Knowledge) who subscribes to the general principle that knowledge must be supported by experience, especially the experience we obtain through the five senses. The kind of mystical or revelatory experiences undergone by charismatic Christians at prayer meetings, when they are overcome by what they call "the holy spirit," are disallowed. The idea is that if we have any knowledge, moral or otherwise, our ideas must be supported by perceptions that are common to all of us. However moving certain religious experiences may be, only relatively few individuals seem privileged to have them.

But what exactly are we supposed to see? What are we to look for in attempting to verify, for example, some moral judgment? Donovan has decided it is right to do away with the Englishmen. Bonaparte and Noble seem to have their doubts. What exactly does Donovan observe that Bonaparte and Noble miss? What special words have the Englishmen uttered, what gestures or movements have they made that Donovan has noticed but Bonaparte and Noble overlooked? If anything, Bonaparte and Noble should be more attuned to the behavior and dispositions of Hawkins and Belcher. The two Irish guards know the British prisoners better than Jeremiah Donovan. And yet, even if Donovan had seen, heard and otherwise experienced everything Bonaparte and Noble perceived, his judgment would still be the same. How then can anyone insist that moral judgments be supported by experience? It seems that even when our experiences are similar, moral judgments differ.

(The influential British philosopher, A. J. Ayer, argued in his early work, *Language, Truth and Logic*, that moral discourse is essentially unverifiable and, hence, empirically meaningless. For more recent discussion of moral skepticism, see the selections by Harman, Kleiman and Brower.)

The teleologist does not claim, however, that there is something special in what we see that marks the difference between right and wrong. Rather, the basic point is that the morality of human action is determined by its consequences. In particular, an act is deemed right if it contributes to human well-being and is wrong otherwise. Since people know by experience what contributes to their well-being and what affects them adversely, the proposed test seems properly empirical. On this view, Donovan's judgment to execute the prisoners is correct, provided that the execution, in a manner of speaking, does more good than harm. The problem then becomes one of specifying how the proposed deed will have an *overall* desirable effect. Otherwise, since almost every action will have a variety of consequences, both good and bad, the general idea, by itself, is inadequate.

Teleologists have struggled to define more precisely the basic intuition, resulting in subtle differences in the approach. Those who favor an approach called *egoism*, for example, have suggested that an individual need only be concerned with the effect an action has on *him*, the person contemplating, ordering, or otherwise carrying out the action. Does this mean that in issuing the order to assassinate the two British soldiers Donovan need only be concerned with himself? If so, not only does egoism seem harsh, raising extreme selfishness to a virtue; it also seems incapable of answering the basic question of why, under certain circumstances, we must do things that we would not otherwise want to do. If a person must always contribute to his or her own well-being, by doing only what he or she wants to do anyway, there should never be a moral conflict.

But people do not always know, nor always want, what is in their best interests. For example, a child with a cinder in her eye might just rub the eye until it gets infected. If egoism is to distinguish between right and wrong, it must first distinguish between what *is* in our interests from what we *think* is in our interests. Somehow short-term gains must be balanced against long-term benefits. A little discomfort now, for example, of having the cinder properly removed, seems a very small price to pay to avoid the greater pain of an eye infection. (Exactly how one fashions the balance, however, is not entirely clear. Sometimes immediate gratification is worth the pain. Depending on circumstances, it may be better to have loved and lost, as some people say, than never loved at all.) As a rational egoist, Donovan might have second thoughts about killing the hostages, especially if this act merely causes the opposition to execute more Irishmen.

A wise egoist would try to integrate the interests of others in the pursuit of his or her own goals, carefully balancing long-term gains against short-term benefits. If egoism is defined in this way, then it is a powerful moral theory. Not only would it explain the appearance of moral conflict as the difference between what actually is, and what we only think is, in our interest, it would also explain why, on occasion, we must do things it seems we would not otherwise want to do. The egoist's answer is that, in the final analysis, there is no ultimate conflict between our moral duty and what we really want.

Can egoism succeed? Ayn Rand, the noted novelist, has suggested that the interests of rational individuals never conflict. (See, for example, her works, *Atlas Shrugged*, *The Fountainhead* or *The Virtue of Selfishness*.) If this is true, then we need search no further. By considering their own rational interests, Noble and Bonaparte, for example, may find no conflict with Donovan's desires. In the long run they would all benefit by a free Ireland.

But what of Belcher and Hawkins? Do *their* interests coincide with that of their Irish captors? Is Hawkins unapprised of certain facts, or, somehow, irrational in pleading for his life? Is Belcher morally better off by not pleading, or has he just resigned himself to his own impending doom? How can it be in the long- *or* short-term interests of either prisoner to die now? How could their sacrifice benefit them? Egoists should be clear about this. Otherwise, the interests of apparently rational individuals do seem to conflict. (Does this mean that, according to the egoist, the prisoners ought and ought not to be put to death? In "Ultimate Principles and Ethical Egoism," Brian Medlin discusses whether egoism is coherent.) In the absence of some account of how conflicting interests are to be reconciled, egoism is as unacceptable as either traditional moralism or authoritarianism.

We are brought back once again to the question, is there a right answer? Despite the apparent drawbacks of egoism, the basic teleological insight seems sound, that the consequences of what we do are morally relevant. What is needed, however, is a standard of right and wrong independent of individual interests. *Utilitarianism*, first proposed by Jeremy Bentham and then defended by John Stuart Mill in the nineteenth century, is intended to satisfy this need. The basic idea is that there is a common good for all mankind, usually thought of as the attainment of happiness and the elimination, as far as possible, of pain and suffering. An act is right, on this view, if it contributes to the general welfare, and wrong otherwise. (Strictly speaking, since even immoral deeds may contribute some good, while a moral act may be the lesser of two evils, the utilitarian should say that an act is right provided that it contributes to the general welfare or contributes no less than any available alternative.) For example, in deciding what's right, Bonaparte need only consider the effect that shooting the two men will have, not just to himself, nor just to himself, Noble, and Donovan, nor just to the three of them and all the other members of the IRA. Following the utilitarian principle, Bonaparte must also consider Belcher and Hawkins, the suffering caused to Hawkins' family, and the ultimate benefit, if any, the deaths will have on the entire British-Irish conflict. In this utilitarian calculation, all individuals affected count for one—no individual counts for more than one—not the soldier, the officer, the general, nor the king.

Assuming we could quantify suffering, as well as happiness, the utilitarian approach is objective, mathematical, and scientific. Just as a scientist may be perplexed as to whether the universe will continue to expand indefinitely, so an individual may be perplexed as to whether a particular course of action is right. And just as Einsteinian relativity tells the scientist that he or she must calculate the sum total of matter in the universe, so utilitarianism tells the individual that he or she must calculate the sum total of happiness over suffering. And just as trying to determine the amount of happiness may seem impractical, so, too, trying to determine the amount of matter may seem impractical. Nevertheless, just as a physicist can estimate matter, so, too, an individual can estimate utility. Therefore, just as a scientist can scientifically judge the behavior of the universe, an individual can morally judge the behavior of human beings.

Utilitarianism has proven to be extremely influential, especially in determining public policy. Its popularity is credited with helping to foster the British social reforms of the nineteenth century, such as restrictions on child labor, and it is also hailed as providing part of the foundation of the modern democratic social welfare state. (There will be more discussion of this in Part V, Justice.)

However, as a moral theory, it has also proven to be extremely controversial. Utilitarians are split between those who favor judging each act individually, a view called *act-utilitarianism,* and those, more akin to traditional moralists, who prefer to appeal to a set of common rules of conduct, a view called *rule-utilitarianism.* The latter group differs from traditional moralists in claiming that the rules of morality, such as the prohibition against killing, are themselves to be judged on utilitarian grounds. For example, if executing Belcher and Hawkins results in more good than harm, everything considered, then the act-utilitarian would approve. However, if executing hostages *as a rule* produced more harm than good, then regardless of the apparent beneficial outcome of this particular execution, the rule-utilitarian would deem it wrong.

How are we to decide between these two apparently different schools? Rather than attempt to assess the comparative merits and drawbacks of each version (for instance, that the rule-utilitarian seems better able to reconcile traditional moralism with the basic tenet of utilitarianism), let us consider whether there is any significant difference between them. Suppose that executing Belcher and Hawkins results in more good than harm. Executing hostages as a rule, *under similar circumstances,* would have similar results. Otherwise, the execution of Belcher and Hawkins would also be wrong. It seems that for any act that satisfies the act-utilitarian, there is a rule governing the same act that satisfies the rule-utilitarian. And vice versa. For any rule that satisfies the rule-utilitarian, for example, killing hostages is permissible when this leads to an overall decrease in pain and suffering, there is an act, presumably the killing of Belcher and Hawkins, that satisfies the act-utilitarian. If there appears to be a conflict, then it seems that either the act is poorly assessed or the rule misdescribed.

Does this mean that the basic problem is solved? If executing two British hostages would effectively halt many more senseless deaths and contribute to a stable peace, then perhaps it ought to be done. But why must *Noble* or *Bonaparte* do it? They are

Irish soldiers, but there are many others who could pull a trigger just as well. Why are they to be singled out to do the job? Can it be because they are guarding the prisoners? But why must guards also be executioners? Neither Noble nor Bonaparte has had any idea it would come to this. They have given no one their word nor have they made any promises that they will, in cold blood, kill anyone. So why them?

Moreover, why Belcher and Hawkins? What did they do to deserve this end? They are, of course, British soldiers. But they, like many, are caught up in a conflict that has been going on for generations, over which neither they nor any other soldier has any control. Why should they pay, especially with their lives? Did they commit any special crimes, any atrocities that set them apart? Apparently not. Why should they suffer?

The utilitarian seems to ignore individuals in favor of a larger social vision. But morality is not just concerned with sum totals. *How* the overall amount of happiness gets increased seems to matter. Are promises ignored? Is some innocent person punished? Are somebody's rights violated? Is justice served? These are important moral questions which often give rise to the toughest moral dilemmas we face. A British soldier vows to fight for his country, forfeiting his life if need be. But he, like everyone, has an obligation not to throw away his life needlessly. Is Hawkins wrong to try to save his life by offering to fight for the Irish cause, something he would not do under other circumstances? The utilitarian does not seem to address Hawkins's particular dilemma, except perhaps to say that by allowing himself to be executed, other people will benefit. Why Hawkins in particular must benefit those other people, however, is not made plain. As a consequence, the utilitarian is not clear how Hawkins is to resolve his moral conflict; nor is the utilitarian any clearer in general how we are to answer our basic moral question: why, under certain circumstances, must we do things that we would not otherwise want to do? It seems that if we are to find an answer to our question, we must turn elsewhere. Let us consider the *deontological* approach.

The deontologist is more of a rationalist (for more on rationalism, see Part I, Knowledge) than empiricist in ethics. Like the traditional moralist, the deontologist recognizes that the moral life is governed by certain rules that specify our duties and obligations. To avoid the problem of conflicting rules, the sophisticated deontologist tries to describe a single, fundamental moral law that serves as a foundation for all the rest. For example, in Judeo-Christian theology, the Golden Rule is often invoked as fundamental to all the other moral commandments. But the law that says treat others as you would be treated is limited in scope. It seems applicable only to individuals that are basically moral to begin with. Otherwise, if employed by some sado-masochist, the results might be bizarre. In addition, not all acts clearly fall under the rule. How, for example, would a person contemplating suicide arrive at a decision on the basis of the Golden Rule, especially if there are no other individuals directly affected, as is sometimes the case? Since the person is not apparently doing anything to anyone else, there is nothing he or she would expect in return.

The most impressive attempt to construct a single, all-encompassing moral law was that of Immanuel Kant in the eighteenth century. His *categorical imperative* has stood as a monument of philosophical acumen. The basic idea is that in assessing the morality of any action, we must ask ourselves, "Could everybody do it?" If the answer is yes, then the contemplated act, or its particular rule, is universalizable, and the act is moral. Otherwise, not. For example, suppose a class of, say, twelve students is to take a short-answer quiz without any supervision, "on their honor," so to speak. Moreover, the desks are arranged in a circle, so that each student could easily peek at (and cheat from) the student to the immediate right. Should Charlie (one of the students in the class) cheat? It is not clear exactly what the egoist or utilitarian would say except that an answer depends on the consequences.

The Kantian would say something very different. First, what if everybody cheated? Consider, for example, what would happen if Charlie, and everybody else, tried to cheat from the person to his or her immediate right. Everybody would be straining to see his or her neighbor's paper, including the student to Charlie's immediate left, who would be straining to see Charlie's paper. But that person would not get an answer because Charlie does not have an answer. And Charlie could not get an answer until the person to his right gets one, and so on around the room. In other words, if everybody tried to cheat, nobody could successfully do it. Cheating, or the rule (or *maxim* as Kant sometimes suggests) that governs this behavior is not universalizable.

But why would this make cheating wrong? So what if the maxim that says "Thou shalt cheat!" is not universalizable? The answer seems to be that to do something when not everybody else could do it, to make an exception in one's own case, is to act like a parasite, an insect, something less than human. Morality, on Kant's view, has less to do with calculating self-aggrandizement or social cost-benefits, than with acting as a full-fledged human being, a *mensch* in Kant's Prussian, a "person" in plain English.

But how exactly is a person to behave? To begin with, we must treat each other with dignity and respect. Human beings are "ends-in-themselves," not to be exploited. More importantly, we must never place our self-interest or communal or social interest above our basic sense of duty and obligation. Otherwise, like the egoist or utilitarian, we would be acting in accordance with a *hypothetical*, rather than categorical, imperative and thus be missing the basic form of the moral life. For example, visitors to foreign countries are warned, "If you don't want to get dysentery, don't drink the water." This warning, "Don't drink the water," is hypothetical because it is issued under (the fairly obvious) assumption that people don't want dysentery.

According to Kant, moral imperatives, such as "Don't cheat," are categorical. Their force need not depend on satisfying some other condition, such as, "If you don't want to get caught . . ." Otherwise, if the only reason Charlie, for example, refrains from cheating is to avoid getting caught, then Charlie is behaving more like a child, not a mature human being. Charlie must refrain from cheating because he understands that cheating is categorically wrong. Only then would Charlie receive full moral credit.

To summarize Kant's view: people act morally provided (1) they act in accordance with a universalizable maxim; (2) they treat themselves and others with dignity and respect; and (3) they act out of a sense of duty in accordance with the moral law.

How might this approach help Bonaparte? To satisfy the Kantian sense of morality, Bonaparte would have to decide whether his action is universalizable. Would he make an exception if he himself were in Hawkins' shoes? Are they treating Hawkins and Belcher with dignity and respect? Have they ascertained that the two captives deserve to be put to death? If the answers to these and other related questions are in the affirmative, the Kantian would recognize Bonaparte's actions as moral.

Does the Kantian solve the basic problem? The answer seems to be yes. (We invite the reader to explore in the literature on Kantian ethics a host of objections to Kant's approach—for example, its apparent lack of moral substance. Not only can some immoral maxims be universalized—for example, "Cheat, at least a little, on your income taxes"—but some moral maxims seem to be not universalizable, such as, "Withdraw your money before there is a run on the bank.") If the question is, "Why, under certain circumstances, must we do things that we would not otherwise want to do?'' the Kantian response is that, in part, that's what acting morally means. However, does the Kantian address Bonaparte's particular dilemma? The young Irish soldier is not just torn between his sense of duty and his own immediate interests. If that were the case, his problem would be solved. The Kantian would say that Bonaparte must rise to the call of duty and do what is right. But what exactly *is* his duty—to follow the orders of a superior officer, or to refrain from harming someone he has come to regard as a friend? Bonaparte seems to be facing a conflict between two imperatives, both of which seem equally categorical. Unless the moralist can explain how apparently conflicting imperatives can be reconciled, the Kantian approach seems no more adequate than any of the others discussed thus far.

In the absence of a clear moral theory, what are we to do? Should we embrace a skeptical attitude (for more on the skeptical attitude, see our discussion of skepticism in Part I, Knowledge) that there is no empirical or rational foundation for moral judgment, that what we call morality is a collection of customs, like rules of etiquette, that differ from culture to culture and are largely accidents of history? If so, then perhaps there is no ultimate answer to the question, Why be moral? (Consider Kurt Baier's discussion of this question.) In the final analysis, perhaps we should each do what we want.

But what *do* we want? The answer many people would give is that we want more for ourselves, more money, a better job, a bigger house, a faster car—this view is called "psychological egoism." Most people who claim to be skeptical of morality embrace this philosophy. Moreover, the skeptical attitude seems to be that, in the absence of an otherwise well-defined moral theory, people ought to look out for themselves. Looking out for number one is our primary obligation, especially in a tough, competitive, and sometimes hostile world. If we don't help ourselves, who will? (Eddy Zemach addresses the issue of self-interest in the context of personal identity. See his article, "Looking Out For Number One," in Part III, Personal Identity.)

But in looking out for our own interests, shouldn't we distinguish between our immediate gains and long term benefits, as the ethical egoist suggests? Otherwise, we might be selling ourselves short. It seems that the skeptic would be wise to embrace ethical egoism, at least as a working strategy. But ethical egoism, however inadequate it may appear, is a moral theory. It seems that even a skeptic can accept at least one moral view, the morality of self-interest. But then the skeptic would know why we should be moral: morality would suit our interests.

Should the skeptic go further? In pursuing our long-term goals, wouldn't we be wise to recognize that other people, too, have interests—if only to enlist others in helping us to succeed? It would be foolish to act otherwise. Moreover, the longer the term, the more difficult it is to distinguish clearly our own interests from those of others. For example, suppose we want a better paying job. Our long-term strategy might be to support political candidates who stand primarily for a strong economy and more public funds for education. A strong economy would help to insure that there are better jobs; public support for education would help individuals, such as ourselves, to improve our qualifications for those jobs. But well-paid jobs and better education would suit, not just our interests, but the interests of the vast majority of other people as well—what we might call "the common good." So it seems that the moral skeptic would be wise to embrace not just ethical egoism, but utilitarianism. The utilitarian goal of increasing the sum total of happiness and minimizing, as much as possible, the harms that can befall us, would seem to suit well the skeptic who ultimately seeks his or her own well-being. It now seems that we have yet another answer that the skeptic could accept to the question, why be moral? Morality serves the common good.

Need we stop here? If we are willing to accept utilitarianism, why not go at least one step further? Cheating and stealing may work in the short run, but as long-term modes of conduct we are all better off to stick to certain traditional rules. The person who might otherwise profess skepticism of morality would be prudent, as we all would, to live by a code that teaches respect for the individual, that punishes only the guilty, and places a premium on trust and integrity. Otherwise, anyone of us, skeptic included, can become the victim of some apparent injustice. It seems we may have another answer to the question, why be moral? The moral way of life seems right.

The skeptic and moralist can agree, although for different reasons. The moralist, such as Kant, would insist that virtue is its own reward; the skeptic would accept the moral life, ultimately, on grounds of prudence. In the absence of a clear moral theory, perhaps we can agree with both

But can we? A moral dilemma seems to be essentially a conflict between one's moral obligations and prudence. If this is so, the conflict appears both rationally and empirically unresolvable. If we appeal to moral reasons to resolve a moral dilemma, we seem to beg the question against prudence. If we appeal to self-interest, we seem to ignore morality. Neither Bonaparte, nor anyone else, could hope rationally to resolve anything under these conditions.

But as our discussion has shown, we do not have an ultimate moral theory, nor can we always be certain about our own interests. In the absence of a more precise definition of the one or the other, there is little reason to suppose that morality and prudence are essentially at odds.

If there is no ultimate conflict between prudence and morality, then there is no need to think that moral dilemmas are hopeless. Bonaparte, for example, does not want to kill Hawkins, and apparently for good reason. Murder is wrong. Moreover, experience confirms that killing hostages does more harm than good, even to one's own cause. Bonaparte's dilemma seems solved. The British hostages should be allowed to live.

Why then does Bonaparte contribute to Hawkins' death? If, under certain circumstances, we must do things that we would not otherwise want to do, under other circumstances—we must not.

ROBERT C. MORTIMER
Moral Authority

THE BIBLE AND ETHICS

The Christian religion is essentially a revelation of the nature of God. It tells men that God has done certain things. And from the nature of these actions we can infer what God is like. In the second place the Christian religion tells men what is the will of God for them, how they must live if they would please God. This second message is clearly dependent on the first. The kind of conduct which will please God depends on the kind of person God is. This is what is meant by saying that belief influences conduct. The once popular view that it does not matter what a man believes so long as he acts decently is nonsense. Because what he considers decent depends on what he believes. If you are a Nazi you will behave as a Nazi, if you are a Communist you will behave as a Communist, and if you are a Christian you will behave as a Christian. At least, in general; for a man does not always do what he knows he ought to do, and he does not always recognize clearly the implications for conduct of his belief. But in general, our conduct, or at least our notions of what constitutes right conduct, are shaped by our beliefs. The man who knows about God— has a right faith—knows or may learn what conduct is pleasing to God and therefore right.

The Christian religion has a clear revelation of the nature of God, and by means of it instructs and enlightens the consciences of men. The first foundation is the doctrine of God the Creator. God made us and all the world. Because of that he has an absolute claim on our obedience. We do not exist in our own right, but only as His creatures, who ought therefore to do and be what He desires. We do not possess anything in the world, absolutely, not even our own bodies; we hold things in trust for God, who created them, and are bound, therefore, to use them only as He intends that they should be used. This is the doctrine contained in the first chapters of Genesis. God created man and placed him in the Garden of Eden with all the animals and the fruits of the earth at his disposal, subject to God's own law. "Of the fruit of the tree of the knowledge of good and evil thou shall not eat." Man's ownership and use of the material world is not absolute, but subject to the law of God.

From the doctrine of God as the Creator and source of all that is, it follows that a thing is not right simply because we think it is, still less because it seems to be expedient. It is right because God commands it. This means that there is a real distinction between right and wrong which is independent of what we happen to think. It is rooted in the nature and will of God. When a man's conscience tells him that a thing is right, which is in fact what God wills, his conscience is true and its judgment correct; when a man's conscience tells him a thing is right which is, in fact, contrary to God's will, his conscience is false and telling him a lie. It is a lamentably common experience for a man's conscience to play him false, so that in all good faith he does what is wrong, thinking it to be right. "Yea the time cometh that whosoever killeth you will think that he doeth God service." But this does not mean that whatever you think is right is right. It means that even conscience can be wrong: that the light which is in you can be darkness.

There is such a thing as human nature, which is the same in all men. It exists, like everything else, in order to become fully itself, to achieve its end. What that end is can be perceived, at any rate to a great extent, by the use of reason alone, unaided by any special divine revelation. For example, everybody has some idea of what is meant by a good man or a noble man. Everybody has some idea of what makes a society "advanced" or developed and what makes it primitive or decadent. Or again, that mind should control matter, the reason order the emotions, is clearly demanded by the very structure of our nature, in which there is a hierarchy of spirit, mind, and body. To make the body obey the reason is in harmony with nature, to allow the body to dominate the mind is to violate nature. Temperance, self-control, has always been recognized as a virtue. Indeed there has always been a general recognition of what the virtues are: justice, courage, temperance, consideration for others. The man who has these is well on the way to realizing his true nature, to becoming a man. The coward, the thief, the libertine, the ruthless oppressor is stunting and maiming himself. He becomes less and less a man, as he becomes more and more the slave of some dominant impulse and obsession. He is unbalanced and only partially developed.

All this means that there is a pattern of general behavior, a code of things to do and not to do, which derives necessarily from nature itself, from the simple fact that man is man. It is what is called natural law. The knowledge of it is not peculiar to Christians: it is common to man. It may make things plainer to give an illustration or two.

It is clear that man's power of memory, by means of which he can use the experience of the past as a guide for the present and can in some measure forecast the future and so provide for coming needs out of present superfluity—it is clear that this power of memory indicates the duty of thrift and prudence and condemns prodigality as unnatural. Man is meant to acquire control of his environment by such use of reason and to live free of the bondage of chance and desperate need. Wilful neglect to make provision for the future is to violate the law of nature and to incur the risk of the penalties which such violations incur.

Again, nature makes it abundantly clear that the survival and education of human offspring require a long and close union of the two parents. Kittens and puppies may survive birth from promiscuous unions, being adequately cared for by the mother alone, and quickly reaching an age of self-sufficiency. Not so human babies, whose slow development to maturity involves them in a long helpless dependence on their parents, and creates for the parents a long period of shared responsibility for the lives they have brought into the world. Hence the institution of marriage, found at all levels of human culture, and the general recognition of the virtue of chastity and of fidelity to the marriage bond.

Again, it is clear that the isolated individual man, the fictional solitary inhabitant of a desert island, cannot, or does not, easily attain to the full development of his personality and power. It is by sharing the fruits of their diverse labour, by each contributing that for which he has a special aptitude, that men accumulate wealth, and by wealth get leisure. It is by mutual intercourse and the exchange of thought that men acquire and distribute wisdom, and are able to practise and appreciate the arts. It is by living together that men develop their spiritual and mental powers and become persons. In other words, as Aristotle said, Man is by nature a political animal. He is not meant to live alone but in society. From this follows the universal recognition of the virtue of justice. Without justice there can be no stable society. Justice demands that all respect each other's rights, so that all may live together in peaceable enjoyment of that which is their own. The particular determinations of justice, the decision as to what are each man's rights has always been difficult, and subject to constant variation; but the general principle that rights are to be respected has been universally admitted and finds expression in such universal prohibitions as "thou shalt not kill," and "thou shalt not steal.". . .

It is certain that human perception of the content and implications of natural law has developed with the emergence of man from his primitive condition—the history of the institution of marriage is but one, if the clearest, illustration of this. It is equally certain that it has also regressed; that from time to time different human societies have lost, or failed to reach, a grasp of certain of the most elementary of its contents. Anthropologists have little difficulty in showing that there is scarcely one of the generally accepted moral axioms which has not somewhere at some time been denied. Cannibalism, thievery, even prostitution have in some societies not merely been practised, but extolled as moral duties. And in our own day we have been amazed at the Nazi moral code, which inculcated cruelty and lies as patriotic virtues.

Some have used these facts as an argument in favour of relativism and against the very existence of the natural law of divinely constituted human behavior. But the facts will not bear this argument, any more than ignorance of the solar system proves that the earth does not go round the sun. Existence of law and knowledge of that law are not the same thing. The law may well exist, and yet men be in ignorance of it. Knowledge of the law of nature in its more delicate implications and determinations demands refinement of moral sensitiveness and a quality of

prophetic insight. Even in its elementary content, in such precepts as the ten commandments, passion, self-interest, long-standing custom can blind men to truths which to others seem self-evident. The elementary right to individual freedom has often been denied to slaves in the name of the law of nature itself. There is no limit to the perversity of the human reason when clouded and weakened by unredeemed sin. It is the fact of universal human selfishness, or as theologians call it, the Fall, which prevents men from attaining a clear and persistent understanding of what constitutes right behavior. And it is this which establishes the permanent need of Revelation, and places Christians in a privileged and especially responsible position.

The pattern of conduct which God has laid down for man is the same for all men. It is universally valid. When we speak of Christian ethics we do not mean that there is one law for Christians and another for non-Christians. We mean the Christian understanding and statement of the one common law for all men. Unbelievers also know or can be persuaded of that law or of part of it: Christians have a fuller and better knowledge. The reason for this is that Christians have by revelation a fuller and truer knowledge both of the nature of God Himself and of the nature of man. As has been well said, "Christian men, in order to learn what is the place of the Natural Law and its products in the economy of salvation, must look to the Bible as the witness of God's operations and as the record of God's supernatural destiny for man, to which the Natural Law is itself orientated and subordinated. Only with such a perspective, and with the will to purification of perception and purpose thereby created, will they be able to perceive or affirm the Natural Law in its completeness as an expression of the Lordship of Jesus Christ."

The Revelation in the Bible plays a threefold part. In the first place it recalls and restates in simple and even violent language fundamental moral judgments which men are always in danger of forgetting or explaining away. It thus provides a norm and standard of human behavior in the broadest and simplest outline. Man's duty to worship God and love the truth, to respect lawful authority, to refrain from violence and robbery, to live in chastity, to be fair and even merciful in his dealings with his neighbor—and all this as the declared will of God, the way man *must* live if he would achieve his end—this is the constant theme of the Bible. The effect of it is not to reveal something new which men could not have found out for themselves, but to recall them to what they have forgotten or with culpable blindness have failed to perceive.

It is not easy to exaggerate the power of human self-deception nor man's ingenuity in persuading himself that black is white; manifest injustice can be depicted as justice, and unchastity acclaimed as "a venture of bold living." For example in times of shortages to exploit the needs and miseries of the poor by a strictly legal use of the markets may easily be represented as a perfectly proper use of one's opportunities, a quite legitimate advancement of oneself and one's family. The complacency born of such long and widespread practice is shattered by the violence of Revelation. "Thus saith the Lord: For three transgressions of Israel, and for four, I will not turn away the punishment thereof; because they sold the righteous for silver and the poor for a pair of shoes . . ." (Amos ii, 6). This, then, is the first work of Revelation; it continuously sets forth the broad paths of right conduct. Lies are lies by whatever name you call them, and injustice is injustice however fairly screened and decked. They who read the Scriptures constantly and with attention cannot fail to ask themselves not only how far they have knowingly and wilfully transgressed the law of God, but also how far even that conduct which has seemed above question and reproach comes under divine condemnation.

And this leads to the second work of Revelation. The conduct which God demands of men, He demands out of His own Holiness and Righteousness. "Be ye perfect, as your Father in Heaven is perfect." Not the service of the lips but of the heart, not obedience in the letter but in the Spirit is commanded. The standard is too high: the Judge too all-seeing and just. The grandeur and majesty of the moral law proclaims the weakness and impotence of man. It shatters human pride and self-sufficiency: it overthrows that complacency with which the righteous regard the tattered robes of their partial virtues, and that satisfaction with which rogues rejoice to discover other men more evil than themselves. The revelation of the holiness of God and His Law, once struck home, drives men to confess their need of grace and brings them to Christ their Saviour.

Lastly, Revelation, by the light which it throws on the nature of God and man, suggests new emphases and new precepts, a new scale of values which could not at all, or could not easily, have been perceived as part of the Natural Law for man without it. Thus it comes about that Christian ethics is at once old and new. It covers the same ground of human conduct as the law of the Old Testament and the "law of the Gentiles written in their hearts." Many of its precepts are the same precepts. Yet all is seen in a different light and in a new perspective—the perspective of God's love manifested in Christ. It will be worth while to give one or two illustrations of this.

Revelation throws into sharp relief the supreme value of each individual human being. Every man is an immortal soul created by God and designed for an eternal inheritance. The love of God effected by the Incarnation the restoration and renewal of fallen human nature in order that all men alike might benefit thereby. The Son of God showed particular care and concern for the fallen, the outcast, the weak and the despised. He came, not to call the righteous, but sinners to repentance. Like a good shepherd, He sought especially for the sheep which was lost. Moreover, the divine drama of Calvary which was the cost of man's redemption, the price necessary to give him again a clear picture of what human nature was designed to be and to provide him with the inspiration to strive towards it and the assurance that he is not irrevocably tied and bound to his sinful, selfish past, makes it equally clear that in the eyes of the Creator His creature man is of infinite worth and value.

The lesson is plain and clear: all men equally are the children of God, all men equally are the object of His love. In consequence of this, Christian ethics has always asserted that every man is a person possessed of certain inalienable rights, that he is an end in himself, never to be used merely as a means to something else. And he is this in virtue of his being a man, no matter what his race or color, no matter how well or poorly endowed with talents, no matter how primitive or developed. And further, since man is an end in himself, and that end transcends this world of time and space, being fully attained only in heaven, it follows that the individual takes precedence over society, in the sense that society exists for the good of its individual members, not those members for society. However much the good of the whole is greater than the good of any one of its parts, and whatever the duties each man owes to society, individual persons constitute the supreme value, and society itself exists only to promote the good of those persons.

This principle of the infinite worth of the individual is explicit in Scripture, and in the light of it all totalitarian doctrines of the State stand condemned. However, the implications of this principle for human living and for the organization of society are not explicit, but need to be perceived and worked out by the human conscience. How obtuse that conscience can be, even when illumined by revelation, is startlingly illustrated by the long centuries in which Christianity tolerated the institution of slavery. In view of the constant tendency of man to exploit his fellow men and use them as the instruments of his greed and selfishness, two things are certain. First, that the Scriptural revelation of the innate inalienable dignity and value of the individual is an indispensable bulwark of human freedom and growth. And second, that our knowledge of the implication of this revelation is far indeed from being perfect; there is constant need of further refinement of our moral perceptions, a refinement which can only emerge as the fruit of a deeper penetration of the Gospel of God's love into human life and thought.

Another illustration of the effect of Scripture upon ethics is given by the surrender of the principle of exact retribution in favor of the principle of mercy. Natural justice would seem to require exact retributive punishment, an eye for an eye, a tooth for a tooth. The codes of primitive peoples, and the long history of blood feuds show how the human conscience has approved of this concept. The revelation of the divine love and the explicit teaching of the Son of God have demonstrated the superiority of mercy, and have pointed the proper role of punishment as correction and not vengeance. Because of the revelation that in God justice is never unaccompanied by mercy, in Christian ethics there has always been an emphasis on the patient endurance of wrongs in imitation of Calvary, and on the suppression of all emotions of vindictive anger. As a means to soften human relations, as a restraint of human anger and cruelty, so easily disguised under the cloak of justice, the history of the world has nothing to show comparable to this Christian emphasis on patience and mercy, this insistence that even the just satisfaction of our wrongs yields to the divine example of forebearance. We are to be content with the reform or at least the restraint of the evil-doer, never to seek or demand vengeance.

It is well known how great a store Aristotle set by the "magnanimous" man, the man who holds himself to be intellectually and morally superior to his fellows, and is so. The concept of humility as a virtue is, I think, peculiar to the Christian code of ethics. It is inspired wholly by the example of the Son of God who came down from Heaven and lived as a man, and suffered the shameful death of the Cross. "The Son of Man came not to be ministered unto but to minister." "He that is greatest among you, let him be as one that serveth."

The duty of the great and highly placed not to seek their own advantage, but to devote themselves to the service of those over whom they bear rule: the conviction that all are equal in the sight of God, though different men have different functions; the recognition that all au thority, power and wealth are from above, held in trust for God to whom account must one day be given; the understanding that respect, deference, prestige, rank are not things to be eagerly grasped at, but authority, power, and wealth are from above, held in trust for God to prize, to be snatched at, their surrender is nobler than their acquisition, their responsibility weightier than their privileges: these are insights not easily gained by the natural man but plain in the Revelation and always emphasized in the Christian tradition. Humility in high and low alike is that virtue by which men are conscious of their own frailty and unworthiness, and grateful for the divine mercy and help upon which they constantly depend; by it they see in their own virtues only the triumph of God's grace and a divine commission to the service of others. This lovely quality is perhaps the noblest of all the gifts of Christianity to the human race. . . .

These are only a few of the matters on which the human conscience is enlightened by the Revelation contained in the Christian tradition. Nor are all the implications of the Revelation anything like fully realized even now after nearly two thousand years. No doubt, so long as humanity exists, among those who humbly and patiently seek to live under the Gospel there will develop an ever clearer and more delicate perception of what the divine pattern for human conduct is. It is certain that where the Revelation is ignored, the darkness of degeneracy and barbarism sets in. Sin-ridden man needs the Scriptures to rebuke his errors, to correct the distortion with which he perceives the natural law, to hold him firmly to its elementary principles and to lighten his eyes to its hidden depths. Christian ethics is the exposition of the moral truths implicit in the Revelation, and the application of them to human living. It interprets to man the natural law on the basis of that superior knowledge of the nature of God, of man, and of the end for which man is created, which Revelation contains.

AUTHORITY AND CONSCIENCE

Because the content of Christian ethics is thus determined by the nature of the divine revelation in Scripture, the Church has always held a high position of authority in the matter of morals. Just as it is her duty and function to define what is the Christian faith, and to guard it from false teaching, so it is her duty to define what is the Christian conduct which follows from that faith, and to denounce practices which are opposed to it. The most important part of her duty in this respect is to proclaim the broad principles and general duties of Christian behavior. It is her duty constantly to remind men of those obvious moral truths which they are always in danger of forgetting under the influence of passion and self-interest. The "duty towards God" and "the duty towards my neighbor" in the English Church Catechism are illustrations of the Church performing this kind of work. The two "duties" set out the ordinary Christian duties. They are stated without argument and on authority—the authority of Scripture and of the Church interpreting Scripture. The clergy, armed with the same authority, preach these duties and expound them.

In addition to this duty of constantly emphasizing general principles, the Church has also the duty of applying these principles to changing circumstances. This is a task of very considerable difficulty—a difficulty not clearly realized by those who glibly call "for a lead from the Church" whenever any fresh moral problem arises. The difficulty is created by the tension between the "magisterium" or "teaching authority" of the Church in faith and morals on the one hand, and the autonomy of every individual conscience on the other.

Once the Church has "pronounced" on any question of morals, there is a prima facie obligation on Christians to obey: for the Church has authority in such matters. Yet if the pronouncement is contrary to a man's own conscientious judgment there is a higher obligation, as we shall see in a moment, to obey one's own con science. It is for this reason, in order to avoid a conflict of this kind, that the Protestant Churches, at least, are reluctant to issue detailed and authoritative statements on new moral problems. After all, the guidance of the Holy Spirit is promised to the Church as a whole, the Spirit dwells in every member of the Church from the highest and most instructed to the lowest and least gifted. Authoritative pronouncements are only properly made when they express and articulate the common mind of the whole Church. To determine what this mind is is a slow and difficult matter. It is not necessarily what those in authority in the Church hold to be true at the moment of the first impact of the new problem; neither is it necessarily the half-instinctive reaction of the general mass of Christians. The common Spirit-guided judgment more often emerges or crystallizes slowly after debate and reflection.

Nevertheless, life has to be lived. And men naturally and rightly demand of the Church help and advice in solving their moral problems and in applying the principles of Christian ethics to the situation in which they daily find themselves. It is much easier to perceive and admit, for example, the claims of justice in general, than to decide what is in fact just within the framework of a given social order. The Church has an undeniable duty to ease this difficulty, sometimes by re-proclaiming the general principles and outline of justice, sometimes by going further and asserting positively that this or that practice is demanded or is condemned by those principles. This duty brings the Church not only into the area of personal ethics but also into the spheres of politics and economics. Her voice is to be heard both declaring and expounding, for example, the duties of marriage and also teaching the laws of war, the requirements of honesty in business or the mutual duties of employer and employed.

In many cases, perhaps in most, the Church does not try so much to lay down the solutions of moral problems or to dictate in detail the moral conduct appropriate to particular circumstances, as to set forth the principles which must be borne in mind by those faced with such problems, and with which conduct must conform in this or that set of circumstances. Thus, in time of war, the Church will not necessarily condemn out of hand any particular method of warfare—for she may have altogether inadequate material for passing a judgment—but she will remind belligerents of the duties of mercy and humanity and of the general claims of justice. And in this way she will call on those in authority to see to it that their conduct of the war does not infringe these principles. Or again, in matters of the marketplace, the Church will not herself lay down what is the just price, or at what point profits turn into profiteering: she will not herself determine what is a fair wage, or what is the proper number of hours to be worked in a day or a week. But she will insist that merchants aim at a just price, that manufacturers be content with a moderate profit, that masters and men have a common Master in Heaven, that the laborer is worthy of his hire, that power and advantage are not rightly used as opportunities to exploit or coerce. And she will call on those engaged in the marketplace to see to it that in their conduct they do not wilfully and flagrantly violate those principles.

When new inventions suddenly create new situations, it becomes the duty of the Church to assist Christians to form their moral judgments by stating clearly the moral issues which are involved. She assists them by showing what is genuinely new in the new situation and what is old, by disentangling the various elements which go to form the situation, and so presenting a clearer picture of the problem which has to be solved.

These are some of the ways in which the Protestant Churches, at least, try to discharge their duty of guiding and teaching Christian people in matters of morals. Occasionally, and in the case of the Roman Church more often, the Church will authoritatively forbid particular practices as certainly contrary to the laws of God. For example, divorce and remarriage is condemned as a violation of the marriage bond. The compulsory sterilization of the mentally defective is forbidden as constituting a denial of an essential human right, and their extermination as an unjustifiable subordination of the individual to the community. The institution of slavery is condemned as unjust in its affront to human dignity and its denial of human rights.

Whether the Church commands or reminds or advises, precisely because she is the divinely constituted guardian and interpreter of the Christian faith in which Christian ethics is rooted, her voice is not to be disregarded. She is not to be carelessly and lightly dismissed as though she had no right to speak, and were guilty of an unwarrantable intrusion into matters outside of the sphere of religion. All Christians are morally bound to pay her the greatest attention; they are to take account in their conduct of those principles which she lays down as governing particular matters, and where she issues a definite command or prohibition, they are under a moral obligation to obey. Yet, because the application of moral principles to particular situations and the consequent determination of where duty lies is the primary task of individual conscience, the Church, however authoritative her teaching, is not the final arbiter. The last word lies with conscience.

The statement that Christians are under a moral obligation to obey the Church in matters of morals presupposes that their own consciences are not at variance with the teaching of the Church. No man lightly sets up his own judgment against that of the Church, nor acquiesces in conscientious disagreement without the most serious and painful effort to understand and make his own the Church's judgment; but in the last resort his own conscience must be allowed to be supreme. Deeply embedded in the heart of Christian ethics is the dictum "Conscience is always to be obeyed."

It must be so. Conscience is a man's reason making moral judgments. It is by the use of this reason that man apprehends truth, if he apprehends it at all. What, therefore, a man perceives to be true he must hold to be true or else deny that he can ever perceive truth at all.

A judgment of conscience is a perception or apprehension of moral truth. It takes the form

"this is right" or "this is wrong." The foundation of all morality is the innate instinctive universal recognition that right is to be done, wrong is not to be done. When, therefore, a man judges, by his reason, that "this is right," at the same moment he recognizes that "this ought to be done." To hold that "this is right, yet it ought not to be done" is the same as to say "this is right, though I know it to be wrong" or "I accept as true what I know to be untrue." In other words, a man can never be acting rightly when he goes against his conscience.

This does not mean . . . that he is necessarily acting rightly whenever he obeys his conscience. It is nonsense to suppose that whatever a man thinks is right must be right. But it does mean that whenever a man disobeys his conscience, whether his conscience is right or wrong, he is acting wrongly. For every time he does so, he says in effect "I am doing what I judge to be wrong." Hence, in the last resort, no matter how much others may denounce my judgment as false, no matter with what authority of tradition and learning the contrary opinion be invested, if my own conscience is clear and certain, it must be followed. For not to follow it would be to refuse to do what I know to be right, what I know to be the will of God.

From this fundamental principle of the supremacy of the individual conscience, as constituting for each individual the norm and standard of moral conduct from which there is no appeal, there flow two important corollaries. The first is that it becomes at times a duty to disobey lawful authority. The second is that it is at all times a duty to take moral problems seriously.

Although . . . it is the teaching of Christian ethics that subjects are under a moral obligation to obey their lawful superiors—that such obedience is the will of God, to be rendered "for conscience sake" and not merely from compulsion—yet the obedience so enjoined is not blind and undiscriminating. It is due to superiors because and in so far as they are the agents of God. It follows, therefore, that no obedience is due where the superiors command anything which is against the will of God. On the contrary, such commands not only may but must be disobeyed. For we are to obey God rather than men. In consequence it is the duty of subjects in every state to scrutinize the laws passed upon them, to make sure that they will not, by obeying them, transgress the laws of God. In a democratic state they have the further duty of taking the appropriate constitutional steps to have such laws repealed and to ensure that no more such laws be enacted.

BRIAN MEDLIN
Ultimate Principles and Ethical Egoism

I believe that it is now pretty generally accepted by professional philosophers that ultimate ethical principles must be arbitrary. One cannot derive conclusions about what should be merely from accounts of what is the case; one cannot decide how people ought to behave merely from one's knowledge of how they do behave. To arrive at a conclusion in ethics one must have at least one ethical premise. This premise, if it be in turn a conclusion, must be the conclusion of an argument containing at least one ethical premiss. And so we can go back, indefinitely but not for ever. Sooner or later, we must come to at least one ethical premise which is not deduced but baldly asserted. Here we must be a-rational; neither rational nor irrational, for here there is no room for reason even to go wrong.

But the triumph of Hume in ethics has been a limited one. What appears quite natural to a handful of specialists appears quite monstrous to the majority of decent intelligent men. At any rate, it has been my experience that people who are normally rational resist the above account of the logic of moral language, not by argument—for that can't be done—but by tooth and nail. And they resist from the best motives. They see the philosopher wantonly unravelling the whole fabric of morality. If our ultimate principles are arbitrary, they say, if those principles came out of thin air, then anyone can hold any principle he pleases. Unless moral assertions are statements of fact about the world and either true or false, we can't claim that any man is wrong, whatever his principles may be, whatever his behaviour. We have to surrender the luxury of calling one another scoundrels. That this anxiety flourishes because its roots are in confusion is evident when we consider that we don't call people scoundrels, anyhow, for being mistaken about their facts. Fools, perhaps, but that's another matter. Nevertheless, it doesn't become us to be high-up. The layman's uneasiness, however irrational it may be, is very natural and he must be reassured.

People cling to objectivist theories of morality from moral motives. It's a very queer thing that by doing so they often thwart their own purposes. There are evil opinions abroad, as anyone who walks abroad knows. The one we meet with most often, whether in pub or parlour, is the doctrine that everyone should look after himself. However refreshing he may find it after the high-minded pomposities of this morning's editorial, the good fellow knows this doc-

"Ultimate Principles and Ethical Egoism" is reprinted from the *Australasian Journal of Philosophy* Vol. 35, No. 2 (1957), by permission of the *Australasian Journal of Philosophy.* **Brian Medlin,** a contemporary Australian philosopher, has contributed much to the study of ethics.

trine is wrong and he wants to knock it down. But while he believes that moral language is used to make statements either true or false, the best he can do is to claim that what the egoist says is false. Unfortunately, the egoist can claim that it's true. And since the supposed fact in question between them is not a publicly ascertainable one, their disagreement can never be resolved. And it is here that even good fellows waver, when they find they have no refutation available. The egoist's word seems as reliable as their own. Some begin half to believe that perhaps it is possible to supply an egoistic basis for conventional morality, some that it may be impossible to supply any other basis. I'm not going to try to prop up our conventional morality, which I fear to be a task beyond my strength, but in what follows I do want to refute the doctrine of ethical egoism. I want to resolve this disagreement by showing that what the egoist says is inconsistent. It is true that there are moral disagreements which can never be resolved, but this isn't one of them. The proper objection to the man who says 'Everyone should look after his own interests regardless of the interests of others' is not that he isn't speaking the truth, but simply that he isn't speaking.

We should first make two distinctions. This done, ethical egoism will lose much of its plausibility.

I. UNIVERSAL AND INDIVIDUAL EGOISM

Universal egoism maintains that everyone (including the speaker) ought to look after his own interests and to disregard those of other people except in so far as their interests contribute towards his own.

Individual egoism is the attitude that the egoist is going to look after himself and no one else. The egoist cannot promulgate that he is going to look after himself. He can't even preach that he *should* look after himself and preach this alone. When he tries to convince me that he should look after himself, he is attempting so to dispose me that I shall approve when he drinks my beer and steals Tom's wife. I cannot approve of his looking after himself and himself alone without so far approving of his achieving his happiness, regardless of the happiness of myself and others. So that when he sets out to persuade me that he should look after himself regardless of others, he must also set out to persuade me that I should look after him regardless of myself and others. Very small chance he has! And if the individual egoist cannot promulgate his doctrine without enlarging it, what he has is no doctrine at all.

A person enjoying such an attitude may believe that other people are fools not to look after themselves. Yet he himself would be a fool to tell them so. If he did tell them, though, he wouldn't consider that he was giving them *moral* advice. Persuasion to the effect that one should ignore the claims of morality because morality doesn't pay, to the effect that one has insufficient selfish motive and, therefore, insufficient motive for moral behaviour is not moral persuasion. For this reason I doubt that we should call the individual egoist's attitude an ethical one. And I don't doubt this in the way someone may doubt whether to call the ethical standards of Satan ''ethical'' standards. A malign morality is none the less a morality for being malign. But the attitude we're considering is one of mere contempt for all moral considerations whatsoever. An indifference to morals may be wicked, but it is not a perverse morality. So far as I am aware, most egoists imagine that they are putting forward a doctrine in ethics, though there may be a few who are prepared to proclaim themselves individual egoists. If the good fellow wants to know how he should justify conventional morality to an individual egoist, the answer is that he shouldn't and can't. Buy your car elsewhere, blackguard him whenever you meet, and let it go at that.

II. CATEGORICAL AND HYPOTHETICAL EGOISM

Categorical egoism is the doctrine that we all ought to observe our own interests, *because that is what we ought to do*. For the categorical egoist the egoistic dogma is the ultimate principle in ethics.

The hypothetical egoist, on the other hand, maintains that we all ought to observe our own interests, because . . . . If we want such and such an end, we must do so and so (look after ourselves). The hypothetical egoist is not a real egoist at all. He is very likely an unwitting utilitarian who believes mistakenly that the general happiness will be increased if each man looks wisely to his own. Of course, a man may believe that egoism is enjoined on us by God and he may therefore promulgate the doctrine and observe it in his conduct, not in the hope of achieving thereby a remote end, but simply in order to obey God. But neither is *he* a real egoist. He believes, ultimately, that we should obey God, even should God command us to altruism.

An ethical egoist will have to maintain the doctrine in both its universal and categorical forms. Should he retreat to hypothetical egoism he is no longer an egoist. Should he retreat to individual egoism his doctrine, while logically impregnable, is no longer ethical, no longer even a doctrine. He may wish to quarrel with this and if so, I submit peacefully. Let him call himself what he will, it makes no difference. I'm a philosopher, not a rat-catcher, and I don't see it as my job to dig vermin out of such burrows as individual egoism.

Obviously something strange goes on as soon as the ethical egoist tries to promulgate his doctrine. What is he doing when he urges upon his audience that they should each observe his own interests and those interests alone? Is he not acting contrary to the egoistic principle? It cannot be to his advantage to convince them, for seizing always their own advantage they will impair his. Surely if he does believe what he says, he should try to persuade them otherwise. Not perhaps that they should devote themselves to his interests, for they'd hardly swallow that; but that everyone should devote himself to the service of others. But is not to believe that someone should act in a certain way to try to persuade him to do so? Of course, we don't always try to persuade people to act as we think they should act. We may be lazy, for instance. But in so far as we believe that Tom should do so and so, we have a tendency to induce him to do so and so. Does it make sense to say: "Of course you should do this, but for goodness' sake don't"? Only where we mean: "You should do this for certain reasons, but here are even more persuasive reasons for not doing it." If the egoist believes ultimately that others should mind themselves alone, then, he must persuade them accordingly. If he doesn't persuade them, he is no universal egoist. It certainly makes sense to say: "I know very well that Tom should act in such and such a way. But I know also that it's not to my advantage that he should so act. So I'd better dissuade him from it." And this is just what the egoist must say, if he is to consider his own advantage and disregard everyone else's. That is, he must behave as an individual egoist, if he is to be an egoist at all.

He may want to make two kinds of objection here:

1. That it will not be to his disadvantage to promulgate the doctrine, provided that his audience fully understand what is to their ultimate advantage. This objection can be developed in a number of ways, but I think that it will always be possible to push the egoist into either individual or hypothetical egoism.

2. That it is to the egoist's advantage to preach the doctrine if the pleasure he gets out of doing this more than pays for the injuries he must endure at the hands of his converts. It is hard to believe that many people would be satisfied with a doctrine which they could only consistently promulgate in very special circumstances. Besides, this looks suspiciously like individual egoism in disguise.

I shall say no more on these two points because I want to advance a further criticism which seems to me at once fatal and irrefutable.

Now it is time to show the anxious layman that we have means of dealing with ethical egoism which are denied him; and denied him by just that objectivism which he thinks essential to morality. For the very fact that our ultimate principles must be arbitrary means they can't be anything we please. Just because they come out of thin air they can't come out of hot air. Because these principles are not propositions about matters of fact and cannot be deduced from propositions about matters of fact, they must be the fruit of our own attitudes. We assert them largely to modify the attitudes of our fellows but by asserting them we express our own desires and purposes. This means that we cannot use moral language cavalierly. Evidently, we cannot say something like 'All human desires and purposes are bad'. This would be to express our own desires and purposes, thereby committing a kind of absurdity. Nor, I shall argue, can we say 'Everyone should observe his own interests regardless of the interests of others'.

Remembering that the principle is meant to be both universal and categorical, let us ask what kind of attitude the egoist is expressing. Wouldn't that attitude be equally well expressed by the conjunction of an infinite number of avowals thus?—

I want myself to come out on top	and	I don't care about Tom, Dick, Harry . . .
and		and
I want Tom to come out on top	and	I don't care about myself, Dick, Harry . . .
and		and
I want Dick to come out on top	and	I don't care about myself, Tom, Harry . . .
and		and
I want Harry to come out on top etc.	and	I don't care about myself, Dick, Tom . . . etc.

From this analysis it is obvious that the principle expressing such an attitude must be inconsistent.

But now the egoist may claim that he hasn't been properly understood. When he says 'Everyone should look after himself and himself alone', he means 'Let each man do what he wants regardless of what anyone else wants'. The egoist may claim that what he values is merely that he and Tom and Dick and Harry should each do what he wants and not care about what anyone else may want and that this doesn't involve his principle in any inconsistency. Nor need it. But even if it doesn't, he's no better off. Just what does he value? Is it the well-being of himself, Tom, Dick and Harry or merely their going on in a certain way regardless of whether or not this is going to promote their well-being? When he urges Tom, say, to do what he wants, is he appealing to Tom's self-interest? If so, his attitude can be expressed thus:

| I want myself to be happy and I want Tom to be happy | *and* | I want myself not to care about Tom, Dick, Harry . . . |

We need go no further to see that the principle expressing such an attitude must be inconsistent. I have made this kind of move already. What concerns me now is the alternative position the egoist must take up to be safe from it. If the egoist values merely that people should go on in a certain way, regardless of whether or not this is going to promote their well-being, then he is not appealing to the self-interest of his audience when he urges them to regard their own interests. If Tom has any regard for himself at all, the egoist's blandishments will leave him cold. Further, the egoist doesn't even have his own interest in mind when he says that, like everyone else, he should look after himself. A funny kind of egoism this turns out to be.

Perhaps now, claiming that he is indeed appealing to the self-interest of his audience, the egoist may attempt to counter the objection of the previous paragraph. He may move into "Let each man do what he wants and let each man disregard what others want when their desires clash with his own''. Now his attitude may be expressed thus:

| I want everyone to be happy | *and* | I want everyone to disregard the happiness of others when their happiness clashes with his own. |

The egoist may claim justly that a man can have such an attitude and also that in a certain kind of world such a man could get what he wanted. Our objection to the egoist has been that his desires are incompatible. And this is still so. If he and Tom and Dick and Harry did go on as he recommends by saying 'Let each man disregard the happiness of others, when their happiness conflicts with his own', then assuredly they'd all be completely miserable. Yet he wants them to be happy. He is attempting to counter this by saying that it is merely a fact about the world that they'd make one another miserable by going on as he recommends. The world could conceivably have been different. For this reason, he says, this principle is not inconsistent. This argument may not seem very compelling, but I advance it on the egoist's behalf because I'm interested in the reply to it. For now we don't even need to tell him that the world isn't in fact like that. (What it's like makes no difference.) Now we can point out to him that he is arguing not as an egoist but as a utilitarian. He has slipped into hypothetical egoism to save his principle from inconsistency. If the world were such that we always made ourselves and others happy by doing one another down, then we could find good utilitarian reasons for urging that we should do one another down.

If, then, he is to save his principle, the egoist must do one of two things. He must give up the claim that he is appealing to the self-interest of his audience, that he has even his own interest in mind. Or he must admit that, although 'I want everyone to be happy' refers to ends, nevertheless 'I want everyone to disregard the hap-

piness of others when their happiness conflicts with his own' can refer only to means. That is, his so-called ultimate principle is really compounded of a principle and a moral rule subordinate to that principle. That is, he is really a utilitarian who is urging everyone to go on in a certain way so that everyone may be happy. A utilitarian, what's more, who is ludicrously mistaken about the nature of the world. Things being as they are, his moral rule is a very bad one. Things being as they are, it can only be deduced from his principle by means of an empirical premise which is manifestly false. Good fellows don't need to fear him. They may rest easy that the world is and must be on their side and the best thing they can do is be good.

It may be worth pointing out that objections similar to those I have brought against the egoist can be made to the altruist. The man who holds that the principle 'Let everyone observe the interests of others' is both universal and categorical can be compelled to choose between two alternatives, equally repugnant. He must give up the claim that he is concerned for the well-being of himself and others. Or he must admit that, though 'I want everyone to be happy' refers to ends, nevertheless 'I want everyone to disregard his own happiness when it conflicts with the happiness of others' can refer only to means.

I have said from time to time that the egoistic principle is inconsistent. I have not said it is contradictory. This for the reason that we can, without contradiction, express inconsistent desires and purposes. To do so is not to say anything like 'Goliath was ten feet tall and not ten feet tall'. Don't we all want to eat our cake and have it too? And when we say we do we aren't asserting a contradiction. We are not asserting a contradiction whether we be making an avowal of our attitudes or stating a fact about them. We all have conflicting motives. As a utilitarian exuding benevolence I want the man who mows my landlord's grass to be happy, but as a slug-a-bed I should like to see him scourged. None of this, however, can do the egoist any good. For we assert our ultimate principles not only to express our own attitudes but also to induce similar attitudes in others, to dispose them to conduct themselves as we wish. In so far as their desires conflict, people don't know what to do. And, therefore, no expression of incompatible desires can ever serve for an ultimate principle of human conduct.

JOHN STUART MILL
Utilitarianism

I. GENERAL REMARKS

There are a few circumstances, among those which make up the present condition of human knowledge, more unlike what might have been expected, or more significant of the backward state in which speculation on the most important subjects still lingers, than the little progress which has been made in the decision of the controversy respecting the criterion of right and wrong. From the dawn of philosophy, the question concerning the *summum bonum* or, what is the same thing, concerning the foundation of morality, has been accounted the main problem in speculative thought, has occupied the most gifted intellects and divided them into sects and schools, carrying on a vigorous warfare against one another. And, after more than two thousand years, the same discussions continue, philosophers are still ranged under the same contending banners, and neither thinkers nor mankind at large seem nearer to being unanimous on the subject than when the youth Socrates listened to the old Protagoras, and asserted (if Plato's dialogue be grounded on a real conversation) the theory of utilitarianism against the popular morality of the so-called Sophist.

It is true that similar confusion and uncertainty, and in some cases similar discordance, exist respecting the first principles of all the sciences, not excepting that which is deemed the most certain of them—mathematics—without much impairing, generally indeed without impairing at all, the trustworthiness of the conclusions of those sciences. An apparent anomaly, the explanation of which is that the detailed doctrines of a science are not usually deduced from, nor depend for their evidence upon, what are called its first principles. Were it not so, there would be no science more precarious, or whose conclusions were more insufficiently made out, than algebra, which derives none of its certainty from what are commonly taught to learners as its elements, since these, as laid down by some of its most eminent teachers, are as full of fictions as English law, and of mysteries as theology. The truths which are ultimately accepted as the first principles of a science are really the last results of metaphysical analysis practiced on the elementary notions with which the science is conversant, and their relation to the science is not that of foundations

Reprinted from John Stuart Mill's *Utilitarianism, Liberty and Representative Government*, (1931) by permission of J. M. Dent & Sons and Everyman's Library. **John Stuart Mill** (1806–1873) was an extremely influential British philosopher of the nineteenth century, making inroads in the philosophy of science and logic, and also, through his defense of utilitarianism, inspiring many political and social reforms.

to an edifice, but of roots to a tree, which may perform their office equally well though they be never dug down to and exposed to light. But though, in science the particular truths precede the general theory, the contrary might be expected to be the case with a practical art, such as morals or legislation. All action is for the sake of some end; and rules of action, it seems natural to suppose, must take their whole character and color from the end to which they are subservient. When we engage in a pursuit, a clear and precise conception of what we are pursuing would seem to be the first thing we need, instead of the last we are to look forward to. A test of right and wrong must be the means, one would think, of ascertaining what is right or wrong, and not a consequence of having already ascertained it.

The difficulty is not avoided by having recourse to the popular theory of a natural faculty, a sense or instinct, informing us of right and wrong. For, besides that the existence of such a moral instinct is itself one of the matters in dispute, those believers in it who have any pretensions to philosophy have been obliged to abandon the idea that it discerns what is right or wrong in the particular case in hand, as our other senses discern the sight or sound actually present. Our moral faculty, according to all those of its interpreters who are entitled to the name of thinkers, supplies us only with the general principles of moral judgments; it is a branch of our reason, not of our sensitive faculty, and must be looked to for the abstract doctrines of morality, not for perception of it in the concrete. The intuitive, no less than what may be termed the inductive, school of ethics, insists on the necessity of general laws. They both agree that the morality of an individual action is not a question of direct perception, but of the application of a law to an individual case. They recognize also, to a great extent, the same moral laws, but differ as to their evidence, and the source from which they derive their authority. According to the one opinion, the principles of morals are evident *a priori,* requiring nothing to command assent, except that the meaning of the terms be understood. According to the other

doctrine, right and wrong, as well as truth and falsehood, are questions of observation and experience. But both hold equally that morality must be deduced from principles, and the intuitive school affirm, as strongly as the inductive, that there is a science of morals. Yet they seldom attempt to make out a list of the *a priori* principles which are to serve as the premises of the science; still more rarely do they make any effort to reduce those various principles to one first principle, or common ground of obligation. They either assume the ordinary precepts of morals as of *a priori* authority, or they lay down as the common groundwork of those maxims some generality much less obviously authoritative than the maxims themselves, and which has never succeeded in gaining popular acceptance. Yet, to support their pretensions, there ought either to be some one fundamental principle or law at the root of all morality, or, if there be several, there should be a determinate order of precedence among them, and the one principle, or the rule for deciding between various principles when they conflict, ought to be self-evident.

To inquire how far the bad effects of this deficiency have been mitigated in practice, or to what extent the moral beliefs of mankind have been vitiated or made uncertain by the absence of any distinct recognition of an ultimate standard, would imply a complete survey and criticism of past and present ethical doctrine. It would, however, be easy to show that whatever steadiness or consistency these moral beliefs have attained has been mainly due to the tacit influence of a standard not recognized. Although the nonexistence of an acknowledged first principle has made ethics not so much a guide as a consecration of men's actual sentiments, still, as men's sentiments, both of favor and of aversion, are greatly influenced by what they suppose to be the effects of things upon their happiness, the principle of utility, or, as Bentham latterly called it, the greatest-happiness principle, has had a large share in forming the moral doctrines even of those who most scornfully reject its authority. Nor is there any school of thought which refuses to admit that the influence of actions on happiness is a most material and even predominant consideration in many of the details of morals, however unwilling to acknowledge it as the fundamental principle of morality and the source of moral obligation. I might go much further, and say that, to all those *a priori* moralists who deem it necessary to argue at all, utilitarian arguments are indispensable. It is not my present purpose to criticize these thinkers, but I cannot help referring, for illustration, to a systematic treatise by one of the most illustrious of them—the *Metaphysics of Ethics*, by Kant. This remarkable man, whose system of thought will long remain one of the landmarks in the history of philosophical speculation, does, in the treatise in question, lay down a universal first principle as the origin and ground of moral obligation. It is this: "So act, that the rule on which thou actest would admit of being adopted as a law by all rational beings." But when he begins to deduce from this precept any of the actual duties of morality, he fails, almost grotesquely, to show that there would be any contradiction, any logical (not to say physical) impossibility, in the adoption by all rational beings of the most outrageously immoral rules of conduct. All he shows is that the *consequences* of their universal adoption would be such as no one would choose to incur.

On the present occasion, I shall, without further discussion of the other theories, attempt to contribute something towards the understanding and appreciation of the Utilitarian or Happiness theory and towards such proof as it is susceptible of. It is evident that this cannot be proof in the ordinary and popular meaning of the term. Questions of ultimate ends are not amenable to direct proof. Whatever can be proved to be good, must be so by being shown to be a means to something admitted to be good without proof. The medical art is proved to be good by its conducing to health, but how is it possible to prove that health is good? The art of music is good, for the reason, among others, that it produces pleasure, but what proof is it

possible to give that pleasure is good? If, then, it is asserted that there is a comprehensive formula, including all things which are in themselves good, and that whatever else is good is not so as an end, but as a mean, the formula may be accepted or rejected, but is not a subject of what is commonly understood by proof. We are not, however, to infer that its acceptance or rejection must depend on blind impulse or arbitrary choice. There is a larger meaning of the word "proof," in which this question is as amenable to it as any other of the disputed questions of philosophy. The subject is within the cognizance of the rational faculty, and neither does that faculty deal with it solely in the way of intuition. Considerations may be presented capable of determining the intellect either to give or withhold its assent to the doctrine, and this is equivalent to proof.

We shall examine presently of what nature are these considerations, in what manner they apply to the case, and what rational grounds, therefore, can be given for accepting or rejecting the utilitarian formula. But it is a preliminary condition of rational acceptance or rejection that the formula should be correctly understood. I believe that the very imperfect notion ordinarily formed of its meaning is the chief obstacle which impedes its reception, and that, could it be cleared even from only the grosser misconceptions, the question would be greatly simplified, and a large proportion of its difficulties removed. Before, therefore, I attempt to enter into the philosophical grounds which can be given for assenting to the utilitarian standard, I shall offer some illustrations of the doctrine itself, with the view of showing more clearly what it is, distinguishing it from what it is not, and disposing of such of the practical objections to it as either originate in, or are closely connected with, mistaken interpretations of its meaning. Having thus prepared the ground, I shall afterwards endeavor to throw such light as I can upon the question, considered as one of philosophical theory.

II. WHAT UTILITARIANISM IS

A passing remark is all that needs be given to the ignorant blunder of supposing that those who stand up for utility, as the test of right and wrong, use the term in that restricted and merely colloquial sense in which utility is opposed to pleasure. An apology is due to the philosophical opponents of utilitarianism for even the momentary appearance of confounding them with any one capable of so absurd a misconception, which is the more extraordinary, inasmuch as the contrary accusation, of referring every thing to pleasure, and that, too, in its grossest form, is another of the common charges against utilitarianism, and, as has been pointedly remarked by an able writer, the same sort of persons, and often the very same persons, denounce the theory "as impracticably dry when the word 'utility' precedes the word 'pleasure,' and as too practicably voluptuous when the word 'pleasure' precedes the word 'utility.' " Those who know any thing about the matter are aware that every writer from Epicurus to Bentham who maintained the theory of utility meant by it, not something to be contradistinguished from pleasure, but pleasure itself, together with exemption from pain, and, instead of opposing the useful to the agreeable or the ornamental, have always declared that the useful means these, among other things. Yet the common herd, including the herd of writers, not only in newspapers and periodicals, but in books of weight and pretension, are perpetually falling into this shallow mistake. Having caught up the word "utilitarian," while knowing nothing whatever about it but its sound, they habitually express by it the rejection or the neglect of pleasure in some of its forms, of beauty, of ornament, or of amusement. Nor is the term thus ignorantly misapplied solely in disparagement, but occasionally in compliment, as though it implied superiority to frivolity and the mere pleasures of the moment. And this perverted use is the only one in which the word is popularly known, and the one from which the new generation are acquiring their sole notion of its meaning. Those who introduced the word, but who had for many years discontinued it as a distinctive appellation, may well feel themselves called upon to resume it, if by doing so they can hope to contribute any thing towards rescuing it from this utter degradation.

The creed which accepts as the foundation of morals Utility, or the Greatest-happiness Principle, holds that actions are right in proportion as they tend to promote happiness, wrong as they tend to produce the reverse of happiness. By happiness is intended pleasure and the absence of pain, by unhappiness, pain and the privation of pleasure. To give a clear view of the moral standard set up by the theory, much more requires to be said, in particular, what things it includes in the ideas of pain and pleasure, and to what extent this is left an open question. But these supplementary explanations do not affect the theory of life on which this theory of morality is grounded—namely, that pleasure and freedom from pain are the only things desirable as ends, and that all desirable things (which are as numerous in the utilitarian as in any other scheme) are desirable either for the pleasure inherent in themselves, or as means to the promotion of pleasure and the prevention of pain.

Now, such a theory of life excites in many minds, and among them in some of the most estimable in feeling and purpose, inveterate dislike. To suppose that life has (as they express it) no higher end than pleasure—no better and nobler object of desire and pursuit—they designate as utterly mean and groveling, as a doctrine worthy only of swine, to whom the followers of Epicurus were, at a very early period, contemptuously likened; and modern holders of the doctrine are occasionally made the subject of equally polite comparisons by its German, French, and English assailants.

When thus attacked, the Epicureans have always answered, that it is not they, but their accusers, who represent human nature in a degrading light, since the accusation supposes human beings to be capable of no pleasures except those of which swine are capable. If this supposition were true, the charge could not be gainsaid but would then be no longer an imputation; for, if the sources of pleasure were precisely the same to human beings and to swine, the rule of life which is good enough for the one would be good enough for the other. The comparison of the Epicurean life to that of beasts is felt as degrading, precisely because a beast's pleasures do not satisfy a human being's conceptions of happiness. Human beings have faculties more elevated than the animal appetites, and, when once made conscious of them, do not regard anything as happiness which does not include their gratification. I do not, indeed, consider the Epicureans to have been by any means faultless in drawing out their scheme of consequences from the utilitarian principle. To do this in any sufficient manner, many Stoic as well as Christian elements require to be included. But there is no known Epicurean theory of life which does not assign to the pleasures of the intellect, of the feelings and imagination, and of the moral sentiments, a much higher value as pleasures than to those of mere sensation. It must be admitted, however, that utilitarian writers in general have placed the superiority of mental over bodily pleasures chiefly in the greater permanency, safety, uncostliness, etc., of the former—that is, in their circumstantial advantages rather than in their intrinsic nature. And, on all these points, utilitarians have fully proved their case, but they might have taken the other, and, as it may be called, higher ground, with entire consistency. It is quite compatible with the principle of utility to recognize the fact that some *kinds* of pleasure are more desirable and more valuable than others. It would be absurd that while, in estimating all other things, quality is considered as well as quantity, the estimation of pleasures should be supposed to depend on quantity alone.

If I am asked what I mean by difference of quality in pleasures, or what makes one pleasure more valuable than another, merely as a pleasure, except its being greater in amount, there is but one possible answer. Of two pleasures, if there be one to which all or almost all

who have experience of both give a decided preference, irrespective of any feeling of moral obligation to prefer it, that is the more desirable pleasure. If one of the two is, by those who are competently acquainted with both, placed so far above the other that they prefer it, even though knowing it to be attended with a greater amount of discontent, and would not resign it for any quantity of the other pleasure which their nature is capable of, we are justified in ascribing to the preferred enjoyment a superiority in quality so far outweighing quantity, as to render it, in comparison, of small account.

Now, it is an unquestionable fact, that those who are equally acquainted with and equally capable of appreciating and enjoying both do give a most marked preference to the manner of existence which employs their higher faculties. Few human creatures would consent to be changed into any of the lower animals for a promise of the fullest allowance of a beast's pleasures; no intelligent human being would consent to be a fool, no instructed person would be an ignoramus, no person of feeling and conscience would be selfish and base, even though they should be persuaded that the fool, the dunce, or the rascal is better satisfied with his lot than they are with theirs. They would not resign what they possess more than he for the most complete satisfaction of all the desires which they have in common with him. If they ever fancy they would, it is only in cases of unhappiness so extreme that, to escape from it, they would exchange their lot for almost any other, however undesirable in their own eyes. A being of higher faculties requires more to make him happy, is capable probably of more acute suffering, and certainly accessible to it at more points, than one of an inferior type, but, in spite of these liabilities, he can never really wish to sink into what he feels to be a lower grade of existence. We may give what explanation we please of this unwillingness: we may attribute it to pride, a name which is given indiscriminately to some of the most and to some of the least estimable feelings of which mankind are capable; we may refer it to the love of liberty and personal independence—an appeal to which was with the Stoics one of the most effective means for the inculcation of it; to the love of power, or to the love of excitement, both of which do really enter into and contribute to it; but its most appropriate appellation is a sense of dignity, which all human beings possess in one form or other, and in some, though by no means in exact, proportion to their higher faculties, and which is so essential a part of the happiness of those in whom it is strong, that nothing which conflicts with it could be, otherwise than momentarily, an object of desire to them. Whoever supposes that this preference takes place at a sacrifice of happiness, that the superior being, in any thing like equal circumstances, is not happier than the inferior—confounds the two very different ideas of happiness and content. It is indisputable that the being whose capacities of enjoyment are low has the greatest chance of having them fully satisfied, and a highly endowed being will always feel that any happiness which he can look for, as the world is constituted, is imperfect. But he can learn to bear its imperfections, if they are at all bearable, and they will not make him envy the being who is indeed unconscious of the imperfections, but only because he feels not at all the good which those imperfections qualify. It is better to be a human being dissatisfied than a pig satisfied, better to be Socrates dissatisfied than a fool satisfied. And if the fool or the pig are of a different opinion, it is because they only know their own side of the question. The other party to the comparison knows both sides.

It may be objected that many who are capable of the higher pleasures occasionally, under the influence of temptation, postpone them to the lower. But this is quite compatible with a full appreciation of the intrinsic superiority of the higher. Men often, from infirmity of character, make their election for the nearer good, though they know it to be the less valuable, and this no less when the choice is between two bodily pleasures than when it is between bodily and mental. They pursue sensual indulgences to the injury of health, though perfectly aware that health is the greater good. It may be further objected, that many who begin with youthful enthusiasm for everything noble, as they advance in years sink into indolence and selfishness. But I do not believe that those who undergo this very common change voluntarily choose the lower description of pleasures in preference to the higher. I believe that, before they devote themselves exclusively to the one, they have already become incapable of the other. Capacity for the nobler feelings is in most natures a very tender plant, easily killed, not only by hostile influences but by mere want of sustenance, and, in the majority of young persons, it speedily dies away if the occupations to which their position in life has devoted them, and the society into which it has thrown them, are not favorable to keeping that higher capacity in exercise. Men lose their high aspirations as they lose their intellectual tastes, because they have not time or opportunity for indulging them, and they addict themselves to inferior pleasures, not because they deliberately prefer them, but because they are either the only ones to which they have access or the only ones which they are any longer capable of enjoying. It may be questioned whether any one who has remained equally susceptible to both classes of pleasures ever knowingly and calmly preferred the lower, though many in all ages have broken down in an ineffectual attempt to combine both.

From this verdict of the only competent judges, I apprehend there can be no appeal. On a question which is the best worth having of two pleasures, or which of two modes of existence is the most grateful to the feelings, apart from its moral attributes and from its consequences, the judgment of those who are qualified by knowledge of both, or, if they differ, that of the majority among them, must be admitted as final. And there needs be the less hesitation to accept this judgment respecting the quality of pleasures, since there is no other tribunal to be referred to even on the question of quantity. What means are there of determining which is the acutest of two pains, or the intensest of two pleasurable sensations, except the general suffrage of those who are familiar with both? Neither pains nor pleasures are homogeneous, and pain is always heterogeneous with pleasure. What is there to decide whether a particular pleasure is worth purchasing at the cost of a particular pain, except the feelings and judgment of the experienced? When, therefore, those feelings and judgment declare the pleasures derived from the higher faculties to be preferable *in kind*, apart from the question of intensity, to those of which the animal nature disjoined from the higher faculties is susceptible, they are entitled on this subject to the same regard.

I have dwelt on this point, as being a necessary part of a perfectly just conception of Utility or Happiness, considered as the directive rule of human conduct. But it is by no means an indispensable condition to the acceptance of the utilitarian standard, for that standard is not the agent's own greatest happiness, but the greatest amount of happiness altogether; and if it may possibly be doubted whether a noble character is always the happier for its nobleness, there can be no doubt that it makes other people happier, and that the world in general is immensely a gainer by it. Utilitarianism, therefore, could only attain its end by the general cultivation of nobleness of character, even if each individual were only benefited by the nobleness of others, and his own, so far as happiness is concerned, were a sheer deduction from the benefit. But the bare enunciation of such an absurdity as this last renders refutation superfluous.

According to the Greatest-happiness Principle, as above explained, the ultimate end with reference to and for the sake of which all other things are desirable (whether we are considering our own good or that of other people) is an existence exempt as far as possible from pain, and as rich as possible in enjoyments, both in point of quantity and quality; the test of quality, and the rule for measuring it against quantity, being the preference felt by those who in their opportunities of experience, to which must be added their habits of self-consciousness and self-observation, are best furnished with the means of comparison. This being, according to the utilitarian opinion, the end of human action is necessarily also the standard of morality; which may accordingly be defined, the rules

and precepts for human conduct by the observance of which an existence such as has been described might be, to the greatest extent possible, secured to all mankind, and not to them only but, so far as the nature of things admits, to the whole sentient creation.

Against this doctrine, however, arises another class of objectors who say that happiness, in any form, cannot be the rational purpose of human life and action, because, in the first place, it is unattainable; and they contemptuously ask, What right has thou to be happy? a question which Mr. Carlyle clinches by the addition, What right, a short time ago, hadst thou even *to be*? Next they say that men can do *without* happiness, that all noble human beings have felt this, and could not have become noble but by learning the lesson of *Entsagen* or renunciation, which lesson, thoroughly learned and submitted to, they affirm to be the beginning and necessary condition of all virtue.

The first of these objections would go to the root of the matter, were it well founded; for, if no happiness is to be had at all by human beings, the attainment of it cannot be the end of morality, or of any rational conduct. Though, even in that case, something might still be said for the utilitarian theory, since utility includes not solely the pursuit of happiness, but the prevention or mitigation of unhappiness; and, if the former aim be chimerical, there will be all the greater scope and more imperative need for the latter, so long at least as mankind think fit to live, and do not take refuge in the simultaneous act of suicide recommended under certain conditions by Novalis. When, however, it is thus positively asserted to be impossible that human life should be happy, the assertion, if not something like a verbal quibble, is at least an exaggeration. If by happiness be meant a continuity of highly pleasurable excitement, it is evident enough that this is impossible. A state of exalted pleasure lasts only moments, or in some cases, and with some intermissions, hours or days, and is the occasional brilliant flash of enjoyment, not its permanent and steady flame. Of this the philosophers who have taught that happiness is the end of life were as fully aware as those who taunt them. The happiness which they meant was not a life of rapture, but moments of such, in an existence made up of few and transitory pains, many and various pleasures, with a decided predominance of the active over the passive, and having, as the foundation of the whole, not to expect more from life than it is capable of bestowing. A life thus composed, to those who have been fortunate enough to obtain it, has always appeared worthy of the name of "happiness." And such an existence is even now the lot of many, during some considerable portion of their lives. The present wretched education and wretched social arrangements are the only real hindrance to its being attainable by almost all.

The objectors, perhaps, may doubt whether human beings, if taught to consider happiness as the end of life, would be satisfied with such a moderate share of it. But great numbers of mankind have been satisfied with much less. The main constituents of a satisfied life appear to be two, either of which by itself is often found sufficient for the purpose—tranquillity and excitement. With much tranquillity, many find that they can be content with very little pleasure; with much excitement, many can reconcile themselves to a considerable quantity of pain. There is assuredly no inherent impossibility in enabling even the mass of mankind to unite both, since the two are so far from being incompatible, that they are in natural alliance, the prolongation of either being a preparation for, and exciting a wish for, the other. It is only those in whom indolence amounts to a vice that do not desire excitement after an interval of repose; it is only those in whom the need of excitement is a disease, that feel the tranquillity which follows excitement dull and insipid, instead of pleasurable in direct proportion to the excitement which preceded it. When people who are tolerably fortunate in their outward lot do not find in life sufficient enjoyment to make it valuable to them, the cause generally is caring for nobody but themselves. To those who have neither public nor private affections, the excitements of life are much curtailed and, in any case, dwindle in value as the time approaches when all selfish interests must be terminated by death; while those who leave after them objects of personal affection, and especially those who have also cultivated a fellow feeling with the collective interests of mankind, retain as lively an interest in life on the eve of death as in the vigor of youth and health. Next to selfishness, the principal cause which makes life unsatisfactory is want of mental cultivation. A cultivated mind—I do not mean that of a philosopher, but any mind to which the fountains of knowledge have been opened, and which has been taught, in any tolerable degree, to exercise its faculties—finds sources of inexhaustible interest in all that surrounds it, in the objects of nature, the achievements of art, the imaginations of poetry, the incidents of history, the ways of mankind past and present, and their prospects in the future. It is possible, indeed, to become indifferent to all this, and that, too, without having exhausted a thousandth part of it, but only when one has had from the beginning no moral or human interest in these things, and has sought in them only the gratification of curiosity.

Now there is absolutely no reason in the nature of things why an amount of mental culture sufficient to give an intelligent interest in these objects of contemplation should not be the inheritance of every one born in a civilized country. As little is there an inherent necessity that any human being should be a selfish egoist, devoid of every feeling or care but those which center in his own miserable individuality. Something far superior to this is sufficiently common even now to give ample earnest of what the human species may be made. Genuine private affections and a sincere interest in the public good are possible, though in unequal degrees, to every rightly brought up human being. In a world in which there is so much to interest, so much to enjoy, and so much also to correct and improve, every one who has this moderate amount of moral and intellectual requisites is capable of an existence which may be called enviable; and unless such a person, through bad laws or subjection to the will of others, is denied the liberty to use the sources of happiness

within his reach, he will not fail to find this enviable existence, if he escape the positive evils
of life, the great sources of physical and mental
suffering—such as indigence, disease, and the
unkindness, worthlessness, or premature loss,
of objects of affection. The main stress of the
problem lies, therefore, in the contest with
these calamities, from which it is a rare good
fortune entirely to escape, which, as things now
are, cannot be obviated, and often cannot be in
any material degree mitigated. Yet no one
whose opinion deserves a moment's consideration can doubt that most of the great positive
evils of the world are in themselves removable,
and will, if human affairs continue to improve,
be in the end reduced within narrow limits.
Poverty, in any sense implying suffering, may
be completely extinguished by the wisdom of
society, combined with the good sense and
providence of individuals. Even that most intractable of enemies, disease, may be indefinitely reduced in dimensions by good physical
and moral education, and proper control of nox-
ious influence, while the progress of science
holds out a promise for the future of still more
direct conquests over this detestable foe. And
every advance in that direction relieves us from
some, not only of the chances which cut short
our own lives but, what concerns us still more,
which deprive us of those in whom our happiness is wrapped up. As for vicissitudes of fortune and other disappointments connected with
worldly circumstances, these are principally the
effect either of gross imprudence, of ill-
regulated desires, or of bad or imperfect social
institutions. All the grand sources, in short, of
human suffering are in a great degree, many of
them almost entirely, conquerable by human
care and effort; and though their removal is
grievously slow, though a long succession of
generations will perish in the breach before the
conquest is completed, and this world becomes
all that, if will and knowledge were not wanting, it might easily be made—yet every mind
sufficiently intelligent and generous to bear a
part, however small and inconspicuous, in the
endeavor will draw a noble enjoyment from the
contest itself, which he would not, for any bribe

in the form of selfish indulgence, consent to be
without.

And this leads to the true estimation of what
is said by the objectors concerning the possibility and the obligation of learning to do without
happiness. Unquestionably, it is possible to do
without happiness; it is done involuntarily by
nineteen-twentieths of mankind, even in those
parts of our present world which are least deep
in barbarism, and it often has to be done voluntarily by the hero or the martyr, for the sake of
something which he prizes more than his individual happiness. But this something—what is
it, unless the happiness of others, or some of
the requisites of happiness? It is noble to be capable of resigning entirely one's own portion of
happiness, or chances of it; but, after all, this
self-sacrifice must be for some end; it is not its
own end, and if we are told that its end is not
happiness but virtue, which is better than happiness, I ask, Would the sacrifice be made if
the hero or martyr did not believe that it would
earn for others immunity from similar sacrifices? Would it be made if he thought that his
renunciation of happiness for himself would
produce no fruit for any of his fellow-creatures
but to make their lot like his, and place them
also in the condition of persons who have renounced happiness? All honor to those who can
abnegate for themselves the personal enjoyment
of life, when by such renunciation they contribute worthily to increase the amount of happiness in the world, but he who does it, or
professes to do it, for any other purpose is no
more deserving of admiration than the ascetic
mounted on his pillar. He may be an inspiring
proof of what men *can* do, but assuredly not an
example of what they *should*.

Though it is only in a very imperfect state
of the world's arrangements that any one can
best serve the happiness of others by the absolute sacrifice of his own, yet, so long as the
world is in that imperfect state, I fully acknowledge that the readiness to make such a sacrifice
is the highest virtue which can be found in
man. I will add that in this condition of the
world, paradoxical as the assertion may be, the
conscious ability to do without happiness gives

the best prospect of realizing such happiness as is attainable. For nothing except that consciousness can raise a person above the chances of life, by making him feel that, let fate and fortune do their worst, they have not power to subdue him; which, once felt, frees him from excess of anxiety concerning the evils of life, and enables him, like many a Stoic in the worst times of the Roman Empire, to cultivate in tranquillity the sources of satisfaction accessible to him, without concerning himself about the uncertainty of their duration, any more than about their inevitable end.

Meanwhile, let utilitarians never cease to claim the morality of self-devotion as a possession which belongs by as good a right to them as either to the Stoic or to the Transcendentalist. The utilitarian morality does recognize in human beings the power of sacrificing their own greatest good for the good of others. It only refuses to admit that the sacrifice is itself a good. A sacrifice which does not increase, or tend to increase, the sum total of happiness, it considers as wasted. The only self-renunciation which it applauds is devotion to the happiness, or to some of the means of happiness, of others, either of mankind collectively, or of individuals within the limits imposed by the collective interests of mankind.

I must again repeat what the assailants of utilitarianism seldom have the justice to acknowledge, that the happiness which forms the utilitarian standard of what is right in conduct is not the agent's own happiness but that of all concerned. As between his own happiness and that of others, utilitarianism requires him to be as strictly impartial as a disinterested and benevolent spectator. In the golden rule of Jesus of Nazareth, we read the complete spirit of the ethics of utility. To do as you would be done by, and to love your neighbor as yourself, constitute the ideal perfection of utilitarian morality. As the means of making the nearest approach to this ideal, utility would enjoin, first, that laws and social arrangements should place the happiness or (as, speaking practically, it may be called) the interest of every individual as nearly as possible in harmony with the interest of the whole; and secondly, that education and opinion, which have so vast a power over human character, should so use that power as to establish in the mind of every individual an indissoluble association between his own happiness and the good of the whole—especially between his own happiness, and the practice of such modes of conduct, negative and positive, as regard for the universal happiness prescribes—so that not only he may be unable to conceive the possibility of happiness to himself consistently with conduct opposed to the general good, but also that a direct impulse to promote the general good may be in every individual one of the habitual motives of action, and the sentiments connected therewith may fill a large and prominent place in every human being's sentient existence. If the impugners of the utilitarian morality represented it to their own minds in this its true character, I know not what recommendation possessed by any other morality they could possibly affirm to be wanting to it, what more beautiful or more exalted developments of human nature any other ethical system can be supposed to foster, or what springs of action, not accessible to the utilitarian, such systems rely on for giving effect to their mandates.

The objectors to utilitarianism cannot always be charged with representing it in a discreditable light. On the contrary, those among them who entertain any thing like a just idea of its disinterested character sometimes find fault with its standard as being too high for humanity. They say it is exacting too much to require that people shall always act from the inducement of promoting the general interests of society. But this is to mistake the very meaning of a standard of morals, and confound the rule of action with the motive of it. It is the business of ethics to tell us what are our duties or by what test we may know them, but no system of ethics requires that the sole motive of all we do shall be a feeling of duty; on the contrary, ninety-nine hundredths of all our actions are done from other motives, and rightly so done, if the rule of duty does not condemn them. It is the more unjust to utilitarianism that this particular misapprehension should be made a ground of ob-

jection to it, inasmuch as utilitarian moralists
have gone beyond almost all others in affirming
that the motive has nothing to do with the morality of the action though much with the worth
of the agent. He who saves a fellow creature
from drowning does what is morally right,
whether his motive be duty or the hope of being
paid for his trouble; he who betrays the friend
that trusts him is guilty of a crime, even if his
object be to serve another friend to whom he is
under greater obligations. But to speak only of
actions done from the motive of duty, and in
direct obedience to principle: it is a misapprehension of the utilitarian mode of thought to
conceive it as implying that people should fix
their minds upon so wide a generality as the
world or society at large. The great majority of
good actions are intended, not for the benefit of
the world but for that of individuals, of which
the good of the world is made up; and the
thoughts of the most virtuous man need not on
these occasions travel beyond the particular persons concerned, except so far as is necessary to
assure himself that, in benefiting them, he is
not violating the rights—that is, the legitimate
and authorized expectations—of any one else.
The multiplication of happiness is, according to
the utilitarian ethics, the object of virtue; the
occasions on which any person (except one in a
thousand) has it in his power to do this on an
extended scale—in other words, to be a public
benefactor—are but exceptional, and on these
occasions alone is he called on to consider public utility; in every other case, private utility,
the interest or happiness of some few persons,
is all he has to attend to. Those alone, the influence of whose actions extends to society in
general, need concern themselves habitually
about so large an object. In the case of absti-
nences indeed—of things which people forbear
to do from moral considerations, though the
consequences in the particular case might be
beneficial—it would be unworthy of an intelligent agent not to be consciously aware that the
action is of a class which, if practised generally, would be generally injurious, and that this
is the ground of the obligation to abstain from
it. The amount of regard for the public interest

implied in this recognition is no greater than is
demanded by every system of morals, for they
all enjoin to abstain from whatever is manifestly
pernicious to society.

The same considerations dispose of another
reproach against the doctrine of utility, founded
on a still grosser misconception of the purpose
of a standard of morality, and of the very meaning of the words "right" and "wrong." It is
often affirmed that utilitarianism renders men
cold and unsympathizing, that it chills their
moral feelings toward individuals, that it makes
them regard only the dry and hard consideration of the consequences of actions, not taking
into their moral estimate the qualities from
which those actions emanate. If the assertion
means that they do not allow their judgment respecting the rightness or wrongness of an action
to be influenced by their opinion of the qualities
of the person who does it, this is a complaint,
not against utilitarianism but against having any
standard of morality at all; for certainly no
known ethical standard decides an action to be
good or bad because it is done by a good or bad
man, still less because done by an amiable, a
brave, or a benevolent man, or the contrary.
These considerations are relevant, not to the estimation of actions, but of persons, and there is
nothing in the utilitarian theory inconsistent
with the fact that there are other things which
interest us in persons besides the rightness and
wrongness of their actions. The Stoics indeed,
with the paradoxical misuse of language which
was part of their system and by which they
strove to raise themselves above all concern
about any thing but virtue, were fond of saying
that he who has that has everything, that he,
and only he, is rich, is beautiful, is a king. But
no claim of this description is made for the virtuous man by the utilitarian doctrine. Utilitarians are quite aware that there are other
desirable possessions and qualities besides virtue, and are perfectly willing to allow to all of
them their full worth. They are also aware that
a right action does not necessarily indicate a
virtuous character, and that actions which are
blamable often proceed from qualities entitled
to praise. When this is apparent in any particu-

lar case, it modifies their estimation, not certainly of the act but of the agent. I grant that they are notwithstanding of opinion that, in the long run, the best proof of a good character is good actions, and resolutely refuse to consider any mental disposition as good, of which the predominant tendency is to produce bad conduct. This makes them unpopular with many people; but it is an unpopularity which they must share with every one who regards the distinction between right and wrong in a serious light, and the reproach is not one which a conscientious utilitarian need be anxious to repel.

If no more be meant by the objection than that many utilitarians look on the morality of actions, as measured by the utilitarian standards, with too exclusive a regard, and do not lay sufficient stress upon the other beauties of character which go towards making a human being lovable or admirable, this may be admitted. Utilitarians who have cultivated their moral feelings but not their sympathies nor their artistic perceptions, do fall into this mistake, and so do all other moralists under the same conditions. What can be said in excuse for other moralists is equally available for them, namely that, if there is to be any error, it is better that it should be on that side. As a matter of fact, we may affirm that among utilitarians, as among adherents of other systems, there is every imaginable degree of rigidity and of laxity in the application of their standard; some are even puritanically rigorous, while others are as indulgent as can possibly be desired by sinner or by sentimentalist. But on the whole, a doctrine which brings prominently forward the interest that mankind have in the repression and prevention of conduct which violates the moral law, is likely to be inferior to no other in turning the sanctions of opinion against such violations. It is true, the question, What does violate the moral law? is one on which those who recognize different standards of morality are likely now and then to differ. But difference of opinion on moral questions was not first introduced into the world by utilitarianism, while that doctrine does supply, if not always an easy, at all events a tangible and intelligible mode of deciding such differences.

It may not be superfluous to notice a few more of the common misapprehensions of utilitarian ethics, even those which are so obvious and gross that it might appear impossible for any person of candor and intelligence to fall into them, since persons even of considerable mental endowments often give themselves so little trouble to understand the bearings of any opinion against which they entertain a prejudice, and men are in general so little conscious of this voluntary ignorance as a defect, that the vulgarest misunderstandings of ethical doctrines are continually met with the deliberate writings of persons of the greatest pretensions both to high principle and to philosophy. We not uncommonly hear the doctrine of utility inveighed against as a *godless* doctrine. If it be necessary to say any thing at all against so mere an assumption, we may say that the question depends upon what idea we have formed of the moral character of the Deity. If it be a true belief that God desires, above all things, the happiness of his creatures, and that this was his purpose in their creation, utility is not only not a godless doctrine but more profoundly religious than any other. If it be meant that utilitarianism does not recognize the revealed will of God as the supreme law of morals, I answer that a utilitarian, who believes in the perfect goodness and wisdom of God, necessarily believes that whatever God has thought fit to reveal on the subject of morals must fulfil the requirements of utility in a supreme degree. But others besides utilitarians have been of opinion that the Christian revelation was intended, and is fitted, to inform the hearts and minds of mankind with a spirit which should enable them to find for themselves what is right and incline them to do it when found, rather than to tell them, except in a very general way, what it is, and that we need a doctrine of ethics, carefully followed out, to *interpret* to us the will of God. Whether this opinion is correct or not, it is superfluous here to discuss, since whatever aid religion, either natural or revealed, can afford to ethical investigation, is as open to the utilitarian moralist as to any other. He can use it as the testimony of God to the usefulness or hurtfulness of any given course of action, by as good a right as others can use it for the indication of a transcendental law, having no connection with usefulness or with happiness.

Again: Utility is often summarily stigmatized as an immoral doctrine by giving it the name of Expediency and, taking advantage of the popular use of that term, to contrast it with Principle. But the Expedient, in the sense in which it is opposed to the Right, generally means that which is expedient for the particular interest of the agent himself, as when a minister sacrifices the interests of his country to keep himself in place. When it means any thing better than this, it means that which is expedient for some immediate object, some temporary purpose, but which violates a rule whose observance is expedient in a much higher degree. The Expedient, in this sense, instead of being the same thing with the useful, is a branch of the hurtful. Thus it would often be expedient, for the purpose of getting over some momentary embarrassment or attaining some object immediately useful to ourselves or others, to tell a lie. But inasmuch as the cultivation in ourselves of a sensitive feeling on the subject of veracity is one of the most useful, and the enfeeblement of that feeling one of those most hurtful, things to which our conduct can be instrumental, and inasmuch as any, even unintentional, deviation from truth does that much towards weakening the trustworthiness of human assertion, which is not only the principal support of all present social well-being, but the insufficiency of which does more than any one thing that can be named to keep back civilization, virtue, every thing on which human happiness on the largest scale depends—we feel that the violation, for a present advantage, of a rule of such transcendent expediency is not expedient, and that he who, for the sake of a convenience to himself or to some other individual, does what depends on him to deprive mankind of the good, and inflict upon them the evil, involved in the greater or less reliance which they can place in each other's word, acts the part of one of their worst enemies. Yet that even this rule, sacred as it is, admits of possible exceptions is acknowledged by all moralists, the chief of which is, when the

withholding of some fact (as of information from a malefactor, or of bad news from a person dangerously ill) would save an individual (especially an individual other than one's self) from great and unmerited evil and when the withholding can only be effected by denial. But in order that the exception may not extend itself beyond the need and may have the least possible effect in weakening reliance on veracity, it ought to be recognized and, if possible, its limits defined, and, if the principle of utility is good for any thing, it must be good for weighing these conflicting utilities against one another, and marking out the region within which one or the other preponderates.

Again: defenders of utility often find themselves called upon to reply to such objections as this—that there is not time, previous to action, for calculating and weighing the effects of any line of conduct on the general happiness. This is exactly as if any one were to say that it is impossible to guide our conduct by Christianity, because there is not time, on every occasion on which any thing has to be done, to read through the Old and New Testaments. The answer to the objection is that there has been ample time, namely, the whole past duration of the human species. During all that time, mankind have been learning by experience the tendencies of actions, on which experience all the prudence as well as all the morality of life are dependent. People talk as if the commencement of this course of experience had hitherto been put off and as if, at the moment when some man feels tempted to meddle with the property or life of another, he had to begin considering for the first time whether murder and theft are injurious to human happiness. Even then, I do not think that he would find the question very puzzling, but at all events the matter is now done to his hand. It is truly a whimsical supposition that, if mankind were agreed in considering utility to be the test of morality, they would remain without any agreement as to what *is* useful, and would take no measures for having their notions on the subject taught to the young and enforced by law and opinion. There is no difficulty in proving any ethical standard whatever to work ill, if we suppose universal idiocy to be conjoined with it;

but on any hypothesis short of that, mankind must by this time have acquired positive beliefs as to the effects of some actions on their happiness, and the beliefs which have thus come down are the rules of morality for the multitude, and for the philosopher, until he has succeeded in finding better. That philosophers might easily do this, even now, on many subjects, that the received code of ethics is by no means of divine right, and that mankind have still much to learn as to the effects of actions on the general happiness—I admit or, rather, earnestly maintain. The corollaries from the principle of utility, like the precepts of every practical art, admit of indefinite improvement and, in a progressive state of the human mind, their improvement is perpetually going on. But to consider the rules of morality as improvable is one thing; to pass over the intermediate generalizations entirely, and endeavor to test each individual action directly by the first principle, is another. It is a strange notion, that the acknowledgment of a first principle is inconsistent with the admission of secondary ones. To inform a traveler respecting the place of his ultimate destination is not to forbid the use of landmarks and direction posts on the way. The proposition that happiness is the end and aim of morality does not mean that no road ought to be laid down to that goal, or that persons going thither should not be advised to take one direction rather than another. Men really ought to leave off talking a kind of nonsense on this subject which they would neither talk nor listen to on other matters of practical concernment. Nobody argues that the art of navigation is not founded on astronomy, because sailors cannot wait to calculate the ''Nautical Almanac.'' Being rational creatures, they go to sea with it ready calculated, and all rational creatures go out upon the sea of life with their minds made up on the common questions of right and wrong, as well as on many of the far more difficult questions of wise and foolish. And this, as long as foresight is a human quality, it is to be presumed they will continue to do. Whatever we adopt as the fundamental principle of morality, we require subordinate principles to apply it by; the impossibility of doing without them, be-

ing common to all systems, can afford no argument against any one in particular; but gravely to argue as if no such secondary principles could be had, and as if mankind had remained till now and always must remain without drawing any general conclusions from the experience of human life, is as high a pitch, I think, as absurdity has ever reached in philosophical controversy.

The remainder of the stock arguments against utilitarianism mostly consist in laying to its charge the common infirmities of human nature, and the general difficulties which embarrass conscientious persons in shaping their course through life. We are told that an utilitarian will be apt to make his own particular case an exception to moral rules and, when under temptation, will see a utility in the breach of a rule greater than he will see in its observance. But is utility the only creed which is able to furnish us with excuses for evil-doing, and means of cheating our own conscience? They are afforded in abundance by all doctrines which recognize as a fact in morals the existence of conflicting considerations, which all doctrines do that have been believed by sane persons. It is not the fault of any creed, but of the complicated nature of human affairs, that rules of conduct cannot be so framed as to require no exceptions, and that hardly any kind of action can safely be laid down as either always obligatory or always condemnable. There is no ethical creed which does not temper the rigidity of its laws by giving a certain latitude, under the moral responsibility of the agent, for accommodation to peculiarities of circumstances and, under every creed, at the opening thus made, self-deception and dishonest casuistry get in. There exists no moral system under which there do not arise unequivocal cases of conflicting obligation. These are the real difficulties, the knotty points both in the theory of ethics and in the conscientious guidance of personal conduct. They are overcome practically with greater or with less success according to the intellect and virtue of the individual, but it can hardly be pretended that any one will be the less qualified for dealing with them, from possessing an ultimate standard to which conflicting rights and duties can be referred. If utility is the ultimate source of moral obligations, utility may be invoked to decide between them when their demands are incompatible. Though the application of the standard may be difficult, it is better than none at all; while in other systems, the moral laws all claiming independent authority, there is no common umpire entitled to interfere between them, their claims to precedence one over another rest on little better than sophistry, and unless determined, as they generally are,

by the unacknowledged influence of considerations of utility, afford a free scope for the action of personal desires and partialities. We must remember that only in these cases of conflict between secondary principles is it requisite that first principles should be appealed to. There is no case of moral obligation in which some secondary principle is not involved and, if only one, there can seldom be any real doubt which one it is, in the mind of any person by whom the principle itself is recognized.

IMMANUEL KANT
Passage from Ordinary Rational Knowledge of Morality to Philosophical

THE GOOD WILL

It is impossible to conceive anything at all in the world, or even out of it, which can be taken as good without qualification, except a *good will*. Intelligence, wit, judgement, and any other *talents* of the mind we may care to name, or courage, resolution, and constancy of purpose, as qualities of *temperament*, are without doubt good and desirable in many respects; but they can also be extremely bad and hurtful when the will is not good which has to make use of these gifts of nature, and which for this reason has the term *'character'* applied to its peculiar quality. It is exactly the same with *gifts of fortune*. Power, wealth, honour, even health

and that complete well-being and contentment with one's state which goes by the name of *'happiness'*, produce boldness, and as a consequence often over-boldness as well, unless a good will is present by which their influence on the mind—and so too the whole principle of action—may be corrected and adjusted to universal ends; not to mention that a rational and impartial spectator can never feel approval in contemplating the uninterrupted prosperity of a being graced by no touch of a pure and good will, and that consequently a good will seems to constitute the indispensable condition of our very worthiness to be happy.

Some qualities are even helpful to this good will itself and can make its task very much easier. They have none the less no inner unconditioned worth, but rather presuppose a good will which sets a limit to the esteem in which they are rightly held and does not permit us to regard them as absolutely good. Moderation in affections and passions, self-control, and sober reflexion are not only good in many respects: they may even seem to constitute part of the *inner* worth of a person. Yet they are far from being properly described as good without qualification (however unconditionally they have been commended by the ancients). For without the principles of a good will they may become exceedingly bad; and the very coolness of a scoundrel makes him, not merely more dangerous, but also immediately more abominable in our eyes than we should have taken him to be without it.

THE GOOD WILL AND ITS RESULTS

A good will is not good because of what it effects or accomplishes—because of its fitness for attaining some proposed end: it is good through its willing alone—that is, good in itself. Considered in itself it is to be esteemed beyond comparison as far higher than anything it could ever bring about merely in order to favour some inclination or, if you like, the sum total of inclinations. Even if, by some special disfavour of destiny or by the niggardly endowment of stepmotherly nature, this will is entirely lacking in power to carry out its intentions; if by its utmost effort it still accomplishes nothing, and only good will is left (not, admittedly, as a mere wish, but as the straining of every means so far as they are in our control); even then it would still shine like a jewel for its own sake as something which has its full value in itself. Its usefulness or fruitlessness can neither add to, nor subtract from, this value. Its usefulness would be merely, as it were, the setting which enables us to handle it better in our ordinary dealings or to attract the attention of those not yet sufficiently expert, but not to commend it to experts or to determine its value.

THE FORMAL PRINCIPLE OF DUTY

Our second proposition is this: An action done from duty has its moral worth, *not in the purpose* to be attained by it, but in the maxim in accordance with which it is decided upon; it depends therefore, not on the realization of the object of the action, but solely on the principle of *volition* in accordance with which, irrespective of all objects of the faculty of desire, the action has been performed. That the purposes we may have in our actions, and also their effects considered as ends and motives of the will, can give to actions no unconditioned and moral worth is clear from what has gone before. Where then can this worth be found if we are not to find it in the will's relation to the effect hoped for from the action? It can be found nowhere but *in the principle of the will,* irrespective of the ends which can be brought about by such an action; for between its *a priori* principle, which is formal, and its *a posteriori* motive, which is material, the will stands, so to speak, at a parting of the ways; and since it must be determined by some principle, it will have to be determined by the formal principle of volition when an action is done from duty, where, as we have seen, every material principle is taken away from it.

REVERENCE FOR THE LAW

Our third proposition, as an inference from the two preceding, I would express thus: *Duty is the necessity to act out of reverence for the law.* For an object as the effect of my proposed action I can have an *inclination,* but *never reverence,* precisely because it is merely the effect, and not the activity, of a will. Similarly for inclination as such, whether my own or that of another, I cannot have reverence: I can at most in the first case approve, and in the second case sometimes even love—that is, regard it as favourable to my own advantage. Only something which is conjoined with my will solely as a ground and never as an effect—something which does not serve my inclination, but outweighs it or at least leaves it entirely out of account in my own choice—and therefore only bare law for its own sake, can be an object of reverence and therewith a command. Now an action done from duty has to set aside altogether the influence of inclination, and along with inclination every object of the will; so there is nothing left able to determine the will except objectively the *law*

and subjectively *pure reverence* for this practical law, and therefore the maxim[1] of obeying this law even to the detriment of all my inclinations.

Thus the moral worth of an action does not depend on the result expected from it, and so too does not depend on any principle of action that needs to borrow its motive from this expected result. For all these results (agreeable states and even the promotion of happiness in others) could have been brought about by other causes as well, and consequently their production did not require the will of a rational being, in which, however, the highest and unconditioned good can alone can be found. Therefore nothing but the *idea of the law* in itself, *which admittedly is present only in a rational being*— so far as it, and not an expected result, is the ground determining the will—can constitute that pre-eminent good which we call moral, a good which is already present in the person acting on this idea and has not to be awaited merely from the result.[2]

THE CATEGORICAL IMPERATIVE

But what kind of law can this be the thought of which, even without regard to the results expected from it, has to determine the will if this is to be called good absolutely and without qualification? Since I have robbed the will of every inducement that might arise for it as a consequence of obeying any particular law, nothing is left but the conformity of actions to universal law as such, and this alone must serve the will as its principle. That is to say, I ought never to act except in such a way *that I can also will that my maxim should become a universal law.* Here bare conformity to universal law as such (without having as its base any law prescribing particular actions) is what serves the will as its principle, and must so serve it if duty is not to be everywhere an empty delusion and a chimerical concept. The ordinary reason of

mankind also agrees with this completely in its practical judgements and always has the aforesaid principle before its eyes.

Take this question, for example. May I not, when I am hard pressed, make a promise with the intention of not keeping it? Here I readily distinguish the two senses which the question can have—Is it prudent, or is it right, to make a false promise? The first no doubt can often be the case. I do indeed see that it is not enough for me to extricate myself from present embarrassment by this subterfuge: I have to consider whether from this lie there may not subsequently accrue to me much greater inconvenience than that from which I now escape, and also—since, with all my supposed *astuteness,* to foresee the consequences is not so easy that I can be sure there is no chance, once confidence in me is lost, of this proving far more disadvantageous than all the ills I now think to avoid—whether it may not be a *more prudent* action to proceed here on a general maxim and make it my habit not to give a promise except with the intention of keeping it. Yet it becomes clear to me at once that such a maxim is always founded solely on fear of consequences. To tell the truth for the sake of duty is something entirely different from doing so out of concern for inconvenient results; for in the first case the concept of the action already contains in itself a law for me, while in the second case I have first of all to look around elsewhere in order to see what effects may be bound up with it for me. When I deviate from the principle of duty, this is quite certainly bad; but if I desert my prudential maxim, this can often be greatly to my advantage, though it is admittedly safer to stick to it. Suppose I seek, however, to learn in the quickest way and yet unerringly how to solve the problem 'Does a lying promise accord with duty?' I have then to ask myself 'Should I really be content that my maxim (the maxim of getting out of a difficulty by a false promise) should hold as a universal law (one valid both for myself and others)? And could I really say to myself that every one may make a false promise if he finds himself in a difficulty from which he can extricate himself in no other way?' I then become aware at once that I can

indeed will to lie, but I can by no means will a universal law of lying; for by such a law there could properly be no promises at all, since it would be futile to profess a will for future action to others who would not believe my profession or who, if they did so over-hastily, would pay me back in like coin; and consequently my maxim, as soon as it was made a universal law, would be bound to annul itself.

Thus I need no far-reaching ingenuity to find out what I have to do in order to possess a good will. Inexperienced in the course of world affairs and incapable of being prepared for all the chances that happen in it, I ask myself only 'Can you also will that your maxim should become a universal law?' Where you cannot, it is to be rejected, and that not because of a prospective loss to you or even to others, but because it cannot fit as a principle into a possible enactment of universal law. For such an enactment reason compels my immediate reverence, into whose grounds (which the philosopher may investigate) I have as yet no *insight,* although I do at least understand this much: reverence is the assessment of a worth which far outweighs all the worth of what is commended by inclination, and the necessity for me to act out of *pure* reverence for the practical law is what constitutes duty, to which every other motive must give way because it is the condition of a will good *in itself,* whose value is above all else.

CLASSIFICATION OF IMPERATIVES

All *imperatives* command either *hypothetically* or *categorically.* Hypothetical imperatives declare a possible action to be practically necessary as a means to the attainment of something else that one wills (or that one may will). A categorical imperative would be one which represented an action as objectively necessary in itself apart from its relation to a further end.

Every practical law represents a possible action as good and therefore as necessary for a subject whose actions are determined by reason. Hence all imperatives are formulae for deter-

mining an action which is necessary in accordance with the principle of a will in some sense good. If the action would be good solely as a means *to something else,* the imperative is *hypothetical*; if the action is represented as good in *itself* and therefore as necessary, in virtue of its principle, for a will which of itself accords with reason, then the imperative is *categorical.*

An imperative therefore tells me which of my possible actions would be good; and it formulates a practical rule for a will that does not perform an action straight away because the action is good—whether because the subject does not always know that it is good or because, even if he did know this, he might still act on maxims contrary to the objective principles of practical reason.

A hypothetical imperative thus says only that an action is good for some purpose or other, either *possible* or *actual*. In the first case it is a *problematic* practical principle; in the second case an *assertoric* practical principle. A categorical imperative, which declares an action to be objectively necessary in itself without reference to some purpose—that is, even without any further end—ranks as an *apodeictic* practical principle.

Everything that is possible only through the efforts of some rational being can be conceived as a possible purpose of some will; and consequently there are in fact innumerable principles of action so far as action is thought necessary in order to achieve some possible purpose which can be effected by it. All sciences have a practical part consisting of problems which suppose that some end is possible for us and of imperatives which tell us how it is to be attained. Hence the latter can in general be called imperatives of *skill*. Here there is absolutely no question about the rationality or goodness of the end, but only about what must be done to attain it. A prescription required by a doctor in order to cure his man completely and one required by a poisoner in order to make sure of killing him are of equal value so far as each serves to effect its purpose perfectly. Since in early youth we do not know what ends may present themselves to us in the course of life, parents seek above all to make their children learn things *of many kinds*; they provide carefully for *skill* in the use of means to all sorts of *arbitrary* ends, of none of which can they be certain that it could not in the future become an actual purpose of their ward, while it is always *possible* that he might adopt it. Their care in this matter is so great that they commonly neglect on this account to form and correct the judgement of their children about the worth of the things which they might possibly adopt as ends.

There is, however *one* end that can be presupposed as actual in all rational beings (so far as they are dependent beings to whom imperatives apply); and thus there is one purpose which they not only *can* have, but which we can assume with certainty that they all *do* have by a natural necessity—the purpose, namely, of *happiness*. A hypothetical imperative which affirms the practical necessity of an action as a means to the furtherance of happiness is *assertoric*. We may represent it, not simply as necessary to an uncertain, merely possible purpose, but as necessary to a purpose which we can presuppose *a priori* and with certainty to be present in every man because it belongs to his very being. Now skill in the choice of means to one's own greatest well-being can be called *prudence*[3] in the narrowest sense. Thus an imperative concerned with the choice of means to one's own happiness—that is, a precept of prudence—still remains *hypothetical*: an action is commanded, not absolutely, but only as a means to a further purpose.

Finally, there is an imperative which, without being based on, and conditioned by, any further purpose to be attained by a certain line of conduct, enjoins this conduct immediately. This imperative is *categorical*. It is concerned, not with the matter of the action and its presumed results, but with its form and with the principle from which it follows; and what is essentially good in the action consists in the mental disposition, let the consequences be what they may. This imperative may be called the imperative of *morality*.

Willing in accordance with these three kinds of principle is also sharply distinguished by a *dissimilarity* in the necessitation of the will. To make this dissimilarity obvious we should, I think, name these kinds of principle most appropriately in their order if we said they were either *rules* of skill or *counsels* of prudence or *commands (laws)* of morality. For only *law* carries with it the concept of an *unconditioned*, and yet objective and so universally valid, *necessity*; and commands are laws which must be obeyed—that is, must be followed even against inclination. *Counsel* does indeed involve necessity, but necessity valid only under a subjective and contingent condition—namely, if this or that man counts this or that as belonging to his happiness. As against this, a categorical imperative is limited by no condition and can quite precisely be called a command, as being absolutely, although practically, necessary. We could also call imperatives of the first kind

technical (concerned with art); of the second kind *pragmatic*[4] (concerned with well-being); of the third kind *moral* (concerned with free conduct as such—that is, with morals).

HOW ARE IMPERATIVES POSSIBLE?

The question now arises 'How are all these imperatives possible?' This question does not ask how we can conceive the execution of an action commanded by the imperative, but merely how we can conceive the necessitation of the will expressed by the imperative in setting us a task. How an imperative of skill is possible requires no special discussion. Who wills the end, wills (so far as reason has decisive influence on his actions) also the means which are indispensably necessary and in his power. So far as willing is concerned, this proposition is analytic: for in my willing of an object as an effect there is already conceived the causality of myself as an acting cause—that is, the use of means; and from the concept of willing an end the imperative merely extracts the concept of actions necessary to this end. (Synthetic propositions are required in order to determine the means to a proposed end, but these are concerned, not with the reason for performing the act of will, but with the cause which produces the object.) That in order to divide a line into two equal parts on a sure principle I must from its ends describe two intersecting arcs—this is admittedly taught by mathematics only in synthetic propositions; but when I know that the aforesaid effect can be produced only by such an action, the proposition 'If I fully will the effect, I also will the action required for it' is analytic; for it is one and the same thing to conceive something as an effect possible in a certain way through me and to conceive myself as acting in the same way with respect to it.

If it were only as easy to find a determinate concept of happiness, the imperatives of prudence would agree entirely with those of skill and would be equally analytic. For here as there it could alike be said 'Who wills the end, wills

also (necessarily, if he accords with reason) the sole means which are in his power'. Unfortunately, however, the concept of happiness is so indeterminate a concept that although every man wants to attain happiness, he can never say definitely and in unison with himself what it really is that he wants and wills. The reason for this is that all the elements which belong to the concept of happiness are without exception empirical—that is, they must be borrowed from experience; but that none the less there is required for the Idea of happiness an absolute whole, a maximum of well-being in my present, and in every future, state. Now it is impossible for the most intelligent, and at the same time most powerful, but nevertheless finite, being to form a determinate concept of what he really wills. Is it riches that he wants? How much anxiety, envy, and pestering might he not bring in this way on his own head! Is it knowledge and insight? This might perhaps merely give him an eye so sharp that it would make evils at present hidden from him and yet unavoidable seem all the more frightful, or would add a load of still further needs to the desires which already give him trouble enough. Is it long life? Who will guarantee that it would not be a long misery? Is it at least health? How often has infirmity of body kept a man from excesses into which perfect health would have let him fall!— and so on. In short, he has no principle by which he is able to decide with complete certainty what will make him truly happy, since for this he would require omniscience. Thus we cannot act on determinate principles in order to be happy, but only on empirical counsels, for example, of diet, frugality, politeness, reserve, and so on—things which experience shows contribute most to well-being on the average. From this it follows that imperatives of prudence, speaking strictly, do not command at all—that is, cannot exhibit actions objectively as practically *necessary*; that they are rather to be taken as recommendations *(consilia)*, than as commands *(praecepta)*, of reason; that the problem of determining certainly and universally what action will promote the happiness of a rational being is completely insoluble; and consequently that in regard to this there is no imperative possible which in the strictest sense could command us to do what will make us happy, since happiness is an Ideal, not of reason, but of imagination—an Ideal resting merely on empirical grounds, of which it is vain to expect that they should determine an action by which we could attain the totality of a series of consequences which is in fact infinite. Nevertheless, if we assume that the means to happiness could be discovered with certainty, this imperative of prudence would be an analytic practical proposition; for it differs from the imperative of skill only in this—that in the latter the end is merely possible, while in the former the end is given. In spite of this difference, since both command solely the means to something assumed to be willed as an end, the imperative which commands him who wills the end to will the means is in both cases analytic. Thus there is likewise no difficulty in regard to the possibility of an imperative of prudence.

Beyond all doubt, the question 'How is the imperative of *morality* possible?' is the only one in need of a solution; for it is in no way hypothetical, and consequently we cannot base the objective necessity which it affirms on any presupposition, as we can with hypothetical imperatives. Only we must never forget here that it is impossible to settle *by an example,* and so empirically, whether there is any imperative of this kind at all: we must rather suspect that all imperatives which seem to be categorical may none the less be covertly hypothetical. Take, for example, the saying 'Thou shalt make no false promises'. Let us assume that the necessity for this abstention is no mere advice for the avoidance of some further evil—as it might be said 'You ought not to make a lying promise lest,

when this comes to light, you destroy your credit'. Let us hold, on the contrary, that an action of this kind must be considered as bad in itself, and that the imperative of prohibition is therefore categorical. Even so, we cannot with any certainty show by an example that the will is determined here solely by the law without any further motive, although it may appear to be so; for it is always possible that fear of disgrace, perhaps also hidden dread of other risks, may unconsciously influence the will. Who can prove by experience that a cause is not present? Experience shows only that it is not perceived. In such a case, however, the so-called moral imperative, which as such appears to be categorical and unconditioned, would in fact be only a pragmatic prescription calling attention to our advantage and merely bidding us take this into account.

We shall thus have to investigate the possibility of a *categorical* imperative entirely *a priori,* since here we do not enjoy the advantage of having its reality given in experience and so of being obliged merely to explain, and not to establish, its possibility. So much, however, can be seen provisionally—that the categorical imperative alone purports to be a practical *law,* while all the rest may be called *principles* of the will but not laws; for an action necessary merely in order to achieve an arbitrary purpose can be considered as in itself contingent, and we can always escape from the precept if we abandon the purpose; whereas an unconditioned command does not leave it open to the will to do the opposite at its discretion and therefore alone carries with it that necessity which we demand from a law.

In the second place, with this categorical imperative or law of morality the reason for our difficulty (in comprehending its possibility) is a very serious one. We have here a synthetic *a priori* practical proposition;[5] and since in theoretical knowledge there is so much difficulty in comprehending the possibility of propositions of this kind, it may readily be gathered that in practical knowledge the difficulty will be no less.

THE FORMULA OF UNIVERSAL LAW

In this task we wish first to enquire whether perhaps the mere concept of a categorical imperative may not also provide us with the formula containing the only proposition that can be a categorical imperative; for even when we know the purport of such an absolute command, the question of its possibility will still require a special and troublesome effort, which we postpone to the final chapter.

When I conceive a *hypothetical* imperative in general, I do not know beforehand what it will contain—until its condition is given. But if I conceive a *categorical* imperative, I know at once what it contains. For since besides the law this imperative contains only the necessity that our maxim[6] should conform to this law, while the law, as we have seen, contains no condition to limit it, there remains nothing over to which the maxim has to conform except the universality of a law as such; and it is this conformity alone that the imperative properly asserts to be necessary.

There is therefore only a single categorical imperative and it is this: 'Act only on that *maxim through which you can at the same time will that it should become a universal law.*'

Now if all imperatives of duty can be derived from this one imperative as their principle, then even though we leave it unsettled whether what we call duty may not be an empty concept, we shall still be able to show at least what we understand by it and what the concept means.

THE FORMULA OF THE END IN ITSELF

The will is conceived as a power of determining oneself to action *in accordance with the idea of certain laws.* And such a power can be found only in rational beings. Now what serves the will as a subjective ground of its self-determination is an *end;* and this, if it is given by reason alone, must be equally valid for all rational beings. What, on the other hand, contains merely the ground of the possibility of an action whose effect is an end is called a *means.* The subjective ground of a desire is an *impulsion (Triebfeder);* the objective ground of a volition is a *motive (Bewegungsgrund).* Hence the difference between subjective ends, which are based on impulsions, and objective ends, which depend on motives valid for every rational being. Practical principles are *formal* if they abstract from all subjective ends; they are *material,* on the other hand, if they are based on such ends and consequently on certain impulsions. Ends that a rational being adopts arbitrarily as *effects* of his action (material ends) are in every case only relative; for it is solely their relation to special characteristics in the subject's power of appetition which gives them their value. Hence this value can provide no universal principles, no principles valid and necessary for all rational beings and also for every volition—that is, no practical laws. Consequently all these relative ends can be the ground only of hypothetical imperatives.

Suppose, however, there were something *whose existence* has *in itself* an absolute value, something which as *an end in itself* could be a ground of determinate laws; then in it, and in it alone, would there be the ground of a possible categorical imperative—that is, of a practical law.

Now I say that man, and in general every rational being, *exists* as an end in himself, *not merely as a means* for arbitrary use by this or that will: he must in all his actions, whether they are directed to himself or to other rational beings, always be viewed *at the same time as an end.* All the objects of inclination have only a conditioned value; for if there were not these inclinations and the needs grounded on them, their object would be valueless. Inclinations themselves, as sources of needs, are so far from having an absolute value to make them desirable for their own sake that it must rather be the universal wish of every rational being to be wholly free from them. Thus the value of all objects that can *be produced* by our action is always conditioned. Beings whose existence depends, not on our will, but on nature, have none the less, if they are non-rational beings, only a relative value as means and are consequently called *things*. Rational beings, on the other hand, are called *persons* because their nature already marks them out as ends in themselves—that is, as something which ought not to be used merely as a means—and consequently imposes to that extent a limit on all arbitrary treatment of them (and is an object of reverence). Persons, therefore, are not merely subjective ends whose existence as an object of our actions has a value *for us:* they are *objective ends*—that is, things whose existence is in itself an end, and indeed an end such that in its place we can put no other end to which they should serve *simply* as means; for unless this is so, nothing at all of *absolute* value would be found anywhere. But if all value were conditioned— that is, contingent—then no supreme principle could be found for reason at all.

If then there is to be a supreme practical principle and—so far as the human will is concerned—a categorical imperative, it must be such that from the idea of something which is necessarily an end for every one because it is an *end in itself* it forms an *objective* principle of the will and consequently can serve as a practical law. The ground of this principle is: *Rational nature exists as an end in itself.* This is the way in which a man necessarily conceives his own existence: it is therefore so far a *subjective* principle of human actions. But it is also the way in which every other rational being conceives his existence on the same rational ground which is valid also for me;[7] hence it is at the same time an *objective* principle, from which, as a supreme practical ground, it must be possible to derive all laws for the will. The practical imperative will therefore be as follows: *Act in such a way that you always treat humanity, whether in your own person or in the person of any other, never simply as a means, but always at the same time as an end.* We will now consider whether this can be carried out in practice.

THE FORMULA OF THE KINGDOM OF ENDS

The concept of every rational being as one who must regard himself as making universal law by all the maxims of his will, and must seek to judge himself and his actions from this point of view, leads to a closely connected and very fruitful concept—namely, that of *a kingdom of ends*.

I understand by a '*kingdom*' a systematic union of different rational beings under common laws. Now since laws determine ends as regards their universal validity, we shall be able—if we abstract from the personal differences between rational beings, and also from all the content of their private ends—to conceive a whole of all ends in systematic conjunction (a whole both of rational beings as ends in themselves and also of the personal ends which each may set before himself); that is, we shall be

able to conceive a kingdom of ends which is possible in accordance with the above principles.

For rational beings all stand under the *law* that each of them should treat himself and all others, *never merely as a means,* but always *at the same time as an end in himself.* But by so doing there arises a systematic union of rational beings under common objective laws—that is, a kingdom. Since these laws are directed precisely to the relation of such beings to one another as ends and means, this kingdom can be called a kingdom of ends (which is admittedly only an Ideal).

A rational being belongs to the kingdom of ends as a *member,* when, although he makes its universal laws, he is also himself subject to these laws. He belongs to it as its *head,* when as the maker of laws he is himself subject to the will of no other.)

A rational being must always regard himself as making laws in a kingdom of ends which is possible through freedom of the will—whether it be as member or as head. The position of the latter he can maintain, not in virtue of the maxim of his will alone, but only if he is a completely independent being, without needs and with an unlimited power adequate to his will.

Thus morality consists in the relation of all action to the making of laws whereby alone a kingdom of ends is possible. This making of laws must be found in every rational being himself and must be able to spring from his will. The principle of his will is therefore never to perform an action except on a maxim such as can also be a universal law, and consequently such *that the will can regard itself as at the same time making universal law by means of its maxim*. Where maxims are not already by their very nature in harmony with this objective principle of rational beings as makers of universal law, the necessity of acting on this principle is practical necessitation—that is, *duty*. Duty does not apply to the head in kingdom of ends, but it does apply to every member and to all members in equal measure.

The practical necessity of acting on this principle—that is, duty—is in no way based on feelings, impulses, and inclinations, but only on the relation of rational beings to one another, a relation in which the will of a rational being must always be regarded as *making universal law*, because otherwise he could not be conceived as *an end in himself*. Reason thus relates every maxim of the will, considered as making universal law, to every other will and also to every action towards oneself: it does so, not because of any further motive or future advantage, but from the Idea of the *dignity* of a rational being who obeys no law other than that which he at the same time enacts himself.

THE DIGNITY OF VIRTUE

In the kingdom of ends everything has either a *price* or a *dignity*. If it has a price, something else can be put in its place as an *equivalent;* if it is exalted above all price and so admits of no equivalent, then it has a dignity.

What is relative to universal human inclinations and needs has a *market price;* what, even without presupposing a need, accords with a certain taste—that is, with satisfaction in the mere purposeless play of our mental powers—has a *fancy price (Affektionspreis);* but that which constitutes the sole condition under which anything can be an end in itself has not merely a relative value—that is, a price—but has an intrinsic value—that is, *dignity*.

Now morality is the only condition under which a rational being can be an end in himself; for only through this is it possible to be a law-making member in a kingdom of ends. Therefore morality, and humanity so far as it is capable of morality, is the only thing which has dignity. Skill and diligence in work have a market price; wit, lively imagination, and humour have a fancy price; but fidelity to promises and kindness based on principle (not on instinct) have an intrinsic worth. In default of these, nature and art alike contain nothing to put in their place; for their worth consists, not in the effects which result from them, not in the advantage or profit they produce, but in the attitudes of mind—that is, in the maxims of the will—which are ready in this way to manifest themselves in action even if they are not favoured by success. Such actions too need no recommendation from any subjective disposition or taste in order to meet with immediate favour and approval; they need no immediate propensity or feeling for themselves; they exhibit the will which performs them as an object of immediate reverence; nor is anything other than reason required to *impose* them upon the will, not to *coax* them from the will—which last would anyhow be a contradiction in the case of duties. This assessment reveals as dignity the value of such a mental attitude and puts it infinitely above all price, with which it cannot be brought into reckoning or comparison without, as it were, a profanation of its sanctity.

What is it then that entitles a morally good attitude of mind—or virtue—to make claims so high? It is nothing less than the *share* which it affords to a rational being *in the making of universal law,* and which therefore fits him to be a member in a possible kingdom of ends. For this he was already marked out in virtue of his own proper nature as an end in himself and consequently as a maker of laws in the kingdom of ends—as free in respect of all laws of nature,

obeying only those laws which he makes himself and in virtue of which his maxims can have their part in the making of universal law (to which he at the same time subjects himself). For nothing can have a value other than that determined for it by the law. But the law-making which determines all value must for this reason have a dignity—that is, an unconditioned and incomparable worth—for the appreciation of which, as necessarily given by a rational being, the word *'reverence'* is the only becoming expression. *Autonomy* is therefore the ground of the dignity of human nature and of every rational nature.

NOTES

1. A *maxim* is the subjective principle of a volition: an objective principle (that is, one which would also serve subjectively as a practical principle for all rational beings if reason had full control over the faculty of desire) is a practical *law*.

2. It might be urged against me that I have merely tried, under cover of the word *'reverence'*, to take refuge in an obscure feeling instead of giving a clearly articulated answer to the question by means of a concept of reason. Yet although reverence is a feeling, it is not a feeling *received* through outside influence, but one *self-produced* by a rational concept, and therefore specifically distinct from feelings of the first kind, all of which can be reduced to inclination or fear. What I recognize immediately as law for me, I recognize with reverence, which means merely consciousness of the *subordination* of my will to a law without the mediation of external influences on my senses. Immediate determination of the will by the law and consciousness of this determination is called *'reverence'*, so that reverence is regarded as the *effect* of the law on the subject and not as the *cause* of the law. Reverence is properly awareness of a value which demolishes my self-love. Hence there is something which is regarded neither as an object of inclination nor as an object of fear, though it has at the same time some analogy with both. The *object* of reverence is the *law* alone—that law which we impose *on ourselves* but yet as necessary in itself. Considered as a law, we are subject to it without any consultation of self-love; considered as self-imposed it is a consequence of our will. In the first respect it is analogous to fear, in the second to inclination. All reverence for a person is properly only reverence for the law (of honesty and so on) of which that person gives us an example. Because we regard the development of our talents as a duty, we see too in a man of talent a sort of *example of the law* (the law of becoming like him by practice), and this is what constitutes our reverence for him. All moral *interest*, so-called, consists solely in *reverence* for the law.

3. The word 'prudence' (*Klugheit*) is used in a double sense: in one sense it can have the name of 'worldly wisdom' *(Weltklugheit)*; in a second sense that of 'personal wisdom' *(Privatklugheit)*. The first is the skill of a man in influencing others in order to use them for his own ends. The second is sagacity in combining all these ends to his own lasting advantage. The latter is properly that to which the value of the former can itself be traced; and of him who is prudent in the first sense, but not in the second, we might better say that he is clever and astute, but on the whole imprudent.

4. It seems to me that the proper meaning of the word *'pragmatic'* can be defined most accurately in this way. For those *Sanctions* are called Pragmatic which, properly speaking, do not spring as necessary laws from the Natural Right of States, but from *forethought* in regard to the general welfare. A *history* is written pragmatically when it teaches *prudence*—that is, when it instructs the world of today how to provide for its own advantage better than, or at least as well as, the world of other times.

5. Without presupposing a condition taken from some inclination I connect an action with the will *a priori* and therefore necessarily (although only objectively so—that is, only subject to the Idea of a reason having full power over all subjective impulses to action). Here we have a practical proposition in which the willing of an action is not derived analytically from some other willing already presupposed (for we do not possess any such perfect will), but is on the contrary connected immediately with the concept of the will of a rational being as something which is not contained in this concept.

6. A *maxim* is a subjective principle of action and must be distinguished from an *objective principle*—namely, a practical law. The former contains a practical rule determined by reason in accordance with the conditions of the subject (often his ignorance or again his inclinations): it is thus a principle on which the subject *acts*. A law, on the other hand, is an objective principle valid for every rational being; and it is a principle on which he *ought to act*—that is, an imperative.

7. This proposition I put forward here as a postulate. The grounds for it will be found in the final chapter.

A. J. AYER
Critique of Ethics and Theology

There is still one objection to be met before we can claim to have justified our view that all synthetic propositions are empirical hypotheses. This objection is based on the common supposition that our speculative knowledge is of two distinct kinds—that which relates to questions of empirical fact, and that which relates to questions of value. It will be said that "statements of value" are genuine synthetic propositions, but that they cannot with any show of justice be represented as hypotheses, which are used to predict the course of our sensations; and, accordingly, that the existence of ethics and aesthetics as branches of speculative knowledge presents an insuperable objection to our radical empiricist thesis.

In face of this objection, it is our business to give an account of "judgements of value" which is both satisfactory in itself and consistent with our general empiricist principles. We shall set ourselves to show that in so far as statements of value are significant, they are ordinary "scientific" statements; and that in so far as they are not scientific, they are not in the literal sense significant, but are simply expressions of emotion which can be neither true nor false. In maintaining this view, we may confine ourselves for the present to the case of ethical statements. What is said about them will be found to apply, *mutatis mutandis,* to the case of aesthetic statements also.

The ordinary system of ethics, as elaborated in the works of ethical philosophers, is very far from being a homogeneous whole. Not only is it apt to contain pieces of metaphysics, and analyses of non-ethical concepts: its actual ethical contents are themselves of very different kinds. We may divide them, indeed, into four main classes. There are, first of all, propositions which express definitions of ethical terms, or judgements about the legitimacy or possibility of certain definitions. Secondly, there are propositions describing the phenomena of moral experience, and their causes. Thirdly, there are exhortations to moral virtue. And lastly, there are actual ethical judgements. It is unfortunately the case that the distinction between these four classes, plain as it is, is commonly ignored by ethical philosophers; with the result that it is often very difficult to tell from their works what it is that they are seeking to discover or prove.

In fact, it is easy to see that only the first of our four classes, namely that which comprises the propositions relating to the definitions of ethical terms, can be said to constitute ethical philosophy. The propositions which describe the phenomena of moral experience, and their causes, must be assigned to the science of psy-

Reprinted from *Language, Truth and Logic* (1936) by permission of Dover Publications, Inc. **Sir Alfred Jules Ayer** (1910–1989), one of the most famous of contemporary British philosophers, inspired more than one generation of philosophy students to be alive to important distinctions in common discourse, such as the emotive use of language.

chology, or sociology. The exhortations to moral virtue are not propositions at all, but ejaculations or commands which are designed to provoke the reader to action of a certain sort. Accordingly, they do not belong to any branch of philosophy or science. As for the expressions of ethical judgements, we have not yet determined how they should be classified. But inasmuch as they are certainly neither definitions nor comments upon definitions, nor quotations, we may say decisively that they do not belong to ethical philosophy. A strictly philosophical treatise on ethics should therefore make no ethical pronouncements. But it should, by giving an analysis of ethical terms, show what is the category to which all such pronouncements belong. And this is what we are now about to do.

A question which is often discussed by ethical philosophers is whether it is possible to find definitions which would reduce all ethical terms to one or two fundamental terms. But this question, though it undeniably belongs to ethical philosophy, is not relevant to our present enquiry. We are not now concerned to discover which term, within the sphere of ethical terms, is to be taken as fundamental; whether, for example, "good" can be defined in terms of "right" or "right" in terms of "good," or both in terms of "value." What we are interested in is the possibility of reducing the whole sphere of ethical terms to non-ethical terms. We are enquiring whether statements of ethical value can be translated into statements of empirical fact.

That they can be so translated is the contention of those ethical philosophers who are commonly called subjectivists, and of those who are known as utilitarians. For the utilitarian defines the rightness of actions, and the goodness of ends, in terms of the pleasure, or happiness, or satisfaction, to which they give rise; the subjectivist, in terms of the feelings of approval which a certain person, or group of people, has towards them. Each of these types of definition makes moral judgements into a sub-class of psychological or sociological judgements; and for this reason they are very attractive to us. For, if either was correct, it would follow that

ethical assertions were not generically different from the factual assertions which are ordinarily contrasted with them; and the account which we have already given of empirical hypotheses would apply to them also.

Nevertheless we shall not adopt either a subjectivist or a utilitarian analysis of ethical terms. We reject the subjectivist view that to call an action right, or a thing good, is to say that it is generally approved of, because it is not self-contradictory to assert that some actions which are generally approved of are not right, or that some things which are generally approved of are not good. And we reject the alternative subjectivist view that a man who asserts that a certain action is right, or that a certain thing is good, is saying that he himself approves of it, on the ground that a man who confessed that he sometimes approved of what was bad or wrong would not be contradicting himself. And a similar argument is fatal to utilitarianism. We cannot agree that to call an action right is to say that of all the actions possible in the circumstances it would cause, or be likely to cause, the greatest happiness, or the greatest balance of pleasure over pain, or the greatest balance of satisfied over unsatisfied desire, because we find that it is not self-contradictory to say that it is sometimes wrong to perform the action which would actually or probably cause the greatest happiness, or the greatest balance of pleasure over pain, or of satisfied over unsatisfied desire. And since it is not self-contradictory to say that some pleasant things are not good, or that some bad things are desired, it cannot be the case that the sentence "x is good" is equivalent to "x is pleasant," or to "x is desired." And to every other variant of utilitarianism with which I am acquainted the same objection can be made. And therefore we should, I think, conclude that the validity of ethical judgements is not determined by the felicific tendencies of actions, any more than by the nature of people's feelings; but that it must be regarded as "absolute" or "intrinsic," and not empirically calculable.

If we say this, we are not, of course, denying that it is possible to invent a language in which all ethical symbols are definable in non-ethical terms, or even that it is desirable to invent such a language and adopt it in place of our own; what we are denying is that the suggested reduction of ethical to non-ethical statements is consistent with the conventions of our actual language. That is, we reject utilitarianism and subjectivism, not as proposals to replace our existing ethical notions by new ones, but as analyses of our existing ethical notions. Our contention is simply that, in our language, sentences which contain normative ethical symbols are not equivalent to sentences which express psychological propositions, or indeed empirical propositions of any kind.

It is advisable here to make it plain that it is only normative ethical symbols, and not descriptive ethical symbols, that are held by us to be indefinable in factual terms. There is a danger of confusing these two types of symbols, because they are commonly constituted by signs of the same sensible form. Thus a complex sign of the form "x is wrong" may constitute a sentence which expresses a moral judgement concerning a certain type of conduct, or it may constitute a sentence which states that a certain type of conduct is repugnant to the moral sense of a particular society. In the latter case, the symbol "wrong" is a descriptive ethical symbol, and the sentence in which it occurs expresses an ordinary sociological proposition; in the former case, the symbol "wrong" is a normative ethical symbol, and the sentence in which it occurs does not, we maintain, express an empirical proposition at all. It is only with normative ethics that we are at present concerned; so that whenever ethical symbols are used in the course of this argument without qualification, they are always to be interpreted as symbols of the normative type.

In admitting that normative ethical concepts are irreducible to empirical concepts, we seem to be leaving the way clear for the "absolutist" view of ethics—that is, the view that statements of value are not controlled by observation, as ordinary empirical propositions are, but only by a mysterious "intellectual intuition." A feature of this theory, which is seldom recognized by its advocates, is that it makes statements of value unverifiable. For it is notorious that what seems intuitively certain to one person may seem doubtful, or even false, to another. So that unless it is possible to provide some criterion by which one may decide between conflicting intuitions, a mere appeal to intuition is worthless as a test of a proposition's validity. But in the case of moral judgements, no such criterion can be given. Some moralists claim to settle the matter by saying that they "know" that their own moral judgements are correct. But such an assertion is of purely psychological interest, and has not the slightest tendency to prove the validity of any moral judgement. For dissentient moralists may equally well "know" that their ethical views are correct. And, as far as subjective certainty goes, there will be nothing to choose between them. When such differences of opinion arise in connection with an ordinary empirical proposition, one may attempt to resolve them by referring to, or actually carrying out, some relevant empirical test. But with regard to ethical statements, there is, on the "absolutist" or "intuitionist" theory, no relevant empirical test. We are therefore justified in saying that on this theory ethical statements are held to be unverifiable. They are, of course, also held to be genuine synthetic propositions.

Considering the use which we have made of the principle that a synthetic proposition is significant only if it is empirically verifiable, it is clear that the acceptance of an "absolutist" theory of ethics would undermine the whole of our main argument. And as we have already rejected the "naturalistic" theories which are commonly supposed to provide the only alternative to "absolutism" in ethics, we seem to have reached a difficult position. We shall meet the difficulty by showing that the correct treatment of ethical statements is afforded by a third theory, which is wholly compatible with our radical empiricism.

We begin by admitting that the fundamental ethical concepts are unanalysable, inasmuch as there is no criterion by which one can test the validity of the judgements in which they occur.

So far we are in agreement with the absolutists. But, unlike the absolutists, we are able to give an explanation of this fact about ethical concepts. We say that the reason why they are unanalysable is that they are mere pseudo-concepts. The presence of an ethical symbol in a proposition adds nothing to its factual content. Thus if I say to someone, "You acted wrongly in stealing that money," I am not stating anything more than if I had simply said, "You stole that money." In adding that this action is wrong I am not making any further statement about it. I am simply evincing my moral disapproval of it. It is as if I had said, "You stole that money," in a peculiar tone of horror, or written it with the addition of some special exclamation marks. The tone, or the exclamation marks, adds nothing to the literal meaning of the sentence. It merely serves to show that the expression of it is attended by certain feelings in the speaker.

If now I generalise my previous statement and say, "Stealing money is wrong," I produce a sentence which has no factual meaning—that is, expresses no proposition which can be either true or false. It is as if I had written "Stealing money!!"—where the shape and thickness of the exclamation marks show, by a suitable convention, that a special sort of moral disapproval is the feeling which is being expressed. It is clear that there is nothing said here which can be true or false. Another man may disagree with me about the wrongness of stealing, in the sense that he may not have the same feelings about stealing as I have, and he may quarrel with me on account of my moral sentiments. But he cannot, strictly speaking, contradict me. For in saying that a certain type of action is right or wrong, I am not making any factual statement, not even a statement about my own state of mind. I am merely expressing certain moral sentiments. And the man who is ostensibly contradicting me is merely expressing his moral sentiments. So that there is plainly no sense in asking which of us is in the right. For neither of us is asserting a genuine proposition.

What we have just been saying about the symbol "wrong" applies to all normative ethical symbols. Sometimes they occur in sentences which record ordinary empirical facts besides expressing ethical feeling about those facts: sometimes they occur in sentences which simply express ethical feeling about a certain type of action, or situation, without making any statement of fact. But in every case in which one would commonly be said to be making an ethical judgement, the function of the relevant ethical word is purely "emotive." It is used to express feeling about certain objects, but not to make any assertion about them.

It is worth mentioning that ethical terms do not serve only to express feeling. They are calculated also to arouse feeling, and so to stimulate action. Indeed some of them are used in such a way as to give the sentences in which they occur the effect of commands. Thus the sentence "It is your duty to tell the truth" may be regarded both as the expression of a certain sort of ethical feeling about truthfulness and as the expression of the command "Tell the truth." The sentence "You ought to tell the truth" also involves the command "Tell the truth," but here the tone of the command is less emphatic. In the sentence "It is good to tell the truth" the command has become little more than a suggestion. And thus the "meaning" of the word "good," in its ethical usage, is differentiated from that of the word "duty" or the word "ought." In fact we may define the meaning of the various ethical words in terms both of the different feelings they are ordinarily taken to express, and also the different responses which they are calculated to provoke.

We can now see why it is impossible to find a criterion for determining the validity of ethical judgements. It is not because they have "absolute" validity which is mysteriously independent of ordinary sense-experience, but because they have no objective validity whatsoever. If a sentence makes no statement at all, there is obviously no sense in asking whether what it says is true or false. And we have seen that sentences which simply express moral judgements do not say anything. They are pure expressions of feeling and as such do not come under the category of truth and falsehood.

They are unverifiable for the same reason as a cry of pain or a word of command is unverifiable—because they do not express genuine propositions.

Thus, although our theory of ethics might fairly be said to be radically subjectivist, it differs in a very important respect from the orthodox subjectivist theory. For the orthodox subjectivist does not deny, as we do, that the sentences of a moralizer express genuine propositions. All he denies is that they express propositions of a unique non-empirical character. His own view is that they express propositions about the speaker's feelings. If this were so, ethical judgements clearly would be capable of being true or false. They would be true if the speaker had the relevant feelings, and false if he had not. And this is a matter which is, in principle, empirically verifiable. Furthermore they could be significantly contradicted. For if I say, "Tolerance is a virtue," and someone answers, "You don't approve of it," he would, on the ordinary subjectivist theory, be contradicting me. On our theory, he would not be contradicting me, because, in saying that tolerance was a virtue, I should not be making any statement about my own feelings or about anything else. I should simply be evincing my feelings, which is not at all the same thing as saying that I have them.

The distinction between the expression of feeling and the assertion of feeling is complicated by the fact that the assertion that one has a certain feeling often accompanies the expression of that feeling, and is then, indeed, a factor in the expression of that feeling. Thus I may simultaneously express boredom and say that I am bored, and in that case my utterance of the words, "I am bored," is one of the circumstances which make it true to say that I am expressing or evincing boredom. But I can express boredom without actually saying that I am bored. I can express it by my tone and gestures, while making a statement about something wholly unconnected with it, or by an ejaculation, or without uttering any words at all. So that even if the assertion that one has a certain feeling always involves the expression of that feeling, the expression of a feeling assuredly does not always involve the assertion that one has it. And this is the important point to grasp in considering the distinction between our theory and the ordinary subjectivist theory. For whereas the subjectivist holds that ethical statements actually assert the existence of certain feelings, we hold that ethical statements are expressions and excitants of feeling which do not necessarily involve any assertions.

We have already remarked that the main objection to the ordinary subjectivist theory is that the validity of ethical judgements is not determined by the nature of their author's feelings. And this is an objection which our theory escapes. For it does not imply that the existence of any feelings is a necessary and sufficient condition of the validity of an ethical judgement. It implies, on the contrary, that ethical judgements have no validity.

There is, however, a celebrated argument against subjectivist theories which our theory does not escape. It has been pointed out by Moore that if ethical statements were simply statements about the speaker's feelings, it would be impossible to argue about questions of value. To take a typical example: if a man said that thrift was a virtue, and another replied that it was a vice, they would not, on this theory, be disputing with one another. One would be saying that he approved of thrift, and the other that *he* didn't; and there is no reason why both these statements should not be true. Now Moore held it to be obvious that we do dispute about questions of value, and accordingly concluded that the particular form of subjectivism which he was discussing was false.

It is plain that the conclusion that it is impossible to dispute about questions of value follows from our theory also. For as we hold that such sentences as "Thrift is a virtue" and "Thrift is a vice" do not express propositions at all, we clearly cannot hold that they express incompatible propositions. We must therefore admit that if Moore's argument really refutes the ordinary subjectivist theory, it also refutes ours. But, in fact, we deny that it does refute even the ordinary subjectivist theory. For we hold that one really never does dispute about questions of value.

This may seem, at first sight, to be a very paradoxical assertion. For we certainly do engage in disputes which are ordinarily regarded as disputes about questions of value. But, in all such cases, we find, if we consider the matter closely, that the dispute is not really about a question of value, but about a question of fact. When someone disagrees with us about the moral value of a certain action or type of action, we do admittedly resort to argument in order to win him over to our way of thinking. But we do not attempt to show by our arguments that he has the "wrong" ethical feeling towards a situation whose nature he has correctly apprehended. What we attempt to show is that he is mistaken about the facts of the case. We argue that he has misconceived the agent's motive: or that he has misjudged the effects of the action, or its probable effects in view of the agent's knowledge; or that he has failed to take into account the special circumstances in which the agent was placed. Or else we employ more general arguments about the effects which actions of a certain type tend to produce, or the qualities which are usually manifested in their performance. We do this in the hope that we have only to get our opponent to agree with us about the nature of the empirical facts for him to adopt the same moral attitude towards them as we do. And as the people with whom we argue have generally received the same moral education as ourselves, and live in the same social order, our expectation is usually justified. But if our opponent happens to have undergone a different process of moral "conditioning" from ourselves, so that, even when he acknowledges all the facts, he still disagrees with us about the moral value of the actions under discussion, then we abandon the attempt to convince him by argument. We say that it is impossible to argue with him because he has a distorted or undeveloped moral sense; which signifies merely that he employs a different set of values from our own. We feel that our own system of values is superior, and therefore speak in such derogatory terms of his. But we cannot bring forward any arguments to show that our system is superior. For our judgement that it is so is itself a judgment of value, and accordingly outside the scope of argument. It is because argument fails us when we come to deal with pure questions of value, as distinct from questions of fact, that we finally resort to mere abuse.

In short, we find that argument is possible on moral questions only if some system of values is presupposed. If our opponent concurs with us in expressing moral disapproval of all actions of a given type t, then we may get him to condemn a particular action A, by bringing forward arguments to show that A is of type t. For the question whether A does or does not belong to that type is a plain question of fact. Given that a man has certain moral principles, we argue that he must, in order to be consistent, react morally to certain things in a certain way. What we do not and cannot argue about is the validity of these moral principles. We merely praise or condemn them in the light of our own feelings.

If anyone doubts the accuracy of this account of moral disputes, let him try to construct even an imaginary argument on a question of value which does not reduce itself to an argument about a question of logic or about an empirical matter of fact. I am confident that he will not succeed in producing a single example. And if that is the case, he must allow that its involving the impossibility of purely ethical arguments is not, as Moore thought, a ground of objection to our theory, but rather a point in favour of it.

Having upheld our theory against the only criticism which appeared to threaten it, we may now use it to define the nature of all ethical enquiries. We find that ethical philosophy consists simply in saying that ethical concepts are pseudo-concepts and therefore unanalysable. The further task of describing the different feelings that the different ethical terms are used to express, and the different reactions that they customarily provoke, is a task for the psychologist. There cannot be such a thing as ethical science, if by ethical science one means the elaboration of a "true" system of morals. For we have seen that, as ethical judgements are mere expressions of feeling, there can be no way of determining the validity of any ethical system, and, indeed, no sense in asking whether any such system is true. All that one may legitimately enquire in this connection is, What are the moral habits of a given person or group of people, and what causes them to have precisely those habits and feelings? And this enquiry falls wholly within the scope of the existing social sciences.

It appears, then, that ethics, as a branch of knowledge, is nothing more than a department of psychology and sociology. And in case anyone thinks that we are overlooking the existence of casuistry, we may remark that casuistry is not a science, but is a purely analytical investigation of the structure of a given moral system. In other words, it is an exercise in formal logic.

When one comes to pursue the psychological enquiries which constitute ethical science, one is immediately enabled to account for the Kantian and hedonistic theories of morals. For one finds that one of the chief causes of moral behaviour is fear, both conscious and unconscious, of god's displeasure, and fear of the enmity of society. And this, indeed, is the reason why moral precepts present themselves to some people as "categorical" commands. And one finds, also, that the moral code of a society is partly determined by the beliefs of that society concerning the conditions of its own happiness—or, in other words, that a society tends to encourage or discourage a given type of conduct by the use of moral sanctions according as it appears to promote or detract from the contentment of the society as a whole. And this is the reason why altruism is recommended in most moral codes and egotism condemned. It is from the observation of this connection between morality and happiness that hedonistic or eudaemonistic theories of morals ultimately spring, just as the moral theory of Kant is based on the fact, previously explained, that moral precepts have for some people the force of inexorable commands. As each of these theories ignores the fact which lies at the root of the other, both may be criticized as being one-sided; but this is not the main objection to either of them. Their essential defect is that they treat propositions which refer to the causes and attributes of our ethical feelings as if they were definitions of ethical concepts. And thus they fail to recognise that ethical concepts are pseudo-concepts and consequently indefinable.

GILBERT HARMAN
Ethics and Observation

I. THE BASIC ISSUE

Can moral principles be tested and confirmed in the way scientific principles can? Consider the principle that, if you are given a choice between five people alive and one dead or five people dead and one alive, you should always choose to have five people alive and one dead rather than the other way round. We can easily imagine examples that appear to confirm this principle. Here is one:

> You are a doctor in a hospital's emergency room when six accident victims are brought in. All six are in danger of dying but one is much worse off than the others. You can just barely save that person if you devote all of your resources to him and let the others die. Alternatively, you can save the other five if you are willing to ignore the most seriously injured person.

It would seem that in this case you, the doctor, would be right to save the five and let the other person die. So this example, taken by itself, confirms the principle under consideration. Next, consider the following case.

> You have five patients in the hospital who are dying, each in need of a separate organ. One needs a kidney, another a lung, a third a heart, and so forth. You can save all five if you take a single healthy person and remove his heart, lungs, kidneys, and so forth, to distribute to these five patients. Just such a healthy person is in room 306. He is in the hospital for routine tests. Having seen his test results, you know that he is perfectly healthy and of the right tissue compatibility. If you do nothing, he will survive without incident; the other patients will die, however. The other five patients can be saved only if the person in Room 306 is cut up and his organs distributed. In that case, there would be one dead but five saved.

The principle in question tells us that you should cut up the patient in Room 306. But in this case, surely you must not sacrifice this innocent bystander, even to save the other five patients. Here a moral principle has been tested and disconfirmed in what may seem to be a surprising way.

This, of course, was a "thought experiment." We did not really compare a hypothesis

From *The Nature of Morality: An Introduction to Ethics* by Gilbert Harman. Copyright © 1977 by Oxford University Press, Inc. Reprinted by permission of Oxford University Press. **Gilbert Harman,** affiliated with Princeton University, has written clearly and with precision on many important issues in ethics, philosophy of science, and language.

with the world. We compared an explicit principle with our feelings about certain imagined examples. In the same way, a physicist performs thought experiments in order to compare explicit hypotheses with his "sense" of what should happen in certain situations, a "sense" that he has acquired as a result of his long working familiarity with current theory. But scientific hypotheses can also be tested in real experiments, out in the world.

Can moral principles be tested in the same way, out in the world? You can observe some-one do something, but can you ever perceive the rightness or wrongness of what he does? If you round a corner and see a group of young hoodlums pour gasoline on a cat and ignite it, you do not need to *conclude* that what they are doing is wrong; you do not need to figure anything out; you can *see* that it is wrong. But is your reaction due to the actual wrongness of what you see or is it simply a reflection of your moral "sense," a "sense" that you have acquired perhaps as a result of your moral upbringing?

II. OBSERVATION

The issue is complicated. There are no pure observations. Observations are always "theory laden." What you perceive depends to some extent on the theory you hold, consciously or unconsciously. You see some children pour gasoline on a cat and ignite it. To really see that, you have to possess a great deal of knowledge, know about a considerable number of objects, know about people: that people pass through the life stages infant, baby, child, adolescent, adult. You must know what flesh and blood animals are, and in particular, cats. You must have some idea of life. You must know what gasoline is, what burning is, and much more. In one sense, what you "see" is a pattern of light on your retina, a shifting array of splotches, although even that is theory, and you could never adequately describe what you see in that sense. In another sense, you see what you do because of the theories you hold. Change those theories and you would see something else, given the same pattern of light.

Similarly, if you hold a moral view, whether it is held consciously or unconsciously, you will be able to perceive rightness or wrongness, goodness or badness, justice or injustice. There is no difference in this respect between moral propositions and other theoretical propositions. If there is a difference, it must be found elsewhere.

Observation depends on theory because perception involves forming a belief as a fairly direct result of observing something; you can form a belief only if you understand the relevant concepts and a concept is what it is by virtue of its role in some theory or system of beliefs. To recognize a child as a child is to employ, consciously or unconsciously, a concept that is defined by its place in a framework of the stages of human life. Similarly, burning is an empty concept apart from its theoretical connections to the concepts of heat, destruction, smoke, and fire.

Moral concepts—Right and Wrong, Good and Bad, Justice and Injustice—also have a place in your theory or system of beliefs and are the concepts they are because of their context. If we say that observation has occurred whenever an opinion is a direct result of perception, we must allow that there is moral observation, because such an opinion can be a moral opinion as easily as any other sort. In this sense, observation may be used to confirm or disconfirm moral theories. The observational opinions that, in this sense, you find yourself with can be in either agreement or conflict with your consciously explicit moral principles. When they are in conflict, you must choose between your explicit theory and observation. In ethics, as in science, you sometimes opt for theory, and say that you made an error in observation or were biased or whatever, or you sometimes opt for observation, and modify your theory.

In other words, in both science and ethics, general principles are evoked to explain particular cases and, therefore, in both science and ethics, the general principles you accept can be tested by appealing to particular judgments that certain things are right or wrong, just or unjust, and so forth; and these judgments are analogous to direct perceptual judgments about facts.

III. OBSERVATIONAL EVIDENCE

Nevertheless, observation plays a role in science that it does not seem to play in ethics. The difference is that you need to make assumptions about certain physical facts to explain the occurrence of the observations that support a scientific theory, but you do not seem to need to make assumptions about any moral facts to explain the occurrence of the so-called moral observations I have been talking about. In the moral case, it would seem that you need only make assumptions about the psychology or moral sensibility of the person making the moral observation. In the scientific case, theory is tested against the world.

The point is subtle but important. Consider a physicist making an observation to test a scientific theory. Seeing a vapor trail in a cloud chamber, he thinks, "There goes a proton." Let us suppose that this is an observation in the relevant sense, namely, an immediate judgment made in response to the situation without any conscious reasoning having taken place. Let us also suppose that his observation confirms his theory, a theory that helps give meaning to the very term "proton" as it occurs in his observational judgment. Such a confirmation rests on inferring an explanation. He can count his making the observation as confirming evidence for his theory only to the extent that it is reasonable to explain his making the observation by assuming that, not only is he in a certain psychological "set," given the theory he accepts and his beliefs about the experimental apparatus, but furthermore, there really was a proton going through the cloud chamber, causing the vapor trail, which he saw as a proton. (This is evidence for the theory to the extent that the theory can explain the proton's being there better than competing theories can.) But, if his having made that observation could have been equally well explained by his psychological set alone, without the need for any assumption about a proton, then the observation would not have been evidence for the existence of that proton and therefore would not have been evidence for the theory. His making the observation supports the theory only because, in order to explain his making the observation, it is reasonable to assume something about the world over and above the assumptions made about the observer's psychology. In particular, it is reasonable to assume that there was a proton going through the cloud chamber, causing the vapor trail.

Compare this case with one in which you make a moral judgment immediately and without conscious reasoning, say, that the children are wrong to set the cat on fire or that the doctor would be wrong to cut up one healthy patient to save five dying patients. In order to explain your making the first of these judgments, it would be reasonable to assume, perhaps, that the children really are pouring gasoline on a cat and you are seeing them do it. But, in neither case is there any obvious reason to assume anything about "moral facts," such as that it really is wrong to set the cat on fire or to cut up the patient in Room 306. Indeed, an assumption about moral facts would seem to be totally irrelevant to the explanation of your making the judgment you make. It would seem that all we need assume is that you have certain more or less well articulated moral principles that are reflected in the judgments you make, based on your moral sensibility. It seems to be completely irrelevant to our explanation whether your intuitive immediate judgment is true or false.

The observation of an event can provide observational evidence for or against a scientific theory in the sense that the truth of that observation can be relevant to a reasonable explanation of why that observation was made. A moral observation does not seem, in the same sense, to be observational evidence for or against any moral theory, since the truth or falsity of the moral observation seems to be completely irrelevant to any reasonable explanation of why that observation was made. The fact that an observation of an event was made at the time it was made is evidence not only about the observer but also about the physical facts. The fact that you made a particular moral observation when you did does not seem to be evidence about moral facts, only evidence about you and your moral sensibility. Facts about protons can affect what you observe, since a proton passing through the cloud chamber can cause a vapor trail that reflects light to your eye in a way that, given your scientific training and psychological set, leads you to judge that what you see is a proton. But there does not seem to be any way in which the actual rightness or wrongness of a given situation can have any effect on your perceptual apparatus. In this respect, ethics seems to differ from science.

In considering whether moral principles can help explain observations, it is therefore important to note an ambiguity in the word "observation." You see the children set the cat on fire and immediately think, "That's wrong." In one sense, your observation is that what the children are doing is wrong. In another sense, your observation is your thinking that thought. Moral observations might explain observations in the first sense but not in the second sense. Certain moral principles might help to explain why it was *wrong* of the children to set the cat on fire, but moral principles seem to be of no help in explaining *your thinking* that that is wrong. In the first sense of "observation," moral principles can be tested by observation—"That this act is wrong is evidence that causing unnecessary suffering is wrong." But in the second sense of "observation," moral principles cannot clearly be tested by observation, since they do not appear to help explain observations in this second sense of "observation." Moral principles do not seem to help explain your observing what you observe.

Of course, if you are already given the moral principle that it is wrong to cause unnecessary suffering, you can take your seeing the children setting the cat on fire as observational evidence that they are doing something wrong. Similarly, you can suppose that your seeing the vapor trail is observational evidence that a proton is going through the cloud chamber, if you are given the relevant physical theory. But there is an important apparent difference between the two cases. In the scientific case, your making the observation is itself evidence for the physical theory because the physical theory explains the proton, which explains the trail, which explains your observation. In the moral case, your making your observation does not seem to be evidence for the relevant moral principle because that principle does not seem to help explain your observation. The explanatory chain from principle to observation seems to be broken in morality. The moral principle may "explain" why it is wrong for the children to set the cat on fire. But the wrongness of that act does not appear to help explain the act, which you observe, itself. The explanatory chain appears to be broken in such a way that neither the moral principle nor the wrongness of the act can help explain why you observe what you observe.

A qualification may seem to be needed here. Perhaps the children perversely set the cat on fire simply "because it is wrong." Here it may seem at first that the actual wrongness of the act does help explain why they do it and therefore indirectly helps explain why you observe what you observe just as a physical theory, by explaining why the proton is producing a vapor trail, indirectly helps explain why the observer observes what he observes. But on reflection we must agree that this is probably an illusion. What explains the children's act is not clearly the actual wrongness of the act but, rather, their belief that the act is wrong. The actual rightness or wrongness of their act seems to have nothing to do with why they do it.

Observational evidence plays a part in science it does not appear to play in ethics, because scientific principles can be justified ultimately by their role in explaining observations, in the second sense of observation—by their explanatory role. Apparently, moral principles cannot be justified in the same way. It appears to be true that there can be no explanatory chain between moral principles and particular observings in the way that there can be such a chain between scientific principles and particular observings. Conceived as an explanatory theory, morality, unlike science, seems to be cut off from observation.

Not that every legitimate scientific hypothesis is susceptible to direct observational testing. Certain hypothesis about "black holes" in space cannot be directly tested, for example, because no signal is emitted from within a black hole. The connection with observation in such a case is indirect. And there are many similar examples. Nevertheless, seen in the large, there is the apparent difference between science and ethics we have noted. The scientific realm is accessible to observation in a way the moral realm is not.

IV. ETHICS AND MATHEMATICS

Perhaps ethics is to be compared, not with physics, but with mathematics. Perhaps such a moral principle as "You ought to keep your promises" is confirmed or disconfirmed in the way (whatever it is) in which such a mathematical principle as "$5 + 7 = 12$" is. Observation does not seem to play the role in mathematics it plays in physics. We do not and cannot perceive numbers, for example, since we cannot be in causal contact with them. We do not even understand what it would be like to be in causal contact with the number 12, say. Relations among numbers cannot have any more of an effect on our perceptual apparatus than moral facts can.

Observation, however, *is* relevant to mathematics. In explaining the observations that support a physical theory, scientists typically appeal to mathematical principles. On the other hand, one never seems to need to appeal in this way to moral principles. Since an observation is evidence for what best explains it, and since mathematics often figures in the explanations of scientific observations, there is indirect observational evidence for mathematics. There does not seem to be observational evidence, even indirectly, for basic moral principles. In explaining why certain observations have been made, we never seem to use purely moral assumptions. In this respect, then, ethics appears to differ not only from physics but also from mathematics. . . .

LOWELL KLEIMAN
Morality as the Best Explanation

Many people are sceptical of moralizers. I share this scepticism with many contemporary philosophers, such as J. L. Mackie and Gilbert Harman. Crime in the New York subways, alcoholism, drug abuse, the spread of AIDS are socio-economic and medical problems, despite what certain religious leaders say.[1]

But moralizing is one thing; morality, it seems, is something else. One need not belong to a special religious group to lament the atrocities of Nazism or condemn the terrorism of the Hezbollah. If we know anything, we know that killing and maiming the innocent is wrong. Or so it seems.

Recently, Mackie, Harman and others have suggested an intriguing and original defense of moral scepticism, what I call "The Best Explanation Approach" ("BEA" for short). They seem to feel that since moral conduct and belief can be explained empirically without assuming "moral facts" or a metaethical theory of meaning such as non-cognitivists espoused, moral judgments and explanations are gratuitous.

The view is compelling. Someone who believes that AIDS is a moral problem, for example, seems to ignore the evidence that many AIDS patients are children. Deep seated religious prejudice against homosexuals seems to have influenced moral attitudes more than any special facts about the disease itself.

Moreover, BEA theorists propose no new theory of the meaning or function of moral discourse. Advocates do not claim that a moral judgment is a disguised psychological or sociological report, as traditional subjectivists and relativists suggested. Nor is it a noise emoted to vent one's feelings, as the positivists argued; a special kind of order, command or request, as proposed by imperativists; or even a crypto-commendation, as prescriptivists urged. For all of that, moral language might just as well be descriptive, since, according to BEA proponents, there are no moral facts anyway. The apparent simplicity is impressive.

Nevertheless, as I shall try to show, the view is excessive. Those who propose BEA are not sceptical of all values. Someone who claims that morality does not provide the best explanation seems to think that there are better ones. But to countenance good, better or best explanations is to accept certain values, especially of science. I shall argue that in the absence of a theory of moral discourse, or additional empirical evidence, a moral explanation, except for subject matter, is not significantly different from any other. In what follows I will try to show, contrary to the assumptions of the BEA theorist, that a moral explanation can be objective, universal and consistent with the rest of science.

"Morality As The Best Explanation" is reprinted from the *American Philosophical Quarterly* Vol. 26, No. 2 (April 1989), by permission of the *American Philosophical Quarterly*. **Lowell Kleiman** teaches philosophy at Suffolk Community College of the State University of New York. He has published articles in the areas of the philosophy of mind, of language, and of religion, as well as in the field of ethics.

But first a word of caution. It may seem that I defend in this paper what has come to be called "Moral Realism." I do not, although I agree with the Moral Realist that some things are right and others wrong. Moral Realism is an ambitious and broad based view which attempts to extend certain doctrines of Scientific Realism, such as a causal theory of reference and a belief in natural kinds, to morality.[2] It seems to me that the jury is still out on these issues.[3] My point is more modest: aside from subject matter, since there is no essential difference between science and morality, as I shall argue, no special argument for or against morality is needed. If judgments of science are descriptive, so are judgments of morality. If scientific theories are observational, so are moral theories. If scientific properties are real, so are moral properties. I realize that there are those who are sceptical of science. I take no issue with them in this paper. The philosophers whose views I wish to examine, however, do not seem to be sceptical of science. On the contrary. J. L. Mackie, Gilbert Harman and others who adopt BEA suggest that *because* of science, especially the social sciences, morality does not provide the best explanation of human conduct or belief. I will try to show how these and other similar views are unwarranted.

What view do I propose? In this paper, I advocate no special view of morality, no special theory of the meaning of moral discourse, no special explanation of moral conduct or belief. On the contrary, my main point is that no special view, theory of meaning or explanation is needed. However, some account is needed of why people, especially when they initially think about morality, seem to feel the need for some special treatment of the subject. Here I can only speculate.

Moral issues, at least those that make the headlines, are dramatic and absorbing. Abortion, euthanasia, surrogate motherhood are fascinating, not only because they reflect advances in technology, but because they are morally complex and confusing. To help settle these issues, as in any controversy, more details are often needed—but that is just what is missing especially in popular moral debates. As a consequence, moralists fall back on platitudes. But platitudes, such as "Life is sacred," are, by themselves practically useless in the face of other equally compelling (at least in the abstract) slogans, for example, "A woman has a right to her own body." It should not be surprising that when apparent moral conflict is reduced to sloganeering, as is often the case, morality appears empty and devoid of significant guidance.

Moreover, since people tend to think of dramatic moral issues when they begin to theorize about morality, it is natural that scepticism would result. The only serious question seems to be how best to explain the apparent emptiness of the field, its apparent lack of factual content, even its lack of making any sense whatsoever. This is one reason why the same individuals, especially students of ethics who may have strong moral convictions outside of the classroom, tend to lose that sense of objectivity when they begin to philosophize about the subject. Moral scepticism, especially for the student, is seductive. The arguments of certain more mature thinkers make it even more tempting. Nevertheless, as I would now like to show, it is a temptation that we ought to resist.

I. OBJECTIVITY

I begin with what I take to be a basic assumption of those who propose the Best Explanation Approach:

(1) An explanation is best only if it can be objective.

The idea is that while there may be certain facts to which a scientist or someone offering a common-sensical explanation can appeal, there are no "objective values" to which a moralist can appeal. As J. L. Mackie argues,

The assertion that there are objective values, or intrinsically prescriptive entities or features of some kind which ordinary moral judgements presuppose, is, I hold, not meaningless but false.[4]

Mackie's thesis seems bold but it is unclear. What exactly is false, (a) that moral judgments presuppose special entities or (b) that there are certain entities that moral judgments presuppose? If Mackie means (a), then he may be correct. But this is the position of traditional metaethicists. For example, if a value judgment is a noise emoted to vent one's feelings, then some such utterance presupposes no special entities. But Mackie's approach is intended to avoid traditional metaethics.

Let us consider (b). According to this interpretation, moral judgments presuppose things that do not exist. If this is correct, then perhaps independent of traditional metaethics, we should be sceptical of moral judgments. But why should we not also be sceptical of other value judgments, including the judgment that there is a good argument for moral scepticism? If Mackie's thesis is to succeed there should be some relevant difference between a moral judgment and other value judgments.

It might be felt that if there were objective moral values they would be peculiar (Mackie calls them "queer") in the sense that anything that had them would be intrinsically prescriptive. The idea seems to be that when people

judge that torturing an animal is cruel, for example, they presuppose that there is something about the action, not just the people judging it, that makes it something that ought not be done. By contrast, it seems, a good reason in science or a good argument in philosophy depends, to some extent, on a community of scholars recognizing it as such. The history of scholarship is replete with changing standards of judgment.

But a moral judgment, too, depends, to some extent, on a community of individuals. As will be discussed in the next section, moral judgments vary from society to society, or within the same society from one historical period to another. If values of science are not prescriptive, or prescriptive in some special way, or if moral values are somehow independent Platonic entities,[5] additional argument is needed to show this. Otherwise, it seems that moralists have no more reason to be sceptical of their judgments than scientists and scholars have to be sceptical of theirs.

What about the connection between the apparent fact that torturing an animal is cruel and the value by which we judge this behavior? As Humeans point out, there appears to be a gap between what is and what ought to be. For example, that an action is cruel does not, by itself, entail that it is wrong (Mackie, p. 41). It seems that some additional explanation is needed for why we judge that cruel behavior ought not be done. But neither does inflicting pain for the fun of it, for example, entail that something is cruel. Some additional explanation seems needed here as well. Yet cruelty exists. Just as the lack of entailment in the second case does not, by itself, support scepticism of cruelty, so the lack of entailment in the first case does not, by itself, support scepticism of morality.

It may be suggested that moral qualities are "supervenient," for example, in the following sense proposed by W. D. Hudson:

You would puzzle your hearers if you said that two things, A and B, are alike in every respect except that A is good and B is not; or if you said that two actions, C and D, were exactly the same except that C was right, or obligatory, and D was not. They would insist that there must be some other difference to account for this one. But if you said, for instance, "This book is exactly like that one except that this has a red cover," no such insistence would be forthcoming. Differences in value have to be accounted for by differences of another kind as other sorts of difference do not.[6]

But what other kind of difference do those who draw this distinction have in mind? Must it be something physical? If so, it seems that differences other than value, including differences in color, are supervenient. If we wish to account for the difference between a book cover that is red and one that is not, for example, we might consider the underlying chemical structure of the dye used in printing. But color dependence alone does not make us sceptical of color.[7] Why should moral dependence make us sceptical of morality?

It might be objected that a person need not know, or have any special beliefs about, the underlying physical structure that accounts for difference in color. By contrast, someone who judges that one action is right and another not must have some idea why this is so. Otherwise, as Hudson suggests, the judgment would puzzle the hearers. But a person who judges that an object is red also has *some* idea why this is so, if only that it *looks* red. Otherwise, this judgment, too, would puzzle the hearers.

Are moral judgments objective? If objectivity means that a judgment presupposes things that exist, then there is reason to think that moral judgments, except perhaps for those of certain religious moralizers, are objective. In the next section let us consider the additional argument from cultural relativism.

II. RELATIVISM

Morality seems to consist in sets of rules intended to guide human conduct, for example, "Promises ought to be kept." We teach, or try to teach, these rules to our children so that, among other things, as they grow up they agree with us in our way of life. A person who abides by no rules or moral principles, like an untutored child, does not seem to know the difference between right and wrong. The significance of rules in morality, it seems, cannot be over-emphasized.

But not all rules are the same. Historians tell us that past cultures developed ways of living which seem not only different from our own, but in apparent conflict with what we believe. For example, the ancient Egyptians, or at least the Pharaohs, practiced incest; the Romans, infanticide. Our own American predecessors accepted slavery, while members of the Kali cult of Northern India still practice human sacrifice. In the face of apparent moral diversity, the following principle presents itself:

(2) An explanation is best only if it is universal.

The idea seems to be that moral belief is a matter of cultural upbringing. For example, we are not racists, sexists or bigots. But sexism, racism and bigotry are out of fashion today, at least in some circles. Had we lived ten, twenty, a hundred years ago, who knows what we would have believed. If belief is a matter of upbringing, a person could be brought up to believe almost anything. How then can we blame the racist for upholding Apartheid, the anti-Semite for discriminating against Jews, the misogynist for hating women? To think that we can seems to commit what is often called the "Ethnocentric Fallacy," the alleged mistake of judging others by standards that are not their own.

But is the "Ethnocentric Fallacy" a fallacy? Judging others by our standards is not always a mistake. Children, for example, add one plus one and sometimes get three. We have no hesitation to correct them. We do not feel that there is some special fallacy in judging, whether in our culture or any other culture, how people add. Why should there be some fallacy in judging how people behave? If the rules of arithmetic are universally valid, why aren't the rules of morality?

The answer seems to be, with the exception of children, most, if not all, people in all cultures share the same principles of mathematics. Jews, gentiles, Greeks, Romans, blacks, whites, Orientals—when they add one plus one they get two. This is no coincidence. The best explanation seems to be that one plus one *equals* two and that human beings, whether through reason, experience or both, have the capacity to recognize this.

By contrast, the best explanation for the apparent diversity of moral belief seems to come from sociology, in conjunction, perhaps, with the related disciplines of anthropology and psychology. According to the ethical relativist (see Mackie, pp. 36–38), however moral belief is to be explained, there is no need to assume the truth of any moral principle.

But scientific belief, too, is diverse. The ancients believed that the earth was the center of the universe, scientists of the 18th and 19th century believed in a universal ether, and today there is no general agreement whether or not the universe will continue to expand or eventually begin to contract. If the social sciences can explain moral diversity, then perhaps they can help to explain scientific diversity as well. But if the sociological explanation of moral belief means that there is no need to assume the truth of any moral principle, then the sociological explanation of scientific belief means that there is no need to assume the truth of any scientific principle. But this cannot be. Otherwise, paradoxically, there is no need to assume the truth of sociology or any of the other social disciplines.

But science is observational, or so it might be suggested. An historian of science, for example, would not completely explain Galileo's belief in the heliocentric theory without mentioning his various celestial observations, for example, of Jupiter's moons. A political historian, it seems, need not mention the observa-

tions of those who favored resettling Japanese-Americans during the Second World War. It is enough to speak of ultra-patriotism, and, perhaps, racism.

But scientific observations need not always be mentioned either. For example, it seems that the Church astronomers of the 16th and early 17th century rejected the Copernican system without looking into a telescope. Part of the explanation seems to be that their own Ptolemaic views were well established. And, among other things, it seems that scientists, not unlike most people, tend to be conservative in their beliefs and reluctant to accept change.

The moral relativist might respond that observation in science provides *evidence* for certain theories. Galileo's telescopic observations helped to prove that the Copernican hypothesis was better than the older Aristotelian approach. Ethical observation does not seem to play a similar role.[8] The U. S. Government's observation of Japanese-Americans did not seem to provide evidence that a resettlement program was needed.

But scientific observation does not always provide evidence either. The Aristotelians who eventually looked into Galileo's telescope saw what they claimed were aberrations of light.[9] Part of the explanation seems to be that they were biased against Galileo. Apparently, those who were against the Japanese communities in the United States were also biased. The reason why we need not assume certain moral facts seems to be similar to why we need not assume certain scientific facts. Some judgments, whether of morality or science, are just false.

Despite controversy and disagreement, scientific explanation seems to have universal application. In the absence of further argument, it seems that moral explanation can have universal application as well. The sceptic might agree, but claim that objectivity and universality in ethics is not enough. Unlike science, where the canons of investigation seem to minimize bias, moral opinions seem less determined by what people actually see than by what they already believe. In the next section, I turn to the BEA sceptic who argues that moral explanations are not scientific.

III. SCIENTISM

The BEA theorist claims that belief in morality, like belief in spirit possession, is unscientific. As science can explain why people appear to be possessed by spirits, so science can explain why people appear to behave morally. And just as there are no "spirit facts" to speak of, so there are no "moral facts" either.

The sceptical principle many be summarized as follows:

> (3) An explanation is best only if it is
>   scientific.

The view is persuasive.[10] Just as there seems little point to theorize about unicorns and spirits, so there seems little point to moralize about the spread of AIDS.

But not every scientific explanation avoids certain facts. For example, color perception is explained, in part, on the basis of the physics of light, the principles of optics, the genetically determined reticular structures of the eye, the physiology of the central nervous system including the optic nerve, and the neurochemistry of the brain, especially the anterior lobe of the cerebral cortex. Yet, when we are looking at a ripe McIntosh apple, it seems, we are seeing something red. Similarly, even if we can explain moral perception physically, optically, genetically, physiologically, neurochemically and cerebrally, when we are observing American families being displaced from their homes into resettlement camps, it seems, we are seeing something wrong.

Colors, as philosophers say, are "secondary" properties, qualities that seem to exist only in perception. If moral qualities too exist only in perception, then, unless there is some external cause, moral judgments would seem to be suspect. Color perception, for example, seems to have some such cause. We see something red, in part, because there is something independent of perception affecting us in a certain way. What, if anything, is there independent of moral perception? Unlike colors, there does not seem to be any special wavelength of light that we associate with the perception of right and wrong.

But not all perceived qualities are associated with some special wavelength of light. We can see something white, for example, because a combination of wavelengths of light is reflected by an object to the eye. Similarly, we can see something wrong for the same reason. Otherwise, in the absence of light, we would not see anything.

But in perceiving something white the wavelengths of red, orange, yellow, green, blue, indigo and violet are all present. There does not seem to be any special spectrum of light needed to explain moral perception. Is this reason to be sceptical? I think not. Moral qualities, unlike colors, are not just visual. We see something wrong when we are affected, not just by electromagnetic radiation, but by something a person does. Human action seems to be the main focus of moral perception.

Is there reason to be sceptical of human action? The BEA theorist is unclear about this. Francis Snare, for example, suggests, "We can more adequately describe, explain, predict the world as it is without the use of moral terms and moral notions. . . . "(p. 216).

If Snare means "the world" as discussed in physics and chemistry texts, he may be right. There seems little need for morality to describe, explain or predict the behavior of electrons or amino acids. But if he means the world of human conduct, then what he says is problematic. We do not need a psycho-social account of Nazi mentality, for example, to explain why genocide is not an acceptable state policy. It seems enough to know that killing the innocent is wrong.

IV. SCEPTICISM, MORALIZING AND MORALITY

The sceptic and moralizer have much in common. They both emphasize diversity. The moralizer looks at the world and sees black and white. Either you are with him or against him. The sceptic sees only neutral gray. There is nothing to be with him or against him about. But not everything in morality is either absolutely black, absolutely white, or absolutely neutral. Though it is often ignored in debates of this kind, there is much more unanimity than moralizers and sceptics seem to admit. With few exceptions, for example, human beings are against genocide. Especially in the aftermath of the Holocaust, no one nowadays is blind to its consequences. In the absence of additional argument, it seems that part of the best explanation for this apparent unanimity is that genocide is wrong. Moreover, genocide is not an isolated example. Rape, extortion, blackmail, treason are all regarded as wrong. If there is a better explanation, it should be made plain.[11]

Some BEA theorists have tried. Francis Snare, for example, suggests that ". . . the best explanation of this uniformity is . . . all alternative cultures were systematically exterminated, along with the deviants and dissenters in our own culture" (Snare, p. 223).

Aside from the glaring omission of evidence to support this speculation, it is difficult to believe that cultures opposed to genocide would systematically exterminate anybody, even deviants and dissenters.

Another suggestion is that ". . . all cultures might happen to socialize and condition individuals to react similarly in regard to certain kinds of conduct. Perhaps the cultures which do so are more likely to survive" (Snare, p.223).

This may be. But why would it "be difficult to see any moral facts behind this uniformity" (Snare, p. 223)? Cultures that are opposed to genocide, and killing in general, are more likely to be at peace with their neighbors. Peace among nations is a moral goal. Why is it difficult to see any moral facts behind the achievement of a moral goal?

The sceptic might look to the sociobiologist to bolster his cause. Edward O. Wilson, for example, has recently suggested that social behavior, including moral conduct such as altruistic activity, can be explained genetically.[12] If Wilson is right, then the common genetic pool of mankind might help to explain apparent common moral belief.

Does sociobiology support moral scepticism? If certain genetic hormonal secretions help to determine moral preferences, similar biological processes, it seems, would influence scientific choices as well. Perhaps sociobiology can help to explain agreement in science as well as in morality. But if sociobiology implies moral scepticism, then it implies scientific scepticism, including, paradoxically, scepticism of sociobiology. If this is so, why accept sociobiology in the first place?

The anti-moralist thinks that morality is not needed to explain or predict human conduct, that the moral idiom is not necessary to describe human behavior. Indeed, we need not talk of wickedness to explain the occurrence of AIDS just as we need not talk of supernatural powers to explain the 4000 witches that apparently live on Long Island today.[13] But the reason is not that we have a better or more scientific explanation of how certain individuals can fly about on broomsticks or why only wicked people get sick. Rather, just as no one flies about on a broomstick, so not all victims of disease are immoral. If the moral idiom is essentially different from the idiom of science, if we cannot explain human conduct morally, or speak of right and wrong matter-of-factly, the BEA theorist has yet to show us why. In the absence of further debate, it seems that morality can be the best explanation.

NOTES

1. The Rev. Charles Stanley, for example, leader of the Southern Baptist Convention, has suggested that "Homosexuality has been going on for a long time, but as it has become an acceptable lifestyle in the minds of many people, we have AIDS. . . . AIDS is God indicating his displeasure . . . toward that form of lifestyle" *Free Inquiry*, vol. 6 (1986), pp. 60–61.

2. Richard Boyd takes on this ambitious task in "How to be a Moral Realist," *Essays on Moral Realism*, Geoffrey Sayre-McCord, ed. (Ithaca: Cornell University Press, 1988).

3. My reservations about a causal theory of reference have been expressed, in collaboration with Ed Erwin and Eddy Zemach, in "The Historical Theory of Reference," *Australasian Journal of Philosophy*, vol 54 (1976) pp. 50–57.

4. J. L. Mackie, *Ethics: Inventing Right and Wrong* (New York: Penguin Books, 1977), p. 35.

5. Mackie suggest that "Platonic Forms give a dramatic picture of what objective values would have to be" (p. 40).

6. W. D. Hudson, *Modern Moral Philosophy* (Garden City, NY: Doubleday & Co., Inc., 1970), p. 165.

7. Alan H. Goldman has recently argued (*Journal of Philosophy*, vol. 84 (1987), pp. 349–62) that the analogy between colors and moral qualities, as a way of demonstrating moral realism, is ineffective since the reality of color is itself questionable. His main argument is that ordinary judgments of color (or shades of some color) vary, not only from one observer to the next, but for the same observer, from one observation to the next. Since there is no nonarbitrary class of "normal" observers or "normal" conditions of observation, the Lockean analysis of secondary qualities, ". . . for each specific color, an object of that color will appear a certain way to normal observers under normal conditions" (p. 352), does not avoid the problem of "ascribing incompatible shades to the same uniformly colored surfaces" (p. 353).

   Goldman, however, seems to confuse the Lockean analysis, correctly described above, with something else, namely, for each specific color an object of that color will appear *the same* to normal observers under normal conditions. If Goldman is correct about variation in color perception, this latter proposition is false. But this is not the Lockean analysis. According to the Lockean, color is not just a phenomenal occurrence but something ultimately determined by an underlying physical structure. Hence, if I have just finished painting my house pure white, for example, it may nevertheless look off-white to you, partly because of the way the sunlight is reflected off the roof, partly for any one of a number of other optical, neurological, or physiological reasons alluded to by Goldman. Some such variation, however, especially when understood as caused by something other than a different paint, provides little or no reason to doubt that the house is really pure white.

8. Gilbert Harman suggests that while moral judgments are observational, we need not assume any moral facts to explain their occurrence. See *The Nature of Morality*, especially Chap. I. "Ethics and Observation" (New York: Oxford University Press, 1977).

9. For a lively and illuminating account of the conflict in the early 17th century between Galileo and his detractors, see Arthur Koestler's *The Sleepwalkers*, Part V (New York: The Universal Library, 1976).

10. Francis Snare defends a similar view in "The Empirical Bases of Moral Scepticism," *American Philosophical Quarterly*, vol. 21 (1984), pp. 215–24.

11. It may be argued that moral judgments are analytic. The apparent unanimity against rape, for example, would be explained as the result of following a linguistic convention. Any who denied that rape is wrong would exhibit linguistic incompetence, not ignorance of certain facts. Stephen Baumrin has suggested this to me.

   But the concept of the analytic is unclear. Does "analytic" mean *true by virtue of meaning* or *necessarily true?* If the former, then moral judgments do not seem to be analytic. "Genocide is wrong" seems true, but not just by virtue of some linguistic convention. The genocide committed during the German holocaust, for example, was unprecedented. There were no established conventions, linguistic or otherwise, governing such extreme behavior. On the other hand, if "analytic" means *necessarily true*, then moral judgments may be analytic. "Rape is wrong," for example, seems necessarily true. But as Kripke and others have argued [see "Naming and Necessity" in Donald Davidson and Gilbert Harman (eds.) *Semantics of Natural Language* (Dordrecht: D. Reidel, 1972)] statements of fact can be necessarily true in the sense that they can be true in all possible worlds.

12. Edward O. Wilson, *Sociobiology* (Cambridge, Mass.: The Belknap Press of Harvard University Press, 1975), especially Chapter 1, "The Morality of the Gene," and the section, "Ethics," in Chapter 27.

13. Sybil Leek, until her death several years ago, was well known as a witch. ("Sybil Leek, 'Ordinary Witch From New Forest,' Dies at 65," *New York Times*, October 29, 1982, II 8:1). A recent article in *Newsday* (October 29, 1979) estimates that there are 4000 witches currently living on Long Island.

BRUCE BROWER
Virtue Concepts and Ethical Realism

Several philosophers have recently suggested that certain concrete ethical concepts, such as those of promising, courage, kindness, and dishonesty, provide rich and finely-grained evaluations.[1] They also hold that such concepts refer to properties about which some form of "ethical realism" is true.

These philosophers assume that the concepts in question are evaluative or have an evaluative component. I disagree. I shall argue that many of these concepts are merely descriptive and do not express an evaluation. I call this position *descriptivism,* even though this term has been overworked. I use antidescriptivism to refer to the opposing view. Descriptivists can be realists about the properties referred to by these concepts, but they are not thereby ethical realists. So a descriptivist can be a realist about courage, for instance, without being an ethical realist.

I shall follow a number of writers by concentrating on concepts of what have been taken to be virtues and vices. As it turns out, strong arguments can be made that certain traditional virtue and vice concepts are evaluative. I hope to show that such arguments are unsound. I shall argue that, for any traditional virtue, we can imagine worlds at which the virtue is of negative value overall. So, for any virtue, we can imagine a world where having that virtue is not good, and acting in accord with that virtue is not right. This conflicts with the most interesting form of antidescriptivism.

Descriptivism can be illustrated by considering a concept that is not of a virtue or a vice. Williams claims that the concept of a lie has an evaluative component (op. cit., p. 140). According to his view, to say that someone lies is not only to say that she states a falsehood with the intent to deceive, but it is also to express a negative evaluation of her or her action. In contrast, the descriptivist holds that to say that someone lies is merely to describe, not to evaluate.

Without at this point arguing for descriptivism, let me compare the concept of lying with the more obviously descriptive concept of kicking other people. Several things are worth noting. First, descriptivism grants that lying is usually of negative value; but the value is not included in the concept of lying. Similarly, kicking others is usually of negative value; but the concept of kicking others is not evaluative. Second, speakers who discuss someone's lying often expect their listeners to form negative evaluations. The descriptivist holds that this is because the speakers take their listeners to have values close to their own, not because the concept of lying is evaluative. Similarly, if I tell you that someone kicks others, I merely describe; but I assume that you will form a negative evaluation of the other person. Third, there

"Virtue Concepts and Ethical Realism" is reprinted from the *Journal of Philosophy* LXXXV 12 (December 1988), by permission of the *Journal of Philosophy*. **Bruce Brower**, a contemporary American philosopher affiliated with the University of Illinois, brings together two major concerns in current ethical theory, the nature of virtue and ethical realism, a doctrine concerning the ultimate status of moral value.

are several senses in which the descriptivist can be a realist about lying, for lying exists, and facts about lying can be true independent of our beliefs. Similarly, one can be a realist about the property of kicking others. Thus, descriptivism is not committed to "antirealism" or "nonrealism" about the properties referred to by concrete ethical concepts.[2] Fourth, it would be easy to give an account of evaluation—say, in terms of emotional responses—from which antidescriptivism immediately follows. So there are "cheap" forms of antidescriptivism according to which both the concept of lying and the concept of kicking others have negative value. But these forms of antidescriptivism would hold true of any concept that refers to properties that, as a matter of fact, we value or do not value. The form of antidescriptivism I wish to consider is more interesting, because it does not easily apply to a broad range of concepts.

The term 'descriptivism' could mislead, since its use may seem to presuppose noncognitivism. Traditional noncognitivists distinguish between *descriptive propositions,* which are held to apply to the world independently of our attitudes, and *evaluations,* which are held to express our attitudes, and are viewed as inapplicable to the world that is independent of our attitudes. The usual noncognitivist view is that descriptive propositions, but not evaluations, can be true or false. In this essay, the distinction between description and evaluation is not meant to imply that evaluations cannot be true or false. So the claim that a concept is evaluative is not meant to imply that propositions containing the concept cannot be true or false. One may use 'descriptive' for all propositions that can be true or false. Within this broadly descriptive set of propositions, one may distinguish between the evaluative and the nonevaluative. This intuitive distinction is worth preserving, even if one wishes to avoid noncognitivism.

I

Let us look at concepts as having conditions of application, such that a concept applies only to objects that meet its conditions. Totally competent speakers must recognize that each condition of application is a necessary condition for applying the concept to an object.[3] If a concept has a condition of application, then, in any possible world, objects in the extension of the concept must meet the condition. Descriptivism holds that concrete ethical concepts have only descriptive conditions of application. Antidescriptivism holds that concrete ethical concepts have both descriptive and evaluative conditions of application.

Before examining the evaluative condition, consider some examples. One sort of example is of cases in which a concept that we might take to be evaluative is applied to actions from which our usual evaluation is withheld. Examples of this kind were discussed by Philippa Foot[4] and R. M. Hare.[5] Foot argued that 'rude' is both descriptive and evaluative. Hare responded that 'rude' is primarily descriptive. He supported this view by citing actions which meet the descriptive conditions for rudeness but which we would not evaluate adversely. Other examples of this sort are easy to imagine. For instance, most of us allow that some actions are honest but wrong, or dishonest but right. Yet such cases show only that there are isolated circumstances in which the concept applies but our normal evaluation is withheld. They are consistent with the view that rudeness is usually of negative value, or the view that honesty is usually of positive value. So, by slightly weakening the position, an antidescriptivist can argue that a concept has an evaluative condition just in case that condition must be met by most actions in the extension of the concept.

A second sort of example involves concepts that refer to properties that are no longer evaluated as they were in the past. For many, chastity is a good example of such a property. Another is pride, which is now often seen as a sign of appropriate self-esteem—especially if the pride is directed at a property that was wrongly denigrated in the past, such as being black. In taking note of these, the antidescriptivist can claim that whether a concept is evaluative is relative to a "form of life," "tradition," "point of view," or "conceptual scheme." I shall say below why I take this move to be inadequate. But the antidescriptivist can also claim that, while some concepts undergo shifts in their evaluative component, such shifts are impossible for central virtue concepts, such as prudence, courage, and kindness.

What we need, then, are examples involving central virtue concepts, such that the virtues in question are shown not merely to have negative value occasionally, but rather to be of negative value in general. Consider these "possible worlds":

World W1: Human beings are enslaved by a physically and intellectually superior species, and are forced to spend their lives constructing spaceships. They have no reasonable hope of successful revolution against this system.

Members of the master species, who are completely informed about humans, regularly review the behavior of each human. If a human overcame fear, ignored fear, or failed to have fear in a situation where most humans would act out of fear, then that human is tortured for the rest of her life. If any other human benefited from the overcoming of fear, the ignoring of fear, or the failure to have fear, then that other human is also tortured. It follows that, if a human acts courageously or benefits from another's courage, she will be tortured for the rest of her life.[6]

If a human does not act courageously, she is allowed to live a moderately fulfilling life.

World W2: As a matter of psychological fact, kind people become weak and powerless. They are indecisive, lose control of their lives, and become ineffective in relations with others. Only those who are not kind can become strong and take charge of their lives. They need not be cruel or vicious, but even isolated kind acts lead to the destruction of one's character.

According to descriptivism, courage has no positive value at W1, and kindness has no positive value at W2. So the concepts of courage and kindness seem to be purely descriptive concepts that apply at other possible worlds to actions that lack positive value.[7]

The descriptivist agrees that courage and kindness have positive value at our world, but holds that our concepts of them are not evaluative. The mere fact that a property is valuable at our world does not imply that a concept that refers to it is evaluative.

One response to descriptivism is that the concept of courage (for example) only requires that courage be valuable at our world. On this view, a speaker understands the concept of courage if she understands that (a) at other worlds, certain acts meet a given descriptive condition, but (b) at our world, a courageous act must both meet the descriptive condition and have positive value. An analogy is provided by revising our concept of gold. Let gold* be a concept just like our concept of gold, except that in order to apply gold* correctly, a speaker must recognize that members of its extension have positive value at our world. At some other world W*, where gold is abundant, iron is scarce, and socio-economic conditions are similar to ours, gold is not valuable. Suppose, however, that as the concept of gold* is understood, it may be applied to gold objects at W*, even though we recognize that gold (and hence gold*) is not valuable at W*.

A similar response is that the evaluative condition varies with the world, such that, if one is considering a world at which the property denoted by the concept is of a certain positive or negative value, then one must recognize that value of the property, at that world. So actions at other worlds may be described by such concepts, yet at these other worlds the property denoted by the concept has a different value than it has at our world. Nevertheless, at the actual world, any competent speaker must recognize the actual value of the property. Thus, if one fully understands the concept of courage, then to describe an action at our world as courageous is thereby to acknowledge the positive value of the action; but one must also recognize certain actions performed at W1 as courageous and yet see that they are not of positive value at W1.

These responses seem ad hoc, and I do not believe they capture the central antidescriptivist intuitions. But there is a further problem: W1 and W2 are not merely possible worlds. Our world might be like them. In the case of W1,

this must occur in the future; but, in the case of W2, we could in principle discover that our current psychological beliefs are wrong, and that our world is at present similar to W2. The descriptivist holds that whether courage and kindness have value depends on how the world is, and that therefore we could discover that they lack value at our world. W1 and W2 are possible states of our world.

Of course, we do not believe our world is like W1 or W2. In daily life we automatically value courage and kindness, because given our basic beliefs about society and psychology (beliefs that we rarely have occasion to doubt), we hold that courage and kindness are valuable. Yet we could find out that these beliefs are false, in which case we would no longer automatically value courage and kindness.

II

Antidescriptivism can be made more defensible by spelling out the evaluative condition of application along certain lines. Most antidescriptivists have cashed out evaluation in terms of there being a reason for action. The clearest account is developed by Williams, on the basis of work by McDowell. Williams holds that concrete ethical concepts are "thick," where this means that they are "both world-guided and action-guiding" (op. cit., 129–130, 140–142). His idea is that the correct application of such concepts depends both on how the world is and on whether they are understood as "characteristically" or "often" providing a reason for action. He holds that it is a plausible "demand on the understanding" that the user of such concepts must accept their evaluative point (op. cit., p. 142). Let us say that a concept is positive if it denotes a property that we ordinarily take to be of positive value. On Williams's view, a positive, thick concept is action-guiding in that it is correctly applied to an action only if there is a reason for the agent to take that action. A competent speaker misapplies a concept if she applies it to an action for which there is no reason. So, if she knows that the concept ap-

plies to an action she is considering, she thereby knows that there is a reason for the action. A negative, thick concept, in contrast, is action-guiding in that it is correctly applied to an action only if there is a reason for not taking the action. If a competent speaker applies the concept to an action, she thereby knows that there is a reason for not taking that action. In general, the evaluative condition of application is provided by this action-guiding element.[8]

Let us interpret the requirement that *there be a reason* in a strong fashion. Accordingly, to say that there is a reason for an action is not merely to say that there is some reason, or that the agent has some reason, for the action. Rather, there is a reason for an action only if there is reason to take the action, all things considered. In this sense, there may be reason for or against an action even if the agent does not recognize the reason.[9]

By construing evaluation in terms of there being reasons, the antidescriptivist can respond to descriptivism. The antidescriptivist will argue that W1, as portrayed above, is misdescribed. To formulate this response, more must be said about courage. Courage is not exhibited by every action in which the agent overcomes fear. If a soldier endures gunfire in order to retrieve a button that has fallen off her uniform, her act is stupid, not courageous. If I cross a busy highway in order to save ten steps, then my act is stupid, not courageous. These acts involve overcoming fear, but they are not courageous, because an act is courageous only if the goal one hopes to attain is worth the risk involved in performing the action.

What is it for an action to be worth the risk? One popular theory holds that an action is rational if, given the values and probabilities of the outcomes of that action and other actions, the action maximizes the expected utility for the agent. If we accept this theory, we might say that an action is worth the risk if it maximizes expected utility; i.e., an action is worth the risk if it is rational. Thus, on this theory, an action is courageous only if it is rational.

Totally aside from a detailed theory of rationality, it would be odd to take an action to be worth the risk, but to hold that there is no reason to take the action. So even on a very intuitive account, an action is courageous only if there is a reason for performing it.

If these views are correct, then it seems the concept of courage requires that an act is courageous only if there is a reason for doing it.[10] Then, given the account of evaluative conditions above, the concept of courage has an evaluative condition of application.

Let us reconsider W1. At W1, it would be irrational to take the risk involved in attempting a slave rebellion, since the result will be the life-long torture of all who rebel or benefit from rebellion. So the above description of W1 seems to be off the mark. Some acts, such are rebellion, are worth the risk at other worlds but not worth the risk at W1. Thus W1 is not a world at which acts of courage lack positive value; rather, it is a world at which acts that would normally be courageous are not courageous because there is no reason for doing them.

We can think of W1 and a world similar to it. At W1, members of the master species are aware of every human action and the psychol-

ogy behind it. Then it is false that courage exists at W1 and lacks value at W1. Courage does not exist at W1, because it is impossible to act courageously at W1. Courageous actions are impossible at W1, because it is never rational—never worth the risk—to overcome fear at W1. But it may be that, at any world where courage is possible, an agent can perform a courageous action only if there is a reason to perform it.

Now consider this similar world:

World W3: This world is exactly like W1, except that the master species does not detect every human action and the psychology behind it. Specifically, the masters sometimes overlook small movements of the thumbs. Humans develop a set of thumb movements, such that they converse in "thumb language." The language is greatly valued by humans, since it provides a realm of freedom beyond the control of their masters. The masters occasionally detect free thumb movements, however, in which case they torture the thumb mover and those around her.

Speaking thumb language is courageous at W3. It is true that, at the actual world, thumb movements are rarely courageous, and it is also true that, at W3, attempting rebellion would not be courageous. This shows that the behaviors that constitute courage at W3 differ significantly from the behaviors that constitute courage at the actual world. It does not show that courage lacks positive value at W3, or that recognizing an action as courageous is not, at all worlds, also recognizing it as an action for which there is a reason.

The concept of courage, then, appears to be both world-guided and action-guiding. But a similar response is not available in the case of kindness. Given that we want people to lead fruitful, satisfying lives, we would not value kindness at W2. At W2, the kind person makes a sacrifice disproportionate to the good done. So, at W2, it is best that people do not act kindly. There is no reason for agents at W2 to act kindly.

The concept of courage appears not to be purely descriptive and the concept of kindness appears to be purely descriptive. Where do other virtue and vice concepts fall? Among traditional virtues and vices, we may distinguish between *character* virtues or vices and *moral* virtues or vices. Character virtues, such as courage, temperance, and prudence, are typically exercised when the agent overcomes a specific type of temptation, desire, or emotion which threatens to interfere with the agent's achievement of an end. (In the case of courage, the agent overcomes fear.) These virtues are not primarily directed toward others or toward a principle that directly mentions behavior toward others. This is not to deny that the exercise of these virtues often affects the well-being of others. Likewise, the exercise of the corresponding vices, such as cowardice, intemperance, and imprudence, can adversely affect others. On the other hand, moral virtues, such as kindness, generosity, and honesty, are primarily directed either toward others or toward principles that directly mention behavior toward others. Their corresponding vices, such as cruelty, greediness, and dishonesty, always have some direct effect on others.

Concepts of character virtues are plausibly construed as action-guiding. Although such virtues are typically exercised when the agent overcomes a temptation, desire, or emotion, the agent must overcome these only to a rational extent. Temperance, for instance, does not require that one never indulge, but only that one not overindulge. That is, it requires that one never indulge to the point at which the negative effects of indulgence fail to be worth the positive gains. Thus, for reasons similar to those discussed in the case of courage, temperance may be held to require that the agent only indulge as much as is rational. So an action is temperate, it may be argued, only if there is a reason for performing it.

Concepts of moral virtues, however, are purely descriptive. Examining these virtues individually would be too lengthy, so I have chosen kindness as a typical example. For any moral virtue, there are possible worlds at which all actions that have the virtue lack positive value. Moreover, the central moral virtues—such as charity, kindness, generosity, and honesty—do not involve a reason-guiding condition of application, since they do not require that an agent perform a certain type of action only to a rational extent. Thus, the antidescriptivist argument that we have been considering applies only to concepts of character virtues.

III

I claimed that, by spelling out the evaluative condition in terms of action guiding, the antidescriptivist can plausibly argue that concepts of character virtues are evaluative. I now want to argue that this antidescriptivist move will not work.

In the case of courage, consider two kinds of examples. First, suppose that false but justified beliefs cause the agent to be misinformed about the possible outcomes of her action. For instance, suppose that soldiers in an isolated bunker believe, on the basis of recent radio reports, that the war is not over. Suppose that they take risks in their attacks on the enemy, yet (unknown to them) the only possible outcome of their actions is the aggravation of a strong enemy that has already won. The soldiers' actions appear to be worth the risk, but they actually have negative value.

The second kind of case occurs when, due to a mistake in complicated reasoning, an agent is misinformed about the utility of an action. Examples are too complex for detailed description; but we can imagine a general, engaged in sophisticated strategic planning, who places her army in a situation that she believes is worth the risk. She could easily reason incorrectly. Again, the action appears to be worth the risk, even if it is not.

Let us say that an agent acts *reasonably* when (a) she attempts to be rational in deciding to act and (b) she succeeds, for the most part, in actually being rational. An agent can act reasonably even if she is misinformed or makes a bad inference. In our examples, we did not imagine soldiers who fought after receiving messages that the war ended; nor did we imagine the general deciding by the flip of a coin. The imagined agents acted reasonably, yet they were mistaken about the value of their actions.

The concept of courage extends to these cases. The case of the soldiers is the clearest. Soldiers are often misinformed about the position or strength of the enemy, and they are often forced to make quick decisions in confusing situations. Thus, they take actions that they would not view as worth the risk, were they able to reflect carefully on all the relevant facts. Yet soldiers can act courageously in performing such actions.

Thus, the soldiers act courageously even when their actions are not worth the risk. Since an agent can act courageously even if her action is not worth the risk, an agent can act courageously even if she does not act in a way that has any actual chance of promoting a worthwhile end.

The consequences are unfortunate for the antidescriptivist. Consider this world:

World W4: This world is like W1, except that the humans mistakenly believe their world is like W3. This is, they mistakenly believe that some actions (e.g., thumb movements) go undetected by the masters. Further, they have very good grounds for this belief. (The masters allow them to speak thumb language for a few years without being punished. The humans notice that people are missing, but the masters tell them that these people were transferred to other workplaces. The masters force those who have been removed to send letters claiming to be well.)

Humans at W4 will reasonably believe that some courageous actions are worth the risk. They will act courageously, even if courage is not of value, and even if, unbeknownst to those who act courageously, courage leads to torture and is therefore of negative value.

At any world where agents can be reasonable but misinformed about whether actions are worth the risk, courageous actions can lack positive value. Thus, the value of courage depends not only on general social and psychological facts, but also on the extent to which agents are well-informed. At W4, agents are poorly informed. Similarly, if soldiers were usually misinformed about the position and strength of the enemy, but reasonably believed they were well-informed, then they would often perform courageous actions that had unfortunate consequences. In such a world, courage would lack positive value.

Let us reexamine the view that the concept of courage has an action-guiding condition of application. Consider three readings of this condition. On the first, weak reading, the condition requires merely that the agent have some reason, whether or not the reason is a good one. On the second, intermediate reading, the condition requires that the agent have a reason, and that the agent be reasonable in accepting that reason. On the third, strong reading, the condition requires that there be a good reason, where this entails that the action is actually worth the risk.

The case of the soldier who endures gun fire in order to retrieve a button shows that the weak reading is not enough. It would not be enough if she had some reason to retrieve the button— for instance, that it would keep her a bit warmer. Unless the soldier reasonably believed her action was worth the risk, she cannot have been courageous. On the other hand, the cases just gone over show that the strong reading demands too much, because an agent can be courageous even if she is wrong about the risk involved.

The action-guiding component in the concept of courage, then, requires only that there be a reason in the intermediate sense—it requires that the agent be reasonable. But, since it does not require that courage be of generally positive value, there can be worlds at which courage has negative value.

The antidescriptivist could object that what has been shown is precisely that there is a sense in which concepts of character virtues are evaluative. For one may hold that, when evaluation is cashed out in the intermediate sense (that is, in terms of reasonableness), the concept of courage and other concepts of character virtues can be shown to have evaluative conditions of application.

The problem with this is that, from the descriptivist point of view, reasonableness itself need not provide value; so there is no ground for holding that a condition which requires being reasonable is an *evaluative* condition. The descriptivist can back up this view by noting that there are possible worlds where being reasonable is generally of great negative value, and where acting on gut intuition, uncontrolled emotion, faith, or in some other unreasonable manner is always of greater value.[11] At W4, being reasonable is of no value whatsoever when contemplating courageous actions. We can, if we wish, imagine that at W4 the masters reward unreasonable behavior, perhaps by rewarding those who act only on emotions. The descriptivist holds that our tendency to believe that reasonableness must have positive value results from our concentration on what we take to be valuable in our world. But reasonableness, like courage and kindness, could turn out to have negative value.

IV

Two related objections may be made to the strategy adopted so far. The first is that, by spelling out evaluation in terms of prima facie reasons, we can treat virtues as valuable at all worlds. On this view, a concept has a positive, evaluative condition of application just in case it may be applied only to actions for which there are prima facie reasons. Then courage, for instance, is of positive value at W4, because (according to the antidescriptivist's intuitions) there is a prima facie reason for acting courageously at W4. This prima facie reason does not give courage the greatest overall value at W4, because the value of courage is outweighed or overridden by other factors. But courage does have value, even at W4.

The second objection is that courage (for instance) may have intrinsic value at worlds like W4, but that the value is outweighed by the intrinsic value of other factors, such as the negative value of the pain suffered by those tortured. If one takes the first objection to presuppose that an action has intrinsic value if and only if there is a prima facie reason for performing it, then the first objection may be treated as a version of the second. (The second objection, unlike the first, can be made without assuming that evaluation is to be explained in terms of reasons for action.)

The first objection remains unclear until the notion of a prima facie reason is explained. On many readings, this account succumbs to the same problems as accounts in terms of reasonableness. For example, suppose that we say there is a prima facie reason for an action just in case there is available a consideration which the agent, were she aware of it, would take to constitute some reason for the action. Then there could be prima facie reasons for actions of a certain sort, even if actions of that sort always had great negative value.

The central problem with both objections, however, is that they beg the question against descriptivism. The claim that courage and other virtues must be valuable is precisely what is being debated. The descriptivist does not share the intuitions that courageous actions are intrinsically valuable, or that an action is courageous only if there is a prima facie reason for performing it.

Moreover, the descriptivist can offer an explanation of why some people have these antidescriptivist intuitions: they believe themselves to live at a world unlike W4, and so they have developed the belief that courage is always valuable. If they believed that their world was one at which courage was not of greater overall value, they would not have developed the intuitions that there are always prima facie reasons for courageous actions and that courage is intrinsically valuable.

Returning to an earlier example, consider the following world:

World W5: Due to an unknown cause, humans have incredibly strong urges to kick others. Moreover, the shins and calves of humans are extremely sensitive. A kick that would result in a barely perceptible tap at our world would lead to excruciating pain at W5.

At W5, kicking others would have great negative value. Refraining from kicking in situations where one had the strong urge to kick would be an important virtue. Parents, educators, and religious leaders would stress that this virtue must be mastered in order to live a good life. Stories would be told about heroes who refrained from kicking. And some philosophers would develop the "intuitions" that the concept of refraining from kicking refers to a trait with intrinsic value, or that the concept must apply only to actions for which there is a prima facie reason. From the descriptivist point of view, they would be mistaken. Clearly, what would make refraining from kicking so valuable at W5 would not be its intrinsic value, but its contribution to the good life of humans, given the total set of facts about the human condition at W5. This contribution to overall value would mislead the philosophers into antidescriptivism regarding the concept of refraining from kicking.

The point here is that, for any descriptive concept, we can imagine a world at which the property referred to by the concept has great value. So we should not let the fact that we happen to live at a world where certain properties have great value mislead us into holding that these properties have intrinsic value.

I turn below to the "holistic" picture of evaluation on which this argument for descriptivism depends. But I want first to note the consequences of descriptivism for realism about virtues.

V

There are many senses of realism about a property. I shall note three. First, realism may be the view that the property plays a causal role in the world. Second, realism could be the theory that propositions containing concepts that refer to the property have truth conditions that depend on how the world is. Third, realism could be construed as the view that these truth conditions can transcend our recognitional capacities; so propositions containing concepts that refer to the property can be true or false even if we cannot verify their truth or falsity.

If, as I have argued, concepts of traditional virtues are descriptive, then realism (in any of these senses) can hold true of the properties referred to by virtue concepts, without moral or ethical realism holding true. Suppose, for example, that realism is true of kindness. In other words, suppose that kindness plays a causal role, that propositions containing the concept of kindness have truth conditions, and that these truth conditions can transcend our recognitional capacities. Since the concept of kindness is purely descriptive, it does not follow that there is any ethical or moral property such that either the property plays a causal role in the world, or propositions containing concepts that refer to the property have truth conditions, or such propositions can have truth conditions beyond our recognitional capacity. In short, one can be a realist about properties to be valued (such as kindness) without being a realist about values themselves.

It is worth noting that realism about values does not follow directly from antidescriptivism about virtue concepts. One may argue that, for any virtue concept, the descriptive and evaluative conditions can be separated. One can then hold that realism is true of properties denoted by the descriptive condition, but not true of properties denoted by the evaluative condition. To avoid this line of argument, the moral realist about virtues must argue that, although a virtue concept is both world-guided and action-guiding, it is impossible to sort out independent descriptive and evaluative conditions of application. So a competent agent cannot apply the descriptive part of the concept to a possible action without taking there to be a reason for the action.[12]

If descriptivism is correct, the question of whether descriptive and evaluative conditions can be sorted is beside the point, since there are no evaluative conditions. But the special connection between virtues of character and reasonableness illuminates how one could be misled into taking virtue concepts to be positively evaluative. If a fully competent agent is considering an action that she takes to be courageous, then she must view the action as reasonable. Generally, an action can be viewed as reasonable even though it is one for which the agent does not give a good reason, where having a good reason entails that the agent is actually correct that there is a reason for the action. Yet, since we are now considering the agent herself as the person who takes the action to be courageous, the agent cannot view the action as one which is reasonable but for which she does

not have a good reason. For, if the agent viewed herself as not having a good reason, she could not view herself as reasonable. So, if an agent believes one of her own possible actions is courageous, then she has, from her own point of view, reason to take the action. Thus, the concept of courage is action-guiding, in the sense that agents who believe their own present or possible actions are courageous must also take themselves to have a good reason for so acting. This could mislead someone into holding that the concept has an evaluative condition of application.

We have seen that the concept of courage lacks an evaluative condition, if this means that it must apply to what is valuable. So, outside of the viewpoint that an agent adopts in considering her present or possible actions, she may recognize that the action is not valuable. Thus, she can view her past actions as courageous but of negative value, or she can view the actions of others as courageous but of negative value. (This was how we viewed human actions at W4.)

Concepts of character virtues other than courage can also refer to properties that have negative value. Agents who competently apply such concepts to their present or possible actions cannot at that point in time recognize the negative value of their actions. I am not suggesting that this has actually misled philosophers into holding that these concepts have a positive evaluative condition, but I am suggesting that it could so mislead.[13]

VI

The argument so far relies on a sort of "holism," according to which whether or not a property is valuable depends on a broad set of social and psychological facts. What we take to be valuable—what we hold there is reason to do, all things considered—depends not only on our conception of particular circumstances, but on our total set of beliefs. Just as we depend on many beliefs in order to predict future experience, so we rely on many beliefs in order to determine what ought to be done. No particular

property of an agent or an action can be evaluated independently of a large number of beliefs.

An antidescriptivist might argue against this that to base our account on such extreme examples as W1–W4 is to fail to understand that virtue concepts can be applied only from within a given "point of view," "form of life," "conceptual scheme," or "tradition" in which certain assumptions and claims are basic.[14] Among these assumptions and claims will be general claims about the nature of human beings and their social situation. So we assume that humans are not weakened by acting kindly and that they are not enslaved by a superior species. Such assumptions, it might be said, are "at the base of our language game"; they have the status, as it were, of synthetic a priori truths that guide our moral life. On this view, our concepts apply only to worlds where the assumptions are true. If so, then our concepts are improperly applied to the possible worlds imagined in this paper. When applied properly, they always refer to properties that are valuable.

This kind of move is a matter of much debate. But, even if we allow that this sort of move is sometimes acceptable, there are two reasons for not accepting it in the case of virtue concepts. First, in this case, the appeal to "points of view" (etc.) and associated implicit assumptions is not sufficiently similar to examples where such appeal is more appropriate. Some cases in the literature—for instance, Wittgenstein's discussion in *On Certainty*[15] of the special role that claims like "Here is my hand" play in our language game—involve assumptions that are so fundamental that, if we gave them up, we would not know how to make any appropriate move in our language game. We do not feel we could make *any* legitimate claims if we could not assert the claims in question.

The claims we have considered are not like that. Although it is somewhat difficult, for instance, to imagine that we are enslaved to a superior species, we can imagine transporting our values and our moral point of view into that situation. We can suppose that the master species leaves us alone to develop our own morality and conception of the good life. We would still care about morality, and we would still have our ideals of human flourishing, whatever those amount to in detail. Indeed, it is because we would still have them that we can judge that, even in this situation, acts that would result in the torture of many people would not be valuable. By transporting our point of view into situations that we believe are different from our actual situation, we are able to pass judgment on what we would value in those other situations.

The cases we have considered are thus different from those in which variations between points of view are so radical that, if we were to accept the claims made from another point of view, we would not know how to make any legitimate claims. Many readers of this essay could not, from within their point of view, allow that the seventeenth-century Samurai warrior is ethically correct in killing a peasant who hesitated two seconds before bowing. If we were to accept the judgment "it is morally acceptable for the Samurai to kill the nondeferential peasant," we would, on the Wittgensteinian sort of view under consideration, not know how to continue using our moral language. It is central to our moral language game that human life is worth more than that. If we allowed this judgment, we would no longer know when to say killing is impermissible; we would not know how to talk about rights to life or just and equal treatment. We would, in other words, have to give up much of our moral language game. But the cases considered in this paper cannot be successfully assimilated to the Samurai warrior case.

There is a second, more pragmatic reason for not holding, on the basis of considerations about points of view, that our ordinary concepts are thick, and for not relying heavily, in our account of the ethical realm, on such thick concepts.[16] This second reason is based on a recognition that there are variations in moral sensibility between cultures. Thick concepts can only be usefully applied from within a particular point of view; they cannot be interestingly applied in arguments between different points of view. Since, in the actual world, there are important conflicts between points of view, treating ethical concepts as thick tends to cut off rational discussion of value, and it leads to uninteresting, nonexplanatory accounts of value.

Consider revenge, for instance. Many of us do not believe that revenge is of positive value, but in some cultures it is regularly used in positive moral evaluations. Suppose it were argued that the concept of revenge applies only to actions for which there is a reason. Then we would not be able to understand how the concept of revenge is applicable to our world, since we hold that there is usually no reason for performing actions that meet the descriptive condition contained in the concept of revenge. If someone takes it to be necessary that the concept of revenge applies only to acts that are of positive value, then we cannot debate with that person about the value of revengeful acts—the issue is already settled. Either we must invent a new concept which has the descriptive component contained in the concept of revenge but which is drained of its evaluative component, or discussion must simply come to an end because we lack a common descriptive concept that can be used in debate. Treating a concrete ethical concept as thick is simply an effective means for cutting discussion short.

NOTES

1. This sort of view is endorsed by Sabina Lovibund, in *Realism and Imagination in Ethics* (Minneapolis: Minnesota UP, 1983); John McDowell, in "Are Moral Requirements Hypothetical Imperatives?," *Proceedings of the Aristotelian Society,* 1.II Supplementary Volume (1978): 13–29; "Virtue and Reason," *The Monist*, LXII, 3 (July, 1979): 331–350; "Non-cognitivism and Rule-following," in Steven H. Holtzman and Christopher M. Leich, eds., *Wittgenstein: To Follow a Rule* (London: Routledge & Kegan Paul, 1981), pp. 141–162; and "Values and Secondary Qualities," in Ted Honderich, ed., *Morality and Objectivity* (London: Routledge & Kegan Paul, 1985), pp. 110–129; Mark Platts, in *Ways of Meaning* (London:Routledge & Kegan Paul, 1979), pp. 243–262; and David Wiggins, in "Truth, Invention and the Meaning of Life," Proceedings of the British Academy, LXII (1976): 331–378.

    Lovibund holds that 'brave', 'malicious', and 'corrupt' are used in "lower-level evaluations" (pp. 14/5). In the first three articles mentioned, McDowell concentrates on 'courage' and 'kindness'. Platts claims to be an ethical realist about language containing the expressions 'sincerity', 'loyalty', 'honesty', 'prudence', 'courage', and 'integrity' (pp. 243/4). Wiggins mentions 'brave', 'dishonest', 'ignoble', 'just', 'malicious', and 'priggish' (p. 359).

    Bernard Williams, in *Ethics and the Limits of Philosophy* (Cambridge: Harvard, 1985), also endorses this view. He argues, however, that the properties referred to by concrete ethical evaluations have no place in the world described by the "absolute conception of reality." Yet he holds that concrete ethical concepts are both evaluative and descriptive, and that judgments using these concepts can be true and known.

2. The expression 'concrete ethical concepts' may suggest concepts that *do* express an ethical evaluation. As used here, however, it is intended to refer to concepts which are relatively concrete and which have traditionally been *thought* to express ethical evaluations. Concepts may be said to be more or less concrete depending on how much determinate descriptive content they have, though this notion must be left intuitive. The concepts of good and right are highly abstract, the concepts of courage and brutality are relatively concrete. I concentrate on concepts of traditional virtues, but I hope that my argument lends support to a skeptical attitude toward antidescriptivism about all concrete concepts.

3. In the last twenty years, philosophers have argued that speakers can acquire the use of a term even if they are wrong about conditions for its application, or even if the term is best looked at as not having any conditions of application. (Cf. Saul Kripke, *Naming and Necessity* (Cambridge: Harvard, 1982); and Hilary Putnam "The Meaning of 'meaning'," in *Mind, Language and Reality* (New York: Cambridge, 1975), pp. 215–271.) I find this view attractive, so I discuss the requirements on a speaker who is "totally competent" with a "concept" (not a term). In any case, it is not clear that concepts of character traits should be treated in the same fashion as proper names and "natural kind" terms. Moreover, the phrase 'condition of application' is used by Williams and others who discuss concrete ethical concepts. I am simply retaining their usage.

4. "Moral Beliefs," in *Virtues and Vices* (Berkeley: California UP, 1978), pp. 110–131.

5. *Moral Thinking* (New York: Oxford, 1981) pp. 17/8, 74/5. Hare argues briefly for a form of what I call descriptivism, but his own use of 'descriptivism' is different than mine.

6. I am not attempting to give a complete account of courage. I do, however, assume that an action is courageous only if the agent overcomes fear, ignores fear, or is fearless in a situation where most people would act out of fear. I express these three in a shorthand manner by saying only that the agent "overcomes fear." My view of courage has been influenced in part by Peter T. Geach, *The Virtues* (New York: Cambridge, 1977); and James D. Wallace, *Virtues and Vices* (Ithaca: Cornell, 1978).

7. In this paper, I do not always distinguish between virtue concepts as they apply to actions and virtue concepts as they apply to agents. The context makes clear which application is intended.

8. This account must be extended in order to apply virtue concepts to agents. A concept of a character trait has a positive, evaluative condition just in case the concept applies only to traits that typically result in actions for which there is a reason. A concept of a character trait has a negative, evaluative condition just in case the concept applies only to traits that typically result in actions that there is reason not to perform.

9. Williams sometimes formulates his view in terms of prima facie reasons. I comment on prima facie reasons in section IV below.

10. The connection between reason and courage has its origin in Greek thought, and the notion that an action is courageous only if it is worth the risk is, on some interpretations, implicit in Aristotle's account of virtues as means.

11. According to some religious conceptions of the relation between faith and reason, we live in this sort of world.
12. McDowell argues for this view in "Virtue and Reason" and "Non-cognitivism and Rule-following."
13. I have been arguing against antidescriptivism, that ordinary virtue concepts are not evaluative; yet philosophers can invent concepts that are both descriptive and evaluative. Nothing said here shows that this is impossible. But, since the concepts are invented, the nonrealist about values may argue that the evaluative and descriptive components can be separated, and then endorse realism only about properties denoted by the descriptive component.
14. Wiggins. *op. cit.*, stresses the importance of points of view. Alasdair MacIntyre, in *After Virtue* (Notre Dame:

University Press, 1984), emphasizes the importance of traditions. I do not have space to examine their arguments in detail.
15. G. E. M. Anscombe and G. H. von Wright, trans. (New York: Harper & Row, 1969).
16. Some philosophers might object that I have given an illegitimate "conceptual analysis." I hold that something like conceptual analysis is acceptable, so long as no claim is made that we have special, a priori access to a realm of meanings. In any case, my argument is in complete accord with the Quinean view that by revising our beliefs, we can apply terms in ways which might have been thought to conflict with "rules of meaning." The pragmatic point made in this section is also consistent with a Quinean view.

KURT BAIER
Why Should We Be Moral?

THE SUPREMACY OF MORAL REASONS

Are moral reasons really superior to reasons of self-interest as we all believe? Do we really have reason on our side when we follow moral reasons against self-interest? What reasons could there be for being moral? Can we really give an answer to "Why should we be moral?" It is obvious that all these questions come to the same thing. When we ask, "Should we be moral?" or "Why should we be moral?" or "Are moral reasons superior to all others?" we ask to be given a reason for regarding moral reasons as superior to all others. What is this reason?

Let us begin with a state of affairs in which reasons of self-interest are supreme. In such a state everyone keeps his impulses and inclinations in check when and only when they would lead him into behavior detrimental to his own

interest. Everyone who follows reason will discipline himself to rise early, to do his exercises, to refrain from excessive drinking and smoking, to keep good company, to marry the right sort of girl, to work and study hard in order to get on, and so on. However, it will often happen that people's interests conflict. In such a case, they will have to resort to ruses or force to get their own way. As this becomes known, men will become suspicious, for they will regard one another as scheming competitors for the good things in life. The universal supremacy of the rules of self-interest must lead to what Hobbes called the state of nature. At the same time, it will be clear to everyone that universal obedience to certain rules overriding self-interest would produce a state of affairs which serves everyone's interest much better than his unaided pursuit of it in a state where everyone does the same. Moral rules are universal rules designed to override those of self-interest when following the latter is harmful to others. "Thou shalt not kill," "Thou shalt not lie," "Thou shalt not steal" are rules which forbid the inflicting of harm on someone else even when this might be in one's interest.

The very *raison d'être* of morality is to yield reasons which overrule the reasons of self-interest in those cases when everyone's following self-interest would be harmful to everyone. Hence moral reasons are superior to all others.

"But what does this mean?" it might be objected. "If it merely means that we do so regard them, then you are of course right, but your contention is useless, a mere point of usage. And how could it mean any more? If it means that we not only do so regard them, but *ought* so to regard them, then there must be *reasons* for saying this. But there could not be any reasons for it. If you offer reasons of self-interest, you are arguing in a circle. Moreover, it cannot be true that it is always in my interest to treat moral reasons as superior to reasons of self-interest. If it were, self-interest and morality could never conflict, but they notoriously do. It is equally circular to argue that there are moral reasons for saying that one ought to treat moral reasons as superior to reasons of self-interest. And what other reasons are there?"

The answer is that we are now looking at the world from the point of view of *anyone*. We are not examining particular alternative courses of action before this or that person; we are examining two alternative worlds, one in which moral reasons are always treated by everyone as superior to reasons of self-interest and one in which the reverse is the practice. And we can see that the first world is the better world, because we can see that the second world would be the sort which Hobbes describes as the state of nature.

This shows that I ought to be moral, for when I ask the question "What ought I to do?" I am asking. "Which is the course of action supported by the best reasons?" But since it has just been shown that moral reasons are superior to reasons of self-interest, I have been given a reason for being moral, for following moral reasons rather than any other, namely, they are better reasons than any other.

But is this always so? Do we have a reason for being moral whatever the conditions we find ourselves in? Could there not be situations in which it is not true that we have reasons for being moral, that, on the contrary, we have reasons for ignoring the demands of morality? Is not Hobbes right in saying that in a state of nature the laws of nature, that is, the rules of morality, bind only *in foro interno* [subjectively]?

Hobbes argues as follows.

(i) To live in a state of nature is to live outside society. It is to live in conditions in which there are no common ways of life and, therefore, no reliable expectations about other people's behavior other than that they will follow their inclination or their interest.

(ii) In such a state reason will be the enemy of co-operation and mutual trust. For it is too risky to hope that other people will refrain from protecting their own interests by the preventive elimination of probable or even possible dangers to them. Hence reason will counsel everyone to avoid these risks by preventive actions. But this leads to war.

(iii) It is obvious that everyone's following self-interest leads to a state of affairs which is desirable from no one's point of view. It is, on the contrary, desirable that everybody should follow rules overriding self-interest whenever that is to the detriment of others. In other words, it is desirable to bring about a state of affairs in which all obey the rules of morality.

(iv) However, Hobbes claims that in the state of nature it helps nobody if a single person or small group of people begins to follow the rules of morality, for this could only lead to the extinction of such individuals or groups. In such a state, it is therefore contrary to reason to be moral.

(v) The situation can change, reason can support morality, only when the presumption about other people's behavior is reversed. Hobbes thought that this could be achieved only by the creation of an absolute ruler with absolute power to enforce his laws. We have already seen that this is not true and that it can also be achieved if people live in a society, that is, if they have common ways of life, which are taught to all members and somehow enforced by the group. Its members have reason to expect their fellows generally to obey its rules, that is, its religion, morality, customs, and law, even when doing so is not, on certain occasions, in their interest. Hence they too have reason to follow these rules.

Is this argument sound? One might, of course, object to step (i) on the grounds that this is an empirical proposition for which there is little or no evidence. For how can we know whether it is true that people in a state of nature would follow only their inclinations or, at best, reasons of self-interest, when nobody now lives in that state or has ever lived in it?

However, there is some empirical evidence to support this claim. For in the family of nations, individual states are placed very much like individual persons in a state of nature. The doctrine of the sovereignty of nations and the absence of an effective international law and police force are a guarantee that nations live in a state of nature, without commonly accepted rules that are somehow enforced. Hence it must be granted that living in a state of nature leads to living in a state in which individuals act either on impulse or as they think their interest dictates. For states pay only lip service to morality. They attack their hated neighbors when the opportunity arises. They start preventive wars in order to destroy the enemy before he can deliver his knockout blow. Where interests conflict, the stronger party usually has his way, whether his claims are justified or not. And where the relative strength of the parties is not obvious, they usually resort to arms in order to determine "whose side God is on." Treaties are frequently concluded but, morally speaking, they are not worth the paper they are written on. Nor do the partners regard them as contracts binding in the ordinary way, but rather as public expressions of the belief of the governments concerned that for the time being their alliance is in the interest of the allies. It is well understood that such treaties may be canceled before they reach their predetermined end or

simply broken when it suits one partner. In international affairs, there are very few examples of *Nibelungentreue*, although statesmen whose countries have kept their treaties in the hope of profiting from them usually make such high moral claims.

It is, moreover, difficult to justify morality in international affairs. For suppose a highly moral statesman were to demand that his country adhere to a treaty obligation even though this meant its ruin or possibly its extinction. Suppose he were to say that treaty obligations are sacred and must be kept whatever the consequences. How could he defend such a policy? Perhaps one might argue that someone has to make a start in order to create mutual confidence in international affairs. Or one might say that setting a good example is the best way of inducing others to follow suit. But such a defense would hardly be sound. The less skeptical one is about the genuineness of the cases in which nations have adhered to their treaties from a sense of moral obligation, the more skeptical one must be about the effectiveness of such examples of virtue in effecting a change of international practice. Power politics still govern in international affairs.

We must, therefore, grant Hobbes the first step in his argument and admit that in a state of nature people, as a matter of psychological fact, would not follow the dictates of morality. But we might object to the next step that knowing this psychological fact about other people's behavior constitutes a reason for behaving in the same way. Would it not still be immoral for anyone to ignore the demands of morality even though he knows that others are likely or certain to do so, too? Can we offer as a justification for morality the fact that no one is entitled to do wrong just because someone else is doing wrong? This argument begs the question whether it *is* wrong for anyone in this state to disregard the demands of morality. It cannot be wrong to break a treaty or make preventive war if we have no reason to obey the moral rules. For to say that it is wrong to do so is to say that we ought not to do so. But if we have no reason for obeying the moral rule, then we have no reason overruling self-interest, hence no reason for keeping the treaty when keeping it is not in our interest, hence it is not true that we have a reason for keeping it, hence not true that we ought to keep it, hence not true that it is wrong not to keep it.

I conclude that Hobbes's argument is sound. Moralities are systems of principles whose acceptance by everyone as overruling the dictates of self-interest is in the interest of everyone alike, though following the rules of a morality is not of course identical with following self-interest. If it were, there could be no conflict between a morality and self-interest and no point in having moral rules overriding self-interest. Hobbes is also right in saying that the application of this system of rules is in accordance with reason only under social conditions, that is, when there are well-established ways of behavior.

The answer to our question "Why should we be moral?" is therefore as follows. We should be moral because being moral is following rules designed to overrule reasons of self-interest whenever it is in the interest of everyone alike that such rules should be generally followed. This will be the case when the needs and wants and aspirations of individual agents conflict with one another and when, in the absence of such overriding rules, the pursuit of their ends by all concerned would lead to the attempt to eliminate those who are in the way. Since such rules will always require one of the rivals to abandon his pursuit in favor of the other, they will tend to be broken. Since, ex hypothesi it is in everyone's interest that they should be followed, it will be in everyone's interest that they should not only be taught as "superior to" other reasons but also adequately enforced, in order to reduce the temptation to break them. A person instructed in these rules can acknowledge that such reasons are superior to reasons of self-interest without having to admit that he is always or indeed ever attracted or moved by them.

But is it not self-contradictory to say that it is in a person's interest to do what is contrary to his interest? It certainly would be if the two expressions were used in exactly the same way.

But they are not. We have already seen that an enlightened egoist can acknowledge that a certain course of action is in his enlightened long-term, but contrary to his narrow short-term interest. He can infer that it is "in his interest" and according to reason to follow enlightened long-term interest, and "against his interest" and contrary to reason to follow short-term interest. Clearly, "in his interest" and "against his interest" here are used in new ways. For suppose it is discovered that the probable long-range consequences and psychological effects on others do not work out as predicted. Even so we need not admit that, in this new and extended sense, the line of action followed merely seemed but really was not in his interest. For we are now considering not merely a single action but a policy.

All the same, we must not make too much of this analogy. There is an all-important difference between the two cases. The calculations of the enlightened egoist properly allow for "exceptions in the agent's favor." After all, his calculus is designed to promote his interest. If he has information to show that in his particular circumstances it would pay to depart from a well-established general canon of enlightened self-interest, then it is proper for him to depart from it. It would not be a sign of the enlightened self-interest of a building contractor, let us say, if he made sacrifices for certain subcontractors even though he knew that they would or could not reciprocate, as subcontractors normally do. By contrast, such information is simply irrelevant in cases where moral reasons apply. Moral rules are not designed to serve the agent's interest directly. Hence it would be quite inappropriate for him to break them whenever he discovers that they do not serve his interest. They are designed to adjudicate primarily in cases where there is a conflict of interests so that from their very nature they are bound to be contrary to the interest of one of the persons affected. However, they are also bound to serve the interest of the other person, hence his interest in the other's observing them. It is on the assumption of the likelihood of a reversal of roles that the universal observation of the rule will serve everyone's interest. The principle of justice and other principles which we employ in improving the moral rules of a given society help to bring existing moralities closer to the ideal which is in the interest of everyone alike. Thus, just as following the canons of enlightened self-interest is in one's interest only if the assumptions underlying it are correct, so following the rules of morality is in everyone's interest only if the assumptions underlying it are correct, that is, if the moral rules come close to being true and are generally observed. Even then, to say that following them is in the interest of everyone alike means only that it is better for everyone that there should be a morality generally observed than that the principle of self-interest should be acknowledged as supreme. It does not of course mean that a person will not do better for himself by following self-interest than by doing what is morally right, when others are doing what is right. But of course such a person cannot *claim* that he is following a superior reason.

It must be added to this, however, that such a system of rules has the support of reason only where people live in societies, that is, in conditions in which there are established common ways of behavior. Outside society, people have no reason for following such rules, that is, for being moral. In other words, outside society, the very distinction between right and wrong vanishes.

WHY SHOULD WE FOLLOW REASON?

But someone might now ask whether and why he should follow reason itself. He may admit that moral reasons are superior to all others, but doubt whether he ought to follow reason. He may claim that this will have to be proved first, for if it is not true that he ought to follow reason, then it is not true that he ought to follow the strongest reason either.

What is it to follow reason? It involves two tasks, the theoretical, finding out what it would be in accordance with reason to do in a certain situation, what contrary to reason, and the practical task, to act accordingly. . . . We must also remind ourselves that there are many different ways in which what we do or believe or feel can be contrary to reason. It may be *irrational,* as when, for no reason at all, we set our hand on fire or cut off our toes one by one, or when, in the face of conclusive evidence to the contrary, someone *believes* that her son killed in the war is still alive, or when someone is *seized by fear* as a gun is pointed at him although he knows for certain that it is not loaded. What we do, believe, or feel is called irrational if it is the case not only that there are conclusive or overwhelming reasons against doing, believing, or feeling these things, but also that we must know

there are such reasons and we still persist in our action, belief, or feeling.

Or it may be *unreasonable,* as when we make demands which are excessive or refuse without reason to comply with requests which are reasonable. We say of demands or requests that they are excessive if, though we are entitled to make them, the party against whom we make them has good reasons for not complying, as when the landlord demands the immediate vacation of the premises in the face of well-supported pleas of hardship by the tenant.

Being unreasonable is a much weaker form of going counter to reason than being irrational. The former applies in cases where there is a conflict of reasons and where one party does not acknowledge the obvious force of the case of the other or, while acknowledging it, will not modify his behavior accordingly. A person is irrational only if he flies in the face of reason, if, that is, all reasons are on one side and he acts contrary to it when he either acknowledges that this is so or, while refusing to acknowledge it, has no excuse for failing to do so.

Again, someone may be *inconsistent,* as when he refuses a Jew admission to a club although he has always professed strong positive views on racial equality. Behavior or remarks are inconsistent if the agent or author professes principles adherence to which would require him to say or do the opposite of what he says or does.

Or a person may be *illogical*, as when he does something which, as anyone can see, cannot or is not at all likely to lead to success. Thus when I cannot find my glasses or my fountain pen, the logical thing to do is to look for them where I can remember I had them last or where I usually have them. It would be illogical of me to look under the bed or in the oven unless I have special reason to think they might be there. To say of a person that he is a logical type is to say that he always does what, on reflection, anyone would agree is most likely to lead to success. Scatterbrains, people who act rashly, without thinking, are the opposite of logical.

When we speak of following reason, we usually mean "doing what is supported by the best reasons because it is so supported" or perhaps "doing what we think (rightly or wrongly) is supported by the best reasons because we think it is so supported." It might, then, occur to someone to ask, "Why should I follow reason?" During the last hundred years or so, reason has had a very bad press. Many thinkers have sneered at it and have recommended other guides, such as the instincts, the unconscious, the voice of the blood, inspiration, charisma, and the like. They have advocated that one should not follow reason but be guided by these other forces.

However, in the most obvious sense of the question "Should I follow reason?" this is a tautological question like "Is a circle a circle?"; hence the advice "You should not follow reason" is as nonsensical as the claim "A circle is not a circle." Hence the question "Why should I follow reason?" is as silly as "Why is a circle a circle?" We need not, therefore, take much notice of the advocates of unreason. They show by their advocacy that they are not too clear on what they are talking about.

How is it that "Should I follow reason?" is a tautological question like "Is a circle a cir-

cle?" Questions of the form "Shall I do this?" or "Should I do this?" or "Ought I do this?" are . . . requests to someone (possibly oneself) to deliberate on one's behalf. That is to say, they are requests to survey the facts and weigh the reasons for and against this course of action. These questions could therefore be paraphrased as follows. "I wish to do what is supported by the best reasons. Tell me whether this is so supported." As already mentioned "following reason" means "doing what is supported by the best reasons." Hence the question "Shall (should, ought) I follow reason?" must be paraphrased as "I wish to do what is supported by the best reasons. Tell me whether doing what is supported by the best reasons is doing what is supported by the best reasons." It is, therefore, not worth asking.

The question "*Why* should I follow reason?" simply does not make sense. Asking it shows complete lack of understanding of the meaning of "why questions." "Why should I do this?" is a request to be given the reason for saying that I should do this. It is normally asked when someone has already said, "You should do this" and answered by giving the reason. But since "Should I follow reason?" means "Tell me whether doing what is supported by the best reasons is doing what is supported by the best reasons," there is simply no possibility of adding "Why?" For the question now comes to this, "Tell me the reason why doing what is supported by the best reasons is doing what is supported by the best reasons." It is exactly like asking, "Why is a circle a circle?"

However, it must be admitted that there is another possible interpretation to our question according to which it makes sense and can even be answered. "Why should I follow reason?" may not be a request for a reason in support of a tautological remark, but a request for a reason why one should enter on the theoretical task of deliberation. As already explained, following reason involves the completion of two tasks, the theoretical and the practical. The point of the theoretical is to give guidance in the practical task. We perform the theoretical only because we wish to complete the practical task in accordance with the outcome of the theoretical. On our first interpretation, "Should I follow reason?" meant "Is the practical task completed when it is completed in accordance with the outcome of the theoretical task?" And the answer to this is obviously "Yes," for that is what we mean by "completion of the practical task." On our second interpretation, "Should I follow reason?" is not a question about the practical but about the theoretical task. It is not a question about whether, given that one is prepared to perform both these tasks, they are properly completed in the way indicated. It is a question about whether one should enter on the whole performance at all, whether the "game" is worth playing. And this is a meaningful question. It might be better to "follow inspiration" than to "follow reason," in this sense: better to close one's eyes and wait for an answer to flash across the mind.

But while, so interpreted, "Should I follow reason?" makes sense, it seems to me obvious that the answer to it is "Yes, because it pays." Deliberation is the only reliable method. Even if there were other reliable methods, we could only tell whether they were reliable by checking them against this method. Suppose some charismatic leader counsels, "Don't follow reason, follow me. My leadership is better than that of reason"; we would still have to check his claim against the ordinary methods of reason. We would have to ascertain whether in following

his advice we were doing the best thing. And this we can do only by examining whether he has advised us to do what is supported by the best reasons. His claim to be better than reason can in turn only be supported by the fact that he tells us precisely the same as reason does.

Is there any sense, then, in his claim that his guidance is preferable to that of reason? There may be, for working out what is supported by the best reasons takes a long time. Frequently, the best thing to do is to do something quickly now rather than the most appropriate thing later. A leader may have the ability to "see," to "intuit," what is the best thing to do more quickly than it is possible to work this out by the laborious methods of deliberation. In evaluating the qualities of leadership of such a person, we are evaluating *his ability to perform correctly the practical task of following reason* without having to go through the lengthy operations of the theoretical. Reason is required to tell us whether anyone has qualities of leadership better than ordinary, in the same way that pencil and paper multiplications are required to tell us whether a mathematical prodigy is genuine or a fraud.

Lastly, it must be said that sometimes it may be better even for an ordinary person without charisma not to follow reason but to do something at once, for quick action may be needed.

QUESTIONS ABOUT ETHICS

1. What is Bonaparte's problem? In what way is this a moral problem? How does it illustrate the deeper philosophical issue about right and wrong?
2. As a soldier, Bonaparte has an obligation to obey orders. Does this mean that he is not in a position even to consider the difference between right and wrong?
3. Does Bonaparte resolve his apparent conflict by allowing Donovan to fire the fatal shot?
4. Need an egoist be self-centered and selfish?
5. What is the apparent difference between act-utilitarianism and rule-utilitarianism? How does rule-utilitarianism appear to be more practical as providing guidance in making a moral decision?
6. What is the basic point of the categorical imperative in opposition to both egoism and utilitarianism?

7. Was Donovan unfair to Bonaparte and Noble not to reveal at the outset the possibility of their having to execute the prisoners? Suppose Donovan thought it better for all concerned not to mention the possibility of killing. Would this have made his actions fair? How does this question illustrate the difference between the utilitarian and Kantian approaches?

8. Describe the Kantian idea of universalizability. How is this part of the categorical imperative related to the idea of treating human beings as "ends-in-themselves"? What is the point of the third part of the categorical imperative, the idea of acting out of a sense of duty?

9. How does the categorical imperative differ from the golden rule?

10. Why should Bonaparte be moral? Why should anyone?

Ethics:
Suggestions for Further Study

The study of ethics, or moral philosophy, is often divided into three closely related but distinct branches: descriptive ethics, normative ethics, and metaethics. The first, descriptive ethics, is primarily concerned with the study of actual moral belief or systems of belief—nineteenth-century slavery in the American South, for example. Many important sociological and anthropological studies have been published depicting ways of life different from that to which we have become accustomed, by such anthropologists as Ruth Benedict and Margaret Mead. Works in descriptive ethics tend to be less philosophical than writings found in the other two categories.

However, the striking differences in moral belief among different ethnic groups raises at least one of the deepest philosophical questions about right and wrong: Is there a universally valid moral code? Cross-cultural studies seem to indicate there is no such code, although ordinary moral judgment, for example, that rape is wrong, seems to indicate the opposite. Both normative ethics and metaethics attempt to come to grips with this fundamental issue, but in different ways. Normative ethics is primarily concerned with describing a universally valid moral code, or at least, the principles underlying such a code—the golden rule, the principle of ethical egoism, act-utilitarianism or rule-utilitarianism, or the categorical imperative. Our discussion in the text, and the selections we have included, fall primarily into this area.

Metaethics, by contrast, is concerned with the foundations of theories in normative ethics, in particular, whether a theory of right and wrong can appeal to any special facts or "objective" values. The dominant trend in Western philosophy, especially since the publication of David Hume's *Treatise of Human Nature* in 1739, and the later publication, in 1751, of *An Enquiry Concerning the Principles of Morals*, has been negative. Hume's own view seems to have been a form of subjectivism, that a moral judgment is a kind of psychological report—to say that an action is right means that we approve of it, for instance. Others have offered variants of this theme. Edward Westermarck, in *Ethical Relativity* (London: Routledge & Kegan Paul, 1932), suggested that moral judgments are disguised sociological reports.

In opposition to the subjectivists and relativists, G. E. Moore (*Principia Ethica* Cambridge: Cambridge University Press, 1903) and other *intuitionists* attempted to provide an objective account by introducing, among other things, a special class of "nonnatural" properties for which value terms allegedly stand. Their attempt proved unsuccessful. Positivists, such as A. J. Ayer, in *Language, Truth and Logic*, second ed., (London: Gollancz, 1946), argued that talk of nonnatural properties and talk of values in general made little sense. Moral judgments, according to this view, are emotive utterances, devoid of truth or falsity. C. L. Stevenson, in *Ethics and Language* (New Haven: Yale University Press, 1946), attempted to extend this analysis to show how moral judgments have an imperative function, especially in ethical disagreement. R. M. Hare, in *Language of Morals* (Oxford: Oxford University Press, 1952), J. O. Urmson, in "On Grading," (*Mind* LIX No. 234, 1950, 145–169), and others have gone further to sketch out more precisely other functions performed by value terms—in commending and grading, for example. Still others, including Stephen Toulmin, in *The Place of Reason in Ethics* (London: Cambridge University Press, 1950) and Kurt Baier, in *The Moral Point of View* (Ithaca, New York: Cornell University Press, 1958), attempted to account for the role of reason in ethics. More recently, John Mackie, in *Ethics: Inventing Right and Wrong* (New York: Penguin Books, 1977), and in "A Refutation of Morals" (*Australasian Journal of Philosophy*, Vol. 24, No. 1, 1946), argued that moral discourse lacks an objective foundation and is gratuitous in attempting to explain human behavior and belief. His position is similar to Gilbert Harman's, reprinted in this text. Both Mackie and Harman are discussed by Lowell Kleiman in "Morality as the Best Explanation." Bruce Brower contributes to this ongoing debate by discussing the reality of moral virtues in "Virtue Concepts and Ethical Realism."

PART
5
Justice

Literary Introduction:
What Is Just?

On a bitterly cold night, a bag lady seeks shelter in a commuter railroad station and spends her last few coins on a hot cup of soup. One of the commuters rushes by her to catch a train that will carry him to a warm house and a full meal. Is there something unjust in this situation? Is it right for there to be such a disparity between the rich and poor?

A recurrent theme in our culture is the aspiration toward a more just society, one in which the rights of the individual are balanced against the needs of society. The starting point for this aspiration is the recognition that in any given society some have more than they need, while others make do with less. From time to time this theme gathers energy and becomes a compelling vision of a more perfect world.

For example, in the eighteenth century, English literature began to manifest the influence of romanticism, an intellectual and artistic movement that emphasized, among other ideas, the innate goodness and perfectibility of the individual. And goodness and perfection arguably are the cornerstones of a concept of a just society.

Romantics, however, were not blind to the obvious fact that many individuals appeared to be neither good nor anywhere close to perfection. These individuals cheated each other, physically and economically abused each other, and generally placed their own interests above those of others. Collectively, the same less-than-perfect behaviors could be observed in the wars between nations and in the indifference of governments to the needs of their own citizens.

These facts argued against the romantics' premise of innate goodness and perfectibility, but they had an answer. In various ways, different romantics asserted that when individuals permitted themselves to be organized into groups, their natural goodness was corrupted, and consequently their sense of justice distorted. One of the thrusts of romanticism, therefore, was to return the individual to his or her natural, uncorrupted, sense of justice.

Among the early English romantics was William Blake, who was intensely aware of the distance between the world as he saw it and as he imagined it could be. He wrote two matched cycles of poems—"The Songs of Innocence" which represented a naive and uncorrupted view of the world, and "Songs of Experience" which recognized the harsh realities of his times. Among the latter group Blake offered "London":

I wander thro' each charter'd street
Near where the charter'd Thames does flow,
And mark in every face I meet
Marks of weakness, marks of woe.

In every cry of every Man,
In every Infant's cry of fear,
In every voice, in every ban,
The mind-forg'd manacles I hear.

How the Chimney-sweeper's cry
Every black'ning Church appalls;
And the hapless Soldier's sigh
Runs in blood down Palace walls.

But most thro' midnight streets I hear
How the youthful Harlot's curse
Blasts the new born Infant's tear,
And blights with plagues the Marriage hearse.

The tone of this poem is controlled outrage. Blake sees the capital city of London as the symbol of all that is wrong in his society. The streets are "charter'd" as is the Thames River flowing through the city, and Blake repeats the word to emphasize the imposition of the government's restrictive presence on the city. From the poet's perspective, society causes the individual to enchain his or her imagination and thereby create rules ostensibly aimed at the common good but in reality the source of oppression.

These "mind-forg'd manacles" are responsible for the poverty that results in the child labor of the chimney sweeps; they motivate the wars that leave a disabled soldier begging for a crust of bread outside the palace in which the monarch for whom he fights lives in luxury; they pervert the institution of marriage through the blights of prostitution and venereal disease. All of these wrongs, according to Blake, are the inevitable consequences of an unjust society in which the few batten on the misery of the many.

Perhaps to the modern sensibility, Blake's criticism might seem overstated. Even, we might say, if we accept his premise that there is a great deal of suffering in the world, his call to return to a state of innocence does not seem very practical. How would it be accomplished? And what would be the nature of such an "innocent" society? Blake seems to argue that in such a society there would be a more equitable distribution of resources, so that children would not lose their childhood to a daily struggle for survival, soldiers would no longer bleed for self-serving monarchs, and young women would not be driven to sell their bodies to live. Although we would probably agree that our world would be a better place without the abuses Blake enumerates, and others of a more contemporary quality we could add to the list, his solution seems vague at best.

More than its vagueness, however, is at issue. Every society of any sophistication seems to provide an opportunity for some individuals to excel and, in the process, to acquire a greater share of the society's resources. Although some, like Blake, might suggest that the desire to prosper materially as a result of one's labors is corrupt, we must nevertheless accept the fact that this "corruption" appears to be a necessary component of human nature. Further, attaining a luxurious lifestyle seems to be a very natural, if not universal, goal. Most of us, on some level, would like to live like the very rich we read about in novels, and see on television and in the movies. Wealth certainly does have its charms.

The American novelist F. Scott Fitzgerald, although with some ambivalence, celebrates the power of extraordinary wealth in such works as *The Great Gatsby*, in which the title character acquires a tremendous fortune in his pursuit of reclaiming his "golden girl," Daisy. We are told in that novel that Daisy's voice "was full of money—that was the inexhaustible charm that rose and fell in it, the jingle of it, the cymbals' song of it." The fact that Fitzgerald gave his hero his fortune through bootlegging during Prohibition only partially detracts from the dazzle of the wealth portrayed in the novel.

Ernest Hemingway, Fitzgerald's sometime-friend, took a far more critical attitude toward this fascination with wealth. In "The Snows of Kilimanjaro," Hemingway parodies Fitzgerald in a character he calls Julian:

> He remembered poor Julian and his romantic awe of them [the very wealthy] and how he had started a story once that began, "The very rich are different from you and me." And how someone had said to Julian, Yes, they have more money. But that was not humorous to Julian. He thought they were a special glamorous race and when he found they weren't it wrecked him just as much as any other thing that wrecked him.

Fitzgerald, according to Hemingway, suffered from an exaggerated envy of the wealthy, so much so that he imagined them a special race of people.

We may agree with Hemingway that the only difference between the very wealthy and the rest of us is a certain amount of money and that in every other way they live lives very similar to ours. Or we may share Fitzgerald's awe of such people. But either way, the simple fact remains that in our society, as in every other, the distribution of wealth is grossly uneven, and therefore possibly unjust, especially if by justice we mean fairness in the allocation of the stuff of material existence.

One writer who explored this unevenness of distribution is Stephen Crane. In the short story, "An Experiment in Misery," Crane presents the gritty details of daily survival in the lives of the homeless of the 1890s. For these people, the focus of a day's activity consists of finding a meal and shelter for the night. The young man who is the hero of the story seems to have decided to spend some time among the street people of New York City, to taste what their lives are like.

He meets a panhandler whom he dubs the "assassin" for the aggressive manner in which he begs. In his company, the young man finds the cheapest lodging available, a bed for seven cents a night, and together they share a meager breakfast the next morning. The other characters are the forgotten poor and homeless who gather in parks during the day and in the rooming houses, if they have found the money, at night. They are a uniformly desperate lot, clinging to survival by their fingernails. Nonetheless, there seems to be a rough camaraderie among them as they try to make it to the next day.

One conclusion the young man draws, however, is that, contrary to what Hemingway asserts, there is a great gulf between the very poor and the rest of society:

> The people of the street hurrying hither and thither made a blend of black figures, changing, yet frieze-like. They walked in their good clothes as upon important missions, giving no gaze to the two wanderers seated upon the benches. They expressed to the young man his infinite distance from all that he valued. Social position, comfort, the pleasures of living, were unconquerable kingdoms. He felt a sudden awe.

The young man's "awe" is strikingly different from that ascribed to Fitzgerald by Hemingway, simply because the vantage point is so different. He is at the bottom of the social heap looking up at the unspeakable distance between himself and the ordinary citizens who are going about their business and who will end the day in their comfortable homes. The narrator's awe is perhaps therefore more poignant than Fitzgerald's fascination with the super rich. Nonetheless, in both cases the awe underscores the gap between the have's and the have-not's.

Crane's story is set in the early 1890's, very possibly during the Panic of 1893 when the economy was in a shambles because of the failing gold standard of our currency. At the very time that Crane's characters were a step away from starvation, the House of Morgan, as described by John Dos Passos, was increasing its already monumental fortune. During the Panic, for example, "at no inconsiderable profit to himself," J. Pierpont Morgan singlehandedly bailed out the U. S. Treasury. This action is one of a long list of details included in Dos Passos's "The House of Morgan," which describes the process by which that famous family achieved its stupendous wealth.

Dos Passos writes in an experimental style that blends the prosaic tone of the journalist with the knowing juxtapositions and jumps of the poet. In "The House of Morgan" this style emphasizes his implied point: that the Morgans exercised their considerable talents to amass an incredible fortune, but in so doing they thrived during times of general misery for the rest of the population. The picture that emerges of success built on others' misfortunes is not so very different from the "charter'd streets" of Blake's London, peopled by the neglected poor.

STEPHEN CRANE
An Experiment in Misery

It was late at night, and a fine rain was swirling softly down, causing the pavements to glisten with hue of steel and blue and yellow in the rays of the innumerable lights. A youth was trudging slowly, without enthusiasm, with his hands buried deep in his trousers' pockets, toward the downtown places where beds can be hired for coppers. He was clothed in an aged and tattered suit, and his derby was a marvel of dust-covered crown and torn rim. He was going forth to eat as the wanderer may eat, and sleep as the homeless sleep. By the time he had reached City Hall Park he was so completely plastered with yells of "bum" and "hobo" and with various unholy epithets that small boys had applied to him at intervals, that he was in a state of the most profound dejection. The sifting rain saturated the old velvet collar of his overcoat, and as the wet cloth pressed against his neck, he felt that there no longer could be pleasure in life. He looked about him searching for an outcast of highest degree that the two might share miseries. But the lights threw a quivering glare over rows and circles of deserted benches that glistened damply, showing patches of wet sod behind them. It seemed that their usual freights had fled on this night to better things. There were only squads of well-dressed Brooklyn people who swarmed toward the Bridge.

The young man loitered about for a time and then went shuffling off down Park Row. In the sudden descent in style of the dress of the crowd he felt relief, and as if he were at last in his own country. He began to see tatters that matched his tatters. In Chatham Square there were aimless men strewn in front of saloons and lodging houses, standing sadly, patiently, reminding one vaguely of the attitudes of chickens in a storm. He aligned himself with these men, and turned slowly to occupy himself with the flowing life of the great street.

Through the mists of the cold and storming night, the cable cars went in silent procession, great affairs shining with red and brass, moving with formidable power, calm and irresistible, dangerful and gloomy, breaking silence only by the loud fierce cry of the gong. Two rivers of people swarmed along the sidewalks, spattered with black mud, which made each shoe leave a scar-like impression. Overhead elevated trains with a shrill grinding of the wheels stopped at the station, which upon its leg-like pillars seemed to resemble some monstrous kind of crab squatting over the street. The quick fat puffings of the engines could be heard. Down an alley there were sombre curtains of purple and black, on which street lamps dully glittered like embroidered flowers.

Stephen Crane's "An Experiment in Misery" is reprinted from *The Works of Stephen Crane*, edited by Fredson Bowers, University of Virginia Edition, by permission of the Rector and Visitors of the University of Virginia. **Stephen Crane** (1871–1900), an American fiction writer and poet, is known for his impressionistic prose and bitingly ironic view of life.

A saloon stood with a voracious air on a corner. A sign leaning against the front of the doorpost announced: "Free hot soup tonight." The swing doors snapping to and fro like ravenous lips, made gratified smacks as the saloon gorged itself with plump men, eating with astounding and endless appetite, smiling in some indescribable manner as the men came from all directions like sacrifices to a heathenish superstition.

Caught by the delectable sign, the young man allowed himself to be swallowed. A bartender placed a schooner of dark and portentous beer on the bar. Its monumental form upreared until the froth a-top was above the crown of the young man's brown derby.

"Soup over there, gents," said the bartender, affably. A little yellow man in rags and the youth grasped their schooners and went with speed toward a lunch counter, where a man with oily but imposing whiskers ladled genially from a kettle until he had furnished his two mendicants with a soup that was steaming hot and in which there were little floating suggestions of chicken. The young man, sipping his broth, felt the cordiality expressed by the warmth of the mixture, and he beamed at the man with oily but imposing whiskers, who was presiding like a priest behind an altar. "Have some more, gents?" he inquired of the two sorry figures before him. The little yellow man accepted with a swift gesture, but the youth shook his head and went out, following a man whose wondrous seediness promised that he would have a knowledge of cheap lodging houses.

On the side-walk he accosted the seedy man. "Say, do you know a cheap place t' sleep?"

The other hesitated for a time, gazing sideways. Finally he nodded in the direction of up the street. "I sleep up there," he said, "when I've got th' price."

"How much?"

"Ten cents."

The young man shook his head dolefully. "That's too rich for me."

At that moment there approached the two a reeling man in strange garments. His head was a fuddle of bushy hair and whiskers from which his eyes peered with a guilty slant. In a close scrutiny it was possible to distinguish the cruel lines of a mouth, which looked as if its lips had just closed with satisfaction over some tender and piteous morsel. He appeared like an assassin steeped in crimes performed awkwardly.

But at this time his voice was turned to the coaxing key of an affectionate puppy. He looked at the men with wheedling eyes and began to sing a little melody for charity.

"Say, gents, can't yeh give a poor feller a couple of cents t' git a bed. I got five and I gits anudder two I gits me a bed. Now, on th' square, gents, can't yeh jest gimme two cents t' git a bed. Now, yeh know how a respecter'ble gentlem'n feels when he's down on his luck an' I—"

The seedy man, staring with imperturbable countenance at a train which clattered overhead, interrupted in an expressionless voice: "Ah, go t'h—!"

But the youth spoke to the prayerful assassin in tones of astonishment and inquiry. "Say, you must be crazy! Why don't yeh strike somebody that looks as if they had money?"

The assassin, tottering about on his uncertain legs, and at intervals brushing imaginary obstacles from before his nose, entered into a long explanation of the psychology of the situation. It was so profound that it was unintelligible.

When he had exhausted the subject the young man said to him: "Let's see th' five cents."

The assassin wore an expression of drunken woe at this sentence, filled with suspicion of him. With a deeply pained air he began to fumble in his clothing, his red hands trembling. Presently he announced in a voice of bitter grief, as if he had been betrayed: "There's on'y four."

"Four," said the young man thoughtfully. "Well, look-a-here, I'm a stranger here, an' if ye'll steer me to your cheap joint I'll find the other three."

The assassin's countenance became instantly radiant with joy. His whiskers quivered with the wealth of his alleged emotions. He seized the young man's hand in a transport of delight and friendliness.

"B'gawd," he cried, "if ye'll do that, b'gawd, I'd say yeh was a damned good feller, I would, an' I'd remember yeh all m' life, I would, b'gawd, an' if I ever got a chance I'd return th' compliment"—he spoke with drunken dignity—"b'gawd, I'd treat yeh white, I would, an' I'd allus remember yeh—"

The young man drew back, looking at the assassin coldly. "Oh, that's all right," he said. "You show me th' joint—that's all you've got t'do."

The assassin, gesticulating gratitude, led the young man along a dark street. Finally he stopped before a little dusty door. He raised his hand impressively. "Look-a-here," he said, and there was a thrill of deep and ancient wisdom upon his face, "I've brought yeh here, an' that's my part, ain't it? If th' place don't suit yeh yeh needn't git mad at me, need yeh? There won't be no bad feelin', will there?"

"No," said the young man.

The assassin waved his arm tragically and led the march up the steep stairway. On the way, the young man furnished the assassin with three pennies. At the top a man with benevolent spectacles looked at them through a hole in the board. He collected their money, wrote some names on a register, and speedily was leading the two men along a gloom shrouded corridor.

Shortly after the beginning of this journey the young man felt his liver turn white, for from the dark and secret places of the building there suddenly came to his nostrils strange and unspeakable odors that assailed him like malignant diseases with wings. They seemed to be from human bodies closely packed in dens; the exhalations from a hundred pairs of reeking lips; the fumes from a thousand bygone debauches; the expression of a thousand present miseries.

A man, naked save for a little snuff colored undershirt, was parading sleepily along the corridor. He rubbed his eyes, and, giving vent to a prodigious yawn, demanded to be told the time.

"Half past one."

The man yawned again. He opened a door, and for a moment his form was outlined against a black, opaque interior. To this door came the three men, and as it was again opened the unholy odors rushed out like released fiends, so that the young man was obliged to struggle as against an overpowering wind.

It was some time before the youth's eyes were good in the intense gloom within, but the man with benevolent spectacles led him skillfully, pausing but a moment to deposit the limp assassin upon a cot. He took the youth to a cot that lay tranquilly by the window, and, showing him a tall locker for clothes that stood near the head with the ominous air of a tombstone, left him.

The youth sat on his cot and peered about him. There was a gas jet in a distant part of the room that burned a small flickering orange hued flame. It caused vast masses of tumbled shadows in all parts of the place, save where, immediately above it, there was a little gray haze. As the young man's eyes became used to the darkness he could see upon the cots that thickly littered the floor the forms of men sprawled out, lying in death-like silence or heaving and snoring with tremendous effort, like stabbed fish.

The youth locked his derby and his shoes in the mummy case near him and then lay down with his old and familiar coat around his shoulders. A blanket he handled gingerly, drawing it over part of the coat. The cot was leather covered and cold as melting snow. The youth was obliged to shiver for some time on this affair, which was like a slab. Presently, however, his chill gave him peace, and during this period of leisure from it he turned his head to stare at his friend, the assassin, whom he could dimly discern where he lay sprawled on a cot in the abandon of a man filled with drink. He was snoring with incredible vigor. His wet hair and beard dimly glistened and his inflamed nose shone with subdued luster like a red light in a fog.

Within reach of the youth's hand was one who lay with yellow breast and shoulders bare to the cold drafts. One arm hung over the side of the cot and the fingers lay full length upon the wet cement floor of the room. Beneath the inky brows could be seen the eyes of the man exposed by the partly opened lids. To the youth it seemed that he and this corpse-like being were exchanging a prolonged stare and that the other threatened with his eyes. He drew back, watching' his neighbor from the shadows of his blanket edge. The man did not move once through the night, but lay in this stillness as of death, like a body stretched out, expectant of the surgeon's knife.

And all through the room could be seen the tawny hues of naked flesh, limbs thrust into the darkness, projecting beyond the cots; up-reared knees; arms hanging, long and thin, over the cot edges. For the most part they were statuesque, carven, dead. With the curious lockers standing all about like tombstones there was a strange effect of a graveyard, where bodies were merely flung.

Yet occasionally could be seen limbs wildly tossing in fantastic, nightmare gestures, accompanied by gutteral cries, grunts, oaths. And there was one fellow off in a gloomy corner, who in his dreams was oppressed by some frightful calamity, for of a sudden he began to utter long wails that went almost like yells from a hound, echoing wailfully and weird through this chill place of tombstones, where men lay like the dead.

The sound, in its high piercing beginnings that dwindled to final melancholy moans, expressed a red and grim tragedy of the unfathomable possibilities of the man's dreams. But to the youth these were not merely the shrieks of a vision pierced man. They were an utterance of the meaning of the room and its occupants. It was to him the protest of the wretch who feels the touch of the imperturbable granite wheels and who then cries with an impersonal eloquence, with a strength not from him, giving voice to the wail of a whole section, a class, a people. This, weaving into the young man's brain and mingling with his views of these vast and somber shadows that like mighty black fingers curled around the naked bodies, made the young man so that he did not sleep, but lay meager experience. At times the fellow in the carving biographies for these men from his corner howled in a writhing agony of his imaginations.

Finally a long lance point of gray light shot through the dusty panes of the window. Without, the young man could see roofs drearily white in the dawning. The point of light yellowed and grew brighter, until the golden rays of the morning sun came in bravely and strong. They touched with radiant color the form of a small, fat man, who snored in stuttering fashion. His round and shiny bald head glowed suddenly with the valor of a decoration. He sat up, blinked at the sun, swore fretfully and pulled his blanket over the ornamental splendors of his head.

The youth contentedly watched this rout of the shadows before the bright spears of the sun and presently he slumbered. When he awoke he heard the voice of the assassin raised in valiant curses. Putting up his head he perceived his comrade seated on the side of the cot engaged in scratching his neck with long finger nails that rasped like files.

"Hully Jee dis is a new breed. They've got can openers on their feet," he continued in a violent tirade.

The young man hastily unlocked his closet and took out his shoes and hat. As he sat on the side of the cot, lacing his shoes, he glanced about and saw that daylight had made the room comparatively commonplace and uninteresting. The men, whose faces seemed stolid, serene or absent, were engaged in dressing, while a great crackle of bantering conversation arose.

A few were parading in unconcerned nakedness. Here and there were men of brawn, whose skins shone clear and ruddy. They took splendid poses, standing massively, like chiefs. When they had dressed in their ungainly garments there was an extraordinary change. They then showed bumps and deficiencies of all kinds.

There were others who exhibited many deformities. Shoulders were slanting, humped, pulled this way and pulled that way. And notable among these latter men was the little fat man who had refused to allow his head to be glorified. His pudgy form, builded like a pear, bustled to and fro, while he swore in fish-wife fashion. It appeared that some article of his apparel had vanished.

The young man, attired speedily, went to his friend, the assassin. At first the latter looked dazed at the sight of the youth. This face seemed to be appealing to him through the cloud wastes of his memory. He scratched his neck and reflected. At last he grinned, a broad smile gradually spreading until his countenance was a round illumination. "Hello, Willie," he cried, cheerily.

"Hello," said the young man. "Are yeh ready t' fly?"

"Sure." The assassin tied his shoe carefully with some twine and came ambling.

When he reached the street the young man experienced no sudden relief from unholy atmospheres. He had forgotten all about them, and had been breathing naturally and with no sensation of discomfort or distress.

He was thinking of these things as he walked along the street, when he was suddenly startled by feeling the assassin's hand, trembling with excitement, clutching his arm, and when the assassin spoke, his voice went into quavers from a supreme agitation.

"I'll be hully, bloomin' blowed, if there wasn't a feller with a nightshirt on up there in that joint!"

The youth was bewildered for a moment, but presently he turned to smile indulgently at the assassin's humor.

"Oh, you're a d— liar," he merely said.

Whereupon the assassin began to gesture extravagantly and take oath by strange gods. He frantically placed himself at the mercy of remarkable fates if his tale were not true. "Yes, he did! I cross m' heart thousan' times!" he protested, and at the same time his eyes were large with amazement, his mouth wrinkled in unnatural glee. "Yes-sir! A nightshirt! A hully white nightshirt!"

"You lie!"

"Nosir! I hope ter die b'fore I kin get anudder ball if there wasn't a jay wid a hully, bloomin' white nightshirt!"

His face was filled with the infinite wonder of it. "A hully white nightshirt," he continually repeated.

The young man saw the dark entrance to a basement restaurant. There was a sign which read, "No mystery about our hash," and there were other age stained and world battered legends which told him that the place was within his means. He stopped before it and spoke to the assassin. "I guess I'll git somethin' t' eat."

At this the assassin, for some reason, appeared to be quite embarrassed. He gazed at the seductive front of the eating place for a moment. Then he started slowly up the street. "Well, goodby, Willie," he said, bravely.

For an instant the youth studied the departing figure. Then he called out, "Hol' on a minnet." As they came together he spoke in a certain fierce way, as if he feared that the other would think him to be weak. "Look-a-here, if yeh wanta git some breakfas' I'll lend yeh three cents t' do it with. But say, look-a-here, you've gota git out an' hustle. I ain't goin' t' support yeh, or I'll go broke b'fore night. I ain't no millionaire."

"I take me oath, Willie," said the assassin, earnestly, "th' on'y thing I really needs is a ball. Me t'roat feels like a fryin' pan. But as I can't git a ball, why, th' next bes' thing is breakfast, an' if yeh do that fer me, b'gawd, I'd say yeh was th' whitest lad I ever see."

They spent a few moments in dexterous exchanges of phrases, in which they each protested what the other was, as the assassin had originally said, a "respecter'ble gentlem'n." And they concluded with mutual assurances they they were the souls of intelligence and virtue. Then they went into the restaurant.

There was a long counter, dimly lighted from hidden sources. Two or three men in soiled white aprons rushed here and there.

The youth bought a bowl of coffee for two cents and a roll for one cent. The assassin purchased the same. The bowls were webbed with brown seams, and the tin spoons wore an air of having emerged from the first pyramid. Upon them were black, moss-like encrustations of age, and they were bent and scarred from the attacks of long forgotten teeth. But over their repast the wanderers waxed warm and mellow. The assassin grew affable as the hot mixture went soothingly down his parched throat, and the young man felt courage flow in his veins.

Memories began to throng in on the assassin, and he brought forth long tales, intricate, incoherent, delivered with a chattering swiftness as from an old woman. "—great job out'n Orange. Boss keep yeh hustlin', though, all time. I was there three days, and then I went an' ask'im t' lend me a dollar. 'G-g-go ter the devil,' he ses, an' I lose me job.

—"South no good. Damn niggers work for twenty-five and thirty cents a day. Run white man out. Good grub, though, Easy livin'.

—"Yas; useter work little in Toledo, raftin' logs. Make two or three dollars er day in the spring. Lived high. Cold as ice, though, in the winter—

"I was raised in northern N'York. O-o-o-oh, yeh jest ough to live there. No beer ner whisky, though, way off in the woods. But all th' good hot grub yeh can eat. B'gawd, I hung around there long as I could till th' ol' man fired me. 'Git t'hell outa here, yeh wuthless skunk, git t'hell outa here an' go die,' he ses. 'You're a hell of a father,' I ses, 'you are,' an' I quit 'em.''

As they were passing from the dim eating place they encountered an old man who was trying to steal forth with a tiny package of food, but a tall man with an indomitable mustache stood dragon fashion, barring the way of escape. They heard the old man raise a plaintive protest. "Ah, you always want to know what I take out, and you never see that I usually bring a package in here from my place of business."

As the wanderers trudged slowly along Park Row, the assassin began to expand and grow blithe. "B'gawd, we've been liven like kings," he said, smacking appreciative lips.

"Look out or we'll have t' pay fer it t' night," said the youth, with gloomy warning.

But the assassin refused to turn his gaze toward the future. He went with a limping step, into which he injected a suggestion of lamb-like gambols. His mouth was wreathed in a red grin.

In the City Hall Park the two wanderers sat down in the little circle of benches sanctified by traditions of their class. They huddled in their old garments, slumbrously conscious of the march of the hours which for them had no meaning.

The people of the street hurrying hither and thither made a blend of black figures, changing, yet frieze-like. They walked in their good clothes as upon important missions, giving no gaze to the two wanderers seated upon the benches. They expressed to the young man his infinite distance from all that he valued. Social position, comfort, the pleasures of living, were unconquerable kingdoms. He felt a sudden awe.

And in the background a multitude of buildings, of pitiless hues and sternly high, were to him emblematic of a nation forcing its regal head into the clouds, throwing no downward glances; in the sublimity of its aspirations ignoring the wretches who may flounder at its feet. The roar of the city in his ear was to him the confusion of strange tongues, babbling heedlessly; it was the clink of coin, the voice of the city's hopes which were to him no hopes.

He confessed himself an outcast, and his eyes from under the lowered rim of his hat began to glance guiltily, wearing the criminal expression that comes with certain convictions.

JOHN DOS PASSOS
The House of Morgan

I commit my soul into the hands of my savior, wrote John Pierpont Morgan in his will, *in full confidence that having redeemed it and washed it in His most precious blood, He will present it faultless before my heavenly father, and I intreat my children to maintain and defend at all hazard and at any cost of personal sacrifice the blessed doctrine of complete atonement for sin through the blood of Jesus Christ once offered and through that alone,*

and into the hands of the House of Morgan represented by his son,

he committed,

when he died in Rome in 1913,

the control of the Morgan interests in New York, Paris and London, four national banks, three trust companies, three life insurance companies, ten railroad systems, three street railway companies, an express company, the International Mercantile Marine,

power.

on the cantilever principle, through interlocking directorates

over eighteen other railroads, U.S. Steel, General Electric, American Tel and Tel, five major industries;

the interwoven cables of the Morgan Stillman Baker combination held credit up like a suspension bridge, thirteen percent of the banking resources of the world.

The first Morgan to make a pool was Joseph Morgan, a hotel keeper in Hartford Connecticut who organized stagecoach lines and bought up AEtna Life Insurance stock in a time of panic caused by one of the big New York fires in the 1830's;

his son Junius followed in his footsteps, first in the drygoods business, and then as a partner to George Peabody, a Massachusetts banker who built up an enormous underwriting and mercantile business in London and became a friend of Queen Victoria;

Junius married the daughter of John Pierpont, a Boston preacher, poet, eccentric, and abolitionist; and their eldest son,

John Pierpont Morgan

arrived in New York to make his fortune

after being trained in England, going to school at Vevey, proving himself a crack mathematician at the University of Göttingen,

a lanky morose young man of twenty,

just in time for the panic of '57.

(war and panics on the stock exchange, bankruptcies, warloans. Good growing weather for the House of Morgan.)

When the guns started booming at Fort Sumter, young Morgan turned some money over reselling condemned muskets to the U. S. army and began to make himself felt in the gold room

John Dos Passos' "House of Morgan" is reprinted by permission of Elizabeth H. Dos Passos. **John Dos Passos** (1896–1970), an American novelist with strong political views, particularly in his earlier work, developed a unique narrative technique that mixed stream of consciousness with factual material.

in downtown New York; there was more in trading in gold then in trading in muskets; so much for the Civil War.

During the Franco-Prussian war Junius Morgan floated a huge bond issue for the French government at Tours.

At the same time young Morgan was fighting Jay Cooke and the German-Jew bankers in Frankfort over the funding of the American war debt (he never did like the Germans or the Jews).

The panic of '75 ruined Jay Cooke and made J. Pierpont Morgan the boss croupier of Wall Street; he united with the Philadelphia Drexels and built the Drexel building where for thirty years he sat in his glassedin office, redfaced and insolent, writing at his desk, smoking great black cigars, or, if important issues were involved, playing solitaire in his inner office; he was famous for his few words, Yes or No, and for his way of suddenly blowing up in a visitor's face and for that special gesture of the arm that meant, *What do I get out of it?*

In '77 Junius Morgan retired; J. Pierpont got himself made a member of the board of directors of the New York Central railroad and launched the first *Corsair*. He liked yachting and to have pretty actresses call him Commodore.

He founded the Lying-in Hospital on Stuyvesant Square, and was fond of going into St. George's church and singing a hymn all alone in the afternoon quiet.

In the panic of '93

at no inconsiderable profit to himself

Morgan saved the U.S. Treasury; gold was draining out, the country was ruined, the farmers were howling for a silver standard, Grover Cleveland and his cabinet were walking up and down in the blue room at the White House without being able to come to a decision, in Congress they were making speeches while the gold reserves melted at the Subtreasuries; poor people were starving; Coxey's army was marching to Washington; for a long time Grover Cleveland couldn't bring himself to call in the representative of the Wall Street moneymasters; Morgan sat in his suite at the Arlington smoking cigars and quietly playing solitaire until at last the president sent for him;

he had a plan all ready for stopping the gold hemorrhage.

After that what Morgan said went; when Carnegie sold out he built the Steel Trust.

J. Pierpont Morgan was a bullnecked irascible man with small black magpie's eyes and a growth on his nose; he let his partners work themselves to death over the detailed routine of banking, and sat in his back office smoking black cigars; when there was something to be decided he said Yes or No or just turned his back and went back to his solitaire.

Every Christmas his librarian read him Dickens' *A Christmas Carol* from the original manuscript.

He was fond of canarybirds and pekinese dogs and liked to take pretty actresses yachting. Each *Corsair* was a finer vessel than the last.

When he dined with King Edward he sat at His Majesty's right; he ate with the Kaiser tête-à-tête; he liked talking to cardinals or the pope, and never missed a conference of Episcopal bishops;

Rome was his favorite city.

He liked choice cookery and old wines and pretty women and yachting, and going over his collections, now and then picking up a jewelled snuffbox and staring at it with his magpie's eyes.

He made a collection of the autographs of the rulers of France, owned glass cases full of Babylonian tablets, seals, signets, statuettes, busts,

Gallo-Roman bronzes,

Merovingian jewels, miniatures, watches, tapestries, porcelains, cuneiform inscriptions, paintings by all the old masters, Dutch, Italian, Flemish, Spanish,

manuscripts of the gospels and the Apocalypse,

a collection of the works of Jean-Jacques Rousseau,

and the letters of Pliny the Younger.

His collectors bought anything that was expressive or rare or had the glint of empire on it, and he had it brought to him and stared hard at it with his magpie's eyes. Then it was put in a glass case.

The last year of his life he went up the Nile on a dahabiyeh and spent a long time staring at the great columns of the Temple Karnak.

The panic of 1907 and the death of Harriman, his great opponent in railroad financing, in 1909, had left him the undisputed ruler of Wall Street, most powerful private citizen in the world

an old man tired of the purple, suffering from gout, he had deigned to go to Washington to answer the questions of the Pujo Committee during the Money Trust Investigation: Yes, I did what seemed to me to be for the best interests of the country.

So admirably was his empire built that his death in 1913 hardly caused a ripple in the exchanges of the world: the purple descended to his son, J. P. Morgan,

who had been trained at Groton and Harvard and by associating with the British ruling class

to be a more constitutional monarch: *J. P. Morgan suggests. . . .*

By 1917 the Allies had borrowed one billion, nine hundred million dollars through the House of Morgan: we went overseas for democracy and the flag;

and by the end of the Peace Conference the phrase *J. P. Morgan suggests* had compulsion over a power of seventy four billion dollars

J. P. Morgan is a silent man, not given to public utterances, but during the great steel strike, he wrote Gary: *Heartfelt congratulations on your stand for the open shop, with which I am, as you know, absolutely in accord. I believe American principles of liberty are deeply involved, and must win if we stand firm.*

(Wars and panics on the stock exchange, machinegun fire and arson, bankruptcies, warloans, starvation, lice, cholera and typhus: good growing weather for the House of Morgan.)

QUESTIONS ABOUT "AN EXPERIMENT IN MISERY" AND "THE HOUSE OF MORGAN"

1. Why is Crane's story called an "experiment"?
2. In an earlier edition of the story, Crane makes it clear that he personally undertook to live among the street people of New York City. If we knew that the young man in the story could leave its environment at any time, would we react to the story differently?
3. Note the color imagery in the story, beginning with the "hue of steel and blue" in the first sentence. How does the imagery shape our response to the young man's experience?
4. The assassin marvels at the man in the boarding house who owns a "hully white nightshirt." What significance are we supposed to attach to this detail?
5. What has the young man learned as a result of his experiment?
6. Dos Passos presents numerous specific facts without seeming to be selective, yet we realize that there are thousands of other facts from the lives of the Morgans he could have included. What appears to be the basis for Dos Passos's choice of detail?

7. The style of "The House of Morgan" uses line breaks unusual in prose, leaving some lines with only one word. How does this device influence our understanding of the description of the Morgans?

8. Dos Passos occasionally offers critical judgments of the Morgans. Find specific instances of these judgments. Are they direct or indirect comments?

9. What does either Crane or Dos Passos have in common with Blake?

10. If we accept the fact that Crane and Dos Passos present extremes, does this recognition change our sense of the great distance between "the assassin" and the Morgans? Must any society contain such extremes?

Philosophical Discussion:
What Is Justice?

J. P. Morgan was very successful. He and his family amassed fortunes and lived like kings. His father, J. Pierpont Morgan, according to John Dos Passos, accumulated four national banks, three trust companies, three life insurance companies, ten railroad systems, the International Mercantile Marine, U.S. Steel, General Electric, American Telephone and Telegraph, and approximately thirteen percent of the banking resources of the world. By the end of the first World War, J. P. Morgan had increased the family's control of assets to approximately seventy-four billion dollars (worth close to a trillion dollars in today's economy).

Most human beings cannot imagine such wealth, let alone dream of controlling this vast financial empire. Others, such as the young man called "Willie" in Stephen Crane's "Experiment in Misery," struggle to exist, living from day to day, in abject poverty. To those at the bottom, like "Willie," ten cents for a cot in a flophouse is "too rich for me."

Dos Passos's "House of Morgan" and Crane's "Experiment In Misery" depict extremes. Most of us are neither millionaires nor destitute. Nevertheless, there seems to be something wrong when one family controls thirteen percent of the banking resources of the world, while others can't rent a bed to sleep on. Is "Willie" just a failure, a "bum," a "hobo," or does the problem go deeper?

Political scientists, economists, and historians have shown that there are many different ways for society to be organized. Monarchies, oligarchies, meritocracies, democracies, authoritarian and totalitarian dictatorships are some of the main forms of political systems that have been tried with varying degrees of success. Most Western countries today, including the United States, are amalgams that may be described as democratic social welfare states. The main alternatives, until recently, have been East European Marxist proletarian dictatorships, but a variety of states do not fall neatly into either camp—contemporary Iran, for instance, seems to be a theocracy.

Each of these systems has its own merits. Western democracies boast of basic freedoms, including those of political and religious expression. Marxist countries emphasize economic security. Others, such as Iran, seem to value a certain form of spiritual purity. Of all of these systems, and others that have yet to be tried, one question seems naturally to present itself: which system is best?

But how can we choose, when each system emphasizes something different? Is there a single yardstick against which each can be measured? Most philosophers grappling with this question appear to come to the same conclusion: any acceptable political system, along with its related social, economic and legal structure, must be just. But what exactly is justice?

The basic idea is that a state is just provided that its members are treated impartially before the law. In *The Republic,* Plato proposes a similar conception. (See the selections from *The Republic*: "Justice as the Interest of the Stronger" and "The Virtues in the State.") Plato makes his proposal in response to Thrasymachus, who advances a more cynical view, sometimes credited to Marxists, that justice is whatever suits the interests of the ruling class. Both suggestions are inadequate. The abolition of slavery, for example, is just, even though freeing slaves does not serve the interests of those who previously owned them. Moreover, a system of slavery would still be unjust even if all slaves were treated equally.

If impartiality is not enough, what more is needed? Several, apparently competing, slogans have been suggested—"To each according to his merit," or "according to his contribution," or "his need," or whatever. Which one, if any, is acceptable as a substantive criterion of justice? If we pick "need," then perhaps Willie and his companion would have a right to a bowl of soup. But then it is difficult to justify J. P. Morgan's seventy-four billion dollars. If we pick "merit," then perhaps the House of Morgan would deserve much of its wealth, but then Willie would have to give up his soup. The question, of course, is not just whether Willie should have his soup or J. P. Morgan his billions. Perhaps everybody should have whatever he or she wants. But when there is not enough to satisfy everybody, as is commonly the case, what then? How should the things people need and want be distributed?

Apparently something more than a mere slogan is called for, especially as so much has been made in recent years of the appeal to justice—in the civil rights movement, in the anti-war protests of the sixties and early seventies, in the feminist movement, and in the conservative efforts of recent years to reduce taxes and cut back on social benefit programs. In addition, we hear cries for gay rights, gray rights, animal rights, environmental rights. All, in one way or another, explicitly or tacitly appeal to justice, whether it be to pass new legislation (as in the Civil Rights Act of 1964), to alter existing law (through attempted passage of the Equal Rights Amendment, for instance), or to clarify present practice (as in the efforts to ensure that, while racial discrimination remains illegal, reverse discrimination is permitted).

How can this idea of justice have the power to support such a variety of claims, some apparently in conflict with others? Philosophers have proposed three main approaches to answer this question: *utilitarianism, egalitarianism* and *libertarianism.* But before we examine these approaches, let us first consider what exactly we are looking for.

Philosophers generally begin the pursuit of justice by distinguishing between *retributive* and *distributive* justice, two related but distinct forms of the same basic concept. Retributive justice is concerned primarily with theories of appropriate punishment for crime, from the Old Testament injunction of an eye for an eye and a tooth for a tooth, to the more commonly expressed rule, let the punishment fit the crime. By contrast, distributive justice is a broader undertaking, primarily concerned with two leading themes: (1) to describe the ideal state (for example, Plato's proposed Republic); and (2) to explain the moral basis of political obligations and rights. In what follows we will focus on distributive justice.

The two themes of distributive justice are related, at least in the sense that if, for example, monarchy is proposed as ideal, then we should expect some account of the obligation to obey the king. Similarly, if democracy is proposed, then an account of the right to vote would seem to be in order.

In addition, there is a third objective. If not everybody can satisfy his or her basic needs and wants, given the available resources, as seems to be the case not only in Stephen Crane's ''Experiment in Misery,'' but in much of the world today, a theory of justice, especially one concerned with the ideal state, should explain either how the goods of social life are to be redistributed or why some people should go without.

Let us now turn to *utilitarianism,* an approach often identified with the so-called *greatest happiness principle,* the idea that our actions are right, provided that they contribute to the greatest good for the greatest number. (We have included two readings on utilitarianism and justice. The first is by John Stuart Mill. The second, by J. J. C. Smart, is a response to the main alternatives to utilitarianism. For a more extensive discussion of utilitarianism as a general theory in ethics, see Part IV, Ethics.) At first glance, the utilitarian would seem to satisfy all the requirements suggested above. In the ideal state, for example, human well-being would be maximized. The necessities of life, such as food, clothing, and shelter would be distributed so as to satisfy every-body's basic needs, or at least the needs of the vast majority of individuals, not just J. P. Morgan but Willie and his Bowery compatriots as well. The ultimate justification is the greatest happiness principle, according to which, if there are two states equal in all respects, such as size, population, and available resources, the one that maximizes the greatest good for the greatest number would be preferable.

Why accept the greatest happiness principle? Although utilitarians do not claim any ultimate proof, the basic idea is morally compelling. John Stuart Mill argues that, just as an object of vision is visible, so an object of desire is desirable. Since happiness is ultimately desired for itself, happiness is ultimately desirable as an end in itself. (See his complete essay on utilitarianism.) As many philosophers have pointed out, however, the argument is flawed. ''Visible'' means *can be* seen; ''desirable'' means *ought to be* desired. Something more is needed for the conclusion to be established.

J. J. C. Smart, for example, suggests that utility appeals to our feelings of ''gener-alized benevolence'' toward fellow human beings. Since indifference to human misery is morally unacceptable, Smart's suggestion is persuasive.

Which system would the utilitarian ultimately recommend? The choice is open. Laissez-faire capitalism, Marxism or some hybrid, such as Great Britain's quasi-socialistic capitalistic monarchy could be picked, depending upon which system proves most useful in lifting society out of misery and deprivation.

What about a slave state? The utilitarian is unclear about this, especially if slavery is only a temporary measure or if the greatest number of people are free. In either case, it would appear that the utilitarian is willing to embrace, if only to a limited extent, at least one form of injustice. But then utilitarianism would fail to account for the third objec-tive listed above: a just redistribution of the wealth in order to achieve the ideal state.

The utilitarian may suggest that slavery is so evil that the misery of those enslaved outweighs whatever benefits others derive. But then the greatest happiness principle is unclear about what ought to be done. If slaves constitute a minority and slavery is abolished, then the greatest good is served, but not for the greatest number. If slavery is maintained, then the greatest number is served, but not the greatest good. In the absence of a more adequate version of the utilitarian principle, utilitarianism cannot account for the injustice of slavery. But slavery is not unique. Like bigotry and prejudice, slavery is possible only if certain fundamental rights are violated. If utilitarianism cannot account for such rights, it cannot provide a theory of justice.

Recognizing the apparent conflict between utilitarianism and justice, philosophers have attempted to formulate a more adequate version of the utilitarian principle. For example, it has been suggested that in assessing the pros and cons of our conduct, we strive to achieve a single quasi-mathematical utility function, arrived at by adding together all the good that a particular action would produce, and then subtracting from that total all the negative effects that that same action would produce. An action would be justified provided that, of all the available alternatives, it has the highest utility rating. (See Part IV, Ethics, for a discussion of the apparent difference between rule-utilitarianism and act-utilitarianism.) In this way, slavery and other apparent injustices would be excluded, since they would inevitably have a low rating when compared to the available alternatives.

However, what if two competing actions have approximately the same rating? Is the choice between them arbitrary? If so, justice would not be served. For example, suppose the owner of the hotel in "Experiment in Misery" charges his friends (approximately half the people who show up for a night's lodging) nothing at all for a place to sleep, while he doubles the rate for everybody else. The owner ends up with the same receipts, the hotel remains in business, and everybody has a place to sleep. The utilitarian would seem to find no relevant difference between this system and one in which everybody pays an equal amount. Although Willie would, in effect, subsidize one of the other patrons, the extra burden would be balanced in the utilitarian calculation by the fact that the subsidized individual has no burden at all. His pleasure makes up for Willie's pain.

This does not seem fair, however, especially for those like Willie, who have to pay twice as much for exactly the same service. Why should Willie pay for the sleeping accommodations of the owner's friends? They are not Willie's friends. What special obligation does the young man have to them? What right do they have to live off of his few pennies? What right does the owner have to show favoritism in this way, especially since those who are forced to pay may even have less than those who get a free bed?

Fairness, an important part of justice, seems missing from the utilitarian approach. In the absence of a more adequate formulation of the utilitarian principle, the utilitarian account does not succeed.

Can fairness provide an adequate foundation for a theory of justice? In 1971, John Rawls, professor of philosophy at Harvard University, published his theory of justice as fairness, in which he intended to go beyond the utilitarian approach by reaching back to an earlier doctrine, the *social contract theory,* favored in the seventeenth and eighteenth centuries by Thomas Hobbes, John Locke, and Jean Jacques Rousseau. The basic idea is that a just state is organized on the basis of an agreement, or contract, between those governing and those governed, as in the British parliamentary model, or between independent individuals in order to form a government, as in America and France immediately after their revolutions. Theorists did not all claim that a state constructed in this way would be ideal. Rather, as Hobbes thought, it would be preferable to living a "brutish" existence of unbridled competition in "a state of nature." However, all seemed to feel that the idea of a social contract could help to explain the foundation of political rights and obligations. Just as independent grain merchants contract to form a grain cooperative, so individuals contract to form a government. And just as the merchants agree in advance of market fluctuations to sell their combined grain stores at a certain price, or in accordance with some formula that defines their rights to profits or their debt due to losses, so the individuals agree in advance to abide by a set of legal, economic, and social regulations that defines their fundamental political rights and obligations in the community. And just as the merchant is morally bound by the agreement, so a member of a state, structured in this way, is bound by the regulations of the state.

There are, however, two main questions that this so-called *contractarian approach* raises. What guarantee, if any, is there that the principles chosen in the contract are just? For example, why wouldn't a utilitarian state be adopted? Second, what exactly are the principles of a just state?

Rawls attempts to answer the first question by specifying carefully the conditions of the "original position": the purely hypothetical circumstances under which a fair agreement is to be reached. Part of his main argument is that if the bargaining is fair, the principles agreed upon will be just. To insure fairness, Rawls makes two basic stipulations: (1) that those charged with drawing up the contract be rational egoists, individuals primarily concerned with creating a society in which they each have an optimum chance of satisfying their own ends; and (2) that they deliberate under a "veil of ignorance," a kind of selective amnesia in which the participants are barred from knowing who they are and what position they will hold in the state they are trying to structure. They don't know whether they are a member of the House of Morgan or a transient in a boarding house on the Bowery. Nor do they know the social or economic situation of the state—whether it is rich in natural resources, or suffers from chronic poverty and over population. They do, however, know general facts about human nature, at least in terms of social science and economic theory.

Part of Rawls's point is that without knowing the position each participant will hold, each will want to structure things in advance so that, when the veil is lifted, the chances of success are optimum, *whatever* position one finds oneself in. This means that if having the opportunity to rise to the financial heights of J. P. Morgan leaves others like Willie in the depths of economic depression, then the system is unfair and would not be chosen. Prudence would demand foregoing the opportunity to become a Morgan to avoid the economic disaster of becoming a Willie. For this reason, utilitarianism, which can encompass great economic disparity, would be ruled out.

What exactly is ruled *in*? What basic principles would rational egoists adopt under a veil of ignorance? Rawls proposes two:

(1) Each person is to have an equal right to the most extensive basic liberty compatible with a similar liberty for others.
(2) Social and economic inequalities are to be arranged so that they are both (a) reasonably expected to be to everyone's advantage, and (b) attached to positions and offices open to all.

The first principle establishes an *egalitarian* **society,** guaranteeing to every citizen the same basic political liberties, such as free speech and assembly, freedom from arbitrary arrest and seizure, and the right to vote and hold public office. The second, called the *difference principle,* applies to the distribution of income and wealth. While economic opportunities must be open to all, economic inequalities are not forbidden. Rather, they are justified, provided that they are to everyone's advantage.

The last proviso, that the unequal distribution of wealth and income must be to everyone's advantage, spells the main difference between Rawls and the utilitarian. In a utilitarian society, some may suffer so that others may prosper, provided that the sum total benefit to the society is higher than it would otherwise be. J. P. Morgan can amass his billions, even at the expense of low-paid workers or a pool of the unemployed, provided that most people are better off. In Rawls's state, the people at the bottom *must* benefit, if anybody does. Otherwise, the system is unjust.

What kind of state is Rawlsian? It may be felt that justice as fairness is best exemplified by some form of socialism, in which basic freedoms are guaranteed, and in which wealth is controlled and distributed by government in order to guarantee employment, subsidize retirement income, education, health and child care, and other programs aimed primarily at benefiting those that would otherwise be the poorest members of the community. But justice as fairness may also be attained in a capitalistic society, provided that political and civil liberties are protected and that the disparity between the haves and have-nots is minimized—by taxation used to fund social welfare programs, for example. In brief, it appears that Rawls's theory of justice as fairness can provide the foundation of the modern democratic social welfare state.

Is the Rawlsian state ideal? Not if the happiness of *every single* individual is to be maximized. The House of Morgan's holdings might be nationalized, or heavily taxed. In either case, J. P. Morgan would be less well off. But others, not just Willie and those bumming a handout on Skid Row, but the working poor, mothers with dependent children, the elderly, those chronically ill, physically handicapped, or mentally incapacitated, would be assured a higher, more humane, standard of living. If Rawls's state is not ideal, it may be the best any rational individual, primarily concerned with satisfying his or her basic needs, could hope for.

But is it just? It has been suggested that any scheme to redistribute wealth, be it utilitarian, contractarian, or what have you, would inevitably interfere with individual rights—not only with J. P. Morgan's apparent right to his properties, but with the young man's freedom as well. For example, suppose a Rawlsian egalitarian state is instituted by means of a unanimous referendum. Everybody, including J. P. Morgan, votes for a system defined by the principles of equality and difference. A social contract is established.

Morgan and others like him are permitted to trade, invest, and own property; they can make as much money as their talents, ingenuity, and good luck will permit, but within limits. They can increase their wealth only if others, especially those at the other end of the economic spectrum, are also better off. So the Morgans are taxed, and jobs, education and welfare are made available. The difference between rich and poor is diminished. An egalitarian state is born.

Now, Willie, too, has money to spend. No longer in abject poverty, he, too, is taxed. This seems only fair. Suppose, however, he decides to improve his lot even more. He goes to school, works very hard, studies writing and produces a very successful story about his former life on the Bowery. He makes millions. What happens now? His fame and popularity increase and he begins to accumulate a disproportionate amount of wealth, more than the social contract would appear to permit. Just as ordinary income is taxed, royalties, too, would have to be taxed, perhaps at a higher rate. Special regulations might be needed to control the income of successful artists, athletes, entertainers—anyone whose earnings, or accumulated wealth, seems to be making too much of a difference. As much as ninety percent of one's income might go to the government.

Willie could stop writing. Nobody is forcing him to write. But suppose the young man's readers are willing to pay a premium on each of his books, an amount that goes directly to him, independent of all other taxed income, just to insure that he keeps writing. Just as nobody is forcing him to write, nobody is forcing anyone to pay. His readers pay the extra amount voluntarily, hoping that he will freely produce more for them to read.

Once again, however, a disparity will appear between a certain class of successful individuals and the rest of society. If the writer and others whose works are in popular demand keep producing, then limits might be needed on how much people will be permitted to pay for them. But then the writer will be compelled to stop writing or others will be forced to stop paying. In either case, the right to receive the value of one's labor or the freedom to dispose of one's own legitimate holdings would be violated.

It might be felt that the problem just described is a rare exception. How many popular and highly paid writers are there? How many successful entertainers, actors, athletes? How many people would be forced to give away ninety percent of their income? Still, does the percentage alone matter? What difference does it make whether a person is compelled to pay ninety percent or nine percent? The point seems to be the same. A certain part of a person's income is taken away, used, in part, to subsidize the income of someone else. If the injustice is not apparent, imagine that instead of paying twenty percent of one's income, an individual is compelled to work one day a week without compensation for the benefit of someone else. The only system that compels labor without compensation is slavery. If the social contract theory encompasses slavery, then the theory cannot be adequate.

If the idea of a social contract, or perhaps Rawls's version of this approach, does not seem to guarantee justice, we should turn elsewhere, perhaps to a more recent attempt by Robert Nozick. See his *Anarchy, State and Utopia* (New York: Basic Books, Inc., 1974). Nozick explains justice within the tradition of Individualism, nowadays called *Libertarianism,* often associated with the nineteenth-century American writers Ralph Waldo Emerson and Henry David Thoreau. These earlier thinkers preached a set of virtues—self-reliance, independence and freedom—that typifies a certain vision of the American dream. Individuals who share this vision today often express the attitude that many people in our society, especially those on welfare, are not entitled to the money they receive. Nozick captures the spirit of this vision in the following three proposed principles of what is called the *entitlement theory:*

(1) A person who acquires a holding in accordance with the principle of justice in acquisition is entitled to that holding.

(2) A person who acquires a holding in accordance with the principle of justice in transfer, from someone else entitled to the holding, is entitled to the holding.

(3) No one is entitled to a holding except by (repeated) applications of 1 and 2.

(Nozick, p. 151)

The basic idea is that people are entitled to what they possess only if they acquire it in a certain manner. This suggestion, by itself, is not essentially different from the basic tenet of the egalitarian, who thinks that people are entitled to what they have, provided they acquire it in a fair manner. How does the entitlement theory differ? In what way exactly can people be entitled to what they have even though their acquisition need not be part of a fair distribution?

According to the first principle of the proposed theory of entitlement, people are entitled to what they have provided they have acquired something that was previously unowned in accordance with what Nozick calls "justice in acquisition." However, Nozick does not tell us clearly what this expression means, an omission that is unfortunate since not every original acquisition is just. During the eighteenth and nineteenth centuries, slave traders who made a business out of acquiring Africans to be sold into slavery, were "original owners," yet their holdings were unjust. There is no justice in the acquisition of a human being as a piece of property. If the entitlement theory is to succeed, some proviso is needed to explain how slave trading, for example, is to be proscribed.

It might be suggested that an individual may acquire something, provided that in the process, other's rights are not violated. Since enslaving a human being violates his or her basic freedoms, the proviso would rule out slavery. But it would also seem to rule out much else. For example, a settler who lays claim to an otherwise unowned parcel of land would seem to interfere with someone else's right to make the same claim. Some additional restriction seems needed; otherwise, it is not clear how the original title to something unowned—whether it be to land, water, to mineral or oil deposits, or to any of the other natural resources that serve as the foundation of wealth in a modern industrial state—can be justly established.

Perhaps the settler is the first to discover the parcel of land, having forged a path through the wilderness and overcome hardships and obstacles that caused others to turn back. It seems that he, more than anyone else, would be entitled to the property. His claim would take precedence over others since he has earned the right to take possession. Shall we say then that the principle of justice in acquisition be interpreted to mean that a person is entitled to original ownership of a thing provided he or she earns the right to possess it? This may be part of what John Locke, the seventeenth-century philosopher, had in mind when he suggested that a person must "mix his labor with it." Working a piece of otherwise unowned property is another way, perhaps, of earning the right to possess it.

However, if the principle of justice in acquisition be interpreted in this way, it is not clear how the entitlement theory offers an alternative to justice as fairness. It seems only fair that a person who blazes a new trail, stakes out a piece of otherwise unowned property, and invests his labor in making the land productive, should be entitled to it—especially if others have had, but have not succeeded in availing themselves of, the same opportunity to acquire the same holding. Unless there is another interpretation, the libertarian approach would not seem to go beyond the egalitarian.

Nozick suggests that a person's apparent right to something may be limited if "the position of those no longer at liberty to use the thing is thereby worsened." Does this mean that the settler is not entitled to his plot of land since the position of those no longer at liberty to use the parcel is worsened, at least to the extent that it is no longer available to them? If this is so, they would still have the same right to possess the property even though the settler invested his own time and energy in finding and improving the resource. According to Nozick's proviso, the settler would have to compensate others before he could take full possession. But this does not seem just. Not only would he receive no compensation for his own efforts, he would incur a debt to others for a piece of property that wasn't theirs to begin with. If slavery consists in working for little or no compensation so that others may benefit, the settler would appear to be a slave. If the principle of justice in acquisition embraces slavery, it seems not to be an adequate principle of justice. Nozick suggests that part of the problem consists in fixing a certain baseline, an estimate of how much worse off people would be if the unowned resource is acquired. But the difficulty is not just in making some hypothetical calculation; rather, the principle itself seems unjust.

Let us assume, however, that the libertarian could formulate an acceptable principle of acquisition that did not depend on the ideas of equality and fairness. Since most questions of social justice seem to involve the transfer of resources from those that have to those that do not, does the libertarian's principle of justice in transfer fare any better?

The idea of justice in transfer is that people are entitled to what they have, provided they receive it in a certain way from someone else who was entitled to it. Ultimately, the historical line of transfer must originate in a just acquisition of something unowned. For example, much of J. P. Morgan's wealth was inherited from his father, J. Pierpont Morgan, who, in turn, received the bulk of his money from his father, Junius, who inherited the estate left to him by Joseph, presumably the first Morgan to strike it rich. But how did Joseph get his initial capital? He must have had some money. Otherwise, how was he able to become a hotel keeper and organize stagecoach lines, let alone buy up Aetna Life Insurance stock during the panic of the 1830s?

Dos Passos does not tell us, perhaps because these details are not known. Indeed, the history of family wealth—any family's not just the Morgans'—can usually be traced back just so far, and then, like the history of the family itself, tends to get lost. Yet most people, including those committed to Marxist ideology, seem to think that despite the murky origins of wealth, individuals are entitled to what they receive as gifts, including, to some extent, what they inherit. In a Marxist regime, instead of individuals inheriting large holdings, the entire proletariat class is the benefactor. But the point seems to be the same. Considerations of historical transfer are not always necessary in determining who is entitled to what. Otherwise, if J. P. Morgan's great grandfather swindled somebody in a horse trade, J. P. Morgan would not be entitled to the family's vast empire—a judgment that seems excessive.

It may be suggested that unless the historical line of transfer is just, the present recipient's holdings are tainted. That the House of Morgan prospered, for example, on the catastrophes of war, famine, and disease seems to confirm a suspicion that no one person or family can be completely entitled to so vast a set of holdings. Just as no one may appropriate the only water hole in a desert and charge what he will for water, so no one family may appropriate all the steel mills in a country and charge what it will for steel.

If this is so, however, it seems that individual rights can be overridden by social or utilitarian considerations. The libertarian approach, by itself, would appear to be insufficient. Nozick suggests that this is not the case, that rights are never overridden by considerations external to the entitlement theory. But the entitlement theory is not well defined. Its necessary provisions have not been worked out. Perhaps Nozick is correct that individual rights cannot be overridden by utilitarian or egalitarian considerations. In the absence of a more adequate formulation, however, this does not seem to be the case.

The utilitarian provides us with a certain vision of the ideal state in which the common good is served. The egalitarian adds fairness as a necessary condition in attaining some such goal, while the libertarian insists that rights must be respected. Yet none of these approaches gives us an adequate account of justice. Nor is it clear how all three might be combined into a unified theory. If fairness is preserved, utility, it seems, cannot be maximized. If rights are respected, equality cannot always be guaranteed. Shall we despair of finding an answer to the question, what is justice?

Marxists apparently think so. Those who follow the teachings of Karl Marx, the nineteenth-century social theorist, do not propose an independent theory of justice, but emphasize a historical struggle between classes, especially the "proletariat" or working class, and the "bourgeoisie," or entrepreneurial class, over the means of production in a modern industrial state. Their idea seems to be that justice is largely a class concept, that a "just wage," for example, makes little sense outside a capitalistic society. According to the Marxist, a theory of justice is not needed, but rather a revolution, not only in economics, but in human consciousness. Only then can the vast majority of human beings be liberated both from their material dependence on economic forces over which they have little or no control, and also from their own slavish mentality that prevents them from appropriating the fruits of their labor.

The impact of Marx's ideas on political, economic, and social upheavals in the twentieth century can hardly be overemphasized. The Russian and Chinese Revolutions, the post-World War II conflict between East and West, the many wars of so-called liberation in Africa, Asia, Cuba, and Central America, even the U.S. involvement in Vietnam, are all inspired, in one way or another, by the call for armed revolt against what is perceived as class oppression. But what exactly is the basis for this call to arms?

If justice is nothing more than class struggle, why favor one side rather than the other? If the meaning of the very term "justice" changes according to which class a person belongs to, then there is no common basis for rationally deciding which side ought to win. *Dialectical materialism,* as Marxism is sometimes called, would seem to be nothing more than a grab for political power, and Marxism no better than the Marxist's own depiction of capitalism.

If members of an oppressed class have a rightful claim to take control of their lives, as Marxist rhetoric strongly suggests, then there is a common sense of justice to which even the Marxist appeals. Marxism, however, is silent on the issue of what that is. (See the selection by Milton Fisk, "Economic Justice.")

Where does this leave us? If utility, equality, and individual rights are not enough to define the concept of justice, the Marxist is not in a position to reject these ideas. Something more, not less, seems needed. What that is, however, remains to be shown.

PLATO
from *The Republic*

CHAPTER III
Thrasymachus: Justice as the Interest of the Stronger

All this time Thrasymachus had been trying more than once to break in upon our conversation; but his neighbours had restrained him, wishing to hear the argument to the end. In the pause after my last words he could keep quiet no longer; but gathering himself up like a wild beast he sprang at us as if he would tear us in pieces. Polemarchus and I were frightened out of our wits, when he burst out to the whole company:

What is the matter with you two, Socrates? Why do you go on in this imbecile way, politely deferring to each other's nonsense? If you really want to know what justice means, stop asking questions and scoring off the answers you get. You know very well it is easier to ask questions than to answer them. Answer yourself, and tell us what you think justice means. I won't have you telling us it is the same as what is obligatory or useful or advantageous or profitable or expedient; I want a clear and precise statement; I won't put up with that sort of verbiage.

I was amazed by this onslaught and looked at him in terror. If I had not seen this wolf before he saw me, I really believe I should have been struck dumb; but fortunately I had looked at him earlier, when he was beginning to get exasperated with our argument; so I was able to reply, though rather tremulously:

Don't be hard on us, Thrasymachus. If Polemarchus and I have gone astray in our search, you may be quite sure the mistake was not intentional. If we had been looking for a piece of gold, we should never have deliberately allowed politeness to spoil our chance of finding it; and now when we are looking for justice, a thing much more precious than gold, you cannot imagine we should defer to each other in that foolish way and not do our best to bring it to light. You must believe we are in earnest, my friend; but I am afraid the task is beyond our powers, and we might expect a man of your ability to pity us instead of being so severe.

Thrasymachus replied with a burst of sardonic laughter.

Good Lord, he said; Socrates at his old trick of shamming ignorance! I knew it; I told the others you would refuse to commit yourself and do anything sooner than answer a question.

Yes, Thrasymachus, I replied; because you are clever enough to know that if you asked someone what are the factors of the number twelve, and at the same time warned him: 'Look here, you are not to tell me that 12 is

Reprinted from *The Republic of Plato*, translated by F. M. Cornford (1941), by permission of Oxford University Press. **Plato** (ca. 428–348 B.C.) epitomizes for many the true philosopher, otherworldy in vision, yet practical in his attempt to address common moral concerns.

twice 6, or 3 times 4, or 6 times 2, or 4 times 3; I won't put up with any such nonsense'—you must surely see that no one would answer a question put like that. He would say: 'What do you mean, Thrasymachus? Am I forbidden to give any of these answers, even if one happens to be right? Do you want me to give a wrong one?' What would you say to that?

Humph! said he. As if that were a fair analogy!

I don't see why it is not, said I; but in any case, do you suppose our barring a certain answer would prevent the man from giving it, if he thought it was the truth?

Do you mean that you are going to give me one of those answers I barred?

I should not be surprised, if it seemed to me true, on reflection.

And what if I give you another definition of justice, better than any of those? What penalty are you prepared to pay?

The penalty deserved by ignorance, which must surely be to receive instruction from the wise. So I would suggest that as a suitable punishment.

I like your notion of a penalty! he said; but you must pay the costs as well.

I will, when I have any money.

That will be all right, said Glaucon; we will all subscribe for Socrates. So let us have your definition, Thrasymachus.

Oh yes, he said; so that Socrates may play the old game of questioning and refuting someone else, instead of giving an answer himself!

But really, I protested, what can you expect from a man who does not know the answer or profess to know it, and, besides that, has been forbidden by no mean authority to put forward any notions he may have? Surely the definition should naturally come from you, who say you do know the answer and can tell it us. Please do not disappoint us. I should take it as a kindness, and I hope you will not be chary of giving Glaucon and the rest of us the advantage of your instruction.

Glaucon and the others added their entreaties to mine. Thrasymachus was evidently longing to win credit, for he was sure he had an admirable answer ready, though he made a show of insisting that I should be the one to reply. In the end he gave way and exclaimed:

So this is what Socrates' wisdom comes to! He refuses to teach, and goes about learning from others without offering so much as thanks in return.

I do learn from others, Thrasymachus; that is quite true; but you are wrong to call me ungrateful. I give in return all I can—praise; for I have no money. And how ready I am to applaud any idea that seems to me sound, you will see in a moment, when you have said your own; for I am sure that will be sound.

Listen then, Thrasymachus began. What I say is that 'just' or 'right' means nothing but what is to the interest of the stronger party. Well, where is your applause? You don't mean to give it me.

I will, as soon as I understand, I said. I don't see yet what you mean by right being the interest of the stronger party. For instance, Polydamas, the athlete, is stronger than we are, and it is to his interest to eat beef for the sake of his muscles; but surely you don't mean that the same diet would be good for weaker men and therefore be right for us?

You are trying to be funny, Socrates. It's a low trick to take my words in the sense you think will be most damaging.

No, no, I protested; but you must explain.

Don't you know, then, that a state may be ruled by a despot, or a democracy, or an aristocracy?

Of course.

And that the ruling element is always the strongest?

Yes.

Well then, in every case the laws are made by the ruling party in its own interest; a democracy makes democratic laws, a despot autocratic ones, and so on. By making these laws they define as 'right' for their subjects whatever is for their own interest, and they call anyone who breaks them a 'wrongdoer' and punish him accordingly. That is what I mean: in all states alike 'right' has the same meaning, namely what is for the interest of the party established in power, and that is the strongest. So the sound conclusion is that what is 'right' is the same everywhere: the interest of the stronger party.

Now I see what you mean, said I; whether it is true or not, I must try to make out. When you define right in terms of interest, you are yourself giving one of those answers you forbade to me; though, to be sure, you add 'to the stronger party.'

An insignificant addition, perhaps!

Its importance is not clear yet; what is clear is that we must find out whether your definition is true. I agree myself that right is in a sense a matter of interest; but when you add 'to the stronger party,' I don't know about that. I must consider.

Go ahead, then.

I will. Tell me this. No doubt you also think it is right to obey the men in power?

I do.

Are they infallible in every type of state, or can they sometimes make a mistake?

Of course they can make a mistake.

In framing laws, then, they may do their work well or badly?

No doubt.

Well, that is to say, when the laws they make are to their own interest; badly, when they are not?

Yes.

But the subjects are to obey any law they lay down, and they will then be doing right?

Of course.

If so, by your account, it will be right to do what is not to the interest of the stronger party, as well as what is so.

What's that you are saying?

Just what you said, I believe; but let us look again. Haven't you admitted that the rulers, when they enjoin certain acts on their subjects, sometimes mistake their own best interests, and at the same time that it is right for the subjects to obey, whatever they may enjoin?

Yes, I suppose so.

Well, that amounts to admitting that it is right to do what is not to the interest of the rulers or the stronger party. They may unwittingly enjoin what is to their own disadvantage; and you say it is right for the others to do as they are told. In that case, their duty must be the opposite of what you said, because the weaker will have been ordered to do what is against the interest of the stronger. You with your intelligence must see how that follows.

Yes, Socrates, said Polemarchus, that is undeniable.

No doubt, Cleitophon broke in, if you are to be a witness on Socrates' side.

No witness is needed, replied Polemarchus; Thrasymachus himself admits that rulers sometimes ordain acts that are to their own disadvantage, and that it is the subjects' duty to do them.

That is because Thrasymachus said it was right to do what you are told by the men in power.

Yes, but he also said that what is to the interest of the stronger party is right; and, after making both these assertions, he admitted that the stronger sometimes command the weaker subjects to act against their interests. From all which it follows that what is in the stronger's interest is no more right than what is not.

No, said Cleitophon; he meant whatever the stronger *believes* to be in his own interest. That is what the subject must do, and what Thrasymachus meant to define as right.

That was not what he said, rejoined Polemarchus.

No matter, Polemarchus, said I; if Thrasymachus says so now, let us take him in that sense. Now, Thrasymachus, tell me, was that what you intended to say—that right means what the stronger thinks is to his interest, whether it really is so or not?

Most certainly not, he replied. Do you suppose I should speak of a man as 'stronger' or 'superior' at the very moment when he is making a mistake?

I did think you said as much when you admitted that rulers are not always infallible.

That is because you are a quibbler, Socrates. Would you say a man deserves to be called a physician at the moment when he makes a mistake in treating his patient and just in respect of that mistake; or a mathematician, when he does a sum wrong and just in so far as he gets a wrong result? Of course we do commonly speak of a physician or a mathematician or a scholar having made a mistake; but really none of these, I should say, is ever mistaken, in so far as he is worthy of the name we give him. So strictly speaking—and you are all for being precise—no one who practises a craft makes mistakes. A man is mistaken when his knowledge fails him; and at that moment he is no craftsman. And what is true of craftsmanship or any sort of skill is true of the ruler: he is never mistaken so long as he is acting as a ruler; though anyone might speak of a ruler making a mistake, just as he might of a physician. You must understand that I was talking in that loose way when I answered your question just now; but the precise statement is this. The ruler, in so far as he is acting as a ruler, makes no mistakes and consequently enjoins what is best for himself; and that is what the subject is to do. So, as I said at first, 'right' means doing what is to the interest of the stronger.

Very well, Thrasymachus, said I. So you think I am quibbling?

I am sure you are.

You believe my questions were maliciously designed to damage your position?

I know it. But you will gain nothing by that. You cannot outwit me by cunning, and you are not the man to crush me in the open.

Bless your soul, I answered, I should not think of trying. But, to prevent any more misunderstanding, when you speak of that ruler or stronger party whose interest the weaker ought to serve, please make it clear whether you are using the words in the ordinary way or in that strict sense you have just defined.

I mean a ruler in the strictest possible sense. Now quibble away and be as malicious as you can. I want no mercy. But you are no match for me.

Do you think me mad enough to beard a lion or try to outwit a Thrasymachus?

You did try just now, he retorted, but it wasn't a success.

Enough of this, said I. Now tell me about the physician in that strict sense you spoke of: is it his business to earn money or to treat his patients? Remember, I mean your physician who is worthy of the name.

To treat his patients.

And what of the ship's captain in the true sense? Is he a mere seaman or the commander of the crew?

The commander.

Yes, we shall not speak of him as a seaman just because he is on board a ship. That is not the point. He is called captain because of his skill and authority over the crew.

Quite true.

And each of these people has some special interest?

No doubt.

And the craft in question exists for the very purpose of discovering that interest and providing for it?

Yes.

Can it equally be said of any craft that it has an interest, other than its own greatest possible perfection?

What do you mean by that?

Here is an illustration. If you ask me whether it is sufficient for the human body just to be itself, with no need of help from without, I should say, Certainly not; it has weaknesses and defects, and its condition is not all that it might be. That is precisely why the art of medicine was invented: it was designed to help the body and provide for its interests. Would not that be true?

It would.

But now take the art of medicine itself. Has that any defects or weaknesses? Does any art stand in need of some further perfection, as the eye would be imperfect without the power of vision or the ear without hearing, so that in their case an art is required that will study their interests and provide for their carrying out those functions? Has the art itself any corresponding need of some further art to remedy its defects and look after its interests; and will that further art require yet another, and so on for ever? Or will every art look after its own interests? Or, finally, is it not true that no art needs to have its weaknesses remedied or its interests studied either by another art or by itself, because no art has in itself any weakness or fault, and the only interest it is required to serve is that of its subject-matter? In itself, an art is sound and flawless, so long as it is entirely true to its own nature as an art in the strictest sense—and it is the strict sense that I want you to keep in view. Is not that true?

So it appears.

Then, said I, the art of medicine does not study its own interest, but the needs of the body, just as a groom shows his skill by caring for horses, not for the art of grooming. And so every art seeks, not its own advantage—for it has no deficiencies—but the interest of the subject on which it is exercised.

It appears so.

But surely, Thrasymachus, every art has authority and superior power over its subject.

To this he agreed, though very reluctantly.

So far as arts are concerned, then, no art ever studies or enjoins the interest of the superior or stronger party, but always that of the weaker over which it has authority.

Thrasymachus assented to this at last, though he tried to put up a fight. I then went on:

So the physician, as such, studies only the patient's interest, not his own. For as we agreed, the business of the physician, in the strict sense, is not to make money for himself, but to exercise his power over the patient's body; and the ship's captain, again, considered strictly as no mere sailor, but in command of the crew, will study and enjoin the interest of his subordinates, not his own.

He agreed reluctantly.

And so with government of any kind: no ruler, in so far as he is acting as ruler, will study or enjoin what is for his own interest. All that he says and does will be said and done with a view to what is good and proper for the subject for whom he practises his art.

At this point, when everyone could see that Thrasymachus' definition of justice had been turned inside out, instead of making any reply, he said:

Socrates, have you a nurse?

Why do you ask such a question as that? I said. Wouldn't it be better to answer mine?

Because she lets you go about sniffling like a child whose nose wants wiping. She hasn't even taught you to know a shepherd when you see one, or his sheep either.

What makes you say that?

Why, you imagine that a herdsman studies the interest of his flocks or cattle, tending and fattening them up with some other end in view than his master's profit or his own; and so you don't see that, in politics, the genuine ruler regards his subjects exactly like sheep, and thinks of nothing else, night and day, but the good he can get out of them for himself. You are so far out in your notions of right and wrong, justice and injustice, as not to know that 'right' actually means what is good for someone else, and to be 'just' means serving the interest of the stronger who rules, at the cost of the subject who obeys; whereas injustice is just the reverse, asserting its authority over those innocents who are called just, so that they minister solely to their master's advantage and happiness, and not in the least degree to their own. Innocent as you are yourself, Socrates, you must see that a just man always has the worst of it. Take a private business: when a partnership is wound up, you will never find that the more honest of two partners comes off with the larger share; and in their relations to the state, when there are taxes to be paid, the honest man will pay more than the other on the same amount of property; or if there is money to be distributed, the dishonest will get it all. When either of them hold some public office, even if the just man loses in no other way, his private affairs at any rate will suffer from neglect, while his principles will not allow him to help himself from the public funds; not to mention the offence he will give to his friends and relations by refusing to sacrifice those principles to do them a good turn. Injustice has all the opposite advantages. I am speaking of the type I described just now, the man who can get the better of other people on a large scale: you must fix your eye on him, if you want to judge how much it is to one's own interest not to be just. You can see that best in the most consummate form of injustice, which rewards wrongdoing with supreme welfare and happiness and reduces its victims, if they won't retaliate in kind, to misery. That form is despotism, which uses force or fraud to plunder the goods of others, public or private, sacred or profane, and to do it in a wholesale way. If you are caught committing any one of these crimes on a small scale, you are punished and disgraced; they call it sacrilege, kidnapping, burglary, theft and brigandage. But if, besides taking their property, you turn all your countrymen into slaves, you will hear no more of those ugly names; your countrymen themselves will call you the happiest of men and bless your name, and so will everyone who hears of such a complete triumph of injustice; for when people denounce injustice, it is because they are afraid of suffering wrong, not of doing it. So true is it, Socrates, that injustice, on a grand enough scale, is superior to justice in strength and freedom and autocratic power; and 'right,' as I said at first, means simply what serves the interest of the stronger party; 'wrong' means what is for the interest and profit of oneself.

Having deluged our ears with this torrent of words, as the man at the baths might empty a bucket over one's head, Thrasymachus meant to take himself off; but the company obliged him to stay and defend his position. I was specially urgent in my entreaties.

My good Thrasymachus, said I, do you propose to fling a doctrine like that at our heads and then go away without explaining it properly or letting us point out to you whether it is true or not? Is it so small a matter in your eyes to determine the whole course of conduct which every one of us must follow to get the best out of life?

Don't I realize it is a serious matter? he retorted.

Apparently not, said I; or else you have no consideration for us, and do not care whether we shall lead better or worse lives for being ignorant of this truth you profess to know. Do take the trouble to let us into your secret; if you treat us handsomely, you may be sure it will be a good investment; there are so many of us to show our gratitude. I will make no secret of my own conviction, which is that injustice is not more profitable than justice, even when left free

to work its will unchecked. No; let your unjust man have full power to do wrong, whether by successful violence or by escaping detection; all the same he will not convince me that he will gain more than he would by being just. There may be others here who feel as I do, and set justice above injustice. It is for you to convince us that we are not well advised.

How can I? he replied. If you are not convinced by what I have just said, what more can I do for you? Do you want to be fed with my ideas out of a spoon?

God forbid! I exclaimed; not that. But I do want you to stand by your own words; or, if you shift your ground, shift it openly and stop trying to hoodwink us as you are doing now. You see, Thrasymachus, to go back to your earlier argument, in speaking of the shepherd you did not think it necessary to keep to that strict sense you laid down when you defined the genuine physician. You represent him, in his character of shepherd, as feeding up his flock, not for their own sake but for the table or the market, as if he were out to make money as a caterer or a cattle-dealer, rather than a shepherd. Surely the sole concern of the shepherd's art is to do the best for the charges put under its care; its own best interest is sufficiently provided for, so long as it does not fall short of all that shepherding should imply. On that principle it followed, I thought, that any kind of authority, in the state or in private life, must, in its character of authority, consider solely what is best for those under its care. Now what is your opinion? Do you think that the men who govern states— I mean rulers in the strict sense—have no reluctance to hold office?

I don't think so, he replied; I know it.

Well, but haven't you noticed, Thrasymachus, that in other positions of authority no one is willing to act unless he is paid wages, which he demands on the assumption that all the benefit of his action will go to his charges? Tell me: Don't we always distinguish one form of skill from another by its power to effect some particular result? Do say what you really think, so that we may get on.

Yes, that is the distinction.

And also each brings us some benefit that is peculiar to it: medicine gives health, for example; the art of navigation, safety at sea; and so on.

Yes.

And wage-earning brings us wages; that is its distinctive product. Now, speaking with that precision which you proposed, you would not say that the art of navigation is the same as the art of medicine, merely on the ground that a ship's captain regained his health on a voyage, because the sea air was good for him. No more would you identify the practice of medicine with wage-earning because a man may keep his health while earning wages, or a physician attending a case may receive a fee.

No.

And, since we agreed that the benefit obtained by each form of skill is peculiar to it, any common benefit enjoyed alike by all these practitioners must come from some further practice common to them all?

It would seem so.

Yes, we must say that if they all earn wages, they get that benefit in so far as they are engaged in wage-earning as well as in practising their several arts.

He agreed reluctantly.

This benefit, then—the receipt of wages—does not come to a man from his special art. If we are to speak strictly, the physician, as such, produces health; the builder, a house; and then each, in his further capacity of wage-earner, gets his pay. Thus every art has its own function and benefits its proper subject. But suppose the practitioner is not paid; does he then get any benefit from his art?

Clearly not.

And is he doing no good to anyone either, when he works for nothing?

No, I suppose he does some good.

Well then, Thrasymachus, it is now clear that no form of skill or authority provides for its own benefit. As we were saying some time ago, it always studies and prescribes what is good for its subject—the interest of the weaker party, not of the stronger. And that, my friend, is why I said that no one is willing to be in a position of authority and undertake to set straight other men's troubles, without demand-ing to be paid; because, if he is to do his work well, he will never, in his capacity of ruler, do, or command others to do, what is best for himself, but only what is best for the subject. For that reason, if he is to consent, he must have his recompense, in the shape of money or honour, or of punishment in case of refusal.

What do you mean, Socrates? asked Glaucon. I recognize two of your three kinds of reward; but I don't understand what you mean by speaking of punishment as a recompense.

Then you don't understand the recompense required by the best type of men, or their motive for accepting authority when they do consent. You surely know that a passion for honours or for money is rightly regarded as something to be ashamed of.

Yes, I do.

For that reason, I said, good men are unwilling to rule, either for money's sake or for honour. They have no wish to be called mercenary for demanding to be paid, or thieves for making a secret profit out of their office; nor yet will honours tempt them, for they are not ambitious. So they must be forced to consent under threat of penalty; that may be why a readiness to accept power under no such constraint is thought discreditable. And the heaviest penalty for declining to rule is to be ruled by someone inferior to yourself. That is the fear, I believe, that makes decent people accept power; and when they do so, they face the prospect of authority with no idea that they are coming into the enjoyment of a comfortable berth; it is forced upon them because they can find no one better than themselves, or even as good, to be entrusted with power. If there could ever be a society of perfect men, there might well be as much competition to evade office as there now is to gain it; and it would then be clearly seen that the genuine ruler's nature is to seek only the advantage of the subject, with the consequence that any man of understanding would sooner have another to do the best for him than be at the pains to do the best for that other himself. On this point, then, I entirely disagree with Thrasymachus' doctrine that right means what is to the interest of the stronger.

CHAPTER XII
The Virtues in the State

So now at last, son of Ariston, said I, your commonwealth is established. The next thing is to bring to bear upon it all the light you can get from any quarter, with the help of your brother and Polemarchus and all the rest, in the hope that we may see where justice is to be found in it and where injustice, how they differ, and which of the two will bring happiness to its possessor, no matter whether gods and men see that he has it or not.

Nonsense, said Glaucon; you promised to conduct the search yourself, because it would be a sin not to uphold justice by every means in your power.

That is true; I must do as you say, but you must all help.

We will.

I suspect, then, we may find what we are looking for in this way. I take it that our state, having been founded and built up on the right lines, is good in the complete sense of the word.

It must be.

Obviously, then, it is wise, brave, temperate, and just.

Obviously.

Then if we find some of these qualities in it, the remainder will be the one we have not found. It is as if we were looking somewhere for one of any four things: if we detected that one immediately, we should be satisfied; whereas if we recognized the other three first, that would be enough to indicate the thing we wanted; it could only be the remaining one. So here we have four qualities. Had we not better follow that method in looking for the one we want?

Surely.

To begin then: the first quality to come into view in our state seems to be its wisdom; and there appears to be something odd about this quality.

What is there odd about it?

I think the state we have described really has wisdom; for it will be prudent in counsel, won't it?

Yes.

And prudence in counsel is clearly a form of knowledge; good counsel cannot be due to ignorance and stupidity.

Clearly.

But there are many and various kinds of knowledge in our commonwealth. There is the knowledge possessed by the carpenters or the smiths, and the knowledge how to raise crops. Are we to call the state wise and prudent on the strength of these forms of skill?

No; they would only make it good at furniture-making or working in copper or agriculture.

Well then, is there any form of knowledge, possessed by some among the citizens of our new-founded commonwealth, which will enable it to take thought, not for some particular interest, but for the best possible conduct of the state as a whole in its internal and external relations?

Yes, there is.

What is it, and where does it reside?

It is precisely that art of guardianship which resides in those Rulers whom we just now called Guardians in the full sense.

And what would you call the state on the strength of that knowledge?

Prudent and truly wise.

And do you think there will be more or fewer of these genuine Guardians in our state than there will be smiths?

Far fewer.

Fewer, in fact, than any of those other groups who are called after the kind of skill they possess?

Much fewer.

So, if a state is constituted on natural principles, the wisdom it possesses as a whole will be due to the knowledge residing in the smallest part, the one which takes the lead and governs the rest. Such knowledge is the only kind that deserves the name of wisdom, and it appears to be ordained by nature that the class privileged to possess it should be the smallest of all.

Quite true.

Here then we have more or less made out one of our four qualities and its seat in the structure of the commonwealth.

To my satisfaction, at any rate.

Next there is courage. It is not hard to discern that quality or the part of the community in which it resides so as to entitle the whole to be called brave.

Why do you say so?

Because anyone who speaks of a state as either brave or cowardly can only be thinking of that part of it which takes the field and fights in its defence; the reason being, I imagine, that the character of the state is not determined by the bravery or cowardice of the other parts.

No.

Courage, then, is another quality which a community owes to a certain part of itself. And its being brave will mean that, in this part, it possesses the power of preserving, in all circumstances, a conviction about the sort of things that it is right to be afraid of—the conviction implanted by the education which the law-giver has established. Is not that what you mean by courage?

I do not quite understand. Will you say it again?

I am saying that courage means preserving something.

Yes, but what?

The conviction, inculcated by lawfully established education, about the sort of things which may rightly be feared. When I added 'in all circumstances,' I meant preserving it always and never abandoning it, whether under the influence of pain or of pleasure, of desire or of fear. If you like, I will give an illustration.

Please do.

You know how dyers who want wool to take a purple dye, first select the white wool from among all the other colours, next treat it very carefully to make it take the dye in its full brilliance, and only then dip it in the vat. Dyed in

that way, wool gets a fast colour, which no washing, even with soap, will rob of its brilliance; whereas if they choose wool of any colour but white, or if they neglect to prepare it, you know what happens.

Yes, it looks washed-out and ridiculous.

That illustrates the result we were doing our best to achieve when we were choosing our fighting men and training their minds and bodies. Our only purpose was to contrive influences whereby they might take the colour of our institutions like a dye, so that, in virtue of having both the right temperament and the right education, their convictions about what ought to be feared and on all other subjects might be indelibly fixed, never to be washed out by pleasure and pain, desire and fear, solvents more terribly effective than all the soap and fuller's earth in the world. Such a power of constantly preserving, in accordance with our institutions, the right conviction about the things which ought, or ought not, to be feared, is what I call courage. That is my position, unless you have some objection to make.

None at all, he replied; if the belief were such as might be found in a slave or an animal—correct, but not produced by education—you would hardly describe it as in accordance with our institutions, and you would give it some other name than courage.

Quite true.

Then I accept your account of courage.

You will do well to accept it, at any rate as applying to the courage of the ordinary citizen; if you like we will go into it more fully some other time. At present we are in search of justice, rather than of courage; and for that purpose we have said enough.

I quite agree.

Two qualities, I went on, still remain to be made out in our state, temperance and the object of our whole inquiry, justice. Can we discover justice without troubling ourselves further about temperance?

I do not know, and I would rather not have justice come to light first, if that means that we should not go on to consider temperance. So if you want to please me, take temperance first.

Of course I have every wish to please you.

Do go on then.

I will. At first sight, temperance seems more like some sort of concord or harmony than the other qualities did.

How so?

Temperance surely means a kind of orderliness, a control of certain pleasures and appetites. People use the expression, 'master of oneself,' whatever that means, and various other phrases that point the same way.

Quite true.

Is not 'master of oneself' an absurd expression? A man who was master of himself would presumably be also subject to himself, and the subject would be master; for all these terms apply to the same person.

No doubt.

I think, however, the phrase means that within the man himself, in his soul, there is a better part and a worse; and that he is his own master when the part which is better by nature has the worse under its control. It is certainly a term of praise; whereas it is considered a disgrace, when, through bad breeding or bad company, the better part is overwhelmed by the worse, like a small force outnumbered by a multitude. A man in that condition is called a slave to himself and intemperate.

Probably that is what is meant.

Then now look at our newly founded state and you will find one of these two conditions realized there. You will agree that it deserves to be called master of itself, if temperance and self-mastery exist where the better part rules the worse.

Yes, I can see that is true.

It is also true that the great mass of multifarious appetites and pleasures and pains will be found to occur chiefly in children and women and slaves, and, among free men so called, in the inferior multitude; whereas the simple and moderate desires which, with the aid of reason and right belief, are guided by reflection, you will find only in a few, and those with the best inborn dispositions and the best educated.

Yes, certainly.

Do you see that this state of things will exist in your commonwealth, where the desires of the inferior multitude will be controlled by the desires and wisdom of the superior few? Hence, if any society can be called master of itself and in control of pleasures and desires, it will be ours.

Quite so.

On all these grounds, then, we may describe it as temperate. Furthermore, in our state, if anywhere, the governors and the governed will share the same conviction on the question who ought to rule. Don't you think so?

I am quite sure of it.

Then, if that is their state of mind, in which of the two classes of citizens will temperance reside—in the governors or in the governed?

In both, I suppose.

So we were not wrong in divining a resemblance between temperance and some kind of harmony. Temperance is not like courage and wisdom, which made the state wise and brave by residing each in one particular part. Temperance works in a different way; it extends throughout the whole gamut of the state, producing a consonance of all its elements from the weakest to the strongest as measured by any standard you like to take—wisdom, bodily strength, numbers, or wealth. So we are entirely justified in identifying with temperance this unanimity or harmonious agreement between the naturally superior and inferior elements on the question which of the two should govern, whether in the state or in the individual.

I fully agree.

Good, said I. We have discovered in our commonwealth, three out of our four qualities, to the best of our present judgment. What is the remaining one, required to make up its full complement of goodness? For clearly this will be justice.

Clearly.

Now is the moment, then, Glaucon, for us to keep the closest watch, like huntsmen standing round a covert, to make sure that justice does not slip through and vanish undetected. It must certainly be somewhere hereabouts; so keep your eyes open for a view of the quarry, and if you see it first, give me the alert.

I wish I could, he answered; but you will do better to give me a lead and not count on me for more than eyes to see what you show me.

Pray for luck, then, and follow me.

I will, if you will lead on.

The thicket looks rather impenetrable, said I; too dark for it to be easy to start up the game. However, we must push on.

Of course we must.

Here I gave the view halloo. Glaucon, I exclaimed, I believe we are on the track and the quarry is not going to escape us altogether.

That is good news.

Really, I said, we have been extremely stupid. All this time the thing has been under our very noses from the start, and we never saw it. We have been as absurd as a person who hunts for something he has all the time got in his hand. Instead of looking at the thing, we have been staring into the distance. No doubt that is why it escaped us.

What do you mean?

I believe we have been talking about the thing all this while without ever understanding that we were giving some sort of account of it.

Do come to the point. I am all ears.

Listen, then, and judge whether I am right. You remember how, when we first began to establish our commonwealth and several times since, we have laid down, as a universal principle, that everyone ought to perform the one function in the community for which his nature best suited him. Well, I believe that that principle, or some form of it, is justice.

We certainly laid that down.

Yes, and surely we have often heard people say that justice means minding one's own business and not meddling with other men's concerns; and we have often said so ourselves.

We have.

Well, my friend, it may be that this minding of one's own business, when it takes a certain form, is actually the same thing as justice. Do you know what makes me think so?

No, tell me.

I think that this quality which makes it possible for the three we have already considered, wisdom, courage, and temperance, to take their place in the commonwealth, and so long as it remains present secures their continuance, must be the remaining one. And we said that, when three of the four were found, the one left over would be justice.

It must be so.

Well now, if we had to decide which of these qualities will contribute most to the excellence of our commonwealth, it would be hard to say whether it was the unanimity of rulers and subjects, or the soldier's fidelity to the established conviction about what is, or is not, to be feared, or the watchful intelligence of the Rulers; or whether its excellence were not above all due to the observance by everyone, child or woman, slave or freeman or artisan, ruler or ruled, of this principle that each one should do his own proper work without interfering with others.

It would be hard to decide, no doubt.

It seems, then, that this principle can at any rate claim to rival wisdom, temperance, and courage as conducing to the excellence of a state. And would you not say that the only possible competitor of these qualities must be justice?

Yes, undoubtedly.

Here is another thing which points to the same conclusion. The judging of law-suits is a duty that you will lay upon your Rulers, isn't it?

Of course.

And the chief aim of their decisions will be that neither party shall have what belongs to another or be deprived of what is his own.

Yes.

Because that is just?

Yes.

So here again justice admittedly means that a man should possess and concern himself with what properly belongs to him.

True.

Again, do you agree with me that no great harm would be done to the community by a general interchange of most forms of work, the carpenter and the cobbler exchanging their positions and their tools and taking on each other's jobs, or even the same man undertaking both?

Yes, there would not be much harm in that.

But I think you will also agree that another kind of interchange would be disastrous. Suppose, for instance, someone whom nature designed to be an artisan or tradesman should be emboldened by some advantage, such as wealth or command of votes or bodily strength, to try to enter the order of fighting men; or some member of that order should aspire, beyond his merits, to a seat in the council-chamber of the Guardians. Such interference and exchange of social positions and tools, or the attempt to combine all these forms of work in the same person, would be fatal to the commonwealth.

Most certainly.

Where there are three orders, then, any plurality of functions or shifting from one order to another is not merely utterly harmful to the community, but one might fairly call it the extreme of wrongdoing. And you will agree that to do the greatest of wrongs to one's own community is injustice.

Surely.

This, then, is injustice. And, conversely, let us repeat that when each order—tradesman, Auxiliary, Guardian—keeps to its own proper business in the commonwealth and does its own work, that is justice and what makes a just society.

I entirely agree.

JOHN STUART MILL
On the Connection Between Justice and Utility

In all ages of speculation, one of the strongest obstacles to the reception of the doctrine that Utility or Happiness is the criterion of right and wrong, has been drawn from the idea of Justice. The powerful sentiment, and apparently clear perception, which that word recalls with a rapidity and certainty resembling an instinct, have seemed to the majority of thinkers to point to an inherent quality in things; to show that the Just must have an existence in Nature as something absolute, generically distinct from every variety of the Expedient, and, in idea, opposed to it, though (as is commonly acknowledged) never, in the long run, disjoined from it in fact.

In the case of this, as of our other moral sentiments, there is no necessary connection between the question of its origin, and that of its binding force. That a feeling is bestowed on us by Nature, does not necessarily legitimate all its promptings. The feeling of justice might be a peculiar instinct, and might yet require, like our other instincts, to be controlled and enlightened by a higher reason. If we have intellectual instincts that prompt us to act in a particular way,

Reprinted from John Stuart Mill's *Utilitarianism, Liberty and Representative Government*, (1931), by permission of J. M. Dent & Sons and Everyman's Library. **John Stuart Mill** (1806–1873) influenced by Jeremy Bentham (1748–1832), developed a system of empirical philosophy, including his own version of utilitarianism, which still inspires many thinkers today.

there is no necessity that the former should be more infallible in their sphere than the latter in theirs: it may as well happen that wrong judgments occasionally suggested by those, as wrong actions by these. But though it is one thing to believe that we have natural feelings of justice and another to acknowledge them as an ultimate criterion of conduct, these two opinions are very closely connnected in point of fact. Mankind are always predisposed to believe that any subjective feeling, not otherwise accounted for, is a revelation of some objective reality. Our present object is to determine whether the reality, to which the feeling of justice corresponds, is one which needs any such special revelation; whether the justice or injustice of an action is a thing intrinsically peculiar and distinct from all its other qualities, or only a combination of certain of those qualities, presented under a peculiar aspect. For the purpose of this inquiry it is practically important to consider whether the feeling itself, of justice and injustice is *sui generis* like our sensations of colour and taste, or a derivative feeling, formed by a combination of others. And thus it is the more essential to examine, as people are in general willing enough to allow, that objectively the dictates of Justice coincide with a part of the field of General Expediency; but inasmuch as the subjective mental feeling of Justice is different from that which commonly attaches to simple expediency, and, except in the extreme cases of the latter, is far more imperative in its demands, people find it difficult to see, in Justice, only a particular kind or branch of general utility, and think that its superior binding force requires a totally different origin.

To throw light upon this question, it is necessary to attempt to ascertain what is the distinguishing character of justice, or of injustice: what is the quality, or whether there is any quality, attributed in common to all modes of conduct designated as unjust (for justice, like many other moral attributes, is best defined by its opposite), and distinguishing them from such modes of conduct as are disapproved, but without having that particular epithet of disapprobation applied to them. If in everything which

men are accustomed to characterise as just or unjust, some one common attribute or collection of attributes is always present, we may judge whether this particular attribute or combination of attributes would be capable of gathering round it a sentiment of that peculiar character and intensity by virtue of the general laws of our emotional constitution, or whether the sentiment is inexplicable, and requires to be regarded as a special provision of Nature. If we find the former to be the case, we shall, in resolving this question, have resolved also the main problem: if the latter, we shall have to seek for some other mode of investigating it.

To find the common attributes of a variety of objects, it is necessary to begin by surveying the objects themselves in the concrete. Let us therefore advert successively to the various modes of action, and arrangements of human affairs, which are classed, by universal or widely spread opinion, as Just or as Unjust. The things well known to excite the sentiments associated with those names are of a very multifarious character. I shall pass them rapidly in review, without studying any particular arrangement.

In the first place, it is mostly considered unjust to deprive any one of his personal liberty, his property, or any other thing which belongs to him by law. Here, therefore, is one instance of the application of the terms just and unjust in a perfectly definite sense, namely, that it is just to respect, unjust to violate, the *legal rights* of any one. But this judgment admits of several exceptions, arising from the other forms in which the notions of justice and injustice present themselves. For example, the person who suffers the deprivation may (as the phrase is) have *forfeited* the rights which he is so deprived of: a case to which we shall return presently. But also,

Secondly; the legal rights of which he is deprived, may be rights which *ought* not to have belonged to him; in other words, the law which confers on him these rights, may be a bad law. When it is so, or when (which is the same thing for our purpose) it is supposed to be so, opinions will differ as to the justice or injustice of infringing it. Some maintain that no law, however bad, ought to be disobeyed by an individual citizen; that his opposition to it, if shown at all, should only be shown in endeavouring to get it altered by competent authority. This opinion (which condemns many of the most illustrious benefactors of mankind, and would often protect pernicious institutions against the only weapons which, in the state of things existing at the time, have any chance of succeeding against them) is defended, by those who hold it, on grounds of expediency; principally on that of the importance, to the common interest of mankind, of maintaining inviolate the sentiment of submission to law. Other persons, again, hold the directly contrary opinion, that any law, judged to be bad, may blamelessly be disobeyed, even though it be not judged to be unjust, but only inexpedient; while others would confine the licence of disobedience to the case of unjust laws: but again, some say, that all laws which are inexpedient are unjust; since every law imposes some restriction on the natural liberty of mankind, which restriction is an injustice, unless legitimated by tending to their good. Among these diversities of opinion, it seems to be universally admitted that there may be unjust laws, and that law, consequently, is not the ultimate criterion of justice, but may give to one person a benefit, or impose on another an evil, which justice condemns. When, however, a law is thought to be unjust, it seems always to be regarded as being so in the same way in which a breach of law is unjust, namely, by infringing somebody's right; which, as it cannot in this case be a legal right, receives a different appellation, and is called a moral right. We may say, therefore, that a second case of injustice consists in taking or withholding from any person that to which he has a *moral right*.

Thirdly, it is universally considered just that each person should obtain that (whether good or evil) which he *deserves;* and unjust that he should obtain a good, or be made to undergo an evil, which he does not deserve. This is, perhaps, the clearest and most emphatic form in which the idea of justice is conceived by the general mind. As it involves the notion of desert, the question arises, what constitutes desert? Speaking in a general way, a person is understood to deserve good if he does right, evil if he does wrong; and in a more particular sense, to deserve good from those to whom he does or has done evil. The precept of returning good for evil has never been regarded as a case of the fulfilment of justice, but as one in which the claims of justice are waived, in obedience to other considerations.

Fourthly, it is confessedly unjust to *break faith* with any one: to violate an engagement, either express or implied, or disappoint expectations raised by our own conduct, at least if we have raised those expectations knowingly and voluntarily. Like the other obligations of justice already spoken of, this one is not regarded as absolute, but as capable of being overruled by a stronger obligation of justice on the other side; or by such conduct on the part of the person concerned as is deemed to absolve us from our obligation to him, and to constitute a *forfeiture* of the benefit which he has been led to expect.

Fifthly, it is, by universal admission, inconsistent with justice to be *partial;* to show favour or preference to one person over another, in matters to which favour and preference do not properly apply. Impartiality, however, does not seem to be regarded as a duty in itself, but rather as instrumental to some other duty; for it is admitted that favour and preference are not always censurable, and indeed the cases in which they are condemned are rather the exception than the rule. A person would be more likely to be blamed than applauded for giving his family or friends no superiority in good offices over strangers, when he could do so without violating any other duty; and no one thinks it unjust to seek one person in preference to another as a friend, connection, or companion. Impartiality where rights are concerned is of course obligatory, but this is involved in the more general obligation of giving to every one his right. A tribunal, for example, must be impartial, because it is bound to award, without regard to any other consideration, a disputed object to the one of two parties who has the right to it. There are other cases in which impartiality means, being solely influenced by desert; as with those who, in the capacity of judges, preceptors, or parents, administer reward and punishment as such. There are cases, again, in which it means, being solely influenced by consideration for the public interest; as in making a selection among candidates for a government employment. Impartiality, in short, as an obligation of justice, may be said to mean, being exclusively influenced by the considerations which it is supposed ought to influence the particular case in hand; and resisting the solicitation of any motives which prompt to conduct different from what those considerations would dictate.

Nearly allied to the idea of impartiality is that of *equality;* which often enters as a component part both into the conception of justice and into the practice of it, and, in the eyes of many persons, constitutes its essence. But in this, still more than in any other case, the notion of justice varies in different persons, and always conforms in its variations to their notion of utility. Each person maintains that equality is the dictate of justice, except where he thinks that expediency requires inequality. The justice of giving equal protection to the rights of all, is maintained by those who support the most outrageous inequality in the rights themselves. Even in slave countries it is theoretically admitted that the rights of the slave, such as they are, ought to be as sacred as those of the master; and that a tribunal which fails to enforce them with equal strictness is wanting in justice; while, at the same time, institutions which leave to the slave scarcely any rights to enforce, are not deemed unjust, because they are not deemed inexpedient. Those who think that utility requires distinctions of rank, do not consider it unjust that riches and social privileges should be unequally dispensed; but those who think this inequality inexpedient, think it unjust also. Whoever thinks that government is necessary, sees no injustice in as much inequality as is constituted by giving to the magistrate powers not granted to other people. Even among those

who hold levelling doctrines, there are as many questions of justice as there are differences of opinion about expediency. Some Communists consider it unjust that the produce of the labour of the community should be shared on any other principle than that of exact equality; others think it just that those should receive most whose wants are greatest; while others hold that those who work harder, or who produce more, or whose services are more valuable to the community, may justly claim a larger quota in the division of the produce. And the sense of natural justice may be plausibly appealed to in behalf of every one of these opinions.

Among so many diverse applications of the term Justice, which yet is not regarded as ambiguous, it is a matter of some difficulty to seize the mental link which holds them together, and on which the moral sentiment adhering to the term essentially depends. Perhaps, in this embarrassment, some help may be derived from the history of the word, as indicated by its etymology.

In most, if not in all, languages, the etymology of the word which corresponds to Just, points distinctly to an origin connected with the ordinances of law. *Justum* is a form of *jussum,* that which has been ordered. Δίκαιον comes directly from δίκη, a suit at law. *Recht,* from which came *right* and *righteous,* is synonymous with law. The courts of justice, the administration of justice, are the courts and the administration of law. *La justice,* in French, is the established term for judicature. I am not committing the fallacy imputed with some show of truth to Horne Tooke, of assuming that a word must still continue to mean what it originally meant. Etymology is slight evidence of what the idea now signified is, but the very best evidence of how it sprang up. There can, I think, be no doubt that the *idée mère,* the primitive element, in the formation of the notion of justice, was conformity to law. It constituted the entire idea among the Hebrews, up to the birth of Christianity; as might be expected in the case of a people whose laws attempted to embrace all subjects on which precepts were required, and who believed those laws to be a direct emanation from the Supreme Being. But other nations, and in particular the Greeks and Romans, who knew that their laws had been made originally, and still continued to be made, by men, were not afraid to admit that those men might make bad laws; might do, by law, the same things, and from the same motives, which if done by individuals without the sanction of law, would be called unjust. And hence the sentiment of injustice came to be attached, not to all violations of law, but only to violations of such laws as *ought* to exist, but do not; and to laws themselves, if supposed to be contrary to what ought to be law. In this manner the idea of law and of its injunctions was still predominant in the notion of justice, even when the laws actually in force ceased to be accepted as the standard of it.

It is true that mankind consider the idea of justice and its obligations as applicable to many things which neither are, nor is it desired that they should be, regulated by law. Nobody desires that laws should interfere with the whole detail of private life; yet every one allows that in all daily conduct a person may and does show himself to be either just or unjust. But even here, the idea of the breach of what ought to be law, still lingers in a modified shape. It would always give up pleasure, and chime in with our feelings of fitness, that acts which we deem unjust should be punished, though we do not always think it expedient that this should be done by the tribunals. We forego that gratification on account of incidental inconveniences. We should be glad to see just conduct enforced and injustice repressed, even in the minutest details, if we were not, with reason, afraid of trusting the magistrate with so unlimited an amount of power over individuals. When we think that a person is bound in justice to do a thing, it is an ordinary form of language to say, that he ought to be compelled to do it. We should be gratified to see the obligation enforced by anybody who had the power. If we see that its enforcement by law would be inexpedient, we lament the impossibility, we consider the impunity given to injustice as an evil, and strive to make amends for it by bringing a strong expression of our own and the public dis-

approbation to bear upon the offender. Thus the idea of legal constraint is still the generating idea of the notion of justice, though undergoing several transformations before that notion, as it exists in an advanced state of society, becomes complete.

The above is, I think, a true account, as far as it goes, of the origin and progressive growth of the idea of justice. But we must observe, that it contains, as yet, nothing to distinguish that obligation from moral obligation in general. For the truth is, that the idea of penal sanction, which is the essence of law, enters not only into the conception of injustice, but into that of any kind of wrong. We do not call anything wrong, unless we mean to imply that a person ought to be punished in some way or other for doing it; if not by law, by the opinion of his fellow-creatures; if not by opinion, by the reproaches of his own conscience. This seems the real turning point of the distinction between morality and simple expediency. It is a part of the notion of Duty in every one of its forms, that a person may rightfully be compelled to fulfil it. Duty is a thing which may be *exacted* from a person, as one exacts a debt. Unless we think that it may be exacted from him, we do not call it his duty. Reasons of prudence, or the interest of other people, may militate against actually exacting it; but the person himself, it is clearly understood, would not be entitled to complain. There are other things, on the contrary, which we wish that people should do, which we like or admire them for doing, perhaps dislike or despise them for not doing, but yet admit that they are not bound to do; it is not a case of moral obligation; we do not blame them, that is, we do not think that they are proper objects of punishment. How we come by these ideas of deserving and not deserving punishment, will appear, perhaps, in the sequel; but I think there is no doubt that this distinction lies at the bottom of the notions of right and wrong; that we call any conduct wrong, or employ, instead, some other term of dislike or disparagement, according as we think that the person ought, or ought not, to be punished for it; and we say, it would be right to do so and so, or merely that it would be desirable or laudable, according as we would wish to see the person whom it concerns, compelled, or only persuaded and exhorted, to act in that manner.

This, therefore, being the characteristic difference which marks off, not justice, but morality in general, from the remaining provinces of Expediency and Worthiness; the character is still to be sought which distinguishes justice from other branches of morality. Now it is known that ethical writers divide moral duties into two classes, denoted by the ill-chosen expressions, duties of perfect and of imperfect obligation; the latter being those in which, though the act is obligatory, the particular occasions of performing it are left to our choice; as in the case of charity or beneficence, which we are indeed bound to practise, but not towards any definite person, nor at any prescribed time. In the more precise language of philosophic jurists, duties of perfect obligation are those duties in virtue of which a correlative *right* resides in some person or persons; duties of imperfect obligation are those moral obligations which do not give birth to any right. I think it will be found that this distinction exactly coincides with that which exists between justice and the other obligations of morality. In our survey of the various popular acceptations of justice, the term appeared generally to involve the idea of a personal right—a claim on the part of one or more individuals, like that which the law gives when it confers a proprietary or other legal right. Whether the injustice consists in depriving a person of a possession, or in breaking faith with him, or in treating him worse than he deserves, or worse than other people who have no greater claims, in each case the supposition implies two things—a wrong done, and some assignable person who is wronged. Injustice may also be done by treating a person better than others; but the wrong in this case is to his competitors, who are also assignable persons. It seems to me that this feature in the case—a right in some person, correlative to the moral obligation—constitutes the specific difference between justice, and generosity or beneficence. Justice implies something which it is not only right to do, and wrong not to do, but which some individual person can claim from us as his moral right. No one has a moral right to our generosity or beneficence, because we are not morally bound to practise those virtues towards any given individual. And it will be found with respect to this as to every correct definition, that the instances which seem to conflict with it are those which most confirm it. For if a moralist attempts, as some have done, to make out that mankind generally, though not any given individual, have a right to all the good we can do them, he at once, by that thesis, includes generosity and beneficence within the category of justice. He is obliged to say, that our utmost exertions are *due* to our fellow-creatures, thus assimilating them to a debt; or that nothing less can be a sufficient *return* for what society does for us, thus classing the case as one of gratitude; both of which are acknowledged cases of justice. Wherever there is a right, the case is one of justice, and not of the virtue of beneficence: and whoever does not place the distinction between justice and morality in general, where we have now placed it, will be found to make no distinction between them at all, but to merge all morality in justice.

Having thus endeavoured to determine the distinctive elements which enter into the composition of the idea of justice, we are ready to enter on the inquiry, whether the feeling, which accompanies the idea, is attached to it by a special dispensation of nature, or whether it could have grown up, by any known laws, out of the idea itself; and in particular, whether it can have originated in considerations of general expediency.

I conceive that the sentiment itself does not arise from anything which would commonly, or correctly, be termed an idea of expediency; but that though the sentiment does not, whatever is moral in it does.

We have seen that the two essential ingredients in the sentiment of justice are, the desire to punish a person who has done harm, and the knowledge or belief that there is some definite individual or individuals to whom harm has been done.

Now it appears to me, that the desire to punish a person who has done harm to some individual is a spontaneous outgrowth from two sentiments, both in the highest degree natural, and which either are or resemble instincts; the impulse of self-defence, and the feeling of sympathy.

It is natural to resent, and to repel or retaliate, any harm done or attempted against ourselves, or against those with whom we sympathise. The origin of this sentiment it is not necessary here to discuss. Whether it be an instinct or a result of intelligence, it is, we know, common to all animal nature; for every animal tries to hurt those who have hurt, or who it thinks are about to hurt, itself or its young. Human beings, on this point, only differ from other animals in two particulars. First, in being capable of sympathising, not solely with their offspring, or, like some of the more noble animals, with some superior animal who is kind to them, but with all human, and even with all sentient, beings. Secondly, in having a more developed intelligence, which gives a wider range to the whole of their sentiments, whether self-regarding or sympathetic. By virtue of his superior intelligence, even apart from his superior range of sympathy, a human being is capable of apprehending a community of interest between himself and the human society of which he forms a part, such that any conduct which threatens the security of the society generally, is threatening to his own, and calls forth his instinct (if instinct it be) of self-defence. The same superiority of intelligence, joined to the power of sympathising with human beings generally, enables him to attach himself to the collective idea of his tribe, his country, or mankind, in such a manner that any act hurtful to them, raises his instinct of sympathy, and urges him to resistance.

The sentiment of justice, in that one of its elements which consists of the desire to punish, is thus, I conceive, the natural feeling of retaliation or vengeance, rendered by intellect and sympathy applicable to those injuries, that is, to those hurts, which wound us through, or in common with, society at large. This sentiment, in itself, has nothing moral in it; what is moral is, the exclusive subordination of it to the social sympathies, so as to wait on and obey their call. For the natural feeling would make us resent indiscriminately whatever any one does that is disagreeable to us; but when moralised by the social feeling, it only acts in the directions conformable to the general good: just persons resenting a hurt to society, though not otherwise a hurt to themselves, and not resenting a hurt to themselves, however painful, unless it be of the kind which society has a common interest with them in the repression of.

It is no objection against this doctrine to say, that when we feel our sentiment of justice outraged, we are not thinking of society at large, or of any collective interest, but only of the individual case. It is common enough certainly, though the reverse of commendable, to feel resentment merely because we have suffered pain; but a person whose resentment is really a moral feeling, that is, who considers whether an act is blamable before he allows himself to resent it—such a person, though he may not say expressly to himself that he is standing up for the interest of society, certainly does feel that he is asserting a rule which is for the benefit of others as well as for his own. If he is not feeling this—if he is regarding the act solely as it affects him individually—he is not consciously just; he is not concerning himself about the justice of his actions. This is admitted even by anti-utilitarian moralists. When Kant (as before remarked) propounds as the fundamental principle of morals, "So act, that thy rule of conduct might be adopted as a law by all rational beings," he virtually acknowledges that the interest of mankind collectively, or at least of mankind indiscriminately, must be in the mind of the agent when conscientiously deciding on the morality of the act. Otherwise he uses words without a meaning; for, that a rule even of utter selfishness could not *possibly* be adopted by all rational beings—that there is any insuperable obstacle in the nature of things to its adoption—cannot be even plausibly maintained. To give any meaning to Kant's principle, the sense put upon it must be, that we ought to shape our conduct by a rule which all rational beings might adopt *with benefit to their collective interest.*

To recapitulate: the idea of justice supposes two things; a rule of conduct, and a sentiment which sanctions the rule. The first must be supposed common to all mankind, and intended for their good. The other (the sentiment) is a desire that punishment may be suffered by those who infringe the rule. There is involved, in addition, the conception of some definite person who suffers by the infringement; whose rights (to use the expression appropriated to the case) are violated by it. And the sentiment of justice appears to me to be, the animal desire to repel or retaliate a hurt or damage to oneself, or to those with whom one sympathises, widened so as to include all persons, by the human capacity of enlarged sympathy, and the human conception of intelligent self-interest. From the latter elements, the feeling derives its morality; from the former, its peculiar impressiveness, and energy of self-assertion.

I have, throughout, treated the idea of a *right* residing in the injured person, and violated by the injury, not as a separate element in the composition of the idea and sentiment, but as one of the forms in which the other two elements clothe themselves. These elements are, a hurt to some assignable person or persons on the one hand, and a demand for punishment on the other. An examination of our own minds, I think, will show, that these two things include all that we mean when we speak of violation of a right. When we call anything a person's right, we mean that he has a valid claim on society to protect him in the possession of it, either by the force of law, or by that of education and opinion. If he has what we consider a sufficient claim, on whatever account, to have something guaranteed to him by society, we say that he has a right to it. If we desire to prove that anything does not belong to him by right, we think this done as soon as it is admitted that society ought not to take measures for securing it to him, but should leave him to chance, or to his own exertions. Thus, a person is said to have a right to what he can earn in fair professional competition; because society ought not to allow any other person to hinder him from endeavouring to earn in that manner as much as he can.

But he has not a right to three hundred a-year, though he may happen to be earning it; because society is not called on to provide that he shall earn that sum. On the contrary, if he owns ten thousand pounds three per cent. stock, he *has* a right to three hundred a-year; because society has come under an obligation to provide him with an income of that amount.

To have a right, then, is, I conceive, to have something which society ought to defend me in the possession of. If the objector goes on to ask, why it ought? I can give him no other reason than general utility. If that expression does not seem to convey a sufficient feeling of the strength of the obligation, nor to account for the peculiar energy of the feeling, it is because there goes to the composition of the sentiment, not a rational only, but also an animal element, the thirst for retaliation; and this thirst derives its intensity, as well as its moral justification, from the extraordinarily important and impressive kind of utility which is concerned. The interest involved is that of security, to every one's feelings the most vital of all interests. All other earthly benefits are needed by one person, not needed by another; and many of them can, if necessary, be cheerfully foregone, or replaced by something else; but security no human being can possibly do without; on it we depend for all our immunity from evil, and for the whole value of all and every good, beyond the passing moment; since nothing but the gratification of the instant could be of any worth to us, if we could be deprived of anything the next instant by whoever was momentarily stronger than ourselves. Now this most indispensable of all necessaries, after physical nutriment, cannot be had, unless the machinery for providing it is kept unintermittedly in active play. Our notion, therefore, of the claim we have on our fellow-creatures to join in making safe for us the very groundwork of our existence, gathers feelings around it so much more intense than those concerned in any of the more common cases of utility, that the difference in degree (as is often the case in psychology) becomes a real difference in kind. The claim assumes that character of absoluteness, that apparent infinity, and incommensurability with all other considerations, which constitute the distinction between the feeling of right and wrong and that of ordinary expediency and inexpediency. The feelings concerned are so powerful, and we count so positively on finding a responsive feeling in others (all being alike interested), that *ought* and *should* grow into *must*, and recognised indispensability becomes a moral necessity, analogous to physical, and often not inferior to it in binding force.

If the preceding analysis, or something resembling it, be not the correct account of the notion of justice; if justice be totally independent of utility, and be a standard *per se,* which the mind can recognise by simple introspection of itself; it is hard to understand why that internal oracle is so ambiguous, and why so many things appear either just or unjust, according to the light in which they are regarded.

We are continually informed that Utility is an uncertain standard, which every different person interprets differently, and that there is no safety but in the immutable, ineffaceable, and unmistakable dictates of Justice, which carry their evidence in themselves, and are independent of the fluctuations of opinion. One would suppose from this that on questions of justice there could be no controversy; that if we take that for our rule, its application to any given case could leave us in as little doubt as a mathematical demonstration. So far is this from being the fact, that there is as much difference of opinion, and as much discussion, about what is just, as about what is useful to society. Not only have different nations and individuals different notions of justice, but in the mind of one and the same individual, justice is not some one rule, principle, or maxim, but many, which do not always coincide in their dictates, and in choosing between which, he is guided either by some extraneous standard, or by his own personal predilections.

For instance, there are some who say, that it is unjust to punish any one for the sake of example to others; that punishment is just, only when intended for the good of the sufferer himself. Others maintain the extreme reverse, contending that to punish persons who have attained years of discretion, for their own benefit, is despotism and injustice, since if the matter at issue is solely their own good, no one has a right to control their own judgment of it; but that they may justly be punished to prevent evil to others, this being the exercise of the legitimate right of self-defence. Mr. Owen, again, affirms that it is unjust to punish at all; for the criminal did not make his own character; his education, and the circumstances which surrounded him, have made him a criminal, and for these he is not responsible. All these opinions are extremely plausible; and so long as the question is argued as one of justice simply, without going down to the principles which lie under justice and are the source of its authority, I am unable to see how any of these reasoners can be refuted. For in truth every one of the three builds upon rules of justice confessedly true. The first appeals to the acknowledged injustice of singling out an individual, and making him a sacrifice, without his consent, for other people's benefit. The second relies on the acknowledged justice of self-defence, and the admitted injustice of forcing one person to conform to another's notions of what constitutes his good. The Owenite invokes the admitted principle, that it is unjust to punish any one for what he cannot help. Each is triumphant so long as he is not compelled to take into consideration any other maxims of justice than the one he has selected; but as soon as their several maxims are brought face to face, each disputant seems to have exactly as much to say for himself as the others. No one of them can carry out his own notion of justice without trampling upon another equally binding. These are difficulties; they have always been felt to be such; and many devices have been invented to turn rather than to overcome them. As a refuge from the last of the three, men imagined what they called the freedom of the will; fancying that they could not justify punishing a man whose will is in a thoroughly hateful state, unless it be supposed to have come into that state through no influence of anterior circumstances. To escape from the other difficulties, a favourite contrivance has been the fiction of a contract, whereby at some unknown period all the members of society engaged to obey the laws, and consented to be punished for any disobedience to them; thereby giving to their legislators the right, which it is assumed they would not otherwise have had, of punishing them, either for their own good or for that of society. This happy thought was considered to get rid of the whole difficulty, and to legitimate the infliction of punishment, in virtue of another received maxim of justice, *Volenti non fit injuria;* that is not unjust which is done with the consent of the person who is supposed to be hurt by it. I need hardly remark, that even if the consent were not a mere fiction, this maxim is not superior in authority to the others which it is brought in to supersede. It is, on the contrary, an instructive specimen of the loose and irregular manner in which supposed principles of justice grow up. This particular one evidently came into use as a help to the coarse exigencies of courts of law, which are sometimes obliged to be content with very uncertain presumptions, on account of the greater evils which would often arise from any attempt on their part to cut finer. But even courts of law are not able to adhere consistently to the maxim, for they allow voluntary engagements to be set aside on the ground of fraud, and sometimes on that of mere mistake or misinformation.

Again, when the legitimacy of inflicting punishment is admitted, how many conflicting conceptions of justice come to light in discussing the proper apportionment of punishments to offences. No rule on the subject recommends itself so strongly to the primitive and spontaneous sentiment of justice, as the *lex talionis,* an eye for an eye and a tooth for a tooth. Though this principle of the Jewish and of the Mahomedan law has been generally abandoned in Europe as a practical maxim, there is, I suspect, in most minds, a secret hankering after it; and when retribution accidentally falls on an offender in that precise shape, the general feeling of satisfaction evinced bears witness how natural is the sentiment to which this repayment in

kind is acceptable. With many, the test of justice in penal infliction is that the punishment should be proportioned to the offence; meaning that it should be exactly measured by the moral guilt of the culprit (whatever be their standard for measuring moral guilt): the consideration, what amount of punishment is necessary to deter from the offence, having nothing to do with the question of justice, in their estimation: while there are others to whom that consideration is all in all; who maintain that it is not just, at least for man, to inflict on a fellow-creature, whatever may be his offences, any amount of suffering beyond the least that will suffice to prevent him from repeating, and others from imitating, his misconduct.

To take another example from a subject already once referred to. In a co-operative industrial association, is it just or not that talent or skill should give a title to superior remuneration? On the negative side of the question it is argued, that whoever does the best he can, deserves equally well, and ought not in justice to be put in a position of inferiority for no fault of his own; that superior abilities have already advantages more than enough, in the admiration they excite, the personal influence they command, and the internal sources of satisfaction attending them, without adding to these a superior share of the world's goods; and that society is bound in justice rather to make compensation to the less favoured, for this unmerited inequality of advantages, than to aggravate it. On the contrary side it is contended, that society receives more from the more efficient labourer; that his services being more useful, society owes him a larger return for them; that a greater share of the joint result is actually his work, and not to allow his claim to it is a kind of robbery; that if he is only to receive as much as others, he can only be justly required to produce as much, and to give a smaller amount of time and exertion, proportioned to his superior efficiency. Who shall decide between these appeals to conflicting principles of justice? Justice has in this case two sides to it, which it is impossible to bring into harmony, and the two disputants have chosen opposite sides; the one looks to what it is just that the individual should receive, the other to what it is just that the community should give. Each, from his own point of view, is unanswerable; and any choice between them, on grounds of justice, must be perfectly arbitrary. Social utility alone can decide the preference.

How many, again, and how irreconcilable, are the standards of justice to which reference is made in discussing the repartition of taxation. One opinion is, that payment to the State should be in numerical proportion to pecuniary means. Others think that justice dictates what they term graduated taxation; taking a higher percentage from those who have more to spare. In point of natural justice a strong case might be made for disregarding means altogether, and taking the same absolute sum (whenever it could be got) from every one: as the subscribers to a mess, or to a club, all pay the same sum for the same privileges, whether they can all equally afford it or not. Since the protection (it might be said) of law and government is afforded to, and is equally required by all, there is no injustice in making all buy it at the same price. It is reckoned justice, not injustice, that a dealer should charge to all customers the same price for the same article, not a price varying according to their means of payment. This doctrine, as applied to taxation, finds no advocates, because it conflicts so strongly with man's feelings of humanity and of social expediency; but the principle of justice which it invokes is as true and as binding as those which can be appealed to against it. Accordingly it exerts a tacit influence on the line of defence employed for other modes of assessing taxation. People feel obliged to argue that the State does more for the rich than for the poor, as a justification for its taking more from them: though this is in reality not true, for the rich would be far better able to protect themselves, in the absence of law or government, than the poor, and indeed would probably be successful in converting the poor into their slaves. Others, again, so far defer to the same conception of justice, as to maintain that all should pay an equal capitation tax for the protection of their persons (these being of equal value to all), and an unequal tax

for the protection of their property, which is unequal. To this others reply, that the all of one man is as valuable to him as the all of another. From these confusions there is no other mode of extrication than the utilitarian.

Is, then, the difference between the Just and the Expedient a merely imaginary distinction? Have mankind been under a delusion in thinking that justice is a more sacred thing than policy, and that the latter ought only to be listened to after the former has been satisfied? By no means. The exposition we have given of the nature and origin of the sentiment, recognises a real distinction; and no one of those who profess the most sublime contempt for the consequences of actions as an element in their morality, attaches more importance to the distinction than I do. While I dispute the pretensions of any theory which sets up an imaginary standard of justice not grounded on utility, I account the justice which is grounded on utility to be the chief part, and incomparably the most sacred and binding part, of all morality. Justice is a name for certain classes of moral rules, which concern the essentials of human well-being more nearly, and are therefore of more absolute obligation, than any other rules for the guidance of life; and the notion which we have found to be of the essence of the idea of justice, that of a right residing in an individual, implies and testifies to this more binding obligation.

The moral rules which forbid mankind to hurt one another (in which we must never forget to include wrongful interference with each other's freedom) are more vital to human well-being than any maxims, however important, which only point out the best mode of managing some department of human affairs. They have also the peculiarity, that they are the main element in determining the whole of the social feelings of mankind. It is their observance which alone preserves peace among human beings: if obedience to them were not the rule, and disobedience the exception, every one would see in every one else an enemy, against whom he must be perpetually guarding himself. What is hardly less important, these are the precepts which mankind have the strongest and the most direct inducements for impressing upon one another. By merely giving to each other prudential instruction or exhortation, they may gain, or think they gain, nothing: in inculcating on each other the duty of positive beneficence they have an unmistakable interest, but far less in degree: a person may possibly not need the benefits of others; but he always needs that they should not do him hurt. Thus the moralities which protect every individual from being harmed by others, either directly or by being hindered in his freedom of pursuing his own good, are at once those which he himself has most at heart, and those which he has the strongest interest in publishing and enforcing by word and deed. It is by a person's observance of these that his fitness to exist as one of the fellowship of human beings is tested and decided; for on that depends his being a nuisance or not to those with whom he is in contact. Now it is these moralities primarily which compose the obligations of justice. The most marked cases of injustice, and those which give the tone to the feeling of repugnance which characterises the sentiment, are acts of wrongful aggression, or wrongful exercise of power over some one; the next are those which consist in wrongfully withholding from him something which is his due; in both cases, inflicting on him a positive hurt, either in the form of direct suffering, or of the privation of some good which he had reasonable ground, either of a physical or of a social kind, for counting upon.

The same powerful motives which command the observance of these primary moralities, enjoin the punishment of those who violate them; and as the impulses of self-defence, of defence of others, and of vengeance, are all called forth against such persons, retribution, or evil for evil, becomes closely connected with the sentiment of justice, and is universally included in the idea. Good for good is also one of the dictates of justice; and this, though its social utility is evident, and though it carries with it a natural human feeling, has not at first sight that obvious connection with hurt or injury, which, existing in the most elementary cases of just and unjust, is the source of the characteristic intensity of the sentiment. But the connection, though less obvious, is not less real. He who accepts benefits, and denies a return of them when needed, inflicts a real hurt, by disappointing one of the most natural and reasonable of expectations, and one which he must at least tacitly have encouraged, otherwise the benefits would seldom have been conferred. The important rank, among human evils and wrongs, of the disappointment of expectation, is shown in the fact that it constitutes the principal criminality of two such highly immoral acts as a breach of friendship and a breach of promise. Few hurts which human beings can sustain are greater, and none wound more, than when that on which they habitually and with full assurance relied, fails them in the hour of need; and few wrongs are greater than this mere withholding of good; none excite more resentment, either in the person suffering, or in a sympathising spectator. The principle, therefore, of giving to each what they deserve, that is, good for good as well as evil for evil, is not only included within the idea of Justice as we have defined it, but is a proper object of that intensity of sentiment, which places the Just, in human estimation, above the simply Expedient.

Most of the maxims of justice current in the world, and commonly appealed to in its transactions, are simply instrumental to carrying into effect the principles of justice which we have now spoken of. That a person is only responsible for what he has done voluntarily, or could voluntarily have avoided; that it is unjust to condemn any person unheard; that the punishment ought to be proportioned to the offence, and the like, are maxims intended to prevent the just principle of evil for evil from being perverted to the infliction of evil without that justification. The greater part of these common maxims have come into use from the practice of courts of justice, which have been naturally led to a more complete recognition and elaboration than was likely to suggest itself to others, of the rules necessary to enable them to fulfil their double function, of inflicting punishment when due, and of awarding to each person his right.

That first of judicial virtues, impartiality, is an obligation of justice, partly for the reason last mentioned; as being a necessary condition of the fulfilment of the other obligations of justice. But this is not the only source of the exalted rank, among human obligations, of those maxims of equality and impartiality, which, both in popular estimation and in that of the most enlightened, are included among the precepts of justice. In one point of view, they may be considered as corollaries from the principles already laid down. If it is a duty to do to each according to his deserts, returning good for good as well as repressing evil by evil, it necessarily follows that we should treat all equally well (when no higher duty forbids) who have deserved equally well of *us,* and that society should treat all equally well who have deserved equally well of *it,* that is, who have deserved equally well absolutely. This is the highest abstract standard of ocial and distributive justice; towards which all institutions, and the efforts of all virtuous citizens, should be made in the utmost possible degree to converge. But this great moral duty rests upon a still deeper foundation, being a direct emanation from the first principle of morals, and not a mere logical corollary from secondary or derivative doctrines. It is involved in the very meaning of Utility, or the Greatest Happiness Principle. That principle is a mere form of words without rational signification, unless one person's happiness, supposed equal in degree (with the proper allowance made for kind), is counted for exactly as much as another's. Those conditions being supplied, Bentham's dictum, "everybody to count for one, nobody for more than one," might be written under the principle of utility as an explanatory commentary.* The equal claim of everybody to happiness in the estimation of the moralist and of the legislator, involves an equal claim to all the means of happiness, except in so far as the inevitable conditions of human life, and the general interest, in which that of every indiv dual is included, set limits to the maxim; and those limits ought to be strictly construed. As every other maxim of justice, so this is by no means applied or held applicable universally; on the contrary, as I have already remarked, it bends to every person's ideas of social expediency. But in whatever case it is deemed applicable at all, it is held to be the dictate of justice. All persons are deemed to have a *right* to equality of treatment, except when some recognised social expediency requires the reverse. And hence all social inequalities which have ceased to be considered expedient, assume the character not of simple inexpediency, but of injustice, and appear so tyrannical, that people are apt to wonder how they ever could have been tolerated; forgetful that they themselves perhaps tolerate other inequalities under an equally mistaken notion of expediency, the correction of which would make that which they approve seem quite as monstrous as what they have at last learnt to condemn. The entire history of social improvement has been a series of transitions, by which one custom or institution after another, from being a supposed primary necessity of social existence, has passed into the rank of a universally stigmatised injustice and tyranny. So it has been with the distinctions of slaves and freemen, nobles and serfs, patricians and plebeians; and so it will be, and in part already is, with the aristocracies of colour, race, and sex.

It appears from what has been said, that justice is a name for certain moral requirements, which, regarded collectively, stand higher in the scale of social utility, and are therefore of more paramount obligation, than any others; though particular cases may occur in which some other social duty is so important, as to overrule any one of the general maxims of justice. Thus, to save a life, it may not only be allowable, but a duty, to steal, or take by force, the necessary food or medicine, or to kidnap, and compel to officiate, the only qualified medical practitioner. In such cases, as we do not call anything justice which is not a virtue, we usually say, not that justice must give way to some other moral principle, but that what is just in ordinary cases is, by reason of that other principle, not just in the particular case. By this useful accommodation of language, the character of indefeasibility attributed to justice is kept up, and we are saved from the necessity of maintaining that there can be laudable injustice.

The considerations which have now been adduced resolve, I conceive, the only real difficulty in the utilitarian theory of morals. It has always been evident that all cases of justice are also cases of expediency: the difference is in the peculiar sentiment which attaches to the former, as contradistinguished from the latter. If this characteristic sentiment has been sufficiently accounted for; if there is no necessity to assume for it any peculiarity of origin; if it is simply the natural feeling of resentment, moralised by being made coextensive with the demands of social good; and if this feeling not only does but ought to exist in all the classes of cases to which the idea of justice corresponds; that idea no longer presents itself as a stumbling-block to the utilitarian ethics. Justice remains the appropriate name for certain social utilities which are vastly more important, and therefore more absolute and imperative, than any others are as a class (though not more so than others may be in particular cases); and which, therefore, ought to be, as well as naturally are, guarded by a sentiment not only different in degree, but also in kind; distinguished from the milder feeling which attaches to the mere idea of promoting human pleasure or convenience, at once by the more definite nature of its commands, and by the sterner character of its sanctions.

NOTE

* This implication, in the first principle of the utilitarian scheme, of perfect impartiality between persons, is regarded by Mr. Herbert Spencer (in his *Social Statics*) as a disproof of the pretensions of utility to be a sufficient guide to right; since (he says) the principle of utility presupposes the anterior principle, that everybody has an equal right to happiness. It may be more correctly described as supposing that equal amounts of happiness are equally desirable, whether felt by the same or by different persons. This, however, is not a *pre*-supposition; not a premise needful to support the principle of utility, but the very principle itself; for what is the principle of utility, if it be not that "happiness" and "desirable" are synonymous terms? If there is any anterior principle implied, it can be no other than this, that the truths of arithmetic are applicable to the valuation of happiness, as of all other measurable quantities.

[Mr. Herbert Spencer, in a private communication on the subject of the preceding Note, objects to being considered an opponent of utilitarianism, and states that he regards happiness as the ultimate end of morality; but deems that end only partially attainable by empirical generalisations from the observed results of conduct, and completely attainable only by deducing, from the laws of life and the conditions of existence, what kinds of action necessarily tend to produce happiness, and what kinds to produce unhappiness. With the exception of the word "necessarily," I have no dissent to express from this doctrine; and (omitting that word) I am not aware that any modern advocate of utilitarianism is of a different opinion. Bentham, certainly, to whom in the *Social Statics* Mr. Spencer particularly referred, is, least of all writers, chargeable with unwillingness to deduce the effect of actions on happiness from the laws of human nature and the universal conditions of human life. The common charge against him is of relying too exclusively upon such deductions, and declining altogether to be bound by the generalisations from specific experience which Mr. Spencer thinks that utilitarians generally confine themselves to. My own opinion (and, as I collect, Mr. Spencer's) is, that in ethics, as in all other branches of scientific study, the consilience of the results of both these processes, each corroborating and verifying the other, is requisite to give to any general proposition the kind and degree of evidence which constitutes scientific proof.]

JOHN RAWLS
from *A Theory of Justice*

THE MAIN IDEA OF THE THEORY OF JUSTICE

My aim is to present a conception of justice which generalizes and carries to a higher level of abstraction the familiar theory of the social contract as found, say, in Locke, Rousseau, and Kant.[1] In order to do this we are not to think of the original contract as one to enter a particular society or to set up a particular form of government. Rather, the guiding idea is that the principles of justice for the basic structure of society are the object of the original agreement. They are the principles that free and rational persons concerned to further their own interests would accept in an initial position of equality as defining the fundamental terms of their association. These principles are to regulate all further agreements; they specify the kinds of social cooperation that can be entered into and the forms of government that can be established. This way of regarding the principles of justice I shall call justice as fairness.

Thus we are to imagine that those who engage in social cooperation choose together, in one joint act, the principles which are to assign basic rights and duties and to determine the division of social benefits. Men are to decide in advance how they are to regulate their claims against one another and what is to be the foundation charter of their society. Just as each person must decide by rational reflection what constitutes his good, that is, the system of ends which it is rational for him to pursue, so a group of persons must decide once and for all what is to count among them as just and unjust. The choice which rational men would make in this hypothetical situation of equal liberty, assuming for the present that this choice problem has a solution, determines the principles of justice.

In justice as fairness the original position of equality corresponds to the state of nature in the traditional theory of the social contract. This original position is not, of course, thought of as an actual historical state of affairs, much less as a primitive condition of culture. It is understood as a purely hypothetical situation characterized so as to lead to a certain conception of justice.[2] Among the essential features of this situation is that no one knows his place in society, his class position or social status, nor does any one know his fortune in the distribution of natural assets and abilities, his intelligence, strength, and the like. I shall even assume that the parties do not know their conceptions of the good or their special psychological propensities. The principles of justice are chosen behind a veil of ignorance. This ensures that no one is advantaged or disadvantaged in the choice of principles by the outcome of natural chance or the contingency of social circumstances. Since all are similarly situated and no one is able to design principles to favor his particular condition, the principles of justice are the result of a fair agreement or bargain. For given the circumstances of the original position, the symmetry of everyone's relations to each other, this initial situation is fair between individuals as moral persons, that is, as rational beings with their own ends and capable, I shall assume, of a sense of justice. The original position is, one might say, the appropriate initial status quo, and thus the fundamental agreements reached in it are fair. This explains the propriety of the name "justice as fairness": it conveys the idea that the principles of justice are agreed to in an initial situation that is fair. The name does not mean that the concepts of justice and fairness are the same, any more than the phrase "poetry as metaphor" means that the concepts of poetry and metaphor are the same.

Justice as fairness begins, as I have said, with one of the most general of all choices which persons might make together, namely, with the choice of the first principles of a conception of justice which is to regulate all subsequent criticism and reform of institutions. Then, having chosen a conception of justice, we can suppose that they are to choose a constitution and a legislature to enact laws, and so on, all in accordance with the principles of justice initially agreed upon. Our social situation is just if it is such that by this sequence of hypothetical agreements we would have contracted into the general system of rules which defines it. Moreover, assuming that the original position does determine a set of principles (that is, that a particular conception of justice would be chosen), it will then be true that whenever social institutions satisfy these principles those engaged in them can say to one another that they are cooperating on terms to which they would agree if they were free and equal persons whose relations with respect to one another were fair. They could all view their arrangements as meeting the stipulations which they would acknowl-

edge in an initial situation that embodies widely accepted and reasonable constraints on the choice of principles. The general recognition of this fact would provide the basis for a public acceptance of the corresponding principles of justice. No society can, of course, be a scheme of cooperation which men enter voluntarily in a literal sense; each person finds himself placed at birth in some particulr position in some particular society, and the nature of this position materially affects his life prospects. Yet a society satisfying the principles of justice as fairness comes as close as a society can to being a voluntary scheme, for it meets the principles which free and equal persons would assent to under circumstances that are fair. In this sense its members are autonomous and the obligations they recognize self-imposed.

One feature of justice as fairness is to think of the parties in the initial situation as rational and mutually disinterested. This does not mean that the parties are egoists, that is, individuals with only certain kinds of interests, say in wealth, prestige, and domination. But they are conceived as not taking an interest in one another's interests. They are to presume that even their spiritual aims may be opposed, in the way that the aims of those of different religions may be opposed. Moreover, the concept of rationality must be interpreted as far as possible in the narrow sense, standard in economic theory, of taking the most effective means to given ends. I shall modify this concept to some extent, as explained later . . . but one must try to avoid introducing into it any controversial ethical elements. The initial situation must be characterized by stipulations that are widely accepted.

In working out the conception of justice as fairness one main task clearly is to determine which principles of justice would be chosen in the original position. To do this we must describe this situation in some detail and formulate with care the problem of choice which it presents. These matters I shall take up in the immediately succeeding chapters. It may be observed, however, that once the principles of justice are thought of as arising from an original agreement in a situation of equality, it is an open question whether the principle of utility would be acknowledged. Offhand it hardly seems likely that persons who view themselves as equals, entitled to press their claims upon one another, would agree to a principle which may require lesser life prospects for some simply for the sake of a greater sum of advantages enjoyed by others. Since each desires to protect his interests, his capacity to advance his conception of the good, no one has a reason to acquiesce in an enduring loss for himself in order to bring about a greater net balance of satisfaction. In the absence of strong and lasting benevolent impulses, a rational man would not accept a basic structure merely because it maximized the algebraic sum of advantages irrespective of its permanent effects on his own basic rights and interests. Thus it seems that the principle of utility is incompatible with the conception of social cooperation among equals for mutual advantage. It appears to be inconsistent with the idea of reciprocity implicit in the notion of a well-ordered society. Or, at any rate, so I shall argue.

I shall maintain instead that the persons in the initial situation would choose two rather different principles: the first requires equality in the assignment of basic rights and duties, while the second holds that social and economic inequalities, for example inequalities of wealth and authority, are just only if they result in compensating benefits for everyone, and in particular for the least advantaged members of society. These principles rule out justifying institutions on the grounds that the hardships of some are offset by a greater good in the aggregate. It may be expedient but it is not just that some should have less in order that others may prosper. But there is no injustice in the greater benefits earned by a few provided that the situation of persons not so fortunate is thereby improved. The intuitive idea is that since everyone's well-being depends upon a scheme of cooperation without which no one could have a satisfactory life, the division of advantages should be such as to draw forth the willing cooperation of everyone taking part in it, including those less well situated. Yet this can be expected only if

reasonable terms are proposed. The two principles mentioned seem to be a fair agreement on the basis of which those better endowed, or more fortunate in their social position, neither of which we can be said to deserve, could expect the willing cooperation of others when some workable scheme is a necessary condition of the welfare of all.[3] Once we decide to look for a conception of justice that nullifies the accidents of natural endowment and the contingencies of social circumstances as counters in quest for political and economic advantage, we are led to these principles. They express the result of leaving aside those aspects of the social world that seem arbitrary from a moral point of view.

The problem of the choice of principles, however, is extremely difficult. I do not expect the answer I shall suggest to be convincing to everyone. It is, therefore, worth noting from the outset that justice as fairness, like other contract views, consists of two parts: (1) an interpretation of the initial situation and of the problem of choice posed there, and (2) a set of principles which, it is argued, would be agreed to. One may accept the first part of the theory (or some variant thereof), but not the other, and conversely. The concept of the initial contractual situation may seem reasonable although the particular principles proposed are rejected. To be sure, I want to maintain that the most appropriate conception of this situation does lead to principles of justice contrary to utilitarianism and perfectionism, and therefore that the contract doctrine provides an alternative to these views. Still, one may dispute this contention even though one grants that the contractarian method is a useful way of studying ethical theories and of setting forth their underlying assumptions.

Justice as fairness is an example of what I have called a contract theory. Now there may be an objection to the term "contract" and related expressions, but I think it will serve reasonably well. Many words have misleading connotations which at first are likely to confuse. The terms "utility" and "utilitarianism" are surely no exception. They too have unfortunate suggestions which hostile critics have been willing to exploit; yet they are clear enough for those prepared to study utilitarian doctrine. The same should be true of the term "contract" applied to moral theories. As I have mentioned, to understand it one has to keep in mind that it implies a certain level of abstraction. In particular, the content of the relevant agreement is not to enter a given society or to adopt a given form of government, but to accept certain moral principles. Moreover, the undertakings referred to are purely hypothetical: a contract view holds that certain principles would be accepted in a well-defined initial situation.

The merit of the contract terminology is that it conveys the idea that principles of justice may be conceived as principles that would be chosen by rational persons, and that in this way conceptions of justice may be explained and justified. The theory of justice is a part, perhaps the most significant part, of the theory of rational choice. Furthermore, principles of justice deal with conflicting claims upon the advantages won by social cooperation; they apply to the relations among several persons or groups. The word "contract" suggests this plurality as well as the condition that the appropriate division of advantages must be in accordance with principles acceptable to all parties. The condition of publicity for principles of justice is also connoted by the contract phraseology. Thus, if these principles are the outcome of an agreement, citizens have a knowledge of the principles that others follow. It is characteristic of contract theories to stress the public nature of political principles. Finally there is the long tradition of the contract doctrine. Expressing the tie with this line of thought helps to define ideas and accords with natural piety. There are then several advantages in the use of the term "contract." With due precautions taken, it should not be misleading.

A final remark. Justice as fairness is not a complete contract theory. For it is clear that the contractarian idea can be extended to the choice of more or less an entire ethical system, that is, to a system including principles for all the virtues and not only for justice. Now for the most part I shall consider only principles of justice and others closely related to them; I make no attempt to discuss the virtues in a systematic way. Obviously if justice as fairness succeeds reasonably well, a next step would be to study the more general view suggested by the name "rightness as fairness." But even this wider theory fails to embrace all moral relationships, since it would seem to include only our relations with other persons and to leave out of account how we are to conduct ourselves toward animals and the rest of nature. I do not contend that the contract notion offers a way to approach these questions which are certainly of the first importance; and I shall have to put them aside. We must recognize the limited scope of justice as fairness and of the general type of view that it exemplifies. How far its conclusions must be revised once these other matters are understood cannot be decided in advance.

THE ORIGINAL POSITION AND JUSTIFICATION

I have said that the original position is the appropriate initial status quo which insures that the fundamental agreements reached in it are fair. This fact yields the name "justice as fairness." It is clear, then, that I want to say that one conception of justice is more reasonable than another, or justifiable with respect to it, if rational persons in the initial situation would choose its principles over those of the other for the role of justice. Conceptions of justice are to be ranked by their acceptability to persons so circumstanced. Understood in this way the question of justification is settled by working out a problem of deliberation: we have to ascertain which principles it would be rational to adopt given the contractual situation. This connects the theory of justice with the theory of rational choice.

If this view of the problem of justification is to succeed, we must, of course, describe in some detail the nature of this choice problem. A problem of rational decision has a definite answer only if we know the beliefs and interests of the parties, their relations with respect to one another, the alternatives between which they are to choose, the procedure whereby they make up their minds, and so on. As the circumstances are presented in different ways, correspondingly different principles are accepted. The concept of the original position, as I shall refer to it, is that of the most philosophically favored interpretation of this initial choice situation for the purposes of a theory of justice.

But how are we to decide what is the most favored interpretation? I assume, for one thing, that there is a broad measure of agreement that principles of justice should be chosen under certain conditions. To justify a particular description of the initial situation one shows that it incorporates these commonly shared presumptions. One argues from widely accepted but weak premises to more specific conclusions. Each of the presumptions should by itself be natural and plausible; some of them may seem innocuous or even trivial. The aim of the contract approach is to establish that taken together they impose significant bounds on acceptable principles of justice. The ideal outcome would be that these conditions determine a unique set of principles; but I shall be satisfied if they suffice to rank the main traditional conceptions of social justice.

One should not be misled, then, by the somewhat unusual conditions which characterize the original position. The idea here is simply to make vivid to ourselves the restrictions that it seems reasonable to impose on arguments for principles of justice, and therefore on these principles themselves. Thus it seems reasonable and generally acceptable that no one should be advantaged or disadvantaged by natural fortune or social circumstances in the choice of principles. It also seems widely agreed that it should be impossible to tailor principles to the circumstances of one's own case. We should insure further that particular inclinations and aspirations, and persons' conceptions of their good do not affect the principles adopted. The aim is to rule out those principles that it would be ratio-

nal to propose for acceptance, however little the chance of success, only if one knew certain things that are irrelevant from the standpoint of justice. For example, if a man knew that he was wealthy, he might find it rational to advance the principle that various taxes for welfare measures be counted unjust; if he knew that he was poor, he would most likely propose the contrary principle. To represent the desired restrictions one imagines a situation in which everyone is deprived of this sort of information. One excludes the knowledge of those contingencies which sets men at odds and allows them to be guided by their prejudices. In this manner the veil of ignorance is arrived at in a natural way. This concept should cause no difficulty if we keep in mind the constraints on arguments that it is meant to express. At any time we can enter the original position, so to speak, simply by following a certain procedure, namely, by arguing for principles of justice in accordance with these restrictions.

It seems reasonable to suppose that the parties in the original position are equal. That is, all have the same rights in the procedure for choosing principles; each can make proposals, submit reasons for their acceptance, and so on. Obviously the purpose of these conditions is to represent equality between human beings as moral persons, as creatures having a conception of their good and capable of a sense of justice. The basis of equality is taken to be similarity in these two respects. Systems of ends are not ranked in value; and each man is presumed to have the requisite ability to understand and to act upon whatever principles are adopted. Together with the veil of ignorance, these conditions define the principles of justice as those which rational persons concerned to advance their interests would consent to as equals when none are known to be advantaged or disadvantaged by social and natural contingencies.

There is, however, another side to justifying a particular description of the original position. This is to see if the principles which would be chosen match our considered convictions of justice or extend them in an acceptable way. We can note whether applying these principles would lead us to make the same judgments about the basic structure of society which we now make intuitively and in which we have the greatest confidence; or whether, in cases where our present judgments are in doubt and given with hesitation, these principles offer a resolution which we can affirm on reflection. There are questions which we feel sure must be answered in a certain way. For example, we are confident that religious intolerance and racial discrimination are unjust. We think that we have examined these things with care and have reached what we believe is an impartial judgment not likely to be distorted by an excessive attention to our own interests. These convictions are provisional fixed points which we presume any conception of justice must fit. But we have much less assurance as to what is the correct distribution of wealth and authority. Here we may be looking for a way to remove our doubts. We can check an interpretation of the initial situation, then, by the capacity of its principles to accommodate our firmest convictions and to provide guidance where guidance is needed.

In searching for the most favored description of this situation we work from both ends. We begin by describing it so that it represents generally shared and preferably weak conditions. We then see if these conditions are strong enough to yield a significant set of principles. If not, we look for further premises equally reasonable. But if so, and these principles match our considered convictions of justice, then so far well and good. But presumably there will be discrepancies. In this case we have a choice. We can either modify the account of the initial situation or we can revise our existing judgments, for even the judgments we take provisionally as fixed points are liable to revision. By going back and forth, sometimes altering the conditions of the contractual circumstances, at others withdrawing our judgments and conforming them to principle, I assume that eventually we shall find a description of the initial situation that both expresses reasonable conditions and yields principles which match our considered judgments duly pruned and adjusted. This state of affairs I refer to as reflective equilibrium.[4] It is an equilibrium because at

last our principles and judgments coincide; and it is reflective since we know to what principles our judgments conform and the premises of their derivation. At the moment everything is in order. But this equilibrium is not necessarily stable. It is liable to be upset by further examination of the conditions which should be imposed on the contractual situation and by particular cases which may lead us to revise our judgments. Yet for the time being we have done what we can to render coherent and to justify our convictions of social justice. We have reached a conception of the original position.

I shall not, of course, actually work through this process. Still, we may think of the interpretation of the original position that I shall present as the result of such a hypothetical course of reflection. It represents the attempt to accommodate within one scheme both reasonable philosophical conditions on principles as well as our considered judgments of justice. In arriving at the favored interpretation of the initial situation there is no point at which an appeal is made to self-evidence in the traditional sense either of general conceptions or particular convictions. I do not claim for the principles of justice proposed that they are necessary truths or derivable from such truths. A conception of justice cannot be deduced from self-evident premises or conditions on principles; instead, its justification is a matter of the mutual support of many considerations, of everything fitting together into one coherent view.

A final comment. We shall want to say that certain principles of justice are justified because they would be agreed to in an initial situation of equality. I have emphasized that this original position is purely hypothetical. It is natural to ask why, if this agreement is never actually entered into, we should take any interest in these principles, moral or otherwise. The answer is that the conditions embodied in the description of the original position are ones that we do in fact accept. Or if we do not, then perhaps we can be persuaded to do so by philosophical reflection. Each aspect of the contractual situation can be given supporting grounds. Thus what we shall do is to collect together into one conception a number of conditions on principles that we are ready upon due consideration to recognize as reasonable. These constraints express what we are prepared to regard as limits on fair terms of social cooperation. One way to look at the idea of the original position, therefore, is to see it as an expository device which sums up the meaning of these conditions and helps us to extract their consequences. On the other hand, this conception is also an intuitive notion that suggests its own elaboration, so that led on by it we are drawn to define more clearly the standpoint from which we can best interpret moral relationships. We need a conception that enables us to envision our objective from afar: the intuitive notion of the original position is to do this for us.

TWO PRINCIPLES OF JUSTICE

I shall now state in a provisional form the two principles of justice that I believe would be chosen in the original position. In this section I wish to make only the most general comments, and therefore the first formulation of these principles is tentative. As we go on I shall run through several formulations and approximate step by step the final statement to be given much later. I believe that doing this allows the exposition to proceed in a natural way.

The first statement of the two principles reads as follows.

First: each person is to have an equal right to the most extensive basic liberty compatible with a similar liberty for others.

Second: social and economic inequalities are to be arranged so that they are both (a) reasonably expected to be to everyone's advantage, and (b) attached to positions and offices open to all. There are two ambiguous phrases in the second principle, namely "everyone's advantage" and "open to all."

By way of general comment, these principles primarily apply, as I have said, to the basic structure of society. They are to govern the assignment of rights and duties and to regulate the distribution of social and economic advantages. As their formulation suggests, these principles presuppose that the social structure can be divided into two more or less distinct parts, the first principle applying to the one, the second to the other. They distinguish between those aspects of the social system that define and secure the equal liberties of citizenship and those that specify and establish social and economic inequalities. The basic liberties of citizens are, roughly speaking, political liberty (the right to vote and to be eligible for public office) together with freedom of speech and assembly; liberty of conscience and freedom of thought; freedom of the person along with the right to hold (personal) property; and freedom from arbitrary arrest and seizure as defined by the concept of the rule of law. These liberties are all required to be equal by the first principle, since citizens of a just society are to have the same basic rights.

The second principle applies, in the first approximation, to the distribution of income and wealth and to the design of organizations that make use of differences in authority and responsibility, or chains of command. While the distribution of wealth and income need not be equal, it must be to everyone's advantage, and at the same time, positions of authority and offices of command must be accessible to all. One applies the second principle by holding positions open, and then, subject to this constraint, arranges social and economic inequalities so that everyone benefits.

These principles are to be arranged in a serial order with the first principle prior to the second. This ordering means that a departure from the institutions of equal liberty required by the first principle cannot be justified by, or compensated for, by greater social and economic advantages. The distribution of wealth and income, and the hierarchies of authority, must be consistent with both the liberties of equal citizenship and equality of opportunity.

It is clear that these principles are rather specific in their content, and their acceptance rests on certain assumptions that I must eventually try to explain and justify. A theory of justice depends upon a theory of society in ways that will become evident as we proceed. For the present, it should be observed that the two principles (and this holds for all formulations) are a special case of a more general conception of justice that can be expressed as follows.

All social values—liberty and opportunity, income and wealth, and the bases of self-respect—are to be distributed equally unless an unequal distribution of any, or all, of these values is to everyone's advantage. Injustice, then, is simply inequalities that are not to the benefit of all. Of course, this conception is extremely vague and requires interpretation.

As a first step, suppose that the basic structure of society distributes certain primary goods, that is, things that every rational man is presumed to want. These goods normally have a use whatever a person's rational plan of life. For simplicity, assume that the chief primary goods at the disposition of society are rights and liberties, powers and opportunities, income and wealth. (Later on in Part Three the primary good of self-respect has a central place.) These are the social primary goods. Other primary goods such as health and vigor, intelligence and imagination, are natural goods; although their possession is influenced by the basic structure, they are not so directly under its control. Imagine, then, a hypothetical initial arrangement in which all the social primary goods are equally distributed: everyone has similar rights and duties, and income and wealth are evenly shared. This state of affairs provides a benchmark for judging improvements. If certain inequalities of wealth and organizational powers would make everyone better off than in this hypothetical starting situation, then they accord with the general conception.

Now it is possible, at least theoretically, that by giving up some of their fundamental liberties men are sufficiently compensated by the resulting social and economic gains. The general conception of justice imposes no restrictions on what sort of inequalities are permissible; it only requires that everyone's position be improved.

We need not suppose anything so drastic as consenting to a condition of slavery. Imagine instead that men forego certain political rights when the economic returns are significant and their capacity to influence the course of policy by the exercise of these rights would be marginal in any case. It is this kind of exchange which the two principles as stated rule out; being arranged in serial order they do not permit exchanges between basic liberties and economic and social gains. The serial ordering of principles expresses an underlying preference among primary social goods. When this preference is rational so likewise is the choice of these principles in this order.

In developing justice as fairness I shall, for the most part, leave aside the general conception of justice and examine instead the special case of the two principles in serial order. The advantage of this procedure is that from the first the matter of priorities is recognized and an effort made to find principles to deal with it. One is led to attend throughout to the conditions under which the acknowledgment of the absolute weight of liberty with respect to social and economic advantages, as defined by the lexical order of the two principles, would be reasonable. Off hand, this ranking appears extreme and too special a case to be of much interest; but there is more justification for it than would appear at first sight. Or at any rate, so I shall maintain. Furthermore, the distinction between fundamental rights and liberties and economic and social benefits marks a difference among primary social goods that one should try to exploit. It suggests an important division in the social system. Of course, the distinctions drawn and the ordering proposed are bound to be at best only approximations. There are surely circumstances in which they fail. But it is essential to depict clearly the main lines of a reasonable conception of justice; and under many conditions anyway, the two principles in serial order may serve well enough. When necessary we can fall back on the more general conception.

The fact that the two principles apply to institutions has certain consequences. Several points illustrate this. First of all, the rights and liberties referred to by these principles are those which are defined by the public rules of the basic structure. Whether men are free is determined by the rights and duties established by the major institutions of society. Liberty is a certain pattern of social forms. The first principle simply requires that certain sorts of rules, those defining basic liberties, apply to everyone equally and that they allow the most extensive liberty compatible with a like liberty for all. The only reason for circumscribing the rights defining liberty and making men's freedom less extensive than it might otherwise be is that these equal rights as institutionally defined would interfere with one another.

Another thing to bear in mind is that when principles mention persons, or require that everyone gain from an inequality, the reference is to representative persons holding the various social positions, or offices, or whatever, established by the basic structure. Thus in applying the second principle I assume that it is possible to assign an expectation of well-being to representative individuals holding these positions. This expectation indicates their life prospects as viewed from their social station. In general, the expectations of representative persons depend upon the distribution of rights and duties throughout the basic structure. When this changes, expectations change. I assume, then, that expectations are connected: by raising the prospects of the representative man in one position we presumably increase or decrease the prospects of representative men in other positions. Since it applies to institutional forms, the second principle (or rather the first part of it) refers to the expectations of representative individuals. As I shall discuss below, neither principle applies to distributions of particular goods to particular individuals who may be identified by their proper names. The situation where someone is considering how to allocate certain commodities to needy persons who are known to him is not within the scope of the principles. They are meant to regulate basic institutional arrangements. We must not assume that there is much similarity from the standpoint of justice between an administrative allotment of goods to specific persons and the appropriate design of society. Our common sense intuitions for the former may be a poor guide to the latter.

Now the second principle insists that each person benefit from permissible inequalities in the basic structure. This means that it must be reasonable for each relevant representative man defined by this structure, when he views it as a going concern, to prefer his prospects with the inequality to his prospects without it. One is not allowed to justify differences in income or organizational powers on the ground that the disadvantages of those in one position are outweighed by the greater advantages of those in another. Much less can infringements of liberty be counterbalanced in this way. Applied to the basic structure, the principle of utility would have us maximize the sum of expectations of representative men (weighted by the number of persons they represent, on the classical view); and this would permit us to compensate for those losses of some by the gains of others. Instead, the two principles require that everyone benefit from economic and social inequalities. It is obvious, however, that there are indefinitely many ways in which all may be advantaged when the initial arrangement of equality is taken as a benchmark. How then are we to choose among these possibilities? The principles must be specified so that they yield a determinate conclusion. I now turn to this problem.

THE TENDENCY TO EQUALITY

I wish to conclude this discussion of the two principles by explaining the sense in which they express an egalitarian conception of justice. Also I should like to forestall the objection to the principle of fair opportunity that it leads to a callous meritocratic society. In order to prepare the way for doing this, I note several aspects of the conception of justice that I have set out.

First we may observe that the difference principle gives some weight to the considerations singled out by the principles of redress. This is the principle that undeserved inequalities call for redress; and since inequalities of birth and natural endowment are undeserved, these inequalities are to be somehow compensated for.[5] Thus the principle holds that in order to treat all persons equally, to provide genuine equality of opportunity, society must give more attention to those with fewer native assets and to those born into the less favorable social positions. The idea is to redress the bias of contingencies in the direction of equality. In pursuit of this principle greater resources might be spent on the education of the less rather than the more intelligent, at least over a certain time of life, say the earlier years of school.

Now the principle of redress has not to my knowledge been proposed as the sole criterion of justice, as the single aim of the social order. It is plausible as most such principles are only as a prima facie principle, one that is to be weighed in the balance with others. For example, we are to weigh it against the principle to improve the average standard of life, or to advance the common good.[6] But whatever other principles we hold, the claims of redress are to be taken into account. It is thought to represent one of the elements in our conception of justice. Now the difference principle is not of course the principle of redress. It does not require society to try to even out handicaps as if all were expected to compete on a fair basis in the same race. But the difference principle would allocate resources in education, say, so as to improve the long-term expectation of the least favored. If this end is attained by giving more attention to the better endowed, it is permissible; otherwise not. And in making this decision, the value of education should not be assessed solely in terms of economic efficiency and social welfare. Equally if not more important is the role of education in enabling a person to enjoy the culture of his society and to take part in its affairs, and in this way to provide for each individual a secure sense of his own worth.

Thus although the difference principle is not the same as that of redress, it does achieve some of the intent of the latter principle. It transforms the aims of the basic structure so that the total scheme of institutions no longer emphasizes social efficiency and technocratic values. We see then that the difference principle represents, in effect, an agreement to regard the distribution of natural talents as a common asset and to share in the benefits of this distribution whatever it turns out to be. Those who have been favored by nature, whoever they are, may gain from their good fortune only on terms that improve the situation of those who have lost out. The naturally advantaged are not to gain merely because they are more gifted, but only to cover the costs of training and education and for using their endowments in ways that help the less fortunate as well. No one deserves his greater natural capacity nor merits a more favorable starting place in society. But it does not follow that one should eliminate these distinctions. There is another way to deal with them. The basic structure can be arranged so that these contingencies work for the good of the least fortunate. Thus we are led to the difference principle if we wish to set up the social system so that no one gains or loses from his arbitrary place in the distribution of natural assets or his initial position in society without giving or receiving compensating advantages in return.

In view of these remarks we may reject the contention that the ordering of institutions is always defective because the distribution of natural talents and the contingencies of social circumstance are unjust, and this injustice must inevitably carry over to human arrangements. Occasionally this reflection is offered as an excuse for ignoring injustice, as if the refusal to acquiesce in injustice is on a par with being unable to accept death. The natural distribution is neither just or unjust; nor is it unjust that persons are born into society at some particular position. These are simply natural facts. What is just and unjust is the way that institutions deal with these facts. Aristocratic and caste societies are unjust because they make these contingencies the ascriptive basis for belonging to more or less enclosed and privileged social classes. The basic structure of these societies incorporates the arbitrariness found in nature. But there is no necessity for men to resign themselves to these contingencies. The social system is not an unchangeable order beyond human control but a pattern of human action. In justice as fairness men agree to share one another's fate. In designing institutions they undertake to avail themselves of the accidents of nature and social circumstance only when doing so is for the common benefit. The two principles are a fair way of meeting the arbitrariness of fortune; and while no doubt imperfect in other ways, the institutions which satisfy these principles are just.

A further point is that the difference principle expresses a conception of reciprocity. It is a principle of mutual benefit. We have seen that, at least when chain connection holds, each representative man can accept the basic structure as designed to advance his interests. The social order can be justified to everyone, and in particular to those who are least favored; and in this sense it is egalitarian. But it seems necessary to consider in an intuitive way how the condition of mutual benefit is satisfied. Consider any two representative men A and B, and let B be the one who is less favored. Actually, since we are most interested in the comparison with the least favored man, let us assume that B is this individual. Now B can accept A's being better off since A's advantages have been gained in ways that improve B's prospects. If A were not allowed his better position, B would be even worse off than he is. The difficulty is to show that A has no grounds for complaint. Perhaps he is required to have less than he might since his having more would result in some loss to B. Now what can be said to the more favored man? To begin with, it is clear that the well-being of each depends on a scheme of social cooperation without which no one could have a satisfactory life. Secondly, we can ask for the willing cooperation of everyone only if the terms of the scheme are reasonable. The difference principle, then, seems to be a fair basis on which those better endowed, or more fortunate in their social circumstances, could expect others to collaborate with them when some workable arrangement is a necessary condition of the good of all.

There is a natural inclination to object that those better situated deserve their greater advantages whether or not they are to the benefit of others. At this point it is necessary to be clear about the notion of desert. It is perfectly true that given a just system of cooperation as a scheme of public rules and the expectations set up by it, those who, with the prospect of improving their condition, have done what the system announces that it will reward are entitled to their advantages. In this sense the more fortunate have a claim to their better situation; their claims are legitimate expectations established by social institutions, and the community is obligated to meet them. But this sense of desert presupposes the existence of the cooperative scheme; it is irrelevant to the question whether in the first place the scheme is to be designed in accordance with the difference principle or some other criterion.

Perhaps some will think that the person with greater natural endowments deserves those assets and the superior character that made their development possible. Because he is more worthy in this sense, he deserves the greater advantages that he could achieve with them. This view, however, is surely incorrect. It seems to be one of the fixed points of our considered judgments that no one deserves his place in the distribution of native endowments, any more than one deserves one's initial starting place in society. The assertion that a man deserves the superior character that enables him to make the effort to cultivate his abilities is equally problematic; for his character depends in large part upon fortunate family and social circumstances for which he can claim no credit. The notion of desert seems not to apply to these cases. Thus the more advantaged representative man cannot say that he deserves and therefore has a right to a scheme of cooperation in which he is permitted to acquire benefits in ways that do not contribute to the welfare of others. There is no basis for his making this claim. From the standpoint of common sense, then, the difference principle appears to be acceptable both to the more advantaged and to the less advantaged individual. Of course, none of this is strictly speaking an argument for the principle, since in a contract theory arguments are made from the point of view of the original position. But these intuitive considerations help to clarify the nature of the principle and the sense in which it is egalitarian.

I noted earlier that a society should try to avoid the region where the marginal contributions of those better off to the well-being of the less favored are negative. It should operate only on the upward rising part of the contribution curve (including of course the maximum). One reason for this, we can now see, is that on this segment of the curve the criterion of mutual benefit is always fulfilled. Moreover, there is a natural sense in which the harmony of social interests is achieved; representative men do not gain at one another's expense since only reciprocal advantages are allowed. To be sure, the shape and slope of the contribution curve is determined in part at least by the natural lottery in native assets, and as such it is neither just nor unjust. But suppose we think of the forty-five degree line as representing the ideal of a perfect harmony of interests; it is the contribution curve (a straight line in this case) along which everyone gains equally. Then it seems that the consistent realization of the two principles of justice tends to raise the curve closer to the ideal of a perfect harmony of interests. Once a society goes beyond the maximum it operates along the downward sloping part of the curve and a harmony of interests no longer exists. As the more favored gain the less advantaged lose, and vice versa. The situation is analogous to being on an efficiency frontier. This is far from desirable when the justice of the basic structure is involved. Thus it is to realize the ideal of the harmony of interests on terms that nature has given us, and to meet the criterion of mutual benefit, that we should stay in the region of positive contributions.

A further merit of the difference principle is that it provides an interpretation of the principle of fraternity. In comparison with liberty and equality, the idea of fraternity has had a lesser place in democratic theory. It is thought to be less specifically a political concept, not in itself defining any of the democratic rights but conveying instead certain attitudes of mind and forms of conduct without which we would lose sight of the values expressed by these rights.[7] Or closely related to this, fraternity is held to represent a certain equality of social esteem manifest in various public conventions and in the absence of manners of deference and servility.[8] No doubt fraternity does imply these things, as well as a sense of civic friendship and social solidarity, but so understood it expresses no definite requirement. We have yet to find a principle of justice that matches the underlying idea. The difference principle, however, does seem to correspond to a natural meaning of fraternity: namely, to the idea of not wanting to have greater advantages unless this is to the benefit of others who are less well off. The family, in its ideal conception and often in practice, is one place where the principle of maximizing the sum of advantages is rejected. Members of a family commonly do not wish to gain unless they can do so in ways that further the interests of the rest. Now wanting to act on the difference principle has precisely this consequence. Those better circumstanced are willing to have their greater advantages only under a scheme in which this works out for the benefit of the less fortunate.

The ideal of fraternity is sometimes thought to involve ties of sentiment and feeling which it is unrealistic to expect between members of the wider society. And this is surely a further reason for its relative neglect in democratic theory. Many have felt that it has no proper place in political affairs. But if it is interpreted as incorporating the requirements of the difference principle, it is not an impracticable conception. It does seem that the institutions and policies which we most confidently think to be just satisfy its demands, at least in the sense that the inequalities permitted by them contribute to the well-being of the less favored. Or at any rate, so I shall try to make plausible in Chapter V. On this interpretation, then, the principle of fraternity is a perfectly feasible standard. Once we accept it we can associate the traditional ideas of liberty, equality, and fraternity with the democratic interpretation of the two principles of justice as follows: liberty corresponds to the first principle, equality to the idea of equality in the first principle together with equality of fair opportunity, and fraternity to the difference principle. In this way we have found a place for the conception of fraternity in the democratic interpretation of the two principles, and we see that it imposes a definite requirement on the basic structure of society. The other aspects of fraternity should not be forgotten, but the difference principle expresses its fundamental meaning from the standpoint of social justice.

Now it seems evident in the light of these observations that the democratic interpretation of the two principles will not lead to a meritocratic society.[9] This form of social order follows the principle of careers open to talents and uses equality of opportunity as a way of releasing men's energies in the pursuit of economic prosperity and political dominion. There exists a marked disparity between the upper and lower classes in both means of life and the rights and privileges of organizational authority. The culture of the poorer strata is impoverished while that of the governing and technocratic elite is securely based on the service of the national ends of power and wealth. Equality of opportunity means an equal chance to leave the less fortunate behind in the personal quest for influence and social position.[10] Thus a meritocratic society is a danger for the other interpretations of the principles of justice but not for the democratic conception. For, as we have just seen, the difference principle transforms the aims of society in fundamental respects. This consequence is even more obvious once we note that we must when necessary take into account the essential primary good of self-respect and the fact that a well-ordered society is a social union of social unions. It follows that the confident sense of their own worth should be sought for the least favored and this limits the forms of hierarchy and the degrees of inequality that justice permits. Thus, for example, resources for education are not to be allotted solely or necessarily mainly according to their return as estimated in productive trained abilities, but also according to their worth in enriching the personal and

social life of citizens, including here the less favored. As a society progresses the latter consideration becomes increasingly more important.

These remarks must suffice to sketch the conception of social justice expressed by the two principles for institutions. Before taking up the principles for individuals I should mention one further question. I have assumed so far that the distribution of natural assets is a fact of nature and that no attempt is made to change it, or even to take it into account. But to some extent this distribution is bound to be affected by the social system. A caste system, for example, tends to divide society into separate biological populations, while an open society encourages the widest genetic diversity.[11] In addition, it is possible to adopt eugenic policies, more or less explicit. I shall not consider questions of eugenics, confining myself throughout to the traditional concerns of social justice. We should note, though, that it is not in general to the advantage of the less fortunate to propose policies which reduce the talents of others. Instead, by accepting the difference principle, they view the greater abilities as a social asset to be used for the common advantage. But it is also in the interest of each to have greater natural assets. This enables him to pursue a preferred plan of life. In the original position, then, the parties want to insure for their descendants the best genetic endowment (assuming their own to be fixed). The pursuit of reasonable policies in this regard is something that earlier generations owe to later ones, this being a question that arises between generations. Thus over time a society is to take steps at least to preserve the general level of natural abilities and to prevent the diffusion of serious defects. These measures are to be guided by principles that the parties would be willing to consent to for the sake of their successors. I mention this speculative and difficult matter to indicate once again the manner in which the difference principle is likely to transform problems of social justice. We might conjecture that in the long run, if there is an upper bound on ability, we would eventually reach a society with the greatest equal liberty the members of which enjoy the greatest equal talent. But I shall not pursue this thought further.

NOTES

1. As the text suggests, I shall regard Locke's *Second Treatise of Government*, Rousseau's *The Social Contract*, and Kant's ethical works beginning with *The Foundations of the Metaphysics of Morals* as definitive of the contract tradition. For all of its greatness, Hobbes's *Leviathan* raises special problems. A general historical survey is provided by J. W. Gough, *The Social Contract*, 2nd ed. (Oxford, The Clarendon Press, 1957), and Otto Gierke, *Natural Law and the Theory of Society*, trans. with an introduction by Ernest Barker (Cambridge, The University Press, 1934). A presentation of the contract view as primarily an ethical theory is to be found in G. R. Grice, *The Grounds of Moral Judgment* (Cambridge, The University Press, 1967).

2. Kant is clear that the original agreement is hypothetical. See *The Metaphysics of Morals*, pt. I (*Rechtslehre*), especially §§47, 52; and pt. II of the essay "Concerning the Common Saying: This May Be True in Theory but It Does Not Apply in Practice," in *Kant's Political Writings*, ed. Hans Reiss and trans. by H. B. Nisbet (Cambridge, The University Press, 1970), pp. 73–87. See Georges Vlachos, *La Pensée politique de Kant* (Paris, Presses Universitaires de France, 1962), pp. 326–335; and J. G. Murphy, *Kant: The Philosophy of Right* (London, Macmillan, 1970), pp. 109–112, 133–136, for a further discussion.

3. For the formulation of this intuitive idea I am indebted to Allan Gibbard.

4. The process of mutual adjustment of principles and considered judgments is not peculiar to moral philosophy. See Nelson Goodman, *Fact, Fiction, and Forecast* (Cambridge, Mass., Harvard University Press, 1955), pp. 65–68, for parallel remarks concerning the justification of the principles of deductive and inductive inference.

5. See Herbert Spiegelberg, "A Defense of Human Equality," *Philosophical Review*, vol. 53 (1944), pp. 101, 113–123; and D. D. Raphael, "Justice and Liberty," *Proceedings of the Aristotelian Society*, vol. 51 (1950–1951), pp. 187f.

6. See, for example, Spiegelberg, pp. 120f.

7. See J. R. Pennock, *Liberal Democracy: Its Merits and Prospects* (New York, Rinehart, 1950), pp. 94f.

8. See R. B. Perry, *Puritanism and Democracy* (New York, The Vanguard Press, 1944), ch. XIX, sec. 8.

9. The problem of a meritocratic society is the subject of Michael Young's fantasy, *The Rise of Meritocracy* (London, Thames and Hudson, 1958).

10. For elaborations of this point to which I am indebted, see John Schaar, "Equality of Opportunity and Beyond," *Nomos IX: Equality*, ed. by J. R. Pennock and J. W. Chapman (New York, Atherton Press, 1967); and B. A. O. Williams, "The Idea of Equality," pp. 125–129.

11. See Theodosius Dobzhansky, *Mankind Evolving* (New Haven, Yale University Press, 1962), pp. 242–252, for a discussion of this question.

J. J. C. SMART
Distributive Justice and Utilitarianism

INTRODUCTION

In this paper I shall not be concerned with the defense of utilitarianism against other types of ethical theory. Indeed I hold that questions of ultimate ethical principle are not susceptible of proof, though something can be done to render them more acceptable by presenting them in a clear light and by clearing up certain confusions which (for some people) may get in the way of their acceptance. Ultimately the utilitarian appeals to the sentiment of generalized benevolence, and speaks to others who feel this sentiment too and for whom it is an over-riding

"Distributive Justice and Utilitarianism" is reprinted from *Justice and Economic Distribution* edited by John Arthur and William H. Shaw (Englewood Cliffs, NJ: Prentice-Hall, 1978), by permission of J. J. C. Smart. **J. J. C. Smart,** contemporary British philosopher, presently affiliated with the Australian National University, helped foster the movement towards materialism in the philosophy of mind and spark renewed interest in utilitarianism.

feeling.[1] (This does not mean that he will always act from this over-riding feeling. There can be backsliding and action may result from more particular feelings, just as an egoist may go against his own interests, and may regret this.) I shall be concerned here merely to investigate certain consequences of utilitarianism, as they relate to questions of distributive justice. The type of utilitarianism with which I am concerned is act utilitarianism.

THE PLACE OF JUSTICE IN UTILITARIAN THEORY

The concept of justice as a *fundamental* ethical concept is really quite foreign to utilitarianism. A utilitarian would compromise his utilitarianism if he allowed principles of justice which might conflict with the maximization of happiness (or more generally of goodness, should he be an "ideal" utilitarian). He is concerned with the maximization of happiness[2] and not with the distribution of it. Nevertheless he may well deduce from his ethical principle that certain ways of distributing the means to happiness (e.g., money, food, housing) are more conducive to the general good than are others. He will be interested in justice in so far as it is a political or legal or quasi-legal concept. He will consider whether the legal institutions and customary sanctions which operate in particular societies are more or less conducive to the utilitarian end than are other possible institutions and customs. Even if the society consisted entirely of utilitarians (and of course no actual societies have thus consisted) it might still be important to have legal and customary sanctions relating to distribution of goods, because utilitarians might be tempted to backslide and favour non-optimistic distributions, perhaps because of bias in their own favour. They might be helped to act in a more nearly utilitarian way because of the presence of these sanctions.

As a utilitarian, therefore, I do not allow the concept of justice as a fundamental moral concept, but I am nevertheless interested in justice in a subordinate way, as a *means* to the utilitarian end. Thus even though I hold that it does not matter in what way happiness is distributed among different persons, provided that the total amount of happiness is maximized, I do of course hold that it can be of vital importance

that the *means* to happiness should be distributed in some ways and not in others. Suppose that I have the choice of two alternative actions as follows: I can either give $500 to each of two needy men, Smith and Campbell, or else give $1000 to Smith and nothing to Campbell. It is of course likely to produce the greatest happiness if I divide the money equally. For this reason utilitarianism can often emerge as a theory with egalitarian consequences. If it does so this is because of the empirical situation, and not because of any moral commitment to egalitarianism as such. Consider, for example, another empirical situation in which the $500 was replaced by a half-dose of a life saving drug, in which case the utilitarian would advocate giving two half-doses to Smith or Campbell and none to the other. Indeed if Smith and Campbell each possessed a half-dose it would be right to take one of the half-doses and give it to the other. (I am assuming that a whole dose would preserve life and that a half-dose would not. I am also assuming a simplified situation: in some possible situations, especially in a society of nonutilitarians, the wide social ramifications of taking a half-dose from Smith and giving it to Campbell might conceivably outweigh the good results of saving Campbell's life.) However, it is probable that in most situations the equal distribution of the means to happiness will be the right utilitarian action, even though the utilitarian has no ultimate moral commitment to egalitarianism. If a utilitarian is given the choice of two actions, one of which will give 2 units of happiness to Smith and 2 to Campbell, and the other of which will give 1 unit of happiness to Smith and 9 to Campbell, he will choose the latter course.[3] It may also be that I have the choice between two alternative actions, one of which gives −1 unit of happiness to Smith and +9 units to Campbell, and the other of which gives +2 to Smith and +2 to Campbell. As a utilitarian I will choose the former course, and here I will be in conflict with John Rawls's theory, whose maximum principle would rule out making Smith worse off.

UTILITARIANISM AND RAWLS'S THEORY

Rawls deduces his ethical principles from the contract which would be made by a group of rational egoists in an 'original position' in which they thought behind a 'veil of ignorance,' so that they would not know who they were or even what generation they belonged to.[4] Reasoning behind this veil of ignorance, they would apply the maximin principle. John Harsanyi earlier used the notion of a contract in such a position of ignorance, but used not the maximin principle but the principle of maximizing expected utility.[5] Harsanyi's method leads to a form of rule utilitarianism. I see no great merit in this roundabout approach to ethics *via* a contrary to fact supposition, which involves the tricky notion of a social contract and which thus appears already to presuppose a moral position. The approach seems also too Hobbesian: it is anthropologically incorrect to suppose that we are all originally little egoists. I prefer to base ethics on a principle of generalized benevolence, to which some of those with whom I discuss ethics may immediately respond. Possibly it might show something interesting about our common moral notions if it could be proved that they follow from what would be contracted by rational egoists in an 'original position,' but as a utilitarian I am more concerned to advocate a normative theory which might replace our common moral notions than I am to explain these notions. Though some form of utilitarianism might be deducible (as by Harsanyi) from a contract or original position theory, I do not think that it either ought to be or need be defended in this sort of way.

Be that as it may, it is clear that utilitarian views about distribution of happiness do differ from Rawls's view. I have made a distinction between justice as a moral concept and justice as a legal or quasi-legal concept. The utilitarian has no room for the former, but he can have strong views about the latter, though *what* these views are will depend on empirical considerations. Thus whether he will prefer a political theory which advocates a completely socialist state, or whether he will prefer one which advocates a minimal state (as Robert Nozick's book does[6]), or whether again he will advocate something between the two, is something which depends on the facts of economics, sociology, and so on. As someone not expert in these fields I have no desire to dogmatize on these empirical matters. (My own private non-expert opinion is that probably neither extreme leads to maximization of happiness, though I have a liking for rather more socialism than exists in Australia or U.S.A. at present.) As a utilitarian my approach to political theory has to be tentative and empirical. Not believing in moral rights as such I can not deduce theories about the best political arrangements by making deductions (as Nozick does) from propositions which purport to be about such basic rights.

Rawls deduces two principles of justice.[7] The first of these is that 'each person is to have an equal right to the most extensive basic liberty compatible with a similar liberty for others,' and the second one is that 'social and economic inequalities are to be arranged so that they are both (a) reasonably expected to be to everyone's advantage, and (b) attached to positions and offices open to all.' Though a utilitarian could (on empirical grounds) be very much in sympathy with both of these principles, he could not accept them as universal rules. Suppose that a society which had no danger of nuclear war could be achieved only by reducing the liberty of one per cent of the world's population. Might it not be right to bring about such a state of affairs if it were in one's power? Indeed might it not be right greatly to reduce the liberty of 100% of the world's population if such a desirable outcome could be achieved? Perhaps the present generation would be pretty miserable and would hanker for their lost liberties. However we must also think about the countless future generations which might exist and be happy provided that mankind can avoid exterminating itself, and we must also think of all the pain, misery and genetic damage which would be brought about by nuclear war even if this did not lead to the total extermination of mankind.

Suppose that this loss of freedom prevented a war so devastating that the whole process of evolution on this planet would come to an end. At the cost of the loss of freedom, instead of the war and the end of evolution there might occur an evolutionary process which was not only long lived but also beneficial: in millions of years there might be creatures descended from *homo sapiens* which had vastly increased talents and capacity for happiness. At least such considerations show that Rawls's first principle is far from obvious to the utilitarian, though in certain mundane contexts he might accede to it as a useful approximation. Indeed I do not believe that restriction of liberty, in our present society, could have beneficial results in helping to prevent nuclear war, though a case could be made for certain restrictions on the liberty of all present members of society so as to enable the government to prevent nuclear blackmail by gangs of terrorists.

Perhaps in the past considerable restrictions on the personal liberties of a large proportion of citizens may have been justifiable on utilitarian grounds. In view of the glories of Athens and its contributions to civilization it is possible that the Athenian slave society was justifiable. In one part of his paper, 'Nature and Soundness of the Contract and Coherence Arguments,'[8] David Lyons has judiciously discussed the question of whether in certain circumstances a utilitarian would condone slavery. He says that it would be unlikely that a utilitarian could condone slav-

ery as it has existed in modern times. However he considers the possibility that less objectionable forms of slavery or near slavery have existed. The less objectionable these may have been, the more likely it is that utilitarianism would have condoned them. Lyons remarks that our judgments about the relative advantages of different societies must be very tentative because we do not know enough about human history to say what were the social alternatives at any juncture.[9]

Similar reflections naturally occur in connection with Rawls's second principle. Oligarchic societies, such as that of eighteenth century Britain, may well have been in fact better governed than they would have been if posts of responsibility had been available to all. Certainly to resolve this question we should have to go deeply into empirical investigations of the historical facts. (To prevent misunderstanding, I do think that in our present society utilitarianism would imply adherence to Rawls's second principle as a general rule.)

A utilitarian is concerned with maximizing total happiness (or goodness, if he is an ideal utilitarian). Rawls largely concerns himself with certain 'primary goods,' as he calls them. These include 'rights and liberties, powers and opportunities, income and wealth.'[10] A utilitarian would regard these as mere means to the ultimate good. Nevertheless if he is proposing new laws or changes to social institutions the utilitarian will have to concern himself in practice with the distribution of these 'primary goods' (as Bentham did).[11] But if as an approximation we neglect this distinction, which may be justifiable to the extent that there is a correlation between happiness and the level of these 'primary goods,' we may say that according to Rawls an action is right only if it is to the benefit of the least advantaged person. A utilitarian will hold that a redistribution of the means to happiness is right if it maximizes the general happiness, even though some persons, even the least advantaged ones, are made worse off. A position which is intermediate between the utilitarian position and Rawls's position would be one which held that one ought to maximize some sort of trade-off between total happiness and distribution of happiness. Such a position would imply that sometimes we should redistribute in such a way as to make some persons, even the least advantaged ones, worse off, but this would happen less often than it would according to the classical utilitarian theory.

UTILITARIANISM AND NOZICK'S THEORY

General adherence to Robert Nozick's theory (in his *Anarchy, State and Utopia*)[12] would be compatible with the existence of very great inequality indeed. This is because the whole theory is based quite explicitly on the notion of *rights:* in the very first sentence of the preface of his book we read 'Individuals have rights. . . .' The utilitarian would demur here. A utilitarian legislator might tax the rich in order to give aid to the poor, but a Nozickian legislator would not do so. A utilitarian legislator might impose a heavy tax on inherited wealth, whereas Nozick would allow the relatively fortunate to become even more fortunate, provided that they did not infringe the *rights* of the less fortunate. The utilitarian legislator would hope to increase the total happiness by equalizing things a bit. How far he should go in this direction would depend on empirical considerations. He would not want to equalize things too much if this led to too much weakening of the incentive to work, for example. Of course according to Nozick's system there would be no reason why members of society should not set up a utilitarian utopia, and voluntarily equalize their wealth, and also give wealth to poorer communities outside. However it is questionable whether such isolated utopias could survive in a modern environment, but if they did survive, the conformity of the behaviour of their members to utilitarian theory, rather than the conformity to Nozick's theory, would be what would commend their societies to me.

SUMMARY

In this article I have explained that the notion of justice is not a fundamental notion in utilitarianism, but that utilitarians will characteristically have certain views about such things as the distribution of wealth, saving for the benefit of future generations and for the third world countries and other practical matters. Utilitarianism differs from John Rawls's theory in that it is ready to contemplate some sacrifice to certain individuals (or classes of individuals) for the sake of the greater good of all, and in particular may allow certain limitations of personal freedom which would be ruled out by Rawls's theory. *In practice,* however, the general tendency of utilitarianism may well be towards an egalitarian form of society.

NOTES

1. In hoping that utilitarianism can be rendered acceptable to some people by presenting it in a clear light, I do not deny the possibility of the reverse happening. Thus I confess to a bit of a pull the other way when I consider Nozick's example of an 'experience machine'. See Robert Nozick, *Anarchy, State and Utopia* (Oxford: Blackwell, 1975), pp. 42–45, though I am at least partially reassured by Peter Singer's remarks towards the end of his review of Nozick, *New York Review of Books*, March 6, 1975. Nozick's example of an experience machine is more worrying than the more familiar one of a pleasure inducing machine, because it seems to apply to ideal as well as to hedonistic utilitarianism.

2. In this paper I shall assume a hedonistic utilitarianism, though most of what I have to say will be applicable to ideal utilitarianism too.

3. There are of course difficult problems about the assignment of cardinal utilities to states of mind, but for the purposes of this paper I am assuming that we can intelligibly talk, as utilitarians do, about units of happiness.

4. John Rawls, *A Theory of Justice* (Cambridge, Mass.: Harvard University Press, 1971).

5. John C. Harsanyi, 'Cardinal Utility in Welfare Economics and the Theory of Risk-Taking', *Journal of Political Economy*, 61 (1953), 434–435, and 'Cardinal Welfare, Individualistic Ethics, and Interpersonal Comparisons of Utility', *ibid.*, 63 (1955), 309–321. Harsanyi has discussed Rawls's use of the maximin principle and has defended the principle of maximizing expected utility instead, in a paper 'Can the Maximin Principle Serve as a Basis for Morality? A Critique of John Rawls' Theory', *The American Political Science Review*, 69 (1975), 594–606. These articles have been reprinted in John C. Harsanyi, *Essays on Ethics, Social*
Behavior, and Scientific Explanation (Dordrecht, Holland: D. Reidel, 1976).

6. Robert Nozick, *Anarchy, State and Utopia.* (See note 1 above.)

7. Rawls, *A Theory of Justice*, p. 60.

8. In Norman Daniels (ed.), *Reading Rawls* (Oxford: Blackwell, 1975), pp. 141–167. See pp. 148–149.

9. Lyons, *op. cit.*, p. 149, near top.

10. Rawls, *op. cit.*, p. 62.

11. On this point see Brian Barry, *The Liberal Theory of Justice* (London: Oxford University Press, 1973), p. 55.

12. See note 1.

MILTON FISK
Economic Justice

Defenders of the capitalist form of society do not defend a right to economic equality. Economic inequality is, they argue, to everyone's advantage. Yet some of these defenders of capitalism are also supporters of liberal democracy. They must then recognize limits to economic inequality beyond which even capitalism should not go. Vast concentrations of economic wealth are sources of political power that strangle the basic liberties of a democratic society. But many defenders of capitalist society maintain that in the US at least these limits to economic inequality have not been reached.

The purpose of this [paper] is to show that the arguments justifying the existing high degree of economic inequality fall apart. To show this it will not be necessary to defend, or to reject, the right to complete economic equality. Nonetheless, this [paper] points in an egalitarian direction. For it shows also that the degree of economic inequality inevitable within even a reformed capitalist society cannot be justified from the perspective of working-class morality.

I. ECONOMIC INEQUALITY

According to many writers on US society, the stage of widespread affluence has been reached within the US. There is, on the one hand, a reduced level of economic inequality, and there is, on the other hand, an elimination of the lower classes as a majority in favour of a large and prosperous middle-class. The misery and inequality that characterized nineteenth- and

"Economic Justice" is reprinted from *Ethics and Society* (New York: New York University Press, 1980), by permission of the publisher. **Milton Fisk,** a contemporary political theorist, argues forcefully for a radical reexaminaton of basic tenets of economic distribution.

early twentieth-century capitalism have been redeemed with the arrival of the 'affluent society'. This picture, however, conceals the urgent problem of economic inequality within the US. As Gabriel Kolko notes in his pathbreaking dissenting work on income distribution, 'The predominantly middle-class society is only an image in the minds of isolated academicians.'[1]

First let us look at the distribution of before-tax personal, as opposed to corporate, income during the period 1910–70 to get some idea as to whether there has been a significant trend toward equality. To do this we can consider families as broken up into five groups of equal size, ranging from those with the highest to those with the lowest income. (People living in families make up roughly 90 per cent of the US population.) *In the sixty-year period considered, families in the highest fifth received between 40 and 45 per cent of all family income.* That is, they received at least two times more than they would have if every family received the same income. Despite variations from year to year, there is no overall trend in this period toward a significantly smaller share of the national income for the richest fifth. The middle fifth has received between 15 and 18 percent of all family income. This means that it received over the entire sixty-year period less than it would have if income were egalitarian. For this group the trend, within these narrow limits, has been for a slight rise in its share of income, but after World War II that rise stopped completely. Finally, what about the families in the poorest quintile? That group has received between 4 and 6 per cent of the national personal income, which runs up to five times less than it would receive under equality. The overall trend has been for families in this bottom group to get proportionately the same during the sixty-year period. As regards income in the US, then, there is significant and continuing inequality.[2] The top fifth as a whole takes six to ten times more of the national family income than does the bottom fifth. (Data for non-family persons shows even greater inequality.)

Our data has so far been taken on before-tax income. Will not taxation make the picture one of greater equality? It does change the picture as regards equality but only in an insignificant way. Many taxes are regressive: they are a larger fraction of lower than of higher incomes. Social security taxes, property taxes, and sales taxes are all regressive. It cannot be expected that these would provide a shift toward equality. But even the federal income tax, which is progressive, has failed to do more than decrease by two per cent the share of national income of the top fifth. The increase in the share of the bottom fifth resulting from federal income taxes has remained a fraction of a per cent. Moreover, the percentage of all taxes coming from the non-owning classes has been rising steadily since World War II. Taxes have, then, failed to equalize income significantly.[3]

We are dealing with a society in which private ownership of the means of production is a fundamental feature. Some personal income comes from ownership, to be sure, but one cannot say exactly how wealth is distributed simply on the basis of knowing how income is distributed. For one thing, a significant but variable share of returns from ownership is invested in new means of production and does not appear as dividend income. Nonetheless, in a capitalist society we can predict that wealth, like income, is unevenly distributed. It is highly concentrated in the hands of a very few owners: they own the plants, the trucks, the warehouses, the mines, the office buildings, the large estates, and the objects of art. The poor are often net holders of 'negative wealth' because of their debts. *Between 1810 and 1969, the concentration of wealth has remained remarkably constant; the top one per cent as regards wealth has held between 20 and 30 per cent of all the wealth in the US.* In 1962 the poorest 20 per cent held less than one-half of one per cent of the nation's wealth.[4]

Nonetheless, some currency has been given to the view that corporate ownership has become widespread and that workers are now significant owners. Stock ownership is, indeed, more widespread, but this has not seriously affected the high degree of concentration of stock ownership in the hands of the wealthiest.

By 1962, the wealthiest one per cent of the population still held 72 per cent of the nation's corporate stock. In that year, the wealthiest one per cent also held 48 per cent of the nation's bonds, 24 per cent of the loans, and 16 per cent of the real estate.[5] Clearly then wealth is even less equitably distributed than income in the US, and the inequality has been one of long duration. Pensions for workers account for nearly ten per cent of corporate stock. This may provide workers with security after retirement, but it does not give them the power of wealth holders. The reason is that they have no control over these pension funds, which merely add power to the financial institutions that manage them. . . .

A large prosperous middle class has by no means replaced the struggling lower classes as the majority class. With more than half of the people living below the modest but adequate budget of the BLS, the underbelly of US capitalist society is a deprived majority, just as it was fifty years ago. 'In advanced capitalist societies, the costs of staying out of poverty (i.e. of satisfying invariant subsistence needs) grows as the economy grows. Consequently, there is no long-term tendency in advanced capitalist societies for the incidence of poverty to decrease significantly as the economy grows.'[6] The economic inequality of US society is not just relative inequality, for it is an inequality that means deprivation for a sizeable chunk of the society.

II. OWNERSHIP AND PRODUCTIVITY

There are several strategies used by spokespersons of the ruling class to defend the situation of inequality described above. The first defence rests on the rights of ownership. The second rests on the need for inequality in order to increase productivity. In the next section, a third strategy will be discussed: it rests on the notion of a fair wage.

According to the *first defence* of inequality, those who have put their hard-earned money into a business enterprise have the right to appropriate the fruits of that enterprise and divide them according to their own decisions. Thus the product that workers have made is controlled by owners and not by the workers. Owners are within their rights to divide the product in such a way that inequality is great and poverty widespread. An entire web of ideology has been woven on this basic frame of the rights of ownership. Part of that web is the system of law, backed by police force, entitling the owner to the fruits of the worker. From the perspective of members of the working class, there are several holes in this defence. These holes show that what is built on the frame of ownership rights is indeed only ideology.

On the one hand, if ownership rights lead to continued inequality and poverty, then from a working-class perspective there simply are no such rights. The attitude that ownership of the means of production is sacred merely protects the owners at the expense of those who suffer the resulting inequality. A right is more than such an attitude; it must be justified and indeed justified from a class standpoint. Economic inequality can be justified by ownership rights only if there are such rights. There may well be such rights from the perspective of the ruling class. Yet the continued inequality and poverty resulting from ownership are evidence favouring the view that relative to the working class owners have no legitimate right to the fruits of enterprise.

On the other hand, the basis given for the justification of the owner's right to the fruits of enterprise is not adequate. That basis was the hard work of the investor. Investment, however, is an on-going process in a viable firm. The initial investment is followed by many subsequent investments. Let us grant that the owner has worked hard—whether in the form of the honest toil of the self-employed person or in the form of the forcible plunder of the syndicated criminal—to accumulate the initial investment. But when the plant is rebuilt or expanded, the new investment will be possible only because of the hard work of the workers. Once new investment has been made, there is no longer the same basis for saying that the original owner has the right to control the entire product of the new investment. The logic of 'hard work' applies here too. If the owner worked hard to accumulate the initial investment, it is equally true that the workers worked hard to make the new investment possible. Thus, in a viable firm, the workers should, on the logic of hard work, have a right to appropriate an ever increasing share of the product. The capitalist's own logic backfires! . . .

According to the *second defence* of inequality, significant inequality with poverty at the bottom is a necessary condition for making the society as affluent as it is. In a widely published newspaper article entitled 'Morality and the Pursuit of Wealth' appearing in July 1974, the President of the US Chamber of Commerce, Arch Booth, said the realization of equality by the transfer of wealth from the haves to the have-nots would lessen the 'work incentive of the most productive members of society' and endanger 'the ability of the economic system to accumulate capital for new productive facilities'. Booth's solution is to let the rich keep on investing in productive facilities thereby increasing the share the poor get through better wages and higher employment.

There is one glaring fallacy in this argument. It is the logical fallacy of an 'incomplete disjunction'. The disjunction Booth offers us is that *either* we have a forced redistribution of income within capitalism *or* we let the income of the non-owners rise naturally by increasing investment. But the disjunction needs to be expanded to include at least one more alternative: beyond capitalism, it is possible to expand productive facilities through the investment of collective rather than of private capital. In one form of collective ownership, workers would manage the investment of collective capital in order to advance their interests. In this case, the inequality in both wealth and income needed for growth under private capitalism becomes unnecessary. Without significant inequality, private capitalism would lack the centres of economic power needed to put large amounts of labour to work in order to produce a surplus for growth. The model here for a system of collective ownership of the means of production is not that of nationalized industry run by a bunch of officials who are not controlled by workers. This would be the bureaucratic model found in places like the USSR which are no longer private capitalist societies. Rather, the model is that of a workers' democracy in which democracy extends down to the workplace and in which workplaces are coordinated by a council of representatives from each. This socialist alternative is sufficient to make Booth's disjunction incomplete. . . .

III. A FAIR WAGE

A *third strategy* for defending the inequality and the poverty that is to be found today in the US introduces the concept of compensation for work. The defence is that labour is sold on the free market and, on the whole, the free market determines a *just* price for things. Thus, since inequality and poverty are, in part, a result of the free market for labour, there is no *right* to economic equality or even to a 'modest budget'. A free market must not involve the use of power by those who exchange their goods and services within it to coerce those with whom they exchange.

This argument seems to leave open the possibility that wages should mount and thus that the worker should come closer to the owner in economic status. But in fact this possibility is not open. As pointed out in Section I, the range of inequality and the degree of poverty in the US have remained remarkably constant. The majority of the people are at or below the level of existence provided by the modest budget. Because of the greater power and organization of the owning class, the wages and salaries of workers remain at a level that allows them merely to perform their jobs well and to raise a new generation of workers. (Differences between the wages of, say, industrial and clerical workers need to be viewed against the background of a general pull toward this subsistence level.) To perform well and to reproduce themselves they have been forced to purchase the ever more elaborate and hence more expensive means of satisfying survival needs and the needs specific to their jobs. Short-term variations in the supply of and demand for labour are only part of this long-term pattern of compensating workers at a subsistence level. At this level, there is nothing much left over for savings and investments that might narrow the gap between them and the owning class. . . .

What, then, is a fair wage from the perspective of the working class? Suppose we are calves who face the prospect of going to slaughter as one-year-olds. The farmers who send us to slaughter find that this is the age at which to realize a maximum profit on us. So one year is the 'fair' time, from the perspective of the farmers, for calves to enjoy themselves before slaughter. An inquisitive calf poses the question, 'What is the true ''fair'' time for cattle to live before slaughter? Is it two years, or even three?' A selfish calf who has no regard for the farmer and the future of cattle farming generally shouts, 'Stop quibbling; we should demand a moratorium on beef eating. An end to the slaughter of cattle!'' Similarly, Marx said that the slogan, 'A fair day's wage for a fair day's work!' should be replaced by the slogan, 'An end to the wage system!'[7] Instead of the wage system, work should be done in such a way that the

workers' compensation is not just a function of the greater power of a non-working ruling class.

The wage system is a system that in advanced industrial countries has been central to the domination of lower classes by a ruling class. Through that system people are set to work in order to preserve or increase the control of wealth by and, thus, the power of a minority class. They are thus given from what they produce only what is needed to reproduce their labour. When part of the product of workers is used in this way to perpetuate and strengthen the domination of a non-working class, workers are properly said to be 'exploited'. Acceptance of the wage system and plans to reform it from within do not face up to the key role wages play in domination. When workers themselves decide how they are to be compensated out of what they produce, the wage system has ceased to exist and along with it exploitation. . . .

The struggle for higher income begins the organization of people for the collective action that is needed to abolish the wage system itself. This long-term perspective has for some time been forgotten by trade unions everywhere. Their leaders advocate accommodation with the existing system of domination of working people. These leaders talk about a fair wage but they mean only the wages and benefits they think they can wheedle out of the owners. Their conception of fairness and rights is no longer a class conception. A class conception makes overthrowing the wage system a right of working people.

IV. A JUST DISTRIBUTION

Let us leave defences of present economic inequality and take up a proposal for limiting inequality. If capitalist arguments justifying present inequality fail, then where is the line to be drawn for an acceptable degree of inequality? Our problem is how to distribute a product that has come about through the combined efforts of people in different roles. Since isolated producers are the exception, we cannot start

with the assumption that there is a product to which an individual producer is 'entitled' because he or she is 'responsible' for that product.[8] In deciding on a principle of just distribution there are two factors to be considered.

On the one hand, there is the average amount of goods per individual in the population, and, on the other hand, there is the degree of inequality with which goods are actually parceled out to individuals. Increasing the average amount of goods per individual might increase the inequality of distribution, whereas decreasing the inequality in distribution might decrease the average per individual. In capitalism we saw that inequality of wealth is a condition of economic growth. Also, inequality of income within the working class weakens solidarity, making possible a greater surplus and hence greater growth. If strict equality means poverty all around, we might recoil from strict equality and look for a balance between a large average amount and considerable equality. But so far we have no clue as to where to strike this balance.

John Rawls has recently proposed an interesting way of balancing a high average amount of goods with a low degree of inequality.[9] The idea is that we are to avoid demanding such a low degree of inequality that the worst off are penalized by getting less than they would with a higher degree of inequality. We are to avoid only those high degrees of inequality that are arrived at by preventing the worst off from getting the most they could get.

Rawls formuated this in his Principle of Difference which tells us to 'maximize the expectations of the least favoured position'. . . .

[But] Rawls talks about distribution without relating it to production. He assumes wrongly that the validity of his principle is absolute, rather than relative to circumstances within production. One thing is certain: in capitalist society there is not the least chance that the Rawlsian scheme could be put into practice. The reason is simply that the organization of production in a capitalist society centres around increasing productive facilities through the making of profits. The class of owners would not advance the interests characteristic of their class by agreeing to maximize the expectations of the least favoured. Given its power, this class would block the realization of the scheme.

Suppose, though, that some mode of production would allow for distribution in accordance with the Principle of Difference. Should not one simply choose to bring about such a mode of production? Certainly—if the Principle of Difference is valid. But its validity is relative to production in the following way. Validity in general is relative to classes, and classes are essential roles in a given mode of production. One should, then, choose to realize the principle only if it is valid relative to one's class. Nonetheless, that class might have to change the existing mode of production in order to realize the new distribution. Even though the capitalist mode of production excludes the application of the Principle of Difference, it may be a valid principle for one of the lower classes within capitalism.

A distributional plan is not just because it is elegant or intuitive but because it answers to needs arising in production. Not only the actual but also the just distribution is dependent on production.

NOTES

1. Gabriel Kolko, *Wealth and Power in America* (Praeger, New York, 1962), p. 108.
2. These data are based on tables in Kolko, *Wealth and Power in America*, p. 14, and in Frank Ackerman and Andrew Zimbalist, "Capitalism and inequality in the United States," in *The Capitalist System*, 2nd ed., p. 298.
3. Kolko, *Wealth and Power in America*, Ch. II, and Ackerman and Zimbalist "Capitalism and inequality in the United States," in *The Capitalist System*, 2nd ed., p. 303. In Sweden, by contrast, taxes change the ratio of the bottom third to that of the top third from 38 to 48 percent.
4. Lititia Upton and Nancy Lyons, *Basic Facts: Distribution of Personal Income and Wealth in the United States* (Cambridge Institute, 1878 Massachusetts Ave., Cambridge, Mass., 1972), p. 6, and Ackerman and Zimbalist, "Capitalism and inequality in the United States," in *The Capitalist System*, 2nd ed., p. 301.
5. Upton and Lyons, *Basic Facts,* p. 31.
6. Bernard Gendron, "Capitalism and Poverty," *Radical Philosophers' Newsjournal,* 4, January 1975, p. 13. This essay appears as Ch. XII of Gendron's *Technology and the Human Condition* (St. Martin's Press, New York, 1977).
7. Karl Marx, *Wages, Price, and Profit* (1865) (Foreign Language Press, Peking, 1970), Ch. XIV.
8. On entitlement, see Robert Nozick, *Anarchy, State, and Utopia* (Basic Books, New York, 1974), Ch. VII.
9. Rawls, *A Theory of Justice,* pp. 78–80.

QUESTIONS ABOUT JUSTICE

1. After considering the utilitarian, egalitarian and libertarian approaches to the problem of justice, how do you react to the suggestion that any society that permits great disparity between rich and poor must be unjust? How would proponents of each of these views respond?

2. What is wrong with the proposed principle of justice that says: people are to be treated equally, except in proportion to their relevant differences?

3. What exactly is Thrasymachus's proposed conception of justice? What is Socrates's point in suggesting that subjects are obliged to obey their rulers even when the "rulers sometimes ordain acts that are to their own disadvantage. . . ."

4. How does Plato explain justice as the "minding of one's own business"?

5. John Stuart Mill suggests that "To have a right, then is, I conceive, to have something which society ought to defend me in the possession of. If the objector goes on to ask, why it ought? I can give him no other reason than general utility." Does this help to reconcile the ideas of utility and justice, especially the idea of respecting individual rights?

6. Mill suggests that certain commonly accepted rules of justice—such as that the innocent should not be punished, or that a person has a right to defend himself—not only appear to conflict with utility but also with each other. Does this help to explain justice as utility?

7. Rawls suggests that " 'justice as fairness' . . . conveys the idea that the principles of justice are agreed to in an initial situation that is fair." Does a fair agreement carried out under a veil of ignorance guarantee justice? Is a person always bound by fair agreements? Can you think of situations in which this is not the case? How might this affect Rawls's approach?

8. Rawls's view is regarded as egalitarian. Yet his system permits social and economic inequality. How do you explain this apparent conflict?

9. Does Milton Fisk subscribe to some theory of justice? What exactly is it and how does it compare with the others discussed?

10. Is the Marxist a moral skeptic? (See Part IV.)

Justice:
Suggestions for Further Study

The question of justice is one of the oldest discussed by philosophers in the Western tradition. The subject of justice is often divided into two parts, retributive justice, concerned primarily with theories of punishment, and distributive or social justice. The latter is the main topic of Part V. Since there is an extensive and growing literature in both areas, we will describe just a few paths that the interested student might care to follow in pursuing the subject further.

The term "retributive justice" is, perhaps, not the most apt to describe treatment of those who violate the law. Retribution, the idea that wrongdoers ought to be punished and that the punishment must be commensurate with the crime, is but one of several aproaches. In 1939, J. D. Mabbott developed this approach in "Punishment" (*Mind,* vol. 48) while in recent years, Ernest van den Haag, in *Punishing Criminals* (New York: Basic Books, 1975), has defended this view in opposition to those who might favor deterrence, restitution, or rehabilitation as appropriate responses to those who violate the law. Deterrence, although closely associated with retribution (since most forms of punishment also deter) is not, however, the same thing. Many people feel, for example, that the death penalty is a fitting punishment for murder whether or not it deters others from committing a capital offense. Moreover, it seems that, under certain circumstances, crime can be deterred by punishing someone who is otherwise innocent of wrongdoing. Richard B. Brandt has presented an interesting discussion of deterrence as a criterion of just punishment in *Ethical Theory* (Englewood Cliffs, New Jersey: Prentice-Hall, 1959). Restitution, the idea that justice requires a wrongdoer to compensate the victim for the wrong done, has been defended recently by Randy E. Barnett in "Restitution: A New Paradigm of Criminal Justice" (*Ethics,* vol. 87, no. 4, 1977), while the noted psychiatrist, Karl Menninger, has argued for rehabilitation as the appropriate reaction to criminal offense; see his *The Crime of Punishment* (New York: Viking Press, 1968).

For more on utilitariansim as an approach to social justice, see Jeremy Bentham, *An Introduction to the Principles of Morals and Legislation* new ed. (Oxford: Oxford University Press, 1832), and Henry Sidgwick, *Methods of Ethics* (New York: Dover, 1966). Rawls's egalitarianism, based on his theory of justice as fairness, has been widely discussed. Most notable among these discussions is the critical review by Robert Paul Wolff, *Understanding Rawls* (Princeton: Princeton University Press, 1977) and the collection of articles on Rawls by Norman Daniels in *Reading Rawls* (New York: Basic Books, DNA). Robert Nozick's *Anarchy, State and Utopia* (New York: Basic Books, 1968) has also been discussed widely. For an interesting critique of one of Nozick's basic ideas—that schemes to redistribute the wealth interfere with rights—see G. A. Cohen, "Robert Nozick and Wilt Chamberlain: How Patterns Preserve Liberty" (*Erkenntnis* II, 1977, 5–23). For an additional discussion of rights, see Ronald Dworkin's *Taking Rights Seriously* (Cambridge: Cambridge University Press, 1977). For more on Marxism, consider *Karl Marx: Early Writings* (New York: McGraw-Hill, 1963) and *Marx, Justice, and History,* edited by Marshall Cohen, Thomas Nagel, and Thomas Scanlon (Princeton: Princeton University Press, 1980).

Religious Belief

Literary Introduction:
Why Is There Evil?

Discovering a basis for belief consistent with the evidence of our senses is one of the fundamental questions raised by those who examine the nature of religion. One answer to the question is to rely on faith. But what do we do when a promise held out to us cannot be reached through the same rational processes we use to attain other goals? Nobody would question the allure of the benefits offered to religious believers. Among other things, such benefits include the hope of immortality and an ideology that not only explains the individual's place in the larger scheme of things, but provides the scheme itself. Therefore, faith seems a good choice. But for some, faith that is not grounded in reason, or in common experience, is inadequate, and it is the search for a rational basis for belief that is one of the enduring puzzles of religious thought.

One way to focus on the problems underlying religious belief is to approach them with the naivety of a child. Mark Twain, best known as the creator of *Huckleberry Finn* and *Tom Sawyer,* had a particular genius for seeing the world through the eyes of a child. In "Little Bessie," a piece written late in his life, Twain creates a precocious three-year-old in whose mouth he places questions and observations that go to the heart of the demands of faith. Bessie mercilessly questions her mother about God with a zealous dedication to rational truth that far outstrips her childish years. In fact, the only thing childish about Bessie is the openmindedness she brings to the questions she asks. In any other sense, she is more intellectually mature than most adults. Her poor mother is clearly outmatched because she has never given these matters serious thought and can rely only on simplistic tenets.

Bessie's mother fails to provide satisfactory answers because she can offer only her faith, but not a reasoned explanation. Of course, it is unlikely that any adult would be able to do much better at grappling with the precocious child's line of inquiry, for Bessie is pushing for answers to the most fundamental and profoundly perplexing of theological questions. For example, the child wants to reconcile the concepts of God's omnipotence with human responsibility, that is, how can we hold a mere mortal responsible for his or her actions when that person was created by, and lives under the control of, an all-powerful deity? Wouldn't it be reasonable, Bessie asserts, to hold God responsible and to see the person as an agent of divine power?

The best response that Bessie's mother can offer is that seeming injustices, such as the fatal illness of a young child, must serve God's justice, perhaps by representing a deserved punishment for a human infraction of God's law. This reasoning—that God punishes those who violate His law, and rewards those who observe it—is the central issue of one of the Bible's most powerful books, the Book of Job.

Job is described as an obedient servant of God, one who observes all of the commandments, major and minor. He is also, however, a prosperous man, raising the question as to whether he is obedient because he anticipates his dutiful observance will earn him material rewards, or whether he serves God out of a pure sense of faith in His goodness. Urged by Satan, God agrees to put Job to the test by depriving him of his wealth, his family, and finally his health.

In this condition, Job is visited by "comforters," friends who insist that his troubles must result from his own iniquities. However, Job steadfastly insists that he has done nothing to warrant God's anger, and finally he demands an explanation from God as to why he has been subjected to such terrible punishment. God's famous nonanswer, delivered as a voice from a whirlwind, consists of a series of questions that demonstrate the ineffable distance between God's power and humans' puny understanding. The "answer" to Job's questions, God asserts, is simply that a mere mortal cannot hope to comprehend God's ways. Job feels compelled to accept this answer and bows his head before the majesty of the Deity.

The excerpts from the Book of Job that follow include the opening sections, showing Job's faith being tested, then Job's questioning of God, and finally, God's response to Job from the whirlwind.

The Book of Job and "Little Bessie" were written approximately 2600 years apart. Although they do so in very different ways, they address the same perplexing questions. God does not actually answer Job, but instead displays His awful power and humbles His servant into submission. Nor does Bessie's mother adequately answer her daughter's questions, offering only an uncritical acceptance of the faith demanded of Job by God. Yet, the question of a rational basis for religious belief remains, and though it seems to elude a completely satisfactory solution, it has stimulated the best efforts of gifted philosophers for thousands of years.

MARK TWAIN
from *Little Bessie*

CHAPTER 1
Little Bessie Would Assist Providence

Little Bessie was nearly three years old. She was a good child, and not shallow, not frivolous, but meditative and thoughtful, and much given to thinking out the reasons of things and trying to make them harmonize with results. One day she said—

"Mamma, why is there so much pain and sorrow and suffering? What is it all for?"

It was an easy question, and mamma had no difficulty in answering it: .

"It is for our good, my child. In His wisdom and mercy the Lord sends us these afflictions to discipline us and make us better."

"Is it *He* that sends them?"

"Yes."

"Does He send *all* of them, mamma?"

"Yes, dear, all of them. None of them comes by accident; He alone sends them, and always out of love for us, and to make us better."

"Isn't it strange!"

"Strange? Why, no, I have never thought of it in that way. I have not heard any one call it strange before. It has always seemed natural and right to me, and wise and most kindly and merciful."

"Who first thought of it like that, mamma? Was it you?"

"Oh, no, child, I was taught it."

"Who taught you so, mamma?"

"Why, really, I don't know—I can't remember. My mother, I suppose; or the preacher. But it's a thing that everybody knows."

"Well, anyway, it does seem strange. Did He give Billy Norris the typhus?"

"Yes."

"What for?"

"Why, to discipline him and make him good."

"But he died, mamma, and so it *couldn't* make him good."

"Well, then, I suppose it was for some other reason. We know it was a *good* reason, whatever it was."

"What do you think it was, mamma?"

"Oh, you ask so many questions! I think it was to discipline his parents."

"Well, then, it wasn't fair, mamma. Why should *his* life be taken away for their sake, when he wasn't doing anything?"

"Oh, *I* don't know! I only know it was for a good and wise and merciful reason."

"What reason, mamma?"

"Little Bessie" is reprinted from *Devil's Race-Track: Mark Twain's Great Dark Writings*, edited by John Tuckey, pgs. 3–13, University of California Press, by permission of the publisher. **Mark Twain,** the pseudonym for Samuel Langhorne Clemens (1835–1910), wrote *Huckleberry Finn*, a masterpiece of realistic fiction, published in 1884. His later work, including "Little Bessie," grew increasingly pessimistic about human nature.

"I think—I think—well, it was a judgment; it was to punish them for some sin they had committed."

"But *he* was the one that was punished, mamma. Was that right?"

"Certainly, certainly. He does nothing that isn't right and wise and merciful. You can't understand these things now, dear, but when you are grown up you will understand them, and then you will see that they are just and wise."

After a pause:

"Did He make the roof fall in on the stranger that was trying to save the crippled old woman from the fire, mamma?"

"Yes, my child. *Wait!* Don't ask me why, because I don't know. I only know it was to discipline some one, or be a judgment upon somebody, or to show His power."

"That drunken man that stuck a pitchfork into Mrs. Welch's baby when—"

"Never mind about it, you needn't go into particulars; it was to discipline the child—*that* much is certain, anyway."

"Mamma, Mr. Burgess said in his sermon that billions of little creatures are sent into us to give us cholera, and typhoid, and lockjaw, and more than a thousand other sicknesses and—mamma, does He send them?"

"Oh, certainly, child, certainly. Of course."

"What for?"

"Oh, to *dis*cipline us! Haven't I told you so, over and over again?"

"It's awful cruel, mamma! And silly! And if I—"

"Hush, oh hush! Do you want to bring the lightning?"

"You know the lightning *did* come last week, mamma, and struck the new church, and burnt it down. Was it to discipline the church?"

(Wearily). "Oh, I suppose so."

"But it killed a hog that wasn't doing anything. Was it to discipline the hog, mamma?"

"Dear Child, don't you want to run out and play a while? If you would like to—"

"Mamma, only think! Mr. Hollister says there isn't a bird or fish or reptile or any other animal that hasn't got an enemy that Providence has sent to bite it and chase it and pester it, and kill it, and suck its blood and discipline it and make it good and religious. Is that true, mother—because if it is true, why did Mr. Hollister laugh at it?"

"That Hollister is a scandalous person, and I don't want you to listen to anything he says."

"Why, mamma, he is very interesting, and *I* think he tries to be good. He says the wasps catch spiders and cram them down into their nests in the ground—*alive,* mamma!—and there they live and suffer days and days and days, and the hungry little wasps chewing their legs and gnawing into their bellies all the time, to make them good and religious and praise God for His infinite mercies. *I* think Mr. Hollister is just lovely, and ever so kind; for when I asked him if *he* would treat a spider like that, he said he hoped to be damned if he would; and then he—"

"My child! Oh, do for goodness' sake—"

"And mamma, he says the spider is appointed to catch the fly, and drive her fangs into his bowels, and suck and suck and suck his blood, to discipline him and make him a Christian; and whenever the fly buzzes his wings with the pain and misery of it, you can see by the spider's grateful eye that she is thanking the Giver of All Good for—well, she's saying grace, as *he* says; and also, he—"

"Oh, aren't you *ever* going to get tired chattering! If you want to go out and play—"

"Mamma, he says himself that all troubles and pains and miseries and rotten diseases and horrors and villainies are sent to us in mercy and kindness to discipline us; and he says it is the duty of every father and mother to *help* Providence, every way they can; and says they can't do it just by scolding and whipping, for that won't answer, it is weak and no good—Providence's way is best, and it is every parent's duty and every *person's* duty to help discipline everybody, and cripple them and kill them, and starve them, and freeze them, and rot them with diseases, and lead them into murder and theft and dishonor and disgrace; and he says Providence's invention for disciplining us and the animals is the very brightest idea that ever was, and not even an idiot could get up anything shinier. Mamma, brother Eddie needs disciplining, right away; and I know where you can get the smallpox for him, and the itch, and the diphtheria, and bone-rot, and heart disease, and consumption, and—*Dear* mamma, have you fainted! I will run and bring help! Now *this* comes of staying in town this hot weather."

CHAPTER 2
Creation of Man

Mamma. You disobedient child, have you been associating with that irreligious Hollister again?

Bessie. Well, mamma, he is interesting, anyway, although wicked, and I can't help loving interesting people. Here is the conversation we had:

Hollister. Bessie, suppose you should take some meat and bones and fur, and make a cat out of it, and should tell the cat, Now you are not to be unkind to any creature, on pain of punishment and death. And suppose the cat should disobey, and catch a mouse and torture it and kill it. What would you do to the cat?

Bessie. Nothing.

H. Why?

B. Because I know what the cat would say. She would say, It's my nature, I couldn't help it; I didn't make my nature, *you* made it. And so you are responsible for what I've done—I'm not. I couldn't answer that, Mr. Hollister.

H. It's just the case of Frankenstein and his Monster over again.

B. What is that?

H. Frankenstein took some flesh and bones and blood and made a man out of them; the man ran away and fell to raping and robbing and murdering everywhere, and Frankenstein was horrified and in despair, and said, *I* made him, without asking his consent, and it makes me responsible for every crime he commits. *I* am the criminal, he is innocent.

B. Of course he was right.

H. I judge so. It's just the case of God and man and you and the cat over again.

B. How is that?

H. God made man, without man's consent, and made his nature, too; made it vicious instead of angelic, and then said, Be angelic, or I will punish you and destroy you. But no matter, God is responsible for everything man does, all the same; He can't get around that fact. There is only one Criminal, and it is not man.

Mamma. This is atrocious! It is wicked, blasphemous, irreverent, horrible!

Bessie. Yes'm, but it's true. And I'm not going to make a cat. I would be above making a cat if I couldn't make a good one.

CHAPTER 3

Mamma, if a person by the name of Jones kills a person by the name of Smith just for amusement, it's murder, isn't it, and Jones is a murderer?

Yes, my child.

And Jones is punishable for it?

Yes, my child.

Why, mamma?

Why? Because God has forbidden homicide in the Ten Commandments, and therefore whoever kills a person commits a crime and must suffer for it.

But mamma, suppose Jones has by birth such a violent temper that he can't control himself?

He *must* control himself. God requires it.

But he doesn't make his own temper, mamma, he is born with it, like the rabbit and the tiger; and so, why should he be held responsible?

Because God *says* he is responsible and *must* control his temper.

But he *can't,* mamma; and so, don't you think it is God that does the killing and is responsible, because it was *He* that gave him the temper which he couldn't control?

Peace, my child! He *must* control it, for God requires it, and that ends the matter. It settles it, and there is no room for argument.

(*After a thoughtful pause.*) It doesn't seem to me to settle it. Mamma, murder is murder, isn't it? And whoever commits it is a murderer? That is the plain simple fact, isn't it?

(*Suspiciously.*) What are you arriving at now, my child?

Mamma, when God designed Jones He could have given him a rabbit's temper if He had wanted to, couldn't He?

Yes.

Then Jones would not kill anybody and have to be hanged?

True.

But He chose to give Jones a temper that would *make* him kill Smith. Why, then, isn't *He* responsible?

Because He also gave Jones a Bible. The Bible gives Jones ample warning not to commit murder; and so if Jones commits it he alone is responsible.

(*Another pause.*) Mamma, did God make the housefly?

Certainly, my darling.

What for?

For some great and good purpose, and to display His power.

What is the great and good purpose, mamma?

We do not know, my child. We only know that He makes *all* things for a great and good purpose. But this it too large a subject for a dear little Bessie like you, only a trifle over three years old.

Possibly, mamma, yet it profoundly interests me. I have been reading about the fly, in the newest science-book. In that book he is called "the most dangerous animal and the most murderous that exists upon the earth, killing hundreds of thousands of men, women and children

every year, by distributing deadly diseases among them." Think of it, mamma, the *most* fatal of all the animals! by all odds the most murderous of all the living things created by God. Listen to this, from the book:

Now, the house fly has a very keen scent for filth of any kind. Whenever there is any within a hundred yards or so, the fly goes for it to smear its mouth and all the sticky hairs of its six legs with dirt and disease germs. A second or two suffices to gather up many thousands of these disease germs, and then off goes the fly to the nearest kitchen or dining room. There the fly crawls over the meat, butter, bread, cake, anything it can find in fact, and often gets into the milk pitcher, depositing large numbers of disease germs at every step. The house fly is as disgusting as it is dangerous.

Isn't it horrible, mamma! One fly produces fifty-two billions of descendants in 60 days in June and July, and they go and crawl over sick people and wade through pus, and sputa, and foul matter exuding from sores, and gaum themselves with every kind of disease-germ, then they go to everybody's dinner table and wipe themselves off on the butter and the other food, and many and many a painful illness and ultimate death results from this loathsome industry. Mamma, they murder seven thousand persons in New York City alone, every year—people against whom they have no quarrel. To kill without cause is murder—nobody denies that. Mamma?

Well?

Have the flies a Bible?

Of course not.

You have said it is the Bible that makes man responsible. If God didn't give him a Bible to circumvent the nature that He deliberately gave him, God would be responsible. He gave the fly his murderous nature, and sent him forth unobstructed by a Bible or any other restraint to commit murder by wholesale. And so, therefore, God is Himself responsible. God is a murderer. Mr. Hollister says so. Mr. Hollister says God can't make one moral law for man and another for Himself. He says it would be laughable.

Do shut up! I wish that that tiresome Hollister was in H—amburg! He is an ignorant, unreasoning, illogical ass, and I have told you over and over again to keep out of his poisonous company.

from the *Book of Job*

CHAPTER 1

There was a man in the land of Uz, whose name was Job, and that man was perfect and upright, and one that feared God, and eschewed evil. And there were born unto him seven sons and three daughters. His substance also was seven thousand sheep, and three thousand camels, and five hundred yoke of oxen, and five hundred she-asses, and a very great household; so that this man was the greatest of all the men of the east. And his sons went and feasted in their houses, every one his day, and sent and called for their three sisters to eat and to drink with them. And it was so, when the days of their feasting were gone about, that Job sent and sanctified them, and rose up early in the morning, and offered burnt offerings according to the number of them all: for Job said, "It may be that my sons have sinned, and cursed God in their hearts." Thus did Job continually.

Now there was a day when the sons of God came to present themselves before the Lord, and Satan came also among them. And the Lord said unto Satan, "Whence comest thou?" Then Satan answered the Lord, and said, "From going to and fro in the earth, and from walking up and down in it." And the Lord said

unto Satan, "Hast thou considered my servant Job, that there is none like him in the earth, a perfect and an upright man, one that feareth God, and escheweth evil?" Then Satan answered the Lord, and said, "Doth Job fear God for nought? Hast not thou made an hedge about him, and about his house, and about all that he hath on every side? Thou hast blessed the work of his hands, and his substance is increased in the land. But put forth thine hand now, and touch all that he hath, and he will curse thee to thy face." And the Lord said unto Satan, "Behold, all that he hath is in thy power, only upon himself put not forth thine hand." So Satan went forth from the presence of the Lord.

And there was a day when his sons and his daughters were eating and drinking wine in their eldest brother's house: and there came a messenger unto Job, and said, "The oxen were plowing, and the asses feeding beside them, and the Sabeans fell upon them, and took them away: Yea, they have slain the servants with the edge of the sword, and I only am escaped alone to tell thee." While he was yet speaking, there came also another, and said, "The fire of God

The Book of Job is a classic story of the Old Testament that attempts to inspire both fear and respect for a diety that can do what He will, but in the end guarantees that justice prevails.

is fallen from heaven, and hath burnt up the sheep, and the servants, and consumed them, and I only am escaped alone to tell thee.'' While he was yet speaking, there came also another, and said, ''The Chaldeans made out three bands, and fell upon the camels, and have carried them away, yea, and slain the servants with the edge of the sword, and I only am escaped alone to tell three.'' While he was yet speaking there came also another, and said, ''Thy sons and thy daughters were eating and drinking wine in their eldest brother's house. And behold, there came a great wind from the wilderness, and smote the four corners of the house, and it fell upon the young men, and they are dead, and I only am escaped alone to tell thee.'' Then Job arose, and rent his mantle, and shaved his head, and fell down upon the ground, and worshipped, and said, ''Naked came I out of my mother's womb, and naked shall I return thither: the Lord gave, and the Lord hath taken away, blessed be the name of the Lord.'' In all this Job sinned not, nor charged God foolishly.

CHAPTER 2

Again there was a day when the sons of God came to present themselves before the Lord, and Satan came also among them to present himself before the Lord. And the Lord said unto Satan, ''From whence comest thou?'' And Satan answered the Lord, and said, ''From going to and fro in the earth, and from walking up and down in it.'' And the Lord said unto Satan, ''Hast thou considered my servant Job, that there is none like him in the earth, a perfect and an upright man, one that feareth God, and escheweth evil? and still he holdeth fast his integrity, although thou movedst me against him, to destroy him without cause.'' And Satan answered the Lord, and said, ''Skin for skin, yea all that a man hath, will he give for his life. But put forth thine hand now, and touch his bone and his flesh, and he will curse thee to thy face.'' And the Lord said unto Satan, ''Behold, he is in thine hand, but save his life.''

So went Satan forth from the presence of the Lord, and smote Job with sore boils, from the sole of his foot unto his crown. And he took him a potsherd to scrape himself withal; and he sat down among the ashes.

Then said his wife unto him, ''Doest thou still retain thine integrity? Curse God, and die.'' But he said unto her, ''Thou speakest as one of the foolish women speaketh; what? shall we receive good at the hand of God, and shall we not receive evil?'' In all this did not Job sin with his lips.

Now when Job's three friends heard of all this evil that was come upon him, they came every one from his own place: Eliphaz the Temanite, and Bildad the Shuhite, and Zophar the Naamathite; for they had made an appointment together to come to mourn with him, and to comfort him. And when they lifted up their eyes afar off, and knew him not, they lifted up their voice, and wept; and they rent every one his mantle, and sprinkled dust upon their heads toward heaven. So they sat down with him upon the ground seven days and seven nights, and none spake a word unto him; for they saw that his grief was very great.

CHAPTER 3

After this, opened Job his mouth, and cursed his day.

And Job spake, and said,

''Let the day perish wherein I was born, and the night in which it was said, 'There is a man-child conceived.'

Let that day be darkness, let not God regard it from above, neither let the light shine upon it.

Let darkness and the shadow of death stain it, let a cloud dwell upon it, let the blackness of the day terrify it.

As for that night, let darkness seize upon it, let it not be joined unto the days of the year, let it not come into the number of the months.

Lo, let that night be solitary, let no joyful voice come therein.

Let them curse it that curse the day, who are ready to raise up their mourning.

Let the stars of the twilight thereof be dark, let it look for light but have none, neither let it see the dawning of the day:

Because it shut not up the doors of my mother's womb, nor hid sorrow from mine eyes.

Why died I not from the womb? why did I not give up the ghost when I came out of the belly?

Why did the knees prevent me? or why the breasts, that I should suck?

For now should I have lain still and been quiet, I should have slept; then had I been at rest,

With kings and counsellors of the earth, which built desolate places for themselves,

Or with princes that had gold, who filled their houses with silver:

Or as an hidden untimely birth, I had not been; as infants which never saw light.

There the wicked cease from troubling: and there the weary be at rest.

There the prisoners rest together, they hear not the voice of the oppressor.

The small and great are there, and the servant is free from his master.

Wherefore is light given to him that is in misery, and life unto the bitter in soul?

Which long for death, but it cometh not, and dig for it more than for hid treasures:

Which rejoice exceedingly, and are glad when they can find the grave?

Why is light given to a man, whose way is hid, and whom God hath hedged in?

For my sighing cometh before I eat, and my roarings are poured out like the waters.

For the thing which I greatly feared is come upon me, and that which I was afraid of is come unto me.

I was not in safety, neither had I rest, neither was I quiet: yet trouble came.''

CHAPTER 31

''I made a covenant with mine eyes; why then should I think upon a maid?

For what portion of God is there from above? and what inheritance of the Almighty from on high?

Is not destruction to the wicked? and a strange punishment to the workers of iniquity?

Doth not he see my ways, and count all my steps?

If I have walked with vanity, or if my foot hath hasted to deceit:

Let me be weighed in an even balance, that God may know mine integrity.

If my step hath turned out of the way, and mine heart walked after mine eyes, and if any blot hath cleaved to my hands:

Then let me sow, and let another eat, yea let my offspring be rooted out.

If mine heart have been deceived by a woman, or if I have laid wait at my neighbour's door:

Then let my wife grind unto another, and let others bow down upon her.

For this is an heinous crime, yea, it is an iniquity to be punished by the judges.

For it is a fire that consumeth to destruction, and would root out all mine increase.

If I did despise the cause of my manservant, or of my maidservant, when they contended with me:

What then shall I do when God riseth up? and when he visiteth, what shall I answer him?

Did not he that made me in the womb, make him? and did not one fashion us in the womb?

If I have withheld the poor from their desire, or have caused the eyes of the widow to fail:

Or have eaten my morsel myself alone, and the fatherless hath not eaten thereof:

(For from my youth he was brought up with me as with a father, and I have guided her from my mother's womb.)

If I have seen any perish for want of clothing, or any poor without covering:

If his loins have not blessed me, and if he were not warmed with the fleece of my sheep:

If I have lifted up my hand against the fatherless, when I saw my help in the gate:

Then let mine arm fall from my shoulder blade, and mine arm be broken from the bone.

For destruction from God was a terror to me: and by reason of his highness I could not endure.

If I have made gold my hope, or have said to the fine gold, 'Thou art my confidence':

If I rejoiced because my wealth was great, and because mine hand had gotten much:

If I beheld the sun when it shined, or the moon walking in brightness:

And my heart hath been secretly enticed, or my mouth hath kissed my hand:

This also were an iniquity to be punished by the judge: for I should have denied the God that is above.

If I rejoiced at the destruction of him that hated me, or lifted up myself when evil found him:

(Neither have I suffered my mouth to sin by wishing a curse to his soul.)

If the men of my tabernacle said not, 'Oh that we had of his flesh! we cannot be satisfied.'

The stranger did not lodge in the street: but I opened my doors to the traveler.

If I covered my transgressions, as Adam, by hiding mine iniquity in my bosom:

Did I fear a great multitude, or did the contempt of families terrify me, that I kept silence, and went not out of the door?

O that one would hear me! Behold, my desire is that the Almighty would answer me, and that mine adversary had written a book.

Surely I would take it upon my shoulder, and bind it as a crown to me.

I would declare unto him the number of my steps, as a prince would I go near unto him.

If my land cry against me, or that the furrows likewise thereof complain:

If I have eaten the fruits thereof without money, or have caused the owners thereof to lose their life:

Let thistles grow instead of wheat, and cockle instead of barley." The words of Job are ended.

CHAPTER 38

Then the Lord answered Job out of the whirlwind, and said,

"Who is this that darkeneth counsel by words without knowledge?

Gird up now thy loins like a man; for I will demand of thee, and answer thou me.

Where wast thou when I laid the foundations of the earth? declare, if thou hast understanding.

Who hath laid the measures thereof, if thou knowest? or who hath stretched the line upon it?

Whereupon are the foundations thereof fastened? or who laid the cornerstone thereof;

When the morning stars sang together, and all the sons of God shouted for joy?

Or who shut up the sea with doors, when it brake forth as if it had issued out of the womb?

When I made the cloud the garment thereof, and thick darkness a swaddling band for it,

And brake up for it my decreed place, and set bars and doors,

And said, 'Hitherto shalt thou come, but no further: and here shall thy proud waves be stayed?'

Hast thou commanded the morning since thy days? and caused the day-spring to know his place,

That it might take hold of the ends of the earth, that the wicked might be shaken out of it?

It is turned as clay to the seal, and they stand as a garment.

And from the wicked their light is withholden, and the high arm shall be broken.

Hast thou entered into the springs of the sea? or hast thou walked in the search of the depth?

Have the gates of death been opened unto thee? or hast thou seen the doors of the shadow of death?

Hast thou perceived the breadth of the earth? Declare if thou knowest it all.

Where is the way where light dwelleth? and as for darkness, where is the place thereof,

That thou shouldest take it to the bound thereof, and that thou shouldest know the paths to the house thereof?

Knowest thou it, because thou wast then born? or because the number of thy days is great?

Hast thou entered into the treasures of the snow? or hast thou seen the treasures of the hail,

Which I have reserved against the time of trouble, against the day of battle and war?

By what way is the light parted, which scattereth the east wind upon the earth?

Who hath divided a watercourse for the overflowing of waters? or a way for the lightning of thunder,

To cause it to rain on the earth, where no man is: on the wilderness wherein there is no man;

To satisfy the desolate and waste ground, and to cause the bud of the tender herb to spring forth?

Hath the rain a father? or who hath begotten the drops of dew?

Out of whose womb came the ice? and the hoary frost of heaven, who hath gendered it?

The waters are hid as with a stone, and the face of the deep is frozen.

Canst thou bind the sweet influences of Pleiades? or loose the bands of Orion?

Canst thou bring forth Mazzaroth in his season, or canst thou guide Arcturus with his sons?

Knowest thou the ordinances of heaven? canst thou set the dominion thereof in the earth?

Canst thou lift up thy voice to the clouds, that abundance of waters may cover thee?

Canst thou send lightnings, that they may go, and say unto thee, 'Here we are'?

Who hath put wisdom in the inward parts? or who hath given understanding to the heart?

Who can number the clouds in wisdom? or who can stay the bottles of heaven,

When the dust groweth into hardness, and the clods cleave fast together?

Wilt thou hunt the prey for the lion? or fill the appetite of the young lions,

When they crouch in their dens, and abide in the covert to lie in wait?

Who provideth for the raven his food? when his young ones cry unto God, they wander for lack of meat.''

CHAPTER 39

''Knowest thou the time when the wild goats of the rock bring forth? or canst thou mark when the hinds do calve?

Canst thou number the months that they fulfill? or knowest thou the time when they bring forth?

They bow themselves, they bring forth their young ones, they cast out their sorrows.

Their young ones are in good liking, they grow up with corn: they go forth, and return not unto them.

Who hath sent out the wild ass free? or who hath loosed the bands of the wild ass?

Whose house I have made the wilderness, and the barren land his dwellings.

He scorneth the multitude of the city, neither regardeth he the crying of the driver.

The range of the mountains is his pasture, and he searcheth after every green thing.

Will the unicorn be willing to serve thee? or abide by thy crib?

Canst thou bind the unicorn with his band in the furrow? or will he harrow the valleys after thee?

Wilt thou trust him because his strength is great? or wilt thou leave thy labour to him?

Wilt thou believe him that he will bring home thy seed? and gather it into thy barn?

Gavest thou the goodly wings unto the peacocks, or wings and feathers unto the ostrich?

Which leaveth her eggs in the earth, and warmeth them in the dust,

And forgetteth that the foot may crush them, or that the wild beast may break them.

She is hardened against her young ones, as though they were not hers: her labour is in vain without fear:

Because God hath deprived her of wisdom, neither hath he imparted to her understanding.

What time she lifteth up herself on high, she scorneth the horse and his rider.

Hast thou given the horse strength? has thou clothed his neck with thunder?

Canst thou make him afraid as a grasshopper? the glory of his nostrils is terrible.

He paweth in the valley, and rejoiceth in his strength: he goeth on to meet the armed men.

He mocketh at fear, and is not affrighted: neither turneth he back from the sword.

The quiver rattleth against him, the glittering spear and the shield.

He swalloweth the ground with fierceness and rage: neither believeth he that it is the sound of the trumpet.

He saith among the trumpets, 'Ha, ha': and he smelleth the battle afar off, the thunder of the captains, and the shouting.

Doth the hawk fly by thy wisdom, and stretch her wings toward the south?

Doth the eagle mount up at thy command? and make her nest on high?

She dwelleth and abideth on the rock, upon the crag of the rock, and the strong place.

From thence she seeketh the prey, and her eyes behold afar off.

Her young ones also suck up blood: and where the slain are, there is she.''

CHAPTER 40

Moreover the Lord answered Job, and said,

"Shall he that contendeth with the Almighty instruct him? he that reproveth God, let him answer it.''

Then Job answered the Lord, and said,

"Behold, I am vile, what shall I answer thee? I will lay my hand upon my mouth.

Once have I spoken, but I will not answer: yea twice, but I will proceed no further.''

Then answered the Lord unto Job out of the whirlwind, and said,

"Gird up thy loins now like a man: I will demand of thee, and declare thou unto me.

Wilt thou also disannul my judgment? wilt thou condemn me, that thou mayest be righteous?

Hast thou an arm like God? or canst thou thunder with a voice like him?

Deck thyself now with majesty and excellency, and array thyself with glory and beauty.

Cast abroad the rage of thy wrath: and behold every one that is proud, and abase him.

Look on every one that is proud, and bring him low: and tread down the wicked in their place.

Hide them in the dust together, and bind their faces in secret.

Then will I also confess unto thee, that thine own right hand can save thee.

Behold now behemoth, which I made with thee, he eateth grass as an ox.

Lo now, his strength is in his loins, and his force is in the navel of his belly.

He moveth his tail like a cedar: the sinews of his stones are wrapped together.

His bones are as strong pieces of brass: his

bones are like bars of iron.

He is the chief of the ways of God: he that made him can make his sword to approach unto him.

Surely the mountains bring him forth food, where all the beasts of the field play.

He lieth under the shady trees, in the covert of the reed, and fens.

The shady trees cover him with their shadow: the willows of the brook compass him about.

Behold, he drinketh up a river, and hasteth not: he trusteth that he can draw up Jordan into his mouth.

He taketh it with his eyes: his nose pierceth through snares.''

CHAPTER 41

''Canst thou draw out leviathan with an hook? or his tongue with a cord which thou lettest down?

Canst thou put an hook into his nose? or bore his jaw through with a thorn?

Will he make many supplications unto thee? will he speak soft words unto thee?

Will he make a covenant with thee? wilt thou take him for a servant for ever?

Wilt thou play with him as with a bird? or wilt thou bind him for thy maidens?

Shall the companions make a banquet of him? shall they part him among the merchants?

Canst thou fill his skin with barbed irons? or his head with fish spears?

Lay thine hand upon him, remember the battle: do no more.

Behold, the hope of him is in vain: shall not one be cast down even at the sight of him?

None is so fierce that dare stir him up: who then is able to stand before me?

Who hath prevented me that I should repay him? whatsoever is under the whole heaven is mine.

I will not conceal his parts, nor his power, nor his comely proportion.

Who can discover the face of his garment? or who can come to him with his double bridle?

Who can open the doors of his face? his teeth are terrible round about.

His scales are his pride, shut up together as with a close seal.

One is so near to another that no air can come between them.

They are joined one to another, they stick together, that they cannot be sundered.

By his neesings a light doth shine, and his eyes are like the eyelids of the morning.

Out of his mouth go burning lamps, and sparks of fire leap out.

Out of his nostrils goeth smoke, as out of a seething pot or caldron.

His breath kindleth coals, and a flame goeth out of his mouth.

In his neck remaineth strength, and sorrow is turned into joy before him.

The flakes of his flesh are joined together: they are firm in themselves, they cannot be moved.

His heart is as firm as a stone, yea as hard as a piece of the nether millstone.

When he raiseth up himself, the mighty are afraid: by reason of breakings they purify themselves.

The sword of him that layeth at him cannot hold: the spear, the dart, nor the habergeon.

He esteemeth iron as straw, and brass as rotten wood.

The arrow cannot make him flee: slingstones are turned with him into stubble.

Darts are counted as stubble: he laugheth at the shaking of a spear.

Sharp stones are under him: he spreadeth sharp pointed things upon the mire.

He maketh the deep to boil like a pot: he maketh the sea like a pot of ointment.

He maketh a path to shine after him; one would think the deep to be hoary.

Upon earth there is not his like, who is made without fear.

He beholdeth all high things: he is a king over all the children of pride.''

CHAPTER 42

Then Job answered the Lord, and said,

"I know that thou canst do every thing, and that no thought can be withholden from thee.

Who is he that hideth counsel without knowledge? therefore have I uttered that I understood not, things too wonderful for me, which I knew not.

Hear, I beseech thee, and I will speak: I will demand of thee, and declare thou unto me.

I have heard of thee by the hearing of the ear: but now mine eye seeth thee.

Wherefore I abhor myself, and repent in dust and ashes."

And it was so, that after the Lord had spoken these words unto Job, the Lord said to Eliphaz the Temanite, "My wrath is kindled against thee, and against thy two friends: for ye have not spoken of me the thing that is right, as my servant Job hath. Therefore take unto you now seven bullocks, and seven rams, and go to my servant Job, and offer up for yourselves a burnt offering, and my servant Job shall pray for you, for him will I accept: lest I deal with you after your folly, in that ye have not spoken of me the thing which is right, like my servant Job." So Eliphaz the Temanite, and Bildad the Shuhite, and Zophar the Naamathite went, and did according as the Lord commanded them: the Lord also accepted Job. And the Lord turned the captivity of Job, when he prayed for his friends: also the Lord gave Job twice as much as he had before.

Then came there unto him all his brethren, and all his sisters, and all they that had been of his acquaintance before, and did eat bread with him in his house: and they bemoaned him, and comforted him over all the evil that the Lord had brought upon him: every man also gave him a piece of money, and every one an earring of gold. So the Lord blessed the latter end of Job more than his beginning: for he had fourteen thousand sheep, and six thousand camels, and a thousand yoke of oxen, and a thousand she-asses. He had also seven sons, and three daughters. And he called the name of the first Jemima, and the name of the second Kezia, and the name of the third Keren-happuch. And in all the land were no women found so fair as the daughters of Job: and their father gave them inheritance among their brethren. After this lived Job an hundred and forty years, and saw his sons, and his sons' sons, even four generations. So Job died, being old, and full of days.

QUESTIONS ABOUT "LITTLE BESSIE" AND THE *BOOK OF JOB*

1. Read the first paragraph of "Little Bessie" carefully, and note Twain's description of how she tried to make "the reasons of things . . . harmonize with results." What does this observation tell us about the way in which Bessie thinks about religions?
2. Study the questions Bessie asks of her mother. How does Twain use a seemingly childish mind to ask very adult questions?
3. What are the bases for Bessie's mother's responses to her daughter's questions? Find places where she relies on doctrine.
4. Bessie's tutor seems to be Mr. Hollister. What do we learn about him and his views on religion?
5. In Chapter Three, Bessie takes a scientific approach by showing how much disease is spread by flies. How does this passage represent a conflict between scientific findings and religious belief?

6. How does the Bible characterize Job?

7. Is there anything in this characterization to suggest that Job's behavior or attitudes deserve punishment?

8. What is the central concern of Job's complaint to God in Chapter 31? Do his complaints seem valid? By what standards?

9. In this chapter, Job states that he has made a covenant with God. What is a covenant, and how does Job's use of this term explain his attitude toward God's justice?

10. When God speaks to Job out of the whirlwind, in Chapters 38–41, He lists many marvelous accomplishments. What is the purpose of this list?

11. Are you satisfied with God's answer to Job?

12. Why does God restore Job in Chapter 42? How does this act comment on the question of Job's faith being rewarded?

Philosophical Discussion:
Does God Exist?

Job is a good man. He works hard, obeys the law, cares for his family, and treats others with dignity and respect. Yet great evils befall him. His properties and possessions are nearly destroyed. Some of the members of his family suffer great hardships; others are killed. He himself is plagued by illness.

Job is not alone in his troubles. Good people suffer. This seems to be as firmly established as any fact of science or common sense. Yet good people believe, as Job does, in God. And they believe that He is all-good, all-knowing, and all-powerful. Their God—the God of Abraham, Isaac, and Moses, of Jesus, and of Mohammed—is an all-perfect being.

How can this be? How can individuals believe in such an all-perfect being, especially in the face of what appears to be unwarranted pain and suffering? The problem of evil, the main obstacle to monotheism in the Judeo-Christian-Islamic tradition, is the task of attempting to reconcile all the bad things that seem to occur in the world with the belief that God, an all-good, all-powerful, and all-knowing diety, exists.

What exactly is the difficulty? If God is all-knowing and all-good, it seems that He is not all-powerful. Otherwise, why would He permit the innocent to suffer? If God is all-good and all-powerful, it seems that He does not fully know or understand what is happening in the world. Otherwise, why do so many prayers apparently go unanswered? If God is all-powerful and all-knowing, it seems that He is not wholly good. Otherwise, how can He see the suffering that takes place, have the power to alleviate it, and not exercise that power? But God *must* be all-good, all-knowing, and all-powerful. Otherwise He would be less than perfect, and hence, no more worthy of worship than the gods of ancient Greece or Rome, or the other mythological beings worshipped by different peoples at one time or another.

Can it be that there is no evil? Perhaps. But this too should be explained. Otherwise, why do innocent people appear to suffer?

The idea of an all-perfect being is a very profound and powerful one. By comparison, all of the important concepts of morality, science, and politics—that people ought to treat others as they themselves would wish to be treated; that there is enormous energy locked in the tiniest particles of matter; that the state above all else must be just—pale to insignificance. If God exists, He devised the golden rule, made matter and energy, invented human rights. He created the world, not in a mindless cataclysmic explosion as proposed by contemporary scientists, but in an act of supreme ingenuity, intelligence, and divine inspiration. He was mindful of the fundamental structure of space and time, of the intimate relationship between the inanimate and organic, of the distinction between human being and beast, of the difference between life and death, and of the ultimate outcome of the entire scheme of things. If God exists, the world has a special purpose, life has a special meaning, and whatever happens must be all the for best.

But *does* God exist? Many things that happen seem in conflict with so all-encompassing a belief. The catastrophes that befall Job appear to be undeserved punishment. Even if God restores Job's health, his property, his family and friends, can that make up for the pain? What about Billy Norris, in Mark Twain's "Little Bessie"? Like Job, he, too, suffers—in this case from typhus. But as Little Bessie points out to her mother, Billy Norris *died*. How can that be made right? Except for the story of Lazarus in the *New Testament*, God does not restore people to life. And even if Billy Norris survived his disease, how would his apparently undeserved pain be meaningful? What good would it do? What purpose would it serve? What good is there in any undeserved suffering? What purpose was served by those who died in the many wars throughout history, of those who perished in the plagues of the middle ages, of those who fell victim to Nazi atrocities in the Holocaust? (Sidney Hook and Yaakov Hominick debate the problem of evil, especially as it pertains to the Holocaust.)

Perhaps, if God exists, then pain and suffering, even when undeserved, are not as bad as they seem. Death may be a welcome relief, if as religious believers say, there is a life after death at which time the scales of justice are finally balanced, when the good are rewarded, and the evil punished. But how can we be assured of God's existence? How can we believe that ultimately all is for the best, especially in the face of so much evidence to the contrary? Must we have the faith of Job?

Moreover, if God exists, why would He demand such loyalty, such blind fidelity? Why would He create creatures intelligent enough to ask questions about their place in the larger scheme of things, yet give them insufficient evidence of His existence? Does he want irrational followers, or does He prefer not to be believed in? Why would an intelligent being act so mysteriously?

Can it be that we do not deserve to know the ultimate truth about the nature of things? As the voice "out of the whirlwind" suggests, Job was not there when the heavens and earth were created, when the plants and animals were first fashioned, when Adam and Eve were molded out of clay. By what right does so insignificant a creature question God's plan? Would a sculptor try to justify his conduct to his clay form even if it were designed in his own image? Why should God try to explain His ways to mankind? Perhaps it is miracle enough that we exist.

But if we are little more than lumps of clay, why does God even speak out of the whirlwind? Can it be that the world and everything within it is beyond reason? Perhaps the attempt to understand God's ways eludes all rational explanation.

But God and evil can't be completely beyond reason. Otherwise, God himself could not explain the human condition, even to Himself. He could not be all-knowing, since He would lack understanding. Or, since He seems ultimately responsible for what happens, He could not be all-good. He would have created a bad situation that even He could not explain. Or perhaps He is not all-powerful, since He would have created a world that, for no apparent reason, seems to have gotten out of hand. That the world is beyond all reason does not solve the problem of evil. It *is* the problem of evil.

Perhaps the appearance of evil is our problem, not God's. We, not God, are incapable of reconciling the appearance of unwarranted suffering with God's noble intentions. The problem of evil is simply beyond our comprehension. But this cannot be true either. There is at least one resolution of the problem that appears well within human reason—the atheist's proposal that God does not exist. If there is no God, then there is little reason to think that the world is just. There would be little puzzle then in why evil befalls those who seem not to deserve it. Both the innocent and the guilty alike would be subject to the same hurricanes, floods, fires, famines, droughts, and diseases—as seems to be the case. The human condition would be as much a matter of luck as design. The main problem of human existence, according to the atheist, would be to find ways of avoiding the natural calamities that affect all people, not to justify disaster or try to explain it away.

Only if we insist on two things do we seem to have a logical impasse: (1) that evil exists; and (2) that God exists. If we accept the first, as seems apparent, then there should be some special reason or argument to accept the second. Otherwise, in the absence of a better explanation of the appearance of evil, atheism would seem to be correct. In part for this reason, theists have long sought independent proof of God's existence and have devised three main approaches: the *ontological, cosmological,* and *teleological* arguments for the existence of God.

Before we examine each of these approaches, however, let us consider first what an acceptable proof should be. To begin with, the premises, or assumptions upon which the conclusion is alleged to rest, should not only be true, but should be known to be true, or at least supported by the available evidence. This may appear obvious, except that many believers argue in favor of God's existence on the basis of scripture alone. If the objective is to establish God's existence, then it should first be shown that the Bible, unlike other quasi-historical religious writings (such as the ancient Hindu *Upanishads*), alone reveals the essential truth about existence. Otherwise, how can we be sure that the basic message of the *Old* and *New Testaments,* any more so than the ideas expressed in the holy writings of other religious traditions (especially those which speak not just of one but of many gods) corresponds to the way things actually are? It seems that in addition to holy writ, independent evidence is needed.

Second, the conclusion of an acceptable argument should be valid, either in the formal sense that the assertion of the premises in conjunction with the denial of the conclusion is a contradiction, or in a less formal sense, that the conclusion does not depend upon what logicians call "informal" fallacies of reasoning. For example, it may be argued validly, at least in the formal sense, that God exists, since the Bible speaks of God, and the Bible, which is divinely inspired, cannot be wrong. There would appear to be a contradiction in admitting that the Bible cannot be wrong, and yet denying that God exists. But this argument commits the fallacy of circular reasoning, the error of assuming among the premises the conclusion to be established. In the above example, the suggestion that the Bible is divinely inspired already assumes that God exists. This does not mean that the argument is formally invalid, but rather, if the conclusion is admissible as a premise, that the argument itself is gratuitous.

Third, it seems that not every acceptable argument need be formally valid. For example, there is no apparent contradiction in suggesting that human beings, in the next few years, will sprout wings and fly like the birds, although given past experience and what we know about human physiology, there is every reason to believe that this will not occur. In the absence of formal validity, why do we find one proposed conclusion more acceptable than another? Logicians have given different answers. One of the most important of these is the suggestion that an argument should be compelling in that if the premises seem to admit of more than one conclusion, there should be additional reason to discount all but the one that is favored. Otherwise the argument is inconclusive. For example, since part of the explanation for human physiognomy is genetic structure, and since it is unlikely that the human gene pool will alter dramatically in the next few years, it is more likely that human beings will remain as wingless in the near future as in the past.

Let us now consider the main arguments theists have given for the existence of God. One of the simplest, and most striking, is a "proof" credited to Anselm, an eleventh-century Benedictine abbot who served in his later years as Archbishop of Canterbury. According to Anselm, the belief in God is so overpowering and certain that one would have to be a virtual fool to deny, either outwardly or even in one's heart, that God exists. Why exactly is the atheist a fool? According to Anselm, the idea of God is the idea of a being than which "none greater can be conceived," or, if you will, the idea of a perfect being, which seems to be the basic idea of deity within the Judeo-Christian-Islamic tradition. Why exactly should we think that there is some such being? Anselm's answer, in what has come to be called the *ontological proof*, is this: if the idea of God is the idea of a being than which none greater can be conceived, then God's existence is undeniable. Otherwise, the idea of a being than which none greater can be conceived is not the idea of a being than which none greater can be conceived—which is a contradiction. In other words, if it be thought or suggested that God does not exist, then it can be suggested that there is a being greater than God, a being that has all of the same attributes *plus* the attribute of existence. But then *that* being would be the one than which none greater can be conceived; that being would be the one Job has in mind in asking for an explanation for his ill-deserved punishment, and also the same being that the atheist has in mind when he says that God does not exist. This is why the atheist is a fool. Only a fool would say that God, a being that exists, does not exist.

Anselm's argument is clever. It seems to capture the element of certainty that many believers feel when God's existence is questioned. Moreover, the main premise would seem to be true—even to an atheist. Otherwise, if the atheist does not have in mind a being than which none greater can be conceived, then the atheist would not be denying that *God* exists, and would not be disagreeing, for example, with Job or other believers.

Is Anselm's argument valid? Many people have felt that the ontological proof is little more than a verbal trick, a scholastic legerdemain, a mere debator's ploy that has little to do with the great issues of life, death, and eternity generally associated with matters of ultimate concern. And to some extent, these critics are correct. Anselm's proof does not attempt to reconcile God's ways to mankind. Rather, its goals are more modest. Anselm's argument is intended merely to prove that God exists, not that His presence in the midst of apparent injustice is anything less than mysterious. If successful, Anselm would not eliminate the problem of evil, but would effectively do away with the atheists's proposed solution. This, by itself, would be a significant achievement.

Is Anselm's argument successful? Many thinkers, beginning with Anselm's contemporary, the monk Gaunilon, have attempted to reject the ontological proof, although pinpointing the error, if any, is not an easy task. The most celebrated attempt was that of Immanuel Kant, who suggested that *existence*, contrary to the apparent assumption of the proof, is not an attribute, or what he called a "real property." If Kant is correct, then, for example, there is no difference in principle between suggesting that the Brooklyn Bridge spans the East River in New York City, and suggesting, by way of apparently adding an additional piece of information, that the Brooklyn Bridge exists. If the first comment is true, the second goes without saying. This is why the atheist's assertion that God does not exist appears paradoxical. It would be just as paradoxical to refer to the Brooklyn Bridge and say that *it* does not exist.

However, there may be this difference. There was a time when the famous Brooklyn span did not exist, and no doubt, there will come a time when it will no longer exist. Can we say the same of God? Could a being than which none greater can be conceived fail to exist? Perhaps God is a being that exists always and everywhere, a being that exists necessarily. Contemporary defenders of Anselm (see the selection by Norman Malcolm) concede that existence may not be a property, but suggest that "necessary existence" is different. On this view, if it is possible that God exists, then God exists necessarily.

Is it possible that God exists? Those who defend Anselms's argument emphasize that there is no apparent incoherence in the idea of a being than which none greater can be conceived. But the idea of God also includes the idea of a being that is all-good, all-knowing, and all-powerful—a conception that does not seem possible in the presence of apparent evil. Unless there is an independent solution to the problem of evil, Anselm's ontological proof, even in its modern formulation, does not seem to work.

Let us turn to the next major attempt to establish God's existence, the *cosmological approach*. Unlike Anselm's argument which is purely conceptual, or *a priori*, the cosmological argument depends, in each of its three related, but slightly different, formulations, on certain basic facts of the universe. Saint Thomas Aquinas, who developed this approach in the thirteenth century, following Aristotle's earlier analysis of the concept of causality, suggested that the appearance of motion, the existence of the universe, and the apparent fact that things in the universe are contingent require special explanation. For instance, according to Aquinas, when an object changes from a state of rest to a state of motion something else is needed to bring about the change, since the same object cannot move itself. Otherwise, the same object can be at rest and not at rest, which seems impossible. For example, a stone on the side of a hill has the potential of rolling, but will not actually do so unless something else, such as another stone, comes along to give it a push. That stone, too, would not have been moving unless something else had pushed it. But the series of potential movers cannot go back through infinity. Otherwise, nothing moves, which is patently false. Consequently, according to Acquinas, there is a *prime mover:* God.

What exactly is a prime mover? Is it something that starts the series of movers moving, or is it something that has motion to begin with? Aquinas is not clear about this. If it is something that starts the series moving, God would be the first in a series of potential movers. But then, like every other member in the series, God could not move Himself. In this sense, the idea of a prime mover would not help to explain how anything gets started. If it is something that has motion to begin with, the idea of a prime mover would be more successful. But if there is something that has motion to begin with, why must it be God? Why can't the universe itself be the prime mover? Some objects move while others rest, and so on. What need is there for some special entity, unless we assume with Aristotle that the universe itself is naturally in a state of rest? However, since the seventeenth century, largely as a result of the work of Galileo,

Kepler, and Newton, physicists no longer believe that motion requires a special explanation. According to Newtonian mechanics, the natural state of things is inertia—the tendency to remain in the same state, whether it be rest or motion, unless acted upon by an external force. In the absence of additional reasons for abandoning modern physical theory and readopting Aristotelian physics, it is not clear why we should accept Aquinas's argument for the prime mover.

Aquinas's second argument seems more in keeping with contemporary physics. According to this argument, when something occurs, whether it be the change from rest to motion or from motion to rest, something else must bring it about, since nothing is its own cause. Otherwise, the same thing would precede itself, which is impossible. But the series of causes cannot go back through infinity. Otherwise, nothing would occur. Consequently, there is a first cause: God.

But the notion of a *first cause* seems as confusing as the idea of a prime mover. Is a first cause something that is its own cause, or something that is uncaused? If the former, according to this version of the cosmological argument, there is no first cause, since nothing can cause itself. If the latter, the universe itself may be uncaused, unless it be further assumed that *everything* is caused. But then God, too, could not be a first cause.

Can God be an uncaused cause? This brings us to the third version of the cosmological argument, which suggests that God is unique. According to this version, while everything else in the universe is *contingent,* God is *necessary.* The idea is that a contingent thing exists only if something else exists. If everything in nature is contingent, then there is something independent upon which everything else depends. If there is not some such thing, then nothing exists, which is absurd. Consequently, there is an independent, or necessary, being: God.

Is God a necessary being? It would appear so, unless the universe, or nature as a whole, is necessary. How could this be? If every part of the universe is contingent, it seems that the universe as a whole is contingent. But logicians point out that we commit a fallacy of composition when we infer that, since all the parts of a thing have a certain property, the whole thing has that same property. For example, just because every brick in a house weighs less than a pound does not mean that the house itself weighs less than a pound. So, it might be suggested that, while every particular thing in the universe is dependent on some other thing *in the universe,* the universe as a whole is not dependent on anything. Unless there is some other reason to think that the universe is contingent, there is little reason to think that there is something upon which the universe as a whole depends.

The cosmological approach is appealing. When we reflect on the existence of the universe we are tempted to conclude that there must be something that started everything going, an ultimate cause, a being upon which everything depends. Yet, upon further reflection, we find that the arguments for a prime mover and first cause are not valid, while the argument from contingency and necessity seems to commit a logical fallacy. Should we concede that, independent of resolving the problem of evil, there is no God?

There is, however, another feature of the universe that is pervasive and striking. The world seems orderly. The regularities of night and day, of seasonal change, of growth and decay, the delicate intracacies of the smallest plant, the functioning of different organs that comprise a single animal, the ecological interdependence of plant and animal life, suggest patterns that occur not by accident but by design. Aquinas suggested what has come to be called the *teleological argument:* that just as the existence of something designed implies a designer, so the apparent design of nature implies the presence of God.

Aristotle, who influenced Aquinas's thinking, believed that everything has a purpose, a final state that it is trying to achieve. On the Aristotelian view, an acorn falls from a tree because, like all unsupported objects composed largely of an earthy substance, it naturally gravitates downward to where most of the earth in the universe is found. Things apparently want to be with like things. On the earth, the acorn could then germinate and take root. Eventually it might achieve its full potential and become a mature oak tree.

Since the seventeenth century, however, physicists have explained the apparent purposeful behavior of inanimate objects mechanistically. An acorn falls at the same acceleration as other objects of different weight and substance—at thirty-two feet second/per second—whether it wants to or not. Newton proposed a universal law of gravitation—that for every two objects in the universe there is a force proportional directly to the product of their masses and indirectly to the square of the distance between them. If the mechanistic approach to the explanation of inanimate behavior is correct, as scientists nowadays believe, there is no need for special Aristotelian purposes.

What about animal behavior? A cat, unlike an acorn, does not just fall but jumps from a table in order to catch a mouse. Its entire physiology seems especially well-designed for it to behave in this way. Are we back with teleology? Apparently not. The nineteenth-century naturalist, Charles Darwin, explained the apparent design of all living forms as the result of evolution, a process of natural selection that was as mechanistic as those proposed by physicists to explain the behavior of inanimate objects. Unless the physicists and biologists are wrong, there seems little need for Aristotelian teleology to explain either living or nonliving forms.

What about the universe as a whole? The teleologist may use the composition fallacy to his advantage and suggest that, since the whole may have properties not possessed by its parts, nature as a whole, unlike its parts, has design. For example, it may be suggested that the so-called Big Bang, the singular event to which scientists point as constituting the origin of the universe, is itself no accident. The laws of nature, whether physical or biological, reflect an ultimate purpose. The theory of evolution may explain particular structures, but the process of evolution itself seems eminently well designed for bringing about and guaranteeing the survival of the great variety of plant and animal species that we find today. Aside from undermining the teleological argument, the discoveries of Darwin and other scientists attest all the more to the ingenuity and brilliance that lies behind the apparent natural order of things.

Does this version of the argument from design work? The design argument is an argument from analogy. The conclusion is as compelling as is the strength of the analogy. For example, if the world is like a watch, as William Paley suggests (see Paley's "The Argument from Design"), then just as we could infer a watchmaker from the presence of a watch, so we could infer a world-maker from the presence of the world. But what kind of a watch is this, and what kind of a world? Is it a Rolex, the best of all possible watches? If so, then the craftsman that designed it must be of the highest calibre. And so, too, for the world and its craftsman.

Is this the best of all possible worlds? One would assume so, if God is the best of all possible gods, as the tradition suggests. But how are we to tell? Part of the problem is that, unlike a watch, there is only one world and so there is nothing else to compare it to. We can try to imagine other worlds that might be better than this one, just as we can try to imagine a watch better than a Rolex. Our failure in either case, however, may just reflect a lack of imagination rather than proof that there can be nothing better.

Moreover, it seems that we can imagine a better world, a world in which the innocent do not suffer. Otherwise, we would not think that there is anything wrong with the appearance of evil, and we would have no need for a special proof, such as the teleological argument, for God's existence.

In addition, a designer is not always a maker. The individual who designs the Rolex mechanism is not the same craftsperson who assembles the separate pieces. Constructing a watch, like putting together any complex structure, often requires special skills and know-how that the designer does not always possess. Robert Moses, for example, is credited with designing the near labyrinth of roads and parkways that crisscross Long Island, yet he was not an engineer. Like all great builders, Robert Moses had teams of technical experts working out the myriad of details needed to make his tunnels and bridges work properly. Should we infer that God had assistants in putting the world together? But then God Himself was not all-knowing.

In addition, just as Robert Moses did not contribute his own labor to the construction of his many edifices, but depended, as all designers of works on a grand scale depend, on armies of laborers to put his design into practice, so God too would have depended on others to forge his designs into a working model. This suggests that God is not all-powerful.

Moreover, if we consider some of the consequences of Robert Moses' designs—for example, that Long Island roadways are among the most congested in the world—we might realize that although the great New York builder was good, he was not perfect. And if, as Little Bessie points out to her mother,

the wasps catch spiders and cram them down into their nests in the ground—*alive*, mamma!—and there they live and suffer days and days and days, and the hungry little wasps chewing their legs and gnawing into their bellies all the time,

We might also think that although the designer of the world is good, he is not perfect either.

The teleological, cosmological, and ontological arguments are among the best attempts to prove that God exists. Yet the conclusion in each case is less than compelling. Should we agree with the atheist that there is no God, or maintain faith with Job that there is? There is another alternative. The agnostic neither denies that God exists, nor accepts the explanation for evil offered to Little Bessie that "In His wisdom and mercy the Lord sends us these afflictions to discipline us and make us better." (Bertrand Russell expresses the agnostic view.) Rather, the agnostic recognizes not only that the world contains much evil but also that it contains much good as well. If we are not to embrace atheism, nor accept blind fideism, perhaps, with the agnostic, we can reserve final judgment.

J. L. MACKIE
Evil and Omnipotence

. . . The problem of evil, in the sense in which I shall be using the phrase, is a problem only for someone who believes that there is a God who is both omnipotent and wholly good. And it is a logical problem, the problem of clarifying and reconciling a number of beliefs: it is not a scientific problem that might be solved by further observations, or a practical problem that might be solved by a decision or an action. These points are obvious; I mention them only because they are sometimes ignored by theologians, who sometimes parry a statement of the problem with such remarks as "Well, can you solve the problem yourself?" or "This is a mystery which may be revealed to us later" or "Evil is something to be faced and overcome, not to be merely discussed."

In its simplest form the problem is this: God is omnipotent; God is wholly good; and yet evil exists. There seems to be some contradiction between these three propositions, so that if any two of them were true the third would be false. But at the same time all three are essential parts of most theological positions: the theologian, it seems, at once *must* adhere and *cannot consistently* adhere to all three. (The problem does not arise only for theists, but I shall discuss it in the form in which it presents itself for ordinary theism.)

However, the contradiction does not arise immediately; to show it we need some additional premises, or perhaps some quasi-logical rules connecting the terms "good," "evil," and "omnipotent." These additional principles are that good is opposed to evil, in such a way that a good thing always eliminates evil as far as it can, and that there are no limits to what an omnipotent thing can do. From these it follows that a good omnipotent thing eliminates evil completely, and then the propositions that a good omnipotent thing exists, and that evil exists, are incompatible.

A. ADEQUATE SOLUTIONS

Now once the problem is fully stated it is clear that it can be solved, in the sense that the problem will not arise if one gives up at least one of the propositions that constitute it. If you are prepared to say that God is not wholly good, or not quite omnipotent or that evil does not exist, or that good is not opposed to the kind of evil that exists or that there are limits to what an omnipotent thing can do, then the problem of evil will not arise for you.

"Evil and Omnipotence" is reprinted from *Mind* Vol. LXIX (1955), by permission of Oxford University Press. **John L. Mackie,** Australian born, taught for many years at Oxford University. He wrote in the philosophy of science but is most widely remembered for his incisive, skeptical approach to ethics and religious belief.

There are, then, quite a number of adequate solutions of the problem of evil, and some of these have been adopted, or almost adopted, by various thinkers. For example, a few have been prepared to deny God's omnipotence, and rather more have been prepared to keep the term "omnipotence" but severely to restrict its meaning, recording quite a number of things that an omnipotent being cannot do. Some have said that evil is an illusion, perhaps because they held that the whole world of temporal, changing things is an illusion, and that what we call evil belongs only to this world, or perhaps because they held that although temporal things *are* much as we see them, those that we call evil are not really evil. Some have said that what we call evil is merely the privation of good, that evil in a positive sense, evil that would really be opposed to good, does not exist. Many have agreed with Pope that disorder is harmony not understood, and that partial evil is universal good. Whether any of these views is *true* is, of course, another question. But each of them

gives an adequate solution of the problem of evil in the sense that if you accept it this problem does not arise for you, though you may, of course, have *other* problems to face.

But often enough these adequate solutions are only *almost* adopted. The thinkers who restrict God's power, but keep the term "omnipotence," may reasonably be suspected of thinking, in other contexts, that his power is really unlimited. Those who say that evil is an illusion may also be thinking, inconsistently, that this illusion is itself an evil. Those who say that "evil" is merely privation of good may also be thinking, inconsistently, that privation of good is an evil. . . .

In addition, therefore, to adequate solutions, we must recognize unsatisfactory inconsistent solutions, in which there is only a half-hearted or temporary rejection of one of the propositions which together constitute the problem. In these, one of the constituent propositions is explicitly rejected, but it is covertly re-asserted or assumed elsewhere in the system.

B. FALLACIOUS SOLUTIONS

Besides these half-hearted solutions, which explicitly reject but implicitly assert one of the constituent propositions, there are definitely fallacious solutions which explicitly maintain all the constituent propositions, but implicitly reject at least one of them in the course of the argument that explains away the problem of evil.

There are, in fact, many so-called solutions which purport to remove the contradiction without abandoning any of its constituent propositions. These must be fallacious, as we can see from the very statement of the problem, but it is not so easy to see in each case precisely where the fallacy lies. I suggest that in all cases the fallacy has the general form suggested above: in order to solve the problem one (or perhaps more) of its constituent propositions is given up, but in such a way that it appears to have been retained, and can therefore be as-

serted without qualification in other contexts. Sometimes there is a further complication: the supposed solution moves to and fro between, say, two of the constituent propositions, at one point asserting the first of these but covertly abandoning the second, at another point asserting the second but covertly abandoning the first. These fallacious solutions often turn upon some equivocation with the words "good" and "evil," or upon some vagueness about the way in which good and evil are opposed to one another, or about how much is meant by "omnipotence." I propose to examine some of these so-called solutions, and to exhibit their fallacies in detail. Incidentally, I shall also be considering whether an adequate solution could be reached by a minor modification of one or more of the constituent propositions, which would, however, still satisfy all the essential requirements of ordinary theism.

1. "Good cannot exist without evil" or "Evil is necessary as a counterpart to good."

It is sometimes suggested that evil is necessary as a counterpart to good, that if there were no evil there could be no good either, and that this solves the problem of evil. It is true that it points to an answer to the question "Why should there be evil?" But it does so only by qualifying some of the propositions that constitute the problem.

First, it sets a limit to what God can do, saying that God *cannot* create good without simultaneously creating evil, and this means either that God is not omnipotent or that there are *some* limits to what an omnipotent thing can do. It may be replied that these limits are always presupposed, that omnipotence has never meant the power to do what is logically impossible, and on the present view the existence of good without evil would be a logical impossibility. This interpretation of omnipotence may, indeed, be accepted as a modification of our original account which does not reject anything that is essential to theism, and I shall in general assume it in the subsequent discussion. It is, perhaps, the most common theistic view, but I think that some theists at least have maintained that God can do what is logically impossible. Many theists, at any rate, have held that logic itself is created or laid down by God, that logic is the way in which God arbitrarily chooses to think. . . . And *this* account of logic is clearly inconsistent with the view that God is bound by logical necessities—unless it is possible for an omnipotent being to bind himself. . . . This solution of the problem of evil cannot, therefore, be consistently adopted along with the view that logic is itself created by God.

But, secondly, this solution denies that evil is opposed to good in our original sense. If good and evil are counterparts, a good thing will not "eliminate evil as far as it can." Indeed, this view suggests that good and evil are not strictly qualities of things at all. Perhaps the suggestion is that good and evil are related in much the same way as great and small. Cer-

tainly, when the term "great" is used relatively as a condensation of "greater than so-and-so," and "small" is used correspondingly, greatness and smallness are counterparts and cannot exist without each other. But in this sense greatness is not a quality, not an intrinsic feature of anything; and it would be absurd to think of a movement in favor of greatness and against smallness in this sense. Such a movement would be self-defeating, since relative greatness can be promoted only by a simultaneous promotion of relative smallness. I feel sure that no theists would be content to regard God's goodness as analogous to this—as if what he supports were not the *good* but the better, and as if he had the paradoxical aim that all things should be better than other things.

This point is obscured by the fact that "great" and "small" seem to have an absolute as well as a relative sense. I cannot discuss here whether there is absolute magnitude or not, but if there is, there could be an absolute sense for "great," it could mean of at least a certain size, and it would make sense to speak of all things getting bigger, of a universe that was expanding all over, and therefore it would make sense to speak of promoting greatness. But in this sense great and small are not logically necessary counterparts; either quality could exist without the other. There would be no logical impossibility in everything's being small or in everything's being great.

Neither in the absolute nor in the relative sense, then, of "great" and "small" do these terms provide an analogy of the sort that would be needed to support this solution of the problem of evil. In neither case are greatness and smallness *both* necessary counterparts *and* mutually opposed forces or possible objects for support and attack.

It may be replied that good and evil are necessary counterparts in the same way as any quality and its logical opposite: redness can occur, it is suggested, only if non-redness also occurs. But unless evil is merely the privation of good, they are not logical opposites, and some further argument would be needed to show that they are counterparts in the same way as genuine logical opposites. Let us assume that this could be given. There is still doubt of the correctness of the metaphysical principle that a quality must have a real opposite: I suggest that it is not really impossible that everything should be, say, red, that the truth is merely that if everything were red we should not notice redness, and so we should have no word "red"; we observe and give names to qualities only if they have real opposites. If so, the principle that a term must have an opposite would belong only to our language or to our thought, and would not be an ontological principle, and, correspondingly, the rule that good cannot exist without evil would not state a logical necessity of a sort that God would just have to put up with. God might have made everything good, though we should not have noticed it if he had.

But, finally, even if we concede that this is an ontological principle, it will provide a solution for the problem of evil only if one is prepared to say, "Evil exists, but only just enough evil to serve as the counterpart of good." I doubt whether any theist will accept this. After all, the *ontological* requirement that non-redness should occur would be satisfied even if all the universe, except for a minute speck, were red, and, if there were a corresponding requirement for evil as a counterpart to good, a minute dose of evil would presumably do. But theists are not usually willing to say, in all contexts, that all the evil that occurs is a minute and necessary dose.

2. "Evil is necessary as a means to good."

It is sometimes suggested that evil is necessary for good not as a counterpart but as a means. In its simple form this has little plausibility as a solution of the problem of evil, since it obviously implies a severe restriction of God's power. It would be a *causal* law that you cannot have a certain end without a certain means, so that if God has to introduce evil as a means to good, he must be subject to at least some causal laws. This certainly conflicts with what a theist normally means by omnipotence.

This view of God as limited by causal laws also conflicts with the view that causal laws are themselves made by God, which is more widely held than the corresponding view about the laws of logic. This conflict would, indeed, be resolved if it were possible for an omnipotent being to bind himself, and this possibility has still to be considered. Unless a favorable answer can be given to this question, the suggestion that evil is necessary as a means to good solves the problem of evil only by denying one of its constituent propositions either that God is omnipotent or that "omnipotent" means what it says.

3. "The universe is better with some evil in it than it could be if there were no evil."

Much more important is a solution which at first seems to be a mere variant of the previous one, that evil may contribute to the goodness of a whole in which it is found, so that the universe as a whole is better as it is, with some evil in it, than it would be if there were no evil. This solution may be developed in either of two ways. It may be supported by an aesthetic analogy, by the fact that contrasts heighten beauty, that in a musical work, for example, there may occur discords which somehow add to the beauty of the work as a whole. Alternatively, it may be worked out in connection with the notion of progress, that the best possible organization of the universe will not be static, but progressive, that the gradual overcoming of evil by good is really a finer thing than would be the eternal unchallenged supremacy of good.

In either case, this solution usually starts from the assumption that the evil whose existence gives rise to the problem of evil is primarily what is called physical evil, that is to say, pain. In Hume's rather half-hearted presentation of the problem of evil, the evils that he stresses are pain and disease, and those who reply to him argue that the existence of pain and disease makes possible the existence of sympathy, benevolence, heroism, and the gradually successful struggle of doctors and reformers to overcome these evils. In fact, theists often seize the opportunity to accuse those who stress the problem of evil of taking a low, materialistic view of good and evil, equating these with pleasure and pain, and of ignoring the more spiritual goods which can arise in the struggle against evils.

But let us see exactly what is being done here. Let us call pain and misery "first order evil" or "evil (1)." What contrasts with this, namely, pleasure and happiness will be called "first order good" or "good (1)." Distinct from this is "second order good" or "good (2)" which somehow emerges in a complex situation in which evil (1) is a necessary component—logically, not merely causally, necessary. (Exactly *how* it emerges does not matter: in the crudest version of this solution good (2) is simply the heightening of happiness by the contrast with misery; in other versions it includes sympathy with suffering, heroism in facing danger, and the gradual decrease of first order evil and increase of first order good.) It is also being assumed that second order good is more important than first order good or evil, in particular that it more than outweighs the first order evil it involves.

Now this is a particularly subtle attempt to solve the problem of evil. It defends God's goodness and omnipotence on the ground that (on a sufficiently long view) this is the best of all logically possible worlds, because it includes the important second order goods, and yet it admits that real evils, namely first order evils, exist. But does it still hold that good and evil are opposed? Not, clearly, in the sense that we set out originally: good does not tend to eliminate evil in general. Instead, we have a modified, a more complex pattern. First order good (e.g., happiness) *contrasts with* first order evil (e.g., misery): these two are opposed in a fairly mechanical way; some second order goods (e.g., benevolence) try to maximize first order good and minimize first order evil; but God's goodness is not this, it is rather the will to maximize *second* order good. We might, therefore, call God's goodness an example of a third order goodness, or good (3). While this account is different from our original one, it might well be held to be an improvement on it, to give a more

accurate description of the way in which good is opposed to evil, and to be consistent with the essential theist position.

There might, however, be several objections to this solution.

First, some might argue that such qualities as benevolence—and *a fortiori* the third order goodness which promotes benevolence—have a merely derivative value, that they are not higher sorts of good, but merely means to good (1), that is, to happiness, so that it would be absurd for God to keep misery in existence in order to make possible the virtues of benevolence, heroism, etc. The theist who adopts the present solution must, of course, deny this, but he can do so with some plausibility, so I should not press this objection.

Secondly, it follows from this solution that God is not in our sense benevolent or sympathetic: he is not concerned to minimize evil (1), but only to promote good (2); and this might be a disturbing conclusion for some theists.

But, thirdly, the fatal objection is this. Our analysis shows clearly the possibility of the existence of a *second* order evil, an evil (2) contrasting with good (2) as evil (1) contrasts with good (1). This would include malevolence, cruelty, callousness, cowardice, and states in which good (1) is decreasing and evil (1) increasing. And just as good (2) is held to be the important kind of good, the kind that God is concerned to promote, so evil (2) will, by analogy, be the important kind of evil, the kind which God, if he were wholly good and omnipotent, would eliminate. And yet evil (2) plainly exists, and indeed most theists (in other contexts) stress its existence more than that of evil (1). We should, therefore, state the problem of evil in terms of second order evil, and against this form of the problem the present solution is useless.

An attempt might be made to use this solution again, at a higher level, to explain the occurrence of evil (2): indeed the next main solution that we shall examine does just this, with the help of some new notions. Without any fresh notions, such a solution would have little plausibility: for example, we could hardly say that the really important good was a good (3), such as the increase of benevolence in proportion to cruelty, which logically required for its occurrence the occurrence of some second order evil. But even if evil (2) could be explained in this way, it is fairly clear that there would be third order evils contrasting with this third order good: and we should be well on the way to an infinite regress, where the solution of a problem of evil, stated in terms of evil (*n*), indicated the existence of an evil (*n* + 1), and a further problem to be solved.

4. "Evil is due to human freewill."

Perhaps the most important proposed solution of the problem of evil is that evil is not to be ascribed to God at all, but to the independent actions of human beings, supposed to have been endowed by God with freedom of the will. This solution may be combined with the preceding one: first order evil (*e.g.* pain) may be justified as a logically necessary component in second order good (*e.g.* sympathy) while second order evil (*e.g.* cruelty) is not *justified*, but is so ascribed to human beings that God cannot be held responsible for it. This combination evades my third criticism of the preceding solution.

The freewill solution also involves the preceding solution at a higher level. To explain why a wholly good God gave men freewill although it would lead to some important evils, it must be argued that it is better on the whole that men should act freely, and sometimes err, than that they should be innocent automata, acting rightly in a wholly determined way. Freedom, that is to say, is now treated as a third order good, and as being more valuable than second order goods (such as sympathy and heroism) would be if they were deterministically produced, and it is being assumed that second order evils, such as cruelty, are logically necessary accompaniments of freedom, just as pain is a logically necessary pre-condition of sympathy.

I think that this solution is unsatisfactory primarily because of the incoherence of the notion of freedom of the will: but I cannot discuss this topic adequately here, although some of my criticisms will touch upon it.

First I should query the assumption that sec-

ond order evils are logically necessary accompaniments of freedom. I should ask this: if God has made men such that in their free choices they sometimes prefer what is good and sometimes what is evil, why could he not have made men such that they always freely choose the good? If there is no logical impossibility in a man's freely choosing the good on one, or on several occasions, there cannot be a logical impossibility in his freely choosing the good on every occasion. God was not, then, faced with a choice between making innocent automata and making beings who, in acting freely, would sometimes go wrong: there was open to him the obviously better possibility of making beings who would act freely but always go right. Clearly, his failure to avail himself of this possibility is inconsistent with his being both omnipotent and wholly good.

If it is replied that this objection is absurd, that the making of some wrong choices is logically necessary for freedom, it would seem that "freedom" must here mean complete randomness or indeterminacy, including randomness with regard to the alternatives good and evil, in other words that men's choices and consequent actions can be "free" only if they are not determined by their characters. Only on this assumption can God escape the responsibility for men's actions; for if he made them as they are, but did not determine their wrong choices, this can only be because the wrong choices are not determined by men as they are. But then if freedom is randomness, how can it be a characteristic of *will*? And, still more, how can it be the most important good? What value or merit would there be in free choices if these were random actions which were not determined by the nature of the agent?

I conclude that to make this solution plausible two different senses of "freedom" must be confused, one sense which will justify the view that freedom is a third order good, more valuable than other goods would be without it, and another sense, sheer randomness, to prevent us from ascribing to God a decision to make men such that they sometimes go wrong when he might have made them such that they would always freely go right.

This criticism is sufficient to dispose of this solution. But besides this there is a fundamental difficulty in the notion of an omnipotent God creating men with free will, for if men's wills are really free this must mean that even God cannot control them, that is that God is no longer omnipotent. It may be objected that God's gift of freedom to men does not mean that he *cannot* control their wills, but that he always *refrains* from controlling their wills. But why, we may ask, should God refrain from controlling evil wills? Why should he not leave men free to will rightly, but intervene when he sees them beginning to will wrongly? If God could do this, but does not, and if he is wholly good, the only explanation could be that even a wrong free act of will is not really evil, that its freedom is a value which outweighs its wrongness, so that there would be a loss of value if God took away the wrongness and the freedom together. But this is utterly opposed to what theists say about sin in other contexts. The present solution of the problem of evil, then, can be maintained only in the form that God has made men so free that he *cannot* control their wills. . . .

CONCLUSION

Of the proposed solutions of the problem of evil which we have examined, none has stood up to criticism. There may be other solutions which require examination, but this study strongly suggests that there is no valid solution of the problem which does not modify at least one of the constituent propositions in a way which would seriously affect the essential core of the theistic position. . . .

JOHN H. HICK
The Problem of Evil

I. CLARIFICATION OF THE PROBLEM
A. The Problem

To many, the most powerful positive objection to belief in God is the fact of evil. Probably for most agnostics it is the appalling depth and extent of human suffering, more than anything else, that makes the idea of a loving Creator seem so implausible and disposes them toward one or another of the various naturalistic theories of religion.

As a challenge to theism, the problem of evil has traditionally been posed in the form of

John H. Hick, *Philosophy of Religion*, 2/E, © 1973, pgs. 36–43. Reprinted by permission of Prentice-Hall, Inc., Englewood Cliffs, New Jersey. **John Harwood Hick,** born in Edinburgh 1922, served as a Presbyterian minister before he turned to teaching. He is widely known for his writings in the philosophy of religion.

a dilemma: If God is perfectly loving, he must wish to abolish evil; and if he is all-powerful, he must be able to abolish evil. But evil exists; therefore God cannot be both omnipotent and perfectly loving.

B. Untenable ''Solutions''

Certain solutions, which at once suggest themselves, have to be ruled out so far as the Judaic-Christian faith is concerned.

To say, for example (with contemporary Christian Science), that evil is an illusion of the human mind, is impossible within a religion based upon the stark realism of the Bible. Its pages faithfully reflect the characteristic mixture of good and evil in human experience. They record every kind of sorrow and suffering, every mode of man's inhumanity to man and of his painfully insecure existence in the world. There is no attempt to regard evil as anything but dark, menacingly ugly, heart-rending, and crushing. In the Christian scriptures, the climax of this history of evil is the crucifixion of Jesus, which is presented not only as a case of utterly unjust suffering, but as the violent and murderous rejection of God's Messiah. There can be no doubt, then, that for biblical faith, evil is unambiguously evil, and stands in direct opposition to God's will.

Again, to solve the problem of evil by means of the theory (sponsored, for example, by the Boston ''Personalist'' School)[1] of a finite deity who does the best he can with a material, intractable and co-eternal with himself, is to have abandoned the basic premise of Hebrew-Christian monotheism; for the theory amounts to rejecting belief in the infinity and sovereignty of God.

Indeed, any theory which would avoid the problem of the origin of evil by depicting it as an ultimate constituent of the universe, coordinate with good, has been repudiated in advance by the classic Christian teaching, first developed by Augustine, that evil represents the going wrong of something which in itself is good.[2] Augustine holds firmly to the Hebrew-Christian conviction that the universe is *good*—that is to say, it is the creation of a good God for a good purpose. He completely rejects the ancient prejudice, widespread in his day, that matter is evil. There are, according to Augustine, higher and lower, greater and lesser goods in immense abundance and variety; but everything which has being is good in its own way and degree, except in so far as it may have become spoiled or corrupted. Evil—whether it be an evil will, an instance of pain, or some disorder or decay in nature—has not been set there by God, but represents the distortion of something that is inherently valuable. Whatever exists is, as such, and in its proper place, good; evil is essentially parasitic upon good, being disorder and perversion in a fundamentally good creation. This understanding of evil as something negative means that it is not willed and created by God; but it does not mean (as some have supposed) that evil is unreal and can be disregarded. Clearly, the first effect of this doctrine is to accentuate even more the question of the origin of evil.

II. SOLUTION TO THE PROBLEM

Theodicy,[3] as many modern Christian thinkers see it, is a modest enterprise, negative rather than positive in its conclusions. It does not claim to explain, nor to explain away, every instance of evil in human experience, but only to point to certain considerations which prevent the fact of evil (largely incomprehensible though it remains) from constituting a final and insuperable bar to rational belief in God.

In indicating these considerations it will be useful to follow the traditional division of the subject. There is the problem of *moral evil* or wickedness: Why does an all-good and all-powerful God permit this? And there is the problem of the *nonmoral evil* of suffering or pain, both physical and mental: Why has an all-good and all-powerful God created a world in which this occurs?

A. Moral Evil

Christian thought has always considered moral evil in its relation to human freedom and responsibility. To be a person is to be a finite center of freedom, a (relatively) free and self-directing agent responsible for one's own decision. This involves being free to act wrongly as well as to act rightly. The idea of a person who can be infallibly guaranteed always to act rightly is self-contradictory. There can be no guarantee in advance that a genuinely free moral agent will never choose amiss. Consequently, the possibility of wrongdoing or sin is logically inseparable from the creation of finite persons, and to say that God should not have created beings who might sin amounts to saying that he should not have created people.

This thesis has been challenged in some recent philosophical discussions of the problem of evil, in which it is claimed that no contradiction is involved in saying that God might have made people who would be genuinely free and who could yet be guaranteed always to act rightly. A quotation from one of these discussions follows:

> If there is no logical impossibility in a man's freely choosing the good on one, or on several occasions, there cannot be a logical impossibility in his freely choosing the good on every occasion. God was not, then, faced with a choice between making innocent automata and making beings who, in acting freely, would sometimes go wrong: there was open to him the obviously better possibility of making beings who would act freely but always go right. Clearly, his failure to avail himself of this possibility is inconsistent with his being both omnipotent and wholly good.[4]

A reply to this argument is suggested in another recent contribution to the discussion.[5] If by a free action we mean an action which is not externally compelled but which flows from the nature of the agent as he reacts to the circumstances in which he finds himself, there is, indeed, no contradiction between our being free and our actions being "caused" (by our own nature) and therefore being in principle predictable. There is a contradiction, however, in saying that God is the cause of our acting as we do but that we are free beings in relation to God. There is, in other words, a contradiction in saying that God has made us so that we shall of necessity act in a certain way, and that we are genuinely independent persons in relation to him. If all our thoughts and actions are divinely predestined, however free and morally responsible we may seem to be to ourselves, we cannot be free and morally responsible in the sight of God, but must instead be his helpless puppets. Such "freedom" is like that of a patient acting out a series of posthypnotic suggestions: He appears, even to himself, to be free, but his volitions have actually been predetermined by another will, that of the hypnotist, in relation to whom the patient is not a free agent.

A different objector might raise the question of whether or not we deny God's omnipotence if we admit that he is unable to create persons who are free from the risks inherent in personal freedom. The answer that has always been given is that to create such beings is logically impossible. It is no limitation upon God's power that he cannot accomplish the logically impossible, since there is nothing here to accomplish, but only a meaningless conjunction of words[6]—in this case "person who is not a person." God is able to create beings of any and every conceivable kind; but creatures who lack moral freedom, however superior they might be to human beings in other respects, would not be what we mean by persons. They would constitute a different form of life which

God might have brought into existence instead of persons. When we ask why God did not create such beings in place of persons, the traditional answer is that only persons could, in any meaningful sense, become "children of God," capable of entering into a personal relationship with their Creator by a free and uncompelled response to his love.

When we turn from the possibility of moral evil as a correlate of man's personal freedom to its actuality, we face something which must remain inexplicable even when it can be seen to be possible. For we can never provide a complete causal explanation of a free act; if we could, it would not be a free act. The origin of moral evil lies forever concealed within the mystery of human freedom.

The necessary connection between moral freedom and the possibility, now actualized, of sin throws light upon a great deal of the suffering which afflicts mankind. For an enormous amount of human pain arises either from the inhumanity or the culpable incompetence of mankind. This includes such major scourges as poverty, oppression and persecution, war, and all the injustice, indignity, and inequity which occur even in the most advanced societies. These evils are manifestations of human sin. Even disease is fostered to an extent, the limits of which have not yet been determined by psychosomatic medicine, by moral and emotional factors seated both in the individual and in his social environment. To the extent that all of these evils stem from human failures and wrong decisions, their possibility is inherent in the creation of free persons inhabiting a world which presents them with real choices which are followed by real consequences.

B. Physical Evil

We may now turn more directly to the problem of suffering. Even though the major bulk of actual human pain is traceable to man's misused freedom as a sole or part cause, there remain other sources of pain which are entirely independent of the human will, for example, earthquake, hurricane, storm, flood, drought, and blight. In practice, it is often impossible to trace a boundary between the suffering which results from human wickedness and folly and that which falls upon mankind from without. Both kinds of suffering are inextricably mingled together in human experience. For our present purpose, however, it is important to note that the latter category does exist and that it seems to be built into the very structure of our world. In response to it, theodicy, if it is wisely conducted, follows a negative path. It is not possible to show positively that each item of human pain serves the divine purpose of good; but, on the other hand, it does seem possible to show that the divine purpose as it is understood in Judaism and Christianity could not be forwarded in a world which was designed as a permanent hedonistic paradise.

An essential premise of this argument concerns the nature of the divine purpose in creating the world. The skeptic's assumption is that man is to be viewed as a completed creation and that God's purpose in making the world was to provide a suitable dwelling-place for this fully formed creature. Since God is good and loving, the environment which he has created for human life to inhabit is naturally as pleasant and comfortable as possible. The problem is essentially similar to that of a man who builds a cage for some pet animal. Since our world, in fact, contains sources of hardship, inconvenience, and danger of innumerable kinds, the conclusion follows that this world cannot have been created by a perfectly benevolent and all-powerful deity.[7]

Christianity, however, has never supposed that God's purpose in the creation of the world was to construct a paradise whose inhabitants would experience a maximum of pleasure and a minimum of pain. The world is seen, instead, as a place of "soul-making" in which free beings grappling with the tasks and challenges of their existence in a common environment may become "children of God" and "heirs of eternal life." A way of thinking theologically of God's continuing creative purpose for man was suggested by . . . Irenaeus [an early Christian theologian and church father]. Following hints from St. Paul, Irenaeus taught that man has been made as a person in the image of God but has not yet been brought as a free and responsible agent into the finite likeness of God, which is revealed in Christ.[8] Our world, with all its rough edges, is the sphere in which this second and harder stage of the creative process is taking place.

III. RELATED ISSUES
A. Consequences If There Were No Evil

This conception of the world (whether or not set in Irenaeus' theological framework) can be supported by the method of negative theodicy. Suppose, contrary to fact, that this world were a paradise from which all possibility of pain and suffering were excluded. The consequences would be very far-reaching. For example, no one could ever injure anyone else: The murderer's knife would turn to paper or his bullets to thin air; the bank safe, robbed of a million dollars, would miraculously become filled with another million dollars (without this device, on however large a scale, proving inflationary); fraud, deceit, conspiracy, and treason would somehow always leave the fabric of society undamaged. Again, no one would ever be injured by accident: The mountain-climber, steeplejack, or playing child falling from a height would float unharmed to the ground; the reckless driver would never meet with disaster. There would be no need to work, since no harm could result from avoiding work; there would be no call to be concerned for others in time of need or danger, for in such a world there could be no real needs or dangers.

To make possible this continual series of individual adjustments, nature would have to work by "special providences" instead of running according to general laws which men must learn to respect on penalty of pain or death. The laws of nature would have to be extremely flexible: Sometimes gravity would operate, sometimes not; sometimes an object would be hard and solid, sometimes soft. There could be no sciences, for there would be no enduring world structure to investigate. In eliminating the problems and hardships of an objective environment, with its own laws, life would become like a dream in which, delightfully but aimlessly, we would float and drift at ease.

One can at least begin to imagine such a world. It is evident that our present ethical concepts would have no meaning in it. If, for example, the notion of harming someone is an essential element in the concept of a wrong action, in our hedonistic paradise there could be no wrong actions—nor any right actions in distinction from wrong. Courage and fortitude would have no point in an environment in which there is, by definition, no danger or difficulty. Generosity, kindness, love, prudence, unselfishness, and all other ethical notions which presuppose life in a stable environment could not even be formed. Consequently, such a world, however well it might promote pleasure, would be very ill adapted for the development of the moral qualities of human personality. In relation to this purpose it would be the worst of all possible worlds.

It would seem, then, that an environment intended to make possible the growth in free beings of the finest characteristics of personal life must have a good deal in common with our present world. It must operate according to general and dependable laws; and it must involve real dangers, difficulties, problems, obstacles, and possibilities of pain, failure, sorrow, frustration, and defeat. If it did not contain the particular trials and perils which—subtracting man's own very considerable contribution—our world contains, it would have to contain others instead.

To realize this is not, by any means, to be in possession of a detailed theodicy. It is to understand that this world, with all its "heartaches and the thousand natural shocks that flesh is heir to," an environment so manifestly not designed for the maximization of human pleasure and the minimization of human pain, may be rather well adapted to the quite different purpose of "soul-making."[9]

These considerations are related to theism as such. Specifically, Christian theism goes further in the light of the death of Christ, which is seen paradoxically both (as the murder of the divine Son) as the worst thing that has ever happened and (as the occasion of man's salvation) as the best thing that has ever happened. As the supreme evil turned to supreme good, it provides the paradigm for the distinctively Christian reaction to evil. Viewed from the standpoint of Christian faith, evils do not cease to be evils; and certainly, in view of Christ's healing work, they cannot be said to have been sent by God. Yet it has been the persistent claim of those seriously and wholeheartedly committed to Christian discipleship that tragedy, though truly tragic, may nevertheless be turned, through a man's reaction to it, from a cause of despair and alienation from God to a stage in the fulfillment of God's loving purpose for that individual. As the greatest of all evils, the crucifixion of Christ, was made the occasion of man's redemption, so good can be won from other evils. As Jesus saw his execution by the Romans as an experience which God desired him to accept, an experience which was to be brought within the sphere of the divine purpose and made to serve the divine ends, so the Christian response to calamity is to accept the adversities, pains, and afflictions which life brings, in order that they can be turned to a positive spiritual use.[10]

B. Life After Death

At this point, theodicy points forward in two ways to the subject of life after death.

First, although there are many striking instances of good being triumphantly brought out of evil through a man's or a woman's reaction to it, there are many other cases in which the opposite has happened. Sometimes obstacles breed strength of character, dangers evoke courage and unselfishness, and calamities produce patience and moral steadfastness. But sometimes they lead, instead, to resentment, fear, grasping selfishness, and disintegration of character. Therefore, it would seem that any divine purpose of soul-making which is at work in earthly history must continue beyond this life if it is ever to achieve more than a very partial and fragmentary success.

Second, if we ask whether the business of soul-making is worth all the toil and sorrow of human life, the Christian answer must be in terms of a future good which is great enough to justify all that has happened on the way to it.

NOTES

1. Edgar Brightman's *A Philosophy of Religion* (Englewood Cliffs, N.J.: Prentice-Hall, Inc., 1940), chaps. 8–10, is a classic exposition of one form of this view.
2. See Augustine's *Confessions*, Book VII, chap. 12; *City of God*, Book XII, chap. 3; *Enchiridion*, chap. 4.
3. The word "theodicy," from the Greek *theos* (God) and *dike* (righteous), means the justification of God's goodness in face of the fact of evil.
4. J. L. Mackie, "Evil and Omnipotence," *Mind* (April 1955), p. 209 [or p. 462 in this volume]. A similar point is made by Antony Flew in "Divine Omnipotence and Human Freedom," *New Essays in Philosophical Theology*. An important critical comment on these arguments is offered by Ninian Smart in "Omnipotence, Evil and Supermen," *Philosophy* (April, 1961), with replies by Flew (January, 1962) and Mackie (April, 1962).
5. Flew, in *New Essays in Philosophical Theology*.
6. As Aquinas said, ". . . nothing that implies a contradiction falls under the scope of God's omnipotence." *Summa Theologica*, part 1, question 25, article 4.
7. This is the nature of David Hume's argument in his discussion of the problem of evil in his *Dialogues*, part 11.
8. See Irenaeus' *Against Heresies*, book IV, chaps. 37 and 38.
9. This brief discussion has been confined to the problem of human suffering. The large and intractable problem

of animal pain is not taken up here. For a discussion of it, see, for example, Nels Ferre, *Evil and the Christian Faith* (New York: Harper & Row, Publishers, Inc., 1947), chap. 7; and Austin Farrer, *Love Almighty and Ills Unlimited (New York: Doubleday & Company, Inc., 1961), chap. 5.*

10. This conception of providence is stated more fully in John Hick, *Faith and Knowledge* (Ithaca: Cornell University Press, 1957), chap. 7, from which some sentences are incorporated in this paragraph.

YAAKOV D. HOMNICK
On God and the Holocaust

The following exchange between Yaakov Homnick and Sidney Hook was provoked by a story Tom Bethell wrote for the American Spectator *(May 1987). Called "A Stroll with Sidney Hook," the story recounted a conversation between Bethell and Hook in which Hook sketches his ideas about religious faith. "At the age of twelve," Hook told Bethell, "I discovered the problem of evil. How can you reconcile God's goodness and infinite power with the suffering of the innocent and the success of the infamous?" Homnick, an Orthodox rabbi, wrote Bethell vigorously contesting Hook's ideas.*

I feel compelled to share with you some of the agitation that was occasioned in me by the report of your stroll with the redoubtable Mr. Hook. As an almost-twenty-nine-year-old whippersnapper, I am hardly in a position to snap a whip at so distinguished a gentleman. Still, as a "plain Jew" of the classical variety, I sense an obligation to respond to the profile of Mr. Hook's apostasy as transcribed by yourself. . . .

. . . I must begin by saying that his remarks left me gaping, utterly amazed and incredulous. Do you mean to say that this eighty-five-year-old laureate, this paragon of reason, this beacon of enlightenment, this symbol of academic courage and integrity, is still basing his lack of faith on the questions he raised at the age of twelve, and that, moreover, are raised by most intelligent children by that age, if not earlier? I feel cheated, like someone who opens his mailorder package and sees that all that glitters in the catalog is not gold up close. Come on. Is this really it? Isn't this an insult to the meanest intelligence?

He talks as if these quibbles are a credit to his penetrating intellect. Bah, humbug! Every line of the Torah, and the Talmud that explicates it, is replete with references to these subjects. We have a massive literature of commentary from the best Jewish minds over three thousand years, incorporating an almost infinite variety of insights into these questions. And Hook, the great philosopher, has the supreme effrontery to build an entire life on his prepubescent grumblings and to write off the magnificent history of his downtrodden, but proud and studious, people. Humph!

"On God and the Holocaust" is reprinted from *Free Inquiry* Vol. 7, No. 4 (Fall 1987), by permission of *Free Inquiry*. **Sidney Hook** (1902–1989), student and colleague of John Dewey (1859–1952), was an advocate of pragmatism throughout his prolific career. **Yaakov Homnick** is an Orthodox rabbi.

Now I admit to being on a fairly high level of Talmudic scholarship, having elected at the age of eighteen to make this my life's work; but my specialties are law and theology, and my grasp of Jewish philosophy is more casual. Still, his points seem so feeble, the potential refutations so numerous and elementary, that I find his presentation inconsistent with his wisdom and openness in other areas of thought, pointing up the existence of an irrational segment of his personality that "just doesn't want to be bothered."

Let's take his charming dialogue with his father (hardly an educated man, and a poor spokesman, indeed, for the faith of his ancestors for millennia). Sid: How do we know there's a G-d? Pop: Who else made the world? Sid: But who made G-d? Pop: You can't ask that. Sid: So then don't ask me who made the world. Here his father, in his pristine simplicity, is absolutely correct by all the standards of recta ratio. The question "who made x?" is only valid if we must assume that x was made. We are entitled to assume that the world was made, since its components are physical, and all manifestations of physical existence that we observe share the characteristic of being made by, or growing from, something. However, we cannot observe G-d, nor do we have any grounds to attribute to Him physical properties or phenomena, and consequently are not entitled to ask who made Him.

Or let's even follow Sid's lead and grant the validity of his question. So what would he have us do? He would like for us to agree that G-d must also be a product and not only a source. So what? Aren't we still dependent on His constant beneficence? Don't we still owe Him our very existence? Doesn't this alone entitle Him to dictate terms for our dwelling on His turf? (Of course, the idea of G-d not being completely autonomous is not acceptable to the Torah; my point is that we can even concede this point and still leave Him with the authority, not to mention the power, to charge a bit of rent for His grace.)

But, of course, what Sid is actually arguing is that since we are forced, ultimately, to concede that there is some force that can exist without being made, why postulate a G-d outside this world instead of assuming that it is the world itself that has this property? Which brings us full circle, because, given a choice between assigning metaphysical powers to the physical world or to a power beyond it, we ought certainly to choose the latter, even if it involves stipulating an existence that we cannot perceive (particularly since our inability to capture a metaphysical entity in the lens of our physical vision is no reflection on its existence at all; just as we have no right to assume that it needs to be made, we cannot demand that it be visible on the physical level that it intrinsically transcends). Furthermore, it is, in reality, impossible to attribute extra-physical qualities to the physical world, as has been noted by the earliest philosophers.

So tell me: Where is this abstruse point that I must be missing hiding?

Hook's next point is that he fails to see enough justice in the world. Before responding to this, it must be pointed out that this argument does not challenge the existence of G-d, because who said G-d must be just? The only way for us to know that G-d is just is through observation or through revelation, i.e., He himself tells us so. Thus, Hook is already in our ballpark when he puts this question. In essence, he is saying: Assuming that G-d exists, that He made the world for a purpose, that He created Man for the task of serving Him and bringing about the purpose of creation, that He did not rely on Man's ability to surmise exactly the nature and guidelines of the purpose and therefore revealed himself to a nation of millions at Sinai, that in the course of this revelation, He explained that kindness and justice were His ultimate goals, then where is the justice? So he is admitting that G-d created the world, granting His right to make demands upon our lives, and just doubting that there was a revelation, or that it still obtains, since justice is not sufficiently evident in Creation.

Once he has painted himself into that corner, he is left with little room to maneuver. First of all, his view of justice is subjective. Remember, the likelihood of three million people in a desert faking revelation is pathetically slim. The likelihood of a stubborn, independent bunch like that being conned is close to nil. There are fake revelations in other cultures, but never with too many real eyewitnesses. So here we have three million men, women, and children who have undergone indescribable hardships and tribulations to merit being the direct recipients of G-d's Word, marching out of the desert and establishing a society marked by standards of charity and justice never dreamed of before. And someone who hasn't really mastered the details of their history and teachings feels entitled, on the basis of a subjective sense of injustice in Creation, to reject all their noble systems of thought and life. Remarkable.

And what is this injustice that he perceives? That a man can live a life of iniquity without ever receiving outstanding punishment. So what? First of all, the Torah recognizes death itself as an unfortunate consequence of man's own actions, and final redemption must bring about its complete elimination (but, meanwhile, everyone dies, so the truly evil man is not distinguished by this punishment). Second, most evil people are really quite miserable, particularly as they get on in years. Their punishment is no less devastating for being subtle and subliminal. Often, their frustrations are compounded by the fact that they must suffer in private, without receiving sympathy and commiseration. Third, it is a basic principle of the Torah that, until the world is elevated through redemption, the payment of reward and punishment is mostly carried out in a world beyond our own. The theological foundation for this is twofold—the purification or corruption of the spirit must be rewarded in a spiritual form, and the system of free choice may not be knocked out of whack by making the cause-and-effect relationship between physical actions and metaphysical consequences too readily discernible. Fourth, it's not even true. Despite everything, most evil men do not die either naturally or easily (at least, not obviously evil men). Nor have evil societies historically prospered for extended periods.

Actually, just to show you how radically removed is the Jewish perspective from Hook's, I would point out that I have always been surprised by just how much justice G-d is able to get away with showing this world without tipping His hand and eliminating free choice. The Jews have got their land back after two thousand years (an event for which there is nothing remotely resembling a historical precedent), and where are the Greeks and Romans who drove them away back then? Where is Babylon? Persia? Fourteen ninety-two was the time of the Spanish Inquisition; by 1588 the Spanish Armada was defeated. And how long did Britain last as a world power once they began pushing the Jews around? Where are the Eastern European countries who ghettoized the Jews for centuries if not enclosed in the most extensive and restrictive ghetto system of history? So where's the problem exactly? Because there are a few prosperous Germans still around? Because a man like Mengele lived forty years like a hunted animal instead of being strung up publicly? Do you want G-d to appear in public on a regular basis and explain all the minutiae of His operation? Should He send out little bulletins explaining why it was more appropriate to make a public example of one evil-doer rather than of another? I, for one, think that it is a mind-boggling testimony to Man's capacity for conceit and self-deceit that there is anyone who still has the nerve to deny Him or His justice.

Yes, without a doubt, the guidance of history by G-d is perceptible even to our limited gaze. The sense of justice, of balance and order, is palpable—and should be doubly so to someone who has lived eighty-five years, particularly these most eventful ones, replete with poetic justice. Especially is the Holocaust a proof of G-d's justice, coming as the climax of a century in which the vast majority of Jews, after thousands of years of loyalty in exile, decided to cast off the yoke of the Torah. But you wouldn't expect Mr. Hook to see that, would you?

I believe these answers to be adequate even without recourse to the Talmudic approach, but I include it here because it does more than deflect criticism; it argues that the dictates of true justice and kindness require that some evil men should have pleasant deaths while some good men should experience difficult ones, because this enables the individual to pass on to his just deserts with a clean slate, as it were. The wicked person is paid off here with a few crumbs for his rare moments of goodness, then he passes on to an unmitigated Hell or an everlasting Limbo. The righteous one, cleansed by physical suffering from the taint of his infrequent infractions, proceeds on to eternal ecstasy.

Lastly, Hook decries what he sees to be pointless suffering. Now, anyone who has lived a little bit and opened his eyes occasionally in the process knows that suffering, in general, is at least as beneficial in the context of our physical existence as is pleasure. It is only through pain and disappointment that we learn the value of things, that we come to recognize our obligations and limitations, and that we develop the fortitude to lead successful and productive lives. Let us take the case of Hook's mother, who lost her two-year-old child through an accident (which, incidentally, reads like a heavy indictment against her supervision). The wisdom, maturity, sensitivity, and, yes, atonement that she and her husband derived (or could have; people miss opportunities, too) from that incident we will assume to be substantial. Now the question arises: Is it just to make the child suffer for the benefit of the parents? Why not, if the child is viewed as an extension of the parents and its whole existence is for their benefit (at least, until he's old enough to call his own shots)?

But even without focusing on the immediate good that suffering can bring, the rationale for the presence of tremendous pain in the world is obvious, inescapably so. First of all, there is a need to provide a scope. Remember, G-d is not playing games here. There are high stakes involved. Good must triumph, must be shown to be superior. By following His commands we bring life. By sinning we bring death and destruction. When we heed His Word, we are bringing the entire world to its realization and

fruition. By ignoring or violating the Word, we undo all His handiwork, we undermine all His plans. BIG things happen when we act. In order to appreciate that, we must be shown a microcosm of the vastness of His power. We must be able to reach magnificent heights of pleasure and frightful depths of pain just to achieve a perspective of the importance, the significance, and the meaningfulness of His enterprise. So there must be suffering, often great suffering, to show the scale of the consequences of our sojourns here.

Then, there must be suffering for balance. It would not be possible to offer Man free choice in a world obviously dominated by good. Evil must be represented, often wreaking great havoc but never quite achieving the ability to either destroy the entire world or corrupt it. There must be destruction so that we can learn to prevent it, to limit it, to gear our lives in a way that will eventually vanquish it completely. We must say, as Hook does, that it would be ideal for no innocent to ever suffer, and we must then say to ourselves that it is in our power to assure that ideal, ultimately, by being sure that we never harm an innocent, that we choose good over evil at every juncture.

My, my, how I've rattled on and on, without even scratching the surface. Sure these are basic areas of human experience, and understanding them (as far as the human mind is capable of doing so) is essential if we are to live, and serve, with intelligence. But methinks that the proper approach here is to examine the broader propositions of balancing the goal of supreme and perfect justice with the prerequisite free choice that is charged with bringing this about. The question that we should be asking is: How else could it possibly be managed? How could someone have free will in a world where no undeserving person ever suffered or prospered? It's truly ridiculous to suggest that a world could feasibly be run in the manner outlined by Mr. Hook and still achieve a fraction of these goals.

Personally, I always welcome discussion of these issues. It is here, more than anywhere, that the triumph of religion over secularism becomes assured. It is the innate sense that suffering cannot be random, in contradiction to the well-organized phenomena of the world, that nudges people toward religion. They want to be sure that the message of their suffering will not be lost on them.

Enough said. It is pitiful and pitiable that an eighty-five-year-old man has rejected the heritage of millennia of intellectual and virtuous forebears because of the questions of a twelve-year-old. As I have often argued, this is a far greater tragedy than all the physically maimed children in the world. As the old Negro College Fund posters so poignantly proclaimed, a mind is a terrible thing to waste.

Lord, says Sidney Hook, You didn't give me enough evidence. So sad, really, that he had to grow up in the religiously impoverished country that was turn-of-the-century America. Grotesque, even, that he should still be wallowing in the mire of secular confusion and directionlessness, while young punks like me have it all handed to us on a platter in the spectacularly well-developed Yeshiva system of today.

I must close by saying ruefully of Sidney what he said about his own father, "If only he had my opportunities. . . ."

SIDNEY HOOK

I asked Paul Kurtz to solicit Rabbi Homnick's permission to reproduce his letter to Tom Bethell for several reasons. First, to give evidence of the absence of discrimination on the part of secular humanists toward obscurantism of any religious variety. In the past some readers may have felt that our criticism was focused too heavily on Christian fundamentalists. Here, we have a specimen of Jewish fundamentalist faith. More important, however, it raises a question about the reasons for the surprising revival of fundamentalist religion in our time. Even those of us who cannot give credence to the supernaturalist dogmas of the religionists of our time have been prepared to grant that the religious revival has been a response to the public and private decline of morality, to the corruption, systematic lying, hypocrisy, and gratuitous cruelties of our time. Although we were never persuaded that the practice of morality could be sustained by the inculcation of religious faith, we have taken for granted that we share a basic agreement with religious fundamentalists about what is good and bad, right and wrong, in the human community.

I have now come to the conclusion that those who, like Rabbi Homnick, believe that every word of the Bible is inspired, that every event inspired or approved by Jehovah is morally good, cannot really share with us a common universe of moral discourse, despite appearances to the contrary. Although I have long suspected this in my past exchanges with Christian fundamentalists, it has become a conviction in consequence of Rabbi Homnick's arguments.

Readers should be told that Mr. Tom Bethell is an Orthodox Catholic layman and that his account of his stroll with me, published in *The American Spectator*, was an interview written by him in a light vein and with a gentle kindness to me. What he reported was my answer to his question: "At what age did you lose the religious faith in which you had been nurtured?" The first question, as to why the world needed a creator instead of being taken as given—which almost every child asks—was not as important to me as were the questions about those biblical incidents that fell short of a boyish sense of fairness, justice, and even honesty. Although Rabbi Homnick makes heavy weather about my obtuseness in not recognizing the necessity of seeing why the world has to have a creator who himself is not created, he is blissfully unaware that every sentence of his reply to my childish question begs the issue. Because the world has components, he assumes that "they must have the characteristic of being made by, or growing from, something"—which is precisely what is being questioned. Nor is it clear that "being made by" and "growing from" are synonymous, or that being made by something (say, rain by clouds, wind, and a drop in temperature) involves being made by *someone* (the airman who seeds the clouds), and that the someone is God. One could say, following this logic, that because something has moved, a person has moved it.

Closing in for the kill, the rabbi is filled with a spirit of magnanimity. Granting the validity of the child's question, Homnick writes, "He would like for us to agree that God must also be a product and not only a source. So what? Aren't we still dependent on his constant beneficence? Don't we still owe him our very existence?" But I am confident the child he is instructing would have retorted: "Hold on! Where is the evidence that whoever created God—if He exists—created me? And where is the evidence of his beneficence?"

But, as I recall his experience, what troubled the child more were the incidents he could not morally accept—even before the larger problem of the existence of evil blotted out any serious notion that the director of human destiny was both all powerful and all good. Our doubts as children really arose originally as much out of a desire to be mischievous and to tease the half-illiterate pedagogue who taught us the Bible as from moral soul-searching. We asked how God could approve of Jacob stealing Esau's blessing, why God hardened Pharaoh's heart when Moses asked him to let the Israelites go and then punished him for acting on the judgment of that hardened heart. And, although we didn't understand too well what was involved in the story of Dinah, Jacob's daughter, we felt, despite the story fobbed off on us by our teacher, that Jacob's sons were thoroughly dishonorable, killing people rendered helpless by circumcision.

All apologists, whether Christian or Jewish, for the divine inspiration of the Bible end up justifying these and all other actions that in or-

dinary moral discourse we should regard as wicked or evil. This should be evidence enough that, in our discussions with them, we are not using terms like *good* and *bad, right* and *wrong* in the same sense.

The same conclusion is suggested when religious fundamentalists try to explain away the problem of evil. They either end up by denying that what we in an ordinary moral context regard as evil is really evil, or they try to interpret it, despite the absence of any evidence, as a necessary part of a greater good. Evil in a world controlled by a loving God either does not exist or is a blessing in the disguise of apparent evil.

What is remarkable about Rabbi Homnick's contribution is the extent to which he is prepared to go to regard as an act of justice an event that in its moral awfulness has been considered unprecedented, at least in scale, in human history. I refer to the holocaust of six million Jews by Hitler and his followers. Accustomed as I am to reading the tortured exegeses of religious fundamentalists trying to square the revelations of the Bible with common sense, reason, and the vestiges of a common universe of moral discourse, I could hardly believe that I was seeing the words correctly:

Especially is the Holocaust a proof of God's justice, coming as the climax of a century in which the vast majority of Jews, after thousands of years of loyalty in exile, decided to cast off the yoke of the Torah.

The Holocaust—an act of a just God, an act of justice? Rabbi Homnick cannot mean by "just" or "justice" what any moral person means. He cannot be unaware that the vast majority of the Jewish victims of the Holocaust were as Orthodox as he is and were still living under "the yoke of the Torah" in their settlements. And even if they constituted only a minority of world Jewry, where is the justice in their punishment or in that of their wives and children? And what a punishment!

The enormity of Rabbi Homnick's sentiment is enhanced by the fact that it is expressed to a believing Christian who, if he accepted God's revelations in the way Rabbi Homnick does, might well have retorted that the fate of the Jews was brought on themselves by their rejection of the final revelation of Christ. This, in effect, was the belief of Edith Stein, a Jewish convert to Catholicism who went to her death at the hands of the Nazis convinced that rejection of Christianity by the Jews was the ultimate cause of their fate. But regardless of her religion, Edith Stein could not believe—nor could any moral person—that the Holocaust was an act of justice. It seems more the act of a satanic Creator than a divine one.

The Holocaust, in its unextenuated horror, is a challenge to the religious faith of all persons, and especially to the faith of religious Jews. I cannot believe that there are many—or any—who, on reflection, are prepared to regard it as an act of justice. If there are, then they are also beyond the reach of the considerations of reason and compassion that move human beings who do not live in the light of revelation. Of course, those who do not accept revelation are, and can be, guilty of lapses of morality. But if they forgo the belief in absurdity, they are less likely to be blind to moral atrocity. And that seems the tragic end to which the absurdities of religious fundamentalism can lead—the acceptance of moral atrocity as integral to the cosmic scene.

I cannot believe that the revival of religious fundamentalism is inspired by a desire to strengthen moral values and principles as we normally understand them. For it can be established that acceptance of the divine inspiration, and therefore justification, of biblical teaching is incompatible with these values and principles. Of course, not all religions or all persons who consider themselves religious accept the fundamentalist creed. They select those teachings that are in accord with standards of good and evil that are autonomous of the Bible. It is these standards that define a common universe of moral discourse.

WILLIAM JAMES
from *The Varieties of Religious Experience*

CONCLUSIONS

The material of our study of human nature is now spread before us; and in this parting hour, set free from the duty of description, we can draw our theoretical and practical conclusions.

In my first lecture, defending the empirical method, I foretold that whatever conclusions we might come to could be reached by spiritual judgments only, appreciations of the signifi-

Reprinted from "Conclusions," *The Varieties of Religious Experience* (New York: The Modern Library-Random House, 1936). **William James** (1842–1910), a luminary in the development of American pragmatism, respected human experience, including religious experience, as an ultimate source of knowledge.

cance for life of religion, taken "on the whole." Our conclusions cannot be as sharp as dogmatic conclusions would be, but I will formulate them, when the time comes, as sharply as I can.

Summing up in the broadest possible way the characteristics of the religious life, as we have found them, it includes the following beliefs:—

1. That the visible world is part of a more spiritual universe from which it draws its chief significance;
2. That union or harmonious relation with that higher universe is our true end;
3. That prayer or inner communion with the spirit thereof—be that spirit "God" or "law"—is a process wherein work is really done, and spiritual energy flows in and produces effects, psychological or material, within the phenomenal world.

Religion includes also the following psychological characteristics:—

4. A new zest which adds itself like a gift to life, and takes the form either of lyrical enchantment or of appeal to earnestness and heroism.
5. An assurance of safety and a temper of peace, and, in relation to others, a preponderance of loving affections.

In illustrating these characteristics by documents, we have been literally bathed in sentiment. In re-reading my manuscript, I am almost appalled at the amount of emotionality which I find in it. After so much of this, we can afford to be dryer and less sympathetic in the rest of the work that lies before us.

The sentimentality of many of my documents is a consequence of the fact that I sought them among the extravagances of the subject. If any of you are enemies of what our ancestors used to brand as enthusiasm, and are, nevertheless, still listening to me now, you have probably felt my selection to have been sometimes almost perverse, and have wished I might have stuck to soberer examples. I reply that I took these extremer examples as yielding the profounder information. To learn the secrets of any science, we go to expert specialists, even though they may be eccentric persons, and not to commonplace pupils. We combine what they tell us with the rest of our wisdom, and form our final judgment independently. Even so with religion. We who have pursued such radical expressions of it may now be sure that we know its secrets as authentically as anyone can know them who learns them from another; and we have next to answer, each of us for himself, the practical question: what are the dangers in this element of life? and in what proportion may it need to be restrained by other elements, to give the proper balance?

But this question suggests another one which I will answer immediately and get it out of the way, for it has more than once already vexed us. Ought it to be assumed that in all men the mixture of religion with other elements should be identical? Ought it, indeed, to be assumed that the lives of all men should show identical religious elements? In other words, is the existence of so many religious types and sects and creeds regrettable?

To these questions I answer "No" emphatically. And my reason is that I do not see how it is possible that creatures in such different positions and with such different powers as human individuals are, should have exactly the same functions and the same duties. No two of us have identical difficulties, nor should we be expected to work out identical solutions. Each, from his peculiar angle of observation, takes in a certain sphere of fact and trouble, which each must deal with in a unique manner. One of us must soften himself, another must harden himself; one must yield a point, another must stand firm—in order the better to defend the position assigned him. If an Emerson were forced to be a Wesley, or a Moody forced to be a Whitman, the total human consciousness of the divine would suffer. The divine can mean no single quality, it must mean a group of qualities, by being champions of which in alternation, different men may all find worthy missions. Each attitude being a syllable in human nature's total message, it takes the whole of us to spell the meaning out completely. So a "god of battles" must be allowed to be the god for one kind of person, a god of peace and heaven and home, the god for another. We must frankly recognize the fact that we live in partial systems, and that parts are not interchangeable in the spiritual life. If we are peevish and jealous, destruction of the self must be an element of our religion; why need it be one if we are good and sympathetic from the outset? If we are sick souls, we require a religion of deliverance; but why think so much of deliverance, if we are healthy-minded?[1] Unquestionably, some men have the completer experience and the higher vocation, here just as in the social world; but for each man to stay in his own experience, whate'er it be, and for others to tolerate him there, is surely best.

But, you may now ask, would not this one-sidedness be cured if we should all espouse the science of religions as our own religion? In answering this question I must open again the general relations of the theoretic to the active life.

Knowledge about a thing is not the thing itself. You remember what Al-Ghazzali told us in the Lecture on Mysticism—that to understand the causes of drunkenness, as a physician understands them, is not to be drunk. A science might come to understand everything about the causes and elements of religion, and might even decide which elements were qualified, by their general harmony with other branches of knowledge, to be considered true; and yet the best man at this science might be the man who found it hardest to be personally devout. *Tout savoir c'est tout pardonner.* The name of Renan would doubtless occur to many persons as an example of the way in which breadth of knowledge may make one only a dilettante in possibilities, and blunt the acuteness of one's living faith. If religion be a function by which either God's cause or man's cause is to be really ad-

vanced, then he who lives the life of it, however narrowly, is a better servant than he who merely knows about it, however much. Knowledge about life is one thing; effective occupation of a place in life, with its dynamic currents passing through your being, is another.

For this reason, the science of religions may not be an equivalent for living religion; and if we turn to the inner difficulties of such a science, we see that a point comes when she must drop the purely theoretic attitude, and either let her knots remain uncut, or have them cut by active faith. To see this, suppose that we have our science of religions constituted as a matter of fact. Suppose that she has assimilated all the necessary historical material and distilled out of it as its essence the same conclusions which I myself a few moments ago pronounced. Suppose that she agrees that religion, wherever it is an active thing, involves a belief in ideal presences, and a belief that in our prayerful communion with them, work is done, and something real comes to pass. She has now to exert her critical activity, and to decide how far, in the light of other sciences and in that of general philosophy, such beliefs can be considered *true*.

Dogmatically to decide this is an impossible task. Not only are the other sciences and the philosophy still far from being completed, but in their present state we find them full of conflicts. The sciences of nature know nothing of spiritual presences, and on the whole hold no practical commerce whatever with the idealistic conceptions towards which general philosophy inclines. The scientist, so-called, is, during his scientific hours at least, so materialistic that one may well say that on the whole the influence of science goes against the notion that religion should be recognized at all. And this antipathy to religion finds an echo within the very science of religions itself. The cultivator of this science has to become acquainted with so many groveling and horrible superstitions that a presumption easily arises in his mind that any belief that is religious probably is false. In the "prayerful communion" of savages with such mumbo-jumbos of deities as they acknowledge, it is hard for us to see what genuine spiritual work—even though it were work relative only to their dark savage obligations—can possibly be done.

The consequence is that the conclusions of the science of religions are as likely to be adverse as they are to be favorable to the claim that the essence of religion is true. There is a notion in the air about us that religion is probably only an anachronism, a case of "survival," an atavistic relapse into a mode of thought which humanity in its more enlightened examples has outgrown; and this notion our religious anthropologists at present do little to counteract.

This view is so widespread at the present day that I must consider it with some explicitness before I pass to my own conclusions. Let me call it the "Survival theory," for brevity's sake.

The pivot round which the religious life, as we have traced it, revolves, is the interest of the individual in his private personal destiny. Religion, in short, is a monumental chapter in the history of human egotism. The gods believed in—whether by crude savages or by men disciplined intellectually agree with each other in recognizing personal calls. Religious thought is carried on in terms of personality, this being, in the world of religion, the one fundamental fact. To-day, quite as much as at any previous age, the religious individual tells you that the divine meets him on the basis of his personal concerns.

Science, on the other hand, has ended by utterly repudiating the personal point of view. She catalogues her elements and records her laws indifferent as to what purpose may be shown forth by them, and constructs her theories quite careless of their bearing on human anxieties and fates. Though the scientist may individually nourish a religion, and be a theist in his irresponsible hours, the days are over when it could be said that for Science herself the heavens declare the glory of God and the firmament showeth his handiwork. Our solar system, with its harmonies, is seen now as but one passing case of a certain sort of moving equilibrium in the heavens, realized by a local accident in an appalling wilderness of worlds where no life

can exist. In a span of time which as a cosmic interval will count but as an hour, it will have ceased to be. The Darwinian notion of chance production, and subsequent destruction, speedy or deferred, applies to the largest as well as to the smallest facts. It is impossible, in the present temper of the scientific imagination, to find in the driftings of the cosmic atoms, whether they work on the universal or on the particular scale, anything but a kind of aimless weather, doing and undoing, achieving no proper history, and leaving no result. Nature has no one distinguishable ultimate tendency with which it is possible to feel a sympathy. In the vast rhythm of her processes, as the scientific mind now follows them, she appears to cancel herself. The books of natural theology which satisfied the intellects of our grandfathers seem to us quite grotesque,[2] representing, as they did, a God who conformed the largest things of nature to the paltriest of our private wants. The God whom science recognizes must be a God of universal laws exclusively, a God who does a wholesale, not a retail business. He cannot accommodate his processes to the convenience of individuals. The bubbles on the foam which coats a stormy sea are floating episodes, made and unmade by the forces of the wind and water. Our private selves are like those bubbles—epiphenomena, as Clifford, I believe, ingeniously called them; their destinies weigh nothing and determine nothing in the world's irremediable currents of events.

You see how natural it is, from this point of view, to treat religion as a mere survival, for religion does in fact perpetuate the traditions of the most primeval thought. To coerce the spiritual powers, or to square them and get them on our side, was, during enormous tracts of time, the one great object in our dealings with the natural world. For our ancestors, dreams, hallucinations, revelations, and cock-and-bull stories were inextricably mixed with facts. Up to a comparatively recent date such distinctions as those between what has been verified and what is only conjectured, between the impersonal and the personal aspects of existence, were hardly suspected or conceived. Whatever you imagined in a lively manner, whatever you thought fit to be true, you affirmed confidently; and whatever you affirmed, your comrades believed. Truth was what had not yet been contradicted, most things were taken into the mind from the point of view of their human suggestiveness, and the attention confined itself exclusively to the aesthetic and dramatic aspects of events.[3]

How indeed could it be otherwise? The extraordinary value, for explanation and prevision, of those mathematical and mechanical modes of conception which science uses, was a result that could not possibly have been expected in advance. Weight, movement, velocity, direction, position, what thin, pallid, uninteresting ideas! How could the richer animistic aspects of Nature, the peculiarities and oddities that make phenomena picturesquely striking or expressive, fail to have been first singled out and followed by philosophy as the more promising avenue to the knowledge of Nature's life? Well, it is still in these richer animistic and dramatic aspects that religion delights to dwell. It is the terror and beauty of phenomena, the "promise" of the dawn and of the rainbow, the "voice" of the thunder, the "gentleness" of the summer rain, the "sublimity" of the stars, and not the physical laws which these things follow, by which the religious mind still continues to be most impressed; and just as of yore, the devout man tells you that in the solitude of his room or of the fields he still feels the divine presence, that inflowings of help come in reply to his prayers, and that sacrifices to this unseen reality fill him with security and peace.

Pure anachronism! says the survival-theory; —anachronism for which deanthropomorphization of the imagination is the remedy required. The less we mix the private with the cosmic, the more we dwell in universal and impersonal terms, the truer heirs of Science we become.

In spite of the appeal which this impersonality of the scientific attitude makes to a certain magnanimity of temper, I believe it to be shallow, and I can now state my reason in comparatively few words. That reason is that, so long as we deal with the cosmic and the general, we deal only with the symbols of reality, but *as soon as we deal with private and personal phenomena as such, we deal with realities in the completest sense of the term.* I think I can easily make clear what I mean by these words.

The world of our experience consists at all times of two parts, an objective and a subjective part, of which the former may be incalculably more extensive than the latter, and yet the latter can never be omitted or suppressed. The objective part is the sum total of whatsoever at any given time we may be thinking of, the subjective part is the inner "state" in which the thinking comes to pass. What we think of may be enormous—the cosmic times and spaces, for example—whereas the inner state may be the most fugitive and paltry activity of mind. Yet the cosmic objects, so far as the experience yields them, are but ideal pictures of something whose existence we do not inwardly possess but only point at outwardly, while the inner state is our very experience itself; its reality and that of our experience are one. A conscious field *plus* its object as felt or thought of *plus* an attitude towards the object *plus* the sense of a self to whom the attitude belongs—such a concrete bit of personal experience may be a small bit, but it is a solid bit as long as it lasts; not hollow, not a mere abstract element of experience, such as the "object" is when taken all alone. It is a *full* fact, even though it be an insignificant fact; it is of the *kind* to which all realities whatsoever must belong; the motor currents of the world run through the like of it; it is on the line connecting real events with real events. That unsharable feeling which each one of us has of the pinch of his individual destiny as he privately feels it rolling out on fortune's wheel may be disparaged for its egotism, may be sneered at as unscientific, but it is the one thing that fills up the measure of our concrete actuality, and any would-be existent that should lack such a feeling, or its analogue, would be a piece of reality only half made up.[4]

If this be true, it is absurd for science to say that the egotistic elements of experience should be suppressed. The axis of reality runs solely through the egotistic places—they are strung upon it like so many beads. To describe the world with all the various feelings of the individual pinch of destiny, all the various spiritual attitudes, left out from the description—they being as describable as anything else—would be something like offering a printed bill of fare as the equivalent for a solid meal. Religion makes no such blunder. The individual's religion may be egotistic, and those private realities which it keeps in touch with may be narrow enough; but at any rate it always remains infinitely less hollow and abstract, as far as it goes, than a science which prides itself on taking no account of anything private at all.

A bill of fare with one real raisin on it instead of the word "raisin," with one real egg instead of the word "egg," might be an inadequate meal, but it would at least be a commencement of reality. The contention of the survival-theory that we ought to stick to nonpersonal elements exclusively seems like saying that we ought to be satisfied forever with reading the naked bill of fare. I think, therefore, that however particular questions connected with our individual destinies may be answered, it is only by acknowledging them as genuine questions, and living in the sphere of thought which they open up, that we become profound. But to live thus is to be religious; so I unhesitatingly repudiate the survival-theory of religion, as being founded on an egregious mistake. It does not follow, because our ancestors made so many errors of fact and mixed them with their religion, that we should therefore leave off being religious at all.[5] By being religious we establish ourselves in possession of ultimate reality at the only points at which reality is given us to guard. Our responsible concern is with our private destiny, after all.

You see now why I have been so individualistic throughout these lectures, and why I have seemed so bent on rehabilitating the element of feeling in religion and subordinating its intellectual part. Individuality is founded in feeling; and the recesses of feeling, the darker, blinder strata of character, are the only places in the world in which we catch real fact in the making, and directly perceive how events happen, and how work is actually done.[6] Compared with

this world of living individualized feelings, the world of generalized objects which the intellect contemplates is without solidity or life. As in stereoscopic or kinetoscopic pictures seen outside the instrument, the third dimension, the movement, the vital element, are not there. We get a beautiful picture of an express train supposed to be moving, but where in the picture, as I have heard a friend say, is the energy or the fifty miles an hour?[7]

Let us agree, then, that Religion, occupying herself with personal destinies and keeping thus in contact with the only absolute realities which we know, must necessarily play an eternal part in human history. The next thing to decide is what she reveals about those destinies, or whether indeed she reveals anything distinct enough to be considered a general message to mankind. We have done as you see, with our preliminaries, and our final summing up can now begin.

I am well aware that after all the palpitating documents which I have quoted, and all the perspectives of emotion-inspiring institution and belief that my previous lectures have opened, the dry analysis to which I now advance may appear to many of you like an anti-climax, a tapering-off and flattening out of the subject, instead of a crescendo of interest and result. I said awhile ago that the religious attitude of Protestants appears poverty-stricken to the Catholic imagination. Still more poverty-stricken, I fear, may my final summing up of the subject appear at first to some of you. On which account I pray you now to bear this point in mind, that in the present part of it I am expressly trying to reduce religion to its lowest admissible terms, to that minimum, free from individualistic excrescences, which all religions contain as their nucleus, and on which it may be hoped that all religious persons may agree. That established, we should have a result which might be small, but would at least be solid; and on it and round it the ruddier additional beliefs on which the different individuals make their venture might be grafted, and flourish as richly as you please. I shall add my own over-belief (which will be, I confess, of a somewhat pallid kind, as befits a critical philosopher), and you will, I hope, also add your over-beliefs, and we shall soon be in the varied world of concrete religious constructions once more. For the moment, let me dryly pursue the analytic part of the task.

Both thought and feeling are determinants of conduct, and the same conduct may be determined either by feeling or by thought. When we survey the whole field of religion, we find a great variety in the thoughts that have prevailed there; but the feelings on the one hand and the conduct on the other are almost always the same, for Stoic, Christian, and Buddhist saints are practically indistinguishable in their lives. The theories which Religion generates, being thus variable, are secondary; and if you wish to grasp her essence, you must look to the feelings and the conduct as being the more constant elements. It is between these two elements that the short circuit exists on which she carries on her principal business, while the ideas and symbols and other institutions form loop-lines which may be perfections and improvements, and may even some day all be united into one harmonious system, but which are not to be regarded as organs with an indispensable function, necessary at all times for religious life to go on. This seems to me the first conclusion which we are entitled to draw from the phenomena we have passed in review.

The next step is to characterize the feelings. To what psychological order do they belong?

The resultant outcome of them is in any case what Kant calls a "sthenic" affection, an excitement of the cheerful, expansive, "dynamogenic" order which, like any tonic, freshens our vital powers. In almost every lecture, but especially in the lectures on Conversion and on Saintliness, we have seen how this emotion overcomes temperamental melancholy and imparts endurance to the Subject, or a zest, or a meaning, or an enchantment and glory to the common objects of life. The name of "faith-state," by which Professor Leuba designates it, is a good one. It is a biological as well as a psychological condition, and Tolstoy is absolutely accurate in classing faith among the

forces *by which men live*. The total absence of it, anhedonia, means collapse.

The faith-state may hold a very minimum of intellectual content. We saw examples of this in those sudden raptures of the divine presence, or in such mystical seizures as Dr. Bucke described. It may be a mere vague enthusiasm, half spiritual, half vital, a courage, and a feeling that great and wondrous things are in the air.[8]

When, however, a positive intellectual content is associated with a faith-state, it gets invincibly stamped in upon belief, and this explains the passionate loyalty of religious persons everywhere to the minutest details of their so widely differing creeds. Taking creeds and faith-state together, as forming "religions," and treating these as purely subjective phenomena, without regard to the question of their "truth," we are obliged, on account of their extraordinary influence upon action and endurance, to class them amongst the most important biological functions of mankind. Their stimulant and anaesthetic effect is so great that Professor Leuba, in a recent article, goes so far as to say that so long as men can *use* their God, they care very little who he is, or even whether he is at all. "The truth of the matter can be put," says Leuba, "in this way: *God is not known, he is not understood; he is used*—sometimes as meat-purveyor, sometimes as moral support, sometimes as friend, sometimes as an object of love. If he proves himself useful, the religious consciousness asks for no more than that. Does God really exist? How does he exist? What is he? are so many irrelevant questions. Not God, but life, more life, a larger, richer, more satisfying life, is, in the last analysis, the end of religion. The love of life, at any and every level of development, is the religious impulse."

At this purely subjective rating, therefore, Religion must be considered vindicated in a certain way from the attacks of her critics. It would seem that she cannot be a mere anachronism and survival, but must exert a permanent function, whether she be with or without intellectual content, and whether, if she have any, it be true or false.

We must next pass beyond the point of view of merely subjective utility, and make inquiry into the intellectual content itself.

First, is there, under all the discrepancies of the creeds, a common nucleus to which they bear their testimony unanimously?

And second, ought we to consider the testimony true?

I will take up the first question first, and answer it immediately in the affirmative. The warring gods and formulas of the various religions do indeed cancel each other, but there is a certain uniform deliverance in which religions all appear to meet. It consists of two parts:—

1. An uneasiness; and
2. Its solution.
1. The uneasiness, reduced to its simplest terms, is a sense that there is *something wrong about us* as we naturally stand.
2. The solution is a sense that *we are saved from the wrongness* by making proper connection with the higher powers.

In those more developed minds which alone we are studying, the wrongness takes a moral character, and the salvation takes a mystical tinge. I think we shall keep well within the limits of what is common to all such minds if we formulate the essence of their religious experience in terms like these:—

The individual, so far as he suffers from his wrongness and criticises it, is to that extent consciously beyond it, and in at least possible touch with something higher, if anything higher exist. Along with the wrong part there is thus a better part of him, even though it may be but a most helpless germ. With which part he should identify his real being is by no means obvious at this stage; but when stage 2 (the stage of solution or salvation) arrives,[9] the man identifies his real being with the germinal higher part of himself; and does so in the following way. *He becomes conscious that this higher part is conterminous and continuous with a* MORE *of the same quality, which is operative in the universe outside of him, and which he can keep in working touch with, and in a fashion get on board of and save himself when all his lower being has gone to pieces in the wreck.*

It seems to me that all the phenomena are accurately describable in these very simple general terms.[10] They allow for the divided self and the struggle; they involve the change of personal centre and the surrender of the lower self; they express the appearance of exteriority of the helping power and yet account for our sense of union with it;[11] and they fully justify our feelings of security and joy. There is probably no autobiographic document, among all those which I have quoted, to which the description will not well apply. One need only add such specific details as will adapt it to various theologies and various personal temperaments, and one will then have the various experiences reconstructed in their individual forms.

So far, however, as this analysis goes, the experiences are only psychological phenomena. They possess, it is true, enormous biological worth. Spiritual strength really increases in the subject when he has them, a new life opens for him, and they seem to him a place of conflux where the forces of two universes meet; and yet this may be nothing but his subjective way of feeling things, a mood of his own fancy, in spite of the effects produced. I now turn to my second question: What is the objective "truth" of their content?[12]

The part of the content concerning which the question of truth most pertinently arises is that "MORE of the same quality" with which our own higher self appears in the experience to come into harmonious working relation. Is such a "more" merely our own notion, or does it really exist? If so, in what shape does it exist? Does it act, as well as exist? And in what form should we conceive of that "union" with it of which religious geniuses are so convinced?

It is in answering these questions that the various theologies perform their theoretic work, and that their divergencies most come to light. They all agree that the "more" really exists; though some of them hold it to exist in the shape of a personal god or gods, while others are satisfied to conceive it as a stream of ideal tendency embedded in the eternal structure of the world. They all agree, moreover, that it acts as well as exists, and that something really is effected for the better when you throw your life into its hands. It is when they treat of the experience of "union" with it that their speculative differences appear most clearly. Over this point pantheism and theism, nature and second birth, works and grace and karma, immortality and reincarnation, rationalism and mysticism, carry on inveterate disputes.

At the end of my lecture on Philosophy I held out the notion that an impartial science of-religions might sift out from the midst of theirdiscrepancies a common body of doctrine which she might also formulate in terms to which physical science need not object. This, I said, she might adopt as her own reconciling hypothesis, and recommend it for general belief. I also said that in my last lecture I should have to try my own hand at framing such an hypothesis.

The time has now come for this attempt. Who says "hypothesis" renounces the ambition to be coercive in his arguments. The most I can do is, accordingly, to offer something that may fit the facts so easily that your scientific logic will find no plausible pretext for vetoing your impulse to welcome it as true.

The "more," as we called it, and the meaning of our "union" with it, form the nucleus of our inquiry. Into what definite description can these words be translated, and for what definite facts do they stand? It would never do for us to place ourselves offhand at the position of a particular theology, the Christian theology, for example, and proceed immediately to define the "more" as Jehovah, and the "union" as his imputation to us of the righteousness of Christ. That would be unfair to other religions, and, from our present standpoint at least, would be an over-belief.

We must begin by using less particularized terms; and, since one of the duties of the science of religions is to keep religion in connection with the rest of science, we shall do well to seek first of all a way of describing the "more," which psychologists may also recognize as real. The *subconscious self* is nowadays a well-accredited psychological entity; and I believe that in it we have exactly the mediating term required. Apart from all religious considerations, there is actually and literally more life in our total soul than we are at any time aware of. The exploration of the transmarginal field has hardly yet been seriously undertaken, but what Mr. Myers said in 1892 in his essay on the Subliminal Consciousness[13] is as true as when it was first written: "Each of us is in reality an abiding psychical entity far more extensive than he knows—an individuality which can never express itself completely through any corporeal manifestation. The Self manifests through the organism; but there is always some part of the Self unmanifested; and always, as it seems, some power of organic expression in abeyance or reserve." Much of the content of this larger background against which our conscious being stands out in relief is insignificant. Imperfect memories, silly jingles, inhibitive timidities, "dissolutive" phenomena of various sorts, as Myers calls them, enters into it for a large part. But in it many of the performances of genius seem also to have their origin; and in our study of conversion, of mystical experiences, and of prayer, we have seen how striking a part invasions from this region play in the religious life.

Let me then propose, as an hypothesis, that whatever it may be on its *farther* side, the "more" with which in religious experience we feel ourselves connected is on its *hither* side the subconscious continuation of our conscious life. Starting thus with a recognized psychological fact as our basis, we seem to preserve a contact with "science" which the ordinary theologian lacks. At the same time the theologian's contention that the religious man is moved by an external power is vindicated, for it is one of the peculiarities of invasions from the subconscious region to take on objective appearances, and to suggest to the Subject an external control. In the religious life the control is felt as "higher"; but since on our hypothesis it is primarily the higher faculties of our own hidden mind which are controlling, the sense of union with the power beyond us is a sense of something, not merely apparently, but literally true.

This doorway into the subject seems to me the best one for a science of religions, for it mediates between a number of different points of view. Yet it is only a doorway, and difficulties present themselves as soon as we step through it, and ask how far our transmarginal consciousness 'carries us if we follow it on its remoter side. Here the over-beliefs begin: here mysticism and the conversion-rapture and Vedantism and transcendental idealism bring in their monistic interpretations and tell us that the finite self rejoins the absolute self, for it was always one with God and identical with the soul of the world.[14] Here the prophets of all the different religions come with their visions, voices, raptures, and other openings, supposed by each to authenticate his own peculiar faith.

Those of us who are not personally favored with such specific revelations must stand outside of them altogether and, for the present at least, decide that, since they corroborate incompatible theological doctrines, they neutralize one another and leave no fixed results. If we follow any one of them, or if we follow philosophical theory and embrace monistic pantheism on non-mystical grounds, we do so in the exercise of our individual freedom, and build out our religion in the way most congruous with our personal susceptibilities. Among these susceptibilities intellectual ones play a decisive part. Although the religious question is primarily a question of life, of living or not living in the higher union which opens itself to us as a gift, yet the spiritual excitement in which the gift appears a real one will often fail to be aroused in an individual until certain particular intellectual beliefs or ideas which, as we say, come home to him, are touched.[15] These ideas will thus be essential to that individual's religion;—which is as much as to say that over-beliefs in various directions are absolutely indispensable, and that we should treat them with tenderness and tolerance so long as they are not intolerant themselves. As I have elsewhere written, the most interesting and valuable things about a man are usually his over-beliefs.

Disregarding the over-beliefs, and confining ourselves to what is common and generic, we have in *the fact that the conscious person is continuous with a wider self through which saving experiences come,*[16] a positive content of religious experience which, it seems to me, *is literally and objectively true as far as it goes.* If I now proceed to state my own hypothesis about the farther limits of this extension of our personality, I shall be offering my own over-belief—though I know it will appear a sorry under-belief to some of you—for which I can only bespeak the same indulgence which in a converse case I should accord to yours.

The further limits of our being plunge, it seems to me, into an altogether other dimension of existence from the sensible and merely "understandable" world. Name it the mystical region, or the supernatural region, whichever you choose. So far as our ideal impulses originate in this region (and most of them do originate in it, for we find them possessing us in a way for which we cannot articulately account), we belong to it in a more intimate sense than that in which we belong to the visible world, for we belong in the most intimate sense wherever our ideals belong. Yet the unseen region in question is not merely ideal, for it produces effects in this world. When we commune with it, work is actually done upon our finite personality, for we are turned into new men, and consequences in the way of conduct follow in the natural world upon our regenerative change.[17] But that which produces effects within another reality must be termed a reality itself, so I feel as if we had no philosophic excuse for calling the unseen or mystical world unreal.

God is the natural appellation, for us Christians at least, for the supreme reality, so I will call this higher part of the universe by the name of God.[18] We and God have business with each other; and in opening ourselves to his influence our deepest destiny is fulfilled. The universe, at those parts of it which our personal being constitutes, takes a turn genuinely for the worse or for the better in proportion as each one of us fulfills or evades God's demands. As far as this goes I probably have you with me, for I only translate into schematic language what I may call the instinctive belief of mankind: God is real since he produces real effects.

The real effects in question, so far as I have as yet admitted them, are exerted on the personal centres of energy of the various subjects, but the spontaneous faith of most of the subjects is that they embrace a wider sphere than this. Most religious men believe (or ''know,'' if they be mystical) that not only they themselves, but the whole universe of beings to whom the God is present, are secure in his parental hands. There is a sense, a dimension, they are sure, in which we are *all* saved, in spite of the gates of hell and all adverse terrestrial appearances. God's existence is the guarantee of an ideal order that shall be permanently preserved. This world may indeed, as science assures us, some day burn up or freeze; but if it is part of his order, the old ideals are sure to be brought elsewhere to fruition, so that where God is, tragedy is only provisional and partial, and shipwreck and dissolution are not the absolutely final things. Only when this farther step of faith concerning God is taken, and remote objective consequences are predicted, does religion, as it seems to me, get wholly free from the first immediate subjective experience, and bring a *real hypothesis* into play. A good hypothesis in science must have other properties than those of the phenomenon it is immediately invoked to explain, otherwise it is not prolific enough. God, meaning only what enters into the religious man's experience of union, falls short of being an hypothesis of this more useful order. He needs to enter into wider cosmic relations in order to justify the subject's absolute confidence and peace.

That the God with whom, starting from the hither side of our own extra-marginal self, we come at its remoter margin into commerce should be the absolute world-ruler, is of course a very considerable over-belief. Over-belief as it is, though, it is an article of almost every one's religion. Most of us pretend in some way to prop it upon our philosophy, but the philosophy itself is really propped upon this faith. What is this but to say that Religion, in her fullest exercise of function, is not a mere illumination of facts already elsewhere given, not a mere passion, like love, which views things in a rosier light. It is indeed that, as we have seen abundantly. But it is something more, namely, a postulator of new *facts* as well. The world interpreted religiously is not the materialistic world over again, with an altered expression; it must have, over and above the altered expression, *a natural constitution* different at some point from that which a materialistic world would have. It must be such that different events can be expected in it, different conduct must be required.

This thoroughly ''pragmatic'' view of religion has usually been taken as a matter of course by common men. They have interpolated divine miracles into the field of nature, they have built a heaven out beyond the grave. It is only transcendentalist metaphysicians who think that, without adding any concrete details to Nature, or subtracting any, but by simply calling it the expression of absolute spirit, you make it more divine just as it stands. I believe the pragmatic way of taking religion to be the deeper way. It gives it body as well as soul, it makes it claim, as everything real must claim, some characteristic realm of fact as its very own. What the more characteristically divine facts are, apart from the actual inflow of energy in the faith-state and the prayer-state, I know not. But the over-belief on which I am ready to make my personal venture is that they exist. The whole drift of my education goes to persuade me that the world of our present consciousness is only one out of many worlds of consciousness that exist, and that those other worlds must contain experiences which have a meaning for our life also; and that although in the main their experiences and those of this world keep discrete, yet the two become continuous at certain points, and higher energies filter in. By being faithful in my poor measure to this over-belief, I seem to myself to keep more sane and true. I *can,* of course, put myself into the sectarian scientist's attitude, and imagine vividly that the world of sensations and of scientific laws and objects may be all. But whenever I do this, I hear that inward monitor of which

W. K. Clifford once wrote, whispering the word "bosh!" Humbug is humbug, even though it bear the scientific name, and the total expression of human experience, as I view it objectively, invincibly urges me beyond the narrow "scientific" bounds. Assuredly, the real world is of a different temperament—more intricately built than physical science allows. So my objective and my subjective conscience both hold me to the over-belief which I express. Who knows whether the faithfulness of individuals here below to their own poor over-beliefs may not actually help God in turn to be more effectively faithful to his own greater tasks?

NOTES

1. From this point of view, the contrasts between the healthy and the morbid mind, and between the once-born and the twice-born types, of which I spoke in earlier lectures cease to be the radical antagonisms which many think them. The twice-born look down upon the rectilinear consciousness of life of the once-born as being "mere morality," and not properly religion. "Dr. Channing," an orthodox minister is reported to have said, "is excluded from the highest form of religious life by the extraordinary rectitude of his character." It is indeed true that the outlook upon life of the twice-born—holding as it does more of the element of evil in solution—is the wider and completer. The "heroic" or "solemn" way in which life comes to them is a "higher synthesis" into which healthy-mindedness and morbidness both enter and combine. Evil is not evaded, but sublated in the higher religious cheer of these persons. But the final consciousness which each type reaches of union with the divine has the same practical significance for the individual; and individuals may well be allowed to get to it by the channels which lie most open to their several temperaments. In the cases which were quoted in Lecture IV, of the mind-cure form of healthy-mindedness, we found abundant examples of regenerative process. The severity of the crisis in this process is a matter of degree. How long one shall continue to drink the consciousness of evil, and when one shall begin to short-circuit and get rid of it, are also matters of amount and degree, so that in many instances it is quite arbitrary whether we class the individual as a once-born or a twice-born subject

2. How was it ever conceivable, we ask, that a man like Christian Wolff, in whose dry-as-dust head all the learning of the early eighteenth century was concentrated, should have preserved such a baby like faith in the personal and human character of Nature as to expound her operations as he did in his work on the uses of natural things? This, for example, is the account he gives of the sun and its utility:—

"We see that God has created the sun to keep the changeable conditions on the earth in such an order that living creatures, men and beasts, may inhabit its surface. Since men are the most reasonable of creatures, and able to infer God's invisible being from the contemplation of the world, the sun in so far forth contributes to the primary purpose of creation: without it the race of man could not be preserved or continued. . . . The sun makes daylight, not only on our earth, but also on the other planets; and daylight is of the utmost utility to us; for by its means we can commodiously carry on those occupations which in the night-time would either be quite impossible, or at any rate impossible without our going to the expense of artificial light. The beasts of the field can find food by day which they would not be able to find at night. Moreover we owe it to the sunlight that we are able to see everything that is on the earth's surface, not only near by, but also at a distance, and to recognize both near and far things according to their species, which again is of manifold use to us not only in the business necessary to human life, and when we are traveling, but also for the scientific knowledge of Nature, which knowledge for the most part depends on observations made with the help of sight, and, without the sunshine, would have been impossible. If any one would rightly impress on his mind the great advantages which he derives from the sun, let him imagine himself living through only one month, and see how it would be with all his undertakings, if it were not day but night. He would then be sufficiently convinced out of his own experience, especially if he had much work to carry on in the street or in the fields. . . . From the sun we learn to recognize when it is midday, and by knowing this point of time exactly, we can set our clocks right, on which account astronomy owes much to the sun. . . . By help of the sun one can find the meridian. . . . But the meridian is the basis of our sun-dials, and generally speaking, we should have no sun-dials if we had no sun" Vernünftige Gedanken von den Absichter der natürlichen Dinge, 1782. pp. 74–84

Or read the account of God's beneficence in the institution of "the great variety throughout the world of men's faces, voices, and hand-writing," given Derham's Physico-theology, a book that had much vogue in the eighteenth century. "Had Man's body," says Dr. Derham, "been made according to any of the Atheistical Schemes, or any other Method than that of the infinite Lord of the World, this wise Variety would never have been: but Men's faces would have been cast in the same, or not a very different Mould, their Organs of Speech would have sounded the same or not so great a Variety of Notes; and the same Direction in Writing. And in this Case, what Confusion, what Disturbance, what Mischiefs would the world eternally have lain under! No Security could have been to our persons; no Certainly, no Enjoyment of our Possessions; no Justice between Man and Man; no Division between Good and Bad, between Friends and Foes, between Father and Child, Husband and Wife, Male or Female; but all would have been turned topsy-turvy, by being exposed to the Malice of the Envious and ill-Natured, to the Fraud and Violence of Knaves and Robbers, to the

Forgeries of the crafty Cheat, to the Lusts of the Effeminate and Debauched, and what not! Our Courts of Justice can abundantly testify the dire Effects of Mistaking Men's Faces, of counterfeiting their Hands, and forging Writings. But now as the infinitely wise Creator and Ruler hath ordered the Matter, every man's Face can distinguish him in the Light, and his Voice in the Dark; his Hand-writing can speak for him though absent, and be his Witness, and secure his Contracts in future Generations. A manifest as well as admirable Indication of the divine Superintendence and Management.''

A God so careful as to make provision even for the unmistakable signing of bank checks and deeds was a deity truly after the heart of eighteenth century Anglicanism.

I subjoin, omitting the capitals, Derham's ''Vindication of God by the Institution of Hills and Valleys,'' and Wolff's altogether culinary account of the institution of Water:—

''The uses,'' says Wolff, ''which water serves in human life are plain to see and need not be described at length. Water is a universal drink of man and beasts. Even though men have made themselves drinks that are artificial, they could not do this without water. Beer is brewed of water and malt, and it is the water in it which quenches thirst. Wine is prepared from grapes, which could never have grown without the help of water; and the same is true of those drinks which in England and other places they produce from fruit. . . . Therefore since God so planned the world that men and beasts should live upon it and find there everything required for their necessity and convenience, he also made water as one means whereby to make the earth into so excellent a dwelling. And this is all the more manifest when we consider the advantages which we obtain from this same water for the cleaning of our household utensils, of our clothing, and of other matters. . . . When one goes into a grinding-mill one sees that the grindstone must always be kept wet and then one will get a still greater idea of the use of water.''

Of the hills and valleys, Derham, after praising their beauty, discourses as follows: ''Some constitutions are indeed of so happy a strength, and so confirmed an health, as to be indifferent to almost any place or temperature of the air. But then others are so weakly and feeble, as not to be able to bear one, but can live comfortably in another place. With some the more subtle and finer air of the hills doth best agree, who are languishing and dying in the feculent and grosser air of great towns, or even the warmer and vaporous air of the valleys and waters. But contrariwise, others languish on the hills, and grow lusty and strong in the warmer air of the valleys.

''So that this opportunity of shifting our abode from the hills to the vales, is an admirable easement, refreshment, and great benefit to the valetudinarian, feeble part of mankind; affording those an easy and comfortable life, who would otherwise live miserably, languish, and pine away.

''To this salutory conformation of the earth we may add another great convenience of the hills, and that is affording commodious places for habitation, serving (as an eminent author wordeth it) as screens to keep off the cold and nipping blasts of the northern and easterly winds, and reflecting the benign and cherishing sunbeams, and so rendering our habitations both more comfortable and more cheery in winter.

''Lastly, it is to the hills that the fountains owe their rise and the rivers their conveyance, and consequently those vast masses and lofty piles are not, as they are charged, such rude and useless excrescences of our ill-formed globe; but the admirable tools of nature, contrived and ordered by the infinite Creator, to do one of its most useful works. For, was the surface of the earth even and level, and the middle parts of its islands and continents not mountainous and high as now it is, it is most certain there could be no descent for the rivers, no conveyance for the waters; but, instead of gliding along those gentle declivities which the higher lands now afford them quite down to the sea, they would stagnate and perhaps stink, and also drown large tracts of land.

''[Thus] the hills and vales, though to a peevish and weary traveler they may seem incommodious and troublesome, yet are a noble work of the great Creator, and wisely appointed by him for the good of our sublunary world.''

3. Until the seventeenth century this mode of thought prevailed. One need only recall the dramatic treatment even of mechanical questions by Aristotle, as, for example, his explanation of the power of the lever to make a small weight raise a larger one. This is due, according to Aristotle, to the generally miraculous character of the circle and of all circular movement. The circle is both convex and concave; it is made by a fixed point and a moving line, which contradict each other; and whatever moves in a circle moves in opposite directions. Nevertheless, movement in a circle is the most ''natural'' movement; and the long arm of the lever, moving, as it does, in the larger circle, has the greater amount of this natural motion, and consequently requires the lesser force. Or recall the explanation by Herodotus of the position of the sun in winter: It moves to the south because of the cold which drives it into the warm parts of the heavens over Libya. Or listen to Saint Augustine's speculations: ''Who gave to chaff such power to freeze that it preserves snow buried under it, and such power to warm that it ripens green fruit? Who can explain the strange properties of fire itself, which blackens all that it burns, though itself bright, and which, though of the most beautiful colors, discolors almost all that it touches and feeds upon, and turns blazing fuel into grimy cinders? . . . Then what wonderful properties do we find in charcoal, which is so brittle that a light tap breaks it, and a slight pressure pulverizes it, and yet is so strong that no moisture rots it, nor any time causes it to decay.'' City of God, book xxi, ch. iv.

Such aspects of things as these, their naturalness and unnaturalness, the sympathies and antipathies of their superficial qualities, their eccentricities, their brightness and strength and destructiveness, were inevitably the ways in which they originally fastened our attention.

If you open early medical books, you will find sympathetic magic invoked on every page. Take, for example, the famous vulnerary ointment attributed to Paracelsus. For this there were a variety of receipts, including usually human fat, the fat of either a bull, a wild boar, or a bear; powdered earthworms, the *usnia*, or mossy growth on the weathered skull of a hanged criminal, and other materials equally unpleasant—the whole prepared under the planet Venus if possible, but never under Mars or Saturn. Then, if a splinter of wood, dipped in the patient's blood, or the blood-stained weapon that wounded him, be immersed in this ointment, the wound itself being tightly bound up, the latter infallibly gets well—I quote now Van Helmont's account—for the blood on the weapon or splinter, containing in it the spirit of the wounded man, is roused to active excitement by the contact of the ointment, whence there results to it a full commission or power to cure its cousin-german, the blood in the patient's body. This it does by sucking out the dolorous and exotic impression from the wounded part. But to do this it has to implore the aid of the bull's fat, and other portions of the unguent. The reason why bull's fat is so powerful is that the bull at the time of slaughter is full of secret reluctancy and vindictive murmurs, and therefore dies with a higher flame of revenge about him than any other animal. And thus we have made it out, says this author, that the admirable efficacy of the ointment ought to be imputed, not to any auxiliary concurrence of Satan, but simply to the energy of the *posthumous character of Revenge* remaining firmly impressed upon the blood and concreted fat in the unguent. J. B. VAN HELMONT: A Ternary of Paradoxes, translated by WALTER CHARLETON, London, 1650.—I much abridge the original in my citations.

The author goes on to prove by the analogy of many other natural facts that this sympathetic action between things at a distance is the true rationale of the case. "If," he says, "the heart of a horse, slain by a witch, taken out of the yet reeking carcase, be impaled upon an arrow and roasted, immediately the whole witch becomes tormented with the insufferable pains and cruelty of the fire, which could by no means happen unless there preceded a conjunction of the spirit of the witch with the spirit of the horse. In the reeking and yet panting heart, the spirit of the witch is kept captive, and the retreat of it prevented by the arrow transfixed. Similarly hath not many a murdered carcase at the coroner's inquest suffered a fresh hæmorrhage or cruentation at the presence of the assassin?—the blood being, as in a furious fit of anger, enraged and agitated by the impress of revenge conceived against the murderer, at the instant of the soul's compulsive exile from the body. So, if you have dropsy, gout, or jaundice, by including some of your warm blood in the shell and white of an egg, which, exposed to a gentle heat, and mixed with a bait of flesh, you shall give to a hungry dog or hog, the disease shall instantly pass from you into the animal, and leave you entirely. And similarly again, if you burn some of the milk either of a cow or of a woman, the gland from which it issued will dry up. A gentleman at Brussels had his nose mowed off in combat, but the celebrated surgeon Tagliacozzus digged a new nose for him out of the skin of the arm of a porter at Bologna.

About thirteen months after his return to his own country, the engrafted nose grew cold, putrefied, and in a few days dropped off, and it was then discovered that the porter had expired, near the same punctilio of time. There are still at Brussels eye-witnesses of this occurrence," says Van Helmont; and adds, "I pray what is there in this of superstition or of exalted imagination?"

Modern mind-cure literature—the works of Prentice Mulford, for example—is full of sympathetic magic.

4. Compare Lotze's doctrine that the only meaning we can attach to the notion of a thing as it is "in itself" is by conceiving it as it is *for* itself; i.e., as a piece of full experience with a private sense of "pinch" or inner activity of some sort going with it.

5. Even the errors of fact may possibly turn out not to be as wholesale as the scientist assumes. We saw in Lecture IV how the religious conception of the universe seems to many mind-curers "verified" from day to day by their experience of fact. "Experience of fact" is a field with so many things in it that the sectarian scientist, methodically declining, as he does, to recognize such "facts" as mind-cures and others like them experience otherwise than by such rude heads of classification as "bosh," "rot," "folly," certainly leaves out a mass of raw fact which, save for the industrious interest of the religious in the more personal aspects of reality, would never have succeeded in getting itself recorded at all. We know this to be true already in certain cases; it may, therefore, be true in others as well. Miraculous healings have always been part of the supernaturalist stock in trade, and have always been dismissed by the scientist as figments of the imagination. But the scientist's tardy education in the facts of hypnotism has recently given him an apperceiving mass for phenomena of this order, and he consequently now allows that the healings may exist, provided you expressly call them effects of "suggestion." Even the stigmata of the cross on Saint Francis's hands and feet may on these terms not be a fable. Similarly, the time-honored phenomenon of diabolical possession is on the point of being admitted by the scientist as a fact, now that he has the name of "hysterodemonopathy" by which to apperceive it. No one can foresee just how far this legitimation of occultist phenomena under newly found scientist titles may proceed—even "prophecy," even "levitation," might creep into the pale.

Thus the divorce between scientist facts and religious facts may not necessarily be as eternal as it at first sight seems, nor the personalism and romanticism of the world, as they appeared to primitive thinking, be matters so irrevocably outgrown. The final human opinion may, in short, in some manner now impossible to foresee, revert to the more personal style, just as any path of progress may follow a spiral rather than a straight line. If this were so, the rigorously impersonal view of science might one day appear as having been a temporarily useful eccentricity rather than the definitively triumphant position which the sectarian scientist at present so confidently announces it to be.

6. Hume's criticism has banished causation from the world of physical objects, and "Science" is absolutely satisfied to define cause in terms of concomitant change—read Mach, Pearson, Ostwald. The "origi-

nal'' of the notion of causation is in our inner personal experience, and only there can causes in the old-fashioned sense be directly observed and described.

7. When I read in a religious paper words like these: ''Perhaps the best thing we can say of God is that he is *the Inevitable Inference*,'' I recognize the tendency to let religion evaporate in intellectual terms. Would martyrs have sung in the flames for a mere inference, however inevitable it might be? Original religious men, like Saint Francis, Luther, Behmen, have usually been enemies of the intellect's pretension to meddle with religious things. Yet the intellect, everywhere invasive, shows everywhere its shallowing effect. See how the ancient spirit of Methodism evaporates under those wonderfully able rationalistic booklets (which everyone should read) of a philosopher like Professor Browne (The Christian Revelation, The Christian Life, The Atonement: Cincinnati and New York, 1898, 1899, 1900). See the positively expulsive purpose of philosophy properly so called:—

''Religion,'' writes M. Vacherot (La Religion, Paris, 1869, pp. 313, 436, et passim), ''answers to a transient state or condition, not to a permanent determination of human nature, being merely an expression of that stage of the human mind which is dominated by the imagination. . . . Christianity has but a single possible final heir to its estate, and that is scientific philosophy.''

In a still more radical vein, Professor Ribot (Psychologie des Sentiments, p. 310) describes the evaporation of religion. He sums it up in a single formula—the ever-growing predominance of the rational intellectual element, with the gradual fading out of the emotional element, this latter tending to enter into the group of purely intellectual sentiments. ''Of religious sentiment properly so called, nothing survives at last save a vague respect for the unknowable x which is a last relic of the fear, and a certain attraction towards the ideal, which is a relic of the love, that characterized the earlier periods of religious growth. To state this more simply, *religion tends to turn into religious philosophy.*—These are psychologically entirely different things, the one being a theoretic construction of ratiocination, whereas the other is the living work of a group of persons, or of a great inspired leader, calling into play the entire thinking and feeling organism of man.''

I find the same failure to recognize that the stronghold of religion lies in individuality in attempts like those of Professor Baldwin (Mental Development, Social and Ethical Interpretations, ch. x) and Mr. H. R. Marshall (Instinct and Reason, chaps. viii. to xii.) to make it a purely ''conservative social force.''

8. Example: Henri Perreyve writes to Gratry: ''I do not know how to deal with the happiness which you aroused in me this morning. It overwelms me; I want to *do* something, yet I can do nothing and am fit for nothing. . . . I would fain do *great things*.'' Again, after an inspiring interview, he writes: ''I went homewards, intoxicated with joy, hope, and strength. I wanted to feed upon my happiness in solitude, far from all men. It was late; but, unheeding that, I took a mountain path and went on like a madman, looking at the heavens, regardless of earth. Suddenly an instinct made me draw hastily back—I was on the very edge of a precipice, one

step more and I must have fallen. I took fright and gave up my nocturnal promenade.'' A. GRATRY: Henri Perreyve, London, 1872, pp. 92, 89.

This primacy, in the faith-state, of vague expansive impulse over direction is well expressed in Walt Whitman's lines (Leaves of Grass, 1872, p. 190):—

''O to confront night, storms, hunger, ridicule, accidents, rebuffs, as the trees and animals do. . . .

Dear Camerado! I confess I have urged you onward with me, and still urge you, without the least idea what is our destination,

Or whether we shall be victorious, or utterly quell'd and defeated.''

This readiness for great things, and this sense that the world by its importance, wonderfulness, etc., is apt for their production, would seem to be the undifferentiated germ of all the higher faiths. Trust in our own dreams of ambition, or in our country's expansive destinies, and faith in the providence of God, all have their source in that onrush of our sanguine impulses, and in that sense of the exceedingness of the possible over the real.

9. Remember that for some men it arrives suddenly, for others gradually, whilst others again practically enjoy it all their life.

10. The practical difficulties are: 1, to ''realize the reality'' of one's higher part; 2, to identify one's self with it exclusively; and 3, to identify it with all the rest of ideal being.

11. ''When mystical activity is at its height, we find consciousness possessed by the sense of a being at once *excessive* and *identical* with the self: great enough to be God; interior enough to be *me*. The ''objectivity'' of it ought in that case to be called *excessivity*, rather, or exceedingness.'' RÉCÉJAC: Essai sur les fondements de la conscience mystique, 1897, p. 46.

12. The word ''truth'' is here taken to mean something additional to bare value for life, although the natural propensity of man is to believe that whatever has great value for life is thereby certified as true.

13. Proceedings of the Society for Psychical Research, vol. vii. p. 305. For a full statement of Mr. Myers's views, I may refer to his posthumous work, ''Human Personality in the Light of Recent Research,'' which is already announced by Messrs. Longmans, Green & Co. as being in press. Mr. Myers for the first time proposed as a general psychological problem the exploration of the subliminal region of consciousness throughout its whole extent, and made the first methodical steps in its topography by treating as a natural series a mass of subliminal facts hitherto considered only as curious isolated facts, and subjecting them to a systematized nomenclature. How important this exploration will prove, future work upon the path which Myers has opened can alone show. Compare my paper: ''Frederic Myers's Services to Psychology,'' in the said Proceedings, part xlii., May, 1901.

14. One more expression of this belief, to increase the reader's familiarity with the notion of it:—

''If this room is full of darkness for thousands of years, and you come in and begin to weep and wail, 'Oh, the darkness,' will the darkness vanish? Bring the light in, strike a match, and light comes in a moment.

So what good will it do you to think all your lives, 'Oh, I have done evil, I have made many mistakes'? It requires no ghost to tell us that. Bring in the light, and the evil goes in a moment. Strengthen the real nature, build up yourselves, the effulgent, the resplendent, the ever pure, call that up in every one whom you see. I wish that every one of us had come to such a state that even when we see the vilest of human beings we can see the God within, and instead of condemning, say, 'Rise, thou effulgent One, rise thou who art always pure, rise thou birthless and deathless, rise almighty, and manifest your nature.' . . . This is the highest prayer that the Advaita teaches. This is the one prayer: remembering our nature." . . . "Why does man go out to look for a God? . . . It is your own heart beating, and you did not know, you were mistaking it for something external. He, nearest of the near, my own self, the reality of my own life, my body and my soul.—I am Thee and Thou art Me. That is your own nature. Assert it, manifest it. Not to become pure, you are pure already. You are not to be perfect, you are that already. Every good thought which you think or act upon is simply tearing the veil, as it were, and the purity, the Infinity, the God behind, manifests itself—the eternal Subject of everything, the eternal Witness in this universe, your own Self. Knowledge is, as it were, a lower step, a degradation. We are It already; how to know It?" SWAMI VIVEKANANDA: Addresses, No. XII., Practical Vendanta, part iv. pp. 172, 174, London, 1897; and Lectures, The Real and the Apparent Man, p. 24, abridged.

15. For instance, here is a case where a person exposed from her birth to Christian ideas had to wait till they came to her clad in spiritistic formulas before the saving experience set in:—

"For myself I can say that spiritualism has saved me. It was revealed to me at a critical moment of my life, and without it I don't know what I should have done. It has taught me to detach myself from worldly things and to place my hope in things to come. Through it I have learned to see in all men, even in those from whom I have most suffered, undeveloped brothers to whom I owe assistance, love, and forgiveness. I have learned that I must lose my temper over nothing, despise no one, and pray for all. Most of all I have learned to pray! And although I have still much to learn in this domain, prayer ever brings me more strength, consolation, and comfort. I feel more than ever that I have only made a few steps on the long road of progress; but I look at its length without dismay, for I have confidence that the day will come when all my efforts shall be rewarded. So Spiritualism has a great place in my life, indeed it holds the first place there." Flournoy Collection.

16. "The influence of the Holy Spirit, exquisitely called the Comforter, is a matter of actual experience, as solid a reality as that of electro-magnetism." W. C. BROWNELL, Scribner's Magazine, vol. xxx. p. 112.

17. That the transaction of opening ourselves, otherwise called prayer, is a perfectly definite one for certain persons, appears abundantly in the preceding lectures. I append another concrete example to reinforce the impression on the reader's mind:—

"Man can learn to transcend these limitations [of finite thought] and draw power and wisdom at will. . . . The divine presence is known through experience. The turning to a higher plane is a distinct act of consciousness. It is not a vague, twilight or semi-conscious experience. It is not an ecstasy; it is not a trance. It is not super-consciousness in the Vedantic sense. It is not due to self-hypnotization. It a perfectly calm, sane, sound, rational, common-sense shifting of consciousness from phenomena of sense-perception to the phenomena of seership, from the thought of self to a distinctively higher realm. . . . For example, if the lower self be nervous, anxious, tense, one can in a few moments compel it to be calm. This is not done by a word simply. Again I say, it is not hypnotism. It is by the exercise of power. One feels the spirit of peace as definitely as heat is perceived on a hot summer day. The power can be as surely used as the sun's rays can be focused and made to do work, to set fire to wood." The Higher Law, vol. iv. pp. 4, 6, Boston, August, 1901.

18. Transcendentalists are fond of the term "Over-soul," but as a rule they use it in an intellectual sense, as meaning only a medium of communion. "God" is a causal agent as well as a medium of communion, and that is the aspect which I wish to emphasize.

SAINT ANSELM and GAUNILON
A Dialogue on the Ontological Proof for the Existence of God

I
Saint Anselm

O Lord, who grants understanding to faith, make me, so far as is good for me, to understand that you exist, as we believe, and that you are what we believe you to be. Now we believe you to be something greater than which we can conceive of nothing. Could it be then that there is no such nature, since "the fool says in his heart, 'There is no God' " [Ps. 13:1]? But surely this same fool, when he hears me say this "something than which we can conceive of nothing greater," understands what he hears and what he understands is in his understanding even if he does not understand it to exist. For it is one thing for something to be in the understanding and quite another to understand that the thing in question exists. When a painter thinks of the work he will make beforehand, he has it in his understanding, but he does not think that what he has yet to make exists. But once he has painted it, he not only has it in his understanding but he understands that what he has made exists. Even the fool then must be convinced that in his understanding at least there is something than which nothing greater

can be conceived, for when he hears this, he understands it and whatever is understood is in the understanding. But surely if the thing be such that we cannot conceive of something greater, it does not exist solely in the understanding. For if it were there only, one could also think of it as existing in reality and this is something greater. If the thing than which none greater can be thought were in the mind alone, then this same thing would both be and not be something than which nothing greater can be conceived. But surely this cannot be. Without doubt then there exists both in the understanding and in reality a being greater than which nothing can be conceived.

So truly does such a thing exist that it cannot be thought of as not existing. For we can think of something as existing which cannot be thought of as not existing, and such a thing is greater than what can be thought not to be. Wherefore, if the thing than which none greater can be thought could be conceived of as not existing then this very thing than which none greater can be thought is not a thing than which

Reprinted with permission of The Free Press, a Division of Macmillan, Inc. from *Medieval Philosophy: from St. Augustine to Nicholas of Cusa*, edited by John F. Nippal and Allen B. Walter. Copyright © 1969 by The Free Press. **Saint Anselm of Canterbury** (1033–1109), a Benedictine, having risen to the rank of Archbishop of Canterbury, was a famous scholar in his day. The monk, **Gaunilon,** was unknown except for his famous exchange with the renowned prelate.

none greater can be thought. But this is not possible. Hence, something greater than which nothing can be conceived so truly exists that it cannot be conceived not to be.

O Lord, our God, you are this being. So truly do you exist that you cannot even be thought of as nonexistent. And rightly so, for if some mind could think of something better than you, then the creature would rise above the Creator and would judge him, which is absurd. It is possible indeed to think of anything other than you as nonexistent. Of all beings then you alone have existence in the truest and highest sense, for nothing else so truly is or has existence in so great a measure. Why then does the fool "say in his heart, 'There is no God,' " when it is so evident to a reasoning mind that of all things you exist in a supreme degree? Why indeed save that he is stupid and a fool!

II
Gaunilon

If one doubts or denies there is some such nature that nothing greater than it can be conceived, he is told that the existence of this being is proved, first, from the fact that in doubting or denying such he already has such a being in his understanding, for in hearing about it, he understands what is said. Next he is told that what he understands must needs exist not only in the intellect but in reality as well. And the proof of this is that a thing is greater if it also exists in reality than if it were in the understanding alone. Were it only in the intellect, even something that once existed would be greater than it. And so what is greater than all is less than something and thus not really greater than everything, which is clearly contradictory. It is necessary then that something greater than all, already proved to exist in the understanding, exists in reality as well, for otherwise it could not be greater than all. To this he might reply: . . .

They say that somewhere in the ocean there is an island, which because of the difficulty, or better, the impossibility of finding what does not exist some call the lost island. And they say this island is inestimably wealthy, having all kinds of delights and riches in greater abundance even than the fabled "Fortunate Islands." And since it has no possessor or inhabitant, it excels all other inhabited countries in its possessions. Now should someone tell me that there is such an island, I could readily understand what he says, since there is no problem there. But suppose he adds, as though it were already implied: "You can't doubt any more that this island, which is more excellent than any land, really exists somewhere, since you don't doubt that it is in your understanding and that it is more excellent not to be in the understanding only. Hence it is necessary that it really exists, for if it did not, any land which does would excel it and consequently the island which you already understand to be more excellent would not be such." If one were to try to prove to me that this island in truth exists and its existence should no longer be questioned, either I would think he was joking or I would not know whether to consider him or me the greater fool, me for conceding his argument or him for supposing he had established with any certainty such an island's existence without first showing such excellence to be real and its existence indubitable rather than just a figment of my understanding, whose existence is uncertain.

This then is an answer the fool could make to your arguments against him. When he is first assured that this being is so great that its nonexistence is inconceivable, and that this in turn is established for no other reason than that otherwise it would not excel all things, he could counter the same way and say: "When have I admitted there really is any such thing, i.e. something so much greater than everything else that one could prove to me it is so real, it could not even be conceived as unreal?" What we need at the outset is a very firm argument to show there is some superior being, bigger and better than all else that exists, so that we can go on from this to prove all the other attributes such a bigger and better being has to have. As for the statement that it is inconceivable that the highest thing of all should not exist, it might be better to say its nonexistence or even its possibility of nonexistence is unintelligible. For according to the true meaning of the word, unreal things are not intelligible, but their existence is conceivable in the way that the fool thinks that God does not exist. I most certainly know I exist, but for all that, I know my nonexistence is possible. As for that supreme being which God is, I understand without doubt both his existence and the impossibility of his nonexistence. But whether I can conceive of my nonexistence as long as I most certainly know I exist, I don't know. But if I am able to, why can I not conceive of the nonexistence of whatever else I know with the same certainty? But if I cannot, then such an inability will not be something peculiar to God . . .

III
Saint Anselm

It was a fool against whom I argued in my little work. But since my critic is far from a fool, and is a Catholic speaking in the fool's behalf, it is enough for me if I can answer the Catholic . . .

But you claim our argument is on a par with the following. Someone imagines an island in the ocean which surpasses all lands in its fertility. Because of the difficulty, or rather impossibility, of finding what does not exist, he calls it "Lost Island." He might then say you cannot doubt that it really exists, because anyone can readily understand it from its verbal description. I assert confidently that if anyone finds something for me, besides that "than which none greater is conceivable," which exists either in reality or concept alone to which the logic of my argument can be applied, I will find and give him his "Lost Island," never to be lost again. But it now seems obvious that a thing such that none greater can be conceived cannot be thought of as nonexistent since it exists on such firm grounds of truth. For otherwise it would not exist at all. If anyone says he thinks it does not exist, then I declare that when he thinks this he either thinks of something than which a greater is inconceivable, or else he does not think at all. If he does not think, then neither does he think that what he is not thinking of is nonexistent. But if he does think, then he thinks of something which cannot be thought of as not existing. For if it could be conceived as nonexistent, it could be conceived as having a beginning and an end. Now this is impossible. Hence if anyone thinks of it, he thinks of something that cannot even be conceived to be nonexistent. Now whoever conceives it thus doesn't think of it as nonexistent, for if he did he would conceive what can't be conceived. Nonexistence is inconceivable, then, of something greater than which nothing can be conceived.

You claim moreover that when we say this supreme reality cannot be conceived of as nonexistent, it would be perhaps better to say that its nonexistence or even the possibility of its nonexistence is not understandable. But it is better to say it cannot be conceived. For had I said that the reality itself could not be understood not to exist, perhaps you, who insist that according to proper usage what is false cannot be understood, would object that nothing existing could be understood not to exist. For it is false to claim that what exists does not exist. Hence it would not be peculiar to God to be unable to be understood as nonexistent. If any one of the things that most certainly exist can be understood to be nonexistent, however, then other certain things can also be understood to be nonexistent. But this objection cannot be applied to "conceiving," if this is correctly understood. For though none of the things that exist can be understood not to exist, still they can all be conceived as nonexistent except the greatest. For all—and only—those things can be conceived as nonexistent which have a beginning or end or consist of parts or do not exist in their entirety in any time or place, as I have said. Only that being which cannot be conceived to be nonexistent must be conceived as having no beginning or end or composition of parts but is whole and entire always and everywhere.

Consequently you must realize that you can conceive of yourself as nonexistent, though you most certainly know that you exist. You surprise me when you say you are not sure of this. For we conceive of many things as nonexistent which we know to exist and of many things as existent which we know do not exist. And we conceive them thus not by judging but by imagining them so. We can indeed conceive of something as existent even while we know it does not exist, because we are able to conceive the one at the same time that we know the other. But we cannot conceive nonexistence while knowing existence, because we cannot conceive existence and nonexistence at the same time. If anyone distinguishes between the two senses of the statement in this fashion, then, he will understand that nothing, as long as it is known to be, can be conceived not to be, and that whatever exists, with the exception of a thing such that no greater is conceivable can be conceived of as nonexistent even when it is known to exist. This inability to be conceived of as nonexistent, then, is peculiar to God, even though there are many objects which cannot be conceived not to be while they are . . .

NORMAN MALCOLM
Anselm's Ontological Arguments

I

I believe that in Anselm's *Proslogion* and *Responsio editoris* there are two different pieces of reasoning which he did not distinguish from one another, and that a good deal of light may be shed on the philosophical problem of "the ontological argument" if we do distinguish them. In Chapter 2 of the *Proslogion*[1] Anselm says that we believe that God is *something a greater than which cannot be conceived.* (The Latin is *aliquid quo nihil maius cogitari posit.* Anselm sometimes uses the alternative expressions *aliquid quo maius nihil cogitari potest, id quo maius cogitari nequit, aliquid quo maius cogitari non valet.*) Even the fool of the Psalm who says in his heart there is no God, when he hears this very thing that Anselm says, namely, "something a greater than which cannot be conceived," understands what he hears, and what he understands is in his understanding though he does not understand that it exists.

"Anselm's Ontological Arguments" appeared in *The Philosophical Review,* Vo. LXIX (1960) and in *Knowledge and Certainty* (Cornell University Press, 1963). Reprinted by permission of Norman Malcolm. **Norman Malcolm** (b. 1911), a well-known student of the influential Austrian philosopher Ludwig Wittgenstein (1889–1951), has written incisively in epistemology, philosophy of mind and philosophy of religion.

Apparently Anselm regards it as tautological to say that whatever is understood is in the understanding (*quidquid intelligitur in intellectu est*): he uses *intelligitur* and *in intellectu est* as interchangeable locutions. The same holds for another formula of his: whatever is thought is in thought (*quidquid cogitatur in cogitatione est*).[2]

Of course many things may exist in the understanding that do not exist in reality; for example, elves. Now, says Anselm, something a greater than which cannot be conceived exists in the understanding. But it cannot exist *only* in the understanding, for to exist in reality is greater. Therefore that thing a greater than which cannot be conceived cannot exist only in the understanding, for then a greater thing could be conceived: namely, one that exists both in the understanding and in reality.[3]

Here I have a question. It is not clear to me whether Anselm means that (a) existence in reality by itself is greater than existence in the understanding, or that (b) existence in reality and existence in the understanding together are greater than existence in the understanding alone. Certainly he accepts (b). But he might also accept (a), as Descartes apparently does in *Meditation III* when he suggests that the mode of being by which a thing is "objectively in the understanding" is *imperfect*.[4] Of course Anselm might accept both (a) and (b). He might hold that in general something is greater if it has both of these "modes of existence" than if it has either one alone, but also that existence in reality is a more perfect mode of existence than existence in the understanding.

In any case, Anselm holds that something is greater if it exists both in the understanding and in reality than if it exists merely in the understanding. An equivalent way of putting this interesting proposition, in a more current terminology, is: something is greater if it is both conceived of and exists than if it is merely conceived of. Anselm's reasoning can be expressed as follows: *id quo maius cogitari nequit* cannot be merely conceived of and not exist, for then it would not be *id quo maius cogitari nequit*. The doctrine that something is greater if it exists in addition to being conceived of, than if

it is only conceived of, could be called the doctrine that existence is a perfection. Descartes maintained, in so many words, that existence is a perfection,[5] and presumably he was holding Anselm's doctrine, although he does not, in *Meditation V* or elsewhere, argue in the way that Anselm does in *Proslogion 2*.

When Anselm says, "And certainly, that than which nothing greater can be conceived cannot exist merely in the understanding. For suppose it exists merely in the understanding, then it can be conceived to exist in reality, which is greater,"[6] he is claiming that if I conceived of a being of great excellence, that being would be *greater* (more excellent, more perfect) if it existed than if it did not exist. His supposition that "it exists merely in the understanding" is the supposition that it is conceived of but does not exist. Anselm repeated this claim in his reply to the criticism of the monk Gaunilo. Speaking of the being a greater than which cannot be conceived, he says:

> I have said that if it exists merely in the understanding it can be conceived to exist in reality, which is greater. Therefore, if it exists merely in the understanding obviously the very being a greater than which cannot be conceived, is one a greater than which can be conceived. What, I ask, can follow better than that? For if it exists merely in the understanding, can it not be conceived to exist in reality? And if it can be so conceived does not he who conceives of this conceive of a thing greater than it, if it does exist merely in the understanding? Can anything follow better than this: that if a being a greater than which cannot be conceived exists merely in the understanding, it is something a greater than which can be conceived? What could be plainer?[7]

He is implying, in the first sentence, that if I conceive of something which does not exist then it is possible for it to exist, and *it will be greater if it exists than if it does not exist.*

The doctrine that existence is a perfection is remarkably queer. It makes sense and is true to say that my future house will be a better one if it is insulated than if it is not insulated; but what could it mean to say that it will be a better house if it exists than if it does not? My future child will be a better man if he is honest than if he is not; but who would understand the saying that he will be a better man if he exists than if he does not? Or who understands the saying that if God exists He is more perfect than if He does not exist? One may say, with some intelligibility, that it would be better (for oneself or for mankind) if God exists than He does not—but that is a different matter.

A king might desire that his next chancellor should have knowledge, wit, and resolution; but it is ludicrous to add that the king's desire is to have a chancellor who exists. Suppose that two royal councilors, A and B, were asked to draw up separately descriptions of the most perfect chancellor they could conceive, and that the descriptions they produced were identical except that A included existence in his list of attributes of a perfect chancellor and B did not. (I do not mean that B put nonexistence in his list.) One and the same person could satisfy both descriptions. More to the point, any person who satisfied A's description would *necessarily* satisfy B's description and *vice versa!* This is to say that A and B did not produce descriptions that differed in any way but rather one and the same description of necessary and desirable qualities in a chancellor. A only made a show of putting down a desirable quality that B had failed to include.

I believe I am merely restating an observation that Kant made in attacking the notion that "existence" or "being" is a "real predicate." He says:

> By whatever and by however many predicates we may think a thing—even if we completely determine it—we do not make the least addition to the thing when we further declare that this thing *is*. Otherwise, it would not be exactly the same thing that exists, but something more than we had thought in the concept; and we could not, therefore, say that the exact object of my concept exists.[8]

Anselm's ontological proof of *Proslogion 2* is fallacious because it rests on the false doctrine that existence is a perfection (and therefore that "existence" is a "real predicate"). It would be desirable to have a rigorous refutation of the doctrine but I have not been able to provide one. I am compelled to leave the matter at the more or less intuitive level of Kant's observation. In any case, I believe that the doctrine does not belong to Anselm's other formulation of the ontological argument. It is worth noting that Gassendi anticipated Kant's criticism when he said, against Descartes:

> Existence is a perfection neither in God nor in anything else; it is rather that in the absence of which there is no perfection. . . . Hence neither is existence held to exist in a thing in the way that perfections do, nor if the thing lacks existence is it said to be imperfect (or deprived of a perfection), so much as to be nothing.[9]

II

I take up now the consideration of the second ontological proof, which Anselm presents in the very next chapter of the *Proslogion*. (There is no evidence that he thought of himself as offering two different proofs.) Speaking of the being a greater than which cannot be conceived, he says:

And it so truly exists that it cannot be conceived not to exist. For it is possible to conceive of a being which cannot be conceived not to exist; and this is greater than one which can be conceived not to exist. Hence, if that, than which nothing greater can be conceived, can be conceived not to exist, it is not that than which nothing greater can be conceived. But this is a contradiction. So truly, therefore, is there something than which nothing greater can be conceived, that it cannot even be conceived not to exist.

And this being thou art, O Lord, our God.[10]

Anselm is saying two things: first, that a being whose nonexistence is logically impossible is "greater" than a being whose nonexistence is logically possible (and therefore that a being a greater than which cannot be conceived must be one whose nonexistence is logically impossible); second, that *God* is a being than which a greater cannot be conceived.

In regard to the second of these assertions, there certainly is *a* use of the word "God," and I think far the more common use, in accordance with which the statements "God is the greatest of all beings," "God is the most perfect being," "God is the supreme being," are *logically* necessary truths, in the same sense that the statement "A square has four sides" is a logically necessary truth. If there is a man named "Jones" who is the tallest man in the world, the statement "Jones is the tallest man in the world" is merely true and is not a logically necessary truth. It is a virtue of Anselm's unusual phrase, "a being a greater than which cannot be conceived,"[11] to make it explicit that the sentence "God is the greatest of all beings" expresses a logically necessary truth and not a mere matter of fact such as the one we imagined about Jones.

With regard to Anselm's first assertion (namely, that a being whose nonexistence is logically impossible is greater than a being whose nonexistence is logically possible) perhaps the most puzzling thing about it is the use of the word "greater." It appears to mean exactly the same as "superior," "more excellent," "more perfect." This equivalence by itself is of no help to us, however, since the latter expressions would be equally puzzling here. What is required is some explanation of their use.

We do think of *knowledge,* say, as an excellence, a good thing. If A has more knowledge of algebra than B we express this in common language by saying that A has a *better* knowledge of algebra than B, or that A's knowledge of algebra is *superior* to B's, whereas we should not say that B has a better or superior *ignorance* of algebra than A. We do say "greater ignorance," but here the word "greater" is used purely quantitatively.

Previously I rejected *existence* as a perfection. Anselm is maintaining in the remarks last quoted, not that existence is a perfection, but that *the logical impossibility of nonexistence is a perfection.* In other words, *necessary existence* is a perfection. His first ontological proof uses the principle that a thing is greater if it exists than if it does not exist. His second proof employs the different principle that a thing is greater if it necessarily exists than if it does not necessarily exist.

Some remarks about the notion of *dependence* may help to make this latter principle intelligible. Many things depend for their existence on other things and events. My house was built by a carpenter: its coming into existence was dependent on a certain creative activity. Its continued existence is dependent on many things: that a tree does not crush it, that it is not consumed by fire, and so on. If we reflect on the common meaning of the word "God" (no matter how vague and confused this is), we realize that it is incompatible with this meaning that God's existence should *depend* on anything. Whether we believe in Him or not we must admit that the "almighty and everlasting God" (as several ancient prayers begin), the "Maker of heaven and earth, and of all things visible and invisible" (as is said in the Nicene Creed), cannot be thought of as being brought into existence by anything or as depending for His continued existence on anything. To conceive of anything as dependent upon something else for its existence is to conceive of it as a lesser being than God.

If a housewife has a set of extremely fragile dishes, then as dishes they are *inferior* to those of another set like them in all respects except that they are *not* fragile. Those of the first set are *dependent* for their continued existence on gentle handling; those of the second set are not. There is a definite connection in common language between the notions of dependency and inferiority, and independence and superiority. To say that something which was dependent on nothing whatever was superior to ("greater than") anything that was dependent in any way upon anything is quite in keeping with the everyday use of the terms "superior" and "greater." Correlative with the notions of dependence and independence are the notions of *limited* and *unlimited*. An engine requires fuel and this is a limitation. It is the same thing to say that an engine's operation is *dependent* on as that it is *limited* by its fuel supply. An engine that could accomplish the same work in the same time and was in other respects satisfactory, but did not require fuel, would be a *superior* engine.

God is usually conceived of as an *unlimited* being. He is conceived of as a being who *could not* be limited, that is, as an absolutely unlimited being. This is no less than to conceive of Him as *something a greater than which cannot be conceived*. If God is conceived to be an absolutely unlimited being He must be conceived to be unlimited in regard to His existence as well as His operation. In this conception it will not make sense to say that He depends on anything for coming into or continuing in existence. Nor, as Spinoza observed, will it make sense to say that something could *prevent* Him from existing.[12] Lack of moisture can prevent trees from existing in a certain region of the earth. But it would be contrary to the concept of God as an unlimited being to suppose that anything other than God Himself could prevent Him from existing, and it would be self-contradictory to suppose that He Himself could do it.

Some may be inclined to object that although nothing could prevent God's existence, still it might just *happen* that He did not exist. And if He did exist that too would be by chance. I think, however, that from the supposition that it could happen that God did not exist it would follow that, if He existed, He would have mere duration and not eternity. It would

make sense to ask, "How long has He existed?," "Will He still exist next week?," "He was in existence yesterday but how about today?," and so on. It seems absurd to make God the subject of such questions. According to our ordinary conception of Him, He is an eternal being. And eternity does not mean endless duration, as Spinoza noted. To ascribe eternity to something is to exclude as senseless all sentences that imply that it has duration. If a thing has duration then it would be merely a *contingent* fact, if it was a fact, that its duration was endless. The moon could have endless duration but not eternity. If something has endless duration it will *make sense* (although it will be false) to say that it will cease to exist, and it will make sense (although it will be false) to say that something will *cause* it to cease to exist. A being with endless duration is not, therefore, an absolutely unlimited being. That God is conceived to be eternal follows from the fact that He is conceived to be an absolutely unlimited being.

I have been trying to expand the argument of *Proslogion* 3. In *Responsio* 1 Anselm adds the following acute point: if you can conceive of a certain thing and this thing does not exist then if it *were* to exist its nonexistence would be *possible*. It follows, I believe, that if the thing were to exist it would depend on other things both for coming into and continuing in existence, and also that it would have duration and not eternity. Therefore it would not be, either in reality or in conception, an unlimited being, *aliquid quo nihil maius cogitari possit*.

Anselm states his argument as follows:

If it [the thing a greater than which cannot be conceived] can be conceived at all it must exist. For no one who denies or doubts the existence of a being a greater than which is inconceivable, denies or doubts that if it did exist its nonexistence, either in reality or in the understanding, would be impossible. For otherwise it would not be a being a greater than which cannot be conceived. But as to whatever can be conceived but-does not exist: if it were to exist its non-existence either in reality or in the understanding would be possible. Therefore, if a being a greater than which cannot be conceived, can even be conceived, it must exist.[13]

What Anselm has proved is that the notion of contingent existence or of contingent nonexistence cannot have any application to God. His existence must either be logically necessary or logically impossible. The only intelligible way of rejecting Anselm's claim that God's existence is necessary is to maintain that the concept of God, as a being a greater than which cannot be conceived, is self-contradictory or nonsensical.[14] Supposing that this is false, Anselm is right to deduce God's necessary existence from his characterization of Him as a being a greater than which cannot be conceived.

Let me summarize the proof. If God, a being a greater than which cannot be conceived, does not exist then He cannot *come* into existence. For if He did He would either have been *caused* to come into existence or have *happened* to come into existence, and in either case He would be a limited being, which by our conception of Him He is not. Since He cannot come into existence, if He does not exist His existence is impossible. If He does exist He cannot have come into existence (for the reasons given), nor can He cease to exist, for nothing could cause Him to cease to exist nor could it just happen that He ceased to exist. So if God exists His existence is necessary. Thus God's existence is either impossible or necessary. It can be the former only if the concept of such a being is self-contradictory or in some way logically absurd. Assuming that this is not so, it follows that He necessarily exists.

It may be helpful to express ourselves in the following way: to say, not that *omnipotence* is a property of God, but rather that *necessary omnipotence* is; and to say, not that omniscience is a property of God, but rather that *necessary omniscience* is. We have criteria for determining that a man knows this and that and can do this and that, and for determining that one man

has greater knowledge and abilities in a certain subject than another. We could think of various tests to give them. But there is nothing we should wish to describe, seriously and literally, as "testing" God's knowledge and powers. That God is omniscient and omnipotent has not been determined by the application of criteria: rather these are requirements of our conception of Him. They are internal properties of the concept, although they are also rightly said to be properties of God. *Necessary existence* is a property of God in the *same sense* that *necessary omnipotence* and *necessary omniscience* are His properties. And we are not to think that "God necessarily exists" means that it follows necessarily from something that God exists *contingently*. The a priori proposition "God necessarily exists" entails the proposition "God exists," if and only if the latter also is understood as an a priori proposition: in which case the two propositions are equivalent. In this sense Anselm's proof is a proof of God's existence.

Descartes was somewhat hazy on the question of whether existence is a property of things that exist, but at the same time he saw clearly enough that *necessary existence* is a property of God. Both points are illustrated in his reply to Gassendi's remark, which I quoted above:

I do not see to what class of reality you wish to assign existence, nor do I see why it may not be said to be a property as well as omnipotence, taking the word property as equivalent to any attribute or anything which can be predicated of a thing, as in the present case it should be by all means regarded. Nay, necessary existence in the case of God is also a true property in the strictest sense of the word, because it belongs to Him and forms part of His essence alone.[15]

Elsewhere he speaks of "the necessity of existence" as being "that crown of perfections without which we cannot comprehend God."[16] He is emphatic on the point that necessary existence applies solely to "an absolutely perfect Being."[17]

III

I wish to consider now a part of Kant's criticism of the ontological argument which I believe to be wrong. He says:

> If, in an identical proposition, I reject the predicate while retaining the subject, contradiction results; and I therefore say that the former belongs necessarily to the latter. But if we reject subject and predicate alike, there is no contradiction; for nothing is then left that can be contradicted. To posit a triangle, and yet to reject its three angles, is self-contradictory; but there is no contradiction in rejecting the triangle together with its three angles. The same holds true of the concept of an absolutely necessary being. If its existence is rejected, we reject the thing itself with all its predicates; and no question of contradiction can then arise. There is nothing outside it that would then be contradicted, since the necessity of the thing is not supposed to be derived from anything external; nor is there anything internal that would be contradicted, since in rejecting the thing itself we have at the same time rejected all its internal properties. "God is omnipotent" is a necessary judgment. The omnipotence cannot be rejected if we posit a Deity, that is, an infinite being; for the two concepts are identical. But if we say, "There is no God," neither the omnipotence nor any other of its predicates is given; they are one and all rejected together with the subject, and there is therefore not the least contradiction in such a judgment.[18]

To these remarks the reply is that when the concept of God is correctly understood one sees that one cannot "reject the subject." "There is no God" is seen to be a necessarily false statement. Anselm's demonstration proves that the proposition "God exists" has the same a priori footing as the proposition "God is omnipotent."

Many present-day philosophers, in agreement with Kant, declare that existence is not a property and think that this overthrows the ontological argument. Although it is an error to regard existence as a property of things that have contingent existence, it does not follow that it is an error to regard necessary existence as a property of God. A recent writer says, against Anselm, that a proof of God's existence "based on the necessities of thought" is "universally regarded as fallacious: it is not thought possible to build bridges between mere abstractions and concrete existence."[19] But this way of putting the matter obscures the distinction we need to make. Does "concrete existence" mean contingent existence? Then to build bridges between concrete existence and mere abstractions would be like inferring the existence of an island from the concept of a perfect island, which both Anselm and Descartes regarded as absurd. What Anselm did was to give a demonstration that the proposition "God necessarily exists" is entailed by the proposition "God is a being a greater than which cannot be conceived" (which is equivalent to "God is an absolutely unlimited being"). Kant declares that when "I think a being as the supreme reality, without any defect, the question still remains whether it exists or not."[20] But once one has grasped Anselm's proof of the necessary existence of a being a greater than which cannot be conceived, no question remains as to whether it exists or not, just as Euclid's demonstration of the existence of an infinity of prime numbers leaves no question on that issue.

Kant says that "every reasonable person" must admit that "all existential propositions are synthetic."[21] Part of the perplexity one has about the ontological argument is in deciding whether or not the proposition "God necessarily exists" is or is not an "existential proposition." But let us look around. Is the Euclidean theorem in number theory, "There exists an infinite number of prime numbers," an "existential proposition"? Do we not want to say that *in some sense* it asserts the existence of something? Cannot we say, with equal justification, that the proposition "God necessarily exists" asserts the existence of something, *in some sense?* What we need to understand, in each case, is the particular sense of the assertion. Neither proposition has the same sort of sense as do the propositions, "A low pressure area exists over the Great Lakes," "There still exists some possibility that he will survive," "The pain continues to exist in his abdomen." One good way of seeing the difference in sense of these various propositions is to see the variously different ways in which they are proved or supported. It is wrong to think that all assertions of existence have the same kind of meaning. There are as many kinds of existential propositions as there are kinds of subjects of discourse.

Closely related to Kant's view that all existential propositions are "synthetic" is the contemporary dogma that all existential propositions are contingent. Professor Gilbert Ryle tells us that "Any assertion of the existence of something, like any assertion of the occurrence of something, can be denied without logical absurdity."[22] "All existential statements are contingent," says Mr. I. M. Crombie.[23] Professor J. J. C. Smart remarks that "Existence is not a property" and then goes on to assert that "There can never be any *logical contradiction* in denying that God exists."[24] He declares that "The concept of a logically necessary being is a self-contradictory concept, like the concept of a round square. . . . No existential proposition can be logically necessary," he maintains, for "the truth of a logically necessary proposition depends only on our symbolism, or to put the same thing in another way, on the relationship of concepts" (p. 38). Professor K. E. M. Baier says, "It is no longer seriously in dispute that the notion of a logically necessary being is self-contradictory. Whatever can be conceived of as existing can equally be conceived of as not existing."[25] This is a repetition of Hume's assertion, "Whatever we conceive as existent, we can also conceive as non-existent. There is no being, therefore, whose non-existence implies a contradiction."[26]

Professor J. N. Findlay ingeniously constructs an ontological *dis*proof of God's existence, based on a "modern" view of the nature of "necessity in propositions": the view, namely, that necessity in propositions "merely reflects our use of words, the arbitrary conventions of our language."[27] Findlay undertakes to characterize what he calls "religious attitude," and here there is a striking agreement between his observations and some of the things I have said in expounding Anselm's proof. Religious attitude, he says, presumes *superiority* in its object and superiority so great that the worshiper is in comparison as nothing. Religious attitude finds it "anomalous to worship anything *limited* in any thinkable manner. . . . And hence we are led on irresistibly to demand that our religious object should have an *unsurpassable* supremacy along all avenues, that it should tower *infinitely* above all other objects" (p. 51). We cannot help feeling that "the worthy object of our worship can never be a thing that merely *happens* to exist, nor one on which all other objects merely *happen* to depend. The true object of religious reverence must not be one, merely, to which no *actual* independent realities stand opposed: it must be one to which such opposition is totally *inconceivable*. . . . And not only must the existence of *other* things be unthinkable without Him, but His own nonexistence must be wholly unthinkable in any circumstances" (p. 52). And now, says Findlay, when we add up these various requirements, what they entail is "not only that there isn't a God, but that the Divine Existence is either senseless or impossible" (p. 54). For on the one hand, "if God is to satisfy religious claims and needs, He must be a being in every way inescapable, One whose existence and whose possession of certain excellences we cannot possibly conceive away." On the other hand, "modern views make it self-evidently absurd (if they don't make it ungrammatical) to speak of such a Being and attribute existence to Him. It was indeed an ill day for Anselm when he hit upon his famous proof. For on that day he not only laid bare something that is of the essence of an adequate religious object, but also some-

thing that entails its necessary non-existence"
(p. 55).

Now I am inclined to hold the "modern" view that logically necessary truth "merely reflects our use of words" (although I do not believe that the conventions of language are always *arbitrary*). But I confess that I am unable to see how that view is supposed to lead to the conclusion that "the Divine existence is either senseless or impossible." Findlay does not explain how this result comes about. Surely he cannot mean that this view entails that nothing can have necessary properties: for this would imply that mathematics is "senseless or impossible," which no one wants to hold. Trying to fill in the argument that is missing from his article, the most plausible conjecture I can make is the following: Findlay thinks that the view that logical necessity "reflects the use of words" implies, not that nothing has necessary properties, but that *existence* cannot be a necessary property of anything. That is to say, every proposition of the form "*x* exists," including the proposition "God exists," must be *contingent*.[28] At the same time, our concept of God requires that His existence be *necessary*, that is, that "God exists" be a necessary truth. Therefore, the modern view of necessity proves that what the concept of God requires *cannot* be fulfilled. It proves that God *cannot* exist.

The correct reply is that the view that logical necessity merely reflects the use of words cannot possibly have the implication that every existential proposition must be contingent. That view requires us to *look at* the use of words and not manufacture a priori theses about it. In the Ninetieth Psalm it is said: "Before the mountains were brought forth, or ever thou hadst formed the earth and the world, even from everlasting to everlasting, thou art God." Here is expressed the idea of the necessary existence and eternity of God, an idea that is essential to the Jewish and Christian religions. In those complex systems of thought, those "languages-games," God has the status of a necessary being. Who can doubt that? Here we must say with Wittgenstein, "This language-game is played!"[29] I believe we may rightly take the existence of those religious systems of thought in which God figures as a necessary being to be a disproof of the dogma, affirmed by Hume and others, that no existential proposition can be necessary.

Another way of criticizing the ontological argument is the following. "Granted that the concept of necessary existence follows from the concept of a being a greater than which cannot be conceived, this amounts to no more than granting the *a priori* truth of the *conditional* proposition, 'If such a being exists then it necessarily exists.' This proposition, however, does not entail the *existence of anything,* and one can deny its antecedent without contradiction." Kant, for example, compares the proposition (or "judgment," as he calls it) "A triangle has three angles" with the proposition "God is a necessary being." He allows that the former is "absolutely necessary" and goes on to say:

> The absolute necessity of the judgment is only a conditional necessity of the thing, or of the predicate in the judgment. The above proposition does not declare that three angles are absolutely necessary, but that, under the condition that there is a triangle (that is, that a triangle is given), three angles will necessarily be found in it.[30]

He is saying, quite correctly, that the proposition about triangles is equivalent to the conditional proposition, "If a triangle exists, it has three angles." He then makes the comment that there is no contradiction "in rejecting the triangle together with its three angles." He proceeds to draw the alleged parallel: "The same holds true of the concept of an absolutely necessary being. If its existence is rejected, we reject the thing itself with all its predicates; and no question of contradiction can then arise."[31] The priest, Caterus, made the same objection to Descartes when he said:

> Though it be conceded that an entity of the highest perfection implies its existence by its very name, yet it does not follow that that very existence is anything actual

in the real world, but merely that the concept of existence is inseparably united with the concept of highest being. Hence you cannot infer that the existence of God is anything actual, unless you assume that that highest being actually exists; for then it will actually contain all its perfections, together with this perfection of real existence.[32]

I think that Caterus, Kant, and numerous other philosophers have been mistaken in supposing that the proposition "God is a necessary being" (or "God necessarily exists") is equivalent to the conditional proposition "If God exists then He necessarily exists."[33] For how do they want the antecedent clause, "*If* God exists," to be understood? Clearly they want it to imply that it is *possible* that God does *not* exist.[34] The whole point of Kant's analysis is to try to show that it is possible to "reject the subject." Let us make this implication explicit in the conditional proposition, so that it reads: "If God exists (and it is possible that He does not) then He necessarily exists." But now it is apparent, I think, that these philosophers have arrived at a self-contradictory position. I do not mean that this conditional proposition, taken alone, is self-contradictory. Their position is self-contradictory in the following way. On the one hand, they agree that the proposition "God necessarily exists" is an a priori truth; Kant implies that it is "absolutely necessary," and Caterus says that God's existence is implied by His very name. On the other hand, they think that it is correct to analyze this proposition in such a way that it will entail the proposition "It is possible that God does not exist." But so far from its being the case that the proposition "God necessarily exists" entails the proposition "It is possible that God does not exist," it is rather the case that they are *incompatible* with one another! Can anything be clearer than that the conjunction "God necessarily exists but it is possible that He does not exist" is self-contradictory? Is it not just as plainly self-contradictory as the conjunction "A square necessarily has four sides but it is possible for a square not to have four sides"? In short, this familiar criticism of the ontological argument is self-contradictory, because it accepts *both* of two incompatible propositions.[35]

One conclusion we may draw from our examination of this criticism is that (contrary to Kant) there is a lack of symmetry, in an important respect, between the propositions "A triangle has three angles" and "God has necessary existence," although both are a priori. The former can be expressed in the conditional assertion "If a triangle exists (and it is possible that none does) it has three angles." The latter cannot be expressed in the corresponding conditional assertion without contradiction.

IV

I turn to the question of whether the idea of a being a greater than which cannot be conceived is self-contradictory. Here Leibniz made a contribution to the discussion of the ontological argument. He remarked that the argument of Anselm and Descartes

is not a paralogism, but it is an imperfect demonstration, which assumes something that must still be proved in order to render it mathematically evident; that is, it is tactily assumed that this idea of the all-great or all-perfect being is possible, and implies no contradiction. And it is already something that by this remark it is proved that, assuming that God is possible, he exists, which is the privilege of divinity alone.[36]

Leibniz undertook to give a proof that God is possible. He defined a *perfection* as a simple, positive quality in the highest degree.[37] He argued that since perfections are *simple* qualities they must be compatible with one another.

Therefore the concept of a being possessing all perfections is consistent.

I will not review his argument because I do not find his definition of a perfection intelligible. For one thing, it assumes that certain qualities or attributes are "positive" in their intrinsic nature, and others "negative" or "privative," and I have not been able clearly to understand that. For another thing, it assumes that some qualities are intrinsically simple. I believe that Wittgenstein has shown in the *Investigations* that nothing is *intrinsically* simple, but that whatever has the status of a simple, an indefinable, in one system of concepts, may have the status of a complex thing, a definable thing, in another system of concepts.

I do not know how to demonstrate that the concept of God—that is, of a being a greater than which cannot be conceived—is not self-contradictory. But I do not think that it is legitimate to demand such a demonstration. I also do not know how to demonstrate that either the concept of a material thing or the concept of *seeing* a material thing is not self-contradictory, and philosophers have argued that both of them are. With respect to any particular reasoning that is offered for holding that the concept of seeing a material thing, for example, is self-contradictory, one may try to show the invalidity of the reasoning and thus free the concept from the charge of being self-contradictory *on that ground*. But I do not understand what it would mean to demonstrate *in general*, and not in respect to any particular reasoning, that the concept is not self-contradictory. So it is with the concept of God. I should think there is no more of a presumption that it is self-contradictory than is the concept of seeing a material thing. Both concepts have a place in the thinking and the lives of human beings.

But even if one allows that Anselm's phrase may be free of self-contradiction, one wants to know how it can have any *meaning* for anyone. Why is it that human beings have even *formed* the concept of an infinite being, a being a greater than which cannot be conceived? This is a legitimate and important question. I am sure there cannot be a deep understanding of that concept without an understanding of the phenomena of human life that give rise to it. To give an account of the latter is beyond my ability. I wish, however, to make one suggestion (which should not be understood as autobiographical).

There is the phenomenon of feeling guilt for something that one has done or thought or felt or for a disposition that one has. One wants to be free of this guilt. But sometimes the guilt is felt to be so great that one is sure that nothing one could do oneself, nor any forgiveness by another human being, would remove it. One feels a guilt that is beyond all measure, a guilt "a greater than which cannot be conceived." Paradoxically, it would seem, one nevertheless has an intense desire to have this incomparable guilt removed. One requires a forgiveness that is beyond all measure, a forgiveness "a greater than which cannot be conceived." Out of such a storm in the soul, I am suggesting, there arises the conception of a forgiving mercy that is limitless, beyond all measure. This is one important feature of the Jewish and Christian conception of God.

I wish to relate this thought to a remark made by Kierkegaard, who was speaking about belief in Christianity but whose remark may have a wider application. He says:

> There is only one proof of the truth of Christianity and that, quite rightly, is from the emotions, when the dread of sin and a heavy conscience torture a man into crossing the narrow line between despair bordering upon madness—and Christendom.[38]

One may think it absurd for a human being to feel a guilt of such magnitude, and even more absurd that, if he feels it, he should *desire* its removal. I have nothing to say about that. It may also be absurd for people to fall in love, but they do it. I wish only to say that there *is* that human phenomenon of an unbearably heavy conscience and that it is importantly connected with the genesis of the concept of God, that is, with the formation of the "grammar" of the word "God." I am sure that this concept is related to human experience in other ways. If one had the acuteness and depth to perceive these connections one could grasp the *sense* of the concept. When we encounter this concept as a problem in philosophy, we do not consider the human phenomena that lie behind it. It is not surprising that many philosophers believe that the idea of a necessary being is an arbitrary and absurd construction.

What is the relation of Anselm's ontological argument to religious belief? This is a difficult question. I can imagine an atheist going through the argument, becoming convinced of its validity, acutely defending it against objections, yet remaining an atheist. The only effect it could have on the fool of the Psalm would be that he stopped saying in his heart "There is no God," because he would now realize that this is something he cannot meaningfully say or think. It is hardly to be expected that a demonstrative argument should, in addition, produce in him a living faith. Surely there is a level at which one can view the argument as a piece of logic, following the deductive moves but not being touched religiously? I think so. But even at this level the argument may not be without religious value, for it may help to remove some philosophical scruples that stand in the way of faith. At a deeper level, I suspect that the argument can be thoroughly understood only by one who has a view of that human "form of life" that gives rise to the idea of an infinitely great being, who views it from the *inside* not just from the outside and who has, therefore, at least some inclination to *partake* in that religious form of life. This inclination, in Kierkegaard's words, is "from the emotions." This inclination can hardly be an *effect* of Anselm's argument, but is rather presupposed in the fullest understanding of it. It would be unreasonable to require that the recognition of Anselm's demonstration as valid must produce a conversion.

NOTES

1. I have consulted the Latin text of the *Proslogion*, of *Gaunilonis Pro Insipiente*, and of the *Responsio editoris*, in S. Anselmi, *Opera Omnia*, edited by F. C. Schmitt (Secovii, 1938), vol. I. With numerous modifications, I have used the English translation by S. N. Deane: *St. Anselm* (La Salle, Illinois, 1948).
2. See *Proslogion* 1 and *Responsio* 2.
3. Anselm's actual words are: "Et certe id quo maius cogitari nequit, non potest esse in solo intellectu. Si enim vel in solo intellectu est, potest cogitari esse et in re, quod maius est. Si ergo id quo maius cogitari non potest, est in solo intellectu: id ipsum quo maius cogitari non potest, est quo maius cogitari potest. Sed certe hoc esse non potest." *Proslogion* 2.
4. Haldane and Ross, *The Philosophical Works of Descartes*, 2 vols. (Cambridge, 1931), I, 163.
5. *Op. cit.*, p. 182.
6. *Proslogion* 2; Deane, p. 8.
7. *Responsio* 2; Deane, pp. 157–158.
8. *The Critique of Pure Reason*, tr. by Norman Kemp Smith (London, 1929), p. 505.
9. Haldane and Ross, II, 186.
10. *Proslogion* 3; Deane, pp. 8–9.
11. Professor Robert Calhoun has pointed out to me that a similar locution had been used by Augustine. In *De moribus Manichaeorum* (Bk. II, ch. xi, sec. 24), he says that God is a being *quo esse aut cogitari melius nihil possit* (*Patrologiae Patrum Latinorum*, ed. by J. P. Migne, Paris, 1841–1845, vol. 32: Augustinus, vol. 1).
12. *Ethics*, pt. I, prop. 11.
13. *Responsio* 1; Deane, pp. 154–155.
14. Gaunilo attacked Anselm's argument on this very point. He would not concede that a being a greater than which cannot be conceived existed in his understanding (*Gaunilonis Pro Insipiente*, secs. 4 and 5; Deane, pp. 148–150). Anselm's reply is: "I call on your faith and conscience to attest that this is most false" (*Responsio* 1; Deane, p. 154). Gaunilo's faith and conscience will attest that it is false that "God is not a being a greater than which is inconceivable," and false that "He is not understood (*intelligitur*) or conceived (*cogitatur*)" (*ibid.*). Descartes also remarks that one would go to "strange extremes" who denied that we understand the words "*that thing which is the most perfect that we can conceive;* for that is what all men call God" (Haldane and Ross, II, 129).
15. Haldane and Ross, II, 228.
16. *Ibid.*, I, 445.
17. E.g., *ibid.*, Principle 15, p. 225.
18. *Op. cit.*, p. 502.
19. J. N. Findlay, "Can God's Existence Be Disproved?," *New Essays in Philosophical Theology*, ed. by A. N. Flew and A. MacIntyre (London, 1955), p. 47.
20. *Op. cit.*, pp. 505–506.
21. *Ibid.*, p. 504.
22. *The Nature of Metaphysics*, ed. by D. F. Pears (New York, 1957), p. 150.
23. *New Essays in Philosophical Theology*, p. 114.
24. *Ibid.*, p. 34.
25. *The Meaning of Life*, Inaugural Lecture, Canberra University College (Canberra, 1957), p. 8.
26. *Dialogues Concerning Natural Religion*, pt. IX.

27. Findlay, *op. cit.*, p. 54.
28. The other philosophers I have just cited may be led to this opinion by the same thinking. Smart, for example, says that "the truth of a logically necessary proposition depends only on our symbolism, or to put the same thing in another way, on the relationship of concepts" (*supra*). This is very similar to saying that it "reflects our use of words."
29. *Philosophical Investigations* (New York, 1953), sec. 654.
30. *Op. cit.*, pp. 501–502.
31. *Ibid.*, p. 502.
32. Haldane and Ross, II, 7.
33. I have heard it said by more than one person in discussion that Kant's view was that it is really a misuse of language to speak of a "necessary being," on the grounds that necessity is properly predicated only of propositions (judgments) not of *things*. This is not a correct account of Kant. (See his discussion of "The Postulates of Empirical Thought in General," *op. cit.*, pp. 239–256, esp. p. 239 and pp. 247–248.) But if he had held this, as perhaps the above philosophers think he should have, then presumably his view would not have been that the pseudo-proposition "God is a necessary being" is equivalent to the conditional "If God exists then He necessarily exists." Rather his view would have been that the genuine proposition "'God exists' is necessarily true" is equivalent to the conditional "If God exists then He exists" (*not* "If God exists then He *necessarily* exists," which would be an illegitimate formulation, on the view imaginatively attributed to Kant).

"If God exists then He exists" is a foolish tautology which says nothing different from the tautology "If a new earth satellite exists then it exists." If "If God exists then He exists" were a correct analysis of "'God exists' is necessarily true," then "If a new earth satellite exists then it exists" would be a correct analysis of "'A new earth satellite exists' is necessarily true." If the *analysans* is necessarily true then the *analysandum* must be necessarily true, provided the analysis is correct. If this proposed Kantian analysis of "'God exists' is necessarily true" were correct, we should be presented with the consequence that not only is it necessarily true that God exists, but also it is necessarily true that a new earth satellite exists: which is absurd.
34. When summarizing Anselm's proof (in part II, *supra*) I said: "If God exists He necessarily exists." But there I was merely stating an entailment. "If God exists" did not have the implication that it is possible He does not exist. And of course I was not regarding the conditional as *equivalent* to "God necessarily exists."
35. This fallacious criticism of Anselm is implied in the following remarks by Gilson: "To show that the affirmation of necessary existence is analytically implied in the idea of God, would be . . . to show that God is necessary if He exists, but would not prove that He does exist" (E. Gilson, *The Spirit of Medieval Philosophy*, New York, 1940, p. 62).
36. *New Essays Concerning the Human Understanding*, Bk. IV, ch. 10; ed. by A. G. Langley (La Salle, Illinois, 1949), p. 504.
37. See *Ibid.*, Appendix X, p. 714.
38. *The Journals*, tr. by A. Dru (Oxford, 1938), sec. 926.

SAINT THOMAS AQUINAS
The Existence of God

. . . The existence of God can be proved in five ways.

The first and more manifest way is the argument from motion. It is certain and evident to our senses, that in the world some things are in motion. Now whatever is moved is moved by another, for nothing can be moved except it is in potentiality to that towards which it is moved; whereas a thing moves inasmuch as it is in act. For motion is nothing else than the reduction of something from potentiality to actuality. But nothing can be reduced from potentiality to ac-

Reprinted from *Introduction to Saint Thomas Aquinas*, edited by Anton C. Pegis (New York: Random House, 1948), by permission of Richard J. Pegis. **St. Thomas Aquinas** (1225–1274) is hailed as one of the intellectual pillars of the Catholic Church, having attempted to reconcile the spiritual and otherworldly aspects of Catholic thinking with the more secular writings of the great pre-Christian philosopher, Aristotle.

tuality, except by something in a state of actuality. Thus that which is actually hot as fire, makes wood, which is potentially hot, to be actually hot, and thereby moves and changes it. Now it is not possible that the same thing should be at once in actuality and potentiality in the same respect, but only in different respects. For what is actually hot cannot simultaneously be potentially hot; but it is simultaneously potentially cold. It is therefore impossible that in the same respect and in the same way a thing should be both mover and moved, i.e., that it should move itself. Therefore, whatever is moved must be moved by another. If that by which it is moved be itself moved, then this also must needs be moved by another, and that by another again. But this cannot go on to infinity, because then there would be no first mover, and, consequently, no other mover, seeing that subsequent movers move only inasmuch as they are moved by the first mover; as the staff moves only because it is moved by the hand. Therefore it is necessary to arrive at a first mover, moved by no other; and this everyone understands to be God.

The second way is from the nature of efficient cause. In the world of sensible things we find there is an order of efficient causes. There is no case known (neither is it, indeed, possible) in which a thing is found to be the efficient cause of itself; for so it would be prior to itself, which is impossible. Now in efficient causes it is not possible to go on to infinity, because in all efficient causes following in order, the first is the cause of the intermediate cause, and the intermediate is the cause of the ultimate cause, whether the intermediate cause be several, or one only. Now to take away the cause is to take away the effect. Therefore, if there be no first cause among efficient causes, there will be no ultimate, nor any intermediate, cause. But if in efficient causes it is possible to go on to infinity, there will be no first efficient cause, neither will there be an ultimate effect, nor any intermediate efficient causes; all of which is plainly false. Therefore it is necessary to admit a first efficient cause, to which everyone gives the name of God.

The third way is taken from possibility and necessity, and runs thus. We find in nature things that are possible to be and not to be, since they are found to be generated, and to be corrupted, and consequently, it is possible for them to be and not to be. But it is impossible for these always to exist, for that which can not-be at some time is not. Therefore, if everything can not-be, then at one time there was nothing in existence. Now if this were true, even now there would be nothing in existence, because that which does not exist begins to exist only through something already existing. Therefore, if at one time nothing was in existence, it would have been impossible for anything to have begun to exist; and thus even now nothing would be in existence—which is absurd. Therefore, not all beings are merely possible, but there must exist something the existence of which is necessary. But every necessary thing either has its necessity caused by another, or not. Now it is impossible to go on to infinity in necessary things which have their necessity caused by another, as has been already proved in regard to efficient causes. Therefore we cannot but admit the existence of some being having of itself its own necessity, and not receiving it from another, but rather causing in others their necessity. This all men speak of as God.

The fourth way is taken from the gradation to be found in things. Among beings there are some more and some less good, true, noble, and the like. But more and less are predicted of different things according as they resemble in their different ways something which is the maximum, as a thing is said to be hotter according as it more nearly resembles that which is hottest; so that there is something which is truest, something best, something noblest, and, consequently, something which is most being, for those things that are greatest in truth are greatest in being. . . . Now the maximum in any genus is the cause of all in that genus, as fire, which is the maximum of heat, is the cause of all hot things, as is said in the same book. Therefore there must also be something which is to all beings the cause of their being, goodness, and every other perfection; and this we call God.

The fifth way is taken from the governance of the world. We see that things which lack knowledge, such as natural bodies, act for an end, and this is evident from their acting always, or nearly always, in the same way, so as to obtain the best result. Hence it is plain that they achieve their end, not fortuitously, but designedly. Now whatever lacks knowledge cannot move towards an end, unless it be directed by some being endowed with knowledge and intelligence; as the arrow is directed by the archer. Therefore some intelligent being exists by whom all natural things are directed to their end; and this being we call God.

SAMUEL CLARKE
A Modern Formulation of the Cosmological Argument

There has existed from eternity some one unchangeable and independent being. For since something must needs have been from eternity; as hath been already proved, and is granted on all hands: either there has always existed one unchangeable and *independent* Being, from which all other beings that are or ever were in the universe, have received their original; or else there has been an infinite succession of changeable and *dependent* beings, produced one from another in an endless progression, without any original cause at all: which latter supposition is so very absurd, that tho' all atheism must in its account of most things (as shall be shown hereafter) terminate in it, yet I think very few atheists ever were so weak as openly and directly to defend it. For it is plainly impossible and contradictory to itself. I shall not argue against it from the supposed impossibility of infinite succession, *barely and absolutely considered in itself;* for a reason which shall be mentioned hereafter: but, if we consider such an infinite progression, as *one* entire endless *series* of *dependent* beings; 'tis plain this whole *series* of beings can have no cause *from without,* of its existence; because in it are supposed to be included *all things* that are or ever were in the universe: and 'tis plain it can have no reason *within itself,* of its existence; because no one being in this infinite succession is supposed to be self-existent or *necessary* (which is the only ground or reason of existence of any thing, that can be imagined *within the thing itself,* as will presently more fully appear), but every one *dependent* on the foregoing: and where *no part* is necessary, 'tis manifest *the whole* cannot be necessary; absolute necessity of existence, not being an outward, relative, and accidental determination; but an inward and essential property of the nature of the thing which so exists. An infinite succession therefore of merely *dependent* beings, without any original independent cause; is a *series* of beings, that has nei-

Reprinted from Samuel Clarke's *A Demonstration of the Being and Attributes of God,* originally published in 1705. **Samuel Clarke** (1675–1725) was an English theologian who attempted to reintroduce within the context of Newtonian physics the older Thomistic proof of God's existence.

ther necessity nor cause, nor any reason *at all* of its existence, neither *within itself* nor *from without:* that is, 'tis an express contradiction and impossibility; 'tis a supposing *something* to be *caused,* (because it's granted in every one of its stages of succession, not to be necessary and from itself); and yet that in the whole it is caused *absolutely by nothing:* Which every man knows is a contradiction to be done *in time;* and because duration in this case makes no diference, 'tis equally a contradiction to suppose it done from eternity: And consequently there must *on the contrary,* of necessity have existed from eternity, *some one* immutable and *independent* Being: Which, what it is, remains in the next place to be inquired.

WILLIAM PALEY
The Argument from Design

In crossing a heath, suppose I pitched my foot against a stone and were asked how the stone came to be there, I might possibly answer that for anything I knew to the contrary it had lain there forever; nor would it, perhaps, be very easy to show the absurdity of this answer. But suppose I had found a watch upon the ground, and it should be inquired how the watch happened to be in that place, I should hardly think of the answer which I had before given, that for anything I knew the watch might have always been there. Yet why should not this answer serve for the watch as well as for the stone; why is it not as admissible in the second case as in the first? For this reason, and for no other, namely, that when we come to inspect the watch, we perceive—what we could not discover in the stone—that its several parts are framed and put together for a purpose, e.g., that they are so formed and adjusted as to produce motion, and that motion so regulated as to point out the hour of the day; that if the different parts had been differently shaped from what they are, or placed after any other manner or in any other order than that in which they are placed, either no motion at all would have been carried on in the machine, or none which would have answered the use that is now served by it. To reckon up a few of the plainest of these parts and of their offices, all tending to one result: we see a cylindrical box containing a coiled elastic spring, which, by its endeavor to relax itself, turns round the box. We next observe a flexible chain—artifically wrought for the sake of flexure—communicating the action of the spring from the box to the fusee. We then find a series of wheels, the teeth of which catch in and apply to each other, conducting the motion from the fusee to the balance and from the balance to the pointer, and at the same time, by the size and shape of those wheels, so regulating that motion as to terminate in causing an index, by an equable and measured progression, to pass over a given space in a given time. We take notice that the wheels are made of brass, in order to keep them from rust; the springs of steel, no other metal being so elastic; that over the face of the watch there is placed a glass, a material

Reprinted from William Paley's *Natural Theology,* originally published in 1802. **William Paley** (1743–1805), British theologian, taught philosophy at Cambridge University before becoming a minister in the Church of England.

employed in no other part of the work, but in the room of which, if there had been any other than a transparent substance, the hour could not be seen without opening the case. This mechanism being observed—it requires indeed an examination of the instrument, and perhaps some previous knowledge of the subject, to perceive and understand it; but being once, as we have said, observed and understood—the inference we think is inevitable, that the watch must have had a maker—that there must have existed, at some time and at some place or other, an artificer or artificers who formed it for the purpose which we find it actually to answer, who completely comprehended its construction and designed its use.

1. Nor would it, I apprehend, weaken the conclusion, that we had never seen a watch made—that we had never known an artist capable of making one—that we were altogether incapable of executing such a piece of workmanship ourselves, or of understanding in what manner it was performed; all this being no more than what is true of some exquisite remains of ancient art, of some lost arts, and, to the generality of mankind, of the more curious productions of modern manufacture. Does one man in a million know how oval frames are turned? Ignorance of this kind exalts our opinion of the unseen and unknown artist's skill, if he be unseen and unknown, but raises no doubt in our minds of the existence and agency of such an artist, at some former time and in some place or other. Nor can I perceive that it varies at all the inference, whether the question arise concerning a human agent or concerning an agent of a different species, or an agent possessing in some respects a different nature.

2. Neither, secondly, would it invalidate our conclusion, that the watch sometimes went wrong or that it seldom went exactly right. The purpose of the machinery, the design, and the designer might be evident, and in the case supposed, would be evident, in whatever way we accounted for the irregularity of the movement, or whether we could account for it or not. It is not necessary that a machine be perfect in order to show with what design it was made: still less

necessary where the only question is whether it were made with any design at all.

3. Nor, thirdly, would it bring any uncertainty into the argument, if there were a few parts of the watch, concerning which we could not discover or had not yet discovered in what manner they conduced to the general effect; or even some parts, concerning which we could not ascertain whether they conduced to that effect in any manner whatever. For, as to the first branch of the case, if by the loss, or disorder, or decay of the parts in question, the movement of the watch were found in fact to be stopped, or disturbed, or retarded, no doubt would remain in our minds as to the utility or intention of these parts, although we should be unable to investigate the manner according to which, or the connection by which, the ultimate effect depended upon their action or assistance; and the more complex the machine, the more likely is this obscurity to arise. Then, as to the second thing supposed, namely, that there were parts which might be spared without prejudice to the movement of the watch, and that we had proved this by experiment, these superfluous parts, even if we were completely assured that they were such, would not vacate the reasoning which we had instituted concerning other parts. The indication of contrivance remained with respect to them, nearly as it was before. . . .

Every observation which was made . . . concerning the watch may be repeated with strict propriety concerning the eye, concerning animals, concerning plants, concerning, indeed, all the organized parts of the works of nature. As, when we are inquiring simply after the existence of an intelligent Creator, imperfection, inaccuracy, liability to disorder, occasional irregularities may subsist in a considerable degree without inducing any doubt into the question; just as a watch may frequently go wrong, seldom perhaps exactly right, may be faulty in some parts, defective in some, without the smallest ground of suspicion from thence arising that it was not a watch, not made, or not made for the purpose ascribed to it. When faults are pointed out, and when a question is started concerning the skill of the artist or the dexterity with which the work is executed, then, indeed, in order to defend these qualities from accusation, we must be able either to expose some intractableness and imperfection in the materials or point out some invincible difficulty in the execution, into which imperfection and difficulty the matter of complaint may be resolved; or, if we cannot do this, we must adduce such specimens of consummate art and contrivance proceeding from the same hand as may convince the inquirer of the existence, in the case before him, of impediments like those which we have mentioned, although, what from the nature of the case is very likely to happen, they be unknown and unperceived by him. This we must do in order to vindicate the artist's skill, or at least the perfection of it; as we must also judge of his intention and of the provisions employed in fulfilling that intention, not from an instance in which they fail but from the great plurality of instances in which they succeed.

But, after all, these are different questions from the question of the artist's existence; or, which is the same, whether the thing before us be a work of art or not; and the questions ought always to be kept separate in the mind. So likewise it is in the works of nature. Irregularities and imperfections are of little or no weight in the consideration when that consideration relates simply to the existence of a Creator. When the argument respects his attributes, they are of weight; but are then to be taken in conjunction—the attention is not to rest upon them, but they are to be taken in conjunction with the unexceptional evidences which we possess of skill, power, and benevolence displayed in other instances; which evidences may, in strength, number, and variety, be such and may so overpower apparent blemishes as to induce us, upon the most reasonable ground, to believe that these last ought to be referred to some cause, though we be ignorant of it, other than defect of knowledge or of benevolence in the author. . . .

DAVID HUME
Reply to the Argument from Design

Not to lose any time in circumlocutions, said Cleanthes, addressing himself to Demea, much less in replying to the pious declamations of Philo; I shall briefly explain how I conceive this matter. Look round the world: contemplate the whole and every part of it: You will find it to be nothing but one great machine, subdivided into an infinite number of lesser machines, which again admit of subdivisions, to a degree beyond what human senses and faculties can trace and

explain. All these various machines, and even their most minute parts, are adjusted to each other with an accuracy, which ravishes into admiration all men, who have ever contemplated them. The curious adapting of means to ends, throughout all nature, resembles exactly, though it much exceeds, the productions of human contrivance: of human designs, thought, wisdom, and intelligence. Since therefore the effects resemble each other, we are led to infer, by all the

Reprinted from David Hume's *Dialogues Concerning Natural Religion,* first published in 1779. **David Hume** (1711–1776) was one of the great critics of religious, moral, and scientific thinking of the eighteenth century.

rules of analogy, that the causes also resemble; and that the Author of Nature is somewhat similar to the mind of man; though possessed of much larger faculties, proportioned to the grandeur of the work, which he has executed. By this argument *a posteriori,* and by this argument alone, do we prove at once the existence of a Deity, and his similarity to human mind and intelligence. . . .

What I chiefly scruple in this subject, said Philo, is not so much that all religious arguments are by Cleanthes reduced to experience, as that they appear not to be even the most certain and irrefragable of that inferior kind. That a stone will fall, that fire will burn, that the earth has solidity, we have observed a thousand and a thousand times; and when any new instance of this nature is presented, we draw without hesitation the accustomed inference. The exact similarity of the cases gives us a perfect assurance of a similar event; and a stronger evidence is never desired nor sought after. But where-ever you depart, in the least, from the similarity of the cases, you diminish proportionably the evidence; and may at last bring it to a very weak *analogy,* which is confessedly liable to error and uncertainty. After having experienced the circulation of the blood in human creatures, we make no doubt that it takes place in Titius and Maevius: but from its circulation in frogs and fishes, it is only a presumption, though a strong one, from analogy, that it takes place in men and other animals. The analogical reasoning is much weaker, when we infer the circulation of the sap in vegetables from our experience, that the blood circulates in animals: and those, who hastily followed that imperfect analogy, are found, by more accurate experiments, to have been mistaken.

If we see a house, Cleanthes, we conclude, with the greatest certainty, that it had an architect or builder; because this is precisely that species of effect, which we have experienced to proceed from that species of cause. But surely you will not affirm, that the universe bears such a resemblance to a house, that we can with the same certainty infer a similar cause, or that the analogy is here entire and perfect. The dissimil-itude is so striking, that the utmost you can here pretend to is a guess, a conjecture, a presumption concerning a similar cause; and how that pretension will be received in the world, I leave you to consider.

It would surely be very ill received, replied Cleanthes; and I should be deservedly blamed and detested, did I allow, that the proofs of a Deity amounted to no more than a guess or conjecture. But is the whole adjustment of means to ends in a house and in the universe so slightly a resemblance? The œconomy of final causes? The order, proportion, and arrangement of every part? Steps of a stair are plainly contrived, that human legs may use them in mounting: and this inference is certain and infallible. Human legs are also contrived for walking and mounting: and this inference, I allow, is not altogether so certain, because of the dissimilarity which you remark: but does it, therefore, deserve the name only of presumption or conjecture? . . .

[Philo replies:]

Were a man to abstract from every thing which he knows or has seen, he would be altogether incapable, merely from his own ideas, to determine what kind of scene the universe must be, or to give the preference to one state or situation of things above another. For as nothing which he clearly conceives, could be esteemed impossible or implying a contradiction, every chimera of his fancy would be upon an equal footing; nor could he assign any just reason, why he adheres to one idea or system, and rejects the others, which are equally possible.

Again; after he opens his eyes, and contemplates the world, as it really is, it would be impossible for him, at first, to assign the cause of any one event; much less, of the whole of things or of the universe. He might set his Fancy a rambling; and she might bring him in an infinite variety of reports and representations. These would all be possible; but being all equally possible, he would never, of himself, give a satisfactory account for his preferring one of them to the rest. Experience alone can point out to him the true cause of any phenomenon.

Now, according to this method of reasoning . . . it follows (and is, indeed, tacitly allowed by Cleanthes himself) that order, arrangement, or the adjustment of final causes is not, of itself, any proof of design; but only so far as it has been experienced to proceed from that principle. For aught we can know *a priori,* matter may contain the source or spring of order originally, within itself, as well as mind does; and there is no more difficulty in conceiving, that the several elements, from an internal unknown cause, may fall into the most exquisite arrangement, than to conceive that their ideas, in the great, universal mind, from a like internal, unknown cause, fall into that arrangement. The equal possibility of both these suppositions is allowed. But by experience we find, (according to Cleanthes) that there is a difference between them. Throw several pieces of steel together, without shape or form; they will never arrange themselves so as to compose a watch: Stone, and mortar, and wood, without an architect, never erect a house. But the ideas in a human mind, we see, by an unknown, inexplicable œconomy, arrange themselves so as to form the plan of a watch or house. Experience, therefore, proves, that there is an original principle of order in mind, not in matter. From similar effects we infer similar causes. The adjustment of means to ends is alike in the universe, as in a machine of human contrivance. The causes, therefore, must be resembling. . . .

That all inferences, Cleanthes, concerning fact, are founded on experience, and that all experimental reasonings are founded on the supposition, that similar causes prove similar effects, and similar effects similar causes; I shall not, at present, much dispute with you. But observe, I entreat you, with what extreme caution all just reasoners proceed in the transferring of experiments to similar cases. Unless the cases be exactly similar, they repose no perfect confidence in applying their past observation to any particular phenomenon. Every alteration of circumstances occasions a doubt concerning the event; and it requires new experiments to prove certainly, that the new circumstances are of no moment or importance. A change in bulk, situation, arrangement, age, disposition of the air, or surrounding bodies; any of these particulars may be attended with

the most unexpected consequences: And unless the objects be quite familiar to us, it is the highest temerity to expect with assurance, after any of these changes, an event similar to that which before fell under our observation. The slow and deliberate steps of philosophers, here, if any where, are distinguished from the precipitate march of the vulgar, who, hurried on by the smallest similitudes, are incapable of all discernment or consideration.

But can you think, Cleanthes, that your usual phlegm and philosophy have been preserved in so wide a step as you have taken, when you compared to the universe houses, ships, furniture, machines; and from their similarity in some circumstances inferred a similarity in their causes? Thought, design, intelligence, such as we discover in men and other animals, is no more than one of the springs and principles of the universe, as well as heat or cold, attraction or repulsion, and a hundred others, which fall under daily observation. It is an active cause, by which some particular parts of nature, we find, produce alterations on other parts. But can a conclusion, with any propriety, be transferred from parts to the whole? Does not the great disproportion bar all comparison and inference? From observing the growth of a hair, can we learn any thing concerning the generation of a man? Would the manner of a leaf's blowing, even though perfectly known, afford us any instruction concerning the vegetation of a tree?

But allowing that we were to take the *operations* of one part of nature upon another for the foundation of our judgement concerning the *origin* of the whole (which never can be admitted) yet why select so minute, so weak, so bounded a principle as the reason and design of animals is found to be upon this planet? What peculiar privilege has this little agitation of the brain which we call *thought,* that we must thus make it the model of the whole universe? Our partiality in our own favour does indeed present it on all occasions; but sound philosophy ought carefully to guard against so natural an illusion.

So far from admitting, continued Philo, that the operations of a part can afford us any just conclusion concerning the origin of the whole, I will not allow any one part to form a rule for another part, if the latter be very remote from the former. Is there any reasonable ground to conclude, that the inhabitants of other planets possess thought, intelligence, reason, or any thing similar to these faculties in men? When Nature has so extremely diversified her manner of operation in this small globe; can we imagine, that she incessantly copies herself throughout so immense a universe? And if thought, as we may well suppose, be confined merely to this narrow corner, and has even there so limited a sphere of action; with what propriety can we assign it for the original cause of all things? The narrow views of a peasant, who makes his domestic œconomy the rule for the government of kingdoms, is in comparison a pardonable sophism. . . .

A very small part of this great system, during a very short time, is very imperfectly discovered to us: and do we then pronounce decisively concerning the origin of the whole?

Admirable conclusion! Stone, wood, brick, iron, brass, have not, at this time, in this minute globe of earth, an order or arrangement without human art and contrivance: therefore the universe could not originally attain its order and arrangement, without something similar to human art. But is a part of nature a rule for another part very wide of the former? Is it a rule for the whole? . . .

How the most absurd argument, replied Cleanthes, in the hands of a man of ingenuity and invention, may acquire an air of probability! Are you not aware, Philo . . . that it is by no means necessary, that Theists should prove the similarity of the works of Nature to those of Art; because this similarity is self-evident and undeniable? The same matter, a like form: what more is requisite to show an analogy between their causes, and to ascertain the origin of all things from a divine purpose and intention? Your objections, I must freely tell you, are no better than the abstruse cavils of those philosophers who denied motion; and ought to be refuted in the same manner, by illustrations, examples, and instances, rather than by serious argument and philosophy.

Suppose, therefore, that an articulate voice were heard in the clouds, much louder and more melodious than any which human art could ever reach: Suppose, that this voice were extended in the same instant over all nations, and spoke to each nation in its own language and dialect: Suppose, that the words delivered not only contain a just sense and meaning, but convey some instruction altogether worthy of a benevolent being, superior to mankind: could you possibly hesitate a moment concerning the cause of this voice? and must you not instantly ascribe it to some design or purpose? Yet I cannot see but all the same objections (if they merit that appellation) which lie against the system of Theism, may also be produced against this inference.

Might you not say, that all conclusions concerning fact were founded on experience: that when we hear an articulate voice in the dark, and thence infer a man, it is only the resemblance of the effects, which leads us to conclude that there is a like resemblance in the cause: but that this extraordinary voice, by its loudness, extent, and flexibility to all languages, bears so little analogy to any human voice, that we have no reason to suppose any analogy in their causes: and consequently, that a rational, wise, coherent speech proceeded, you know not whence, from some accidental whistling of the winds, not from any divine reason or intelligence? You see clearly your own objections in these cavils; and I hope too, you see clearly, that they cannot possibly have more force in the one case than in the other.

But to bring the case still nearer the present one of the universe, I shall make two suppositions, which imply not any absurdity or impossibility. Suppose, that there is a natural, universal, invariable language, common to every individual of human race, and that books are natural productions, which perpetuate themselves in the same manner with animals and vegetables, by descent and propagation. Several expressions of our passions contain a universal language: all brute animals have a natural speech, which, however limited, is very intelligible to their own species. And as there are infinitely fewer parts and less contrivance in the finest composition of eloquence, than in the coarsest organized body, the propagation of an *Iliad* or *Æneid* is an easier supposition than that of any plant or animal.

Suppose, therefore, that you enter into your library, thus peopled by natural volumes, containing the most refined reason and most exquisite beauty: could you possibly open one of them, and doubt, that its original cause bore the strongest analogy to mind and intelligence? When it reasons and discourses; when it expostulates, argues, and enforces its views and topics; when it applies sometimes to the pure intellect, sometimes to the affections; when it collects, disposes, and adorns every consideration suited to the subject: could you persist in asserting, that all this, at the bottom, had really no meaning, and that the first formation of this volume in the loins of its original parent proceeded not from thought and design? Your obstinacy, I know, reaches not that degree of firmness: even your sceptical play and wantonness would be abashed at so glaring an absurdity.

But if there be any difference, Philo, between this supposed case and the real one of the universe, it is all to the advantage of the latter. The anatomy of an animal affords many stronger instances of design than the perusal of Livy or Tacitus: and any objection which you start in the former case, by carrying me back to so unusual and extraordinary a scene as the first formation of worlds, the same objection has place on the supposition of our vegetating library. Choose, then, your party, Philo, without ambiguity or evasion; assert either that a rational volume is no proof of a rational cause, or admit of a similar cause to all the works of nature.

Let me here observe too, continued Cleanthes, that this religious argument, instead of being weakened by that scepticism, so much affected by you, rather acquires force from it, and becomes more firm and undisputed. To exclude all argument or reasoning of every kind is either affectation or madness. The declared profession of every reasonable sceptic is only to reject abstruse, remote and refined arguments; to adhere to common sense and the plain instincts of nature; and to assent, where-ever any reasons strike him with so full a force, that he cannot,

without the greatest violence, prevent it. Now the arguments for Natural Religion are plainly of this kind; and nothing but the most perverse, obstinate metaphysics can reject them. Consider, anatomize the eye; Survey its structure and contrivance; and tell me, from your own feeling, if the idea of a contriver does not immediately flow in upon you with a force like that of sensation. The most obvious conclusion surely is in favor of design; and it requires time, reflection and study, to summon up those frivolous, though abstruse objections, which can support Infidelity. Who can behold the male and female of each species, the correspondence of their parts and instincts, their passions and whole course of life before and after generation, but must be sensible, that the propagation of the species is intended by Nature? Millions and millions of such instances present themselves through every part of the universe; and no language can convey a more intelligible, irresistible meaning, than the curious adjustment of final causes. To what degree, therefore, of blind dogmatism must one have attained, to reject such natural and such convincing arguments? . . .

But to show you still more inconveniences, continued Philo, in your Anthropomorphism; please to take a new survey of your principles. *Like effects prove like causes.* This is the experimental argument; and this, you say too, is the sole theological argument. Now it is certain, that the liker the effects are, which are seen, and the liker the causes, which are inferred, the stronger is the argument. Every departure on either side diminishes the probability, and renders the experiment less conclusive. You cannot doubt of the principle: neither ought you to reject its consequences.

All the new discoveries in astronomy, which prove the immense grandeur and magnificence of the works of Nature, are so many additional arguments for a Deity, according to the true system of Theism; but according to your hypothesis of experimental Theism, they become so many objections, by removing the effect still farther from all resemblance to the effects of human art and contrivance. . . .

The discoveries by microscopes, as they open a new universe in miniature, are still objections, according to you; arguments, according to me. The farther we push our researches of this kind, we are still led to infer the universal cause of all to be vastly different from mankind, or from any object of human experience and observation.

And what say you to the discoveries in anatomy, chymistry, botany? . . . These surely are no objections, replied Cleanthes: they only discover new instances of art and contrivance. It is still the image of mind reflected on us from innumerable objects. Add, a mind *like the human*, said Philo. I know of no other, replied Cleanthes. And the liker the better, insisted Philo. To be sure, said Cleanthes.

Now, Cleanthes, said Philo, with an air of alacrity and triumph, mark the consequences. *First*, By this method of reasoning, you renounce all claim to infinity in any of the attributes of the Deity. For as the cause ought only to be proportioned to the effect, and the effect, so far as it falls under our cognisance, is not infinite; what pretensions have we, upon your suppositions, to ascribe that attribute to the divine Being? You will still insist, that, by removing him so much from all similarity to human creatures, we give in to the most arbitrary hypothesis, and at the same time weaken all proofs of his existence.

Secondly, You have no reason, on your theory, for ascribing perfection to the Deity, even in his finite capacity; or for supposing him free from every error, mistake, or incoherence in his undertakings. There are many inexplicable difficulties in the works of Nature, which, if we allow a perfect author to be proved *a priori*, are easily solved, and become only seeming difficulties, from the narrow capacity of man, who cannot trace infinite relations. But according to your method of reasoning, these difficulties become all real; and perhaps will be insisted on, as new instances of likeness to human art and contrivance. At least, you must acknowledge, that it is impossible for us to tell, from our limited views, whether this system contains any great faults, or deserves any considerable

praise, if compared to other possible, and even real systems. Could a peasant, if the Æneid were read to him, pronounce that poem to be absolutely faultless, or even assign to it its proper rank among the productions of human wit; he, who had never seen any other production?

But were this world ever so perfect a production, it must still remain uncertain, whether all the excellences of the work can justly be ascribed to the workman. If we survey a ship, what an exalted idea must we form of the ingenuity of the carpenter, who framed so complicated, useful, and beautiful a machine? And what surprise must we feel, when we find him a stupid mechanic, who imitated others, and copied an art, which, through a long succession of ages, after multiplied trials, mistakes, corrections, deliberations, and controversies, had been gradually improving? Many worlds might have been botched and bungled, throughout an eternity, ere this system was struck out: much labour lost: many fruitless trials made: and a slow, but continued improvement carried on during infinite ages in the art of world-making. In such subjects, who can determine, where the truth; nay, who can conjecture where the probability, lies; amidst a great number of hypotheses which may be proposed, and a still greater number which may be imagined?

And what shadow of an argument, continued Philo, can you produce, from your hypothesis, to prove the unity of the Deity? A great number of men join in building a house or ship, in rearing a city, in framing a commonwealth: why may not several deities combine in contriving and framing a world? This is only so much greater similarity to human affairs. By sharing the work among several, we may so much further limit the attributes of each, and get rid of that extensive power and knowledge, which must be supposed in one deity, and which, according to you, can only serve to weaken the proof of his existence. And if such foolish, such vicious creatures as man can yet often unite in framing and executing one plan; how much more those deities or daemons, whom we may suppose several degrees more perfect?

To multiply causes, without necessity, is indeed contrary to true philosophy: but this principle applies not to the present case. Were one deity antecedently proved by your theory, who were possessed of every attribute, requisite to the production of the universe; it would be needless, I own (though not absurd) to suppose any other deity existent. But while it is still a question, Whether all these attributes are united in one subject, or dispersed among several independent beings: by what phenomena in nature can we pretend to decide the controversy? Where we see a body raised in a scale, we are sure that there is in the opposite scale, however concealed from sight, some counterpoising weight equal to it: but it is still allowed to doubt, whether that weight be an aggregate of several distinct bodies, or one uniform united mass. And if the weight requisite very much exceeds any thing which we have ever seen conjoined in any single body, the former supposition becomes still more probable and natural. An intelligent being of such vast power and capacity, as is necessary to produce the universe, or, to speak in the language of ancient philosophy, so prodigious an animal, exceeds all analogy, and even comprehension.

But farther, Cleanthes; men are mortal, and renew their species by generation; and this is common to all living creatures. The two great sexes of male and female, says Milton, animate the world. Why must this circumstance, so universal, so essential, be excluded from those numerous and limited deities? Behold then the theogony of ancient times brought back upon us.

And why not become a perfect Anthropomorphite? Why not assert the deity or deities to be corporeal, and to have eyes, a nose, mouth, ears, etc.? Epicurus maintained, that no man had ever seen reason but in a human figure; therefore the gods must have a human figure.

And this argument, which is deservedly so much ridiculed by Cicero, becomes, according to you, solid and philosophical.

In a word, Cleanthes, a man, who follows your hypothesis, is able, perhaps, to assert, or conjecture, that the universe, sometime, arose from something like design: but beyond that position he cannot ascertain one single circumstance, and is left afterwards to fix every point of his theology, by the utmost license of fancy and hypothesis. The world, for aught he knows, is very faulty and imperfect, compared to a superior standard: and was only the first rude essay of some infant deity, who afterwards abandoned it, ashamed of his lame performance: it is the work only of some dependent, inferior deity; and is the object of derision to his superiors: it is the production of old age and dotage in some superannuated deity; and ever since his death, has run on at adventures, from the first impulse and active force, which it received from him. You justly give signs of horror, Demea, at these strange suppositions: but these, and a thousand more of the same kind, are Cleanthes's suppositions, not mine. From the moment the attributes of the Deity are supposed finite, all these have place. And I cannot, for my part, think, that so wild and unsettled a system of theology is, in any respect, preferable to none at all.

These suppositions I absolutely disown, cried Cleanthes: they strike me, however, with no horror: especially, when proposed in that rambling way in which they drop from you. On the contrary, they give me pleasure, when I see, that, by the utmost indulgence of your imagination, you never get rid of the hypothesis of design in the universe; but are obliged, at every turn, to have recourse to it. To this concession I adhere steadily; and this I regard as a sufficient foundation for religion.

BERTRAND RUSSELL
What is an Agnostic?

ARE AGNOSTICS ATHEISTS?

No. An atheist, like a Christian, holds that we can know whether or not there is a God. The Christian holds that we can know there is a God; the atheist, that we can know there is not. The agnostic suspends judgment, saying that there are not sufficient grounds either for affirmation or for denial. At the same time, an agnostic may hold that the existence of God, though not impossible, is very improbable; he may even hold it so improbable that it is not worth considering in practice. In that case, he is not far removed from atheism. His attitude may be that which a careful philosopher would have toward the gods of ancient Greece. If I were asked to prove that Zeus and Poseidon and Hera and the rest of the Olympians do not exist, I should be at a loss to find conclusive arguments. An agnostic may think the Christian God as improbable as the Olympians; in that case, he is, for practical purposes, at one with the atheists.

SINCE YOU DENY "GOD'S LAW," WHAT AUTHORITY DO YOU ACCEPT AS A GUIDE TO CONDUCT?

An agnostic does not accept any "authority" in the sense in which religious people do. He holds that a man should think out questions of conduct for himself. Of course, he will seek to profit by the wisdom of others, but he will have to select for himself the people he is to consider wise, and he will not regard even what they say as unquestionable. He will observe that what passes as "God's law" varies from time to time. The Bible says both that a woman must not marry her deceased husband's brother, and that, in certain circumstances, she must do so. If you have the misfortune to be a childless widow with an unmarried brother-in-law, it is logically impossible for you to avoid disobeying "God's law."

"What is an Agnostic?" is reprinted from *Religions of America*, edited by Leo Rosten (New York: Simon & Schuster, Inc., 1975), by permission of Cowles Magazines, Inc., renewed © 1983 by Cowles Broadcasting, Inc. **Bertrand Russell** (1872–1970) is one of the great thinkers of the twentieth century, having written influential tracts on everything from the foundation of mathematics and logic to marriage and the family.

DOES AN AGNOSTIC DO WHATEVER HE PLEASES?

In one sense, no; in another sense, everyone does whatever he pleases. Suppose, for example, you hate some one so much that you would like to murder him. Why do you not do so? You may reply: "Because religion tells me that murder is a sin." But as a statistical fact, agnostics are not more prone to murder than other people, in fact, rather less so. They have the same motives for abstaining from murder as other people have. Far and away the most powerful of these motives is the fear of punishment. In lawless conditions, such as a gold rush, all sorts of people will commit crimes, although in ordinary circumstances they would have been law-abiding. There is not only actual legal punishment: there is the discomfort of dreading discovery, and the loneliness of knowing that, to avoid being hated, you must wear a mask even with your closest intimates. And there is also what may be called "conscience": If you ever contemplated a murder, you would dread the horrible memory of your victim's last moments or lifeless corpse. All this, it is true, depends upon your living in a law-abiding community, but there are abundant secular reasons for creating and preserving such a community.

I said that there is another sense in which every man does as he pleases. No one but a fool indulges every impulse, but what holds a desire in check is always some other desire. A man's anti-social wishes may be restrained by a wish to please God, but they may also be restrained by a wish to please his friends, or to win the respect of his community, or to be able to contemplate himself without disgust. But if he has no such wishes, the mere abstract precepts of morality will not keep him straight.

QUESTIONS ABOUT RELIGIOUS BELIEF

1. According to J. L. Mackie, "There seems to be some contradiction" between the propositions that "God is omnipotent; God is wholly good; and yet evil exists." An explicit contradiction is usually of the form "p and not p" where "p" is any proposition. Is Mackie's claim that there is a contradiction correct?

2. What exactly is the difference between moral and physical evil as discussed by John Hick? How does he respond to both?

3. Of what significance is the belief in life after death to the problem of evil, according to Hick? Does the appearance of evil help to establish that there is life after death?

4. Yaakov Homnick asks rhetorically, "Is it just to make the child suffer for the benefit of the parents?" How does his answer compare with the responses given by Little Bessie's mother?

5. What exactly is Sidney Hook's point concerning the Holocaust, in response to Homnick? What special significance does the Holocaust have in the debate over the existence of God and the appearance of evil?

6. What is Gaunilon's answer to Anselm's first formulation of the ontological proof? Does Anselm's second formulation succeed in avoiding Gaunilon's criticism?

7. According to Norman Malcolm, "Athough it is an error to regard existence as a property of things that have contingent existence, it does not follow that it is an error to regard necessary existence as a property of God." What exactly is the difference between "existence" and "necessary existence"? How does this distinction help to prove that God exists?

8. What is the difference between the ontological and cosmological proofs? Is there one formulation of the cosmological proof which seems stronger than the others? Which version does Samuel Clarke favor?

9. The design argument is an argument from analogy. Can you think of other analogies between the universe and objects that appear to have design but which are not human artifacts? What conclusion, if any, could we draw about the ultimate origin of the universe? Is Paley's proposed analogy better than any alternatives we might consider?

10. Is Philo defending the argument from design in suggesting that "Like effects prove like causes"? How does the teleological approach lead to conclusions that seem unacceptable to the theist, according to David Hume?

Religious Belief:
Suggestions for Further Study

The philosophy of religion, especially within the Western tradition, focuses primarily on the question of God's existence, which is why we have emphasized in the text the traditional proofs and the problem of evil. However, there are other threads in the complex fabric of religious debate that the reader might find of interest. Earlier in this century, A. J. Ayer, in his book *Language, Truth and Logic* (New York: Dover, 1952), launched a powerful attack on the whole enterprise of religious discussion as practiced by both believers and traditional skeptics. (See particularly Chapter VI, "Critique of Ethics and Theology" in Ayer's book.) According to Ayer's postivist approach, religious utterances are neither true nor false. Unlike statements of science, they are essentially unverifiable and hence, strictly speaking, are meaningless. (A section of Ayer's book is included in our discussion of ethics, Part IV.)

The idea of verification as a theory of meaning came under severe attack, in part because some generalizations in science are themselves not completely verifiable. See, for example, Carl Hempel's "Problems and Changes in the Empiricist Criterion of Meaning," in *Semantics and the Philosophy of Language,* edited by Leonard Linsky (Urbana: Univ. of Illinois Press, 1952). Following the work of Sir Karl Popper, *Logic of Scientific Discovery* (London: Hutchinson, 1959) attention turned to the question of whether religious utterances are falsifiable. The famous debate involving Antony Flew, R. M. Hare, and Basil Mitchell in *New Essays in Philosophical Theology* (New York: Macmillan, 1964), explored this approach. An alternate response to positivism, influenced largely by the later work of Ludwig Wittgenstein, especially his *Philosophical Investigations* (Oxford: Basil Blackwell, 1953) is *Wittgensteinian fideism,* the view that the meaning of religious language, as used in prayer, for example, can only be understood within the rules of the religious "language-game" itself, independent of whatever criterion of meaning may apply in science. D. Z. Phillips developed this idea in *The Concept of Prayer* (New York: Schocken Books, 1966). See also, Kai Nielsen's "Wittgensteinian Fideism" (*Philosophy* 42, July 1967, 191–209).

Other approaches have included the pragmatist's attempt to account for the special significance of religious experience and belief—William James's *Varieties of Religious Experience,* for example, and his essay, "The Will to Believe," in *The Will to Believe and Other Essays* (New York: Dover, 1956). In sharp contrast is the Freudian critique of religion. See, for example, "The Religious World View" in *New Introductory Lectures on Psychoanalysis* edited by James Strachey (New York: Norton, 1965) or *The Future of An Illusion* translated by W. D. Robson-Scott (New York: Liveright, 1953) which has been critically discussed by Jon Pashman and Lowell Kleiman in "Freud and the Genetic Fallacy" and "Pashman on Freud and the Genetic Fallacy" (*The Southern Journal of Philosophy*, Vol. 8, No. 1, Spring 1970). Also, in recent years, the Judeo-Christian tradition especially has come under feminist attack. See, for example, Mary Daly's *Beyond God the Father: Toward a Philosophy of Women's Liberation* (Boston: Beacon Press, 1973).

PART
7

Freedom, Fatalism, and Determinism

Literary Introduction:
What Will Be, Will Be.

What ultimately determines the paths we choose? Are there laws of human behavior like those that govern animals, plants, and inanimate objects, or are we free to select our own destinies? Almost 2500 years ago, in *Oedipus the King*, the Greek playwright Sophocles explored the idea that some events are fated, and therefore not only immune to the power of the human will, but beyond the realm of scientific law as well. We will begin our discussion with this ancient and intriguing possibility.

Oedipus the King really involves two stories, both of which draw our attention to questions of free will, determinism, and fatalism. In what we can call the pre-play story—the events that had already occurred before the action of the play proper—we hear of a prophesy delivered to Laius and Jocasta, king and queen of Thebes, that their infant son will grow up to kill his father and marry his mother. In order to prevent this prophesy from happening, the parents order that the baby be killed by exposure to the elements on a mountaintop. However, the servant who is entrusted with this mission is kind-hearted, and instead of leaving the baby on the mountain, he gives him to a shepherd from the neighboring city of Corinth, where Oedipus is adopted by the childless king and queen, Polybos and Merope. Oedipus grows to manhood believing that Polybos and Merope are his parents.

But at a feast, a reveler tells Oedipus that he is not the natural son of the king and queen. Made angry by this, Oedipus consults the gods to question the accuracy of the accusation. However, in stead of a reply to his question, he hears the same prophesy his real parents had heard when he was an infant. He, too, wants to prevent these terrible events, and so he leaves Corinth. On the road, he fights with a stranger about right of way and kills the man. The man is King Laius, Oedipus's true father. Before he reaches Thebes, he solves the riddle of the Sphinx, a creature who has caused a plague to fall on the land until someone solves her riddle. Oedipus is welcomed into Thebes as a savior, installed as king, and given the hand of Jocasta, the recently widowed queen, in marriage. She, of course, is his mother.

All of this is the background to the play, which opens some years later when Oedipus has already fathered children with his wife/mother. Unbeknownst to him, the prophesy has been fulfilled. In this respect, the pre-play story seems clearly to suggest a fatalistic view of life: all the important characters have done everything they could to escape the prophesy, yet the prophesied events have occurred. These terrible events, it appears, were simply meant to be, not because anybody willed them to happen, and not even as a consequence of previous actions, but simply because they were, in some sense, inescapable, inevitable, or fated.

The action of the play proper centers on Oedipus's attempt to discover the truth about himself. As the play opens, Thebes is once again experiencing a plague, one which the gods say will not be lifted until the murderer of Laius is discovered and cast out of the community. Oedipus, as king and protector of his people, resolves to find the culprit and sets out on an investigation that ultimately reveals the terrible truth: he himself is the man he seeks. Discovering that he has, indeed, fulfilled the prophecy by murdering his father and marrying his mother, Oedipus punishes himself by gouging out his eyes, and goes into exile as a blind beggar.

The plot of the play seems to involve something other than the fatalism of the pre-play story. Although we can say that Oedipus was fated to kill his father and marry his mother, he was not, it would seem, similarly fated to discover the horrible truth. The play, therefore, concerns Oedipus's self-motivated search for the truth, and in this respect, he seems to be exercising his free will. In the course of the play, he has exercised several choices. In the beginning, he could have chosen to do nothing, and let the city suffer the plague. Later, he could have stopped his investigation when he knew he was the murderer. At that point, he might have satisfied the gods and thereby lifted the plague by going into exile. But Oedipus's decision is to push on until he knows the full truth. At the conclusion, he blinds himself, an awful punishment since he will receive no new images to replace the ones of his father, mother, and children locked in his memory. All of these choices appear to be ones that result from the exercise of Oedipus's will. However, they may actually be determined by Oedipus's character. Only the man he is, stubborn and proud, would have made such decisions, and followed his road to its bitter terminus.

Which is it? Is Oedipus free or determined? Can he be both? Can anyone? The play raises this deeper philosophical puzzle. Although Oedipus solves the riddle of the Sphinx, does *Oedipus the King* help solve the riddle of free-will?

SOPHOCLES
Translated by Anthony Burgess
Oedipus the King

Characters

OEDIPUS, king of Thebes
JOCASTA, his wife
CREON, Jocasta's brother
TIRESIAS, a blind prophet
Messenger from Corinth
An old shepherd
An officer of the court
Elders
Children
Chorus of citizens

PART ONE

(A bare stage, but there should be a simple shrine down left. Before the palace of King Oedipus at Thebes. A chorus representative of the citizenry comes on, with four elders leading a group of children.)

CHORUS

Oedipus, Oedipus, king,
Solver of riddles,
Slayer of monsters,
Savior of the people,
Hear.

Hear the voice of the agony
Of the city.
Leave your palace.
Come among us.
Hear.

(Oedipus comes out toward the end of the speech)

OEDIPUS

Sons and daughters of the city-state of Thebes,
I was ready for the voice of your supplication.
I do not cling to my kingly right

Of hearing the city's wrongs through messen-
gers.
Messengers distill, abstract, smooth over.
Avoiding violent speech they do violence
To the truth. And there is a truth here
That will not yield to words.
It is in the ears and nostrils—
A stench of decay countered in vain by your
incense,
Groans undrowned by holy hymns.
I, Oedipus, whom men have called the Great,
Come not now to you in greatness,
But in humility, as the city's servant,
To hear—hear what? You elders—
Speak for the rest. If it is sickness,
My physicians await; if it is simple need,
My granaries are open. Before you even ask,
I spend pity, dispense compassion.

FIRST ELDER

Ruler of our country, I, a priest of Zeus,
I and my fellow priests, at the shrine of Pal-
las,
At the temple where the oracle speaks in fire,
Have done sacrifice, have prayed, have led
Others in prayer, crowned with garlands
Of supplication, hair and garments torn,
All over Thebes.

SECOND ELDER

Your subjects wail,
Wonder, ask why of the gods.
You have seen it yourself already—
Our city, thrashing, heaving, reeling in ship-
wreck,
Scarcely able to thrust its prow
Up from the surge of blood—

THIRD ELDER

A blight is on our fields and on
The cattle of our fields. A blight
Lies on our women. What children they bear
Are dead or deformed. The fire has struck.
A god that carries fire worries our roofs.
We grow poor while death grows rich.

FOURTH ELDER

Oedipus,
We have not come to you as one goes to a
god.

You are no more than a man, though our first
of men.
But we remember—and to these children here
It is a lesson at school as well as a bedtime
story—
How you came one day and saved this city.
You freed us from the tribute which we paid
In blood and bones to the Sphinx,
The lion-woman with her cruel song, her riddle
Which you alone could answer.

THIRD ELDER

It was said,
And it is said still, that what you did
You did through God's aid, that God
Shone over you then. I and others believe
That God walks with you now.

SECOND ELDER

Though some say
God nods in a chair behind you, or has
His chin on your shoulder, dozing, and that
you
Must shake him awake.

FIRST ELDER

Oedipus,
Who helped us in days that grow already fa-
bled,
Give us your strength now. Let not the word
Savior
Be a mere formal word struck on a medal,
An empty honorific of dead ceremony.

SECOND ELDER

Save us.
A savior is one who saves, not one who
Has saved.

THIRD ELDER

Find us some means of salvation,
From god or some superior man. We know
that
Long knowledge of trials past lends strength
To the acts of the present.

FOURTH ELDER

Restore us to life,
Restore our city to life. And, if I may say this,
Look to your honor, your fame. Let none be
able

To say that under your rule we were raised up
   high
Only to fall low.

THIRD ELDER

Save the city
And keep it safe. That star that shone over
   you
In the day of your coming, that gave us for-
   tune then,
Surely must shine still, though in hiding.

SECOND ELDER

If you are to be our king—

ALL FOUR

If you are to be our king,
Be king of the living not
Of dead stone and empty air,
A city is a city, a ship
A ship only when men possess them.
King of nothingness—
There is no kingship there.

OEDIPUS

Need I tell my grief, my brothers, my chil-
   dren?
I know what you suffer, believe me, I know
What you wish of me. You suffer, yes, but
None suffers more than I. For each of you
Is confined to his own grief, but I
Bear the intolerable weight of yours
And that of all my people. I am not blind,
I am not asleep. Sleep indeed is a rare
Visitant. But tears oppress me and the
Wide night is a labyrinth I tread
With no thread of useful thought to
Lead me to the light.
But I have done
A little more than weep and wander
In a circle of thought. There was, is,
A source of hope and I sought it. The Lord
   Creon,
Brother of my queen, has been
Sent to the shrine of golden Apollo, there
To seek of the oracle what word or deed of
   mine
May help you, may help us all. Today
He is due to return, not long after sunrise
According to his undertaking. Watch for him.

Give me news of his approach. Upon my
   honor
As a king and a man, all that the god enjoins
Shall be done, shall be promptly done.

FIRST ELDER

Well spoken.

(Oedipus leaves. A child speaks.)

CHILD

Tell us about the Sphinx.

SECOND ELDER

You've heard the story too often.

CHILD

But tell us again.

FIRST ELDER

The Sphinx—she is so far back in the past
As to seem a mere fable, a fairy-tale ogre
To frighten infants. But she existed.
Her body was a lion's body—

SECOND ELDER

Her face the face of a virgin girl.

FIRST ELDER

She ravaged our country, roaring up
To the unwary wanderer in a swirl
Of dust.

SECOND ELDER

To any she met
She put a riddle. None
Could ever answer it.

FIRST ELDER

Then
She would leap on the ignorant one
And eat him.

CHILD

What was the riddle?

SECOND ELDER

You know the riddle, you all
Know the riddle.

FIRST ELDER

Bear with the child,
Bear with the children.
They all love to hear it

And answer it. Each of them gains that way
A little of the substance of Oedipus.

SECOND ELDER

Very well, then. Which animal
Walks on four legs in the morning,
Two legs at noon, and three legs
In the evening?

CHILD

The animal is man.
As a baby he crawls on all fours.
In the noon of his life he walks
Upright on two legs. And in old age
Of evening he walks with a stick.
It's an easy riddle.

FIRST ELDER

Easy or not, not one could solve it
Except our king. Trudging toward our city,
A stranger, unknown, seeking his fortune,
He met the Sphinx and answered
The unanswerable. In chagrin
She killed herself, our scourge was gone
And, as a reward, Oedipus our lord
Gained the crown and the hand
Of our widowed queen.

CHILD

And yet it's an easy riddle.

SECOND ELDER

The point about the riddle was
That it was unanswerable.
Difficult or easy—that was never the point.
The riddle was unanswered because
It was unanswerable.

CHILD

Why?

FIRST ELDER

He is coming. Creon is coming.
Call the king.

*(One elder goes in to fetch the king. The others
call.)*

CHORUS

(severally) Oedipus—King Oedipus!

(Oedipus enters)

THIRD ELDER

Creon is smiling. The news is good.

FOURTH ELDER

He has crowned his head with ripe berries
Of the bay tree. The news must be good.

OEDIPUS

Welcome to our royal brother.

(Enter Creon)

Creon,
The times, our agony, your mission—all
Forbid the delay of a private audience,
A public announcement to follow. It is
In the presence of the people that you must
Deliver what comes from God's mouth. Tell
    us, then:
Is it good or bad news?

CREON

Good news.
Or shall I say that good may come
Even from what seems evil, if things go right.

OEDIPUS

But the answer? What was the answer?

CREON

May I speak before all?

OEDIPUS

The plight is theirs. They have first right to an
    answer.

CREON

This then is what Phoebus Apollo our lord
Said and commanded. There is something un-
    clean
That was born and nourished on our soil and
    now
Corrupts and makes filthy our soil. It is
Destroying us. It must be driven away,
Or must itself be destroyed.

OEDIPUS

This is another riddle. What unclean thing?
What manner of expulsion or destruction?

CREON

The unclean thing is a man. The god
Decrees the banishment of a man or else

Or also the shedding of blood.
From the shedding of blood comes our city's
    agony,
Our city's peril. Blood calls for blood, he
    says.
Blood must be paid with blood,
Or loss with banishment. Or both.

OEDIPUS

What blood does he mean? Whose blood
Was shed?

CREON

Before you took the throne, the throne
That I as regent offered to the slayer of the
    Sphinx,
We were ruled by King Laius.

OEDIPUS

I know of Laius
Though I never knew him. He died.
That was why the throne was empty.

CREON

Laius was killed. The meaning of the god's
    command
Is that the unknown killer of Laius be made
    known;
Made known, be brought to justice.

OEDIPUS

But how
Is that possible? Where would that murderer
    be?
It is so long ago. How can we hope to
Trace those buried footprints now?
There was a murder, and that murder grows to
    a fable
Like the Sphinx herself. Where can we even
    begin
To look?

CREON

Here—the god said.
Seek. There is no doubt
That all will be found out.
If blood is not sought,
Blood will not be bought.
Those are the words.

OEDIPUS

When I took the crown from your hands I
    knew
You mourned a dead king, but I have never yet
Inquired into the precise
Manner of his death. Was it here at home,
Or on the field of battle, or abroad
On the soil of the stranger that he
Met this death, this violent death?

CREON

Laius set forth on a holy pilgrimage
To some distant shrine, some distant god.
And from that day of his leaving he was dis-
    tant forever.
We never saw him again.

OEDIPUS

Did no word come back
From fellow traveler, from retinue
Of accompanying officers or servants—
From any who saw what happened?

CREON

There were servants with Laius. All died,
All were killed with him—except one who
Fled the carnage in terror. He had nothing to
    tell,
Nothing for certain—except for one thing.

OEDIPUS

One thing would be something—a clue
Pointing to other clues.

CREON

This man's story was
That a band of robbers, not one robber but
    many,
Fell on the king's party and slew them.

OEDIPUS

Robbers—it seems unlikely. To kill a king.
Unless they were under high orders—orders
    from here,
High money, protection from on high.

CREON

This too has been thought of. But there was
Much to harass us. Too much trouble in the
    state

To seek to seek out the murderers or the
Arch-murderer behind them—

OEDIPUS

Is that possible?
Surely no trouble in the state could be so great
As to hinder a state inquiry into
A royal death, a royal murder?

CREON

You forget the Sphinx,
You who slew the Sphinx and delivered us.
The Sphinx was very much alive in those
    days.
She took up all our attention.

OEDIPUS

We will start,
As from now. We will seek
To bring everything to light that has been too
    long hidden.
All thanks to you, Lord Creon, and all praise
To Phoebus Apollo, for telling us what our
    duty is
To the dead. Be sure you will find me
Untiring in this cause—God's cause.
Our country's cause. My own cause also,
Since it is from myself as well as my subjects
That this stain must be cleaned away. After all,
The killer of Laius, secure in his ability
To kill a king and go unpunished because
Undetected—might he not, whoever he is,
Turn against this king?
Serving the cause of Laius, I serve myself.
People of Thebes, there is nothing I will not do
To douse the fire, to smite the demons,
Deliver our city, with God's help, from the
Blood that is bred of blood. Now let me
Enjoin you, the faithful, to show your faith.
Pray to the gods for guidance, revelation,
The lifting of the curse. That they
May bless you is my own prayer. I take my
    leave.

(He and Creon go into the palace.)

FIRST ELDER

Come, children. You heard the voice of the
    king.
He has promised us all that we came to ask.

Let us go and add our prayers to his efforts,
That we may be saved.

CHILDREN

Oedipus, Oedipus, King,
Solver of riddles,
Slayer of monsters.
Seek out the monster
That killed a king.
Answer this riddle,
Unwind
The tangled string.

*(The first elder takes the children away. The re-
maining elders mingle with the chorus, which is
now totally adult. The chorus chants.)*

CHORUS

Strophe

To Thebes, the city of light, from out of the
    gold
Shrine of the golden god the word has come.
It is not a word of deliverance that is told.
Fear cleaves our hearts, fear renders us dumb.
Hear, O hearer, healer of Delos, hear,
Tell us in our fear what you will do.
Will it be something new?
Will it be something old as the wheeling year?
Daughter of hope, we call on you.

Antistrophe

There are three divinities
Whose task it is
To avert
Adversities.
Artemis, Artemis,
Daughter of the father of
The gods, who
In majesty but with a special love
Sits above our city.
Next, from her sister Athena, we
Seek pity. Last
From Phoebus, lord of the bow, the far
Shooter, we ask
Aid in our task.
O, in the past
You drove away fire, plague, famine
    from the state.
Be great as then,
Help us again.

Strophe

Our sorrows are so many they cannot be told.
Sickness holds the land. The hand is numb
That drives the useless plow. The shepherd's
     fold
Is stricken. The city soon will become
Empty of life, the ship is beached, its wood
Rotting, rotten. No seed takes hold
In the earth or in the womb. Like flocks of
     birds
The hopeless leave the city, seeking some
     good
On the shore of an alien god. Words,
Words of prayer are all that is left to us,
But our mouths grow cold.

Antistrophe

               Death in the streets,
               Children lying
               Dead in the streets, spreading
               Contagion of death.
               The breath of the mourners,
               The suppliants, freezes
               On the altar. Alter
               Our condition, Golden Athena,
               Golden Apollo, grant
               Remission to our pain.
               The night wind,
               The morning breeze is
               Sour with pain.
               Once you listened.
               Listen again.

Strophe

There is war, but not a war of brazen shields,
No clash of armor lifts the heart. Our war
Is with the god of war himself. He strikes our
     fields,
Our homes, a savage god, a god of fire,
     whose roar
Is louder than the cries of the dying. O Zeus,
Exile the war god to some northern shore,
For we can no longer abide the tortured night,
The agony of the morning. Let your bright
Lightning strike him, turn loose
Your steeds of thunder under whose fiery feet
He will be beaten and crushed and seen no
     more.

Slay him, Apollo,
You of the golden bow.
Artemis, slay him, flashing
In torchlight
Over our hills. And you,
Bacchus, splashing
Wine in boisterous revelry,
With your torch of pinewood
Scorch him, burn him,
Send him screaming away,
The enemy,
The god whom all the gods
Abhor and loathe to see,
Restoring joy
To the bright day!

(Oedipus comes out from the palace)

OEDIPUS

You have prayed, and your prayers will be an-
     swered
If you will but hear my words and obey them.
A remedy is at hand and we must
Put it in hand. Listen to me now
With close attention. Though your king,
I am in many ways a stranger—a stranger es-
     pecially
To the story of Laius's death as much as to
The black deed itself. I need a beginning,
A fact, the start of the thread which will
Lead me through the labyrinth. Therefore,
A citizen speaking to his fellow citizens,
I ask you, Thebans: if any of you knows,
If any of you thinks that he knows who the
Murderer of Laius was or is—let him speak.
Let him declare the truth fully to me—
In public, or in secrecy if he wishes.

(There is no reply)

Let me say more. If any man's conscience is
     guilty,
He may give himself up without fear. His fate
Will be instant banishment, no more.
He who was merciless shall know the taste of
     mercy.

(silence still)

Or if it was some foreigner you know
To have been the assassin, declare this openly.
The informant shall be rewarded, not only
     with thanks.

(silence still)

But—let me speak plainly—if one among you
Is found to be hiding himself or another in
    fear,
In lack of faith in my clemency, I here
Pronounce his sentence. Whoever he be,
I forbid him shelter in my land, the hand
Of human friendship, the comfort of
Religion, of prayer or sacrifice or the right
To the lustral rites of cleansing. Thereby
Excommunicate him. He shall be totally
Homeless, friendless, godless, cursed and un-
    clean.
I follow the divine oracle in this, doing
My duty to the god as well as to the dead.
And I pray in all solemnity that the
Unknown murderer and his accomplices,
If accomplices there be, shall wear
The badge of shame, the brand of infamy
On the very skin to life's end, world's end.
I seek no royal exemption from this curse.
If, in full knowledge, I have harbored
In house, on hearth, this man of blood,
Then on my head lie the evil and the
Consequences of the evil. We have, all of us,
A duty to see that these duties to the god,
To our suffering country, be faithfully carried
    out.
A stranger in so many ways, I am a stranger
In my failure to understand why, when he
    died,
Your late king, there were no voluntary acts
Of purification—acts unprompted by the gods,
    I mean.
So good a king—his death went by
With no more perturbation in the state
Than might be occasioned by the death of a
    beggar.
I cannot understand why the most
Rigorous inquiries were not undertaken.
So good a king. But enough of this.
I stand in his place, having inherited
Not only his crown but his bed,
His dear wife, now my dear wife.
Had there been children of his, they would
    have been
A further bond of blood between us.
But there are enough bonds. His cause is
    mine.

I will fight for him as I would fight
For my own father. No corner of the labyrinth
Shall lack the probing of light till the light
    bring forth
The slayer of Laius,
Laius, the son of Labdacus, the son of
Polydorus, the son of Cadmus, the son of
    Agenor.
The curse of the gods light on all who
Disobey our royal charge. May the earth
Be empty of seed for them, and empty of seed
The women they lie with. May the curse of
    heaven
Pursue them to the gates of hell. For you,
My friends and brothers, brothers in suffering,
May justice be your ally, may the gods
Grant blessing.

CHORUS LEADER

I speak, King Oedipus,
But only to ask. If the god Apollo said so
    much,
Why cannot he say more?

OEDIPUS

I do not quite—

CHORUS LEADER

If asked, would not the god
Say who the murderer is?

OEDIPUS

One does not ask again. The god's silence
Would be a rebuke and a new disappointment.
There is no path there.

CHORUS LEADER

I have another thing,
A second thought.

OEDIPUS

Second, third—let me have them all.

CHORUS LEADER

Tiresias—I was thinking of Tiresias. He, it is
    said,
Stands nearest to Phoebus Apollo. The divine
    fire
Burned out his eyes and killed his manhood,
    so they say.
For the rest, he withstood it, and

It stays within him.

OEDIPUS

So they say, and for that reason—

CHORUS LEADER

He surely could help more than any in the
     state.

OEDIPUS

For that reason, I say, he has been sent for.
It was on Creon's advice. I stressed the ur-
     gency.
He should be here now to meet me.

A CHORUS MEMBER

Tiresias?

CHORUS LEADER

A bundle of myths, and very old.
And very irritable.

CHORUS MEMBER

Blind, you said?

CHORUS LEADER

So many stories. He was believed to have seen
The goddess Athena bathing. A deadly sin
And he lost his sight for it. Or so some say.
Some say that the gods took pity and
Gave him in recompense the power of
     prophecy.

ANOTHER CHORUS MEMBER

He has another gift too, they say, unless
It was really a calamity of birth.

CHORUS LEADER

You mean:
He is both man and woman? Who knows?
He is past the pleasures of both, though he
     may
Suffer with both. There. See the suffering.
See the irritability.

(Tiresias is led on by a boy)

OEDIPUS

Tiresias, it was good of you to come.
We know, the whole world knows, that there
     is
Nothing beyond your sphere of knowledge.
In your heart, if not in your eyes, you see

The wretched state of our city. Only you
Can help us. You will have heard
That we have sent to Apollo for the
Guidelines of help, and Apollo has answered.
The only way of deliverance from the plague
That has struck us is to find the murderer
Of Laius, your late king, and kill or banish
     him.
Him or them. Sir, your gifts are great.
You have worked in all the modes of divina-
     tion— Scrying, astrology, probing the en-
     trails of birds.
Save us, save yourself, you too are of Thebes.
Show us the way of cleansing. To help man
Is the noblest work of man.

TIRESIAS

Very wise words.
But when wisdom brings no profit to the wise,
Wisdom is a mode of suffering. Why did I
     forget this?
I who knew it so well. It was useless to send
     for me.
I should never have come.

OEDIPUS

This is no help.

TIRESIAS

Let me go home. It will be easier, believe me,
For you to bear your suffering, me mine.

OEDIPUS

You are great in Thebes, but you show your-
     self
No friend of Thebes if you refuse to answer.
Son of Thebes, it is the king of Thebes who
     speaks to you.

TIRESIAS

I refuse to answer, yes. Refuse because
Your words tend to no good. So I guard my
     own.

OEDIPUS

You know something, yet you refuse to speak.
Let this king be a beggar and beg again.

TIRESIAS

Beg in vain. You sin by asking. I will not
Divulge my heavy secrets—your heavy secrets.

OEDIPUS

More riddles. All I take your words to mean
Is that you know and will not tell. All I take
Your intention to mean is that you will fail us,
See with your blind eyes the city perish.

TIRESIAS

I wish to spare you, I wish to spare myself.
Ask nothing more. I will tell nothing more.

OEDIPUS

Nothing? This is insolence. You would lash
A heart of stone to anger. You are obstinate
Like stone. I command you to speak.

TIRESIAS

You anger is misplaced. Reserve it
For yourself. Put your own house in order.

OEDIPUS

You hear these insults? My anger is
The anger of the state. It is the state
You insult.

TIRESIAS

Things will be
As we shall see. Fate's engine
Is beyond the control of man's hands.
You need no prophet to tell you this.

OEDIPUS

What fate will bring to birth—
It is your art or trade to know this
And to say it. Practice your trade.

TIRESIAS

Prepare what new rage you will,
You whose great fault is rage,
I say no more.

OEDIPUS

If you want more rage you shall have it.
I speak openly, I say unflinchingly
What I must now believe. I believe that you
Had some hand in the plot to kill a king.
If you had eyes, I would say that those eyes
Instructed the hand. I say that
In your darkness murder coiled and writhed.

TIRESIAS

You would say that? Very well then, hear.

You have stung me out of silence. On your
    head
And your head only let the curse fall
That fell from your own lips. You are excom-
    municate,
Cut off from men. Speak no more to me or
    any. It is you,
You who are the defiler of this land.

OEDIPUS

You dare to say this? You—shameless,
Treacherous—you know the consequence—
You think you can escape the—

TIRESIAS

I have
Already escaped. The truth is my door.

OEDIPUS

But—it is treason. Who put you up to this?

TIRESIAS

You were, shall I say, the instigator.
You asked, you taunted, you stung. What I
    said
You made me say. It was against my will.

OEDIPUS

Say it again. Say what you said
Against your will. Let me be clear, let there be
No mistake.

TIRESIAS

It was plain enough.

OEDIPUS

Say it loud,
I will know it beyond all doubt. Say it once
    more.

TIRESIAS

I say that the murderer you seek
Is yourself.

OEDIPUS

Madman—

TIRESIAS

It is your voice
That grows to the voice of a madman. Now I
    have started,

At your request, at your order, remember
    that—
Will you hear more?

OEDIPUS

Spew all your madness out.
Fly to, the limits of treason. You will suffer.
Say all you know.

TIRESIAS

This I know. This you do not know.
Your marriage is a sin. Your love is a sin.
Your bed is stained with sin.

OEDIPUS

Impunity—
You think your blindness and age grant you—

TIRESIAS

The truth grants it, not I, the mere
Bearer of the truth.

OEDIPUS

Bearer of lies, infamy,
Blind, senseless, brainless—

TIRESIAS

Cast no taunts,
You who must yet live in a thunder of them,
Swim in a torrent of them—

OEDIPUS

Do not threaten me,
You, who lack power to make flesh and blood
    of threats,
You who live in the dark. But men in the light
Lack equal power. My throne is of rock.

TIRESIAS

Rocks, you mean. Your throne rocks. No, I
    admit
I cannot harm you. But the gods can. Apollo
    can.

OEDIPUS

Apollo—Creon—it is Creon, then? Creon—
His idea, not yours—?

TIRESIAS

Creon is not your enemy.
You are your own.

OEDIPUS

The shadow of success
Is always envy. It is the scorpion over the
    royal bed,
The headache under the crown. Creon, my
    friend,
Trusted so long, standing in the shadow,
With the claw of dispossession ready to
    strike—
Is it possible? I took the crown from his hand,
A crown unsought by me, freely given
By him. And now—is it possible?—
He sets this cheating monger of magic on to
    me,
The light of cupidity in the blind eyes.
You, sir—I call your craft into question.
That famous gift was notably lacking when
The Sphinx fed on Theban flesh. That riddle
Which none could answer save I—surely a
    seer,
A prophet, a special being walking under
The equivocal canopy of the gods, surely he
Should have answered it? But the stars were
    silent,
The lees in the wine cup yielded no pattern,
The flight of the birds spelled nothing. I,
I, Oedipus, ignorant Oedipus gave the answer
And stopped the riddler's mouth forever,
With no benefit of the prophet's lore. I,
Oedipus, whom you would now dispossess
To feel in your blindness the embossed gold
Of a royal counselor's chair. Tiresias,
Though blind, the seeing eye of Creon.
Make no mistake, you shall regret this,
Creon shall regret it. To make me, your king,
The sacrificial goat—such impiety to the gods,
Such treason.

CHORUS LEADER

King Oedipus, we hear too much anger
On both sides. If I may say so, the true impi-
    ety
Is to waste time in anger, to neglect
The command of Apollo.

TIRESIAS

I accept that you
Wear the crown and stand above me, but I
    claim

No less than what you claim—the right of
speech.
Moreover, it was more out of courtesy that I
came
Than from a subject's duty. I am not your sub-
ject.
Apollo is my one master, him I serve.
Nor is Creon my patron. I answer freely,
As a free being should. You mock my blind-
ness.
First think of your own. You have eyes
That can see and will not. You shut them to
Your own state of sin and impending damna-
tion.
Ask yourself whose son you are. Consider that
A man sins no less for being blind to his sin.
The curse of a father and a mother will yet
Send you packing from this palace and from
this land.
Then you shall be blind like me but lack no
voice
To cry aloud the horror of the truth
I know but you are yet to learn. Believe me,
You who use your voice to decry
Creon and myself, you shall be struck dumb
yet
Before you find the air for lamentation.
You shall be stamped in the ground
But bear no fruit other than bitterness,
The bitterness of men's scorn.

OEDIPUS

I have stood enough. Leave me. Go back
Whither you came.

TIRESIAS

I came at your bidding,
Not from my own wish.

OEDIPUS

If only I had known
What slanderous madness I was to listen to,
I would have spared us both the trouble.

TIRESIAS

You talk of my madness. It is not the word
Your father would have used.

OEDIPUS

Would have used?

My father lives.

TIRESIAS

Today you find your father.
Today you are born. Today you die.

OEDIPUS

Riddles.
I am sick of riddles.

TIRESIAS

Strange words from a man
Whose pride lay in solving them. But, as you
Shall learn, what was your pride must be your
ruin.

OEDIPUS

Ruin, ruin. Let us think of the city's ruin.
I saved it once. I will again. I am Oedipus.

TIRESIAS

And I am going. Give me your hand, boy.

OEDIPUS

Give it, boy. We can well spare him.

TIRESIAS

Wait. This is the last time you will see my
face.
The rest of you will see and will remember.
Remember these words. This is the man you
seek,
The killer of Laius. He passes for a stranger
But, as he will know to his cost, he is Theban
born.
He came here seeing. He shall go blind.
He is rich now, but will soon beg his bread.
A stick shall tap his way into exile.
Where he enters, he once came out.
For the ones he loves, new names are needed,
Names against nature, sphinx-names.
He laid his father low to sleep in his bed.
Remember these things. Blind you called me.
You will not call me blind when you learn to
see.
And when you learn to see, it is you—
You who will be blind. Lead me away.

(He goes. Oedipus enters the palace.)

CHORUS

Out of the rock of golden Apollo

A voice calls: where is the slayer,
Where is the doer of a deed without a name?
Phoebus, sweet singer, golden harp-player,
Strike strings no longer. Follow, follow
With swift wings, with avenging flame.
The hunt is up. A man in hiding
Skulks in caves, roams the wood,
Lonely as the mountain lion or the wild ox,
Cut off from kindliness, bereft of good.
In every shadow his pursuers are striding.
He whimpers through the snow like a maimed
    fox.
Tiresias the prophet has unleashed terror
Into our darkness, but darkness it remains.
We lack knowledge, but we do not lack fear.
We ask and hear no answer, beating our
    brains.
Soothsayers are so often the sayers of error,
Surely it was ghastly error that was spoken
    here?
The gods know all, but men know so little,
Even the greatest of prophets. Prove blame
On our king and then we will believe.
We stand aghast, aghast at the frail and brittle
Fabric of accusation we watched him weave,
With sure fingers in his blindness. But can that
    shame
Really attach to our king, whose goodness is a
    flame,
Whose wisdom is wonder? We will wonder
    and not grieve,
Unbelieving that the deed without a name
Came from his hand, continuing to proclaim
His goodness, wisdom, trumpeting his fame.

*(Creon comes on toward the end of the chorus.
He is angry.)*

CREON

Citizens of Thebes, it has been brought to my
    knowledge
That the king, King Oedipus, has laid
A most serious and slanderous accusation
    against me.
I come to you, my brothers, in anger and sor-
    row.
To think that he should harbor such a thought,
The thought that I have sought his harm, in
Word or act. I do not wish to live

In the odor of such scandal. If you, my
    friends,
The voices and ears of my country, are, like
    him,
Ready to cry treason, then I will end it now,
A life already too long.

CHORUS LEADER

My lord Creon,
Our king is distressed. Take it that his words
Were spoken in an anger so great
It seized on the first object, one close to him,
One dear to him.

CREON

Enough of that. Did he say
What I heard that he said: that under my
    prompting
The prophet Tiresias lied?

CHORUS LEADER

I must admit
That he cried out in those terms—but
With what intention I cannot say.

CREON

Spoken directly, coherently, deliberately,
With none of the stumbling of distress—was
    this so?
Was the accusation clear and unequivocal?

CHORUS LEADER

Who am I to say more of the deeds or words
Of our master? He has heard you. He is here.
Let him speak.

*(Oedipus comes from the palace and confronts
Creon)*

OEDIPUS

You, sir, you have the effrontery to stand in
The shadow of my door, brazening it all out,
Pretending sanctimonious shock, as I
Heard and now see, when you are the
Proved plotter against my life, the
Foiled thief of my crown? For God's sake,
Did you take me for a fool or a coward
Or one lacking eyes like your precious
Senile confederate? Did you think I lacked
    means
To uncover a conspiracy as puerile as yours?

A childish plot and a hopeless one. How could
  you
Hope to succeed without powerful friends or
The backing of the people or, yes, money?
Money wins thrones when talent and virtue
  fail,
When talent and virtue are lacking—

CREON

You cannot know what you are saying. Listen.
I have a right to be heard.

OEDIPUS

I have a right
To justice.

CREON

Judge when I have spoken.

OEDIPUS

Quick to speak and, as I know, eloquent.
You cannot cloud in words what you are—
An enemy, a bitter and cunning—

CREON

First let me tell you—

OEDIPUS

Anything you will, except that you're not
Guilty.

CREON

If you think that unenlightened obstinacy
Will do you any good—

OEDIPUS

And if you think
That you're safe from justice just because
You're a kinsman—

CREON

Would I be such a fool?
Why are you such a fool as to think it?
Enough of this nonsense. Tell me—I've a right
  to know—
The precise nature of the harm I'm supposed
  to have done you.

OEDIPUS

Was it you, or was it not you,
Who persuaded me to send for that
Prophetic humbug, that canting mumbler?

CREON

If you mean Tiresias, yes.
And I would do it again.

OEDIPUS

Doubtless. Now then, tell me—
How long ago is it that Laius, King Laius—

CREON

Laius? What has Laius to do with it?

OEDIPUS

How long is it since Laius—disappeared,
Died, was murdered?

CREON

That you should know, common knowledge.
A little longer ago than your crowning,
Your marriage. The event's a year older
Than your eldest child.

OEDIPUS

Was Tiresias at his profession then,
If you can call it a profession?

CREON

He was an honored prophet.
As honored as now.

OEDIPUS

In those days,
Did he ever—mention me?

CREON

Not to my knowledge.

OEDIPUS

Was there
No inquest into the king's death,
No search for his body?

CREON

We inquired, we searched. There was nothing.

OEDIPUS

And why was our professional wise man,
Our state soothsayer, so silent then?

CREON

I don't know.

OEDIPUS

You don't know, but
There is something that you know.

And you'd be wise to confess it now.

CREON

I will always confess what I know.
What do I know?

OEDIPUS

This—
That Tiresias would not have said,
Said to my very face, that I
Was the murderer of Laius, if you, sir,
Had not prompted him—

CREON

If he said that, you know best that he said it.
But, since you've pounded questions at me,
Give me leave to ask you something.

OEDIPUS

Ask all you wish. You will never prove me
Guilty of Laius's murder.

CREON

Leave that.
Answer this: are you my sister's husband?

OEDIPUS

You know I am.

CREON

Is she your equal partner
In the rule and revenues of the kingdom?

OEDIPUS

This you know too.

CREON

Do I share your honor?
Am I an equal partner?

OEDIPUS

Yes, you are,
And being so you are all the more a traitor.

CREON

I deny it, and I could be hot in the denial,
I could counter-rage. But I prefer reason,
And I ask reason from you. Consider this:
I have royal rank, royal honor, but I lack
One thing I am glad to lack—I mean
The unquiet head of a king, the specious
Glint of the crown. I do not wish
To be king—what more could it give me?

Certainly my sleep would be uneasier,
The night shadows more full of menace.
No, I have what I want—royalty and rule
Unqualified by the final responsibility.
Would I not be a fool to snatch from you
The thing I am—selfishly, if you wish—
Least disposed to possess? I have honors
    enough.
I am liked, I am friend to all men. It is to me
That suppliants for your help or favor come.
Who would seek to exchange this comfortable
    life
For yours that is so comfortless? Treason?
If you want treason look elsewhere for it,
Among men who grope for power. I have
    power.
All you need do, you on whose face doubt
    rides,
Unslowed by reason, is to go yourself
To the shrine of Apollo. Ask if the message
I brought back was the message given. Do that
    first.
Then I am ready, under due process of law,
To be proved guilty or innocent of any
Conspiracy with our state soothsayer.
If I am guilty let me choose
My own mode of death. It will be far more
    terrible
Than any that our statutes hold for treason.
Hold me to this, citizens of Thebes.
But I will not be charged in this manner,
On suspicion, on blind suspicion,
Hissing and writhing behind my back. You, sir,
Are guilty of two crimes. The first is little,
Compared with the other—it is this dreary
    crime of slander.
But the other crime is inexcusable in a king—
The crime of mistaking a good man for a bad.
Throw away a friend and you throw away
Your own life. Time teaches this, but the les-
    son is a
Long and slow one. Years prove the good man;
The evil man is known in a single day.

CHORUS LEADER

Listen to those words, King Oedipus.
Slow thoughts aim best. Anger hits nothing.
Your quickness of temper is a fault

That has undone lesser men.

OEDIPUS

I pride myself on quickness. I was quick
With the Sphinx, when slowness earned others
　　death.
I am quick at countering quick treason.
What must I do—wait till I am in the net
And the rope tightens?

CREON

Be quick then
With your condemnation. What will you do
　　with me?
Banish me, Oedipus?

OEDIPUS

Ah no, no banishment.
Death. Quick death.

CREON

Think. Be a king.
Show me the wrongs I am said to have done
　　or be doing.
Evidence.

OEDIPUS

Obstinate still. Reasonable obstinacy.

CREON

I am obstinate in saying you are wrong.

OEDIPUS

I know I am right.

CREON

In your own knowledge,
Not in the knowledge of the gods
Or of reasonable men. Not in mine.

OEDIPUS

You are a traitor.

CREON

And if I am not?
If you are wrong?

OEDIPUS

Kings must rule.

CREON

Not if they rule unjustly.

OEDIPUS

Do you hear this,
Thebes, my city?

CREON

Your city? Is she not my city too?

CHORUS LEADER

With respect, sirs—this is enough.
You need a woman's calm. Now you will get
　　it.
The queen, Jocasta, is coming.

(Jocasta comes out from the palace)

JOCASTA

Your noise awoke me. Quarreling, quarreling.
Is this a time to shout out private grievances?
You should be ashamed. There are larger is-
　　sues
To engage our passions—must I remind you?

CREON

None larger than this. Your husband here,
Our lord the king, is engaged in condemning
Me to death.

OEDIPUS

It is true. He is guilty
Of plotting against my life.

CREON

He will not cease
In his wild accusations. I, Jocasta,
The easy-living, who shuddered in your wid-
　　owhood
When I feared the crown must come to me—

JOCASTA

Believe him, Oedipus. Believe him for your
　　own sake,
For all our sakes.

CHORUS

　　　Listen, O King, consent.
　　　May your anger be spent.
　　　Let mercy flower.

OEDIPUS

　　　Why should I relent,
　　　Repent of the truth?

CHORUS

> Truth, like a flower,
> Blooms for all men.
> You nourish a sour
> Weed of your own planting.

OEDIPUS

> Do you know what you are saying?

CHORUS

> We are saying that Creon swore
> His friendship, never before
> Showed falseness, said
> Falsehood. The betrayal is your
> Betrayal. On your own head
> Be the crime.

OEDIPUS

> In asking me to relent
> You ask for my own death,
> Or my own banishment.

CHORUS

> Let the breath
> That carried that word
> Be eaten by the wind.
> All we say is that we have heard
> Too much in too evil a time.
> You have sinned,
> King, in imputing sin.
> We are sick of the wrangling
> Of princes. Let mercy in.

OEDIPUS

If it is your wish that I let him go, then so be
  it.
This may encompass my own end. Neverthe-
  less,
I say yes to your plea. But you have no power
To quell my hate. I hate him forever.

CREON

It is harsh mercy, the other face of anger.
You build yourself a cell, cut off from the sun,
And furnish it with engines for your own
Torture.

OEDIPUS

Out of my sight. Take your last leave.

CREON

I am going, wrapped in a traveling cloak.
Of injustice woven by your hands alone.
Wherever I go, I walk in innocence.

(He leaves. Oedipus moves away from him, turns his back. The chorus addresses Jocasta.)

CHORUS

> Persuade him, Majesty,
> Of the wrong he has done.

JOCASTA

> How did all this begin?

CHORUS

> Surmise, suspicion, calumny.
> The heat and stress of the time.

JOCASTA

> Each blamed the other one.
> How? For what fault?

CHORUS

> It is best that we take
> The story as done.
> Let us not make
> More wretched
> This wretchedness of our own.
> Best to leave well alone.
> But talk to him, Majesty.

OEDIPUS

Ignorant peacemakers, you will consider
That you have done well. I tremble for the
  consequences.

CHORUS

> King Oedipus,
> Hear us once more.
> Who are we to wish harm
> To the man who saved us,
> The man who will yet
> Steer us out of the storm?
> We wished good to goodness,
> To rightness of choice.
> Our voice was raised in this
>   cause.

JOCASTA

My brother banished. Surely I have a right
To know the sudden spring of this hatred.

OEDIPUS

Your brother is your brother. But I am the
  king.
He plotted against me. He put into the mouth
Of that blind old monger of lies that it was I
Who murdered Laius.

JOCASTA

Is it from his own pretended knowledge,
Or from what others have said and he has
  heard?

OEDIPUS

He kept himself cunningly clean of the accusa-
  tion,
Using a soothsayer. Could anything be filthier,
More underhand?

JOCASTA

What has shaken you
Is that a soothsayer may speak truth, after all,
May have said truth now, against all evidence.
We are all superstitious. But let me give you
One instance to show that human prophecies
Can dismally fail. To Laius one day I remem-
  ber,
An oracle uttered a dismal prophecy. It was
  not
The god himself of course—God forbid
I should think such a thing—but one of his
Least reliable servants. He said to Laius
That he should die at the hands of his own
  son,
A son to be born of Laius and me.
But the whole world knows what happened.
Laius was killed by robbers, foreign men,
At a place where three roads meet. As for our
  son—
And there was a son, the prophet was right in
  that—
In fear of the prophecy, the king gave orders—
It was a terrible thing to do, I had no part in
  it,
But necessary, I see that it was necessary—
Gave orders to pierce the ankles of the child
With an iron spike and cast him forth
To die on a barren hillside—

OEDIPUS

Pierce his ankles?

JOCASTA

So he could not crawl
Out of the deadly cold. Laius could be cruel,
But he could not directly kill. A winter night
Was the murderer. The point though is this—
That the prophecy failed. Laius's son
Did not kill his father. Prophecies *can* fail.
What God intends He prefers to show
In His own time. Pay no heed to prophets.

OEDIPUS

My wife, my dear wife—something
Terrifies me. Something in your words.
My mind wanders back then stops,
Fearful to look—

JOCASTA

Something in my words?

OEDIPUS

You said that Laius was murdered
At a point where three roads meet.

JOCASTA

That is the story.

OEDIPUS

Where is the place, Jocasta?
Where did it happen?

JOCASTA

Phocis—the road divides there,
Leading to Delphi one way, to Daulia another.

OEDIPUS

And the news of his death came when?

JOCASTA

As you know—just prior to your coming,
Your crowning, our marriage. What is it,
What is in your mind?

OEDIPUS

Oh God God,
To do this to me—

JOCASTA

To do what? What is the trouble?
For God's sake tell me—

OEDIPUS

Laius—
What did he look like?

JOCASTA

Tall, about your height.
Older, of course. White-haired.

OEDIPUS

Is it possible?
To curse oneself in ignorance?

JOCASTA

You're ill,
You frighten me—

OEDIPUS

I have a sudden fear
That that blind man had eyes. Tell me one
  more thing,
Then, God help me, I shall know.
How was he attended—Laius, King Laius?
Many officers? Many servants? A full
Royal retinue?

JOCASTA

There were five men all told,
Including a herald. One carriage for the king.
The details were clear.

OEDIPUS

All too clear. Who told you?
Who told you all this?

JOCASTA

The one servant
Who escaped and ran home.

OEDIPUS

And is he at home still?

JOCASTA

No. When he returned and saw you king,
He said his life was rooted in the old way.
He could not serve a new master. He asked me
To let him leave the service of the palace
And go into the fields to work as a shepherd.
He wanted no more of the city. I let him go.
He was good and honest. He could have
Begged a far greater favor. But
I granted what he asked.

OEDIPUS

Is it known where he is?
Could he be brought here quickly?

JOCASTA

He could.

His hovel is near enough. Why do you want
  him?

OEDIPUS

I am full of fear. I fear I have spoken too
  much.
I must see him.

JOCASTA

See him you shall. But
Meantime tell me everything. I am your wife,
I have a right to know.

OEDIPUS

You have the first right.
For the first time now I tell my whole story.
Listen, my dear wife, who, God help us both,
Are, I fear, all too deeply involved. But listen.
My father was a Corinthian—King Polybus—
And my mother a Dorian: Merope was her
  name.
I, as prince, was held by the citizens of
  Corinth
To be their greatest next to the king. Until one
  day
A strange thing happened. There was a dinner,
And a man who'd been drinking too much
Suddenly and insolently said that I
Was not the son of the man I called father.
I was hurt and angry but, rather than show
  anger,
I kept silence. I went to my parents
And told them what had been said and they
Were quick to quiet my fears, angry in their
  turn
That such a story should be put about.
But the story was put about, and put about
  widely.
I did what I had to do, though without
My parents' knowledge. I went to the shrine
Of Apollo at Pytho and asked,
But to that question received no answer. In-
  stead
I was given, without asking, some information
So wretched, so terrible I could hardly sustain
The telling. For the god said I was doomed
To marry my own mother and bring to the
  daylight
A misbegotten brood, a breed of monsters
That men would shun as they shunned the
  Sphinx.

Add to this that I must also kill my father,
And there was but one way open to me—
To leave both father and mother, to flee from
    Corinth,
Never see home again, so that those ghastly
Prophecies should never be fulfilled.
This is what I did. I started
The longest possible journey, and on this jour-
    ney
I came to that very neighborhood, the place
Where three roads meet. There I encountered
A herald followed by a carriage with a man in
    it,
A man like the man you described. This her-
    ald,
In a surly way, a way unfitted to my rank
Or indeed to anyone's, ordered me off the
    road.
I refused, then this venerable one in the car-
    riage
Joined in with equal surliness—he even of-
    fered
To thrust me bodily off the road. I became
    angry
And struck the coachman. The old man
Watched for his moment and, as he passed,
Leaned out with a two-pronged goad and hit
    me
Full on the head. What could I do except
Seek payment in full for the pain and insult?
My stick struck him backwards from his car-
    riage
And he fell out. The others attacked me
And I—need I go on? If this was Laius,
See then what I have done: rendered myself
Hateful to gods and to men. I was born evil,
I am utterly unclean, murderer and polluter
Of my victim's bed. Was it not enough
To have to leave my country in wretchedness,
Never again to see the parents I had at least,
Have at least, spared from the ultimate horror?
The gods have at least saved me from
Patricide and incest, but, for the rest,
They have spent themselves in malignancy.
As for that other—O God, may that day not
    dawn.
May I be lost to men's sight forever before
That final corruption visits me. But is not this

Enough, to know I am the murderer
Of the man whose crown I wear, whose queen
    I love?

CHORUS LEADER

Sir, if I may speak—everything depends
On the testimony of the man you have still to
    meet.
There is surely still ground for hope.

OEDIPUS

That is true. I can hope. I can wait in hope
For the coming of the shepherd.

JOCASTA

But when he comes
What do you want of him?

OEDIPUS

If his story
Is of robbers, of highway robbers, more than
    one—
That is the point, a plurality of killers—
Then I am safe. But if he speaks
Of a man traveling alone, then the guilt
Points clearly toward one man who already
    fears,
Already fears—

JOCASTA

But that was always his story,
A story told and retold, now part of our his-
    tory.
He cannot now go back on it. But even
If in some small point he changes it,
He will never be able to allay my disbelief—
A disbelief I enjoin on you—in prophecies.
A child of mine should kill him: that was how
    it went.
But it was the child himself that died.
Poor child. Divination, soothsaying—
I would not cross the street to
Hear any of that nonsense.

OEDIPUS

You're right.
It is nonsense. Let us have hard fact, the
    record
Of a simple man's mind. Send for him.

JOCASTA

Without delay. Let us go in, out of this

Burning day. Out of the stench of decay,
The distant murmur of laments. Wait, my love,
My lord, and rest while you wait.
You have need of rest.

(They leave)

CHORUS

A Chorale

It is enough to love the law proceeding
 Out of high heaven's light,
Born of the Lord, flawed with no mortal
 breeding,
 A paradigm of right.

Only the tyrant, blown with insolence,
 Dreams of a higher flight.
Seeking the sky but not the light from
 hence,
 He finds an endless night.

Ambition is a good in kings and princes,
 May heaven prosper it,
When every deed that breeds from it
 evinces
 The subject's benefit.

But now we fear the radiance may be
 clouded
 That issues from the sky,
The visage of divinity be shrouded,
 The truth be proved a lie.

The living voice of heaven that we cher-
 ish—
 Is it of little worth?
Shall piety and faith and honor perish

And evil stalk the earth?

Awaken, Zeus, and show your power in
 thunder,
 Say that the voice speaks true.
If heaven errs, then is it any wonder
 We fail and falter too?
 And know not what to do?

*(Jocasta comes on, carrying a garlanded branch
and incense. A girl is with her.)*

JOCASTA

Elders of the city, citizens,
It seems that I must do homage
To the gods, and not solely because of
The plague and the other calamities
We suffer together. I may speak freely,
As to a family, I trust.
You must know, then, that the king
Suffers from stress and unwholesome fancies
I can do little to heal, by either
Advice or soothing words. He is too much
At the mercy of man's speech,
No longer, it seems, able to make sound judg-
 ments.
These things will pass, but not without
Help from the gods. Help from the gods
I seek, then—first from you, golden Apollo.
Lift our uncleanness, restore to our ship's mas-
 ter
The skill to steer us all to safe haven.

(A messenger enters)

MESSENGER

Great news.

END OF THE FIRST PART

PART TWO

*(As before, but the quality of the light shows it
is much later in the day. By the end of the scene
night will have fallen. Jocasta comes on.)*

JOCASTA

These things will pass, but not without
Help from the gods. Help from the gods
I seek, then—first from you, golden Apollo.
Lift our uncleanness, restore to our ship's mas-
 ter

The skill to steer us all to safe haven.

(A messenger enters)

MESSENGER

Peace on you, madam, and men of Thebes.
I am come from Corinth, seeking the house of
 Oedipus,
With a message for the king himself.

CHORUS LEADER

This is the palace, the king is within.
That lady is the queen, his consort.

MESSENGER

God's blessings on you and on your household,
Noble lady, worthy of such a man.

JOCASTA

From Corinth, you say?

MESSENGER

A message from Corinth. Great news, I may
tell you,
But tinged with sadness.

JOCASTA

Leave the sadness till after. We have
Enough of our own. What is your good news?

MESSENGER

The people of Corinth wish to make
Oedipus their king—king of all the Isthmus.

JOCASTA

But surely Polybus is their king there, unless—

MESSENGER

You have hit on the sadness, madam.
Polybus is dead. Old age has claimed him.
It was a long good life—perhaps sadness
Is out of place.

JOCASTA

Dead? Oedipus's father?
Dead of mere age? Quick, girl, go to your
master,
Tell him the news.

(Her servant leaves)

So much, now, for your oracles.
The father Oedipus fled, fearing to be his
murderer—
Dead by nature's stroke, not by his.
Who again can credit these voices, these
Distillations through fallible men?

(Oedipus comes quickly out)

OEDIPUS

What is this I hear? What news, dearest Jocasta,

Am I summoned to—

JOCASTA

Listen to this gentleman,
A royal messenger of your own country. Say
then
What all this holy prophesying is worth.

OEDIPUS

Who is he? What is his message?

JOCASTA

A royal officer of the court, I take him to be,
Who says your father, King Polybus, is dead.

OEDIPUS

Is this true, sir? Let me hear it from your own
lips.

MESSENGER

This is part of my message, the part
You seem most anxious to hear. It is all too
true.
King Polybus is dead.

OEDIPUS

By sickness?
By man's treachery?

MESSENGER

By accident. A small
Accident can put an old body to sleep.

OEDIPUS

Of sickness, then. My father, my poor father.

MESSENGER

Sickness and age. He had had many years.

OEDIPUS

So, well then, we see, dearest Jocasta,
How little trust to repose in booming oracles,
In smoke from the sacrificial hearth,
From the pattern of the birds screaming over
our heads,
That solemn prophecy—and now he lies,
His body unmarked by any weapon of mine,
At peace in his grave. Unless, unless, of
course,
He died of grief at my absence, with an
Old man's longing to see his son. Does that
Make me his murderer? No, the oracle

Spoke of killing, of the shedding of a father's
  blood.
Oracles are not to be trusted. This
We know now, we know for certain.

OEDIPUS

This we knew before. You have forgotten my
  words.

OEDIPUS

Indeed yes. I was misled by fear.

JOCASTA

Fear no more.

OEDIPUS

No more. And yet there is one,
One fear more. My mother lives, sleeps
In an empty bed.

JOCASTA

And you will dream
Of your body's imprint upon it. Enough of
  this.
Chance is everything, foreknowledge nothing.
Best to live in that knowledge, in lack of
  knowledge.
Take the days as they come, live easy.
Dreams have been taken for oracles. If you
  dream,
As many a man has done, of lying with his
  mother,
It is but a memory of lying with her once
In babyhood. Put off these imaginings.
Let us live.

OEDIPUS

I would not wish her dead,
A father dead is enough for now. But, while
  she lives,
Jocasta, I must still travel in fear.

JOCASTA

Take some comfort at least from the bitter
  news
Of your father's death.

OEDIPUS

There is a small candle of comfort there.
But I still fear the living. I am not safe.

MESSENGER

Fear the living, you say, sir? Whom do you
  fear?

OEDIPUS

Queen Merope, your queen. Widow of Polybus.

MESSENGER

She is a danger to you? In what way a danger?

OEDIPUS

There was this terrible oracle, known to me,
Unknown to the people of Corinth.

MESSENGER

Can it be told,
Or does some sacred law forbid your
Divulging it to me, a stranger though a Corin-
  thian?

OEDIPUS

It may be told. When I was a younger man,
The oracle of Phoebus Apollo said that I
Must kill my father, lie with my mother.
This drove me out of Corinth. I regret noth-
  ing—
I have married happily, raised a family, known
The sweetness of power—nothing save
That long estrangement. It is good
To know the embrace of a father, a mother—

MESSENGER

That fear, you say, drove you away from
  Corinth?

OEDIPUS

Drove me away from the chance of killing my
  father.

MESSENGER

That is all over. As for the other fear,
I can make you rest easy.

OEDIPUS

If you can,
You will not find me ungrateful.

MESSENGER

To be honest,
And I have got where I have through honesty,
I had in mind some sort of tangible gratitude

When you return to Corinth, to rule in
   Corinth.

OEDIPUS

Of course, I had forgotten. But the crown
Must go elsewhere. I will never set foot
In my parents' house.

MESSENGER

No reason why you should not.

OEDIPUS

You are old. The old forget quickly,
Even sometimes while they are being told.

MESSENGER

I know, I know—you mentioned your fear.
But it's any empty one.

OEDIPUS

Empty?

MESSENGER

Yes. Polybus was not your father.

OEDIPUS

Polybus—?

MESSENGER

Was not your father.

OEDIPUS

He was not my—why then did he call me his
   son?
Doubting you now, I wonder whether I should
   not
Doubt you on your other news.

MESSENGER

Doubt all you will. Truth is truth.
It is truth, for instance, that both Polybus and
   his queen
Longed for a son, but remained childless.
If my manner to you, sir, seems somewhat
   more familiar
Than is fitting, it is because—doubt this too if
   you wish—
Because it was from my hands that King Poly-
   bus
Received his son. You were given to him by
   me.

OEDIPUS

Given? What was I? Something you bought for
   a drachma
From a family rich only in children?
Something you found in a gutter?

MESSENGER

You were found in a wood, a thicket
On the slope of Cithaeron.

OEDIPUS

Found by you?

MESSENGER

I was a shepherd then. I became
More than a shepherd later.

OEDIPUS

I cannot understand
How a child could come to be—exposed is the
   term.
A child unwanted, left to die in the cold.
   Whose child?

MESSENGER

Your ankles had been riveted. I loosed you.
A child's ankles, pierced and fettered.

OEDIPUS

I carry the stigma.

MESSENGER

And the stigma is in your name,
Oedipus. A man's name always means some-
   thing,
Though the something be lost in time.

OEDIPUS

Who did this to me—my father or my mother?
This I must know.

MESSENGER

I cannot tell you,
But the shepherd who brought you to me—
He would know.

OEDIPUS

So it was not you yourself—

MESSENGER

No, I was guarding my flocks. This other
   shepherd,
He was, I remember, called Laius's man.

OEDIPUS

Laius? Laius of Thebes?

MESSENGER

Why, yes. This man
Was Laius's own shepherd, or one of them.
  The chief one.
Kings have large flocks.

OEDIPUS

Is this man still alive?
Could I see him?

MESSENGER

This is Thebes,
And I live in Corinth. These people here
  would know.

OEDIPUS

Do any of you indeed know the man he speaks
  of?
An old shepherd I take him to be. Has he
  been seen
In the city or the pastures outside the city?
For God's sake speak if you know.

CHORUS LEADER

I think he is none other than the one you
Have already demanded to see. But the queen
Surely can best tell you.

OEDIPUS

Jocasta,
You know the man we have sent for. Is it the
Same man?

JOCASTA

(frightened)

Does it matter? Is it worth while
Probing into the past, defiling the present?

OEDIPUS

I must follow the clue to the end,
To the heart of the labyrinth.

JOCASTA

In God's name I beg you—no. If you wish to
  live,
Do not go on like this. Have I not
Suffered enough?

OEDIPUS

Courage, Jocasta. It is a

Matter of my honor, not of yours. If I am
  proved
To be the son of a slave, of slave's stock
To the third generation—you are what you
  are.
Your lineage is not brought low.

JOCASTA

Don't do this.
I beg you. Be persuaded by me.

OEDIPUS

I cannot.
I must bring this whole thing to the light.

JOCASTA

It is for your own good—

OEDIPUS

My own good.
If ignorance is for my own good, then I
Want no more of my own good.

JOCASTA

Oh, God help you.
God keep you ignorant of who you are.

OEDIPUS

Go, someone. Bring this shepherd to me.
As for our lady the queen, leave her to bask
In her pride of birth.

JOCASTA

Lost. Condemned.
What more can I say? Go forward to your
Damnation. There is no turning back now.
I have no more words. I have spoken
My last word.

(She leaves, terribly distraught)

CHORUS LEADER

Why, sir, does she go in this grief?
She leaves us the thought of her silence.
What wild beast will rush out of this silence?

OEDIPUS

Let it rush out. Let the silent world,
Silent too long, spew out its secrets.
I must unlock this last door to the last room
Where I myself am lodged. I must look on
  myself.
What I am or may be already shames her,

The high-born woman. Let it come out.
At worst, I am the son of the goddess Fortune.
Who would not have such a mother? I am
Kin to the seasons—four-legged spring,
Summer upright in its pride, tottering winter,
I rise and fall and rise and fall with the
Rising and falling and rising year. This is my
    breed.
I ask no other. I am not ashamed
To ask who I am. I will know who I am.

CHORUS

The secret will out in the full moon—
The secret of our master's birth. The earth
Will sound with it, and one spot of earth
Will be honored above any other—
Cithaeron, mother to our king.
Let new flowers spring on Cithaeron,
Bring honor to Cithaeron.

Was he begotten in a summer noon
By Pan, lover of the mountains? Fountains
Sacred to Apollo saw the act of love, perhaps,
Between our god of the sun
And some favored one of the daughters of
    earth.
Did Bacchus rejoice in his birth,
His wine-stained hands receiving him in joy
From a nymph on Helicon?
Let new flowers spring on Cithaeron.
Bring honor to Cithaeron.

OEDIPUS

Is this the man approaching? A stranger to me,
But much of an age with this Corinthian mes-
    senger.
Is it the man?

CHORUS LEADER

It is. Well-known to us all,
Laius's shepherd, faithful in his service,
A good man.

*(An old shepherd is brought in by two of Oedi-
pus's men)*

OEDIPUS

Now, sir, you, our friend of Corinth—
Is this the one you spoke of?

MESSENGER

This is the one.
It has been many years, but—this is the one.

OEDIPUS

Old shepherd, look at me and listen.
You were, I hear, a servant of King Laius.

SHEPHERD

Yes. A servant but no slave.
Reared in the king's own house.

OEDIPUS

You have always been his shepherd?

SHEPHERD

Most of my life I have tended the king's
    flocks.

OEDIPUS

In what part of the country?

SHEPHERD

Many parts.

OEDIPUS

Name one part.

SHEPHERD

Cithaeron—and the places near to Cithaeron.

OEDIPUS

And in Cithaeron you knew this man, did you
    not?

SHEPHERD

Who? Him? I don't know. What was his
    trade?

OEDIPUS

Forget the trade. You had dealings with this
    man.

SHEPHERD

It's so long ago—I can't remember.

MESSENGER

It *is* a long time ago. But wait, sir.
I'll make him remember. Don't you remember
A shepherd neighbor on the slopes of
    Cithaeron?

You had two flocks—I one only.
We had three seasons together—spring to fall.
I would fold my flock in Corinth for the winter,
You would drive yours to Thebes, to the steadings
Of King Laius. Surely you remember?

SHEPHERD

A long time ago. But it comes back, a little.

MESSENGER

Then perhaps you will remember the day
You gave a child to me—a baby boy—
To bring up as my own?

SHEPHERD

(frightened)

I don't know.
I don't know what you mean. Why was I
    brought here?

MESSENGER

To see that child. Or the man who was that
    child.
Here he is.

SHEPHERD

Damn you, fool. Can't you keep your—

OEDIPUS

Come on now. He's spoken honestly.
More honestly than you.

SHEPHERD

I've done nothing wrong.
Why do you look at me as if I've done—

OEDIPUS

It's wrong
Not to answer a straight question. You were
    asked
A straight question—

SHEPHERD

This one here
Knows nothing about it, nothing about anything.

OEDIPUS

Look, old man, if you won't speak

Of your own free will, we must use
Ways to make you speak.

SHEPHERD

Don't torture me. I'm only a poor old man.

OEDIPUS

(to attendants)

Twist his arms behind him.

SHEPHERD

No, no, leave me. What do you want to know?

OEDIPUS

That child. You gave a child to him,
That child he spoke about.

SHEPHERD

All right, I did.
And I wish to God I'd died the day I did.

OEDIPUS

You'll die now if you don't tell me the truth.

SHEPHERD

And if I do, I'll die. I'll die worse.

OEDIPUS

Come on, out with it. You're wasting time.

SHEPHERD

I said I gave it to him, didn't I?
What more can I say?

OEDIPUS

Where did the child come from?
Your home or someone else's?

SHEPHERD

It wasn't my child, if that's what you mean.
It was another man's.

OEDIPUS

Whose?

SHEPHERD

Please don't ask me any more—please—

OEDIPUS

I'll drag the answer out with your tongue.
Whose?

SHEPHERD

It was a—the child came from the house

Of King Laius.

OEDIPUS

A slave? Or one of his own?

SHEPHERD

Must I say?

OEDIPUS

You must say. I must know.

SHEPHERD

It was his child—so they said, anyway.
Your wife, the queen I mean, could tell you
More about it—

OEDIPUS

She gave it to you?

SHEPHERD

Yes, sir.

OEDIPUS

Why?

SHEPHERD

To—to do away with it.

OEDIPUS

To—kill it? To kill her own child?

SHEPHERD

There was this evil spell put on it, sir.
She cried terribly. But there was this evil
   spell,
You see.

OEDIPUS

What evil spell?

SHEPHERD

The child was going to kill his own father.

OEDIPUS

But the child was not destroyed.
You disobeyed an order.

SHEPHERD

I couldn't do it, sir. Could you do it?
Could anybody here? I gave it to this one here
Who's so high up now. I thought to myself:
He comes from another country, he'll take him
   there,
Right over the hills, miles away.
And now you're here, if it is you.

If it is you, O my God. O my God—

OEDIPUS

All out. Oozed out, to the last drop.
There's a sort of joy in it. No more.
No more to fear. No more to—
Oh, what sin. Oh, what unspeakable—
What filth. To see this in a mirror.
The stain on the bed. The wound in the earth,
Festering. My children, my poor children.
The light is stained. Never again.
The last sunset. No more dawns, no noon.
The light shall not be stained
By my looking on it.
There's a knife to be taken somewhere—
Here, the fountain of seed?
But I would still see. No, the light will look.
The light shall not look. No.
The light has seen enough.

(*He totters out. The messenger and shepherd,
talking under the chorus that follows, go out together.*)

CHORUS

What does it mean? What does it all amount
   to?
Here was a man the world called happy,
Oedipus, pattern of earthly happiness.
Who, after this, can be called happy?
Who would wish for happiness?

Consider his life. Consider his deeds of hero-
   ism.
He shot his arrows straight, favored by Zeus.
He saw the Sphinx, foiled and cursing,
Choke in her own blood. He steered our ship,
His arm was strong against disaster.

Our hearts are torn with this story, with this
   sight
Of affliction unspeakable, for it is our afflic-
   tion.
We are all Oedipus, but to some heaven is
   merciful,
Forbidding the unfolding of the pattern
To the ultimate horror, the thing we have seen.

Time sees everything, suffers everything,
Suffers what must now be inscribed forever
On stone unperishable. Curse after curse,

Begetter and begotten cursed. Son of Laius,
Would to God I had never seen you, you
Who were my light and must now be my dark-
    ness.

Our king, our king—stamped like ash into the
    earth.
But the story is stamped forever in our brains,
In our books, in our very loins. It is
Woven into the light of the sky,
Beats in the blood of the yet unborn,
Is with us, is with you. God forgive us all.

(An officer of the court comes on)

OFFICER

Citizens of Thebes—

(He finds it difficult, in his distress, to continue)

CHORUS LEADER

My lord
High Steward of the Court, we know.
We have heard. You may spare yourself
The distress of a formal announcement.

OFFICER

Heard? You cannot have heard? I have
But just now—

CHORUS LEADER

There can be no new horror.
We have tasted the last of its wine—

OFFICER

Our queen— Dead by her own hand. Note
    what I say,
Preserve what happened before the horror
Rushes into full realization and
Makes me tongueless—

CHORUS LEADER

How? How?

OFFICER

She went raging into her bedroom, fell
Screaming onto the marriage bed, tearing
Her hair, her very skin, crying out the name
Of Laius, cursing the bed in which she
Had brought forth children of her own child,
    she said.
And then Oedipus entered, calling, begging
For a sword to, as he put it, blast to death

The field of such foul sowing. He raved,
Seeking the queen, hammering on her door.
He wrenched the bolts from their sockets,
And fell into the room. There he saw,
And we saw from behind him—

CHORUS LEADER

Courage, courage.

OFFICER

Hanging from a roofbeam, the rope twisted
About her neck, her body circling, circling.
He cried out like a mad thing and used the
    sword
To cut her down. And then—

CHORUS LEADER

Himself?

OFFICER

He was prevented. He was prevented from
Tearing in his passion what had no more life.
For her to die once was enough. He ripped
The very brooches from her robe, his hands
Are fists about them. But for his own harm,
He has been made impotent. His sword was
    taken,
He is under guard. He claims his royal right,
He says, to blazon the unclean thing that is
    himself
Before the eyes of the wronged. I came
To warn you why he comes and of his
Manner of coming.

*(Oedipus enters, distraught, attendants with
him)*

OEDIPUS

Let him be cursed, the man who sought
To do good to a dying child, the life-bringer.
I should have died innocent. Here he is,
Sons and daughters of Thebes, your shame,
The author of your pestilence. Cithaeron,
My foster mother, your winds should have
    blown
Chill on this body, your snows should have
Buried it. You will remember, you will
Carry a curse in your stone barren of grass
And your stunted trees. And you too,
Crossroad in the clearing, at least that forest
Has not been nourished by a father's blood

Split by his son's hand. But wayfarers
Will catch a shiver as of an evil memory
And death sits forever on the signpost. Now,
Let me be hidden from all eyes. Let me go
   hence.
I am unworthy of death, the benison
Of innocent sufferers. Let me wander
And keep my hell alive.

(Creon enters)

CREON

I, Oedipus,
Must dispose all things, under God.
You must know that I have not come to
Gloat or reproach. Ask nothing yet. First,
Consider that it would be seemly
To hide such grief from the generality.
We must mourn in private. Let him be
Conducted in.

OEDIPUS

Let me leave now.
I do not wish to enter that house again
That rang with laughter once and is now,
Through my doing, a house of death. Cast me
   out.
Or do worse, or better—

CREON

The gods must instruct me,
I await the word.

OEDIPUS

You were given the word.
The god pronounced death on the defiler.
Here he stands, though all unworthy of
So light a sentence.

CREON

Death or banishment.
But we must await more guidance.
A king is a king.

OEDIPUS

A queen a queen.
You, as her brother, will do what is fitting
For her burial and the accompanying rites.
As for me, I entreat you again—let me go.
I will not quit the kingdom. I will return
To the place my parents chose to be my death-
   bed—

The mountain Cithaeron. I will wait there
Till death comes. As for my children,
Let the boys stay here in Thebes. They will do
Service in good time. But my daughters,
Girls who shared their father's cup,
Ate from his plate, what can become of them?
What men will seek them? The god of mar-
   riage
Will turn his back. Let them be with their fa-
   ther.

CREON

Over your children I must claim control.
The disposal of their future is in my hands.
Come, let us go in.

OEDIPUS

One prayer at this shrine
That saw so often a united family
Give praise and thanks. Let me go.
A man can do no harm there.

(He is allowed to move toward the altar. He pierces his eyes with the brooches he holds in his hands.)

Dark dark. The sun has burst there
For the last time.

CHORUS

   Horror. Horror of horrors.
   The eyes of the world are out.
   The gods scream,
   Finding poison in the wine cup.
   The mountains are molten,
   The sea blood.
   The mounting moon
   Turns her face away.
   Day will never return.

(During the above Oedipus is led within, Creon going also. The stage is lighted only by an uncertain moon.)

CHORUS

The night has come. But who will sleep
   tonight?
   Only the innocent.
Yet even children will cry out in fright,
   Or dream's bewilderment.

The wolves will howl, seeing inside the

moon
 Ciphers of fear.
In unborn lands, under some distant
 noon
 It will be now and here.

But is there not some sweetness to be
 wrung
 Out of such bitterness?
Drive out the sin—so said the prophet's
 tongue,
 And drive out the distress.

And so the blind defiler cleanses us,
 Grants us new sight.
Restore the savior's crown to Oedipus
 After this night.

(We hear a shepherd's pipe. The dawn comes up. An elder leads in children with votive offerings which they place on the altar. This goes on until the end of the scene.)

CHORUS LEADER

You come in some sort of rejoicing?

ELDER

It is early to offer thanks in person
To the king. But the god is always awake.

CHORUS LEADER

You have heard no news?

ELDER

We live away.
Little of the city's news reaches us.
But we have good news of our own.
A cow calved safely. We heard the crying
Of a newborn human child. The blight
Has lifted from one of our fields.
It seems we are to be delivered
From our afflictions. Praise to the gods.
Praise also to the king.
He has found a way.

(Oedipus, blind, comes from the palace, escorted by his daughters Ismene and Antigone. He makes his exit through the theatre.)

CHILD

What has happened to his eyes?

CHORUS LEADER

It is a long story. You will hear it some day.

(to the chorus)

Creon has relented. He goes into exile
With his daughters.

CHILD

Who did it to him?
He had only one enemy. And that was the
 Sphinx.
But he killed the Sphinx.

CHORUS LEADER

Perhaps it was better to be killed by it.
The riddle was not meant to be answered.

CHILD

But he answered it. He saved us.
That's the story we're told.

CHORUS LEADER

It is dangerous to answer riddles,
But some men are born to answer them.
It is the gods' doing. They hide themselves in
 riddles.
We must not try to understand too much.

CHILD

Why?

CHORUS

Citizens of Thebes, this was Oedipus,
 A man strong in war, gentle in peace.
 God gave him joy, God gave his loins
  increase.
 His happy lot was fire to the envious,
 But now the flutes are stilled, the
  trumpets cease.
 Misfortune's waves have crashed,
  tumultuous,
 Over that head endowed with masteries.
 He yields to the Destroyer's animus.
 A last day is reserved to all of us.
 Look to it always. Human happiness
 Is not for human error to assess.
 Call no man happy till his days surcease,
 Till all the gods of pain declare release,
 Fate turns her back upon his obsequies,
 And happiness may rest with him in peace.

THE END

QUESTIONS ABOUT *OEDIPUS THE KING*

1. Light is traditionally associated with knowledge, and darkness with ignorance. How does Sophocles's play reverse this usual pattern? What references to light and dark do you find, and how do they emphasize Oedipus's state of awareness?

2. Creon is a foil character, one who stands in contrast to the hero. How does his argument, that he does not want to be king, help us better understand Oedipus?

3. Give examples from the play that define Oedipus's character. Does he appear to be a good leader? Why?

4. Because Oedipus has such a strong character, it appears that his actions result from the exercise of his will. How does this characterization make us empathize with Oedipus? Would we care as much about him if we felt that he was the simple toy of fate?

5. Much of the play's effectiveness depends on irony—the discrepancy between what is and what seems to be. What examples of irony can you find, and how do they connect to the question of Oedipus's knowledge of who he is?

6. A tragedy, such as this play, involves the fall of the hero. What causes Oedipus to fall?

7. The chorus warns, at the very end of the play, "Call no man happy till his days surcease," suggesting that we do not know what the future holds in store for us, and that although we are content now, we may end our lives in misery. Is this a fatalistic, or deterministic attitude? Does it deny free will? Why?

Philosophical Discussion:
Can We Be Fated, Determined, and Free?

Oedipus's fate was sealed. In his infancy it was prophesied that he would grow up to kill his father and marry his mother. And that is exactly what happened—he killed his father, Laius, king of Thebes and married his mother, queen Jocasta.

But how could such a tragedy be allowed to happen? Couldn't Oedipus or others familiar with the prophesy have taken precautions to thwart its fulfillment? The irony is that the more Oedipus and others tried to avoid their fate, the closer they came to realizing it. Laius, for example, ordered that the infant be killed. What more could he do? Surely with the child dead, there would be no chance of patricide or incest. But the servant charged with carrying out the deed could not bring himself to commit murder. So the child lived and was brought up thinking that Corinth was his true home, and King Polybus and Queen Merope his true parents.

Oedipus, too, tried to avoid his predicted destiny. Upon learning of the prophecy, he left Corinth so there would be no chance of his killing Polybus or sleeping with Merope. A wise decision, or so it would seem. But these futile efforts only lead to his fatal encounter with Laius, an apparent stranger, and his subsequent marriage to Jocasta, a woman apparently unrelated to him in any way.

Could Oedipus, or the others associated with the tragic set of events, have done otherwise? No one forced Laius to order that his son be killed, or to pick this particular servant to carry out the deed. Perhaps, had some other servant been chosen, or had Laius committed the act himself, subsequent events would not have taken place.

Nor did anyone compel Oedipus to leave Corinth. Had he stayed there it seems, things might have been different. But the Oedipal prophecy seems impossible to avoid, as if those most intent on thwarting it are also most responsible for ensuring its ultimate success.

What if the envisioned events had not been foretold? Laius would not have been motivated to do away with Oedipus, who, in turn, would have been brought up knowing his true parentage. Would Oedipus still have killed his father and sired children by his own mother? Who can say in matters of this kind? Part of the point of the story, however, is that even when we are apprised of our fate, still we cannot avoid it. How then could ignorance make any difference? It seems that what will be, will be—whether or not we want, or are even aware of, what fate holds in store.

Most of us are not fatalists. We tend to eschew the idea that there are a set of events waiting to unfold. Nor do we believe with the ancients that human destiny is controlled by the gods, or Fates: Clotho who spins the thread of life; Lachesis who determines its length; and Atropos who makes the final cut. Of course, we know that sooner or later we all must die, just as we all must pay taxes. But a person can reduce his financial liability by changing investments; so, too, a test pilot could increase his longevity by changing professions.

How can we dismiss an apparent truism, that what will be will be? The alternative, that what will be will *not* be, seems absurd. The idea of fate, in the story of Oedipus, however, is more than just a truism. Otherwise, *anything* that happens to Oedipus— kills his father, does not kill his father, marries his mother, does not marry his mother—is fated to happen, which is uninteresting. If prophesying is compatible with *whatever* happens, then prophesies would be trivially true.

What more is needed? In part, fatalism seems interesting because it suggests that there are some events that *must* occur—necessary events, if you will, such as Oedipus's commiting patricide. But even this characterization is insufficient, since not all necessary events are fated. For example, once Laius's servant decided not to kill the infant it became necessary that someone would have to raise it. But this necessity, by itself, did not mean that Polybus and Merope were to be the adoptive parents. The servant could have raised the infant himself, or given it to someone other than the shepherd of Polybus. The idea that certain events must occur *if* certain other events take place—what we might call "hypothetically necessary" events—is the basic idea of determinism. Fatalism is more than this. It is the idea that certain events must occur *whether or not* certain other events take place—what we might call "categorically necessary" events. For example, if Oedipus is fated to commit incest, then he will do so whether or not he is reared by Merope.

Are there categorically necessary events? A person misses a flight that crashes several hours later. Was missing the flight an act of fate? Perhaps, although the tardiness may just have been a lucky coincidence or necessitated by inordinately heavy traffic on the way to the airport. In either case, the person's being alive would not seem to be fated. Somehow, if fated, the person would have missed the plane no matter what route he took to the airport, just as Oedipus fulfilled the prophecy no matter how he tried to avoid doing so. But most of us, unlike Oedipus, do not have our future lives foretold, so it is difficult to determine on the basis of experience alone whether some events are categorically unavoidable. (Richard Taylor argues that future events are fated in the sense that they are as fixed and unavoidable as are events of the past. But Taylor does not show that historical events are categorically necessary.)

In the absence of successful soothsayers, seers, or oracles, is there some other reason to interpret the things that happen to us fatalistically? It may be suggested that fatalism poses a logical dilemma. For example, either Oedipus will kill his father or he will not. If he will, then anything he does to avoid performing the deed will be insufficient. If he will not, then anything he does will be unnecessary. In either case, Oedipus's actions would seem to be irrelevant to the future course of events. Since the argument may be generalized to include any future event, fatalism would appear to be logically inescapable.

One of the main responses among philosophers has been to challenge the first premise, in particular to question whether propositions about the future can be true or false. Aristotle, for example, suggested that while a certain sea battle either will or will not occur tomorrow, it is neither true nor false that it will (or will not) occur. (The same point is sometimes expressed by suggesting that one of Aristotle's three basic laws of thought, the law of excluded middle—that every proposition is either true or false—does not apply to propositions about the future.)

But Aristotle's suggestion is unclear. Did he mean that the truth or falsity of a proposition about the future is not determined by events of the past or present, or that the truth or falsity of a proposition about the future is not determined at all? If the former, he may be correct. The truth of the proposition that there will be a sea battle tomorrow depends, it seems, on whether or not tomorrow there *is* a sea battle. Fatalists do not deny this. On the contrary, they urge that since the truth or falsity of certain propositions depends on future events—on whether or not Oedipus kills his father, for example—neither we nor Oedipus can affect the truth of such propositions. Interpreted in this way, Aristotle's suggestion would seem to be consistent with fatalism.

On the other hand, if Aristotle meant that the truth or falsity of a proposition about the future is not determined at all, then fatalism would be refuted. But then how could Aristotle, or anybody, suggest truly that either there will or there will not be a sea battle tomorrow? If the individual propositions of which a disjunction (an either/or proposition) is composed are neither true nor false, how can the disjunction itself be true? Perhaps the truth of a disjunction is independent of the truth (or falsity) of the individual propositions of which it is composed. Aristotle, however, did not show this. (See Part II, Truth, for a broader discussion of the concept of truth.)

Gilbert Ryle has suggested that a disjunction of propositions of *particular* future events does not appear to be true or false. For example, while it makes sense to suggest that by leaving Corinth Oedipus will either avoid or not avoid killing his father, it does not make sense that there is some particular act of killing his father that Oedipus will either avoid or fail to avoid.

Ryle's point is well taken, but is it because certain propositions about the future are neither true nor false, or just that we do not know precisely where or when certain events will take place? If the latter, Ryle may be right that it makes little sense to speak of certain future events of which we have no knowledge, just as it makes little sense to speak of past or present events of which we have no knowledge. But propositions about past or present events are either true or false. If propositions about the future are neither true nor false, Ryle would need an additional argument to show this.

It may be suggested that particular future events do not exist. For example, if Oedipus will kill his father, he has not yet done so. Past events by contrast *do* exist—they exist *in the past.* If Oedipus killed his father, the event occurred. But then why can't future events exist as well—*in the future?* If Oedipus will kill his father, then the event will occur. That, in part, is what the fatalist claims: what will be will be. In the absence of additional argument, it is not clear why the fatalist is wrong.

Thus far we have considered and rejected some of the main arguments against fatalism. Does this mean that we should all be fatalists? We think not. Let us recall that the fatalist does not just claim that what will be will be, nor that there are necessary events. The fatalist claims that there are categorically necessary events. The fatalist's argument, however, does not show this.

Let us consider a slightly different example. Either Oedipus will discover the truth about the killer of Laius or he will not. According to the fatalist's dilemma, if he does not discover the truth, then his efforts to do so are insufficient. And if he does discover the truth, then his efforts are unnecessary. Consequently, according to the fatalist, Oedipus's efforts to discover the truth are irrelevant. This may be. But why does this mean that some events are fated? No seer or oracle prophesied that Oedipus would learn the ugly truth about himself (nor was it foretold that he would remain blissfully ignorant). There is nothing in the story of Oedipus to indicate that *everything* that happens to Oedipus, or anybody else, is fated to occur. On the contrary, the story of Oedipus is of particular interest, in part because it picks out certain events that are prophesied in advance and shows how those events occur despite the best efforts of all concerned to avoid their occurrence. If it were not for this feature, the story of Oedipus would illustrate little more than the truism that what will be will be—which we have already dismissed.

Moreover, Oedipus's discovery of the truth about himself does not seem inevitable. The details of his life are revealed gradually and it is only because of his stubborn insistence that the truth is at last uncovered. If the fatalist's argument implies that this event is fated, then there seems something wrong with the argument.

But what can that be? The fatalist's premises are unclear. If a person fails to achieve a certain goal despite his or her best efforts, then, as the fatalist would suggest, the person's efforts are insufficient. But people do not always fail to achieve their goals. Oedipus, for example, succeeds in discovering Laius's true killer. If his efforts were inadequate some additional argument is needed to show this.

Moreover, the fatalist is correct to suggest that if some events occur independently of our efforts, then human effort is unnecessary. But it seems that some things would not occur if it were not for our attempts to bring them about. For example, had Oedipus followed Jocasta's advice and given up the search, he would have remained ignorant of his patricide and incest. If the fatalist suggests otherwise, some additional reason should be offered.

The above reasoning may help to explain why we tend to eschew fatalism. But why do we embrace the idea of freedom? At the end of the story Oedipus deliberately blinds himself, presumably as punishment for his unforgiveable sins. Why should he do this unless he believes that somehow *he* is responsible, personally and morally culpable, for the tragic events that have occurred? And if he *is* responsible, if he is truly blameworthy, then it seems he has acted of his own free will. Otherwise, he could not have prevented what actually took place. He would be no more guilty of a crime than a tree that falls and kills a woodcutter.

A fatalist, or someone like Oedipus who apparently believes in the power of prophecy, should not feel free. The idea that our actions are determined, or, if you will, "pre-determined," should make us feel more like a piece of wood. Yet we do not, anymore than does Oedipus. As human beings, we feel that we have the power to control things, to determine our own destiny, if you will. Like Oedipus, we feel that if things do not turn out as planned, then we are at fault.

But *feeling* free is one thing. *Being* free is something else. Oedipus may have been treated as a god, a being that is essentially free of physical influence. His followers seem to have felt that in defeating the Sphinx he performed a miracle. But Oedipus like the rest of us is a physical being, a creature of flesh and bone, subject to the same laws and physical forces that determine the behavior of every other physical object in the universe. If, as an infant, he had been thrown from the slopes of Cithaeron, he would have fallen at the rate of thirty-two feet second/per second, the same rate at which an acorn plummets from a tree. Will-power would have had nothing to do with it. Try as he might, he would have had as much success as an acorn in decreasing his rate of descent.

The determinist, unlike the fatalist, does not claim that things are essentially unavoidable. Rather, the basic idea is that every event is caused, what is called the *universal law of causality*. According to the determinist, anything that happens is the outcome of a set of antecedent conditions sufficient for bringing the event about. For example, if an acorn grows into an oak tree, then the soil, nutrients, water, sunshine were all of the proper proportion and combination to insure this result. Had the soil been more acidic, had there been less rainfall, more shade, the acorn would not have sprouted. There would not have been a tree. The event would not have occurred.

The difference between fatalism and determinism is significant. While fatalism is highly problematic, determinism is widely accepted and apparently well supported. When the AIDS epidemic first became apparent, medical investigators were at a loss to explain its cause. Nevertheless, *something* was causing it. That seemed plain enough. Otherwise, so the reasoning goes, a growing number of so many different individuals would not have been exhibiting the same symptoms.

The universal law of causality seems to be a basic assumption of common sense, as well as a fundamental principle of science. Unless every event is caused, there would be little point in investigating the source and etiology of the AIDS virus, the apparent depletion of ozone in the atmosphere, the reasons for the famine in Ethiopia, the effect of cocaine on brain chemistry, or any of the other major phenomena for which an explanation is sought. In the absence of causality, the fields of physics, chemistry, biology, sociology, economics, and psychology would be unthinkable. Unless we are prepared to abandon modern science, it seems that we are all determinists.

How then can we believe in freedom? It seems that if a person acts of his own free will, he could have acted otherwise. But if every event is the outcome of a set of conditions sufficient for bringing it about, then given the same conditions, the outcome would be the same. To accept both freedom and determinism, it seems, is to believe that things can be otherwise and cannot be otherwise—which is a contradiction. What shall we do? Should we accept science and give up the basic idea of human freedom and with it the related ideas of personal responsibility, morality, and systems of law? Or, with the moralist, should we maintain that some events are uncaused, and thus abandon a fundamental precept of science? (C. A. Campbell defends the libertarian view that freewill implies uncaused events.)

Some philosophers accept determinism and give up the idea of freedom. (Baron d'Holbach expresses this view, which is often called *hard determinism*.) Others accept freedom and abandon determinism. (William James advocates what has come to be called *indeterminism*.) The trick, however, is to accept both, if possible—an approach called *compatibilism*. How does it work? It has been suggested that there is no conflict between freewill and determinism, since acting freely is simply doing what we want to do. When we act in accordance with our own unimpeded desires, our conduct becomes the result of a set of antecedent psychological conditions sufficient for action. As long as no one else is forcing, coercing, or compelling us to act, we could do otherwise. Hence, it seems, our actions can be both determined and free. (Moritz Schlick proposes a similar view, what is sometimes called *soft determinism*.) For example, for defeating the Sphinx, Oedipus was offered the throne of Thebes and the hand of Jocasta in marriage. He could have refused both, or so it seems. No one forced, coerced, or compelled him to accept. Jocasta was widowed and apparently in need of someone with whom she could share the rule of Thebes. Oedipus had demonstrated his skills at outwitting the Sphinx and eliminating its scourge from the people. He was born and raised a prince, groomed to lead a country. Moreover, he was unmarried and ready to accept his husbandly duties. He accepted both offers freely. He did what he wanted to do.

However, is acting in accordance with our own psychological motivation enough? In contrast to the Cartesian tradition (see Part I for more on René Descartes's philosophy of mind, especially in regard to the idea that we are necessarily aware of what we have in mind, including our basic wants and desires), Sigmund Freud introduced in the late-nineteenth century the concept of the unconscious, the idea that we have feelings, thoughts, beliefs, wants, and desires of which we are unaware. If Freud was right, much of our own motivation is hidden from us in the way that the causes of other people's behavior are closed, so to speak, to direct inspection. We might infer the basic reasons for another person's actions as well as our own. And just as we can be mistaken about others, so we can be wrong about ourselves as well. In brief, we do not always know what we want.

Part of the problem is this. The compatibilist claims that we act freely provided that we do what we want to do. But what do we want to do? Oedipus, for example, thinks that he wants to marry Jocasta. But he does not. Jocasta is his mother, someone with whom he wants to avoid a conjugal relationship, which is why he left Corinth. In the absence of knowledge, he appears to be giving in to his passions. He could refuse to marry Jocasta, if his passions were different, just as a branch of a tree could avoid killing the woodcutter if a different wind were blowing. But just as there is no wind to blow the branch in a different direction, so Oedipus has no apparent motivation to refuse Jocasta's offer. Just as a branch does not act of its own free will, neither does Oedipus. (John Hospers criticizes compatibilism from the Freudian point of view.)

It might be suggested, however, that we can become aware of what might otherwise be our unconscious desires. Oedipus, for example, becomes aware that he did something he did not want to do. Had he found out sooner that Jocasta was his mother, he would have acted otherwise. Does this mean that the compatibilist's view is vindicated?

It seems that we are free, provided we act in accordance with what we know. But are cognitive states needed to explain human behavior? The behaviorist thinks not. (B. F. Skinner has pioneered the development of behaviorism and its implications for the freewill debate. A selection of his is reprinted below.) According to the behavioral school of thought, a person's behavior is essentially a set of responses to the environment that are either random, as in the case of an untrained fledgling chick, or apparently purposeful, as in the case of a laboratory rat that successfully negotiates its passage through a maze. Ivan Pavlov is credited with introducing in the nineteenth century the concept of what is called "classical conditioning," the technique made famous in his successful attempt to train a dog to salivate in the absence of food at the sound of a bell. More recent practitioners, such as J. B. Watson and B. F. Skinner, have gone beyond Pavlov to demonstrate, using a method called "instrumental conditioning," that a laboratory animal can be trained to behave in any one of a variety of ways by judiciously reinforcing certain physical movements and discouraging others.

Instrumental conditioning is an important innovation, with both practical and theoretical application to human behavior. First, it provides a basic line of therapy—to help a person with a tendency to experience claustrophobia to ride in an elevator, for example. Second, it suggests a general explanation of all human conduct. If the behaviorist is correct, the psychoanalyst's motivations, hidden or otherwise, are unnecessary in the explanation of human conduct. Conditioning is enough. For example, there seems little need to ask what, if anything, Oedipus has in mind as he rages against the blind Tiresias who suggests that Oedipus is the ultimate source of Thebes's woes. Oedipus is a king, conditioned to respond harshly, especially when accused of murder. Like a laboratory animal caught in a maze, Oedipus responds accordingly.

But an animal, experimental or otherwise, is not an automaton. Even Pavlov's dog could not have been conditioned to salivate at the sound of a bell had it not initially been aware of food. So, too, Oedipus would not have responded so harshly had he not thought that he was falsely accused. Perhaps, as the behaviorist suggests, much of our behavior is conditioned. But unless it can be shown that our conduct is more pigeon-like than it appears to be, behaviorism, by itself, does not undermine our sense of freedom.

We seem to be left with what might be called *cognitivism*, the idea that we can be motivated by our beliefs. Oedipus, it seems, could have resisted killing Laius had he believed that the man was his father, just as he could have refused marrying Jocasta had he known she was his mother. But what exactly is a belief and how can having a certain belief effect a change in a person's behavior? These are difficult questions. Suffice it to say that the main approach today to answering these questions is *functionalism*, the view that having a belief or having a thought is to have one's brain functioning in a certain way.

But how exactly *does* the brain function? Unfortunately, this is not clear, although different models have been proposed. At one extreme, we might think of the brain as a kind of self-regulating mechanical device like a thermostat. But this would not be enough, since thermostats do not think. If a thermostat, on occasion, seems to have a mind of its own, for example, making the temperature in a room too hot or too cold, it is more likely that the device has malfunctioned.

Another, more promising, suggestion is that the brain is like a computer, a complex system that can perform intelligent tasks. However, given the current state of our technology, computers must be programmed to perform their many functions, while human beings, or the brain, need not be programmed. For example, no one apparently programmed Oedipus to mutilate himself when he discovered that Jocasta was his mother. Nor did he behave in accordance with a specific set of instructions that might have been wired into his brain through evolution. The efficacy of the incest taboo among human beings is difficult to explain on the basis of evolution alone. The offspring of animals that engage in close family interbreeding tend to die off, which may help to explain why animals in the wild avoid such behavior. But human beings, such as Oedipus, find the practice immoral, not simply in conflict with the survival of the species. Otherwise, Oedipus would have little to feel guilty about since his daughters, Isemene and Antigone, are not genetically deficient.

How then does having a certain belief affect our behavior? At present, this question poses an unsolved mystery. But need we unlock the inner workings of the human brain in order to illuminate the problem of freewill? Perhaps Oedipus himself can help solve the riddle.

Oedipus was determined to get to the bottom of the puzzle surrounding the events of his life, just as he was determined to thwart the prophecy. In so doing his conduct seems to have been controlled by metaphysical, social and psychological forces over which he had little control. But he acted out of a moral sense that patricide and incest are wrong as well as the conviction that as King of Thebes he was obliged to help solve its woes. If he failed to thwart the prophecy or ultimately brought doom upon himself, he did so, in part, of his own freewill. In brief, in the absence of some additional theory of human behavior, Oedipus's conduct seems both determined and free.

Oedipus is not alone. Although many of us, for example, have been conditioned by our upbringing to pay our debts, nevertheless, we choose to return a neighbor's favor because we know that doing so is right. We, like Oedipus, are both determined and free. If the common explanations of our conduct are unacceptable, if Oedipus did not act out of a sense of duty, or if he was not determined in his conduct, the incompatibilist has yet to show us why.

ARISTOTLE
The Sea Battle

. . . An affirmation is a positive assertion of something about something, a denial a negative assertion. . . .

We will call such a pair of propositions a pair of contradictories. Those positive and negative propositions are said to be contradictory which have the same subject and predicate. The identity of subject and of predicate must not be "equivocal." . . .

In the case of that which is or which has taken place, propositions, whether positive or negative, must be true or false. . . . When the subject . . . is individual, and that which is predicated of it relates to the future, the case is altered. For if all propositions whether positive or negative are either true or false, then any given predicate must either belong to the subject or not, so that if one man affirms that an event of a given character will take place and another denies it, it is plain that the statement of the one will correspond with reality and that of the other will not. For the predicate cannot both belong and not belong to the subject at one and the same time with regard to the future.

Thus if it is true to say that a thing is white, it must necessarily be white; if the reverse proposition is true, it will of necessity not be white. Again, if it is white, the proposition stating that it is white was true; if it is not white, the proposition to the opposite effect was true. And if it is not white, the man who states that it is is making a false statement; and if the man who states that it is white is making a false statement, it follows that it is not white. It may therefore be argued that it is necessary that affirmations or denials must be either true or false.

Reprinted from *The Oxford Translation of Aristotle*, edited by W. D. Ross, Vol. 1 (1928), by permission of Oxford University Press. **Aristotle** (384–322 B.C.) analyzed and discussed with precision every major branch of learning in antiquity. It is remarkable that although his work was lost to Western scholars after the sixth century A.D., his writings survived in the East and were reintroduced in the twelfth and thirteenth centuries to inspire new respect for scientific thought.

Now if this be so, nothing is or takes place fortuitously, either in the present or in the future, and there are no real alternatives; everything takes place of necessity and is fixed. For either he that affirms that it will take place or he that denies this is in correspondence with fact, whereas if things did not take place of necessity, an event might just as easily not happen as happen; for the meaning of the word "fortuitous" with regard to present or future events is that reality is so constituted that it may issue in either of two opposite directions.

Again, if a thing is white now, it was true before to say that it would be white, so that of anything that has taken place it was always true to say "it is" or "it will be." But if it was always true to say that a thing is or will be, it is not possible that it should not or not be about to be, and when a thing cannot not come to be, it is impossible that it should not come to be, and when it is impossible that it should not come to be, it must come to be. All, then, that is about to be must of necessity take place. It results from this that nothing is uncertain or fortuitous, for if it were fortuitous it would not be necessary.

Again, to say that neither the affirmation nor the denial is true, maintaining, let us say, that an event neither will take place nor will not take place, is to take up a position impossible to defend. In the first place, though facts should prove the one proposition false, the opposite would still be untrue. Secondly, if it was true to say that a thing was both white and large, both these qualities must necessarily belong to it; and if they will belong to it the next day, they must necessarily belong to it the next day. But if an event is neither to take place nor not to take place the next day, the element of chance will be eliminated. For example, it would be necessary that a sea-fight should neither take place nor fail to take place on the next day.

These awkward results and others of the same kind follow, if it is an irrefragable law that of every pair of contradictory propositions, whether they have regard to universals and are stated as universally applicable, or whether they have regard to individuals, one must be true and the other false, and that there are no real alternatives, but that all that is or takes place is the outcome of necessity. There would be no need to deliberate or to take trouble, on the supposition that if we should adopt a certain course, a certain result would follow, while, if we did not, the result would not follow. For a man may predict an event ten thousand years beforehand, and another may predict the reverse; that which was truly predicted at the moment in the past will of necessity take place in the fullness of time.

Further, it makes no difference whether people have or have not actually made the contradictory statements. For it is manifest that the circumstances are not influenced by the fact of an affirmation or denial on the part of anyone. For events will not take place or fail to take place because it was stated that they would or would not take place, nor is this any more the case if the prediction dates back ten thousand years or any other space of time. Wherefore, if through all time the nature of things was so constituted that a prediction about an event was true, then through all time it was necessary that that prediction should find fulfillment; and with regard to all events, circumstances have always been such that their occurrence is a matter of necessity. For that of which someone has said truly that it will be, cannot fail to take place; and of that which takes place, it was always true to say that it would be.

Yet this view leads to an impossible conclusion; for we see that both deliberation and action are causative with regard to the future, and that, to speak more generally, in those things which are not continuously actual there is a potentiality in either direction. Such things may either be or not be; events also therefore may either take place or not take place. There are many obvious instances of this. It is possible that this coat may be cut in half, and yet it may not be cut in half, but wear out first. In the same way, it is possible that it should not be cut in half; unless this were so, it would not be possible that it should wear out first. So it is therefore with all other events which possess this kind of potentiality. It is therefore plain that it is not of necessity that everything is or takes place; but in some instances there are real alternatives, in which case the affirmation is no more true and no more false than the denial; while some exhibit a predisposition and general tendency in one direction or the other, and yet can issue in the opposite direction by exception.

Now that which is must needs be when it is, and that which is not must needs not be when it is not. Yet it cannot be said without qualification that all existence and non-existence is the outcome of necessity. For there is a difference between saying that that which is, when it is, must needs be, and simply saying that all that is must needs be, and similarly in the case of that which is not. In the case, also, of two contradictory propositions this holds good. Everything must either be or not be, whether in the present or in the future, but it is not always possible to distinguish and state determinately which of these alternatives must necessarily come about.

Let me illustrate. A sea-fight must either take place tomorrow or not, but it is not necessary that it should take place tomorrow, neither is it necessary that it should not take place, yet it is necessary that it either should or should not take place tomorrow. Since propositions correspond with facts, it is evident that when in future events there is a real alternative, and a potentiality in contradictory directions, the corresponding affirmation and denial have the same character.

This is the case with regard to that which is not always existent or not always non-existent. One of the two propositions in such instances must be true and the other false, but we cannot say determinately that this or that is false, but must leave the alternative undecided. One may indeed be more likely to be true than the other, but it cannot be either actually true or actually false. It is therefore plain that it is not necessary that of an affirmation and a denial one should be true and the other false. For in the case of that which exists potentially but not actually, the rule which applies to that which exists actually does not hold good.

GILBERT RYLE
It Was To Be

I want now to launch out without more ado into the full presentation and discussion of a concrete dilemma. It is a dilemma which, I expect, has occasionally bothered all of us, though, in its simplest form, not very often or for very long at a time. But it is intertwined with two other dilemmas, both of which probably have seriously worried nearly all of us. In its pure form it has not been seriously canvassed by any important Western philosopher, though the Stoics drew on it at certain points. It was, however, an ingredient in discussions of the theological

"It Was To Be" is reprinted from *Dilemmas* (Cambridge: University Press, 1964), by permission of Cambridge University Press. **Gilbert Ryle** (1900–1976), Waynflete Professor of Metaphysical Philosophy at Oxford University, brought not only fresh insight to every philosophical issue he addressed, but also clarity and often a touch of humor.

doctrine of Predestination and I suspect that it has exerted a surreptitious influence on some of the champions and opponents of Determinism.

At a certain moment yesterday evening I coughed and at a certain moment yesterday evening I went to bed. It was therefore true on Saturday that on Sunday I would cough at the one moment and go to bed at the other. Indeed, it was true a thousand years ago that at certain moments on a certain Sunday a thousand years later I should cough and go to bed. But if it was true beforehand—forever beforehand—that I was to cough and go to bed at those two moments on Sunday, 25 January 1953, then it was impossible for me not to do so. There would be a contradiction in the joint assertion that it was true that I would do something at a certain time and that I did not do it. This argument is perfectly general. Whatever anyone ever does, whatever happens anywhere to anything, could not *not* be done or happen, if it was true beforehand that it was going to be done or was going to happen. So everything, including everything that we do, has been definitively booked from any earlier date you like to choose. Whatever is, was to be. So nothing that does occur could have been helped and nothing that has not actually been done could possibly have been done.

This point, that for whatever takes place it was antecedently true that it was going to take place, is sometimes picturesquely expressed by saying that the Book of Destiny has been written up in full from the beginning of time. A thing's actually taking place is, so to speak, merely the turning up of a passage that has for all time been written. This picture has led some fatalists to suppose that God, if there is one, or, we ourselves, if suitably favoured, may have access to this book and read ahead. But this is a fanciful embellishment upon what in itself is a severe and seemingly rigorous argument. We may call it 'the fatalist argument'.

Now the conclusion of this argument from antecedent truth, namely that nothing can be helped, goes directly counter to the piece of common knowledge that some things are our own fault, that some threatening disasters can be foreseen and averted, and that there is plenty of room for precautions, planning and weighing alternatives. Even when we say nowadays of someone that he is born to be hanged or not born to be drowned, we say it as a humorous archaism. We really think that it depends very much on himself whether he is hanged or not, and that his chances of drowning are greater if he refuses to learn to swim. Yet even we are not altogether proof against the fatalist view of things. In a battle I may well come to the half-belief that either there exists somewhere behind the enemy lines a bullet with my name on it, or there does not, so that taking cover is either of no avail or else unnecessary. In card-games and at the roulette-table it is easy to subside into the frame of mind of fancying that our fortunes are in some way prearranged, well though we know that it is silly to fancy this.

But how can we deny that whatever happens was booked to happen from all eternity? What is wrong with the argument from antecedent truth to the inevitability of what the antecedent truths are antecedently true about? For it certainly is logically impossible for a prophecy to be true and yet the event prophesied not to come about.

We should notice first of all that the premiss of the argument does not require that anyone, even God, *knows* any of these antecedent truths, or to put it picturesquely, that the Book of Destiny has been written by anybody or could be perused by anybody. This is just what distinguishes the pure fatalist argument from the mixed theological argument for predestination. This latter argument does turn on the supposition that God at least has foreknowledge of what is to take place, and perhaps also preordains it. But the pure fatalist argument turns only on the principle that it was true that a given thing would happen, before it did happen, i.e. that what is, was to be; not that it was known by anyone that it was to be. Yet even when we try hard to bear this point in mind, it is very easy inadvertently to reinterpret this initial principle into the supposition that before the thing happened it was known by someone that it was booked to happen. For there is something intolerably vacuous in the idea of the eternal but unsupported pre-existence of truths in the future tense. When we say 'a thousand years ago it was true that I should now be saying what I am', it is so difficult to give any body to this 'it' of which we say that it was then true, that we unwittingly fill it out with the familiar body of an expectation which someone once entertained, or of a piece of foreknowledge which someone once possessed. Yet to do this is to convert a principle which was worrying because, in a way, totally truistic, into a supposition which is unworrying because quasi-historical, entirely without evidence and most likely just false.

Very often, though certainly not always, when we say 'it was true that . . .' or 'it is false that . . .' we are commenting on some actual pronouncement made or opinion held by some identifiable person. Sometimes we are commenting in a more general way on a thing which some people, unidentified and perhaps unidentifiable, have believed or now believe. We can comment on the belief in the Evil Eye without being able to name anyone who held it; we know that plenty of people did hold it. Thus we can say 'it was true' or 'it was false' in passing verdicts upon the pronouncements both of named and of nameless authors. But in the premiss of the fatalist argument, namely that it was true before something happened that it would happen, there is no implication of anyone, named or unnamed, having made that prediction.

There remains a third thing that might be meant by 'it was true a thousand years ago that a thousand years later these things would be being said in this place', namely that *if* anybody had made a prediction to this effect, though doubtless nobody did, he would have been right. It is not a case of an actual prediction having come true but of a conceivable prediction having come true. The event has not made an actual prophecy come true. It has made a might-have-been prophecy come true.

Or can we say even this? A target can be hit by an actual bullet, but can it be hit by a might-have-been bullet? Or should we rather say only that it could have been hit by a might-have-been bullet? The historical-sounding phrases 'came true', 'made true' and 'was fulfilled' apply well enough to predictions actually made, but there is a detectable twist, which may be an illegitimate twist, in saying that a might-have-been prediction did come true or was made true by the event. If an unbacked horse wins a race, we can say that it would have won money for its backers, if only there had been any. But we cannot say that it did win money for its backers, if only there had been any. There is no answer to the question 'How much money did it win for them?' Correspondingly, we cannot with a clear conscience say of an event that it has fulfilled the predictions of it which could have been made, but only that it would have fulfilled any predictions of it which might have been made. There is no answer to the question 'Within what limits of precision were these might-have-been predictions correct about the time and the loudness of my cough?'

Let us consider the notions of truth and falsity. In characterizing somebody's statement, for example a statement in the future tense, as true or as false, we usually though not always, mean to convey rather more than that what was forecast did or did not take place. There is something of a slur in 'false' and something honorific in 'true', some suggestion of the insecurity or sincerity of its author, or some suggestion of his rashness or cautiousness as an investigator. This is brought out by our reluctance to characterize either as true or as false pure and avowed guesses. If you make a guess at the winner of the race, it will turn out right or wrong, correct or incorrect, but hardly true or false. These epithets are inappropriate to avowed guesses, since the one epithet pays an extra tribute, the other conveys an extra adverse criticism of the maker of the guess, neither of which can he merit. In guessing there is no place for sincerity or insincerity, or for caution or rashness in investigation. To make a guess is not to give an assurance and it is not to declare the result of an investigation. Guessers are neither reliable nor unreliable.

Doubtless we sometimes use 'true' without intending any connotation of trustworthiness and, much less often, 'false' without any connotation of trust misplaced. But, for safety's sake, let us reword the fatalist argument in terms of these thinner words, 'correct' and 'incorrect'. It would now run as follows. For any event that takes place, an antecedent guess, if anyone had made one, that it was going to take place, would have been correct, and an antecedent guess to the contrary, if anyone had made it, would have been incorrect. This formulation already sounds less alarming than the original formulation. The word 'guess' cuts out the covert threat of foreknowledge, or of there being budgets of antecedent forecasts, all meriting confidence before the event. What, now, of the notion of guesses in the future tense being correct or incorrect?

Antecedently to the running of most horse-races, some people guess that one horse will win, some that another will. Very often every horse has its backers. If, then, the race is run and won, then some of the backers will have guessed correctly and the rest will have guessed incorrectly. To say that someone's guess that Eclipse would win was correct is to say no more than that he guessed that Eclipse would win and Eclipse did win. But can we say in retrospect that his guess, which he made before the race, was already correct before the race? He made the correct guess two days ago, but was his guess correct during those two days? It certainly was not incorrect during those two days, but it does not follow, though it might seem to follow, that it was correct during those two days. Perhaps we feel unsure which we ought to say, whether that his guess was correct during those two days, though no one could know it to be so, or only that, as it turned out, it was during those two days going to prove correct, i.e. that the victory which did, in the event, make it correct had not yet happened. A prophecy is not fulfilled until the event forecast has happened. Just here is where 'correct' resembles 'fulfilled' and differs importantly from 'true'. The honorific connotations of 'true' can certainly attach to a person's forecasts from the moment at which they are made, so that if these forecasts turn out incorrect, while we withdraw the word 'true', we do not necessarily withdraw the testimonials which it carried. The establishment of incorrectness certainly cancels 'true' but not, as a rule, so fiercely as to incline us to say 'false'.

The words 'true' and 'false' and the words 'correct' and 'incorrect' are adjectives, and this grammatical fact tempts us to suppose that trueness and falseness, correctness and incorrectness, and even, perhaps, fulfilledness and unfulfilledness must be qualities or properties resident in the propositions which they characterize. As sugar is sweet and white from the moment it comes into existence to the moment when it goes out of existence, so we are tempted to infer, by parity of reasoning, that the trueness or correctness of predictions and guesses must be features or properties which belong all the time to their possessors, whether we can detect their presence in them or not. But if we consider that 'deceased', 'lamented' and 'extinct' are also adjectives, and yet certainly do not apply to people or mastodons while they exist, but only after they have ceased to exist, we may feel more cordial towards the idea that 'correct' is in a partly similar way a merely obituary and valedictory epithet, as 'fulfilled' more patently is. It is more like a verdict than a description. So when I tell you that if anyone had guessed that Eclipse would win today's race his guess would have turned out correct, I give you no more information about the past than is given by the evening newspaper which tells you that Eclipse won the race.

I want now to turn to the fatalist conclusion, namely that since whatever is was to be, therefore nothing can be helped. The argument seems to compel us to say that since the antecedent truth requires the event of which it is the true forecast, therefore this event is in some disastrous way fettered to or driven by or bequeathed by that antecedent truth—as if my coughing last night was made or obliged to occur by the antecedent truth that it was going to occur, perhaps in something like the way in which gunfire makes the windows rattle a moment or two after the discharge. What sort of necessity would this be?

To bring this out let us by way of contrast suppose that someone produced the strictly parallel argument, that for everything that happens, it is true for ever *afterwards* that it happened.

I coughed last night, so it is true today and will be true a thousand years hence that I coughed last night. But these posterior truths in the past tense, could not be true without my having coughed. Therefore my coughing was necessitated or obliged to have happened by the truth of these posterior chronicles of it. Clearly something which disturbed us in the original form of the argument is missing in this new form. We cheerfully grant that the occurrence of an event involves and is involved by the truth of subsequent records, actual or conceivable, to the effect that it occurred. For it does not even seem to render the occurrence a product or effect of these truths about it. On the contrary, in this case we are quite clear that it is the occurrence which makes the posterior truths about it true, not the posterior truths which make the occurrence occur. These posterior truths are shadows cast by the events, not the events, shadows cast by these truths about them, since these belong to the posterity, not to the ancestry of the events.

Why does the fact that a posterior truth about an occurrence requires that occurrence not worry us in the way in which the fact that an anterior truth about an occurrence requires that occurrence does worry us? Why does the slogan 'Whatever is, always was to be' seem to imply that nothing can be helped, where the obverse slogan 'Whatever is, will always have been' does not seem to imply this? We are not exercised by the notorious fact that when the horse has already escaped it is too late to shut the stable door. We are sometimes exercised by the idea that as the horse is either going to escape or not going to escape, to shut the stable door beforehand is either unavailing or unnecessary. A large part of the reason is that in thinking of a predecessor making its successor necessary we unwittingly assimilate the necessitation to causal necessitation. Gunfire makes windows rattle a few seconds later, but rattling

windows do not make gunfire happen a few seconds earlier, even though they may be perfect evidence that gunfire did happen a few seconds earlier. We slide, that is, into thinking of the anterior truths as *causes* of the happenings about which they were true, where the mere matter of their relative dates saves us from thinking of happenings as the effects of those truths about them which are posterior to them. Events cannot be the effects of their successors, any more than we can be the offspring of our posterity.

So let us look more suspiciously at the notions of *necessitating, making, obliging, requiring* and *involving* on which the argument turns. How is the notion of *requiring* or *involving* that we have been working with related to the notion of *causing?*

It is quite true that a backer cannot guess correctly that Eclipse will win without Eclipse winning and still it is quite false that his guessing made or caused Eclipse to win. To say that his guess that Eclipse would win was correct does logically involve or require that Eclipse won. To assert the one and deny the other would be to contradict oneself. To say that the backer guessed correctly is just to say that the horse which he guessed would win, did win. The one assertion cannot be true without the other assertion being true. But in this way in which one truth may require or involve another truth, an event cannot be one of the implications of a truth. Events can be effects, but they cannot be implications. Truths can be consequences of other truths, but they cannot be causes of effects or effects of causes.

In much the same way, the truth that someone revoked involves the truth that he had in his hand at least one card of the suit led. But he was not forced or coerced into having a card of that suit in his hand by the fact that he revoked. He could not both have revoked and not had a card of that suit in his hand, but this 'could not' does not connote any kind of duress. A proposition can imply another proposition, but it cannot thrust a card into a player's hand. The questions, what makes things happen, what prevents them from happening, and whether we can help them or not, are entirely unaffected by the logical truism that a statement to the effect that something happens, is correct if and only if it happens. Lots of things could have prevented Eclipse from winning the race; lots of other things could have made his lead a longer one. But one thing had no influence on the race at all, namely the fact that if anyone guessed that he would win, he guessed correctly.

We are now in a position to separate out one unquestionable and very dull true proposition from another exciting but entirely false proposition, both of which seem to be conveyed by the slogan 'What is, always was to be'. It is an unquestionable and very dull truth that for anything that happens, if anyone had at any previous time made the guess that it would happen, his guess would have turned out correct. The twin facts that the event could not take place without such a guess turning out correct and that such a guess could not turn out correct without the event taking place tell us nothing whatsoever about how the event was caused, whether it could have been prevented, or even whether it could have been predicted with certainty or probability from what had happened before. The menacing statement that what is was to be, construed in one way, tells us only the trite truth that if it is true to say (a) that something happened, then it is also true to say (b) that that original statement (a) is true, no matter when this latter comment (b) on the former statement (a) may be made.

The exciting but false proposition that the slogan seems to force upon us is that whatever happens is inevitable or doomed, and what makes it sound even worse, *logically* inevitable or *logically* doomed—somewhat as it is logically inevitable that the immediate successor of any even number is an odd number. So what does 'inevitable' mean? An avalanche may be, for all practical purposes, unavoidable. A mountaineer in the direct path of an avalanche can himself do nothing to stop the avalanche or get himself out of its way, though a providential earthquake might conceivably divert the avalanche or a helicopter might conceivably lift him out of danger. His position is much worse,

but only much worse, than that of a cyclist half a mile ahead of a lumbering steam-roller. It is extremely unlikely that the steam-roller will catch up with him at all, and even if it does so it is extremely likely that its driver will halt or that the cyclist himself will move off in good time. But these differences between the plights of the mountaineer and the cyclist are differences of degree only. The avalanche is practically unavoidable, but it is not logically inevitable. Only conclusions can be logically inevitable, given the premises, and an avalanche is not a conclusion. The fatalist doctrine, by contrast, is that everything is absolutely and logically inevitable in a way in which the avalanche is not absolutely or logically inevitable; that we are all absolutely and logically powerless where even the hapless mountaineer is only in a desperate plight and the cyclist is in no real danger at all; that everything is fettered by the Law of Contradiction to taking the course it does take, as odd numbers are bound to succeed even numbers. What sort of fetters are these purely logical fetters?

Certainly there are infinitely many cases of one truth making necessary the truth of another proposition. The truth that today is Monday makes necessary the truth of the proposition that tomorrow is Tuesday. It cannot be Monday today without tomorrow being Tuesday. A person who said 'It is Monday today but not Tuesday tomorrow' would be taking away with his left hand what he was giving with his right hand. But in the way in which some truths carry other truths with them or make them necessary, events themselves cannot be made necessary by truths. Things and events may be the topics of premises and conclusions, but they cannot themselves be premises or conclusions. You may preface a statement by the word 'therefore', but you cannot pin either a 'therefore' or a 'perhaps not' on to a person or an avalanche. It is a partial parallel to say that while a sentence may contain or may be without a split infinitive, a road accident cannot either contain or lack a split infinitive, even though it is what a lot of sentences, with or without split infinitives in them, are about. It is true that an avalanche may be practically inescapable and the conclusion of an argument may be logically inescapable, but the avalanche has not got—nor does it lack—the inescapability of the conclusion of an argument. The fatalist theory tries to endue happenings with the inescapability of the conclusion of valid arguments. Our familiarity with the practical inescapability of some things, like some avalanches, helps us to yield to the view that really everything that happens is inescapable, only not now in the way in which some avalanches are inescapable and others not, but in the way in which logical consequences are inescapable, given their premises. The fatalist has tried to characterize happenings by predicates which are proper only to conclusions of arguments. He tried to flag my cough with a Q.E.D.

Before standing back to draw some morals from this dilemma between *whatever is was to be* and *some things which have happened could have been averted,* I want briefly to discuss one further point which may be of only domestic interest to professional philosophers. If a city-engineer has constructed a roundabout where there had been dangerous cross-roads, he may properly claim to have reduced the number of accidents. He may say that lots of accidents that would otherwise have occurred have been prevented by his piece of road improvement. But suppose we now ask him to give us a list of the particular accidents which he has averted. He can do nothing but laugh at us. If an accident has not happened, there is no 'it' to put down on a list of 'accidents prevented'. He can say that accidents of such and such kinds which used to be frequent are now rare. But he cannot say 'Yesterday's collision at midday between the fire-engine and that milk-float at this corner was, fortunately, averted'. There was no such collision, so he cannot say *'This* collision was averted'. To generalize this, we can never point to or name a particular happening and say of it 'This happening was averted', and this logical truism seems to commit us to saying 'No happenings can be averted' and consequently 'it's no good trying to ensure or prevent anything happening'. So when we try to say that some

things that happen could have been prevented; that some drownings, for example, would not have occurred had their victims learned to swim, we seem to be in a queer logical fix. We can say that a particular person would not have drowned had he been able to swim. But we cannot quite say that his lamented drowning would have been averted by swimming lessons. For had he taken those lessons, he would not have drowned, and then we would not have had for a topic of discussion just that lamented drowning of which we want to say that *it* would have been prevented. We are left bereft of any 'it' at all. Averted fatalities are not fatalities. In short, we cannot, in logic, say of any designated fatality that it was averted—and this sounds like saying that it is logically impossible to avert any fatalities.

The situation is parallel to the following. If my parents had never met, I should not have been born, and had Napoleon known some things that he did not know the Battle of Waterloo would not have been fought. So we want to say that certain contingencies would have prevented me from being born and the Battle of Waterloo from being fought. But then there would have been no Gilbert Ryle and no Battle of Waterloo for historians to describe as not having been born and as not having been fought. What does not exist or happen cannot be named, individually indicated or put on a list, and cannot therefore be characterized as having been prevented from existing or happening. So though we are right to say that some sorts of accidents can be prevented, we cannot put this by saying that this designated accident might have been prevented from occurring—not because it was of an unpreventable sort, but because neither 'preventable' nor 'unpreventable' can be epithets of designated occurrences, any more than 'exists' or 'does not exist' can be predicated of designated things or persons. As 'unborn' cannot without absurdity be an epithet of a named person, so 'born' cannot without a queerly penetrating sort of redundancy be an epithet of him either. The question 'Were you born or not?' is, unless special insurance-policies are taken out, an unaskable question.

Who could be asked it? Nor could one ask whether the Battle of Waterloo was fought or unfought. That it was fought goes with our having an *it* to talk about at all. There could not be a list of unfought battles, and a list of fought battles would contain just what a list of battles would contain. The question 'Could the Battle of Waterloo have been unfought?', taken in one way, is an absurd question. Yet its absurdity is something quite different from the falsity that Napoleon's strategic decisions were forced upon him by the laws of logic.

I suspect that some of us have felt that the fatalist doctrine is unrefuted so long as no remedy has been found for the smell of logical trickiness that hangs about such arguments as 'Accidents can be prevented; therefore *this* accident could have been prevented' or 'I can bottle up my laughter; therefore I could have bottled up *that* hoot of laughter'. For it would not have been a hoot at all, and so not *that* hoot, had I bottled up my laughter. I could not, logically, have bottled *it* up. For *it* was an unbottled up hoot of laughter. The fact that it occurred is already contained in my allusion to 'that hoot of laughter'. So a sort of contradiction is produced when I try to say that the hoot of laughter need not have occurred. No such contradiction is produced when I say 'I did not have to hoot with laughter.' It is the demonstrative word '*that . . .*' which refused to consort with '. . . did not occur' or '. . . might not have occurred'.

This point seems to me to bring out an important difference between anterior truths and posterior truths, or between prophecies and chronicles. After 1815 there could be true and false statements mentioning the Battle of Waterloo in the past tense. After 1900 there could be true and false statements in the present and past tenses mentioning me. But before 1815 and 1900 there could not be true or false statements giving individual mention to the Battle of Waterloo or to me, and this not just because our names had not yet been given, nor yet just because no one happened to be well enough equipped to predict the future in very great detail, but for some more abstruse reason. The

prediction of an event can, in principle, be as specific as you please. It does not matter if in fact no forecaster could know or reasonably believe his prediction to be true. If gifted with a lively imagination, he could freely concoct a story in the future tense with all sorts of minutiae in it and this elaborate story might happen to come true. But one thing he could not do— logically and not merely epistemologically could not do. He could not get the future events themselves for the heroes or heroines of his story, since while it is still an askable question whether or not a battle will be fought at Waterloo in 1815, he cannot use with their normal force the phrase 'the Battle of Waterloo' or the pronoun 'it'. While it is still an askable question whether my parents are going to have a fourth son, he cannot use as a name the name 'Gilbert Ryle' or use as a pronoun designating their fourth son the pronoun 'he'. Roughly, statements in the future tense cannot convey singular, but only general propositions, where statements in the present and past tense can convey both. More strictly, a statement to the effect that something will exist or happen is, in *so far,* a general statement. When I predict the next eclipse of the moon, I have indeed got the moon to make statements about, but I have not got her next eclipse to make statements about. Perhaps this is why novelists never write in the future tense, but only in the past tense. They could not get even the semblances of heroes or heroines into prophetic fiction, since the future tense of their would-be-prophetic mock-narratives would leave it open for their heroes and heroines not to be born. But as my phrase 'I have not got it to make statements about' stirs up a nest of logical hornets, I shall bid farewell for the present to this matter.

I have chosen to start with this particular dilemma for moderately sustained discussion for two or three connected reasons. But I did not do so for the reason that the issue is or ever has been of paramount importance in the Western world. No philosopher of the first or second rank has defended fatalism or been at great pains to attack it. Neither religion nor science wants it. Right-wing and Left-wing doctrines borrow nothing from it. On the other hand we do all have our fatalist moments; we do all know from inside what it is like to regard the course of events as the continuous unrolling of a scroll written from the beginning of time and admitting of no additions or amendments. Yet though we know what it is like to entertain this idea, still we are unimpassioned about it. We are not secret zealots for it or secret zealots against it. We are, nearly all of the time, though also aware that the argument for them is hard to rebut, cheerfully sure that the fatalist conclusions are false. The result is that we can study the issue in the spirit of critical playgoers, not that of electors whose votes are being solicited. It is not a burning issue. This is one reason why I have started with it.

Next, so little has the issue been debated by Western thinkers that I have been free to formulate for myself not only what seem to me the false steps in the fatalist argument from antecedent truth, but even that argument itself. I have not had to recapitulate a traditional controversy between philosophical schools, since there has been next to no such controversy, as there have, notoriously, existed protracted controversies about Predestination and Determinism. You know, from inside your own skins, all that needs to be known about the issue. There are no cards of erudition up my sleeve.

Thirdly, the issue is in a way a very simple one, a very important one and an illuminatingly tricky one. It is simple in that so few pivot-concepts are involved—just, in the first instance, the untechnical concepts of *event, before* and *after, truth, necessity, cause, prevention, fault* and *responsibility*—and of course we all know our ways about in them—or do we? They are public highway concepts, not craftsmen's concepts; so none of us can get lost in them—or can we? It is important in that if the fatalist conclusion were true, then nearly the whole of our normal religious, moral, political, historical, scientific and pedagogic thinking would be on entirely the wrong lines. We cannot shape the world of tomorrow, since it has already been shaped once and for all. It is a tricky issue because there is not any regulation or argumen-

tative manoeuvre by which it can be settled. I have produced quite an apparatus of somewhat elaborate arguments, all of which need expansion and reinforcement. I expect that the logical ice is pretty thin under some of them. It would not trouble me if the ice broke, since the stamp of the foot which broke it would itself be a partially decisive move. But even this move would not be the playing of any regulation logical manoeuvre. Such regulation maneouvers exist only for dead philosophical issues. It was their death which promoted the decisive moves up to the status of regulation manoeuvres.

Now for some general morals which can be drawn from the existence of this dilemma and from attempts to resolve it. It arose out of two seemingly innocent and unquestionable propositions, propositions which are so well embedded in what I may vaguely call 'common knowledge' that we should hardly wish to give them the grand title of 'theories'. These two propositions were, first, that some statements in the future tense are or come true, and, second, that we often can and sometimes should secure that certain things do happen and that certain other things do not happen. Neither of these innocent-seeming propositions is as yet a philosopher's speculation, or even a scientist's hypothesis or a theologian's doctrine. They are just platitudes. We should, however, notice that it would not very often occur to anyone to state these platitudes. People say of this particular prediction that it was fulfilled and of that particular guess that it turned out correct. To say that some statements in the future tense are true is a generalization of these particular concrete comments. But it is a generalizaton which there is not usually any point in propounding. Similarly people say of particular offences that they ought not to have been committed and of particular catastrophes that they could or could not have been prevented. It is relatively rare to stand back and say in general terms that people sometimes do wrong and that mishaps are sometimes our own fault. None the less, there are occasions, long before philosophical or scientific speculations begin, on which people do deliver generalities of these sorts. It is part of the business of the teacher and the preacher, of the judge and the doctor, of Solon and Æsop, to say general things, with concrete examples of which everyone is entirely familiar. In one way the generality is not and cannot be news to anyone that every day has its yesterday and every day has its tomorrow; and yet, in another way, this can be a sort of news. There was the first occasion on which this generality was presented to us, and very surprising it was—despite the fact that on every day since infancy we had thought about its particular yesterday and its particular tomorrow. There is, anyhow at the start, an important sort of unfamiliarity about such generalizations of the totally familiar. We do not yet know how we should and how we should not operate with them, although we know quite well how to operate with the daily particularities of which they are the generalizations. We make no foot-faults on Monday morning with 'will be' and 'was'; but when required to deal in the general case with the notions of *the future* and *the past*, we are no longer sure of our feet.

The two platitudes from which the trouble arose are not in direct conflict with one another. It is real or seeming deductions from the one which quarrel with the other, or else with real or seeming deductions from it. They are not rivals such that before these deductions had been noticed anyone would want to say 'I accept the proposition that some statements in the future tense are fulfilled, so naturally I reject the proposition that some things need not and should not have happened'. It is because the former proposition seems indirectly to entail that what is was from all eternity going to be and because this, in its turn, seems to entail that nothing is anybody's fault, that some thinkers have felt forced to make a choice between the two platitudes. Aristotle, for example, rejected, with reservations, the platitude that statements in the future tense are true or false. Certain Stoics rejected the platitude that we are responsible for some things that happen. If we accept both platitudes, it is because we think that the fatalist deductions from 'it was true . . .' are fallacious or else that certain de-

ductions drawn from 'some things are our fault' are fallacious, or both.

But this raises a thorny general question. How is it that in their most concrete, ground-floor employment, concepts like *will be, was, correct, must, make, prevent* and *fault* behave, in the main, with exemplary docility, but become wild when employed in what are mere first-floor generalizations of their ground-floor employments? We are in very little danger of giving or taking the wrong logical change in our daily marketing uses of 'tomorrow' and 'yesterday'. We know perfectly well how to make our daily sales and purchases with them. Yet in the general case, when we try to negotiate with 'what is', 'what is to be', 'what was' and 'what was to be' we very easily get our accounts in a muddle. We are quite at home with 'therefore' and all at sea with 'necessary'. How is it that we get our accounts in a muddle when we try to do wholesale business with ideas with which in retail trade we operate quite efficiently every day of our lives? Later on I hope to give something of an answer to this question. For the moment I merely advertise it.

Meanwhile there is another feature of the issue to which we should attend. I have indicated that the quandary, though relatively simple, does depend upon a smallish number of concepts, namely, in the first instance, upon those of *event, before* and *after, truth, necessity, cause, prevention, fault* and *responsibility*. Now there is not just one of these concepts which is the logical trouble-maker. The trouble arises out of the interplay between all of them. The litigation between the two initial platitudes involves a whole web of conflicting interests. There is not just a single recalcitrant knot in the middle of one of the concepts involved. All the strings between all of them are implicated in the one tangle.

I mention this point because some people have got the idea from some of the professions though not, I think, the practices of philosophers, that doing philosophy consists or should consist of untying logical knots one at a time— as if, to burlesque the idea, it would have been quite proper and feasible for Hume on Monday to analyse the use of the term 'cause', and then on Tuesday, Wednesday and Thursday to move on to analyse *seriatim* the uses of the terms 'causeway', 'cautery' and 'caution', in alphabetical order.

I have no special objection to or any special liking for the fashion of describing as 'analysis' the sort or sorts of conceptual examination which constitute philosophizing. But the idea is totally false that this examination is a sort of garage inspection of one conceptual vehicle at a time. On the contrary, to put it dogmatically, it is always a traffic-inspector's examination of a conceptual traffic-block, involving at least two streams of vehicles hailing from the theories, or points of view or platitudes which are at cross-purposes with one another.

One other point arises in connexion with this last one. The child can be taught a lot of words, one after another; or, when consulting the dictionary to find out the meanings of some unfamiliar words in a difficult passage, he can look up these words separately in alphabetical or any other order. This fact, among others, has encouraged the notion that the ideas or concepts conveyed by these words are something like separately movable and examinable chessmen, coins, counters, snapshots—or words. But we should not think of what a word conveys as if it were, like the word, a sort of counter, though unlike the word, an invisible counter. Consider a wicket-keeper. He is an individual, who can be fetched out of the team and separately interviewed, photographed or massaged. But his role in the game, namely the wicket-keeping that he does, so interlocks with what the other cricketers do, that if they stopped playing, he could not go on keeping wicket. He alone performs his particular role, yet he cannot perform it alone. For him to keep wicket, there must be a wicket, a pitch, a ball, a bat, a bowler and a batsman. Even that is not enough. There must be a game in progress and not, for example, a funeral, a fight or a dance; and the game must be a game of cricket and not, for example, a game of 'Touch Last'. The same man who keeps wicket on Saturday may play tennis on Sunday. But he cannot keep wicket in a game of

tennis. He can switch from one set of sporting functions to another, but one of his functions cannot be switched to the other game. In much the same way, concepts are not things, as words are, but rather the functionings of words, as keeping wicket is the functioning of the wicket-keeper. Very much as the functioning of the wicket-keeper interlocks with the functioning of the bowler, the batsman and the rest, so the functioning of a word interlocks with the functioning of the other members of the team for which that word is playing. One word may have two or more functions; but one of its functions cannot change places with another.

Let me illustrate. A game like Bridge or Poker has a fairly elaborate and well-organized technical vocabulary, as in different degrees have nearly all games, crafts, professions, hobbies and sciences. Naturally the technical terms peculiar to Bridge have to be learned. How do we learn them? One thing is clear. We do not and could not master the use of one of them without yet having begun to learn the use of any of the others. It would be absurd to try to teach a boy how to use the concept of *crossruff*, without yet having introduced him to the notions of *following suit, trump* and *partner*. But if he has been introduced to the way these terms function together in Bridge talk, then he has begun to learn some of the elements of Bridge. Or consider the technical dictions of English lawyers. Could a student claim to understand one or seven of its specialist terms, though knowing nothing of the law? or claim to know the law while not understanding at least a considerable fraction of its terminological apparatus? The terminological apparatus of a science is in the same way a team and not a mere mob of terms. The part played by one of them belongs, with the parts played by the others, to the particular game or work of the whole apparatus. A person who had merely memorized the dictionary-paraphrases of a thousand technical terms of physics or economics would not yet have begun to be a physicist or an economist. He would not yet have learned how to operate with those terms. So he would not yet understand them. If he cannot yet think of any of the thoughts of economic theory, he has not yet got any of its special concepts.

What is true of the more or less highly technical terms of games, the law, the sciences, the trades and professions is true also, with important modifications, of the terms of everyday discourse. These stand to the terms of the specialists very much as civilians stand to the officers, non-commissioned officers and private soldiers of different units in the Army. The rights, duties and privileges of soldiers are carefully prescribed; their uniforms, badges, stripes and buttons show their ranks, trades and units; drill, discipline and daily orders mould their movements. But civilians too have their codes, their habits, and their etiquettes; their work, pay and taxes tend to be regular; their social circles, their apparel and their amusements, though not regimented, are pretty stable. We know, too, how in this twentieth century of ours the distinctions between civilians and soldiers are notoriously blurred. Similarly the line between untechnical and technical dictions is a blurred line, and one frequently crossed in both directions; and though untechnical terms have not got their functions officially imposed upon them, they have their functions, privileges and immunities none the less. They resemble civilians rather than soldiers, but most of them also resemble rate-payers rather than gipsies.

The functions of technical terms, that is, the concepts conveyed by them, are more or less severely regimented. The kinds of interplay of function for which they are built are relatively definite and circumscribed. Yet untechnical terms, too, though they belong to no single organized unit, still have their individual places in indefinitely many overlapping and intermingling *milieus*.

It can be appreciated, consequently, that the functions of terms become narrower and better prescribed as they become more official. Their roles in discourse can be more strictly formulated as their commitments are reduced in number and in scope. Hence, the more exactly their duties come to being fixed by charters and commissions, the further they move from being philosophically interesting. The official con-

cepts of Bridge generate few if any logical puzzles. Disputes could not be settled or rubbers won if they were generated. Logical puzzles arise especially over concepts that are uncommissioned, namely the civilian concepts which, instead of having been conscripted and trained for just one definite and appointed niche in one organized unit, have grown up into their special but unappointed places in a thousand unchartered groups and informal associations. This is why an issue like the fatalist issue, though starting with a quite slender stem, ramifies out so swiftly into seemingly remote sectors of human interests. The question whether statements in the future tense can be true swiftly opened out into, among a thousand others, the question whether anything is gained by learning to swim.

Certain thinkers, properly impressed by the excellent logical discipline of the technical concepts of long-established and well consolidated sciences like pure mathematics and mechanics, have urged that intellectual progress is impeded by the survival of the unofficial concepts of unspecialized thought; as if there were something damagingly amateurish or infantile in the businesses and avocations of unconscripted civilians. Members of the Portland Club, the M.C.C., or the Law Faculty of a University might, with even greater justice, contrast their own scrupulously pruned and even carpentered terms of art with the undesigned dictions of everyday discourse. It is, of course, quite true that scientific, legal or financial thinking could not be conducted only in colloquial idioms. But it is quite false that people could, even in Utopia, be given their first lessons in talking and thinking in the terms of this or that technical apparatus. Fingers and feet are, for many special purposes, grossly inefficient instruments. But to replace the infant's fingers and feet by pliers and pedals would not be a good plan—especially as the employment of pliers and pedals themselves depends upon the employment of fingers and feet. Nor does the specialist when he comes to use the designed terms of his art cease to depend upon the concepts which he began to master in the nursery, any more than the driver, whose skill and interests are concentrated on the mechanically complex and delicate works of his car, cease to avail himself of the mechanically crude properties of the public highway. He could not use his car without using the roads, though he could, as the pedestrian that he often is, use these same roads without using his car.

RICHARD TAYLOR
Fate

We all, at certain moments of pain, threat, or bereavement, are apt to entertain the idea of fatalism, the thought that what is happening at a particular moment is unavoidable, that we are powerless to prevent it. Sometimes we find ourselves in circumstances not of our own making, in which our very being and destinies are so thoroughly anchored that the thought of fatalism can be quite overwhelming, and sometimes consoling. One feels that whatever then happens, however good or ill, will be what those circumstances yield, and we are helpless. Soldiers, it is said, are sometimes possessed by such thoughts. Perhaps all men would feel more inclined to them if they paused once in a while to think of how little they ever had to do with bringing themselves to wherever they have arrived in life, how much of their fortunes and destinies were decided for them by sheer circumstance, and how the entire course of their lives is often set, once and for all, by the most trivial incidents, which they did not produce and could not even have foreseen. If we are free to work out our destinies at all, which is doubtful, we have a freedom that is at best exercised within exceedingly narrow paths. All the important things—when we are born, of what parents, into what culture, whether we are loved or rejected, whether we are male or female, our temperament, our intelligence or stupidity, indeed everything that makes for the bulk of our happiness and misery—all these are decided for us by the most casual and indifferent circumstances, by sheer coincidences, chance encounters, and seemingly insignificant fortuities. One can see this in retrospect if he searches, but few search. The fate that has given us our very being has given us also our pride and conceit, and has thereby formed us so that, being human, we congratulate ourselves on our blessings, which we call our achievements, blame the world for our blunders, which we call our misfortunes, and scarcely give a thought to that impersonal fate which arbitrarily dispenses both. . . .

A fatalist . . . is someone who believes that whatever happens is and always was unavoidable. He thinks it is not up to him what will happen a thousand years hence, next year, tomorrow, or the very next moment. Of course he does not pretend always to *know* what is going to happen. Hence, he might try sometimes to read signs and portents, as meteorologists and astrologers do, or to contemplate the effects upon him of the various things that might, for

Richard Taylor, *Metaphysics*, 3/E, © 1983, pgs. 51–62. Reprinted by permission of Prentice-Hall, Inc., Englewood Cliffs, New Jersey. **Richard Taylor,** a contemporary American philosopher, writes clearly and effectively on metaphysical issues, defending, in this piece, a doctrine not otherwise widely examined.

all he knows, be fated to occur. But he does not suppose that whatever happens could ever have really been avoidable.

A fatalist thus thinks of the future in the way we all think of the past, for all men are fatalists as they look *back* on things. To a large extent we know what has happened—some of it we can even remember—whereas the future is still obscure to us, and we are therefore tempted to invest it, in our imagination, with all sorts of "possibilities." The fatalist resists this temptation, knowing that mere ignorance can hardly give rise to any genuine possibility in things. He thinks of both past and future "under the aspect of eternity," the way God is supposed to view them. We all think of the past this way, as something settled and fixed, to be taken for what it is. We are never in the least tempted to try to modify it. It is not in the least up to us what happened last year, yesterday, or even a moment ago, any more than are the motions of the heavens or the political developments in Tibet. If we are not fatalists, then we might think that past things once were up to us, to bring about or prevent, as long as they were still future—but this expresses our attitude toward the future, not the past.

Such is surely our conception of the whole past, whether near or remote. But the consistent fatalist thinks of the future in the same way. We say of past things that they are no longer within our power. The fatalist says they never were.

A fatalistic way of thinking most often arises from theological ideas, or from what are generally thought to be certain presuppositions of science and logic. Thus, if God is really all-knowing and all-powerful, it is not hard to suppose that He has arranged for everything to happen just as it is going to happen, that He already knows every detail of the whole future course of the world and there is nothing left for you and me to do except watch things unfold, in the here and hereafter. But without bringing God into the picture, it is not hard to suppose, as we have seen, that everything that happens is wholly determined by what went before it, and hence that whatever happens at any future time is the only thing that can then happen, given

what precedes it. Or even disregarding that, it seems natural to suppose that there is a body of truth concerning what the future holds, just as there is such truth concerning what is contained in the past, whether or not it is known to any man or even to God, and hence, that everything asserted in that body of truth will assuredly happen, in the fullness of time, precisely as it is described therein.

No one needs to be convinced that fatalism is the only proper way to view the past. That it is also the proper way to view the future is less obvious, due in part, perhaps, to our vastly greater ignorance of what the future holds. The consequences of holding such fatalism are obviously momentous. To say nothing of the consolation of fatalism, which enables a person to view all things as they arise with the same undisturbed mind with which he contemplates even the most revolting of history's horrors, the fatalist teaching also relieves one of all tendency toward both blame and approbation of others and of both guilt and conceit in himself. It promises that a perfect understanding is possible, and removes the temptation to view things in terms of human wickedness and moral responsibility. This thought alone, once firmly grasped, yields a sublime acceptance of all that life and nature offer, whether to oneself or one's fellows; and although it thereby reduces one's pride, it simultaneously enhances the feelings, opens the heart, and expands the understanding. . . .

Let us suppose that God has revealed a particular set of facts to a chosen scribe who, believing (correctly) that they came from God, wrote them all down. The facts in question then turned out to be all the more or less significant episodes in the life of some perfectly ordinary man named Osmo. Osmo was entirely unknown to the scribe, and in fact to just about everyone, but there was no doubt concerning whom all these facts were about, for the very first thing received by the scribe from God, was: "He of whom I speak is called Osmo." When the revelations reached a fairly voluminous bulk and appeared to be completed, the scribe arranged them in chronological order and assembled them into a book. He at first gave it the title *The Life of Osmo, as Given by God,* but thinking that people would take this to be some sort of joke, he dropped the reference to God.

The book was published, but attracted no attention whatsoever, because it appeared to be nothing more than a record of the dull life of a very plain man named Osmo. The scribe wondered, in fact, why God had chosen to convey such a mass of seemingly pointless trivia.

The book eventually found its way into various libraries, where it gathered dust until one day a high school teacher in Indiana, who rejoiced under the name of Osmo, saw a copy on the shelf. The title caught his eye. Curiously picking it up and blowing the dust off, he was thunderstruck by the opening sentence: "Osmo is born in Mercy Hospital in Auburn, Indiana, on June 6, 1942, of Finnish parentage, and after nearly losing his life from an attack of pneumonia at the age of five, he is enrolled in the St. James school there." Osmo turned pale. The book nearly fell from his hands. He thumbed back in excitement to discover who had written it. Nothing was given of its authorship nor, for that matter, of its publisher. His questions of the librarian produced no further information, he being as ignorant as Osmo of how the book came to be there.

So Osmo, with the book pressed tightly under his arm, dashed across the street for some coffee, thinking to compose himself and then examine the book with care. Meanwhile he glanced at a few more of its opening remarks, at the things said there about his difficulties with his younger sister, how he was slow in learning to read, of the summer on Mackinac Island, and so on. His emotions now somewhat quieted, Osmo began a close reading. He noticed that everything was expressed in the present tense, the way newspaper headlines are written. For example, the text read, "Osmo is born in Mercy Hospital," instead of saying he was born there, and it recorded that he quarrels with his sister, is a slow student, is fitted with dental braces at age eight, and so on, all in the journalistic present tense. But the text itself made quite clear approximately when all these various things happened, for everything was in chronological order, and in any case each year of its subject's life constituted a separate chapter, and was so titled—"Osmo's Seventh Year," "Osmo's Eighth Year," and so on through the book.

Osmo became absolutely engrossed, to the extent that he forgot his original astonishment, bordering on panic, and for a while even lost his curiosity concerning authorship. He sat drinking coffee and reliving his childhood, much of which he had all but forgotten until the memories were revived by the book now before him. He had almost forgotten the kitten, for example, and had entirely forgotten its name, until he read, in the chapter called "Osmo's Seventh Year," this observation: "Sobbing, Osmo takes Fluffy, now quite dead, to the garden, and buries her next to the rose bush." Ah yes! And then there was Louise, who sat next to him in the eighth grade—it was all right there. And how he got caught smoking one day. And how he felt when his father died. On and on. Osmo became so absorbed that he quite forgot the business of the day, until it occurred to him to turn to Chapter 26, to see what might be said there, he having just recently turned twenty-six. He had no sooner done so than his panic returned, for lo! what the book said was *true!* That it rains on his birthday for example, that his wife fails to give him the binoculars he had hinted he would like, that he receives a raise in salary shortly thereafter, and so on. Now how in God's name, Osmo pondered, could anyone know that, apparently before it had happened? For these were quite recent events, and the book had dust on it. Quickly moving on, Osmo came to this: "Sitting and reading in the coffee shop across from the library, Osmo, perspiring copiously, entirely forgets, until it is too late, that he is supposed to collect his wife at the hairdresser's at four." Oh my god! He had forgotten all about that. Yanking out his watch, Osmo discovered that it was nearly five o'clock—too late. She would be on her way home by now, and in a very sour mood.

Osmo's anguish at this discovery was nothing, though, compared to what the rest of the day held for him. He poured more coffee, and it now occurred to him to check the number of chapters in this amazing book. Only twenty-nine! But surely, he thought, that doesn't mean anything. How anyone could have gotten all this stuff down so far was puzzling enough, to be sure, but no one in God's earth could possibly know in advance how long this or that man is going to live. (Only God could know that sort of thing, Osmo reflected.) So he read along; though not without considerable uneasiness and even depression, for the remaining three chapters were on the whole discouraging. He thought he had gotten that ulcer under control, for example. And he didn't see any reason to suppose his job was going to turn out that badly, or that he was really going to break a leg skiing; after all, he could just give up skiing. But then the book ended on a terribly dismal note. It said: "And Osmo, having taken Northwest flight 569 from O'Hare, perishes when the aircraft crashes on the runway at Fort Wayne, with considerable loss of life, a tragedy rendered the more calamitous by the fact that Osmo had neglected to renew his life insurance before the expiration of the grace period." And that was all. That was the end of the book.

So *that's* why it had only twenty-nine chapters. Some idiot thought he was going to get killed in a plane crash. But, Osmo thought, he just wouldn't get on that plane. And this would also remind him to keep his insurance in force.

(About three years later our hero, having boarded a flight for St. Paul, went berserk when the pilot announced they were going to land at Fort Wayne instead. According to one of the stewardesses, he tried to hijack the aircraft and divert it to another airfield. The Civil Aeronautics Board cited the resulting disruptions as contributing to the crash that followed as the plane tried to land.)

Osmo's extraordinary circumstances led him to embrace the doctrine of fatalism. Not quite completely, perhaps, for there he was, right up to the end, trying vainly to buck his fate—trying, in effect, to make a fool of God, though he did not know this, because he had no idea of the book's source. Still, he had the overwhelm-

ing evidence of his whole past life to make him think that everything was going to work out exactly as described in the book. It always had. It was, in fact, precisely this conviction that terrified him so.

But now let us ask these questions, in order to make Osmo's experiences more relevant to our own. First, why did he become, or nearly become, a fatalist? Second, just what did his fatalism amount to? Third, was his belief justified in terms of the evidence he had? And finally, is that belief justified in terms of the evidence we have—or in other words, should we be fatalists too?

This last, of course, is the important metaphysical question, but we have to approach it through the others.

Why did Osmo become a fatalist? Osmo became a fatalist because there existed a set of true statements about the details of his life, both past and future, and he came to know what some of these statements were and to believe them, including many concerning his future. That is the whole of it.

No theological ideas entered into his conviction, nor any presuppositions about causal determinism, the coercion of his actions by causes, or anything of this sort. The foundations of Osmo's fatalism were entirely in logic and epistemology, having only to do with truth and knowledge. Ideas about God did not enter in, for he never suspected that God was the ultimate source of those statements. And at no point did he think God was *making* him do what he did. All he was concerned about was that someone seemed somehow to *know* what he had done and was going to do.

What, then, did Osmo believe? He did not, it should be noted, believe that certain things were going to happen to him, *no matter what*. That does not express a logically coherent belief. He did not think he was in danger of perishing in an airplane crash even in case he did not get into any airplane, for example, or that he was going to break his leg skiing, whether he went skiing or not. No one believes what he considers to be plainly impossible. If anyone believes that a given event is going to happen, he does not doubt that those things necessary for its occurrence are going to happen too. The expression, "no matter what," by means of which some philosophers have sought an easy and even childish refutation of fatalism, is accordingly highly inappropriate in any description of the fatalist conviction.

Osmo's fatalism was simply the realization that the things described in the book were unavoidable.

Of course we are all fatalists in this sense about some things, and the metaphysical question is whether this familiar attitude should not be extended to everything. We know the sun will rise tomorrow, for example, and there is nothing we can do about it. Each of us knows he is sooner or later going to die, too, and there is nothing to be done about that either. We normally do not know just when, of course, but it is mercifully so! For otherwise we would simply sit checking off the days as they passed, with growing despair, like a man condemned to the gallows and knowing the hour set for his execution. The tides ebb and flow, and heavens revolve, the seasons follow in order, generations arise and pass, and no one speaks of taking preventive measures. With respect to those things each of us recognizes as beyond his control, we are of necessity fatalists.

The question of fatalism is simply: Of all the things that happen in the world, which, if any, are avoidable? And the philosophical fatalist replies: None of them. They never were. Some of them only seemed so.

Was Osmo's fatalism justified? Of course it was. When he could sit right there and read a true description of those parts of his life that had not yet been lived, it would be idle to suggest to him that his future might, nonetheless, contain alternative possibilities. The only doubts Osmo had were whether those statements could really be true. But here he had the proof of his own experience, as one by one they were tested. Whenever he tried to prevent what was set forth he of course failed. Such failure, over and over, of even the most herculean efforts, with never a single success, must surely suggest, sooner or later, that he was *destined* to

fail. Even to the end, when Osmo tried so desperately to save himself from the destruction described in the book, his effort was totally in vain—as he should have realized it was going to be had he really known that what was said there was true. No power in heaven or earth can render false a statement that is true. It has never been done, and never will be.

Is the doctrine of fatalism, then, true? This amounts to asking whether our circumstances are significantly different from Osmo's. Of course we cannot read our own biographies the way he could. Only men who become famous ever have their lives recorded, and even so, it is always in retrospect. This is unfortunate. It is too bad that someone with sufficient knowledge—God, for example—cannot set down the lives of great men in advance, so that their achievements can be appreciated better by their contemporaries, and indeed, by their predecessors—their parents, for instance. But mortals do not have the requisite knowledge, and if there is any god who does, he seems to keep it to himself.

None of this matters, as far as our own fatalism is concerned. For the important thing to note is that, of the two considerations that explain Osmo's fatalism, only one of them was philosophically relevant, and that one applies to us no less than to him. The two considerations were: (1) there existed a set of true statements about his life, both past and future, and (2) he came to know what those statements were and to believe them. Now the second of these two considerations explains why, as a matter of psychological fact, Osmo became fatalistic, but it has nothing to do with the validity of that point of view. Its validity is assured by (1) alone. It was not the fact that the statements happened to be written down that rendered the things they described unavoidable: that had nothing to do with it at all. Nor was it the fact that, because they had been written, Osmo could read them. His reading them and coming to believe them likewise had nothing to do with the inevitability of what they described. This was ensured simply by there being such a set of statements, whether written or not, whether read by anyone or not, and whether or not known to be true. All that is required is that they should be true.

Each of us has but one possible past, described by that totality of statements about us in the past tense, each of which happens to be true. No one ever thinks of rearranging things there; it is simply accepted as given. But so also, each of us has but one possible future, described by that totality of statements about oneself in the future tense, each of which happens to be true. The sum of these constitutes one's biography. Part of it has been lived. The main outlines of it can still be seen, in retrospect, though most of its details are obscure. The other part has not been lived, though it most assuredly is going to be, in exact accordance with that set of statements just referred to. Some of its outlines can already be seen, in prospect, but it is on the whole more obscure than the part belonging to the past. We have at best only premonitory glimpses of it. It is no doubt for this reason that not all of this part, the part that awaits us, is perceived as given, and men do sometimes speak absurdly of altering it—as though what the future holds, as identified by any true statement in the future tense, might after all *not* hold.

Osmo's biography was all expressed in the present tense because all that mattered was that the things referred to were real events; it did not matter to what part of time they belonged. His past consisted of those things that preceded his reading of the book, and he simply accepted it as given. He was not tempted to revise what was said there, for he was sure it was true. But it took the book to make him realize that his future was also something given. It was equally pointless for him to try to revise what was said there, for it, too, was true. As the past contains what has happened, the future contains what will happen, and neither contains, in addition to these things, various other things that did not and will not happen.

Of course we know relatively little of what the future contains. Some things we know. We know the sun will go on rising and setting, for example, that taxes will be levied and wars rage, that men will continue to be callous and greedy, and that people will be murdered and robbed. It is just the details that remain to be discovered. But the same is true of the past; it is only a matter of degree. When I meet a total stranger I do not know, and will probably never know, what his past has been, beyond certain obvious things—that he had a mother, and things of this sort. I know nothing of the particulars of that vast realm of fact that is unique to his past. And the same for his future, with only this difference—that *all* men are strangers to me as far as their futures are concerned, and here I am even a stranger to myself.

Yet there is one thing I know concerning any stranger's past and the past of everything under the sun; namely, that whatever it might hold, there is nothing anyone can do about it now. What has happened cannot be undone. The mere fact that it has happened guarantees this.

And so it is, by the same token, of the future of everything under the sun. Whatever the future might hold, there is nothing anyone can do about it now. What will happen cannot be altered. The mere fact that it is going to happen guarantees this. . . .

BARON d'HOLBACH
Are We Cogs in the Universe?

In whatever manner man is considered, he is connected to universal nature, and submitted to the necessary and immutable laws that she imposes on all beings she contains, according to their peculiar essences or to the respective properties with which, without consulting them, she endows each particular species. Man's life is a line that nature commands him to describe upon the surface of the earth, without his ever being able to swerve from it, even for an instant. He is born without his own consent; his organization does in nowise depend upon himself; his ideas come to him involuntarily; his habits are in the power of those who cause him to contract them; he is unceasingly modified by causes, whether visible or concealed, over which he has no control, which necessarily regulate his mode of existence, give the hue to his way of thinking, and determine his manner of acting. He is good or bad, happy or miserable, wise or foolish, reasonable or irrational, without his will being for anything in these various states. Nevertheless, in spite of the shackles by which he is bound, it is pretended he is a free agent, or that independent of the causes by which he is moved, he determines his own will, and regulates his own condition.

However slender the foundation of his opinion, of which everything ought to point out to him the error, it is current at this day and passes for an incontestable truth with a great number of people, otherwise extremely enlightened; it is the basis of religion, which supposing relations between man and the unknown being she has placed above nature, has been incapable of imagining how man could merit reward or deserve punishment from this being, if he was not a free agent. Society has been believed interested in his system; because an idea has gone abroad, that if all the actions of man were to be contemplated as necessary, the right of punishing those who injure their associates would no longer exist. At length human vanity accommodated itself to a hypothesis which, unquestionably, appears to distinguish man from all other physical beings, by assigning to him the special privilege of a total independence of all other causes, but of which a very little reflection would have shown him the impossibility.

The will, as we have elsewhere said, is a modification of the brain, by which it is disposed to action, or prepared to give play to the organs. This will is necessarily determined by the qualities, good or bad, agreeable or painful, of the object or the motive that acts upon his sense, or of which the idea remains with him, and is resuscitated by his memory. In consequence, he acts necessarily, his action is the result of the impulse he receives either from the motive, from the object, or from the idea which has modified his brain, or disposed his will. When he does not act according to this impulse, it is because there comes some new cause, some new motive, some new idea, which modified

Reprinted from Baron d'Holbach's *The System of Nature*, translated by H. D. Robinson (1868). **Paul Henri Thiry Baron d'Holbach** (1723–1789) was a controversial anti-religionist and outspoken materialist during the French Enlightenment.

his brain in a different manner, gives him a new impulse, determines his will in another way, by which the action of the former impulse is suspended; thus, the sight of an agreeable object, or its idea, determines his will to set him in action to procure it; but if a new object or a new idea more powerfully attracts him, it gives a new direction to his will, annihilates the effect of the former, and prevents the action by which it was to be procured. This is the mode in which reflection, experience, reason, necessarily arrests or suspends the action of man's will: without this he would of necessity have followed the anterior impulse which carried him towards a then desirable object. In all this he always acts according to necessary laws from which he has no means of emancipating himself.

In short, the actions of man are never free; they are always the necessary consequence of his temperament, of the received ideas, and of the notions, either true or false, which he has formed to himself of happiness; of his opinions, strengthened by example, by education, and by daily experience. So many crimes are witnessed on the earth only because every thing conspires to render man vicious and criminal; the religion he has adopted, his government, his education, the examples set before him, irresistibly drive him on to evil: under these circumstances, mo-

rality preaches virtue to him in vain. In those societies where vice is esteemed, where crime is crowned, where venality is constantly recompensed, where the most dreadful disorders are punished only in those who are too weak to enjoy the privilege of committing them with impunity, the practice of virtue is considered nothing more than a painful sacrifice of happiness. Such societies chastise, in the lower orders, those excesses which they respect in the higher ranks; and frequently have the injustice to condemn those in the penalty of death, whom public prejudices, maintained by constant example, have rendered criminal.

Man, then, is not a free agent in any one instant of his life; he is necessarily guided in each step by those advantages, whether real or fictitious, that he attaches to the objects by which his passions are roused: these passions themselves are necessary in a being who unceasingly tends towards his own happiness; their energy is necessary, since that depends on his temperament; his temperament is necessary, because it depends on the physical elements which enter into his composition; the modification of this temperament is necessary, as it is the infallible and inevitable consequence of the impulse he receives from the incessant action of moral and physical beings.

WILLIAM JAMES
The Dilemma of Determinism

[1] A common opinion prevails that the juice has ages ago been pressed out of the freewill controversy, and that no new champion can do more than warm up stale arguments which ev-

ery one has heard. This is a radical mistake. I know of no subject less worn out, or in which inventive genius has a better chance of breaking open new ground,—not, perhaps, of forcing a

William James' "The Dilemma of Determinism" was first published in 1884. **William James** (1842–1910) was an influential and original thinker, contributing to the science of psychology as well as to the broader development of pragmatism.

conclusion or of coercing assent, but of deepen-
ing our sense of what the issue between the two
parties really is, of what the ideas of fate and of
freewill imply. At our very side almost, in the
past few years, we have seen falling in rapid
succession from the press works that present the
alternative in entirely novel lights. Not to speak
of the English disciples of Hegel, such as Green
and Bradley; not to speak of Hinton and Hodgson, nor of Hazard here,—we see in the writings of Renouvier, Fouillée, and Delboeuf how
completely changed and refreshed is the form of
all the old disputes. I cannot pretend to vie in
originality with any of the masters I have
named, and my ambition limits itself to just one
little point. If I can make two of the necessarily
implied corollaries of determinism clearer to
you than they have been made before, I shall
have made it possible for you to decide for or
against that doctrine with a better understanding
of what you are about. And if you prefer not to
decide at all, but to remain doubters, you will
at least see more plainly what the subject of
your hesitation is. I thus disclaim openly on the
threshold all pretension to prove to you that the
freedom of the will is true. The most I hope is
to induce some of you to follow my own example in assuming it true and acting as if it were
true. If it be true, it seems to me that this is
involved in the strict logic of the case. Its truth
ought not to be forced willy-nilly down our indifferent throats. It ought to be freely espoused
by men who can equally well turn their backs
upon it. In other words, our first act of freedom, if we are free, ought in all inward propriety to be to affirm that we are free. This should
exclude, it seems to me, from the freewill side
of the question all hope of a coercive demonstration,—a demonstration which I, for one, am
perfectly contented to go without.

[2] With this much understood at the outset, we can advance. But not without one more
point understood as well. The arguments I am
about to urge all proceed on two suppositions:
first, when we make theories about the world
and discuss them with one another, we do so in
order to attain a conception of things which
shall give us subjective satisfaction; and, sec-

ond, if there be two conceptions, and the one
seems to us, on the whole, more rational than
the other, we are entitled to suppose that the
more rational one is the truer of the two. I hope
that you are all willing to make these suppositions with me; for I am afraid that if there be
any of you here who are not, they will find little
edification in the rest of what I have to say. I
cannot stop to argue the point; but I myself believe that all the magnificent achievements of
mathematical and physical science—our doctrines of evolution, of uniformity of law, and
the rest—proceed from our indomitable desire
to cast the world into a more rational shape in
our minds than the shape into which it is thrown
there by the crude order of our experience. The
world has shown itself, to a great extent, plastic
to this demand of ours for rationality. How
much farther it will show itself plastic no one
can say. Our only means of finding out is to try;
and I, for one, feel as free to try conceptions of
moral as of mechanical or of logical rationality.
If a certain formula for expressing the nature of
the world violates my moral demand, I shall
feel as free to throw it overboard, or at least to
doubt it, as if it disappointed my demand for
uniformity of sequence, for example; the one
demand being, so far as I can see, quite as subjective and emotional as the other is. The principle of causality, for example,—what is it but a
postulate, an empty name covering simply a demand that the sequence of events shall some
day manifest a deeper kind of belonging of one
thing with another than the mere arbitrary jux-
taposition which now phenomenally appears? It
is as much an altar to an unknown god as the
one that Saint Paul found at Athens. All our scientific and philosophic ideals are altars to unknown gods. Uniformity is as much so as is
freewill. If this be admitted, we can debate on
even terms. But if any one pretends that while
freedom and variety are, in the first instance,
subjective demands, necessity and uniformity
are something altogether different, I do not see
how we can debate at all.

[3] To begin, then, I must suppose you acquainted with all the usual arguments on the
subject. I cannot stop to take up the old proofs

from causation, from statistics, from the certainty with which we can foretell one another's conduct, from the fixity of character, and all the rest. But there are two *words* which usually encumber these classical arguments, and which we must immediately dispose of if we are to make any progress. One is the eulogistic word *freedom,* and the other is the opprobrious word *chance.* The word "chance" I wish to keep, but I wish to get rid of the word "freedom." Its eulogistic associations have so far overshadowed all the rest of its meaning that both parties claim the sole right to use it, and determinists today insist that they alone are freedom's champions. Old-fashioned determinism was what we may call *hard* determinism. It did not shrink from such words as fatality, bondage of the will, necessitation, and the like. Nowadays, we have a *soft* determinism which abhors harsh words, and, repudiating fatality, necessity, and even predetermination, says that its real name is freedom; for freedom is only necessity understood, and bondage to the highest is identical with true freedom. Even a writer as little used to making capital out of soft words as Mr. Hodgson hesitates not to call himself a "freewill determinist."

[4] Now, all this is a quagmire of evasion under which the real issue of fact has been entirely smothered. Freedom in all these senses presents simply no problem at all. No matter what the soft determinist means by it,—whether he means the acting without external constraint; whether he means the acting rightly, or whether he means the acquiescing in the law of the whole,—who cannot answer him that sometimes we are free and sometimes we are not? But there *is* a problem, an issue of fact and not of words, an issue of the most momentous importance, which is often decided without discussion in one sentence,—nay, in one clause of a sentence,—by those very writers who spin out whole chapters in their efforts to show what "true" freedom is; and that is the question of determinism, about which we are to talk tonight.

[5] Fortunately, no ambiguities hang about this word or about its opposite, indeterminism.

Both designate an outward way in which things may happen, and their cold and mathematical sound has no sentimental associations that can bribe our partiality either way in advance. Now, evidence of an external kind to decide between determinism and indeterminism is, as I intimated a while back, strictly impossible to find. Let us look at the difference between them and see for ourselves. What does determinism profess?

[6] It professes that those parts of the universe already laid down absolutely appoint and decree what the other parts shall be. The future has no ambiguous possibilities hidden in its womb: the part we call the present is compatible with only one totality. Any other future complement than the one fixed from eternity is impossible. The whole is in each and every part, and welds it with the rest into an absolute unity, an iron block, in which there can be no equivocation or shadow of turning.

> With earth's first clay they did the last
> 	man kneed,
> And there of the last harvest sowed the
> 	seed.
> And the first morning of creation wrote
> What the last dawn of reckoning shall
> 	read.

[7] Indeterminism, on the contrary, says that the parts have a certain amount of loose play on one another, so that the laying down of one of them does not necessarily determine what the others shall be. It admits that possibilities may be in excess of actualities, and that things not yet revealed to our knowledge may really in themselves be ambiguous. Of two alternative futures which we conceive, both may now be really possible; and the one becomes impossible only at the very moment when the other excludes it by becoming real itself. Indeterminism thus denies the world to be one unbending unit of fact. It says there is a certain ultimate pluralism in it; and, so saying, it corroborates our ordinary unsophisticated view of things. To that view, actualities seem to float in a wider sea of possibilities from out of which

they are chosen; and, *somewhere*, indeterminism says, such possibilities exist, and form a part of truth.

[8] Determinism, on the contrary, says they exist *nowhere*, and that necessity on the one hand and impossibility on the other are the sole categories of the real. Possibilities that fail to get realized are, for determinism, pure illusions: they never were possibilities at all. There is nothing inchoate, it says, about this universe of ours, all that was or is or shall be actual in it having been from eternity virtually there. The cloud of alternatives our minds escort this mass of actuality withal is a cloud of sheer deceptions, to which "impossibilities" is the only name that rightfully belongs.

[9] The issue, it will be seen, is a perfectly sharp one, which no eulogistic terminology can smear over or wipe out. The truth *must* lie with one side or the other, and its lying with one side makes the other false.

[10] The question relates solely to the existence of possibilities, in the strict sense of the term, as things that may, but need not, be. Both sides admit that a volition, for instance, has occurred. The indeterminists say another volition might have occurred in its place: the determinists swear that nothing could possibly have occurred in its place. Now, can science be called in to tell us which of these two point-blank contradicters of each other is right? Science professes to draw no conclusions but such as are based on matters of fact, things that have actually happened; but how can any amount of assurance that something actually happened give us the least grain of information as to whether another thing might or might not have happened in its place? Only facts can be proved by other facts. With things that are possibilities and not facts, facts have no concern. If we have no other evidence than the evidence of existing facts, the possibility-question must remain a mystery never to be cleared up.

[11] And the truth is that facts practically have hardly anything to do with making us either determinists or indeterminists. Sure enough, we make a flourish of quoting facts this way or that; and if we are determinists, we talk about the infallibility with which we can predict one another's conduct; while if we are indeterminists, we lay great stress on the fact that it is just because we cannot foretell one another's conduct, either in war or statecraft or in any of the great and small intrigues and businesses of men, that life is so intensely anxious and hazardous a game. But who does not see the wretched insufficiency of this so-called objective testimony on both sides? What fills up the gaps in our minds is something not objective, not external. What divides us into possibility men and anti-possibility men is different faiths or postulates,—postulates of rationality. To this man the world seems more rational with possibilities in it,—to that man more rational with possibilities excluded; and talk as we will about having to yield to evidence, what makes us monists or pluralists, determinists or indeterminists, is at bottom always some sentiment like this.

[12] The stronghold of the deterministic sentiment is the antipathy to the idea of chance. As soon as we begin to talk indeterminism to our friends, we find a number of them shaking their heads. This notion of alternative possibility, they say, this admission that any one of several things may come to pass, is, after all, only a roundabout name for chance; and chance is something the notion of which no sane mind can for an instant tolerate in the world. What is it, they ask, but barefaced crazy unreason, the negation of intelligibility and law? And if the slightest particle of it exists anywhere, what is to prevent the whole fabric from falling together, the stars from going out, and chaos from recommencing her topsy-turvy reign?

[13] Remarks of this sort about chance will put an end to discussion as quickly as anything one can find. I have already told you that "chance" was a word I wished to keep and use. Let us then examine exactly what it means, and see whether it ought to be such a terrible bugbear to us. I fancy that squeezing the thistle boldly will rob it of its sting.

[14] The sting of the word "chance" seems to lie in the assumption that it means something positive, and that if anything happens by

chance, it must needs be something of an intrinsically irrational and preposterous sort. Now, chance means nothing of the kind. It is a purely negative and relative term, giving us no information about that of which it is predicated, except that it happens to be disconnected with something else,—not controlled, secured, or necessitated by other things in advance of its own actual presence. As this point is the most subtile one of the whole lecture, and at the same time the point on which all the rest hinges, I beg you to pay particular attention to it. What I say is that it tells us nothing about what a thing may be in itself to call it "chance." It may be a bad thing, it may be a good thing. It may be lucidity, transparency, fitness incarnate, matching the whole system of other things, when it has once befallen, in an unimaginably perfect way. All you mean by calling it "chance" is that this is not guaranteed, that it may also fall out otherwise. For the system of other things has no positive hold on the chance-thing. Its origin is in a certain fashion negative: it escapes, and says, Hands off! coming, when it comes, as a free gift, or not at all.

[15] This negativeness, however, and this opacity of the chance-thing when thus considered *ab extra*, or from the point of view of previous things or distant things, do not preclude its having any amount of positiveness and luminosity from within, and at its own place and moment. All that its chance-character asserts about it is that there is something in it really of its own, something that is not the unconditional property of the whole. If the whole wants this property, the whole must wait till it can get it, if it be a matter of chance. That the universe may actually be a sort of joint-stock society of this sort, in which the sharers have both limited liabilities and limited powers, is of course a simple and conceivable notion.

[16] Nevertheless, many persons talk as if the minutest dose of disconnectedness of one part with another, the smallest modicum of independence, the faintest tremor of ambiguity about the future, for example, would ruin everything, and turn this goodly universe into a sort of insane sand-heap or nulliverse, no universe at all. Since future human volitions are as a matter of fact the only ambiguous things we are tempted to believe in, let us stop for a moment to make ourselves sure whether their independent and accidental character need be fraught with such direful consequences to the universe as these.

[17] What is meant by saying that my choice of which way to walk home after the lecture is ambiguous and matter of chance as far as the present moment is concerned? It means that both Divinity Avenue and Oxford Street are called; but that only one, and that one *either* one, shall be chosen. Now, I ask you seriously to suppose that this ambiguity of my choice is real; and then to make the impossible hypothesis that the choice is made twice over, and each time falls on a different street. In other words, imagine that I first walk through Divinity Avenue, and then imagine that the powers governing the universe annihilate ten minutes of time with all that it contained, and set me back at the door of this hall just as I was before the choice was made. Imagine then that, everything else being the same, I now make a different choice and traverse Oxford Street. You, as passive spectators, look on and see the two alternative universes,—one of them with me walking through Divinity Avenue in it, the other with the same me walking through Oxford Street. Now, if you are determinists you believe one of these universes to have been from eternity impossible: you believe it to have been impossible because of the intrinsic irrationality or accidentality somewhere involved in it. But looking outwardly at these universes, can you say which is the impossible and accidental one, and which the rational and necessary one? I doubt if the most ironclad determinist among you could have the slightest glimmer of light on this point. In other words, either universe *after the fact* and once there would, to our means of observation and understanding, appear just as rational as the other. There would be absolutely no criterion by which we might judge one necessary and the other matter of chance. Suppose now we relieve the gods of their hypothetical task and assume

my choice, once made, to be made forever. I go through Divinity Avenue for good and all. If, as good determinists, you now begin to affirm, what all good determinists punctually do affirm, that in the nature of things I *couldn't* have gone through Oxford Street,—had I done so it would have been chance, irrationality, insanity, a horrid gap in nature,—I simply call your attention to this, that your affirmation is what the Germans call a *Machtspruch,* a mere conception fulminated as a dogma and based on no insight into details. Before my choice, either street seemed as natural to you as to me. Had I happened to take Oxford Street, Divinity Avenue would have figured in your philosophy as the gap in nature; and you would have so proclaimed it with the best deterministic conscience in the world.

[18] But what a hollow outcry, then, is this against a chance which, if it were present to us, we could by no character whatever distinguish from a rational necessity! I have taken the most trivial of examples, but no possible example could lead to any different result. For what are the alternatives which, in point of fact, offer themselves to human volition? What are those futures that now seem matters of chance? Are they not one and all like the Divinity Avenue and Oxford Street of our example? Are they not all of them *kinds* of things already here and based in the existing frame of nature? Is any one ever tempted to produce an *absolute* accident, something utterly irrelevant to the rest of the world? Do not all the motives that assail us, all the futures that offer themselves to our choice, spring equally from the soil of the past; and would not either one of them, whether realized through chance or through necessity, the moment it was realized, seem to us to fit that past, and in the completest and most continuous manner to interdigitate with the phenomena already there?*

[19] The more one thinks of the matter, the more one wonders that so empty and gratuitous a hubbub as this outcry against chance should have found so great an echo in the hearts of men. It is a word which tells us absolutely

nothing about what chances, or about the *modus operandi* of the chancing; and the use of it as a war cry shows only a temper of intellectual absolutism, a demand that the world shall be a solid block, subject to one control,—which temper, which demand, the world may not be bound to gratify at all. In every outwardly verifiable and practical respect, a world in which the alternatives that now actually distract *your* choice were decided by pure chance would be by *me* absolutely undistinguished from the world in which I now live. I am, therefore, entirely willing to call it, so far as your choices go, a world of chance for me. To *yourselves,* it is true, those very acts of choice, which to me are so blind, opaque, and external, are the opposites of this, for you are within them and effect them. To you they appear as decisions; and decisions, for him who makes them, are altogether peculiar psychic facts. Self-luminous and self-justifying at the living moment at which they occur, they appeal to no outside moment to put its stamp upon them or make them continuous with the rest of nature. Themselves it is rather who seem to make nature continuous; and in their strange and intense function of granting consent to one possibility and withholding it from another, to transform an equivocal and double future into an inalterable and simple past.

[20] But with the psychology of the matter we have no concern this evening. The quarrel which determinism has with chance fortunately has nothing to do with this or that psychological detail. It is a quarrel altogether metaphysical. Determinism denies the ambiguity of future volitions, because it affirms that nothing future can be ambiguous. But we have said enough to meet the issue. Indeterminate future volitions *do* mean chance. Let us not fear to shout it from the housetops if need be; for we now know that the idea of chance is, at bottom, exactly the same thing as the idea of gift,—the one simply being a disparaging, and the other a eulogistic, name for anything on which we have no effective *claim*. And whether the world be the better or the worse for having either chances or gifts

in it will depend altogether on *what* these uncertain and unclaimable things turn out to be.

[21] And this at last brings us within sight of our subject. We have seen what determinism means: we have seen that indeterminism is rightly described as meaning chance; and we have seen that chance, the very name of which we are urged to shrink from as from a metaphysical pestilence, means only the negative fact that no part of the world, however big, can claim to control absolutely the destinies of the whole. But although, in discussing the word "chance," I may at moments have seemed to be arguing for its real existence, I have not meant to do so yet. We have not yet ascertained whether this be a world of chance or no; at most, we have agreed that it seems so. And I now repeat what I said at the outset, that, from any strict theoretical point of view, the question is insoluble. To deepen our theoretic sense of the *difference* between a world with chances in it and a deterministic world is the most I can hope to do; and this I may now at last begin upon, after all our tedious clearing of the way.

[22] I wish first of all to show you just what the notion that this is a deterministic world implies. The implications I call your attention to are all bound up with the fact that it is a world in which we constantly have to make what I shall, with your permission, call judgments of regret. Hardly an hour passes in which we do not wish that something might be otherwise; and happy indeed are those of us whose hearts have never echoed the wish of Omar Khayam—

*That we might clasp, ere closed, the book
    of fate,
And make the writer on a fairer leaf
Inscribe our names, or quite obliterate.
Ah! Love, could you and I with fate
    conspire
To mend this sorry scheme of things
    entire,
Would we not shatter it to bits, and
    then
Remould it nearer to the heart's desire?*

[23] Now, it is undeniable that most of these regrets are foolish, and quite on a par in point of philosophic value with the criticisms on the universe of that friend of our infancy, the hero of the fable The Atheist and the Acorn,—

Fool! had that bough a pumpkin bore,
Thy whimsies would have worked no
more. . . .

Even from the point of view of our own ends, we should probably make a botch of remodelling the universe. How much more then from the point of view of ends we cannot see! Wise men therefore regret as little as they can. But still some regrets are pretty obstinate and hard to stifle,—regrets for acts of wanton cruelty or treachery, for example, whether performed by others or by ourselves. Hardly any one can remain *entirely* optimistic after reading the confession of the murderer at Brockton the other day: how, to get rid of the wife whose continued existence bored him, he inveigled her into a desert spot, shot her four times, and then, as she lay on the ground and said to him, "You didn't do it on purpose, did you, dear?" replied, "No, I didn't do it on purpose," as he raised a rock and smashed her skull. Such an occurrence, with the mild sentence and self-satisfaction of the prisoner, is a field for a crop of regrets, which one need not take up in detail. We feel that, although a perfect mechanical fit to the rest of the universe, it is a bad moral fit, and that something else would really have been better in its place.

[24] But for the deterministic philosophy the murder, the sentence, and the prisoner's optimism were all necessary from eternity; and nothing else for a moment had a ghost of a chance of being put into their place. To admit such a chance, the determinists tell us, would be to make a suicide of reason; so we must steel our hearts against the thought. And here our plot thickens, for we see the first of those difficult implications of determinism and monism which it is my purpose to make you feel. If this Brockton murder was called for by the rest of-

the universe, if it had to come at its preap-
pointed hour, and if nothing else would have
been consistent with the sense of the whole,
what are we to think of the universe? Are we
stubbornly to stick to our judgment of regret,
and say, though it *couldn't* be, yet it *would* have
been a better universe with something different
from this Brockton murder in it? That, of
course, seems the natural and spontaneous thing
for us to do; and yet it is nothing short of deliberately espousing a kind of pessimism. The
judgment of regret calls the murder bad. Calling
a thing bad means, if it means anything at all,
that the thing ought not to be, that something
else ought to be in its stead. Determinism, in
denying that anything else can be in its stead,
virtually defines the universe as a place in
which what ought to be is impossible,—in other
words, as an organism whose constitution is afflicted with an incurable taint, an irremediable
flaw. The pessimism of a Schopenhauer says no
more than this,—that the murder is a symptom;
and that it is a vicious symptom because it belongs to a vicious whole, which can express its
nature no otherwise than by bringing forth just
such a symptom as that at this particular spot.
Regret for the murder must transform itself, if
we are determinists and wise, into a larger regret. It is absurd to regret the murder alone.
Other things being what they are, *it* could not
be different. What we should regret is that
whole frame of things of which the murder is
one member. I see no escape whatever from this
pessimistic conclusion, if, being determinists,
our judgment of regret is to be allowed to stand
at all.

[25] The only deterministic escape from
pessimism is everywhere to abandon the judgment of regret. That this can be done, history
shows to be not impossible. The devil, *quoad
existentiam,* may be good. That is, although he
be a *principle* of evil, yet the universe, with
such a principle in it, may practically be a better universe than it could have been without. On
every hand, in a small way, we find that a certain amount of evil is a condition by which a
higher form of good is bought. There is nothing
to prevent anybody from generalizing this view,

and trusting that if we could but see things in
the largest of all ways, even such matters as this
Brockton murder would appear to be paid for by
the uses that follow in their train. An optimism
quand même, a systematic and infatuated optimism like that ridiculed by Voltaire in his Can-
dide, is one of the possible ideal ways in which
a man may train himself to look on life. Bereft
of dogmatic hardness and lit up with the expression of a tender and pathetic hope, such an optimism has been the grace of some of the most
religious characters that ever lived.

> *Throb thine with Nature's throbbing
>   breast,*
> *And all is clear from east to west.*

[26] Even cruelty and treachery may be
among the absolutely blessed fruits of time, and
to quarrel with any of their details may be blasphemy. The only real blasphemy, in short, may
be that pessimistic temper of the soul which lets
it give way to such things as regrets, remorse,
and grief.

[27] Thus, our deterministic pessimism may
become a deterministic optimism at the price of
extinguishing our judgments of regret.

[28] But does not this immediately bring us
into a curious logical predicament? Our determinism leads us to call our judgments of regret
wrong, because they are pessimistic in implying
that what is impossible yet ought to be. But
how then about the judgments of regret themselves? If they are wrong, other judgments,
judgments of approval presumably, ought to be
in their place. But as they are necessitated,
nothing else *can* be in their place; and the universe is just what it was before,—namely, a
place in which what ought to be appears impossible. We have got one foot out of the pessimistic bog, but the other one sinks all the deeper.
We have rescued our actions from the bonds of
evil, but our judgments are now held fast.
When murders and treacheries cease to be sins,
regrets are theoretic absurdities and errors. The
theoretic and the active life thus play a kind of
seesaw with each other on the ground of evil.
The rise of either sends the other down. Murder

and treachery cannot be good without regret being bad: regret cannot be good without treachery and murder being bad. Both, however, are supposed to have been foredoomed; so something must be fatally unreasonable, absurd, and wrong in the world. It must be a place of which either sin or error forms a necessary part. From this dilemma there seems at first sight no escape. Are we then so soon to fall back into the pessimism from which we thought we had emerged? And is there no possible way by which we may, with good intellectual consciences, call the cruelties and the treacheries, the reluctance and the regrets, *all* good together?

[29] Certainly there is such a way, and you are probably most of you ready to formulate it yourselves. But, before doing so, remark how inevitably the question of determinism and indeterminism slides us into the question of optimism and pessimism, or, as our fathers called it, "the question of evil." The theological form of all these disputes is the simplest and the deepest, the form from which there is the least escape,—not because, as some have sarcastically said, remorse and regret are clung to with a morbid fondness by the theologians as spiritual luxuries, but because they are existing facts of the world, and as such must be taken into account in the deterministic interpretation of all that is fated to be. If they are fated to be error, does not the bat's wing of irrationality still cast its shadow over the world? . . .

[30] We have thus clearly revealed to our view what may be called the dilemma of determinism, so far as determinism pretends to think things out at all. A merely mechanical determinism, it is true, rather rejoices in not thinking them out. It is very sure that the universe must satisfy its postulate of a physical continuity and coherence, but it smiles at any one who comes forward with a postulate of moral coherence as well. I may suppose, however, that the number of purely mechanical or hard determinists among you this evening is small. The determinism to whose seductions you are most exposed is what I have called soft determinism,—the determinism which allows considerations of good

and bad to mingle with those of cause and effect in deciding what sort of a universe this may rationally be held to be. The dilemma of this determinism is one whose left horn is pessimism and whose right horn is subjectivism. In other words, if determinism is to escape pessimism, it must leave off looking at the goods and ills of life in a simple objective way, and regard them as materials, indifferent in themselves, for the production of consciousness, scientific and ethical, in us. . . .

[31] The only consistent way of representing a pluralism and a world whose parts may affect one another through their conduct being either good or bad is the indeterministic way. What interest, zest, or excitement can there be in achieving the right way, unless we are enabled to feel that the wrong way is also a possible and a natural way,—nay, more, a menacing and an imminent way? And what sense can there be in condemning ourselves for taking the wrong way, unless we need have done nothing of the sort, unless the right way was open to us as well? I cannot understand the willingness to act, no matter how we feel, without the belief that acts are really good and bad. I cannot understand the belief that an act is bad, without regret at its happening. I cannot understand regret without the admission of real, genuine possibilities in the world. Only *then* is it other than a mockery to feel, after we have failed to do our best, that an irreparable opportunity is gone from the universe, the loss of which it must forever after mourn.

[32] If you insist that this is all superstition, that possibility is in the eye of science and reason impossibility, and that if I act badly 'tis that the universe was foredoomed to suffer this defect, you fall right back into the dilemma, the labyrinth, of pessimism and subjectivism, from out of whose toils we have just wound our way.

[33] Now, we are of course free to fall back, if we please. For my own part, though, whatever difficulties may beset the philosophy of objective right and wrong, and the indeterminism it seems to imply, determinism, with its alternative of pessimism or romanticism, contains difficulties that are greater still. But you

will remember that I expressly repudiated awhile ago the pretension to offer any arguments which could be coercive in a so-called scientific fashion in this matter. And I consequently find myself, at the end of this long talk, obliged to state my conclusions in an altogether personal way. This personal method of appeal seems to be among the very conditions of the problem; and the most any one can do is to confess as candidly as he can the grounds for the faith that is in him, and leave his example to work on others as it may.

[34] Let me, then, without circumlocution say just this. The world is enigmatical enough in all conscience, whatever theory we may take up toward it. The indeterminism I defend, the freewill theory of popular sense based on the judgment of regret, represents that world as vulnerable, and liable to be injured by certain of its parts if they act wrong. And it represents their acting wrong as a matter of possibility or accident, neither inevitable nor yet to be infallibly warded off. In all this, it is a theory devoid either of transparency or of stability. It gives us a pluralistic, restless universe, in which no single point of view can ever take in the whole scene; and to a mind possessed of the love of unity at any cost, it will, no doubt, remain forever inacceptable. A friend with such a mind once told me that the thought of my universe made him sick, like the sight of the horrible motion of a mass of maggots in their carrion bed.

[35] But while I freely admit that the pluralism and the restlessness are repugnant and irrational in a certain way, I find that every alternative to them is irrational in a deeper way. The indeterminism with its maggots, if you please to speak so about it, offends only the native absolutism of my intellect,—an absolutism which, after all, perhaps, deserves to be snubbed and kept in check. But the determinism with its necessary carrion, to continue the figure of speech, and with no possible maggots to eat the latter up, violates my sense of moral reality through and through. When, for example, I imagine such carrion as the Brockton murder, I cannot conceive it as an act by which the uni-

verse, as a whole, logically and necessarily expresses its nature without shrinking from complicity with such a whole. And I deliberately refuse to keep on terms of loyalty with the universe by saying blankly that the murder, since it does flow from the nature of the whole, is not carrion. There are *some* instinctive reactions which I, for one, will not tamper with. The only remaining alternative, the attitude of gnostical romanticism, wrenches my personal instincts in quite as violent a way. It falsifies the simple objectivity of their deliverance. It makes the gooseflesh the murder excites in me a sufficient reason for the perpetration of the crime. It transforms life from a tragic reality into insincere melodramatic exhibition, as foul or as tawdry as any one's diseased curiosity pleases to carry it out. And with its consecration of the "roman naturaliste" state of mind, and its enthronement of the baser crew of Parisian *littérateurs* among the eternally indispensable organs by which the infinite spirit of things attains to that subjective illumination which is the task of its life, it leaves me in presence of a sort of subjective carrion considerably more noisome than the objective carrion I called it in to take away.

[36] No! better a thousand times, than such systematic corruption of our moral sanity, the plainest pessimism, so that it be straightforward; but better far than that the world of chance. Make as great an uproar about chance as you please, I know that chance means pluralism and nothing more. If some of the members of the pluralism are bad, the philosophy of pluralism, whatever broad views it may deny me, permits me, at least, to turn to the other members with a clean breast of affection and an unsophisticated moral sense. And if I still wish to think of the world as a totality, it lets me feel that a world with a *chance* in it of being altogether good, even if the chance never came to pass, is better than a world with no such chance at all. That "chance" whose very notion I am exhorted and conjured to banish from my view of the future as the suicide of reason concerning it, that "chance" is—what? Just this,—the chance that in moral respects the future may be

other and better than the past has been. This is the only chance we have any motive for supposing to exist. Shame, rather, on its repudiation

and its denial! For its presence is the vital air which lets the world live, the salt which keeps it sweet. . . .

NOTE

* A favorite argument against free will is that if it be true, a man's murderer may as probably be his best friend as his worst enemy, a mother be as likely to strangle as to suckle her firstborn, and all of us be as ready to jump from fourth-story windows as to go out of front doors, etc. Users of this argument should properly be excluded from debate till they learn what the real question is. "Free will" does not say that everything that is physi-

cally conceivable is also morally possible. It merely says that of alternatives that really *tempt* our will more than one is really possible. Of course, the alternatives that do thus tempt us are vastly fewer than the physical possibilities we can coldly fancy. Persons really tempted often do murder their best friends, mothers do strangle their firstborn, people do jump out of fourth-story windows, etc.

MORITZ SCHLICK
The Free Will-Determinism Issue is a Pseudoproblem

THE PSEUDOPROBLEM OF FREEDOM OF THE WILL

With hesitation and reluctance I prepare to add this chapter to the discussion of ethical problems. For in it I must speak of a matter which, even at present, is thought to be a fundamental ethical problem, but which got into ethics and has become a much discussed problem only because of a misunderstanding. This is the so-called problem of the freedom of the will. Moreover, this pseudoproblem has long since been settled by the efforts of certain sensible persons; and, above all, the state of affairs just described has been often disclosed—with exceptional clarity by Hume. Hence it is really one of the greatest scandals of philosophy that again and again so much paper and printer's ink is devoted to this matter. . . . Thus I should

truly be ashamed to write a chapter on "freedom." In the chapter heading, the word "responsible" indicates what concerns ethics, and designates the point at which misunderstanding arises. Therefore the concept of responsibility constitutes our theme, and if in the process of its clarification I must also speak of the concept of freedom I shall, of course, say only what others have already said better; consoling myself with the thought that in this way alone can anything be done to put an end at last to that scandal.

The main task of ethics is to explain moral behavior. To explain means to refer back to laws: every science, including psychology, is possible only in so far as there are such laws to

Reprinted from *Problems of Ethics*, translated by David Rynin (New York: Dover Publications, 1962), by permission of Dover Publications, Inc. **Moritz Schlick** (1882–1936) was one of the founders in the 1920s of the Vienna Circle, a philosophical school whose main tenet was that the physical sciences serve as the only acceptable model of rational discourse.

which the events can be referred. Since the assumption that all events are subject to universal laws is called the principle of causality, one can also say, "Every science presupposes the principle of causality." Therefore every explanation of human behavior must also assume the validity of causal laws; in this case the existence of psychological laws. All of our experience strengthens us in the belief that this presupposition is realized, at least to the extent required for all purposes of practical life in intercourse with nature and human beings, and also for the most precise demands of technique. Whether, indeed, the principle of causality holds universally, whether, that is, determinism is true, we do not know; no one knows. But we do know that it is impossible to settle the dispute between determinism and indeterminism by mere reflection and speculation. . . .

Fortunately, it is not necessary to lay claim to a final solution of the causal problem in order to say what is necessary in ethics concerning responsibility; there is required only an analysis of the concept, the careful determination of the meaning which is in fact joined to the words "responsibility" and "freedom," as these are actually used. If men had made clear to themselves the sense of these propositions, which we use in everyday life, that pseudoargument which lies at the root of the pseudoproblem, and which recurs thousands of times within and outside philosophical books, would never have arisen.

The argument runs as follows: "If determinism is true, if, that is, all events obey immutable laws, then my will too is always determined, by my innate character and my motives. Hence my decisions are necessary, not free. But if so, then I am not responsible for my acts, for I would be accountable for them only if I could do something about the way my decisions went; but I can do nothing about it, since they proceed with necessity from my character and the motives. And I have made neither, and have no power over them: the motives come from without, and my character is the necessary product of the innate tendencies and the external influences which have been effective during my lifetime. Thus determinism and moral responsibility are incompatible. Moral responsibility presupposes freedom, that is, exemption from causality."

This process of reasoning rests upon a whole series of confusions, just as the links of a chain hang together. We must show these confusions to be such, and thus destroy them.

TWO MEANINGS OF THE WORD "LAW"

It all begins with an erroneous interpretation of the meaning of "law." In practice this is understood as a rule by which the state prescribes certain behavior to its citizens. These rules often contradict the natural desires of the citizens (for if they did not do so, there would be no reason for making them), and are in fact not followed by many of them; while others obey, but under compulsion. The state does in fact compel its citizens by imposing certain sanctions (punishment) which serve to bring their desires into harmony with the prescribed laws.

In natural science, on the other hand, the word "law" means something quite different. The natural law is not a prescription as to how something should behave, but a formula, a description of how something does in fact behave. The two forms of "laws" have only this in common: both tend to be expressed in formulae. Otherwise they have absolutely nothing to do with one another, and it is very blameworthy that the same word has been used for two such different things; but even more so that philosophers have allowed themselves to be led into serious errors by this usage. Since natural laws are only descriptions of what happens, there can be in regard to them no talk of "compulsion." The laws of celestial mechanics do not prescribe to the planets how they have to move, as though the planets would actually like to move quite otherwise, and are only forced by-these burdensome laws of Kepler to move in orderly paths; no, these laws do not in any way "compel" the planets, but express only what in fact planets actually do.

If we apply this to volition, we are enlightened at once, even before the other confusions are discovered. When we say that a man's will "obeys psychological laws," these are not civic laws, which compel him to make certain decisions, or dictate desires to him, which he would in fact prefer not to have. They are laws of nature, merely expressing which desires he actually has under given conditions; they describe the nature of the will in the same manner as the astronomical laws describe the nature of planets. "Compulsion" occurs where man is prevented from realizing his natural desires. How could the rule according to which these natural desires arise itself be considered as "compulsion?"

COMPULSION AND NECESSITY

But this is the second confusion to which the first leads almost inevitably: after conceiving the laws of nature, anthropomorphically, as order imposed *nolens volens* upon the events, one adds to them the concept of "necessity." This word, derived from "need," also comes to us from practice, and is used there in the sense of inescapable compulsion. To apply the word with this meaning to natural laws is of course senseless, for the presupposition of an opposing desire is lacking, and it is then confused with something altogether different, which is actually an attribute of natural laws. That is, universality. It is of the essence of natural laws to be universally valid, for only when we have found a rule which holds of events without exception do we call the rule a law of nature. Thus when we say "a natural law holds necessarily" this has but one legitimate meaning: "It holds in all cases where it is applicable." It is again very deplorable that the word "necessary" has been applied to natural laws (or, what amounts to the same thing, with reference to causality), for it is quite superfluous, since the expression "universally valid" is available. Universal validity is something altogether different from "compulsion"; these concepts belong to spheres so remote from each other that once insight into the error has been gained one can no longer conceive the possibility of a confusion.

The confusion of two concepts always carries with it the confusion of their contradictory opposites. The opposite of the universal validity of a formula, of the existence of a law, is the nonexistence of a law, indeterminism, acausality; while the opposite of compulsion is what in practice everyone calls "freedom." Here emerges the nonsense, trailing through centuries, that freedom means "exemption from the causal principle," or "not subject to the laws of nature." Hence it is believed necessary to vindicate indeterminism in order to save human freedom.

FREEDOM AND INDETERMINISM

This is quite mistaken. Ethics has, so to speak, no moral interest in the purely theoretical question of "determinism or indeterminism," but only a theoretical interest, namely: in so far as it seeks the laws of conduct, and can find them only to the extent that causality holds. But the question of whether man is morally free (that is, has that freedom which, as we shall show, is the presupposition of moral responsibility) is altogether different from the problem of determinism. . . . Freedom means the opposite of compulsion; a man is free if he does not act under compulsion; and he is compelled or unfree when he is hindered from without in the realization of his natural desires. Hence he is unfree when he is locked up, or chained, or when someone forces him at the point of a gun to do what otherwise he would not do. This is quite clear, and everyone will admit that the everyday or legal notion of the lack of freedom is thus correctly interpreted, and that a man will be considered quite free and responsible if no such external compulsion is exerted upon him. There are certain cases which lie between these clearly described ones, as, say, when someone acts under the influence of alcohol or a narcotic. In such cases we consider the man to be more or less unfree, and hold him less accountable, because we rightly view the influence of the drug as "external," even though it is found within the body; it prevents him from making decisions in the manner peculiar to his nature. If he takes the narcotic of his own will, we make him completely responsible for this act and transfer a part of the responsibility to the consequences, making, as it were, an average or mean condemnation of the whole. In the case of a person who is mentally ill we do not consider him free with respect to those acts in which the disease expresses itself, because we view the illness as a disturbing factor which hinders the normal functioning of his natural tendencies. We make not him but his disease responsible.

THE NATURE OF RESPONSIBILITY

But what does this really signify? What do we mean by this concept of responsibility which goes along with that of "freedom," and which plays such an important role in morality? It is easy to attain complete clarity in this matter; we need only carefully determine the manner in which the concept is used. What is the case in practice when we impute "responsibility" to a person? What is our aim in doing this? The judge has to discover who is responsible for a given act in order that he may punish him. We are inclined to be less concerned with the inquiry as to who deserves reward for an act, and we have no special officials for this; but of course the principle would be the same. But let us stick to punishment in order to make the idea clear. What is punishment, actually? The view still often expressed, that it is a natural retaliation for past wrong, ought no longer to be defended in cultivated society; for the opinion that an increase in sorrow can be "made good again" by further sorrow is altogether barbarous. Certainly the origin of punishment may lie in an impulse of retaliation or vengeance; but what is such an impulse except the instinctive desire to destroy the cause of the deed to be avenged, by the destruction of or injury to the malefactor? Punishment is concerned only with the institution of causes, of motives of conduct, and this alone is its meaning. Punishment is an educative measure, and as such is a means to the formation of motives, which are in part to prevent the wrongdoer from repeating the act (reformation) and in part to prevent others from committing a similar act (intimidation). Analogously, in the case of reward we are concerned with an incentive.

Hence the question regarding responsibility is the question: Who in a given case, is to be punished? Who is to be considered the true wrongdoer? This problem is not identical with that regarding the original instigator of the act; for the great-grandparents of the man, from whom he inherited his character, might in the end be the cause, or the statesmen who are responsible for his social milieu, and so forth. But the "doer" is the one upon whom the motive must have acted in order, with certainty, to have prevented the act (or called it forth, as the case may be). Consideration of remote causes is of no help here, for in the first place their actual contribution cannot be determined, and in the second place they are generally out of reach. Rather, we must find the person in whom the decisive junction of causes lies. The question of who is responsible is the question concerning the correct point of application of the motive. . . . It is a matter only of knowing who is to be punished or rewarded, in order that punishment and reward function as such—be able to achieve their goal.

Thus, all the facts connected with the concepts of responsibility and imputation are at once made intelligible. We do not charge an insane person with responsibility, for the very reason that he offers no unified point for the application of motive. It would be pointless to try to affect him by means of promises or threats,'when his confused soul fails to respond to such influence because its normal mechanism is out of order. We do not try to give him mo-tives, but try to heal him (metaphorically, we make his sickness responsible, and try to remove its causes). When a man is forced by threats to commit certain acts we do not blame him, but the one who held the pistol at his breast. The reason is clear: the act would have been prevented had we been able to restrain the person who threatened him; and this person is the one whom we must influence in order to prevent similar acts in the future.

THE CONSCIOUSNESS OF RESPONSIBILITY

But much more important than the question of when a man is said to be responsible is that of when he himself feels responsible. Our whole treatment would be untenable if it gave no explanation of this. It is, then, a welcome confirmation of the view here developed that the subjective feeling of responsibility coincides with objective judgment. It is a fact of experience that, in general, the person blamed or condemned is conscious of the fact that he was "rightly" taken to account—of course, under the supposition that no error has been made, that the assumed state of affairs actually occurred. What is this consciousness of having been the true doer of the act, the actual instigator? Evidently not merely that it was he who took the steps required for its performance; but there must be added the awareness that he did it "independently," "of his own initiative," or however it be expressed. This feeling is simply the consciousness of freedom, which is merely the knowledge of having acted on one's own desires. And "one's own desires" are those which have their origin in the regularity of one's character in the given situation, and are not imposed by an external power, as explained above. The absence of the external power expresses itself in the well-known feeling (usually considered characteristic of the consciousness of freedom) that one could also have acted otherwise. How this indubitable experience ever came to be an argument in favor of indeterminism is incomprehensible to me. It is of course obvious that I should have acted differently had I willed something else; but the feeling never says that I could also have willed something else, even though this is true, if, that is, other motives had been present. And it says even less that under exactly the same inner and outer conditions I could also have willed something else. How could such a feeling inform me of anything regarding the purely theoretical question of whether the principle of causality holds or not? Of course, after what has been said on the subject, I do not undertake to demonstrate the principle, but I do deny that from any such fact of consciousness the least follows regarding the principle's validity. This feeling is not the consciousness of the absence of a cause, but of something altogether different, namely, of freedom, which consists in the fact that I can act as I desire.

Thus the feeling of responsibility assumes that I acted freely, that my own desires impelled me; and if because of this feeling I willingly suffer blame for my behavior or reproach myself, and thereby admit that I might have acted otherwise, this means that other behavior was compatible with the laws of volition—of course granted other motives. And I myself desire the existence of such motives and bear the pain (regret and sorrow) caused me by my behavior so that its repetition will be prevented. To blame oneself means just to apply a motive of improvement to oneself, which is usually the task of the educator. But if, for example, one does something under the influence of torture, feel ings of guilt and regret are absent, for one knows that according to the laws of volition no other behavior was possible—no matter what ideas, because of their feeling tones, might have functioned as motives. The important thing, al-ways, is that the feeling of responsibility means the realization that one's self, one's own psy-chic processes constitute the point at which mo-tives must be applied in order to govern the acts of one's body.

CAUSALITY AS THE PRESUPPOSITION OF RESPONSIBILITY

We can speak of motives only in a causal con-text; thus it becomes clear how very much of the concept of responsibility rests upon that of causation, that is, upon the regularity of voli-tional decisions. In fact if we should conceive of a decision as utterly without any cause (this would in all strictness be the indeterministic presupposition) then the act would be entirely a matter of chance, for chance is identical with the absence of a cause; there is no other oppo-site of causality. Could we under such condi-tions make the agent responsible? Certainly not. Imagine a man, always calm, peaceful and blameless, who suddenly falls upon and begins to beat a stranger. He is held and questioned re-garding the motive of his actions, to which he answers, in his opinion truthfully, as we as-sume: "There was no motive for my behavior. Try as I may I can discover no reason. My vo-lition was without any cause—I desired to do so, and there is simply nothing else to be said about it." We should shake our heads and call him insane, because we have to believe that there was a cause, and lacking any other we must assume some mental disturbance as the only cause remaining; but certainly no one would hold him to be responsible. If decisions were causeless there would be no sense in try-ing to influence men; and we see at once that this is the reason why we could not bring such a man to account, but would always have only a shrug of the shoulders in answer to his behav-ior. One can easily determine that in practice we make an agent the more responsible the more motives we can find for his conduct. If a man guilty of an atrocity was an enemy of his victim, if previously he had shown violent ten-dencies, if some special circumstance angered him, then we impose severe punishment upon him; while the fewer the reasons to be found for an offense the less do we condemn the agent, but make "unlucky chance," a momentary ab-erration, or something of the sort, responsible. We do not find the causes of misconduct in his character, and therefore we do not try to influ-ence it for the better: this and only this is the significance of the fact that we do not put the responsibility upon him. And he too feels this to be so, and says, "I cannot understand how such a thing could have happened to me."

In general we know very well how to dis-cover the causes of conduct in the characters of our fellow men; and how to use this knowledge in the prediction of their future behavior, often with as much certainty as that with which we know that a lion and a rabbit will behave quite differently in the same situation. From all this it is evident that in practice no one thinks of ques-tioning the principle of causality, that, thus, the attitude of the practical man offers no excuse to the metaphysician for confusing freedom from compulsion with the absence of a cause. If one makes clear to himself that a causeless happen-ing is identical with a chance happening, and that, consequently, an indetermined will would destroy all responsibility, then every desire will cease that might be father to an indeterministic thought. No one can prove determinism, but it is certain that we assume its validity in all our practical life, and that in particular we can ap-ply the concept of responsibility to human con-duct only in as far as the causal principle holds of volitional processes. . . .

C. A. CAMPBELL
Is "Free Will" A Pseudoproblem?

I

. . . Here . . . is Schlick's theory. Let us now examine it.

In the first place, it is surely quite implausible to suggest that the common assumption that moral freedom postulates some breach of causal continuity arises from a confusion of two different types of law. Schlick's distinction between descriptive and prescriptive law is, of course, sound. It was no doubt worth pointing out, too, that descriptive laws cannot be said to "compel" human behavior in the same way as prescriptive laws do. But it seems to me evident that the usual reason why it is held that moral freedom implies some breach of causal continuity, is not a belief that causal laws "compel" as civil laws "compel," but simply the belief that the admission of unbroken causal continuity entails a *further* admission which is directly incompatible with moral responsibility; *viz.* the admission that no man could have acted otherwise than he in fact did. Now it may, of course, be an error thus to assume that a man is not morally responsible for an act, a fit subject for moral praise and blame in respect of it, unless he could have acted otherwise than he did. Or, if *this* is not an error, it may still be an error to assume that a man could not have acted otherwise than he did, in the sense of the phrase that

is crucial for moral responsibility, without there occurring some breach of causal continuity. Into these matters we shall have to enter very fully at a later stage. But the relevant point at the moment is that these (not *prima facie* absurd) assumptions about the conditions of moral responsibility have very commonly, indeed normally, been made, and that they are entirely adequate to explain why the problem of Free Will finds its usual formulation in terms of partial exemption from causal law. Schlick's distinction between prescriptive and descriptive laws has no bearing at all upon the truth or falsity of these assumptions. Yet if these assumptions are accepted, it is (I suggest) really inevitable that the Free Will problem should be formulated in the way to which Schlick takes exception. Recognition of the distinction upon which Schlick and his followers lay so much stress can make not a jot of difference.

As we have seen, however, Schlick does later proceed to the much more important business of disputing these common assumptions about the conditions of moral responsibility. He offers us an analysis of moral responsibility which flatly contradicts these assumptions; an analysis according to which the only freedom demanded by morality is a freedom which is

"Is 'Free Will' A Pseudoproblem?" is reprinted from *Mind*, Vol. 60 (1951), by permission of Oxford University Press. **C. A. Campbell** (1897–1974) wrote in the areas of theory of knowledge and concept of the self, but is best known for his analysis of free will as implying the lack of universal causality.

compatible with Determinism. If this analysis can be sustained, there is certainly no problem of "Free Will" in the traditional sense.

But it seems a simple matter to show that Schlick's analysis is untenable. Let us test it by Schlick's own claim that it gives us what we mean by "moral responsibility" in ordinary linguistic usage.

We do not ordinarily consider the lower animals to be morally responsible. But *ought* we not to do so if Schlick is right about what we mean by moral responsibility? It is quite possible, by punishing the dog who absconds with the succulent chops designed for its master's luncheon, favourably to influence its motives in respect of its future behavior in like circumstances. If moral responsibility is to be linked with punishment as Schlick links it and punishment conceived as a form of education, we should surely hold the dog morally responsible? The plain fact, of course, is that we don't. We don't, because we suppose that the dog "couldn't help it": that its action (unlike what we usually believe to be true of human beings) was simply a link in a continuous chain of causes and effects. In other words, we do commonly demand the contra-causal sort of freedom as a condition of moral responsibility.

Again, we do ordinarily consider it proper, in certain circumstances, to speak of a person no longer living as morally responsible for some present situation. But *ought* we to do so if we accept Schlick's essentially "forward-looking" interpretation of punishment and responsibility? Clearly we cannot now favourably affect the dead man's motives. No doubt they could *at one time* have been favourably affected. But that cannot be relevant to our judgment of responsibility if, as Schlick insists, the question of who is responsible "is a matter only of knowing who is to be punished or rewarded." Indeed he expressly tells us, as we saw earlier, that in asking this question we are not concerned with a "great-grandparent" who may have been the "original instigator," because, for one reason, this "remote cause" is "out of reach." We cannot bring the appropriate educative influence to bear upon it. But the

plain fact, of course, is that we do frequently assign moral responsibility for present situations to persons who have long been inaccessible to any punitive action on our part. And Schlick's position is still more paradoxical in respect of our apportionment of responsibility for occurrences in the distant past. Since in these cases there is no agent whatsoever whom we can favourably influence by punishment, the question of moral responsibility here should have no meaning for us. But of course it has. Historical writings are studded with examples.

Possibly the criticism just made may seem to some to result from taking Schlick's analysis too much *au pied de la lettre*. The absurd consequences deduced, it may be said, would not follow if we interpreted Schlick as meaning that a man is morally responsible where his motive is such as can *in principle* be favourably affected by reward or punishment—whether or not we who pass the judgment are in a position to take such action. But with every desire to be fair to Schlick, I cannot see how he could accept this modification and still retain the essence of his theory. For the essence of his theory seems to be that moral responsibility has its whole meaning and importance for us in relation to our potential control of future conduct in the interests of society. (I agree that it is hard to believe that anybody *really* thinks this. But it is perhaps less hard to believe today than it has ever been before in the history of modern ethics.)

Again, we ordinarily consider that, in certain circumstances, the *degree* of a man's moral responsibility for an act is affected by considerations of his inherited nature, or of his environment, or of both. It is our normal habit to "make allowances" (as we say) when we have reason to believe that a malefactor had a vicious heredity, or was nurtured in his formative years in a harmful environment. We say in such cases "Poor chap, he is more to be pitied than blamed. We could scarcely expect him to behave like a decent citizen with *his* parentage or upbringing." But this extremely common sort of judgment has no point at all if we mean by moral responsibility what Schlick says that we mean. On *that* meaning the degree of a man's moral responsibility must presumably be dependent upon the degree to which we can favourably affect his future motives, which is quite another matter. Now there is no reason to believe that the motives of a man with a bad heredity, or a bad upbringing are either less or more subject to educative influence than those of his more fortunate fellows. Yet it is plain matter of fact that we do commonly consider the degree of a man's moral responsibility to be affected by these two factors.

A final point. The extremity of paradox in Schlick's identification of the question "Who is morally blameworthy?" with the question "Who is to be punished?" is apt to be partially concealed from us just because it is our normal habit to include in the meaning of "punishment" an element of "requital for moral transgression" which Schlick expressly denies to it. On that account we commonly think of "punishment," in its strict sense, as implying moral blameworthiness in the person punished. But if we remember to mean by punishment what Schlick means by it, a purely "educative measure," with no retributive ingredients, his identification of the two questions loses such plausibility as it might otherwise have. For clearly we often think it proper to "punish" a person, in *Schlick's* sense, where we are not at all prepared to say that the person is morally blameworthy. We may even think him morally commendable. A case in point would be the unmistakably sincere but muddleheaded person who at the cost of great suffering to himself steadfastly pursues as his "duty" a course which, in our judgment, is fraught with danger to the common weal. We should most of us feel entitled, in the public interest, to bring such action to bear upon the man's motives as might induce him to refrain in future from his socially injurious behavior: in other words, to inflict upon him what Schlick would call "punishment." But we should most of us feel perfectly clear that in so "punishing" this misguided citizen we are not proclaiming his moral blameworthiness for moral wickedness.

Adopting Schlick's own criterion, then, looking simply "to the manner in which the concept is used," we seem bound to admit that constantly people to assign moral responsibility where Schlick's theory says they shouldn't, don't assign moral responsibility where Schlick's theory says they should, and assign degrees of moral responsibility where on Schlick's theory there should be no difference in degree. I think we may reasonably conclude that Schlick's account of what we mean by moral responsibility breaks down.

The rebuttal of Schlick's arguments, however, will not suffice of itself to refute the pseudoproblem theory. The indebtedness to Schlick of most later advocates of the theory may be conceded; but certainly it does not comprehend all of significance that they have to say on the problem. There are recent analyses of the conditions of moral responsibility containing sufficient new matter, or sufficient old matter in a more precise and telling form, to require of us now something of a fresh start. In the section which follows I propose to consider some representative samples of these analyses—all of which, of course, are designed to show that the freedom which moral responsibility implies is not in fact a contra-causal type of freedom.

But before reopening the general question of the nature and conditions of moral responsibility there is a *caveat* which it seems to be worth while to enter. The difficulties in the way of a clear answer are not slight; but they are apt to seem a good deal more formidable than they really are because of a common tendency to consider in unduly close association two distinct questions: the question "Is a contra-causal type of freedom implied by moral responsibility?" and the question "Does a contra-causal type of freedom anywhere exist?". It seems to me that many philosophers (and I suspect that Moritz Schlick is among them) begin their enquiry with so firm a conviction that the contra-causal sort of freedom nowhere exists, that they find it hard to take very seriously the possibility that it is *this* sort of freedom that moral responsibility implies. For they are loth to abandon the commonsense belief that moral responsibility itself is something real. The implicit reasoning I take to be this. Moral responsibility is real. If moral responsibility is real, the freedom implied in it must be a fact. But contra-causal freedom is not a fact. Therefore contra-causal freedom is not the freedom implied in moral responsibility. I think we should be on our guard against allowing this or some similar train of reasoning (whose premises, after all, are far from indubitable) to seduce us into distorting what we actually find when we set about a direct analysis of moral responsibility and its conditions.

II

The pseudoproblem theorists usually, and naturally, develop their analysis of moral responsibility by way of contrast with a view which, while it has enjoyed a good deal of philosophic support, I can perhaps best describe as the common view. It will be well to remind ourselves, therefore, of the main features of this view.

So far as the *meaning,* as distinct from the *conditions,* of moral responsibility is concerned, the common view is very simple. If we ask ourselves whether a certain person is morally responsible for a given act (or it may be just "in general"), what we are considering, it would be said, is whether or not that person is a fit subject upon whom to pass moral judgment; whether he can fittingly be deemed morally good or bad, morally praiseworthy or blameworthy. This does not take us any great way: but (*pace* Schlick) so far as it goes it does not seem to me seriously disputable. The really interesting and controversial question is about the *conditions* of moral responsibility, and in particular the question whether freedom of a contra-causal kind is among these conditions.

The answer of the common man to the latter question is that it most certainly *is* among the conditions. Why does he feel so sure about this? Not, I argued earlier, because the common man supposes that causal law exercises "compulsion" in the sense that prescriptive laws do, but simply because he does not see how a person can be deemed morally praiseworthy or blameworthy in respect of an act which he could not help performing. From the standpoint of moral praise and blame, he would say—though not necessarily from other standpoints—it is a matter of indifference whether it is by reason of some external constraint or by reason of his own given nature that the man could not help doing what he did. It is quite enough to make moral praise and blame futile that in either case there were no genuine alternatives, no open possibilities, before the man when he acted. He could not have acted otherwise than he did. And the common man might not unreasonably go on to stress the fact that we all, even if we are linguistic philosophers, do in our actual practice of moral judgment appear to accept the common view. He might insist upon the point alluded to earlier in this paper, that we do all, in passing moral censure, "make allowances" for influences in a man's hereditary nature or environmental circumstances which we regard as having made it more than ordinarily difficult for him to act otherwise then he did: the implication being that if we supposed that the man's heredity and environment made it not merely very *difficult* but actually *impossible* for him to act otherwise than he did, we could not properly assign moral blame to him at all.

Let us put the argument implicit in the common view a little more sharply. The moral "ought" implies "can." If we say that A morally ought to have done X, we imply that in our opinion, he could have done X. But we assign moral blame to a man only for failing to do what we think he morally ought to have done. Hence if we morally blame A for not having done X, we imply that he could have done X even though in fact he did not. In other words, we imply that A could have acted otherwise than he did. And that means that we imply, as a necessary condition of a man's being morally blameworthy, that he enjoyed a freedom of a kind not compatible with unbroken causal continuity.

III

Now what is it that is supposed to be wrong with this simple piece of argument?—For, of course, it must be rejected by all these philosophers who tell us that the traditional problem of Free Will is a mere pseudoproblem. The argument looks as though it were doing little more than reading off necessary implications of the fundamental categories of our moral thinking. One's inclination is to ask "If one is to think morally at all, how else than this *can* we think?"

In point of fact, there is pretty general agreement among the contemporary critics as to what is wrong with the argument. Their answer in general terms is as follows. No doubt *A*'s moral responsibility does imply that he could have acted otherwise. But this expression "could have acted otherwise" stands in dire need of analysis. When we analyze it, we find that it is not, as is so often supposed, simple and unambiguous, and we find that in *some* at least of its possible meanings it implies *no* breach of causal continuity between character and conduct. Having got this clear, we can further discern that only in one of these *latter* meanings is there any compulsion upon our moral thinking to assert that if *A* is morally blameworthy for an act, *A* "could have acted otherwise than he did." It follows that, contrary to common belief, our moral thinking does *not* require us to posit a contra-causal freedom as a condition of moral responsibility.

So much of importance obviously turns upon the validity or otherwise of this line of criticism that we must examine it in some detail and with express regard to the *ipsissima verba* of the critics.

In the course of a recent article in *Mind*, entitled "Free Will and Moral Responsibility," Mr. Nowell-Smith (having earlier affirmed his belief that "the traditional problem has been solved") explains very concisely the nature of the confusion which, as he thinks, has led to the demand for a contra-causal freedom. He begins by frankly recognizing that "It is evident that one of the necessary conditions of moral action is that the agent 'could have acted otherwise'" and he adds "it is to this fact that the Libertarian is drawing attention." Then, after showing (unexceptionably, I think) how the relationship of "ought" to "can" warrants the proposition which he has accepted as evident, and how it induces the Libertarian to assert the existence of action that is "uncaused," he proceeds to point out, in a crucial passage, the nature of the Libertarian's error:

The fallacy in the argument (he contends) lies in supposing that when we say "A could have acted otherwise" we mean that A, being what he was and being placed in the circumstances in which he was placed, *could have done something other than what he did. But in fact we never do mean this.*

What then *do* we mean here by "*A* could have acted otherwise"? Mr. Nowell-Smith does not tell us in so many words, but the passage I have quoted leaves little doubt how he would answer. What we really mean by the expression, he implies, is not a *categorical* but a *hypothetical* proposition. We mean "*A* could have acted otherwise, *if he did not happen to be what he in fact was,* or *if he were placed in circumstances other than those in which he was in fact placed.*" Now, *these* propositions, it is easy to see, are in no way incompatible with acceptance of the causal principle in its full rigour. Accordingly the claim that our fundamental moral thinking obliges us to assert a contra-causal freedom as a condition of moral responsibility is disproved.

Such is the "analytical solution" of our problem offered (with obvious confidence) by one able philosopher of today, and entirely representative of the views of many other able philosophers. Yet I make bold to say that its falsity stares one in the face. It seems perfectly plain that the hypothetical propositions which Mr. Nowell-Smith proposes to substitute for the categorical proposition cannot express "what we really mean" in this context by "*A* could have acted otherwise,'' for the simple reason that these hypothetical propositions have no bearing whatsoever upon the question of the moral responsibility of *A*. And it is *A* whose moral responsibility we are talking about—a definite person *A* with a definitive character and in a definitive set of circumstances. What conceivable significance could it have for our attitude to *A*'s responsibility to know that someone with a *different* character (or *A* with a different character, if that collocation of words has any meaning), or *A* in a different set of circumstances from those in which *A* as we are concerned with him was in fact placed, ''could have acted otherwise''? No doubt this supposititious being *could* have acted otherwise than the definitive person *A* acted. But the point is that where we are reflecting, as we are supposed in this context to be reflecting, upon the question of *A*'s moral responsibility, our interest in this supposititious being is precisely *nil*.

The two hypothetical propositions suggested in Mr. Nowell-Smith's account of the matter do not, however, exhaust the speculations that have been made along these lines. Another very common suggestion by the analysts is that what we really mean by ''*A* could have acted otherwise'' is ''*A* could have acted otherwise *if he had willed, or chosen, otherwise*.'' This was among the suggestions offered by G. E. Moore in the well-known chapter on Free Will in his *Ethics*. It is, I think, the suggestion he most strongly favoured: though it is fair to add that neither about this nor about any other of his suggestions is Moore in the least dogmatic. He does claim, for, I think, convincing reasons, that ''we *very often* mean by 'could' merely 'would, *if* so-and-so had chosen.''' And he concludes ''I must confess that I cannot feel certain that this may not be all that we usually mean and understand by the assertion that we have Free Will.''

This third hypothetical proposition appears to enjoy also the support of Mr. C. L. Stevenson. Mr. Stevenson begins the chapter of *Ethics and Language* entitled ''Avoidability-Indeterminism'' with the now familiar pronouncement of his School that ''controversy about freedom and determinism of the will . . .

presents no permanent difficulty to ethics, being largely a product of confusions.'' A major confusion (if I understand him rightly) he takes to lie in the meaning of the term ''avoidable,'' when we say ''*A*'s action was avoidable''—or, I presume, ''*A* could have acted otherwise.'' He himself offers the following definition of ''avoidable,''—'' '*A*'s action was avoidable' has the meaning of 'If *A* had made a certain choice, which in fact he did not make, his action would not have occurred.' '' This I think we may regard as in substance identical with the suggestion that what we really mean by ''*A* could have acted otherwise'' is ''*A* could have acted otherwise *if* he had chosen (or willed) otherwise.'' For clarity's sake we shall here keep to this earlier formulation. In either formulation the special signficance of the third hypothetical proposition, as of the two hypothetical propositions already considered, is that it is compatible with strict determinism. If this be indeed all that we mean by the ''freedom'' that conditions moral responsibility, then those philosophers are certainly wrong who hold that moral freedom is of the contra-causal type.

Now this third hypothetical proposition does at least possess the merit, not shared by its predecessors, of having a real relevance to the question of moral responsibility. If, *e.g.*, *A* had promised to meet us at 2 p.m., and he chanced to break his leg at 1 p.m., we should not blame him for his failure to discharge his promise. For we should be satisfied that he *could not* have acted otherwise, even if he had so chosen; or *could not* at any rate, in a way which would have enabled him to meet us at 2 p.m. The freedom to translate one's choice into action, which we saw earlier is for Schlick the *only* freedom required for moral responsibility, is without doubt *one* of the conditions of moral responsibility.

But it seems easy to show that this third hypothetical proposition does not exhaust what we mean, and *some*times is not even *part* of what we mean, by the expression ''could have acted otherwise'' in its moral context. Thus it can hardly be even part of what we mean in the case of that class of wrong actions (and it is a large class) concerning which there is really no question whether the agent could have acted otherwise, *if* he had chosen otherwise. Take lying, for example. Only in some very abnormal situation should it occur to one to doubt whether *A*, whose power of speech was evinced by his telling a lie, was in a position to tell what he took to be the truth *if* he had so chosen. Of *course* he was. Yet it still makes good sense for one's moral thinking to ask whether *A*, when lying, "could have acted otherwise": and we still require an affirmative answer to this question if *A*'s moral blameworthiness is to be established. It seems apparent, therefore, that in this class of cases at any rate one does *not* mean by "*A* could have acted otherwise," "*A* could have acted otherwise *if* he had so chosen."

What then *does* one mean in this class of cases by "*A* could have acted otherwise"? I submit that the expression is taken in its simple, categorical meaning, without any suppressed "if" clause to qualify it. Or perhaps, in order to keep before us the important truth that it is only as expressions of *will* or *choice* that acts are of moral import, it might be better to say that a condition of *A*'s moral responsibility is that he could have *chosen* otherwise. We saw that there is no real question whether *A* who told a lie could have acted otherwise *if* he had chosen otherwise. But there is a very real question, at least for any person who approaches the question of moral responsibility at a tolerably advanced level of reflexion, about whether *A* could have *chosen* otherwise. Such a person will doubtless be acquainted with the claims advanced in some quarters that causal law operates universally: or/and with the theories of some philosophies that the universe is throughout the expression of a single supreme principle; or/and with the doctrines of some theologians that the world is created, sustained and governed by an Omniscient and Omnipotent Being. Very understandably such worldviews awaken in him doubts about the validity of his first, easy, instinctive assumption that there are genuinely open possibilities before a man at the moment of moral choice. It thus becomes for him a real question whether a man could have chosen otherwise than he actually did, and, in consequence, whether man's moral responsibility is really defensible. For how can a man be morally responsible, he asks himself, if his choices, like all other events in the universe, could not have been otherwise than they in fact were? It is precisely against the background of worldviews such as these that for reflective people the problem of moral responsibility normally arises.

Furthermore, to the man who has attained this level of reflexion, it will in *no* class of cases be a sufficient condition of moral responsibility for an act that one could have acted otherwise *if* one had chosen otherwise—not even in these cases where there *was* some possibility of the operation of "external constraint." In these cases he will, indeed expressly recognize freedom from external constraint as a *necessary condition*, but not as a *sufficient* condition. For he will be aware that, even granted *this* freedom, it is still conceivable that the agent had no freedom to choose otherwise than he did, and he will therefore require that the latter sort of freedom be added if moral responsibility for the act is to be established.

I have been contending that, for persons at a *tolerably advanced level of reflexion*, "*A* could have acted otherwise," as a condition of *A*'s moral responsibility, means "*A* could have chosen otherwise." The qualification italicised is of some importance. The unreflective or unsophisticated person, the ordinary "man in the street," who does not know or much care what scientists and theologians and philosophers have said about the world, sees well enough that *A* is morally responsible only if he could have acted otherwise, but in his intellectual innocence he will, very probably, envisage nothing capable of preventing *A* from having acted otherwise except some material impediment—like the broken leg in the example above. Accordingly, for the unreflective person, "*A* could have acted otherwise," as a condition of moral responsibility, *is* apt to mean no more than "*A* could have acted otherwise *if* he had so chosen."

It would appear, then, that the view now favoured by many philosophers, that the freedom required for moral responsibility is merely freedom from external constraint, is a view which they share only with the less reflective type of layman. Yet it should be plain that on a matter of this sort the view of the unreflective person is of little value by comparison with the view of the reflective person. There are some contexts, no doubt, in which lack of sophistication is an asset. But this is not one of them. The question at issue here is as to the kind of impediments which might have prevented a man from acting otherwise than he in fact did: and on this question knowledge and reflexion are surely prerequisites of any answer that is worth listening to. It is simply on account of the limitations of his mental vision that the unreflective man interprets the expression "could have acted otherwise," in its context as a condition of moral responsibility, solely in terms of external constraint. He has failed (as yet) to reach the intellectual level at which one takes into account the implications for moral choices of the worldviews of science, religion, and philosophy. If on a matter of this complexity the philosopher finds that his analysis accords with the utterances of the uneducated he has, I suggest, better cause for uneasiness than for self-congratulation. . . .

JOHN HOSPERS
Meaning and Free Will

Perhaps the most obvious conception of freedom is this: an act is free if and only if it is a voluntary act. A response that occurs spontaneously, not as a result of your willing it, such as a reflex action, is not a free act. I do not know that this view is ever held in its pure form, but it is the basis for other ones. As it stands, of course, it is ambiguous: does "voluntary" entail "premeditated?", are acts we perform semiautomatically through habit to be called free acts? To what extent is a conscious decision to act required for the act to be classified as voluntary? What of sudden outbursts of feeling? They are hardly premeditated or decided upon, yet they may have their origin in the presence or absence of habit-patterns due to self-discipline which may have been consciously decided upon. Clearly the view needs to be refined.

Now, however we may come to define "voluntary." It is perfectly possible to maintain that all voluntary acts are free acts and vice versa; after all, it is a matter of what meaning we are giving to the word "free" and we can give it this meaning if we choose. But it soon becomes apparent that this is not the meaning which most of us *want* to give it: for there *are* classes of actions which we want to refrain from calling "free" even though they are voluntary (not that we have this denial in mind when we use the

"Meaning and Free Will" is reprinted from *Philosophy and Phenomenological Research* 10 (March 1950), by permission of *Philosophy and Phenomenological Research*. **John Hospers** (b. 1918) is a contemporary American philosopher who has published in the areas of ethics and political thought. In 1972 he ran for the presidency of the United States as a candidate of the Libertarian Party.

word "free"—still, it is significant that we do not use the word in some situations in which the act in question is nevertheless voluntary).

When a man tells a state secret under torture, he does choose voluntarily between telling and enduring more torture; and when he submits to a bandit's command at the point of a gun, he voluntarily chooses to submit rather than to be shot. And still such actions would not generally be called free; it is clear that they are performed under compulsion. Voluntary acts performed under compulsion would not be called free; and the cruder view is to this extent amended.

For some persons, this is as far as we need to go. Schlick, for example, says that the free will issue is the scandal of philosophy and nothing but so much wasted ink and paper, because the whole controversy is nothing but an inexcusable confusion between compulsion and universal causality. The free act is the uncompelled act, says Schlick, and controversies about causality and determinism have nothing to do with the case. When one asks whether an act done of necessity is free, the question is ambiguous: if "of necessity" means "by compulsion," then the answer is no; if, on the other hand, "of necessity" is a way of referring to "causal uniformity" in nature—the sense in which we may misleadingly speak of the laws of nature as "necessary" simply because there are no exceptions to them—then the answer is clearly yes; every act is an instance of some causal law (uniformity) or other, but this has nothing to do with its being free in the sense of uncompelled.

For Schlick, this is the end of the matter. Any attempt to discuss the matter further betrays a failure to perceive the clarifying distinctions that Schlick has made.

Freedom means the opposite of compulsion; a man is *free* if he does not act under *compulsion*, and he is compelled or unfree when he is hindered from without in the realization of his natural desires. Hence he is unfree when he is locked up, or chained, or when someone forces him at the point of a gun to do what otherwise he would not do. This is quite clear, and everyone will admit that the everyday or legal notion of the lack of freedom is thus correctly interpreted, and that a man will be considered quite free . . . if no such external compulsion is exerted upon him.

This all seems clear enough. And yet if we ask whether it ends the matter, whether it states what we "really mean" by "free," many of us will feel qualms. We remember statements about human beings being pawns of their environment, victims of conditions beyond their control, the result of causal influences stemming from parents, etc., and we think, "Still, are we really free?" We do not want to say that the uniformity of nature itself binds us or renders us unfree; yet is there not something in what generations of wise men have said about man being fettered? Is there not something too facile, too sleight of hand, in Schlick's cutting of the Gordian knot?

It will be noticed that we have slipped from talking about acts as being free into talking about human beings as free. Both locutions are employed, I would say about 50–50. Sometimes an attempt is made to legislate definitely between the two: Stebbing, for instance, says that one must never call acts free, but only the doers of the acts.

Let us pause over this for a moment. If it is we and not our acts that are to be called free, the most obvious reflection to make is that we are free to do some things and not free to do other things; we are free to lift our hands but not free to lift the moon. We cannot simply call ourselves free or unfree *in toto;* we must say at best that we are free in respect of certain actions only. G. E. Moore states the criterion as follows: we are free to do an act if we can do it *if* we want to, that which we can do if we want to is what we are free to do. Some things certain people are free to do while others are not: most of us are free to move our legs, but paralytics are not; some of us are free to concentrate on philosophical reading matter for three hours at a stretch while others are not. In general, we could relate the two approaches by saying that a *person* is free *in respect of* a given action if he can do it if he wants to, and in this case his *act* is free.

Moore himself, however, has reservations that Schlick has not. He adds that there is a sense of "free" which fulfills the criterion he has just set forth; but that there may be *another* sense in which man cannot be said to be free in all the situations in which he could rightly be said to be so in the first sense.

And surely it is not necessary for me to multiply examples of the sort of thing we mean. In practice most of us would not call free many persons who behave voluntarily and even with calculation aforethought, and under no compulsion either of any obvious sort. A metropolitan newspaper headlines an article with the words "Boy Killer Is Doomed Long before He Is Born" and then goes on to describe how a twelve-year-old boy has just been sentenced to thirty years in Sing Sing for the murder of a girl; his family background includes records of drunkenness, divorce, social maladjustment, epilepsy, and paresis. He early displays a tendency to sadistic activity to hide an underlying masochism and "prove that he's a man"; being coddled by his mother only worsens this tendency, until, spurned by a girl in his attempt on her, he kills her—not simply in a fit of anger, but calculatingly, deliberately. Is he free in respect of his criminal act, or for that matter in most of the acts of his life? Surely to ask this question is to answer it in the negative. Perhaps I have taken an extreme case; but it is only to show the superficiality of the Schlick analysis the more clearly. Though not everyone has criminotic tendencies, everyone has been moulded by influences which in large measure at least determine his present behavior; he is literally the product of these influences, stemming from periods prior to his "years of discretion," giving him a host of character traits that he cannot change now even if he would. So obviously does what a man is depend upon how a man comes to be, that it is small wonder that philosophers and sages have considered man far indeed from being the master of his fate. It is not as if man's will were standing high and serene above the flux of events that have moulded him; it is itself caught up in this flux, itself carried along on the current. An act is free when it is

determined by the man's character, say moralists; but when there was nothing the man could do to shape his character, and even the degree of will power available to him in shaping his habits and disciplining himself to overcome the influence of his early environment is a factor over which he has no control, what are we to say of this kind of "freedom?" Is it not rather like the freedom of the machine to stamp labels on cans when it has been devised for just that purpose? Some machines can do so more efficiently than others, but only because they have been better constructed.

It is not my purpose here to establish this thesis in general, but only in one specific respect which has received comparatively little attention, namely, the field referred to by psychiatrists as that of unconscious motivation. In what follows I shall restrict my attention to it because it illustrates as clearly as anything the points I wish to make.

Let me try to summarize very briefly the psychoanalytic doctrine on this point. The conscious life of the human being, including the conscious decisions and volitions, is merely a mouthpiece for the unconscious—not directly for the enactment of unconscious drives, but of the compromise between unconscious drives and unconscious reproaches. There is a Big Three behind the scenes which the automaton called the conscious personality carries out: the id, an "eternal gimme," presents its wish and demands its immediate satisfaction; the superego says no to the wish immediately upon presentation, and the unconscious ego, the mediator between the two, tries to keep peace by means of compromise.

To go into examples of the functioning of these three "bosses" would be endless; psychoanalytic case books supply hundreds of them. The important point for us to see in the present context is that it is the unconscious that determines what the conscious impulse and the conscious action shall be. Hamlet, for example, had a strong Oedipus wish, which was violently counteracted by superego reproaches; these early wishes were vividly revived in an unusual adult situation in which his uncle usurped the coveted position from Hamlet's father and won his mother besides. This situation evoked strong strictures on the part of Hamlet's superego, and it was this that was responsbile for his notorious delay in killing his uncle. A dozen times Hamlet could have killed Claudius easily; but every time Hamlet "decided" not to: a free choice, moralists would say—but no, listen to the superego: "What you feel such hatred toward your uncle for, what you are plotting to kill him for, is precisely the crime which you yourself desire to commit: to kill your father and replace him in the affections of your mother. Your fate and your uncle's are bound up together." This paralyzes Hamlet into inaction. Consciously all he knows is that he is unable to act; this conscious inability he rationalizes, giving a different excuse each time.

We have always been conscious of the fact that we are not masters of our fate in every respect—that there are many things which we cannot do, that nature is more powerful than we are, that we cannot disobey laws without danger of reprisals, etc. Lately we have become more conscious, too, though novelists and dramatists have always been fairly conscious of it, that we are not free with respect to the emotions that we feel—whom we love or hate, what types we admire, and the like. More lately still we have been reminded that there are unconscious motivations for our basic attractions and repulsions, our compulsive actions or inabilities to act. But what is not welcome news is that our very acts of volition, and the entire train of deliberations leading up to them, are but facades for the expression of unconscious wishes, or rather, unconscious compromises and defenses.

A man is faced by a choice: shall he kill another person or not? Moralists would say, here is a free choice—the result of deliberation, an action consciously entered into. And yet, though the agent himself does not know it, and has no awareness of the forces that are at work within him, his choice is already determined for him: his conscious will is only an instrument, a slave, in the hands of a deep unconscious motivation which determines his action. If he has a great deal of what the analyst calls "free-floating guilt," he will not; but if the guilt is such as to demand immediate absorption in the form of self-damaging behavior, this accumulated guilt will have to be discharged in some criminal action. The man himself does not know what the inner clockwork is; he is like the hands on the clock, thinking they move freely over the face of the clock.

A woman has married and divorced several husbands. Now she is faced with a choice for the next marriage: shall she marry Mr. A, or Mr. B, or nobody at all? She may take considerable time to "decide" this question, and her decision may appear as a final triumph of her free will. Let us assume that A is a normal, well-adjusted, kind and generous man, while B is a leech, an impostor, one who will become entangled constantly in quarrels with her. If she belongs to a certain classifiable psychological type, she will inevitably choose B, and she will do so even if her previous husbands have resembled B, so that one would think that she "had learned from experience." Consciously, she will of course "give the matter due consideration," etc., etc. To the psychoanalyst all this is irrelevant chaff in the wind—only a camouflage for the inner workings about which she knows nothing consciously. If she is of a certain kind of masochistic strain, as exhibited in her previous set of symptoms, she *must* choose B: her superego, always out to maximize the torment in the situation, seeing what dazzling possibilities for self-damaging behavior are promised by the choice of B, compels her to make the choice she does, and even to conceal the real basis of the choice behind an elaborate facade of rationalizations.

A man is addicted to gambling. In the service of his addiction he loses all his money, spends what belongs to his wife, even sells his property and neglects his children. For a time perhaps he stops; then, inevitably, he takes it up again, although he himself may think he chose to. The man does not know that he is a victim rather than an agent; or, if he sometimes senses that he is in the throes of something-he-knows-not-what, he will have no inkling of its character and will soon relapse into the illusion that he (his conscious self) is freely deciding the course of his own actions. What he does not know, of course, is that he is still taking out on his mother the original lesion to his infantile narcissism, getting back at her for her fancied refusal of his infantile wishes—and this by rejecting everything identified with her, namely education, discipline, logic, common sense, training. At the roulette wheel, almost alone among adult activities, chance—the opposite of all these things—rules supreme; and his addiction represents his continued and emphatic reiteration of his rejection of Mother and all she represents to his unconscious.

This pseudo-aggression of his is of course masochistic in its effects. In the long run he always loses; he can never quit while he is winning. And far from playing in order to win, rather one can say that his losing is a *sine qua non* of his psychic equilibrium (as it was for example with Dostoyevsky): guilt demands punishment, and in the ego's "deal" with the superego the superego has granted satisfaction of infantile wishes in return for the self-damaging conditions obtaining. Winning would upset the neurotic equilibrium.

A man has wash-compulsion. He must be constantly washing his hands—he uses up perhaps 400 towels a day. Asked why he does this, he says, "I need to, my hands are dirty"; and if it is pointed out to him that they are not really dirty, he says "They feel dirty anyway, I feel better when I wash them." So once again he washes them. He "freely decides" every time; he feels that he must wash them, he deliberates for a moment perhaps, but always ends by washing them. What he does not see, of course, is the invisible wires inside him pulling him inevitably to do the thing he does: the infantile id-wish concerns preoccupation with dirt, the superego charges him with this, and the terrified ego must respond, "No, I don't like dirt, see how clean I like to be, look how I wash my hands!" . . .

Let us take, finally, a less colorful, more everyday example. A student at a university, possessing wealth, charm, and all that is usually considered essential to popularity, begins to develop the following personality pattern: although well taught in the graces of social conversation, he always makes a *faux pas* somewhere, and always in the worst possible situation; to his friends he makes cutting remarks which hurt deeply—and always apparently aimed in such a way as to hurt the most: a remark that would not hurt A but would hurt B he invariably makes to B rather than to A, and so on. None of this is conscious. Ordinarily he is considerate of people, but he contrives always (unconsciously) to impose on just those friends who would resent it most, and at just the times when he should know that he should not impose: at 3 o'clock in the morning, without forewarning, he phones a friend in a nearby city demanding to stay at his apartment for the weekend; naturally the friend is offended, but the person himself is not aware that he has provoked the grievance ("common sense" suffers a temporary eclipse when the neurotic pattern sets in, and one's intelligence, far from being of help in such a situation, is used in the interest of the neurosis), and when the friend is cool to him the next time they meet, he wonders why and feels unjustly treated. Aggressive behavior on his part invites resentment and aggression in turn, but all that he consciously sees is other's behavior toward him—and he considers himself the innocent victim of an unjustified "persecution."

Each of these choices is, from the moralist's point of view, free: he chose to phone his friend at 3 a.m; he chose to make the cutting remark that he did, etc. What he does not know is that an ineradicable masochistic pattern has set in. His unconscious is far more shrewd and clever than is his conscious intellect; it sees with uncanny accuracy just what kind of behavior will damage him most, and unerringly forces him into that behavior. Consciously, the student "doesn't know why he did it"—he gives different "reasons" at different times, but they are all, once again, rationalizations cloaking the unconscious mechanism which propels him willy-nilly into actions that his "common sense" eschews.

The more of this sort of thing you see, the more you can see what the psychoanalyst means when he talks about "the illusion of free will." And the more of a psychiatrist you become, the more you are overcome with a sense of what an illusion this precious free will really is. In some kinds of cases most of us can see it already: it takes no psychiatrist to look at the epileptic and sigh with sadness at the thought that soon this person before you will be as one possessed, not the same thoughtful intelligent person you knew. But people are not aware of this in other contexts, for example when they express surprise at how a person whom they have been so good to could treat them so badly. Let us suppose that you help a person financially or morally or in some other way, so that he is in your debt; suppose further that he is one of the many neurotics who unconsciously identify kindness with weakness and aggression with strength, then he will unconsciously take your kindness to him as weakness and use it as the occasion for enacting some aggression against you. He can't help it, he may regret it himself later; still, he will be driven to do it. If we gain a little knowledge of psychiatry, we can look at him with pity, that a person otherwise so worthy should be so unreliable—but we will exercise realism too and be aware that there are some types of people that you cannot be good to in "free" acts of their conscious volition, they will use your own goodness against you.

Sometimes the persons themselves will become dimly aware that "something behind the scenes" is determining their behavior. The divorcee will sometimes view herself with detachment, as if she were some machine (and indeed the psychoanalyst does call her a "repeating-machine"): "I know I'm caught in a net, that I'll fall in love with this guy and marry him and the whole ridiculous merry-go-round will start all over again."

We talk about free will, and we say, yes, the person is free to do so-and-so if he can do so *if* he wants to—and we forget that his wanting to is itself caught up in the stream of determinism, that unconscious forces drive him into the wanting or not wanting to do the thing in question. The idea of the puppet whose motions are manipulated from behind by invisible wires, or

better still, by springs inside, is no mere figure of speech. The analogy is a telling one at almost every point. . . .

Now, what of the notion of responsibility? What happens to it on our analysis?

Let us begin with an example, not a fictitious one. A woman and her two-year-old baby are riding on a train to Montreal in midwinter. The child is ill. The woman wants badly to get to her destination. She is, unknown to herself, the victim of a neurotic conflict whose nature is irrelevant here except for the fact that it forces her to behave aggressively toward the child, partly to spite her husband whom she despises and who loves the child, but chiefly to ward off superego charges of masochistic attachment. Consciously she loves the child, and when she says this she says it sincerely, but she must behave aggressively toward it nevertheless, just as many children love their mothers but are nasty to them most of the time in neurotic pseudo-aggression. The child becomes more ill as the train approaches Montreal; the heating system of the train is not working, and the conductor advises the woman to get off the train at the next town and get the child to a hospital at once. The woman says no, she must get to Montreal. Shortly afterward, as the child's condition worsens, the mother does all she can to keep it alive, without, however, leaving the train, for she declares that it is absolutely necessary that she reach her destination. But before she gets there the child is dead. After that, of course, the mother grieves, blames herself, weeps hysterically, and joins the church to gain surcease from the guilt that constantly overwhelms her when she thinks of how her aggressive behavior has killed her child.

Was she responsible for her deed? In ordinary life, after making a mistake, we say, "Chalk it up to experience." Here we say, "Chalk it up to the neurosis." No, she is not responsible. She could not help it if her neurosis forced her to act this way—she didn't even know what was going on behind the scenes, she merely acted out the part assigned to her. This is far more true than is generally realized: criminal actions in general are not actions for which their agents are responsible; the agents are passive, not active—they are victims of a neurotic conflict. Their very hyperactivity is unconsciously determined.

To say this is, of course, not to say that we should not punish criminals. Clearly, for our own protection, we must remove them from our midst so that they can no longer molest and endanger organized society. And, of course, if we use the word "responsible" in such a way that justly to hold someone responsible for a deed is by definition identical with being justified in punishing him, then we can and do hold people responsible. But this is like the sense of "free" in which free acts are voluntary ones. It does not go deep enough. In a deeper sense we cannot hold the person responsible: we may hold his neurosis responsible, but he is not responsible for his neurosis, particularly since the age at which its onset was inevitable was an age before he could even speak.

The neurosis is responsible—but isn't the neurosis a part of *him*? We have been speaking all the time as if the person and his unconscious were two separate beings; but isn't he one personality, including conscious and unconscious departments together?

I do not wish to deny this. But it hardly helps us here; for what people want when they talk about freedom, and what they hold to when they champion it, is the idea that the *conscious* will is the master of their destiny. "I am the master of my fate, I am the captain of my soul"—and they surely mean their conscious selves, the self that they can recognize and search and introspect. Between an unconscious that willy-nilly determines your actions, and an external force which pushes you, there is little if anything to choose. The unconscious is just *as if* it were an outside force; and indeed, psychiatrists will assert that the inner Hitler can torment you far more than any external Hitler can. Thus the kind of freedom that people want, the only kind they will settle for, is precisely the kind that psychiatry says that they cannot have. . . .

Let us . . . put the situation schematically in the form of a deductive argument.

1. An occurrence over which we had no control is something we cannot be held responsible for.
2. Events E, occurring during our babyhood, were events over which we had no control.
3. Therefore events E were events which we cannot be held responsible for.
4. But if there is something we cannot be held responsible for, neither can we be held responsible for something that inevitably results from it.
5. Events E have as inevitable consequence Neurosis N, which in turn has as inevitable consequence Behavior B.
6. Since N is the inevitable consequence of E and B is the inevitable consequence of N, B is the inevitable consequence of E.
7. Hence, not being responsible for E, we cannot be responsible for B.

B. F. SKINNER
Freedom and the Control of Men

The second half of the twentieth century may be remembered for its solution of a curious problem. Although Western democracy created the conditions responsible for the rise of modern science, it is now evident that it may never fully profit from that achievement. The so-called "democratic philosophy" of human behavior to which it also gave rise is increasingly in conflict with the applications of the methods of science to human affairs. Unless this conflict is somehow resolved, the ultimate goals of democracy may be long deferred.

Just as biographers and critics look for external influences to account for the traits and achievements of the men they study, so science ultimately explains behavior in terms of "causes" or conditions which lie beyond the individual himself. As more and more causal relations are demonstrated, a practical corollary becomes difficult to resist: it should be possible to *produce* behavior according to plan simply by arranging the proper conditions. Now, among the specifications which might reasonably be submitted to a behavioral technology are these: Let men be happy, informed, skillful, well behaved, and productive.

This immediate practical implication of a science of behavior has a familiar ring, for it recalls the doctrine of human perfectibility of eighteenth- and nineteenth-century humanism.

A science of man shares the optimism of that philosophy and supplies striking support for the working faith that men can build a better world and, through it, better men. The support comes just in time, for there has been little optimism of late among those who speak from the traditional point of view. Democracy has become "realistic," and it is only with some embarrassment that one admits today to perfectionistic or utopian thinking.

The earlier temper is worth considering, however. History records many foolish and unworkable schemes for human betterment, but almost all the great changes in our culture which we now regard as worthwhile can be traced to perfectionistic philosophies. Governmental, religious, educational, economic, and social reforms follow a common pattern. Someone believes that a change in a cultural practice—for example, in the rules of evidence in a court of law, in the characterization of man's relation to God, in the way children are taught to read and write, in permitted rates of interest, or in minimal housing standards—will improve the condition of men: by promoting justice, permitting men to seek salvation more effectively, increasing the literacy of a people, checking an inflationary trend, or improving public health and family relations, respectively. The underlying hypothesis is always the same: that a different physical or cultural environment will make a different and better man.

The scientific study of behavior not only justifies the general pattern of such proposals; it promises new and better hypotheses. The earliest cultural practices must have originated in sheer accidents. Those which strengthened the group survived with the group in a sort of natural selection. As soon as men began to propose and carry out changes in practice for the sake of possible consequences, the evolutionary process must have accelerated. The simple practice of making changes must have had survival value. A further acceleration is now to be expected. As laws of behavior are more precisely stated, the changes in the environment required to bring about a given effect may be more clearly specified. Conditions which have been neglected because their effects were slight or unlooked for may be shown to be relevant. New conditions may actually be created, as in the discovery and synthesis of drugs which affect behavior.

This is no time, then, to abandon notions of progress, improvement, or, indeed, human perfectibility. The simple fact is that man is able, and now as never before, to lift himself by his own bootstraps. In achieving control of the world of which he is a part, he may learn at last to control himself.

Timeworn objections to the planned improvement of cultural practices are already losing much of their force. Marcus Aurelius was probably right in advising his readers to be content with a haphazard amelioration of mankind. "Never hope to realize Plato's republic," he sighed, ". . . for who can change the opinions of men? And without a change of sentiments what can you make but reluctant slaves and hypocrites?" He was thinking, no doubt, of contemporary patterns of control based upon punishment or the threat of punishment which, as he correctly observed, breed only reluctant slaves of those who submit and hypocrites of those who discover modes of evasion. But we need not share his pessimism, for the opinions of men can be changed. The techniques of indoctrination which were being devised by the

early Christian Church at the very time Marcus Aurelius was writing are relevant, as are some of the techniques of psychotherapy and of advertising and public relations. Other methods suggested by recent scientific analyses leave little doubt of the matter.

The study of human behavior also answers the cynical complaint that there is a plain "cussedness" in man which will always thwart efforts to improve him. We are often told that men do not want to be changed, even for the better. Try to help them, and they will outwit you and remain happily wretched. Dostoevsky claimed to see some plan in it. "Out of sheer ingratitude," he complained, or possibly boasted, "man will play you a dirty trick, just to prove that men are still men and not the keys of a piano. . . . And even if you could prove that a man is only a piano key, he would still do something out of sheer perversity—he would create destruction and chaos—just to gain his point. . . . And if all this could in turn be analyzed and prevented by predicting that it would occur, then man would deliberately go mad to prove his point." This is a conceivable neurotic reaction to inept control. A few men may have shown it, and many have enjoyed Dostoevsky's statement because they tend to show it. But that such perversity is a fundamental reaction of the human organism to controlling conditions is sheer nonsense.

So is the objection that we have no way of knowing what changes to make even though we have the necessary techniques. That is one of the great hoaxes of the century—a sort of booby trap left behind in the retreat before the advancing front of science. Scientists themselves have unsuspectingly agreed that there are two kinds of useful propositions about nature—facts and value judgments—and that science must confine itself to "what is," leaving "what ought to be" to others. But with what special sort of wisdom is the nonscientist endowed? Science is only effective knowing, no matter who engages in it. Verbal behavior proves upon analysis to be composed of many different types of utterances, from poetry and exhortation to logic and factual description, but these are not all equally useful in talking about cultural practices. We may classify useful propositions according to the degrees of confidence with which they may be asserted. Sentences about nature range from highly probable "facts" to sheer guesses. In general, future events are less likely to be correctly described than past. When a scientist talks about a projected experiment, for example, he must often resort to statements having only a moderate likelihood of being correct; he calls them hypotheses.

Designing a new cultural pattern is in many ways like designing an experiment. In drawing up a new constitution, outlining a new educational program, modifying a religious doctrine, or setting up a new fiscal policy, many statements must be quite tentative. We cannot be sure that the practices we specify will have the consequences we predict, or that the consequences will reward our efforts. This is in the nature of such proposals. They are not value judgments—they are guesses. To confuse and delay the improvement of cultural practices by quibbling about the word *improve* is itself not a useful practice. Let us agree, to start with, that health is better than illness, wisdom better than ignorance, love better than hate, and productive energy better than neurotic sloth.

Perhaps the most crucial part of our democratic philosophy to be reconsidered is our attitude toward freedom—or its reciprocal, the control of human behavior. We do not oppose all forms of control because it is . . . "human nature" to do so. The reaction is not characteristic of all men under all conditions of life. It is an attitude which has been carefully engineered, in large part by what we call the "literature" of democracy. With respect to some methods of control (for example, the threat of force), very little engineering is needed, for the techniques or their immediate consequences are objectionable. Society has suppressed these methods by branding them "wrong," "illegal," or "sinful." But to encourage these attitudes toward objectionable forms of control, it has been necessary to disguise the real nature of certain indispensable techniques, the commonest examples of which are education, moral discourse,

and persuasion. The actual procedures appear harmless enough. They consist of supplying information, presenting opportunities for action, pointing out logical relationships, appealing to reason or "enlightened understanding," and so on. Through a masterful piece of misrepresentation, the illusion is fostered that these procedures do not involve the control of behavior; at most, they are simply ways of "getting someone to change his mind." But analysis not only reveals the presence of well-defined behavioral processes, it demonstrates a kind of control no less inexorable, though in some ways more acceptable, than the bully's threat of force.

Let us suppose that someone in whom we are interested is acting unwisely—he is careless in the way he deals with his friends, he drives too fast, or he holds his golf club the wrong way. We could probably help him by issuing a series of commands: don't nag, don't drive over sixty, don't hold your club that way. Much less objectionable would be "an appeal to reason." We could show him how people are affected by his treatment of them, how accident rates rise sharply at higher speeds, how a particular grip on the club alters the way the ball is struck and corrects a slice. In doing so we resort to verbal mediating devices which emphasize and support certain "contingencies of reinforcement"—that is, certain relations between behavior and its consequences—which strengthen the behavior we wish to set up. The same consequences would possibly set up the behavior without our help, and they eventually take control no matter which form of help we give. The appeal to reason has certain advantages over the authoritative command. A threat of punishment, no matter how subtle, generates emotional reactions and tendencies to escape or revolt. Perhaps the controllee merely "feels resentment" at being made to act in a given way, but even that is to be avoided. When we "appeal to reason," he "feels freer to do as he pleases." The fact is that we have exerted *less* control than in using a threat; since other conditions may contribute to the result, the effect may be delayed or, possibly in a given instance, lacking. But if we have worked a change in his behavior at all, it is because we have altered relevant environmental conditions, and the processes we have set in motion are just as real and just as inexorable, if not as comprehensive, as in the most authoritative coercion.

"Arranging an opportunity for action" is another example of disguised control. The power of the negative form has already been exposed in the analysis of censorship. Restriction of opportunity is recognized as far from harmless. As Ralph Barton Perry said in an article which appeared in the Spring, 1953, *Pacific Spectator,* "Whoever determines what alternatives shall be made known to man controls what that man shall choose *from.* He is deprived of freedom in proportion as he is denied access to *any* ideas, or is confined to any range of ideas short of the totality of relevant possibilities." But there is a positive side as well. When we present a relevant state of affairs, we increase the likelihood that a given form of behavior will be emitted. To the extent that the probability of action has changed, we have made a definite contribution. The teacher of history controls a student's behavior (or, if the reader prefers, "deprives him of freedom") just as much in *presenting* historical facts as in suppressing them. Other conditions will no doubt affect the student, but the contribution made to his behavior by the presentation of material is fixed and, within its range, irresistible.

The methods of education, moral discourse, and persuasion are acceptable not because they recognize the freedom of the individual or his right to dissent, but because they make only *partial* contributions to the control of his behavior. The freedom they recognize is freedom from a more coercive form of control. The dissent which they tolerate is the possible effect of other determiners of action. Since these sanctioned methods are frequently ineffective, we have been able to convince ourselves that they do not represent control at all. When they show too much strength to permit disguise, we give them other names and suppress them as energetically as we suppress the use of force. Education grown too powerful is rejected as propaganda or "brainwashing," while really

effective persuasion is described as "undue influence," "demagoguery," "seduction," and so on.

If we are not to rely solely upon accident for the innovations which give rise to cultural evolution, we must accept the fact that some kind of control of human behavior is inevitable. We cannot use good sense in human affairs unless someone engages in the design and construction of environmental conditions which affect the behavior of men. Environmental changes have always been the condition for the improvement of cultural patterns, and we can hardly use the more effective methods of science without making changes on a grander scale. We are all controlled by the world in which we live, and part of that world has been and will be constructed by men. The question is this: Are we to be controlled by accident, by tyrants, or by ourselves in effective cultural design?

The danger of the misuse of power is possibly greater than ever. It is not allayed by disguising the facts. We cannot make wise decisions if we continue to pretend that human behavior is not controlled, or if we refuse to engage in control when valuable results might be forthcoming. Such measures weaken only ourselves, leaving the strength of science to others. The first step in a defense against tyranny is the fullest possible exposure of controlling techniques. A second step has already been taken successfully in restricting the use of physical force. Slowly, and as yet imperfectly, we have worked out an ethical and governmental design in which the strong man is not allowed to use the power deriving from his strength to control his fellow men. He is restrained by a superior force created for this purpose—the ethical pressure of the group, or more explicit religious and governmental measures. We tend to distrust superior forces, as we currently hesitate to relinquish sovereignty in order to set up an international police force. But it is only through such counter-control that we have achieved what we call peace—a condition in which men are not permitted to control each other through force. In other words, control itself must be controlled.

Science has turned up dangerous processes and materials before. To use the facts and techniques of a science of man to the fullest extent without making some monstrous mistake will be difficult and obviously perilous. It is no time for self-deception, emotional indulgence, or the assumption of attitudes which are no longer useful. Man is facing a difficult test. He must keep his head now, or he must start again—a long way back.

J. L. AUSTIN
from *Ifs and Cans*

Consider the case where I miss a very short putt and kick myself because I could have holed it. It is not that I should have holed it if I had tried: I did try, and missed. It is not that I should have holed it if conditions had been different: that might of course be so, but I am talking about conditions as they precisely were, and asserting that I could have holed it. There is the rub. Nor does 'I can hole it this time' mean that I shall hole it this time if I try or if anything else: for I may try and miss, and yet not be convinced that I could not have done it; indeed, further experiments may confirm my belief that I could have done it that time although I did not.

But if I tried my hardest, say, and missed, surely there *must* have been *something* that caused me to fail, that made me unable to succeed? So that I *could not* have holed it. Well, a modern belief in science, in there being an explanation of everything, may make us assent to this argument. But such a belief is not in line with the traditional beliefs enshrined in the word *can:* according to *them*, a human ability or power of capacity is inherently liable not to produce success, on occasion, and that for no reason (or are bad luck and bad form sometimes reasons?).

J. L. Austin's account of sinking a putt is taken from "Ifs and Cans," *Philosophical Papers* (Oxford: At The Clarendon Press, 1962). **J. L. Austin** (1911–1960), an influential British proponent of ordinary language philosophy, had a knack for picking surprisingly simple but often illuminating examples.

QUESTIONS ABOUT FREEDOM, FATALISM, AND DETERMINISM

1. Aristotle suggests that, ''A sea-fight must either take place tomorrow or not, but it is not necessary that it should take place tomorrow, neither is it necessary that it should not take place, yet it is necessary that it either should or should not take place tomorrow.'' Does this formulation of his proposed answer to the fatalist's argument help to clarify the issue?
2. Gilbert Ryle suggests that, ''The fatalist theory tries to imbue happenings with the inescapability of the conclusions of valid arguments.'' Explain what Ryle means by this. Do you think that Ryle is correct?

3. According to Ryle, ". . . statements in the future tense cannot convey singular, but only general propositions, where statements in the present and past tense can convey both." How does this suggestion compare with Aristotle's proposed solution to the fatalist's argument and with our discussion of this issue?

4. Richard Taylor suggests that, "A fatalist thus thinks of the future in the way we all think of the past, for all men are fatalists as they look *back* on things." Is Taylor clear about what he means by "all men are fatalists as they look back on things"? Does it make any difference, in looking back on things, whether we feel that we *cannot* do anything about the past, or *could not have done* anything about some past event? How might this distinction affect what Taylor says about the future?

5. William James distinguishes between "hard" and "soft" determinism. What is this distinction? Does James accept either view? If not, what is James' view about free will?

6. Explain why Baron d'Holbach's views on free will fall into the category of "hard determinism."

7. What does Moritz Schlick mean by a "pseudoproblem"? Does he show that the debate over free will is a pseudoproblem?

8. What is C. A. Campbell's main argument against the "soft" determinist? Do you think that he is correct?

9. Part of John Hosper's argument is that our basic motivations are fixed at an early age, before we can have any control over the influences that affect our lives. Do his examples support this suggestion? If Hosper is correct, is his argument against the "soft" determinist or the libertarian?

10. What exactly is J. L. Austin's point about sinking a putt?

Freedom, Fatalism, and Determinism:
Suggestions for Further Study

The debate over free will has served as a crossroads for a host of deeply troublesome metaphysical, physical, psychological, social, moral, and theological issues. Among these are the meaning of personal responsibility, causality and the explanation of human action, moral insight and duty, questions concerning the foundations of political and social theory, and the relationship between God's foreknowledge and human free choice. Since the main debate in modern philosophy has focused on the issue of compatibility, the following recommendations for further study are intended to augment that part of the discussion.

Following established convention, we can divide the field into four basic approaches: *libertarianism, hard determinism, soft determinism* and, most recently, *action theory*. Beginning with libertarianism—the view that moral conduct implies a break in causal law—we recommend, in addition to the writings of William James and C. A. Campbell, the works of the existentialists, especially Jean-Paul Sartre's main contribution, *Being and Nothingness* (New York: Philosophical Library, 1956). Action theorists, too, have expressed libertarian views, but from a different perspective, which will be described briefly below.

Among modern writers, social theorists are often the strongest proponents of hard determinism, the view that causality implies the lack of free will. See, for example, Freud's "Repression" and "The Unconscious" in his *Collected Papers,* Vol. IV, (Honolulu, Hawaii: Hogarth Press, 1959) and his *The Interpretation of Dreams* (Toronto: Hogarth Press, 1980). In addition, see Ernest Jones's *Sigmund Freud: Life and Work,* Vols. I and II (London: Hogarth Press, 1953), as well as A. C. MacIntyre's *The Unconscious* (London: Routledge & Kegan Paul, 1962). B. F. Skinner's views have been best expressed in his *Beyond Freedom and Dignity* (New York: Random House, 1972) and *Walden Two* (New York: Macmillan, 1948). For an extended cognitivist critique of the theory and practice of behaviorism, see Edward Erwin's *Behavior Therapy* (Cambridge: Cambridge University Press, 1978). For more on cognitivism, see Owen Flanagan's "Cognitive Psychology" in *The Science of Mind*, reprinted in *Twenty Questions,* edited by G. Lee Bowie, Meredith W. Michaels, and Robert C. Solomon (New York: Harcourt Brace Jovanovich, 1988). For a philosophical defense of determinism, seeAdolf Grunbaum's "Causality and the Science of Human Behavior" (*American Scientist* Vol. 39, No. 1, Jan. 1951).

Compatibilism, the view that there need be no conflict between free will and determinism, has a rich history, beginning perhaps with David Hume's "Of Liberty and Necessity," in *An Enquiry Concerning Human Understanding,* Section VIII. Among recent theorists, one of the best expositions of the view can be found in Paul Edward's "Hard and Soft Determinism" in *Determinism and Freedom,* edited by Sidney Hook (New York: New York University Press, 1958). See also Gerald Dworkin's "Acting Freely" (*Nous,* Vol. 4, 1970).

The most recent development in the history of the free will debate has been action theory: the view that human conduct can be best understood by reference to reasons for action (or, as J. L. Austin has suggested, reasons for failing to act) rather than in terms of psychological or social causes. See Austin's influential papers, "A Plea for Excuses" and "Ifs and Cans," in *Philosophical Papers* (Oxford: Clarendon Press, 1962). See also A. I. Melden's *Free Action* (London: Routledge & Kegan Paul, 1961), Alvin Goldman's *A Theory of Human Action* (Princeton: Princeton University Press, 1976), and Michael Simon's *Understanding Human Action* (Albany: State University of New York Press, 1982). Is rational action incompatible with determinism? Donald Davidson has defended a new form of compatibilism in "Mental Events," in his *Essays on Action and Events* (Oxford: Oxford University Press, 1980).